EDWARD II

SEYMOUR PHILLIPS is Emeritus Professor of Medieval History, University College, Dublin, former president of the Irish Historical Society, a fellow of the Society of Antiquaries of London and of the Royal Historical Society, and a member of the Royal Irish Academy. Among his publications are *Aymer de Valence, Earl of Pembroke* (1972) and *The Medieval Expansion of Europe* (1988; 2nd edn 1998). He was a member of the editorial team of the Parliament Rolls of Medieval England project (PROME) (2005).

EDWARD II

Seymour Phillips

YALE UNIVERSITY PRESS
NEW HAVEN AND LONDON

Copyright © 2010 Seymour Phillips

First printed in paperback in 2011

All rights reserved. This book may not be reproduced in whole or in part, in any form (beyond that copying permitted by Sections 107 and 108 of the U.S. Copyright Law and except by reviewers for the public press) without written permission from the publishers.

For information about this and other Yale University Press publications, please contact:
U.S. Office: sales.press@yale.edu   yalebooks.com
Europe Office: sales @yaleup.co.uk   www.yalebooks.co.uk

Set in Baskerville by IDSUK (DataConnection) Ltd
Printed in Great Britain by Hobbs the Printers Ltd, Totton, Hamshire

Library of Congress Cataloging-in-Publication Data

Phillips, Seymour.
  Edward II / Seymour Phillips.
    p. cm.
  Includes bibliographical references and index.
  ISBN 978–0–300–15657–7 (cl: alk. paper)
    1. Edward II, King of England, 1284–1327. 2. Great Britain—Kings and rulers—Biography. 3. Great Britain—History—Edward II, 1307–1327. I. Title.
  DA230.P48 2010
  942.03'6092—dc22
  [B]

2009038959

A catalogue record for this book is available from the British Library.

ISBN 978–0–300–17802–9 (pbk)

10 9 8 7 6 5 4 3 2 1

For Nuala, Eoin and Catherine

CONTENTS

LIST OF ILLUSTRATIONS	viii
PREFACE & ACKNOWLEDGEMENTS	x
ABBREVIATED REFERENCES	xiii
Introduction	1
1 The Reputation of a King	5
2 The Nature of a King	33
3 Preparation for the Crown, 1297–1307	77
4 Conflict and Reform, 1307–1312	125
5 From Blacklow Hill to Bannockburn: June 1312 to June 1314	192
6 War, Politics, Money and Weather: June 1314 to August 1316	238
7 Peace by Ordeal, August 1316 to August 1318	280
8 From Settlement to Civil War, 1318–1322	328
9 Edward Victorious, 1322–1324	410
10 Edward Vanquished, 1324–1326	455
11 Deposition and Death	520
12 Afterlives	577
CONCLUSION	607
BIBLIOGRAPHY	614
INDEX	643

ILLUSTRATIONS

Plates

1. Eagle Tower, Caernarfon castle. Cadw, Welsh Assembly Government (Crown Copyright).
2. Edward I creating Edward Prince of Wales in 1301, Cotton Ms. Nero D.II, f. 19v. © All Rights Reserved. British Library Board.
3. Marriage agreement between Edward and Isabella, 1303. Courtesy of the Royal Institution of South Wales, held at the West Glamorgan Archive Service (RISW DOC 5/3).
4. Isabella kneeling between the shields of England and France, from the Psalter of Queen Isabella of England, *c*. 1303–8. Bayerische Staatsbibliothek, Munich, Cod.gall. 16 f. 94r.
5. Silver-gilt casket with royal armorials, *c*. 1303–8. © Trustees of the British Museum.
6. Wedding of Edward and Isabella, illustration in Jean de Wavrin's *Chroniques d'Angleterre*. © British Library Board (Royal Ms. 15.E.iv, f. 295v).
7. Ms. illustration of Edward II seated in majesty, 1308. Courtesy of the Master and Fellows of Corpus Christi College, Cambridge (Ms. 20 f. 68).
8. Edward II holding a sword and a sceptre, Chaworth Roll. Courtesy of Sam Fogg, London.
9a. Sabrina Lenzi as Isabella in David Bintley's ballet *Edward II*. Photograph: Bill Cooper.
9b. Wolfgang Stollwitzer as Edward in David Bintley's ballet *Edward II*. Photograph: Bill Cooper; Birmingham Royal Ballet.
10a, b and c. Miniatures showing Philip IV and Edward II girding Philip's sons with their swords and riding out, preceded by trumpets, from a translation of the *Livre de Kalila et Dimna* by Raymond de Béziers. Bibliothèque Nationale de France, Paris (Ms. Latin 8504, f. 1v).
11. Miniature showing the opening of the sixth vial, Apocalypse Ms. of 1313. Bibliothèque Nationale de France, Paris (Ms. Fr. 13096, f. 50).
12. The Battle of Bannockburn. Courtesy of the Master and Fellows of Corpus Christi College, Cambridge (Ms. 171, f. 265).
13. Execution of Hugh Despenser the Younger, illustration in the Chronicles of Jean Froissart. Bibliothèque Nationale de France, Paris (Ms. Fr. 2643, f. 197).

14. King and queen kneeling, illustration in the Taymouth Hours. © British Library Board (Yates Thompson Ms. 13, f. 18).
15. Illustration from Walter de Milemete, *De nobilitatibus sapientiis et prudentiis regum*, 1326–7. Governing Body of Christ Church, Oxford (Ms. 92, f. 4v).
16. Berkeley castle, Gloucestershire. © Crown Copyright NMR (Wingham Collection).
17. Letter of 24 September 1327 from Edward III at Lincoln to John de Bohun, earl of Hereford, announcing the death of Edward II. The National Archives (DL 10/253).
18. Edward's tomb, Gloucester cathedral. © Angelo Hornak Picture Library.
19. Castle of Melazzo near Acqui Terme, Italy. Author's photograph.
20. Monastery of S. Alberto di Butrio, near Cecima, Italy. Author's photograph.
21. Alleged tomb of Edward II in the monastery of S. Alberto di Butrio, near Cecima, Italy. Author's photograph.
22. Cathédrale Saint-Pierre-de-Maguelone, near Montpellier, France. Photograph © David Merlin.
23. Letter from Manuel Fieschi to Edward III, *c.* 1336–8 containing the alleged confession of Edward II. Archives départementales de l'Hérault, Montpellier, France (G 1123, f. 86r).
24. The 'Oxwich Brooch', early fourteenth-century set gold ring brooch. National Museum of Wales.

Maps

1. England and Scotland in the reign of Edward II.   xvii
2. Ireland at the time of Edward Bruce's invasion (1315–18).   xviii
3. Wales: the Principality and the March.   xix
4. France, the Low Countries, parts of the Rhineland and northwest Italy.   xx

PREFACE & ACKNOWLEDGEMENTS

This book has been a long time in the making. At one level its origins go back to the time when, as a schoolboy visiting the Royal Institution of South Wales in Swansea, I saw a framed document recording the betrothal of the future Edward II and Isabella in 1303 on the wall of the library and wondered how it could possibly have ended up in such an unlikely place. In practice however it stems from my first book, *Aymer de Valence Earl of Pembroke, 1307–1324: Baronial Politics in the Reign of Edward II*, which showed me both the complexity of the reign of Edward II and how much more research was still required to produce a fully rounded treatment of the period. My researches since then have progressed via a lengthy digression into the history of medieval Europe's relations with the outer world and a number of papers on the early fourteenth century, including the biography of Edward II published in the *Oxford DNB* in 2004, and most recently in my contributions to the *Parliament Rolls of Medieval England* (*PROME*) project published in 2005. In writing this volume for the Yale English Monarchs series I have drawn on my own published work and researches, as well as on the published work of many previous scholars such as J.C. Davies, Hilda Johnstone, H.G. Richardson, G.O. Sayles, T.F. Tout and Bertie Wilkinson, and of the numerous other scholars who have been active more recently in the field of late thirteenth- and early fourteenth-century history, notably Michael Altschul, Geoffrey Barrow, Paul Binski, Elizabeth Brown, Mark Buck, the late Pierre Chaplais, Wendy Childs, the late George Cuttino, the late Sir Rees Davies, Jeffrey Denton, Sean Duffy, Archie Duncan, Robin Frame, the late Edmund Fryde, Natalie Fryde, Chris Given-Wilson, Antonia Gransden, Roy Haines, Elizabeth Hallam, Jeffrey Hamilton, Gerald Harriss, the late Geoffrey Holmes, Michael Jones, Richard Kaeuper, Maurice Keen, Colm McNamee, John Maddicott, Ian Mortimer, Mark Ormrod, Edward Peters, Michael Prestwich, Nigel Saul, Beverley Smith, the late Lionel Stones, Matthew Strickland, John Taylor, Malcolm Vale, Claire Valente and Scott Waugh. I have also made use of unpublished work, in particular the outstanding D.Phil. thesis by Paul Doherty on the life and career of Isabella, Edward II's wife and queen; the Ph.D. theses by Arthur Echerd Jr on the cult of 'St' Thomas of Lancaster, and Alistair Tebbit on Edward II's household knights; and two papers on English coronations by John Carmi Parsons. I should also like to thank the many scholars who have helped me with information or offered encouragement, notably my fellow editors on the *PROME* project; James Lydon and the late F.X. Martin, o.s.a., who encouraged my interest in Anglo-Irish relations; Brenda Bolton, the late Leonard Boyle, O.P., John Henderson and Eileen Kane who helped me in my quest for the lost book of Edward II's miracles; Paul Brand, Boyd Breslow, the late Pierre Chaplais, Martin Cunningham, Gwilym Dodd, Paul Drybugh, John Gillingham, Jeffrey Hamilton, Jill Hughes, Donald Logan, Mark Ormrod, Guilhem Pépin, Richard Pfaff, Michael Prestwich, Brendan Smith, Shelagh Sneddon, Alistair Tebbit and Bernadette Williams. David Smith, the former county archivist of Gloucestershire and archivist for Berkeley Castle, and Lowinger Maddison, the librarian of Gloucester Cathedral, gave me invaluable help during my researches in Gloucester and at Berkeley. I am also greatly indebted to the staff of the former Public Record Office in Chancery Lane and The National Archives at Kew; the British Library and Bodleian Library; the Archivio Segreto Vaticano and Biblioteca Apostolica Vaticana in Rome; the Archives Nationales and Bibliothèque Nationale in Paris; and the Archives départementales de l'Hérault, Montpellier; and to the staff of the library at University College Dublin, especially in the inter-library loans department, whose help was invaluable and sometimes crucial.

I was also greatly assisted by the award of a Fellowship at the National Humanities Center, North Carolina, in 1987–8, and a President's Fellowship from University College Dublin in 2000–1, which enabled me to plan my research and to begin writing; by British Academy-Royal Irish Academy Exchange Fellowships in 1984 and 1998, which allowed me to undertake research in London and in Gloucester and Berkeley Castle; by grants at an early stage from the British Academy and the Isobel Thornley Bequest which enabled me to gather material on microfilm; and by travel grants from the former Faculty of Arts in University Dublin in 1997 and 1999 which facilitated research in France and in Italy. I should also like to thank Carolyn Heighway for sending me the report on the recent refurbishment of the tomb of Edward II in Gloucester Cathedral, and Canon Celia Thomson for inviting me to give a lecture in the cathedral in September 2008 to mark the completion of the refurbishment.

My former colleagues and students in the Combined Departments of History (now the School of History and Archives) at University College Dublin offered support and encouragement over many years, even when they must have got tired of hearing me talk about Edward II. I should also like to thank Robert Baldock, my editor at Yale University Press, for his encouragement and for his patience while I was writing this book. The long wait for my biography of Edward II has I hope been less of a burden to him than the fate suffered by his namesake, Robert Baldock archdeacon of Middlesex and Edward II's last chancellor, who died weighed down by chains in prison in 1327. Elizabeth Bourgoin, Candida Brazil, Sarah

Faulkner, Rachael Lonsdale and their colleagues have also shown great patience and skill in piloting a very long text through the press. The reader for Yale University Press also made valuable suggestions and saved me from a number of errors. Those that remain are of course entirely my responsibility.

Above all I owe my heartfelt thanks to my wife Nuala and to my son Eoin and daughter Catherine who kept me going at times when it must have seemed as if the book would never be completed. The finished work is appropriately dedicated to them.

Monkstown, County Dublin

ABBREVIATED REFERENCES

The following abbreviations for frequently cited publications are used in the footnotes. The complete title is given for the first reference and short titles are used thereafter. The full details are given in the bibliography.

All manuscript references are to documents preserved in The National Archives (TNA), Kew, unless otherwise stated.

AN: Archives Nationales, Paris.
Ann. Lond.: *Annales Londonienses*, in *Chronicles of the Reigns of Edward I and Edward II*, i, ed. W. Stubbs (London, 1882).
Ann. Paul.: *Annales Paulini*, in *Chronicles of the Reigns of Edward I and Edward II*, i, ed. W. Stubbs (London, 1882).
Anonimalle: *Anonimalle Chronicle 1307 to 1334*, ed. W.R. Childs & J. Taylor, Yorkshire Archaeological Society, Record Series, cxlvii, for the year 1987 (Leeds, 1991).
ASV: Archivio Segreto Vaticano.
Barrow: Barrow, G.W.S., *Robert Bruce and the Community of the Realm of Scotland*. Unless stated otherwise, the edition cited is the 3rd edn (Edinburgh, 1988).
BIHR: *Bulletin of the Institute of Historical Research*.
BL: British Library.
Blaneford: *Johannis de Trokelowe et Henrici de Blaneforde, Chronica et Annales*, ed. H.T. Riley, Rolls Series (London, 1866).
BN: Bibliothèque Nationale, Paris.
Brown & Regalado: Brown, E.A.R & Regalado, N.F., 'La Grant feste: Philip the Fair's celebration of the knighting of his sons in Paris at Pentecost of 1313', in *City and Spectacle in Medieval Europe*, ed. B.A. Hanawalt & K.L. Reyerson (Minneapolis, 1994).
Bruce: *The Bruce*, ed. A.A.M. Duncan (Edinburgh, 1997). Unless stated otherwise, this edition is the one cited.
Brut: *The Brut*, ed. F.W.D. Brie, Early English Text Society, cxxxi, part i (London, 1906).
Buck: Buck, M., *Politics, Finance and the Church in the Reign of Edward II: Walter Stapeldon Treasurer of England*, Cambridge Studies in Medieval Life and Thought, 3rd ser., xix (Cambridge, 1983).
CCCC: Corpus Christi College, Cambridge.
CChR: *Calendar of Charter Rolls* (1903—)

CCR: *Calendar of Close Rolls* (1892—)
CCW: *Calendar of Chancery Warrants, 1244–1326* (London, 1927).
CDI: *Calendar of Documents relating to Ireland*, iv, *1292–1301*, ed. H.S. Sweetman (London & Dublin, 1881).
CDS: *Calendar of Documents relating to Scotland*, ii, iii, iv, ed. J. Bain (Edinburgh, 1884–7); v, ed. G.G. Simpson & J.D. Galbraith (Edinburgh, 1986).
CFR: *Calendar of Fine Rolls* (1911—)
Chaplais: Chaplais, P., *Piers Gaveston: Edward II's Adoptive Brother* (Oxford, 1994)
Chroniques de Sempringham: *Chroniques de Sempringham: Livere des Reis de Britannie*, ed. J. Glover, Rolls Series (London, 1865).
CIM: *Calendar of Inquisitions, Miscellaneous* (1916—).
CIPM: *Calendar of Inquisitions Post Mortem* (1898—)
CMR, 1326–27: *Calendar of Memoranda Rolls (Exchequer), Michaelmas 1326–Michaelmas 1327*, ed. R.A. Latham (London, 1968).
CPL: *Calendar of Papal Letters, 1305–42*, ed. W.H. Bliss (London, 1895).
CPMR: *Calendar of the Plea and Memoranda Rolls of the City of London, 1324–1457*, ed. A.H. Thomas, i (London, 1926).
CPR: *Calendar of Patent Rolls* (1891—)
Doherty (D.Phil.): Doherty, P.C., 'Isabella, Queen of England, 1296–1330' (D.Phil., Oxford, 1977).
EHR: *English Historical Review*.
English Historical Documents: *English Historical Documents, 1184–1327*, ed. H. Rothwell (London, 1975).
Flores: *Flores Historiarum*, iii, ed. H.R. Luard, Rolls Series (London, 1890).
Foedera: *Foedera, Conventiones, Litterae et Acta Publica*, ed. T. Rymer, Record Commission edition, vols I, II (London, 1816–20).
French Chron.: *French Chronicle of London*, ed. G.J. Aungier, Camden Society, xxviii (London, 1844).
Froissart: Jean Froissart, *Oeuvres de Froissart*, ed. K. de Lettenhove, ii (Brussels, 1867).
Fryde: N. Fryde, *The Tyranny and Fall of Edward II, 1321–1326* (Cambridge, 1979).
Gesta Edwardi: *Gesta Edwardi de Carnarvon Auctore Canonico Bridlingtoniensi*, in *Chronicles of the Reigns of Edward I and Edward II*, ii, ed. W. Stubbs, Rolls Series (London, 1883).
GR: *Gascon Rolls, 1307–1317*, ed. Y. Renouard (London, 1962).
Gransden: Gransden, A., *Historical Writing in England*, i, *c.550–c.1307*; ii, *c.1307 to the Early Sixteenth Century* (London, 1974; 1982).
Guisborough: *Chronicle of Walter of Guisborough*, ed. H. Rothwell, Camden, 3rd series, lxxix (London, 1989).
Hamilton: Hamilton, J.S., *Piers Gaveston: Earl of Cornwall, 1307–1312: Politics and Patronage in the Reign of Edward II* (Detroit & London, 1988).
Harriss: Harriss, G.L., *King, Parliament and Public Finance in England to 1369* (Oxford, 1975).

Historia Anglicana: Thomas Walsingham, *Historia Anglicana*, ed. H.T. Riley, Rolls Series, i (London, 1863).
HMC: *Historical Manuscripts Commission*.
IHS: *Irish Historical Studies*.
Johnstone: Johnstone, H., *Edward of Carnarvon, 1284–1307* (Manchester, 1946).
Knighton: *Chronicon Henrici Knighton*, i, ed., J.R. Lumby, Rolls Series (London, 1889).
KW: Brown, R.A., Colvin, H.M. & Taylor, A.J., *The History of the King's Works*, i, ii, *The Middle Ages* (London, 1963).
Lanercost: *Chronicon de Lanercost*, ed. J. Stevenson, Maitland Club (Edinburgh, 1839).
Lay Taxes: Jurkowski, M., Smith, C.L. & Crook, D., *Lay Taxes in England and Wales, 1186–1688*, Public Record Office Handbook no. 31 (London, 1998).
Le Baker: *Chronicon Galfridi le Baker de Swynebroke*, ed. E.M. Thompson (Oxford, 1889).
Le Bel: Jean le Bel, *Chronique de Jean le Bel*, ed. J. Viard & E. Deprez, i, Société de l'Histoire de France (Paris, 1904).
McNamee: McNamee, C., *The Wars of the Bruces: Scotland, England and Ireland, 1306–1328* (East Linton, 1997).
Maddicott: Maddicott, J.R., *Thomas of Lancaster, 1307–1322: A Study in the Reign of Edward II* (Oxford, 1970).
Melsa: *Chronica Monasterii de Melsa*, ii, ed. E.A. Bond, Rolls Series (London, 1867).
Murimuth: *Adæ Murimuth Continuatio Chronicarumi*, ed. E.M. Thompson (London, 1889).
NHI: ed. A. Cosgrove, ed., *A New History of Ireland*, ii, *Medieval Ireland, 1169–1534* (Oxford, 1987).
Oxford DNB: *Oxford Dictionary of National Biography* (printed and online editions, Oxford, 2004).
Parliamentary Texts: *Parliamentary Texts of the Later Middle Ages*, ed. N. Pronay & J. Taylor (Oxford, 1980).
Phillips: Phillips, J.R.S., *Aymer de Valence, Earl of Pembroke, 1307–24: Baronial Politics in the Reign of Edward II* (Oxford, 1972).
Polychronicon: *Polychronicon Ranulphi Higden*, viii, ed. J.R. Lumby, Rolls Series (London, 1882).
PROME: *Parliament Rolls of Medieval England, 1275–1504*, general editor C. Given-Wilson, digital edition (CD-ROM and online), Scholarly Digital Editions & The National Archives (Leicester, 2005). Printed edition in 16 vols (Woodbridge, Suffolk & Rochester, NY, 2005).
PW: *Parliamentary Writs and Writs of Military Summons, Edward I and Edward II*, ed. F. Palgrave, Record Commission (London, 1827–34).
RDP: *Reports from the Lords' Committees touching the Dignity of a Peer of the Realm*, iii, (London, 1820–29).

Regesta Regum Scottorum: *Regesta Regum Scottorum*, v, *The Acts of Robert I*, ed. A.A.M. Duncan (Edinburgh, 1988).
RP: *Rotuli Parliamentorum*, i, ii, ed. J. Strachey et al. (London, 1767).
Saint-Sardos: *The War of Saint-Sardos (1323–25): Gascon Correspondence and Diplomatic Documents*, ed. P. Chaplais, Camden, 3rd ser., lxxxvii (London, 1954).
SAL: Society of Antiquaries of London.
Scalacronica: Sir Thomas Gray, *Scalacronica, 1272–1363*, ed. and trans. A. King, Surtees Society, ccix (Woodbridge, Suffolk, & Rochester, NY, 2005). Unless stated otherwise, this edition is the one cited.
Scotichronicon: *Scotichronicon by Walter Bower*, vi, viii, ed. D.E.R. Watt (Aberdeen, 1991, 1987).
Select Documents: *Select Documents of English Constitutional History, 1307–1485*, ed. S.B. Chrimes & A.L. Brown (London, 1961).
SHR: *Scottish Historical Review*.
SR: *Statutes of the Realm*, i, ed. A. Luders et al. (Record Commission, London, 1810).
TRHS: *Transactions of the Royal Historical Society*.
Trivet (Cont.): *Nicolai Triveti Annalium Continuatio*, ed. A. Hall (Oxford, 1722).
Trokelowe: *Johannis de Trokelowe et Henrici de Blaneforde, Chronica et Annales*, ed. H.T. Riley, Rolls Series (London, 1866).
Vale: Vale, M., *The Angevin Legacy and the Hundred Years War, 1250–1340* (Oxford, 1990).
VCH: *Victoria County History*.
Vita: *Vita Edwardi Secundi*, ed. W.R. Childs (Oxford, 2005). Unless stated otherwise, this edition is the one cited and not the older edition, ed. N. Denholm-Young (London, 1957).
Vita et Mors: *Vita et Mors Edwardi Secundi*, in *Chronicles of the Reigns of Edward I and Edward II*, ii, ed. W. Stubbs, Rolls Series (London, 1883).

Map 1 England and Scotland in the reign of Edward II.

Map 2 Ireland at the time of Edward Bruce's invasion (1315–18).

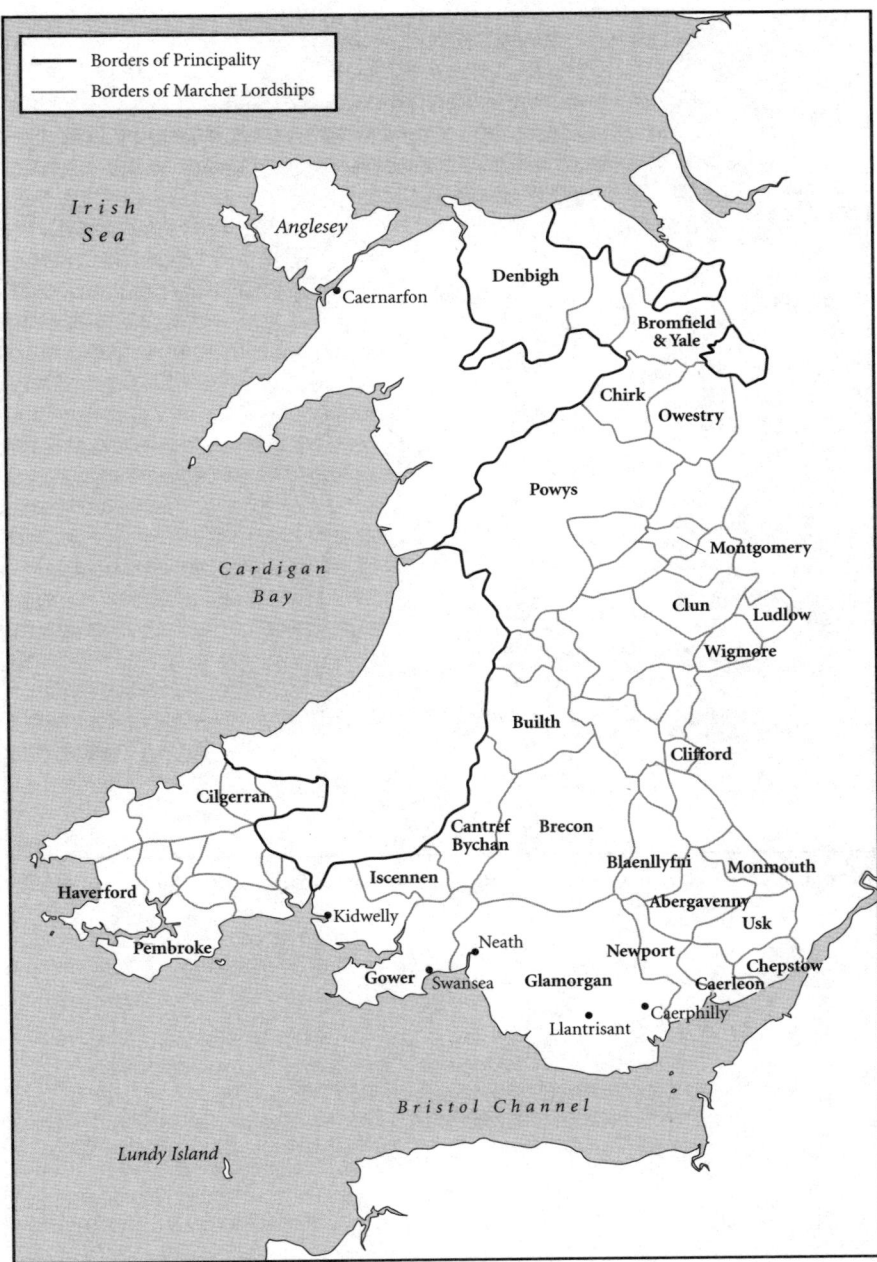

Map 3 Wales: the Principality and the March.

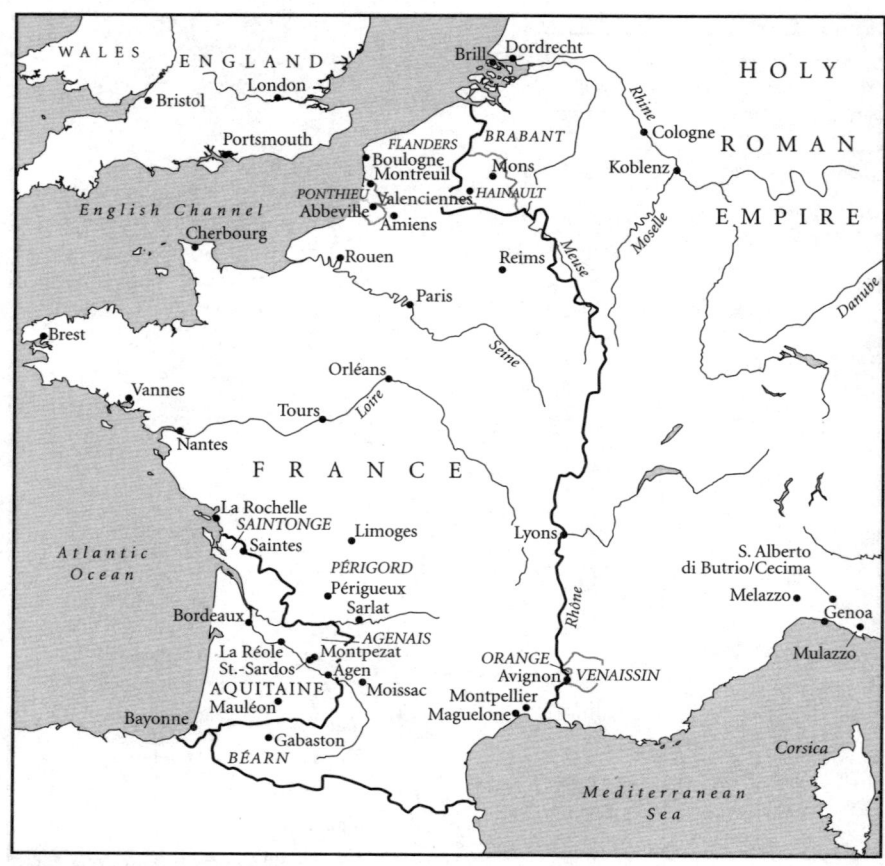

Map 4 France, the Low Countries, parts of the Rhineland and northwest Italy.

INTRODUCTION

To all outward appearances Edward II was a founder member of that select band of rulers who seem to have been doomed to disaster and to ignominy almost from the moment of their birth; about whom little that was good was said in their lifetime, and little to their credit has been written since. Lacking even the aura of incarnate evil that has traditionally been attributed to John and to Richard III, Edward II is depicted as worthless, incapable of any sustained policy, and influencing events only by sporadic displays of ill-directed energy or by a stubborn adherence to greedy and ambitious favourites. He is seemingly the *locus classicus* of the *rex inutilis* discussed by such diverse authorities as canon lawyers and the writers of Arthurian romances, who was fit only to be deposed and replaced by someone more worthy of the throne.[1]

While kings can normally be expected to die and be buried in readily confirmed circumstances, even the fact of Edward's death in 1327 is open to challenge: rumours circulated that he had escaped from his prison cell and led a life as a wanderer and ultimately as a hermit in a remote Italian castle.[2] Edward II thus had an 'afterlife' which makes an assessment of him even more complicated. These ambiguities are somehow typical of Edward and his reign. Edward II was a man who did not fit neatly into the traditional and acceptable categories of medieval monarch: the great warrior, the lawgiver, or the man of God. Some of his personal tastes and behaviour were not what was expected of a king. In consequence he was misunderstood in his own day and has been maligned ever since, his only real value being to demonstrate to his successors the awful consequences of relying on favourites and of falling out with their leading subjects.

---

[1] See E. Peters, *The Shadow King* (New Haven & London, 1970), esp. chs 3, 5; and idem, 'Henry II of Cyprus, "*Rex inutilis*"', *Speculum*, lxxii (1997), esp. 769–74.

Had Edward II ruled a generation earlier he might have joined his grandfather Henry III in Dante's gallery of negligent rulers: Dante, *The Divine Comedy: Purgatory*, canto VII, trans. D.L. Sayers (London, 1949), where, ironically, Henry III is described as having a better issue among his branches. See also E. Peters, 'I Principi negligenti di Dante e le concezioni medievali del *Rex Inutilis*', *Rivista Storica Italiana*, lxxx (1968), 741–58.

[2] I believe that Edward II did indeed die and was buried in 1327 but for an examination of the controversies surrounding his afterlife see ' "Edward II" in Italy', in *Thirteenth Century England*, x, ed. M. Prestwich, R. Britnall & R. Frame (Woodbridge, Suffolk & Rochester, NY, 2005), 209–26; and see below, Chapter 12.

Edward II was not however alone among medieval rulers in attracting abuse. In his *Divine Comedy* the poet Dante depicted Pope Nicholas III (1277–80) head down in a pit in the eighth circle of hell reserved for those guilty of simony, the buying and selling of ecclesiastical offices, and with flames playing on the soles of his feet. But Nicholas was, so to speak, keeping the spot warm only until the time when his place would be taken by Dante's contemporary and *bête noire*, Pope Boniface VIII (1294–1303).[3] Boniface was also to be accused in 1303 by King Philip IV of France of a multitude of offences, ranging from heresy to sodomy, idolatry, murder, and other crimes.[4] In 1320 a French friar, Brother Pierre Girovart, prior of St Géréon in Nantes, said that the reigning pope John XXII (1316–34) was melancholic, frenetic and mad (*melanconicus, freneticus seu furiosus*), that he did not know what he was doing, and that he would no more obey this pope than he would an ass.[5] Kings also came in for their share of attacks. In the late 1270s, for example, Philip III of France was charged with committing unnatural sexual acts by a canon of Laon and two holy women of Liège, while in a separate scandal his second wife Marie de Brabant was accused of killing her two stepsons by poison.[6] In 1301 Philip IV, Philip III's son and successor and later to become the father-in-law of Edward II, was allegedly described by Bernard Saisset, the bishop of Pamiers in southern France, as 'neither man nor beast, but only image'; and, he added 'he did nothing but gaze at men'. The bishop then gave further offence 'by comparing Philip to the large, handsome, and worthless owl, who does not respond but simply passes air'.[7] By comparison the remarks of the Florentine chronicler Giovanni Villani, written after Philip's death in 1314, are no more than modest criticisms, for he said that, although Philip devoted himself to his pleasures – chiefly those of the hunt – neglected the work of government, leaving it to others, and was badly advised, he was 'a wise and good man, for a layman'.[8] Even Edward II's father, Edward I, who was eulogized after his death in 1307 and who is still generally regarded as one of the most successful of the medieval kings of England, was abused on occasion. In 1294 one Irish magnate Sir William de Vescy is said to have told another, Sir John Fitz Thomas, that 'the people of Ireland were the most miserable he knew ... If they

---

[3] Dante, *The Divine Comedy: Hell*, canto XIX. An illustration of Nicholas III's predicament, taken from a fifteenth-century Sienese manuscript of the *Divine Comedy*, is reproduced in G. Barraclough, *The Medieval Papacy* (London, 1968), 137.

[4] B. Tierney, *The Crisis of Church and State, 1050–1300* (New York, 1964; repr. Toronto, 1988), 190.

[5] *Additiones agli 'Instrumenta Miscellanea' dell'Archivio Segreto Vaticano (7945–8802)*, Collectanea AV, 57, ed. S. Pagano (Vatican City, 2005), 7–8 (no. 7952).

[6] E.A.R. Brown, 'The prince is father of the king', *Mediaeval Studies*, xlix (Toronto, 1987), 325–6.

[7] E.A.R. Brown, 'The case of Philip the Fair', in *Persona et Gesta*, *Viator*, xix (Berkeley & Los Angeles, 1988), 228; A. Brachet, *Pathologie mentale des Rois de France* (Paris, 1903), 444.

[8] Cited in J. Calmette, *Textes et documents d'histoire*, ii, *Moyen Age*, 2nd edn (Paris, 1953), 166.

knew as much about the King as he knew, they would value the King very little, for he is the most perverse and dastardly knight of his kingdom';[9] and in 1297 a London goldsmith, John Pater Noster, was drinking in a local tavern when a certain William of Gloucester 'despised the king' and said that he wished the king's head was on a nearby spike alongside that of the Welsh rebel, Llywelyn.[10] One of Edward I's chief ministers, his treasurer, Walter Langton bishop of Coventry and Lichfield, who fell from office spectacularly as soon as his master and protector was dead, was accused of murder, adultery, simony, pluralism, and intercourse with the devil.[11]

In most if not all of these statements, on the other hand, the loud grinding of axes can be heard in the background. The poet Dante, for example, was caught up in the politics of his native Florence and in the continuing battles between empire and papacy, and so was hardly an impartial observer;[12] the French friar Pierre Girovart was probably a member of the spiritual wing of the Franciscan order which was then involved in a desperate battle of its own with the papacy;[13] William de Vescy was engaged in a bitter dispute with John Fitz Thomas which almost ended in a trial by battle before the king;[14] Walter Langton was certainly guilty of many things but devil worship was not one of them.[15] To take one's sources at face value, especially when they are dramatic and lend themselves to easy quotation, can often therefore be highly misleading.

The same is true of Edward II. Just as everybody 'knows', for example, that he was homosexual and that he was cruelly put to death in Berkeley castle in 1327 by a red-hot iron inserted into his bowels,[16] in reality neither statement can be confirmed by clear and unambiguous evidence. Edward's reputation, especially at the time of his deposition and in the

---

[9] *CDI*, iv, *1292–1301*, 71.

[10] *CCW*, 76. The Welshman in question was probably Madoc ap Llywelyn who had rebelled in 1294–5.

[11] T.F. Tout, *The Place of the Reign of Edward II in English History* (Manchester, 1914; 2nd edn, revised by H. Johnstone, 1936), 13–14.

[12] See P. Partner, 'Florence and the papacy, 1300–1370', in *Europe in the Late Middle Ages*, ed. J. Hale, R. Highfield & B. Smalley (London, 1965), 76–121.

[13] See M.D. Lambert, *Franciscan Poverty* (2nd edn, Oxford, 1998).

[14] De Vescy's remarks referred to Edward I's alleged cowardice shortly before the battle of Evesham in 1265, at the end of the civil war in the reign of Henry III: CDI, IV, nos 62–4; M. Prestwich, *Edward I*, 353–4.

[15] On Langton and his career see A. Beardwood, 'The trial of Walter Langton, bishop of Lichfield, 1307–1312', *Trans. American Philosophical Society*, new ser., liv, part 3 (Philadelphia, 1964), 1–45.

[16] The report of the excavation of the remains of the Rosary, a former royal house on the south bank of the River Thames in the *News and Observer*, Raleigh, North Carolina, on Sunday, 22 May 1988, which I read while a Fellow at the nearby National Humanities Center, says it all: 'Archaeologists have unearthed the fourteenth-century remains of King Edward II's palace where he relaxed with his homosexual lover before being deposed by his wife and murdered, as tradition has it, with a red-hot poker.' The Rosary was not however built until 1324–5, long after Gaveston's death: *KW*, i, 508, n. 10.

years after his death, was to some degree a manufactured one, influenced by the extremes of hostility on the one hand and of sympathy on the other. There were a few who stayed loyal to him after his fall and who tried repeatedly to free him from captivity, while there were others, including his great-grandson Richard II, who saw him as a figure worthy of veneration and even of canonization.

This book is not an attempt to present Edward II as a heroic or successful king: the mere fact of his deposition after a turbulent reign of nearly twenty years is proof enough that something went terribly wrong. But it is an attempt to rehabilitate him to some degree. The more one looks at the multitude of available sources for the reign the more apparent it becomes that the traditional view of Edward II needs to be qualified and a more complex picture presented, in line with the complexity of events and of the man himself. If Edward II was not a successful king, neither was he a nullity; in many respects he was not fundamentally different from most of his predecessors and successors on the English throne.[17]

Somewhere a balance has to be struck between the extremes of the calamitous and incompetent Edward II on the one hand and the holy man on the other. What follows is an attempt to achieve such a balance.

---

[17] See J.R.S. Phillips, 'The Place of the Reign of Edward II', in *The Reign of Edward II*, ed. G. Dodd & A. Musson (Woodbridge, Suffolk & Rochester, NY, 2006), 220–33; and the Conclusion to this book.

Chapter 1

THE REPUTATION OF A KING

The general opinion of Edward II from his own day to the present has been that he was a failure: as a king he was incompetent and neglectful of his duties, leaving the business of government to ill-chosen and self-serving councillors; and as a man he had a fatal ability to create enemies through his attachment to favourites, through his hostility to the English magnates, and finally through his alienation of Isabella, his wife and queen. Even the weather appeared to conspire against him. The combination of these failings was to prove disastrous to the peace and stability of his kingdom and ultimately fatal to Edward II himself. With the significant exception of Geoffrey le Baker's *Chronicon*, the contemporary and near-contemporary chronicles were usually critical of him, when they were not openly hostile.[1]

COMPARISONS OF EDWARD I AND EDWARD II

Part of Edward II's problem both with his contemporaries and with posterity was the very fact that he succeeded a powerful and, by contemporary standards, highly successful king. The *Commendatio Lamentabilis*, a lengthy eulogy of Edward I composed by John of London at the time of Edward's funeral in 1307, claimed that 'Once with Alexander, king of Macedon, we defeated the kings of the Medes and the Persians and subdued the provinces of the East. Now, at the end of time, with great King Edward, we have borne a ten-year war with Philip, famous king of France; we have won back Gascony, taken by guile, with force of arms; we have got Wales by slaughter; we have invaded Scotland and cut down her tyrants at the point of the sword.'[2] Edward I's powerful treasurer, Walter

---

[1] For a discussion of the value and the authorship of the chronicles of the reign of Edward II see Gransden, ii, esp. ch. 1, 'Chroniclers of the reign of Edward II', but also chs 2, 3, 4, *passim*. There is also some material in Gransden, i, esp. ch. 19, 'Chronicles in the reign of Edward I', and chs 20, 21, *passim*. Two other very valuable studies of historical writing are J. Taylor, *English Historical Literature in the Fourteenth Century* (Oxford, 1987), and C. Given-Wilson, *Chronicles* (London & New York, 2004).
[2] B. Smalley, *English Friars and Antiquity in the Early Fourteenth Century* (Oxford, 1960), 9, 14 (trans. is from her ch. 1, 'The English public'); for full Latin text of the *Commendatio* see *Chronicles of the Reigns of Edward I and Edward II*, ed. W. Stubbs, ii, Rolls ser. (London, 1883),

Langton, bishop of Coventry & Lichfield, with whom the future Edward II quarrelled bitterly in 1305 and who was to be dismissed and put on trial for peculation early in the new reign, had scenes from the life and campaigns of his royal patron painted on the walls of his magnificent new episcopal palace, which was itself designed as a smaller version of Caernarfon castle.[3] Whoever followed Edward I on the English throne would be hard put to match the glowing opinions of his predecessor, all the more so since they conveniently glossed over the many problems Edward I had bequeathed to his son. To take but two: although a peace treaty was made with France in 1303 by which the duchy of Aquitaine was formally restored to English control, England and France had really fought one another to a standstill, while in 1307 Edward I was still far from achieving his ambition to conquer the Scots.[4]

Edward II also suffered because he was so different in character from both his more readily understood and infinitely more successful father and his own son and successor, Edward III. As the fourteenth-century chronicler, Jean le Bel of Liège, an admirer of the English crown who had first-hand knowledge of England and who wrote after the victories of Edward III, was to remark, 'it was commonly believed in England, and had often happened since the time of King Arthur, that a less able king would often come

---

3–21. See also B. Weiler, 'The *Commendatio Lamentabilis* for Edward I and Plantagenet kingship', in *War, Government and Aristocracy in the British Isles, c. 1150–1500*, ed. C. Given-Wilson, A. Kettle & L. Scales (Woodbridge, Suffolk & Rochester, NY, 2008), 114–30; the Anglo-Norman 'Lament on the Death of Edward I' and the closely related English poem 'Elegy on the Death of Edward I' in *The Political Songs of England from the Reign of John to that of Edward II*, ed. T. Wright, Camden Soc. (London, 1839), 241–50 (Royal Historical Society edn with an introduction by Peter Coss, (Cambridge, 1996)).

The unidentified author of the legal treatise known as *Fleta*, which was written in the early 1290s, remarked: 'How finely, how actively, how skilfully in time of hostilities our most worthy king Edward has waged armed war against the malice of his enemies there is none to doubt, for now his praise has gone forth to all the world and his mighty works to every border thereof, and marvellously have his words resounded far and wide to the ends of the earth': prologue of *Fleta*, ed. H.G. Richardson & G.O. Sayles, Selden Soc., lxii, 1953 (London, 1955).

Similar praise was expressed between 1305 and 1307 by the French crusading propagandist Pierre Dubois when he dedicated his *De Recuperatione Terrae Sanctae* to 'the illustrious and most Christian prince Edward, by the grace of God king of England and Scotland, lord of Ireland and duke of Aquitaine, renowned more for his military prowess than for all his titles': P. Dubois, *The Recovery of the Holy Land*, ed. W. I. Brandt (New York, 1956), 70.

[3] Smalley, 11, citing J. Evans, *English Art, 1307–1461* (Oxford, 1949), 116, and T. Harwood, *The History and Antiquities of the Church and City of Lichfield* (Gloucester, 1806), 288–9. The scenes were painted after the death of Edward I, which would make the contrast between the two reigns even more pointed: Evans, 116; *KW*, i, 508, citing S. Erdeswick, *Survey of Staffordshire*, ed. T. Harwood (1844), 281; J. B. Hughes, 'Walter Langton, bishop of Coventry and Lichfield, 1296–1321, and his register', *Staffordshire Studies*, ix (1997), 7.

[4] On the Anglo-French war of 1294–1303 and its consequences see M. Vale, *The Angevin Legacy and the Hundred Years War, 1250–1340* (Oxford, 1990), 224–8. On Scotland see M. Prestwich, *Edward I* (2nd edn, London & New Haven, 1997), ch. 18, 'The Scottish wars, 1296–1307'.

between two valiant monarchs'.⁵ Thus Edward I, who was wise, a man of prowess, bold and enterprising and fortunate in war, who conquered the Scots three or four times, was succeeded by Edward II, who did not resemble him either in wisdom or in prowess, who governed savagely and with the advice of others, and who was defeated with all his barons by King Robert of Scotland at the battle of Bannockburn.⁶ Another factor was that, unlike France, where the *Grandes Chroniques*, for example, provided a carefully structured and lavishly illustrated account of French history which was intended to reflect and to embellish the glory of the monarchy,⁷ there was no tradition in early fourteenth-century England of official history writing. The nearest to such a work in Edward II's time was the continuation down to the year 1306 by a monk at Westminster of Matthew Paris's St Alban's chronicle, the *Flores Historiarum*. This praised Edward I and was possibly intended for presentation to Edward II at his coronation in 1308.⁸ In contrast, Edward II's father-in-law, Philip IV of France, went to great lengths during his reign to present himself to his subjects and the world at large through images of majesty and power.⁹ Edward II was certainly very conscious of his royal dignity, but there is nothing comparable to this systematic use of propaganda during his own reign.

EDWARD II AND WESTMINSTER ABBEY

Despite the fact that Westminster Abbey 'in some respects stood in a relation to the English kings similar to that of St. Denis to the French ones', since 'its patron was the king, it was the scene of coronations, a royal mausoleum, and situated close to the scene of government',¹⁰ it was not to

---

⁵ Le Bel, *Chronique de Jean Le Bel*, ed. J. Viard & E. Deprez, i (Paris, 1904), 4.

⁶ Le Bel, 4–6: my paraphrase of the text.

⁷ See the important study by A. D. Hederman, *The Royal Image* (Berkeley, 1991).

⁸ A. Gransden, 'The uses made of history by the kings of medieval England', in *Collection de l'Ecole française de Rome*, lxxxii (Rome, 1985), 469; Gransden, 'The continuation of the *Flores Historiarum* from 1265 to 1327', in *Legends, Traditions and History in Medieval England* (London, 1992); A. Hollaender, 'The pictorial work in the "Flores Historiarum" of the so-called Matthew of Westminster', *Bulletin of the John Rylands Library*, xxviii (Manchester, 1944), 377 and plate 6.b (a representation of Edward II at his coronation). The author of the continuation of the *Flores* may have been the John of London (possibly to be identified with the Westminster monk John Bever) who also wrote the *Commendatio Lamentabilis* on the death of Edward I: Gransden, i, 457, 459–60. John Taylor suggests that the continuation may actually have been commissioned by Edward II: *English Historical Literature*, 79.

⁹ E.A.R. Brown, 'The case of Philip the Fair', in *Persona et Gesta*, *Viator*, xix (Berkeley & Los Angeles, 1988), 222–30. See also M. Barber, 'The world picture of Philip the Fair', *Journal of Medieval History*, viii, no. 1 (Amsterdam, March 1982), 13–27.

¹⁰ Gransden, 'The uses made of history', 469. The role played in the affairs of the English monarchy by Westminster Abbey was even greater than that played by Saint Denis in France, since in the latter case coronations took place at the cathedral of Reims. Cf. D.M. Palliser, 'Royal mausolea in the long fourteenth century (1272–1422)', in *Fourteenth-century England*, iii, ed. W.M. Ormrod (Woodbridge Suffolk & Rochester, NY, 2004), 1–8.

be the source of historical writing favourable to the crown. This is all the more remarkable given the attention lavished on the abbey church and on the shrine of the royal saint, Edward the Confessor, by the crown from the reign of Henry III onwards.[11]

Even before the accession of Edward II the monks of Westminster were already in bad odour with the crown because of their complicity in the theft in 1303 of the royal treasure stored in the abbey.[12] Edward II's own bad personal relations with them began in January 1308, a month before his coronation in the abbey, with his intervention in the bitterly contested election of a new abbot, and were to be reflected later in his retention of the manor of Eye, covering the area of the modern Pimlico and Mayfair, from 1316 until the end of his reign, and in his occupation and retention in 1320 of a cottage and large garden within the precincts known as 'Burgoyne'.[13] More seriously for his posthumous reputation, they were also reflected in the further continuation, from 1306 to 1327, of the *Flores Historiarum* by the Westminster monk, Robert of Reading, who probably wrote to justify the seizure of power by Isabella and Mortimer in 1326 and was unsparing in his vilification of Edward II, accusing him of being paralyzed by sloth, of cowardice in battle, of failing to keep his word, of rapacity and avarice, and of stupidity and tyranny.[14] When describing Isabella's mission to France in 1325, for example, Robert denounced Edward's cruelty to his queen: 'Oh! The insane stupidity of the king of the English, condemned by God and men, who should not love his own infamy and illicit bed, full of sin, and should never have removed from his side his noble consort and her gentle wifely embraces, in contempt of her noble birth.'[15] On another occasion the author poured scorn on the fact that in early September 1315 Edward II was nearly drowned when a boat overturned while he was rowing in Cambridgeshire, to which he had gone with 'a great company of simple people'.[16] In describing the great wind,

---

[11] See esp. P. Binski, *Westminster Abbey and the Plantagenets* (New Haven & London, 1995).

[12] See P. Doherty, *The Great Crown Jewels Robbery of 1303* (London, 2005).

[13] J.R. Maddicott, *Thomas of Lancaster, 1307–1322* (Oxford, 1970), 85–6; Gransden, ii, 18 and n. 88. The source of this information is *Flores*, iii, ed. H.R. Luard, Rolls ser. (London, 1890) 191, which, as indicated below, is not favourable to Edward II. For further details of Burgoyne and its location see *KW*, ii, 508.

[14] See Gransden, ii, 17–20, 22, citing *Flores*, 192–3, 201, 210, 214, 218, 221–2, 228.

[15] *Flores*, 229; trans. from Gransden, 21.

The continuation of the *Flores* was not the only chronicle written in the capital city and its vicinity. Other important examples (which are also influenced by the *Flores*) are the *Annales Londonienses* (1301–16), usually attributed to Andrew Horn an alderman and chamberlain of London from c. 1320–28; the *Annales Paulini* (1306–41), written at St Paul's by an unidentified author or authors; and the *Continuatio Chronicarum* (1303–47) by Adam Murimuth, a canon of St Paul's: see discussion in Gransden, ibid., 23–31.

[16] *Flores*, 173: cited in H. Johnstone, *Edward of Carnarvon, 1284–1307* (Manchester, 1946), 130. The author makes it appear that Edward was behaving irresponsibly when he should have been preparing for the parliament that was to be held at Lincoln. In fact Edward had just come from an important meeting with the leading magnates at Lincoln at which they

accompanied by sudden darkness and a water-spout, which struck the manor of Cowick in Yorkshire in May or June 1323 while Edward and the Younger Despenser, 'his evil councillor and parasite', were having breakfast[17] the author treated the event as if it were a supernatural judgment on both men.[18] This was part of a deliberate attempt to use religious imagery to blacken Edward's name, and it follows a passage in which Edward is described as being more evil than Pontius Pilate and as being a tyrant in his oppression of the people and the Church and in his shedding of the blood of the innocent at York. The passage is preceded and followed by accounts of miracles at Thomas of Lancaster's tomb and of an account of Roger Mortimer's escape which the author likens to St Peter's miraculous deliverance from prison.

Writing of Edward II's deposition, the author was at pains to make it appear, contrary to most other evidence, that the king resigned the throne of his own free will: 'I greatly lament that I have so utterly failed my people, but I could not be other than I am; I am pleased that my son who has been thus accepted by all the people should succeed me on the throne'.[19] It is also likely that the hostility that had grown up between Westminster Abbey and the crown during the reign of Edward II was one reason why Edward III refused the monks' request that he should be buried there, and instead chose St Peter's abbey, Gloucester, which he probably then endowed with a magnificent royal tomb and with other patronage.[20]

EDWARD II AND ENGLISH CHRONICLERS

There was no shortage of comment and criticism among other contemporary or near-contemporary writers in England. In a memorable passage of his *Polychronicon*, probably begun in or soon after 1327, Ranulf Higden produced a description of the personality and character of Edward,[21] which was to be quoted by several other fourteenth-century

---

had discussed the defence of northern England and of Ireland against the Scots. The Lincoln parliament did not meet until late Jan. 1316, nearly five months after Edward's boating expedition.

[17] *Flores*, 216–17.

[18] *Flores*, 216, 213–15, 217.

[19] *Flores*, 235; the translation is that in Gransden, ii, 17.

[20] The request from Westminster is referred to in T.F. Tout, 'The captivity and death of Edward of Caernarvon', in *Collected Papers of Thomas Frederick Tout*, iii (Manchester, 1933–34), 168, n. 1, and 169, n. 1, citing Westminster Abbey Munimenta 20344. See further discussion of this episode in ch. 11 of this book.

[21] *Polychronicon Ranulphi Higden*, ed. J.R. Lumby, viii, Rolls Ser. (London, 1882), 298–300. Since Higden did not finish writing until the 1340s this allows for the possibility that his own opinions about Edward II were influenced by Edward's developing reputation as well as influencing those of other writers: on Higden's work see Gransden, ii, 43–5, 55–7.

chroniclers,[22] and which has strongly influenced much subsequent opinion:

> King Edward was a man handsome in body and of outstanding strength, but, if common opinion is to be believed, most inconsistent in behaviour. For, shunning the company of the nobles, he sought the society of jesters, singers, actors, carriage drivers, diggers, oarsmen, sailors, and the practitioners of other kinds of mechanical arts. He indulged in drink, betrayed confidences lightly, struck out at those standing near him for little reason and followed the counsel of others rather than his own. He was extravagant in his gifts, splendid in entertainment, ready in speech, but inconsistent in action. He was unlucky against his enemies, violent with members of his household, and ardently attached to one of his familiars, whom he sustained above all, enriched, preferred, and honoured. From this obsession opprobrium came upon the lover and obloquy to the loved one; scandal was brought upon the people and the kingdom was damaged. He also promoted unworthy and incapable men to office in the church, a practice which was to be like a beam in his eyes and a lance in his side. In his days there was also a dearth of grain and a constant mortality among farm animals, such as had scarcely been seen before.[23]

The description of Edward II in Sir Thomas Gray of Heton's *Scalacronica*, begun in 1355, was one of those influenced by the *Polychronicon*, but was rather more sympathetic towards him, noting in the description of Edward at his accession that 'he was not hard-working, and nor was he loved by the magnates of his realm; on the other hand, he was generous, and genial well beyond measure to those whom he loved, and very affable to his close companions. And physically he was one of the strongest men in the realm.' In his account of Edward at the time of his deposition in 1327 Gray remarked that 'he was wise, charming and affable in conversation, but malevolent in deed. He was clever at whatever he fancied to turn his hand to. He was overly friendly with his intimates, reserved with strangers, and he loved too much a certain person in partic-

---

[22] The passage in the chronicle (begun in about 1390) of the Augustinian canon Henry Knighton of St Mary's abbey, Leicester, is identical to the *Polychronicon*: *Knighton*, i, 407; Gransden, ii, 159–60. The passage in the chronicle of Meaux abbey in Yorkshire, composed by one of its monks Thomas Burton before 1399, is also derived from the *Polychronicon*: *Chronica Monasterii de Melsa*, ed. E.A. Bond ii, Rolls Ser. (London, 1867), 286; Gransden, ii, 355–7. The version which is in the chronicle written by a canon of Bridlington towards the end of the reign of Edward III differs considerably from that of the *Polychronicon* in some places and slightly in others: *Gesta Edwardi de Carnarvon Auctore Canonico Bridlingtoniensi*, in *Chronicles*, ed. Stubbs, ii, 91; Gransden, ii, 9, 113. The translation in Gransden, ii, 1, which is described as of the *Polychronicon* passage, is in fact of the *Gesta* version.

[23] My translation.

ular.' Gray also commented on Edward II's display of physical courage at the battle of Bannockburn in 1314 and his extreme reluctance to leave the battlefield.²⁴

Thomas of Otterbourne, the probable author of the chronicle of the Franciscan house at Lanercost in Cumberland, who had becamc lector of the Franciscans at Oxford some time before 1350, supplied a graphic account of Edward II's rustic activities: 'From his youth he devoted himself in private to the art of rowing and driving carts, of digging ditches and thatching houses, as was commonly said, and also with his companions at night to various works of ingenuity and skill, and other pointless and trivial occupations unsuitable for the son of a king.'²⁵ The anonymous *Brut* chronicle quotes some verses allegedly sung by Scottish maidens after Edward II's defeat by the Scots in 1314. The occasion of the lines was the discomfiture of Sir Edmund Mauley, the steward of the royal household, who

> for drede went and drenchede him-self in a fresshe ryver that is callede Bannokesbourn; therefore the Scottes saide, in reprofe and in despite of Kyng Edward, foralsemiche as he lovede forto go by waters, and also for he was descomfitede at Bannokesbor(n)e, therfore maidenes made a songe therof, in that contre, of Kyng Edward of Engeland, and in this manner thai songe:
>
> > Maidens of England, sore may you mourn,
> > For you have lost your men at Bannockburn with
> >   'Heavalow'.
> > What, would the king of England have won Scotland with
> >   'Rumbalow'?. .²⁶

---

²⁴ *Scalacronica*, xviii–xix, 65, 77, 229, n. 17, 95, 226, n. 1, 234, n. 66.

²⁵ *Lanercost*, 236: trans. from Gransden, 13. This passage forms part of the account of the appearance of the impostor John of Powderham at Oxford in 1318. Some of those present believed John's claim to be the king since Edward II was so different in character from his father: *Lanercost*, 256. On Thomas of Otterbourne and the Lanercost chronicle see Gransden, 12–13. On Edward II's pastimes see A. Richardson, ' "Hedging, ditching and other improper occupations" ', in *Fourteenth Century England*, iv, ed. J.S. Hamilton (Woodbridge, Suffolk & Rochester, NY, 2006), 26–42, esp. 29–32; W.R. Childs, ' "Welcome my brother" ', in *Church and Chronicle in the Middle Ages*, ed. I. Wood and G.A. Loud (London, 1991), 160–1.

²⁶ *Brut*, i, 208. The original text is:

> Maydenes of Engelande, sare may ye morne,
> For tynt ye have [lost] youre lemmans at Bannokesborn
>   with hevalogh.
> What wnde the Kyng of Enge*land* have ygete Scotlande
>   with Rombylogh.

The translation of the verses is cited from M. Prestwich, *The Three Edwards* (London, 1980), 81. '*Heavalow*' and '*Rumbalow*' were the chants used by oarsmen.

This is, however, only a small part of the information and opinion contained in the *Brut*, which survives in many manuscripts; in a short version which ended in 1333 and in a long version ending in 1377; and in French, English and Latin.[27] Although the identity of the author or authors is unknown, the account of the reign of Edward II shows a definite bias towards the side of Edward's first cousin and inveterate opponent, Thomas earl of Lancaster;[28] the author also described the cult which sprang up after the execution of Lancaster in 1322;[29] and in his account of the deposition of Edward II he went to great lengths to demonstrate that the disasters of Edward II's reign were the fulfilment of the prophecies of Merlin.[30]

At least three chroniclers wrote works devoted in whole or in part to Edward II's life.[31] The well informed and extremely perceptive author of the *Vita Edwardi Secundi*, who appears to have written at intervals during the reign and to have finished his work shortly before the disasters of 1326–7,[32] described Edward II at his accession as 'a strong young man'

---

[27] Gransden, ii, 73–6. There is an extensive scholarly literature on the *Brut*. See esp. J. Taylor, 'The French prose *Brut*', in *England in the Fourteenth Century*, ed. W.M. Ormrod (Woodbridge, Suffolk, 1986); idem, *English Historical Literature*, esp. ch. 6, 'The French prose *Brut* and its continuations', and App. i.

[28] Gransden, 73–6. A continuation of the short French *Brut* from 1307 to 1334, which shows both a London and a northern interest, has been published from University of Leeds, Brotherton Ms. 29 by Dr W.R. Childs and Dr J. Taylor: *The Anonimalle Chronicle 1307 to 1334*, Yorkshire Archaeological Soc., Record ser., cxlvii, 1987 (Leeds, 1991).

[29] Gransden, 73–6; *Brut*, i, 221–4, 228–30. On the cult of 'St' Thomas of Lancaster see the very important unpublished Ph.D. thesis by A. R. Echerd, Jr., 'Canonization and politics in late medieval England' (Univ. of North Carolina–Chapel Hill, 1983); and J. T. McQuillan, 'Who was St Thomas of Lancaster?', in *Fourteenth Century England*, iv, 1–25.

[30] *Brut*, i, 242–7. For the importance of prophetic writings in forming the contemporary and posthumous reputation of Edward II, see J.R.S. Phillips, 'Edward II and the prophets', in *England in the Fourteenth Century*, ed. W.M. Ormrod (Woodbridge, Suffolk, 1986), 189–201.

[31] These, and all the other chronicles discussed here, have long been in print, even if sometimes in inadequate editions. There are however several unpublished chronicles which throw light on particular aspects of the reign. These include the chronicle, 1287–1323 (BL, Cotton Ms. Nero D.X), attributed to Nicholas Trivet, which is particularly valuable for the events of 1321–2 and which was used in the sixteenth century by Holinshed for his *Chronicles of England, Scotland and Ireland*; the chronicle, AD 303 to 1385 (Trinity College Cambridge Ms. R.5.41), connected with Canterbury and apparently a continuation of the *Chronica* of Gervase of Canterbury, which is also well informed on 1321–2, has an otherwise unknown record of the deposition of Edward II, and was made use of in the 16th century by John Leland for his *Collectanea*; and the short annals, written in the early 1330s by a member of the Cistercian abbey of Newenham in south Devon (BL, Arundel Ms. 17), under the title *Memorabilia facta tempore Regis Edwardi secundi in Anglia*, which have valuable information on the events between 1326 and 1330.

[32] The standard edition of the *Vita Edwardi Secundi* was until 2005 that by N. Denholm-Young (London, 1957). In his introduction, xxiv–xxvii, and more fully in 'The authorship of the *Vita Edwardi Secundi*', *EHR*, lxxi (1956) (repr. in his *Collected Papers*, Cardiff, 1969, 267–89), he suggested that the author could have been Master John Walwayn, DCL, a canon of Hereford and of St Paul's. Denholm-Young later suggested that Walwayn may

who 'did not achieve the ambition that his father had set before himself, but directed his mind to other things', most notably his favourite, Piers Gaveston, who lorded it over the English magnates 'like a second king, to whom all were subject and none equal'.[33] 'If he had practised the use of arms, he would have exceeded the prowess of King Richard. Physically this would have been inevitable, for he was tall and strong, a handsome man with a fine figure. But why linger over this description of him? If only he had given to arms the attention that he expended on rustic pursuits, he would have raised England on high; his name would have resounded through the land. Oh! What hopes he raised as prince of Wales! All hope vanished when he became king of England.'[34]

Another apparent attempt at a biography is the *Vita et Mors Edwardi Secundi*, traditionally attributed to the Oxfordshire knight Sir Thomas (Laurence) de la More, a nephew of John Stratford, archbishop of Canterbury, who was a witness to many of the dramatic events attending the deposition of Edward II in 1327.[35] The *Vita et Mors* is actually an abbreviated version of the *Chronicon* written by Geoffrey le Baker of Swinbrook in Oxfordshire, who probably obtained much of his information from More but did not begin writing until after 1341.[36] Although unsparing in their

---

have lived in retirement at Malmesbury abbey and that this would explain the erroneous belief of earlier scholars that the *Vita* was composed by a monk of that abbey: Denholm-Young, *The Country Gentry in the Fourteenth Century* (Oxford, 1969), 39–40. His conclusions about Walwayn's authorship are however cautiously rejected in Gransden, ii, 31–7. In his important study, '*Vita Edwardi Secundi*', Professor C. Given-Wilson argues that 'there are strong indications that on several occasions the author brought his narrative up to date before laying down his pen for a year or more' (i.e. 1310–11; summer 1313; late 1315; late 1318; summer 1320; spring 1322;? 1323; and before Sept. 1326) *Thirteenth-Century England*, vi, ed. M. Prestwich, R. Britnell & R. Frame (Woodbridge, Suffolk, 1997), 175–6. This view is broadly accepted by W. R. Childs in her new edition of the *Vita Edwardi Secundi* (Oxford, 2005), xix–xxiii. While not accepting Denholm-Young's conclusion that the author was John Walwayn, she agrees that 'Walwayn fits a substantial number of the criteria in training, west country connections, and career. If it is not he, then someone with a career very like his is needed to fit the bill': Childs, xxiv–xxv.

[33] *Vita*, 4–5. References to the *Vita Edwardi Secundi* in this book are to the 2005 edition by Dr Wendy Childs.

[34] *Vita*, 68–9: this forms part of an assessment of Edward II in the year 1313. Edward II's apparent fondness for digging has a curious parallel in the career of his cousin, King Dinis of Portugal (1279–1325), whose nickname of 'El Labrador' is usually translated as 'The Farm Labourer'. In the case of Dinis, however, the fondness for the soil related to his encouragement of agriculture rather than any personal involvement with the land of his kingdom: there is a brief discussion of him in R.S. Lopez, *The Birth of Europe* (New York, 1967), 308–9.

[35] See the discussion in Gransden, ii, 37–42; R.M. Haines, *The Church and Politics in Fourteenth-century England* (Cambridge, 1978), 102–5; and Haines, *Archbishop John Stratford* (Toronto, 1986), esp. 178–9, 264–5 (where the link with Stratford is indicated). The text of the *Vita et Mors* is published in *Chronicles*, ed. Stubbs, ii.

[36] For the text of the *Chronicon* see *Chronicon Galfridi le Baker de Swynebroke*, ed. E.M. Thompson (Oxford, 1889); for discussions of the text see Gransden, ii, 37–42; Haines, *The Church and Politics*, 102–11; Haines, *Stratford*, 178–80.

criticism of the royal favourites, Piers Gaveston and the Despensers,[37] these two works are sympathetic to Edward II, especially in the predicament he faced after his deposition, and are the source of the tales of Edward's ill-treatment while a prisoner and of his brutal murder at Berkeley castle.[38] Le Baker's gruesome account of the death of Edward II, which has coloured all subsequent accounts of the reign, both literary and historical,[39] seems to have been designed to give the impression that Edward's sufferings were a sign of sanctity and probably played a part in the development of the cult of Edward II which culminated in the attempts by Richard II to have his predecessor canonized. The red-hot iron story and the use made of it by other authors could also, however, be taken as part of an attempt to blacken Edward's posthumous reputation by portraying him as a sodomite.[40]

The remaining work, the *Gesta Edwardi de Carnarvon*,[41] was 'written in its present form towards the end of Edward III's reign' by a canon of the Augustinian priory at Bridlington in Yorkshire. It was, however, derived from 'a lost chronicle begun late in Edward II's reign'.[42] Part of the chronicle's interest lies in the prophetic writings, drawn from the works of John of Bridlington, which are inserted at intervals in the text. The prophetic verses about Edward II, which were included at the end of the account of his reign, were intended (like the *Brut* author's use of the prophecies of Merlin) to show that the disasters he experienced had been foretold,[43] and are immediately preceded by a character sketch of Edward II derived

---

[37] E.g. *Vita et Mors*, 297–9, 301–2, 305–6; *Le Baker*, 4–6, 10–12, 16–17.

[38] *Vita et Mors*, 313–19; *Le Baker*, 25–34.

[39] Geoffrey le Baker claimed to have learned the details of Edward II's ill-treatment and murder 'after the great plague [of 1349] from William Bishop, who was in charge of Edward's guards, which he confessed and repented, hoping for some mercy': Gransden, 39, citing *Le Baker*, 31. There are several references to a William 'Bisshop', who was a sergeant-at-arms in the royal household while Edward III was in the Low Countries between 1338 and 1340: *The Wardrobe Book of William de Norwell, 12 July 1338 to 27 May 1340*, ed. M. Lyon, B. Lyon, H. S. Lucas & J. de Sturler (Brussels, 1983), 11, 281, 304, 351, 391.

Le Baker, 30–4, was the ultimate source of some of the information used in the 16th century by Holinshed for his historical writing and, via Holinshed, by Christopher Marlowe in his play *Edward II*: see Gransden, ii, 40, n. 248. Le Baker was not the only chronicler to record the story of Edward II's murder by means of a red-hot iron thrust into his bowels. It also appears in the *Brut*, i, 252–3; and in the *Polychronicon* of Ranulf Higden, 324. However, Higden mentions only that Edward was murdered with a hot iron, omitting the circumstantial details provided by Le Baker and the unknown author of the *Brut*. Even if Edward II was murdered, which is very likely, it is still questionable whether le Baker's story should be taken literally. See discussion in ch. 11.

[40] E.g., *Le Baker*, 27, 30, 34. This topic is discussed more fully in ch. 11.

[41] *Gesta Edwardi*.

[42] Gransden, ii, 113.

[43] *Gesta Edwardi*, 91–2. The verses, 18 lines in all, begin:

> Transmittent Britones hircum sed non rationes,
> Hircus barbatus erit in sensu quasi mutus.
> Anglorum terra non regnabit sine guerra,
> Dapsilis et gratus sed in actibus infatuatus.

from, but not identical to, the passage in the *Polychronicon* of Ranulf Higden which has already been cited.[44]

OTHER CRITICS OF EDWARD II

The chronicles are not the only sources of comment on and criticism of Edward II. The Exchequer Memoranda Roll for 1315–16 records that in July 1314 Robert de Newington in Kent, a messenger in the royal household, remarked that Edward could not be expected to win battles (he had been defeated by the Scots at Bannockburn the month before) if he spent the time when he should have been hearing mass in 'idling and applying himself to making ditches and digging and other improper occupations'.[45] These criticisms were echoed in the articles of his deposition in 1327 when Edward was accused, among other failings and inadequacies, of devoting himself to unsuitable work and occupations instead of to the affairs of his kingdom.[46] In January 1315 a London goldsmith, John Bonaventure, complained that he had been imprisoned by the marshals of the king's household on an accusation by John of Lincoln of having said 'certain evil and shameful things about the king'.[47]

On two or three occasions during the reign an impostor appeared. On 22 May 1313, when Edward II and Isabella were on the point of crossing to France for a state visit to Paris, a certain Richard de Neueby, described as a yeoman from Gascony, came to the royal court at Eltham, claiming that he was the king's brother. Rather than throwing him into prison or worse, Edward II gave him £13, after which nothing more is heard of him.[48] There is also the episode in 1316 when a clerk named Thomas de Tynwelle was accused of saying publicly in the park of north Oxford on 19 December 1315 that Edward II was not his father's son.[49]

The best known and the most serious of these episodes also took place in Oxford. This was the humiliating occasion in late June 1318 when a certain John of Powderham, from Exeter, appeared, claiming that

---

[44] Ibid., 91.

[45] H. Johnstone, 'The eccentricities of Edward II', *EHR*, xlviii (1933), 264–7, citing the Memoranda Roll for 1315–16, E 368/86, m.32d. A modern observer might have commented that Edward should have been training for war rather than saying his prayers!

[46] *Select Documents of English Constitutional History, 1307–1485*, ed. S.B. Chrimes & A.L. Brown (London, 1961), 37.

[47] '*de rege sinistra aliqua et inhonesta dixisse in contemptu regis*': *PROME*, Parliament of 1315, items 145, 120. See also ch. 6 of this book.

[48] P. Chaplais, *Piers Gaveston* (Oxford, 1994), 111–12, citing E 101/375/8, f. 29d. 'Did he claim to be a blood-brother, in other words an illegitimate son of Edward I, or an adoptive brother as Gaveston had been? Was he a madman like those who from time to time went around the country pretending to be the true king?': Chaplais, 112. On whether or not Gaveston was an adoptive brother of Edward II, as Dr Chaplais argues, see ch. 3 of this book.

[49] Memoranda Roll, 9 Edward II, E 368/86, m.94. The episode was first noted by H. Johnstone in *Edward of Carnarvon*, 130, where it is taken literally. See also ch. 6 of this book.

Edward II was an impostor and that he was the rightful king. John was taken to Northampton where he was brought before the king, who was at first inclined towards leniency. After Edward was advised very strongly that such a public challenge to his royal status could not go unpunished, John was summarily tried and executed on about 23 July. Ironically, although the incident took place at a very delicate stage in the negotiations between Edward II and Thomas of Lancaster, which resulted in the Treaty of Leake in early August 1318, it does not appear to have had any political context. John of Powderham was a deranged individual acting for reasons of his own.[50] In the 1330s this incident was referred to by the Dominican scholar Robert Holcot in his lectures on the *Book of Wisdom*[51] and was to be quoted from that source by Walter Bower, the author of the *Scotichronicon*, in the 1440s when he was writing about James I of Scotland.[52]

Sermons were another device for expressing criticism or comment on Edward II and his regime. Those preached by three of the leading clergy before the session of parliament assembled at Westminster in January 1327 apparently formed a carefully graduated progression, preparing the way for the actual deposition of the king imprisoned at Kenilworth. According to the Lanercost chronicler, on 13 January Adam Orleton, the bishop of Hereford, preached on the theme 'A foolish king destroys his people'; on 14 January John Stratford, bishop of Winchester, used the text 'my head is sick'; and finally on 15 January Walter Reynolds, the archbishop of Canterbury and a former close ally of the king, began by stating that 'the voice of the people is the voice of God'.[53] Less well known are the sermons in which itinerant preachers in Scotland in 1307 foretold that after the coming death of Edward I, *le Roy Coveytous*, the Scots and the Welsh would join together in an alliance against the English;[54] a similar pattern of events occurred around 1315 at the time of the Scottish invasion of Ireland, when Irish Franciscans preached against English rule.[55] In or about 1310 an Irish Franciscan named Malachy had apparently even

---

[50] A full account can be found in W.R. Childs, ' "Welcome my brother" '. Chroniclers who reported the episode were influenced by Edward II's reputation for eccentricity. The Lanercost author remarked that many believed John of Powderham's claims 'because Edward II was so manifestly different from Edward I', while the abbot of Meaux 'repeated the pretender's claims that his case was proved because Edward naturally enjoyed the work of countrymen which reflected the activities of his true father': Childs, 152.

[51] Smalley, *English Friars*, 325. It is possible that Holcot, whose home was in Northampton, witnessed the execution: ibid., n.3.

[52] *Scotichronicon by Walter Bower*, ed. D.E.R. Watt, viii (Aberdeen, 1987), 331.

[53] See Haines, *Stratford*, 183, using the evidence of the Lanercost chronicler. The Canterbury chronicle, Trinity College, Cambridge, Ms. R.5.41, has a slightly different version of the texts employed: Haines, 185–6. It is more likely however that the three sermons were preached on the same day: see C. Valente, 'The deposition and abdication of Edward II', *EHR*, cxiii (1998), 858–60.

[54] Phillips, 'Edward II and the prophets', 191, n. 13.

[55] J.A. Watt, *The Church and the Two Nations in Medieval Ireland* (Cambridge, 1970), 185–6.

preached before Edward II, his court, and the bishops, and had strongly condemned the vices of the age.[56]

In late December 1314, the chancellor of Oxford University, Mr Henry Harclay, apparently referred to Edward II when he preached a sermon to commemorate the murder in December 1170 of Archbishop Thomas Becket at the hands of Henry II's knights and implied that final punishment for Becket's death might be visited upon the fourth generation.[57] Another ecclesiastical protest, in the form of a letter addressed by 'a certain regular of admitted authority' to the king's confessor, is recorded by the author of the *Vita Edwardi Secundi* under the year 1316; the letter complained about such matters as the abuse of purveyance by the king for the use of his household, failure to pay his debts, and his habit of staying too long in religious houses.[58]

A more public form of protest took place at Pentecost, 22 May 1317, when a woman dressed as a theatrical player rode into Westminster Hall while Edward II was feasting with his magnates and presented a letter to the king. Under questioning she revealed that she had been induced to do this by one of Edward II's own household knights: they were annoyed that the king was neglecting knights who had served his father and himself in battle and was promoting others 'who had not borne the heat of the day'.[59] This episode certainly relates to the marriages in late April of Roger Damory and Hugh Audley the Younger to Elizabeth and Margaret de Clare, two of the three heiresses to the lands of the earldom of Gloucester, and to the partition of their inheritance which had been ordered on 17 April.[60]

A further category of comment is the literary genre often referred to as 'political songs', many of which survive in English, French or Latin from the thirteenth and fourteenth centuries and relate to various reigns and political situations. One of them, the *Poem on the Evil Times of Edward II*, was written in the 1320s. While the author is critical of what he sees as the oppressive government of Edward II, he also bemoans the state of society in general: 'The Church, from pope and cardinals to parish priest, is corrupt. Money rules in the ecclesiastical courts, the parson has a mistress, abbots and priors ride to hounds, friars fight for the corpses of the rich and leave the poor unburied. Chivalry is in decay; instead of going on crusade,

---

[56] L. Wadding, *Annales Minorum*, vi (Rome, 1733), 176; *Materials for the History of the Franciscan Province of Ireland AD 1230–1450*, ed. E.B. Fitzmaurice & A.G. Little (Manchester, 1920), 54–8. Malachy may have been the famous Malachy of Limerick who was the probable author of the treatise *De Veneno* on the seven deadly sins. It is not clear whether Malachy had the specific failings of Edward II in mind or was just issuing a general condemnation of the wickedness of the world. No precise occasion for this sermon has been identified.

[57] E.W. Kemp (the bishop of Chichester), 'History and action in the sermons of a medieval archbishop', in *The Writing of History in the Middle Ages*, ed. R.H.C. Davis & J.M. Wallace-Hadrill (Oxford, 1981), 349–53. See also ch. 6 of this book.

[58] *Vita*, 128–31. The text breaks off at this point. See also ch. 6 of this book.

[59] *Trokelowe*, 98–9.

[60] J.R.S. Phillips, *Aymer de Valence Earl of Pembroke, 1307–1324* (Oxford, 1972), 131–3, 146.

earls, barons and knights war among themselves. Justices, sheriffs, and those who raise taxes for the king are all bribable, so that the poor are taxed while the rich escape. Physicians charge too much, lawyers and traders cheat their clients. The poor are perennial victims.'[61] Shortly before the end of the reign of Edward II, one of his Gascon subjects, the troubadour poet Pey de Ladils, composed the *sirventés, El dugat (The Duchy)*, in which he criticized the king-duke for his failure to defend Gascony against French encroachments and declared that the only answer was for the king to come in person. This was written in the context of the Anglo-French war of St Sardos in 1324–5 in which the French had gained the upper hand and had forced Edward's half-brother, Edmund earl of Kent, into a humiliating surrender at La Réole.[62] Other poems from the reign of Edward II include two celebrating the death of Gaveston in 1312, which are composed as parodies of familiar church hymns; and another marking the death of the courageous young earl of Gloucester, allegedly betrayed by one of his knights, named Bartholomew, at the battle of Bannockburn in 1314.[63] Another poem on the battle was allegedly composed by the English Carmelite friar Robert Baston, who had been taken along by Edward II to mark the expected English triumph over the Scots and was instead taken prisoner and required to write verses in praise of the Scottish victory. The fifteenth-century Scottish chronicler Walter Bower gave them an honoured place in his *Scotichronicon*, since 'in view of their excellence these verses are certainly not to be hidden under a bushel, but should be set forth on a candlestick'.[64] The execution of the earl of Lancaster in 1322 was followed by the composition of an office of 'St' Thomas of Lancaster which was intended to demean the authority of the king who had executed him as much as to extol the merits of the martyred

---

[61] This summary of the poem is in the words of Dr J.R. Maddicott in his important paper, 'Poems of social protest in early fourteenth-century England', in *England in the Fourteenth Century*, ed. W.M. Ormrod (Woodbridge, Suffolk, 1986), 132–3. See also Maddicott, 'The English peasantry and the demands of the crown, 1294–1341', *Past & Present, Supplement No. 1* (Oxford, 1975), 13–14.

Other valuable discussions of poems of protest can be found in Taylor, *English Historical Literature*, ch. 12, 'Political poems and ballads'; in the introduction by Peter Coss to the reissue (Cambridge, 1995) of *Political Songs*, ed. T. Wright and in T. Turville-Petre, *England the Nation* (Oxford, 1996), esp. 11–13, 131–4, 195–6. The text of the *Poem on the Evil Times of Edward II* is published in *Political Songs*, xxxvii–xli, 323–45.

[62] G. Pépin, ' Le sirventés *El dugat* ... Une chanson méconnue de Pey de Ladils sur l'Aquitaine Anglo-Gasconne', *Les Cahiers du Bazadais*, clii (Bazas, 2006), 5–28. The *sirventés* was a form of poetry used to discuss current events and was often highly critical.

[63] *Political Songs*, xxxv, 258–61; 262–7. The knight was Bartholomew de Badlesmere. The poem, *On the King's breaking his confirmation of Magna Charta*, which Wright dated to late 1311, was probably composed in 1306–7, as a commentary on Edward I's failure to observe his promises rather than on Edward II: *Political Songs*, xxxiii, 253–8; and *Anglo-Norman Political Songs*, Anglo-Norman Texts, xi, ed. I.S.T. Aspin (Oxford, 1953), 53–66.

[64] *Scotichronicon by Walter Bower*, D.E.R. Watt, vi (Aberdeen, 1991), 367. The Latin text, with a facing translation, is published in ibid., 366–75.

earl.⁶⁵ Such poems were probably far more influential than the attempt possibly made by the royal administration at the time of the great famine of 1316–17 to present Edward II 'as the wise king, dealing with the famine with aplomb and rectitude, like the pharaoh who had put Joseph in charge of the granaries of Egypt in the time of the patriarchs'.⁶⁶

Poems of social protest are usually anonymous but it has been suggested that, although they often purport to represent the voice of the 'common people', they were probably the work of educated writers, possibly including such clerics as the distinguished Oxford scholars Mr Ralph Acton and the Dominican friar William of Pagula.⁶⁷ The author of the *Vita Edwardi Secundi* also falls to some extent into the same category. While unsparing in his criticism of the personal failings of Edward II and the inadequacies of his government, he is also at pains to describe the failings of others, such as Edward's cousin and long-time opponent, Thomas of Lancaster, as well as the papal curia.⁶⁸

The charges that were laid against Edward II at the time of his deposition in January 1327 were broadly in line with the comments of chroniclers and other critics. He was accused, among other things, of being personally incapable of governing, of allowing himself to be led and governed by others, who advised him badly; of devoting himself to unsuitable work and occupations, while neglecting the government of his kingdom; of exhibiting pride, covetousness and cruelty; and of putting to death, imprisoning, exiling and disinheriting the great men of his kingdom; of failing to observe his coronation oath through the influence of his evil councillors; of abandoning his kingdom and doing all in his power to cause the loss both of it and of his people; and of being incorrigible and without hope of improvement.⁶⁹

---

⁶⁵ *Political Songs*, xxxvi–xxxvii, 268–72. See Echerd, 'Canonization and politics' (Ph.D.).

⁶⁶ W. C. Jordan, *The Great Famine* (Princeton, 1996), 177, 258, n. 4; citing K. Smith, 'History, typology and homily', *Gesta*, xxxii (1993), 147–59.

⁶⁷ Maddicott, 'Poems of social protest', 135–6. These two men are not however suggested as the authors of the particular poems mentioned here.

⁶⁸ E.g. *Vita*, 48–51, 168–71 (Lancaster); 170–5 (ills of the times); 76–83 (papal curia).

⁶⁹ *Select Documents*, 37–8: the original text is in French. In some respects similar remarks were made about Philip IV of France, Edward II's father-in-law and supposedly a 'successful' king. In his account of Philip's death in 1314 the Florentine chronicler Giovanni Villani says that, although Philip was 'a wise and good man, for a layman', he devoted himself to his pleasures, chiefly those of the hunt, neglected the work of government, leaving it to others, and was badly advised: Calmette, *Textes et documents d'histoire*, ii: *Moyen Age*, 2nd edn, 166. On his deathbed Philip IV of France allegedly admitted that he had committed many errors as a result of bad counsel, but that he was to blame for that bad counsel: cited in a report preserved in the archives of the kingdom of Aragon: C. Baudon de Mony, 'La Mort et les funerailles de Philippe le Bel', *Bibliothèque de l'Ecole des Chartes*, lviii (1897), 42. Contemporaries expected a king to rule in person and found it very difficult to draw a line between a king's need for advice and assistance from his councillors and professional administrators and the influence and possible dominance of favourites: see J.R. Strayer, 'Philip the Fair – a "constitutional" king', in Strayer, *Medieval Statecraft and the Perspectives of History* (Princeton, 1971); and E.A.R. Brown, 'The case of Philip the Fair', 219–46.

'ST' EDWARD II

Virtually all the evidence cited so far is critical, sometimes venomously so, of Edward II both as a person and as a king. This was not however the whole story, since there were also counter-opinions. One of the elements was the cult of the royal saint, Edward the Confessor (canonized in 1162 during the reign of Henry II), which had been consciously developed by the English monarchy in the years before 1307, and which was given significant emphasis in Edward II's coronation in 1308.[70] Another possible source of inspiration, although there is no specific evidence to support this suggestion, is the life and death of an earlier king and saint, Edward the Martyr, who was foully murdered at Corfe in Dorset in the year 978.[71] Just as Edward II himself was very conscious that his name bore the connotations of sanctity, so too were those who tried to promote Edward II's own claims to sanctity and even to canonization after 1327. The cult of Edward the Confessor also helped to inspire the otherwise unknown Adam Davy to write his English poem, *Five Dreams of Edward II*, at about the time of Edward II's coronation in March 1308, and with the apparent intention of presenting the poem to the new king. In the poem Edward II is depicted variously as a knight standing before the shrine of St Edward in Westminster Abbey (a conscious echo of the ceremony of Edward's knighting in 1306); as a pilgrim entering Rome upon an ass (as Christ had entered Jerusalem before the Crucifixion); as a crusader accompanied on crusade by Christ himself; and, finally, standing before the high altar at Canterbury, clad all in red, a colour suggestive of martyrdom.[72]

---

[70] This theme is more fully discussed in ch. 4. See Binski, *Westminster Abbey*; and two important unpublished papers by J.C. Parsons, 'Saints' cults and kingship', and 'Rethinking English coronations, 1220–1308'. I am grateful to Professor Parsons for allowing me to see these papers.

[71] F.M. Stenton, *Anglo-Saxon England* (Oxford, 1955), 367–8; C. Fell, *Edward, King and Martyr* (Leeds, 1971). One wonders if the appearance of Corfe in the stories both of Edward the Martyr and of the supposed survival of Edward II after 1327 is more than just a coincidence.

[72] Phillips, 'Edward II and the prophets', 191–4. The text of the poem, from Bod., Laud Misc. Ms. 622, was edited by F.J. Furnivall, in *Five Dreams about Edward II*, Early English Text Society, old ser., lxix (1878), 7–16. The most detailed discussion of the subject is V.J. Scattergood, 'Adam Davy's *Dreams* and Edward II', *Archiv für das Studium der neueren Sprachen und Literaturen*, ccvi (Braunschweig, 1970), 253–60, repr. Scattergood, *Reading the Past* (Dublin, 1996). It is not known whether Adam Davy, who describes himself as the marshal, of Stratford-at-Bow, just outside the city of London, did present his poem to Edward II.

The author of the *Lament on the Death of Edward I*, also writing at the start of the new reign, ended his poem: 'The young Edward of England is anointed and crowned king: may God grant that he follow such counsel, that the country may be governed; and so to keep the crown, that the land may be entire, and himself to increase in goodness, for his father was a worthy man': *Political Songs*, 244–5. This was clearly an expression of hope for the future rather than any real assessment of Edward II.

An even more extraordinary prophecy is contained in a work known as the *Verses of Gildas*,[73] which was composed by an unknown author apparently writing around the middle of the reign of Edward II. Although the subject of the prophecy is described only as *Rex noster nunc regnans*, it is clearly intended to refer to Edward II. The prophecy begins, not with a great achievement in the Holy Land, but with Ireland, to which the king will go in 1320 after a certain grave crisis.[74] Once in Ireland, Edward will bring about peace between the English and the Irish, who will then all live together under one English law. From Ireland, Edward will travel to Scotland, in company with the English, Irish and Welsh, and there defeat the Scottish rebels and put Robert Bruce to flight. *Rex noster* will then go to Gascony and kill all the French found there, after which the son and heir of the king of England by his French queen, *quae nunc est*,[75] will become king of Scotland and reign there for the lifetime of his father. On his return from Scotland, the king will honour the magnates of England who come to seek his grace, and will exile all the greatest rebels. As if these prophecies were not fantastic enough, Edward II will then conquer France, pass through Spain, defeat the rulers of Africa, receive the submission of Egypt, and advance to Babylon in Persia. After Edward has reconquered the Holy Land, the pope will three times offer him the crown of the world, which he will finally graciously accept. Edward's career will culminate in the defeat of the emperor of Constantinople, the conquest of the world, the subjection of the pope and cardinals, who will be forced to live by the apostolic rule, and the abolition of the very name of pope.[76]

Neither Adam Davy nor the author of the *Verses of Gildas* is known to have had any direct contact with Edward II, and the prophecies embodied in their writings may be regarded as the triumph of hope over experience. However, between 1317 and 1319 there was the strange episode of the Holy Oil of St Thomas of Canterbury, allegedly given to Thomas Becket by the Virgin Mary while Becket was in exile in France after 1164. According to an accompanying legend, the fifth king of England after the reigning king

---

[73] BL, Arundel Ms. 57, ff 4v–5v. See discussion in Phillips, 'Edward II and the prophets', 194–6, and idem, 'Edward II and Ireland (in fact and in fiction)', *IHS*, xxxiii, no. 129 (May 2002), 1–18.

[74] Presumably a reference to the Scottish invasion of Ireland led by Edward Bruce, between 1315 and 1318.

[75] I.e. Edward of Windsor, the future Edward III, and his mother, Queen Isabella.

[76] Phillips, 'Edward II and the prophets', 194–6. This was a period of intense crusading propaganda, often featuring the king of France as a likely crusading leader, but also involving the English monarchy, especially Edward I. Edward II was an unlikely crusader, but he did take the cross, together with Philip IV of France and his sons, in Paris in 1313. See S. Schein, *Fideles Crucis* (Oxford, 1991) and N. Housley, *The Avignon Papacy and the Crusades, 1305–1378* (Oxford, 1986). Whoever wrote the *Verses of Gildas* appears to have been deeply hostile to the papacy. Possibly the author was one of the Spiritual Franciscans who were then in conflict with the pope over the question of apostolic poverty: see Lambert, *Franciscan Poverty*.

(i.e. Henry II) would be a good man and a champion of the Church, and by virtue of the Holy Oil he would succeed in recovering the Holy Land from the infidel. Edward II became personally involved in this after he was persuaded that he was the prophesied king and that the oil would be the answer to his political troubles, if he were to be anointed with it. Edward's efforts to persuade the pope to allow this were firmly rejected by John XXII, and the incident resulted only in Edward II's embarrassment, and in the arrest and subsequent flight from captivity of the apparent instigator of the whole idea, an English Dominican, Nicholas of Wisbech, who had earlier been the confessor of Edward II's sister, Margaret, the duchess of Brabant.[77] As Edward himself remarked in 1319, in a very frank letter to the pope, which is revealing both of the king's piety and of his gullibility in religious matters, he had through his own 'imbecility' allowed the unscrupulous friar to take advantage of his 'dovelike simplicity'.[78]

After his death Edward II became the subject of contrasting interpretations among the chroniclers. After telling the red-hot iron story, Ranulf Higden, the author of the *Polychronicon*, remarked that some people thought that Edward II should be placed among the saints, but countered this view with an account of Edward's vices and the failure of his government. However, he also made a very interesting choice of religious imagery in referring to Edward's promotion of unworthy churchmen, whom he described as 'a beam in his eyes and a lance in his side'.[79] In contrast, Geoffrey le Baker's account of Edward II's death, in which he is presented as a martyr, seems positively designed to prepare the way for a cult of royal sanctity.[80]

[77] Phillips, 'Edward II and the prophets', 196–201.
[78] C 70/4, m.6d.
[79] *Polychronicon*, 300. Cf. *Annals of Osney*, *Annales Monastici*, iv, ed. H.R. Luard, Rolls ser. (London, 1889), 348.
[80] See *Le Baker*, 9, 27, 30–4. This theme is discussed further in ch. 11 of this book.
There are two literary curiosities which also at first sight appear to be part of a posthumous rehabilitation of Edward II. The first is the English poem *Somer Soneday (Summer Sunday)*, which has sometimes been identified as a lament for Edward II, written soon after his deposition: see *Historical Poems of the XIVth and XVth Centuries*, ed. R. H. Robbins (New York, 1959), 98–102, 301–3, from Bod. Ms. Laud Misc. 108, f. 107. However there is no reason to connect the poem, which is based on the theme of the wheel of fortune, either with Edward II or with any particular king: see D. Gray, 'Songs and Lyrics', in *Literature in Fourteenth-century England*, ed. P. Boitani & A. Torti (Tübingen & Cambridge, 1983), 85; and T. Turville-Petre, *Alliterative Poetry of the Later Middle Ages* (London, 1989), 140–7. The wheel of fortune is given both verbal and pictorial expression in the genealogy of English kings known as the Chaworth Roll which was produced in the closing years of the reign of Edward II, but again only as a general theme: *The Chaworth Roll*, ed. A. Bovey (London, 2005), frontispiece and 14, 17.
The second poem is *The Lament of Edward II*, written in French (entitled *De le Roi Edward le Fiz Roi Edward, le Chanson qe il fist mesmes*) and supposedly composed by Edward himself while in prison. In the poem Edward laments his fate and shows repentance for his past

Geoffrey le Baker was writing in the 1340s, by which time a movement to present Edward II as a holy figure and even to have him canonized may have been gathering strength. The now famous letter written to Edward III by the Genoese cleric, Manuel Fieschi, in which Edward II appears as a hermit offering prayers for his own redemption and that of others, might have had the same effect if it had circulated more widely. An exceptionally interesting example of writing which was certainly designed to enhance Edward's reputation, if only among the academic community, can be found in the work of the Dominican scholar Thomas Ringstead, who was bishop of Bangor between 1357 and 1366, but who was teaching in Cambridge in the 1340s. In one of his lectures on the Book of Proverbs Ringstead told of how Edward I had cast Prince Edward off under the influence of evil counsellors. 'He bore the injury patiently and came to his father's help on a winter's night, when the king was riding along a muddy, dangerous road. Fearing for his safety, Prince Edward took the horse's bridle and walked beside him until the danger was over. The king did not know who had come to his rescue.' And so, according to Ringstead, *Talis filius fuit Christus*.[81]

The magnificent tomb erected in memory of Edward II in his burial place in Gloucester abbey showed Edward as a figure of great nobility, in contrast to the tragedy and humiliation with which he met his end.[82] The tomb attracted a steady flow of pilgrims whose offerings contributed to the remodelling of the abbey. Royal patronage, by Edward III,

---

misdeeds. The poem exists in two separate 14th-century versions, in Longleat Ms. 26, ff. 76v–77r, published in Aspin, *Anglo-Norman Political Songs*, no. 9; and in BL, Royal Ms. 20. A.II, f. 10r, 10v, published in T. Smallwood, 'The lament of Edward II', *Modern Language Review*, lxviii (1973), 521–9. There is also a closely related Latin version in a 15th-century manuscript, College of Arms, Arundel Ms. 48, ff. 153r–154r, part of which was cited in the 16th-century chronicle by Fabyan: see Johnstone, 20; D. Tyson, 'Lament for a dead king', *Journal of Medieval History*, xxx, no. 4 (Dec. 2004), 359–75, esp. 360–1, 363, 367–70; and Cl. Valente, 'The "Lament of Edward II"', *Speculum*, lxxvii (2002), 422–39. As in the case of *Summer Sunday*, the idea of the wheel of fortune may lie behind the poem, although it is possible that the author was also consciously trying to cast Edward II in a sympathetic light. There is also an Italian edition of the poem by A. Benedetti, 'Una canzone francese di Edoardo II d'Inghilterra', *Nuova studi medievali*, i, part 2 (1923), 283 ff.

[81] Smalley, *English Friars*, 211–15, 219, 338. As Dr Smalley points out, the story clearly originates in the events of 1305, but must be apocryphal since, although Edward did follow his father around in 1305, their quarrel and final reconciliation took place in the summer and autumn, not in winter.

[82] Edward's tomb effigy contrasts sharply with another depiction of him, the drawing of a king and queen, possibly intended to be Edward II and Isabella, looking at one another with unhappy expressions. This appears in Walter de Milemete's treatise, *De Nobilitatibus, Sapientiis, et Prudentiis Regum*, composed early in 1327 (shortly after the deposition of Edward II but before his death) and presented to Edward III: Christ Church, Oxford, Ms. 92, f. 4v. There is a reproduction of this drawing in the edition of *The Treatise of Walter de Milemete* edited by M.R. James for the Roxburghe Club (Oxford, 1913), plate 8; and also in E. Hallam, *The Plantagenet Encyclopaedia* (London, 1996), 105.

Queen Philippa and the Black Prince encouraged the growth of Gloucester abbey as a pilgrimage centre with a special royal connection.[83] There is, however, no clear evidence of a systematic attempt, whether by Dominican enthusiasts or by royal authority, to start a formal process for the canonization of Edward II until the reign of Richard II.[84] But despite intense efforts by Richard himself and others acting on his behalf nothing had been achieved by the time of his deposition in 1399, after which no further action is known.[85]

However much Richard II and others may have tried to enhance the memory and reputation of Edward II, others were working against them. Several of the chroniclers writing shortly before or during the reign of Richard II, such as the Bridlington author of the *Gesta Edwardi de Carnarvon*, Henry Knighton in Leicester, and Thomas Burton at Meaux in Yorkshire, quoted Ranulf Higden's unflattering portrait of Edward II,[86] while Burton also expressed a sharply critical opinion of Edward II's morals in his remark that Edward delighted greatly in the vice of sodomy.[87] Indeed, it has been argued plausibly that Edward II's reputation for sodomy and specifically the story of his murder by red-hot iron, a form of anal rape, was developed after his death as a way of discrediting him.[88]

Those involved in politics at the highest level were also conscious that Edward II's deposition had created a precedent for future action. In 1387, during the 'Wonderful Parliament', Richard II's opponents pointedly reminded him of his great-grandfather's fate. When Richard II was

---

[83] D. Welander, *The History, Art and Architecture of Gloucester Cathedral* (Stroud, 1991), 144–50. See also Evans, *English Art*, 164–5, and most recently Palliser, 'Royal mausolea', 8–9; and R.M. Bryant, G.N.H. Bryant, and C.M. Heighway, *The Tomb of Edward II* (Stonehouse, Glos., 2007). Although it is assumed that Edward III approved the making of his father's tomb, it is not known whether he actually commissioned it; neither is it known who paid for it. For further discussion of the tomb see ch. 11 of this book.

[84] The best and most detailed study of the reign is N. Saul, *Richard II* (New Haven & London, 1997): see esp. ch. 13, 'Piety and orthodoxy'. See also C. Given-Wilson, 'Richard II, Edward II, and the Lancastrian inheritance', *EHR*, cix (June 1994), 553–71.

[85] E. Perroy, *L'Angleterre et le Grand Schisme d'Occident* (Paris, 1933), 301, 330, 341–2.

[86] *Polychronicon*, 298–300; *Knighton*, i, 407. The Augustinian canon Henry Knighton of St Mary's abbey, Leicester, began writing in about 1390: Gransden, ii, 159–60. *Melsa*, 280–1, 286. The chronicle of Meaux abbey in Yorkshire was composed by one of its monks Thomas Burton before 1399: Gransden, ii, 355–7. *Gesta Edvardi*, 91. The *Gesta* was written by an unidentified canon of Bridlington towards the end of the reign of Edward III: Gransden, ii, 9, 113.

[87] '*Ipse quidem Edwardus in vitio sodomitico nimium delectabat, et fortuna ac gratia omni suo tempore carere videbatur*': *Melsa*, 355. Burton introduced these remarks expressly to contradict the opinion that Edward II's cruel death suggested to some people that he was a saint.

[88] See W.M. Ormrod, 'The sexualities of Edward II' and I. Mortimer, 'Sermons of sodomy', in *The Reign of Edward II*, ed. G. Dodd & A. Musson (Woodbridge, Suffolk & Rochester, NY, 2006).

eventually deprived of his throne in 1399 the dramatic events of 1327, and probably also the likely fate of a deposed king, were very much in the mind of everyone involved.[89]

EDWARD II IN LITERATURE: SIXTEENTH TO EIGHTEENTH CENTURIES

Although the cult of Edward II as a prospective saint does not appear to have survived the fourteenth century,[90] in later centuries an extensive literary tradition developed around him, variously expressed by historians, playwrights, poets and political commentators, and deriving its energy from the adverse opinions of the chroniclers as well as from the political precedents set by Edward II's deposition and death. Most concentrated on the relations between Edward and his favourites, especially Gaveston. Gaveston even played a role in French political controversy when in 1588 Jean Boucher drew a parallel between Gaveston and another Gascon gentleman, the duc d'Epernon, the favourite of the French king Henry III.[91]

In sixteenth-century England Holinshed's *Chronicles*, for example, were distinguished by their author's critical but also sympathetic and balanced judgement of Edward, and by his understanding of the implications of Edward's overthrow for the future of English politics.[92] Holinshed also thought that there had been a sexual relationship between Edward II and

---

[89] Saul, *Richard II* 157–8, 418–19, 430–4. The Kirkstall abbey chronicler and Adam of Usk also made pointed comparisons between the failings of Edward II and Richard II: M. Lawrence, ' "Too flattering sweet to be substantial" ', in Hamilton, ed., *Fourteenth Century England*, iv, 146, n. 2.

[90] It is possible, and indeed likely, that a local cult survived around Edward II's tomb in St Peter's abbey, Glos., but there is nothing to indicate anything of wider significance.

[91] Jean Boucher, *Histoire tragique et memorable de Pierre de Gaverston, gentilhomme Gascon jadis le mignon d'Édouard 2 Roy d'Angleterre* (Paris, 1588). Boucher used the chronicles of Thomas Walsingham as his source. Cf. J.S. Hamilton, *Piers Gaveston: Earl of Cornwall, 1307–1312* (Detroit & London, 1988), 130–1.

[92] After telling the story of Edward II's murder, with the usual details of the ambiguous letter and the hot iron, Holinshed makes the following remarks: 'Hee had surely good cause to repent his former trade of lyving, for by his undiscreete and wanton misgovernance, there were headed and put to death during his raigne (by iudgement of law) to the number of XXVIII barons and knights, over and beside such as were slaine in Scotlande by hys unfortunate conduct. And all these mischiefes and many more happened not only to him, but also to the whole state of the realm, in that he wanted iudgement and prudent discretion to make choyse of sage and discrete counsaylers, receyving those into his favour, that abused the same to their pryvate gaine and advantage, not respecting the advancement of the common wealth, so they themselves might attaine to riches and honour, for which they onely sought, insomuch that by their covetous rapine, spoyle and immoderate ambition, the heartes of the common people and nobilitie were quite estranged from the dutifull love and obedience which they ought to have shewed to their soveraigne': Raphael Holinshed, *The Chronicles of England, Scotland and Ireland*, 2 vols (London, 1577), ii, 883–4.

Holinshed's *Chronicles* are also distinguished by their use of original material, such as the still unpublished chronicle ascribed to Nicholas Trivet (BL, Cotton Ms. Nero D.X), which is an important source for the events of 1321–2.

Gaveston,[93] but it was only in Christopher Marlowe's famous play, *Edward II*, written in about 1592, that such a relationship was made explicit.[94] More frequently, its nature was hinted at cautiously or cited as a dreadful example and warning of the fate that had befallen kings who allowed themselves to be influenced by favourites and so estranged themselves from their subjects.

In 1596 the poet Michael Drayton published his *Mortimeriados; the Lamentable Civil Wars of Edward the Second and the Barons*, which he revised and republished in 1603 under its more familiar title, *The Barons' Wars*.[95] In the seventeenth century several works on Edward II (whose career was often treated in parallel with that of Richard II) were published at times of political excitement. A tortuous poem of 4,060 lines by Sir Francis Hubert, *The Deplorable Life and Death of Edward II*, was published in 1628, at about the time of the murder of Charles I's favourite, the duke of Buckingham.[96] An anonymous pamphlet of 1648, *The People Informed of their Oppressors and Oppressions*, compared the power of Gaveston under Edward II with that of Buckingham, and justified the deposition of Edward II and by implication that of Charles I as well.[97]

---

[93] 'through whose company and societie hee was suddainely so corrupted, that he burst out into heinous vices ... he gave himself to wantonnes, passing time in voluptuous pleasure and riotous excesse ... [and] filthy and dishonourable exercises': Holinshed, *Chronicles*, ii, 847.

[94] Christopher Marlowe, *Doctor Faustus and other Plays*, ed. D. Bevington & E. Rasmussen (Oxford, 1995), Intro., xxi–xxiv. See, for example, the opening of the play with Gaveston reading what amounts to a love letter from Edward (I. i, ll. 1–15), and Gaveston's speech in ll. 49–70.

Although Shakespeare did not write a play of his own about Edward II, some scholars have argued that the play *Edward III*, composed in the mid-1590s, was the work in part or as a whole of Shakespeare. The play does not have anything to say about the end of Edward II's reign and the accession of his son, but concentrates on Edward III's campaigns in France during the 1340s and 1350s. The only reference to Edward II is to present him and his wife, Isabella of France, 'as solemn sureties of sovereignty over both realms'. See *Shakespeare's Edward III*, ed. E. Sams (New Haven & London, 1996), 1–3, 147–51.

[95] *The Oxford Companion to English Literature*, ed. M. Drabble (Oxford, 1995), 295. See also B.H. Newdigate, *Michael Drayton and his Circle* (Oxford, 1961). Drayton had also published a poem on Gaveston, *c.* 1593.

[96] F. Hubert, *The Deplorable Life and Death of Edward the Second, King of England, together with the Downefall of the two Unfortunate Favorits, Gavestone and Spencer, Storied in an Excellent Poem* (London, 1628).

[97] Anon., *The People Informed of their Oppressors and Oppressions with a Remedy Against Both. Unto which is added the sentence of Deposition against King Richard the Second, and Edward the Second; with the happiness that ensued to this Nation thereupon*, 4, 7–8: 'Upon the deposing of these two Kings, I shall make this observation, That it pleased God to place in their Thrones (as a sure sign of his approbation) two such Princes, as were not else in all Europe to be found; Edward the third, and Henry the fourth, the latter of which (besides the great advantage that His reign brought to the Kingdom in general) was the happy father of Henry the fift. That Kings may be deposed, is clear by the forementioned Precedent, and that Precedents are Law will not be denied by any man that deserves to wear a bare gown.' See also

The *History of the Most unfortunate Prince King Edward II*, attributed to Henry Cary, Viscount Falkland, Lord Deputy of Ireland, but probably in fact by his wife, Elizabeth Cary, may have been composed in 1626/7, but was not published until the time of the Exclusion Crisis in 1680. It was then provided with a thoughtful introduction by Sir Winston Churchill (father of the future duke of Marlborough), displaying sympathy for Edward II,[98] and was republished in 1689, after the deposition of James II.[99] In the same year there also appeared Sir Robert Howard's *Historical Observations upon the Reigns of Edward I, II, III, and Richard II*, in which the virtues and achievements of Edward I and Edward III are treated in parallel and contrasted with the errors and failings of Edward II and Richard II.[100] Howard also had something to do with a work published in 1713, *The History of the Life and reign of Edward II*,[101] while a further reminder of Edward and Gaveston was provided in an anonymous pamphlet, published in London in 1720, *The Prime Minister and King*.[102]

A significant contrast to the general condemnation of Edward II is *The History of Edward III*, by Joshua Barnes, which was published early in 1688

D. Clarke, ' "The sovereign's vice begets the subject's errour" ', in *Sodomy in Early Modern Europe*, ed. T. Bettridge (Manchester, 2002), 46–64.

By coincidence Edward II and Gaveston were alluded to at about the same time in France, in an anonymous warning addressed to Cardinal Mazarin, in the 15-page pamphlet, Anon., *Histoire Remarquable de la vie et mort d'un favory du roy d'Angleterre* (Paris, 1649). On the theme of rulers and favourites in general see J.H. Elliott, 'Introduction', in *The World of the Favourite*, ed. J.H. Elliott & L.W.B. Brockliss (New Haven & London, 1999).

[98] E. Cary, *The History of the Most unfortunate Prince King Edward II, with Choice Observations on Him and his unhappy Favourites, Gaveston and Spencer* (London, 1680): a book of 77 pages, plus the Preface by Sir Winston Churchill.

On Henry and Elizabeth Cary see the separate entries in the *Oxford DNB*.

[99] Published as E. Cary, *The History of the Life, Reign, Deposition and Death of King Edward the Second, with an Account of his Favourites, P. Gaveston and the Spencers* (London, 1689). (A note at the end indicates that this was first written by E.F. in 1627, published in 1680, and then again in 1689.)

[100] R. Howard, *Historical Observations upon the Reigns of Edward I, II, III, and Richard II. With Remarks upon their Faithful Counsellors and False Favourites. Written by a Person of Honour* (identified in the BL catalogue as Sir Robert Howard); licensed 17 Jan. 1688/9 (just in time for the Convention which assembled at Westminster on 22 Jan. 1689).

[101] Howard, *The History of the Life and Reign of Edward II, containing a Full Account of the Tyrannical Government of his Favourites and Minions. The several Struggles of the Barons for Liberty in his Time. The Bloody Executions when the Minions prevail. Their ill Treatment of the Queen and the Prince. The Deposing of Edward II and the Election of Edward III, By the Author of the Life and Reign of Henry VI. To which are added the Political Reflections of a Person of Quality* (p. 63 names him as Sir Robert Howard) (London, 1713).

[102] Anon., *The Prime Minister and King, with Political remarks, by way of Caution to all Crowned Heads and Evil Ministers*, 43. The Preface begins: 'The Subject of the following Sheets is the infamous Life and deserved Death of PIERCE GAVESTON, that overgrown Favourite and evil Prime Minister to that unfortunate Prince, KING EDWARD the Second; who for his immoderate Love to him, was hated by the Nobles and despised by the Commons.'

and dedicated to James II, and which is also distinguished by the amount of original research undertaken by its author. Having argued that Edward II was, at the last, truly repentant of 'all his former vanities', he noted the worthy things which Edward II had done in his lifetime, such as the foundation of Oriel College and St Mary's Hall at Oxford, and the houses of Carmelite friars at Oxford and of the Dominicans at King's Langley in Hertfordshire, 'and might have done more, had he not been so miserably interrupted'.[103]

EDWARD II IN THE NINETEENTH AND TWENTIETH CENTURIES

The fascination with Edward II and his fate lived on into the nineteenth century when it became part of an increasingly public debate on the nature of male sexuality, fuelled by such episodes as Marcus Stone's painting of Edward II and Gaveston, which was exhibited at the Royal Academy in 1872, and the trial of Oscar Wilde in 1895. In 1887 Havelock Ellis had published the first modern unexpurgated edition of Marlowe's play, *Edward II*, which drew attention, although in a somewhat defensive way, to the sexual implications of the text. Despite a growing interest in the play among literary societies from the 1880s, it remained unperformed until 1903; and as late as 1908 the Board of Education 'advised that in school history lessons the story of Edward II "be passed over in discreet silence"'.[104]

---

[103] Joshua Barnes (Bachelor of Divinity and one of the senior fellows of Emmanuel College, Cambridge), *The History of that Most Victorious Monarch Edward III etc., etc.* (Cambridge, 1688). The Preface is dated at Emmanuel College, 16 April 1688. Barnes goes to great lengths to clear Edward III of any responsibility for his father's murder and describes in detail the splendours of Edward II's tomb at Gloucester: Barnes, 3, 22–3. The account of Edward II's deposition, imprisonment, death and burial is on pp. 18–23. After printing a translation of the Lament supposedly composed by Edward II after his deposition, Barnes comments: 'Thus did this poor King repent all his former Vanities most heartily, no way repining at this punishment and heavy stroak of Gods Hand; but made so good use of these Afflictions that 'tis more than hoped, he fitted himself for a Kingdom more durable: to which his Enemies long'd to send him': Barnes, 19.

Another work which also shows a certain sympathy for Edward II, while not ignoring his failings, is the play by William Mountford, performed in London in 1691, *King Edward the Third, with the Fall of Mortimer Earl of March*. In the dedication of the play to Henry, Lord Viscount Sydney of Sheppey, Mountford says it is 'an English Story so fam'd for the reign of its Monarch, and the management of the few good Men about him, who with great difficulty preserv'd this Prince from the evill Machinations of Mortimer and his Faction, from the Potent Enemies of an Interested State; and the unnatural Connivance of a Mother (who design'd as much to usurp his Right as she really did destroy his Fathers) and the delivering their Country from the Tyranny and Oppression it had long been afflicted with, and which in all probability threatned the totall overthrow of the Established Liberties of the Subject.'

[104] P. Horne, 'The besotted king and his Adonis', *History Workshop Journal*, 47 (Oxford, 1999), 31–48, esp. 31–3, 42–5.

The serious academic study of the reign of Edward II which began in the late nineteenth and early twentieth centuries was influenced by the increasing availability of both administrative records and chronicle narratives, the growth of history as an academic discipline, and by the progress of political reform, and tended to concentrate on the implications of Edward II's reign for the constitutional development of England. Over and above the constant political crises and the chaos and bitterness of civil war, the reign was seen by historians such as William Stubbs, T.F. Tout and J.C. Davies as exhibiting a struggle between the king and the magnates on issues of constitutional principle, with the king seeking in the last resort to build up the power of his household as an inner bastion of government secure from baronial control and with attempts by the magnates to reform the royal administration and to manage royal policy in the interests of some greater ideal of constitutional liberty. The importance of parliament was also seen as being greatly enhanced by its role in the operation of the Ordinances, in the Statute of York and in the final deposition of Edward II.[105] Edward's perceived ineffectiveness was, in turn, seen almost as a blessing: 'A strong successor to Edward I might have made England a despotism; his weak and feckless son secured the permanence of Edwardian constitutionalism.'[106] The 'constitutional' view of the reign held sway until the 1970s when it was challenged in detailed studies of two of the leading magnates, Thomas, earl of Lancaster (Edward II's first cousin and his most bitter opponent) and Aymer de Valence, earl of Pembroke (also a cousin of Edward II and generally a loyal ally).[107] These and other studies[108] have shown the complexity of the politics of this

[105] W. Stubbs, *Constitutional History of England*, ii (Oxford, 1875), and in his historical introduction to the *Chronicles*, i. T.F. Tout expressed his views in his *DNB* article on Edward II (London, 1888); *The Political History of England, 1216–1377* (London, 1905); the classic statement of his views in *The Place of the Reign of Edward II*; and finally in *Chapters in the Administrative History of Mediaeval England*, ii (Manchester, 1933). J.C. Davies, *The Baronial Opposition to Edward II* (Cambridge, 1918; repr. London, 1967).

[106] Tout, *Place* (1936), 30.

[107] Maddicott; Phillips. Although the work of earlier scholars, notably that of Tout and Davies, was based on a very thorough examination of the resources of the Public Record Office which were then becoming accessible, more material, some of it very important, has since come to light and has been fully used in recent work on the period.

[108] Haines, *The Church and Politics*; N. Fryde, *The Tyranny and Fall of Edward II, 1321–1326* (Cambridge, 1979); J.H. Denton, *Robert Winchelsey and the Crown* (Cambridge, 1980); M. Buck, *Politics, Finance and the Church in the Reign of Edward II* (Cambridge, 1983); Haines, *Stratford*; Hamilton; Chaplais. To this list should be added two of Michael Prestwich's books, *The Three Edwards* and *Edward I*. Among recent studies of the reign are R. M. Haines, *King Edward II: Edward of Caernarfon, his Life, his Reign, and its Aftermath, 1284–1330* (Montreal & London, 2003); Prestwich's *Plantagenet England, 1225–1360* (Oxford, 2005); and S. Raban, *England under Edward I and Edward II, 1259–1327* (Oxford, 2000). A great deal of other important work has also been published in journals and collections of articles, such as *The Reign of Edward II*, ed. G. Dodd & A. Musson (Woodbridge, Suffolk & Rochester, NY, 2006) and in the volumes published under various editors since 2000 in the *Fourteenth Century England* series (Woodbridge, Suffolk, & Rochester, NY).

period, and the importance of understanding individual behaviour and motivations, as well as wider problems and issues of policy. As a result many of the earlier certainties have largely dissolved.[109]

Edward II has not however been the subject only of recent specialized research monographs. The range of interest in and of reference to him is extraordinary. A number of writers have produced accounts of the reign for a general audience;[110] and there have been some notable historical novels on the period.[111] In Italy there are plaques to commemorate Edward II's 'presence' at the castle of Melazzo, north of Genoa, and another at the former Benedictine abbey of Butrio, marking the supposed 'tomb' of Edward II.[112] Edward II has been made the subject of medical analysis, one early twentieth-century medical author going so far as to argue that the incompetence and peculiarities of behaviour of Edward II were the result of a physical degeneration of the brain.[113] There has been particular interest in Christopher Marlowe's *Edward II*, which has been staged many times both in its original form, and also in Bertolt Brecht's adaptation made in 1922–23.[114] Sidney Lumet's 1966 film of a John le Carré spy novel set in London, *The Deadly Affair*, reached its climax during a Royal Shakespeare Company production of

---

[109] An important step towards the dissolution of earlier certainties was taken, by implication, in Johnstone's pioneering monograph, *Edward of Carnarvon*, in which she provided a detailed treatment of Edward's character and early career, making full use of the extensive archive sources for this period of Edward's life.

[110] H. F. Hutchison, *Edward II* (London, 1971); C. Bingham, *The Life and Times of Edward II* (London, 1973); and M. Saaler, *Edward II, 1307–1327* (London, 1997). Of these three books Bingham's is probably the best, although (like Hutchison's) it was written before the publication of most of the new research.

[111] See, for example, Paul Doherty's novel on the imprisonment, death and 'escape' of Edward II, *The Death of a King* (London, 1985). Since Dr Doherty is also the author of an important unpublished doctoral thesis, 'Isabella, Queen of England, 1296–1330' (Oxford, 1977), now partially published as *Isabella and the Strange Death of Edward II* (London, 2003), this is a particularly well-informed novel. See also the series of six novels by the French author and member of the Académie Française, Maurice Druon, published under the general title of *Les Rois maudits* (Paris, 1955–60) (*The Accursed Kings*, London, 1956–61), and covering the period from 1314 to 1343. These well-written novels contain a great deal of material about events both in France and in England, and about the relations between the French and English courts. The novels were dramatized for a highly acclaimed series shown on French television in 1971–72, and are now available on DVD.

[112] The website for Melazzo states as a fact that Edward II stayed there between 1330 and 1333; the abbey of S. Alberto has been occupied by a modern religious community since 1899, while the local tourist website records the tradition that Edward II had also been there as a hermit. I have examined the subject in ' "Edward II" in Italy', 209–26. See also Ch. 11 of this book.

[113] C. Robinson, 'Was Edward the Second a degenerate?', *American Journal of Insanity*, lxvi (1909–10), 445–64. Cf. V. Green, *The Madness of Kings* (Stroud, 1993), 47–53.

[114] J. Willet & R. Manheim, eds, *Bertolt Brecht Collected Plays*, i, x–xi, and text of *The Life of King Edward II of England* (London, 1970).

Edward II.[115] The sexual connotations of the play have made it the focus of numerous doctoral theses and of much other critical writing,[116] and were emphasized in Derek Jarman's very explicit 1992 film version of the play.[117] More recently, the depiction of Edward and of Gaveston in Mel Gibson's film *Braveheart* (1995) has brought the story of Marlowe's play to an even wider audience. In the late 1980s the English composer Peter Tranchell (1922–93) projected an opera on Edward II,[118] while David Bintley used Marlowe's play for his full-length ballet, *Edward II*, which he produced for the Stuttgart Ballet in the Württemberg State Theatre in April 1995 and again for the Birmingham Royal Ballet in Birmingham in October 1997. The music for the ballet was written by John McCabe, who also reworked the music in his symphony number 5, 'Edward II' (2000).[119] Edward's modern musical associations also extend to a 'folk/reggae' band, variously known under the evocative name of Edward II and the Red Hot Polkas or simply as Edward II, which was appropriately formed in Gloucestershire and was active between 1985 and 1999. In Rome there is even a nightclub named after him, La Taverna di Edoardo Secondo, 'formerly a medieval torture chamber theme bar', and in San Francisco an Edward II hotel.[120]

EDWARD II TODAY

Part of the problem of Edward II, and therefore also a major problem for any modern biographer, is that he has in a sense been in the 'possession' of so many people both in his own day and down to the present time. While he was alive he was the subject of much criticism, some of it justified but much of it unfair. At the time of his deposition in 1327, and in the seventy years or so following, his reputation was manipulated both by those who wished to blacken his name in order to justify the change of regime and by others who sought to present him as a holy figure and even as a candidate for canonization. Even today Edward II is one of the few English kings (together with 'bad' King John and Henry VIII and his

---

[115] D. Willis, 'Marlowe our contemporary', *Criticism*, xl, no. 4 (Detroit, 1999), 599–622, esp. 599.

[116] For a selection of modern interpretations of Marlowe's play see Marlowe, *Doctor Faustus*, xxxiv.

[117] Jarman gave further emphasis to this approach by his simultaneous publication of a book on the making of the film, *Queer Edward II* (London, 1991). Edward II and his reputation became a part of the sexual politics of the late 20th century.

[118] Cambridge University Library, Ms. Tranchell 1.15. The opera would presumably have given emphasis to the relationship between Edward and Gaveston under the conventions of that time.

[119] Notes on the website of Novello & Co. Ltd.

[120] M. Dunford, *The Rough Guide to Rome* (New York & London, 2005), 238; and hotel website.

six wives) about whom nearly everyone still 'knows' something: in Edward's case that he was homosexual and that he was murdered with a red-hot iron. Whether either piece of information is necessarily true and whether it is possible for the historian faced with so many centuries of received opinion and prejudice to reach a more balanced conclusion on Edward II and his reign is another matter entirely.[121]

---

[121] The task is not made any easier by the fact that any characteristic of behaviour or event in the life of Edward II, from playing at dice for recreation and drinking with companions to his conduct of affairs of state and military campaigns, which can be interpreted to his discredit or disadvantage has usually been so interpreted. Two excellent illustrations of the problem can be found in the accounts of Edward II's chamber for 1326 when, on two separate occasions, he made a generous gift to a royal servant who had made him laugh: on 11 March he gave 50 shillings to his painter James of St Albans who had danced on a table; and on 30 July, while he was stag hunting near the royal lodge in Woolmer forest on the borders of Surrey and Hampshire, he gave 20 shillings to Maurice one of his cooks who was evidently not a good rider and had kept falling off his horse: SAL, Ms. 122, pp. 55, 79. These incidents could be interpreted simply as demonstrating Edward II's enjoyment of the society of low-born companions and his frivolity at a critical time in his reign when fears were growing of an invasion of England by his estranged wife Isabella and her lover Roger Mortimer of Wigmore; or as showing that Edward had a sense of humour and could find relaxation even at stressful moments in his life; or as evidence of his concern with other people's welfare – in the first instance Edward gave the money in order to help James's wife and children.

Chapter 2

THE NATURE OF A KING[1]

EDWARD'S BIRTH

Edward of Caernarfon, the future Edward II, king of England, was born on St Mark's Day, 25 April 1284,[2] at Caernarfon castle in North Wales,[3] and was baptized there on 1 May.[4] Even in its present ruined state, the massive bulk of Caernarfon castle, set against the backdrop of the mountains of Snowdonia, is an impressive and even awe-inspiring sight. At the time of Edward's birth however the construction of the castle had only recently begun. Although the Eagle Tower in which Edward is traditionally said to have been born may already have been sufficiently complete to house such an important event, the actual birthplace was probably the king and queen's lodgings, a wooden building which had recently been provided with glazed windows for additional comfort. Caernarfon castle as a whole was little more than a vast building site strewn with wood, earth and stone, and, to all appearances, a most unlikely location for the birth of a new royal child.[5] Royal children did of course come into the world wherever

---

[1] The classic account of Edward's early years by Johnstone in *Edward of Carnarvon* drew extensively on the substantial surviving household records both for Edward of Caernarfon and for Edward I. Although I disagree with some of her conclusions, much of what she wrote retains its value. I shall not attempt to emulate the detail of her study. The much older work of Dr J. Doran, *The Book of the Princes of Wales* (London, 1860) is of little value.

[2] Edward shared his birth date with St Louis IX of France. Liturgically St Mark's Day was celebrated by the carrying of black crosses in procession and by 'prayers for good weather, good harvests and good health in the ensuing year'. Louis IX's biographer, Joinville, saw the date as prophetic of all those who would die with Louis while on crusade and of the king's own tragic end. No one in England noted the possible gloomy significance for Edward's own life of his birth date, which was celebrated annually during Edward's youth by rejoicing and the entertaining of 'hundreds of poor people in honour of St. Mark': Johnstone, 7–8.

[3] Twelve shillings were paid for feeding 100 poor people, as the private alms of Edward I, and a sum of £9 was distributed at Caernarfon to mark the birth of 'the lord Edward, the king's son': E 101/351/15, m.2. Edward I was clearly present at Caernarfon on the date of the birth and not at Rhuddlan as stated elsewhere: cf. ibid., 8, n. 3. The birth was recorded by several chroniclers, one of whom remarked that at the news of his birth 'many rejoiced, especially the Londoners': ibid., 8, n. 1.

[4] £10 in alms was distributed at Caernarfon on the day of the baptism: E 101/351/15, m.2.

[5] E 101/351/9, m.12; A. J. Taylor, *Caernarfon Castle*, 4th edn (Cardiff, 1997), 10; *KW*, i, 372. The famous tower with its triple turrets, each surmounted by an eagle, was not finished until much later. The first evidence of any of the eagles being put in place dates from

their mother happened to be at the time, sometimes in very unlikely places,[6] yet in this case there is little doubt that Edward I deliberately chose Caernarfon as the birthplace of his latest offspring.[7]

Edward of Caernarfon's birth was but one detail, and probably at the time not the most important, in the process by which his father Edward I took final control of the territory of the principality of Wales. In December 1282 the first native Prince of Wales,[8] Llywelyn ap Gruffudd, had been killed in a skirmish near Builth, while in June 1283 his brother Dafydd was betrayed and captured, and in October suffered a cruel death as a traitor to the English crown. In the spring and summer of 1283 Edward I sealed his victory by beginning the construction of a series of great fortresses at Conwy, Caernarfon and Harlech; in March 1284 at Rhuddlan he issued the Statute of Wales which laid down the practicalities of the future English government of Wales;[9] and in July of 1284 he celebrated his conquest with a splendid tournament and Arthurian 'round table' at Nefyn, south-west of Caernarfon on the Lleyn peninsula.[10]

Edward I was however concerned to do much more than simply achieve a military conquest and the introduction of a new administrative framework for Wales. As he was to do later in Scotland, he also took possession of the religious and political centres, the holy relics, and the symbols of Welsh independence. The surviving children of Llywelyn ap Gruffudd and his brother, Dafydd, were dispatched for safekeeping in England, the sons to imprisonment in castles and the daughters to convents.[11] In the summer and autumn of 1284 Edward I and Queen Eleanor made a triumphal tour of Wales and of Welsh places of

---

1316–17, in the middle of the reign of Edward II. In 1321 a statue of Edward II was erected on the King's Gate, one of the last sections of the castle to see building works: Taylor, 10–17.

[6] A good example is the birth in 1300 of Edward I's son, Thomas, at Brotherton in Yorkshire instead of at the archbishop of York's manor at Cawood, when Edward's new wife, Margaret of France, went into labour unexpectedly: Prestwich, *Edward I*, 131.

[7] Here I am in fundamental disagreement with Hilda Johnstone, *Edward*, 6.

[8] And the last native Prince of Wales until the revolt of Owain Glyndŵr in 1400.

[9] R.R. Davies, *Conquest, Coexistence and Change* (Oxford & Cardiff, 1987), 353–6, 364–5; J.B. Smith, *Llywelyn ap Gruffudd, Prince of Wales* (Cardiff, 1998), 562–7, 575–9.

[10] Although the site had first to be cleared of nettles and thistles by two small boys, who were paid 4d for two days' work (E 101/351/9, m.13), it was a highly successful occasion which effectively demonstrated the English victory. The choice of Nefyn, the site of one of the former courts of Llywelyn ap Gruffudd, was deliberate on the part of Edward who 'took a particular delight in appropriating the residences of the Gwynedd dynasty': Davies, *Conquest*, 355; Davies, *The First English Empire* (Oxford, 2000), 31–2. For Edward I's interest in the legends of King Arthur see R.S. Loomis, 'Edward I', *Speculum*, xxviii (1953), 114–27, and the more sceptical views in Prestwich, *Edward I*, 120–2.

[11] Smith, *Llywelyn ap Gruffudd*, 579–80. Llywelyn had no sons but his daughter, Gwenllian, lived as a nun at Sempringham in Lincolnshire for over fifty years; one of Dafydd's sons, Owain, lived until at least 1325; Llywelyn's brother Rhodri lived until about 1315: Smith, 580; Prestwich, *Edward I*, 203; Davies, *Conquest*, 438.

pilgrimage;[12] the sacred possession of the dynasty of Llywelyn ap Gruffudd, the relic of the True Cross, *Y Groes Naid*, was sent to England, as were Llywelyn's crown and the 'crown of King Arthur'; while his seal was melted down to make a chalice.[13] Edward I pointedly arranged for Alfonso, his elder son and heir to the throne of England, to present the Welsh treasures to the shrine of Edward the Confessor, the dynastic saint and protector of the English monarchy, in Westminster Abbey.[14] The author of the annals of Waverley abbey, commenting on the event, remarked aptly: 'and thus the glory of the Welsh was transferred to the English'.[15] In all possible ways Edward I sought to appropriate for himself and his successors every claim to legitimacy over the newly conquered 'land of Wales'.[16]

Within Wales, Caernarfon was a place of particular significance because of its associations with imperial Rome, both through the remains of the nearby Roman fortress of Segontium and, more powerfully, in Welsh legend. Magnus Maximus, a Roman commander in late fourth-century Britain who was proclaimed emperor by his troops, had later become immortalized as Macsen Wledig who had dreamt of 'a great fortified city at the mouth of the river, and a great fort in the city, the fairest man ever saw, and great towers of many colours on the fort; and in its hall a chair of ivory, and the image of two eagles in gold thereon'.[17] He was also believed to have been the father of the emperor Constantine and, very conveniently for Edward I's purposes, a body was discovered at Caernarfon in 1283 and identified either as that of Magnus Maximus or even of Constantine himself.[18] On this slender but alluring foundation

---

[12] On 5 Aug., for example, the king and queen visited Bardsey Island, a famous place of pilgrimage off the tip of the Lleyn peninsula; they were at St David's cathedral in November: these and other details appear in the Alms Roll of 1283–4 (E 101/351/15). This is discussed in A.J. Taylor, 'Royal alms and oblations in the late thirteenth century', in *Tribute to an Antiquary*, ed. F. Emmison & R. Stephens (London, 1976), 93–125.

[13] Davies, *Conquest*, 354–5; Smith, *Llywelyn ap Gruffudd*, 580–1; Prestwich, *Edward I*, 203–4.

[14] Davies, *First English Empire*, 27. For a detailed study of the relationship between St Edward, Westminster Abbey and the English monarchy see Binski, *Westminster Abbey*, esp. ch. 2, 'The cult of St Edward'. See also Prestwich, *Edward I*, 4–5. On 18 July 1297 the Stone of Scone, which Edward I had seized at Scone Abbey in Scotland in 1296, was dedicated in Westminster Abbey to St Edward. By 27 March 1300 the Stone had been incorporated in a specially made chair, 'intended as the sacred reliquary of a sacred relic', which was placed in the chapel of St Edward beside the shrine of the saint. The Stone remained at Westminster until its recent return to Scotland: S. S. Jervis, President, Anniversary Address 1997, in *Society of Antiquaries of London: Annual Report: Proceedings 1997* (London, 1997), 12–13.

[15] *Annales Monasterii de Waverleia*, *Annales Monastici*, ii, ed. H.R. Luard, Rolls ser. (London, 1865), 401–2.

[16] Davies, *Conquest*, 356.

[17] Phillips, 'Edward II and the prophets', 190; Davies, *Conquest*, 360; Prestwich, *Edward I*, 120.

[18] Davies, *Conquest*, 360. The finding of the body and its ideological significance could be compared with the convenient discovery of the Holy Lance by the crusaders besieging Antioch in 1098. The legend confused another Constantine, the early fifth-century claimant of the Roman Empire, with the historical emperor Constantine of a century earlier: see Edward James, *Britain in the First Millennium* (London, 2001), 92–3.

Edward I determined to build a magnificent fortress of his own, which would be the focus of royal authority and the administrative centre of the new English order in Wales.[19]

EDWARD AND WALES

There is no apparent basis for David Powel's late sixteenth-century statement that the newly born Edward of Caernarfon was presented to the Welsh nobility as a prince 'that was borne in Wales and could speake never a word of English'.[20] On the other hand it is possible that Edward I may have considered setting up in Wales a new ruling house, subordinate to that of England and taking its legitimacy both from the fact of English conquest and from the signs and symbols of Welsh authority which Edward I had gone to such lengths to take over. Edward's new son would have been the obvious candidate to found such a dynasty.[21]

This is of course speculation since there is nothing in the records of the time to indicate what immediate plans, if any, Edward I had for his youngest son, Edward. In the event Edward spent little time in Wales. Within a few months of his birth he left Wales, together with his sisters Eleanor and Joan, via Chester for Acton Burnell in Shropshire and thence to rejoin his parents at Bristol.[22] He did not return until his progress through Wales in 1301 after his creation as Prince of Wales, and after that not until the tragic autumn of 1326 when he fled to Wales for refuge from his enemies in England.

Nonetheless Wales played an important part in the life and career of Edward, first simply as Edward 'the king's son', later as Prince of Wales and finally as Edward II. From his birthplace he was forever to be known as Edward of Caernarfon. Even if the claim by the St Albans chronicler William Rishanger that in 1301 the Welsh rejoiced, from the highest to the lowest, and accepted him as their legitimate lord because he had been

---

[19] Davies, *Conquest*, 360; Taylor, *Caernarfon Castle*, 39–41. The striking resemblance between the polygonal towers and bands of light and dark stone at Caernarfon and Constantinople suggested to Taylor that it could only have been intentional. The great tower known as the Eagle Tower also reinforced the imperial associations. Very little of this elaborate plan of construction had of course been realized when Edward II was born in 1284. Recent research has confirmed the imperial association in respect of Magnus Maximus, while calling into question the suggested connection with Constantine and the parallel with the walls of Constantinople: A. Wheatley, *The Idea of the Castle in Medieval England* (Woodbridge, Suffolk & Rochester, NY, 2007), ch. 4, 'The imperial castle'.

[20] D. Powel, *The Historie of Cambria* (London, 1584), 377. The legend was duly repeated, with some embellishment, in J. Doran, *The Book of the Princes of Wales* (London, 1860), 15–16. This story was firmly discarded by Hilda Johnstone in *Edward of Carnarvon*, 6–7. However, modern research has shown that earlier material preserved in 16th- and 17th-century sources can sometimes be of great importance for writing the history of medieval Wales: J.B. Smith, 'Gruffydd Llwyd and the Celtic alliance, 1315–1318', *Bulletin of the Board of Celtic Studies*, xxvi, part 4 (May 1976), 469–71, 477–8.

[21] Edward was not at the time of his birth the immediate heir to the English throne.

[22] E 101/351/12, m.2; Johnstone, 10.

born in Wales,[23] is certainly an exaggeration,[24] there is no doubt that Edward enjoyed a remarkable degree of loyalty from his Welsh subjects. At critical moments, such as the English civil war of 1321–2, they stayed loyal and helped to defeat his enemies,[25] while in 1327 Welsh conspiracies threatened for a time to release him from his captivity in Berkeley castle and even to restore him to his throne.[26] The opinion quoted by several fourteenth-century English chroniclers that Edward II's one great fortune was that Wales never revolted against him was amply borne out by events.[27] It was somehow appropriate that even the impostor, who turned up at Cologne in 1338 claiming to be the long-dead Edward II, should apparently have been a Welshman.[28]

How Edward in his turn regarded Wales and the Welsh is impossible to know with any certainty, although there are some clues. His first wet-nurse, Mariota or Mary Maunsel, may have been Welsh, but her connection with Edward was so short that no influence upon her royal charge can be inferred.[29] Edward may have enjoyed Welsh music, since in September 1305 he sent a member of his household, Richard the Rhymer, to Shrewsbury abbey to learn the Welsh stringed instrument, the *crwth*.[30] It is

---

[23] *Annales Regis Edwardi Primi, Fragmentum I*, in *Chronica Monasterii S. Albani*, ed. H.T. Riley, Rolls ser. (London, 1865), 464; also cited by a later St Albans historian, Thomas Walsingham, in his *Historia Anglicana*, ed. H.T. Riley, Rolls ser., i (London, 1863), 83. For whatever motive, Edward was remembered in his birthplace. On 2 August 1290, 6s 8d was given to 'certain men of Caernarfon' who had brought him four herons. These were probably the two Welshmen, Iorwerth and Dafydd, who were given the same sum on 15 Aug. for their return home: C 47/3/22, m.1. In Jan. 1301 the bishop of Bangor sent Edward presents of two falcons and a palfrey from Powys: E 101/360/10, m.2. See also Johnstone, 10, n. 4.

[24] One reason for Welsh loyalty was the fact that royal power in the principality of Wales was seen by the Welsh as a source of protection against the abuses of power by the English lords in the Welsh March, the borderland between Wales and England: cf. Davies, *Conquest*, 386–8, 394–7; and J.B. Smith, 'Edward II and the allegiance of Wales', *Welsh History Review*, viii (1976–7), 139–71.

[25] Phillips, *Aymer de Valence*, 221–2; Davies, *Conquest*, 397.

[26] Phillips, 'Edward II and Ireland'; Davies, *Conquest*, 397.

[27] E.g. *Polychronicon*, 300–1. The same comment can also be found in *Gesta Edwardi*, in *Melsa*, and in *Knighton*. According to Thomas Walsingham, who was however writing long after the death of Edward II and in an abbey which had strong ties with the crown, the Welsh attachment to Edward went much further: 'When Scotland would openly rebel against him and all England would rid herself of him, then the Welsh in a wonderful manner cherished and esteemed him, and, as far as they were able, stood by him grieving over his adversities both in life and in his death, and composing mournful songs about him in the language of their country, the memory of which lingers to the present time, and which neither the dread of punishment nor the passage of time has destroyed': G.C. Coulton, *Medieval Panorama* (Cambridge, 1943), 560, citing *Historia Anglicana*, i, 83.

[28] *The Wardrobe Book of William de Norwell*, ed. Lyon et al., 178–9. The impostor's name was apparently William le Galeys (i.e. literally 'William the Welshman'). On William see Phillips, ' "Edward II" in Italy', 222–6, and ch. 11 of this book.

[29] E 101/351/12, m.2; Johnstone, 9. She fell ill at Rhuddlan in Sept. 1284.

[30] Johnstone, 64; *Letters of Edward Prince of Wales, 1304–1305*, ed. H. Johnstone, Roxburghe Club (Cambridge, 1931), 114. This is an edition of E 163/5/2, a roll containing

also known that he possessed, although he could not possibly have read, a manuscript in Welsh, which may have been an anthology of Welsh religious and secular poetry by bardic poets. The manuscript 'may not even have predated 1300', although the poems it contained were probably already old.[31] This has been described as one of 'the chance spoils of war',[32] but it is perhaps more likely to have been produced by a Welsh scribe for presentation to Edward, the newly created English Prince of Wales, during his tour of Wales in 1301 to accept the homage of his Welsh subjects.[33] Another hint of his attitude to Wales and the Welsh can be found in the well-known letter he addressed in May 1305 to Count Louis of Évreux,[34] which has variously been described as displaying petulance or frivolity on the part of Edward.[35] What it really shows is that Edward had a wry affection for Wales and also that he had a sense of humour:

> We send you a big trotting palfrey which can hardly carry its own weight, and some of our bandy-legged harriers from Wales, who can well catch a hare if they find it asleep, and some of our running dogs, which go at a gentle pace; for well we know that you take delight in lazy dogs.[36] And dear cousin, if you want anything else from our land of Wales, we can

---

transcripts of over 600 privy seal letters sent on behalf of Edward in 33 Edward I, i.e. Nov. 1304–Nov. 1305. The roll throws a great deal of light on Edward's affairs and personality, but it is unfortunately a unique survival and also does not cover the entire year, there being a gap of six months between Langley on 27 Nov. 1304 and Sunbury on 18 May 1305.

[31] The manuscript's former existence is known only from the first line which is recorded in an inventory of books owned by Edward II in 1320: *The Antient Kalendars and Inventories of His Majesty's Exchequer*, ed. F. Palgrave (London, 1836), i, 106, 116; R. I. Jack, *Medieval Wales* (London, 1972), 53–4. The possible nature of the manuscript has been identified in a brilliant piece of linguistic detective work by Andrew Breeze in 'A manuscript of Welsh poetry in Edward II's library', *National Library of Wales Journal*, xxx, part 2 (Winter 1997), 129–31.

[32] Jack, *Medieval Wales*, 54.

[33] This is entirely speculation on my part but it seems a plausible way to account for Edward's possession of the manuscript.

[34] Louis of Evreux (1276–1319) was the half-brother of Philip IV of France and became Edward's uncle when his sister Margaret (1282–1318) married Edward I in 1299. There is evidence both here and elsewhere that Edward was on close and friendly terms with Louis, who was perhaps almost a father figure at a time when Edward was on bad terms with his own father. In 1305 Louis was visiting England, together with his mother, Marie, the queen-mother of France, at about the time of the start of Edward's quarrel with his father: Johnstone, 99

[35] Johnstone, 64; Prestwich, *Edward I*, 227. The modern reaction to this letter, especially that of Johnstone, is a very good example of the unfairness with which Edward has often been treated both in his own day and since. In this letter Edward is simply sharing a joke with someone he knew well. In her introduction to the *Letters of Edward Prince of Wales*, xxxvii, Johnstone made the very odd remark that the letter 'seems to suggest that Edward himself was far from content with his position and his sporting equipment'. In fairness, her translation of the letter on this occasion (1931) is much less considered than in *Edward of Carnarvon* (1946).

[36] Edward may well have been thinking of the two greyhounds sent to him by the constable of Conway in 1300: *Liber Quotidianus Garderobae, 28 Edward I*, ed. J. Topham (London, 1787), 166 (an edn of SAL Ms. 119); Johnstone, 10, n. 4.

send you plenty of wild men (*gentz sauvages*)[37] if you like, who will know well how to teach breeding to the young heirs or heiresses of great lords.[38]

The best indication however of how Edward regarded Wales is in his careful cultivation after he became Prince of Wales of influential figures in native Welsh society and their employment in important administrative posts, especially as sheriffs. Men like Gruffydd Llwyd, Rhys ap Gruffudd, and others came into Edward's service at this time, stayed with him when he became king and showed their loyalty in the years to come.[39] Sadly Edward was not to show the same ability to manage and to sustain loyalties on the greater and even more complex stage of English political life.

EDWARD AND HIS FAMILY

Edward was the last of at least fourteen (and possibly as many as sixteen) children born to Edward I (1272–1307) and his first wife, Eleanor of Castile.[40] The choice of Edward for his Christian name was significant. Edward I's father, Henry III (1216–72), had, for the first time since the Norman Conquest, given English names to his two sons, Edward and Edmund. This was in token of Henry's devotion to the cult of the Anglo-Saxon king, Edward the Confessor (1042–66), whose body was buried in Westminster Abbey and who had been canonized in 1161.[41] Edward I had at first followed earlier royal tradition in his choice of names. His eldest son John was called after his grandfather King John, while his second son Henry[42] was named after both Edward I's own father and his great-grandfather Henry II (1154–89), the founder of the Plantagenet dynasty. Alfonso, his third son, was named after Alfonso X, king of Castile (1252–84), the half-brother of Edward I's wife Eleanor.[43] Only with his last-born son did Edward I revert to the English name, which he himself bore.[44]

---

[37] Literally this means 'men of the woods': '*homines silvatici*', and by extension 'wild men'. The 'wild man' was a familiar theme in medieval tradition and folklore: see Phillips, 'The outer world of the European middle ages', in *Implicit Understandings*, ed. St. B. Schwartz (Cambridge, 1994), 48.
[38] Johnstone, 64, citing *Letters of Edward Prince of Wales*, 11.
[39] Davies, *Conquest*, 386–7, 409–10, 415–16.
[40] J.C. Parsons, *Eleanor of Castile* (New York & London, 1995), 33; Prestwich, *Edward I*, 125–6.
[41] Henry III had the abbey entirely rebuilt between 1245 and 1272 as a setting for the shrine of St Edward and for the royal tombs grouped around it: see Binski, *Westminster Abbey*, esp. ch. 2, 'The cult of St Edward'. Henry III's other surviving son was named after another Anglo-Saxon ruler, the martyred Edmund, king of the East Angles (d. 869): see Prestwich, *Edward I*, 4–5.
[42] J.C. Parsons, 'The year of Eleanor of Castile's birth and her children by Edward I', *Mediaeval Studies*, xlvi (1984), 258–60.
[43] Ibid., 261–2.
[44] When it came to family names, Edward I's devotion to the Angevin origins of his dynasty was greater than to the Anglo-Saxon.

By the time of Edward of Caernarfon's birth at least seven of the children of Edward I and Eleanor of Castile were already dead, including their two elder sons John (1266–71) and Henry (1268–74).[45] The surviving children were Alfonso (born in 1273) who was the heir to the throne, and five sisters, Eleanor (born in 1269), Joan (born in 1272), Margaret (born in 1275), Mary (born in 1279), and Elizabeth (born in August 1282 at Rhuddlan in Wales).[46] The death of Alfonso in August 1284 left the newly born Edward both as the only surviving son and as heir to the throne; with unpredictable consequences for the future of the kingdom of England should he too die in infancy.[47] Childhood illnesses therefore took on a more than usual importance. While there is nothing to suggest that Edward experienced any life-threatening illness as a child, it is known that he and his sister Margaret suffered a bout of 'tertian fever', lasting more than a month, early in 1294.[48] A few years earlier, probably in September 1290, Edward I's mother, the formidable Eleanor of Provence, expressed her alarm at the possible consequences if the king were to take his son into *le mauveis air* of the north of England.[49] Although the young Edward of Caernarfon seems in fact to have been strong and athletic, and also to have been a good horseman, the need to preserve his life remained paramount. This may, in part, explain why, unlike his father in his own youth or his first cousins, Thomas and Henry of Lancaster, he is never known to have taken part in a tournament.[50] Lack of interest or aptitude may also have been a reason, as is usually assumed, but it is just as likely that it was simply too dangerous to risk the life or health of the heir to the throne, and hence also the life and health of the kingdom itself, in such a sport.[51]

[45] Edward's own existence had been threatened by the fire in the king and queen's chamber at Hope castle near Chester in Aug. 1283, at about the time when he must have been conceived: Parsons, *Eleanor of Castile*, 33, 267, n. 77.

[46] The fullest treatment of the children of Edward I and Eleanor of Castile is in Parsons, 'The year of Eleanor of Castile's birth', 249–65.

[47] Ibid., 261–2. Alfonso was buried in Westminster Abbey next to the shrine of St Edward. See Binski, *Westminster Abbey*, 93, 100; Sally Badham, 'Edward the Confessor's chapel, Westminster Abbey', *Antiquaries Journal*, lxxxvii (2007), 197–208.

[48] Johnstone, 12; M.A.E. Green, *Lives of the Princesses of England*, ii (London, 1850), 375–6. Of Edward I's children by his first marriage only two, his daughters Mary (1279–1332) and Margaret (1275–c.1333), lived to be over fifty: Parsons, 'The year of Eleanor of Castile's birth', 262, 264. The remaining daughters survived only into their late twenties or mid-thirties. In this company Edward of Caernarfon's life-span of 43 years was above average. Although Edward I was to live to the age of sixty-eight, his health in childhood often gave cause for concern; he had one brother, Edmund, but four other brothers and sisters died in infancy: Prestwich, *Edward I*, 6.

[49] SC 1/16/170: 1 Sept., 1286–90; prob. 1290: Johnstone, 24. There is nothing to suggest any other cause of concern for Edward's health at this time.

[50] Johnstone, 17. He apparently intended to hold a tournament at Wark in Northumberland in Jan. 1307 but gave up the plan: BL, Add. Ms. 22923, f. 14v; Johnstone, 117. It has also been suggested that he held a tournament at Roxburgh on 29 Oct. 1306, but Hamilton, 33, 138, n. 50, thinks this is unlikely. In any case arranging a tournament did not necessarily imply actual participation.

The death of Duke John I of Brabant, the father-in-law of Edward's sister Margaret, in a tournament in 1294 was a close family example of what might so easily happen.

It is not therefore surprising that the issue of the succession to the crown became of increasing concern to Edward I as he grew older. The death without a male heir of Alexander III of Scotland in 1286 was a further warning of how easily a kingdom could be plunged into uncertainty.[52] The question came to centre stage in 1290, when Edward I was completing his plans for a new crusade. Because of the possibility that he might die during the expedition, he held a gathering of family members, leading churchmen, nobles and administrators on 17 April at the convent of Amesbury in Wiltshire, to which Eleanor of Provence had withdrawn in 1286. The six-year-old Edward of Caernarfon was among those present on this important occasion. Gilbert de Clare, earl of Gloucester, who was about to marry Edward I's daughter, Joan of Acre (1272–1307), took an oath that he would recognize the young Edward as king, if Edward I should die.[53] On the same day Edward I, as he thought, copper-fastened the succession by writing to the king of Norway to complete arrangements for a marriage between Edward and Margaret of Norway, the heiress to the throne of Scotland.[54] Edward I however knew that he too might not be succeeded by a male heir when he ensured the rights of succession in turn of each of his surviving daughters and any future offspring: Eleanor (1269–98); Joan of Acre; Margaret (1275–c.1333); and Elizabeth (1282–1316) then eight years old.[55]

The plans for Edward of Caernarfon's own marriage and for the succession to the English throne were celebrated soon after by a tournament held not far from Amesbury, at Winchester on 20 April 1290. The centrepiece of the feast held afterwards was the 'Round Table' of King Arthur, which today hangs on the wall of the former Great Hall of Winchester castle.[56]

---

[51] On the other hand, Edward did take part in a considerable number of military campaigns and was several times in imminent danger.

[52] The Capetian dynasty, which had ruled England's powerful neighbour and rival the kingdom of France since 987, had been blessed with an unbroken succession of male heirs to the throne. However, in 1328 that succession too was to end, with disastrous consequences for France.

[53] *Foedera*, I, ii, 742; Prestwich, *Edward I*, 348–9; C. Given-Wilson, 'Legitimation, designation and succession to the throne in fourteenth-century England', in *Building Legitimacy*, ed. I. Alfonso, H.N. Kennedy and J. Escalona, The Medieval Mediterranean, liii (Leiden & Boston, 2004), 99–100.

[54] See the papers by G.W.S. Barrow, 'A kingdom in crisis', and M. Prestwich, 'Edward I and the Maid of Norway', *Scottish Historical Review*, lxix (Oct. 1990), 121–41, and 157–74. The negotiations had begun seriously in April 1289 but a marriage may have been considered even earlier: Prestwich, 'Maid of Norway', 165–8.

[55] F.M. Powicke, *Henry III and the Lord Edward* (Oxford, 1947), 732–3, 788–90; M. Howell, *Eleanor of Provence* (Oxford & Malden, Mass., 1998), 305; M. Biddle, ed., *King Arthur's Round Table* (Woodbridge, Suffolk & Rochester NY, 2000), 361–4.

[56] Biddle, ed., *King Arthur's Round Table*, 361–4, 390–1. The conclusion is that the most likely date of manufacture was 1289 but dates earlier in the reign of Edward I cannot be ruled out.

Within months of the agreement Edward I's plans were thrown into disarray by the death of Edward of Caernarfon's intended wife, the 'Maid of Norway', in September 1290, followed by the loss of his own wife and devoted companion, Eleanor of Castile, in November that year.

It is easy, but probably misleading, to argue that Edward's childhood was a very unsatisfactory one, that he lacked contact with and affection from his family, and that such factors go far to explain many of his personal problems in later life. His parents travelled a great deal in the course of royal business so that for long periods they would have seen neither Edward nor their other children. As already noted, for several months after Edward's birth in 1284 both parents were touring Wales. For three years, between May 1286 and August 1289 Edward I and Eleanor of Castile were absent in Gascony,[57] and from the summer of 1291 to late 1292 the recently widowed Edward I was in the north of England about the business of the Scottish 'Great Cause'.[58]

The young Edward also lost several members of his family to whom he had been close. On 19 August 1284, when he was only a few months old, the death of his ten-year-old brother Alfonso deprived him of future companionship and a possible role model.[59] On 15 August 1285 his five-year-old sister Mary entered the convent of Amesbury in Wiltshire, the English daughterhouse of the great abbey of Fontevraud in France where Henry II and Richard I were buried.[60] A year later, on 7 July 1286, Edward's grandmother, Eleanor of Provence, the widow of Henry III, also entered the convent at Amesbury.[61] On 30 April 1290 Edward's eighteen-year-old sister Joan was married in Westminster Abbey to Gilbert de Clare, the earl of Gloucester, and so left the family circle.[62] On 9 July another sister, the fifteen-year-old Margaret, was also married in Westminster Abbey, to John de Brabant, the heir to the duchy of Brabant in the Low Countries. John had lived in England since 1285, awaiting the time of his marriage, and seems to have been treated as one of the English royal family, staying on occasions both with Edward I and with Edward of Caernarfon, whom he clearly knew well.[63] On 20 September 1293 a third sister, Eleanor, at the mature age of twenty-four, married count Henry of Bar at Bristol. She left England and lived only a few more years, dying in 1298 probably in Ghent.[64] Edward's last

---

[57] J.P. Trabut-Cussac, *L'Administration anglaise en Gascogne sous Henry III et Édouard I de 1254 à 1307* (Paris & Geneva, 1972), 79; Prestwich, *Edward I*, 307.

[58] Prestwich, *Edward I*, 364–9.

[59] Parsons, 'The year of Eleanor of Castile's birth', 261.

[60] Prestwich, *Edward I*, 128; A large family gathering, which appears to have included Edward himself, took place at Amesbury to mark the occasion. There is a detailed account of the event in Green, *Lives*, ii, 409–10.

[61] Howell, *Eleanor*, 300.

[62] Parsons, 'The year of Eleanor of Castile's birth', 261.

[63] Ibid., 262; there is a detailed account in Green, *Lives*, ii, 368–73. Edward and his sister Elizabeth made offerings of 2s 2d at the wedding: C47/3/22, m.1.

[64] Parsons, 'The year of Eleanor of Castile's birth', 260.

remaining sister, Elizabeth, born in 1282 and the one nearest to him in age, was married in January 1297 at Ipswich to John, count of Holland and Zeeland. She was, however, widowed in 1299 and returned to the English scene in 1302 when she married Humphrey de Bohun, the earl of Hereford and Essex.[65]

More serious for Edward's childhood and his future emotional development was the loss in quick succession of both his mother, Eleanor of Castile and his grandmother, Eleanor of Provence. Eleanor of Castile died on 28 November 1290 at Harby in Nottinghamshire and was buried in Westminster Abbey on 17 December.[66] Except for great occasions, she rarely saw her children when they were young and not yet able to join the court on its travels. Nonetheless she was devoted to them and concerned about their welfare. During her long separations from her children she kept in regular contact with them by messenger. In 1282 she joined her mother-in-law in protesting against Edward I's plans for the marriage of the thirteen-year-old Eleanor on the grounds that she was still too young; in 1285 she was very reluctant for Mary to enter the convent at Amesbury; and in 1290 she sent Dominican friars and one of her scribes to the young Edward's household to ensure his spiritual and intellectual formation.[67]

During October 1290 Edward and his household had been at the royal manor of Clipstone in Nottinghamshire, and on 16 November he was at *Laxinton* (probably Laxton) where he and his sister Elizabeth attended mass for the soul of Henry III.[68] It seems at any rate that he was not far away when news of his mother's death came. As a child of six Edward cannot have understood the depth of his father's grief at the loss of Eleanor or have appreciated the 'state progress of unprecedented splendour followed by a majestic funeral' which marked the passage of his mother's body from Lincoln cathedral via several stopping places until her final burial in Westminster Abbey on 17 December.[69] We do not know whether the young Edward was present at his mother's funeral, but as he grew up his own loss would have gradually been borne in upon him. Eleanor of Castile's death was followed only a few months later, on 24 June 1291, by

---

[65] Ibid., 265.

[66] Parsons, *Eleanor*, 59–60; Prestwich, *Edward I*, 125.

[67] Parsons, *Eleanor of Castile*, 37–42, and esp. 37–8. In 1285 she was resisting her mother-in-law's pressure. See also Parsons, 'Eleanor of Castile (1241–1290)', in *Eleanor of Castile, 1290–1990*, ed. D. Parsons (Stamford, 1991), 38–40.

[68] C47/3/22, m.2. This roll of daily expenses finishes on 19 Nov., the end of Edward I's regnal year. There is no surviving evidence to show Edward of Caernarfon's movements in the days immediately following. See also Johnstone, 24.

[69] Parsons, *Eleanor*, 58–60; Howell, *Eleanor*, 307–8; E. Hallam, 'The Eleanor crosses and royal burial customs', in *Eleanor of Castile, 1290–1990*, ed. D. Parsons (Stamford 1991) 15–18. Between 1291 and 1294 Edward I gave further expression to his grief by erecting elaborate stone crosses at the twelve places at which his wife's body had rested on its way to Westminster: N. Coldstream, 'The commissioning and design of the Eleanor Crosses', in D. Parsons, ed., *Eleanor*, 55–67.

that of his grandmother. Eleanor of Provence was given a solemn burial at Amesbury on 8 September in the presence of Edward I and a great gathering of nobles and clergy. With her passed not only a great figure in the history of thirteenth-century England but also the last female member of the older generation to take an interest in Edward of Caernarfon.[70]

This is not however the whole picture. While the deaths of Edward's mother and grandmother in quick succession were probably severe blows, the departure of his sisters from the family circle was more apparent than real. Mary, the nun of Amesbury, was far from being an exponent of the enclosed religious life. She led an independent and often extravagant existence, which included a love of gambling; she frequently visited either the royal court or her brother Edward, travelling in style with many companions and servants. She was herself often visited at Amesbury by her father, by her brother Edward, and by other members of her family.[71] It was no accident that Mary should have become a nun at Amesbury. Eleanor of Provence had apparently been planning to retire there since the early 1280s and as part of her arrangements for her future comfort and companionship she made sure that Mary and another granddaughter, Eleanor the daughter of Beatrice of Brittany, entered the abbey first, together with twenty other girls drawn from aristocratic families. Mary's admission to Amesbury on 15 August 1285 was a great family occasion, attended by Edward I and Queen Eleanor and by many of the leading nobility and clergy of the kingdom. Even the one-year-old Edward of Caernarfon was there, probably making his first appearance at a major public event. Although her two granddaughters eventually became professed nuns, they probably did so only after Eleanor's death in 1291 and it is likely that she herself never took vows. Amesbury, in close proximity to Salisbury and to the royal palace at Clarendon, thus became like an extension of the royal court and a regular port of call. The abbess of the mother house of Amesbury at Fontevraud steadfastly hoped that Mary would transfer there after the death of Eleanor of Provence, but she refused, and Edward I refused to allow it. Mary was having too good a time.[72]

Two of Edward's other sisters also remained within his social circle for a time, even after they were married. Edward I was so reluctant for the fifteen-year-old Elizabeth to leave court after her marriage to the count of Holland in 1296 that nine months later her anxious husband had to plead

---

[70] Howell, *Eleanor*, 310–12. She had shown her concern in the letter mentioned earlier in which she expressed anxiety about Edward's health if he were taken to the north of England: Johnstone, 24. It was no coincidence either that the family conference in April 1290 at which allegiance was sworn to Edward of Caernarfon as Edward I's successor was held at Amesbury: Howell, 305.

[71] Prestwich, *Edward I*, 124. There is a detailed account of her long life and doings in Green, *Lives*, ii, esp. 408–42.

[72] Howell, *Eleanor*, 300–5; Green, *Lives*, ii, 408–10. Mary's cousin Eleanor of Brittany, did however go to Fontevraud, of which she became abbess in 1304.

with the king to let his wife join him.[73] Edward's sister Margaret and her husband John de Brabant both stayed in England after their marriage in 1290 until her husband returned to Brabant in 1294 after the death of his father. During this period she and her husband continued to have frequent social contact with Edward of Caernarfon. Even in 1294 Margaret remained in England and did not finally rejoin her husband until 1297.[74]

Despite his loss of close relatives through death and, to a lesser extent through marriage, Edward of Caernarfon's childhood was not a lonely one. There is really nothing to suggest the conclusion that 'ease and confidence, as a member of a happy family circle, played no part in Edward's childish experience'.[75] As his household accounts and many other records indicate, he had extensive social contacts, with his own sisters, with his older cousins Thomas and Henry of Lancaster, and with other children; and also, as he grew up, with adults.[76] His childhood experiences were not untypical of his social class and time.[77] Edward was probably more fortunate than his future father-in-law, Philip IV of France, who as a child 'lived in the shadow of St. Louis, the perfect king, a daunting example and challenge'.[78]

EDWARD AND HIS FATHER

The young Edward of Caernarfon also lived in the shadow of a great king, but Edward I was at least still alive, all too obviously human, and never likely to be declared a saint. Nonetheless Edward I was a difficult father for any of his children, not least for the heir to the throne who

[73] Prestwich, *Edward I*, 128.
[74] E 101/353/18; Phillips, 'Edward II and the prophets', 198; Green, *Lives*, ii, 373–5.
[75] Johnstone, 128.
[76] In 1290, e.g., when he was six, Edward had the company of his sisters, Eleanor, Margaret and Elizabeth, and of numerous other children, including Eleanor de Burgh, Matilda de Chaworth (the daughters of Richard de Burgh, the earl of Ulster, and of Payn de Chaworth, the lord of Kidwelly in Wales and one of Edward I's leading commanders in the conquest of Wales), and Humphrey de Bohun (the future earl of Hereford, who was born in about 1276 and therefore some years older than Edward): C47/3/22, m.1. Edward's contacts with other children were very similar to those of his father: Prestwich, *Edward I*, 5.
[77] My conclusions are essentially the same as those of Johnstone, 21–2. Her remark that 'there is no doubt that in many respects Edward's boyish environment and experience have been seen askew by later writers, who viewed them through lenses coloured by the preconceptions, prejudices and patriotic convictions, of their own age' is a very apposite one. Many modern comments have been unfair, when they have not been inaccurate.
[78] Philip IV grew up starved of affection after his mother died in childbirth when he was only three years old. He also had a poor relationship with his stepmother Marie de Brabant, unlike Edward who appears to have been on very friendly and easy terms with his own stepmother, Marie de Brabant's daughter Margaret, after she married Edward I in 1299. See Brown, 'The prince is father of the king', esp. 332–4. To make matters worse, Marie was more closely descended from the former Carolingian rulers of France than was Philip himself, so there was the nagging doubt that in a sense his claim to the French throne was weaker than that of his younger half-brother Louis of Evreux: Brown, 321, 332–4.

would be expected to match his achievements in war and in government. Edward I's loss of his wife in 1290, when he was already fifty years old, and, in the years to come, the frustrations of prolonged and ultimately unsuccessful warfare and of political difficulties at home, amid the growing evidence of his own mortality, made difficult relations with his son all the more likely at some stage. The bitter and violent quarrel between father and son which ultimately occurred in 1305 is of course well known and will be examined in the next chapter, but it would be unwise to assume that the roots of the quarrel were connected in any simple and straightforward fashion to the events of Edward of Caernarfon's childhood in the 1280s and 1290s, or even of his young manhood in the early 1300s.[79] If Edward I was disappointed in or dissatisfied with his son at this early stage of his career, there is nothing obvious in the records or in the chronicles of the time to suggest it. Edward I is known to have had a violent temper,[80] but whatever disagreements he may have had with the younger Edward they did not yet lead to pulling his son's hair out by the roots, as allegedly happened in 1307.[81] Edward nonetheless had an underlying respect for his father, which he showed in 1324 when he ordered Master John of St Albans to paint the walls of the Lesser Hall of Westminster Palace with scenes, probably martial and heroic in character, from the life of Edward I, 'whom God assoil'. Perhaps at the last Edward felt reconciled with his father and that in destroying his internal enemies during the civil war of 1321–2 he had somehow matched Edward I's greatness in war.[82]

Ironically, Edward II was to match his father in another way in June 1326 when he received news of his son's intended betrothal without his permission to Philippa of Hainault. Edward was greatly angered and, in an echo of the scenes between himself and his own father, wrote to his son that unless he obeyed 'he will ordain in such wise that Edward shall feel it all the days of his life, and that all other sons shall take example thereby of disobeying their lords and fathers'.[83] In his own youth Edward I had had a number of serious, and sometimes angry, disagreements with his father, Henry III; while in the twelfth century the disputes between Henry II and his sons had led to open civil war.[84] Too much should not be

---

[79] This will be discussed in ch. 3. It is too simple to assume that after his mother's death 'the little boy was left to become accustomed to a father, hitherto unknown, who never fully recovered from the loss of his wife, and who daily became more irascible and terrifying': Johnstone, 128.

[80] Prestwich, *The Three Edwards*, 36.

[81] Johnstone, 123–4, citing the account of Walter of Guisborough. Cf. ibid., 97–8, for the breach between Edward and his father in 1305.

[82] P. Binski, *The Painted Chamber at Westminster* (London, 1986), 112. *KW*, i, 508, n. 7.

[83] *CCR, 1323–27*, 577.

[84] Disputes between Edward I and Henry III are recorded in 1255 (over Gascony) in 1257 (over Wales), and in 1260 (during the baronial period of reform): Prestwich, *Edward I*, 14,

made of the mere fact of differences between father and son: these were almost par for the course.[85]

EDWARD AND HIS HOUSEHOLD

Although in his earliest years Edward of Caernarfon was frequently in the company of other of the royal children,[86] a separate household especially established for him already seems to have existed in the year 1284–5.[87] His personal needs were looked after by his nurse, Mariota Maunsel's successor, Alice de Leygrave, who may earlier have served as *berceresse* or 'rocker' for Edward's elder brother Henry.[88] Alice remained close to Edward even in adult life. In 1313 she was described as 'the king's mother ... who suckled him in his youth' and in the same year was in the service of Queen Isabella.[89] The financial management of Edward's household was at first the responsibility of an experienced royal clerk, Giles of Oudenarde, who accounted for £832 expenditure for 1284–5,[90] and for

---

18–19, 21, 33. On another occasion Edward clashed with his father when he wished to give the island of Oléron in Gascony to his uncle Guy de Lusignan. This can be compared with the bitter row between Edward I and his own son Edward in 1307 when the latter allegedly wanted to give the county of Ponthieu to his favourite, Piers Gaveston: Johnstone, 124, n. 2. These disagreements came as Edward grew to maturity and wished to exercise a degree of real as opposed to nominal power rather than because of any fundamental differences between father and son. The causes of dispute between Edward I and his own son and successor were very similar. My view of Edward of Caernarfon's relations with his father at this early stage contrasts sharply with that of Prestwich: *Edward I*, 127.

[85] Ironically, the only evidence of violence directed by Edward I against a member of his family at this period is in relation to his daughters. In a famous incident in 1297 he threw his daughter Elizabeth's coronet into the fire; while at the wedding of his daughter Margaret in 1290 he struck a page on the head and badly wounded him: C 47/3/25; Prestwich, *Edward I*, 111; Prestwich, *The Three Edwards*, 36. However, Prestwich also argues that 'Edward appears to have been fonder of his daughters than of his sons': *Edward I*, 127–9. My opinion is that there is no strong evidence one way or the other.

[86] There are numerous references to Edward and his sisters, Elizabeth and Joan, in E 101/351/9, m.14: in Oct. 1284 a feeding bowl, a ewer and basin for washing, a 'little pot', and a curtain and cord were bought for Edward and buttons for sewing on to his sister Elizabeth's smock.

[87] *Records of the Wardrobe and Household, 1285–1286*, ed. B. F. & C. R. Byerly (London, 1977), 194. (These are records of Edward I's household.)

[88] Johnstone, 9.

[89] *CCR, 1307–13*, 581; Johnstone, 9. Isabella was herself only about seventeen years old in 1313 and the mother of a young baby, the future Edward III.

[90] *Records*, ed. Byerly & Byerly, 194. Giles was described as 'keeper of the wardrobe of Edward, the king's son'. The accounting period was Nov. 1284–Nov. 1285, covering the 13th year of the reign of Edward I. The figures quoted in this chapter have usually been rounded up or down to the nearest pound to avoid the confusion of pre-decimal pounds, shillings and pence.

The extant household records for Edward of Caernarfon preserved in the Public Record Office are recorded in *List of Documents relating to the Household and Wardrobe: John to Edward I*

£686 in 1285–6.[91] Giles was still in charge in 1288–9 when the household expenses rose to over £2,140, and included the wages of seven knights and nine serjeants, as well as the expenses of Edward himself and 'other children living with him in the keeping of the king'.[92] Another experienced royal administrator, William of Blyborough, who had served with Edward I in the Holy Land, was already a member of Edward's household in 1290, and succeeded Giles as its keeper in 1293.[93] By this time the household appears to have become definitively Edward's own personal establishment rather than indifferently 'the household of the king's children' or 'the household of the king's son' as in the past.[94] It was evidently now assumed that Edward's sisters would be less regularly in his company. In 1292–3 the household expenses reached £3,896,[95] and in the following year £3,785.[96] William of Blyborough probably remained in office until 1301 when Edward became Prince of Wales. That event brought great changes both to Edward and to those who served him, but as early as November 1295 another important change had taken place. From that date Edward's household received its income from and accounted directly to the exchequer rather than his father's household. Between 1295 and 1299 the annual income averaged about £1,300. The total expenditure during this period on the other hand was over £10,813.[97] Some of this additional cost may have arisen from the increasingly public role which Edward was then assuming, especially while he was Regent of England in 1297–8 during his

---

(London, 1964), 94–5. Some of Edward's household records are preserved elsewhere: e.g. BL, Harleian Ms. 5001 and Add. Ms. 22923.

For a detailed account of the organization and operations of Edward of Caernarfon's household before he became king see T.F. Tout, 'The wardrobe and household of the Prince of Wales', in Tout, *Chapters*, ii, 165–87.

[91] Tout, *Chapters*, ii, 242: this sum included the expenses of Edward's sisters when they were in his company. There was no clear-cut division as yet between the households of Edward and other royal children.

[92] Johnstone, 11. This was clearly a large household for a five-year-old child. On the other hand Edward I and Eleanor of Castile were absent in Gascony for the three years 1286–9, so their son's household in England inevitably gained in size and responsibility. The money to run it came from the revenues of the king's household and continued to do so until Nov. 1295 when Edward began to be funded from the exchequer: Johnstone, 11.

[93] C 47/3/22, *passim*: Roll of necessaries of the household of the Lord Edward, Son of the King, 18 Edward I; Tout, *Chapters*, ii, 166. Since Giles of Oudenarde ceased to act in Feb. 1290, William may have become keeper from this earlier date: Tout, ii, 165. On Blyborough see *Records*, ed. Byerly & Byerly, xx–xxi.

[94] Tout, *Chapters*, ii, 166–7.

[95] E 101/353/18, m.10: this figure includes a sum of £285 for gifts, offerings and other expenses (which accounts for the different figure quoted in Johnstone, 11).

[96] Tout, *Chapters*, ii, 166. There is some difficulty in distinguishing between receipts and expenses. It appears that the royal household paid out the sum accounted for by Blyborough, so that receipts and expenses remained in balance.

[97] The total of the receipts for 1295–9 was £5,264: ibid., ii, 167, and nn. 2, 3, 4; Johnstone, 11–12.

father's absence in Flanders. But it also seems likely that at a time of great financial stringency the exchequer was systematically supplying Edward's household with less than it needed to function efficiently.[98]

Even while his household was still adequately financed, Edward's presence could impose stresses upon the local community through a combination of steady pressure on resources and slowness in payment. This is well illustrated by the complaints recorded in 1294 by the author of the Annals of Dunstable who remarked:

> Two hundred dishes a day were not sufficient for his kitchen. Whatever he spent on himself or his followers he took without paying for it. His officials carried off all the victuals that came to market, even cheese and eggs, and not whatever was for sale, but even things not for sale, in the houses of the townsfolk. They scarcely left anybody a tally. They seized bread from the bakers and beer from the ale-wives, or if they had none, forced them to brew and bake.[99]

Too much should not be made of this one reference, since the lengthy periods spent at King's Langley in Hertfordshire by Edward and his household made it likely that sometimes their needs would exceed the resources available locally, or ill-feeling would arise if payments were not prompt. There were also occasions, as will be seen later, when Edward was entertaining large numbers of visitors at Langley and would have required substantial quantities of food and drink at short notice. On the other hand, this is but one example of the multitude of complaints about the purveyance of food supplies by royal officials, delays in payment by the royal household and the exchequer, and excessive taxation by the crown which accumulated during the later years of the reign of Edward I. These grievances contributed to the political crises of 1297 and 1300 while Edward I was still king and were a foretaste of what Edward of Caernarfon was himself to face as king after 1307. In embryo the demands for reform of the royal administration made by the Ordainers in 1310 were already present at a local level in 1294. The complaints by the Dunstable annalist are also an indication of how Edward's own personal reputation could have developed in his early years. Edward's continued close proximity to centres of population like St Albans and Dunstable and to the main route between London and the north, made it natural that all kinds of gossip and innuendo about the doings of the heir to the throne and his companions would have spread, while the existence of locally based monastic chroniclers gave local rumour the chance of a much wider circulation.

---

[98] On the crown's financial problems during this period see M. Prestwich, *War, Politics and Finance under Edward I* (London, 1972); and idem, *Edward I*, ch. 16, 'The years of crisis, 1294–8'.

[99] *Annales Prioratus de Dunstaplia, Annales Monastici*, ed. H.R. Luard, Rolls ser. (London, 1869), iii, 392; Johnstone, 26–7. Viewed from another perspective, the presence of Edward and his followers was good for business.

The expense roll for 1292–3, which records a total expenditure of nearly £3,900,[100] also reveals a great deal about the young Edward of Caernarfon and his activities. For over four months of this period, between 23 November and 12 April, Edward was at Langley,[101] the manor near St Albans where he had already spent much time as a small child,[102] which was given to him by his father in 1302, and became one of his favourite residences[103] as king. Edward then set out on a series of travels,[104] which took him, for example, to Westminster in late April and to Mortlake and Kennington in Surrey for the months of May and June. In early July he was at Canterbury, where on 7 July he was present for the celebration of the feast of the Translation of St Thomas Becket, a saint to whom in later life he appears to have had a particular devotion. He was briefly at Windsor Park in early August, after which he was almost constantly on the move until his return to Mortlake in October. His travels took him through Hampshire and Wiltshire, to cathedral cities such as Winchester, Salisbury and Bath, to the royal manor of Clarendon, and to country towns such as Melksham and Devizes. On 8 September he went from Clarendon to attend mass in Salisbury cathedral; on 9 September he was at Amesbury, where his grandmother Margaret of Provence was buried and where his sister Mary was a nun; and on 20 September he was in Bristol for the wedding of his sister Eleanor to Count Henry of Bar.[105]

The marginal notes, which were added to the roll in order to explain days of unusual expense and which sometimes show a degree of impatience or even exasperation, name the people who visited Edward and dined with him during the period of this account. The nine-year-old Edward's social circle in 1293 was already a sophisticated one, drawn chiefly from the upper levels of the English nobility and with a considerable leavening from among the clergy and the religious. Langley was a very convenient stopping-place for visitors because of its proximity both to Westminster and to the main route north via St Albans, so it is hardly surprising that many people called there, sometimes staying for several

---

[100] E 101/353/18; Tout, *Chapters*, ii, 166 and n. 6.

[101] E 101/353/18, mm.1–4.

[102] E.g., for much of 1288–9: E 101/352/16. It was from Langley that Edward and his sisters left for Dover on 28 July 1289 to meet their parents on their return from Gascony: E 101/352/16; Johnstone, 11, n. 2.

[103] On Langley see Johnstone, 28–30, 65. Johnstone, 28, plausibly but rather coyly suggests that his long residences at Langley were influential in 'the formation of young Edward's tastes and habits', presumably thinking of his notorious interests in swimming, hedging and ditching, but not being any more specific.

[104] For the details of his itinerary during this year see the table ibid., 26, derived from E 101/353/18.

[105] A much-delayed wedding since Eleanor had been betrothed to Alfonso, the son of King Peter of Aragon, in 1282. The 1293 wedding suited the changed diplomatic needs of Edward I: Prestwich, *Edward I*, 320, 389. The county of Bar was situated in north-eastern France near the border with the Empire in Germany.

days. From 22 to 24 January Edward was visited by the countess of Gloucester (his sister Joan), with her knights, ladies, clerk and squires;[106] on 7 February by the castellan of *'Bergles'* with four knights and the two sons of Sir Robert de Tibetot; from 11 to 13 February by Sir Hugh de Vere (brother of the earl of Oxford), Sir Stephen Fitz Walter and Sir Peter and Sir John de Stratling.[107] On Thursday, 12 February, it was the turn of Sir John de Brabant, the son and heir of the duke of Brabant who had married Edward's sister Margaret in 1290, and of Edward's first cousins, Thomas and Henry of Lancaster, with 'a great company', who had come from a tournament at nearby Dunstable. Sir John left on Sunday, 15 February, to go to Canterbury, but left the boys behind; he returned from Canterbury on 22 February and went again on the Tuesday following, taking Thomas and Henry with him.[108] On 3 March the earl and countess of Gloucester came with a 'decent company' of knights, ladies, damsels and squires, and stayed for two days. On 7 March he entertained at dinner his father's close friend and counsellor, Anthony Bek, bishop of Durham, together with a bishop of the Friars Minor who was with him and an important royal clerk Sir John de Berwick. The two bishops left after dinner but Sir John stayed the night.[109] The Franciscan was probably the bishop of Jebail in Syria who dined with Edward and the bishop of Durham at Mortlake on Sunday, 24 May.[110] On 24 April the 'arrival of the lords' was recorded, presumably for the celebration of Edward's ninth birthday the following day and probably included Edmund of Lancaster, the king's brother, who was certainly present on 28 April.[111]

The transfer of Edward and his household to Mortlake led to another stream of visitors: on 7 May the bishop of Durham, Thomas and Henry of Lancaster, and John de Brabant;[112] at Whitsun (17 May) Edward Balliol,

---

[106] E 101/353/18, m.2d.

[107] E 101/353/18, m.3d.

[108] Ibid. On the links between England and Brabant, which were to be of great importance to the personal life of Edward as king, see Phillips, 'Edward II and the prophets', 198–200.

[109] E 101/353/18, m.3d. For the career of Bek see C.M. Fraser, *A History of Anthony Bek* (Oxford, 1957). Bek died in March 1310, just as the demands for administrative and financial reform were about to force Edward II to appoint the Ordainers. The Bridlington chronicler remarked that many considered that if Bek had survived, the dissension between the king and the magnates would not have lasted: *Gesta Edwardi*, 38–9.

[110] E 101/353/18, mm.3d, 5d; in 1306 Bek was appointed as the nominal patriarch of Jerusalem by Clement V: Fraser, *Bek*, 164–5. These two visits to Edward in 1293 took place only two years after the loss of Acre and the virtual extinction of the crusader states in Syria and Palestine. In 1293 Edward I was still hoping to realize his long-standing ambition to lead another crusade to the East. It is more than likely that the young Edward of Caernarfon's two visitors tried to inspire him with stories of the crusade. Edward did eventually take the cross himself in 1313, although he never fulfilled his vow: see J.R.S. Phillips, *The Medieval Expansion of Europe*, 2nd edn (Oxford, 1998), 129.

[111] E 101/353/18, mm.4, 4d.

[112] E 101/353/18, m.4d.

the son of the king of Scots John Balliol; the lady Agnes de Valence, the daughter of Edward of Caernarfon's great-uncle William de Valence; the prior of Merton; Master John de Lacy, a son of the earl of Lincoln; the Leyburn brothers; and the lady Isabella de Vescy. Several of these were again present on 18 and 19 May, while Henry de Lacy, the earl of Lincoln, and four knights were there on 20 May. On the 21st there was another large gathering at dinner: Sir John de Bar, whose brother Count Henry of Bar was shortly to marry Edward's sister Eleanor; Sir Roger de Mohaut, Sir Roger de Leyburn, the castellan of *'Bergles'* with three knights, and the wife of Sir Walter de Beauchamp with one knight. All those in attendance on 21 May, and presumably many of the others as well, were there to attend the wedding of Eleanor, the daughter of Sir John de Mereworth. Three days later came the visit of the bishop of Durham and the bishop of Jebail in Syria.[113]

Another round of entertaining began in June, with the arrival on the 12th of Edward's sister, the lady Mary, 'nun of Amesbury with a great company of nuns',[114] and Thomas and Henry of Lancaster with their following. All of them appear to have stayed until 14 June. Only three days later, John de Brabant arrived with thirty horses and twenty-four boys, while Thomas and Henry were back again with thirty horses and twenty-one boys, all of them staying 'at our expense'. They remained until 22 June when John, Thomas and Henry breakfasted at Kingston on the way to jousting at Fulham, and caused great expense to Edward's household 'because many strangers came to them'. Day by day during this period, Edward's household clerk noted their presence with growing annoyance: 'they are staying', 'they are still here', and, on the final day, 'here they are still. And this day is burdensome'. Having to pay for the breakfast of so many guests was clearly the last straw. The three weeks of entertaining itinerant nuns and tournament-goers between Sunday 7 June and Saturday 27 June cost Edward's household about £370, almost 10 per cent of the whole year's expenditure.[115]

Edward's travels began again in early July. On 7 July he gave a reception in the Great Hall of Archbishop Robert Winchelsey at Canterbury;[116] on 27 July at Otford in Kent he entertained two of Edward I's administrators, John de Berwick and the keeper of the royal household, Walter Langton, 'a man of great ability and little principle', who in 1305 was to be the cause of a bitter dispute between Edward and his father.[117] On

---

[113] All these details are in E 101/353/18, mm.4d, 5. In Nov. 1292 Edward I had declared Edward Balliol's father John the rightful successor to the vacant Scottish throne at the end of the 'Great Cause': Prestwich, *Edward I*, 363–70. Agnes de Valence, who had been married to Edward's uncle, Hugh de Balliol (d. 1271), was the sister (not the wife) of Aymer de Valence the future earl of Pembroke: Phillips, *Aymer de Valence*, 2. cf. Johnstone, 27.

[114] Mary was only just fourteen in 1293 and had been a nun since 1285.

[115] E 101/353/18/ m.6; and Johnstone, 28.

[116] E 101/353/18, m.6.

[117] E 101/353/18, m.7d; Prestwich, *Edward I*, 139–40.

17 and 18 August, while he was at Ashley near Winchester, in company with John de Brabant and Thomas and Henry of Lancaster, he was visited by his father Edward I 'and many others' who had come to hunt in Ashley forest. This was the beginning of a series of family gatherings. Between 27 and 29 August Edward was his father's guest at Clarendon; from 31 August to 2 September he was joined at Downton by the steward of the royal household, some Welsh huntsmen and many of the king's household 'at our expense'; the next day the king dined there with his son; and on 4 September Thomas and Henry of Lancaster were again with Edward. Thomas left the following day but Henry stayed because of illness. After attending High Mass at Salisbury cathedral on 8 September, the feast of the Nativity of the Virgin Mary, Edward entertained to dinner the canons, and many others. The following day at Amesbury he was joined by his sister Mary and other nuns, all of whom plus their servants were with him again on the 10th.[118] Edward was in his father's company in Bristol between 20 and 26 September, at the time of the wedding of his sister Eleanor to Henry of Bar,[119] after which he moved back again by stages to Surrey. On 13 October he celebrated the feast of St Edward the Confessor at Kennington; on Saturday, 24 October, and again on the 31st, he was joined at Mortlake by the count of Bar, John de Brabant and a large number of the knights and squires of the king's household.[120] Thus ended a remarkably eventful year.

EDWARD'S OWN EDUCATION

Little is known in detail about the young Edward's education and personal formation, although much has been said on the theme in the past and sweeping conclusions have been drawn on slender evidence. One thing that is known is the identity of Edward's 'master', a veteran Gascon knight named Guy Ferre, who had previously been a prominent household knight and administrator of Eleanor of Provence, as well as acting as one of her executors. He was also closely connected to the queen, Eleanor of Castile, whom he had accompanied to the Holy Land in 1270–1. Guy's uncle John Ferre was steward of her household until 1288; in the mid-1280s Guy was a member of her council and was himself steward of her household in 1289–90, the final year of her life.[121] Guy was therefore a man of great experience who was clearly trusted by both the queens whom he served and, by implication, by Edward I as well. He should have been a very suitable person to act as a kind of father figure for Edward of Caernarfon, providing discipline, and instilling in him an appreciation of the ideals of the crusade

---

[118] All these details are in E 101/353/18, mm.8, 8d.
[119] E 101/353/18, m.8.
[120] E 101/353/18, m.9, 9d.
[121] Prestwich, *Edward I*, 127; Johnstone, 16–17; Howell, *Eleanor*, 292–3; Parsons, *Eleanor*, 88.

and of the rules of behaviour in noble society, as well as the skills of horsemanship and the use of arms that would be needed on future battlefields.[122] Guy's service with Edward of Caernarfon had probably begun before 1295; it ended with Guy's death in 1303.[123] It is not known how well Edward and Guy got on together, but in 1299 there is a hint, which suggests that Guy was a hard master to serve but which also reflects well on Edward personally. On 16 November, at Langley, Edward gave one mark (13s 4d) to Guy Ferre's chamberlain, Roger, 'to acquit him of a silver dish of his lord which he lost and for which he ought to have lost his service, until he was able to restore its value'.[124] In later life, at the battle of Bannockburn and in other tight spots, Edward had good cause to be grateful that, whatever else Guy failed to instil in him, he taught him to ride well. When Guy died at Durham in 1303 Edward showed at least his formal respect by attending mass in Guy's memory on 14 April.[125] Any influence Guy had exerted on the character and behaviour of his royal charge was at an end. Ironically, a new and much more powerful influence upon Edward was already present and growing rapidly, in the form of another Gascon knight, Piers Gaveston.

The traditional assumption that Edward of Caernarfon's formal education was inadequate and, in particular, that he was 'illiterate' in the sense of knowing little or no Latin rests on two pieces of evidence.[126] The first is the fact that in 1308 Edward took his coronation oath in French, in a form allegedly devised for a king who did not know Latin.[127] From this circumstance and from evidence that in 1300 a primer was bought for Edward from William the Bookbinder of London at a cost of £2, V.H. Galbraith concluded damningly that 'It was thus stupidity or laziness, and not want of opportunity to learn Latin, that made it necessary for Edward II to take his coronation oath in French'.[128] The second piece of evidence

---

[122] S.D. Lloyd, *English Society and the Crusade, 1216–1307* (Oxford, 1988), 124. Experience of the crusade may have been a particular qualification for Guy's role as tutor to the future king. Two earlier crusaders, William Marshal and Philip Daubeny, had acted as tutor to Henry II's eldest son, the Young Henry, and to the future Henry III respectively: Lloyd, 100.

[123] Johnstone, 17. There is no surviving list of the members of Edward's household between 1288–9, when Guy does not appear, and 1300–1, when Guy is listed fourth in order of importance after Edward himself: E 101/360/17.

[124] E 101/355/17. On the same occasion Edward gave 40s to his hunter Edmund to buy a 'rouncey' or 'nag' 'which the king's son had promised him for a long time'.

[125] E 101/363/18, f. 2; Johnstone, 17. Guy's son, also named Guy, was to have a distinguished career in royal service in his native Gascony, of which he was seneschal for both Edward I (1298–9) and Edward II (1308–10). This may suggest that Edward of Caernarfon appreciated the services that his father had rendered him and other members of his family. See J.L. Boehm, 'The maintenance of ducal authority in Gascony', in *Essays in History*, xxxiv (Univ. of Virginia, Charlotteville, 1992) (although there is some confusion between the careers of father and son).

[126] For a valuable summary of the debates on Edward's education see Johnstone, 18–21.

[127] Ibid., 19.

[128] *Liber Quotidianus Garderobae*, 55; Johnstone, 18; V.H. Galbraith, 'The literacy of the medieval English kings', *Proceedings of the British Academy*, xxi (1935), 2–5.

is a letter of 1317 in which Pope John XXII thanked the archbishop of Canterbury for translating a papal letter from Latin into French 'so that what is the better understood may bear the richer fruit'.[129] Such evidence may seem conclusive, but it is seriously misleading and has been substantially undermined by more recent scholarship.[130]

The damage caused to Edward's posthumous reputation by the coronation oath was brought about by a roll produced at Canterbury in 1311 and still preserved there. In it there are two versions of the oath, the first in Latin and headed 'if the king shall be literate', and the second in French and headed 'if the king shall not be literate'.[131] The implication seems clear enough, and the appropriate conclusions were drawn by scholars from William Stubbs to Vivian Galbraith. However, H.G. Richardson and G.O. Sayles, writing in 1938–9, concluded that the references to literacy and illiteracy had been added as a gloss by the clerk who produced the roll and were of no authority, and that Edward took the oath in French in order to use 'the common idiom of all those assembled in the abbey'.[132] This is clearly correct. The Canterbury clerk, who presumably was highly educated in Latin, was being too clever. French was the spoken language of the upper levels of English society as well as a language of record and it was entirely appropriate that it should be used on a great public occasion such as a coronation. Richardson and Sayles also pointed out, quite properly, that if Edward had needed to take the oath in Latin, he could easily have been taught the appropriate responses, whether he knew Latin or not.[133] Later kings, from Edward III in 1327, also took their oath in French, but have not been charged with illiteracy.[134] Furthermore, the

---

[129] Johnstone, 19–20.

[130] Ibid.

[131] *'Si Rex fuerit litteratus talis est'* & *'si Rex non fuerit litteratus'*: Roll K11 in the Canterbury cathedral archives: this text was used by the editors of the Statutes of the Realm: *SR*, i, 168.

[132] Johnstone, 19; H.G. Richardson & G.O. Sayles, 'Early coronation records', *BIHR*, xvi (1938–39), 140; Richardson, 'The English coronation oath', *TRHS*, 4th ser., xxii (1940), 135, 144–5.

[133] Just as Prince Charles was coached in Welsh before his inauguration as Prince of Wales in 1968.

In the official records of the coronation, the Latin version of the oath appears on the Coronation Roll (C 57/1) and the French as a schedule to the Close Roll (C 54/125, m.10) which shows that they were regarded as equally authentic. The Close Roll text is omitted in the calendared version (*CCR, 1307–13*, 53) but is printed in *Foedera*, II, i, 36, which also includes the Latin text.

[134] Johnstone, 19. Edward III took the same oath as his father, both in language and in content: *CCR, 1327–30*, 100; *Foedera*, II, ii, 684. It is worth adding that, in the absence of official records of Edward I's coronation in 1274, it is unknown whether he also took the oath in French: see Richardson, 'English coronation oath', 131. A Latin version of his oath has however recently been discovered by Dr Bernadette Williams of Trinity College Dublin. See 'The coronation oath of Edward I', in *Medieval Dublin*, ix, ed. S. Duffy (Dublin, 2009), 84–90.

Canterbury roll containing Edward II's coronation oath included the text as a postscript to the Ordinances of 1311, another great public document which was of course also composed in French.[135] The language of the coronation oath of 1308 thus has no bearing whatsoever on Edward's knowledge of Latin.

Pope John XXII's letter to the archbishop of Canterbury in 1317 is equally fragile as evidence.[136] The fact that the pope was writing to persuade Edward II to engage himself more seriously in his duties as king has probably made the translation of his words from Latin into French seem even more pointed to modern observers. However, none of this necessarily proves that Edward knew little or no Latin. As Hilda Johnstone wisely remarked, 'the stately periods of the papal chancery were no easy reading, even for a scholar'.[137] The problems of comprehension were not confined to Edward II, since in 1326 he himself wrote to John XXII in Latin rather than in French, on the assumption that the pope, as a speaker of the *langue d'oc*, would find Latin easier to understand. In 1323 the pope had also written to Charles IV of France telling him that he had a recent letter translated for him from French into Latin because his reading knowledge of the French vernacular was inadequate, and asking him to write in Latin in future.[138]

With the grosser charges of illiteracy out of the way, it is arguable that Edward's level of education has been underestimated. Although the belief that Walter Reynolds, the future archbishop of Canterbury, who was a prominent member of Edward's household from 1297 to 1307, was his

---

[135] *SR*, i, 157–67.

[136] Johnstone, 19–20, citing f. 218 of the still unpublished Register of Archbishop Walter Reynolds in Lambeth Palace Library. The register is the basis of a major study by J.R. Wright, *The Church and the English Crown, 1305–1334* (Toronto, 1980). See also P. Chaplais, *English Medieval Diplomatic Practice* (London, 1982), i, 22, n. 126.

Another example, albeit at a different social level, occurred in Nov. 1317 when two French clerks first of all read out letters from Philip V of France to Gilbert Pecche, the seneschal of Gascony, in Latin before explaining them in French because he did not understand Latin: AN, J 633, no. 37.

[137] Johnstone, 20. The specialized language of papal documents was devised as a way of ensuring that papal letters could not readily be forged, but also to couch what was sometimes a blunt message in diplomatic language. A good example is another letter sent by John XXII to Edward II in 1318, in which he asked Edward to remedy the grievances of the Irish against English rule: *CPL, 1305–42*, 440; A. Theiner, *Vetera monumenta Hibernorum et Scotorum historiam illustrantia* (Rome, 1864), 201. A more recent example, which shows how readily an unpractised reader or hearer could lose the message of a complicated document, is Henry VIII's proclamation of 20 Feb. 1537 which began by rehearsing the many reasons why there should be a legislative union between Wales and England. Only towards the end does it become apparent that the 'Act of Union' of 1536, which provided for this, was in fact being suspended: *Tudor Royal Proclamations*, i, *The Early Tudors, 1485–1553*, ed. P.L. Hughes & J.F. Larkin (New Haven & London, 1964), no. 172, 254.

[138] Chaplais, *Diplomatic Practice*, 21–2, n. 126. The problem of language is more complicated than I have suggested here: ibid.

intellectual mentor has long since been disproved,[139] there is evidence to suggest that Edward's education was given special attention, especially by his mother, Eleanor of Castile. She had been brought up in her native Castile in an atmosphere of learning. Her half-brother, Alfonso X, was deeply interested in literature and in law, and fully merited his nickname, 'the Wise'.[140] She herself may have been educated by Dominican friars at the court of her father Ferdinand III, and it has been suggested that she may have 'developed a command of the written word that went beyond the decorative or pious accomplishment it is often said to have been for medieval women of rank'.[141] During her time in England she is known to have owned a library of romances, and to have employed scribes to write books for her and a painter to illuminate them.[142] She appears to have tried to pass on something of her own education and cultural appreciation to her children: her daughters Eleanor and Mary, for example, were probably both literate,[143] and there is no reason to suppose that she treated the young Edward in any different manner. In 1290 she sent one of her scribes named Philip to join Edward's household at Woodstock. If Philip transcribed books for the use of his royal master, some attempt was presumably made to put them to practical use, perhaps under the guidance of the Dominican friars who were already in Edward's household in 1289–90.[144] It is also likely that one of the tasks of Edward's magister, Guy Ferre, an experienced administrator who must therefore have been literate himself, was to ensure that his royal charge acquired some degree of learning along with the ability to ride a horse.

EDWARD'S BOOKS AND MANUSCRIPTS

It is known that Edward possessed a few books, such as the 'book of romance', probably in French and formerly the property of Eleanor of Provence which he was given in 1298–9;[145] this might even have been the

---

[139] Johnstone, 20–1. In 1297 Reynolds was responsible for purchasing supplies for the household, of which he was joint controller from 1301 to 1307: Johnstone, 21. Although he was not a university graduate, Reynolds was a patron and promoter of learning and was certainly not illiterate as his enemies claimed: see Wright, *The Church and the English Crown*, 250–7; idem, 'The supposed illiteracy of Archbishop Walter Reynolds', *Studies in Church History*, v (1969), 58–68.

[140] See R.I. Burns, ed., *The Worlds of Alfonso the Learned and James the Conqueror: Intellect and Force in the Middle Ages* (Princeton, 1985).

[141] Parsons, *Eleanor*, 9.

[142] Prestwich, *Edward I*, 123.

[143] The Wardrobe Book of 14 Edward I (1285–6) records the purchase of 'writing tablets for Eleanor the king's daughter': Galbraith, 'Literacy', 215. This immediately follows Galbraith's remarks about Edward's laziness and stupidity and makes Edward's lack of education seem even more improbable.

[144] Parsons, *Eleanor*, 41–2, 271, n. 120; and idem, 'Eleanor of Castile', 38–9, 51, n. 64.

[145] BL, Add. Ms. 24509, f. 61 (vol. 1 of Joseph Hunter's collections); Johnstone, 18.

big book containing a Tristram romance which Edward loaned to Hugh Despenser the Younger in the autumn of 1326 when they were fleeing to Wales in the hope of safety.[146] He also owned a primer or prayer book and a copy of Geoffrey of Monmouth's *Historia regum Britanniae* which were bought for him in 1300 and 1301, and the French Life of St Edward which he obtained in 1302.[147] Later in life Edward borrowed a manuscript containing the Lives of St Anselm and St Thomas from the library of Christ Church, Canterbury, and did not return it.[148] In 1324 fourteen romances and a French psalter were issued by the privy wardrobe, possibly for Edward's use.[149] In 1320 the survey of the contents of the treasury made on the instructions of the treasurer, Walter Stapeldon, bishop of Exeter, revealed a number of books, which included the book of Welsh poetry alluded to earlier and which the English clerks described simply as written in a language unknown to the English ('*de Ydiomata Anglicis ignorata*).[150] The rest of the collection was made up of 'a book called *De Regimine Principum* (On Royal Rule) bound in red leather, a "little book" of the rules of the Knights Templar, a quire (that is part of an unbound book) of the life of St Patrick . . . and a book of the chronicles of Roderick archbishop of Toledo'.[151] The fact that these manuscripts were all kept in the treasury rather than among the household records suggests however that they were not part of the everyday reading material available to Edward. The book on the rule of the Templars might, for example, have been consulted at the time of the arrest of the Templars in England in 1308.

Edward does not appear to have been active as a patron of manuscript production, with two possible exceptions. The first is the Isabella Psalter, which is now preserved in the Staatsbibliothek in Munich.[152] According to one opinion, the psalter was written in Paris and illuminated in England

---

[146] SAL Ms. 122, p. 92; M. Prestwich, 'The court of Edward II'. in *The Reign of Edward II: New Perspectives*, ed. G. Dodd & A. Musson (Woodbridge, Suffolk & Rochester, NY, 2006), 69.

[147] Johnstone, 18.

[148] The manuscript was recorded as missing from the library in 1337: *Ancient Libraries of Canterbury and Dover*, ed. M.R. James (Cambridge, 1903), xlv–xlvi, 148. There is no indication of when Edward II had borrowed the manuscript but it could have been during the period 1317–19, when he was trying to make political use of the legend of the Holy Oil of St Thomas of Canterbury.

[149] Prestwich, 'The court of Edward II'.

[150] *Antient Kalendars*, ed. Palgrave, i, 106, 116; Jack, *Medieval Wales*, 53–4.

[151] M. Clanchy, *From Memory to Written Record*, 2nd edn (Oxford, 1993), 162. The latter work was *De Rebus Hispaniae*, by a former chancellor of the kingdom of Castile who had also been present at the battle of Las Navas de Tolosa in 1213, which had determined once and for all that the future of Spain was to lie in Christian rather than Muslim hands. It seems highly probable, as Clanchy suggests, that Eleanor of Castile had brought the book to England.

[152] Codex Gall. 16. The manuscript should not be confused with another Isabella Psalter, which was made before 1270 for Isabella, the sister of Louis IX of France and is now Ms. 300 in the collection of the Fitzwilliam Museum, Cambridge.

and was made for Isabella either on or before her marriage to Edward II in 1308,[153] but a more recent view is that the psalter was entirely English in origin, probably being made in the vicinity of Nottingham between the betrothal of Isabella and Edward in 1303 and their marriage.[154] The other manuscript, now known as the Queen Mary Psalter, is even more tentatively connected with Edward.[155] Joan Evans considered that this was also commissioned by Edward (who appears in gold in the calendar) for presentation to Isabella but that it was made a little later than the Isabella Psalter.[156] More recent opinion is divided on the subject of a possible connection with either Edward II or Isabella.[157]

But possession of books or the possible commissioning of manuscripts does not prove that he read them: Geoffrey of Monmouth was after all a very appropriate text to present to the newly created Prince of Wales, while the Life of St Edward was copiously illustrated.[158] As Michael Clanchy has remarked, 'In having no library and in leaving little evidence of possessing books, the English kings were no different from other contemporary rulers . . . The explanation for the dearth of libraries is not primarily that kings were ignorant laymen, more interested in fighting and hunting than in study. Rather it is that the business of government, whether ecclesiastical or secular, only gradually became associated with book-learning and written precedents.'[159]

The French poem, supposedly written by Edward while in prison after his deposition in 1327, and which appears in two fourteenth-century manuscripts, has no bearing on Edward's literacy or lack of it. It was almost certainly composed by another and anonymous author and embodied the idea of the wheel of fortune, as did another fourteenth-century work,

---

[153] Evans, *English Art*, 15.

[154] D. D. Egbert, 'Sister to the Tickhill Psalter: the Psalter of Queen Isabella of England', *Bulletin of the New York Public Library*, xxxix (1935), 759–88, esp. 760. But, even if Edward nominally commissioned it, he is unlikely to have had much if anything to do with the finished manuscript. Lewis argues however in 'The Apocalypse of Isabella of France: Paris, Bibl. Nat. ms. Fr. 13096', *Art Bulletin*, lxxii (New York, 1990), 234, that the psalter was commissioned by Edward I's widow, Queen Margaret, who was also Isabella's aunt, but presents no evidence other than 'Edward's scarcely disguised indifference to his bride in preference to his favourite Gaveston'.

[155] The psalter later came into the possession of Queen Mary Tudor and is now in the British Library as Ms. Royal 2 B.VII.

[156] Evans, *English Art*, 15–16.

[157] Nigel Morgan in his article in the *Grove Dictionary of Art* (online version) argues that the manuscript was produced in England in the decade between c. 1310 and 1320 but can find no evidence of patronage or ownership. Kathryn Smith, 'History, typology and homily', suggests the ms. was made for Isabella, while the lengthy discussion of the subject by Anne Rudloff Stanton in *The Queen Mary Psalter: A Study of Affect and Audience*, *Transactions of the American Philosophical Society*, xci, part 6 (Philadelphia, 2001) argues for but provides no conclusive evidence of a link with Isabella.

[158] Johnstone, 18–19.

[159] Clanchy, *From Memory*, 162.

the English poem *Somer Soneday (Summer Sunday)*.[160] Although Edward was closely related to two kings, who were practised poets, his cousin and contemporary, Dinis of Portugal (1279–1325), and Edward's uncle and Dinis's grandfather, Alfonso X of Castile (1252–84), there is no reason to suppose that Edward possessed any of their literary skill.[161] The safest conclusion about Edward of Caernarfon's educational achievements is that, like his father Edward I, 'his main language was ... French, more specifically the Anglo-Norman dialect, but [that] he had some understanding of Latin and could speak English'.[162] Although, again like his father, it cannot be certain whether Edward learned to read, it seems probable that he did.[163] Neither is it known whether, like his son Edward III, he could write, but again the possibility should not be ruled out.[164]

[160] See ch. 1 of this book; Valente, 'The Lament of Edward II', and Tyson, 'Lament for a dead king'. Neither argues that Edward II was the actual author of the poem.

[161] See H.R. Lang, *Das Liederbuch des Königs Denis von Portugal* (Halle, 1894; repr. Hildesheim & New York, 1972); Burns, ed., *The Worlds of Alfonso the Learned and James the Conqueror*; and S. R. Ackerlind, *King Dinis of Portugal and the Alfonsine Heritage* (New York, 1990). Ironically, Dinis was also nicknamed *el labrador*, 'the farm labourer', but this referred to his encouragement of agriculture in his kingdom rather than to any interest in hedging and ditching which he might have shared with his English cousin.

[162] Prestwich, *Edward I*, 6. I have deliberately quoted this description of Edward I, since even less is known of his education than of his son's, yet it has never been assumed that he was ignorant and untrained. The most thorough discussion of the languages spoken in thirteenth-century England is in Clanchy, *From Memory*, 197–211.

On the ability of Edward I and of some of his leading officials to speak English see J.R.S. Phillips & E.L.G. Stones, 'English in the public records', *Nottingham Medieval Studies* (1988), 1–10; see also N. Denholm-Young, *History and Heraldry, 1254–1310* (Oxford, 1965), 54, on Edward I and English as well as his knowledge of Latin and French.

[163] It is interesting that Galbraith argued that from the time of Henry II 'all our kings were taught letters in their youth, and their literacy, as distinct from their culture, has no particular importance ... How far they were literate, in the strict sense of the word, that is to say to what extent they were Latin scholars, is hard to know; but, and this is much more important, we can hardly doubt that henceforth they could all read French': Galbraith, 'Literacy', 215. He also notes that from the time of Edward I, for about a century, wills were normally written in French: ibid., 234, n. 35. It is worth adding, in relation to Edward II, that of the 719 items in his roll of letters in 1304–5, 676 were in French and only 43 in Latin. 'A form of French, perfectly comprehensible to both Frenchmen and Englishmen alike, was the normal language of secular correspondence': Vale, 43–4. The relaxed tone of the language of Edward's letters also suggests that, although he would have had clerks to do the actual writing, he understood perfectly what was set down in his name.

[164] As with knowledge of English, so with writing: the problem is 'catching them at it'. It is only through the chance survival in the Vatican Archive of the young Edward III's 1330 letter to the pope with the words '*pater sancte*' written in his own hand that we know he could write. It is also possible that Edward III wrote the response to a petition of 1350 in his own hand: Galbraith, 'Literacy', 222–3 & 236, n. 47. It seems unlikely that Edward III possessed a skill, even in a very basic form, which his father had not also possessed. For the text and comment on the '*pater sancte*' letter see Chaplais, *Diplomatic Practice*, i, no.18, 21–3. The original document is ASV, AA, Arm. C, fasc.79.

EDWARD AS A PUBLIC SPEAKER

The opinion expressed by Ranulf Higden in his *Polychronicon* that Edward II was 'ready in speech' is borne out by contemporary evidence. In January 1312 at York he dictated the French text of a proclamation announcing the return of Gaveston from exile.[165] In July that year he gave a powerful speech to the mayor and citizens of London, calling upon their loyalty against Thomas of Lancaster and the other opposition magnates.[166] In January 1320 he apparently addressed parliament on the arrangements for him to perform homage to Philip V of France for the duchy of Aquitaine.[167] This was a prelude to the speech he gave at Amiens in June 1320 when he bluntly refused the French suggestion that he should perform liege homage rather than simple homage;[168] he gave another speech concerning Aquitaine to an assembly of knights, prelates and magnates in London in October 1324;[169] and according to the *Vita Edwardi Secundi* he delivered a speech before the Westminster parliament of November 1325 concerning Isabella's refusal to return from France.[170]

Edward did not need to achieve the heights of scholarship of a university master or the skills in reading and writing of an experienced royal clerk, but there is little doubt that he had sufficient education to perform his duties as king. He was, in other words, probably no better and no worse educated than his predecessor and successor on the English throne.

EDWARD AND EDUCATION

For a king who is supposed to have been illiterate and ignorant, if not stupid,[171] Edward contributed significantly to the development of the English universities during his lifetime. Even allowing for motives of national prestige and the need to educate trained administrators for the royal service, this says something positive about Edward's intellectual interests. In January 1301, for example, he gave a certain Richard, one of the boys of his household, 5s 4d to keep him for eight weeks at the school

---

[165] *Foedera*, II, i, 153; *CCR, 1307–13*, 448–9; J. Masschaele, 'The public space of the marketplace in medieval England', *Speculum*, lxxvii (2002), 393.

[166] *Ann. Lond.*, 208; G.A. Williams, *Medieval London*, 2nd edn (London, 1970), 272.

[167] 'Apparently', since it is possible that the speech was delivered on his behalf. The speech itself is not recorded but is reported in the proceedings of the Oct. 1320 parliament: C 49/43/20: see *Rotuli Parliamentorum Hactenus Inediti*, ed. H. G. Richardson & G. O. Sayles, Camden, 3rd ser., li (London, 1935), 87, and *PROME*, *sub* Oct. 1324, in the CD-ROM edition or online version or in the print edition, iii, 420.

[168] Vale, 51.

[169] E 30/1582 (in *Rotuli Parliamentorum Hactenus Inediti*, ed. Richardson & Sayles, 94–8, where it is wrongly dated to June 1325). See *PROME*, *sub* Oct. 1324.

[170] *Vita*, 242–5.

[171] Marc Bloch's verdict, for example, that Edward II 'seems to have been a prince of second-rate character and intelligence', is very like that of Galbraith: Bloch, *The Royal Touch* (London, 1973), 59.

of St Martin's in London; while in 1302–3 two scholars, Richard of Nottingham and Thomas Duns were sent at Edward's orders to study at the schools of Oxford, for which Edward gave them 6d a week each for their maintenance there for an entire year, and also provided them with 32 shillings for their clothing, shoes and other necessaries.[172] Earlier English kings had also supported individual clerks at the English universities,[173] but Edward II's involvement went far beyond this. Although his petition in 1317 to Pope John XXII to grant Oxford graduates the same *ius ubique docendi* as had recently been given to the university of Paris, was unsuccessful, another petition from Edward on behalf of the university of Cambridge brought its confirmation by the pope as a *studium generale* in 1318.[174] Edward also supported the creation of a new university in Dublin under the auspices of the archbishop of Dublin; this was formally established by Pope Clement V in 1312 and functioned briefly from 1320.[175]

The Dominican priory which Edward II established at King's Langley in or before 1308 included a school for preparatory studies for the universities. Many of the members of the Carmelite priory he founded in Oxford after 1314 studied at the university, while it is likely that the priory also accommodated secular students.[176] Several of Edward's administrators were directly involved in the development of the university. Roger de Northburgh, keeper of the wardrobe and bishop of Coventry and Lichfield, planned to found halls for the study of logic and theology; between 1314 and 1316 Walter Stapeldon, Edward's treasurer and bishop of Exeter, founded Stapeldon Hall, the future Exeter College; in 1324 Adam de Brome, a chancery clerk, founded Oriel College with royal licence.[177] The latter college was so closely associated with Edward that it was later re-established with the king as the nominal founder. After his death in 1327 prayers were regularly said for his soul, and his tomb in the former Gloucester abbey (a cathedral since the Reformation) was restored on several occasions at the college's expense.[178]

Edward's association with Cambridge University was to be even more significant. Apart from obtaining papal recognition of the university, in 1317 he established his Society of the King's Scholars for the education in

---

[172] E 101/360/10, m.2 (Roll of Edward's household expenses in Jan. 1301); E 101/363/18, f. 2 (wardrobe book of Edward of Caernarfon for 31 Edward I).

[173] A.B. Cobban, *The King's Hall within the University of Cambridge in the Later Middle Ages* (Cambridge, 1969), 11.

[174] Cobban, 'Edward II, Pope John XXII and the university of Cambridge', *Bulletin of the John Rylands Library*, xlvii (1964–5), 49, 62–3, 66–8; Cobban, *The Medieval English Universities* (Aldershot, 1988), 58–9.

[175] A. Gwynn, 'The medieval university of St Patrick's, Dublin', *Studies*, xvii (Dublin, 1938), 199–200, 207–8, 442–3.

[176] D. Knowles & R.N. Hadcock, *Medieval Religious Houses* (London, 1953), 185, 198.

[177] Buck, *Politics, Finance and the Church*, 100–8.

[178] Cobban, *Medieval English Universities*, 129; Evans, *English Art*, 164, n. 4. The prayers for Edward II have continued into modern times.

Cambridge of twelve children of the Chapel Royal. Although in 1337 the Society was to be absorbed into Edward III's foundation of King's Hall, Edward II was regarded as the true founder and under the university statute, *De exequiis annuatim celebrandis*, the regent masters of the university were required to attend mass in memory of Edward of Caernarfon every year on 5 May in the church of Great St Mary. King's Hall existed down to 1546 when it was amalgamated with Michaelhouse to form the present Trinity College.[179] The scholars of King's Hall were 'the first royal colony of clerks to be located in the English Universities and constituted the initial institutional link forged between the latter and the royal household', and 'until the foundation of King's College, Cambridge, in 1441, [King's Hall] remained the only truly royal establishment at either of the English Universities'.[180] Edward's patronage of Cambridge made it attractive to other intending benefactors of university education, such as Hervey de Stanton, a leading official of the exchequer (Michaelhouse, 1324), and to wealthy noblewomen such as Elizabeth de Clare (Clare Hall, 1326) and Marie de St Pol, countess of Pembroke (Pembroke Hall, 1347).[181]

EDWARD AND RELIGION

Like his father and his son, Edward of Caernarfon was probably in most respects 'a man of unsophisticated piety'[182] and 'conventional and predictable in his personal devotions'.[183] It is known, for example, that he inherited a very large collection of relics from his father and passed them on intact to his son, Edward III.[184] Edward II does not appear to have added significantly to this collection, unless we include the ampoule containing the Holy Oil of St Thomas of Canterbury; but even this had originally belonged to Edward I and was simply brought to greater public attention by his son.[185]

---

[179] Cobban, *The King's Hall*, 9–13, 302.

[180] Cobban, *Medieval English Universities*, 128–9. Cobban also suggests that Edward II's foundation of King's Hall in 1317 was part of an attempt to develop the independent power of the royal household by educating future administrators who would, presumably, be loyal to the king rather than to his baronial opponents: Cobban, *The King's Hall*, 19–23. While the monarchy no doubt did hope to gain the future services of graduates of the university, such benefits would be in the long term and would have no bearing on the immediate state of English politics.

[181] Cobban, *Medieval English Universities*, 128–9.

[182] Prestwich, *Edward I*, 111. For a discussion of Edward I's religious proclivities and practices see ibid., 111–14, and, in more detail, Prestwich, 'The piety of Edward I', in *England in the Thirteenth Century*, ed. W.M. Ormrod (Grantham, 1986), 120–8.

[183] W.M. Ormrod, 'The personal religion of Edward III', *Speculum*, lxiv (1989), 853.

[184] Ibid., 855–6, where the most important ones are listed. The details are derived from the list of royal relics in 1331–2 preserved in E 101/385/19, f. 10r. It is unlikely that so early in his reign Edward III would have made many additions of his own.

[185] Phillips, 'Edward II and the prophets', 198–9.

As one would expect, the records of Edward's household, both in childhood and in adult life, contain many references to conventional acts of piety: his attendance at masses on saints' days and other religious festivals, his feeding of the poor and his donations to religious houses. On 12 January 1301, for example, Edward offered 4s 7d at the funeral mass for his cousin Edmund, earl of Cornwall, at Ashridge in Hertfordshire; and 10s 10d at the threshold of St Thomas the Martyr; and on 24 January in Lincoln cathedral he made offerings totalling 20s 6d at the mass for the soul of his dead mother, Eleanor of Castile, at the shrine of Hugh of Avalon (bishop of Lincoln, 1186–1200) and at the tomb of Robert Grosseteste (bishop of Lincoln, 1235–53).[186] Edward's household records for the year 1302–3 give a detailed picture of the extent and purposes of his alms-giving and are not untypical.[187] During the year he attended masses for the souls of his mother, Queen Eleanor, in the church of Bradfield in Berkshire; for his grandmother Queen Eleanor, at Amesbury where she was buried; at South Warnborough in Hampshire for his clerk, John de Haneworth; at Chalfont near Amersham in Buckinghamshire for Edward I's steward, Walter de Beauchamp; at Langley for a member of his own household, William Comyn, on the day he heard of the latter's death; and for Sir Guy Ferre, his 'magister', at Durham. He gave alms to the prioress and nuns of Amesbury, to the Dominican, Franciscan, Augustinian, Carmelite and Crutched friars, and to the friars of the Sack, all of London; the Augustinian friars of Tickhill; the monks (unidentified) of Derby, and the Dominicans of Roxburgh. On Maundy Thursday 1303 (4 April) he gave a pair of slippers and a penny each with his own hands to thirty poor people at Strelley in Northants (one for each completed year of Edward I's reign); and on his birthday, 25 April, at Byland in Yorkshire he gave a penny to each of 300 poor people.[188] A similar pattern of behaviour continued after he became king. From 1315 to 1316, for example, he made a daily oblation in his private chapel of 7d, except for the feast of the Epiphany (6 January) when he offered gold, frankincense and myrrh. In the same year he gave £38 6s 8d to the Carmelites of Sheen to celebrate masses for the souls of his ancestors.[189]

Edward's religious formation, like his education, was probably begun by the Dominican friars whom his mother sent to join his household in 1290. She had a particular devotion to the Dominicans, to whom she gave

---

[186] E 101/360/10, m.2. The reference to St Thomas must relate to a chapel at Ashridge since Edward was certainly not at Canterbury at this time.

[187] E 101/363/18: Book of Peter of Abingdon, controller of Edward's wardrobe.

[188] E 101/363/18, f.2. In all Edward spent £23 2s 9d on alms in that year. His gifts to the friars of London were all made on 13 March, the day he left London to campaign in Scotland.

[189] M. Vale, *The Princely Court* (Oxford, 2001), 236–7, 307 (Table 7). This material comes from E 101/376/7, ff.5r, 5v (a wardrobe book which covers only the period 8 July 1315 to 31 Jan. 1316). However, as Dr Vale points out, much more was spent (£334 18s 11d) on New Year's gifts for members of the court.

generous endowments in her lifetime and in her will, and whose religious practices, including the saying of the rosary, she followed.[190] In 1300, just before his sixteenth birthday, Edward was given an expensive primer, at a cost of £2. This has sometimes been interpreted as a textbook for Edward to learn Latin but it was probably a book of devotions. The book itself is no longer extant, so it is impossible to say whether the prayers which it contained would have been in accordance with his mother's wishes and those of her Dominican mentors.[191] Both Eleanor of Castile and her husband had Dominican confessors in their households, and this practice was to be followed by their son, Edward of Caernarfon.[192] John of Lenham was Edward's confessor as early as 1301 and remained until his retirement in 1315, when he was succeeded by John of Warefield who had been in Edward's service since at least 1303. Later in his reign Edward employed Luke of Wodeford and Robert of Duffeld as his confessors. Edward sometimes used Dominicans such as John of Wrotham in 1311 and Nicholas of Wisbech in 1317–19 for particularly delicate royal business at the papal curia. The records of Edward's household are full of gifts and donations made to individual Dominicans or to their houses, notably the house at King's Langley which he founded and where the body of Edward's favourite, Gaveston, was finally buried in 1315.[193]

As early as 1305, in a letter to the mayor of Northampton on behalf of the local Dominicans, Edward had expressed 'a great affection for the order of friars preacher, for many reasons', and showed his affection for them in practical ways both then and on many other occasions during his life.[194] It is not surprising that in 1327 Dominicans were involved in plots to release Edward from captivity, first at Kenilworth and then at Berkeley, or that in later years they were instrumental in spreading tales of Edward's sanctity. Edward's most striking involvement with the order was the episode of the Holy Oil of St Thomas of Canterbury between 1317 and 1319 when Nicholas of Wisbech, a former confessor to Edward's sister Margaret the duchess of Brabant, persuaded Edward to ask the pope to

[190] C 47/4/5, ff.13, 29; Parsons, *Eleanor*, 41–2. See also Parsons, 'Eleanor of Castile', 38–40, and 51, nn. 64 & 65.

[191] Johnstone, 18; cf. Galbraith, 'Literacy', 215.

[192] Parsons, 'Eleanor', 38. The role of Dominicans as confessors to English kings has been studied by R.D. Clarke in an unpublished MA thesis, 'Some secular activities of the English Dominicans during the reigns of Edward I, Edward II and Edward III, 1272–1377' (London, 1930). See also W.A. Hinnebusch, *The Early English Friars Preachers* (Rome, 1951).

[193] For Edward's confessors see, for example (Lenham) E 101/359/5, f. 5v; E 101/376/7, f. 4; E 101/363/18, f. 6. When Lenham was dying in Aug. 1316 Edward took particular care for his comfort: E 101/376/7, f. 5v; SAL, Ms.120, f. 8v. (Wodeford and Duffeld): SAL, Ms.120, f.11v; BL, Add. Ms. 17362, f. 5; Add. Ms. 9951, f. 2. (Wrotham): BL, Cotton Ms. Nero C.VIII, f. 54v; E 101/373/26, f. 90. For royal gifts in aid of building work at Langley see BL, Add. Ms. 35293, f. 8v (1307); BL, Cotton Ms. C.VIII, f. 51 (1311); for the burial of Gaveston see Phillips, 63.

[194] *Letters of Edward Prince of Wales*, 1 & 21. A number of examples are cited.

allow him to be anointed with the oil in the hope that the ceremony would end the political troubles in which he was then immersed. The pope refused to sanction what would, in effect, have been a second coronation, and the attempt ended in the imprisonment and subsequent flight of Nicholas of Wisbech and in the deep embarrassment of Edward himself. These events, however, suggest that in religious matters Edward combined a greater piety than either his father or his son with a certain gullibility. In a remarkably frank letter, which he addressed to the pope in the summer of 1319, Edward admitted that through his own weakness (*'imbecillitatem'*) he had allowed the unscrupulous friar to take advantage of his 'dovelike simplicity'.[195]

Apart from his bad experience with Nicholas of Wisbech, Edward appears to have enjoyed the company of religious men and to have been at ease with them. He was so much at ease that in 1316 an unidentified monk cited by the author of the *Vita Edwardi Secundi* complained that Edward II spent too much time in monasteries.[196] In May 1300, when he was on his way to Scotland for his first taste of warfare, he and his father stayed at the abbey of Bury St Edmund's in Suffolk. Edward remained after his father had left, 'enjoying the seclusion of the monastery. He became our brother in chapter. The magnificence of the place and the frequent recreation of the brethren pleased him greatly. Every day, he asked to be served with a monk's portion, such as the brothers take in the refectory. Some say that he declared that he had never enjoyed the pleasant company of monks so much. But on the twelfth day, he said farewell to the monks and hurried to join his father.'[197] Although there is no connection between the two, this report anticipates the story of Edward's going into seclusion as a hermit, which was contained in the famous letter of Manuel Fieschi composed some time in the late 1330s.[198] When he visited the cathedral abbey of Ely at Easter 1314 and debated with the monks over whether they or the monks of St Albans possessed the true relics of St Alban, he seems to have been greatly enjoying himself, even if his hosts were embarrassed.[199] On another occasion when Edward was dining with Abbot Thoky of St Peter's abbey in Gloucester, the king is supposed to have looked at the painted figures of his predecessors around the hall. The abbot asked Edward whether he would like to be

---

[195] For details see Phillips, 'Edward II and the prophets', 196–201; C 70/ 4, m.6d. Even allowing for the rhetorical use of language in a letter to the pope, this is still an interesting choice of words. A fuller account appears in ch. 7 of this book.

[196] *Vita*, 128–31. Whatever spiritual benefits Edward obtained from his visits to monastic houses, his hosts would have been put to considerable expense in entertaining Edward and his household.

[197] V.H. Galbraith, 'The St Edmundsbury Chronicle, 1296–1301', *EHR*, lviii (1943), 75. The translation is that of Mary Saaler in her book *Edward II, 1307–1327* (London, 1997), 17.

[198] See Phillips, ' "Edward II" in Italy'.

[199] *Historia Anglicana*, 138–9.

portrayed among them, only for Edward to reply 'more in prophecy than in jest' that he hoped he would occupy a more honourable place, 'and so it turned out'.[200] One of Edward's close personal friends was William, the abbot of the Premonstratensian house at Langdon in Kent. In 1321 Edward II's favourite, Hugh Despenser the Younger, fled the country allegedly disguised as a monk of Langdon, while in October 1323 Edward wrote to the pope asking (unsuccessfully) for the appointment of William as bishop of Bath and Wells in place of John Droxford who had opposed the king in 1321–2; in late August 1325 Edward spent time at Langdon debating whether to cross to France to do homage. William's loyalty to Edward II survived the king's deposition: in 1330 he was one of those implicated in the earl of Kent's doomed plot to free Edward II, as they hoped, from captivity.[201]

Edward's piety and his tendency to turn to religion for help when in a tight corner were expressed on a number of other significant occasions. The Dominican house at King's Langley was said to have been founded by Edward in fulfilment of a vow he had made 'when in peril'. It is not known to what this refers, but it was probably during one of the Scottish campaigns between 1300 and 1307. The first friars arrived at Langley in late October 1307, presumably in the wake of a decision taken by Edward very soon after his accession to the throne in July; they were to have numbered 100 but in 1311 there were only 45. Edward also intended the house to be built in the park at his manor of King's Langley but until 1311 the friars were staying 'at Langley in another place', the king's lodge known as Little London. In March that year Edward granted them 700 marks for the construction of their house 'in which to celebrate prayers daily for the souls of his ancestors, and for himself and his state'. The money was however to be provided by the abbey of St Albans at the rate of £100 a year, in payment of a debt to the king. The church, which was the first building to be constructed, was consecrated as 'Christ Church' or 'St Saviour' in the summer of 1312 and was the scene of the solemn burial of Edward II's former favourite Piers Gaveston in January 1315.[202] Edward II made the tomb of Gaveston a focal point of his

---

[200] *Historia et Cartularium Monasterii Sancti Petri Gloucestriae*, i, ed. W.H. Hart, Rolls ser. (London, 1863), 44. This tale was recorded in the context of the later death and burial of Edward II at Gloucester. It is not clear whether 'painted figures' (*depictas figures*) means two-dimensional images of kings or statues (see *Historia*, Introduction, lx). It is not known when this visit to Gloucester by Edward II took place. Edward was in Gloucester on a number of occasions, all of them late in his reign: in 1321, 1322, 1324, and in May and Oct. 1326: see the Index of Places in *The Itinerary of Edward II and his Household, 1307–1327*, ed. E.M. Hallam (London, 1984). Edward did not necessarily go to the abbey on each occasion, although as the biggest local source of hospitality, it would be the obvious place for the king to stay.

[201] Phillips, 206; *Foedera*, II, ii, 86; Haines, *The Church and Politics*, 137–8, 153 n. 95, 188 n. 51.

[202] *Victoria County History, Hertfordshire*, iv, ed. W. Page (Oxford, 1971), 46–51; Chaplais, 30, 110–11.

spiritual life, and both then and for the rest of his reign he made regular and generous offerings at it. On 31 January 1325, for example, he attended mass for Gaveston's soul at Langley, during which he made offerings of 9s 4d and placed two cloths of gold, one red and one white, and worth £5, on the tomb.[203] The church was not however complete in 1315; the buildings of the priory were not finished for another sixty or seventy years and Little London remained the home of the friars. Edward also intended to found a house of Dominican nuns subject to the priory of King's Langley, but this did not become reality until its establishment by Edward III at Dartford in Kent in 1346.[204] At the time Edward II made the grant to the Dominicans in 1311 he was in another tight spot, one of a political kind, following the recent appointment of the Ordainers to reform his administration.

Edward's second religious foundation in the wake of a narrow escape was an addition to the Carmelite house which had existed at Oxford since 1256. When Edward was in danger of capture at Bannockburn in 1314 he is said to have vowed to the Virgin Mary that if he escaped he would found a house for twenty-four Carmelites to study at Oxford. The twenty-four friars were initially installed in 1315 at Edward's manor of Sheen near London (the present-day Richmond) and moved to Oxford in 1318 after Edward had given them his manor, known as the palace of Beaumont, by the North Gate of Oxford. Each friar was to receive five marks per year for his support. Edward apparently made this foundation despite attempts by Hugh Despenser the Younger to dissuade him on grounds of cost.[205]

On two other occasions Edward's attempts to invoke divine assistance came to nothing. On Palm Sunday 1314 (31 March), when he was beginning his journey north for a new campaign in Scotland, he stopped at St Alban's abbey where he made an offering to the saint of a gold cross set with precious stones and containing relics of various other saints. Edward commended himself and his affairs to the protection of St Alban and to the prayers of the monks.[206] On Easter Sunday (7 April) he was at Ely where he caused great embarrassment to the bishop and to the monks, who claimed to possess the body of St Albans, by telling them that his brothers at St Albans sincerely believed that they had the body.

[203] *Proceedings of His Majesty's Commissioners on the Public Records*, ed. C.P. Cooper, i (London, 1833), 502, citing E 101/381/4.
[204] Knowles & Hadcock, *Medieval Religious Houses*, 185; *CPR, 1307–13*, 453; *KW*, i, 257–9 (King's Langley), 264 (Dartford).
[205] Knowles & Hadcock, *Medieval Religious Houses*, 198. The story of Edward II's vow is recorded in the *Chronicon* of Geoffrey le Baker: see Gransden, ii, 38. The details are confirmed by a petition to Edward III by the Carmelites in 1330 in which they complained that their financial support was in arrears: SC 8/11/512, printed in *RP*, ii, 35, no. 23.
[206] *Historia Anglicana*, 138. Edward was also reminded by the monks of an alleged promise by his father to help rebuild the choir of the abbey, and donated 100 marks and a supply of timber, urging that no expense be spared for the honour of God and of St Alban, the protomartyr of the English.

Edward, who seems to have been greatly interested in the question, then ordered an inquiry which proved that the true relic was indeed at St Albans.[207] Whatever benefit he might have hoped for from the various relics of St Alban was not forthcoming since he led his army to disaster at Bannockburn on 24 June. His final quest for divine aid came in South Wales in October 1326 when he was fleeing from the advancing forces of Queen Isabella. Having set sail from Chepstow with the Younger Despenser in an attempt to reach Lundy and possibly even Ireland, Edward made an offering to Despenser's confessor in return for prayers to St Anne for a fair wind. Sadly both the prayers and the wind failed and Edward had to land at Cardiff and seek refuge in Caerphilly castle.[208]

EDWARD'S PERSONAL DEVOTIONS

One of his devotions was to his name saint and that of his dynasty, St Edward the Confessor, whose cult was central to the rebuilt abbey of Westminster and who was to figure prominently in the ceremonial of Edward's coronation in 1308. On that occasion the first clause of his coronation oath was a promise to uphold the laws, customs and liberties granted by St Edward to the Church and people. He was crowned with the crown of St Edward which was afterwards placed upon the altar in the saint's shrine; the sword of St Edward (*curtana*) was carried before him in procession; he made an offering of a pound weight of gold fashioned to represent St Edward offering a ring; and the chalice, patten, sceptre and rod of St Edward were used in the ritual. Edward II was in other words surrounded at his coronation by reminders of St Edward and of his own intermediate place between God and mankind.[209] Throughout his reign the feast of St Edward the Confessor was routinely observed by Edward and his household, nowhere more significantly than in the chapel of St Edward at Windsor. This chapel was already old in Edward II's day, having been built by Henry III between 1240 and 1245/6 and matching Henry's rebuilding of Westminster Abbey as a shrine to St Edward.[210] In the summer of 1313 Edward ordered the refurbishment of the chapel, the appointment of four chaplains to serve there and to say two masses daily, one for the Virgin Mary and the other for the soul of Edward I. The king's chancellor was to inspect

---

[207] *Historia Anglicana*, 138–9. On inspection the relic of St Alban possessed by the monks of Ely turned out to be the cloak given to Alban by St Amphibalus to mark his conversion: ibid. The story of Edward's visit to Ely was reported by Thomas Walsingham, a St Albans chronicler.

[208] SAL, Ms. 122, p.90.

[209] See Binski, *Westminster Abbey*, 130–1; *Foedera*, II, i, 33–6; H.G. Richardson, 'English coronation oath', 149; idem & Sayles, 'Early coronation records', *BIHR*, xvi (1938–39), 7,10.

[210] *KW*, ii, 868–9.

the chapel and its fittings once a year.[211] A few months earlier the chapel had been the scene of the baptism on 16 November 1312 of the future Edward III, who was born at Windsor on 13 November.[212]

Edward's other devotion to the cult of a particular saint was to that of St Thomas of Canterbury,[213] a practice he inherited from his father Edward I who visited the shrine of St Thomas at Canterbury on six occasions between 1279 and 1305.[214] Edward himself was there in July 1293 on the feast of the Translation of St Thomas, for the second marriage of Edward I and Margaret of France in September 1299, and visited Canterbury on sixteen occasions between December 1307 and April 1323.[215] As noted earlier, a Life of St Thomas was one of the manuscripts which Edward later borrowed from Canterbury and failed to return. More significant, however, was his choice of the martyrdom of St Thomas as the theme of the painting he commissioned from William of Northampton in April 1301 for the chapel of Chester castle shortly after he became Prince of Wales.[216] Although there are many surviving representations of Becket, this appears to be the only recorded medieval reference to an actual commission.[217] The later episode

---

[211] *Foedera*, II, i, 193; *CCR, 1307–13*, 586. No date is given but the entry appears at the very end of the roll, in company with entries for late June and early July 1313. The chapel had been served by four chaplains from its foundation.

[212] *Foedera*, II, i, 187; *CCR, 1307–13*, 558.

[213] In 1320, in the course of trying to resolve a dispute between the archbishop of Canterbury and the prior of St Martin's, Dover, Edward remarked on his special devotion to St Thomas: *RP*, i, 370.

[214] A. J. Duggan, 'The cult of St. Thomas Becket in the thirteenth century', in *St. Thomas Cantilupe, Bishop of Hereford*, ed. M. Jancey (Hereford, 1982), 31.

[215] 1293: E 101/353/18, m.6. His visits to Canterbury as king are listed in the Index of Places, in E.M. Hallam, *The Itinerary of Edward II*. It does not of course follow that Edward went to St Thomas's shrine on each of these occasions but it is likely that he made a considerable number of visits.

Edward was also interested in encouraging the process for the canonization of another Thomas, Thomas Cantilupe bishop of Hereford (d. 1282). The bull of canonization was finally issued on 17 April 1320 during a mission to Avignon by Adam Orleton, bishop of Hereford and other royal envoys. Orleton then attended the ceremony on 27 May. Edward II expressed his pleasure at the canonization and stated that he would attend the translation of the remains of the new saint. In Nov. he gave orders for the collection of alms for the construction of St Thomas's shrine: Haines, *The Church and Politics*, 24–5; P. H. Daly, 'The process of canonization in the late thirteenth and early fourteenth centuries', and P. E. Morgan, 'The effect of the pilgrim cult of St. Thomas Cantilupe on Hereford cathedral', in M. Jancey, ed., *St Thomas Cantilupe*, 135, 150–1.

[216] William was asked for 'a picture of blessed Thomas the martyr with the four knights who slew him': Johnstone, 61, citing the account roll of William Melton, chamberlain of Chester, 1301 (National Library of Wales, Wynnstay Ms. 86), ed. R.S. Brown in *Cheshire in the Pipe Rolls, 1158–1301*, Lancashire & Cheshire Record Soc., xcii (Manchester, 1938): see App., 209, 219. The painting is no longer extant.

[217] This was the opinion expressed to Professor Johnstone by Professor C.T. Borenius, the author of *St Thomas Becket in Art* (London, 1932). The Chester painting was not however previously known to him and does not figure in the list of English wall-paintings of the martyrdom: ibid., 98–9.

of the Holy Oil of St Thomas and Edward's unsuccessful attempt to make use of it and the accompanying legend for his own propaganda purposes is another highly significant example.[218] Edward did, however, involve St Thomas in another practice which was also designed to emphasize and to extend the sacred powers of the monarchy. This was the *chevage* or annual payment at the shrine of St Thomas at Canterbury which is first recorded in 1316 and which closely resembles the offerings that French kings had made at the abbey of St Denis since the time of Philip I or Louis VI.[219]

These examples suggest that Edward II was very conscious of the sacred character of monarchy and of the indefinable yet very real power he derived from it. This was inherent in the ceremony of coronation which he had undergone in March 1308 and was always a bulwark against the power of his opponents. Only in the exceptional circumstances attending Edward's deposition in 1327 could this first and last line of defence of his royal power be breached, and even then with dubious legality. It should not be thought, for example, that when Edward sought to be anointed with the Holy Oil of St Thomas he was acting simply out of political weakness. There is little doubt that he genuinely believed that the oil had the magical powers ascribed to it. Another aspect of sacred monarchy was the 'sacred touch', the miraculous ability to cure scrofula (a tubercular inflammation of the lymph nodes) which was believed to be possessed by both the French and the English kings. In his study of the phenomenon Marc Bloch presented evidence from the royal household records suggesting that Edward II performed the ritual far less frequently than either his father or his son and that this indicated that his subjects were not inclined 'to come for healing to a monarch lacking in prestige'.[220] He also concluded that even within the reign of Edward II there was a marked decline in the numbers presenting themselves for healing, from 214 in 1316 to 93 in 1320, and only 79 in 1320–1: in a 'good year' during the reign of Edward I, 1296–7, 725 persons were touched by the king. However, Bloch examined the records for only those three years of the reign of Edward II.[221] On the other hand too much weight should not be attached to statistics alone, as Bloch himself observed.[222] Edward II also appears to have been responsible for introducing a new royal miracle, first recorded in 1323 (and possibly reflecting his new-found confidence since his defeat of his enemies in 1322),

---

[218] Bloch, *Royal Touch*, 137–9.
[219] Ibid., 352, n. 116.
[220] Ibid., 56–60.
[221] Ibid., 56–9, 310, n. 18, and 311, n. 25. Between 8 July and 19 Oct. 1322 he blessed a mere 36 sick poor men: BL, Stowe Ms. 553, f. 118; Prestwich, 'The court of Edward II', 67. Edward III continued the practice but it is recorded only between 1336 and 1344; the lack of further evidence may, as Mark Ormrod suggests, be the result of changes in record-keeping practice rather than disuse of the royal touch: Ormrod, 'The personal religion of Edward III', 862–3. Perhaps something of the kind also happened during Edward II's reign.
[222] Bloch, *Royal Touch*, 57–8.

which had no parallel in France. After the adoration of the cross during the Good Friday ceremonies the king would place upon the altar a number of gold and silver coins which would then be 'redeemed' and made into wonder-working rings or 'cramp rings' which were supposed to cure the wearer of certain unspecified diseases.[223]

LEISURE ACTIVITIES

Edward II's interest in rustic activities 'and other pointless and trivial occupations unsuitable for the son of a king' was well known and commented on by, for example, the authors of the Lanercost chronicle,[224] the *Brut*[225] and the *Vita Edwardi Secundi*,[226] by a household messenger in 1314,[227] in the articles of his deposition in 1327,[228] and in Ranulf Higden's *Polychronicon*.[229]

There is some evidence to support these statements. His liking of rowing, for example, is attested in September 1315 when he had a narrow escape from drowning while rowing at Fen Ditton near Cambridge;[230] while a year earlier the Scots allegedly made fun of his engagement in this sport.[231] The 'great company of simple people' who accompanied him at Fen Ditton is one indication that he enjoyed the near-presence of the low-born, as are the records in 1325 showing that the master of the royal barge, along with royal sailors and carpenters dined in the royal chamber.[232] There is no direct evidence to support the claims about Edward II's interest in hedging and ditching,[233] but the recent suggestion that the objections to these practices may have been to the enclosure of land for hunting and should be seen in the context of poems of social protest rather than taken literally is not convincing.[234] If Edward really did

---

[223] Ibid., 92–3, 250–2. The practice is referred to in the household ordinance of 1323 but it was probably already in use: ibid., 327, n. 5.

[224] *Lanercost*, 236 (rowing, driving carts, hedging, ditching, 'various works of ingenuity and skill').

[225] *Brut*, i, 208 (rowing).

[226] *Vita*, 69 (rustic pursuits).

[227] H. Johnstone, 'Eccentricities of Edward II', 264–7, citing the Memoranda Roll for 1315–16, E 368/86, m.32d. ('making ditches and digging and other improper occupations').

[228] *Select Documents*, 37 (unsuitable work and occupations).

[229] *Polychronicon*, 298: 'he forsook the company of lords and sought out the company of harlots, singers, jesters, carters, delvers, ditchers, rowers and other craftsmen'.

[230] *Flores*, 173. Fen Ditton is today the scene of the annual rowing races or 'bumps' held by the university of Cambridge, in which the object is to make physical contact with a rival boat. This form of rowing can lead to accidents and makes one wonder whether Edward's narrow escape was the result of a similar boisterous sport.

[231] *Brut*, i, 208.

[232] SAL, Ms. 122, pp. 4, 6, 7, 30; Prestwich, 'The court of Edward II', 72.

[233] Except of course, E 368/86, m.32d, cited above: but this is a report of someone else's comment about Edward rather than an official record *per se*.

[234] Richardson, ' "Hedging, ditching" ', 40–2. Dr Richardson draws particular attention to the creation of the 1,737-hectare deer park at Clarendon in 1317.

engage in hedging or ditching or any of the other improper occupations, it is likely that he did so first at Langley, his favourite manor.

He had an interest in building at places of personal importance to him. Surprisingly, there is least evidence of royal building at Langley. The main construction work here was centred instead on the Dominican priory which Edward founded.[235] When he was on his tour of Wales after being made Prince of Wales in 1301 he appears to have taken a personal interest in the refurbishing of Chester castle.[236] There is particular evidence that in 1308 he was directly concerned in the preparation of Westminster Palace for his coronation. Two new chambers, one between the Green Chamber and the 'queen's bridge' and the other alongside the Painted Chamber for use as Edward's bedroom were constructed *per proprium divisamentum Regis*. Edward was also involved in the fitting out of the royal ship, the *Margaret of Westminster*, which was to fetch his bride and queen from France.[237] There is also evidence that Edward played some part in the design of the great tower of Knaresborough castle and of buildings in Nottingham castle.[238] He certainly influenced the details of work carried out, but there is nothing to suggest he was involved in the work itself at any of these places. The purchase in 1310–11 of iron and plaster for 'the private works of the king' suggests that Edward sometimes got his hands dirty, but even this does not prove that he did so.[239]

Edward did not engage in tournaments, which were in any case discouraged for political reasons during much of his reign;[240] and showed only an occasional interest in hunting,[241] despite his huntsman William Twiti's dedication to him late in the reign of a treatise on the subject, *The Art of*

---

[235] *KW*, i, 972–3.
[236] *Cheshire in the Pipe Rolls*, 189–90.
[237] *KW*, i, 506.
[238] Prestwich, 'The court of Edward II', 67; *KW*, i, 698, 761.
[239] BL, Cotton Mss, Nero C.VIII, f. 57; Prestwich, 'The court of Edward II', 71–2. See also Richardson, ' "Hedging, ditching" ', 31.
[240] However J.S. Hamilton cites a number of occasions when, as Prince of Wales, Edward gave assistance to others who engaged in them. There were also the tournaments early in his reign in which Gaveston and his companions showed off their prowess, much to the annoyance of other barons. J.S. Hamilton, 'The character of Edward II', in *The Reign of Edward II: New Perspectives*, ed. G. Dodd and A. Musson (Woodbridge, Suffolk & Rochester, NY, 2006), 6.
[241] Prestwich, 'The court of Edward II', 72. In June 1312 Edward was shooting with a bow in Hatfield park. However, he had to borrow the bow and arrows for the occasion from a valet of the earl of Pembroke, so this may not have been a regular occurrence. It is also not clear whether he was using the bow for hunting or target practice: Vale, *The Princely Court*, 180.
[242] The most recent edition is by B. Daniellsson, Stockholm Studies in English, XXXVII, Cynegetica Anglica, i (Stockholm, 1977). The role of Twyti (who died in about 1328) seems to have been to feed the royal household rather than guide his royal master on the hunting field. The royal hunt in Clarendon park in August 1326, when 88 great bucks were taken in a single day, is more likely to have been of this kind rather than a personal outing by the king: cf. Richardson, ' "Hedging, ditching" ', 37, citing C 145/106/8/2.

Hunting.[242] He was, however, very interested in horses and clearly was a good judge of their quality. In 1304–5 Edward came into possession of the stud which had belonged to the late earl of Surrey and also asked the archbishop of Canterbury for assistance in obtaining a good breeding stallion.[243] When Anthony Bek the bishop of Durham died in 1311 Edward II reserved for his own use Bek's famous Weardale stud of 240 horses and ten *stabuli* for destriers and other horses.[244] Edward was also a connoisseur of dogs, which figure on several occasions in his correspondence for 1304–5.[245] It was an interest he was to share with Isabella, his future wife and queen, who left her hunting dogs in the custody of the monks of Christ Church, Canterbury during her stay in France in 1325–6, much to the annoyance of the prior, Henry of Eastry.[246] Hawking was another activity closely associated with the court. While Edward on occasions gave or received hawks as special gifts, again he does not seem to have engaged in hawking in person. Compared with the reign of Edward I, hawking declined during that of Edward II but revived under Edward III.[247]

There is ample evidence of Edward's interest in music, which included the Welsh stringed instrument, the *crwth*;[248] and also the organ. He had an organ at Langley which was repaired in 1303 'against the coming of the king and queen',[249] while in 1305 he sent another organ to his sister Mary, the nun of Amesbury.[250] At the feast held in May 1306, after Edward was knighted the guests were entertained by eighty minstrels, fourteen of whom were provided by Edward himself, including two trumpeters, five boy minstrels, one taborer (the tabor was a small drum), one harper, one player of the *vielle* (a four-stringed instrument), two crowders (who played the *crwth*), and one guitarist.[251] During Edward's reign as king there are many references to the performances of minstrels and others for the entertainment of Edward and his court, including John de Colon, from Lombardy, who used snakes in his act at Canterbury in August 1312; Cardinal Luke Fieschi's minstrel who performed before the king in December 1317; and John de Trentham the king's harper who went into honourable retirement at Muchelney abbey in 1328.[252] Edward II was not in any way exceptional

---

[243] *Letters of Edward Prince of Wales*, 31; Hamilton, 'The character of Edward II', 7.

[244] Article by C.M. Fraser in the *Oxford DNB*. Edward also kept the pick of his jewels, and later bought from his executors his gold plate for 2,075 marks (£1,383). He also bought for £500 Bek's campaign tents, consisting of two *aulae*, three *camerae*, and a chapel.

[245] *Letters of Edward Prince of Wales*, 83, 116–17; Hamilton, 'The character of Edward II', 8.

[246] *Literae Cantuarienses*, i, ed. J.B. Sheppard, (London, 1887), 164–71.

[247] R. S. Oggins, *The Kings and their Hawks* (New Haven & London, 2004), 86, 89, 91, 108, 185.

[248] *Letters of Edward Prince of Wales*, 114.

[249] *KW*, i, 973.

[250] *Letters of Edward Prince of Wales*, 134; Hamilton, 'The character of Edward II', 9.

[251] C. Bullock-Davies, '*Multitudo*' (Cardiff, 1978), 1–13.

[252] Bullock-Davies, *A Register of Royal and Baronial Minstrels, 1272–1327* (Woodbridge, Suffolk & Dover, NH, 1986), 32, 53, 209.

in having minstrels in his service. The records show that members of the royal family, the nobility and the clergy all employed minstrels.[253] They were an international fraternity, part of a cultural area in which French was the common literary language: when Edward's sisters Joan and Margaret married in 1290 minstrels came from all over northern France and the Low Countries; the same thing occurred when Edward I married Margaret of France at Canterbury in July 1299.[254] However, not all of the performances witnessed by Edward II were of evident cultural merit. The most extraordinary took place at Pontoise in France in 1313 when he and Isabella were visiting the French court. On 19 June, ironically the first anniversary of his former favourite Gaveston's death, Edward and Isabella were entertained 'with jubilation' (*cum tripudio*) by Bernard le Fol and fifty-four naked dancers.[255] Whether we are to interpret this event as 'a decadent extravagance, fitting the familiar stereotype of the king',[256] or simply as something appropriate to a stay in France (for they were apparently French performers),[257] there is little to be gained from pursuing the point.

Minstrelsy was not the only form of entertainment available to Edward. He kept a camel at Langley, both in his childhood and adulthood;[258] and he had a pet lion which he even took with him on campaign to Scotland in 1303.[259] Malcolm Vale has also commented that 'the future Edward II of England, was already an experienced player of games of skill and chance in July 1299 when he was given 40s. by his father to meet the costs of his wagering *in diversos ludos*'.[260] These probably included dice, chess and 'tables', international games which were part of the knightly way of life.[261] Edward played such games regularly with Piers Gaveston: in Scotland, for example, in 1302–3 and at Christmas 1310, and sometimes for high stakes.[262]

---

[253] See Bullock-Davies, *Register*.

[254] Vale, *The Princely Court*, 292–3.

[255] E 101/375/8. f. 32; Bullock-Davies, *Register*, xiii, 9; E. A. R. Brown & N. F. Regalado, 'La grant feste', in *City and Spectacle in Medieval Europe*, ed. B. A. Hanawalt & K. L. Reyerson (Minneapolis, 1994), 71–2.

[256] Prestwich, 'The court of Edward II', 61. Edward was more tolerant of such displays than 'the prudish Henry VI of England' who 'was said to have fled when naked dancers appeared at a Christmas feast': Brown & Regalado, 84, n. 107.

[257] As Constance Bullock-Davies mischievously puts it, 'The entry is an unconscious confirmation of the waywardness of humanity, common to all men at all times; yet it cannot fail to raise a smile of amusement. *Plus ça change, plus la même chose*. The *Folies Bergères* has a long pedigree': Bullock-Davies, *Register*, xiii. In any case 'naked' may mean scantily clad rather than nude.

[258] In 1290 and again between 1322 and 1325: *KW*, i, 973.

[259] *CDS*, ii, 364–67.

[260] Vale, *The Princely Court*, 171.

[261] Ibid., 171–4.

[262] *CDS*, ii, 368; Vale, *The Princely Court*, 171–2. In 1307–8 Edward twice received sums of over £80 to pay for his gambling: ibid., 172; E 101/375/15, ff. 9r, 9v. The large sums involved may indicate that Edward II was a poor gambler or simply that he enjoyed the social contacts involved and did not mind too much whether he won or lost.

In many ways Edward II was typical of his class and time, in his level of education, religious practices, social relations and forms of relaxation. His experience of war was also considerable, as the next chapter will show. But it was in the wider realm of politics and kingship that he proved to be very different from both his father and his son. Some of the reasons lay beyond his control but the difference also lay within himself, not least in his obsessive friendships and eccentricities of behaviour.

Chapter 3

PREPARATION FOR THE CROWN, 1297–1307

EDWARD'S PUBLIC CAREER

Edward's public career began in a sense with such events as meeting his father and mother at Dover on their return from Gascony in August 1289, the family gathering at Amesbury in April 1290 to settle the succession to the crown, and the plans in the same year for his marriage to Margaret, 'the Maid of Norway'. This never took place but in July 1290 the wedding of Edward's sister Margaret to John de Brabant in Westminster Abbey was a splendid occasion attended, among many other leaders of society, by the six-year-old Edward who was reportedly accompanied by a train of eighty knights.[1] In November that year Edward acquired his first territorial possession when he succeeded to the county of Ponthieu and Montreuil on the Channel coast of France after his mother's death. This small but valuable territory, with its administrative centre in the cloth-making town of Abbeville, had been Eleanor's personal inheritance from her own mother, and provided a ready means of access to the continent. Ponthieu was efficiently administered on Edward's behalf until he came of age, but possession of the county gave him the beginnings of a status other than simply that of the 'king's son'. In 1307 Ponthieu was also to be Piers Gaveston's place of exile when Edward and his father fell out bitterly over him.[2]

Although he was still a child, from the mid-1290s Edward's life became increasingly affected by both national and international affairs. In 1294 England and France went to war when Philip IV confiscated the duchy of Aquitaine after years of friction.[3] While peace negotiations were still continuing, Edward I had preferred a French marriage for his son, but now, as part of Edward's diplomatic offensive against France, a marriage was proposed between Edward of Caernarfon and a daughter of the count of Flanders, who was both a leading vassal and a political opponent of Philip IV of France. Under intense pressure from the French king, the

---

[1] Parsons, 'The year of Eleanor of Castile's birth', 262. Edward's presence was noted by the chronicler, Bartholomew Cotton, *Historia Anglicana*, ed. H.R. Luard, Rolls ser. (London, 1859), 177.

[2] Prestwich, *Edward I*, 316–17; Johnstone, 65–7, 124–5; Johnstone, 'The county of Ponthieu, 1279–1307', *EHR*, xxix (1914), 435–52; Vale, 71–3, 286 (map).

[3] For the background to the war see Vale, ch. 6, 'Anglo-French conflict'.

count was forced in 1295 to send his daughter to Paris for safekeeping and for the moment the marriage plans lapsed.[4] In 1296 England and Scotland also went to war and, while Edward I campaigned in the north, his son was given nominal command of the defence of the south coast of England against a possible French invasion in support of the Scots.[5]

In 1297 the Anglo-French conflict intensified. In January the plan for a Flemish marriage was revived and in February Edward I travelled to the shrine of Our Lady of Walsingham to meet proctors of the count of Flanders to agree on an alliance against France and to announce formally the betrothal of the young Edward to the count's daughter Philippa or, if she were not available, to her sister Isabella. The prospective bridegroom in the meantime remained at Windsor.[6] In August Edward I crossed to Flanders with a large army to conduct operations against the French, leaving his son Edward as his lieutenant in England. For the young Edward this should again have been an experience of nominal command, but events turned out very differently, since 1297 was a year of crisis in both England's internal affairs and international relations. The pressure of royal taxation for the wars with France and Scotland led to the refusal to pay further taxes by the English Church, with the support of the papacy, and by the laity, led by the earls of Hereford and Norfolk. The further refusal of these two magnates to join the royal army in Flanders on the eve of Edward I's departure brought matters to a head.[7]

This was the situation in which the young Edward now found himself. On 14 July and during the days immediately following, the prelates of the English Church and the leading members of the English nobility, including the earls of Hereford and Norfolk, had sworn fealty to Edward as his father's successor, in a solemn ceremony held at Westminster in the presence of Edward I. The occasion was emotionally as well as politically charged, since it also marked the public reconciliation between the king and the archbishop of Canterbury, Robert Winchelsey.[8] During his father's absence in Flanders Edward was officially in charge of the affairs of the realm. Edward I left England on 22 August, and on 27 August the

[4] Johnstone, 32; Prestwich, *Edward I*, 388. A Flemish marriage had been under discussion since 1292 and was part of a wider diplomatic scheme which saw the marriages of Edward I's daughters, Margaret, Elizabeth and Eleanor to the future duke of Brabant and to the counts of Holland and Bar respectively.

[5] Johnstone, 33.

[6] Ibid., 32; Prestwich, *Edward I*, 388–9. There are no household records for Edward of Caernarfon at this period but the chronicler Bartholomew Cotton reports that he was at Windsor with his sister Elizabeth, countess of Holland: Cotton, *Historia Anglicana*, 316–17 (cited in Johnstone, 35).

[7] For the most recent survey of the events of 1297 see Prestwich, *Plantagenet England*, 165–72.

[8] *Documents Illustrating the Crisis of 1297–98 in England*, ed. Prestwich, Camden, 4th ser., xxiv (London, 1980), 106–7 (no. 91); Johnstone, 35; J.H. Denton, *Robert Winchelsey and the Crown, 1294–1313: a Study in the Defence of Ecclesiastical Liberty* (Cambridge, 1980), 131–2.

seal that Edward I had previously used during his absences in Gascony was formally handed over to his son at Tonbridge castle in Kent. Documents were consistently described as having been witnessed by 'Edward the king's son'.[9] The political tensions remained unresolved until on 10 October Edward and his advisers, without consulting Edward I, made concessions on taxation to the opposition earls and agreed to the confirmation of Magna Carta as a token of their sincerity. On the same date Edward issued letters patent offering a pardon to the earls. Edward I probably disapproved of these decisions but confirmed them at Ghent on 5 November.[10] One of the reasons for the final compromise was the humiliating defeat of an English army at Stirling Bridge in Scotland on 11 September, which was followed by Scottish raids into northern England. On 21 October a new English army was summoned to be at Newcastle on 6 December to go to Scotland under the nominal command of the young Edward.[11] Edward was not however to gain his first taste of warfare on this occasion since the next English campaign in Scotland was led by Edward I in person after his return from Flanders in March 1298. His son's only encounter with things Scottish at this stage of his career was with the son of John Balliol, the king of Scots deposed by Edward I in 1296. Also named Edward, and like his namesake Edward of Caernarfon, also destined for a turbulent career, the younger Balliol was placed in Edward's household for safekeeping and was to remain there with intervals in the Tower of London until 1299.[12] One of his stays in the Tower was in September 1297 at the time when 'Edward, the king's son' was staying within the walls of the city of London for greater security.[13]

Although the thirteen-year-old Edward was formally in control of the government of England during the critical months between August 1297 and March 1298, he was still only his father's son and heir. His position was therefore not strictly comparable even with that of his son, Edward III, or of his great-grandson, Richard II, who each found themselves succeeding to the throne at a tender age. The letters patent which Edward issued on 10 October reveal the names of the councillors

[9] *CCR, 1296–1302*, 58–9 and *passim*.
[10] Prestwich, *Plantagenet England*, 170; idem, *Edward I*, 427–9; *Documents*, ed. Prestwich, 155–6 (no. 153), 158–60 (no. 155).
[11] Prestwich, *Edward I*, 427, 477–9.
[12] Article by Bruce Webster on Edward Balliol in *Oxford DNB*; *CCR, 1296–1302*, 142, 288.
[13] *CCR, 1296–1302*, 142; Johnstone, 39. Writs issued at this time were dated at St Paul's. This may well be the occasion when Edward gave a cloth with a purple ground to St Paul's cathedral on the anniversary of its dedication; in 1299 a red altar cloth with images of St Peter holding the cross and the keys was presented to St Paul's by William Blyborough on behalf of Edward: O. Lehmann-Brockhaus, *Lateinische Schriftquellen zur Kunst in England, Wales und Schottland vom Jahre 901 bis zum Jahre 1307*, 5 vols (Munich, 1955–60), iii, 209–10 (no. 2932).
The two young men had already met as children, at Mortlake on Whit Sunday, 17 May 1293: E 101/353/18, m.5.

whom Edward I had left to advise his son during his absence: three bishops (Ely, London, and Coventry & Lichfield); the archbishop-elect of York; three earls (Cornwall, Surrey and Warwick); and three barons (John Giffard, Reginald Grey and Alan Plukenet); as well as other unnamed advisers. All were men of administrative experience or military reputation and above all loyal to the king.[14] After the excitements of the autumn months, which Edward had spent at Westminster, London, or the nearby palace of Eltham, he passed much of the early weeks of 1298 at his favourite country retreat of Langley near St Albans. Although no longer at the centre of the routine of government, he did not lack advice here either: on 3 January a valuable grant of £7,000 worth of tin to the earl of Cornwall, in repayment of loans to the king, was read and approved there by the three bishops, Reginald Grey, and Guncelin Badlesmere (whose son Bartholomew was to play an important role in Edward II's reign) and William Blyborough (the keeper of Edward's household).[15] Nonetheless Edward had lived through and been closely involved in a period of intense political crisis and of near civil war, which proved to be a prelude to a further crisis in 1300–1. In some respects these crises were also a prelude to the upheavals of Edward II's own reign after 1307, when similar issues concerning taxation and royal exactions of food and other supplies for war again came to the fore.[16] It is impossible to say what effect the experience had on the young Edward, but it cannot have been a negligible one. At a personal level he had seen how magnates who had sworn loyalty could appear in opposition to the crown only a few weeks later. Although the leaders of 1297 were long dead by 1307, it is possible that their actions helped to instil a certain wariness towards the magnates in the future king and turn him towards a close circle of individuals whose loyalty was unquestioned and in whom he could put his trust.

A STEPMOTHER AND A BETROTHAL

After his father's return to England in March 1298 the young Edward reverted to his position simply as 'the king's son'. He took no part in Edward I's campaign in Scotland in the summer of 1298 which culminated in the hard-fought victory over the Scots under William Wallace at Falkirk on 22 July.[17] However, the fourteen-year-old Edward was about to make his entrance on a wider stage. In June 1299 English and French envoys meeting at Montreuil agreed on a treaty which in effect brought an

---

[14] *Documents*, ed. Prestwich, 155–6 (no. 153); Johnstone, 36–7.
[15] *CCR, 1296–1302*, 142; Johnstone, 37.
[16] Prestwich, *Edward I*, 425, and Johnstone, 40–1, on the threat of civil war. On the aftermath of the crisis of 1297–8 see Prestwich, *Plantagenet England*, 172–7.
[17] Prestwich, *Edward I*, 479–82; G.W.S. Barrow, *Robert Bruce and the Community of the Realm of Scotland*, 3rd edn (Edinburgh, 1988), 98–104.

end to the Anglo-French conflict in Gascony and Flanders. One of the terms of the treaty was that Edward I should marry Margaret, the sister of Philip IV, and the younger Edward should promise to marry Philip's daughter Isabella.[18] The planned Flemish marriage was therefore abandoned[19] and, although Edward and Isabella did not marry until 1308, their lives were now fatefully entwined.[20] Edward I and Margaret were married on 10 September 1299 at Canterbury and lost no time in further guaranteeing the succession to the English crown by producing children: two sons, Thomas, who was born at Brotherton in Yorkshire on 1 June 1300, and Edmund, born at the royal palace of Woodstock near Oxford on 5 August 1301.[21] Both survived into manhood and as earls of Norfolk and Kent respectively were to play a political role in the later years of the reign of their elder brother Edward. Edmund of Woodstock was indeed to play an unwitting and tragic role in the vicious politics of the early years of Edward III's reign and met his death on the scaffold in 1330. In the meantime, had Edward of Caernarfon not outlived his father, Thomas or Edmund could have found himself king.

The new queen, Margaret of France, could never replace her predecessor Eleanor of Castile in Edward I's affections, but despite the forty years' difference in their ages the marriage appears to have been a happy one. She probably helped to soothe the temper of her increasingly irascible and ailing husband and, from the point of view of her stepson Edward, who was only a few years her junior, she provided a sense of family life and companionship which he had lacked since his mother's death in 1290. Margaret was also to mediate between father and son when they had their famous falling-out in 1305.[22] Edward and his stepmother spent time together early in her stay in England. On 2 November 1299, very soon after his marriage, Edward I left Margaret and the ladies of her household with his son at Langley,[23] where they remained until 20 November. Edward's

---

[18] Prestwich, *Edward I*, 396–7. The documents concerning the proposed marriages are preserved in AN, J 632, nos 33–36. The earl of Lincoln acted on behalf of the young Edward.

[19] The marriage contract had already been annulled by Pope Boniface VIII in June 1298: *Foedera*, I, ii, 894.

[20] Their formal betrothal did not however take place until 20 May 1303: Doherty, *Isabella*, 13, 15–16, 18. There is some confusion about the age of Isabella. Her age is given in Doherty, 16, 18, as two in 1298 and nine in 1303, which is impossible. Elsewhere however he cites convincing evidence (AN, J 435, no. 18) that she was born in the winter of 1295–6, which would make her aged seven in 1303: P.C. Doherty, 'The date of the birth of Isabella, queen of England (1308–58)', *BIHR*, xlviii (London, 1975), 246–8. This date is accepted by J.C. Parsons, the author of the *Oxford DNB* article on Isabella.

[21] Prestwich, *Edward I*, 129–31, 520–1; E.B. Fryde et al., *Handbook of British Chronology*, 3rd edn (London, 1986), 38–9.

[22] Prestwich, *Edward I*, 129–31.

[23] Edward I had celebrated All Saints' Day at Langley before leaving for Berwick-upon-Tweed with the intention of mounting another invasion of Scotland, which did not take place because of magnate opposition: Johnstone, 44.

sister Mary, the nun of Amesbury, was also present and the young people would have had a good opportunity to get to know one another. Supplies of apples, pears, nuts and other fruit were brought from London for the young queen and her stepson; Master Peter the queen's apothecary supplied two dozen pomegranates and also medicines for the queen and her ladies, who were sick on various occasions (perhaps homesick as much as unaccustomed to the English food and way of life); and a London apothecary provided 12 pounds of sugar for Edward and Margaret and their households. Entertainment was provided by Henry, the 'fool' of the count of Savoy, while Edward borrowed 10d from William Hertfield to play dice. Edward also made the acquaintance of Agnes de la Croix and other unnamed ladies of Queen Margaret's household.[24] Although there is no evidence to prove this supposition, it is possible that Edward had an affair with one of them then or later which led to the birth of his illegitimate son Adam. Edward had other opportunities to enjoy the company of Margaret and her ladies. They were at Windsor together from Christmas 1299 until February 1300 when they were rejoined by the king; towards the end of February, Edward, his father and stepmother visited the shrines at Canterbury, notably that of Thomas Becket, at which the young Edward made an offering on behalf of his yet unborn half-brother, Thomas. The family then returned to Westminster for the meeting of parliament. Edward probably remained in contact with both his father and his stepmother until early May when Margaret left for the birth of her baby. When Edward received the news of the birth on 2 June he rewarded the messenger handsomely and also sent a present to the infant's nurses.[25]

FIRST EXPERIENCE OF WAR

In 1299 and the first part of 1300 Edward had, for the first time since his mother's death in 1290, enjoyed something very like a stable family life, in close contact with his father and also with a young stepmother whom he appears to have liked.[26] However, his life was about to change. By the time his stepbrother was born Edward was already on his way north to take part in his first campaign in Scotland. Altogether Edward was in Scotland on four occasions, 1300–1, 1302–3, 1303–4 and 1306, and was on the point of entering Scotland when his father died in July 1307. There is no obvious

---

[24] E 101/355/17 (a single membrane of Edward's household expenses); E 101/ 355/30 (a single membrane of the queen's household expenses).

[25] Johnstone, 44–6.

[26] Ibid., 44, n. 9, cites William of Rishanger's remark that the family lived in 'leisured security'. In Feb. 1303 Edward entertained the king and queen for a week at Langley and probably then visited them at Westminster in early March. As a New Year's present for Queen Margaret he had bought a gold ring mounted with a ruby: E 101/363/18, ff.4v, 20, 29; Johnstone, 85.

sign of any lack of military zeal or capacity on Edward's part before he became king. As king, he campaigned in Scotland on another four occasions, in 1310, 1314, 1319 and 1322, with, as we shall see, very different fortunes.

His early experiences in Scotland brought favourable comments from the herald who composed the Roll of Arms describing the siege of Caerlaverock in July 1300:

> The fourth squadron with its train, Edward the king's son led, A youth of seventeen years of age (*recte* in his seventeenth year), and newly bearing arms. He was of a well-proportioned and handsome person, of a courteous disposition and well bred, and desirous of finding an occasion to make proof of his strength. He managed his steed wonderfully well, and bore with a blue label the arms of the good king his father. Now God give him grace that he be as valiant and no less so; then may fall into his hands those who never expect to do so.[27]

This was hardly surprising but approval also came later from a writer who might be expected to be hostile, John Barbour, archdeacon of Aberdeen, the author in the 1370s of a poem on the career of Robert Bruce. In his account of Edward's part in the siege of Kildrummy castle in Scotland in September 1306 Barbour described Edward as 'a fine young batchelor' and 'the strongest man of any that you could find in any country.'[28]

In May 1300, on their way north, both Edward and his father stayed at the abbey of Bury St Edmunds. Edward remained for a week after his father and greatly enjoyed himself, becoming, as the abbey chronicler remarked, 'our brother in chapter'. Edward I also took the precaution of having his banner touched by all the relics in the abbey.[29] The young Edward had reached Carlisle, where the army was gathering, before the end of June.[30] On 4 July the army advanced into Scotland with the intention of invading Galloway and in mid-July settled down to besiege the castle of Caerlaverock. Edward was placed by his father in a position of safety as the commander of the rearguard and with an experienced knight, John de St John, at his side to see that he could distinguish himself without too much danger. The castle duly fell after a few days, but through the work of engineers who undermined the walls rather than a frontal attack. Edward I took his revenge on the garrison by hanging a number of them, giving his son a first taste of the horrors of war to set alongside the

---

[27] *Roll of Arms of the Princes, Barons and Knights who attended Edward I at the Siege of Caerlaverock*, ed. T. Wright (London, 1864), 17–18. For the latest discussion of the roll see D.B. Tyson, 'The *Siege of Caerlaverock*', *Nottingham Medieval Studies*, xlvi (Nottingham, 2002), 45–69.

[28] *Bruce*, book 4, 154–5 (ll. 72–7); Johnstone, 114–15.

[29] Galbraith, 'The St. Edmundsbury Chronicle'; Johnstone, 46.

[30] Edward's movements up to 9 June can be followed in E 101/355/28.

splendours of banners, coats of arms[31] and shining armour. Little was achieved by the campaign since thousands of the infantry deserted, food supplies ran short and the Scots did not allow themselves to be brought to battle.[32] In September Edward I gave up and returned to Carlisle. His son had however taken part in a skirmish on the banks of the River Cree on 8 August. After the earl of Hereford had misunderstood the king's orders and crossed the river to attack a Scottish force, an engagement developed on swampy ground and in heavy rain. The divisions commanded by the king and by Edward then joined the fight and drove off the Scots. The fighting in the end achieved little, but it was an indication to the young Edward that war could be dangerous as well as exciting.[33] After the skirmish at Cree, Edward followed his father to Dumfries, but by early November both were back at Carlisle where the queen dined with her stepson on 6 November. Edward I was furious at the failure of his campaign and threatened to devastate Scotland from sea to sea.[34]

PRINCE OF WALES

Edward's public role was now starting to grow. On 12 January 1301 he represented his father at the burial of the heart of his father's first cousin, Edmund, earl of Cornwall, at the Augustinian house at Ashridge in Buckinghamshire. Edmund, who had died without an heir the previous September while Edward and his father were in Scotland, was the last of the older members of the royal family, Edward I's brother Edmund, earl of Lancaster having died in 1296.[35] Although no one could have foreseen it, the eventual granting of the vacant earldom of Cornwall to Edward's favourite Piers Gaveston in August 1307 was to be the cause of many of the troubles of his reign as king.[36] From Ashridge he made his way to

---

[31] This was the first occasion on which Edward bore a coat of arms. In *c.* 1295, when he was about eleven, Edward was listed simply as *filius Regis* on Collin's Roll of Arms. His brother Alfonso had been assigned a coat of arms as a child, in about 1280, though he did not live to be knighted, and his half-brother, Edmund of Woodstock, was given an armorial seal in 1303, when aged two: N. Denholm-Young, *History and Heraldry, 1254–1310* (Oxford, 1965), 62, n. 4. For details of Collin's Roll see A.R. Wagner, *Catalogue of English Medieval Rolls of Arms* (Oxford, 1950), 24.

[32] Whatever else may have been in short supply, there was evidently plenty of wine. Edward was provided with 59 casks of red wine at Ayr, Turnberry and Lochryan for his use and for that of his household: *CDS*, ii, no. 1233.

[33] I have drawn on the accounts of the campaign and of the events at the River Cree in Prestwich, *Edward I*, 487–90; Barrow, 113; Johnstone, 48–51.

[34] Prestwich, *Edward I*, 490; E 101/28/16.

[35] E 101/360/10, m.2. On 23 March Edmund's bones were interred in the presence of Edward I at the Cistercian abbey of Hailes in Gloucestershire, which the earl's father, Richard of Cornwall, had founded: Johnstone, 54. The young Edward was by this time on his way to Wales.

[36] See article on Edmund of Cornwall by Nicholas Vincent in the *Oxford DNB*.

Lincoln, where a parliament was about to be held, and on 7 February 1301, Edward, now almost seventeen, was granted all the royal lands in Wales as well as the earldom of Chester.[37] The earldom alone was a substantial endowment, comprising the county of Chester and extensive lands in other parts of England.[38] Edward received all the lands under royal control in North Wales, as well as Anglesey and the Four Cantreds; in the south he was granted the counties of Carmarthen and Cardigan, the castles and lordships of Haverford and Builth, the lands which had been forfeited by Rhys ap Meredudd in 1287, and all other lands in royal hands except the castle and town of Montgomery which had been assigned to Queen Margaret as part of her dower. In return Edward was to perform for his father the same services as Edward I had performed for his father, Henry III, for the same lands. The title of Prince of Wales was not used in the documents dated 7 February, which refer to him simply as 'the king's son', but Edward was already being described as prince on 1 March, when orders were issued for a new campaign in Scotland. It is likely, although there is no specific evidence, that Edward was invested with the title and insignia of Prince of Wales at the same time as the grants of land.[39] The golden coronet belonging to Llywelyn ap Gruffudd, the first and last Welsh Prince of Wales, which had been seized in 1283 and presented to Westminster Abbey in 1284, could have been used for this purpose.[40]

The question is why Edward I chose to endow his son at this particular time and with these particular lands. Nothing in the documents provides any answers and there is nothing to indicate what discussions Edward I and his advisers had held on the matter. At the time of the Lincoln parliament Edward I was heavily involved in several other major issues – resistance to his demands for taxation to fight the war in Scotland, the war itself, and problems with the papacy and with France – so there must have been pressing reasons for the attention paid to his son.[41] There is an obvious analogy with Henry III's granting of royal possessions in Wales to the future Edward I in 1254, although their extent was then much less. Many of the lands that Edward of Caernarfon now acquired had been conquered from their native Welsh rulers since 1277. On the other hand in

---

[37] *CChR 1300–1326*, 6.

[38] See Johnstone, 59–60.

[39] Davies, *Conquest*, 386; Johnstone, 60. There are depictions of Edward I creating Edward Prince of Wales in the manuscript of a fourteenth-century Rochester chronicle (BL, Cotton Ms. Nero D.II, f. 191v.) and in a series of pictures of English kings from William the Conqueror to Edward I preceding a fourteenth-century text of Peter Langtoft's chronicle (BL, Royal Ms. 20.A.II, f. 10).

[40] Davies, *Conquest*, 252–4, 354–5; Johnstone, 60, n. 2. In 1343 the next English Prince of Wales, Edward the Black Prince, was invested 'according to custom' with 'a circlet for the head, a ring for the finger, and a silver rod', which implies but does not prove that this was also done in 1301: Johnstone, 60.

[41] See the Introduction to the Hilary Parliament of 1290 in *PROME*.

1254 Edward had also been given the lordship of Ireland and the duchy of Aquitaine in south-western France, neither of which was given to his own son in 1301.[42] After 1254 however Henry had retained the titles of Lord of Ireland and Duke of Aquitaine and his son remained 'the Lord Edward' as he had been before.[43]

In 1301 Edward I was probably expressing his approval of his son's achievements to date, limited as they necessarily were at his age. But there was surely more to it than this. When Edward I had been endowed by his father in 1254 he was fifteen and on the verge both of marriage and of knighthood. The younger Edward was now almost seventeen, had seen service in war, and plans for his marriage to Isabella of France were in progress. It was therefore high time to provide him with an appropriate endowment. A grant of the Welsh lands was suitable in 1301, since they were substantial in extent and Edward I would not need even to consider whether to give up one of his own titles as Lord of Ireland or Duke of Aquitaine. In any case the duchy of Aquitaine was still effectively in French hands while negotiations continued for a final peace treaty.[44]

The Welsh lands had other advantages. Although there is no evidence of any deeply laid plans by Edward I to create his son Prince of Wales, least of all any promise at his birth in 1284 to give the Welsh a prince who spoke no English,[45] Edward I probably saw it as an opportunity to ensure the future allegiance of the Welsh to English rule by binding them with ties of personal allegiance. The last major Welsh revolt against English rule had taken place as recently as 1294–5 and had caused Edward I serious problems when he was also fighting a war with France. Now that he was also heavily engaged in the war with Scotland, any measure that might help to prevent another outburst in Wales was to be welcomed. There was no precedent in English usage for calling any son of the king by the title of prince: only in Wales had it become an established usage in the course of the thirteenth century. Its adoption now by Edward 'the king's son' would not only enhance his own status but would provide the Welsh with 'a focus of service and reward to fill the vacuum created by the extinction of their native dynasties'.[46]

The importance of the young Edward's new position was indicated by the speed with which he went to Wales. On 6 April he left his father at Feckenham in Worcestershire[47] and arrived in Chester six days later where he lost no time in getting down to business. On 12 April he appointed William Trussell to the office of Justice of Chester as his general administrator and on 17 April William Melton as chamberlain with responsibility

[42] Prestwich, *Edward I*, 11; Johnstone, 60.
[43] Prestwich, *Edward I*, 11–12.
[44] See Vale, 219–21.
[45] See above Ch. 2, 'The nature of a king'.
[46] Davies, *Conquest*, 386; Johnstone, 60.
[47] BL, Add. Ms. 7966A, f. 155; E 101/360/16.

for the revenues.[48] Both men were to play an important role both now and in the future. Melton had already been a member of Edward's household since 1297; when Edward succeeded as king in 1307 Melton was appointed keeper of the privy seal and was elected archbishop of York in 1316 through royal influence; he remained loyal to Edward's memory after his deposition and death in 1327 and ordered prayers to be said for his soul.[49] In January 1327 William Trussell led the delegation to Kenilworth castle to inform Edward II of the withdrawal of the allegiance of his subjects.[50]

On 13 April 1301 the new Prince of Wales received the homage and fealty of his English tenants of the earldom of Chester, and on 21 April he crossed the bridge over the River Dee at Chester and entered Wales.[51] On the following day more than 200 Welshmen performed homage and fealty at Flint castle; twenty-five at Rhuthun (Ruthin) on 23 April; and on 26 April in the church of the Dominicans at Rhuddlan nearly sixty more came in. Conwy was the scene of the largest numbers: over seventy on 28 April; a similar number on the 29th; over sixty on 1 May; over fifty on 2 May; six on 3 May; and another twelve on the 5th of the month.[52] Ironically, Edward did not visit his birthplace at Caernarfon: instead nearly sixty of the Welsh population of that area came to him at Flint and a few more at Conwy.[53] However, a very large number of native Welshmen, many of whom had travelled considerable distances for the purpose, had seen their new prince, had knelt before him and placed their hands between his in the ceremony of homage, and had sworn fealty to him on holy relics. There could be no doubt as to the nature of the allegiance of Wales to the new order. One of those who did homage and

---

[48] *Cheshire in the Pipe Rolls, 1158–1301*, ed. Brown, 189–90.

[49] See the article on Melton by Hill in the *Oxford DNB*; and *Letters from Northern Registers*, ed. J. Raine, Rolls ser. (London, 1883), 355–6.

[50] There were, however, at least two men of this name.

[51] E 101/360/16.

[52] There is no surviving contemporary record of these proceedings at Chester and in Wales. The names are known because in 1343 Edward III inquired into precedents when he created his own son as Prince of Wales and had the results recorded on the Patent Roll: *CPR, 1343–45*, 227–34. Edward Owen used this material as the basis of his work, *A List of those who did Homage and Fealty to the First English Prince of Wales in AD 1301* (privately printed, 1901), produced to mark the creation of the future George V as Prince of Wales in Nov. 1901. My calculations of the numbers of people involved differ slightly from those of Johnstone, who included Hope as a separate place at which homages and fealties were taken: Johnstone, 62. These were in fact taken at Flint.

[53] The incomplete castle and adjoining borough at Caernarfon had been seriously damaged in the Welsh revolt of 1294–5 and their reconstruction was far from complete in 1301. Some building work is recorded in 1301–2, possibly on the orders or with the encouragement of the new prince: Taylor, *Caernarfon Castle*, 13–15. In any case Welshmen would not have been allowed to live in the borough of Caernarfon: see Davies, *Conquest*, 370–3, and idem, 'Colonial Wales', *Past & Present*, 65 (Oxford, 1974), 3–23.

fealty at Flint on 22 April was a certain Sir Gruffydd Llwyd, who was destined to show a particular loyalty to his new lord.[54]

SCOTLAND AGAIN

Edward rejoined his father at Kenilworth on 24 May,[55] and between then and 31 May he received the homage and fealty of a number of the Anglo-Norman lords of the Welsh March: his cousin Henry of Lancaster for the lordship of Monmouth, Reginald Grey for Rhuthun, William Martin for Cemaes in West Wales, and Roger Mortimer for Chirk.[56] While Edward was in Wales plans were being completed for a new campaign in Scotland. On 1 March, at Lincoln, orders were issued for two armies to assemble by 24 June, one at Berwick under the command of the king and the other at Carlisle under the Prince of Wales.[57] The advance into Scotland by east and west would start from these two bases. The orders which summoned the armies made it clear that the new prince was to be given the chance to distinguish himself.[58] Five earls were assigned to his force: Henry de Lacy, earl of Lincoln, a man of great military experience who was to play an important political role in the early years of Edward II's reign; Richard Fitz Alan, earl of Arundel, another experienced soldier; Thomas, earl of Lancaster, Edward's first cousin, now his friend and collaborator but to become his bitter enemy after 1307; Ralph de Monthermer, titular earl of Gloucester and Edward's brother-in-law through marriage to his sister Joan of Acre, the widowed countess of Gloucester; and Humphrey de Bohun, hereditary constable of England, son of the opposition earl of 1297 and soon to marry Edward's sister Elizabeth, the widowed countess of Holland. Many of the other magnates who were to accompany Edward were men with interests in the Welsh March, some of them Edward's own vassals who were soon to perform their homage and fealty to him or had already done so. These included Henry of Lancaster, the younger brother of the earl of Lancaster, William Martin, Reginald Grey, and Roger and Edmund Mortimer; as well as John Hastings, lord of Abergavenny and

[54] Though even his loyalty was put under strain in the middle years of the reign of Edward II. See the article on him by J.B. Smith in the *Oxford DNB*.

[55] BL, Add. Ms. 7966A, f. 155; E 101/360/16.

[56] *CPR, 1343–45*, 228, 231. Others performed their homage later, sometimes much later. Henry de Lacy, the earl of Lincoln, did so on 19 July 1301 for his lands held from the earldom of Chester, and for Rhos and Rhufoniog in Wales on 6 Jan. 1303; John de Warenne, the earl of Surrey, did homage and fealty for the lordships of Bromfield and Yale in the Welsh March on 25 July 1301; on 6 Nov. Edmund de Mortimer for his lands of Ceri and Cydewain before the prince's council in London, and on the following day Sir Jean de Fiennes, one of Edward's tenants from across the Channel in the county of Ponthieu, also came in to do his duty: ibid., 228, 231.

[57] *CCR, 1296–1302*, 480.

[58] Prestwich, *Edward I*, 493; Johnstone, 73. The chief honour was to accrue to the king's son (*quod proinde prefato filio nostro principalis honor armorum accrescat*): *PW*, I, 357.

Cilgerran; and Theobald de Verdon, lord of Weobley and Ewyas Lacy who was also lord of half the liberty of Meath in Ireland.[59]

As a mark of his increased status Edward now had a substantial household of his own, numbering in 1300–1 one hundred and forty members, including Edward himself.[60] The senior members consisted of nine knights, several of whom have already been noted: John de St John, Reginald de Grey, and Guy Ferre, his master.[61] There were ten boys or young men from noble or knightly families in custody as royal wards, nine of them accompanied by a master. These included Gilbert de Clare, lord of Thomond in the south-west of Ireland who had recently come of age but had been a ward since the death of his father Thomas in 1287.[62] The tenth, the only one without a master, was Piers Gaveston. Much more would soon be heard of him.[63]

The fourteen household clerks, who included Walter Reynolds, a future chancellor and archbishop of Canterbury under Edward II, were to be closely involved in the administration of the Scottish campaign, in the supply of money and stores of all kinds.[64] The rest of the household was made up of men described as 'valets and serjeants', some of whom were active in a military role while others performed a variety of services within the household: the latter included a fowler, named only as *Papegay perdricator*.[65]

The knights and squires of Edward's household, like his clerks, played a prominent part in the 1301 campaign, but their numbers were supplemented by the nobles and their retainers who joined the army. Altogether the contingent directly under the command of the Prince of Wales amounted to a little over 300, consisting of ten bannerets (knights in command of other knights), about seventy knights, and over 200 squires.[66] In addition to the heavy cavalry, there were lightly armed horsemen known as hobelars and large numbers of foot soldiers. After he reached

---

[59] For the magnates summoned to join Edward see *PW*, I, 357. Biographies of each of the five earls and several of the others mentioned can be found in the *Oxford DNB*.

[60] E 101/360/17: this is the first such list since 1289–90, so it is difficult to know whether the substantial size was the result of a recent increase in numbers, marking Edward's changed status, or of a more gradual process. See also Johnstone, 75–7.

[61] The other knights were John Fitz Simon the elder, John de Wolverton, Robert de Haustede the younger, Giles Fineles, Bertram de Montboucher and Gilbert de Brideshale.

[62] See the article on Thomas de Clare by Robin Frame in the *Oxford DNB*.

[63] The other *pueri in custodia* were Robert de Scales, John de Leyburn, John Fitz Waryn, Philip de Courtenay, Robert de Clavering, Thomas Botetourt, Robert Fitz Waryn and William de Munchensey.

[64] Johnstone, 75–6.

[65] E 101/360/17: one wonders if he had his Papagena tucked away somewhere. Papegay appears again in the prince's household roll for 1302–3 when he bought a net for catching partridges and also a setter dog in London for fowling and hunting: *CDS*, ii, no. 1413, pp. 366, 368, citing E 101/363/18, ff. 8d,12.

[66] BL, Add. Ms. 7966A, ff. 84–7. My total comes to 308; Johnstone's to 314: Johnstone, 76–7.

Newcastle-on-Ayr Edward was joined by a significant contingent of knights, hobelars and archers from Ireland, led by the head of the royal administration in Dublin, the justiciar John Wogan, and including two of the most important of the Anglo-Norman magnates of Ireland, John Fitz Thomas and Peter de Bermingham.[67] Among the knights under Edward's overall command were many whose careers would continue into his reign, but there were some who would be of special importance. Bartholomew de Badlesmere, who was a member of Robert de Monthaut's retinue, was to be a prominent supporter of Edward II until his rebellion and execution in 1321–2. Maurice de Berkeley was accompanied by Thomas Gurney, who later won notoriety as one of Edward II's jailers and murderers at Berkeley castle in 1327.[68]

The king's army advanced from Berwick as far as Glasgow by 23 August. Edward I then prepared for the siege of Bothwell castle, which was captured by 24 September; after this he went into winter quarters at Linlithgow.[69] Despite all the surviving detail on Prince Edward's preparations for the campaign, little is really known about what happened once his army left Carlisle. His force probably headed for the Firth of Forth via Nithsdale and then besieged Turnberry castle, which had fallen by early September. Edward then returned to Carlisle[70] before joining his father at Linlithgow on 14 November for the winter.[71] The Prince of Wales had not disgraced himself during the campaign but neither he nor his father had achieved anything very significant. The Scots had not been brought to battle; there had been serious shortages both of money and of supplies, which resulted in the desertion of many of the troops and the death of many of the horses. Extensive preparations were made for a renewal of the campaign in the spring of 1302 but came to nothing in January when Edward I, who was under intense diplomatic pressure both from the pope and from the king of France, agreed to a truce until November 1302.[72]

---

[67] BL, Add. Ms. 7966A, ff. 89–91 (no date is given, but it was possibly towards the end of Aug.); Johnstone, 77–8.

[68] On all these men, except Gurney, see the relevant articles in the *Oxford DNB*. On Gurney see the article on Aymer de Valence, earl of Pembroke. Roger Mortimer of Chirk had another Roger Mortimer with him but the latter was probably too young to be the Roger Mortimer of Wigmore who instigated the murder of Edward II.

[69] Prestwich, *Edward I*, 493.

[70] Edward was at Carlisle on 5 Oct.: *CDS*, ii, no. 1239.

[71] Prestwich, *Edward I*, 493–4. There is a more detailed account in Johnstone, 77–80. For a map showing the conjectured movements of the English armies and of their Scottish opponents and for another account of the 1301 campaign see Barrow, 111, 120–1.

[72] Prestwich, *Edward I*, 494–5; Johnstone, 80–1. Prince Edward's health may also have suffered from the rigours of the campaign. Although he reported to his father from Carlisle on 5 Oct. that he was 'in good estate and health', on the 20th he sent his physician, Master Robert de Oydisterne, to London 'for certain matters required for his [the Prince's] body': *CDS*, ii, nos 1239, 1249.

BETROTHED AT LAST

On 20 May 1303 at Paris a peace treaty was finally agreed, bringing a formal end to the hostilities between England and France which had existed since 1294. Territory in Gascony which had been occupied by the French was to be restored to English control, Edward I abandoned his Flemish allies, and in return was given a free hand in Scotland. The two kings were to meet at Amiens by 8 September for Edward I to perform homage as duke of Aquitaine. If Edward were unable to go in person, the Prince of Wales should go in his place with full powers to act on his behalf.[73] The way was now open for the betrothal of the Prince of Wales and Isabella of France, which was also settled on 20 May by the English envoys, the bishop of Winchester, the count of Savoy, the earl of Lincoln, and Otto de Granson, Edward having given them full powers on 16 May to make an agreement on his behalf.[74] Their letters patent recorded that the pope had pronounced that there should be a marriage between the two as soon as Isabella reached the age for marriage or within four months of the king of France requesting it. A dispensation for the marriage had been received from the pope;[75] the terms of Isabella's dower had been agreed (18,000 *livres tournois* of annual revenues);[76] and the envoys had promised to carry out the terms of the marriage agreement. On 12 June 1303 the bishop of Winchester and earl of Lincoln, acting on behalf of Prince Edward, affianced him and Isabella in the hand of Giles, archbishop of Narbonne, in the presence of the king and queen of France.[77]

SCOTLAND YET AGAIN

In the meantime Edward had been preparing himself for the planned renewal of the war in Scotland in May 1303.[78] His wardrobe book for

---

[73] Prestwich, *Edward I*, 397; Johnstone, 88.

[74] *Foedera*, I, ii, 952, 955; AN, J 633, no. 17bis (20 May). Letters patent of the count of Évreux, duke of Burgundy and duke of Brittany, dated 20 May 1303, and rehearsing the same details concerning the proposed marriage as were contained in the document of 12 June, formerly displayed in the Royal Institution of South Wales, Swansea, are now preserved in the West Glamorgan archives, Swansea. The document seems to be the counterpart of the letters patent of the English envoys. See G.G. Francis, 'Original contract of affiance between Edward Prince of Wales and Isabella of France', *Archaeologia Cambrensis*, iii (Cardiff, 1848), 150–5.

[75] The dispensation was needed on the grounds of affinity.

[76] Around £4,500 sterling, a substantial sum.

[77] AN, J 633, no.17 (12 June). However, there is evidence as late as 10 April 1303 of an earlier attempt to arrange a marriage between Edward and another Isabella, sister of the reigning king of Castile, Ferdinand IV: *CCR, 1302–1307*, 83; Johnstone, 88. The initiative appears to have come from the Castilian side but it is also possible that Edward I had seen the proposal either as an alternative should the French marriage fall through or as a way of bringing Philip IV to the conference table. There was to be an echo of this plan as late as Jan. 1307: Linehan, 'The English mission', 618–19.

[78] The army was summoned to be at Berwick on 26 May: *CPR, 1301–7*, 98.

1302–3 contains many interesting details, showing the warlike equipment required by the well-dressed prince.[79] In March, Manekin the armourer of London supplied three *bacinets* (a light steel headpiece often worn under the great helm), two pairs of *jambers* (armour for the legs), an iron headpiece with crest, another round one, a helmet with visor, and another close one (the most expensive item at £15) at a total cost of nearly £36. In the same month another London armourer, Bernard of Devon, provided two more pairs of *jambers*, a pair of plate *quisses* (armour for the thigh), a pair of *poleyns* (protection for the knee) and two pairs of *sabaters* (armoured covering for the foot), and a pair of gloves of plate, totalling 70 shillings; and Sir Guy Ferre and Walter Reynolds were sent to London to buy chargers and hackneys for Edward to ride in Scotland. In April twenty cart tilts (at 14d each) and thirty sacks (7d each) and other things for carrying the prince's armour and baggage were bought from a London merchant, Henry de Preston; and William Conrad, bowyer of the Tower of London, provided glue, sinews and other items for repairing crossbows and longbows (13s 2d).[80] Between January and March the prince's armourer, Hugh de Bungeye, had his hands full with a multitude of details: these included the making of banners and *pennoncels* (a small pennant for the head of a lance or for a helmet) for Edward and his squires; the provision of six ounces of silk in various colours for pointing two *aketons* (a quilted cotton jacket or leather jacket worn under chain mail); five pairs of gilt spurs; iron thread for mending the prince's two suits of mail; a *pisan* (a mail collar extending over the shoulders) for the prince's body; the embroidering of two *gambesons* (a thick cloth tunic worn under a sleeveless coat of mail) with the prince's arms; and much else including four war swords, and scabbards embroidered with the arms of Gloucester and Hereford. Hugh also saw to repairing and painting a shield with the prince's arms; the provision of four lances and *pennoncels*, a gilt copper crest and parchment and peacock feathers for decorating it; and making forty-two banners of *sindon* (a fine linen) with the prince's arms, together with thirty-six banners with the arms of St Edmund, St Edward and St George (twelve for each saint). The total cost for all the items came to over £31. *Pennoncels* were also specially made for Edward's trumpeters, a leather box bound with iron for holding his *bacinet*, and another for his crests, as well as boxes to hold his linen and his iron armour.[81]

---

[79] E 101/363/18. Johnstone made extensive use of this source in her *Edward of Carnarvon*, 83–7. The sections dealing with military matters and with Scotland were also printed by Bain in *CDS*, ii, no. 1413 (pp. 364–70), where the source is wrongly described as a roll.

[80] *CDS*, ii, 365; E 101/363/18, ff. 5, 5d. Altogether a sum of just over £568 was spent on chargers and hackneys for the prince's household in 1302–3: *CDS*, ii, 368; E 101/363/18, f. 16. The most expensive horse cost 110 marks (£73 6s 8d), which suggests it was good enough to ride in battle. On the cost of warhorses see Andrew Ayton, *Knights and Warhorses* (Woodbridge, Suffolk & Rochester, NY, 1994), ch. 6, 'The horse inventories'; Michael Prestwich, *Armies and Warfare in the Middle Ages* (London & New Haven, 1996), 34–5.

[81] *CDS*, ii, 367; E 101/363/18, ff. 9d, 10.

The creature comforts of Edward and his immediate followers were not forgotten. A team of sixty-three tentmakers, led by John de Somerset, made twenty-eight tents and pavilions, including one to serve as a great hall, another as Edward's chamber, two more for stables, one as a chapel, one as a council chamber, and the remainder for various members of his household.[82] Among other things provided were two leather coffers to carry Edward's urinals in Scotland, a brass cauldron for the prince's kitchen, and an iron oven (bought in London in June and forwarded to him at Dundee). On 27 April Edward's physician, Master Robert de Cisterne, was paid over £9 for syrups, powders, herbs, ointments and medicines for the care of the prince and his household during the campaign. Even the prince's lion was included in the preparations. It was fed at a cost of 4d a day by its keeper, Adam of Lichfield, had its own cart to carry it, and was provided with a chain and collar costing 2s 9d.[83]

Edward left London for the north on 13 March 1303, was at Tickhill near Doncaster by 28 March, in Durham on 14 April, when he attended mass for the soul of his master, Sir Guy Ferre, and had reached Roxburgh in Scotland by 25 May.[84] By this time he had 180 men in his pay, compared with 450 under his father.[85] Edward also had a personal bodyguard of nine Spaniards: seven crossbowmen and two with lances.[86] Edward did not however exercise a separate command in this campaign. The whole army advanced into Scotland, crossing the Firth of Forth on a pontoon bridge, and then moved northwards, spreading devastation everywhere it went.[87] According to the English chronicler Peter Langtoft, Prince Edward played a full part in this.[88] The army then settled down to besiege Brechin castle, which duly fell in mid-August.[89] The young prince no doubt rode up and down before the castle at a safe distance and looking suitably splendid, but does not appear to have performed any personal feats of arms. He did however possess his own siege engine, which was in action against the castle on 8 August, the day before its garrison surrendered.[90] Despite his own exalted status Edward apparently showed concern for the welfare of his men: David Gough, one of his Welsh foot

[82] E 101/363/18, f. 20.
[83] *CDS*, ii, 364–7; E 101/363/18, ff. 6d, 10, 5, 5d, 8d.
[84] E 101/363/18, ff. 2, 2d.
[85] Other magnates served in the army without pay, and there were about 7,500 foot soldiers: Prestwich, *Edward I*, 498.
[86] *CDS*, ii, no. 1599.
[87] For a map showing the path of the English army during 1303–4 see Barrow, 125.
[88] *The Chronicle of Pierre de Langtoft*, ed. T. Wright, Rolls ser. (London, 1886), ii, 348. Edward was at Perth on 7 July and it was probably from there that he and a small raiding party spent two weeks in the neighbouring district of Strathearn: E 101/363/18, ff. 2d, 8.
[89] Prestwich, *Edward I*, 498–9; Johnstone, 90.
[90] The slings of the machine, which was operated by the prince's engineer, Robert of Glasham, first had to be repaired, using a horsehide bought locally at a cost of 5s: *CDS*, ii, 366; E 101/363/18, f. 8.

soldiers, who was wounded in the attack on Brechin, was sent home on 15 August with 6s 8d for his expenses.[91] The English army then made an armed progress via Aberdeen as far north as Kinloss abbey, on the shores of the Moray Firth, which it reached on 14 September. This was the furthest north that any English army had been in Scotland. Edward I then turned south again, as much because of a lack of supplies as for the lack of an enemy to oppose him in the field. On 5 November 1303 he reached Dunfermline in Fife, where he went into winter quarters.[92]

Prince Edward stayed with him until 24 November, when he moved to Perth, remaining there until 7 March 1304, after which he rejoined his father at Dunfermline.[93] On the great religious festivals, Christmas Day, the Feast of the Circumcision (1 January), the Epiphany (6 January), and the Purification (2 February) he entertained important English magnates, such as the earls of Lancaster (his first cousin) and Warwick, the earl of Ulster (the leader of the Irish contingent in the army), Scottish allies such as the earls of Atholl and Strathearn, and numerous other magnates, such as John of Brittany (the future earl of Richmond), and Hugh le Despenser (one of Edward I's leading advisers and soon to play a major part in Edward's own reign). The Christmas feast was especially lavish, including eight and a quarter oxen, forty lambs, twelve swans, two cranes and five casks of the king's wine.[94] Other notable gatherings took place on 4, 10, 11 and 21 February, 1 March and 14 April.[95] This entertaining was partly social, but also had a political dimension which was emphasized by the supplies for the dinners coming from the king's own stores and not from those of the prince.

Although there had been little serious fighting during the Scottish campaign, one of Edward I's purposes in making such an extensive military demonstration had been to try to force the submission of the leaders of Scottish resistance who had now effectively been abandoned by their former French ally.[96] Under his father's close supervision,[97] Prince Edward was to play a role in what followed. Edward was empowered to receive on the king's behalf any of the Scottish leaders who wished to

---

[91] *CDS*, ii, 369; E 101/363/18, f. 21. At the standard rate of 2d a day for a foot soldier, this would have represented 40 days' wages. See Prestwich, *Armies and Warfare*, 126.

[92] Prestwich, *Edward I*, 498–9; Johnstone, 90–1.

[93] Prince Edward's movements from 20 Nov. 1303 until 18 April 1304 can be traced from his daily household roll: E 101/365/12, which is calendared in *CDS*, ii, no. 1516 (pp. 392–4). Edward was with his father briefly between 15 and 18 Feb. E 101/ 365/13 is a duplicate of the portion covering 17 Dec.–17 Jan.

[94] *CDS*, ii, 392–3; E 101/365/12, mm.1–3. Not all these magnates were present on every occasion.

[95] *CDS*, ii, 392–4; E 101/365/12, mm.3–5.

[96] Barrow, 127–8.

[97] The envoys were entertained by Edward on 4 Feb. and again on 10 and 11 Feb.: *CDS*, ii, 394; E 101/365/12, m.3.

submit by 2 February.[98] His father then sent Aymer de Valence, Henry de Percy, Robert Fitz Payn and John Binstead from Dunfermline to perform the negotiations, and on 5 February 1304 the four envoys met John Comyn of Badenoch, the Guardian of Scotland, at Strathord near Perth. On 9 February a formal agreement was made by which Comyn and other Scottish magnates submitted to the authority of the English crown.[99] Edward I's terms were relatively generous, but there were significant exceptions to the general pardon offered to the Scots, the most important being William Wallace. This and the fact that a defiant Scottish garrison still held the strategically placed castle of Stirling in the Scottish Lowlands ensured that the war would continue.[100]

Edward I made careful preparations for the siege of Stirling. Great supplies of crossbows, longbows and their ammunition were gathered, and siege engines brought from Brechin and Aberdeen. Prince Edward was ordered on 12 April to collect the lead from churches around Perth and Dunblane for use in the siege, sparing only the roofs over the altars.[101] Edward had earlier won his father's approval for having sent out Sir Alexander de Abernethy and forty men-at-arms into the countryside around Perth where it was thought that Wallace might be hiding.[102] The king pursued the siege with ruthless determination, employing an early form of gunpowder and refusing to let the garrison surrender until he had tried out a new war machine appropriately called Warwolf. Edward I's determination was no doubt only increased when he was struck but not injured by a crossbow bolt fired from the castle. The siege lasted until 24 July and with the surrender of Stirling it seemed as if at last the conquest of Scotland was complete, with the exception of Wallace who remained at large.[103] Prince Edward was present at the siege and presumably at the surrender, having joined his father at Cambuskenneth, very near Stirling, on 21 April, the day before the siege began. Even the queen and her ladies were present.[104] The young Edward could not however have anticipated that ten years later Stirling would again be under siege and that on 24 June 1314 the marshy ground near the castle would be the scene of one of the greatest English defeats since 1066 and a turning-point in his own reign.

---

[98] *Documents and Records illustrating the History of Scotland*, ed. F. Palgrave, i (London, 1837), 278–82.

[99] *RP*, i, 212–13; *Documents*, ed. Palgrave, 282–3. There is no evidence that Prince Edward was present, as stated in Johnstone, 92. On 22 Feb. Comyn and his knights dined with Edward in Perth: *CDS*, ii, 394; E 101/365/12, m.3.

[100] Prestwich, *Edward I*, 500; Johnstone, 92; Barrow, 127–8.

[101] *CDS*, ii, no.1504; Prestwich, *Edward I*, 500–2; Johnstone, 93–4; Barrow, 128–9.

[102] *CDS*, ii, no. 1462 (2 Mar.) and no. 1463 (3 Mar.).

[103] Prestwich, *Edward I*, 501–2; Johnstone, 93; Barrow, 129.

[104] *CDS*, ii, no. 1509; Prestwich, *Edward I*, 501. Edward was certainly at Stirling on 29 June: *CDS*, ii, no. 1550.

EDWARD AND GAVESTON

One of the squires in Edward's company at Stirling in 1304 was Piers Gaveston.[105] Although his spectacular career in the reign of Edward II certainly made it seem the case, he was not 'raised up as if from nothing', as one of the English chroniclers Walter of Guisborough remarked,[106] but was the son of Arnaud de Gabaston, one of the leading barons of the county of Béarn in south-western France, on the borders of the English dominions in Gascony.[107] Arnaud had been in the service of Edward I since 1282–3, when he fought in Wales and commanded a contingent of knights, archers and foot soldiers from his native Béarn. He was a hostage on behalf of the English crown in the hands of the king of France from 1294 until 1296 when he escaped and made his way to England. He served in Gascony in 1297–8, and in August 1300 returned to England, where he became a knight of the royal household and served in Scotland, before dying in May 1302.[108] Two of Arnaud's sons, Arnaud-Guillaume de Marsan and Guillaume-Arnaud de Gabaston, were with him in England, so that it was hardly surprising that a third son, Piers de Gabaston, or Gaveston as he became known, should also have entered royal service. Piers Gaveston probably first arrived in England in 1296–7, at the time of his father's escape from France. His first active service was not however in Gascony but in the Flemish campaign of 1297, where he first appears to have come to the king's attention. By November 1297 he was already a squire in the royal household, served in the Falkirk campaign in Scotland in this capacity in 1298 and was again in Scotland in 1300.[109] By the end of 1300 Gaveston had transferred to the household of Prince Edward, first as one of the boys in custody and then as one of Edward's squires. He was with Edward in Scotland in 1301–2 and again in 1303–4, so there was plenty of opportunity for the two young men to get to know one another.[110] By 1303 he was no longer being referred to in household records as Edward's squire (*scutifer*), but as his *socius*, which can mean a servant but also carries the sense of a companion.[111] Too much should not be made of the choice of word, since it was common for a knight to be accompanied by a *socius*, but it does imply some degree of closeness.[112]

---

[105] On Gaveston's life and career see J.S. Hamilton's article in the *Oxford DNB*; Hamilton; and Chaplais. The evidence that Gaveston was at Stirling is to found in BL, Add. Ms. 35293, f. 79.

[106] *Guisborough*, 382.

[107] Hamilton, 19, 132. For a map showing the location of Gabaston and the other family possessions see ibid., 23.

[108] Ibid., 22–5, 134–5. Arnaud was buried in Winchester cathedral.

[109] Ibid., 28–31, 135–7.

[110] E 101/360/17; Hamilton, 29–31, 136. He is first described as a squire in July 1301: BL, Add. Ms. 7966A, f. 101. Gaveston was closely involved in Edward's social life: at Christmas 1302 and again in early Jan. 1303 Gaveston delivered two separate sums of 100s for Edward to play at dice: E 101/363/18, f. 12; *CDS*, ii, 368.

[111] E 101/612/11, m.5d; Hamilton, 30, 136, n. 20.

[112] E.g., in 1302 Gaveston's *socius* was William de Bourdon: E 101/357/28/ m.4.

How close is of course the question. The initiative for bringing Gaveston into Edward's household appears to have come from Edward I who had clearly been impressed by the young Gascon's demeanour on campaign and as a member of his own household. Gaveston was a little older than Prince Edward,[113] already had considerable experience in war, possessed good manners, and may have been seen as a potential role model for his royal master.[114] It is also possible that Gaveston was in effect an assistant to or potentially even a substitute for Edward's own '*magister*', another but much older Gascon, Sir Guy Ferre, who had been with Edward since before 1295 and remained until his death in April 1303.[115] Edward and Gaveston clearly got on extremely well, so well indeed that on one occasion when they visited the abbey of Peterborough, possibly in 1302, Edward created a very embarrassing situation by refusing to accept a gift from the abbot of a cup worth £50 until one of comparable value (£40) was offered to Gaveston.[116] Writing in the 1320s, an anonymous chronicler of the civil wars of Edward's reign remarked that 'upon looking on him the son of the king immediately felt such love for him that he entered into a covenant of constancy, and bound himself with him before all other mortals with a bond of indissoluble love, firmly drawn up and fastened with a knot'.[117] Such comments[118] have led to the modern assumption that their relationship was definitely sexual. The evidence for this is however far from clear. While some of the chroniclers' remarks about Edward II can be interpreted as implying homosexuality, too many of them are either much later in date or the product of hostility or a combination of the two to be accepted at face

[113] Gaveston's date of birth is unknown but his service in Flanders in 1297 suggests he was at least a year or two older than Edward, who was then in his fourteenth year.

[114] The unknown author of the unpublished Canterbury chronicle, the *Polistorie del Eglise de Christ de Caunterbyre*, contained in BL, Harley Ms. 636, explained the choice of Gaveston on the grounds that being from 'the region of fine manners he was courteous': Harley Ms. 636, f. 232; Hamilton, 30, 136, n. 12. Another chronicler, Geoffrey le Baker, writing after the reign of Edward II, described Gaveston as 'graceful and agile in body, sharp witted, refined in manners, [and] sufficiently well versed in military matters': *Le Baker*, 4; Hamilton, 13.

[115] Johnstone, 17.

[116] *Historia Coenobii Burgensis auctore Waltero de Whitlesey, Historiae Coenobii Burgensis Scriptores*, ed. J. Sparks (London, 1723), 171–2. The date of this incident is not clear, except that it evidently occurred before Edward became king. The king and queen visited Peterborough in 1302 and it may be that the younger Edward was there at about the same time. It is also interesting in the light of his later reputation that Gaveston appears to have played a tactful role in mediating between Edward and the abbot. The passage is also published in Lehmann-Brockhaus, *Lateinische Schriftquellen*, iii, 308 (no. 6270).

[117] G.L. Haskins, 'A chronicle of the civil wars of Edward II', *Speculum*, xiv (1939), 75, trans. in Hamilton, 13.

[118] Other examples are the reports by the St Albans chronicler, John Trokelowe, that when Edward returned to England on 7 Feb. 1308 after his wedding to Isabella, he ran to greet Gaveston: 'giving him kisses and repeated embraces, he was adored with a singular familiarity'; and by the St Paul's chronicler of the outrage caused at the coronation banquet on 25 Feb. by Gaveston's behaviour and the king's preference for Gaveston's couch over Isabella's: *Trokelowe*, 65; *Ann. Paul.* 262; Hamilton, 46–8, 142, nn. 82, 90.

value.[119] There is nothing overt or even implicit in any of the strictly contemporary criticism of Edward II that would suggest homosexual behaviour, until the very end of the reign, in October and December 1326, when Adam Orleton, bishop of Hereford, allegedly accused Edward in sermons preached at Oxford and Wallingford of being a tyrant and a sodomite, in order to detach Edward's subjects from their allegiance and so help to prepare the way for the act of deposition which followed.[120]

Edward II was to have other favourites after the death of Gaveston in 1312, such as the household knights Roger Damory, Hugh Audley the Younger and William de Montacute, and most notable of all Hugh Despenser the Younger. Other than their perceived influence on royal patronage, there was no suggestion of any sexual relationship in the case of the first three.[121] Nor is there any convincing evidence even in the case of Despenser, who had a major influence both on the flow of patronage and on the work of government in general during the final years of Edward II's reign.[122] While the remark by the unknown author of the annals composed at the Cistercian abbey of Newenham in Devon that in 1326 *rex et maritus eius* fled to Wales to escape Mortimer and Isabella may be an indication of contemporary opinion on the nature of Edward II's relationship with Despenser, it should perhaps be understood ironically or satirically rather than literally.[123] On the contrary, any sexual relationship that existed[124] may instead have been between Edward II and Despenser's wife, Eleanor de Clare, who was also Edward's niece. A chronicler writing in Hainault in the Low Countries, who recorded events in England in the 1320s in great detail, claimed that she was Edward II's mistress and that after her husband was executed in 1326 she was even kept under surveillance in case she might be pregnant by the king.[125]

---

[119] See ch. 1 of this book and Ormrod, 'The sexualities of Edward II', and Mortimer, 'Sermons of sodomy'. Charges of homosexuality were often used as a way of blackening the reputations of individuals or groups. Other examples, of which Orleton was certainly aware in 1326, were the charges laid against Pope Boniface VIII in 1303 and those against the Templars in 1308, in both cases in France and by agents of the French crown: Mortimer, 51–2.

[120] See Mortimer, 'Sermons of sodomy', 50–6, 58–60. However, the articles of his deposition in 1327 accuse him, among other things, of devoting himself to unsuitable work and occupations but do not suggest any sexual failings; nor was Edward accused of tyranny.

[121] See Phillips, 131–3.

[122] Ibid., 132–3, 177, 227, 273, 280; and Fryde, *Tyranny*, esp. chs 3 and 8.

[123] These short annals, which have valuable information on the events between 1326 and 1330, appear in BL, Arundel Ms. 17, ff. 40–4, under the title *Memorabilia facta tempore Regis Edwardi secundi in Anglia*.

[124] The chronicler Jean Froissart implied a sexual relationship between Edward and Despenser, but he was writing many years later when the literary tradition surrounding Edward II's character was already developing: *Chroniques de Jean Froissart*, ed. S. Luce, i, Société de l'Histoire de France (Paris, 1869), 34.

[125] *Willelmi Capellani in Brederode postea Monachi et Procuratoris Egmondensis Chronicon*, ed. C. Pijnacker Hordijk, Werken uitgegeven door het Historisch Genootschap, 3rd ser., xx (Amsterdam, 1904), 177.

It is significant that Edward I does not appear to have seen anything improper in the relationship of Edward and Gaveston, who continued to receive royal favours after 1303. In July 1304 Gaveston was given custody of the lands of Edmund Mortimer of Wigmore, during the minority of Edmund's heir. The grant was made at the request of Prince Edward and was a notable acquisition for a man who was still only a squire.[126] On 26 May 1306 Gaveston's social status was improved when he was knighted (together with a large number of other young men), four days after Edward himself.[127] If Edward I had disapproved of Gaveston he could at any stage have removed him from his son's household and even sent him home to his native Gascony.[128] The famous quarrel between Edward I and his son, which led to Edward's banishment from court between June and October 1305, had nothing directly to do with Edward's relationship with Gaveston.[129] Gaveston did leave Edward's household at this time, but this was really a consequence of the sharp reduction in the amount of money allocated to Edward by the king and in the number of household members who could be supported rather than an action directed against Gaveston himself.[130] Although in a letter written to his sister Elizabeth in August 1305 Edward expressed his eagerness for Gaveston's return, it was also clear that there were others whose company he particularly wanted.[131] Even in February 1307, when Edward I ordered Gaveston to leave the realm, the real reason appears to have been Prince Edward's desire to grant Gaveston the county of Ponthieu (or more probably the earldom of Cornwall) rather than any specific offence committed by Gaveston himself. Gaveston was exiled but not permanently and was granted an annuity of 100 marks 'for as long as he shall remain in parts beyond the sea during the king's pleasure and awaiting his recall'.[132] The

---

[126] *CPR, 1301–07*, 244. It is deeply ironic that the heir in question was the same Roger Mortimer who was to play a leading part in the deposition and murder of Edward II and was himself to become a royal favourite on a scale far exceeding Gaveston and even Despenser.

[127] Chaplais, 21 and n. 77 (which make it clear that the knighting of Edward and Gaveston did not take place on the same day, as is often assumed); Hamilton, 32–3, 137; Johnstone, 107–9.

[128] Gascony was supposed to be Gaveston's destination when he was exiled in Feb. 1307, although in fact he went to Ponthieu instead: Hamilton, 34–5.

[129] See Johnstone, 97–101; Hamilton, 31–2, 137. It seems more likely that the growing cost of maintaining his household and the refusal of the treasurer, Walter Langton, to give Edward extra money at a time of great financial difficulty were the real causes: Prestwich, *Edward I*, 549.

[130] On Edward's household expenses at this time see Johnstone, 99–100.

[131] *Letters of Edward Prince of Wales*, 70; Johnstone, 100. The others were two yeomen, John de Haustede and John de Weston who had already been permitted to return, and Edward's cousin, Gilbert de Clare, son of Thomas de Clare.

[132] Hamilton, 34–7, 138–9; Johnstone, 122–5; Prestwich, *Edward I*, 552 (who considers that Edward's relationship with Gaveston was homosexual in nature but that this was not the issue in 1307). Gaveston was also permitted to stay in England until after a forthcoming tournament on 30 April, and Edward I was prepared, at his pleasure, to increase

anger and anxieties of an ageing king at his son's extravagance and the knowledge that his task in Scotland was still unfinished probably explain the quarrels between Edward I and Prince Edward rather than any question of the relations between Edward and Gaveston.

It is possible that, initially at least, Edward saw Gaveston as the accomplished and experienced elder brother whom he had never had, but it has also been very plausibly, though not conclusively, argued by Pierre Chaplais that Edward and Gaveston entered into a compact of brotherhood, comparable with the relationship between David and Jonathan in the Old Testament, between Achilles and Patroclus in the *Iliad*, and between Roland and Oliver in *The Song of Roland*, or with the practice of brotherhood-in-arms between members of the nobility in fourteenth- and fifteenth-century Europe.[133] Chaplais cites a number of chronicle sources in which Gaveston was reportedly described by Edward in terms of brotherhood, including the *Vita Edwardi Secundi*, the Lanercost chronicle, the *Annales Paulini*, the chronicle of Walter of Guisborough, and the *Polistorie* of Christ Church, Canterbury,[134] and also a privy seal writ of July 1308 in which he is addressed as 'our dear brother and faithful', the same language Edward used to his true half-brothers, Thomas of Brotherton and Edmund of Woodstock.[135] In his account of the death of Gaveston in 1312 the author of the *Vita* remarks that the earls had 'killed a great earl whom the king had adopted as brother'; the 'Chronicle of the Civil Wars of Edward II' refers specifically to Edward and Gaveston entering upon a compact of brotherhood (*fraternitatis fedus*); and the writer of the *Annales Paulini* records how in 1308 Edward could not bring himself to send into exile the person of Piers Gaveston, his adoptive brother (*adoptivi fratris sui*). Chaplais concludes that if any document was drawn up containing such a compact between the two men it was produced at some point between Gaveston's first entry into the royal household in 1297 and the death of Edward I in 1307, and that it was probably destroyed at Edward I's command on the occasion of the Lanercost oaths of 26 February 1307 when Gaveston swore to go into exile

---

Gaveston's income from the revenues of his lands in England or abroad: Johnstone, 122. Gaveston had earlier (in Oct. 1306) fallen into disfavour because he had left the army in Scotland without permission to take part in a tournament, but he was only one of a group of 22 young knights, many of whom were closely associated with Prince Edward, who had done so: Hamilton, 33–4, 137; Johnstone, 115–17; Prestwich, 505–10.

[133] Chaplais, esp. 3, 6–22, 109–14. See also E.A.R. Brown, 'Introduction' and 'Ritual brotherhood in western medieval Europe', in *Ritual Brotherhood in Ancient and Medieval Europe: A Symposium, Traditio*, lii (New York, 1997), 261–83, 357–81, esp. 359–60; M. Keen, 'Brotherhood in arms', *History*, xlvii (London, 1983), repr. in Keen, *Nobles, Knights and Men-at-arms in the Middle Ages* (London & Rio Grande, 1996), 43–62. Prestwich also accepts the likelihood that Edward and Gaveston made a brotherhood agreement: *Armies and Warfare*, 45.

[134] Chaplais, 10–11.

[135] Ibid., 11. The text of the writ is given ibid, n. 33, citing E 159/81, m.34d, and is also cited in Davies, *Baronial Opposition*, 84, n. 14.

and Edward swore not to have him near him.¹³⁶ There is however another possible date at which a compact of brotherhood might have been drawn up. The reference to Gaveston as Edward II's adoptive brother in the *Annales Paulini* forms part of an account of the crisis in March and April 1308 when the opposition magnates were attempting to force Gaveston into exile once more. The political situation became so tense that there was a real danger of civil war. Edward II and Gaveston withdrew to Windsor castle at Easter and prepared its defences against a possible baronial attack. A compact of brotherhood might have been seen not only as giving formal recognition to a relationship that already existed between the two men, but also as a legal device to protect Gaveston from the expected baronial attempts to oust him.¹³⁷ This is of course speculation as is the further possibility that, if a compact of brotherhood was created either in 1308 or at any other time, it could have been among Edward II's private documents which were plundered and lost from Swansea castle in South Wales in November 1326.¹³⁸

Edward II and Gaveston were both to marry early in the new reign, at a time when the closeness of their relationship was much remarked upon. Although each of their marriages had a social and a political dimension, it is improbable that Philip IV of France, who had a strong aversion to homosexuality¹³⁹ and also hoped that the children of the union would bind the English possessions in France to both the French and the English crowns,¹⁴⁰ would have allowed the marriage with his daughter Isabella, which had been under negotiation since 1298, if her future husband's sexual proclivities had been clearly proclaimed over so long a period.¹⁴¹ Nor might the young Gilbert de Clare, earl of Gloucester and Edward II's nephew, have agreed to the marriage between his sister Margaret and Gaveston. Both marriages produced children. Gaveston's daughter Joan was born at York on 12 January 1312, Gaveston having returned from exile at great risk to himself in order to be present.¹⁴² Gaveston also appears to have had a second daughter, Amy or Amie, probably illegitimate, whose date of birth is unknown but who was to serve as a lady of the bedchamber in the households of both Queen Isabella and Queen

---

¹³⁶ Chaplais, 12–13.

¹³⁷ *Ann. Paul.*, 263; Introductions to the parliaments of March and April 1308 in *PROME*.

¹³⁸ The document of 20 May 1303 relating to Edward's betrothal which is now in the Swansea Museum is probably a chance survival of many more important documents now lost. See Francis, 'Original contract', 150–5.

¹³⁹ See J.R. Strayer, *The Reign of Philip the Fair* (Princeton, 1980), 288–9; and Brown, 'The prince is father of the king', 290–1. Philip IV's actions against the Templars had started only a few weeks before Edward II and Isabella were finally married in Jan. 1308 so that possible charges of immorality were very much on Philip's mind. See Barber, 'World picture', 14–16.

¹⁴⁰ E.A.R. Brown, 'The political repercussions of family ties in the early fourteenth century', *Speculum*, lxiii (Cambridge, Mass., 1988), 574, 576, 584.

¹⁴¹ Chaplais, 9–10.

¹⁴² Hamilton, 93–4, 101–2, 167; Chaplais, 78–9.

Philippa.[143] Edward's son, the future Edward III, was born at Windsor on 13 November 1312, a few months after Gaveston's death and must have been conceived while the latter was still alive. As is well known, Edward II's wife Isabella was only twelve years old at the time of their marriage and could not have been expected to bear children much earlier than she did. Edward II and Isabella also produced three more children: John, born at Eltham on c. 15 August 1316; Eleanor, born at Woodstock on 18 June 1318; and Joan, born in the Tower of London on 5 July 1321. There is nothing to suggest that Edward II was not the father of any of these children. He is also known to have had an illegitimate son Adam, who died during the 1322 Scottish campaign and was probably born before Edward's marriage in 1308 at a time when his relationship with Gaveston was already established.[144]

It is impossible to be certain of the true nature of the relationship between Edward II and Gaveston, whether sexual, a formal bond of brotherhood,[145] or simply a very close friendship.[146] The contemporary evidence is often ambiguous or capable of different interpretations; the later traditions too contaminated by distortions or by deliberate propaganda.[147] But, whether or

[143] Hamilton, 102; idem, 'Another daughter for Piers Gaveston? Amie de Gaveston, damsel of the Queen's Chamber', *Medieval Prosopography*, xix (Kalamazoo, 1998), 177–86.

[144] F.D. Blackley, 'Adam, the bastard son of Edward II', *BIHR*, xxxvii (London, 1964), 76–7, citing BL, Stowe Ms. 553, f. 27. In 1322 Edward II openly recognized Adam as his bastard son, although it is surprising that there is no mention of Adam in any earlier records. Assuming he was at least as old as Edward II when he had first gone to war (i.e. in his seventeenth year in 1300), Adam would have been born in about 1305 or 1306. This seems to me more likely than the date of about 1310 suggested by Given-Wilson and Curteis in *The Royal Bastards of Medieval England* (London, 1984), 136. Although I have speculated above as to the possible identity of Adam's mother, there is no positive evidence.

[145] At a symposium entitled 'History in the Comic Mode', in honour of Professor Charles T. Wood in May 1998 Jeffrey Hamilton argued, entertainingly and with tongue very firmly in cheek, that Gaveston was not Edward II's brother by adoption but was in fact his illegitimate older brother.

[146] See Ch. 1 of this book and the papers referred to above by Ormrod, 'The sexualities of Edward II', and Mortimer, 'Sermons of sodomy'. Accusations of sodomy were closely akin to accusations of heresy and were widely used in the fourteenth century as a way of blackening the reputations of individuals or vulnerable groups, while the term 'sodomy' could cover a range of sexual practices, not just homosexuality. See, for example, V.L. Bullough, *Sexual Variance in Society and History* (New York & London, 1976), ch. 14, 'The later middle ages'; idem, 'The sin against nature and homosexuality', in *Sexual Practices and the Medieval Church*, ed. V.L. Bullough & J. Brundage (Buffalo, NY, 1982), 55–71, 239–44; W. Johansson and W.A. Percy, 'Homosexuality', in *Handbook of Medieval Sexuality*, ed. V.L. Bullough & J.A. Brundage (New York & London, 1996), 155–89. One of the leading scholars of homosexuality in the medieval period was certain that Edward II was homosexual: J. Boswell, *Christianity, Social Tolerance, and Homosexuality* (Chicago, 1980), 298–300. Another writer on the same theme is just as certain that he was not: A. Lumsden, 'The fairy tale of Edward II', *Gay and Lesbian Review*, xi, no. 2 (London, March–April 2004), 27–9.

[147] If the analogy of David and Jonathan seemed appropriate to the author of the *Vita Edwardi Secundi* as a way of describing the relationship between Edward and Gaveston, we should not forget David's other famous relationship, that with Bathsheba.

not an actual document containing a compact of brotherhood ever existed, the most likely explanation is that Edward really did regard Gaveston as if he were his brother by blood and that this goes to the heart of their relationship. As brothers, this would allow for a strong emotional tie but would also rule out a physical sexual relationship. Whatever the truth of the matter, Gaveston was perceived during his short career as wielding a degree of influence over Edward both as prince and as king which excluded others who considered they had a right of access to Edward or a right to be consulted. Both he and ultimately Edward II himself were to pay the penalty for their offence.

EDWARD'S QUARREL WITH HIS FATHER

After the conclusion of the siege of Stirling in July 1304 Edward became involved once more in England's relations with France. Under the terms of the Treaty of Paris in May 1303 either Edward I or his son was to go to France to perform homage for the duchy of Aquitaine. This was originally to have taken place at Amiens by 8 September 1303. In the meantime the duchy was formally restored to English control at a solemn ceremony at St Emilion in June 1303.[148] French envoys had visited Edward I at St Andrews in Scotland in March 1304 asking that Prince Edward should go to France to perform homage. This was agreed and on 27 September Edward was appointed to be at Amiens on 1 November. On 25 October Edward arrived at Dover, ready to cross to France for what would have been his first and also highly significant visit. Instead he was forced to abandon his plans after waiting in vain until 1 November to receive letters of safe conduct from Philip IV and for the arrival at Wissant of the king's brothers and the dukes of Burgundy and Brittany to escort him to Amiens.[149] There is no obvious explanation as to why the proposed ceremony failed to take place, but the answer probably lies somewhere in the tangle of Anglo-French relations over Aquitaine, which was constantly throwing up new problems. Even the possibility of a renewed war between England and France could not be ruled out at this time.[150]

Until the spring of 1305 Edward's career seemed to be advancing steadily towards his succession to the crown, which could not now be long delayed. Although Edward I was never lavish with praise, he appears to have been generally satisfied with his son's progress. So far as we can now

---

[148] Vale, 224; Prestwich, *Edward I*, 397; Johnstone, 88.

[149] *Foedera*, I, ii, 966–7, and C 47/27/5; Johnstone, 94–5. See also C. Johnson, 'The homage for Guienne in 1304', *EHR*, liii (1938), 728–9; P. Chaplais, 'Le Duché-Pairie de Guyenne', *Annales du Midi*, lxix (Toulouse, 1957), 104–5.

[150] See, for example, Vale, 224–5; Elizabeth Lalou, 'Les Négociations diplomatiques avec l'Angleterre sous le règne de Philippe le Bel', in *La 'France Anglaise' au Moyen Age* (Poitiers, 1986), Section d'histoire médiévale et de philologie (Paris, 1988), 343–4. On another occasion, in Oct. 1306, an English commissioner arrived in Paris to meet his French counterparts, but failed to make any contact with them: Prestwich, *Edward I*, 397.

tell, the younger Edward had acquitted himself well on campaign in Scotland. He had not fought in any major battle but he had at least gained considerable experience both of the splendours and the horrors of war. While we should not exaggerate the role he had played in, for example, the events of 1297, when as a boy of thirteen he was nominally in charge of the government of the realm, he had gained a degree of experience of the affairs of state. On 16 March 1302 he had 'held a "parliament" with the magnates of England at London on behalf of his father'.[151] The purpose of this meeting is not apparent but Edward was clearly trusted at least to represent his father, if not actually to conduct business. The first parliament to meet since the Lincoln parliament of 1301, during which Edward had been created Prince of Wales, assembled at Westminster in July 1302. This was followed by another at Westminster in October. Edward was duly summoned to both.[152] When parliament next met, at Westminster in late February and March 1305, Edward and his council were at Kennington busily dealing with and answering the petitions from his Welsh subjects which had accumulated since 1301.[153] As one modern commentator has remarked, in later years the Welsh were to regard the favourable replies they received in 1305 as if they were their Magna Carta.[154]

The period of steady progress ended dramatically and with no apparent advance warning on 14 June 1305, at Midhurst in Sussex, where Edward exchanged bitter words with his father's treasurer, Walter Langton, the bishop of Coventry & Lichfield, after allegedly being accused of breaking into one of the latter's woods.[155] Whatever the truth of this particular story, events of this kind were often symptomatic of some deeper problem.[156] It is important to remember that even though Edward had access to some of the revenues of the principality of Wales and of the counties of Chester and Ponthieu, these did not cover his household expenses. He was therefore still dependent on the royal exchequer, and hence on Langton's co-operation, for much of his

---

[151] Johnstone, 82. The meeting is referred to in *Ann. Lond.*, 127. The nature of the business is not stated.

[152] *PW*, i, 112, 116. For a discussion of the business of these two parliaments see *PROME*. Petitions were only a small part of the business of this parliament: see *PROME*, Lent Parliament 1305.

[153] The petitions are printed in *The Record of Carnarvon*, ed. H. Ellis, Record Commission (London, 1838), 212–25. For a discussion of the business of this parliament see *PROME*.

[154] *Calendar of Ancient Petitions relating to Wales*, ed. W. Rees (Cardiff, 1975), 17. However, the petitions of 1305 and those submitted by the communities of North and West Wales in 1316 showed that there were many grievances and considerable potential for unrest: Davies, *Conquest*, 387.

[155] Johnstone, 97; Prestwich, *Edward I*, 549–50; *Ann. Lond.*, 138.

[156] Another good example is the breaking into and plundering of the earl of Pembroke's manor of Painswick in Gloucestershire in 1318 by disaffected members of Pembroke's retinue: Phillips, 261–6.

income.[157] Edward had just passed his twenty-first birthday and may have felt that this required a reduction in his financial dependence. There is also some evidence that Edward had been annoyed by his treatment at the hands of royal administrators during the Scottish campaign in 1304.[158] Langton for his part was very conscious of the strains that the war in Scotland had been placing on the royal finances and was likely to resist any requests for more money and to complain to the king about the extravagance of Edward and his companions.[159] Whatever the explanation, the outburst was probably the result of an accumulation of petty irritations rather than one single event.

Edward I, who was very sensitive about any criticism of his ministers and was heavily dependent upon Langton and his financial and administrative expertise, immediately came to Langton's aid and banished his son from court.[160] The possibility that Edward I's attitude to Edward was influenced more by a sense of duty than by enduring personal anger is hinted at in a statement by the council later that year that he had 'removed his own eldest and dearest son, Edward, prince of Wales, from his household, . . . because he had uttered certain gross and harsh words to a certain minister of his'.[161]

---

[157] See the very valuable discussions of Edward's revenues in Johnstone, 67–71; and in Tout, *Chapters*, ii, 174–7. Tout shows that the earldom of Chester provided the greater part of the revenue received from Edward's personal domains: £1,007 in 1301–2, £1,696 in 1302–3, and £1,514 in 1303–4; Wales provided much less, while from 1299 Ponthieu was under the receivership of the Florentine bankers, the Frescobaldi: Tout, ii, 174–6.

[158] On 4 May 1304 John Droxford, the keeper of the wardrobe, wrote to his colleague, Richard de Bremesgrave, that Prince Edward was 'much annoyed' at Richard's refusal to deliver wine for the use of his household and at other acts 'done against him since he came to Scotland': *CDS*, ii, 397 (no. 1527).

[159] Prestwich, *Edward I*, 549. Edward I was certainly very conscious of the costs of his family at this time. In April he had paid £200 in debts owed by his daughter, Mary, the nun of Amesbury, and in May he had added revenues worth £433 6s 8d to the dower of £2,000 *livres tournois* (£500) assigned to his wife, Queen Margaret: *CCR, 1302–07*, 262, 276. It is very hard to know whether Edward was spending excessively at this time. In any case extravagance can be very much in the eye of the beholder. In 1301–2 and 1302–3 Edward's household expenditure amounted to £10,199 and £5,653 respectively, admittedly at a time of war when there were many exceptional costs: *CDS*, ii, 370 (E 101/363/18); Tout, *Chapters*, ii, 173 (citing E 101/360/16). He is likely to have spent less in 1305–6, when there was no campaign in Scotland. On the other hand, as Edward grew older and became increasingly involved in public events, his financial needs probably also grew.

[160] Johnstone, 97–8; Prestwich, *Edward I*, 549; *Abbreviatio Placitorum*, Record Commission (London, 1811), 256–7. In a letter to Pope Boniface VIII in 1303 Edward I had strongly defended Langton against various charges: *CCR, 1302–7*, 81–2; Prestwich, 549.

[161] The occasion of the statement was the punishment of a leading baron, William de Braose, who had 'uttered gross and contumelious words' at the exchequer, with Langton presumably once again the target: *Abbreviatio Placitorum*, 256–7. Edward I was to refer to Edward as 'our dear son' in a letter to the pope early in 1307: *Foedera*, I, ii, 1007. There is of course a formality about such language, especially since this latter example occurred at the time of Edward I's violent anger over Edward and Gaveston, but there is probably also an underlying truth in the words.

Some sense of what occurred can be gleaned from the unique roll of Prince Edward's letters which survives for much of the year 1304–5.[162] On the very day of the incident Edward wrote to Henry de Lacy, the earl of Lincoln, and an old and trusted friend, to tell him what had happened. Edward recounted that he had come to join his father at Midhurst on Sunday, 13 June, and that on the following day the king had become angry with him 'on account of some words spoken between him and the bishop of Chester [Coventry & Lichfield]'. The king had then forbidden him or any of his followers to enter his presence, and had ordered his household and exchequer officials not to make any payments for the support of Edward and his household. Edward said that he was remaining at Midhurst while awaiting his father's 'goodwill and grace', and would follow behind him as best he could at a distance of ten or twelve leagues, until he was restored to his father's favour. Edward ended by asking the earl to come to him on his return from Canterbury, since he had great need of his help and counsel.[163] It is known that the young Edward did in fact follow his father around at a distance, although not so far away as ten or twelve leagues;[164] and that, despite the king's orders, small sums of money were forthcoming from the king's almoner, Henry Blunsdon, and with the assistance of Walter Reynolds, the treasurer of Edward's household.[165] Within little more than a month there were signs that Edward I's anger was beginning to diminish. On 16 July the constable of Windsor was ordered to place seven tuns of wine in the cellars of the king's houses in Windsor Park for his son's use; and on 22 July the mayor of London and all the sheriffs of England were told that they could now provide assistance to Edward and his household.[166] On the previous day Edward wrote to his sister, Joan, countess of Gloucester, from the archbishop of Canterbury's palace at Lambeth, telling her that the king's anger had abated and thanking her for giving him her goods and the use of her seal, which he now returned to her.[167] It is clear from this letter and also from the king's orders of 22 July, which had been issued at the request of Queen Margaret, that a great deal of activity on Edward's behalf had been going on behind the scenes on the part of his family and friends. By 24 July Edward was installed in Windsor Park, where he was to remain at his father's orders for most of the time until late September.[168] On 4 August

---

[162] *Letters of Edward Prince of Wales*. See the discussion in ch. 2 of this book.
[163] Ibid., 30.
[164] Edward's movements can be traced from his daily household roll, E 101/368/4, covering the period 20 Nov. 1304 to 9 Oct. 1305. The reality of Edward's following of his father was later transmuted into the story told by Bishop Ringstead of Bangor which made Edward appear a Christlike figure. See ch. 1 and B. Smalley, *English Friars*, 211–15, 219, 338.
[165] *Letters of Edward Prince of Wales*, 31–2; Johnstone, 98–9.
[166] *CCR, 1302–7*, 279, 342.
[167] *Letters of Edward Prince of Wales*, 60–1.
[168] Ibid., 63–130.

he wrote to his sister Elizabeth, the former countess of Holland and now countess of Hereford, telling her that his father had allowed him the company of John de Haustede and John de Weston, two valets whom he especially valued, and asking his sister to talk to the queen in the hope she would persuade the king to let him have the company of two more valets, namely Gilbert de Clare and Piers Gaveston. This would go far towards relieving 'the anguish which we have endured, and still suffer daily, through the ordinance and pleasure of our lord the king'.[169] The breach between father and son could not continue indefinitely without causing further public scandal and disrupting the necessary flow of official business. Already it seems that Edward, although summoned to the parliament which began at Westminster on 15 September, did not attend.[170]

Edward I's temper gradually cooled, aided by family and friends and by Prince Edward's studied good behaviour, and no doubt helped further by the execution at Smithfield on 23 August, with all the gruesome accompaniments, of Edward I's old enemy William Wallace.[171]

There was no formal end to the estrangement but on 12 October Prince Edward moved to Westminster palace, where on 13 October (appropriately the feast of the Translation of St Edward the Confessor) he presided at a banquet on behalf of his father, but significantly did not occupy the high seat.[172] Father and son were now apparently reconciled, but how far this was the reality and how far for public consumption we shall never know. The younger Edward certainly knew by now who his friends were and who his enemies. He had good friends and supporters within his own family; in his household he had Walter Reynolds, for example; outside it he had the help and sympathy of influential figures such as the earl of Lincoln, Hugh Despenser, and the bishop of Durham.[173] His one real enemy remained the king's treasurer, Walter Langton. One day there would be a settling of accounts between the two men and that day could not be long delayed.

EDWARD'S MARRIAGE AGAIN

The long-delayed marriage of Edward and Isabella once again became an issue at the end of 1305. This was probably one of the reasons for the visit to England in the summer of 1305 of Queen Marie of France, the mother of Queen Margaret, and Margaret's brother Louis, count of Évreux. Even after the beginning of the estrangement from his father, Edward had still

---

[169] Ibid., 70; the translation is that in Johnstone, 100.
[170] Johnstone, 100–1.
[171] A. Fisher, *William Wallace* (Edinburgh, 1986 & 2002), 123–30; Prestwich, *Edward I*, 503.
[172] *Ann. Lond.*, 143; Johnstone, 101; Prestwich, *Edward I*, 549.
[173] *Letters of Edward Prince of Wales*, 62, 133–4; Johnstone, 101–2.

expected to meet and escort them on their arrival and on 22 June wrote to Walter Reynolds asking him to buy two riding horses for his personal use and the finest cloth to be found in London to make two or three new outfits.[174] It must have been personally embarrassing for Edward not to be allowed to meet the royal visitors, who were also of course close relatives of his betrothed, Isabella,[175] and no doubt diplomatically embarrassing for Edward's father to have to explain what was happening at the English court.

A further stimulus to action was the election of the archbishop of Bordeaux, Bertrand de Got, as Pope Clement V in June 1305. The new pope was a subject of the English crown and a former royal clerk, and could be expected to be favourable to English interests and demands.[176] But he was also anxious to launch a new crusade to recover the territories in the Holy Land lost in 1291, an expedition for which the military resources of England and France would be essential.[177] To achieve this aim a resolution of the remaining disputes between England and France over the duchy of Aquitaine was needed and Clement hoped that the marriage of Edward and Isabella would be the necessary catalyst. On 25 August 1305 Clement wrote to Edward I proposing that the Prince of Wales should go to Lyons for the papal coronation in November and that while there he and Isabella should be married. To avoid a repeat of the fiasco of 1304 when Edward had waited in vain at Dover for permission to enter France, Clement took the precaution of ensuring that Philip IV issued a safe conduct in advance.[178] On 4 October Edward I replied, excusing both himself and his son from attending the coronation on the grounds of lack of time to make the necessary preparations but stating that he would soon be sending envoys of his own to the pope.[179] It is likely that Edward I was concerned that if he and his son were present in person he would be put under pressure by both the French representatives and the pope to make unacceptable concessions; the king was also, although he could scarcely admit this, ageing rapidly and ailing and in no condition to make such an arduous journey;[180] and above all, arrangements for the future government of Scotland were absorbing all his time and energy.[181] Edward I however sent an impressive delegation, consisting of the bishops of Coventry & Lichfield and of Worcester, the earl of Lincoln, Hugh Despenser and other

---

[174] *Letters of Edward Prince of Wales*, 34; Johnstone, 99.

[175] They were Isabella's stepmother and half-brother respectively.

[176] On Clement V's family background and his connections with the English crown see S. Menache, *Clement V* (Cambridge, 1998), 7–8, 247–8.

[177] Ibid., 17–18; Schein, 'Fideles Crucis', 181–3.

[178] SC 6/44/16; *The Gascon Calendar of 1322*, ed. G.P. Cuttino, Camden, 3rd ser., lxx (London, 1949), 30, nos 270, 274, 275; Doherty (D.Phil.), 14–15.

[179] *CCR, 1302–07*, 348.

[180] On Edward I's health in the latter stages of his reign see Prestwich, *Edward I*, 506–7.

[181] Ibid., 503–5.

nobles and administrative experts, one of whose duties was to arrange a proxy marriage between the Prince of Wales and Isabella.[182] On 11 November Philip IV gave Isabella authority to appoint proctors; on 28 November the pope issued a dispensatio for Isabella to marry while still under the canonical age; and on 3 December she appointed her uncle, Count Louis of Évreux and two other nobles to act for her.[183]

The coronation of Clement V had already taken place at Lyons amidst great splendour on 14 November 1305, attended by Philip IV of France, Charles of Valois, Louis of Evreux, John II, duke of Brittany, and count Henry of Luxemburg (soon to be the emperor Henry VII), and on the English side by the earl of Lincoln and the other members of the English delegation who brought presents valued at £1,343.[184] The proxy marriage was not however celebrated, probably because the French and English envoys could not agree on the terms of the marriage settlement.[185]

SCOTLAND, FRANCE AND KNIGHTHOOD

The war in Scotland, which had appeared to be at an end with the capture and execution of William Wallace, was dramatically reignited in February 1306 when Robert Bruce, earl of Carrick murdered John Comyn of Badenoch before the high altar of the Greyfriars' church at Dumfries. This was followed in March by the inauguration at Scone of Bruce as Robert I, king of Scots.[186] Edward I responded by ordering his army to muster on 8 July. Edward himself initially intended to lead the army but in April it was decided that Prince Edward would be in overall command and that his father would join him later.[187] Meanwhile, on 5 April it was announced that Edward would be knighted at the feast of Pentecost, 22 May. The sheriffs were ordered to proclaim that anyone whose father was a knight and who wished himself to be knighted on that occasion should come to London beforehand and be provided with the necessary equipment from the royal wardrobe.[188] On 7 April Edward, who was now almost twenty-two, was granted the duchy of Aquitaine, the island of Oléron and the Agenais. This was done ostensibly to maintain Edward in

---

[182] On 15 Oct. Prince Edward gave his father's envoys authority to agree to this: *Letters of Edward Prince of Wales*, 144–5; Johnstone, 104.

[183] AN, J 408, no. 11; and Doherty (D.Phil.), 15, citing Bibliothèque Nationale, Collection Brienne, 7007, f. 1.

[184] Menache, *Clement V*, 16–17; Johnstone, 104–5.

[185] The English envoys demanded the return of the castle of Mauléon before they would agree on the terms of the marriage settlement and this the French refused. Clement V's dispensation is endorsed with the words *dispensatio matrimonii reginae Angliae non valeat*, which indicates that it was not used: Doherty (D.Phil.), 15.

[186] Prestwich, *Edward I*, 505–6; Barrow, 145–9.

[187] *CCR, 1302–07*, 438; *CPR, 1301–07*, 428; Johnstone, 106.

[188] *PW*, i, 164; *CCR, 1302–07*, 434, 438; *Flores*, 131; Johnstone, 106–7. In 1254 Henry III had originally planned to knight the future Edward I and a large number of other young

his impending status of knighthood,[189] but it was certainly also a further stage in the developing relations with France. The young Edward would now have a higher status if his marriage with Isabella were to take place before his accession to the English throne, while at the same time ensuring that the necessary homage for Aquitaine would be performed by Edward for himself and not by or in the name of his father.[190]

The future knights spent the night before in church, many of them in the Temple church but the more distinguished, including the Prince of Wales, in Westminster Abbey. Supposedly they were composing themselves in prayer for the chivalric duties they were about to assume: in fact there was so much noise and general excitement that the monks of Westminster were scarcely able to say their office in the choir of the abbey.[191] On the following day, 22 May, Edward I knighted his son in the chapel of the palace of Westminster; the young Edward's spurs were attached to his heels by the two senior earls of the kingdom, the vastly experienced and statesmanlike Henry de Lacy of Lincoln and the constable of England, Humphrey de Bohun, earl of Hereford.[192] At the same time the king formally invested his son with the duchy of Aquitaine.[193] Afterwards Edward went to Westminster Abbey where he knighted all the other young men, amounting altogether to about three

---

men in Westminster Abbey. In the event Edward was knighted by his father-in-law, Alfonso X of Castile, in the abbey of Las Huelgas at Burgos: Prestwich, *Edward I*, 9–10. Although Edward I's attempt to levy the traditional aid to cover the costs of knighting his son was not approved by the parliament which assembled at Westminster on 30 May 1306, he nonetheless obtained a grant of taxation: Prestwich, 455; *PROME*, Lent Parliament, 1306. Edward I had also in effect abandoned his previous attempts to force those with land of sufficient value to take up the responsibilities of knighthood at their own expense and was now trying to persuade them to do so at his own expense: cf. Prestwich, *War, Politics and Finance*, 83–91.

[189] *CPR, 1301–07*, 424; Johnstone, 107.

[190] There was a parallel with the early career of Edward I. He too had been granted Aquitaine on the eve of his knighting and marriage in 1254: Powicke, *Henry III and the Lord Edward* (Oxford, 1947; repr. 1966), 232–3; Prestwich, *Edward I*, 10–11. Cf. Johnstone, 109.

[191] *Flores*, 131–2; Johnstone, 108; Bullock-Davies, '*Multitudo*', xxvi. For the proper preparation of a young man for knighting see M. Keen, *Chivalry* (New Haven & London, 1984), 64–82; R. Barber, *The Knight and Chivalry* (Woodbridge, Suffolk & Rochester, NY, revised edn, 1995), 23–37.

[192] *Flores*, 132; *Ann. Lond.*, 146; Johnstone, 108; Bullock-Davies, '*Multitudo*', xxvi. The ceremony presumably occurred in the palace rather than in the abbey because Edward I was now too infirm to attend: ibid., xviii. The daily account roll of Prince Edward says laconically: 'on this Sunday the Prince was knighted and therefore the expenses were great for the following week': Bod., Ms. Latin Hist. c.4, m.5.

[193] Control of the duchy was not however handed over to the prince's own officials until the early months of 1307: see Trabut-Cussac, *L'administration anglaise*, 132–4. In Aug. 1306 Edward I also made provision for Edward's young half-brothers, Thomas and Edmund, whom he endowed with lands worth 10,000 and 7,000 marks a year respectively: *Foedera*, I, ii, 998; Maddicott, 23.

hundred.[194] The ceremony was marred by the great crowds of people within the abbey. Two knights were crushed to death, while other knights inside the abbey had to clear a way on horseback. The Prince of Wales meanwhile had to retreat to the high altar for safety.[195]

The ceremonies were followed by a great feast in Westminster Hall,[196] during which the guests were entertained by over eighty minstrels drawn from the households of the king, queen and prince, and from the service of many other nobles and clergy.[197] The highlight of the feast, and the detail which most interested the chroniclers, was the oaths taken upon two swans by Edward I and the prince, followed by the other nobles and knights, that they would defeat Robert Bruce and so avenge 'the injury done to Holy Church, the death of John Comyn and the broken faith of the Scots'.[198] Prince Edward allegedly also swore that he would not rest two nights in the same place until this was achieved.[199]

The mass knighting and the subsequent feast were exciting social events, some of the most exciting that England had ever known, but there was far more to them than that. At one level they were intended by Edward I to raise support for yet another campaign in Scotland, this time to pull down Robert Bruce from the throne which he had obtained through an act of sacrilege. It is an exaggeration to place the occasion on the same level as Pope Urban II's sermon at Clermont in 1095 which launched the First Crusade, but in the combination of religious piety and military enthusiasm, the comparison does carry some weight. There was,

---

[194] The best estimate of the numbers knighted is 297–300, derived from a variety of chronicle sources and from the official record of the men who received robes in aid of their knighting: E 101/362/20; E 101/369/4 (fragmentary); there was also another roll, now lost: see Bullock-Davies, '*Multitudo*', xix–xxi.

[195] *Flores*, 132; Bullock-Davies, '*Multitudo*', xxvii; Johnstone, 108; Hamilton, 32.

[196] There is no detailed record of the arrangements for the feast or of the food served, apart from the four lengths of gold-threaded cloth which were hung on the wall behind the king and the prince during the banquet: Bullock-Davies, '*Multitudo*', xxvii–xxviii.

[197] The names of the minstrels, the instruments on which they performed and the people in whose service they were are recorded in E 101/369/6 and E 101/370/21. The details are given in Bullock-Davies, '*Multitudo*', 1–13. Her book contains a detailed examination of the personal histories and connections of the individual minstrels and a description of their instruments.

[198] *Flores*, 132; Bullock-Davies, '*Multitudo*', xxx.

[199] Nicholas Trevet, *Annales Sex Regum Angliae*, ed. Th. Hog, English Historical Soc. Publications, ix (London, 1845), 408–9; Bullock-Davies, '*Multitudo*', xxix–xxx; Johnstone, 108–9. For a discussion of the available information on the oaths taken and on whether the swans were decorated roasted birds or (more probably) ornamental objects see Bullock-Davies, xxix–xxxviii. On oaths in general and more specifically those taken on birds (such as a peacock, a heron or a sparrowhawk), see Bullock-Davies, xxxv–xxxvi; Prestwich, *Edward I*, 121. Despite the remarks of the chronicler Peter Langtoft that no more splendid occasion had occurred since the crowning of King Arthur at Caerleon, there is no evidence that on this occasion Edward I was trying to follow Arthurian traditions: Bullock-Davies, xxxvii–xxxviii; Prestwich, 121.

too, an element of desperation in Edward I's strategy. He was now almost sixty-seven years of age and in failing health. The Scottish campaign was for him personally a last throw of the dice.[200]

The knightings could also be described as a bonding exercise. For the newly made knights the war would be a test of their individual prowess and of how they would support one another on campaign. But it might also give a foretaste of how they would behave under a new king when Edward I had passed from the scene. Many of those knighted with the Prince of Wales in May 1306 were to play a prominent role for good or ill in the new reign.[201] They included Piers Gaveston,[202] Edmund Fitz Alan, soon to become earl of Arundel; Humphrey de Bohun, son of the earl of Hereford; Hugh Despenser the Younger, son of Hugh Despenser one of Edward I's most trusted baronial advisers; Gilbert de Clare, Edward II's first cousin and heir to the earldom of Gloucester; John Maltravers, who was to be one of Edward II's jailers in 1327; Roger Mortimer of Wigmore, future lover of Edward II's queen and instigator of the king's murder; William Trussell, who was to give Edward II the news of his subjects' withdrawal of allegiance in 1327; and John de Warenne, earl of Surrey. The social bonding was further emphasized by the marriages in 1305/6 of Edmund Fitz Alan to the earl of Surrey's sister; of the earl of Surrey to Prince Edward's niece Joan, daughter of his deceased sister Eleanor, countess de Bar on 25 May 1306; and on the following day of Hugh Despenser the Younger and another of Prince Edward's nieces, Gilbert de Clare's sister Eleanor.[203]

SCOTLAND

On 8 June 1306 Prince Edward left London to visit his stepmother, Queen Margaret, at Winchester,[204] and from there made his way north to join the army summoned to assemble at Carlisle on 8 July. Edward I also went

---

[200] Malcolm Vale has suggested that Edward I's choice of swans should be seen as symbolic of Edward I's 'swan song' since he knew that he was nearing death: Vale, *The Princely Court*, 218–20; see also M. Strickland, 'Treason, feud and the growth of state violence: Edward I and the "War of the Earl of Carrick, 1306–7" ', in *War, Government and Aristocracy in the British Isles, c.1150–1500*, ed. C. Given-Wilson, A. Kettle & L. Scales (Woodbridge, Suffolk & Rochester, NY, 2008), 104–8.

[201] For a list of their names see Bullock-Davies, '*Multitudo*', 185–7.

[202] Who was apparently not knighted on 22 May with Edward but four days later: Bod., Ms. Latin Hist. c.4, m.5; Chaplais, 21. It is not clear why this delay should have occurred but the source is very clear on the point.

[203] For further details on each of these see the *Oxford DNB*. Among those knighted with the Prince of Wales were John Comyn, son of the murdered John Comyn, and Edward Balliol, son of the deposed John Balliol king of Scots and briefly king of Scots himself after 1332. Comyn, who was also the nephew of the earl of Pembroke, was killed fighting against his father's murderer at the battle of Bannockburn in 1314. Balliol was held in honourable custody in England until he went to his family lands in France after his father's death in 1314.

[204] *Ann. Lond.*, 146.

north but at a slower pace, reaching the Carlisle area in late September and establishing himself in the nearby Augustinian priory at Lanercost. The 1306 campaign had begun well. Already, on 19 June, an English army led by Aymer de Valence, the future earl of Pembroke, had severely defeated Robert Bruce at Methven near Perth.[205] In early July 1306 Prince Edward entered Scotland with the main force, receiving the surrender of the castle of Lochmaben in Annandale on 11 July.[206] From there he moved in the direction of Perth which he reached on about 1 August.[207] He was then present at the siege of Kildrummy castle north-west of Aberdeen, which fell before 13 September, yielding one of Robert Bruce's brothers, Neil, as a prisoner.[208] Little is known in detail about the force commanded by the Prince of Wales, but it apparently included his cousins the earls of Lancaster and Gloucester and his brother-in-law the earl of Hereford, as well as many of the young men who had just been knighted.[209]

On Edward I's orders the campaign was conducted with great savagery since Robert Bruce and his supporters were regarded as rebels against their lawful king rather than the leaders of another nation.[210] Many of those taken prisoner were executed as traitors, including Neil Bruce. Two other brothers, Thomas and Alexander, were captured in Galloway in February 1307 and sent as prisoners to the Prince of Wales at Wetheral in Cumberland, together with the heads of some of their companions. The Bruce brothers were then sent to Edward I at Carlisle for execution.[211]

According to the chronicler William Rishanger, the prince took a full part in the punishment of the Scots: Edward, moving a day's march ahead of his father, 'would spare neither sex nor age. Wherever he went, he set fire to villages and hamlets and laid them waste without mercy. This is said to have displeased the king his father, the more so as the hapless populace were paying the penalty for their betters, as the rich had taken to flight.'[212]

---

[205] Phillips, 24; Prestwich, *Edward I*, 507; Barrow, 153–4. The events of 1306 can be followed on the map in Barrow, 147.

[206] *CDS*, ii, no. 1803.

[207] *CDS*, ii, no. 1809: dated at Forteviot near Perth on 1 Aug.

[208] *CDS*, ii, no. 1829; Barrow, 160–1.

[209] *Bruce*, book 4, 154–5 (ll. 75–9); *Scalacronica of Thomas Gray of Heton*, ed. J. Stevenson, Maitland Club (Edinburgh, 1836), 131; Prestwich, *Edward I*, 506.

[210] Edward I's intentions were made very clear in the 'Ordinances by the King and Council for better assuring the peace of Scotland' which were issued at some point between Nov. 1306 and March 1307. 'The king and Council order that all present at the death of Sir John Comyn, or of counsel and assent thereto, shall be drawn and hanged. Those ... found in Scotland without the King's permission, shall be hanged or their heads cut off.': *CDS*, ii, no. 1908. See also Strickland, 'A law of arms or a law of treason?' in *Violence in Medieval Society*, ed. R. W. Kaeuper (Woodbridge, Suffolk & Rochester, NY, 2000), 39–41, 76–7.

[211] Prestwich, *Edward I*, 508–10; Barrow, 161–2, 169–71; *CDS*, iv, 489 (no. 6), citing BL, Add. Ms. 22923, f. 14.

[212] William of Rishanger, *Chronica et Annales*, ed. H.T. Riley, Rolls ser. (London, 1865), 230: cited and trans. in Johnstone, 114. See also Bullock-Davies, '*Multitudo*', 179, and Strickland, 'A law of arms', 57–8.

Hilda Johnstone also cited another apparently damning passage, this time from Barbour's *Bruce*, as evidence for the young Edward's cruelty and lack of human feeling.[213] 'Barbour,' she says, 'writes of the vindictive spirit shown by the prince when he got the news of the rout of Methven':

> And to the king of England sone
> Thai wrate haly as thai had done;
> And he wes blyth of that tithing,
> And for dispyte had draw and hing
> All the prisoneris, thouct thai war ma,
> Bot Schyr Amery did nocht sua.

There is indeed some evidence that Edward I became concerned that ordinary people who had not been directly involved in Robert Bruce's actions or who had been forced to join him against their will were suffering unduly, since in March 1307 he wrote to Aymer de Valence and his other officials in Scotland reminding them to spare such people from punishment.[214]

But there are also some indications that the younger Edward was less brutal in his behaviour than would appear. In the first place, the passage from Barbour's *Bruce* has been misread. If the word 'sone' is understood as 'son', which was Johnstone's interpretation, then the passage is indeed highly critical of Edward's behaviour and character. If, on the other hand, 'sone' is translated as 'soon', which it is in the latest edition of Barbour's *Bruce*, then Edward I and not his son becomes the focus of attention and of criticism.[215] If Barbour's remarks really had been intended to refer to Prince Edward, they would sit very oddly with his strong approval of Edward in his account of the siege of Kildrummy only three months after the battle of Methven:

> The eldest and apperande air
> A yhoung bachiller, stark and fair,
> Schyr Edward callit of Carnarvinane,
> Thet was the starkest man off ane
> That men fynd mycht in ony cuntre;
> Prynce of Walys that tym wes he.[216]

The quotation from Rishanger is also subject to some doubt. His claim that Edward I stayed one day's march behind his son is nonsense, since Edward I did not set foot in Scotland during the 1306–7 campaign. If Rishanger was wrong in this, one may question the reliability of his other

---

[213] Johnstone, 113–14, citing an earlier edition of Barbour, *The Bruce*, ed. W.W. Skeat, 2 vols, Scottish Text Soc., 31–3 (Edinburgh, 1894), ii, book 2, ll. 452–7.
[214] *CDS*, ii, 508 (no. 1909).
[215] *Bruce*, book 2, 102–3 (ll. 455–60).
[216] *Bruce*, book 4, 154–5 (ll. 72–7).

statements. Some evidence of Edward's actual behaviour is contained in two letters he wrote to Aymer de Valence, the king's lieutenant in Scotland, on 13 July and 1 August 1306. In the first he reported that the garrison of Lochmaben castle had surrendered to him unconditionally and were to have a fair trial; in the second Edward thanked Aymer for the protection given to the abbot and convent of Coupar Angus, for which they had much commended him, as he esteemed them as his own. Edward also begged Aymer to see that no damage came to their crops and other goods and to befriend them in all matters.[217] It is also worth adding that after he became king Edward relaxed the terrifying conditions of imprisonment of Bruce's sister Mary and the countess of Buchan, who had been confined in specially built cages on the orders of Edward I.[218] This is not to argue that the Prince of Wales's behaviour in Scotland was exemplary, or that he did not participate in any of the destruction caused by the English armies; but the extreme charges against him cannot be supported. The prime responsibility for what happened in Scotland was and remained that of Edward I.[219]

The Prince of Wales was still in Scotland in September when he supplied miners to assist in the siege of Dunaverty castle on the isle of Mull, where it was hoped that Robert Bruce himself might be.[220] When the campaign ended for the winter shortly afterwards Edward returned to England, visiting Langley, Canterbury and Dover, and then spending Christmas with his half-brothers, Thomas and Edmund, at Northampton.[221] Edward I had already gone into winter quarters at

[217] *CDS*, ii, 483, 485 (nos 1803, 1809). The close working relationship between Aymer de Valence and Edward in 1306–7 was probably the foundation of their relations when Edward became king: cf. Phillips, and the article on Aymer in the *Oxford DNB*. In August 1307 he gave compensation to two brothers of Melrose abbey and to a 'poor Scot' for damage his army had inflicted on their property: E 101/373/17, f. 19. Edward was however in a particularly good mood at the time, having just become king.

[218] Barrow, 162, 360; Prestwich, *Edward I*, 508–9. Whether Edward II's actions were taken on compassionate grounds or for reasons of political convenience is however debatable. See the discussion of the behaviour of Edward I and Edward II in Prestwich, 509, n. 164, and in the 2nd edition of Barrow (Edinburgh, 1976), 230, 233. Ironically, Bruce's queen, who was the daughter of the earl of Ulster, a close ally of Edward I, was not subjected to the same treatment. She was initially confined in the manor house of Burstwick in Holderness in Yorkshire, with two elderly women as companions, and under Edward II was sent to the convent of Barking in Essex: Barrow, 162; *Foedera*, II, i, 244.

[219] It is likely that as his temper cooled Edward I became shocked at the devastation he had unleashed in Scotland. Edward II did however show a capacity for the ruthless pursuit of his enemies at the time of the civil war of 1321–2. Here his opponents were executed as traitors or imprisoned in much the same way as Edward I's Scottish enemies in 1306.

[220] A letter of 22 Sept. from the king to Sir John Botetourt refers to Edward and the miners: *CDS*, ii, 491 (no. 1833). On the siege and Bruce's movements see Barrow, 163–4. In Oct. 1306 Edward was in Kintyre when he sent crossbowmen, miners and masons to aid the defence of the castle of Ayr: *CDS*, iv, 391 (no. 11).

[221] Johnstone, 115, citing BL, Add. Ms. 22923, Edward's wardrobe book for 1306–7.

Lanercost priory in Cumberland by 29 September 1306. This fact, combined with the prince's departure from Scotland, probably explains why twenty-two young knights, including Gaveston and others closely associated with Prince Edward, felt that their duty was performed for the time being and left the army in Scotland without permission, to take part in a tournament overseas.[222] Edward I was furious and on 18 October ordered the seizure of their lands.[223] He eventually relented after mediation by Queen Margaret and on 23 January 1307 he pardoned most of the offenders.[224] The episode had no real significance except to emphasize once again the growing gap between an ailing and increasingly frustrated king and an exuberant younger generation.

EDWARD'S MARRIAGE YET AGAIN

The main reason for Edward's return to England at the end of the campaigning season in Scotland was that negotiations concerning Aquitaine and his marriage had been continuing between English and French envoys at the papal curia at Lyons. The unwillingness of the French to surrender the castle of Mauléon in advance of the marriage of Edward and Isabella had held up agreement in 1305. It appears that negotiations on this subject and on Edward I's demand that the marriage should take place in England rather than France had reached some sort of conclusion by the end of November 1306 when Clement V appointed Cardinal Peter of Spain to go to England to settle the final details of an agreement.[225] The cardinal was expected to arrive in England in early December: Prince Edward was at Dover on 8 December, presumably to meet him but there is no evidence that he did so.[226] Whenever the cardinal did arrive, he was still in the south of England in mid-February.[227] Edward I was meanwhile anxiously awaiting him in Carlisle,[228] where he had been

---

[222] Hamilton, 33–4, 137; Johnstone, 115–17; Prestwich, *Edward I*, 509–10. The knights connected with Edward included Gaveston, Gilbert de Clare (son of Thomas de Clare, lord of Thomond in Ireland), John Chandos, John Haudlo and Giles of Argentein. Robert of Kendal and Henry Leyburn were members of Gaveston's own household: Hamilton, 138, n. 52. The group also included Henry and Humphrey de Bohun, and Roger Mortimer of Wigmore; and two more knights with an Irish connection, Walter de Bermingham and Thomas de Verdon.

[223] *CFR, 1272–1307*, 543–4: there is no suggestion however that the Prince of Wales should not have left Scotland since the young knights were accused of 'deserting the king and his son in those parts, in contempt of the king and to the retarding of the king's business there'.

[224] *CCR, 1302–07*, 481–2.

[225] Doherty (D.Phil.), 15–16, citing C 47/29/5/25; *Vitae Paparum Avenionensium*, ed. E. Baluze, iii (Paris, 1921), 43–4, 46, 54–5.

[226] *CCR, 1302–07*, 521; BL, Add. Ms. 22923, f. 14v.

[227] *Registrum Simonis de Gandavo*, ed. C.T. Flower & M.C.B. Dawes (London, 1934), 243; Johnstone, 118.

[228] *CCR, 1302–07*, 525.

holding a parliament since 25 January. Although some of the parliament's business concerned the situation in Scotland, relations with France and the prince's marriage would seem to have been the major items. Until the cardinal put in an appearance, there was little to be done.[229] Peter of Spain eventually joined Edward I at Carlisle on 12 March and dined with him on 13 and 14 March.[230] On the 15th the cardinal announced the terms which had been agreed between the pope and Philip IV of France. They were apparently simple and straightforward: if Edward I gave final approval to the marriage between Edward and Isabella, then Philip would restore the whole of the duchy of Aquitaine, without reservation, saving only the homage due for these lands.[231] On the following day the archbishop of York announced Edward I's acceptance of the terms, despite continuing concerns about the castle of Mauléon.[232] On 22 March orders were given to the bishops of Worcester and Coventry & Lichfield, the earls of Lincoln, Warwick and Richmond, and seventeen others to join the Prince of Wales in London on 22 May and to accompany him to France to meet the French king and to bring the peace 'lately treated under a certain form and not yet finally concluded . . . to a happy and prosperous ending'.[233] Nothing further is stated about the purpose of the proposed visit, but it is clear that no binding promises had been made at Carlisle and that further, possibly tough, negotiations lay ahead.[234] In the persons of the bishop of Coventry & Lichfield, the earl of Lincoln, and Hugh Despenser, amongst others, Edward would be accompanied by negotiators with long experience of Anglo-French relations, who would not give away anything of importance. While it is possible that, if the planned negotiations in France had been successful, they would then have been followed by his homage as duke of Aquitaine for the lands he held from the king of France, and perhaps even by his marriage, it is unwise to assume either of these outcomes. The surviving documents do not make any mention of an actual wedding or of any preparations for one. It is also unwise to assume

---

[229] The parliament was due to meet on 20 Jan. but its start was delayed because of poor attendance: Johnstone, 117. For the business of the parliament see Prestwich, *Edward I*, 551–2; *PROME*, Hilary Parliament, 1307.

[230] *Foedera*, I, ii, 1009; E 101/684/11, no. 7; E 101/370/15, m.3; Doherty (D.Phil.), 16.

[231] H.G. Richardson, 'The Parliament of Carlisle, 1307', *EHR*, liii (1938), 430, 436. The details of the cardinal's message are contained in a newsletter, headed *Noveles du Parlement*, preserved in C 49/3/18. See also *Lanercost*, 206.

[232] *Guisborough*, 370–1; Richardson, 'Parliament of Carlisle', 436; Prestwich, *Edward I*, 551; Johnstone, 120.

[233] *CCR, 1302–07*, 530–1.

[234] This explains why Johnstone could find no trace of the tripartite indenture she supposed was drawn up to embody the terms of an agreement made at Carlisle (one part for each of the three interested parties (England, France and the papacy) in the National Archives in England: Johnstone, 119–20. There is also no trace of such a document in the AN in France, or in the ASV in the Vatican City. This surely implies that since Prince Edward did not in the end go to France in 1307 the agreement was never completed.

that if there had been a wedding it would have been held at Poitiers in the presence of Philip IV and Clement V.[235] The two rulers did meet at Poitiers in April but both had long departed the city before Edward and his companions could even have left England.[236] It is also known that orders were given to the sheriffs of seven English counties to purvey supplies of wheat, some of it to be delivered to Le Crotoy in Ponthieu by 22 May and some to a place described as '*Poyteres* in Ponthieu' by 25 June.[237] Large quantities of poultry were bought by Ralph of Wendover, the yeoman of the prince's poultry for delivery in Ponthieu, amounting to 105 swans and twenty-eight herons,[238] presumably in anticipation of feasting on a large scale. If alive, it is hard to imagine these birds being taken all the way to Poitiers; if dead, they would scarcely be edible after such a long journey.[239] At a guess, it seems more likely that they were for consumption somewhere closer at hand and that Edward planned to perform his homage and perhaps even to be married at a place in French territory adjacent to Ponthieu, such as Boulogne, where his homage to Philip IV and marriage to Isabella were to take place in January 1308, or Amiens, where he did homage to Philip V in 1320.

Whatever the original intentions, Edward was at Dover from 26 April to 5 May, after which he returned to London; also on 5 May, the bishop of Coventry & Lichfield, who would have played a leading part in the negotiations in France, left for Scotland; by 27 May preparations were already being made for his own return to Scotland, and on 6 June the expedition to France was cancelled altogether.[240] The reasons for the change of plan are not known in any detail but it is clear from a letter which Edward I sent to Clement V in early July that once again the French failure to hand over the castle of Mauléon was at the heart of the problem.[241] There were

---

[235] Doherty (D.Phil.), 16.

[236] Menache, *Clement V*, 26, 178. Clement V left Poitiers on 15 May 1307. Doherty (D.Phil.), 16, and Johnstone, 122, both assume that the prince's intended destination was Poitiers. Doherty argues that the marriage was to take place there but does not cite any specific evidence for this.

[237] Johnstone, 122, n. 2. She suggests that '*Poyteres* in Ponthieu' is a slip in place of 'Poitiers', due either to the chancery scribe or to the editor of *CPR, 1301–07*, 509, which might after all indicate that Edward had planned to go to Poitiers. However, the text in the original roll, C 66/128, m.23, clearly reads '*Poyteres in Pontivio*'. It is also noticeable that Crotoy, although mentioned several times in the same set of entries on the roll, is not specified as being in Ponthieu, whereas '*Poyteres*' is. This suggests that there was a danger of its being confused with Poitiers and that the location was therefore described carefully. It has not however been possible to find a place in Ponthieu with a name like '*Poyteres*'.

[238] BL, Add. Ms. 22923, f. 4; Johnstone, 124.

[239] Two of the swans died in a murrain, so the birds were previously alive: BL, Add. Ms. 22923, f. 4; Johnstone, 124.

[240] BL, Add. Ms. 22923, ff. 3v,15v; E 101/370/15, m.4; E 101/370/16, f. 66; *CCR, 1302–7*, 506; Doherty (D.Phil.), 18.

[241] C 47/29/5/25, reproduced in Doherty (D.Phil.), App. 3. The letter was sent only days before Edward I's death on 7 July.

so many twists and turns in Anglo-French relations, so many failures in communication, and so much mutual mistrust that no outcome was ever certain.[242] Edward and Isabella's eventual marriage at Boulogne-sur-Mer in January 1308, after Edward had become king, was achieved only after intensive and difficult last-minute negotiations which continued even as the marriage was celebrated.[243]

The plans for Edward's marriage had been the main reason for Cardinal Peter of Spain's visit to Carlisle. This was a duty he was performing on behalf of the pope, but there was an unexpected element in his mission, which suggests he may have been playing another game entirely. Peter was well aware of the connections between Prince Edward and Spain through his mother Eleanor of Castile. In a letter to the pope in early 1307 Edward I spoke of Peter of Spain as someone 'who, we hear, should have a special affection for our dear son Edward, since he is of Spanish descent and from that land the cardinal also originated'.[244] The young Edward was also conscious of the value of the connection, having sent the cardinal a cope embroidered with pearls and valued at £60 in 1302–3.[245] According to a newsletter, the cardinal had brought with him to Carlisle an indenture to which the 'counts and barons of the land of Spain' were party, to the effect that in event of Ferdinand IV of Castile dying childless, then as his mother's son the next king of Castile should be Prince Edward of England.[246] There was some plausibility in this story, since Fernando, though married, was still childless, and the kingdom of Castile was in a very disturbed state. On the other hand, whether Peter of Spain had really been authorized to make such a proposal by a group of Castilian nobles, or whether, as Peter Linehan suggests, Edward I had been fishing in troubled Spanish waters for his own possible advantage,[247] there is no way of knowing. In any event the claim to the Castilian throne was not pursued,

---

[242] The process conducted by English and French commissioners at the town of Montreuil-sur-Mer in May and June of 1306 was a recent example of another unsuccessful attempt to resolve Anglo-French differences: see G.P. Cuttino, *English Diplomatic Administration, 1259–1339*, 2nd edn (Oxford, 1971), 13–14, 62–84. The final outcome of these unresolved problems, together with other new ones, was to be the Hundred Years War.

[243] See Brown, 'Repercussions', 573–95; and idem, 'The marriage of Edward II of England and Isabelle of France: a postscript', *Speculum*, lxiv (1989), 373–9.

[244] *Foedera*, I, ii, 1007; Johnstone, 128 (cited in trans.).

[245] E 101/363/18, f. 21v and *CDS*, ii, 369; Johnstone, 128.

[246] Johnstone, 120–1. Richardson, 'Parliament of Carlisle', 436; Linehan, 'The English mission', 615–16. There was no accompanying suggestion that Edward should marry Ferdinand's sister, Isabella, as had been proposed in 1303: Johnstone, 88–9.

[247] Linehan, 'The English mission', 618. Linehan also suggests that the chronicle of Archbishop Roderick of Toledo which was found in the exchequer in 1320 had been used by Edward I to support a possible claim: Linehan, 618, n. 62. It is more likely however that it had belonged to Eleanor of Castile. As Linehan remarks, Pedro Rodriguez, the cardinal bishop of Sabina, better known as Peter of Spain was 'an operator on the grand scale' and 'everyone's friend', so there is no knowing what personal motives he may have had: Linehan, 612–13.

and Ferdinand IV of Castile died in 1312, having at last produced an heir, who succeeded him as Alfonso XI.[248]

THE FIRST EXILE OF GAVESTON

There was one further dramatic turn of events in 1307, which occurred at Lanercost in February and is known principally through the highly coloured but possibly suspect account of the chronicler Walter of Guisborough. According to Guisborough, the Prince of Wales persuaded the bishop of Chester (i.e. Coventry & Lichfield), against his better judgement, to go to the king and ask for the county of Ponthieu to be granted to Gaveston. Edward I was furious and summoned his son, whom he described as the son of a whore and abused roundly for wanting to give away royal lands, allegedly saying that but for the threat to the unity of the kingdom he would have disinherited him. The episode supposedly ended with the king seizing Edward's hair in both hands and tearing out as much as he could before throwing him out of the room. The king then summoned his barons and with their advice ordered that Gaveston should never receive any lands from his son, and decided to send Gaveston into perpetual exile, under pain of death. Edward was made to swear that he would never grant any lands to Gaveston.[249]

It seems extraordinary that Walter Langton, bishop of Coventry & Lichfield, the king's treasurer and most influential adviser, should have been prepared in any circumstances to convey such a request from Edward to his father. If however Edward was determined to promote Gaveston's career, he could not do so without his father's agreement and could not obtain that without first winning Langton's support. It would be a very risky strategy which put his fate in the hands of a man with whom he had quarrelled bitterly less than two years earlier. Edward I's anger at his son's wish to give away the county of Ponthieu, which had been the personal inheritance of Eleanor of Castile, would be all too predictable. By this stage in his life, Edward I's temper was on a knife edge. If the hair-pulling incident really did occur it was while Edward I was awaiting the arrival of Cardinal Peter of Spain with the latest proposals concerning the marriage of Edward and Isabella. One of the details to be agreed was

---

[248] Wendy Childs has shown that in the early 14th century the English government was well informed about Spanish affairs and maintained close relations with the kingdoms of the Iberian peninsula. See W.R. Childs, 'England in Europe in the reign of Edward II', in *The Reign of Edward II*, ed. G. Dodd & A. Musson (Woodbridge, Suffolk & Rochester, NY, 2006), 104–10.

[249] *Guisborough*, 382–3. For a translation of Guisborough's account see Hamilton, 35. I have deliberately not quoted Guisborough's words directly since, as we shall see, they are exaggerated and in most major respects inaccurate or cannot be confirmed. No other chronicler speaks of the incident with the same amount of circumstantial detail: Johnstone, 123. Another chronicler claims that the king knocked his son down and kicked him: Haskins, 'A chronicle', 75.

the dower to be bestowed upon Isabella. This had not been settled in early 1307 but it is possible that Edward I considered using Ponthieu for this purpose and would therefore be even more angry if his son had tried to divert it to his friend Gaveston. It is probably no coincidence that on the day of their marriage, 24 January 1308, Edward II assigned dower to his new wife, Isabella, from the revenues of Ponthieu.[250]

The official record of the events of February 1307 confirms that Gaveston was to be sent into exile but differs from the picture given by Walter of Guisborough in every other significant detail. The memorandum entered on the Close Roll reports that at Lanercost on Sunday, 26 February, the king ordained and ordered 'for certain reasons' that three weeks after the next tournament, which would be held a fortnight after Easter (30 April), Sir Peter de Gaveston should be ready to cross the sea at Dover for Gascony, and to remain there without returning 'until he shall be recalled by the king and by his permission'. On the same day, 26 February, Gaveston swore a solemn oath 'upon God's body, the cross of Neit[251] and upon the other relics of the king'. The Prince of Wales swore on the same relics that 'he would not receive or retain Sir Peter near him or with him contrary to the ordinance . . . unless he be recalled or granted leave by the king'. Gaveston was to receive 100 marks sterling (£66 13s 4d) per year from the revenues of Gascony to cover his expenses while he remained overseas 'during the king's pleasure and awaiting his recall'. The first year was to commence the day after Gaveston had crossed from Dover to Wissant on the way to Gascony, and Gaveston would continue to receive this sum until the king had time to enquire into Gaveston's resources in England; after which the king would 'increase or decrease the estate of Sir Peter according to his pleasure and as shall seem good to him'.[252] There is no mention of the specific reason for Gaveston's exile, so we are left to speculate on what precisely the Prince of Wales had sought to do. There is nothing to confirm Walter of Guisborough's claim that Gaveston was to go into permanent exile. Instead Gaveston would clearly be able to live in modest comfort, against the day when he would be recalled to England. Neither was Gaveston to leave the country immediately: he was to have over two months to prepare and evidently was to be allowed to attend the forthcoming tournament. Finally, there is no mention in the Lanercost oaths of 26 February of Gaveston being forbidden in the future to receive any lands from the Prince of Wales.

Edward I may well have hoped that once Gaveston had been sent to Gascony he would go home to his native Béarn and stay there. In the

---

[250] Brown, 'Repercussions', 588, 592–3 (printing the text of AN, JJ 44, f. 67, no. 103).

[251] *Y Groes Naid*, the relic of the True Cross seized from the Welsh in 1283 and presented to Westminster Abbey in 1284: Davies, *The First English Empire*, 27. The relic was in the king's chapel in 1300 and was evidently taken around with the king: *Liber Quotidianus Garderobae*, 27.

[252] *CCR, 1302–07*, 526–7; the original French text is printed in *Foedera*, I, ii, 1010.

event Gaveston's exile proved to be comfortable and of short duration. Prince Edward lavished presents on him prior to his departure, including two outfits each bearing Gaveston's coat of arms, for wearing at tournaments, five horses and £260 in cash.[253] He also gave Gaveston some of the swans and herons which had been bought in anticipation of Edward's own intended visit to France.[254] Gaveston was accompanied to Dover by Prince Edward and two minstrels,[255] but instead of going to Gascony, he went to Crécy in Ponthieu at the prince's orders and remained there or in its vicinity for the duration of his stay.[256]

The generous treatment of Gaveston strongly supports Hilda Johnstone's conclusion that 'Edward, not Peter, was at this stage the prime offender'.[257] However, in one of her early publications Johnstone made a half-suggestion which might go to the heart of the matter, when she remarked that Gaveston's stay in Ponthieu in 1307 'gave Hemingburgh [i.e. Walter of Guisborough] the ground for a highly-coloured story of the prince requesting his father to make Peter count of Ponthieu in his stead'.[258] This raises the intriguing but unprovable possibility that the story was not true and that there was another reason for Edward I's anger with his son in 1307. If Ponthieu was not the territory which Edward proposed to give to Gaveston, could it not instead have been the earldom of Cornwall, which was closely associated with the crown,[259] which Edward I intended to give to one of his sons, Thomas or Edmund, and which Gaveston did indeed receive only a few months later in August 1307?[260]

[253] BL, Add. Ms. 22923, ff. 12v, 17v; E 101/369/16, f. 12v.; Hamilton, 35–6, 138.

[254] BL, Add. Ms. 22923, f. 4.; Johnstone, 124. Gaveston was given 13 of the 105 swans bought for Edward's stay in France; six more were given to the patriarch of Jerusalem, the bishop of Durham, when he passed through Ponthieu on his way to England, and 84 were handed over to the receiver of Ponthieu; Gaveston got 22 of the 28 herons, and the patriarch the remaining six: Johnstone, 124.

[255] Edward was at Dover on 5 May, but whether this was the actual day of Gaveston's departure or whether Edward was still waiting there to know if he was to go to France himself to settle the final terms of his marriage is not clear: BL, Add. Ms. 22923, ff. 7v, 15v; Hamilton, 35, 138.

[256] BL, Add. Ms. 22923, ff. 5, 12v; Hamilton, 36, 139. He attended two tournaments while he was in Ponthieu and also entertained Anthony Bek, bishop of Durham and patriarch of Jerusalem. Gaveston's household while in exile consisted of two knights, seven yeomen, and seven other servants, as well as one of Prince Edward's yeomen, John de Baldwin, and six of his grooms: Hamilton, 36, 139. See also Johnstone, 'The county of Ponthieu', 452.

[257] Johnstone, 122–5; her opinion is followed in Hamilton, 34–6.

[258] Johnstone, 'The county of Ponthieu', 452, n. 108.

[259] The previous holder of the earldom was Edward's cousin, Edmund of Cornwall, who had died in 1301. If Edward had wanted to give this to Gaveston, his father's anger would have been even more certain than over Ponthieu.

[260] The nominal date of the charter was 6 Aug. but it could have been sealed as late as 17 Aug.: see Chaplais, 27–9. On Edward I's plans for the earldom see ibid., 30–1, n. 49; Maddicott, 71. The statement by the anonymous author of a chronicle composed in the 1320s that Prince Edward had wanted to give Cornwall and not Ponthieu to Gaveston in Feb. 1307 has been discounted, but perhaps the writer was correct: Haskins, 'A chronicle', 75; Johnstone, 124, n. 1.

The fact that the charter granting the earldom to Gaveston was the very first one to be issued in the reign of Edward II strongly suggests that the grant had already been considered before Edward became king. It is likely that, just as Edward's own knighting had been accompanied by his investiture as duke of Aquitaine, so he felt that Gaveston's knighthood should be accompanied by an appropriate territorial endowment, whether Ponthieu, as is generally believed, or Cornwall, as seems more probable. If Edward really did consider Gaveston as his brother, this would also help to explain why he wished to grant him lands of such significance.

With Gaveston safely installed in Ponthieu and having abandoned his own planned visit to France, Prince Edward prepared to rejoin the war in Scotland. In May Robert Bruce defeated Aymer de Valence and the earl of Gloucester in separate encounters, forcing them to retreat to the castle of Ayr. The English position in Scotland was still apparently formidable in terms of strongpoints held,[261] but the balance of opinion was starting to shift against them. Everyone knew that Edward I would soon be dead and supporters of the English crown in Scotland feared for what might follow him. 'False preachers' were prophesying that after the death of '*le Roi Coveytous*' the Scottish people and the Britons (i.e. the Welsh) would ally against the English and live together in accord until the end of the world.[262] Edward I was determined to lead one more campaign in Scotland. The army was summoned to gather at Carlisle in early July. On 6 July Edward I reached Burgh-on-Sands, ready to enter Scotland, and on the following day he died. For good or ill, his son, Edward of Caernarfon, Prince of Wales, Duke of Aquitaine, Earl of Chester and Count of Ponthieu, was now King of England.

Edward was also twenty-three years old, younger and less experienced than his father had been at his own succession in 1272, but considerably more mature than any other thirteenth- and fourteenth-century king of England: Edward's grandfather Henry III, for example, was only nine years old when he succeeded in 1216 and Edward's own son Edward III was fourteen in 1327. But like any other heir to the throne, his suitability for the task could not be fully tested in advance. As long as his father lived and remained physically capable of governing, the young Edward would have to wait. Inevitably some of his time was spent in leisure pursuits with close friends and companions, such as Gaveston and others; just as inevitably, leisure pursuits which were unaccompanied by major responsibility were bound to appear to an unsympathetic observer as frivolous and the money

---

[261] For the situation in 1307-8 see the map in Barrow, 167.

[262] *CDS*, ii, 513 (no. 1926), 536-7: this is a letter written from Forfar on 15 May 1307 by an unknown author to a high official, which gives a vivid impression of the situation in Scotland. The 'false preachers' were probably mendicant friars spreading anti-English propaganda. This pattern can be observed in both Scotland and Ireland at this period: Phillips, 'Edward II and the prophets', 191; idem, 'The Remonstrance revisited', in *Men, Women and War, Historical Studies*, 18, ed. T.G. Fraser & K. Jeffrey (Dublin, 1993), 19, 26-7.

spent on them as extravagance. He had however gained some limited experience of government in his early years when he represented his father during the crisis of 1297, and later through the routine activities of his own household and council. The surviving roll of letters for 1304–5, for example, suggests that he was engaged with and active in business which concerned him. There is nothing to suggest either, as Hilda Johnstone argued, that 'his childhood and early youth had entirely lacked that atmosphere of affection and security which had surrounded Edward I'.[263] In fact he had abundant contacts within his own family and with the nobility, and appears to have possessed good social skills. When he made friends, he showed loyalty to them in times of difficulty, such as during the estrangement from his father in 1305. If anything he was too loyal, as his attachment to Gaveston showed all too clearly. His level of education was probably no more and no less than that of his father Edward I or of his son Edward III. By the time he succeeded to the throne he had gained substantial military experience. While there is nothing to suggest any special abilities as a commander in the field, neither is there anything to suggest ineptitude. He was always ready to go to war and remained so when king.

No 'king-in-waiting' could ever be completely ready for the task, but there is no reason to suppose that Edward 'would feel the obligations of kingship to be uncongenial' or that he might decline to accept them altogether.[264] Although some of the personal weaknesses that were to dog his reign as king were already apparent, most notably his reliance on favourites, Edward's readiness for the throne in 1307 should not be judged in the knowledge of the disasters which lay ahead of him and which led to his deposition and death in 1327. In 1307 Edward was reasonably well prepared both in character and experience for the responsibilities he was about to undertake.[265] What neither he nor his contemporaries fully understood or allowed for were the problems he inherited from his father: an almost empty treasury and administrative confusion; an intractable war with Scotland; difficult relations with France; growing problems of law and order; and a restless nobility.[266] It would take very little for any of these problems to blow up into a major crisis early in the new reign.

---

[263] Johnstone, 128.
[264] Ibid., 127.
[265] My assessment of Edward's personal qualities and experience is more positive than, for example, those of Johnstone, 127–31, and Prestwich, *Plantagenet England*, 178.
[266] See the discussion of the legacy of problems left by his father in Prestwich, *Edward I*, 565–6; idem, *War, Politics and Finance*, 221–3; R.W. Kaeuper, *War, Justice and Public Order* (Oxford, 1988), 139–40, 174–6.

Chapter 4

CONFLICT AND REFORM, 1307–1312

PART ONE

THE ACCESSION OF EDWARD II

Edward I died on 7 July 1307, the feast of the Translation of St Thomas of Canterbury.[1] On the following day, which counted as the first day of the new reign, urgent messages were sent to Prince Edward, the queen, and the earl of Lincoln to tell them the news.[2] Edward was in or near London when he received the news of his father's death on 11 July,[3] and immediately set out for Carlisle which he reached on the 18th. In the meantime the old king's death was kept secret, presumably to avoid giving encouragement to the Scots, and anyone who spread news of it was imprisoned.[4] On 19 July Edward went to Burgh-on-Sands 'to weep for his father',[5] and on the following day he was proclaimed king at Carlisle castle. 'And therefore the younger Edward succeeded the elder, but in the way in which Rehoboam succeeded Solomon, as events were to prove.'[6]

Despite the speed with which Edward learned of his accession, the news did not reach the capital formally until Tuesday, 25 July. Until then Edward I's chancellor, Ralph Baldock, the bishop of London, continued to seal writs with the Great Seal, 'because he had no certain knowledge of the king's death before that day'. The chancellor acted with the advice of

---

[1] Prestwich, *Edward I*, 556–7 (morning); Chaplais, 23 (afternoon).

[2] E 101/370/16; Prestwich, *Edward I*, 557. According to *Lanercost*, 207, fast messengers (*nuncii festini*) were sent to the prince. It would be understandable if their messages were primarily oral rather than written. Something similar happened in 1327 when Edward III was informed 'during the night' (*de deinz la nuyt*) of his father's death at Berkeley on 21 Sept.: DL 10/253 (dated at Lincoln, 24 Sept.: letter from Edward III to John de Bohun, earl of Hereford).

[3] E 101/373/15, f. 43v. Edward is recorded at both Lambeth and London on 10 July. The daily household roll, E 101/373/7, m.1, shows he was at Lambeth on 8 July.

The movements of Edward II during his reign can be followed in *Itinerary*, ed. Hallam, which makes use of evidence from the records of the royal household and other sources. When reference is made to the royal itinerary, it may be assumed that this publication is the source, unless otherwise stated.

[4] *Guisborough*, 379 (not *Lanercost*, 207, as stated in Johnstone, 127, n. 1); Prestwich, *Edward I*, 557.

[5] *Lanercost*, 207. This was also the day on which a collection of silver vessels and plate was handed over to Walter Reynolds for Edward's use: E 101/369/19.

[6] *Lanercost*, 209.

members of the old king's council but, significantly, was also assisted by the two senior members of Prince Edward's household, William of Blyburgh his chancellor and Walter Reynolds, keeper of his wardrobe. On Saturday, 29 July, Baldock received letters from Edward recording that Anthony Bek the bishop of Durham, Henry de Lacy the earl of Lincoln, and other earls and barons who had gathered at Carlisle in readiness for the planned campaign in Scotland had done homage and fealty to him there as king, and ordering the chancellor to send him his father's seal. This was duly done on Tuesday, 2 August.[7] In the meantime, on 22 July, at Carlisle Edward II had issued his first document as king under 'the privy seal which we used before we undertook the government of the kingdom'.[8]

On 31 July Edward II left Carlisle for Scotland and on 4 August arrived in Dumfries where he took the homage and fealty of the remaining Scottish supporters of the English crown.[9] Also at Dumfries, on 6 August, Edward issued the first charter of his reign, creating his friend and 'brother' Piers Gaveston earl of Cornwall. It was to be one of the most fateful decisions of his career.

THE RETURN AND PROMOTION OF GAVESTON

When Edward I died Gaveston was still in comfortable exile in Ponthieu. The question immediately arose of what would happen to him next. The oaths which Gaveston and Edward had taken the previous February provided for the possibility of Gaveston's recall to England at the king's pleasure. But according to the anonymous author of the *Brut* chronicle, Edward I had on his deathbed enjoined the earls of Lincoln, Warwick and Pembroke, and Robert de Clifford, to look after the welfare of his son and, above all, not to allow Gaveston to return and lead Edward into a life of riot.[10] While it is possible that Edward I's attitude towards Gaveston had hardened during his brief period of exile, this statement should not necessarily be taken at its face value any more than Walter of Guisborough's highly misleading account of the circumstances leading up to the exile. The earl of Lincoln and the others were in any case among Edward I's main councillors and it was to be expected that they would be asked to give their support to the new king. The new king's pleasure was of course all too

---

[7] These and other details are recorded on the Fine Rolls and the Patent Rolls: *CFR, 1272–1307*, 558–9; *CPR, 1301–07*, 537. The homage of the bishop and the earl was also reported on 30 July in a letter written from Scrooby in Nottinghamshire to Sir Hugh de Neville by one of his valets, DL 34/12.

[8] *Itinerary*, ed. Hallam, citing C 47/24/3, no.1b.

[9] *Lanercost*, 209. The chronicler also remarked that 'despite the fearful vengeance inflicted upon the Scots who adhered to Bruce, the number of those willing to strengthen him in his kingship increased daily': *Lanercost*, 207; Barrow, 173.

[10] *Brut*, i, 202–3. Aymer de Valence did not in fact become earl of Pembroke until Oct. 1307: Phillips, 25.

certain. Edward II's letters recalling Gaveston were probably sent on or soon after 11 July when Edward first heard of his father's death; and Gaveston himself probably arrived back in England in early August.[11] From London he travelled swiftly to Carlisle and from there to Scotland, where he rejoined Edward. Gaveston does not appear to have been at Dumfries on 6 August, the date of his creation as earl of Cornwall, but he was certainly at Sanquhar, 25 miles north-west of Dumfries, by 17 August.[12]

Despite claims in the *Annales Paulini* that the earls burnt it when Gaveston went into exile for the second time in 1308, the original charter creating Gaveston earl of Cornwall still survives.[13] In a brilliant piece of research Pierre Chaplais discovered that the charter was not written by a clerk of the chancery, as would be usual, but by Thomas de Neuhay, a clerk of Edward II's wardrobe. He also deduced that, although the charter was probably ordered on 6 August and may even have been written on that date, it could not have been sealed then, since the seal used was Edward I's Great Seal, which had been sent from London on 2 August at the king's orders. On arrival in Scotland the seal had been modified, probably by a local goldsmith, for use in the new reign, and was employed for Gaveston's charter. The latest possible date on which this could have been done was 17 August, after which the Great Seal was no longer with the king.[14] Chaplais is surely right in his conclusion that Edward II ordered the Great Seal to be sent from London to Scotland with the sole purpose of using it to authenticate Gaveston's creation as earl. This implies that Edward had decided that the promotion of Gaveston would be his first act when he became king,[15] and supports the suggestion in the previous chapter that the earldom of Cornwall rather than the county of Ponthieu was the source of the estrangement between Edward and his father earlier in 1307. Gaveston's charter was witnessed by no fewer than seven earls: Lincoln, Lancaster, Surrey, Hereford, Arundel, Richmond and Pembroke. It is hard to believe that they would have allowed their names to be attached if they had not actively approved or at least consented to Gaveston's elevation.[16] However,

---

[11] Chaplais, 23–6 (who suggests 6–13 Aug. as the time of his return); Hamilton, 37, 139 (who suggests that Gaveston was in London within two weeks of Edward I's death).

[12] Chaplais, 26: in June 1308 Edward II told both the pope and Philip IV that Gaveston had been absent at the time of the grant and was unaware of it: *Foedera*, II, i, 49–50; Chaplais, 28. Hamilton, 37, implies that Gaveston was at Dumfries on 6 Aug. but this does not seem possible.

[13] Chaplais, 27; Hamilton, 146–7, n. 1. The original document is E 41/460; in its enrolled form it is recorded on the Charter Roll, C 53/94, m.9. Photographs of different portions of the charter are published in *English Royal Documents*, ed. P. Chaplais (Oxford, 1971), 61, plate 8b, and Chaplais, facing 18.

[14] Chaplais, 27–9. While the seal was in the king's custody it was used to authenticate only four documents in total, all of them concerned with the grant of the earldom of Cornwall to Gaveston.

[15] Ibid., 28.

[16] Ibid., 31. This has been a general opinion among modern scholars: Phillips, 27, n. 1; Hamilton, 37; Maddicott, 70–1; Tout, *Place of the Reign*, 14 and n. 5.

the absence of the earl of Warwick from the witness list may have been an early indication of his future hostility to Gaveston.[17] On 17 August Gaveston celebrated his new status with a feast at Sanquhar which was attended by the king, the earls of Lincoln and Hereford, and the earl of Lancaster, one of whose minstrels also performed.[18] On 1 November Gaveston's status was even further enhanced when he married Edward II's niece, Margaret, the sister of Gilbert de Clare the young earl of Gloucester. The ceremony held at Berkhamsted was attended by the king and a number of leading magnates, and was followed by another lavish feast.[19]

TAKING UP THE THRONE

From Sanquhar Edward II moved to nearby Cumnock on about 20 August. According to a later and unreliable tradition, Edward I had called his son to his side and made him swear that on his death 'he would have his body boiled in a large cauldron until the flesh could be separated from the bones; that he would have the flesh buried, and the bones preserved, and that every time the Scots should rebel against him he would summon his people, and carry with him the bones of his father; for he believed most firmly, that as long as his bones should be carried against the Scots, those Scots would never be victorious'.[20] As Michael Prestwich has remarked, this reflects Edward's later reputation, rather than recording a genuine deathbed scene.[21] Edward II's movements were not however the prelude to the great campaign which his father had planned. By early September he was back at Carlisle, having first appointed Aymer de Valence as the English commander in Scotland and then on 13 September replacing him with the earl of Richmond.[22] Edward left Carlisle and moved south via York, spending most of the second part of September at the royal manor of Clipstone in Nottinghamshire. In mid-October he spent some days at his favourite retreat, Langley in Hertfordshire, and was back at Westminster by 27 October.

Edward II did not appear in Scotland again for another three years and in the meantime the English position there had begun the almost irreversible slide which ultimately led to Scottish independence. Yet it was not, as Geoffrey Barrow has argued, the result of exchanging 'the masterful directing hand' of Edward I for 'the wilful *insouciance* of the new king'.[23]

---

[17] Maddicott, 71.

[18] E 101/373/15, f. 19; Chaplais, 26–7.

[19] Hamilton, 38, 140. It is likely, as Pierre Chaplais suggested, that Gaveston and Margaret de Clare had been betrothed earlier, perhaps even before his creation as earl of Cornwall: Chaplais, 32–3.

[20] Prestwich, *Edward I*, 557, citing the chronicles of Jean Froissart composed much later in the fourteenth century.

[21] Ibid., 557.

[22] Phillips, 25.

[23] Barrow, 173.

Edward II was not a reluctant warrior but he had good and urgent political, financial and personal reasons for abandoning the campaign in Scotland.

THE FALL OF LANGTON

Political and financial concerns overlapped in the person of Walter Langton, bishop of Coventry & Lichfield, who had been treasurer and one of the most influential royal advisers since 1295. During that period the royal finances and their administration had deteriorated under the pressures of war into a state of confusion. Although the overall picture could not then be known, it is now estimated that the crown had debts of about £200,000 at the time of Edward I's death and that as much as £60,000 of this was outstanding as late as the 1320s.[24] What could not be in any doubt was that the king owed money to many people, ranging 'from his officials and bankers at one end of the spectrum to infantry soldiers and workmen at the other'. While they might tolerate this situation under a king whom they respected and feared and in aid of a war in Scotland, for which there was general support,[25] their toleration was unlikely to extend to a new and untried king. No individual, however powerful, could really be blamed for the mounting financial problems, but Walter Langton was an obvious target, especially since the new king had personal scores of his own to settle with him.

Edward II's determination to bring down Langton therefore came second only to his determination to promote Gaveston. Langton was arrested by three knights acting on the direct orders of the king on about 7 August at Waltham in Essex.[26] He ceased to act formally as treasurer on 19 August and was replaced three days later by Walter Reynolds, Edward's old ally and the keeper of his wardrobe as Prince of Wales.[27] Langton was

---

[24] Prestwich, *Plantagenet England*, 175–7. The classic account of the financial problems of the reign of Edward I and their consequences is Prestwich, *War, Politics and Finance*.
On 1 Oct. Edward II gave orders for the treasurer to pay two separate sums of 20,000 marks, one for the expenses of the royal household and the other to Edward I's executors for the expenses of executing his will and of his funeral: C 81/58/ 22, 23. It is not clear whether either order was fulfilled. The order to the chancellor on 25 March 1308 to be at the exchequer daily to decide with the treasurer and other members of his council how the royal household could be kept supplied with money suggests that the situation was desperate: C 81/59/120.

[25] Prestwich, *Plantagenet England*, 176.

[26] *Records of the Trial of Walter Langton, Bishop of Coventry and Lichfield, 1307–1312*, ed. A. Beardwood, vi (London, 1969), 1.

[27] Ibid., 1; Fryde et al., *Handbook*, 104 (when changes in the holding of offices of state are noted, this is the source unless otherwise stated). At about the same time Ralph Baldock, bishop of London, who had been chancellor only since April 1307, was replaced by John Langton, bishop of Chichester, who had held the same office between 1292 and 1302. Another major office in the articulation of royal government, that of keeper of the privy seal, was filled by William Melton, another confidant of the new king who had earlier served the Prince of Wales as controller of his wardrobe and as chamberlain of Chester. For a more detailed account and discussion of the administrative appointments made at the beginning of the new reign see Tout, *Place of the Reign*, 69–72.

first imprisoned at Wallingford, then at Windsor, and finally in the Tower of London; his lands were seized and his personal treasure found and paid into the wardrobe;[28] his debts were collected on behalf of the crown; and on 4 October a proclamation was issued in the names of Gaveston and Reynolds inviting individuals to present their grievances against Langton. The proceedings that followed lasted until 1310–11 and produced ample evidence of corruption and abuse of office.[29] This completed the fall of a mighty minister, who had exercised power on a scale comparable with a Tudor official, and who had even built himself a palace modelled on Edward II's birthplace at Caernarfon.[30]

Langton's treasure was not sufficient to meet Edward II's financial needs. Writs of summons for a parliament to meet at Northampton on 13 October had already been issued at Cumnock on 26 August even before the new king left Scotland.[31] The first item of business appears to have been to secure a grant of taxation, which was duly made by the laity on 13 October. The clergy made a separate grant, possibly following an agreement by the king that Robert Winchelsey, the archbishop of Canterbury, who had gone into exile after falling out with Edward I, could return to England.[32] The taxation was urgently needed to finance the continuing war with Scotland,[33] to which the earl of Hereford and fifteen other magnates were sent on 18 October.[34] But money was also necessary to pay for the costs first of Edward I's funeral, the date of which was probably settled at Northampton,[35] and then of Edward II's marriage and coronation which were also discussed there.[36]

THE FUNERAL OF EDWARD I

Edward I's body had first been brought from Burgh-on-Sands to Richmond in Yorkshire and afterwards to Waltham abbey in Essex where it lay for over

[28] According to *Guisborough*, 383, the lands were worth 5,000 marks p.a. and the treasure amounted to £50,000 in silver plus gold and jewels. The exact sums are unknown but these figures are certainly much exaggerated: *Records*, ed. Beardwood, 2, n. 5. In the month of Oct., for example, sums of money totalling nearly 2,000 marks, which Langton had deposited in the abbeys of Thorney and Leicester, and the priory and castle of Kenilworth, were paid into the king's wardrobe: E 101/373/15, f. 2v.
[29] *Records*, ed. Beardwood, 1–7. The details of Langton's debts are preserved in E 13/31, and the complaints against him in JI 1/1344. These are all edited in Beardwood. For a commentary on Langton's trial see Beardwood, 'Trial of Walter Langton', 1–45.
[30] Hughes, 'Walter Langton', 7.
[31] *PW*, II, ii, 1–14. For further details see *PROME*, Parliament of Oct. 1307.
[32] The archbishop had been suspended from office by Pope Clement V in Feb. 1306 and was still in exile in France: Denton, *Robert Winchelsey*, 231–6, 244–6.
[33] *Lay Taxes*, 29; *PW*, II, ii, 15–16; Maddicott, 71–2.
[34] *CCR, 1307–13*, 43.
[35] *Guisborough*, 379.
[36] The writs of summons state that the funeral, marriage and coronation would all be on the agenda: *PW*, II, ii, 1.

two months.[37] On about 18 October the body was taken to London and then to Westminster Abbey,[38] where the funeral service was held on 27 October.[39] The ceremony was presided over and the eulogy delivered by Anthony Bek, the bishop of Durham and patriarch of Jerusalem, an old companion and a recent adversary of Edward I,[40] but also a good friend of Edward II who was to play an important role in the early years of the new reign.[41] He was assisted by the bishops of Winchester and Lincoln who read the Gospel and the Epistle.[42] Edward I was remembered elsewhere: the news of his death on 7 July reached Pope Clement V at Poitiers two weeks later and here the pope performed solemn obsequies for him, exalting 'the strength of his rule, his sense of justice and clemency, his crusading fervour, and his many successes against all enemies'. This was a unique papal tribute in honour of a secular ruler.[43] In sharp contrast to the fine effigy and elaborate tomb which were to be constructed over Edward II's body in the 1330s, Edward I was laid in a simple tomb of polished Purbeck marble without an effigy, except for a wooden figure which may have lain on the coffin during the funeral service. Wax candles were kept burning around the tomb and were maintained both by Edward II and by his successors.[44] The reason for the simplicity of the tomb is unknown, but it was 'plainly intentional' and 'cannot be attributed to Edward II's fecklessness'.[45] There is nothing to tell us of Edward's behaviour or demeanour at his father's funeral but for him

---

[37] DL 34/12; Prestwich, *Edward I*, 558.

[38] On its arrival in London the body had lain for successive nights in the church of Holy Trinity, then in St Paul's cathedral, before being taken to the churches of the Franciscan and Dominican friars. Masses were said for the former king in each of these, before his body was taken to Westminster Abbey where solemn masses were said by five bishops and by Cardinal Peter of Spain: *Guisborough*, 379.

[39] By comparison, Edward II's funeral in 1327 took place three months after his death. The organization of a royal funeral would have taken some considerable time and would also, as in 1327, have to yield place to other pressing events. There is nothing to suggest that Edward II delayed his father's funeral through any lack of feeling.

[40] Prestwich, *Edward I*, 558, where it is suggested that the eulogy known as the *Commendatio Lamentabilis* and written by John of London contains material from Bek's sermon. See also Weiler, 'The Commendatio', 114–30. For the text see *Chronicles*, ed. Stubbs, ii, 3–21.

[41] The young Edward of Caernarfon had known Bek since at least 1293. On 4 Sept. 1307 Edward II showed his regard for the bishop by restoring to him the liberties of the diocese of Durham: *Foedera*, I, i, 5. On Bek's career see the article by C.M. Fraser in *Oxford DNB*.

[42] *Guisborough*, 379–80. There are no other details of who was present.

[43] Menache, *Clement V*, 248; Prestwich, *Edward I*, 558. See also Walter Ullmann, 'The curial exequies for Edward I and Edward III', *Ecclesiastical History Review*, vi (1955), 26, 30–2; and D. L. D'Avray, *Death and the Prince* (Oxford, 1994), 70–9, 168–71.

[44] Prestwich, *Edward I*, 566. P. Lindley, *Gothic to Renaissance* (Stamford, 1995), 102, however argues that the suggestion of a wooden figure is mistaken.

[45] Binski, *Westminster Abbey*, 120. The funeral cost a total of £473, but nothing is known about the making of the tomb. It contrasted in its simplicity with the tombs of his father, his first wife Eleanor of Castile, and his younger brother Edmund of Lancaster, all of whom were buried at Westminster: see M. Duffy, *Royal Tombs of Medieval England* (Stroud, 2003), 92–9; Binski, *Westminster Abbey*, 107–20.

it was the second family bereavement in a few months, his sister Joan of Acre, countess of Gloucester, to whom he was very close, having died the previous April.[46]

MARRIAGE AT LAST

Edward II's marriage to Isabella of France was also a major issue. It had first been agreed in the Treaty of Montreuil in 1299; Edward and Isabella had been betrothed in 1303 following the Treaty of Paris; and twice, in 1305 and earlier in 1307, it had appeared that the marriage would soon take place. On each occasion it had been delayed because of the failure of English and French negotiators to settle outstanding problems over Aquitaine and over the details of the marriage agreement. To make matters even more urgent, Isabella would soon be twelve years old and the canonical age to marry. Edward II would have to make good his promise to marry her or repudiate the contract and provoke a crisis in Anglo-French relations which might even lead to a renewal of war in Gascony.

There is nothing to suggest that Edward II was for any reason unwilling to proceed with the marriage, whether through personal antipathy, the influence of Gaveston or the opinion of any of his advisers.[47] But, like his father, he first wanted to be sure that the terms offered by France would be sufficient, and a final period of intensive negotiation therefore began. A memorandum drawn up by Philip IV's advisers and sent to England early in the autumn of 1307 shows that Edward II had hoped that Isabella would bring with her a handsome marriage portion and that he hoped that Philip would compromise over such long-standing problems as appeals to the Paris *parlement* against the decisions of Gascon judges. Philip IV replied bluntly that he was giving with his daughter the duchy of Aquitaine and all Edward's continental lands, which had been properly forfeited to the French crown. This was her portion, and the king of England should be pleased to have it. Had it not been for the marriage and the French king's hopes to see a grandchild hold the lands, he would never have considered relinquishing them. Philip even threatened to charge Edward with the costs of administering his continental territories while they were in French hands and in the last resort to declare the duchy of Aquitaine forfeit once more, as he had done in 1294.[48]

---

[46] Joan's funeral at Clare priory in Suffolk was attended by Edward and many of the nobility: BL, Cotton Ms., Cleopatra, C.III, f. 293 (extracts from the Dunmow Chronicle).

[47] As implied in Doherty, *Isabella*, 42–3.

[48] Brown, 'Repercussions', 575–8, citing AN, J 654, no. 8 (the text is printed in ibid., 589–92). Cardinal Peter of Spain, who was present at Edward I's funeral, appears to have continued to offer mediation, while the French were represented by Louis of Évreux, who was Isabella's uncle but also on good personal terms with Edward II. Louis probably brought the memorandum just referred to. His meeting with Edward in London in early Nov. was clearly the prelude to the mission appointed by Edward II on 6 Nov.: E 101/373/7, m.2.

On 6 November Edward appointed the bishops of Durham and Norwich, the earls of Lincoln and Pembroke, and others to go to France to agree the terms of Isabella's dower and to conclude other outstanding matters. The delegation arrived at Boulogne, which had evidently already been agreed as the location of the marriage ceremony, on 25 November, at the same time as a section of the royal household which had been sent ahead to make the necessary arrangements.[49] In December Edward made his way to the Channel coast in preparation for the crossing to France. He spent Christmas with Gaveston at Wye in Kent, a manor belonging to the abbot of Battle, and on 26 December appointed Gaveston to be *custos regni* in his absence.[50] A letter from Edward II to Philip IV dated at Canterbury on 30 December shows that discussions about the marriage were continuing until the last moment. In reply to a proposal from Philip, whom he already addressed as 'our most dear lord and father', Edward agreed that they should both arrive at Boulogne on Sunday, 21 January, and that the marriage should take place on Wednesday, 24 January 1308.[51]

By the middle of January Edward was at Dover where he made a series of important decisions preparatory to leaving for France. On 18 January Gaveston's authority as *custos regni* was defined as including the power 'to issue licences to elect, grant royal assents, make restitution of temporalities, collate and present to prebends and other ecclesiastical offices, and deal with wardships and marriage during the king's absence from the kingdom'.[52] On the same date the leading clergy, earls and barons were commanded to attend Edward II's coronation at Westminster on 18 February; and on 19 January further orders were issued for a parliament to meet at Westminster on 3 March.[53]

In the event the king crossed to France on 22 January, a day later than planned.[54] The slight delay in the crossing was probably caused by something as simple as the weather or by last-minute bargaining on the dower that Edward II would present to his wife on their wedding day, and there is no reason to suppose any deliberate discourtesy on Edward's part.[55] On 24 January Edward II agreed to increase the value of Isabella's dower from the sum of 18,000 *livres tournois* (£4,500), initially agreed as far back

---

[49] *Foedera*, II, i, 11–12; E 101/624/15, m.1; Phillips, 25. See also Lalou, 'Les Négociations', 346. Boulogne was a convenient meeting place, in French territory but near to the English-controlled county of Ponthieu.

[50] *Foedera*, II, i, 24; *CPR, 1307–13*, 31; *Ann. Paul.*, 258.

[51] 'notre trescher seigneur e pere': *Foedera*, II, i, 25. A facsimile of the enrolled copy of the letter (C 70/2, m.8) is printed in E. M. Hallam, *English Royal Marriages* (London, 1981), doc. v. The possible failure of the marriage negotiations had been allowed for in the powers assigned to the envoys appointed by Edward II on 6 Nov.: E.A.R. Brown, *Customary Aids and Royal Finance in Capetian France* (Cambridge, Mass., 1992), 15, n. 9.

[52] *Foedera*, II, i, 28; *CPR, 1307–13*, 43.

[53] *Foedera*, II, i, 27; *PW*, II, ii, 18–19.

[54] *CCR, 1307–13*, 18.

[55] Cf. Doherty, *Isabella*, 43.

as 1299, to 20,000 *livres tournois* (£5,000). The dower was to be drawn from the revenues of the county of Ponthieu, with the addition of revenue from the Agenais in Aquitaine and in England if these were insufficient. Philip IV tried unsuccessfully to make Edward seal a document in which the undertakings concerning the dower were to be made to Philip himself and not to Isabella.[56] On 31 January Edward II performed his long-delayed homage to Philip IV for the duchy of Aquitaine and also for the county of Ponthieu, and the Treaty of Paris of 1303 was confirmed.[57] A commission was appointed to settle mutual problems arising from the recent war, but for his pains Edward was also presented with a lengthy list of complaints about the government of his continental lands.[58]

In the midst of all this hard and probably acrimonious bargaining a wedding ceremony did in fact take place on 25 January in the cathedral church of Notre Dame in Boulogne.[59] The details of the occasion are not recorded but it is known that it was attended by many European figures of the highest rank: as well as Philip IV himself, there were three future kings of France, his three sons, Louis, Philip and Charles, and their wives; Philip IV's brothers, Charles of Valois and Louis of Evreux; Louis de Clermont, Hugh de Bourgogne and his brothers, Robert count of Flanders and his brothers, the lord of Nesle, the count of Namur, John duke of Brabant and his wife Margaret (Edward II's sister), the count of Hainault, Robert of Artois, Louis count of Nevers, Guy count of St Pol, the count of Dreux, and the count of Savoy; as well as many archbishops and bishops.[60] Those present on the English side are not named directly but certainly included important figures such as Edward I's widow, Queen Margaret who was Philip IV's sister and Isabella's aunt; Anthony Bek, the bishop of Durham and patriarch of Jerusalem; Aymer de Valence, earl of Pembroke (who

---

[56] Brown, 'Repercussions', 578–80. The relevant documents are AN, J 633, nos. 29, 29 bis (no. 29 is printed in Brown, 'The marriage', 377–9), and AN, JJ 44, f. 67, no. 103 (printed in Brown, 'Repercussions', 592–3). The permanent assignment of dower lands to the value of the original £4,500 was not completed until March 1318, after the death of Edward I's widow, Margaret, made some of her own dower lands available for reassignment: *CPR, 1292–1301*, 451–3; *CPR, 1317–21*, 115–16.

[57] Brown, 'Repercussions', 578; AN, J 633, no. 26. The document states that Edward performed the homage '*personellement*' to Philip IV '*solonc les fourmes du pees et des acors*', but does not make any mention of his also performing fealty. When Edward II performed homage to Philip V in 1320 he was also asked to perform an act of fealty and refused to do so, saying that he had neither been asked for nor had done fealty at Boulogne in 1308: Chaplais, *Diplomatic Practice*, vol. i, 359–60 (no. 199), citing C 47/29/9/25. See also the record of the five acts of homage performed by English kings between 1259 and 1320 in *Chartulary of Winchester Cathedral*, ed. A.W. Goodman (Winchester, 1927), 62–5 (no. 127).

[58] Brown, 'Repercussions', 578, 580–2 (the demands are preserved in C 47/29/6/4).

[59] *Ann. Paul.*, 258; *Flores*, 141; E 101/373/7, m.3. There is a depiction of Edward and Isabella at their wedding in a manuscript of Jean de Wavrin's *Chroniques d'Angleterre* (ending in 1336), made in Flanders, c. 1470–80, for Edward IV: BL, Royal Ms. 15. E.iv, f. 295v.

[60] Lalou, 'Les Négociations', 346, n. 120.

had close French connections of his own); the earls of Lincoln, Surrey and Hereford; and important baronial figures and royal councillors such as Hugh Despenser and Robert de Clifford. Edward II hosted a celebration of the marriage (*festum generale post nupcias Regis*) on Sunday, 28 January, and on Tuesday, 30 January, the brothers of the king of France and many French nobles dined with him and his new queen.[61] Philip IV presented his daughter with lavish wedding gifts of jewels, plate, furs, robes and other furnishings, worth a total of over 21,000 *livres*,[62] and gave the cathedral a gilded silver reliquary containing a fragment of the True Cross,[63] while Edward's wedding gift to his new wife was probably the fine illuminated manuscript now known as the Isabella Psalter.[64]

GAVESTON AND EDWARD: 'TWO KINGS IN ONE REALM'?

Edward and Isabella left Boulogne on 2 or 3 February and crossed in separate vessels to Dover, where they landed on the 7th. On 9 February Gaveston's term of office as *custos regni* formally ended when the Great Seal, which Edward had taken with him to France, was restored to the chancellor.[65] However Gaveston's arrogant behaviour, his relations with the king and his supposed influence over the government of the kingdom were such lively issues that the author of the *Vita Edwardi Secundi* remarked of Gaveston's appointment as *custos regni*, 'What an astonishing thing, he who was lately an exile and outcast from England has now been made governor and keeper of the same land.'[66] The St Paul's annalist wrote that there were 'two kings reigning in one kingdom, one in name

---

[61] E 101/373/6, m.2. A facsimile of this portion of Edward II's household accounts is printed in Hallam, *English Royal Marriages*, doc. vi. See also E 101/373/7, m.3.

[62] The wedding gifts are described and their value given in AN, J 631, no. 4: for the text see W.E. Rhodes, 'The inventory of the jewels and wardrobe of Queen Isabella (1307–8)', *EHR*, xii (1897), 517–21; see also Lewis, 'Apocalypse', 225–6. There is no evidence to support claims that Philip the Fair paid Edward II enormous sums as the marriage portion of Isabella or that these sums came from the confiscated treasure of the Templars. Philip was parsimonious in his dealings both with Edward I and Edward II and despite the lavish wedding gifts did not provide Isabella with a traditional marriage portion. This did not prevent him from trying, with mixed success, to obtain an aid for the marriage from his subjects: Brown, *Customary Aids*, 19, 25–33, and *passim*. Examples of the resistance encountered by Philip IV can be found in the 34 documents from communities in the diocese of Cahors: AN, J 356 (all dated 1309).

[63] Lewis, 'Apocalypse', 232: the fragment probably came from the Sainte-Chapelle in Paris.

[64] Now preserved as Codex Gall. 16 in the Staatsbibliothek in Munich. See also ch. 2. Lewis, 'Apocalypse', 234, however argues that the psalter was commissioned by Edward I's widow, Queen Margaret, who was also Isabella's aunt, but presents no evidence other than 'Edward's scarcely disguised indifference to his bride in preference to his favourite Gaveston'.

[65] The details are recorded in *CFR, 1307–19*, 14. See facsimile from C 60/106, m. 8 in Hallam, *English Royal Marriages*, doc. vii. In the light of later controversies it is significant that one of those present on 9 Feb. was Edward II's first cousin and future opponent Thomas, earl of Lancaster.

[66] *Vita*, 8–9.

and the other in deed', while the *Vita* spoke of Gaveston as 'a second king'.[67] The chroniclers were uniformly hostile and, like today's tabloids, fed on any gossip about Gaveston that was going and when in doubt exaggerated or made it up. Gaveston was accused of having pillaged the royal treasury, with the active connivance of the king, and of sending vast sums of money to his native Gascony, with the connivance of foreign merchants.[68] It was also believed that the taxation granted by parliament in August 1307 had been misused and squandered by Gaveston[69] and that the treasure and other valuables seized from the disgraced treasurer, Walter Langton, had been given to him by the king.[70] Much was also made of the fact that Edward had sent Philip IV's wedding presents to Gaveston in England, even before his own return from France.[71] Gaveston's appointment as *custos regni* was in itself a cause of outrage among the nobility, since this was a position that was usually reserved for a king's son or other close relative.[72] Gaveston was also accused of using his authority to his own advantage, most notably by interfering in the election of a new abbot of Westminster.[73] Gaveston did himself no good in the eyes of his fellow earls when on 2 December 1307 he held a tournament at his castle of Wallingford to celebrate his marriage, at which he and 'almost all the younger and harder knights of the kingdom, whom persuasion or reward could bring together' roundly defeated the earls of Arundel, Hereford and Surrey and their followers.[74]

Some of the charges that were levelled against Gaveston were inaccurate and malicious. There is no evidence that he plundered royal treasure and sent money abroad, or that he profited financially from the fall of Walter Langton, although he did receive sums of money from the wardrobe at intervals in 1308.[75] There are a few examples of Gaveston using his access to the king to influence the flow of patronage, but he appears to have exer-

---

[67] *Ann. Paul.*, 259; *Vita*, 4–5 ('for the great men of the land hated him, because he alone found favour in the king's eyes and lorded it over them like a second king, to whom all were subject and none equal'). Hugh Despenser the Younger was also accused later in the reign of behaving like a second king: Chaplais, 103, n. 62.

[68] *Trokelowe*, 64–5, 8; Haskins, 'A chronicle', 75–6; *Guisborough*, 383; Chaplais, 99–101.

[69] *Lay Taxes*, 29; Maddicott, 71–2.

[70] *Ann. Paul.*, 257; *Guisborough*, 383; Hamilton, 38, 139; Chaplais, 100–1.

[71] *Ann. Paul.*, 257–8.

[72] Chaplais, 34–40.

[73] Hamilton, 45, 144; Chaplais, 61–4.

[74] *Vita*, 6–7; *Ann. Paul.*, 258–9; Hamilton, 45,144. According to the St Paul's annalist, Gaveston caused further anger among the earls and barons at another tournament which he held at Faversham in Kent to celebrate the king's marriage. A third tournament, due to be held at Stepney to mark the coronation, was cancelled by the king when Gaveston reported that the earls would have him killed if he took part: *Ann. Paul.*, 259.

[75] Hamilton, 38, 139–40; Chaplais, 99–104. In 1311 the Ordainers also claimed that Gaveston had appropriated the royal treasure, even though they must have known this to be untrue: Chaplais, 99, 101, 105.

cised his powers as *custos regni* during the king's absence in France in late January and early February 1308 with caution and circumspection.[76] Yet his behaviour towards his fellow earls at this time aroused great enmity against him. 'He adopted such a proud manner of bearing towards them, that the earls coming before him to discuss business were forced to kneel in order to bring their reasons before him, because he did not value them and did not heed the advice of the sage who said: "A sudden reverse awaits those who, raised high in pride from poverty, know neither reason nor measure and have no care" '.[77] When Edward II was greeted by his leading magnates at Dover on his return from France he caused offence and added still further to the hostility against Gaveston by allegedly running to him and 'giving him kisses and repeated embraces'.[78] Even allowing for some exaggeration, there is no reason to doubt the general accuracy of the picture recorded by the chroniclers.

Pierre Chaplais has convincingly argued that the description in some of the chronicles of Gaveston as Edward II's *camerarius*[79] should be understood as referring to Gaveston's formal appointment to the office of chamberlain, or administrative head of the king's chamber, rather than simply to a position of familiarity. He also suggests that this appointment took place between Gaveston's creation as earl of Cornwall in August 1307 and the holding of parliament at Northampton the following October, and that it formed a precedent for the appointment of the Younger Despenser to the same office later in the reign.[80] If this were the case, it would then be legitimate for valuables, such as Philip IV's wedding gifts, to be sent to Gaveston, 'who also happened to be at the time keeper of the realm', for safe lodgement in the king's chamber. Chaplais also argues that in doing so Edward II did not intend to insult Philip IV.[81] This may have been the case, but it is also worth remembering Philip IV's parsimony towards his daughter and son-in-law: Edward may therefore have been making a point after all.[82] On the other hand Edward II's judgement was seriously at fault if he thought that he could make the man he regarded as his brother into the holder of an earldom closely associated with the crown, appoint him as chamberlain with custody of his most valuable possessions,

---

[76] Hamilton, 45–6, 144–5. He may however have become too closely involved in the Westminster dispute for his own good: Hamilton, 144, n. 67; Chaplais, 61–4.

[77] Hamilton, 46, citing the *Polistorie* of Christ Church, Canterbury, BL, Harley Ms. 636, f. 232. The translation is Professor Hamilton's.

[78] *Trokelowe*, 65; Hamilton, 47.

[79] *Vita*, 4–5; *Ann. Paul.*, 258–9; Chaplais, 101–3.

[80] Ibid., 103–4. In 1308 special stables to house Gaveston's horses were built in the section of the palace of Westminster known as the privy palace, the area inhabited by the king and queen, their immediate servants, and any noblemen who enjoyed particular royal favour, such as Gaveston then and Roger Mortimer under Queen Isabella after 1327: *KW*, i, 534.

[81] Chaplais, 104.

[82] Brown, *Customary Aids*, 19, 25.

and also give him the office of *custos regni*, without arousing hostility both among the English nobility and among a wider public. It was also all too easy for opponents to place whatever spin they wished on Gaveston's activities, especially when Gaveston himself went out of his way to create animosity. To make matters even worse, Edward II had succeeded in arousing the anger of his father-in-law, who was becoming determined that Gaveston should be removed from England, and probably also the hostility of his new wife Isabella.

THE BEGINNINGS OF REFORM

On 31 January 1308, the day on which Edward II performed homage for the duchy of Aquitaine, another significant event took place at Boulogne when the bishop of Durham, the earls of Lincoln, Surrey, Pembroke and Hereford, Robert de Clifford and several other magnates and royal administrators sealed an agreement in which they declared that they were bound by fealty to preserve the king's honour and the rights of his crown, undertook to do everything possible to protect and maintain the king's honour, and promised to redress and amend everything that had been done against the king's honour in the past (*avant ces heurs*) and all forms of oppression against the king's subjects which had occurred and were still happening from day to day.[83] None of the parties to the agreement was personally hostile to the king and it is likely that they were thinking chiefly of the consequences of the continuing inconclusive war with Scotland, which had overstretched the royal administration, left the monarchy heavily in debt, and created political tensions between the king and his subjects, who objected to excessive taxation and administrative abuses. These were serious issues, which had been partially suppressed in the closing years of the reign of Edward I but which were bound to resurface in a new reign with a less experienced and less formidable monarch at the helm. It was a good moment, with the coronation due in a few weeks' time, to offer Edward the possibility of achieving financial and administrative reform with the support and encouragement of a group of experienced and loyal subjects. There is nothing to suggest that the Boulogne Declaration was directed against Edward II personally. Neither was it aimed directly against Gaveston in any obvious way, although his behaviour and influence must certainly have been in the minds of those who agreed to it. It is possible too that, in promising to preserve the king's honour and the rights of his crown, they also had in mind the pressures which were then being applied against Edward II by his new father-in-law,

---

[83] For the text of the Boulogne Declaration see Phillips, 316–17. An original once existed as Cotton Charters, Faustina 24, but is no longer extant; a copy was found in the archives of the earl of Lancaster in 1322 (DL 41/1/37, m.7), but also no longer exists. It is known only through two seventeenth-century transcripts in Bod., Dugdale Ms. 18, ff. 1v and 80.

Philip IV.[84] The Boulogne Declaration was essentially designed to help Edward rather than impose restraints upon him, but the warning signs were there and the benign reform programme foreshadowed at Boulogne and possibly, as suggested below, acceptable to Edward II was soon followed by demands for reform of a much more far-reaching and personal kind.[85]

PREPARATIONS FOR THE CORONATION

Edward II's plans for his coronation began with splendid intentions but ended in discord and scandal. The palace of Westminster had suffered damage in a fire in 1298 and from subsequent neglect arising from Edward I's lack of money and frequent absences in Scotland. When Edward II succeeded to the throne in 1307 'he inherited a half-ruined palace': everywhere, apart from the Great Hall and the king's own chamber, 'there were blackened walls, rotten timbers, broken windows and mouldering plaster'.[86] Repair work began at once and continued even after dark by the light of candles. 'So many men were at work that a great horn had to be blown to summon them in the morning and to dismiss them in the evening.'[87] The Painted Chamber was retiled and work began, under the supervision of the king's painter Thomas of Westminster, on the restoration of its wall paintings depicting the coronation of St Edward the Confessor and scenes from the Old Testament. Master Thomas also painted two wooden leopards which stood on the gables of the Lesser Hall of the palace and which held metal banners bearing the king's arms. Around the same time a temporary chapel of St Stephen was set up in a building attached to the exchequer to provide a place of worship for the palace. Statues of St Mary and St Stephen were painted and gilded by Master Adam the Imager and placed on two standards.[88] Altogether more than £3,000 was spent on repairs and embellishments to Westminster Palace during the first year of Edward II's reign.[89]

[84] Brown, 'Repercussions', 574–82. As already indicated, these pressures related to the duchy of Aquitaine and to Isabella's dower, but Edward II's initial refusal to follow Philip IV's arrest of the Templars in Nov. 1307 should be added to them: ibid., 585–6, 594–5. The best account of Edward II's attitude to the Templars and of the proceedings against them is in M. Barber, *The Trial of the Templars*, 2nd edn (Cambridge, 2006), 217–29, esp. 217–20.

[85] Phillips, 26–8. See also Maddicott, 72–3; Hamilton, 46–7; Prestwich, *Plantagenet England*, 179.

[86] *KW*, i, 505.

[87] *KW*, i, 506.

[88] *KW*, i, 507, 513. On the history of the Painted Chamber and the details of the paintings (which are known only from 19th-century copies made before their destruction in the fire of 1834) see Binski, *Painted Chamber*, 17–24, 96–103, between 83 and 84, and at the end of the volume. See also Binski, *Westminster Abbey*, 127.

[89] *KW*, i, 507. Details of the work were recorded in a book of almost 100 folios, now in E 101/468/21. A summary of the repairs made to the palace, 1307–11, is contained in E 101/468/15: *KW*, ii, App. D, 1041–4. Over £400 was still owed in 1324 for the repairs carried out in 1308: SC 1/17/28.

Temporary buildings were constructed for the day of the coronation. A timber hall extending the whole length of the river wall by the palace and at least 500 feet long was built for the ceremony of the king's enthronement, and was specially strengthened to withstand the pressure of people wishing to see the king upon his throne. The throne was repaired and above it in an arch stood a statue of a king cast in copper and gilded. Fourteen smaller halls were built parallel to the 'strong and solemn hall' and extended almost to the gate of the palace, leaving only just enough room for men on foot and on horseback to enter. Forty ovens were built to cook the coronation banquet and 'every vacant space in the palace and the nearby abbey was filled with forms, trestles and tables'. A fountain, 'flowing day and night with red and white wine and a spiced drink known as *pimento*', and fed by underground lead pipes, was installed.[90] For the banquet in Westminster Hall there were two high tables, each with a marble top, one of which was renewed for the occasion.[91] Inside Westminster Abbey itself a wooden staging was built in the middle of the choir. The chairs in which Edward II and Isabella would be crowned were set up on this platform which was so high 'that men at arms could ride on horseback beneath it without stooping'.[92] The sedilia paintings in Westminster Abbey, depicting two unidentified kings, were probably also made by Master Thomas of Westminster for Edward II's coronation.[93]

THE CORONATION

The ceremony was originally due to take place in Westminster Abbey on 18 February, a significant date since it was also the feast of the Translation of St Edward the Confessor and probably chosen for that reason. The coronation was however delayed at the last moment until 25 February. This was ostensibly to allow the archbishop of Canterbury more time to come back to England in order to perform the ceremony[94] but, according

---

[90] *KW*, i, 506–7.

[91] The tables were already present during the reign of Edward I and were apparently permanent fixed structures rather than trestle tables which could be moved away after use: Biddle, ed., *Round Table*, 41; *KW*, i, 544.

[92] *KW*, i, 507. The elevated staging was one of the requirements of the new Coronation Order used in 1308: Binski, *Westminster Abbey*, 130. The chair used by Edward presumably contained the Scottish Stone of Destiny. Edward II was the first English king to be crowned upon it, but it is not clear whether he believed this gave him an additional claim to rule over Scotland.

[93] Evans, *English Art*, 22, n. 1. She suggests that one of the kings is meant to be Edward the Confessor. Binski, *Westminster Abbey*, 124–6 (incl. a photograph on p. 125), suggests that the kings may represent founders of the abbey, such as Sebert and Edgar. The *sedilia* painting is reproduced in Saaler, *Edward II*, facing p. 82, as a depiction of Edward II, and in Prestwich, *Edward I*, front cover and facing p. 144, where it is described as a 'figure of a king, very probably either representing, or modelled on, Edward I'.

[94] Denton, *Robert Winchelsey*, 246–7; Hamilton, 47. In the event the archbishop's return was to be delayed through illness until 24 March and the coronation was performed by the bishop of Winchester, deputizing for Winchelsey.

to the *Annales Paulini*, the leading English magnates and the French magnates who had come to England for the coronation refused to allow the ceremony to proceed unless Gaveston was first banished from the kingdom. Edward II was not prepared to concede this but he temporized by allegedly agreeing 'in good faith to undertake whatever they sought in the next parliament', which was due to meet on 3 March.[95] It has also been suggested that another reason for the delay was a disagreement between the king and the magnates about the form of the oath which Edward II would take at his coronation. This topic has exercised historians for many years and this is not the place to rehearse all the arguments put forward.[96] Briefly, the debate centres on the purpose of the clause which was added to the oath in 1308, and in which Edward swore to uphold 'the rightful laws and customs which the community of the realm shall have chosen'.[97] The wording could mean that Edward was being asked to promise that he would accept future legislation which might be imposed upon him and limit his freedom of action. On the other hand, the clause might be intended to avoid a repetition of the actions of Edward I, who had a habit of going back on his promises and who in 1305 had obtained a papal decree releasing him from his undertakings.[98]

There is however an alternative view of the coronation and of the coronation oath.[99] It is possible that the position of Gaveston and the need for

---

[95] *Ann. Paul.*, 260; Hamilton, 47; Maddicott, 73, 83. A letter written to Edward II by Philip IV on 9 Feb. says that Charles of Valois and the other French representatives at the coronation would inform him more fully by word of mouth concerning 'certain matters which greatly touch our honour and your own': SC 1/34/7. The business could of course also have concerned the outstanding issues surrounding Isabella's dower and the duchy of Aquitaine as well as Gaveston.

[96] In chronological order, some of the main contributions to this debate are: B. Wilkinson, 'The coronation oath of Edward II', in *Historical Essays in Honour of James Tait*, ed. J.G. Edwards, V.H. Galbraith & E.F. Jacob (Manchester, 1933), 405–16; Richardson & Sayles, 'Early coronation records', *BIHR* (1936, 1936–7, 1938); Richardson, 'English coronation oath', *TRHS* (1940); B. Wilkinson, 'The coronation oath of Edward II and the Statute of York', *Speculum*, xix (1944), 445–69; Richardson, 'The English coronation oath', *Speculum*, xxiv (1949), 44–75; R.S. Hoyt, 'The coronation oath of 1308', *Traditio*, xi (1955), 235–57; Hoyt, 'The coronation oath of 1308', *EHR*, lxxi (1956), 353–83; Richardson, 'The coronation in medieval England', *Traditio*, xvi (1960), 111–202; D. Sturdy, ' "Continuity" versus "change" ', in *Coronations*, ed. J. M. Bak (Berkeley, 1990), 228–45, esp. 235–8.

[97] For the text of the oath see *Foedera*, II, i, 33 (Latin), 36 (French); *Select Documents*, 4 (both Latin and French versions).

[98] In Dec. 1305 Clement V released Edward I from the pledges he had made to the nobility in the *Confirmatio Cartarum* of 1297 and the *Articuli super Cartas* of 1300: Menache, *Clement V*, 251–3; Prestwich, *Plantagenet England*, 179. Professor Prestwich makes the point that 'at the time, as later, the clause meant different things to different people': ibid. However, H.G. Richardson long ago suggested that the actions of Edward I rather than Edward II were the real reason for adding the clause in 1308: 'English coronation oath' (*TRHS*), 135; Tout also argued that it was necessary to take into account the events of Edward I's reign when assessing the beginning of that of Edward II: Tout, *Place of the Reign*, 71–6.

[99] I have radically changed my views on the coronation oath since writing the article on Edward II for the *Oxford DNB* and the Introduction to the March 1308 parliament in *PROME*.

reform were initially at least two entirely separate matters; that, as R.S. Hoyt argued, there was 'no certain connexion between political events and the oath';[100] and that 'Edward II, in an attempt to foster an atmosphere of political amity and cooperation at the beginning of his reign, sought means to restore the rapport between crown and magnates which had been eroded under Edward I.'[101] Although H.G. Richardson's suggestion that a clause similar to the one added to the oath taken by Edward II in 1308 had already been part of his father's oath in 1274 can now be shown to be incorrect,[102] his argument that the revision of the coronation order which is known to have taken place at the beginning of Edward II's reign, and consequently of the coronation oath as a part of the order, was undertaken in a leisurely and considered manner should be taken seriously.[103] It is possible, for example, that the Boulogne Declaration of 31 January arose out of a discussion between the king and some of his leading councillors on the form of the forthcoming coronation and in particular of the coronation oath. It may be significant that several of those who were parties to the Boulogne agreement, the earls of Lincoln, Pembroke and Hereford, played a formal part in the coronation ceremony, while Robert de Clifford, who had been appointed marshal of England on about 3 September 1307 was responsible for the organization of

---

[100] Hoyt, 'Coronation oath' (*EHR*), 383.

[101] Sturdy, ' "Continuity" ', 237, following the lines of argument developed by Richardson and Hoyt.

[102] Richardson argued that a clause in which the king promised to do nothing affecting the rights of the crown without the counsel of the prelates and great men of the realm had been added in 1274: Richardson, 'English coronation oath' (*TRHS*), 131–5; Richardson & Sayles 'Early coronation records', 11 (citing a letter from Edward I to Pope Gregory X, 19 June 1275: *PW*, I, 381–2). However, the recent discovery by Dr Bernadette Williams of Trinity College Dublin of a copy of Edward I's oath suggests that there was no such additional clause on that occasion. I should like to thank Dr Williams for sharing her important discovery with me before publication: Williams, 'Coronation oath'.

[103] Richardson, 'English coronation oath' (*TRHS*), 141–4. On the newly revised Coronation Order used for Edward II, technically known as the Fourth Recension, see ibid., 99–102, 107, 110; J. Brückmann, 'The *Ordines* of the Third Recension of the Medieval English Coronation Order', in *Essays in Medieval History presented to Bertie Wilkinson*, ed. T.A. Sandquist & M. R. Powicke (Toronto, 1969), 99–102. For a description of the Coronation Order, as laid down in the Fourth Recension, see Binski, *Westminster Abbey*, 130–1. One of the early manuscript copies of the Fourth Recension, which may even be the service book carried by Edward II's confessor John de Lenham, for use at the coronation, is BL, Harleian Ms. 2901. This is not to be confused with the more famous manuscript of the Fourth Recension, the *Liber Regalis*, made later in the fourteenth century, and now preserved as Westminster Abbey Ms. 38. As Richardson noted, there is no sign in Harleian Ms. 2901 of the coronation oath being added in haste or modified as an afterthought: Richardson, 'English coronation oath' (*TRHS*), 143–4. The royal government's record of the Coronation Order is contained in the Coronation Roll, C 57/1. Again, there is no sign of any last-minute modification of the coronation oath. The oath appears twice in Harleian 2901, once in its Latin form in the main body of the text (ff. 4v–5r) and again at the end in its French form (ff. 49v–50v).

Edward II's coronation.[104] In effect they were offering the new king their support in reforming the royal administration and removing the sources of grievance left over from the reign of Edward I. In return Edward II would accept a new form of coronation oath. In addition to swearing to uphold the existing laws, described symbolically as the laws of St Edward the Confessor,[105] he would also agree to maintain future legislation provided that it was properly approved by himself and the community of the realm. If this line of argument is correct, the coronation oath was not revised with any revolutionary intention but by agreement and without external political pressure from the English magnates. Edward II was in effect offering a coronation charter, such as earlier kings up to Henry III had issued at their accession.[106] This would mean that he would not try to evade his undertakings as his father Edward I had done and that he would offer hope for an orderly redress of grievances in the future. It is therefore arguable that Edward II hoped to make his coronation an occasion of reconciliation as well as one of public display.

Although it is impossible to demonstrate any personal contribution by Edward II to the coronation order and its revision, it is likely that he also wanted the coronation to give a particular emphasis to the sacred quality of his monarchy: not only by his choice of 18 February as the original date for the coronation, but by the reference to the laws of St Edward in his coronation oath, the fact that he would take his oath in close proximity to the shrine of St Edward, and the use of items of regalia associated with St Edward in the coronation ceremony.[107] It has also been suggested that the music associated with the coronation was intended to lay further stress on the holiness of the English monarchy, especially perhaps in the presence of members of the French royal house, whose own family saint, Louis IX, had been canonized as recently as 1297.[108]

---

[104] Denholm-Young, *History and Heraldry*, 116, 131. He held office until March 1308, when forced to resign by the opposition magnates at the Council of Northampton. The planning of the coronation and the revision of the Coronation Order presumably therefore began no later than Clifford's appointment as marshal.

[105] The clause referring to the laws of St Edward was in itself an addition to the coronation oath. Cf. Richardson, 'English coronation oath' (*TRHS*) 149–50; F.W. Maitland, *Constitutional History of England* (Cambridge, 1908), 99–100.

[106] Richardson, 'English coronation oath' (*TRHS*), 129–30.

[107] See also the discussion of Edward II and St Edward in ch. 2 of this book. The shrine of St Edward and the regalia were not of course in themselves new in 1308, but gained in significance when combined with other 'Edwardian' elements. I have also benefited from an unpublished paper by J.C. Parsons, 'Rethinking English coronations, 1220–1308'.

[108] A. Hughes, 'The origins and descent of the Fourth Recension of the English Coronation', in Bak, ed., *Coronations*, 197–216. The melody of the Magnificat antiphon was drawn from that for St Edmund, king and martyr; the chant of *Unxerunt Salamonem* (the coronation anthem now known as Zadok the Priest) was restored to the order after its omission in the previous recension, and gave special emphasis to the anointing of the king with holy oil. Another significant change was the restoration, after two centuries, of *Vivat rex*, the acclamation of the new king, and its placing at the beginning of the service: ibid., 197–8. See also Hughes, 'Antiphons and acclamations', *Journal of Musicology*, vi, no. 2 (Spring 1988), 150–68.

The coronation may have been delayed, as the *Annales Paulini* claims, following threats from some of the English and French magnates, but the account in the annals is inclined to exaggeration and tends to telescope fast-moving and highly emotive events.¹⁰⁹ It is also both interesting and probably very significant that the well-informed and perceptive author of the *Vita Edwardi Secundi*, who is scathing in his criticism of Gaveston's behaviour before the coronation and gives a detailed account of the baronial movement against Gaveston in its immediate aftermath, provides a very different description of the event itself. He says nothing about the coronation being postponed because of dissension between the king and the magnates, and reports that the ceremony was conducted by the bishop of Winchester 'at the command and with the assent of the archbishop of Canterbury' who was 'prevented from being present by illness or continued absence abroad'. All that the *Vita* says of the occasion is that 'at the conclusion of the ceremony and the joyful wedding feast everyone went home'.¹¹⁰ The ceremony may genuinely have been postponed in the hope that the archbishop of Canterbury might still return to England in time to preside. But if Edward had intended his coronation to bring peace and harmony, he was to be disappointed. In practice it was impossible to separate the two great issues of Gaveston and reform. Edward was soon to find himself faced with demands which went beyond what he believed he had sworn to at his coronation.¹¹¹

The coronation took place amidst the crush of people that was inseparable from great events and probably took away some of its intended dignity and majesty. John Bakewell, a knight and former seneschal of Ponthieu, was killed when a wall collapsed; the king himself was allegedly forced to leave the palace via a back door on his way to the abbey in order to avoid the crowds; and the ceremony was, again allegedly, conducted in haste by the bishop of Winchester, assisted by the bishops of Salisbury and

Edward decided, after consulting his council, not to undergo a second anointing at his coronation with the Holy Oil of St Thomas, which his sister Margaret, duchess of Brabant, and her husband had brought with them and offered for his use: Phillips, 'Edward II and the prophets', 196–7.

¹⁰⁹ Richardson has shown that the account of the events of 1307–8 in the *Ann. Paul.* is often unreliable: 'The *Annales Paulini*', *Speculum*, xxiii (1948), 630–40.

¹¹⁰ *Vita*, 8–9 (for the coronation itself) and 7–9, 9–13 (for the comments on Gaveston). The *Vita* also says of Edward's marriage that 'when the marriage had been duly celebrated the king of England returned joyfully to England with his wife', again giving a picture at variance with that of the *Ann. Paul.*: *Vita*, 8–9. See also the discussion of the accounts of the coronation given by the contemporary chroniclers in Hoyt, 'Coronation oath of 1308' (*EHR*), 371–7.

¹¹¹ On 1 April, when political tensions were already fast developing, the chancellor was ordered to write to the Dominicans (an order especially favoured by Edward) who were about to assemble in their general chapter at Padua, asking them to pray for the soul of his late father 'and also to pray for the king that God may give him grace to govern his realm and people to the honour of God and their profit'. While such statements are usually taken as formalities, it is possible that Edward II really was anxious about his ability to govern well. This side of his character should not be as lightly dismissed as it usually is.

Chichester.¹¹² It was attended by many distinguished foreign guests including Isabella's uncles, Charles count of Valois and Louis count of Évreux; her brother Charles, the future Charles IV of France; John duke of Brabant and his wife Margaret, Edward II's sister; the duke of Brittany; Count Henry of Luxemburg (soon to become the emperor Henry VII); and the counts of St Pol and Savoy.¹¹³ Edward's half-brothers Thomas and Edmund were there, as was his sister Mary.¹¹⁴ The English earls, barons and knights of the shire and their wives were also present in force by royal summons. Many of the earls played a part in the coronation itself: the king's sceptre was borne by the earl of Hereford, the sword *curtana* by the earl of Lancaster and two other swords by the earls of Lincoln and Warwick; the royal vestments were carried by the earl of Arundel and others including Hugh Despenser and Roger Mortimer of Wigmore; Charles of Valois put the boot and spur on Edward's right foot. Some of those who took such a public part were to play just as conspicuous a role in the politics of the reign as they unfolded in the weeks and months to come, none more so than the earls of Lincoln and Lancaster, and of course the bitterly resented earl of Cornwall, Piers Gaveston, whose involvement in the coronation was all too conspicuous. He redeemed the sword *curtana* after the king made an offering of a pound of gold at the high altar; he carried the crown of St Edward before the king; the earl of Pembroke placed the boot on the king's left foot but it was Gaveston who then attached the spur.¹¹⁵

The annoyance that was probably caused by Gaveston's prominent place in the coronation ceremony was magnified by his behaviour during the banquet which followed. Gaveston was clothed in purple trimmed with pearls; the king allegedly preferred the company of Gaveston to that

---

¹¹² *Ann. Lond.*, 261. The author of the *Annales* may have an axe to grind in his emphasis on everything that he considered to have gone wrong with the coronation and the banquet that followed. Difficulties with crowd control on occasions of great excitement seem to have been common. A wall also collapsed when Clement V was crowned at Lyons in Nov. 1305, killing 12 people including the duke of Brittany; and two knights had been crushed to death when Edward was knighted in Westminster Abbey in May 1306: Menache, *Clement V*, 16–17; *Flores*, 132.

¹¹³ *Ann. Lond.*, 260; *Flores*, 141.

¹¹⁴ E 101/373/7, m.4. They had joined Edward and Isabella, at Eltham and the Tower of London respectively, a few days earlier. Mary had also been at Dover to meet her new sister-in-law, Isabella, on her arrival from France: E 101/373/15, f. 26v.

¹¹⁵ The liturgy of the coronation ceremony and the details of who performed what function are printed in *Foedera*, II, i, 33–6, from the text in the Coronation Roll, C 57/1. An abbreviated version appears in *CCR, 1307–13*, 53. See also Chaplais, 42–3. There is a representation of a king at his coronation, which is usually identified as either Edward II or Edward III and depicting a 'Glory of Regality', in Corpus Christi College Cambridge Ms. 20, f. 68. This manuscript which contains texts of the Apocalypse and the Coronation Order was made for Henry de Cobham *c.* 1330–9? (reproduced in J. Alexander & P. Binski, eds, *Age of Chivalry* (London, 1987), 201). Binski however argues that CCCC, Ms. 20 (and, by extension, the illustration) does represent the coronation of Edward II: *Westminster Abbey*, 130–1.

of his new wife and queen;[116] while above them hung specially made tapestries bearing not the arms of England and France but those of Edward II and Gaveston.[117] Isabella's relatives were enraged by her treatment, and one of the English earls allegedly wished to kill Gaveston on the spot.[118]

THE EXILE OF GAVESTON

By the end of February 1308 a major crisis in the affairs of the English crown was fast developing, a crisis for which Edward II bore much of the responsibility. It is possible to show that many of the more extravagant charges against Gaveston were ill founded and that the relationship between him and Edward was probably based on a deeply felt sense of brotherhood. It is also fair to note that although Edward had been expecting to marry Isabella since 1299, his new wife and queen was little more than a child whom he still barely knew. Isabella could not for some time to come be a companion and partner in either the emotional or sexual sense. Edward also had outstanding problems in his relations with Isabella's father, over her dower and over Aquitaine. Nonetheless Edward's lavishing of favour upon Gaveston, Gaveston's behaviour and Edward's neglect of Isabella were bound to lead to disaffection in England and to a souring of relations with France. All of this was avoidable. Edward II had spent the early months of his reign with good intentions with regard to reconciliation and reform yet he dissipated goodwill and turned friends into potential enemies by his obsessive attachment to Gaveston.

The intense excitement, the crowds of people gathered in and around Westminster, and the tensions generated during the coronation and the festivities which followed ensured that any crisis would swiftly come to a head. Such a situation arose almost at once with the parliament that had been summoned to meet at Westminster on 3 March. The earls and barons who were to attend were already of course at Westminster for the coronation and so had plenty of opportunity to lay their plans.[119]

The *Annales Paulini* records that the parliament met on 28 February and not 3 March,[120] which suggests that the heated atmosphere created by the events surrounding the coronation forced the king to allow parliament to start several days earlier than planned. The fact that it met in the monks'

[116] *Ann. Paul.*, 262; Hamilton, 48.

[117] Chaplais, 42–3, citing E 101/325/4, m.2; E 101/373/15, f. 51. The tapestries had been ordered from Ralph de Stoke on 26 Oct. 1307, and were clearly another part of Edward's detailed preparation for his coronation.

[118] *Ann. Paul.*, 262. It is necessary to keep saying 'allegedly' in relation to this account because of the possibility of exaggeration.

[119] See *PROME* for an account of the Westminster parliament of March 1308. This was an assembly consisting of the magnates, the higher clergy and royal administrators. Knights and burgesses were not summoned.

[120] *Ann. Paul.*, 262. The date is given as 28 Feb. in Hamilton, 48; Maddicott, 74.

refectory of Westminster Abbey rather than within the king's Palace of Westminster also suggests that the magnates went ahead with a meeting at a place and time of their own choosing, and that the king had no option but to agree. It appears that the king, continuing in the spirit of goodwill with which he had approached his coronation, invited the magnates to discuss 'the state of the Church, the state of the Crown which he had newly assumed and how it ought to be governed according to God and to justice, and how the peace of the land might be preserved for his people'. The magnates apparently refused to do this unless they were given a written commission and the king promised to accept their proposals. The parliament ended inconclusively on or shortly before 10 March, when it was ordered to reconvene on 28 April.[121] It appears that the earl of Lincoln, who had earlier been a supporter of the king, was already beginning to take a leading role in opposing him, while his son-in-law the earl of Lancaster who was later to lead the opposition was still loyal.[122] The real target of the magnates' actions was obviously Gaveston, and his removal from England would have to be conceded before they were prepared to consider any other issues.

Political tension increased sharply in the weeks before the reconvened parliament on 28 April and for a time there was a very real danger of civil war. Between 12 and 18 March Edward II appointed new and loyal custodians, including Gaveston and Hugh Despenser the Elder, to a dozen important castles, and on 19 March repairs were hastily put in hand to the Tower of London. On 31 March the king arrived at Windsor castle, where he remained until his return to Westminster for the meeting of parliament on 28 April. Windsor itself was put in a state of defence, while the bridges across the Thames at Staines and Kingston were broken. From his own stronghold at nearby Wallingford, where the king had spent two days on the way to Windsor, Gaveston was also gathering his forces. He then joined Edward for Easter (14 April) at Windsor, where if necessary he and Edward could hold out against a baronial army. The king controlled many of the strongest fortresses in the kingdom but few of the leading magnates supported him, with the exception of the earl of Lancaster and the uninfluential earls of Richmond and Oxford.[123] In the meantime the earls had gathered at the earl of Lincoln's castle at Pontefract in Yorkshire to debate what to do next. The result of their deliberations was a document, which was to be presented at the forthcoming parliament. Lincoln was however a moderating influence and it was largely due to him that civil war did not break out in the spring of 1308.[124]

[121] *Guisborough*, 381–2; cf. *Ann. Paul.*, 262–3.
[122] Cf. Hamilton, 48–9; Maddicott, 74.
[123] For the details see Maddicott, 77–80; Hamilton, 49–50. The timber so recently used for temporary buildings during the coronation was taken downriver to repair the defences of the Tower of London: *KW*, i, 507.
[124] Maddicott, 80.

According to the *Annales Paulini*, the earls and barons came to parliament fully armed, but only for self-defence. The king remained in the palace of Westminster while the earls, as on the previous occasion in February, were in Westminster Abbey.[125] There was an immediate demand for the exile of Gaveston and the confiscation of his lands; and in order to provide a legal justification for this, the earl of Lincoln presented the document that had been drawn up at Pontefract. The first of the three articles distinguished between the king and his office by declaring that 'homage and the oath of allegiance (*homage et serment*) are more in respect of the crown than in respect of the king's person . . . And, therefore, if it should befall that the king is not guided by reason, then, in order that the dignity of the crown may be preserved the lieges are bound by the oath made to the crown to reinstate the king in the dignity of the crown'. Since it was not possible to reinstate the king by recourse to legal action, because the judges were the king's, 'the evil must be removed by constraint'. The second article stated that 'as regards the person who is talked about [i.e. Gaveston], the people ought to judge him as one not to be suffered because he disinherits the crown and, as far as he is able, impoverishes it. By his counsel he withdraws the king from the counsel of his realm and puts discord between the king and his people, and he draws to himself the allegiance of men by as stringent an oath as does the king, thereby making himself the peer of the king and so enfeebling the crown. . . .' The third article concluded that

> Since the lord king has undertaken to maintain him against all men on every point, entirely without regard to right reason, as behoves the king, he cannot be judged or attainted by an action brought according to law, and therefore, seeing that he is a robber of the people and a traitor to his liege lord and his realm, the people rate him as a man attainted and judged, and pray the king that, since he is bound by his coronation oath to keep the laws that the people shall choose, he will accept and execute the award of his people.[126]

The document is highly significant since it provided a legal and constitutional means for the earl of Lincoln and the other earls to attack Gaveston for encroaching on the power of the crown and to oppose Edward II's support of Gaveston, while at the same time upholding their own oaths of allegiance to the crown which they had so recently affirmed at the corona-

---

[125] *Ann. Paul.*, 263.
[126] *English Historical Documents, 1189–1327*, ed. H. Rothwell (London, 1975), 525–6; Maddicott, 81–2; Hamilton, 50–1. Since there is no roll for the April 1308 parliament, there is no 'official' record of the articles presented by the earl of Lincoln. The complete French text is known only from BL, Burney Ms. 277, f. 5v; a French version of the first article is preserved in the *Ann. Lond.*, 153–4, and a Latin version of the same in the *Gesta Edwardi*, 33–4, written at Bridlington in Yorkshire: cf. Maddicott, 81.

tion. The allusion to the coronation oath shows that, whatever Edward may have thought it meant, the fourth clause of the oath was already being invoked by his opponents. The first article of the declaration, concerning 'homage and the oath of allegiance', is doubly significant since it was to be used again in 1321 as part of the proceedings against Hugh Despenser the Younger, another favourite of Edward II.[127]

Edward refused to accept the articles presented by the earl of Lincoln and strongly resisted the attempt to force Gaveston into exile. As suggested in the previous chapter, Edward and Gaveston's withdrawal at Easter 1308 behind the defences of Windsor castle could have been the occasion for the production of a compact of brotherhood between them, as a legal device to protect Gaveston against the expected baronial attempts to oust him. If such an agreement was made in April 1308, Edward's belief that it might provide a shelter against the increasingly determined opposition of the earls was naïve in the extreme. With the significant exception of the earl of Lancaster, whose loyalty was rewarded and, Edward hoped, ensured for the future by his being granted the office of steward of England on 9 May, virtually all the earls, led by Lincoln, were firmly opposed to the king and to Gaveston.[128] Edward had also been under intense pressure from Philip IV of France since the time of the coronation over issues concerning Isabella's dower and the Templars.[129] The future of Gaveston was now added to these problems. In the spring of 1308 Philip sent Pierre de Courpalay, the abbot of Saint-Germain-des-Prés and three knights to England. According to two anonymous newsletters, written on 12 and 14 May, they were sent *pro statu de Gaveston deteriorando*, while Philip also let it be known that unless Edward expelled Piers Gaveston, whom he regarded as his mortal enemy, from the realm of England, he would also treat all Gaveston's supporters as his enemies. It was rumoured that Philip IV and his sister Margaret, the widow of Edward I, had sent £40,000 to the earls of Lincoln and Pembroke to assist them in their proceedings against Gaveston.[130] Opposed by nearly all of the leading English magnates, by his father-in-law, stepmother, and also by his wife, Edward II finally gave way on 18 May and agreed that Gaveston should go into perpetual exile on 24 June, and that he should restore the lands of the earldom of Cornwall to the crown.[131] Four days earlier, on 14 May, in a

[127] *PROME*, Parliament of 1321, SC 9/24, item 2. On that occasion however Despenser was accused of having employed the declaration for his own purposes.

[128] Maddicott, 86–7, where it is argued that Lancaster was neutral, awaiting developments.

[129] Brown, 'Repercussions', 585–7, citing AN, J 654, no. 25 (the text is printed in ibid., 593–5.

[130] Brown, 'Repercussions', 587–8. The newsletters are preserved in Lincoln, Dean and Chapter Muniments, D ii/56/1, nos 39 & 42, and may be part of the papers of Robert Darcy, one of Gaveston's retainers. No. 39 is printed in Maddicott, App. 1, no. ii. See also Maddicott, 84; Phillips, 28. It is not clear whether the sum of £40,000 was in sterling or in *livres tournois* (equivalent to £10,000 sterling).

[131] Hamilton, 50–3; Maddicott, 83–8; Phillips, 28.

clear concession to Philip IV, Edward assigned to Isabella all the revenues and debts accruing from the county of Ponthieu.[132] The king wished Gaveston to retain the title of earl, which continued to be used in royal letters of privy seal relating to Gaveston, but was systematically omitted in instruments under the Great Seal, which referred to him simply as Sir Peter de Gaveston, knight. On 19 May the archbishop of Canterbury passed sentence of excommunication on Gaveston should he return. The earls did not however trust Edward II to keep his word and, according to the Lanercost chronicle, gathered an army at Northampton on about 2 June and demanded Gaveston's immediate departure from England.[133]

The sentence of exile had not specified where Gaveston should be sent. One of Edward II's possessions in France was the most obvious destination. The county of Ponthieu on the Channel coast of France, where Gaveston had spent his brief exile in 1307, was the nearest, but was ruled out since its revenues had just been granted to Isabella and it was soon full of French and English officials surveying its value.[134] An obvious alternative was to establish him somewhere in Edward II's duchy of Aquitaine in south-west France. On 24 May he was granted lands in Aquitaine worth £2,000 sterling, the grant being replaced on 7 June by another of the same value, which included the island of Oléron and the county of Gaure, close to Gabaston in the neighbouring county of Béarn, from which Gaveston took his name. These lands, together with another £2,000 of revenues from lands in England granted to Gaveston at about the same time, would have given him an income equivalent to that of a substantial earldom in England.[135] It was presumably intended that he would go to Aquitaine. But the depth of Philip IV's hostility to him might have made any part of France, even a part under English rule, too dangerous a place for him.[136] Edward therefore looked farther afield for somewhere where Gaveston might be relatively safe from his domestic and French enemies and where he might play a role of some dignity and importance. On 16 June Edward appointed Gaveston as his lieutenant in Ireland, with wide powers. This was clearly a last-minute appointment since the earl of

---

[132] Brown, 'Repercussions', 588; Maddicott, 84. The French envoys and the earls of Lancaster and Richmond dined with Edward II on that date: E 101/373/7 (daily household roll, 1 Edward II).

[133] Hamilton, 53; Maddicott, 87–8; Phillips, 28. On the question of Gaveston's title see Chaplais, 45–6. The gathering at Northampton in early June mentioned in *Lanercost*, 211, is not confirmed by any other source and may be confused with the 'parliament' held at Northampton on 4 Aug.

[134] Brown, 'Repercussions', 588.

[135] Hamilton, 53–5, 146–7.

[136] Edward II was concerned in 1308 that French agents were about to enter Gascony in order to seize the possessions of the Templars: Brown, 'Repercussions', 585–6. The report of John Hastings, seneschal of Gascony, in about 1311, suggests that this did in fact happen: *Gascon Register A (Series of 1318–19)*, ed. G.P. Cuttino, 3 vols (Oxford, 1975), ii, 691–6 (item no. 331). Their presence could also pose an obvious danger to Gaveston.

Ulster, the leading member of the Irish nobility, had been appointed to the same office only the day before. On 25 June 1308 Edward saw Gaveston off to Ireland from Bristol and, for the moment at least, the political crisis in England was over and the threat of civil war removed.[137]

RECONCILIATION AND REFORM

In the months that followed Gaveston's departure for Ireland a gradual process of reconciliation between the king and the magnates began. This was greatly aided by Gaveston's absence, and by the wish of many of the earls to restore peace to the kingdom, but was also hindered by a residual distrust of the king's motives. On 21 June Edward II issued a general military summons in which the army was ordered to muster at Carlisle on 22 August for a new campaign in Scotland,[138] where during the past twelve months Robert Bruce had been taking English-held castles and defeating and expelling English supporters.[139] The campaign, which would have been the first of Edward II's reign, was urgently needed, but its purpose was probably as much to restore Edward's authority over his magnates as to prevent further advances by Robert Bruce. The campaign did not however take place and, while there was no order cancelling it and there is no recorded evidence of any refusal by the magnates to take part in it, the reason may have been that the earls had unfinished business with the king. This may explain the meeting, understandably but incorrectly called a 'parliament' by the *Annales Paulini*, which was held on 4 August at Northampton. There is evidence from the witness lists of royal charters that a number of earls, including Gloucester, Hereford, Richmond, Warwick and the all-important Lincoln, and royalist barons such as Hugh Despenser the Elder, were present. According to the *Annales Paulini* the king and the earls were reconciled. The king allegedly took an oath that he would remove Hugh Despenser and five others from his council and that he would abide by the decisions of the earls and barons at the next parliament, which was summoned on 16 August to meet on 20 October. This suggests that the earls intended to prepare a programme of reform which they would present to parliament in October.[140]

Even before the Northampton meeting in August there were signs that the king was trying to reconcile himself with individual earls by the careful

---

[137] Hamilton, 55–6, 147; Maddicott, 83–4, 88.
[138] *CCR, 1307–13*, 70.
[139] For an account of events in Scotland see Barrow, 178–82.
[140] *Ann. Paul.*, 264; *PW*, II, ii, 22–3; Hamilton, 69; Maddicott, 90. There is no record of any summons being issued by the king to the earls and barons to attend at Northampton on 4 Aug. It was evidently an informal, though highly significant gathering. The other councillors whom the barons wanted to remove were William Inge, William de Bereford, Nicholas de Segrave (a retainer of the earl of Lancaster, who was clearly still regarded as an ally of the king), and two others unnamed.

application of royal patronage and favour, notably towards his nephew the earl of Gloucester and the earl of Hereford. The earls of Lincoln and Warwick were being courted from August, and the earl of Pembroke, who appears to have been strongly opposed to Gaveston, was receiving royal favours by the autumn of 1308.[141] This pattern of reconciliation was however counterbalanced by other developments. When Edward II arranged a tournament at great expense at Kennington in the autumn, the earls apparently shunned it.[142] Of much greater importance was the increasing distance between the king and his first cousin, the earl of Lancaster, who had earlier in the reign either been aligned with the king or had at least played a neutral role in the disputes over Gaveston. Lancaster was absent from the meeting at Northampton in August 1308 and disappears altogether from the witness lists to royal charters between early November 1308 and March 1310. The reasons for this estrangement are obscure but its existence seems clear. Whatever the cause, Lancaster was now embarked on the road which led him into open opposition from 1309.[143]

In the summer of 1308 Edward II was playing a skilful yet risky game. While he was attempting, with considerable success, to appease the earls, he was actively preparing the ground for the return of Gaveston to England. Whether the earls were aware of what was happening is unknown but they may well have had their suspicions. As early as 16 June, even before Gaveston had left for Ireland, Edward II wrote to Pope Clement V, asking him to lift the archbishop of Canterbury's sentence of excommunication on Gaveston should he return. On the same day Edward wrote to his father-in-law, Philip IV of France.[144] Both the pope and the king of France responded by sending envoys to England. Arnaud d'Aux, bishop of Poitiers and a future cardinal, and Gaveston's nephew, Bertrand Caillau, came on behalf of the pope and were in England in time for the Westminster parliament in October. Bishop Guy of Soissons and Louis, count of Évreux, the half-brother of Philip IV and a close personal friend of Edward II, were sent on behalf of France and reached England in mid-September.[145]

---

[141] *Ann. Paul.*, 26; Maddicott, 90–2; Hamilton, 67–9, 152–3; Phillips, 28–9. The author of the *Vita* commented on what he described as the fickleness and lack of principle of the earls: *Vita*, 15–17. On the other hand Gaveston's departure for Ireland had removed the major cause of grievance. None of the magnates at this stage wanted a renewed danger of civil war.

[142] *Ann. Paul.*, 264.

[143] Maddicott, 92–4. The latest suggested explanation is that the estrangement had no connection with Gaveston or any of his retainers, as might seem likely, but arose from an initially trivial dispute involving Gerard Salveyn, escheator north of the Trent, and the manor of Wilton near Pickering in Yorkshire, held by one of Lancaster's knights: A. King, 'Thomas of Lancaster's first quarrel with Edward II', in *Fourteenth-century England*, iii, ed. W. M. Ormrod (Woodbridge, Suffolk & Rochester, NY 2004), 31–45, esp. 36–40.

[144] *Foedera*, II, i, 49–50.

[145] *Foedera*, II, i, 54, 63–4. Louis of Évreux dined with the king on 12 Sept.: Bod., Ms. Latin Hist. c. 4, m.3

There is no indication that any of the issues that were raised at the meeting at Northampton on 4 August were pursued further when parliament met in late October. This may indicate that the earls were not ready to present the detailed demands for reform which were to be a major feature of the parliaments of 1309, at Westminster in April and at Stamford in July. With the removal of Gaveston, the atmosphere in October 1308 was also largely free of the tensions which had dogged relations between the king and the magnates earlier in the year and had effectively prevented two successive parliaments from conducting any serious business. Although the leading earls were now reconciled to the crown, it is unlikely that Edward formally raised the question of their approval of Gaveston's return to England in the near future. But this issue was certainly uppermost in Edward's mind and had a bearing on some of the decisions that were taken either during or around the time of the parliament. In order to placate both the pope and Philip IV, he gave formal approval to the suppression of the order of the Knights Templar, which he had been resisting since December 1307.[146] He agreed to the release from prison of the former treasurer, Walter Langton, who was duly freed on 9 November.[147] Two Scottish bishops, William Lamberton of St Andrews and Robert Wishart of Glasgow, who had been imprisoned in England since 1306, were also released at papal request.[148] As well as hoping for future assistance from the pope in obtaining Gaveston's return, Edward was hoping for a grant of taxation by the Church, as eventually happened early in 1309. The consecration at Canterbury on 13 October, in the presence of Edward II, of Edward's old ally and treasurer, Walter Reynolds, as bishop of Worcester,[149] was a further sign that relations between the king and the Church were improving. The French envoys, who had arrived in England in September in order to assist in reconciling Edward and his barons, instead arranged a truce between England and Scotland which came into force in November 1308.[150] The truce superseded a decision taken by the king's council, and presumably made during

---

[146] Edward had begun their suppression on 10 Jan. 1308 but had not been convinced of their guilt and delayed taking further action against them: *Foedera*, II, i, 16–20, 55; Lalou, 'Les Négociations', 348. During the summer English envoys had been conducting negotiations concerning Gascony and the Templars with Philip IV at Poitiers. Since the papal curia was then at Poitiers, the envoys were subject to influences from both Philip IV and Clement V: Lalou, 348.

[147] This was done in deference to both the pope and the archbishop of Canterbury: Menache, *Clement V*, 80–1; Maddicott, 94.

[148] *Foedera*, II, i, 53, 65; *CPR, 1307–13*, 94; Maddicott, 94. This was a major concession since Edward II regarded them both as bitter enemies for their support of Bruce: Barrow, 151–3.

[149] *Ann. Paul.*, 264. Reynolds had been elected bishop in Nov. 1307 after considerable pressure from Edward II on the chapter of Worcester and the use of royal influence at the papal curia: Menache, *Clement V*, 61–2.

[150] *Foedera*, II, i, 63; *Ann. Paul.*, 265.

the parliament, to send the earls of Gloucester and Hereford with a large force to Scotland.[151] This brought welcome relief but French mediation with the Scots was a two-edged sword, since Philip IV could always threaten to renew the former French alliance with the Scots if Edward II did not do what he wanted. It also brought French approval of Gaveston's return from exile no nearer.[152]

EDWARD AND GAVESTON

Edward continued to pursue his ambition to obtain the recall and reinstatement of Gaveston. Early in January 1309 he called an assembly of bishops and royal administrators, predominantly consisting of earls and barons, to meet at Westminster on 23 February. Altogether nine earls, Gloucester, Lincoln, Lancaster, Surrey, Hereford, Pembroke, Richmond, Warwick and Arundel, and forty-two barons were summoned, a total very similar in number to those called to each of the three parliaments in 1308. These presumably were the men whom Edward II really wished to consult,[153] and the king must have used the occasion to discover whether the magnates were now prepared to consider allowing Gaveston to return to England. It is also possible that as a quid pro quo, the king promised or hinted that he would be receptive to any proposals for reform that might be put to him in the future. This would have made it all the more urgent for the earls to formulate a detailed plan of reform, for presentation at the next parliament which was summoned on 4 March to meet at Westminster on 27 April.

Also on 4 March Edward wrote to the pope and to the cardinals to announce that he was sending an embassy to Avignon, consisting of the earl of Pembroke (now fully reconciled to the king), the ever-loyal earl of Richmond, Edward's close ally Walter Reynolds the bishop of Worcester and royal treasurer, the bishop of Norwich and others.[154] The business of the embassy was not specified but its purpose was certainly to obtain an annulment by the pope of the sentence of excommunication to be imposed upon Gaveston. Edward probably hoped he could then present the remainder of the earls and their supporters with a *fait accompli*. The

---

[151] *Ann. Paul.*, 265. This expedition was presumably intended to replace the general summons for a muster at Carlisle on 22 Aug. which had been issued in June 1308: Maddicott, 106.

[152] According to the Annals of St Pauls, Philip IV of France even summoned both Edward II and Robert Bruce to attend a 'parliament' in France: *Ann. Paul.*, 266.

[153] *PW*, II, ii, 23–4. See also the Introduction to the Westminster parliament of April 1309 in *PROME*. It is not known how many of the earls actually attended the meeting. The earls of Lincoln, Richmond and Gloucester were there, since they dined with the king on 3 March (Bod., Ms. Latin Hist. C.5, m.10), and Pembroke must have been present as well, before setting off for Avignon. It is not known whether Lancaster attended.

[154] *Foedera*, II, i, 69. On the same date, in a gesture directed towards Philip IV, he ordered the collection of the 'queen's gold' (the queen's share) of fines levied in the lands of the earldom of Chester since the king's marriage: *CCR, 1307–13*, 106.

embassy set out for Avignon in early March,¹⁵⁵ visiting Philip IV of France on the way to try to win his approval for the return of Gaveston. The negotiations with France were still incomplete as late as the end of April,¹⁵⁶ but the mission to Avignon was more successful and on about 21 May the pope issued a bull annulling the sentence of excommunication.¹⁵⁷ The pope stated that he had done so because the archbishop of Canterbury had not followed the proper procedures in canon law before passing sentence, and because the king had assured him that he was now reconciled with the English magnates, who were prepared to accept Gaveston's return. Gaveston had however appealed against the sentence before it came into force, and the pope had yet to give a final ruling on the appeal. This left the possibility that if it failed, Gaveston could still be excommunicated.¹⁵⁸

AN AGENDA FOR REFORM

In the meantime the earls were making extensive preparations of their own for the forthcoming parliament. At some point between 20 March and 7 April a tournament took place at Dunstable, which was attended by the earls of Gloucester, Hereford, Lancaster, Warwick, Surrey and Arundel, together with large retinues. The earl of Lincoln was not present, but there is no evidence that this signified disapproval of the actions of his fellow earls.¹⁵⁹ It has been suggested, though it cannot be proved, that the earl of Lancaster was responsible for convening the tournament and that he was therefore beginning to assume leadership of the movement for reform. Whether or not this was the case, it is likely that the occasion was used either to compose or to perfect an existing draft of the articles that were presented at the Westminster parliament on 27 April. There is also evidence that, of those who attended the Dunstable tournament, all six of the earls, at least twenty-five barons, and four or five knights later attended parliament.¹⁶⁰

---

¹⁵⁵ Pembroke's account for the mission ran from 6 March until 17 July: E 101/372/23. On the embassy see also Chaplais, 54–8.

¹⁵⁶ *Foedera*, II, i, 71; Hamilton, 71, 154.

¹⁵⁷ *Registrum Ricardi de Swinfield, Bishop of Hereford*, ed. W.W. Capes (London, 1909), 451, gives the date of the bull as 25 April. However, Chaplais argues convincingly that the date was more probably *c.* 21 May: Chaplais, 58–9. This seems likely since Pembroke was still at Avignon on 24 May, after which he made a short stay at his estates at Rancon in Poitou before returning to England: Phillips, 29, n. 4.

¹⁵⁸ *Reg. Swinfield*, 452–3; Hamilton, 73, 155; Chaplais, 59–60; Maddicott, 103. On 27 May the pope also announced his intention of sending an embassy of his own to England: SC 7/10/33.

¹⁵⁹ Ill health is a possible explanation, since Lincoln was now nearly sixty and died early in 1311.

¹⁶⁰ On the Dunstable tournament see especially Maddicott, 95–7, 99–102; and A. Tomkinson, 'Retinues at the tournament of Dunstable, *EHR*, lxxiv (1959), 70–89; and also Hamilton, 72; Chaplais, 60.

Edward II's request for the return of Gaveston was rejected.[161] His other request for a grant of taxation in aid of the war in Scotland was agreed on 27 April by the lay and ecclesiastical magnates and by the knights and burgesses, who granted him a twenty-fifth of the value of moveable goods. The grant was however conditional on the king's acceptance of a document containing eleven articles of reform.[162] This document was of the greatest significance, since, as Dr Maddicott has remarked, 'The eleven articles presented in parliament represent a halfway stage between the *Articuli super Cartas* of 1300 and the much fuller plan of reform embodied in the Ordinances of 1311.' The petition began with a complaint that the country was not governed in accordance with Magna Carta. Articles 1 and 7 protested at the abuse of purveyance; articles 4 and 5 at the unjust extension of the jurisdiction of the steward and marshal of the household; and article 8 at the wrongful use of royal protections and writs of privy seal to delay the course of common law. These five articles were very similar to complaints which had been made to Edward I's government in 1300 and had then been answered in the second, third, and sixth clauses of the *Articuli super Cartas*. Two more of the 1309 articles were derived at one remove from the *Articuli*. Article 10 in 1309, which protested that constables of royal castles illegally held common pleas before the gates of their castles, stemmed from article 7 in 1300, which ascribed this offence to the constable of Dover castle alone; and article 11 in 1309, which stated that the king's escheators unjustly seized the lands of tenants-in-chief and then refused them the right of appeal to the king's court, may have been based on articles 18 and 19 of 1300, which protested at similar, though not identical, abuses committed by the escheators. Thus five of the 1309 articles were directly based on the *Articuli super Cartas* of 1300 and another two indirectly. Only the remaining four articles of 1309, which called for the abolition of the new customs of 1303 (article 2); an end to the depreciation of the coinage (article 3); the provision of receivers of petitions in parliament to deal with unheard petitions (article 6), and greater control of the issue of pardons to criminals (article 9), appear to have been substantially new.[163]

[161] Hamilton, 72, 154. In some quarters however opinion on Gaveston appears to have been changing and becoming more favourable: Chaplais, 60–8, citing a letter to Gaveston from the bishop of Winchester and another from Roger de Aldenham, a monk of Westminster Abbey and previously bitterly opposed to Gaveston.

[162] Maddicott, 97–8; *Lay Taxes*, 30. For the form of taxation see *PW*, II, ii, 38–9.

[163] Here I have drawn heavily on the summary and discussion of the articles in Maddicott, 97–8, 102. See also Hamilton, 72. The original document, written in French, was enrolled as a schedule on the dorse of membrane 22 of the Close Roll for 3 Edward II (C 54/ 127; *CCR, 1307–13*, 175). The text is not calendared in the Calendar of Close Rolls, apart from the heading 'Articles for the good government of the kingdom presented by the barons to the king for his acceptance'. The full French text was however published from the Close Roll in *RP*, i, 443–5 (Appendix to vol. i). The annotated copy of *RP* in the Public Record Office Library notes that these articles are also to be found in

The enrolment of the articles on the Close Roll states that the document was presented to the king by the community of his realm (*par la communalte de son roialme*). The term 'community' should not however be understood as 'Commons' in the sense of the knights and the burgesses. While some of the grievances complained of in the articles were of interest to the knights and burgesses, notably article 6 concerning the hearing of petitions, which states that it came specifically from them, there is no doubt that the articles were substantially the work of the earls and barons, probably with the practical help of legally and administratively experienced advisers who were familiar with such earlier documents as the *Articuli super Cartas*. To a very large extent the earls and barons still were the 'community of the realm', speaking for themselves but also beginning to take into account the interests and grievances of a wider political community.[164] The articles of 1309 also bear a close resemblance both in their form and in the kind of grievances expressed to the petitions of the community (*la commune*) which were received and answered by Edward III in the parliaments of 1327, 1333 and 1334.[165] The big difference between 1309 and these later occasions was in the political atmosphere: on the one hand a king who was outwardly willing to consider reforms while in the last resort determined to resist anything which affected the exercise of his prerogative; on the other, a king who was conscious of his need for support, and who was receptive and prepared to accept reforms. According to several of the chroniclers, Edward II did not reject the articles but refused to give an immediate answer.[166]

GAVESTON'S RETURN AND THE BEGINNING OF REFORM

The papal bull annulling the archbishop of Canterbury's sentence of excommunication on Piers Gaveston should he return to England did not have any effect on the political situation in England until its arrival in early June.[167] On 11 June it was read, on the orders of the king, before the arch-

---

SC 8/294/14698 and that SC 8/14/698 is a fragmentary copy of part of these articles. The French text of the articles was reprinted from the *RP* edition, but with the omission of articles 3, 7, 9 and 11, in *Select Documents*, 6–8. The title given in *Select Documents*, 'The Stamford Articles', is somewhat misleading since, although Edward II gave his answers to the articles at the Stamford parliament in July–Aug. 1309, the articles were, as the text makes clear, originally presented at the Westminster parliament of 27 April 1309.

[164] See the discussion in Maddicott, 98–102, and also in G.L. Harriss, *King, Parliament and Public Finance in England to 1369* (Oxford, 1975), 119–20.

[165] See *PROME*, Westminster Parliament of Jan.–Feb. 1327, C 65/1; York Parliament of Jan. 1333, C 49/6/20; and the York Parliament of Feb. 1334, C 65/4. The Latin word *communitas* and the French words *commune* and *communalte* are consistently translated in the 1307–37 section of *PROME* as 'community' in order to avoid giving a premature and probably misleading rendering of them as 'Commons'.

[166] Maddicott, 97, n. 3.

[167] Chaplais, 58–9.

bishop of Canterbury and the bishops of London, Winchester and Chichester. Archbishop Winchelsey was unhappy with the bull and sought the written opinions of the bishops of his province, but found little support and was left with no choice but to accept the pope's decree.[168] Winchelsey's attempt to retaliate by ordering John Droxford, the keeper of the king's wardrobe, to be at Canterbury for his consecration as bishop of Bath & Wells two weeks after the planned opening of the Stamford parliament, was met with fury by the king. In the event the consecration did not take place because of Droxford's attendance at parliament. Winchelsey himself did not attend, partly because of ill health, but also because he was deeply unhappy about Gaveston's return and did not want to debate the matter in parliament.[169] Without even waiting for parliament to meet, Edward II set off from Westminster and met Gaveston at Chester on 27 June, the day of his arrival from Dublin.[170]

The king was aware that he would have to pay a political price for Gaveston's return. On 18 June and 14 July he ordered measures to prevent the abuses of purveyance (goods requisitioned by the king), which had been bitterly complained of in the articles presented in the Westminster parliament in April, and to expedite the payment of royal debts.[171] On 12 June 1309 the sheriffs of England had been ordered to proclaim the 'Statute of Prises', forbidding the taking of undue prises (goods taken by a lord from his dependants) from ecclesiastical and lay persons. Like the Statute of Stamford of the following month, it was in effect a rehearsal and confirmation of legislation belonging to the reign of Edward I, in this case of chapter 1 of the Statute of Westminster I of 1275.[172] The proclamation on prises was however counterbalanced on 14 June when the earls of Gloucester, Hereford, Lancaster, Surrey, Warwick and Arundel were ordered not to engage in tournaments. Edward II was evidently afraid of the possibility of the earls bringing armed retainers to the coming parliament,[173] which had been summoned on 11 June to meet at Stamford on 27 July.[174]

---

[168] Hamilton, 73, 155.

[169] Maddicott, 103, 105; Denton, *Robert Winchelsey*, 257–8. On 8 July the king told his chancellor to write to the archbishop forbidding him to perform the consecration during the meeting of parliament and adding that the order was to be issued in such a way that if the archbishop disobeyed he could be attached to answer before the king's court: *CCW*, 291.

[170] Bod., Ms. Latin Hist. C.5, m.10.

[171] Maddicott, 103. Edward put a brave face on things in a letter of 8 July in which he said he had summoned the prelates and nobles to Stamford where 'with the aid of God and the counsel of the said nobles' he would 'ordain much business touching the honour and profit of himself and his crown and realm': *CCW*, 291.

[172] *SR*, i, 153–4. Hamilton, 73, 155; Maddicott, 103.

[173] *CCR, 1307–13*, 158–9.

[174] *PW*, II, ii, 37–8. The only reference to the assembly as a parliament is in the Close Roll enrolment of the articles presented to Edward II at the Westminster parliament in April 1309 together with the answers provided by the king at Stamford in July. The writs of summons were issued on the day on which the papal bull concerning Gaveston was read out.

When the parliament assembled, Gaveston's return was already a *fait accompli*, although his full reinstatement as earl of Cornwall was still to be approved. Edward had the support of at least five of the earls, Pembroke, Richmond, Gloucester, Hereford and Lincoln.[175] At least six of the bishops present, Durham, Chichester, London, Worcester, Winchester and Norwich, as well as the bishop-elect of Bath & Wells, were royalist or had royalist sympathies. Since the beginning of the reign Edward had been successful in getting three of his clerks elected to the episcopate, Walter Reynolds to Worcester, Walter Stapeldon to Exeter and, most recently, Droxford to Bath & Wells.[176] Edward finally gave his answers to each of the articles which had been presented during the Westminster parliament in April 1309. The Statute of Stamford then gave legislative effect to those answers. Five of the complaints made to the king at Westminster in April were answered by reciting the relevant causes of the *Articuli super Cartas*. These concerned purveyance: the quantities which purveyors should take, punishment for excessive purveyance and purveyance without warrant, methods of payment, and the production of warrants. The statute then promised to limit the authority of the steward and marshal of the royal household and that no privy seal writ affecting the common law would be issued. Edward also promised to curb the powers of the constables of royal castles and to give up temporarily the new customs of 1303 to see what the effects were. The king instructed the chancellor and other royal officials to observe the remaining two articles in the April petition without reciting them specifically. On 20 August the county sheriffs were ordered to proclaim the statute.[177]

Edward II had answered the articles of April 1309 at the least possible personal cost by issuing what amounted to a confirmation of the *Articuli super Cartas* granted by his father in 1300. He also got his wish over Gaveston, who was restored to the title of earl and to the lands of the earldom of Cornwall at Stamford on 5 August. On 26 July and 4 August respectively he had surrendered the lands in England and France which he had been granted by Edward II in compensation for the loss of his earldom at the time of his exile in 1308. The form of Gaveston's tenure was however changed. When he was first created earl of Cornwall in August 1307 he received the earldom in fee simple to himself and his heirs; the re-grant of August 1309 was made in fee-tail to Gaveston and his wife and to the heirs of their bodies. The restoration of the earldom of Cornwall to Gaveston was witnessed by many of the most powerful men in the kingdom: the bishop of Durham, the chancellor the bishop of Chichester, the treasurer the bishop of Worcester, and the bishop of London; by the earls of Gloucester, Lincoln, Surrey, Pembroke, Hereford

---

[175] Maddicott, 103.

[176] Denton, *Robert Winchelsey*, 259.

[177] For the articles and the king's replies see *RP*, i, 443–45, and *Select Documents*, 6–8. For the Statute of Stamford see *SR*, i, 154–6. The text of the statute also appears in the annals of London: *Ann. Lond.*, 158–61. See also Maddicott, 103–4; Prestwich, *Plantagenet England*, 181.

and Warwick; Hugh Despenser the Elder, Henry de Percy and Robert Fitz Payn, the steward of the king's household.[178]

On 30 July Edward II turned to Scotland, the business for which the parliament had ostensibly been called, and issued a summons for the army to meet at Newcastle upon Tyne on 29 September 1309.[179] On the same day he wrote to Philip IV of France politely turning down the latter's request, recently brought by a French envoy, Mathew de Varennes, for a meeting with Edward, on the grounds that he would shortly be going to Scotland. On 3 August he wrote more firmly to Philip objecting to one of the letters carried by Varennes in which Robert Bruce of Scotland had been given the title of king.[180]

The new-found harmony between the king and the earls and barons was marked by the decision taken during the Stamford parliament to send a letter from the barons to the pope protesting against the practice of papal provisions to benefices and other alleged abuses of papal authority in England. Edward II gave effect to this decision on 6 August when he wrote to the earls and barons asking them to append their seals to the letter when they received it. Twelve earls, Gloucester, Lancaster, Lincoln, Cornwall, Ulster, Surrey, Hereford, Richmond, Pembroke, Warwick, Arundel and Oxford, and thirty-four barons sealed the letter.[181]

With the restoration of Gaveston settled and the Statute of Stamford agreed, Edward II finally obtained the grant of taxation which had provisionally been given to him in April, and on 26 August commissions were issued to the assessors and collectors to begin their work.[182] But there were still ominous signs. The earls of Lancaster and Arundel, and the archbishop of Canterbury had all been absent from Stamford; and it has been suggested that the partnership of Lancaster and Winchelsey as Ordainers in 1310–11 first came into being at the time of the Stamford Parliament. It had still to be proved whether Edward II was willing or even able to implement the promised controls on purveyance and on royal officials; and there was also the question of how Gaveston would behave in the future.[183]

---

[178] Chaplais, 68; Hamilton, 73, 75, 155; Maddicott, 104. The various documents relating to Gaveston's surrender of lands and the re-granting of the earldom are in *CCR, 1307–13*, 225–6.

[179] *CCR, 1307–13*, 224–5; *Foedera*, II, i, 78.

[180] *Foedera*, II, i, 79.

[181] *Foedera*, II, i, 84; *CPR, 1307–13*, 180. The full text of the letter, with the names of those who sealed it, appears to be recorded only in *Ann. Lond.*, 161–5. The letter was circulated for sealing, which explains the inclusion of the seals of the earls of Lancaster and Ulster, who were not present at Stamford. The letter was written in response to a list of grievances brought to England and delivered to the king in February 1309 by the papal envoy, Arnald d'Aux, bishop of Poitiers: *Ann. Paul.*, 161, 165–7. The letter is also an indication that the interests of the lay magnates and the prelates did not by any means coincide, even when they were both in conflict with the crown. It also shows how the king was determined to preserve his rights vis-à-vis the papacy, even when he was looking for papal support for the return of Gaveston from exile.

[182] *Lay Taxes*, 30.

[183] Maddicott, 104–5. Denton is however sceptical of the argument that Lancaster and Winchelsey were in effect joint leaders of the political movement which led to the

PART TWO

CRISIS RENEWED: THE APPOINTMENT OF THE ORDAINERS

Within months of the settlement which had apparently been achieved at Stamford in July–August 1309 the political situation in England was again deteriorating rapidly. Although Gaveston's influence over the flow of royal patronage was less evident and exercised more circumspectly than it had been before his exile, his influence was nonetheless widely believed to be extensive and was deeply resented.[184] The well informed author of the *Vita Edwardi Secundi* recorded that Gaveston had one of the earl of Lancaster's retainers replaced in office by one of his own.[185] This may refer to the dispute over the succession to the lordship of Powys in Wales between Gruffudd de la Pole, who was an important member of Lancaster's retinue, and John Charlton, one of Gaveston's adherents, which began in the summer of 1309 and was to continue far beyond the end of Gaveston's life in 1312.[186] His arrogant behaviour towards his fellow earls was also a cause of resentment, especially when he allegedly chose to bestow offensive nicknames upon the earls of Warwick, Gloucester, Lincoln, Lancaster and Pembroke.[187] Only the earls of Gloucester, Richmond, Surrey and, initially, Lincoln appear to have remained on good personal terms with him.[188] The first overt sign of renewed trouble came on 18 October 1309 when the earls

---

appointment of the Ordainers, and argues that 'whatever Winchelsey's influence in the background, and whatever his involvement in 1310 and after, the opposition which was building up in 1309 was essentially baronial': Denton, *Robert Winchelsey*, 260–4.

[184] Hamilton, 75–6, 155–6. As Professor Hamilton points out, the real problem was not so much the gifts Gaveston received from the king for himself as the favours he procured for others which set him apart from his peers.

[185] *Vita*, 16–17.

[186] There are problems in identifying who was involved in this dispute. See Dr Wendy Childs's discussion in *Vita*, 16, n. 31; Chaplais, 69–71; Maddicott, 93–4, 138–41. The dispute tended to flare up whenever relations between Edward II and Lancaster were strained. See the article on Charlton by J.F.A. Mason in the *Oxford DNB*.

[187] Warwick was described as 'the black dog of Arden'; Gloucester as 'whoreson'; Lincoln as 'burst belly'; Lancaster as 'churl'; and Pembroke as 'Joseph the Jew': see Hamilton, 75, 155; Chaplais, 69; Maddicott, 109. The only contemporary chronicles to record Gaveston's behaviour are the *Vita*, 16–17, which speaks only of 'base nicknames', without giving any details, and the *Flores*, 152, which cites Warwick's nickname. The earliest sources for the other names all date from early in the reign of Edward III. Even though Gaveston was himself the victim of slander, not all of it merited, there is no reason to doubt the general nature of his behaviour and his extreme foolishness. There is a very thorough discussion of Gaveston's use of nicknames and the sources in which they are recorded in Tout, *Place of the Reign*, 12–13, n. 2. The description of Gloucester as 'whoreson' was particularly foolish since it reflected on Joan of Acre, the king's sister, and the mother both of the earl of Gloucester and of Gaveston's own wife. The reference was to Joan's marriage in 1290, to Ralph de Monthermer, which Edward I had strongly disapproved of.

[188] Hamilton, 74, 155.

of Lancaster, Lincoln, Warwick, Arundel and Oxford refused to attend a *secretum parliamentum* at York because Gaveston would be there.[189] This meeting was the occasion of Edward II's decision to issue the summons on 26 October for a parliament to meet at York on 8 February.[190] On 4 November the king wrote to the earl of Lincoln, alluding to the recent council at York and seeking his advice on the order of business for the coming parliament. The king also made the very significant remark that it would not be convenient for him to attend parliament for more than ten to twelve days at the most. When February came his hopes were to be seriously disappointed.[191]

Apart from the rapidly growing enmity between Gaveston and the other earls, the issue that caused the most serious problems in late 1309 was that of prises and purveyance – the practice by which agents of the king took 'something for the use of the king by virtue of the royal prerogative'.[192] A system which had originally come into being to provide supplies of food for the use of the royal household as it moved around the kingdom was extensively used from the 1290s by both Edward I and Edward II to provide grain and livestock and transport for royal armies and garrisons in Scotland. As well as the inconvenience that this system caused to those affected, payment was often inadequate and frequently long delayed. The burden of war was thus carried by those who were least able to bear it. By the accession of Edward II in 1307 the accumulated unpaid royal debts resulting from prises and the social stress caused by the system were already acute. Prises and purveyance, together with the rapacity of the royal officials who imposed them, had been bitterly complained of during the reign of Edward I and were one of the major issues in the *Articuli super Cartas* in 1300. Edward II's use of prises and the protests against them both continued. Matters were made even worse when in 1308 and 1309 the king ordered purveyance of supplies on a vast scale for campaigns in Scotland which never took place.[193] Even on his own doorstep, his favourite manor of Langley in Hertfordshire, the king and his household were being abused by the local population for their failure to pay their debts.[194]

The Statute of Stamford of July 1309 had attempted to address the problem, but with little success. In part this was because prises were a part of the royal prerogative and, unlike taxes on moveables or customs duties,

[189] *Guisborough*, 384; Maddicott, 110; Hamilton, 76–7.

[190] *PW*, II, ii, 40–42.

[191] Davies, *Baronial Opposition*, 548–9, App.7. The meeting of 18 Oct. is described as a 'parliamentum' only in *Guisborough*, 384; in his letter to the earl of Lincoln the king describes it as a council.

[192] Maddicott, 106, citing W.S. Thomson, *A Lincolnshire Assize Roll for 1298*, Lincolnshire Record Soc., xxxvi (Lincoln, 1944), lxvi. See also the important study by Maddicott, *English Peasantry*.

[193] For an excellent summary of the issues see Maddicott, 106–8.

[194] Maddicott, citing E 404/5.

legally did not require the approval of parliament.[195] It was therefore in the interests of the king to resist legal control of prises for as long as he could. Without an alternative system of supply, it would be impossible to continue to wage war in Scotland. A modern observer might think that, if the available resources were inadequate, then the war should be brought to an end and the machinery of government and English society in general given a chance to recover. However, although a truce might be agreed from time to time, there was no doubt in the minds of either the king or his magnates that the war should continue. The prestige of the monarchy and national pride demanded that it should. But even if Edward II had been entirely sincere in agreeing to curb prises and assuming that royal officials changed the habits of a lifetime, it was unlikely in practice that much would or could be done. A system which had been in widespread use for so long could not be replaced overnight. Prises were therefore an important part of all the political crises in the early years of the reign of Edward II and they were to be a central issue in the crisis which led to the appointment of the Ordainers in March 1310. The government's acute shortage of ready cash, the result of accumulated debts from the reign of Edward I and the difficulty in obtaining agreement in parliament for taxes on moveables, made prises and purveyance even more essential. Where it was imperative to have ready cash, this was increasingly being obtained through borrowing from the Florentine banking company, the Frescobaldi, who had been dealing with the English crown since the late 1290s. By 1310 Edward II owed them in the region of £22,000.[196]

Although the mustering of the army at Newcastle on 29 September which had been ordered at Stamford on 30 July never took place, Edward II continued to use prises. On 9 November orders were issued for the purveyance of supplies in Ireland and in the counties of Chester and Gloucester, enough for the support of English garrisons but not for a full-scale campaign.[197] On 10 December the collection of the twenty-fifth granted at the Stamford Parliament in July was suspended between 29 December and 16 February 1310 because of the failure to enforce the Statute of Stamford. The collectors were nevertheless to proceed with the assessment of the twenty-fifth and to bring any money already received to the exchequer by 29 December. Significantly, the suspension of the tax was made at the request of the earls of Gloucester, Lincoln and Cornwall, in a rare display of political unity.[198] In the background there were fears of popular resistance to the burden of prises, even to

[195] Prises were subject only to the customary definition that they should be 'reasonable', in much the same way as feudal incidents had been in the reign of John, until these were forcibly defined by Magna Carta in 1215: Maddicott, 106–8.
[196] Prestwich, *Plantagenet England*, 181–2.
[197] *CCW, 1244–1326*, 303–4; Maddicott, 108–9.
[198] *PW*, II, i, 41; Maddicott, 108; *Lay Taxes*, 30.

the extent of a possible peasants' revolt.[199] On 12 December, amid these growing signs of political and social unrest, Edward II ordered a change of venue for the forthcoming parliament from York to Westminster.[200]

The assembly was originally intended to consider how to deal with the 'enemy, rebel and traitor', Robert Bruce, and his breach of the recently made truce, but by the time it was due to begin on 8 February the continued tensions over Gaveston and over prises had produced a serious deterioration in the political situation. Edward II and Gaveston had in the meantime spent a convivial Christmas at Langley, where according to the *Vita Edwardi Secundi* they 'fully made up for former absence by their long wished-for sessions of daily and intimate conversation'.[201] Just how serious matters had become is shown very clearly in the account in the *Vita* that the earls came in answer to the king's summons, as they were legally bound to do, but only as far as London, refusing to attend parliament at Westminster while Gaveston, 'their chief enemy, who had set the kingdom and themselves in an uproar, was skulking in the king's chamber'. They added that, 'if it was absolutely necessary to present themselves before the king', they would do so armed, claiming that they were acting for their own safety and not in order to threaten the king.[202] Edward's immediate response was to write on 7 February to the earls of Lancaster, Hereford, Pembroke and Warwick, who were the most hostile to the king and to Gaveston, forbidding them to bring armed retainers to parliament. The earls of Gloucester, Lincoln, Surrey and Richmond, who were more sympathetic to the king, were charged by the king with providing for the safe conduct of those attending parliament, with arresting anyone who broke the king's commands, and with settling any quarrels that might arise during parliament.[203] The king eventually sent Gaveston away to a safe place,[204] and the parliament finally began on 27 February, after a delay of almost three weeks.[205]

The king was at once given a petition in the name of the prelates, earls and barons, which may have been presented by the earl of Lancaster himself. Like the Boulogne agreement of January 1308 and the articles against Gaveston of April 1308 there is no record of the petition in the royal archives. Instead it is known from transcripts in the *Annales Londonienses*,

---

[199] Maddicott, 107–8, citing the preamble to the ordinance of 1311 demanding an end to prises: 'It is to be feared that the people of the land will rise by reason of the prises and the diverse oppressions made in these times'; Maddicott, *English Peasantry*, 22–4. On 18 Dec. Edward ordered the arrest of those who were spreading false rumours and sowing discord: *Foedera*, II, i, 101.

[200] *PW*, II, ii, 40–2.
[201] *Vita*, 16–17.
[202] *Vita*, 18–19.
[203] *CPR, 1307–13*, 206–7.
[204] *Vita*, 18–19.
[205] *Ann. Lond.*, 167–8; Maddicott, 110; Hamilton, 77.

the muniments of the Guildhall, London, and elsewhere.[206] All the issues that had been complained of since Edward II's accession in 1307 were contained in the petition. The king was guided by unsuitable and evil counsellors; he was so impoverished that he could neither defend the realm nor maintain his household except through the extortions of his ministers, who took from both Church and people without paying, in breach of Magna Carta. His father had left him all his lands, in England, Ireland and most of Scotland in peace, but he had lost Scotland and dismembered the possessions of the crown in England and Ireland, without baronial assent. The taxes granted to him by the community of the realm at Northampton in October 1307 in aid of the war and at Stamford in July 1309 in return for the relief of prises and other exactions were still being levied and wasted. But the war had made no progress and the people had not been relieved, and were more heavily burdened than ever. The petition concluded by humbly praying the king that these and other dangers should be redressed by the ordinance of the barons, who were bound by their allegiance to maintain the crown.[207]

Then, according to the *Vita* a battle of wills began:

This at length, I heard, had been asked for by the barons: namely that, as the state of the king and the kingdom had much deteriorated since the death of the elder king Edward of happy memory, and the whole kingdom had been not a little injured by this, they asked that, with the agreement and consent of the lord king and his barons, twelve discreet and powerful men of good reputation should be elected, by whose judgment and decree the situation should be reformed and settled; and if anything should be found a burden on the kingdom, their ordinance should destroy it; and if there was to be provision for any deficiency in the kingdom, the decision should be taken at their complete discretion.[208]

Edward at first refused to accept their demands, and did not give way until the barons accused him of breaking his coronation oath and threatened him with deposition.[209]

---

[206] *Ann. Lond.*, 168–9; *Munimenta Gildhallae Lond.*, ed. H. T. Riley (London, 1860) II, i, 198–9; Maddicott, 111, nn. 1 & 2. Of the various documents of protest and grievance received by Edward II in 1307–10, the only one to be recorded officially is the articles presented at the Westminster parliament of April 1309 and answered at the Stamford parliament in the following July. As noted above, this document was entered on the Close Roll.

[207] *Ann. Lond.*, 168–9; cf. Maddicott, 111.

[208] *Vita*, 18–19. In the Denholm-Young edition of the *Vita Edwardi Secundi*, 9, the translation of the last part of this passage reads 'and if in any emergency the realm should be threatened, by their discretion adequate and appropriate action should be taken'. This is the result of a different editorial reading of the text. See *Vita*, 18, note.

[209] *Vita*, 18–21. Although there is no direct confirmation of the *Vita* account from other sources, it probably reports accurately the sense of what happened between 27 Feb. and 16 March when Edward II agreed to the appointment of the Ordainers.

On 16 March Edward issued letters patent in which he agreed to the election of Ordainers from among the prelates, earls and barons, and others whom they might decide to summon before them during the period of their authority, which was to last from 29 September 1310 until 29 September 1311. The Ordainers were to have full powers to reform the state both of the kingdom and of the king's household, for the honour of the king and his people, and according to right reason and the king's coronation oath. One weakness in these concessions by the king was that, although he claimed to have acted 'of his free will', it was clear to everyone that he had done so only under the most severe duress. Another was the reference to his coronation oath, which raised the possibility that he might repudiate the reforms agreed by the Ordainers if he considered that they were contrary to his oath. These loopholes were to be used with great determination by Edward after the publication of the Ordinances in September 1311.[210]

On the day following Edward's concession, 17 March 1310, the prelates, earls and barons replied with letters patent of their own in which they rehearsed the king's consent to the appointment of Ordainers and undertook that this would not be made a precedent for any future action. The document was dated at London, which suggests that they were keeping at arm's length from the parliament at Westminster until everything had been settled to their satisfaction. The letter was issued in the names of the archbishop of Canterbury Robert Winchelsey and of ten bishops, London, Lincoln, Salisbury, Winchester, Norwich, Bath & Wells, Chichester, Worcester, Exeter, and St David's; eight earls, Gloucester, Lancaster, Lincoln, Hereford, Richmond, Pembroke, Warwick and Arundel; and thirteen barons: Henry of Lancaster, Henry de Percy, Hugh de Vere, Robert de Clifford, Robert Fitz Payn, William Marshal, John Lovel, Ralph Fitz William, Payn Tybetot, John Botetourt, Bartholomew de Badlesmere, John de Grey and John Cromwell.[211]

On 20 March the twenty-one Ordainers were elected and sworn in: the archbishop of Canterbury, the bishops of London, Salisbury, Chichester, Norwich, St David's and Llandaff; the earls of Gloucester, Lancaster, Lincoln, Pembroke, Hereford, Warwick, Richmond and Arundel; and six barons, Hugh de Vere, Hugh de Courtenay, Robert Fitz Roger, John de Grey, William Marshal and William Martin. Within the group of earls there was an even balance between those who were strongly in favour of reform, the earls of Lancaster, Hereford, Pembroke and Warwick, and those with more royalist inclinations, Gloucester, Lincoln, Richmond and Arundel. Of all the earls, only Oxford and Surrey, and, of course, Piers Gaveston earl of

---

[210] Edward's letters patent were enrolled on the Patent Roll and are also recorded in the *Annales Londonienses*: *CPR, 1307–13*, 215 (the full text is in *Foedera*, II, i, 105); *Ann. Lond.*, 169–70. Edward II's attempts to have the Ordinances annulled began as early as 12 Oct. 1311: see Phillips, 40–1, 46–8.

[211] The letter is preserved only in *Ann. Lond.*, 170–1, and in *Munimenta Gildhallae Lond.*, II, i, 200–2. See also Maddicott, 111–12.

Cornwall took no part in the events of March 1310. Of the bishops elected, the archbishop of Canterbury had long been an opponent of the misuse of royal authority so far as it applied to the Church. Although his name came first on the list of Ordainers, this was probably more a matter of dignity than an indication that he was their real leader. His primary role in 1310 was that of leader of the English Church and guardian of its interests. The bishops elected included only one of the four bishops closely associated with the crown – Chichester, Bath & Wells, Worcester, and Exeter – whose names had appeared in the letters patent of 17 March. The bishop of Chichester was however replaced as chancellor on 11 May by a close ally of the king, Walter Reynolds bishop of Worcester. Of the barons with connections with the king who had participated in composing that letter, Henry de Percy, Robert Fitz Payn (steward of the household), and John Cromwell (constable of the Tower of London), only Henry de Percy was elected as an Ordainer.[212] Finally, on 1 April, after all the upheavals of the past weeks, Edward II obtained some additional revenue when orders were issued to the assessors and collectors to finish the assessment of the twenty-fifth conditionally granted in the parliament of April 1309 and to proceed with its collection.[213]

EDWARD AND GAVESTON IN THE NORTH

The situation in Scotland had changed significantly since the accession of Edward II in 1307. By the end of 1309 Robert Bruce had greatly strengthened his position compared with two years earlier. He had now won control over Buchan, Ross and Argyll, and would soon add Galloway; he had resumed contact with France, raising the possibility of an active alliance; he had won over many prominent nobles; and he had held a parliament at St Andrews at which his authority as king of Scots had been more widely accepted than ever before. 'If Scotsmen still wanted to fight against Bruce, they must now do so as individual members of the English

---

[212] Maddicott, 111–12; Hamilton, 80, 157; Phillips, 30. There is a detailed analysis of the backgrounds and political alignments of the Ordainers in J.H. Trueman, 'The personnel of medieval reform', *Mediaeval Studies*, xxi (1959), 247–71. On the role played by the archbishop of Canterbury in 1310 see Denton, *Robert Winchelsey*, 261–2. Winchelsey took an oath to uphold the work and the decisions of the Ordainers, 'saving my estate and order and the liberty of the Church of Rome': Denton, 261. The names of the Ordainers are listed in *Ann. Lond.*, 172. For the form of election see *PW*, II, ii, 43. A notarial certificate of 17 March relating to the appointment of the Ordainers survives as BL, Cotton Charter XVI. 58. Robert de Clifford replaced Robert Fitz Roger after the latter's death.

Evidence that the French court was kept well informed about events in England in March 1310 can be found in BL, Add. Charter 11241, which contains the barons' petition for the reform of the realm, Edward II's letters patent of 16 March allowing the election of the Ordainers, the five preliminary ordinances issued shortly after their election, and the names of the Ordainers: see P. Chaplais, 'Chartes en déficit', *Bibliothèque de l'Ecole des Chartes*, cix (1951), 96–103.

[213] *Lay Taxes*, 30.

forces.'²¹⁴ Nonetheless there was a considerable English presence in Scotland. A few Scottish earls, Angus, Atholl, Dunbar and Strathearn, and other nobles, such as Alexander Abernethy and John Mowbray, were still loyal to the English crown, while there were English garrisons as far north as Perth, Dundee and Banff; at Edinburgh and Stirling in the Lowlands; in the south-west at Dumfries and Caerlaverock; and in the south-east at Jedburgh, Roxburgh and Berwick. Many of these were powerful fortresses whose garrisons could easily be supplied by sea.²¹⁵

If Edward had been able to mount a concerted campaign in Scotland, he should have maintained or even improved this position. But this was the problem. Ever since his accession Edward had been preoccupied with domestic issues, complicated by the difficulties in his relations with France. The material and financial resources were not available for warfare in Scotland on the scale of the campaigns mounted by his father, and, as events would show, there was the question of whether the English magnates would be willing to fight in Scotland. Edward had already planned a Scottish campaign in both 1308 and 1309, but without success. Now, in 1310, a new campaign was more than ever necessary. Matters came to a head on or just before 16 June when Edward was told at a council meeting by Alexander Abernethy, Alexander of Argyll and other loyal Scottish magnates that unless he went north in person and quickly, 'we should lose both the land and those who still remain faithful to us by reason of our default and our laxity'.²¹⁶ A decision was therefore taken to summon the army to Berwick for 8 September.²¹⁷ The proposed campaign also suited Edward personally, since it was a convenient way of putting a distance between himself and the activities of the Ordainers in London while at the same time ensuring the continued safety of Gaveston.²¹⁸

Edward had left Westminster for Scotland by the end of July, but he was joined on campaign only by the earls of Gloucester, Richmond, Surrey,

---

²¹⁴ Barrow, 173–87. For a map of the situation in Scotland, 1307–9, see ibid., 167.
²¹⁵ Ibid., 186, 190–2.
²¹⁶ Letter from Edward II to the earl of Pembroke: SC 1/49/6, cited in Maddicott, 113, and Phillips, 31, n. 2. The letter is published in *CDS*, iii, no. 95. SC 1/49/6 is part of a rich vein of material concerning the earl of Pembroke preserved in vol. 49 of Ancient Correspondence (SC 1) and elsewhere in TNA, which I used extensively in writing my biography of Aymer de Valence. The preservation of this material is probably the result of Pembroke's personal archives coming into royal hands after his death in 1324.
²¹⁷ According to Edward, the earls of Gloucester, Surrey, Cornwall and Richmond had all agreed to serve in Scotland, and he hoped that Pembroke would join them: SC 1/49/6. It is possible that Edward wrote in similar vein to the other absent earls.
²¹⁸ Gaveston had left court in Feb. and was supposed to be somewhere in the north at Easter (19 April). He was again with the king on 11 May, but had left to prepare for the coming campaign by mid-July. He rejoined the king, by the middle of Sept., possibly as early as the 7th: Hamilton, 82, 158. The *Vita*, 22–3, reports that Gaveston was even in danger of assassination in 1310–11. Hamilton, 91 & 162, n. 2, (citing *CPR, 1307–13*, 277) suggests that the Thomas de Walkingham of Yorkshire, for whose death Gaveston and six others had been pardoned in Sept. 1310, might have made an attempt on Gaveston's life.

and of course Cornwall. The earl of Lincoln was to be detained at Westminster by his duties as *custos regni*,[219] but four others, Lancaster, Hereford, Pembroke and Warwick, refused to join the campaign in person.[220] They did however send the minimum service they were legally obliged to provide, representing eight knights' fees in the case of Lancaster and five knight's fees for each of the other three earls.[221] Their refusal was justified on the pretext that they were too busy in their work as Ordainers, but the unspoken truth was that they knew that Gaveston would also be in the king's company.

Of the campaign itself the author of the *Vita Edwardi Secundi* remarked that 'the king entered Scotland with his army, but not a rebel was found to lay a hand upon him or to ambush his men, except that a few from the army, out foraging or on a plundering raid, were cut off'.[222] Although it was not a major campaign in terms of the size of the royal army and its objectives, it was not a negligible undertaking and showed some foresight and planning. With greater resources and a certain amount of luck much more might have been achieved.[223] The army consisted of about 3,000 infantry, most of them Welsh; 100 crossbowmen paid by the City of London for the defence of Berwick; the retinues of the four English earls and those of other magnates such as the Scottish earls of Angus and Strathearn, John de Segrave, John de St John, Henry de Percy, Roger Mortimer, John Cromwell, Henry de Beaumont, Hugh Audley and Bartholomew de Badlesmere; and the men of the royal household, about 50 knights and bannerets, and 200 men-at-arms. Altogether the mounted force totalled about 1,700. There were also large contingents in the garrisons of Berwick and Roxburgh.[224]

In October 1309 a plan had been devised to land a force of nearly 3,000 men from Ireland, led by the earl of Ulster, to help English allies in Argyll on the west coast of Scotland. Transported in Irish ships, supplemented by forty-five vessels from ports in the west of England, this army was intended to arrive in late June 1310, but was delayed and finally cancelled because of bad weather. Instead the earl of Ulster's men were diverted to the defence of the Isle of Man.[225] Despite this serious setback, which

[219] His appointment may have been discussed at the council meeting in June, but the actual appointment was not made until 1 Sept. when the king was at Newcastle upon Tyne: *Foedera*, II, i, 116.

[220] *Ann. Lond.*, 174; *Ann. Paul.*, 269; Maddicott, 114.

[221] C 47/5/8; *Ann. Lond.*, 174; *Vita*, 21–3; Phillips, 31; Maddicott, 114.

[222] *Vita*, 22–3.

[223] There are detailed accounts of the 1310–11 campaign in C. McNamee, *The Wars of the Bruces* (East Linton, 1997), 47–53; and D. Simpkin, 'The English army and the Scottish campaign of 1310–1311', in *England and Scotland in the Fourteenth Century*, ed. A. King & M. Penman (Woodbridge, Suffolk & Rochester, NY, 2007), 14–39.

[224] E 101/374/5, ff. 76–7; McNamee, 49, 69; Simpkin, 'English army', 22–3.

[225] McNamee, 48–9, 69; Barrow, 192–3. In the meantime Robert Bruce had also made important advances in Argyll.

undermined the strategy of the campaign, Edward entered Scotland in mid-September, reached Roxburgh on about 16 September, Selkirk on about the 23rd, and Biggar on about the 26th. He was at Renfrew and Glasgow in mid-October, then Linlithgow, and briefly at Edinburgh at the end of the month. Having ensured, so far as he could, the security of the English-held castles south of the Forth, he returned to Berwick-upon-Tweed on about 11 November.[226] Apart from a brief foray with a small force when Bruce made a raid into Lothian,[227] Edward was to remain at Berwick until the end of July 1311.

With the exception of the attack on an English foraging expedition, which is described by the *Vita*, little offensive action was carried out by either side. Bruce gave no opportunity for the English to bring him to battle.[228] The nearest Edward II and his army came to Bruce was in October when spies informed Edward that Bruce's army was on a moor near Stirling, but nothing came of this.[229] Ironically, when Edward did eventually make contact with Bruce and his army at Bannockburn in June 1314, it was in this very same area. During the winter of 1310–11, the English earls followed the king's example by retiring to bases just inside Scotland or near the English border, the earl of Gloucester at Norham, the earl of Surrey at Wark, and the earl of Cornwall at Roxburgh.[230] But it was also during this period that some contacts were made between Edward II and Robert Bruce. According to a letter written in February 1311, Robert de Clifford and Robert Fitz Payn had met Bruce with Edward II's approval at Selkirk on 17 December 1310. A second meeting between Bruce and the earls of Gloucester and Cornwall near Melrose did not however occur because Bruce was warned of possible treachery.[231] It was also reported in February, in a letter to the earl of Richmond, that Master John Walwayn, a royal clerk, had been arrested and was imprisoned in Berwick 'because he suddenly went towards those parts [the vicinity of Perth] to speak with Robert Bruce'.[232] The purpose of the contacts is unclear, but it is possible, as was to be alleged in 1311–12, that Edward was hoping that Robert Bruce would be prepared to offer Gaveston a place of refuge from his enemies in England in return for a truce or even peace.[233]

---

[226] Details taken from *Itinerary*, ed. Hallam. It is often difficult to distinguish the king's movements from those of his privy seal and of his court and household. McNamee, 49, suggests that Edward had already reached Berwick by 3 Nov. He could have travelled from Edinburgh to Berwick by sea.

[227] *Lanercost*, 214.

[228] *Vita*, 22–5; McNamee, 49–50.

[229] *CDS*, iii, no. 33; Hamilton, 84, 158.

[230] *Lanercost*, 214; Hamilton, 84, 158.

[231] *CDS*, iii, no. 197; McNamee, 51; Hamilton, 84, 158.

[232] *CDS*, v, no. 554; McNamee, 51–2. As Dr McNamee suggests, Walwayn may have been imprisoned to prevent the news of Edward's secret contacts with Bruce leaking out.

[233] *Vita*, 38–41. This report very clearly refers to late 1311 and early 1312, after Gaveston's return to England from his final exile.

With the failure of negotiations with Bruce – if that is really what they were – English campaigning resumed in early 1311. In January Gaveston left Roxburgh for Perth, via Dundee, in order to defend the area from Bruce and to prevent him from using it as a recruiting ground. In February the earls of Gloucester and Surrey passed through the forest of Selkirk to receive any of its inhabitants who were prepared to make peace with the king.[234] Gaveston remained at Perth until late March when he returned briefly to Berwick for a meeting with the king, apparently concerning the work of the Ordainers, after which he went back to Perth. Gaveston gave up command at Perth to Henry de Percy and the earl of Angus in early May and moved to Dundee.[235] According to the chronicle of Walter of Guisborough, the king had sent Gaveston against the Scots with a strong army so that he might make a name for himself and win praise. If so, he was to be disappointed, since the Scots kept their distance.[236]

This was effectively the end of Edward II's campaigning in the north. Money and supplies were running short;[237] Edward's attempt in May to obtain a grant of one foot soldier from every vill in England for a period of seven weeks at their own expense and without the approval of a parliament met with resistance and was soon abandoned, while his attempt to raise a force of nearly 4,000 men in Ireland and have them shipped to Ayr in Scotland in June 1311 in sixty-two English and Irish vessels was also a failure.[238] Edward had stayed in the north in order to fight the Scots, but also in order to evade the Ordainers and their demands for as long as possible. By July 1311 he could no longer resist the pressures to return to Westminster. In the meantime Edward had placed Gaveston for his personal safety in the powerful coastal fortress of Bamburgh in Northumberland, there to await the outcome of events in the south.[239] No sooner had Edward left Berwick than 'Robert [Bruce] unleashed a savage destruction of northern England'.[240]

THE MAKING OF THE ORDINANCES

The Ordainers had begun their work even before their formal election on 20 March, with the issuing on 19 March at the house of the Carmelites in London of six preliminary ordinances. These were later incorporated into

---

[234] Hamilton, 84–5, 158–9; McNamee, 51.

[235] Hamilton, 84–5, 158–9. There is valuable information about these events in two letters written from Berwick on 27 March, one from an unknown writer probably to the chancellor, the other from the king to the chancellor: C 47/22/10/8.

[236] *Guisborough*, 386.

[237] On 28 Feb. the king wrote demanding 4,000 marks from the executors of the earl of Lincoln; even the money owed to Gaveston for his men's wages was slow in payment: Hamilton, 159–60, n. 54.

[238] McNamee, 52–3, 69.

[239] *Ann. Paul.*, 269; Hamilton, 87, 160.

[240] McNamee, 53.

the Ordinances of 1311 but reflected the issues of greatest urgency in 1310. The first ordinance concerned the protection of the liberties of the Church. The second decreed that the Ordainers were to sit in London, where they would have the protection of the mayor and aldermen of the city, and from where they would have ready access to legal and other expert advice and to the records of the chancery and exchequer. The third stated that no gifts of land, revenue, franchises, or wardships and marriages were to be made without the approval of the Ordainers. The fourth ordered that the revenues of the customs duties were to be paid directly into the exchequer to be used for the maintenance of the king's household and for other proper purposes, so that the king could live from his own resources and not have to resort to prises. The fifth ordered that the foreign merchants who had received the profits of the customs since the death of Edward I should be arrested and their goods seized until they had accounted fully at the exchequer before the treasurer and barons of the exchequer and others to be appointed by the Ordainers. The final ordinance required the upholding of Magna Carta in all its points. Although the king ordered the city of London to protect the Ordainers and their work on 29 May,[241] he did not promulgate the preliminary ordinances until 2 August.[242]

Little is known about how the Ordainers carried out their work or who, if anyone, was the major contributor to the Ordinances which were finally published on 27 September 1311. Several of the earls among the Ordainers, in particular Lancaster, Warwick, Hereford and Pembroke, played an active role;[243] but it has also been suggested that 'some royal officials, sympathetic to the point of view of the Ordainers' may have contributed their expert knowledge of the workings of the royal administration and legal system.[244] The support of the Church for the promulgation and enforcement of the Ordinances after their publication in 1311 was to be important, but there is little in the Ordinances themselves to suggest that the clergy made any significant contribution to their formulation, least of all that the archbishop of Canterbury, Robert Winchelsey, was a prime mover.[245] Until recently no draft or other intermediate document had been known to suggest how the Ordinances developed. However, Michael Prestwich has discovered what appears to be a draft of the Ordinances in the archives of Durham cathe-

[241] *Ann. Lond.*, 173–4.
[242] The preliminary ordinances are recorded in *Ann. Lond.*, 172–3, and in *Foedera*, II, i, 113 (proclamation of 2 Aug.) and *RP*, i, 446–7. See also Maddicott, 112–13; Hamilton, 79.
[243] In Feb. 1311 these four earls were said to be in process of deciding certain matters about which the unnamed writer could not yet tell his correspondent: C 47/22/10/10. The four were also present together in London in July 1311: *Councils and Synods*, ed. F.M. Powicke & C.R. Cheney ii, part 2 (Oxford, 1964), 1314; Phillips, 31; Maddicott, 113; M. Prestwich, 'The Ordinances of 1311 and the politics of the early fourteenth century', in *Politics and Crisis in Fourteenth-century England*, ed. J. Taylor & W. R. Childs (Gloucester, 1990), 12–14.
[244] Prestwich, 'Ordinances of 1311', 14.
[245] Denton, *Robert Winchelsey*, 263–4.

dral. The document is undated, but it is likely that it is either a copy of a draft taken to the king by John Botetourt on behalf of the other Ordainers at the end of May 1311, or that it is the text of the Ordinances sent to the king for his approval on 3 August 1311.[246] The Durham text contains thirty-two clauses, only one of which is not to be found in the published text of the Ordinances. In addition to numerous minor variations in wording and the division of clause 35 of the Ordinances into two parts, the first six clauses, together with clauses 12 and 18, and the last four clauses do not appear in the Durham version. Clause 11 of the Durham version of the Ordinances, which is not in the official text, provides for the appointment in every parliament of a committee composed of a bishop, two earls and two barons to oversee the receipt of revenue at the exchequer, and required the treasurer and the keeper of the wardrobe to report there annually. Another significant difference between the Durham text and the Ordinances is in the language used to describe Gaveston, who is referred to in the former as an 'open enemy of the king', and whose deeds were committed 'traitorously as a traitor'. In the final published version of the Ordinances the only suggestion that Gaveston was guilty of treason is in the statement that his deeds were committed *treiterousement*.[247] These two differences between the draft and the final version may reflect second thoughts on the part of the Ordainers about, for example, the future role of parliament, but it is more likely that they were the result of resistance to their proposals by the king.[248]

Edward II had done his best to frustrate the work of the Ordainers by, for example, appointing his close ally Walter Reynolds, bishop of Worcester as chancellor in July 1310 without the consent of 'the community of England';[249] by failing to promulgate the preliminary Ordinances until 2 August;[250] and by ordering on 28 October the removal of the exchequer and both benches from Westminster to York by the following Easter.[251] This latter move, which was an attempt to remove the practical levers of power from possible influence by the Ordainers,[252] caused them great annoyance, including the moderate earl of Lincoln who reportedly

---

[246] M. Prestwich, 'A new version of the Ordinances of 1311', *BIHR*, lvii (1984), 193; Maddicott, 116. Botetourt was sent from London by the *custos regni* and the king's council on 27 May to visit the king at Berwick in order to expound certain matters especially concerning the king. He returned to London on 5 July: Bod., Tanner Ms. 197, f. 44. The Ordinances are not mentioned by name but this is clearly the business involved.

[247] Prestwich, 'New version', 190, 192–3.

[248] Edward was especially resistant to any language that described Gaveston as a traitor. He maintained this opposition after Gaveston's death in June 1312 and eventually won his point in the peace made between himself and Gaveston's former enemies in Nov. 1313.

[249] *Ann. Paul.*, 268–9; Maddicott, 113. Another royal ally, John Sandal, replaced Reynolds as treasurer.

[250] *Foedera*, II, i, 113.

[251] E 159/84, m.13d; Maddicott, 114.

[252] This in effect countered the second of the preliminary ordinances by which the Ordainers were to do their work in London.

threatened to resign from his position as *custos regni* during the king's absence in the north.[253] Earlier in October the king had shown his continued commitment to Gaveston by appointing him to the influential positions of justice of the forest north of the Trent and constable of Nottingham castle.[254] On 27 March 1311 the king wrote to the chancellor, Walter Reynolds, ordering him to see that anything decided by the Ordainers should be submitted to Reynolds and to do nothing concerning these matters without the king's advice and consent.[255]

Edward's situation was made more difficult by the death of Henry de Lacy the earl of Lincoln on 5 February.[256] Lincoln was a man of great experience who was trusted by both the magnates and the king, who had known him well since childhood. Lincoln's death, followed on 3 March by that of Anthony Bek, bishop of Durham another senior figure who had also been close to the king since his early years, removed a moderating force.[257] The appointment of Gilbert de Clare the earl of Gloucester as *custos regni* on 4 March[258] was no substitute for Lincoln. Although an Ordainer, Gloucester was young and inexperienced, as well as being Edward II's nephew and Gaveston's brother-in-law. There was therefore little chance that he could persuade his fellow Ordainers to be more sympathetic towards the king.

Gloucester soon found himself at odds with the earl of Lancaster,[259] who inherited Lincoln's two earldoms of Lincoln and Salisbury through his wife, Alice de Lacy, and also regarded himself as the earl of Lincoln's political heir. As the holder of the earldom of Leicester, Lancaster also saw himself as the political heir of Simon de Montfort. Altogether Lancaster was now in the unique position of holding five earldoms, those of Lancaster, Leicester and Derby, as well as the two inherited from Lincoln.[260] The value of his estates has been estimated at about £11,000 a

---

[253] *CDS*, iii, no. 177; Maddicott, 114.

[254] *Foedera*, II, i, 116; *CFR, 1307–19*, 73; Hamilton, 82, 158. These appointments were made on 1 Oct. when Gaveston and the king were at Biggar in Scotland.

[255] *CDS*, iii, no. 204; Maddicott, 116.

[256] *Ann. Lond.*, 175; *Ann. Paul.*, 269. The earl was buried 'with great honour' in the Lady Chapel of St Paul's cathedral of which he had been a benefactor.

[257] Bek does not appear to have played any major part in the events of 1310–11, although his death took place at Eltham in Kent, close to London. He was buried in his cathedral at Durham on 3 May. Since Edward II was still at Berwick, he may well have attended, although there is no record of this. Earlier, on 20 Feb., he had made an offering of a gold cloth at the tomb of St Cuthbert: Bod., Tanner Ms. 197, f. 63v. After the bishop's death the king reserved for his own use Bek's famous Weardale stud of 240 horses and the pick of his jewels, and later bought from his executors his gold plate for 2,075 marks (£1,383). He also bought for £500 Bek's campaign tents, and ten *stabuli* for destriers and other horses: see the article on Bek by C. M. Fraser in *Oxford DNB*.

[258] *Foedera*, II, i, 129.

[259] Apart from the delicate political situation, there was a feud between one of Lancaster's retainers, Henry de Segrave, and one of Gloucester's, Walter de Berningham: Maddicott, 116.

[260] Maddicott, 114–15, 321–2; idem, *Simon de Montfort* (Cambridge, 1994), 365–6.

year, which placed him far ahead of his nearest rival among the earls, Gloucester, whose lands were worth about £6,000 at his death in 1314. This gave Lancaster the ability to recruit and pay retainers on a large scale and an exceptional opportunity to influence politics at both a local and a national level. All he needed in addition was a measure of personal ability and political skill, and in these he proved to be lacking.[261]

Lancaster was soon at odds with Edward II as well, refusing to join him in Scotland to perform fealty for his newly inherited lands. Lancaster eventually met the king near Berwick, just south of the border, and performed fealty, while at the same time pointedly ignoring Gaveston's presence with the king and causing further offence.[262]

PARLIAMENT AND THE PUBLICATION OF THE ORDINANCES

On 4 April an anonymous letter writer sent a message from Alnwick in Northumberland in which he commented that 'the king is in no mood yet for a parliament, but when the earl of Gloucester and the council meet in London, he will have to do what they order'.[263] Edward had little choice. Sooner or later a parliament would have to be called in order to publish the results of the work of the Ordainers, whose commission was due to expire on 29 September. A parliament was also the only answer to his desperate need of funds. Edward bowed to the inevitable at Berwick on 16 June and summoned a parliament to meet at London on 8 August.[264] He left Berwick in late July, arrived in London on 13 August where he lodged with the Dominicans, and on 16 August he met parliament.[265] According to the *Vita Edwardi Secundi*, the business of parliament was then delayed by the absence of some of the notables and in the meantime Edward visited the shrine of St Thomas at Canterbury before returning to London at the end of August.[266]

By this time the power of prayer was about all that was left to Edward. The *Vita* records that

> when all those concerned had gathered together, the year's work was produced and the chapters were recited one by one, and a copy was

---

[261] Maddicott, 5, 9, 22–3.

[262] *Lanercost*, 215; and the account given in the unpublished chronicle, BL, Nero D.X, f. 109v; Maddicott, 115. Lancaster did not perform homage for his lands until 26 Aug. when he did so in London: ibid.

[263] *CDS*, iii, no. 202; Maddicott, 115.

[264] *PW*, II, ii, 44–56, and Appendix 37–9, 41.

[265] *Vita*, 30–1. The mayor and aldermen of the city of London took precautions for the safekeeping of the city during the parliament: Davies, *Baronial Opposition*, 366.

[266] *Vita*, 30–1. Edward II's itinerary does not record a visit to Canterbury but it is possible.

made available to the king's counsellors.[267] But the king and his council protested that some things were disadvantageous to him, some devised out of hatred, and he argued and pleaded that he was not bound to give his consent to these, since in the commission granted to them matters touching the king's sovereignty had been excluded. The barons knew, however, that the king's excuses were frivolous and invented and always meant to gain time; they therefore firmly stood their ground, setting the common good above the king's loss. There was, however, one of these Ordinances that distressed the king more than the rest, namely the expulsion of Piers Gaveston and his exile; to this the king could in no way be persuaded or brought to agree. Nevertheless, to satisfy the barons he offered these terms: 'whatever things have been ordained or decided on', he said, 'however much they may redound to my private disadvantage, shall be established at your request and remain in force for ever. But you shall stop persecuting my brother Piers, and allow him to have the earldom of Cornwall.' The king sought this time and again, now coaxing them with flattery, now hurling threats; but the barons firmly stood their ground putting forward many arguments as the king's faithful subjects consulting the king's interests, and finally, as if with one mind and voice, they added at the end of their reply that either Piers should suffer exile according to the judgement of the Ordainers, or each man would consider how to defend his own life.[268]

Faced with the threat of civil war and under pressure from his advisers, Edward II finally gave way. On 27 September, only two days before the expiry of the Ordainers' mandate, the Ordinances were published in St Paul's churchyard by the bishop of Salisbury, acting on behalf of the archbishop of Canterbury, in the presence of several bishops, the earls of Lancaster, Pembroke, Hereford, Oxford, Warwick and Arundel, and many barons.[269] On 5 October the leading members of the king's council, the earl of Gloucester, Henry de Percy, Hugh Despenser, the chancellor and treasurer, and others also came to St Paul's churchyard and announced the king's acceptance of the Ordinances.[270] On the same date a copy of the Ordinances under the king's Great Seal was delivered to the mayor and sheriffs to be published in the city and then to be deposited in a safe place.[271] On 8 October, the day before the end of the first session of parliament, writs

[267] The statements in Davies, *Baronial Opposition*, 366, 591; Maddicott, 116; Hamilton, 87, that a copy of the Ordinances was sent to Edward on 3 Aug. 1311 are incorrect. The evidence cited, SC 1/37/110, refers to the preliminary ordinances of 1310 and is dated 3 Aug. that year. See *PROME*, Westminster Parliament of 1310, App.

[268] *Vita*, 30–3. The translation is that of the editor. While there is no official record of the proceedings of the 1311 parliament, the *Vita* account probably gives a fair representation of what took place.

[269] *Liber de Antiquis Legibus*, ed. T. Stapleton, Camden Soc., xxxiv (London, 1846), 251.

[270] Ibid., 251; *SR*, i, 167.

[271] *Munimenta Gildhallae Lond.*, ed. Riley, II, i, 203.

were issued ordering the reconvening of the parliament at Westminster on 5 November;[272] and on 10 October a copy of the Ordinances was sent into each county for proclamation by the sheriff.[273] Measures were also taken to implement the Ordinances. On 9 October writs were issued 'by the king and the whole council' revoking all grants made in Scotland and Ireland; on the same day orders were given for the collection of the new customs to cease; and on 11 October detailed schedules were sent to the escheators north and south of the Trent ordering them to seize all lands granted since the appointment of the Ordainers on 16 March 1310.[274] On 18 October new sheriffs were appointed at the exchequer in the presence of the chancellor and treasurer and other members of the council.[275]

THE ORDINANCES[276]

The Ordinances were contained in a lengthy document of forty-one clauses which dealt with a wide range of grievances. In a clear reference to the Scottish campaign of 1310–11, the king was forbidden to go to war or to leave the kingdom without the consent of the baronage in parliament.[277] The king was not to make any gifts of land or other grants without the approval of the baronage in parliament and all grants made since the appointment of the Ordainers were to be revoked, until the king's debts had been paid off.[278] Prises, i.e. the seizure of foodstuffs for royal use and without immediate payment, which were deeply resented and which the Ordainers had feared might lead to popular revolt, were to cease.[279] The customs duties were to be paid directly into the exchequer and not to be collected by aliens (a reference

[272] *PW*, II, ii, 57–68.
[273] *Liber de Antiquis Legibus*, 251–2; *CCR, 1307–13*, 439; *Foedera*, II, i, 146.
[274] *Foedera*, II, i, 145; *CFR, 1307–19*, 108–9; Davies, *Baronial Opposition*, 386–7. Gaveston's lands were not seized until 30 Nov., which may indicate resistance on the part of the king.
[275] E 368/82, m.20 (schedule); Phillips, 31–2. This was in accordance with clause 39 of the Ordinances. The offices of chancellor, treasurer and keeper of the privy seal remained in the hands of loyal supporters of Edward II (Walter Reynolds, John Sandal and William Melton), until 23 Oct. when Walter of Norwich, one of the barons of the exchequer, was appointed as acting treasurer. The Great Seal itself remained in the hands of the king from 28 Sept. 1311 (the day after the first publication of the Ordinances) until 9 Dec. when it was returned to its baronial keepers: Chaplais, 75, n. 26.
[276] For a general assessment of the Ordinances see Prestwich, 'Ordinances of 1311', esp. 9–15. For a clause by clause discussion see Davies, *Baronial Opposition*, 368–82, and *passim* (see index). There are also valuable discussions of the Ordinances in general and of particular clauses in Maddicott (see index). For a convenient English translation of the Ordinances see *English Historical Documents*, 529–39. The complete French text of the Ordinances can be found both in *RP*, i, 281–6, and *SR*, i, 157–67. A more readily available, but incomplete text (some clauses have only a descriptive heading, while others are abbreviated), is available in *Select Documents*, 11–17. On the texts of the Ordinances see App. to the Westminster parliament of 1311 in *PROME*.
[277] Clause 9.
[278] Clause 7.
[279] Clause 10.

to the Italian merchant company, the Frescobaldi of Florence);[280] no revenues were to be collected for the direct use of the royal household, which was to be maintained by the exchequer.[281] These provisions reflected the financial confusion into which the royal government had fallen under the pressures of the Scottish war and had their roots both in the reign of Edward I and in current practice. But they were also designed to ensure that the king could not evade control of his expenditure by collecting revenue locally. In each parliament one bishop, two earls, and two barons were to be assigned to hear the protests of all those who wished to complain of any contraventions of the Ordinances by any of the king's officers, whoever they might be.[282] Parliament should meet at least once a year, and if necessary twice, and in a convenient location. This was to ensure that legal cases might be brought to a proper conclusion and that men could bring forward complaints about the activities of royal officials.[283] It is likely that this provision of the Ordinances was intended to address the grievance expressed in the parliament of April 1309 that petitions were no longer being received and answered in parliament. All the leading members of the royal administration, the chancellor and treasurer, the chief justices, the steward, keeper and controller of the king's household, the keeper of the king's privy seal, and other officials were to be appointed in parliament with the advice and approval of the magnates.[284] County sheriffs were to be appointed by the chancellor and treasurer and other members of the council then present.[285] All royal officials, from the most senior to the most junior, were to swear to uphold the Ordinances when they were appointed.[286]

Up to this point the Ordinances 'to a very considerable extent restated familiar questions which had been debated under Edward I' and which had continued into the reign of Edward II.[287] However, what gave the Ordinances a distinctive flavour was their insistence on 'evil and deceptive counsel' and on 'evil counsellors' as causes of the troubles of the king and his kingdom: this was the reason for the appointment of the chancellor, etc. only with baronial advice and approval; [288] 'all the evil counsellors' were to 'be ejected and dismissed altogether' and replaced by other more suitable persons.[289] Gaveston was especially singled out for attention: he 'has acted badly towards and has badly advised our lord the king and has

[280] Clauses 4, 5 & 8.
[281] Clause 8.
[282] Clause 40.
[283] Clause 29. Prestwich, 'Ordinances of 1311', 10–11. As Prestwich points out, 'There was no suggestion that biennial meetings were needed so as to ensure that baronial advice prevailed.'
[284] Clause 14.
[285] Clause 17.
[286] Clause 39.
[287] Prestwich, 'Ordinances of 1311', 10.
[288] Clause 14.
[289] Clause 13.

incited him to do wrong in divers and deceptive ways; in taking possession for himself of all of the kingdom's treasure and sending it out of the kingdom; in drawing to himself royal power and royal dignity; in lording it over the estate of the king and of the crown, to the ruin of the king and of the people; and especially in estranging the heart of the king from his lieges'.[290] Gaveston 'as the evident enemy of the king and of his people' was to 'be completely exiled as well from the kingdom of England, Scotland, Ireland and Wales as from the whole lordship of our lord the king overseas as well as on this side, forever without ever returning'. He was to leave England from the port of Dover no later than 1 November 1311. In a chilling anticipation of Gaveston's eventual fate, the Ordinances added that if he were found anywhere in the king's dominions after that date he would be treated as an enemy of the king and his people.[291]

From 1311 until their annulment at the York parliament of May 1322 the Ordinances and their enforcement on the one hand and the king's attempts to evade them or to have them annulled on the other were to be a constant source of political tension between the king and his baronial opponents. The most notable of these was the king's first cousin, Thomas, earl of Lancaster, who erected a tablet in St Paul's cathedral to commemorate Edward II's acceptance of the Ordinances.[292] One chronicler even went so far as to talk about 'the Ordinances of the Earl of Lancaster'.[293] This element of personal animosity was present right from the start and it was to colour English politics for the next decade. No resolution was possible until either Lancaster and his (diminishing) band of supporters were victorious over the king or Edward II succeeded in destroying both Lancaster and the Ordinances. But even without such enmities, it is unlikely that the Ordinances could have achieved a successful end to the administrative and, above all, financial problems facing the government of England, whether the king or the magnates were in charge. As Michael Prestwich has perceptively remarked, 'No regime proved capable of carrying out the programme [of the Ordinances]. What was desirable in the Ordinances was impractical, and what was practical was undesirable. In part, the Ordinances proved unworkable because the administrative mechanisms proposed, notably the payment of all the revenues of the

---

[290] The charges against Gaveston are very general and do not stand up to detailed scrutiny. See Hamilton, 88, 161, n. 72; Chaplais, 73–4.

[291] Clause 20. The translation is taken from *English Historical Documents*, 532. Three other individuals or groups of people were also singled out in the Ordinances. Henry de Beaumont and his sister Isabella de Vescy, who had obtained or procured grants from the king contrary to the Ordinances, were to be removed from the court. Henry was to leave the king's council and not to come near the king except in parliament or during wartime. Amerigo and other members of the company of the Frescobaldi were to render accounts for the money they had received from the crown and their lands and goods were to be seized: clauses 21–3.

[292] Bod., Lyell Ms.17, f. 115v; Maddicott, 117.

[293] *Chroniques de Sempringham*, 344; Maddicott, 119.

land through the Exchequer, could not be put into effect at a time when the government was placed under very considerable strain. There was no proper mechanism suggested for the day-to-day supervision of government, and the concept of baronial parliamentary consent for many matters was difficult to put into effect.'[294]

PART THREE

GAVESTON'S LAST EXILE

Soon after the publication of the Ordinances Edward left London for Windsor and Langley, where he spent the next month, probably in a state of mental and physical exhaustion but also determined to fight back. On about 2 October he had a boatload of jewels moved from Westminster to the Tower of London, probably in order to give himself an independent source of revenue through pawning individual items as needed.[295] On 12 October, only two days after the general publication of the Ordinances, he sent Robert de Newington and William de Lughtebergh to the pope and to seven English representatives at the Council of Vienne to deliver a protestation asking for the Ordinances to be annulled if they should prove prejudicial to him.[296] These or later envoys took a letter asking the pope to absolve Edward from his oath to uphold the Ordinances and to send envoys to England.[297] It is also possible that Edward hoped that papal intervention would allow Gaveston's return to England.[298]

Gaveston did not leave England from Dover on 1 November as required in the Ordinances;[299] instead he departed on 3 November from an unidentified place on the Thames. He landed at a place *inter Rutenos*, which was

---

[294] Prestwich, 'Ordinances of 1311', 14.

[295] BL, Cotton Ms. Nero C.VIII, f. 82v; Chaplais, 94–5, 106–7. It was not uncommon for kings to pawn some of their valuables to raise money or act as collateral for loans. Edward I, for example, did so in Brabant in 1297 and Edward III did the same in 1339 when he pledged the Great Crown to the archbishop of Trier: Chaplais, 97; E.B. Fryde, 'Financial resources of Edward III in the Netherlands, 1337–40', in Fryde, *Studies in Medieval Trade and Finance* (London, 1983), item VII, 1165.

[296] BL, Cotton Ms. Nero C.VIII, ff. 55, 55v; Phillips, 40–1. The English delegation at Vienne was an impressive one, consisting of the archbishop of York, the bishops of London, Winchester and Carlisle, Otto de Grandison (an ally of the English crown of long standing), Amanieu d'Albret (from Gascony), and Master Adam Orleton, canon of Hereford (destined to play a major role in Edward II's reign, especially at its end). Three copies of the protestation were made by public notaries who were paid 40s for their work on 13 Oct.

[297] *Liber Epistolaris of Richard of Bury*, ed. N. Denholm-Young, Roxburghe Club (Oxford, 1950), 104–5: an undated letter but before 14 May 1312. Cf. *CPL, 1305–42*, 104.

[298] There is some evidence for this. Gaveston's nephew Bertrand Caillau was sent to the pope for this purpose, but was arrested and held by Philip IV of France to prevent him from doing so: E 101/375/8, f. 12; Hamilton, 163, n. 10.

[299] On 8 Oct. the king had given him a safe conduct lasting until 1 Nov.: *CPR, 1307–13*, 393.

probably somewhere on the coast of northern France or in Flanders.[300] Although the author of the *Annales Paulini* states that Gaveston went to Bruges in the county of Flanders,[301] it is not known for certain where he spent his final exile. It is likely that Edward had intended him to go to the comparative safety of the duchy of Brabant.[302] Already, on 9 October, he had written to his brother-in-law and his sister Margaret, the duke and duchess of Brabant, asking them to receive Gaveston kindly and treat him honourably; and on 13 October Edward sent one of his household knights, Gerald Salveyn, to Philip IV asking him to give Gaveston safe conduct.[303] Gaveston himself had sent Blasius de Siena, a merchant of the Frescobaldi, to Brabant 'and elsewhere' to make financial arrangements. It seems that even Queen Isabella, who might have been expected to be hostile to Gaveston, showed sympathy by offering him financial assistance from the revenues of the county of Ponthieu.[304] On the other hand there is nothing to suggest that the king either attempted or was able to provide Gaveston with the financial support he received during his previous exile in 1308–9. It is likely that, for all the commands of the Ordainers, Edward and Gaveston did not expect to be parted for very long.[305]

Having got Gaveston out of the country, some at least of the former Ordainers then decided to move against his followers and everyone associated with him. At some point between 25 and 30 November a document which is sometimes described as a second set of Ordinances was presented to the king, having apparently been drawn up by the earls of Lancaster and Warwick.[306] Although the articles have usually been regarded primarily as an attempt to impose further reform on the king's

---

[300] *Ann. Lond.*, 202; Chaplais, 74; Hamilton, 91. There is no evidence that the king, who appears to have been at Windsor in early Nov., saw Gaveston off on his travels.

[301] *Ann. Paul.*, 271; Hamilton, 91, 162, 163, n. 11.

[302] Brussels, the capital of the duchy, although in a different political jurisdiction, is not far from Bruges.

[303] *Foedera*, II, i, 144; BL, Cotton Ms. Nero C.VIII, f. 65; Chaplais, 75; Phillips, 41; Maddicott, 117; Hamilton, 91–2.

[304] BL, Cotton Ms. Nero C.VIII, f. 83; Chaplais, 75–6.

[305] On 22 Oct. Gaveston nominated attorneys to act for him in England for a period of five years: *CPR, 1307–13*, 397. This does not however mean that he intended to be absent for this long.

[306] The rubric in *Ann. Lond.*, 198, describes the document as *Ordinationes comitum secundae*, but there is nothing in the document itself to suggest that they were supplementary ordinances with the same validity as the original Ordinances. They were in any case drawn up after the expiry of the Ordainers' commission on 29 Sept. There is consequently no official text of the document, which is preserved only in *Ann. Lond.*, 198–202; in the *Munimenta Gildhallae Lond.*, ed. Riley, II, ii, 682–90; and in Canterbury Cathedral Library Ms. K.11, dorse. The text in the *Munimenta* begins with the rubric *Ces sunt les articles qe les countes de Lancastre e de Warrewyke maunderent au roi*. The likely date of the document is given by Tout in *Chapters*, ii, 198, n. 1. For the text of the articles see also *Select Documents*, 18–19. However this edition omits much of the detail, especially the names of Gaveston's followers.

household,[307] the real thrust of the document was the removal from royal service of anyone connected with Gaveston. Of the twenty-seven persons named in the articles, eighteen had links with him, including his nephews Bertrand and Arnaud Caillau who were to follow their uncle into exile.[308] It was probably no coincidence that on 30 November the sheriffs of Cornwall, Berkshire and of seven other counties were ordered to take all Gaveston's castles, lands and other possessions into the king's hands. To emphasize the depths of his humiliation he was referred to not as the former earl of Cornwall or even as a knight but simply as Peter de Gaveston.[309] All of this happened against a background of extreme tension between the king and the barons, which led to Edward's order on 28 November that the earls of Gloucester, Lancaster, Hereford, Pembroke, Warwick and Arundel should remove the armed men whom they had brought to parliament.[310] There were even rumours that Gaveston had not left the country at all but was lurking somewhere in the West of England. In order to lay the rumours to rest two former Ordainers, Hugh de Courtenay and William Martin, were ordered on 30 November to search everywhere in Cornwall, Devon, Somerset and Dorset where Gaveston might possibly be hiding.[311]

GAVESTON'S RETURN

What followed appears to have been the result of a deliberate decision by Edward II to defy the Ordainers by recalling Gaveston to England and reinstating him in his former position as earl of Cornwall; and to accompany this act of defiance with a public repudiation of the Ordinances. For Gaveston there was the knowledge that his wife Margaret de Clare was at York and about to give birth to their first child. For both Edward II and Gaveston the events of the early months were a desperate gamble, which were to lead to the death of Gaveston and a very real possibility of civil war.

The last act in the tragedy of Gaveston opened on 1 December 1311 when Gerard Salveyn was sent back to the continent by the king. Initially Salveyn's mission was to seek an extension of Gaveston's safe conduct from the king of France, but the length of his absence from England may,

---

[307] See Tout, *Place of the Reign*, 86–7; Davies, *Baronial Opposition*, 382–5.
[308] For the full details see Hamilton, 88–9, 161–2.
[309] *CFR, 1307–19*, 117.
[310] *Foedera*, II, i, 151.
[311] Ibid., 151; Chaplais, 77; Hamilton, 92, 163. A variant of this rumour was reported by the author of the *Vita*, who said that, after his return to England from exile, Gaveston was thought to be either in the king's apartments, at his former castle of Wallingford, or at Tintagel in Cornwall: *Vita*, 38–9. The stories are remarkably like the false reports of Edward II's survival at Corfe and later escape to Italy which circulated after his death at Berkeley in 1327: see Phillips, ' "Edward II" in Italy', 209–26.

as Chaplais suggests, indicate that something more was afoot.[312] On 19 December, the day after the conclusion of the 1311 parliament, writs of summons were issued for a new meeting of parliament at Westminster on 13 February to consider business left unfinished in the previous parliament.[313] So far there was no hint of what was to come, but over Christmas, which Edward spent at Westminster,[314] he appears to have decided to trust both his own fate and that of Gaveston to the north of England.[315] Edward set out from Westminster soon after Christmas and on 8 January 1312 arrived at Knaresborough in Yorkshire, where he was joined by Salveyn on 13 January.[316] It is highly probable that Salveyn was accompanied by Gaveston,[317] since a draft newsletter addressed to the archbishop of York recorded that on the same date the king, Gaveston (described as earl of Cornwall), and others arrived in York, only 18 miles away from Knaresborough.[318] It is likely that the king then rushed to York as soon as Gaveston joined him at Knaresborough.[319] Whether Gaveston had been directly summoned back to England by the king or whether he had decided that the risk of returning was better than the prospect of a miserable and uncertain exile there is no way of knowing. Gaveston had in any case good reason for hastening to York on 13 January, since his wife Margaret de Clare had just given birth to a daughter, Joan.[320] On 20 February Edward II gave Margaret 40 marks to celebrate her churching and held a feast in the house of the Friars Minor at York, at which the guests were entertained by 'King Robert' and other minstrels.[321] This was to be the last celebration enjoyed by Edward and Gaveston.

It seems unlikely that Gaveston intended returning to his place of exile on the continent after celebrating the birth of his daughter,[322] or indeed

---

[312] BL, Cotton Ms. Nero C.VIII, f. 65r; Chaplais, 77. Salveyn was away from 1 Dec. until 13 Jan.

[313] *PW*, II, ii, 70–1. This parliamentary summons is not noted in Fryde et al., *Handbook of British Chronology*.

[314] Gaveston was not with the king at Christmas either here or elsewhere, as some of the chroniclers claimed: Hamilton, 92–3, 163, n. 18; Chaplais, 79.

[315] His decision may have been influenced by the letter he received from Gaveston and replied to on 23 Dec.: BL, Cotton Ms. Nero C.VIII, f. 84; Hamilton, 93, 163, n. 19.

[316] BL, Cotton Ms. Nero C.VIII, f. 65r; Chaplais, 77–8.

[317] On his journey from the south of England Gaveston (and probably also Salveyn) had stayed for two days in Nottingham: E 101/375/8, f. 25; Hamilton, 93, 163, n. 20.

[318] SC 1/37/218 (cited and trans. in Maddicott, 122–3); Chaplais, 78. The others included Walter Langton, the bishop of Coventry & Lichfield, and Henry de Beaumont.

[319] Chaplais, 78.

[320] Ibid., 78–9. Chaplais worked out that the birth probably occurred on 12 Jan., 40 days before Margaret was churched on 20 Feb.: ibid.

[321] BL, Cotton Ms. Nero C.VIII, f. 84v; Hamilton, 94; Chaplais, 78.

[322] As suggested in Chaplais, 79. On the other hand there is some evidence that in Feb. and March 1312 Gaveston was making preparations for a possible return to the continent: Hamilton, 94, 163–4, nn. 33–4.

that Edward would have allowed him to go. The die was now cast and after 13 January events unfolded quickly. On 16 January the king informed a gathering of Yorkshire knights and other notables that he had consented to the Ordinances under duress and that he had therefore revoked them.[323] On 18 January the king announced officially that Peter de Gaveston, earl of Cornwall, had joined him at York on his orders, that Gaveston had been exiled against law and custom, and that he was ready to justify himself before the king, who regarded him as good and loyal.[324] On 20 January orders were given for the restoration of all Gaveston's lands.[325] On the same day the king wrote to the earls of Lancaster, Gloucester, Pembroke, Hereford, Surrey, Warwick, Arundel and Oxford, cancelling the summons to parliament, since he could not come to Westminster 'for certain reasons'.[326] The proclamation of Gaveston's return from exile and reinstatement was read at the Guildhall on 29 January.[327] The anger of the earls at this news cannot have been assuaged by the duplicity of another royal order on the 26th that the Ordinances should continue to be observed 'so far as they are not prejudicial to the king',[328] or by the appointment of Walter Langton as treasurer on the 23rd.[329] Langton's volte-face was particularly infuriating. Having been first dismissed from office and imprisoned by Edward II in 1307, he had been released from prison under pressure from the Ordainers, to whose secrets he was privy, and was now once more a close confidant of the king, who undoubtedly needed his experience and financial skills.[330]

In the meantime the earl of Lancaster had written to the king demanding either the surrender of Gaveston to the barons or his renewed exile. Edward received and replied to these letters on 30 January, no doubt reacting with a display of defiance.[331] Edward was also making limited preparations for the possibility of war. On 28 January he ordered ten castles to be inspected and put in a state of defence,[332] and also gathered men and horses at York.[333] This was probably the reason for the summons

---

[323] SC 1/37/218; Maddicott, 122. See the discussion of the date of this meeting in Chaplais, 80, where both 9 and 16 Jan. are given as possibilities.

[324] *Foedera*, II, i, 153–4; *CCR, 1307–13*, 448–9. The king had control of the Great Seal which had been brought north on 7 Jan. by the three chancery clerks in whose custody it had been: *CCR, 1307–13*, 448. According to a note on the Close Roll the king had personally drafted the proclamation of Gaveston's return. See also Chaplais, 80, n. 40.

[325] *Foedera*, II, i, 154; *CCR, 1307–13*, 449.

[326] *PW*, II, ii, 71–2.

[327] *Ann. Paul.*, 271.

[328] *Foedera*, II, i, 154; *CCR, 1307–13*, 449.

[329] *CPR, 1307–13*, 413.

[330] According to the newsletter mentioned above (SC 1/37/218) Langton was, after Gaveston, the closest man to the king. The author of the *Flores* was scathing about Langton's duplicity: *Flores*, 148–9; Chaplais, 83.

[331] BL, Cotton Ms. Nero C.viii, f. 87v; *Trokelowe*, 74–5; Maddicott, 124.

[332] *CPR, 1307–13*, 469–70.

[333] BL, Cotton Ms. Nero C.VIII, ff. 63–4, 85; Hamilton, 93, 163, n. 29.

of forty-five notables from the north of England to be at York on 20 February to discuss 'certain arduous and special matters'.[334] There is nothing however to suggest that the king could have held out unaided against a full-scale onslaught if the magnates had decided to exert all their power. This may help to explain the rumour reported by the author of the *Vita Edwardi Secundi* that Edward had made overtures to Robert Bruce, even offering to recognize him as king of Scots, in return for refuge and protection to Gaveston.[335]

THE PURSUIT AND SURRENDER OF GAVESTON

Meanwhile in London the anger of the earls was given free rein at a meeting of prelates and magnates summoned by the archbishop of Canterbury at St Paul's on 13 March.[336] So little did the king appreciate the seriousness of the situation that on 8 March he had written to the archbishop asking him to give a hearing to a number of royal judges and clerks whom Edward was sending to discuss aspects of the Ordinances of especial importance to him.[337] Instead the archbishop excommunicated Gaveston,[338] and the earls then devised a plan for Gaveston's capture. According to the *Vita*, the earls of Lancaster, Pembroke, Hereford, Arundel and Warwick bound themselves by a mutual oath to act against Gaveston but kept their plans secret to avoid warning the king and Gaveston. The earl of Gloucester, the king's nephew and Gaveston's brother-in-law, was not a party to the plan but agreed to approve whatever the earls did. The earl of Lancaster then went to the north while the other earls proclaimed tournaments in various places as a way of gathering men without causing alarm.[339] The author of the *Annales Londonienses* gives a more specific account of their plans. The earl of Gloucester was to look after the south (where he would be least likely to come into contact with the king); the earl of Hereford was put in charge of Essex and the east; Lancaster would look after North Wales (*Venedocia*) and the west; Robert de Clifford and Henry de Percy were to go to the Scottish March to prevent any possible contact between the king and Robert Bruce; and, most crucially, the earls of Pembroke and Surrey were deputed to capture

---

[334] *PW*, II, ii, 71–2.

[335] *Vita*, 38–41; Maddicott, 123–4. Bruce is said to have replied that if Edward II could not keep faith with his liege men, whose homage and fealty he had received, he could not possibly do so with him. There is no evidence to support this report but it is possible that Edward did consider such a move. It may also be significant that on 6 Feb. 1312 orders were given for the transfer of Robert Bruce's wife Elizabeth and her followers to more comfortable imprisonment in Windsor castle: *CCR, 1307–13*, 394.

[336] *Registrum Simonis de Gandavo*, ed. Flower & Dawes, 418–19; *Ann. Lond.*, 203–4.

[337] *que quamplurimum insident cordi nostro*: *PW*, II, ii, 71; Maddicott, 124.

[338] *Vita*, 40–1, and n. 74. The earls however wanted to avoid open war: *Trokelowe*, 69.

[339] *Vita*, 40–3.

Gaveston and then inform the king.³⁴⁰ The earls of Pembroke and Hereford and John Botetourt were also instructed by the council to prevent Walter Langton from presiding as treasurer at the exchequer, which they succeeded in doing on 3 and 4 April. Langton was told firmly that since he had taken an oath to uphold the Ordinances and he had now accepted appointment from the king as treasurer in breach of their provisions, he had committed perjury. The chamberlains of the exchequer were also told that they were not to deliver any money or treasure to anyone through whom it could reach 'the enemy of the kingdom'.³⁴¹

Edward and Gaveston were making their own preparations in the north. At the end of February the king was briefly at Scarborough before returning to York where he remained until early April. This was probably when Gaveston was first placed for safety in Scarborough castle, which was on the coast and offered the possibility of reinforcement if besieged or of escape by sea to the continent or to Scotland.³⁴² From the middle of March the garrison and the defences of Scarborough were both strengthened.³⁴³

Gaveston briefly rejoined Edward at York on 31 March when he was given custody of both Scarborough and Carlisle castles.³⁴⁴ On 3 April he was reappointed to the office of justice of the forest north of the Trent, from which he had been removed after the publication of the Ordinances, and was made constable of Nottingham castle.³⁴⁵ On 4 April Edward ordered Gaveston, on pain of forfeiture not to surrender Scarborough to anyone except the king, even if the king himself were brought there a prisoner; and if the king were to die, he should hold the castle for his heirs.³⁴⁶ This was an extraordinary command which shows that Edward was prepared to meet any fate himself, while ironically not allowing for the possibility of Gaveston's own capture and death. It is probably no coincidence that on 28 March Edward had granted 700 marks to the Dominicans for the construction of a house for themselves in the park of the palace of Langley. This fulfilled a vow that Edward had made when in peril to found a house at Langley in which the Dominicans could 'celebrate prayers daily for the souls of his ancestors, for himself, and for

---

³⁴⁰ *Ann. Lond.*, 203–4 (*Venedocia* has the sense of North Wales, where Lancaster held the lordship of Denbigh, rather than Wales as a whole); Phillips, 32; Hamilton, 95; Maddicott, 123–4.

³⁴¹ E 159/85, m.52 (see also Davies, *Baronial Opposition*, 551–2); Phillips, 32; Chaplais, 85–6. Although Langton may have attended the council on 13 March and have gathered a lot of information, it is unlikely that he would have been allowed to know of the earls' plans and pass them on to the king: cf. Chaplais, 83.

³⁴² *Itinerary*, ed. Hallam. A disadvantage was that the castle was then in poor condition: *KW*, ii, 831.

³⁴³ Hamilton, 94, 164; Maddicott, 124.

³⁴⁴ *CPR, 1307–13*, 454; *CFR, 1307–19*, 129.

³⁴⁵ *Foedera*, II, i, 163; *CPR, 1307–13*, 450–1; *CFR, 1307–19*, 129.

³⁴⁶ *CPR, 1307–13*, 454.

his state'.³⁴⁷ Edward was never more in need of prayer than now, but a further sign of his desperation was his order on 5 April for Gaston de Béarn, count of Foix and over 100 other Gascon lords to come to him with a 'decent company' of armed men. No date or place was set for their assembly, nor was it explained how they were to reach England.³⁴⁸ If Edward hoped that they would rally to the aid of their fellow Gascon, he was to be grievously disappointed.³⁴⁹

In early April Edward and Gaveston left York for Newcastle, which they reached on about 10 April and where they remained until early May. It is not clear why they did so. Possibly Edward hoped to make an agreement with Robert Bruce for the protection of Gaveston, but it was more likely an act of desperation not unlike the flight to Wales of Edward II and Hugh Despenser in the autumn of 1326.³⁵⁰ Edward and Gaveston were simply waiting for things to happen, and happen they did. On the afternoon of 4 May Thomas of Lancaster, Robert de Clifford, Henry de Percy and a large body of troops entered Newcastle, hot on the heels of Edward, Gaveston and the pregnant Queen Isabella, who fled for safety to Tynemouth, just downriver. Edward left Newcastle in such a hurry that he was forced to abandon his war-horses and a large quantity of arms and valuables.³⁵¹ On 5 April the fugitives left Tynemouth by sea for Scarborough, which they reached on 10 April and where they left Gaveston. Edward and Isabella then made their way to Knaresborough on 14 May and returned to York on 17 May.³⁵²

By this date the siege of Scarborough by the earls of Pembroke and Surrey, Henry de Percy and Robert de Clifford was already well under way.³⁵³ Gaveston's isolation was complete. Apart from the besieging army, Lancaster placed himself and his men between Scarborough and York,

---

³⁴⁷ *CPR, 1307–13*, 453. On the Dominicans of Langley see Ch. 2 of this book.
³⁴⁸ *Foedera*, II, i, 163; Chaplais, 86–7.
³⁴⁹ Gaston was also count of Béarn, Gaveston's home territory.
³⁵⁰ On 1 April Edward wrote to Philip IV of France saying that he was about to move towards Scotland in order to counter an expected attack by Robert Bruce on Berwick. On the same date he sent two experienced envoys, Mr Thomas Cobham and Henry de Canterbury, to Philip on unspecified business: *Foedera*, II, i, 163. Perhaps Edward was hoping that Philip would intervene with the magnates on his behalf, but by this time Edward had run out of rational policy options.
³⁵¹ *Vita*, 42–3, according to which Lancaster initially intended restoring them to the king. For the details of what was captured see Chaplais, App. 2, 'The Newcastle Jewels', citing C 66/138, m.3 and *Foedera*, II, i, 203–5. In the event they became a bargaining counter in the protracted peace negotiations between the king and the earls in 1312–13: see Phillips, 54–61. It is likely, as Chaplais suggests, that although some of the valuables belonged to Gaveston, most of them came from the royal treasury, and were probably the jewels moved from Westminster to the Tower in Oct. 1311: Chaplais, 91–5, 106–7.
³⁵² The chronology and much of the detail of the events from 4 to 19 May are given in a memorandum on the Close Roll: *CCR, 1307–13*, 459–60.
³⁵³ *CCR, 1307–13*, 460: on this date Pembroke, etc., were ordered to stop the siege, which had probably begun almost as soon as the king left Scarborough.

and also contributed men to the siege, so that there was no chance of the king's coming to his aid.[354] The king remained in contact with Gaveston by letter during the siege, and may have tried to buy off the besiegers by offering bribes or other inducements.[355] According to the *Vita*, the king took the initiative in offering detailed terms on which Gaveston would surrender, while Gaveston then persuaded Pembroke and the others to accept them.[356] On 19 May Gaveston surrendered to the earls of Pembroke and Surrey and the other besiegers. Making it clear that they believed they were acting with full authority, Pembroke and the others promised on behalf of the community of the realm to take Gaveston to St Mary's abbey, York, where they would present the surrender terms to the king and to Lancaster or his representative. If the king were not willing to continue negotiations over Gaveston's future with the prelates, earls and barons between then and 1 August, Pembroke and the others promised to restore Scarborough to Gaveston's custody and to guarantee his safety until that date. Pembroke, Surrey and Percy agreed that they would forfeit all their property if any harm came to Gaveston, who promised in turn not to try to persuade the king to alter any of the terms of the agreement.[357]

By 26 May Gaveston's captors had joined the king at York, as stipulated in the agreement. There is no mention of Gaveston being with them, but it is reasonable to assume that he was. There is also no reference to the presence of either Lancaster or a representative. This may indicate, as the author of the *Vita* was to claim, that Pembroke had after all negotiated on his own initiative and without sufficiently consulting the other earls, and that Lancaster therefore did not feel bound by the terms.[358] However, it is also likely that, if Lancaster were indeed absent, he already had other plans for Gaveston's fate.[359]

Lancaster was probably right in suspecting the hand of the king in the generous terms offered to Gaveston. The author of the *Vita* claimed that Edward hoped that before the August deadline the king of France and the pope would intervene to secure Gaveston's freedom, and that in return Edward was prepared to give up Gascony.[360] While there is no evidence to

---

[354] SC 8/205/10204; *Vita*, 42–3; Phillips, 32–3; Maddicott, 125.

[355] BL, Cotton Ms. Nero C.VIII, ff. 88, 107v; *Flores*, 150.

[356] *Vita*, 42–3; *Ann. Lond.*, 204.

[357] Phillips, 33–4; Maddicott, 125–6; Hamilton, 96, 165. There is no copy of the agreement in the National Archives. It is known from two sources: *Ann. Lond.*, 204–6; *Literae Cantuarienses*, iii, ed. Sheppard, 388–93. The latter text is derived from Canterbury Register I, ff. 365v–366, which is probably also the source of the text in another Canterbury Ms., BL, Harleian Ms. 636, f. 233.

[358] C 53/98, m.2; *Vita*, 42–3.

[359] Lancaster had left before the end of the siege, ostensibly to prevent such a large besieging force running short of food, but perhaps so that he could repudiate the surrender terms if he wished to.

[360] *Vita*, 42–3.

confirm the latter part of the claim, it is known that a royal embassy had been sent to the papal curia in February 1312 and that in May two papal envoys had been appointed to try to make peace in England; a secret royal mission had been sent to France, probably for a similar purpose, between 15 May and 2 June, when the crisis over Gaveston was at its height.[361]

THE DEATH OF GAVESTON

During the meeting with the king at York after Gaveston's surrender Edward allegedly attempted to placate his opponents by promising to satisfy all the earls' demands, while for their part Pembroke, Surrey and Percy renewed their oaths to forfeit their lands if any harm came to Gaveston.[362] On 3 June Edward summoned a parliament to meet at Lincoln on 23 July, presumably to discuss Gaveston's status further and still within the period laid down in the surrender agreement.[363] At the end of the York meeting Gaveston was placed in the personal custody of Pembroke, who took him south in early June.[364] According to the St Albans chronicler John Trokelowe, they were heading for Wallingford, where there was a powerful castle belonging to the earldom of Cornwall and which had been restored to Gaveston the previous February.[365] If this was their real destination, it would have been enough to arouse suspicion in the minds of Gaveston's enemies among the earls, since Wallingford was close to the royal fortress of Windsor and was much more defensible than Scarborough had been.

On 9 June Pembroke and Gaveston reached Deddington in Oxfordshire. Pembroke then left Gaveston there to rest with a few of his retainers and went to visit his wife at his manor of Bampton about twenty miles away.[366] In the meantime Edward and Gaveston had remained in contact by letter.[367] When the earl of Warwick learned of Gaveston's presence so close at hand he raised a strong force and came to Deddington early in the morning of the 10th. The vivid details in the account of the event given by the *Vita Edwardi Secundi* cannot be vouched for, but the basic outline of the story is confirmed by the declaration made on 18 June, the eve of Gaveston's execution, by John Botetourt who had been present at his capture:[368]

> Coming to the village ... he [Warwick] entered the gate of the courtyard and surrounded the chamber. Then the earl called out in a loud

---

[361] BL, Cotton Ms. Nero C. VIII, ff. 57–8; *CPL, 1305–42*, 103–4, 106, 117.
[362] *Trokelowe*, 76.
[363] *PW*, II, ii, 72.
[364] *Trokelowe*, 76; *Vita*, 42–5; *Flores*, 150, 336; *Murimuth*, 17.
[365] *Trokelowe*, 76; *CChR, 1300–26*, 131; *CPR, 1307–13*, 429; Phillips, 35.
[366] *Ann. Lond.*, 206; *Flores*, 151; H.M. Colvin, *A History of Deddington* (London, 1963), 33–4.
[367] BL, Cotton Ms. Nero C. VIII, ff. 86, 105.
[368] *Vita*, 44–5; Bod., Tanner Ms. 90, p. 1 (Botetourt's declaration).

voice: 'Arise, traitor, thou art taken.' And Piers, hearing the earl, also seeing the earl's superior force and that the guard which he had been allotted was not resisting, putting on his clothes came down from the chamber. In this fashion Piers is taken and is led forth not as an earl but as a thief; and he who used to ride palfreys is now forced to go on foot.

When they had left the village a little behind, the earl ordered Piers to be given a mare so that their journey might proceed more quickly. Blaring trumpets, yelling people, and savage shouting followed Piers. Now Piers has laid aside his belt of knighthood, he travels to Warwick like a thief and a traitor, and coming there he is thrown into prison.[369]

On the face of it, the earl of Pembroke's action in leaving Gaveston in a weakly defended place was at worst a deliberate act of treachery and at best one of extreme foolishness. Understandably, several chroniclers reported their suspicions or implied that Pembroke had connived in Gaveston's capture,[370] but the vehemence with which Pembroke denied any responsibility and his siding with Edward II after Gaveston's death suggest that he was no more than extremely careless and failed to appreciate the ruthlessness of his former magnate allies.[371]

After lodging Gaveston in Warwick castle, the earl of Warwick awaited the arrival of the earls of Lancaster, Hereford and Arundel before taking further action. On 18 June Lancaster, Hereford, Warwick and John Botetourt individually gave their approval of Gaveston's coming execution and gave one another guarantees of mutual support.[372] A semblance of a trial may even have been held before two royal justices, William Inge and Henry Spigurnel, who were then hearing cases in Warwick, and Gaveston condemned to death on the grounds that the Ordinances had declared him to be a traitor.[373] The magnates were determined that Gaveston should not escape yet again but they were equally determined to provide themselves with legal justification for their action. On 19 June Gaveston was taken from his prison in Warwick castle[374] and led in the direction of the earl of Lancaster's lands at nearby Kenilworth. Gaveston was taken to the top of Blacklow Hill, about two miles north of Warwick, and there Lancaster handed him over to two Welshmen

---

[369] *Vita*, 44–5.

[370] *Trokelowe*, 76; *Vita*, 46–7; *Melsa*, 327; *Vita et Mors*, 298; Phillips, 36; Maddicott, 127.

[371] Pembroke's attempts to regain custody of Gaveston between 10 and 19 June and his appeals for help and vindication were turned down or ignored. The earl of Gloucester reputedly told him that Warwick had acted with Pembroke's counsel and aid (referring to the St Paul's meeting in March) and advised him to be more careful in future, while the clerks and the burgesses of Oxford University and town refused to help him: *Vita*, 44–7. Pembroke was in a desperate situation since he stood to forfeit all his property.

[372] Bod., Laud Misc. Ms. 529, f. 104; Dugdale Ms. 15, p. 293 (Botetourt); Tanner Ms. 90, p. 1 (Botetourt); DL 25/1982 (Warwick); DL 34/13 (Lancaster); Phillips, 35; Maddicott, 127–8; Hamilton, 98.

[373] *Vita*, 46–7; *Gesta Edwardi*, 39, 43–4; Maddicott, 127–8.

[374] Warwick himself stayed behind in his castle and took no further part: *Vita*, 48–9.

for execution. One of them ran him through the body and the other cut off his head. Lancaster was informed but refused to believe that Gaveston was dead until he had seen his head. The earls then went their separate ways. Afterwards the Dominicans came and gathered up the body, sewing the head back on, and took it to their house at Oxford; but they dared not bury it because Gaveston had died excommunicate.[375]

Gaveston's life and death were a tragedy for himself, for his family and for all with whom he came into contact, not least the king. Edward II had begun his reign with the best of intentions but his persistent loyalty to Gaveston led him to make ill-judged and even dangerous decisions, the consequences of which were often complex and unforeseeable. At the same time many of the financial and administrative problems which Edward had inherited from his father and which the Ordainers had sought to resolve continued to defy solution. In the wider world of English politics and government, the death of Gaveston now created an undying enmity between Edward and the earls who were primarily responsible, Lancaster and Warwick. The earls of Pembroke and Surrey, whose reputations had been profoundly damaged, returned permanently to the king's side; and Edward became more than ever determined to annul the Ordinances. The scene was now set for another round of bitterness and upheaval.

---

[375] This is the account given by the *Vita*, 48–9. Another account, in *Ann. Lond.*, 207, states that after Gaveston's execution his body lay until four shoemakers from Warwick collected it and carried it to the earl of Warwick, who refused to accept it. Whether this detail is true or not, it is certain that a group of Dominicans eventually took custody of the body and carried it to Oxford: Hamilton, 99, 166. There is a memorial on Blacklow Hill, known as 'Gaveston's Cross' (Ordnance Survey, SP 289 675): *Vita*, 48, n. 90.

Chapter 5

FROM BLACKLOW HILL TO BANNOCKBURN: JUNE 1312 TO JUNE 1314

AFTER GAVESTON'S DEATH

According to the *Vita Edwardi Secundi*, the king was deeply saddened and grieved when he heard the news of Gaveston's death, but commented that Gaveston was foolish to let himself fall into the hands of the earls. Some reacted with derision to the king's moderation. But the author added that he was certain that 'the king grieved for Piers as a father at any time grieves for his son. For the greater the love, the greater the sorrow.' Edward's apparent moderation however concealed a determination to destroy Gaveston's killers when the opportunity arose.[1] There was no doubting the depth of Edward's grief for Gaveston, whose embalmed body, dressed in cloth of gold, remained where it lay in the house of the Dominicans in Oxford. During June and July 1312 it was watched over by Thomas de London and Philip de Eyndon who had been appointed by the king and by Gaveston's widow, Margaret de Clare.[2] Edward II also dealt generously with Gaveston's widow and children. Margaret, who was Edward's niece, was granted lands worth 2,000 marks a year in September 1312; while Gaveston's daughter Joan was brought up among the nuns at Amesbury in Wiltshire, a convent with the closest of royal associations since the time of Eleanor of Provence. A suitably aristocratic marriage was also arranged later for Joan. Amy, another, and probably illegitimate, daughter of Gaveston, was to serve as a lady of the bedchamber for both Queen Isabella and Queen Philippa.[3]

The political situation in the summer of 1312 was very tense, with a real danger of civil war. The immediate effect of Gaveston's death, regarded by some as a judicial execution and by others as an act of murder,[4] was to divide the magnates. The earls of Lancaster, Warwick and Hereford and their supporters withdrew to Worcester to make their own plans, in case it

---

[1] *Vita*, 52–3.
[2] These details are taken from Hamilton, 99–100, 166–7. The body was to stay in Oxford until Dec. 1314 when it was moved to the king's palace at Langley and finally buried amidst great splendour in the Dominican church there in Jan. 1315.
[3] Hamilton, 100–2, 167; Hamilton, 'Another daughter?' On the fate of other members of Gaveston's family and his former retainers see Hamilton, 102, 167.
[4] For the text of a poem written in approval of his death, see Hamilton, 102–3.

came to open warfare.[5] Here, on 3 July, Henry de Percy, one of the three magnates who had accepted Gaveston's surrender at Scarborough, formally threw in his lot with them.[6] The other two, the earls of Pembroke and Surrey, allied themselves definitively with the king, whom they had rejoined in Lincolnshire by 6 July.[7] Until Edward's defeat at Bannockburn in June 1314 Pembroke was to be the most prominent and influential member of the king's council.[8]

The king's own strong inclination was to fight.[9] Some of his advisers, notably the earl of Pembroke, 'whose interest it was to vanquish the earls', Hugh Despenser a councillor of long standing 'who was perhaps even less deserving than Piers', Henry de Beaumont another controversial figure whose removal from court had been ordered by the Ordainers, Edmund Mauley steward of the royal household, and some of Gaveston's former knights were in favour of attacking the magnates. Allegedly they argued that the king 'would surely triumph since he was lawfully striving for his rights' against faithless men who could not be victorious.[10] If Edward had decided to fight, he could have called on the immediate services of his own household knights, numbering nearly fifty in 1312, as well as the retinues of the earls of Pembroke and Surrey and others.[11] Some warned of the dangers to the kingdom if the king embarked on open civil war: he might be captured by his enemies and even if he defeated the earls, this would benefit only Robert Bruce who had already occupied the whole of Scotland and would soon have forced Northumbria to pay tribute.[12]

Edward first made sure of the loyalty and security of the city of London.[13] Stopping briefly at the earl of Pembroke's castle of Hertford, the king rode into London on about 20 July and summoned the mayor and citizens before him and his council at Blackfriars, the house of the London

---

[5] *Vita*, 52–3. The earl of Warwick was already at Worcester on 22 June, three days after Gaveston's death: BL, Add. Ms. 28024, ff. 122, 122d (Beauchamp cartulary).

[6] DL 25/1900. In this document Percy gave his support to the earl of Hereford 'in the quarrel touching Sir Piers de Gaveston'. It is likely that he gave similar guarantees to the other earls. When Percy's change of sides became known, orders were given on 30 and 31 July for his arrest and for the seizure of his lands into royal hands: *Foedera*, II, i, 173.

[7] C 53/98, m.2; E 101/375/8, f. 27; E 101/374/17; *Ann. Lond.*, 208.

[8] See Phillips, chs 2 & 3; Maddicott, 132–3. Significantly, Pembroke was instrumental in ordering the arrest of Percy: *Foedera*, II, i, 173.

[9] *Vita*, 54–5.

[10] *Flores*, 336–7; *Vita*, 54–5.

[11] *Flores*, 337. The figure of 1,000 men-at-arms suggested by *Flores* may be exaggerated but between them the king and his magnate supporters could probably have put together an effective force: Phillips, 39. Dr Alistair Tebbit has made a detailed study of Edward II's household knights and their numbers in his 2006 Bristol Ph.D. thesis, 'The household knights of Edward II, 1307–1326', and in his paper 'Household knights and military service under the direction of Edward II', in Dodd & Musson, eds, *The Reign of Edward II*, 76–96.

[12] *Vita*, 54–5.

[13] In sharp contrast with the autumn of 1326 when the loss of London helped to ensure Edward II's loss of his throne.

Dominicans. Here the king personally delivered a powerful speech. 'These are wondrous times' (*Le secle se mene mervylousement*), he said; the magnates were in arms against him; he ordered the mayor and citizens to pledge to hold the city for him; and threatened that, if they were unable or unwilling to do so, the king's men would do it for them. After a day's debate the mayor, aldermen and the entire community of London came before the king and promised that they would not open the gates of the city to the king's enemies. Whereupon the king complimented them on their loyalty, they acknowledged him and left.[14]

Hoping that London was secured, in early August Edward went to Dover,[15] where he fortified the castle and took the fealty of the Cinque Ports.[16] This was presumably to ensure diplomatic and potentially also military communications with France, as well as local defence. On 16 August, as the opposition earls were advancing towards London,[17] he ordered the constables of Oxford and Wallingford castles to raise as many foot soldiers as they could and bring them to London on 27 August; some men were also summoned from the county of Ponthieu in France.[18]

Having ensured that he could defend himself against a possible baronial attack, Edward decided to gain his revenge upon Lancaster and his allies by political and diplomatic means. On 4 August Edward summoned the earls of Lancaster, Hereford and Warwick, in their capacity as former Ordainers, to appear before him at Westminster or London on 27 August 'to treat of the Ordinances and to correct the same'. He claimed that some of the Ordinances were damaging and prejudicial to him as king while others went beyond the powers of the commission given to the Ordainers in 1310.[19]

At about the same time Edward enlisted papal and French aid in his attack on the Ordinances. The embassies which he had sent to the papal curia in October 1311 and February 1312 had already resulted in the appointment in May 1312 of two envoys, Arnaud Nouvel cardinal-priest of St Prisca and Arnaud d'Aux bishop of Poitiers (soon to become cardinal-bishop of Albano), with authority to restore peace in England

---

[14] *Ann. Lond.*, 208, which has the French texts of the king's speech and the citizens' reply; Williams, *Medieval London*, 272.

[15] He was at Dover between about 7 and 9 Aug. and at Canterbury and other places in Kent until the middle of Aug.

[16] *Ann. Lond.*, 209; Maddicott, 133. The earl of Surrey also organized the defences of Sussex which were under threat from the men of the earl of Arundel and others: SC 1/50/63; SC 1/49/8 & 103.

[17] Although the earls were ordered on 4 Aug. not to bring armed retainers to the parliament which had been summoned to meet at Westminster on 20 Aug., it was probably clear then that they would defy the command: *CPR, 1307–13*, 489–90.

[18] E 101/375/8, f. 38; *CPR, 1307–13*, 486.

[19] *CPR, 1307–13*, 489–90. The language of the Latin original is much stronger: see *PW*, II, ii, App., 53, and *Foedera*, II, i, 175. Edward's envoy, John Benstede, met Lancaster near Blackburn on 19 Aug.: E 101/309/18.

and with specific powers to annul the Ordinances.[20] These two envoys reached London on 29 August and were to play an important mediating role in English affairs during the coming months.[21] On 6 August Edward had sent three more envoys to the pope. The purpose of this mission is not stated but it probably marked the beginning of the negotiations, concluded in 1314, for a large papal loan which helped for a time to give Edward some financial security.[22]

Edward had already sent an embassy to France in the middle of May, just before Gaveston's surrender at Scarborough.[23] Now, on 6 August, he sent two of his closest baronial allies, the earl of Pembroke and Henry de Beaumont, to visit Philip IV.[24] Their business, which they also explained to the papal envoys who were still in France awaiting an opportunity to cross to England, was not described specifically but there is little doubt that it too concerned the earl of Lancaster and the Ordinances. On 17 August Pembroke and Beaumont rejoined the king at Faversham in Kent, bringing with them two of Philip IV's clerks, William de Novo Castro and Master Raymond Subiran.[25] They were soon supplemented by a French envoy, Count Louis of Évreux, the half-brother of Philip IV and already well known in England, who arrived in London on 13 September.[26] Like their papal counterparts, the French clerks and envoy were to play an important part in the negotiations between Edward and the English magnates.[27]

The magnates were not however prepared to allow Edward to gain his ends by diplomacy. They were no doubt well aware of the precedents set by Louis IX in the Mise of Amiens of 1264 and by Clement V in 1305 and did not want a repetition of either.[28] Instead of attending the opening of

---

[20] Phillips, 40–1. Arnaud Nouvel was a Cistercian monk and master of Roman law from the Languedoc; he was also papal vice-chancellor; Arnaud d'Aux came from Gascony and had close ties to Clement V: Menache, *Clement V*, 44–5, 80.

[21] *Ann. Paul.*, 271–2; Phillips, 43.

[22] *Foedera*, II, i, 175, 196, 203; Phillips, 71–2. One of the envoys was Bertrand de Sauviac, count of Campania, a nephew of Clement V.

[23] Phillips, 41.

[24] Both men were French magnates in their own right. Pembroke held Montignac and other lands in Poitou and was married to Beatrice, daughter of Ralph de Clermont, constable of France. Henry de Beaumont was the younger son of Louis de Brienne, viscount of Beaumont in Maine, and distantly related to Edward II's mother, Eleanor of Castile: Phillips, 3–5; article on Beaumont by J.R. Maddicott in *Oxford DNB*.

[25] *Foedera*, II, i, 175; *CPL, 1305–42*, 104, 107; E 101/375/8, ff. 7, 9; Phillips, 40. Raymond entered Edward II's service on 15 Aug.: E 101/375/8, f. 10.

[26] *Ann. Paul.*, 271–2; Phillips, 43, 47, 65–6.

[27] With Gaveston out of the way, Philip IV was now much more prepared to help his fellow ruler and son-in-law: cf. Maddicott, 136–7.

[28] In 1264 Louis had ruled against the baronial plan of reform of 1258 and in favour of Henry III, while in 1305 Clement V had absolved Edward I of his oath to uphold the *Articuli super Cartas* of 1300: Maddicott, *Simon de Montfort*, 258–65; Menache, *Clement V*, 251–3. The barons had good reason to be cautious since the French clerks who drew up the objections to the Ordinances later in 1312 raised these precedents: *Ann. Lond.*, 212.

parliament on 20 August, Lancaster and the others kept both their distance and their armed retainers. They had no intention of discussing the Ordinances either then or on 27 August. Instead the baronial army advanced as far as Ware in Hertfordshire, where they halted and remained for two weeks.[29] It is not clear whether the army then advanced further, but there was evidently a fear that they would do so and perhaps even occupy London.[30] In order to prevent this, the bishops of Norwich and Bath & Wells, and the earl of Richmond were ordered on 3 September to prohibit the earls of Lancaster, Warwick and Hereford from appearing armed before the king.[31]

There was good reason to fear a Lancastrian entry into London. Despite Edward's words to its citizens in July, the city was still extremely volatile. Suspecting that some of the Londoners were preparing to open the gates to Lancaster, the constable of the Tower of London, John Cromwell, arrested and imprisoned several of them in the Tower.[32] On 20 September, after the king had withdrawn to Windsor, the earl of Pembroke, Hugh Despenser, Edmund Mauley the steward of the royal household, Nicholas de Segrave the marshal of the household, and John Cromwell went to the Guildhall to ask for further security for holding the city against the king's enemies. The citizens replied that they had already given their word and need do no more, and then produced a list of complaints against the steward, the marshal and Cromwell. Pembroke and the others promised to deal with these matters at Westminster the following day, but as they were leaving a riot broke out when it was falsely rumoured that they intended to arrest John de Gisors, the mayor of London, and they barely escaped without injury. That night Cromwell sent members of the Tower garrison to attack the Tower ward, to which the Londoners responded by destroying the wall of an enclosure next to the Tower and arresting Cromwell's men. When the mayor appeared before the council at Westminster the following day, Pembroke and the other councillors accused the citizens of having attacked the enclosure in order to break open the Tower prison and loot the royal treasury.[33] Relations between the king and London were therefore left in a delicate state. It was not surprising that on 30 September the king ordered the raising of 1,000 foot soldiers in Kent and Sussex, or that on 5 October he stated that, despite their safe conducts, the baronial negotiators were not to be allowed to stay in or even pass through London.[34]

---

[29] *Trokelowe*, 78; *Ann. Lond.*, 210; *Vita*, 56–7; Maddicott, 133.
[30] Although the *Vita*, 56–7, says that the magnates reached London, there is nothing to suggest that Lancaster and his colleagues did in fact enter the city: cf. Maddicott, 133.
[31] *CPR, 1307–13*, 490.
[32] Williams, *Medieval London*, 273.
[33] *Ann. Lond.*, 215–17; *Ann. Paul.*, 272; Williams, 273; Phillips, 44–5.
[34] *CPR, 1307–13*, 498; *CCR, 1307–13*, 481; *Foedera*, II, i, 181. These orders were issued 'on the information of Pembroke', i.e. at his instigation.

NEGOTIATIONS FOR A TREATY

Little is known about the early meetings between the magnates and the various mediators. On 23 August the earl of Gloucester passed through London with his retinue, probably to make initial contact with them.[35] Gloucester and later the papal envoys as well based themselves in the town and abbey of St Albans.[36] There is mention of an attempt by Cardinal Arnaud Nouvel and Bishop Arnaud d'Aux to send some of their clerks to meet the barons at Wheathampstead near St Albans; but they were rebuffed on the facetious grounds that England already had enough clerks capable of negotiating. The papal envoys then withdrew in alarm and returned to London.[37] A more significant meeting took place at Markyate near St Albans in late September.[38] As a result safe conducts until 13 October were granted on 28 September at the request of the papal envoys, Louis of Évreux and the earls of Gloucester and Richmond for the earl of Hereford, Robert de Clifford, John Botetourt, John de Heslarton, Adam de Herwynton, and Michael de Meldon to meet the cardinal, earls and other members of the council.[39]

A treaty was finally agreed between Edward II and the magnates on 20 December 1312 after long and tortuous negotiations. The king's negotiators were the earl of Pembroke, Hugh Despenser and Nicholas de Segrave. The earl of Hereford was the chief baronial negotiator, while the earl of Lancaster was represented throughout the negotiations by his steward, Michael de Meldon. Neither Lancaster nor Warwick came near the king during this period, no doubt because they feared treachery if they did so. Mediation between the two sides was provided by the moderate earls of Gloucester and Richmond, by the two papal envoys and by the French envoy, Louis of Évreux.[40] On 30 September the papal and French envoys in London wrote to Hereford and the other baronial representatives enclosing letters from the king proposing a meeting. They said that they would be remaining in London until a date suggested by the king and that if Hereford and the others came within that period they would find the envoys at the Temple. Hereford evidently responded to the invitation and it is likely that the subsequent negotiations were held at the Temple. Although it was then in royal hands, following the seizure of the Templars'

---

[35] *CCR, 1307–13*, 475. The earl of Gloucester's mediating role is particularly emphasized in the *Vita*, 58–9.

[36] *Trokelowe*, 77–8.

[37] *Trokelowe*, 77–8; Phillips, 44; Maddicott, 134.

[38] This probably explains the presence of the bishop of Norwich at St Albans on 24 Sept.: Norfolk and Norwich Record Office, Register of John Salmon, f. 48.

[39] *CPR, 1307–13*, 498. As each safe conduct expired, it was renewed for a further period. A stimulus for the opening of negotiations was probably given by the presence in the king's company at Windsor of the papal envoys on 15 Sept., the earls of Gloucester and Richmond on 16 Sept., and of Pembroke on 26 Sept.: E 101/375/2, m.3.

[40] Phillips, 43–4; Maddicott, 135.

property, the Temple was a neutral point, conveniently placed between London and the royal palace at Westminster.[41]

It is not possible to provide a chronology for the negotiations between their beginning in September and conclusion in December 1312. The tentative early stages are probably represented by the account given in the *Vita* of the king's complaints that the magnates had infringed his royal prerogative by cruelly putting to death the man to whom he had granted peace, and that they wished to seize the crown and set up for themselves another king. To which Lancaster allegedly replied that the magnates had acted lawfully according to the Ordinances which had been approved and issued with the assent of the king and his barons. He protested that they had committed no crime against the crown and 'that it had never entered their heads to wish to set up another as king'.[42]

The main negotiations are recorded in three documents, all of them undated, which make it possible to say what issues were raised and how they were finally resolved. These are a list of royal objections to the Ordinances, the *Prima Tractatio ad Pacem Confirmandam* and the *Rationes Baronum*.[43] The objections to the Ordinances were drawn up by the two French royal clerks, William de Novo Castro and Raymond Subiran, who had come to England with the earl of Pembroke in August.[44] They argued, for example, that the Ordinances were invalid because the Ordainers had not been elected by the prelates, earls and barons as a whole but by a small committee; that the Ordinances were uncertain and doubtful in all respects; that the Ordainers had exceeded their powers, thereby diminishing the legal rights and the revenues of the king; that the Ordinances had offended against Magna Carta, the Charter of the Forest, and the king's coronation oath, and the Ordainers were for that reason excommunicate; they also noted that Louis IX of France and Pope Clement V had previously quashed very similar ordinances. The document then continued with a list of objections to eleven specific ordinances.[45] This document was so legalistic and unrealistic politically that the barons promptly rejected it on the grounds that England was not

---

[41] DL 36/2/208. Clifford is known to have stayed at his hospice next to St Dunstan's in Fleet Street: E 403/164, m.2.

[42] *Vita*, 58–61. On baronial threats to restrain or even to remove the king see *Vita*, lvi–lvii.

[43] The first two are known only from the *Ann. Lond.*, 210–15. Stubbs's marginal date of July 1312 for both documents appears to be a guess which is not supported by other evidence. The *Rationes Baronum* are known from the report on the negotiations of 1312–13 compiled by the papal envoys and preserved in ASV, Instrumenta Miscellanea, 5947. The document has been edited by R.A. Roberts as *Edward II, the Lords Ordainers and Piers Gaveston's Jewels and Horses*, Camden 3rd ser., xli (London, 1929). There is also a transcript of the document in The National Archives: PRO 31/9/59.

[44] Both men were also involved in the making of the treaty of 20 Dec.: *Foedera*, II, i, 191–2.

[45] *Ann. Lond.*, 211–15.

governed by written law but by ancient laws and customs, which could be changed only by agreement between the king, prelates, earls and barons. This they said applied to the Ordinances as a whole which should therefore retain their validity. The document could never have formed the basis of negotiations, since it invited the magnates to agree to an unconditional surrender to the crown.[46] Nonetheless, the objections give an insight into Edward II's views of his rights as king, while it is possible that the document was put aside in the royal archives against further use in the future.[47]

The second document, the *Prima Tractatio*, is more significant but also much more difficult to interpret. The *Prima Tractatio* begins by stating that since the earls of Gloucester, Lancaster, Richmond, Pembroke, Surrey, Hereford, Warwick and Arundel had heard that the king was angry with them (*est engrossi devers eux*), they were willing, if the king gave them sufficient security and agreed to receive them as his lieges, to come to Westminster and humbly beg his pardon. They also offered to provide 400 men-at-arms for six months at their own expense for the next Scottish campaign and to persuade parliament to grant an aid for the same purpose, as well as to restore all the goods seized from Gaveston at Newcastle. In return the king would promise to maintain the Ordinances, remove all evil councillors, return all seized lands, and release all persons illegally imprisoned. All rancour and ill-feeling should be forgiven by both sides, except for those who had contravened the Ordinances.[48] On the face of it, these were moderate terms for a political settlement, and there are certain similarities between it and the treaty that was eventually agreed in December.[49] It is just possible that in the autumn of 1312 all eight earls – ranging from the royal supporters Pembroke and Surrey to the mediators Gloucester and Arundel, and the king's opponents, Lancaster, Warwick, Hereford and Arundel – were prepared to co-operate in presenting terms to the king and to join in seeking pardons for their actions as if they were all equally guilty. It is hard to believe, however, given the bitterness between Pembroke and Lancaster and Warwick resulting from Gaveston's death, that such an act of baronial solidarity could have taken place. One possible explanation of the *Prima Tractatio* is that it was a draft treaty put forward by the earls of Gloucester and Richmond as a basis for further negotiations. It is more likely however that it was presented on behalf of the opposition earls themselves. This suggestion fits the account given in the *Vita Edwardi Secundi*, whose author states that at some stage the king asked the magnates to draw up a list of their demands, and that they then did so, asking for the confirmation of the Ordinances and for pardons for the death of Gaveston. Edward's reaction to these demands, and so we

[46] *Ann. Lond.*, 215; Phillips, 47; Maddicott, 136–7.
[47] There is no evidence that this was the case, but the document, or something like it, would have been useful in trying to persuade the pope to annul the Ordinances.
[48] *Ann. Lond.*, 210–11; Phillips, 47; Maddicott, 135.
[49] Phillips, 47; Maddicott, 135.

may suppose to the *Prima Tractatio*, was to accept all the Ordinances except those concerning finance, to agree to pardon the earls, but to refuse to accept that Gaveston should be declared a traitor to prevent his widow or daughter from claiming possession of his lands. Edward remained adamant on this last point and proceeded to wear down his opponents by dragging out the negotiations.[50]

Further light is thrown on the negotiations which led to the December treaty by the third document, the *Rationes Baronum*, which forms part of the report sent to Clement V in 1313 by his two envoys.[51] The *Rationes* shows that the magnates were dissatisfied with the security and safe conduct which the king claimed to have offered them only *propter necessitatem*. They argued that this implied the king had acted under compulsion and that he might therefore repudiate his guarantees. The form of security was also deficient since it suggested that they had murdered Gaveston and not executed him as an enemy of the king and the realm. The barons continued to insist on the removal from court under the terms of the Ordinances of twenty objectionable persons, including Henry de Beaumont, Edmund Mauley, and a number of former associates of Gaveston, whose names were inserted after the *Rationes*.[52]

On 20 December a treaty was finally made between the king and the barons. The agreement was sealed in Cardinal Arnaud's room in London, in the presence of the two papal envoys, Count Louis of Évreux, and the earls of Gloucester and Richmond, all of whom had acted as mediators. The earl of Hereford, Robert de Clifford, and John Botetourt represented Lancaster and Warwick, both of whom were absent, while the earl of Pembroke, Hugh Despenser the Elder, and Nicholas de Segrave represented the king. Under its terms the barons were to come to Westminster to receive the king's pardon; the jewels and horses seized at Newcastle on 4 May were to be restored to royal envoys at St Albans on 13 January 1313; and a parliament, for which a form of security for the barons was included, was to be summoned for 18 March. All offences committed against Gaveston were to be pardoned, and in return no action was to be taken against Gaveston's followers. The barons also promised that the coming parliament would discuss the granting to the king of an aid for the Scottish war and would also consider measures to ensure that no one brought armed retainers to future parliaments. The king promised to investigate the grievances of two of Lancaster's retainers, Gruffudd de la Pole and Fulk Lestrange, and to restore the lands of Henry de Percy.[53] The

---

[50] *Vita*, 62–5; *Lanercost*, 219; Phillips, 47–8; Maddicott, 135.

[51] The first 12 membranes of the report refer wholly to events in 1313; the next three, which include the *Rationes Baronum* and the treaty of 20 Dec., refer to problems which were no longer issues in 1313 but do fit the context of late 1312: *Edward II*, ed. Roberts.

[52] *Edward II*, ed. Roberts, 15–17; Phillips, 48–9.

[53] For the text of the treaty see *Edward II*, ed. Roberts, 17–21; *Foedera*, II, i, 191–2; *Ann. Lond.*, 221–5. There are several other copies in manuscript: see Phillips, 49, n. 4.

treaty appeared to be a considerable victory for the king since, unlike the *Rationes Baronum*, it made no direct mention of the Ordinances and contained no reference to the baronial demands that Gaveston should be declared the king's enemy or for the removal of 'evil councillors'. The treaty was however a paper victory since it could not be assumed that these major issues would not be heard of again. Much would also depend on whether its terms were performed and especially on whether the earls of Lancaster and Warwick, who were not present when the treaty was agreed, would give it their approval.[54]

THE BIRTH OF AN HEIR TO THE THRONE

Edward II could feel some degree of satisfaction with what had been achieved by December 1312. Without giving away anything of vital importance to himself, he had apparently, with the aid of papal and French mediation, as well as several of the English earls, worn down his opponents. All the while a parliament had been going about its business but without making the grant of taxation which Edward so badly needed. In place of such a grant and perhaps as a way of showing his confidence Edward used his royal prerogative to impose a tallage at the rate of a tenth of revenues and a fifteenth of the value of moveable goods on 16 December, the last day of the parliament.[55]

An even greater source of satisfaction and of personal happiness was the birth at Windsor on 13 November of Edward and Isabella's first child, the future Edward III. The infant boy was baptized by Cardinal Arnaud Nouvel in the chapel of St Edward at Windsor on 16 November. His godfathers were the other papal envoy, Arnaud d'Aux, bishop of Poitiers, the bishops of Bath & Wells and of Worcester, Louis count of Évreux, the earls of Pembroke and Richmond, and Hugh Despenser.[56] The happiness of the occasion was almost marred by the insistence of Louis of Évreux, probably acting on instructions from Philip IV, that the child should be named after a French king, therefore Philip or Louis. The English magnates present refused to accept this. There is no reason to think that Edward II disagreed with them, and so Edward was the name

---

[54] Phillips, 49–50; Maddicott, 137–9.

[55] *Lay Taxes*, 30–1. A tallage, which was a tax imposed on royal lands and on boroughs at the king's discretion, did not require the approval of parliament, but such levies were now very rare and met with increasing resistance. The 1312 tallage yielded less than the 1304 tallage. Payments were slow and were still being received in May 1316. In June 1332 Edward III also attempted to levy a tallage but was forced to abandon it during the parliament of the following Sept.: *Lay Taxes*, 37. For fuller details of the 1312 parliament see *PROME*.

[56] The details of the birth and baptism are given in *CCR, 1307–13*, 558; *Foedera*, II, i, 187. Edward II had a special veneration for the chapel of St Edward, which had originally been built by Henry III, but which was refurbished and re-established by Edward II in 1313. See ch. 2 of this book.

chosen.[57] The news of the birth had immediately been proclaimed in London where it was received with rejoicing. On 4 February 1313 Edward and Isabella came to Westminster. From there they went to the city of London where they were greeted by the members of the London guild of fishmongers, who staged an elaborate pageant in Isabella's honour, in which the arms of England and France were conspicuous, and afterwards accompanied her from Westminster to the royal palace at Eltham.[58] The birth of an heir to the throne was clearly a great relief to everyone and raised the prospect of greater political stability in the future. But that was a long way off and in the meantime the young Edward would have to survive the perils of childhood. If the child were to die, there were still however Edward II's half-brothers, Thomas of Brotherton and Edmund of Woodstock, now twelve and eleven years old. Partly in recognition of his status as heir presumptive and partly perhaps to give Edward the renewed comfort of having an earldom in the hands of someone to whom he was close, Thomas was made earl of Norfolk on 16 December 1312.[59]

EDWARD AND ISABELLA

Although the marriage of Edward and Isabella had begun inauspiciously after a long delay since their betrothal in 1303, and was overshadowed by wrangling between England and France over the duchy of Aquitaine and Isabella's dower, as well as the tensions over Gaveston, it appears to have been a successful one. Isabella was only a child of twelve when she first came to England in 1308 and was understandably ill at ease in a new and unfamiliar environment. Isabella's biographer has shown that she spent most of her time in her husband's company, apart from occasional absences, such as her pilgrimages to Canterbury in July 1308 and in October 1311.[60] Once the initial problems over her dower were settled in the summer of 1308, she was treated with generosity both financially and in grants of land. Although this may in part have been to win the agreement of Isabella and her father to the return of Gaveston from Ireland, a growing intimacy between the youthful Isabella and her much older and more experienced husband was probably also starting to develop.[61] By the year 1311–12, for which Isabella's household records survive, her

---

[57] *Trokelowe*, 79; *Historia Anglicana*, 134–5; Maddicott, 152. In a marginal note the editor of Walsingham identifies the proposed name as Louis, but there is nothing in the text to indicate whether Louis or Philip was intended. This episode may help to explain the bitter words exchanged between the French envoys and the English magnates at the Christmas feast: *Historia Anglicana*, 135.

[58] *Ann. Lond.*, 221; Doherty (D.Phil.), 49–50; idem, *Isabella*, 55. Isabella had been given the manor of Eltham in Nov. 1311: *CPR, 1307–13*, 395, 398.

[59] Edmund had to wait until 1321 for his promotion, when he was made earl of Kent.

[60] Doherty (D.Phil.), 33, 39; idem, *Isabella*, 48–50.

[61] Doherty (D.Phil.), 35, 39; idem, *Isabella*, 48–9.

establishment numbered over 200 people; her tailor, John Faleise, employed sixty seamstresses to maintain and repair the queen's robes, and also guarded her jewels, plate and valuable clothing, which were stored in the Tower of London.[62] Isabella's attitude towards Gaveston and his relations with her husband is harder to determine. Her initial hostility to Gaveston may have been dictated as much by her father's attitude as by any personal antipathy. As she became more established at the English court and in her husband's affections, and a property holder in her own right, her attitude may well have changed. Although there is some evidence that she contacted the opposition earls in early 1312, this may have been an attempt to try to reduce the tension between them and the king rather than an indication of any sympathy with them. Isabella's closest companions included Henry de Beaumont and his sister Isabella de Vescy, associates of Gaveston, whose removal the barons were also demanding.[63]

Isabella and her husband spent the Christmas of 1311 at Westminster before leaving for the reunion with Gaveston at York on 13 January. She was there for the festivities that followed the birth of Gaveston's daughter and it was probably at this time of happiness that she became pregnant.[64] The jollities continued on the morning of Easter Monday, 27 March, when the ladies of Isabella's chamber followed a customary practice by hauling Edward II out of his bed.[65] On 4 May Isabella became caught up in the events which led to Gaveston's capture and death when she and Edward were forced to flee from Newcastle to Tynemouth to escape the followers of the earl of Lancaster and his allies. Contrary to the report in Trokelowe's chronicle, written at St Albans, the pregnant Isabella was not abandoned at Tynemouth; instead she left there with her husband on 5 May and accompanied him to Scarborough before returning to York on 17 May.[66]

Isabella remained in York until the end of July when Edward sent members of his household to escort her south, first to Westminster and

---

[62] Doherty (D.Phil.), 39; Doherty, *Isabella*, 49. Her household records for 1311–12, in BL, Cotton Ms. Nero C.VIII, ff. 121–52, have been edited by F.D. Blackley & G. Hermansen as *The Household Book of Queen Isabella of England for the Fifth Regnal Year of Edward II* (Edmonton, Alberta, 1971). In the previous year, 1310–11, her household expenses were still accounted for as part of Edward II's household. At that time only 60 people were listed as members of her household: E 101/374/5, ff. 32–33v.

[63] Doherty (D.Phil.), 40–1; Doherty, *Isabella*, 49–50. Cf. Maddicott, 124–5.

[64] Isabella was still only sixteen and unlikely to have been able to have children much earlier than 1312.

[65] Bod., Tanner Ms. 197, f. 54; Doherty (D.Phil.), 41; Doherty, *Isabella*, 51. The practice was associated with Christ's resurrection. Any man found still in bed on Easter Monday morning could be 'taken prisoner' and made to pay for his release. The amount of Edward's 'ransom' in 1312 was £20. The custom went back to the reign of Edward I: Prestwich, 'The court of Edward II', 66.

[66] *CCR, 1307–13*, 459–60; *Trokelowe*, 75–6; Isabella's *Household Book*, xxvi; Maddicott, 125. Trokelowe's account confuses the events of 1312 with those of October 1322 when Isabella was left at Tynemouth after Edward II's defeat by the Scots at Byland.

then to Windsor, which she had probably reached by 17 September.[67] She and Edward then remained there for the rest of her pregnancy.[68] On 20 October Edward gave leave to *nostre treschiere Compoingne Isabel . . . Royne Dangleterre* to make her last will and testament. Edward granted her all the moveable goods 'which are and will be hers, and all the gold and silver vessels, and all her jewels in whatever place they are or shall be found'. After her death these would all be sold by her executors to perform the terms of her will. Edward also granted her all the county of Ponthieu and the land of Montreuil and all the other lands which she held or would hold in the kingdom of England or in France or elsewhere, to be exploited by her executors for three years after her death. Lastly her executors were given powers to purchase land worth £1,500 sterling to found a hospital for the relief of poor people and for the salvation of the souls of herself and Edward.[69] It is possible that Isabella had had a difficult pregnancy, that there was a real possibility of her dying in childbirth, and that Edward was showing his concern for his wife's spiritual welfare. This may have been the case, but the existence of a copy of the document in Paris[70] strongly suggests that it was made partly at the suggestion and perhaps at the insistence of the French envoys, in order to ensure that the terms of Isabella's dower were continued after her death. It would be interesting to know the details of Isabella's will, but it has not survived in either the English or the French archives.[71] In the event, all went well and on 13 November two members of Isabella's household, John Launge and his wife, informed the king that he had a son.[72]

MORE NEGOTIATIONS

Despite the treaty which had been agreed on 20 December 1312, mutual suspicion between the king and the barons remained strong, causing delays in performing the terms of the treaty and also contributing to the failure of the parliaments which were summoned for 18 March and 8 July 1313. At first, however, attempts were made to implement the treaty. On 16 December, four days before the final agreement, a general safe conduct

---

[67] Doherty (D.Phil.), 47; idem, *Isabella*, 54.

[68] According to Doherty (D. Phil.), 47, n. 4, during this period Edward left Windsor on *c.* 25 Oct., returned on the 30th, left again on 9 Nov. and returned on 12 Nov., the day before his son's birth: citing E 101/375/2, m.4. However, the details given in *Itinerary*, ed. Hallam, suggest that Edward was at Windsor for most if not all of this time. This seems more likely, since Edward probably did not want to be too close to the scene of the negotiations with the opposition magnates at the Temple.

[69] This document is calendared very briefly in *CPR, 1307–13*, p. 508, but the full text is given from the Patent Roll in *Foedera*, II, i, 184.

[70] AN, J 633, no. 34.

[71] AN, J 403, which contains French royal wills does not include any mention of that of Isabella.

[72] E 159/89, m.15; Doherty (D.Phil.), 47; idem, *Isabella*, 54.

until 3 June 1313 was issued for Lancaster and his supporters to move freely about the country. On the 18th Henry de Percy's lands were restored until the coming parliament. On 26 December a commission was issued to investigate Gruffudd de la Pole's complaints about the seizure of his lands,[73] but went beyond the terms of the treaty by including complaints against Gruffudd by the king's chamberlain, John Charlton.[74] Fulk Lestrange's complaints were brought within the terms of the commission on 31 December. On 7 January John Sandal and Ingelard Warley were appointed to receive Gaveston's property at St Albans on 13 January, and on 8 January parliament was summoned, as had been agreed, for 8 March.[75] Almost at once, difficulties began to appear. The imprisonment of one of Henry de Percy's knights, Edmund Darel, led the barons to conclude that their safe conducts were worthless, to their refusal to confirm the treaty and their failure to restore the jewels and horses at St Albans on 13 January.[76] The king's envoys, Sandal and Warley, remained at St Albans until the 15th, when, in righteous indignation, they drew up a formal protestation before witnesses, which they sent to Cardinal Arnaud. The earl of Hereford then attempted to mediate between the king and the magnates, telling the cardinal that he had asked Lancaster, Warwick and Clifford, for the sake of their own honour and the common good, to restore the goods as soon as possible. Hereford also promised that when he next met the other magnates he would do all in his power to persuade them to observe the terms of the treaty.[77]

Darel's release was ordered on 18 January,[78] but this announcement had no immediate effect since in the meantime events had moved on. Soon after 13 January Lancaster sent his chaplain Hugh Skillehare from Pontefract to the cardinal with a further list of demands to be passed on orally to the king. Lancaster said that he was still prepared to return the jewels and horses to the king, but the offer contained a major regression since he described the restoration of the property as if it were the forfeit of a felon's goods to the crown.[79] Lancaster and his allies knew perfectly well that the property captured at Newcastle on 4 May 1312 had really belonged to the king and not to Gaveston, but by maintaining the fiction that it had been Gaveston's Lancaster was trying to force the king to accept that Gaveston had been a criminal and a

---

[73] *CPR, 1307–13*, 516, 546–7; *PW*, II, ii, 93.

[74] For the background to the dispute between De la Pole and Charlton, which erupted every time there was a national crisis, see R. Owen, 'Welsh Pool and Powys-Land', *Collections relating to Montgomeryshire*, xxix (Welshpool, 1929), 257–60; and M.C. Jones, 'The feudal barons of Powys', ibid., i (1868). For the immediate situation see Maddicott, 140–2.

[75] *CPR, 1307–13*, 546; *Foedera*, II, i, 194; *PW*, II, ii, 80.

[76] For the complicated details of this episode see Phillips, 54–5, citing *Edward II*, ed. Roberts, 1–2, 4–5, 8; Maddicott, 139.

[77] *Edward II*, ed. Roberts, 2–7; Phillips, 55; Maddicott, 143.

[78] *CCR, 1307–13*, 504; Phillips, 55, n. 3.

[79] *Edward II*, ed. Roberts, 7; Phillips, 56; Maddicott, 142–3.

traitor.[80] Lancaster's attitude to Gaveston made the December treaty for all practical purposes a dead letter, since Gaveston's status had been a major issue in the negotiations leading up to the agreement. Edward II flatly refused to accept the implication that Lancaster and his colleagues had legally executed Gaveston. After adding several other lesser demands, Lancaster's envoy concluded by stating that Lancaster and Warwick were planning to meet other magnates before 23 February to discuss the terms of the treaty and decide whether or not to give final approval. Their approval would of course depend on the king's acceptance of the new demands.[81]

The papal envoys reacted by asking the earls of Gloucester, Richmond and Hereford to meet them in London. Here they decided that they should meet members of the king's council before replying to Lancaster. In the talks that followed the king was represented by the earl of Pembroke, Hugh Despenser and John Sandal. Pembroke and his fellow councillors ignored Lancaster's claim that Gaveston was a felon and an enemy of the king on the grounds that it contained no request for them to answer.[82] They were able to deal with most of Lancaster's other demands without much difficulty, except for one relating to the appointment of royal justices to investigate the dispute between Gruffudd de la Pole and John Charlton. This proved so intractable that the talks almost broke down because of it. The matter was referred to the king by Hugh Despenser after intense attempts at persuasion by the papal envoys, who themselves met Edward at Sheen on 29 January.[83] Two other matters also remained unresolved: the restoration of the jewels and horses, and the confirmation by Lancaster and Warwick of the December treaty. On 10 February the papal envoys wrote to Lancaster, Warwick, Hereford, John Botetourt and Robert de Clifford to announce that they were sending the bishop of St David's, Master Walter de Thorp and two of their chaplains to discuss these questions.[84]

The focus of the mediation between the king and the magnates now moved from London further north, possibly to Lancaster's castle of Kenilworth in Warwickshire.[85] In the instructions to their messengers the papal envoys made it clear to Lancaster and the others that by their failure to restore the jewels and horses in accordance with the treaty they were harming the king's honour and endangering the safety of the kingdom, already threatened by the Scots and by disturbances in Gascony, as well as causing unease to the pope and to the French king. They were told firmly

---

[80] See the discussion of this issue in Chaplais, 90–1.
[81] *Edward II*, ed. Roberts, 7–9. For further details see Phillips, 56. There is no evidence that Lancaster and Warwick did hold such a meeting.
[82] *Edward II*, ed. Roberts, 9–10, 12, 15.
[83] Ibid., 9–12; SC 1/49/21; Phillips, 57; Maddicott, 144.
[84] *Edward II*, ed. Roberts, 12–13.
[85] Lancaster was probably there on 16 Feb.: DL 25/2253.

that if they continued to act in this way, the king would be justified in acting against them.[86] The pressure seems to have been successful, since by 27 February Hereford, Clifford and Botetourt had delivered the jewels to the bishop of Worcester and John Sandal and received acquittance for them.[87] However this still left unsettled the question of the confirmation of the treaty as a whole by Lancaster and Warwick.

Parliament had been summoned to meet at Westminster on 18 March, but the king remained at Windsor, allegedly because of an illness, which was generally thought to be feigned,[88] while the magnates failed to appear in person.[89] For the moment there was stalemate and on 7 April parliament was adjourned until 6 May. Negotiations however continued outside parliament. The state of affairs was summed up in a document sent to the king by his opponents shortly after parliament opened on 18 March.[90] The document listed points in the December treaty which had been implemented or on which both sides were agreed, but also listed those on which agreement had still to be reached. The earls recalled that they had now restored the jewels and other property taken at Newcastle 'by reason of Gaveston',[91] as the treaty required; they reaffirmed their readiness to come to Westminster to ask for the king's pardon and their willingness to grant an aid in parliament for the Scottish war; and they repeated their promise not to bring armed followers to parliament after their pardon, since the problems concerning Henry de Percy and Gruffudd de la Pole were now being settled in accordance with the treaty. The magnates expressed themselves satisfied that after they had been pardoned the king would act towards them as a faithful lord. Tacitly they also returned to the form of the treaty by omitting any reference to Gaveston as a felon or as an enemy of the king, in contrast to Lancaster's position in February. These concessions in themselves would do much to produce a settlement. However the magnates demanded a fuller form of acquittance for Gaveston's goods than they had received in February, and objected to the form of pardon to them as Gaveston's enemies which they had been offered in the December treaty, since it would then appear to have been extorted from the king, contrary to his coronation oath and their homage to him. The magnates included a new form of pardon, to be held in the custody of the

---

[86] *Edward II*, ed. Roberts, 13–15; Phillips, 58; Maddicott, 145.

[87] *Edward II*, ed. Roberts, 13–15; *Foedera*, II, i, 203–5 (text of the letters patent in French of Edward II acknowledging receipt of the jewels and horses, and including a detailed inventory of all the items). For a copy of the French text see Chaplais, 125–34; and for an English translation see Hamilton, 119–27. The king's letters of acquittance were dated at Windsor on 27 Feb. The actual delivery of the jewels took place c. 23 Feb.; the horses were returned during the following month: *Edward II*, ed. Roberts, 16–17.

[88] *Vita*, 66–7.

[89] *Ann. Lond.*, 225, 227.

[90] *Ann. Lond.*, 225–9. The document is known only from this source.

[91] '*par encheson de Pieres de G.*': *Ann. Lond.*, 226; i.e. they did not claim that the goods necessarily belonged to Gaveston personally.

archbishop of Canterbury, the bishops of London and Chichester, and the earls of Gloucester, Richmond and Arundel, until the magnates had made their submission. The magnates also declared that there was no need to give special pardons to Gaveston's former adherents, since, they argued, only the king would have power to bring any suit against them. They attributed their failure to appear in parliament on 18 March to the fact that the summons had not been made in the usual form, and they therefore asked for a correct form of summons so that they might attend parliament and make their submission.[92] The king's objections to this document probably centred on the demand that Gaveston's followers should not be specially pardoned, since there might then be a baronial demand for their exile under the terms of the Ordinances. Apart from this point there seems to have been relatively little to prevent an early settlement.

By the time parliament reassembled on 6 May there were signs that another attempt to achieve a settlement would soon be made. On 3 May, at the request of Cardinal Arnold, Louis count of Clermont a newly arrived French envoy, and the earls of Gloucester and Richmond, the earl of Lancaster and his followers were given a safe conduct until 24 June to meet the papal envoys and the king's councillors at Bedford; the current parliament came to an end on 19 May and four days later a new parliament was summoned to meet at Westminster on 8 July.[93] There is however no evidence that any more meetings between the king's representatives and those of the magnates did take place, and a further six months were to elapse before a settlement was finally achieved.

ENGLAND AND FRANCE

While the delicate negotiations were going on between king and barons, other important business was also being conducted. This consisted of a sustained attempt by Edward II to improve relations with France, partly in order to resolve existing problems over the English-ruled duchy of Aquitaine but also with the intention of obtaining French support in Edward's continuing disputes with his baronial opponents.

In November 1312 the bishop of Exeter had been ordered to prepare Edward II's legal defence at the Paris *parlement* to appeals against English officials in Aquitaine;[94] he was also to represent Edward in the problems arising out of the Process of Périgueux, which had begun in 1311 and was the latest attempt to resolve Anglo-French differences.[95] On 15 January

---

[92] *Ann. Lond.*, 225–9; Phillips, 59.

[93] *CPR, 1307–13*, 569; *PW*, II, ii, 94.

[94] The most pressing appeal had been made by a leading Gascon nobleman, Amanieu d'Albret, against John de Ferrers, the former seneschal of Gascony. The dispute between the two men had led in 1312 to open war in the duchy and to the murder of Ferrers: *GR, 1307–17*, no. 834; Vale, 164–73.

[95] The Process of Périgueux was the successor to the inconclusive Process of Montreuil in May and June 1306: see Cuttino, *English Diplomatic Administration*, 87–100.

1313 the king's council met at Westminster to discuss these issues and it was probably here that a decision was taken to send a high-ranking embassy to Paris.[96] On 4 February the earl of Pembroke, the bishop of Exeter and Master Thomas de Cobham were appointed to be the king's proctors in Paris and were given full powers to answer on any matters concerning Gascony.[97] On 14 February, several days after the departure of Pembroke and Exeter,[98] a most important addition was made to their business when Pembroke was authorized to arrange a personal meeting between Edward II and Philip IV to resolve outstanding Anglo-French disputes.[99]

Edward was in two minds as to whether he should allow Pembroke to leave England at such a critical juncture in the negotiations with the magnates. On 9 February the papal envoys had written to Philip IV, telling him of the dangers to England from internal dissension and external enemies and asking him to deal promptly with Pembroke's business so that he could return quickly to England where his services were badly needed; and on 14 February Edward II himself went so far as to write to Pembroke recalling him to England because royal affairs there were even more pressing.[100] Pembroke did not however return immediately and continued to Paris where on 14 March he reached an agreement for Edward II to meet Philip IV at Amiens on 20 May.[101] The plan was changed when Philip IV's cousin Louis de Clermont arrived in England at the end of April with an invitation for Edward and Isabella to attend the knighting of Philip's sons in Paris.[102] The intended meeting at Amiens was therefore abandoned in favour of a great social occasion in Paris.

EDWARD AND ISABELLA IN FRANCE

The opposition earls were unhappy about Edward's going to France and advised against it, ostensibly because of rumours that the Scots had invaded England and might even march on London, but probably because they feared – with good reason – the consequences for themselves of a closer friendship between England and France.[103] Edward II and Isabella,

---

[96] *CCR, 1307–13*, 488, 496; *Foedera*, II, i, 190.

[97] For further details of the problems the embassy (esp. Pembroke) had to deal with see Phillips, 60–1; Vale, 164–73.

[98] Pembroke left London on 10 or 11 Feb. and reached Paris by 2 March: *CCR, 1307–13*, 567; E 101/375/8, f. 19; *GR, 1307–17*, no. 1171.

[99] AN, J 918, no. 18 (the original letters patent under the seal of Edward II); a copy is preserved in BL, Cotton Ms. Julius E. I, f. 45 (a register of Gascon documents).

[100] *Edward II*, ed. Roberts, 21–2; *GR, 1307–17*, no. 846.

[101] AN, J 633, no. 35 (original letters patent of the earl of Pembroke). Pembroke then returned to England, probably in order to attend the parliament which was due to start on 18 March; he left behind the bishop of Exeter and Thomas de Cobham to continue the embassy's other business: E 101/375/8, ff. 19–20; Phillips, 61.

[102] E 101/375/2, m.9; *Vita*, 66–7; *CCR, 1307–13*, 579.

[103] *Vita*, 66–7; Maddicott, 149.

accompanied by the earls of Pembroke and Richmond, Hugh Despenser, Henry de Beaumont and many others, duly left for France from Dover on 23 May and reached the outskirts of Paris on 1 June.[104] The royal party remained there until 9 June, when they moved to Pontoise where they stayed until 30 June.[105] Their visit to Paris was marked by high ceremony and scenes of lavish display.[106] On their entry into Paris on 2 June Edward and Isabella were, according to one chronicler, received with solemnity and joy as 'the whole city rose up and went forth to meet them'.[107] In a ceremony reminiscent of Edward's own knighting at Westminster Abbey in 1306, the three sons of Philip IV – Louis king of Navarre, Philip and Charles – were knighted in Notre Dame on 3 June, together with almost 200 other young men;[108] on 6 June Philip IV and Edward II, and many other nobles, took the cross and made crusading vows in Notre Dame. Isabella also took the cross with other royal and noble wives, on 9 June, on condition that she would go to the Holy Land only in the company of her husband.[109] A series of six celebratory banquets was given between 2 and 7 June by Philip IV and Edward II, and by the king of Navarre, Louis of Évreux and Charles of Valois.[110]

Edward's banquet was held at noon on 5 June inside richly appointed tents set up in the meadows surrounding Saint-Germain-des-Prés on the Left Bank, where he and Isabella were lodging.[111] According to the chronicler Godefroy de Paris, the guests were served by attendants on horseback and the tents were lit by great torches even though it was the middle of the day.[112] Edward II's minstrel, the *crwth* player and singer William Craddock, performed for his guests; while another attraction was a 'castle of love' constructed by the armourer of Louis of Navarre and used to provide further entertainment between courses. The scale of the entertainment can be judged by the quantity of food donated to Edward by his father-in-law for his banquet alone, amounting to 94 oxen, 189 pigs, 380 rams, 200 pike, 160 carp and 80 barrels of wine. Altogether Philip IV gave his son-in-law more than £2,000 worth of supplies during his

---

[104] *CCR, 1307–13*, 583; E 101/375/2, m.9. The English contingent amounted to about 220 people in all: *Foedera*, II, i, 212–13.

[105] E 101/375/8, f. 30v; E 101/375/2, mm.9, 10.

[106] For a detailed account see Brown & Regalado. For a timetable of the events in Paris between 2 and 10 June, see ibid., 60–1, table 3.1.

[107] Ibid., 59; 76, n. 22.

[108] Ibid., 59–62.

[109] E 101/375/8, ff. 20, 30v; E 30/1422 (certificate of taking the cross by Edward and Isabella); *Grandes Chroniques de France*, ed. J. Viard, viii (Paris, 1934), 288–9; Brown & Regalado, 60, 64. Philip IV was acting in fulfilment of a vow he had made at the Council of Vienne in April 1312: ibid., 63.

[110] *Chronique métrique de Godefroy de Paris*, ed. J.-A. Buchon (Paris, 1827), 186–7; Brown & Regalado, 60–1.

[111] Brown & Regalado, 62–3, 66. See also the map of Paris in 1313, ibid., 65.

[112] *Godefroy de Paris*, ed. Buchon, 186.

stay.¹¹³ No doubt overcome by all the good living, on the morning of 7 June Edward did not get up in time to meet the French king, preferring to lie in bed with Isabella.¹¹⁴

The display and the generosity surrounding Edward's state visit to Paris were of course designed to show off the splendour of the French monarchy and especially of Philip IV the great king of France, who had put down the power of the papacy and of the Templars, and who was now to be seen surrounded in his capital city by his sons and brothers, and attended by his son-in-law and vassal Edward II and his French queen.¹¹⁵ The occasion was commemorated by the presentation to Philip of a translation from Castilian into Latin by the physician Raymond of Béziers of the text of *Kalila and Dimna*, a collection of tales featuring animals as protagonists and embodying moral lessons for princes as well as other humans.¹¹⁶ The manuscript was embellished with six miniatures,¹¹⁷ one of which shows Edward II girding the king of Navarre with his sword while Philip IV extends his hand as if giving a blessing; another shows Philip IV and Edward II riding out with trumpets preceding them, while a caption states that on the third day of Pentecost the kings of France and of England and a great force of nobles received the banner of the heavenly angel (*vexillum angeli celestis*) from the Dominican Nicholas de Fréauville, cardinal priest of St Eusebius, who was Philip IV's former confessor. This must be a reference to their taking of the cross. In another illumination the cardinal is shown bestowing blessings upon Philip IV, Edward II and the king of Navarre. In order to emphasize his importance, Philip IV is depicted slightly larger than those around him, including Edward.¹¹⁸

A second manuscript associated with the visit to Paris is the elaborately illuminated text of the Apocalypse which was commissioned for presentation

---

¹¹³ Brown & Regalado, 59, 62–3; 77, n. 24; 78–9, nn. 37–41. On 14 June Edward had to pay a Paris citizen 60s for the grass eaten by the oxen given to him by Philip IV: E 101/375/8, f. 32; Brown & Regalado, 77, n. 24.

¹¹⁴ This is the tactful description of the event by Godefroy de Paris: ed. Buchon, 194; Brown & Regalado, 60. Later in the day, however, he did make an offering in the Sainte-Chapelle.

¹¹⁵ See Brown & Regalado, 72–3.

¹¹⁶ The ms. is preserved as BN, Latin Ms. 8504. The tales originated in India in a Sanskrit book of fables of about the third century and were passed via Persian and Arabic across the Muslim world to Muslim and Christian Spain. They were translated from Arabic into Castilian under the auspices of Edward II's uncle, Alfonso X of Castile in about 1251: *Dictionary of the Middle Ages*, ed. J.R. Strayer, iii (New York, 1983), 31–2. For a more detailed study of this very interesting text see N. F. Regalado, '*Kalila et Dimna, Liber regius*', in *Satura: Studies in Medieval Literature in Honour of Robert R. Raymo*, ed. N.M. Reale & R.E. Sternglantz (Donington, Lincs, 2001), 103–23 (note that in the list of contents the title of this paper is given as 'Raymond de Béziers's *Kalila et Dimna* (Paris, BNF Ms. Lat. 8504): inscribing a tutorial performance in a primer for princes').

¹¹⁷ BN, Latin Ms. 8504, ff. 1v–2.

¹¹⁸ For a discussion of the manuscript and a description of the miniatures see Brown & Regalado, 58, 61.

to Isabella by her father. In another obvious reference to the taking of the cross by Philip IV and Edward II one of the illustrations shows a French monarch and an English prince leading the kings of the East gathered together for the battle of Armageddon.[119]

The formal business of Edward's visit to France began after the move to Pontoise, where he was visited by deputations of his Gascon subjects and where negotiations took place with Philip IV.[120] Having brought Edward II to France, and comfortable in the knowledge that Gaveston was no more and that Isabella had produced a half-French heir to the English throne, Philip IV was in a benign and conciliatory mood. The discussions ended on 2 July when Philip, as a mark of esteem for Edward's personal visit and taking the cross, remitted all penalties incurred by Edward and his subjects in Gascony for alleged offences against France. Philip also confirmed his letters patent of 1286 regulating all appeals to Paris by subjects of the duchy.[121] A settlement between Amanieu d'Albret, one of the most rebellious of those subjects, and the seneschal of Gascony was also achieved by giving d'Albret 20,000 *livres tournois* 'for his good services'.[122] Edward for his part could be well satisfied with his visit to France. He could now rely on the support of his father-in-law in the battles which lay ahead with the Scots and the English magnates; he had apparently reached a settlement of the problems concerning Gascony; and he had not been forced to accept anything he did not want, notably the provision of military assistance for Philip against his rebellious subjects in the county of Flanders.[123] Edward had however agreed, at Philip's instigation, to

[119] Philip and Edward are shown followed by the rulers of Castile and the German Empire, 'as they face the enemy in the apocalyptic guise of dragon, beast and false prophet': Lewis, 'Apocalypse'; see esp. 224–7. The illustration is reproduced in ibid., 227, from f. 50 of this ms.

[120] Brown & Regalado, 72; 85, n. 110.

[121] *Foedera*, II, i, 220; E 30/52 & 612; C 47/27/8/29; C 47/29/7/19; C 47/30/4/26; Phillips, 63–4.

[122] C 47/29/7/17; *GR, 1307–17*, no. 979; Phillips, 64; Vale, 172–3.

[123] Cf. Lalou, 'Les Négociations', 349. As vassals of the French crown, kings of England could technically be called upon to provide military service to their overlord in respect of their duchy of Aquitaine. Service had never in fact been provided, although Edward II was to give Louis X some naval assistance against Flanders in 1315: Vale, 59. Edward had his own problems with Flanders, which was providing food supplies to the Scots: *Foedera*, II, i, 210.

Edward had however made one important concession concerning Flanders even before leaving for France when he issued the Ordinance of the Staple, which ordered that all English wool merchants should sell their wool at a single 'staple town' on the continent, rather than in a variety of places as in the past. Tout believed that this decision was somehow connected with the Ordinances of 1311 and with the attempts of the Ordainers to impose a greater degree of control on the royal system of administration. A more likely explanation is that it was a gesture to Philip IV of France, who was anxious not to see the staple at Bruges, in the county of Flanders, and also an attempt to persuade the Flemings to cease their assistance of the Scots. By May 1314 the staple was located at Saint Omer, in the county of Artois, a loyal part of the kingdom of France: Tout, *Place of the Reign*, 221–6; W. S. Reid, 'The Scots and the Staple Ordinance of 1313', *Speculum*, xxxiv (1959), 598–610.

renew for a further year the truce with the Scots, which expired on 10 June; but for the moment this probably suited him. Edward was not ready for a military confrontation with the Scots.[124]

On 2 July Edward and Isabella left Pontoise for Poissy where both they and Philip IV spent the next three days. This was a highly symbolic location since it was where the French crusading saint and king, Louis IX, had been born and baptized, and where Philip IV had founded a Dominican priory in his memory.[125] While there, the two kings were visited by Guillaume de Villeneuve, the Franciscan bishop of an unnamed diocese in Persia, who came to Edward as the messenger of 'the emperor of the Tartars'. Guillaume was the latest and probably the last in a line of envoys from the Mongol rulers of Persia who had been visiting the kings of England and of France in the quest for an alliance since the middle of the thirteenth century. Given that Edward II and Philip IV had just taken the cross, it was an appropriate moment for such a visit. Nothing more however is heard of Guillaume.[126]

The other recorded incident at Poissy was potentially much more serious. During the night a fire started in Edward's wardrobe, destroying many of Edward and Isabella's belongings and forcing them to escape 'naked' into the 'street'.[127] Godefroy de Paris was as effusive in his praise of Edward's courage in saving Isabella as he was of Isabella's beauty. Whatever the truth of Edward's behaviour, Isabella suffered burns to one of her hands, for which she required extensive medical treatment after her return to England.[128]

'PEACE' AT LAST

Singed but otherwise largely intact, Edward and Isabella returned to England at the port of Sandwich on 16 July and reached London on

---

[124] Brown & Regalado, 72; 85, n. 109; C 47/29/8/2, a protest by the English parliament later in the summer of 1313.

[125] Brown & Regalado, 72; 85, n. 114.

[126] E 101/375/8, f. 30; Phillips, *Medieval Expansion*, 129; and, more generally, ch. 7, 'The lost alliance: European monarchs and Mongol "crusaders" '; Brown & Regalado, 72; 85, n. 115. Whether Guillaume's visit to France was more than a coincidence and was part of another attempt by the Mongol ruler of Persia (although himself now a Muslim) to engage France and England in a joint campaign against Muslim Egypt is unknown. The most recent Mongol efforts to achieve this had taken place in 1307, just as Edward II became king: Phillips, 128–9.

[127] *Chronique métrique de Godefroy de Paris*, ed. Buchon, 196–7: '*Oduard car nus toute nue / la royne mist en la rue*'. This probably means in their nightclothes, rather than literally naked: Brown & Regalado, 71.

[128] Doherty (D. Phil.), 53; idem, *Isabella*, 56–7. Doherty rightly discounts Trease's suggestion that a miscarriage some time in 1313 is the explanation of Isabella's illness: H. Trease, 'The spicers and apothecaries of the royal household in the reigns of Edward I and Edward II', *Nottingham Medieval Studies*, iii (1959), xlvi.

23 July.[129] Edward II had originally promised that he would be back in England in time for the opening of parliament on 8 July[130] and for further negotiations with the magnates. Whether because of the importance of the diplomatic business he was conducting in Paris, or because he wanted to wear down the barons by further delay, or because he was enjoying himself too much in France, or a combination of all these factors, it soon became clear that Edward would not be back in time. On 1 July the earls of Gloucester and Richmond and the bishops of Bath & Wells and Worcester were appointed to open and to continue the parliament until the king's arrival.[131] The earls of Gloucester and Richmond and some other magnates and prelates had waited in London as instructed, but the opposition magnates who had attended (it is not known who these were) gave up and left before the king's return, claiming that the king's advisers had persuaded him to delay his return in order to weaken his opponents.[132] As late as 19 July Edward appears to have expected a parliament to be held, since he advised the Kent justices to delay any cases involving the earl of Pembroke whose presence in parliament was urgently needed.[133] The parliament ended on 25 or 27 July without, so far as is known, achieving anything. Although no useful contact had been made with the opposition leaders, it is likely that the king's advisers, and perhaps Edward himself, felt that it was at last time to resolve the deadlock between the king and his opponents. Edward's position was now stronger than it had been earlier in the year. He could rely on support from France, and he was strengthened by the death of his old opponent, Archbishop Robert Winchelsey of Canterbury, on 11 May 1313. This also gave Edward the opportunity to influence the appointment of Winchelsey's successor. Edward had been in Canterbury on 20 and 21 May, but did not attend Winchelsey's funeral in the cathedral on the 23rd. The earl of Gloucester, the bishops of Worcester and Exeter, and four other bishops were however present. On the very day of the funeral Edward wrote secretly to the pope from Dover to inform him that he intended to approach him with his own nominee for the vacant see of Canterbury.[134] Although in the meantime the monks of Christ Church, Canterbury had elected the distinguished scholar Master Thomas Cobham as archbishop, Edward II got his way and on 1 October 1313 his old ally, Walter Reynolds, the bishop of Worcester and keeper of the Great Seal, was provided to Canterbury by Clement V.[135] The enthronement of Reynolds at Canterbury on

[129] *CCR, 1313–18*, 66; *Foedera*, II, i, 222; Phillips 64.
[130] *PW*, II, ii, 94; *Vita*, 66–7.
[131] *CPR, 1307–13*, 594; Phillips, 64; Maddicott, 150.
[132] *Vita*, 72–3; Phillips, 64; Maddicott, 150.
[133] C 81/85/2746A; Phillips, 64.
[134] Denton, *Robert Winchelsey*, 15–16.
[135] Menache, *Clement V*, 63–4; Wright, *The Church and the English Crown*, 245–6; *Vita*, 76–9.

17 February 1314 was to be attended by Edward and Isabella, the bishops of Winchester, Bath & Wells, Norwich and Worcester, the earls of Gloucester and Pembroke, as well as by other dignitaries.[136]

The next phase in the tortuous politics of 1313 began when Edward held a council at Eltham on 22 July, followed on 26 July by the summons of a new parliament to meet at Westminster on 23 September.[137] This decision was made in the presence and presumably with the advice of the earls of Pembroke and Richmond, Hugh Despenser the Elder, and the bishops of Bath & Wells, Worcester (the chancellor), and Exeter. The events of the next few weeks are obscure, until on 28 August Edward wrote asking Pembroke to meet other members of the council at Chertsey on 17 September to discuss the business of the coming parliament. On the same date Edward also requested his father-in-law, Philip IV, to send Enguerrand de Marigny, his chamberlain and in effect chief minister, and Louis of Évreux to assist in negotiating with the magnates.[138]

On their way to parliament the earls of Arundel, Lancaster, Gloucester, Hereford and Warwick met at Brackley on 19 September, ostensibly to hold a tournament, but in reality to plan a common baronial approach to the king when they arrived at Westminster. The king tried unsuccessfully to prohibit the planned tournament but may also have sent the earl of Pembroke to meet the earls and report back to the council on their intentions.[139]

According to the *Vita*, the magnates came to London on 23 September, the day parliament was due to begin, but for some time had no contact with the king, who was reluctant to meet them. The magnates then demanded that Edward should fulfil his promises of pardon and finally, under pressure, the king gave way.[140] It is not known what further demands the magnates made or whether these differed from their earlier ones in March, but there was certainly a period of further negotiation and mediations between the magnates' arrival and the issue of pardons by the king. As in 1312, the mediation was performed by the papal envoys and by the earls of Gloucester and Richmond. Louis of Évreux is also said to have taken part, but this must have been at a later stage of the negotiations, since he and Enguerrand de Marigny were still awaited on 14 October.[141]

The first sign of an impending agreement came on 4 October, when the sections of the Ordinances dealing with Henry de Beaumont and his

---

[136] Trinity College Cambridge, Ms. R.5.41, f. 112d (a continuation of the chronicle of Gervase of Canterbury); *Trivet (Cont.)*, 11; *Ann. Paul.*, 275; *Trokelowe*, 82; Phillips, 72.

[137] SC 1/49/22; C 53/100, m.7; *PW*, II, ii, 114.

[138] SC 1/49/23; *Foedera*, II, i, 226; Philips, 65. The dispatch of French envoys had probably been discussed while Edward was in Paris. The two papal envoys had been seeking the return of Louis of Évreux since the previous Feb.: *Edward II*, ed. Roberts, 22. On de Marigny see J. Favier, *Un conseiller de Philippe le Bel* (Paris, 1963).

[139] *Foedera*, II, i, 227–8; Phillips, 65; Maddicott, 150.

[140] *Vita*, 74–5.

[141] Ibid.; *Flores*, 337; E 101/375/9, f. 33; Phillips, 66; Maddicott, 150.

sister Isabella de Vescy were abrogated as being prejudicial to the king.[142] By 14 October the negotiations were sufficiently far advanced for the magnates to make a formal submission to the king: on this date Lancaster, Warwick, Hereford, Arundel, Henry de Percy, Robert de Clifford and John Botetourt came before Edward in Westminster Hall and asked for and received his pardon. To mark the settlement the earls dined with the king that night and returned the honour the following night.[143] The magnates attended parliament for the first time on 15 October[144] and the king's pardons to them were published the next day. The list was headed by Lancaster and the others just mentioned, together with two of Lancaster's leading retainers, Robert de Holland and Gruffudd de la Pole. The earl of Surrey's name was also included, presumably because of his role in the pursuit and surrender of Gaveston in 1312. As the king's leading councillor, the earl of Pembroke did not require a pardon, but at least eleven of his retainers were included in the list.[145]

No further decisions emerged from parliament until the end of October, suggesting that hard bargaining was still in progress. On 30 October the prelates, earls and barons declared in parliament that it was the king's prerogative alone to bear arms. This was an important concession, which fulfilled the magnates' promise in the treaty of December 1312 that they would stop bringing their armed retainers to parliaments once they had received pardon.[146] On 5 November the magnates were given a formal acquittance for their restoration of Gaveston's property, as they had demanded after the first acquittance in February 1313.[147] On 6 November the king confirmed his earlier ordinance giving a full pardon the earls for Gaveston's death, but in return they had to agree to a pardon for Gaveston's former adherents, which they had previously refused to concede.[148] The dispute between Lancaster's two retainers, Gruffudd de la Pole and Fulk Lestrange, and the king's chamberlain, John Charlton, which had been a major problem in January and February 1313, was settled on 3 November by the appointment of new justices in place of those of December 1312, and by the pardoning of all three parties on 6 November.[149] As in the treaty of December 1312, the Ordinances were not mentioned in the settlement,[150] nor was the removal of any royal

[142] *CPR, 1313–17*, 27, 29; Phillips, 66.
[143] *Liber de Antiquis Legibus*, ed. Stapleton, 252 (this is a London chronicle); *Vita*, 74–5; Phillips, 67; Maddicott, 151.
[144] *Liber de Antiquis Legibus*, 252.
[145] *CPR, 1313–17*, 21–6; Phillips, 66–7; Maddicott, 150–1.
[146] *CPR, 1313–17*, 26; *Ann. Lond.*, 224; Phillips, 67.
[147] *CPR, 1313–17*, 25; *Ann. Lond.*, 227; Phillips, 67.
[148] *CPR, 1313–17*, 26; *Ann. Lond.*, 227; Phillips, 67; Maddicott, 150.
[149] *Edward II*, ed. Roberts, 15; *CPR, 1307–13*, 546–7; *CPR, 1313–17*, 26, 66; Phillips, 67; Maddicott, 150–1.
[150] Except for the removal of the clauses concerning Henry de Beaumont: *CPR, 1313–17*, 27, 29; Phillips, 67.

ministers required;[151] and Gaveston and his supporters were not described as enemies of the king and the kingdom.[152] With these problems at last removed from political debate, at least in public, the king had regained some of the freedom of action within his own kingdom for which he had been striving since the death of Gaveston in June 1312.

The settlement reached in October 1313 was essentially the same as the treaty of December 1312, and, so far as its details were concerned, there was no good reason why it should not have been made earlier. The delay was caused on the one hand by the king's reluctance to give any final pardon to the magnates responsible for the death of Gaveston and by his hope that he might succeed in using diplomatic means to improve his position against his opponents. On the other hand the behaviour of Lancaster in particular in raising new causes of dispute with Edward in January 1313 does not suggest that he and his allies were seeking an early settlement either. Yet neither side was willing or strong enough to risk a military confrontation, with the result that most of 1313 was spent in arguing over the details of a settlement which neither could ultimately avoid. The agreement of October 1313 was a compromise, symbolized by the magnates' lack of unity and by their failure to enforce and the king's inability to destroy the Ordinances.[153] By dint of persistence and the skilful use of both domestic and external[154] political support Edward had achieved a great deal. The appointment of his old ally and friend, Walter Reynolds, bishop of Worcester and chancellor, as archbishop of Canterbury in succession to Winchelsey was another indication of his success, as was the great improvement in Edward's financial position.

ROYAL FINANCES

Edward had begun his reign suffering from an acute shortage of ready money. This was a major reason for the continued exploitation of prises and purveyance and for the political and social tensions which these produced. It also went far to explain Edward II's failure to mount any concerted campaign in Scotland. A solution to his financial problems was therefore just as important as a peace settlement with the magnates. In May 1313, for

[151] The *Vita*, 74–7, emphasizes the unpopularity of Hugh Despenser together with Lancaster's inability to have him removed from the council.

[152] Phillips, 68; Maddicott, 151.

[153] Phillips, 68–9; Maddicott, 151. During the most difficult period of the negotiations with the king in early 1313 both Lancaster and Warwick spent much of their time on their own personal estates, making communication between them and the magnates who were negotiating very difficult: Maddicott, 152–3. It is also significant that after agreement was finally reached in Oct. 1313 the earl of Hereford, who had negotiated on the magnates' behalf, stayed with the king, while the other magnates went home: *Vita*, 76–7.

[154] The two papal envoys were in England continuously from late Aug. 1312 until late Nov. 1313. On 19 Nov. the queen gave the envoys each a gold ring, valued at £50 and £35 respectively before their departure for Avignon: E 101/375/9, f. 35.

example, Cardinal William Testa, the papal chancellor who was then visiting England as a papal envoy, loaned Edward 2,000 marks, to be repaid on 10 June when the king was in Paris.[155] Also in May the Genoese merchant and banker Antonio Pessagno was authorized to borrow £20,000 on Edward's behalf;[156] in June Edward borrowed £33,000 from Philip IV while he was in Paris; and in July, at Ibouvillers in France, Pessagno borrowed a further £15,000 from Enguerrand de Marigny.[157] These sums were probably all needed to meet the substantial costs of Edward's stay in France. Much more was needed and this gradually became available over the coming months. One of the terms of the agreement between the king and the magnates was a grant of taxation, the first since 1309. This was forthcoming in November 1313 with the approval of a twentieth and a fifteenth on moveables, to be used for the war in Scotland.[158] Earlier in the year, in late July and August, Edward had attempted to borrow sums totalling nearly £8,000 for use in the war from the bishops of the Canterbury province and the prelates and abbots of the province of York.[159]

Edward's finances were greatly assisted by a loan which he negotiated with the pope. This had been under discussion since August 1312 and had originally been intended to help Edward hold out against the demands of his opponents. Details of the loan were not agreed until 28 October 1313, making it an important factor in the political situation which emerged from the 1313 settlement. Clement V agreed to make a private loan of 160,000 florins to be secured on the revenues of the duchy of Aquitaine. Since Edward needed the approval of Philip IV, as suzerain of Aquitaine, he crossed to Boulogne on 12 December, accompanied by the earl of Pembroke and Hugh Despenser, for a meeting with Philip at Montreuil. Edward returned to England on 20 December.[160] The loan agreement was confirmed on 20 January 1314 in the king's chamber at Westminster, in the presence of Pembroke and other councillors, and the money amounting to 160,000 florins, equivalent to £25,000 sterling, was received by Pessagno on the king's behalf in March, just in time for the coming campaign in Scotland.[161] This

---

[155] *CPR, 1307–13*, 573. Edward did not however pay on the due date and in Oct. 1313 Testa appointed proctors to reclaim the money from the earl of Pembroke and other guarantors: E 329/69; Phillips, 71.

[156] *CPR, 1307–13*, 571.

[157] *CPR, 1313–17*, 4; Phillips, 71; Brown & Regalado, 59, 77, n. 25. It is not clear whether these sums were denominated in pounds sterling or *livres tournois*.

[158] *CPR, 1313–17*, 49–51; *Ann. Lond.*, 227.

[159] *Foedera*, II, i, 223, 225. It is not clear how much of the money was actually collected.

[160] Phillips, 71–2. Edward's orders in Nov. 1313 for the handing over of the former possessions of the Templars to the Knights Hospitaller were also intended to meet with the approval of both the pope and Philip IV; so too was the safe conduct granted to the bishop of Glasgow: *Foedera*, II, i, 234–7.

[161] *CPR, 1313–17*; Phillips, 71–2. There is a detailed account of the negotiating of this loan in Y. Renouard, 'Édouard II et Clément V d'après les rôles gascons', in Renouard, *Études d'histoire médiévale*, ii (Paris, 1968), 935–57.

was not the only financial assistance which Edward obtained from the pope. During the Council of Vienne in 1312 Clement V had imposed a universal sexennial tenth upon the Church in aid of the crusade which he was then proposing. This enabled Edward to take advantage of his new-found status as a crusader to 'borrow' much of the money collected, nominally to assist his crusading plans but in fact for his own use. Edward ultimately obtained about £18,500 from this source.[162]

Antonio Pessagno's role was crucial in the king's financial arrangements.[163] From modest beginnings as a supplier of spices and small loans to the royal household in 1311, Pessagno was officially designated 'the king's merchant' in April 1312. By this time he was already owed over £2,000 by the crown. In February 1313 an agent of the Frescobaldi wrote that Pessagno 'is now in such a condition that he fears nobody ... and is so generous in the court ... that everybody likes him'.[164] He had the further advantage that he was connected by marriage with the Fieschi, one of the ruling families in his native Genoa and also powerful in the Church. In addition, through the Fieschi he could claim a connection with the English ruling family itself.[165]

Between 1312 and 1319 he was the king's chief financier, taking over the role previously performed by the Frescobaldi until their bankruptcy and exclusion from England by the Ordainers in 1311. During these seven years he advanced at least £144,000 to the king for the expenses of the royal household and of warfare, an annual average of approximately £20,500, which was higher than the annual average of any other royal banker between 1272 and 1337. Promises of 'gifts' to him in return for the use of his money amounted to almost £7,000. In 1314 Pessagno provided more than half the supplies needed for the English army in Scotland as well as large amounts of cash: at least £21,000 between March and June 1314. It was not through lack of resources that the English army was disastrously defeated at Bannockburn on 24 June 1314.[166] In November 1314 Pessagno acknowledged that he had recovered £104,900 from the king, while a balance of £6,605 was still due to him.[167]

---

[162] See W.E. Lunt, 'Clerical tenths levied in England by papal authority during the reign of Edward II', in *Anniversary Essays in Mediaeval History by Students of Charles Homer Haskins*, ed. C.H. Taylor (Boston & New York, 1929), 166–71. Most of the money borrowed was never repaid.

[163] What follows draws heavily on the article on Pessagno by E.B. Fryde in the *Oxford DNB*.

[164] R.W. Kaeuper, 'The Frescobaldi of Florence and the English crown', *Studies in Medieval and Renaissance History*, x (1973), 82–3.

[165] On the link between the Fieschi and the English crown see Phillips, ' "Edward II" in Italy', 218–19.

[166] Fryde in the *Oxford DNB*.

[167] Fryde in the *Oxford DNB*. The details of repayments and the sources from which they came are recorded in the acquittance given to him on 27 Nov. 1314: *CPR, 1313–17*, 203–6.

A MID-TERM ASSESSMENT

In a famous assessment of Edward II in 1313 the author of the *Vita Edwardi Secundi* remarked:

> Behold, our King Edward has now reigned six full years and up until now he has achieved nothing praiseworthy or memorable, except that he has made a splendid marriage and has produced a handsome son and heir to the kingdom . . . Oh! If our King Edward had borne himself as well [as King Richard the Lionheart] at the outset of his reign, and not accepted the counsels of wicked men, not one of his predecessors would have been more renowned than he. For God had endowed him with gifts of every virtue, and had made him equal to or indeed more excellent than other kings. Certainly if anyone cared to describe those qualities which ennoble our king, he could not find his like in the land. His ancestry, stretching back to the tenth generation, shows his nobility. At the beginning of his reign he had wealth, a land of abundance, and the goodwill of his people . . . If he had followed the advice of the barons, he would have humbled the Scots with ease. Oh! If he had practised the use of arms, he would have exceeded the prowess of King Richard. Physically this would have been inevitable, for he was tall and strong, a handsome man with a fine figure. But why linger over this description of him? If only he had given to arms the attention that he expended on rustic pursuits, he would have raised England on high; his name would have resounded through the land. Oh! What hopes he raised as prince of Wales! All hope vanished when he became king of England. Piers Gaveston led the king astray, threw the country into confusion, consumed its treasure, was exiled three times, and then returning lost his head. But there still remain at the king's court those from Piers's intimates and members of his household, who disturb the peace of the whole country and persuade the king to seek vengeance. Give peace in our time, O Lord, and may the king be at one with his barons![168]

From what has already been written in this book, it should be clear that, despite all his faults and especially his adherence to Gaveston, Edward II showed considerable ability when it came to exploiting divisions among his enemies and mobilizing the diplomatic and financial support of powerful allies, such as the king of France and the pope. This talent was shown to good effect in the political and financial settlement that had been achieved by the end of 1313. The *Vita*'s mid-term assessment of Edward underestimated both his abilities and the difficulties he faced when he first became king. He most certainly did not inherit wealth; nor was there any easy military option which would have defeated the Scots and brought

---

[168] *Vita*, 68–71.

them securely under English rule. The *Vita*'s anxiety about the future peace of the kingdom was however well founded, since the peace between Edward and the barons was an uneasy one. Above all, the personal hostility between Edward and Lancaster remained. It was also highly unlikely that the last had been heard of the Ordinances. The mutual distrust was expressed by the authors of the *Flores Historiarum* and of the Lanercost chronicle who remarked that 'the king always kept his distance from the earls, as before, led on by false counsel' and that 'the king promised many things to them, which afterwards he did not fulfil'.[169]

A SCANDAL AT THE FRENCH COURT

As was usual in the history of Anglo-French relations in this period, agreements had a habit of starting to unravel almost as soon as they were made. The successes achieved during Edward's visit to Paris in the summer of 1313, when the two kings had met face to face, had shown the value of personal contacts. But after Edward returned home, when Philip IV was perhaps in a less benign mood and his officials resumed control of affairs, problems concerning Gascon appeals to the Paris *parlement* and other matters soon resurfaced. It is likely that these were among the reasons for Edward's brief meeting with Philip at Montreuil in December 1313, but more diplomacy was clearly needed.[170] In January 1314 Edward II and his council decided to resort to personal diplomacy once more and to send Isabella to present a set of petitions at the next session of the *parlement*.[171] Isabella set out from Dover on 28 February with an impressive entourage, including the earl of Gloucester, Henry de Beaumont and his sister, Isabella de Vescy, and a large number of royal clerks.[172] She stopped at Boulogne on 3 March to make an offering at the church where she and Edward had been married in 1308, and reached Paris by 16 March. She remained in and around Paris until 18 April, when she began her return journey.[173] In the meantime much had happened. Isabella had presented the petitions as planned and obtained a number of concessions from her father.[174] The most important was Philip's acceptance that appeals lodged

---

[169] *Flores*, 337; *Lanercost*, 223; Maddicott, 151.

[170] E.A.R. Brown, 'Diplomacy, adultery and domestic politics at the court of Philip the Fair', in *Documenting the Past*, ed. J.S. Hamilton & P. J. Bradley (Woodbridge, Suffolk & Wolfeboro, NH, 1989), 62–3.

[171] Ibid., 62–5. The reasoning behind the decision to send Isabella is given in a memorandum prepared for the council: C 47/27/8/31: the text is printed in Brown, 78–80. The petitions presented by Isabella are contained in E 30/1530: Brown, 80–3.

[172] Brown, 'Diplomacy', 65–6. To carry them across the Channel 26 ships and 13 barges were required.

[173] Brown, 'Diplomacy', 66–7. Isabella's itinerary during her stay in France can be traced in E 101/375/9 (Isabella's wardrobe book for 7 Edward II, 1313–14).

[174] For a detailed assessment of the issues raised in the petitions and the manner in which they were answered see Brown, 'Diplomacy', 69–73.

at the Paris *parlement* by subjects of the English crown in Aquitaine could be withdrawn without prejudice, provided that the appellants did so of their own free will and the cases did not prejudice the French king's rights.[175] Even so, the gains reaped by Isabella's visit were modest and, as usual, many issues were left unsettled.

What made her visit even more significant was a major scandal which erupted at the French court while she was in Paris. The city was already in a state of high excitement, following the execution by burning on 15 March of Jacques de Molay, the Grand Master of the Knights Templar. Allegedly de Molay had pronounced a curse as he died upon Philip IV and all his family, and upon the pope. Within days of de Molay's execution it was discovered that the wives of Philip IV's three sons, Louis, Philip and Charles were engaged in adulterous affairs with two young knights, the brothers Philippe and Gautier d'Aunay. In April 1314 the young women were disgraced and sentenced to life imprisonment, while the two knights were broken on the wheel at Pontoise.[176] Several chroniclers claimed that Isabella was instrumental in the discovery of the affairs: it was alleged, for example, that she had given purses to two of her sisters-in-law, who had then given them to their lovers. When Isabella saw the purses in the possession of Philippe and Gautier she secretly told her father of her suspicions.[177] The facts that Isabella was personally very close to her father and that she had several meetings with him during her stay in Paris[178] lend plausibility to the claim that she played some role in revealing the scandal. On the other hand most of the chroniclers wrote well after the events and did not have any particularly close connections with the French court.[179] The only near-contemporary source with any possible bearing on the question is the metrical chronicle of Godefroy de Paris, cited earlier for its account of Edward and Isabella's visit to France in 1313. Having described Isabella as 'the most beautiful woman in the kingdom and the Empire' and 'as wise and prudent as any woman could be', Godefroy went on to say that 'through her many things were later disclosed and revealed in France', without stating exactly what these were.[180] The mystery therefore remains.

---

[175] Ibid., 71–2. The usual rule was that an appeal, once lodged, could not be withdrawn and had to proceed to a final decision by the *parlement*. This could often be seriously to the disadvantage of the duke of Aquitaine, i.e. the king of England.

[176] Ibid., 73–7

[177] Ibid., 74–6. The story of the purses comes from the *Myreur des Histors* by Jean d'Outremeuse, ed. S. Bormans, 7 vols (Brussels, 1964–8), vi, 196–8.

[178] E 101/375/9, ff. 3v, 5, 24; Brown, 'Diplomacy', 66. Jean d'Outremeuse, for example, not only wrote much later in the fourteenth century but is also notorious for embroidering or even inventing the stories he told. See G. Kurth, *Etude critique sur Jean d'Outremeuse*, 2nd ser., vii (Brussels, 1910), and Phillips, 'The quest for Sir John Mandeville', in *The Culture of Christendom*, ed. M.A. Meyer (London, 1993), 246–7.

[179] Brown, 'Diplomacy', 74–7.

[180] *Chronique métrique de Godefroy de Paris*, ed. Buchon, 211; Brown, 'Diplomacy', 76–7.

The scandal was only the first of a series of disasters to afflict the French monarchy, seeming to bear out the Templar's curse all too evidently. In November 1314 Philip IV died at the age of forty-six, having reigned since 1285; by January 1328 all three of Philip's sons had succeeded to the throne in turn and each had died without a male heir. Isabella retained her place in her father's affections to the end. In a codicil to his will, dated at Fontainebleau on 28 November, the day before he died, Philip IV left his daughter (*carissime filie nostre Regine Anglie*) two rings, one containing a large lodestone, the other set with a ruby called 'the cherry', which she had given to him. He also left 'a beautiful cup', which *carissima Ysabella Regina Anglie carissima filia nostra* had also given him, to the sisters of Poissy; and a golden fleur-de-lys worth £1,000 *tournois* to the church of St Mary, Boulogne, where Isabella and Edward had been married.[181]

DISASTER IN SCOTLAND

After her return from France, Isabella made an offering for her safe arrival at Canterbury on 29 May. She then travelled north to join her husband, reaching Berwick on the border with Scotland on 14 June.[182] Edward was already there, preparing to enter Scotland with his army for the campaign which led to the fateful encounter with his nemesis, Robert Bruce, at Bannockburn on 24 June.

The traditional view of Edward II's 1314 Scottish campaign is that it was undertaken in response to news received in the summer of 1313 that Philip de Mowbray, the Scottish commander of the English-held castle of Stirling in the Scottish Lowlands, had agreed to surrender to the Scots if he were not relieved by 24 June 1314.[183] The threat to Edward II's honour was too great even for such an unwarlike king to resist the challenge, and the defeat at Bannockburn was the inevitable result. The reality was however very different since, as Professor Archie Duncan has shown, the Scottish siege of Stirling began in late March 1314 and not a year earlier; Mowbray's agreement with Edward Bruce was not made until mid-May 1314; and Edward II first heard of it on 26–27 May, when he was already at Newminster in Northumberland and well on his way to join his army mustering at Berwick.[184]

Much had happened in the north since Edward II's last campaign in 1310–11. Little had been achieved by that campaign except to ensure that English garrisons continued to hold on to a number of strongly fortified

---

[181] AN, J 403. no. 18. There is no mention of Isabella in Philip's main will, drawn up at Royaumont in May 1311: J 403, nos 17, 17 bis. No bequests were made to his son-in-law, Edward II, but this probably is not particularly significant.
[182] E 101/375/9, ff.3, 37, 37v; Brown, 'Diplomacy', 67; Doherty (D. Phil.), 59.
[183] Barrow, 195, 202; McNamee, 60–1.
[184] *Bruce*, 376, note; 402, note; 406, note; McNamee, 60–1.

castles in strategic positions in Scotland, such as Perth, Stirling and Edinburgh, as well as key bases on or near the border, at Carlisle, Berwick-upon-Tweed and Newcastle upon Tyne. The situation began to change rapidly once Edward withdrew to deal with the demands of the Ordainers in 1311 and the prolonged crisis caused by the pursuit and death of Gaveston in 1312.

Within days of Edward's departure from Berwick in July 1311 Robert Bruce began raiding the north of England, bringing devastation to the counties of Northumberland, Cumberland and Westmorland. Unable to defend themselves, and receiving no assistance from the king, local communities bought truces with the Scots. The 'men of Northumberland', for example, are recorded as having bought a truce from the Scots in three successive years, 1311, 1312 and 1313, in return for payments of £2,000 in each of the first two years and 'a very large sum' in 1313.[185] These payments also enabled the Scots to pay for the costs of besieging English-held castles in Scotland.[186] By the end of 1313 this system of local truces was breaking down, probably because the northern counties were having difficulty in raising any more money.[187] In retaliation Edward Bruce invaded England in April 1314, ravaging the lands of the bishop of Carlisle and briefly attacking the city of Carlisle itself.[188]

Since 1311 the Scots had also captured several of the Scottish castles remaining under English control. Berwick, the first great Scottish fortress to fall to the English in 1296 and now the key to any future invasion of Scotland, was attacked on the night of 6 December 1312. The Scots were frustrated only by the timely barking of a dog inside the walls. Perth was taken early in 1313 after the Scots pretended to have broken off their siege and then scaled the walls at night; Dumfries fell a month later after a long siege, and Linlithgow when a loaded haywain concealing eight Scots was jammed into the gateway; Roxburgh was captured on 19–20 February 1314 by another surprise night attack; while Edinburgh was taken in March, again at night, after attackers had climbed the castle rock.[189] The captured castles were then demolished, to prevent the English reoccupying them and to avoid the need for the Scots to divert scarce resources in money and manpower. Finally, in March 1314, Stirling castle, the key to the Scottish Lowlands, which Edward I had captured in 1304, came under siege by Robert Bruce and his brother Edward.[190] If this fell, the English

---

[185] McNamee, 131.

[186] Ibid., 53–6. For a map of the Scottish raids see ibid., 54, and for a detailed discussion of 'the purchase of peace', see 129–40.

[187] Ibid., 56–7. By this time 'the Scots were exacting tribute at double the rate of "normal" English taxation': ibid., 56–7, 132.

[188] Ibid., 57.

[189] Ibid., 59–60; Barrow, 193–5. The date of Perth's fall is given by McNamee and Barrow respectively as 8 Jan. and 7 Feb. 1313.

[190] *Bruce*, 402, 440. On the loss of Scottish castles see *Vita*, 82–5.

position in Scotland would be fatally undermined and their remaining Scottish supporters left with little option but to change sides or to flee.

Edward II's plans for a new Scottish campaign were already far advanced by this time. Although his military achievements were few and far between when compared with those of his father Edward I and his son Edward III, there is no reason to believe that Edward II was a reluctant warrior. Before 1314 he had campaigned in Scotland on five occasions, four times in his father's reign and once during his own. There is little doubt that he would have fought there more often if the financial and material resources had been available and if he had not been constantly distracted by his disputes with Lancaster and the other opposition magnates. In the summer of 1313 Edward's thoughts were again turning towards Scotland. The abortive parliament held in July 1313 was intended to consider the war, but the continuing negotiations between Edward and the magnates prevented any progress on this occasion. Once the negotiations were concluded in October and early November Edward's plans were developed steadily and with deliberation. The taxation granted to him by parliament in November 1313 was due to be collected by 24 June 1314.[191] On 28 November Edward announced his intention to be at Berwick with his army, also on 24 June 1314, and called upon his loyal subjects in Scotland to continue their support.[192] This was probably Edward's response to an assembly held by Robert Bruce at Dundee in October 1313, at which Bruce gave his enemies a year in which to swear fealty to him or lose their lands. At about the same time the Anglo-Scots of Lothian appealed to Edward for help and protection.[193] On 26 November Edward summoned a parliament to meet at Westminster on 21 April 1314, and presumably intended to discuss Scotland further,[194] and on 23 December he summoned the earl of Lancaster, seven other earls and eighty-seven barons to be at Berwick with their military service on 10 June 1314.[195] Edward even interceded with the emperor at Constantinople to ensure that an English knight, Sir Giles d'Argentein, the third best knight in Christendom according to John Barbour, would be released from captivity in Salonika in time to fight against the Scots.[196]

The coming campaign was planned to be on a large scale. For the first time in the reign money was no problem: taxation, borrowings and Antonio Pessagno's credit operations ensured that. Edward was concerned that the purveyance of victuals should be made with all possible haste 'as

---

[191] *CPR, 1313–17*, 49–51.

[192] *Foedera*, II, i, 237.

[193] *Bruce*, 440; Barrow, 203; McNamee, 6. Robert Bruce's decree disinheriting those who had not come to his peace was finally issued at Cambuskenneth on 6 Nov. 1314: *Regesta Regum Scottorum*, v, *The Acts of Robert I*, ed. A.A.M. Duncan (Edinburgh, 1988), 330, no. 41.

[194] *PW*, II, ii, 120–5. The parliament was not in the end held. See *PROME*, Westminster Parliament of April 1314.

[195] *CCR, 1313–18*, 86; Barrow, 204.

[196] *Foedera*, II, i, 229; *Bruce*, 496–7; Prestwich, *Armies and Warfare*, 234–5.

in the time of the king's father'.[197] The outcome was that supplies of grain and other foodstuffs were stockpiled at Carlisle and Berwick on a scale that exceeded anything achieved during the reign of Edward I.[198]

By 26 February Edward had decided to go to Scotland shortly after Easter (7 April) and from then on the pace of events accelerated.[199] On 24 March he cancelled the parliament due to meet on 21 April because the Scots were threatening to invade the north of England and to attack Berwick, and replaced it with a summons to the earl of Lancaster and twenty-one other magnates to be at Newcastle on 1 June.[200] The earl of Pembroke was appointed as keeper of Scotland and to act as the king's lieutenant in the north until his arrival; by 16 April he was already at Berwick.[201] Another loyal supporter of the king, Edmund Mauley the steward of the royal household, was given custody of the castle of Cockermouth in Cumberland.[202]

In March and April 1314 orders were sent out for the mustering of 17,000 infantry from English counties and 3,000 from Wales, to assemble at Berwick by 19 May.[203] Edward II's own personal retinue amounted to thirty-two bannerets and eighty-nine knights, over seventy of whom were recruited for the campaign and had not served him before.[204] The earl of Pembroke also greatly enlarged his retinue for the occasion, having a total of about eighty knights and men-at-arms in his service, including the followers of two important magnates, his nephew John Hastings of Abergavenny and Maurice de Berkeley.[205] With the followers of the earls of Gloucester and Hereford, Hugh Despenser, Robert de Clifford and other barons, it is likely that over 2,000 knights and men-at-arms were present in the army which fought at Bannockburn.[206] The army as a whole did not however reach the size expected. The infantry contingent from England and Wales may have numbered as many as 15,000 of the 20,000

---

[197] *CCW*, 395.
[198] McNamee, 125–7 (incl. charts 3 & 4).
[199] *CCW*, 395; Phillips, 73.
[200] *CCR, 1313–18*, 95.
[201] Phillips, 73.
[202] McNamee, 61.
[203] *Rotuli Scotiae*, i, Record Commission (London, 1874), 118–21; McNamee, 61.
[204] Prestwich, *Armies and Warfare*, 40; Tebbit, 'The Household Knights' (Ph.D.) 58–9. See also Dr Tebbit's paper, 'Household knights', in Dodd & Musson eds, *The Reign of Edward II*, 76–96.
[205] Phillips, 307. A year earlier his retinue had numbered only 34.
[206] The author of the *Vita Edwardi Secundi*, 88–9, estimated the numbers at 2,000, but the total could have been as many as 2,500: *Vita*, 87, n. 168. There is no way of knowing with certainty since there are no royal household records for 1313–14 and no muster roll for the Bannockburn campaign. It is possible that the records were lost at Bannockburn: Prestwich, 'Cavalry service in early fourteenth-century England', in *War and Government in the Middle Ages*, ed. J. Gillingham & J.C. Holt (Woodbridge, Suffolk & Totowa, NJ, 1984), 148. See also the discussion in Barrow, 206–7.

expected.²⁰⁷ Altogether Edward II may have had 15,000–20,000 infantry and cavalry under his command, still a very substantial force, and probably the largest army put into the field since Edward I's Falkirk campaign in 1298.²⁰⁸ Even the author of the *Vita Edwardi Secundi*, usually scathing in his criticism of Edward, was moved to remark that 'all who were present agreed that never in our time has such an army marched out of England'.²⁰⁹

The only immediate fly in the ointment, apart from the uncertainty attaching to any military enterprise, however well prepared, was the failure to serve in person of four of the leading magnates, the earls of Lancaster, Warwick, Arundel and Surrey, who followed the precedent of 1310–11 and sent the minimum service required by law, possibly amounting to as few as sixty knights and men-at-arms in all.²¹⁰ Their argument that the campaign had not been decided upon in parliament was a transparent excuse,²¹¹ since a Scottish campaign had implicitly been part of the business of the parliament held in the autumn of 1313, when a subsidy had been granted for that purpose. The real cause of the absence of Lancaster and Warwick was their fear that if Edward were victorious in Scotland he would then turn against them in England,²¹² while a royal defeat would naturally strengthen their hand against the king. The earl of Surrey's absence may have been caused partly by his efforts to annul his marriage to Edward's niece, Joan de Bar, which probably put him on bad terms with the king,²¹³ but also by fear of Lancaster, who was an uncomfortably near neighbour of his in Yorkshire.²¹⁴ The earl of Arundel may have been influenced by the example of his brother-in-law, Surrey, or, as is more likely, he simply followed what he thought was the more powerful party. Of the magnates who accompanied the king to Scotland only Hereford's presence is of any special interest. Although a Lancastrian supporter in 1312, his part in persuading Lancaster to accept the outcome

---

²⁰⁷ Prestwich, *Armies and Warfare*, 117, citing the estimates in Barrow, 204–7. McNamee, 62, suggests that the infantry might have been as few as half the expected figure.

²⁰⁸ Prestwich, *Armies and Warfare*, 117.

²⁰⁹ *Vita*, 88–9.

²¹⁰ *Vita*, 86–9; Phillips, 73–4; Maddicott, 157–8; Barrow, 206. J.E. Morris's suggestion in *Bannockburn* (Cambridge, 1914), 34, followed by Barrow, 206, that there was no formal summons of the feudal host is incorrect: such a summons was issued on 23 Dec. 1313: *PW*, II, ii, 421–2.

²¹¹ *Vita*, 86–7.

²¹² *Knighton*, i, 410. Lancaster stayed at his castle of Pontefract in Yorkshire during the campaign and Warwick was certainly at Warwick castle early in May: *Knighton*, i, 410; BL, Add. Ms. 28024, f. 70; Phillips, 73.

²¹³ F.R. Fairbank, 'The last earl of Warenne and Surrey', *Yorks. Arch. Journal*, xix (1906–7), 198–9. This may explain why Surrey reluctantly gave up the honour of High Peak in Derbyshire to the queen in Feb. 1314: *CPR, 1313–17*, 38; *CCR, 1313–18*, 38; *CFR, 1307–19*, 182. Apart from his change of allegiance in June 1312, when he and Pembroke rejoined the king, Surrey's influence on politics at this time appears to have been minimal: Phillips, 74.

²¹⁴ This may explain why he spent June 1314 at his Yorkshire castle of Sandal, not far from Pontefract: Lambeth, Register of Walter Reynolds, f. 107.

of the peace negotiations in 1312 and 1313 marked him out as a moderate. He was the king's brother-in-law, having married Edward's sister Elizabeth, the widowed countess of Holland, in 1302, and held the hereditary office of constable of England, which gave him a leading role in time of war. After the 1313 settlement he had remained at court and may even have made an indenture to serve the king in the 1314 campaign.[215]

TO LOSE A BATTLE

Edward left Westminster to join his army in late March, was at St Albans abbey between 30 March and 1 April, and at Ely cathedral for Easter, 7 April, where he prepared himself spiritually for the coming campaign. He was probably in high spirits at the prospect of defeating Robert Bruce in battle: when shown the relics of St Alban kept at Ely he jokingly remarked that he had already seen them at St Albans.[216] After Easter Edward moved north, reaching York in early May, Durham on 21 May, Newminster in Northumberland on 26 May, and finally Berwick-upon-Tweed, where the army was gathering, on about 11 June.[217]

While he was at Newminster Edward received the fateful news that Philip de Mowbray, the constable of Stirling had promised to surrender to the Scots unless relieved by Midsummer's Day (the Nativity of St John the Baptist), 24 June; and that 'the Scots are striving to assemble great numbers of foot in strong and marshy places, extremely hard for cavalry to penetrate, between us and our castle of Stirling'.[218] The information at once determined the direction of the English advance and the location of any likely battlefield, but also gave the Scots ample time to prepare themselves. Edward thought about the implications and on 27 May ordered his infantry to be pushed forward as quickly as possible to prevent the fall of Stirling.[219]

So far Edward and his military advisers had acted sensibly. Having carefully organized and planned the coming campaign, they were now reacting rationally to news of the enemy's activities and likely intentions and were aware of some at least of the dangers they were facing. They were also aware, momentarily at least, of the advantage that the employment of English and Welsh infantry, mostly archers, might have over the English heavy cavalry in any battle before Stirling. Despite the absence of Lancaster and the other earls, there were many experienced commanders in the army: the earls of Hereford and Pembroke (the latter had beaten

---

[215] *Vita*, 76–7; E 101/68/2/34 (badly damaged); Phillips, 74.

[216] *Historia Anglicana*, 138–9.

[217] The details of his movements can be found in *Itinerary*, ed. Hallam. Isabella reached Berwick on 10 June, when her husband was nearby at Fenham.

[218] *Bruce*, 376, note; 402, note; 406, note; McNamee, 60–1; Barrow, 209, citing *Rotuli Scotiae*, i, 126–7 (trans. Professor Barrow).

[219] Barrow, 209; *Rotuli Scotiae*, i, 126–7.

Robert Bruce in battle at Methven in 1306), Robert de Clifford, and others, including the king himself. They had not however fought any serious actions against the Scots for several years and were in a sense 'out of practice'. What they did not yet know, and possibly Robert Bruce himself did not yet know, was whether there would be a pitched battle at all. Edward also failed to foresee the danger that would be caused by discord between leading members of his own army and by his own over-confidence.

The English army set out from Berwick on 17 or 18 June.

> There were in that company quite sufficient to penetrate the whole of Scotland, and some thought that if the whole strength of Scotland had been gathered together, they would not have stayed to face the king's army... The great number of wagons, if they had been placed end to end, would have stretched for twenty leagues.[220] The king therefore took confidence and courage from so great and fine an army and hurried day after day to the appointed place, not as if he was leading an army to battle but rather as if he were going [on pilgrimage] to Santiago. Short were the halts for sleep, shorter still were those for food; hence horses, horsemen, and infantry were worn out with toil and hunger.[221]

After a march of about 50 miles from Berwick, Edward and his army reached the vicinity of Stirling on 23 June.[222] Robert Bruce's army of about 500 light cavalry and 5,000–6,000 infantry, armed mainly with long spears,[223] was drawn up in the 'New Park', a wooded hunting preserve through which the main road to Stirling passed. At the entrance to the New Park the road was about half a mile to the north of a stream flowing between steep banks, called the Bannock Burn,[224] which was tidal at the point where it flowed into a bend of the River Forth. Much of the surrounding land was intersected by streams, known locally as *pols* or *pows*[225] and was boggy. The high road along

---

[220] *Vita*, 88–9. The army was also to be kept supplied by sea, ships calling at ports such as Edinburgh and sailing into the Firth of Forth (from which it would be easy to replenish both the army and the garrison of Stirling): Barrow, 204; A. Nussbacher, *The Battle of Bannockburn, 1314* (Stroud, 2000), 57.

[221] *Vita*, 88–9; Barrow, 209–10. The classic analysis of the battle of Bannockburn is that of Morris, *Bannockburn*, which has formed the starting point for later scholars. What follows is based mainly on Barrow, and on the 'Bannockburn Commentary' and notes, in *Bruce*, 440–7. Apart from falling into the traditional error that the siege of Stirling began in 1313, Nussbacher's book is a well written and clearly presented account of the battle and its circumstances, but differs in its assessment both of the site of the battle and of Edward II's intentions and competence.

[222] Barrow, 209, and Nussbacher, *Battle*, 81, give a very clear idea of the route followed and the distances involved in each stage of the journey.

[223] Barrow, 208–9.

[224] Ibid., 210.

[225] Barrow emphasizes that although the *pols* often flowed through 'deep peaty pools with crumbling, overhanging banks', the word *pol* itself referred to a stream and not to a pool. Failure to appreciate this distinction has, in Professor Barrow's view, led to a

which the English army had to pass was raised above the surrounding land and extremely constricting for a large force with a long baggage train. In order to make life even more difficult for an advancing army Bruce had in effect laid a minefield by honeycombing 'the ground on either side of the road with small pits or "pots", covered with sticks and grass'.[226]

Two days of fighting ensued, on 23 and 24 June. The first day's action consisted of two skirmishes between English cavalry and the Scottish cavalry and infantry. Neither was decisive in itself, but together they provided an ill portent for the main battle that followed. The English vanguard was under the joint or rather competing control of two earls: Edward II's nephew, the twenty-three-year-old Gilbert de Clare, earl of Gloucester, eager for glory in his first battle, who claimed that his forebears had always commanded the vanguard; and Edward's brother-in-law, the veteran Humphrey de Bohun, earl of Hereford, hereditary constable of England, who believed that the command was his by right and was deeply offended by Edward's support of Gilbert's claim.[227]

As the vanguard advanced over the Bannock Burn and approached the Scottish lines, they saw Robert Bruce himself appear ahead of and separated from his followers. The earl of Hereford's nephew, Sir Henry de Bohun, took this as a golden opportunity to kill Bruce in single combat, and charged with the lance. Skilfully, Bruce avoided his opponent and with one blow of his battleaxe split Sir Henry's helmet and head in two. Bohun died on the spot. It was a telling moment of drama and was followed by a general mêlée, in which the earl of Gloucester was knocked off his horse.[228]

In the other engagement of the day, a division of English cavalry, led by Sir Thomas Gray and Sir Henry de Beaumont, headed directly for Stirling castle, either to discover whether the way was open for the main body of the army to follow or to relieve the castle. A well disciplined body of Scottish spearmen advanced to meet them. With no archers to attack the Scottish troops, who were in a close formation (or schiltrom), the English cavalry were helpless against the hedge of spears. Grey's horse was killed under him and he was captured; other English knights were killed too. The remainder withdrew, some making for Stirling castle and others for the main body of the army.[229]

Overnight the rest of the English cavalry force, and probably some of the infantry, crossed the Bannock Burn with difficulty and made camp. It

---

misplacing by modern commentators of the location of the battlefield and a misunderstanding of how the battle was fought: ibid., 212.

[226] Ibid., 217; *Bruce*, 422–3. For a detailed discussion of the likely battlefield and the various suggested locations see Barrow, 210–16 (incl. a map on 213).

[227] *Flores*, 158; *Vita*, 92–3; Barrow, 217.

[228] Barrow, 218; *Vita*, 88–9; *Bruce*, 448–51.

[229] Barrow, 219–21; *Vita*, 90–1; *Bruce*, 452–7; *Scalacronica*, 72–5. Gray, the son of the Thomas Gray captured at Bannockburn, began to write in 1355 while he himself was a prisoner of the Scots in Edinburgh castle.

was an anxious time since the English were disturbed by the events of the day before and were afraid of a Scottish night attack.[230] The English high command suffered from deeply divided counsels. According to the *Vita*, the earl of Gloucester, together with the veteran and more experienced knights, advised the king not to fight the next day, but to rest and let his army recuperate as much as possible. Edward, who had been with the rearguard and had not witnessed the previous day's fighting at first hand, was furious and 'scorned the earl's advice, and grew very heated with him, charging him with treachery and deceit. "Today", said the earl, "it will be clear that I am neither a traitor nor a liar" '.[231] Had the English but known it, the Scots were also unsure of themselves. Bruce wished to avoid the risk of defeat in a pitched battle and was considering a withdrawal into rough country where the English army could not easily follow him. Allegedly his mind was changed by Sir Alexander Seton, a Scottish knight in English service, who saw how demoralized and divided the English were and changed sides during the night.[232]

On the following day, 24 June, the feast of the Nativity of St John the Baptist, the English army advanced from their uncomfortable overnight encampment on to an area of ground, identified by Professor Barrow as lying between Balquiderock and Broomridge.[233] Here the battle would be fought. It was at least firm ground, but it was too small to allow full deployment of the English cavalry and infantry. The steep-sided Bannock Burn and marshy ground lay behind and the Firth of Forth on their flank. If anything went wrong, there would be no easy escape.[234] It is arguable, however, that Edward and his commanders had no intention of fighting on this constricted piece of ground, since they did not seriously expect the Scots to fight and were deployed in a line of advance designed to bring them along the road to Stirling castle but not for battle. When the Scots attacked unexpectedly on the English flank, Edward II and his army were therefore not well placed to fight back.[235]

---

[230] Barrow, 222–4.

[231] *Vita*, 90–1. Ingram de Umfraville, a Scottish nobleman, who was serving with Edward II, apparently also advised a delay: Barrow, 226. Earlier, Philip de Mowbray, the constable of Stirling, had come to Edward II, under a flag of truce, and had told him that the Scots were in a strong position which would make an attack on them difficult. He also apparently said that Stirling was already saved from having to surrender since Edward had relieved it by reaching the vicinity of the castle by the appointed date: Barrow, 217. One may suspect, however, that Mowbray was also safeguarding his own position. He may already have been planning to change sides, as he did immediately after the battle.

[232] Barrow, 222–3; *Bruce*, 456, note.

[233] Barrow, 224; see also the map on p. 213. This identification is accepted by Duncan, in his 'Bannockburn commentary,' *Bruce*, 440, 444, but not by Nussbacher, *Battle*, 102–6, who argues for a site at a lower level.

[234] Barrow, 224, 226.

[235] Nussbacher, *Battle*, 104–6.

Instead of melting away, the Scots advanced. Their infantry first emerged from the New Park where they had been hidden and then stopped and knelt down to pray. When Edward II saw this he thought at first that they were kneeling in submission and refused to believe that the Scots intended to fight[236] until after an exchange of arrows between both sides.[237] The English vanguard, led by the earl of Gloucester, then charged the Scottish infantry, but could not break through the mass of spears. Determined to maintain his honour and his claim to command, the earl of Gloucester charged ahead of the rest, was cut off and killed.[238] Had he been wearing a surcoat bearing his arms, he might have been recognized and saved for ransom, but the press of men and horses was so great that nothing was likely to preserve him.[239]

The Scottish infantry then advanced in close formation on the rest of the English cavalry, who were so tightly bunched together that they were pressed against the Scottish spears and suffered severely.[240] In a similar critical situation at the battle of Falkirk in 1298, Edward I had saved the day by introducing his archers, who shot down the Scottish spearmen in their thousands.[241] This would not happen again. In 1314 the archers were kept in the rear instead of protecting the flanks of the cavalry.[242] By the time some archers were brought up to the front of the battle, it was too late. The small force of Scottish cavalry charged them and drove them in confusion from the battlefield. The battle then turned into a grim slaughter of the English cavalry.[243]

Edward II gave no speech to his troops before the battle[244] and appears to have played little part in its direction, apart from his determination to fight an army which he regarded as little more than a rabble.[245] Once the fighting started, the very constricted space in which the battle was fought soon took its conduct beyond the control of Edward or any of his commanders. Edward stayed with a division of cavalry, and was flanked for his immediate protection by the earl of Pembroke and Sir Giles

---

[236] Barrow, 225–6; *Bruce*, 472–3.

[237] Barrow, 226; *Bruce*, 482, note.

[238] Barrow, 226; *Vita*, 90–3; *Bruce*, 480–1, note.

[239] Prestwich, *Armies and Warfare*, 223, 233.

[240] Barrow, 226, 228; *Bruce*, 475–83: a situation not unlike that of the French knights and men-at-arms at Agincourt in 1415 when the crush was so great that many men died of suffocation: Prestwich, *Armies and Warfare*, 328.

[241] Prestwich, *Armies and Warfare*, 306, 329.

[242] If the English army was arranged in line of advance rather than in line of battle, this might explain the absence of archers in significant numbers.

[243] Barrow, 227. The Scottish cavalry were far fewer in numbers and less heavily equipped than their English counterparts whom they could not expect to defeat in open battle.

[244] Unless we include the remarks of astonishment ascribed by Barbour to Edward II when he realized that the Scots were going to fight a pitched battle on open ground: *Bruce*, 470–1.

[245] *Bruce*, 472–3.

d'Argentein. At all costs Edward had to be saved, since his capture by the Scots would have turned disaster into catastrophe. As soon as defeat became obvious Pembroke seized the reins of the king's horse and led him away from the battle 'against his will, for it pained him to leave'. 'When the Scottish knights, who were on foot, grabbed the caparison of the king's warhorse with their hands to bring him to a halt, he struck behind him with a mace, so forcefully that there were none that he hit, whom he did not beat to the ground.' Edward's horse was wounded in the belly and could go no further, but he was remounted on a riding horse. Once he was sure that Edward could reach safety, Sir Giles d'Argentein, like the blind king John of Bohemia at the battle of Crécy in 1346, rode back into the thick of the fight and was killed.[246] The death of Sir Edmund Mauley, the steward of the king's household, and the capture of one of his household clerks, the keeper of his privy seal, Sir Roger de Northburgh, together with both the seal and the king's shield, are another indication of just how close a call Edward experienced.[247] It was no wonder that Edward made a vow to the Virgin Mary that if he escaped he would found a house for twenty-four Carmelites at Oxford.[248]

Edward and his escort of about 500 men first went to Stirling castle, where the constable Philip de Mowbray according to different reports either told Edward that if he came inside he would be besieged and captured by the Scots or refused to admit him.[249] Edward then made his way to Dunbar castle, pursued by a troop of Scottish cavalry led by Sir James Douglas, who captured any English knights who lagged behind through fatigue or to relieve themselves.[250] Edward was lucky that Patrick, the earl of Dunbar, who held Dunbar castle and who had upheld the English cause in Lothian, decided to help. Instead of taking Edward prisoner,[251] he performed one last service for the English crown. From Dunbar Edward escaped by sea to Berwick,[252] which he reached on 27 June. There he was met by Isabella, who supervised the cleaning of his armour and

---

[246] Phillips, 74; Barrow, 229; *Bruce*, 494–7; *Scalacronica*, 76–7. There is no indication of how Sir Thomas Gray, the author of the *Scalacronica*, learned the details of Edward's experiences in the battle. Sir Thomas's father, also Sir Thomas, was present at Bannockburn but was already a prisoner by this stage.

[247] Barrow, 229. Northburgh's usual function was as keeper of the king's privy seal: Tout, *Chapters*, ii, 294–5. The loss of records makes it very difficult to work out just how many of Edward II's household knights and clerks were killed or captured at Bannockburn.

[248] SC 8/11/512, printed in *RP*, ii, 35, no. 23; Knowles and Hadcock, *Medieval Religious Houses*, 198. See also ch. 2 of this book.

[249] *Vita*, 94–5; *Bruce*, 498–9; Barrow, 230–1.

[250] *Vita*, 94–5; *Bruce*, 498–9, 508–11; Barrow, 230–1.

[251] *Bruce*, 510–13; *Scalacronica*, 76–7; Barrow, 231. Patrick's loyalty to England was suspect however since his lands were declared forfeit as of 24 June 1314 and he was later confirmed in his earldom by Robert Bruce: *Bruce*, 512, note.

[252] *Bruce*, 513–15; *Scalacronica*, 76–7; *Lanercost*, 227–8; Barrow, 230–1; Phillips, 74–5.

loaned him her privy seal, in place of his own.[253] From the time he left Berwick, at the head of a splendidly equipped and confident army, to his return in humiliation, only ten days had elapsed.

With Edward's departure from the battlefield the English army dissolved into panic-stricken flight. Many men and horses were lost trying to cross the Bannock Burn; others were drowned in the River Forth. Of those who escaped, one force of Welsh infantry, numbering several thousand, kept its order and managed to reach Carlisle; many other members of the English army made their way back to Berwick.[254] In the absence of muster rolls for the Scottish campaign, there is no way of knowing the total English losses:[255] Barbour's figure of 30,000 dead is greater than the numbers engaged on both sides combined, while his figure of 200 spurs taken from dead knights and men-at-arms might even be an underestimate.[256] But there are some indications. Apart from the deaths of the earl of Gloucester, Giles d'Argentein and Edmund Mauley, others killed included Sir Robert de Clifford, a prominent political figure and one of the leading commanders in the battle, Sir Payn Tybetot, and Sir William Marshal, a former Ordainer.[257] The *Annales Londonienses*, probably reflecting a contemporary newsletter, lists about forty knights among the dead, including those already mentioned.[258] The earl of Pembroke narrowly escaped with his life, but at least four of the knights in his retinue were killed, either in the battle itself or in covering Edward's flight to Dunbar through Linlithgow and Winchburgh.[259] One of those who died was John Comyn, Pembroke's nephew and son of John Comyn of Badenoch who had been murdered by Robert Bruce in 1306, a reminder that the Anglo-Scottish war embraced a civil war within Scotland as well as a war for an independent Scotland.[260]

Many others were taken captive by the Scots. The most notable prisoner was the earl of Hereford, who fled with many others to Bothwell castle, believing it still to be under English control, only to find that its Scottish constable, Walter Fitz Gilbert, had decided to change sides.[261] Other prisoners included the earl of Angus, Robert de Umfraville, and Ingram de Umfraville, both Scots in the English service; John de Segrave; Anthony de Lucy; Ralph de Monthermer, the stepfather of the dead earl

---

[253] E 101/375/9, ff. 19, 25; Doherty (D.Phil.), 59; idem, *Isabella*, 59–60; Tout, *Chapters*, ii, 294–5.

[254] *Vita*, 94–7; *Bruce*, 494–7; Barrow, 229, 231; Phillips, 74–5.

[255] These records were probably among those lost in the battle.

[256] *Bruce*, 500–1, 504–5.

[257] *Vita*, 92–3; *Bruce*, 504–5.

[258] *Ann. Lond.*, 231; Phillips, 75; Barrow, 230. The fullest casualty list in a chronicle appears to be the one in the continuation of Nicholas Trivet: *Trivet (Cont.)*, 15.

[259] *Bruce*, 494–7; Phillips, 74–5.

[260] Phillips, 75.

[261] *Bruce*, 514–15; Barrow, 231. Bothwell had nominally belonged to the earl of Pembroke after 1301 but had since been taken into royal hands: *Bruce*, 500, note; Phillips, 74.

of Gloucester and formerly titular earl of Gloucester himself; and John Giffard.²⁶² At least ten of the earl of Pembroke's retainers, including several members of the Berkeley family, were also captured.²⁶³

Material losses were enormous.

> Amongst all their misfortunes this one thing at least turned to the advantage of our army, that, while our people sought safety in flight, a great part of the Scottish army turned to plunder; because, if all the Scots had been equally intent on the pursuit of our men, few of our men would have escaped the Scots... Oh! day of vengeance and misfortune, day of ruin and dishonour, evil and accursed day, not to be reckoned in our calendar, that stained the reputation of the English, and robbed the English and enriched the Scots, in which our men's costly belongings, valued at two hundred thousand pounds, were snatched away! So many fine noblemen, [and] strong young men, so many noble horses, so much military equipment, costly garments, and gold plate – all lost in one harsh day, one fleeting hour.²⁶⁴

While the author of the *Vita Edwardi Secundi* spoke of the shame and dishonour and the human and material losses brought about by the battle, he was also aware that it had a wider significance in the history of warfare. 'Indeed I think it is unheard of in our time for such an army to be scattered so suddenly by infantry, unless when the flower of France fell before the Flemings at Courtrai [in 1302].'²⁶⁵ He was perfectly right in his perception that something was shifting in the balance between cavalry and infantry. For the well armed and heavily armoured man on horseback war was an exciting and sometimes dangerous sport, but he did not expect to be killed, least of all by his despised social inferiors, the infantry armed

---

[262] *Vita*, 96–7; *Lanercost*, 228; Barrow, 231.

[263] Phillips, 75: Thomas de Berkeley senior, and Thomas and Maurice de Berkeley the sons of Maurice de Berkeley senior, but not Maurice de Berkeley senior himself: cf. Barrow, 231.

[264] *Vita*, 96–7. See also *Bruce*, 502–3. According to the fifteenth-century Scottish chronicler Walter Bower, Edward II had brought with him a Carmelite friar and poet, Robert Baston, to celebrate his expected victory over the Scots. Baston was captured at Bannockburn and, in return for his release, required to write Latin verses in honour of the Scottish victory. The verses are however more a record of death and destruction than praise for the achievements of Robert Bruce, beginning 'Grief is the theme on which I compose this song in unadorned verse' and ending 'I am a Carmelite, surnamed Baston. I grieve that I am left to outlive such a carnage.' The verses make no mention of Edward II and his conduct in the battle. The Latin text, with a facing translation, is published in *Scotichronicon*, 366–75. A.G. Rigg doubts whether Baston was either present at Bannockburn or the author of the verses: 'Antiquaries'. However, Edward II's vow to found a house of Carmelites at Oxford was clearly made to a Carmelite who was present at the battle and it seems likely that Baston was the one.

[265] *Vita*, 96–7. The comparison with Courtrai was also noted by Sir Thomas Gray, writing in 1355, when knights had become accustomed to fighting on foot rather than on horseback: *Scalacronica*, 74–5.

with spears or with bows. The battle of Courtrai[266] and now the battle fought near Stirling[267] had shown that even the most noble of men was in danger of losing his life at the hands of infantry. Within a few years English tactics were to change dramatically: knights and men-at-arms would now fight on foot alongside archers and would win great victories against both the Scots and the French.[268]

English armies were not used to being defeated by the Scots, whom they had overwhelmed in previous encounters such as the battles of the Standard in 1138, Dunbar in 1296 and Falkirk in 1298. English expectations were coloured by these experiences, making it all too easy to forget their embarrassing defeat by William Wallace at Stirling Bridge in 1297 (Edward I was not present, so perhaps this did not count as a 'real' trial of arms between the English and the Scots) and the close-run battle at Falkirk, when the intervention of the English archers turned the tide. Robert Bruce understood as well as anyone else that to challenge the king of England in open battle was to take a grave risk. This is why he appears to have delayed his decision to fight Edward II before Stirling until the last possible moment, knowing finally that the English were both over-confident of victory and divided in their counsels and that the choice of battlefield was favourable to the Scots. But it also explains why most of the Scottish campaigning during the war with England consisted either of surprise attacks on English-held castles or of swiftly moving raiding parties made up of the light cavalry known as hobelars.[269]

There was no escaping the scale and the significance of the disaster suffered by the English at Bannockburn. The largest and best equipped English army in a generation had been routed by a much smaller Scottish force. The battle gave the Scots a great advantage in their war with England. The fortress of Stirling, for whose relief the battle was nominally fought, swiftly fell into Scottish hands and was demolished.[270] The position of Scottish supporters of the English crown was now untenable. Only

---

[266] J.F. Verbruggen, *The Battle of the Golden Spurs (Courtrai, 11 July 1302)* (Woodbridge, Suffolk & Rochester, NY, 2002); and *The Art of Warfare in Western Europe during the Middle Ages* (Woodbridge, Suffolk, 1998), 190–4 and ch. 3, 'The foot-soldiers'.

[267] At first the battle had no name at all or was referred to as the battle for the relief of Stirling; but by the 1320s it was coming to be known as the battle fought at Bannockburn: Barrow, 215. On the tactics employed by the Scots and the English at Bannockburn see Prestwich, *Armies and Warfare*, 317–18.

[268] Ibid., 318–23. One of the first indications of a change was the battle of Boroughbridge fought between Edward II and the earl of Lancaster in March 1322 when a royal commander, Andrew Harclay, made use both of the Scottish schiltrom and the English tactic of archery.

[269] McNamee, 23–4; Prestwich, *Armies and Warfare*, 52. Hobelars were also familiar in Ireland and had been used by Edward I in Scotland on several occasions. They were to be reintroduced in 1315 to defend the north of England in the aftermath of Bannockburn: McNamee, 24; Phillips, 91.

[270] Barrow, 231.

those who were attached to the English court, such as Robert de Umfraville and David de Strathbogie, the earls of Angus and Atholl, could continue their allegiance, while Donald, earl of Mar, a Scottish prisoner in England who was released as a consequence of Bannockburn, elected to stay in England and to serve the English crown.[271] Robert Bruce was now free, if he wished, to resume raiding the northern counties of England with renewed ferocity and also to consider opening a new front against England in the lordship of Ireland. Bruce used his victory to obtain good value from his most prominent prisoners, obtaining the release of his wife, daughter and sister in return for the earl of Hereford.[272] Bruce could also afford to be generous in victory. The bodies of the earl of Gloucester and Robert de Clifford were returned to their families for burial, while two of his prisoners, the Yorkshire knight Sir Marmaduke de Tweng and Sir Ralph de Monthermer, were released without any demand for ransom.[273] The latter brought back with him Edward II's privy seal which had been captured in the battle.[274]

However, Bruce's victory did not win the war or secure the independence of Scotland. Edward II was defeated in battle in 1314 but there was no indication that either he or any of his leading subjects believed that the war itself was lost and that Bruce should be formally recognized as king of the Scots. If Edward II had even thought of ending the war by recognizing Robert Bruce – and there is not the slightest evidence that he did so – his deposition from the throne might have occurred even sooner than it did. Only the capture of Edward at Bannockburn and a subsequent deal to ransom him might have given Bruce what he wanted, and even then such an agreement under duress would probably have been repudiated the moment Edward set foot back on English soil.[275] The war between England and Scotland was doomed to drag on with no end in sight.

[271] On all three earls see the articles in the *Oxford DNB*.
[272] *Vita*, 100–1; *Lanercost*, 229; Barrow, 231.
[273] Barrow, 231.
[274] The keeper of the privy seal, Roger de Northburgh, was released by Nov. 1314: Tout, *Chapters*, ii, 294–5.
[275] Cf. Barrow, 229, which expresses a more optimistic view for the Scots of such an outcome.

Chapter 6
WAR, POLITICS, MONEY AND WEATHER, JUNE 1314 TO AUGUST 1316

AFTER BANNOCKBURN

For Edward II the defeat in Scotland was a profound personal humiliation, which showed that despite his extensive experience of campaigning, he had, unlike his father, little capacity as a military commander.[1] He did not lead another campaign against the Scots until 1319 but in the meantime the war continued, inflicting misery on the inhabitants of the northern counties of England and also, from May 1315, in Ireland. The misery was compounded by a prolonged period of wet weather, which began in the late summer of 1314, resumed on a much greater scale in 1315,[2] and led in succeeding years to food shortages, high prices, disease among humans and their livestock, and famine. The defeat at Bannockburn also undid completely the political and financial stability which Edward had achieved in 1313. As a result the kingdom of England was to undergo a further period of internal upheaval and external conflict which lasted until yet another political settlement was achieved in the autumn of 1318.

Edward reached Berwick on 27 June and remained there until about 9 July. No doubt stragglers from the battle were continuing to arrive there by whatever means were available. Leaving a strong garrison to defend this key position, he then made his way back to York, where he arrived on about 17 July, accompanied by the earl of Pembroke, Hugh Despenser, Henry de Beaumont, and Bartholomew de Badlesmere, the leading retainer of the dead earl of Gloucester. It was a measure of the insecurity of the time that he apparently began his journey by sea, landing at Hartlepool before making his way inland.[3]

---

[1] For all his experience of warfare, Edward I fought in only three pitched battles (at Lewes and Evesham in 1264 & 1265; and at Falkirk in 1298). Edward III's only full-scale battles on land were at Halidon Hill in 1333 and Crécy in 1346. This is an indication of the rarity of such engagements: Prestwich, *Armies and Warfare*, 306.

[2] *Vita*, 110–11, which indicates that the 1314 harvest was impeded by heavy rain, but that much worse was to follow in 1315. See also Jordan, *Great Famine*, 18–19, 194; I. Kershaw, 'The Great Famine and Agrarian Crisis in England 1315–1322', *Past & Present*, 59 (May 1973), 6; Maddicott, 162–3.

[3] C 53/101, m.22; *Vita*, 98–9; Phillips, 76.

One of Edward's first actions, on 29 July, was to summon a parliament to meet at York on 9 September to discuss the threat from the Scots.[4] On 7 September the earl of Pembroke and the bishop of Exeter were authorized to open the assembly and to continue its business in the king's name until his arrival, since for 'arduous and special affairs touching the king' Edward could not be present at the beginning.[5] Edward had good reason to absent himself since he immediately came under pressure from the earl of Lancaster and others to restore the Ordinances, which by this time had been in abeyance for over two years. According to the *Vita Edwardi Secundi*, Edward said that 'he was prepared to do everything ordained for the common good, and promised that he would observe the Ordinances in good faith'. There then followed a wholesale removal and replacement of royal officers, following the procedures laid down in the Ordinances.[6] On 26 September John Sandal was appointed as chancellor in place of Walter Reynolds the new archbishop of Canterbury, and was replaced as treasurer by Walter of Norwich. The sheriffs of thirty counties were also replaced between 8 October and 16 January.[7] There were also substantial changes within the royal household. These were assisted by the death of Edmund Mauley, the steward of the household, at Bannockburn. Ingelard Warley, whose removal as keeper of the wardrobe had been demanded by the barons three years earlier, was succeeded in November by William Melton, the former controller and a royal household clerk who had not attracted any baronial criticism in the past; John of Ockham, the cofferer of the wardrobe, another official whose removal had been sought, left office at the same time.[8] But the new appointments were not in reality to the king's disadvantage. John Sandal, for example, was a royal clerk of long standing and had, as acting treasurer, been very active in royal affairs in 1312 and 1313. It also made practical sense for the newly consecrated archbishop of Canterbury to step down from the office of chancellor. William Melton was a trusted royal supporter, who had served Edward both as Prince of Wales and as king, and was to become archbishop of York with royal support in 1317. Edmund Mauley had already been replaced as steward in July by a royal knight, John Cromwell; while Roger de Northburgh, the keeper of the privy seal, had resumed office by November 1314 after his release from captivity in Scotland.[9] The king was even able to resist the removal of some of his closest advisers,

[4] *PW*, II, ii, 126–35; C 219/3/4.

[5] *CPR, 1313–17*, 169. Initially Henry de Beaumont was also to assist at the opening, but his name was then omitted on the same day, probably because his presence would have been too provocative to the earl of Lancaster and his allies.

[6] *Vita*, 98–101; *Lanercost*, 229.

[7] *CCR, 1313–18*, 197–8; *CPR, 1313–17*, 178; *CFR, 1307–19*, 220–1; Phillips, 76; Maddicott, 164–5. Although Reynolds had been appointed as chancellor in 1310, he was generally described from early 1312 by the lesser title of keeper of the Great Seal.

[8] Maddicott, 165; Tout, *Place of the Reign*, 316–17.

[9] Tout, *Chapters*, ii, 294–5.

Hugh Despenser the Elder, and Henry de Beaumont, although Despenser was apparently forced to keep out of the way for a time.[10] So far the changes were more symbolic than real. The impression one gets is that baronial pressure on Edward II was growing but was not yet strong enough to force him to agree to anything he did not wish to accept. It may be significant that, although the Ordinances were clearly in the forefront of everybody's mind, no formal confirmation of them was issued on this occasion.[11]

According to the *Vita Edwardi Secundi*, discussion of the struggle against Robert Bruce and the recovery of Scotland was postponed until the next parliament because the earl of Hereford and the other barons held captive had not yet returned. The king's sister, Elizabeth, meanwhile 'lamented for her husband, the earl of Hereford'.[12] There were however considerable contacts between the English and the Scots. In late August and early September 1314 Robert Bruce and his brother Edward Bruce wrote to Edward II with a view to negotiating peace between the two kingdoms. On 20 October Scottish envoys met John de Botetourt and other English representatives in Durham; in November the archbishop of York, the bishop of Durham and the abbot of St Mary's, York, went to Scotland. Other unnamed English envoys went to Dumfries but had returned to England by 26 December. It is likely that the English entered negotiations partly at the instigation of Philip IV of France and partly in order to obtain a truce which would prevent a threatened Scottish invasion of England: a truce of sorts did come into force in the Scottish March on 6 October.[13] Just as urgent was the need to secure the freedom of English prisoners. In October 1314 the most important of these, the earl of Hereford, was finally released after lengthy negotiations but in return Edward had to free Robert Bruce's wife Elizabeth de Burgh, his daughter and sister, as well as Edward I's and Edward II's *bête noire* the aged Robert Wishart, bishop of Glasgow.[14]

GAVESTON AGAIN

Since his death in June 1312 Gaveston's body, embalmed and covered in cloth of gold, had remained in the custody of the Dominican friars of

[10] *Flores*, 339; *Vita*, 100–1; Maddicott, 165.
[11] I have modified the views I expressed in *Aymer de Valence*, 76; cf. also Maddicott, 164–5; and Tout, *Place of the Reign*, 90–2.
[12] *Vita*, 100–1. Edward allegedly gave his sister all the Scottish captives, some of whom had been held in England since the time of Edward I, as bargaining counters for the return of her husband, but the situation cannot have been as simple as this.
[13] Lambeth Ms. 1213, f. 32; *Foedera*, II, i, 254–6; *Letters from Northern Registers*, nos cl, clii, cliii (pp. 233–8); McNamee, 77–8. The mission of the three clergy may have been an attempt to gain protection for their localities against Scottish raiding. But it is also known that between Sept. 1314 and March 1315 the archbishop paid out about 1,250 marks to ransom prisoners held by the Scots: *Letters from Northern Registers*, no. clx (pp. 1248–9).
[14] *Vita*, 100–1; *Lanercost*, 229; Barrow, 231.

Oxford, who watched over it and cared for it. Gaveston was remembered regularly both there and in the king's chapels; and in 1313, on the king's orders, a Dominican friar, Brother Walter de Ashridge, made a tour of abbeys and other religious houses, lasting 122 days and covering nine counties to ask for prayers for Gaveston's soul.[15] Gaveston could not be buried since he had died excommunicate, while it was also rumoured that Edward would not allow the burial until he had avenged himself on Gaveston's killers.[16] It is possible, as the *Vita* remarked, that Edward proceeded with the burial when he did since 'those from whom the king seemed to seek vengeance have been readmitted to friendship', however uneasy that reconciliation might have been in reality.[17] It is also possible, as has been suggested, that Gaveston had been granted a posthumous papal absolution from the sentence of excommunication imposed upon him by Archbishop Winchelsey.[18] On the other hand there is no known evidence to support this conclusion. Pope Clement V, who had been so accommodating to the needs of the English crown, had died in April 1314, and no successor had yet been elected.[19] The presence at the funeral of the new archbishop of Canterbury Walter Reynolds, Edward II's close ally, and other leading clergy strongly suggests that the way had been cleared by Reynolds acting on his own authority.[20]

On 2 January 1315 the burial of Gaveston took place in the church of the Dominicans at the king's palace of Langley, the body being wrapped in three cloths of gold costing £300.[21] Altogether Edward II spent over £600 on preserving Gaveston's body and on prayers for his soul between the time of his death and burial.[22] The ceremony took place in the presence of the king, the archbishop of Canterbury, the bishops of London, Winchester, Worcester, and Bath & Wells, thirteen abbots, 'innumerable religious of the order of mendicants',[23] the earls of Pembroke and

---

[15] E 101/375/8, f. 15; Hamilton, 166, n. 79.

[16] *Vita*, 100–3; Hamilton, 99–100; Chaplais, 110–11.

[17] *Vita*, 100–3.

[18] Hamilton, 99–100; 166, n. 81.

[19] Edward II expressed his concern for the early election of a new pope in letters to the cardinals on 29 June 1314: *Foedera*, II, i, 249–50. Allegedly Edward was concerned because the continued vacancy would delay the crusade he and Philip IV of France had undertaken in 1313. But Edward probably had other matters in mind, such as the affairs of Aquitaine and the rehabilitation of Gaveston. The new pope, John XXII, was not chosen until Aug. 1316.

[20] Cf. Hamilton, 166, n. 8; Chaplais, 111.

[21] E 101/375/16, m.1; E 101/375/15; E 101/376/2; Hamilton, 100; 166, n. 82. Hamilton gives the date as 3 Jan. but 2 Jan. seems more likely: Phillips, 83. Chaplais, 111, suggests that the date may have been chosen since it fell within the octave of the Holy Innocents, 'a point which would have appealed to Edward: what had Piers done which merited death?'

[22] Hamilton, 100; 166, n. 84.

[23] Presumably these were the Dominicans of Langley, but friars from other orders may well have been present.

Hereford, Hugh Despenser the Elder, Henry de Beaumont, Bartholomew de Badlesmere, and over fifty knights (presumably royal household knights), together with the chancellor, treasurer, royal household officers, royal justices, and the mayor of London.[24] The guests were also entertained with large quantities of wine and food.[25]

Despite the large attendance it appears that Edward had wanted many more of the barons to be present than in fact appeared: enmity towards Gaveston still remained even in death.[26] The extent of the absences is unknown, but certainly included the earls of Lancaster and Warwick, who had been responsible for Gaveston's death. It is also not clear whether Edward II's queen, Isabella, was present. Gaveston's burial was really an act of defiance at a time when Edward's enemies abroad and at home were closing in on him once more. The number and rank of those present show clearly that Edward II was making a statement that, no matter what his opponents may have thought of Gaveston, he was still devoted to his memory. Edward was to continue to commemorate Gaveston through prayers and through the careful maintenance of his burial place at Langley up to the very end of his reign.[27]

Among those who attended Gaveston's funeral was Hugh Despenser the Younger, the son of one of Edward II's most influential and most disliked counsellors, who was married to Eleanor de Clare, the king's niece and one of the three sisters of the earl of Gloucester who had been killed at Bannockburn. The earl had died leaving a widow who claimed to be pregnant. Should this turn out to be true and she not give birth to a son, Despenser and his wife would inherit a third share of the most valuable earldom in England. Despenser was also intensely ambitious, and within a few years became a new royal favourite, exerting political power and influence on a scale far beyond either his father or even Gaveston. More than any other factor, Despenser was to be responsible for Edward II's eventual downfall in 1326–7. Had anyone but known it, Edward II's living nemesis was also present at Langley on 2 January 1315.[28]

---

[24] BL, Cotton Mss. Cleopatra D.III, f. 56d (Hailes abbey chronicle); *Trokelowe*, 88; E 101/375/17, m.1.

[25] Hamilton, 100, 166, n. 82. On 25 Dec. 1314 the king's butler was ordered to send 23 tuns of wine to Langley for use at the funeral: *CCR, 1313–18*, 139.

[26] *Trokelowe*, 88.

[27] For the details see Hamilton, 100; 166, n. 85. The last reference to prayers for Gaveston is on 28 June 1326: *CPR, 1324–27*, 281. There is nothing to indicate the nature of Gaveston's tomb or even whether Edward II intended Langley to be Gaveston's permanent resting place.

[28] An indication of what was to come had already appeared in the list of summons to the York parliament of Sept. 1314. The parliament was not only the first occasion on which Hugh Despenser the Younger received a personal summons but he and his father also appeared together almost at the head of the list of barons summoned: *RDP*, iii, 241. The only baron whose name appeared above them was Henry de Percy.

A NEW POLITICAL ORDER

The York parliament of September 1314 was only the beginning of the political upheavals which the defeat at Bannockburn brought in its train, with the stage now set for a return to political influence by the most prominent of the former opposition magnates, the earls of Lancaster and Warwick. One early sign of changing times had come in October 1314 when separate letters supporting the urgent collection of the clerical tenth were sent to the bishops of Bath & Wells and of Exeter by both the king and Lancaster, almost as if the latter were vetting and approving royal acts.[29] Shortly before 27 November Edward II also made a detailed account of his debts to Antonio Pessagno, and on 4 December, in response to a demand which had been made at the York parliament, the exchequer was ordered to list all gifts and grants made contrary to the Ordinances since March 1310.[30]

On 20 January 1315, less than three weeks after Gaveston's burial, a new parliament met to continue on the course begun at York.[31] Although it was summoned to Westminster the account in the *Vita Edwardi Secundi* speaks of the earls and barons meeting at London 'to discuss the state of the king and the realm, and the conquest of the Scots', which may indicate that the magnates had a preliminary meeting before they attended at Westminster. All the chronicles are however agreed on the length of the parliament which, according to the *Vita*, dragged on almost to the end of Lent.[32] Two of the most objectionable of the king's councillors, Hugh Despenser the Elder and the unpopular former treasurer Walter Langton, bishop of Coventry & Lichfield, were removed from the council, steps were taken to reduce the expenditure of the royal household,[33] and on 14 February orders were given for the reobservance of the Ordinances, followed on 3 March by orders to resume grants made since 1310.[34] Before the end of the session on 9 March a grant of taxation was approved in aid of the war in Scotland;[35] and on 14 March a royal ordinance on prices was issued.[36]

---

[29] *HMC, Tenth Report*, part 3, 300; *Register of Walter Stapeldon, Bishop of Exeter, 1307–1326*, ed. F.C. Hingeston-Randolph (London, 1892), 429–30; Phillips, 82; Maddicott, 165–6.

[30] *CPR, 1313–17*, 203–6; *CCW*, 407.

[31] For details of the parliament, which had been summoned on 24 Oct. 1314 shortly after the end of the York parliament, see the Westminster parliament of Jan. 1315 in PROME.

[32] *Vita*, 102–3. *Ann. Lond.*, 232; *Ann. Paul.*, 278, both give Westminster as the place of meeting.

[33] *Vita*, 102–3; 102, n. 198; Phillips, 83; Maddicott, 167.

[34] 'Deeds enrolled on the de Banco Rolls', ed. E.A. Fry (National Archives typescript, 1927), 58; *CFR, 1309–19*, 240, 243–4; Phillips, 83; Maddicott, 167, 179. According to *Gesta Edwardi*, 47, Edward II confirmed the Ordinances 'so that he would be better able to win the earls' sympathies'.

[35] *Lay Taxes*, 32–3.

[36] *Foedera*, II, i, 263, 266; Maddicott, 163. The pressure in parliament for such an ordinance was the result of price inflation in the years since about 1300 rather than of any immediate shortages of food supplies: Kershaw, *Great Famine*, 6; H.E. Hallam, ed., *The Agrarian History of England and Wales*, ii, *1042–1350* (Cambridge, 1988), 718–19, 753, 794.

The parliament was also marked by the receipt and the answering by the king and his council of over 200 petitions on a great variety of subjects. With the exception of the parliament held in August 1312, this was the first occasion during the reign of Edward II when such business was transacted and might almost be regarded as a sign of normality. A large number of pent-up grievances could now be aired by individuals and local communities, as well as by the community of the realm. Most of the petitions have no obvious connection with the 'grand politics' which had occupied most of Edward II's reign since 1307, but a few do. One such item was the common petition from the archbishops, bishops, earls, barons and others of the community of the realm, complaining about the high prices that were being charged for oxen, sheep and pigs, and other food items. The ordinance on prices was issued in response to this.[37] Another common petition, which does not appear to have survived, asked for the observation of the Ordinances, Magna Carta, the Charter of the Forest, the perambulations of the forest, and other matters concerning the welfare of the people. In a letter to the sheriffs on 20 April the king indicated that he had conceded these requests and asked for them to be observed.[38] In another petition the prelates, earls and barons complained that scutage was being levied on the number of knights' fees for which their ancestors had owed military service rather than the much smaller number for which they currently provided service to the king.[39] This was clearly a reference to the king's attempt to levy scutages for the campaigns of 1305 and 1306 in November of 1314 and helps to explain Edward's lack of success in collecting them.[40] On 11 June, after the end of the parliament, but arising out of complaints made during it, the king issued orders to curb the abuse of purveyance and also for the observance of the Statute of Westminster the First.[41]

On the face of it the king's opponents were now in the ascendant. However, the reality was probably more complex. Although it is not possible to specify the influence of Lancaster and Warwick, their frequent appearance as witnesses to royal charters during the time of the parliament suggests that they were active both in parliament and as members of the king's council.[42] The author of the *Annales Londonienses* went so far as to claim that Warwick was appointed as head of the king's council.[43] Certainly he

---

[37] *PROME*, Parliament Roll of 1315, SC9/18, item 35.
[38] Harriss, 120 and 120, n. 2.
[39] *PROME*, Parliament Roll of 1315, item 23.
[40] *PROME*, Parliament Roll of 1315, item 23; *Lay Taxes*, 31–2.
[41] *Ann. Lond.*, 234–6.
[42] C 53/101, mm.5, 6; Phillips, 84; Maddicott, 166.
[43] *Ann. Lond.*, 232: Phillips, 84, n. 3; Maddicott, 166. The chronicler was possibly anticipating Lancaster's formal appointment as head of the council in 1316. Davies dates this reference to Warwick to 1314: *Baronial Opposition*, 395. Tout saw Warwick as replacing the incompetent Lancaster, but the latter had not yet taken a leading role in government and his abilities were as yet untested: *Place of the Reign*, 93.

seems to have been involved in the royal administration until the first half of June 1315, after which he withdrew because of illness, dying at Warwick castle on 12 August.[44] Warwick had probably been more active than Lancaster, who left Westminster soon after parliament was prorogued for Easter on 15 March but did not return when the session was resumed on 13 April.[45] Lancaster's appetite for and application to administrative work seem to have been limited, very much like his first cousin Edward II himself.

But other members of the council, such as the earls of Pembroke and Hereford, the chancellor, treasurer, and the archbishop of Canterbury, were no less active.[46] During the parliament, for example, the earls of Pembroke and Hereford, together with Lancaster's steward, Michael de Meldon, were deputed by the other magnates and prelates present to make a formal complaint at the exchequer about the king's attempts to collect scutage.[47] On 15 March the archbishop of Canterbury, the chancellor and the earl of Warwick assigned a notary to make a copy of the 'Great Cause' recording Edward I's determination of the succession to the Scottish throne after the death of Margaret of Norway in 1290.[48] On the following day the king sent instructions concerning payment of a royal debt to the earls of Richmond and Hereford, following advice from Pembroke, Warwick and Arundel;[49] and orders issued on 6 and 7 May were made in the presence of the archbishop, Pembroke, Hereford and Warwick.[50] There are also some indications of Lancaster's influence in, for example, the granting of a pardon on 17 March, the appointment of a sheriff in Ireland on 20 May, and the granting of safe conducts on the same date for the men of Bristol to discuss their dispute with Bartholomew de Badlesmere, the royal constable and warden of Bristol castle and town.[51] On 8 June Lancaster, Warwick and the chancellor John Sandal mediated on the king's behalf between Badlesmere and the citizens of Bristol.[52] Their activity in England was balanced by the appearance on the same date of Pembroke, the bishop of Exeter and others before the council of Louis X

[44] He had probably returned to Warwick by 11 July; his will was dated there on 28 July but his death was already expected on 18 July: BL, Add. Ms. 28024, f. 70; Bod., Dugdale Ms. 12, ff. 478–9; *CFR, 1307–19*, 255; Phillips, 92, n. 1.

[45] *CCR, 1313–18*, 163; *Trokelowe*, 90; Phillips, 83; Maddicott, 166, 168. Many other magnates also failed to return. Lancaster was at Kenilworth on 20 March, Donington on 14 May, Warwick on 8 June, and Melbourne on 13 June: Maddicott, 168.

[46] *CCW, passim*; C 53/101, mm.1–17; Phillips, 84.

[47] E 159/88, m.144; Phillips, 85.

[48] E 101/376/7, f. 18; Phillips, 85; Maddicott, 166–7. For a study of the 'Great Cause' see *Edward I and the Throne of Scotland, 1290–1296*, ed. E.L.G. Stones & G.G. Simpson, 2 vols (Oxford, 1978).

[49] E 101/376/7, f. 18; SC 1/45/ 186; Phillips, 85.

[50] *CPR, 1313–17*, 279; SC 1/45/186 (endorsement); Phillips, 85.

[51] *CPR, 1313–17*, 263, 289; *CFR, 1307–19*, 248; Phillips, 85.

[52] SC 1/35/135, 135A; Phillips, 87; Maddicott, 169. This meeting took place at Warwick.

of France at Vincennes in the latest attempt to improve Anglo-French relations.[53]

The likelihood is that although Lancaster and Warwick were clearly exercising influence in the spring and early summer of 1315 there was an uneasy political balance, in which the realignments brought about by the events of 1314 were still working themselves out. It was too much to expect that magnates who had so recently been bitterly at odds, not only with the king but also among themselves, should suddenly find the means to work together in harmony. There are indeed hints that a certain amount of bargaining was going on between the king, his sympathizers and opponents. While, for example, the Ordinances were being applied to revoke royal grants and to order a perambulation of the forests, there were a few cases in which grants which had been revoked in March were restored a month or two later.[54] Another factor may have been that, apart from the earl of Warwick who was soon removed from the scene by death, the earl of Lancaster had few friends or even allies. Among the clergy, Archbishop Winchelsey had been replaced by Walter Reynolds, a friend of the king; among the barons, Henry Percy, for example, had died in the autumn of 1314. The earls of Hereford and especially Pembroke were close allies and valued councillors of the king, while the loyalty of Arundel and Surrey was unreliable.[55]

There were also signs of bitterness and suspicion between Lancaster and his fellow earls and between him and the king. There was ill-feeling, for example, between Pembroke and Lancaster over their rival claims to possession of lands at Thorpe Waterville in Northamptonshire, which Lancaster had forced Pembroke to give up during the York parliament in September 1314. Retainers of the two earls had nearly come to blows in February 1314. The whole episode was typical of the way in which Lancaster managed to settle disputes in his own favour through threats of violence,[56] and is a further explanation of his lack of true friends. When Lancaster's only real ally, the earl of Warwick, died in August 1315 it was rumoured that he had been poisoned by persons close to the king.[57] Nor is it surprising that Edward II built himself a fortified tower or peel in the

---

[53] C 47/27/8/34; Phillips, 87.

[54] *CPR, 1313–17*, 296; *CFR, 1307–19*, 240, 251 (grant to Hugh Audley); Phillips, 85. The fresh confirmation of the Ordinances and the perambulation of the forest ordered during the Lincoln parliament in Jan. 1316 might also imply that these had not been fully enforced in 1315.

[55] Maddicott, 158–9, 161.

[56] Phillips, 77–82, 226–7; Maddicott, 154–7. Lancaster did not want an ally of the king to control Thorpe Waterville which was close to one of Lancaster's holdings at Higham Ferrers. Other examples are Lancaster's dispute with the earl of Surrey in 1317–18 over lands in the Welsh March and in Yorkshire and the long-running contest between John Charlton and Lancaster's retainer, Gruffudd de la Pole, over possession of the lordship of Powys: Maddicott, 156.

[57] *Walsingham*, 137; Maddicott, 170. There is no evidence to support the rumour.

grounds of his palace of Clipstone in Nottinghamshire to provide added security against Lancaster's castles in the area.[58]

RELATIONS WITH FRANCE

No matter how preoccupied Edward and his government were with internal politics and problems, relations with France were never off their agenda. In early May 1315 it was decided that the earl of Pembroke and bishop of Exeter should go to Paris to present a set of petitions relating to the duchy of Aquitaine.[59]

The mission was intended to secure confirmation by the new king of France, Louis X, of the concessions made by his father during Isabella's mission to France in March 1314, as well as the continuation of the Process of Périgueux begun in 1311.[60] Accompanied by Antonio Pessagno and an expert adviser, Master Henry de Canterbury, Pembroke and the bishop set out for France in mid-May and probably reached Paris before the end of the month.[61] At Vincennes on 8 June the bishop of Saint-Malo gave the French replies to the English requests.[62] Louis X agreed that commissioners should be appointed by himself and Edward II to implement the peace treaties between England and France, that written law should continue to be the basis of Edward II's rule in the lands he held from the French crown, as Philip IV had granted in 1313, and that appeals from Edward II's subjects in Aquitaine should be adjourned until the next session of the Paris *parlement* or beyond. On behalf of the English delegation, the bishop of Exeter replied that English commissioners would be appointed as soon as possible,[63] and successfully requested that Louis X withdraw his summons to Edward II

[58] The peel tower had first been planned in Jan. 1312 after Gaveston's final return from exile and construction took place in 1316–17. Lancaster had important castles at Leicester and Castle Donington in Leicestershire, Kenilworth in Warwickshire, Tutbury in Staffordshire, and a new castle built at Melbourne in Derbyshire in 1313–14. These added to pressure on the important royal castle at Nottingham and also made Clipstone vulnerable: see D. Crook, 'Clipstone peel', in *Thirteenth Century England*, x, ed. M. Prestwich, R. Britnell & R. Frame (Woodbridge, Suffolk & Rochester, NY, 2005), 187–95, esp. 190–1.

[59] Phillips, 86–7; the petitions are recorded in E 36/187, p. 53 published as *Gascon Calendar of 1322*, ed. Cuttino: see items 442–6.

[60] See Brown, 'Diplomacy,' 71–3. On the Process of Périgueux see Cuttino, *English Diplomatic Administration*, 87–100. In 1315 it suited the English to continue the process indefinitely and in the summer of 1314 an English clerk, Elias de Joneston, had twice gone to France to ensure that this was the case. The reasoning behind Pembroke's mission in 1315 was laid out in a memorandum recorded in E 175/2/5/ [1], and in C 47/27/8/31: Brown, 'Diplomacy', 72–3; 73, n. 91; 78–80.

[61] Phillips, 86–7.

[62] The French and English replies are all contained in C 47/27/8/34; Phillips, 87.

[63] The French appointed their commissioners on 26 June: *Foedera*, II, i, 270. Although it was intended that the earl of Warwick and Hugh de Vere should act as commissioners, the death of both men and the pressure of the war with Scotland prevented the appointment of English commissioners until early in 1316: *CCW*, 423; SC 1/37/33; Brown, 'Diplomacy', 73; Chaplais, *Diplomatic Practice*, i, no.152 (text of SC 1/37/33).

to send troops to serve in the French campaign in Flanders.[64] On 15 June Louis X also remitted punishments for alleged offences committed by English officials in Aquitaine, revoked all acts by his own ministers which contravened Philip IV's concessions of 1313, and limited the number of adherents whom Gascon appellants could bring to Paris.[65] Another possible issue, the need for Edward II to perform homage once more for his French lands, Aquitaine and the county of Ponthieu, does not appear to have been raised by either side.[66]

SCOTLAND

The English embassy to Paris was important but it was only a passing interlude in the most urgent problem facing Edward II and his government: the war with Scotland. Within weeks of his victory at Bannockburn Robert Bruce resumed raids on the northern counties of England,[67] both Northumberland and the area around Carlisle coming under attack in August 1314.[68] But there were significant differences from the raiding in which the Scots had engaged after 1311. Their attacks were now conducted over longer distances, using the mobility given by their light cavalry forces, and were also designed to put pressure on Carlisle and Berwick, the two key points at either end of the Anglo-Scottish border which were essential both for the defence of England and for launching and sustaining any future English attacks upon Scotland. In May 1315 the Scots added a new theatre of warfare when they invaded the lordship of Ireland, one of the most important possessions of the English crown, whose resources were also vital for the English war effort in Scotland.[69]

Apart from the measures to ensure the defence of Berwick and the appointment in August 1314 of the earl of Pembroke as captain of the royal forces between Berwick and the Trent, Edward's government did little in the immediate aftermath of Bannockburn to secure the north

[64] This was an important symbolic concession since Edward II was prepared to perform homage for Aquitaine to the king of France but did not want this to have any practical results such as providing military service. However in September 1315 Edward ordered all the Flemings in England to be banished, in accordance with a decree issued by Louis X in July, and also offered France naval assistance against Flanders: *Foedera*, II, i, 272, 277; Vale, 58–9. Edward had good reason to do this since in May the Scots had invaded Ireland with assistance from Flanders.

[65] *Foedera*, II, i, 269–70; C 47/32/11/2; Phillips, 87; Brown, 'Diplomacy', 73.

[66] Edward II never did perform homage to Louis X, who died in June 1316.

[67] For details of the Scottish raids into England, 1314–15, see the maps in McNamee, 73, and Barrow, 234–5 (this covers the whole period 1311–27).

[68] McNamee, 72–4; Maddicott, 160–1.

[69] McNamee, 74; Barrow, 236–8. On the crucial role of Ireland in financing, supplying and fighting English wars in Scotland see, for example, J. Lydon, 'Edward I, Ireland and the war in Scotland, 1303–1304', in *England and Ireland in the Later Middle Ages*, ed. J. Lydon (Dublin, 1981), 43–61; repr. in P. Crooks, ed., *Government, War and Society in Medieval Ireland* (Dublin, 2008).

against the Scots.⁷⁰ It was also unfortunate that in 1314–15 deaths in battle or from natural causes removed several magnates with long military experience and with a personal interest in the defence of the north: Robert de Clifford whose lands were in Cumberland and Westmorland and included the castle of Appleby, and who also held the important castle of Skipton-in-Craven in Yorkshire; Henry de Percy who held extensive lands in Yorkshire and Northumberland, including Alnwick castle; and the earl of Warwick, who was lord of the powerful castle at Barnard's Castle in Durham. Other magnates with northern interests, such as Anthony Lucy, John de Clavering and John de Eure, had been held prisoner after Bannockburn.⁷¹ In January 1315 twelve of the northern lords were excused attendance at parliament to allow them to concentrate on defence against the Scots, while on 3 January the archbishop of York and bishop of Durham held an assembly of clergy and magnates at York for the same purpose.⁷² In February the earl of Pembroke made a personal commitment to the defence of the north when he purchased the castle of Mitford in Northumberland.⁷³

These were all temporary measures and something more substantial had to be done as soon as possible. Important decisions were taken during the Westminster parliament. On 15 March the heads of ninety religious houses were asked to loan sums totalling almost £9,000, and on the same date the bishops were asked to hasten the collection of the tenth they had just granted in aid of the war.⁷⁴ On 28 May the earl of Warwick, the chancellor John Sandal and Bartholomew de Badlesmere were authorized by the king to discuss the defence of the Scottish March with Lancaster, whom they met at Kenilworth or Warwick in early June.⁷⁵ Warwick, Sandal and Lancaster joined the king on 11 or 12 June, and on the 20th it was announced that Pembroke, Badlesmere, Robert de Monthaut and Richard de Grey had undertaken to go to Newcastle upon Tyne for service between 1 July and 1 November.⁷⁶ Between them they produced a total of just over 300 cavalry,⁷⁷ fewer than the 500 men recorded by the *Vita* but still a very valuable mobile force.⁷⁸ Pembroke was given further responsi-

---

⁷⁰ *Vita*, 98–9; *PW*, II, ii, 122; Phillips, 88.
⁷¹ Maddicott, 161.
⁷² *PW*, II, i, 138–9, 435; SC 1/35/ 142, 142A; *CCR*, *1313–18*, 205; *Register of William Greenfield, Archbishop of York, 1306–1315*, ed. W. Brown & A. Hamilton Thompson, Surtees Soc., cxlv (Durham, 1931), i, no. 359; Maddicott, 167–8; Phillips, 88.
⁷³ E 163/4/1/2; *CPR*, *1313–17*, 254; Phillips, 88.
⁷⁴ *Foedera*, II, i, 263–4.
⁷⁵ SC 1/35/135, 135A; *CPR*, *1313–17*, 291; *CCR*, *1313–18*, 233; Phillips, 88; Maddicott, 169.
⁷⁶ *PW*, II, ii, 158; E 403/174, mm.2, 4; E 101/376/7, ff. 60, 60v; Phillips, 88–9; Maddicott, 169.
⁷⁷ E 101/376/7, ff. 60, 60v; E 101/15/6; C 81/1736/46, 51; Phillips, 89; Maddicott, 169.
⁷⁸ *Vita*, 104–5. The *Vita* may have been broadly right since at various times in 1315 Pembroke was accompanied by 70 extra men-at-arms, 400 hobelars and 170 archers: Phillips, 89.

bility on 5 July when he was appointed keeper and lieutenant between the Trent and Roxburgh.[79] Earlier, on 18 April, Maurice de Berkeley, one of his leading retainers, had been appointed by the council to command Berwick for one year from 11 May, and set to work without delay.[80]

Pembroke's force reached Newcastle in early August but was then diverted to the relief of Carlisle which the Scots had been besieging since 22 July. They forced the Scots to break off the siege and pursued them with the aid of Andrew Harclay, the commander of Carlisle, as far as Lanercost to the north of Carlisle by 16 August.[81] The threat to Carlisle had been averted for the time being but the city had been shown to be vulnerable. In response the earl of Lancaster was appointed as captain of all the royal forces in the area on 8 August. Pembroke was ordered to recognize his authority but this was probably because he happened to be in the vicinity at the time. In practice it seems more likely that the two earls were intended to share the defence of the north, one at the western end of the border and the other in the east.[82]

After returning to Newcastle in late August Pembroke's force advanced northwards to counter an expected Scottish raid into Northumberland. He briefly entered Scotland before returning to the Newcastle area in early October.[83] Lancaster meanwhile was more vocal in expressing his desire for a campaign against the Scots than active in pursuing one. He appears to have done nothing after his appointment in August, and in October his attention was diverted to suppressing the revolt in Lancashire by Adam Banaster, one of his own retainers.[84]

Between 30 August and 1 September Edward held an assembly of magnates, senior clergy and royal officials at Lincoln to consider the situation in the north of England and the recent Scottish landing in Ireland. Pembroke was still absent in the north but the presence can be identified of the earls of Lancaster, Hereford, Richmond and Surrey, the justice of Wales Roger Mortimer of Chirk, Henry of Lancaster the brother of the earl, the archbishop of Canterbury, and the bishops of Norwich and Carlisle, as well as the keeper of the privy seal and the chancellor.[85] On 30 August Edward announced that, with the advice of the earls, he had

---

[79] *PW*, II, ii, 159; Phillips, 89.

[80] E 101/68/2/35; Davies, *Baronial Opposition*, 566–7; *Vita*, 104–5; Phillips, 87–8. Since Berkeley succeeded Simon Ward, who was possibly a follower of Lancaster, and his appointment was made in the presence of the earls of Pembroke, Richmond and Hereford and in the absence of both Lancaster and Warwick, there may have been some element of politics in it: Maddicott, 165; Phillips, 88.

[81] *Lanercost*, 230–2; *Guisborough*, 397; Phillips, 89; Maddicott, 169–70; McNamee, 80–1.

[82] *PW*, II, ii, 159, 161; Phillips, 89–90; Maddicott, 170.

[83] Phillips, 90.

[84] Maddicott, 170, 172, 174–7. There is a detailed account of this episode in G.H. Tupling, *South Lancashire in the Reign of Edward II*, Chetham Soc., 3rd ser., i (Manchester, 1949).

[85] E 101/376/7, ff. 11, 11v; C 53/102, mm.16, 17; Phillips, 92; Maddicott, 171.

decided to remain in the north for the winter and that they and the other magnates present had agreed to stay with him with their retinues at their own expense. Edward summoned sixty-six other magnates to join him on 1 November on the same terms,[86] while orders were given for the raising of men to resist the Scots, under the terms of the Statute of Winchester, and for the collection of the subsidy in aid of the Scots war which had been granted by the clergy.[87] Since the contracts of Pembroke and Badlesmere were due to expire on 1 November, Henry de Beaumont was appointed on their advice as commander of the eastern March during the coming winter.[88] This impressive-sounding military effort turned out to be more show than substance. Little or nothing was achieved during the winter of 1315–16 beyond holding the line. It was fortunate that the end of the siege of Carlisle proved to be the beginning of a lull in Scottish raids into England lasting for almost a year.[89]

MONEY

One of the limitations on English military activity in 1315 was lack of money. With the single exception of the Bannockburn campaign in 1314, Edward II and his government had battled against a shortage of ready money since the beginning of the reign; and they were to continue to do so until after Edward's crushing victory over his baronial opponents in the civil war of 1321–2. The financial resources which had made it possible to recruit and sustain such a large army in 1314 had been exhausted and could not easily be replenished. This is why Edward attempted in the late summer of 1314 and in 1315 to obtain unpaid infantry service from several English counties;[90] and why in the autumn of 1315 the magnates summoned to the defence of the north had been asked to serve without pay.[91] Money in aid of the Scottish war was raised in 1315, principally in the form of the subsidy granted in parliament in January which yielded about £37,000, the clerical tenth which produced nearly £16,000, and the loans from religious houses amounting to about £9,000.[92] In June Edward and his council decided to send Thomas of Cambridge and Sir John Benstede to Gascony in an attempt to persuade Edward's subjects there to

---

[86] *Foedera*, II, i, 275; Phillips, 92–3; Maddicott, 171.
[87] *CPR, 1313–17*, 350; *PW*, II, ii, 162–3; Phillips, 92–3; Maddicott, 171.
[88] This is recorded in a letter from Edward II to Pembroke on 18 Oct.: SC 1/49/32; Phillips, 90, n. 7.
[89] McNamee, 81.
[90] In Aug. 1314, for example, the infantry forces of Yorkshire had been assigned to the command of the earl of Pembroke but at the expense of the vills from which they came. These and other attempts to extend the bounds of military obligation met with mixed success and became a source of grievance: Maddicott, 171–2; M.R. Powicke, *Military Obligation in Medieval England* (Oxford, 1962), 142.
[91] *Foedera*, II, i, 275; Phillips, 92–3; Maddicott, 171.
[92] *Foedera*, II, i, 263–4; Maddicott, 172.

provide a subsidy in aid of the war with Scotland. But any revenues from this source would inevitably take a long time to win approval and even longer to collect.[93] An attempt was also made to raise money in Ireland to aid the Scottish war but with little success.[94] All of the money received from the parliamentary subsidy and the clerical tenth, and more, was allegedly used up by the force led by the earl of Pembroke in the summer and early autumn of 1315.[95] Edward still of course had to repay the money he had borrowed from the pope and from Antonio Pessagno to fund the Bannockburn campaign.[96] It was hardly surprising that English commanders in the north, such as John de Castre a member of the Carlisle garrison, Maurice de Berkeley the constable of Berwick, and Richard de Grey one of Pembroke's companions in the Scottish March, complained bitterly about the government's failure to send adequate supplies of money or even to pay their wages.[97] Berkeley managed to beat off a Scottish attack on Berwick on 7 January 1316 but in March that year he warned the king that Berwick was in grave danger and 'if you lose it you lose all the remainder of the north'.[98]

WEATHER

In England the late summer of 1314 was wet; the rains began again in 1315 around Pentecost (11 May) and were still falling in October; the summer, such as it was, was also abnormally cold. After another harsh winter, the pattern repeated itself in 1316; 1317 was better but conditions then deteri-

[93] See E.A.R. Brown, 'Gascon subsidies and the finances of the English dominions, 1315–1324', *Studies in Medieval and Renaissance History*, viii (Lincoln, NB, 1971), 33–163. By the end of January 1316 Edward's commissioners had obtained pledges amounting to £12,500 sterling from the towns, communities, nobility and clergy of the duchy, equivalent to about one third of the subsidies granted by the English parliament in 1315 and 1316: Brown, 63–113. The sums pledged are listed in ibid., App. ii, 154–63. In the event collection was slow and Edward received much less than had been pledged; the tactics used by Edward's commissioners were also resented and helped to create feelings of disloyalty to the English crown which surfaced during the Anglo-French war of 1324–5: Brown, 98–9, 114–15, 142–5.
[94] Phillips, 'Mission', 66; 80, n. 38.
[95] *PW*, II, ii, 96–7; Maddicott, 172. This was claimed by Edward in Sept. when he asked the clergy to hasten collection of their promised subsidy. The large sums of money just cited took time to collect and were not necessarily available when most urgently needed.
[96] Pessagno was rewarded for his service to the crown by being made a royal knight on 1 Nov. 1315: E 101/376/7, f. 41v. In Aug. 1315 Edward II had appointed Charles Fieschi, Pessagno's relative by marriage and one of the leading figures in Genoa, to be a member of his council. Fieschi's role was probably to ensure the future smooth flow of Genoese finance and shipping in the direction of England: *Foedera*, II, ii, 274.
[97] E 101/14/5; *CCW*, 422, 428, 435; E 404/483/17/7; *CDS*, iii, 89–91; Phillips, 91; Maddicott, 162.
[98] E 101/376/7, f. 41v; *CCW*, 438; *CDS*, iii, 91 (no. 477); Phillips, 91; Maddicott, 162. Berwick eventually did fall to the Scots in April 1318.

orated again after another wet autumn in 1320 and a disastrous harvest in 1321. Only from 1322 did the situation return to normal. The rains were followed by floods, crop failure, high mortality among animals from starvation and disease, food shortages, high prices, and sickness and famine among the human population. England was badly affected; so too were Scotland, Wales and Ireland, as well as most of north-western Europe. The bad weather was the harbinger of disaster and suffering on a scale which was to be remembered for generations.[99]

If it was a hard time for the population of England,[100] it was also a difficult time for Edward II and his government. Royal finances were affected, for example, by disease among sheep, which led in turn to a sharp decline in England's major export, raw wool, and to a fall in customs receipts at a time when the crown could least afford it. Revenue from wool exports fell from £12,200 in 1312–13 to £7,100 in 1315–16, when the garrison of Berwick was, in theory at least, costing about £8,000 per year.[101] Shortages of food and increased prices, together with the lack of ready money, made it difficult to supply English garrisons, such as Berwick and Carlisle.[102] Some grain for the support of English castles along the Scottish border was imported from the Mediterranean through the agency of Antonio Pessagno, but this of course placed a further strain on the king's financial resources.[103] The attempt at price control made during the 1315 parliament was a failure and had to be repealed only a year later at the Lincoln parliament of 1316.[104] English armies were not the only ones to suffer privation from the bad weather and lack of food. Their Scottish enemies also experienced great hardship,[105] as did the armies of France: the French invasion of Flanders in the summer of 1315 was practically immobilized by flooding and roads which had turned into quagmires.[106]

THE SCOTS AND IRELAND

It was small comfort to Edward II and his government that friends and enemies were also facing problems, since a new and major crisis had begun to unfold on 26 May 1315: the landing at Larne in the north-east of Ireland by a Scottish army led by Robert Bruce's brother, Edward Bruce,

---

[99] Jordan, *Great Famine*, 18–19, 194; and the earlier work of H.S. Lucas, 'The great European famine of 1315, 1316, and 1317', in *Essays in Economic History*, ii, ed. E.M. Carus-Wilson (London, 1962), 49–72. On the situation in England see Kershaw, 'Great Famine', 6–16; Maddicott, 162–3.
[100] See Maddicott, *English Peasantry*, 69–75.
[101] This draws heavily on Maddicott, 163.
[102] Phillips, 91; Maddicott, 162–3.
[103] E.g., *CPR, 1313–17*, 603 (16 Dec. 1316), 636 (1 Apr. 1317).
[104] *Foedera*, II, i, 263, 266, 286.
[105] The famine was to be one of the major reasons for the failure of the Scottish invasion of Ireland between 1315 and 1318.
[106] Jordan, *Great Famine*, 20.

earl of Carrick. This was the reason for the reduction in Scottish raids against the north of England. The army was probably small, but what it may have lacked in numbers, it made up for in quality and determination. In addition to Edward Bruce himself, it included other experienced commanders, such as Thomas Randolph the earl of Moray, John Soules and Philip de Mowbray, the former constable of Stirling who had changed sides after Bannockburn.[107] On 6 June 1315 Edward Bruce was inaugurated as king of Ireland, with the support of Donal O'Neill of Tyrone and others.[108] The Scottish intention was nothing less than the conquest of the lordship of Ireland, which the English crown had held since the time of Henry II, and with it the removal of the Irish resources in manpower, money and food supplies which had played a vital part in English military operations against both Wales and Scotland since the time of Edward I.[109] About £30,000, for example, of the estimated £80,000 total cost of building Edward I's castles in Wales came from the Irish exchequer.[110]

The Bruce invasion of Ireland is one of the most important and yet until recently one of the most neglected aspects of the reign of Edward II.[111] Just as Edward I had sought to create an 'English empire' through his

---

[107] McNamee, 169–71. Larne on the Antrim coast, where the Bruce family held lands, is the most likely landing place but Glendun is also mentioned by some chronicle sources.

[108] Professor Duncan has shown convincingly in his paper 'The Scots' invasion of Ireland, 1315', in *The British Isles, 1100–1500*, ed. R.R. Davies (Edinburgh & Atlantic Highlands, NJ, 1988), 109–10, that Bruce's inauguration took place in June 1315 and not in May 1316, as used to be thought. The exact circumstances of the Scottish invasion of Ireland will probably never be known. While the Irish tract *Cath Fhocairte Brighite*, which refers to an invitation from Ireland, has now been shown to be a 19th-century fabrication, this does not rule out such an invitation. The fact that Edward Bruce was inaugurated as king of Ireland so soon after his arrival is in itself a strong indication of a previously laid plan: see S. Duffy, 'The Gaelic account of the Bruce invasion *Cath Fhochairte Brighite*', *Seanchas Ard Mhacha*, xiii, no. 1 (Dundalk, 1988–9); J.R.S. Phillips, 'The Irish remonstrance of 1317', *Irish Historical Studies*, xxvii (1990), 126, n. 57; S. Duffy, 'The "Continuation" of Nicholas Trevet', *Proceedings of the Royal Irish Academy*, xci, Section C, no. 12 (Dublin, 1991), 308–9, 314. In apparently inviting Edward Bruce to come to Ireland in 1315 Donal O'Neill was playing a political game in his own interests, but the Bruces had close connections of their own with Ireland and had been in contact with local Irish rulers (presumably including O'Neill) since at least 1306–7: see S. Duffy, 'The Bruce brothers and the Irish sea-world, 1306–29', *Cambridge Medieval Celtic Studies*, xxi (1991), 64–5, 70–6.

[109] For a discussion of the possible Scottish motives and intentions, which are not as straightforward as I have presented them, see R. Frame, 'The Bruces in Ireland, 1315–18', in Frame, *Ireland and Britain, 1170–1450* (London, 1998), 71–8.

[110] J. Lydon, 'The impact of the Bruce invasion', in *New History of Ireland*, ii, ed. Art Cosgrove (Oxford, 1987) 196; and Lydon, 'Edward II and the revenues of Ireland in 1311–12', *IHS*, xiv (1964), 56–7.

[111] There is a short but perceptive account in M. McKisack, *The Fourteenth Century, 1307–1399* (Oxford, 1959), 41–5, but surprisingly little about the Irish campaign in, for example, Barrow's *Robert Bruce*. There is now however a substantial body of work on the subject, most notably Frame's classic paper, 'The Bruces in Ireland', reprinted with revisions to take account of advances in scholarship in Frame, *Ireland and Britain*, which

conquest of Wales and attempted conquest of Scotland,[112] the Scottish attacks on northern England after Bannockburn and the Scots intervention in Ireland in 1315 'inaugurated a period of over four years when English power in the British Isles was challenged in a fashion which had not been witnessed since the reign of Stephen, if even then'.[113] As Rees Davies has also noted, both England and Scotland 'were expansionist and acquisitive kingdoms in the twelfth and thirteenth centuries; both were bringing their northern and western outer zones within the reach of their military and political power'.[114] As well as threatening Edward II's ability to govern and especially to tax the northern counties of his own kingdom,[115] the Scots now wished to deprive him of his lordship of Ireland and also sought to raise revolt against his rule in his own principality of Wales.[116] 'It is hardly too much to say that during this brief period [1315–18] the future political shape of the British Isles depended on the outcome of an often obscure series of campaigns and alliances in Ireland.'[117] In the end the Bruce invasion of Ireland failed, in part because of a lack of support in Ireland and the effects of the period of severe weather and famine with which it coincided, but also to a significant extent because of the way in which Edward II's government both in Ireland and in England handled the crisis.

One of Edward Bruce's first actions after landing was to besiege the strategically placed castle of Carrickfergus which protected English communications between Ireland and Scotland and conversely threatened his own. Although the castle did not fall until over a year later, it was in the

---

provides an overall interpretation of the origins, course and significance of the Bruce invasion of Ireland; the best narrative account of the war in Ireland, 1315–18, is now to be found in McNamee's *Wars of the Bruces*, which also has valuable maps of the various stages of the war (172, 178, 183); for an analysis of the complex relationships between Gaelic Ireland and Scotland see Duffy, 'The Bruce brothers', 55–86.

[112] See Davies, *The First English Empire*. This superb study is of course about far more than Edward I.

[113] Ibid., 173–4.

[114] Ibid., 189. On this process in Scotland see, for example, 'The winning of the West', in G.W.S. Barrow, *Kingship and Unity* (London, 1981).

[115] By the summer of 1315 no less than a fifth of the kingdom was paying tribute to Robert Bruce of Scotland with the tacit approval of Edward II: Phillips, 'Mission', 62, citing J. Scammell, 'Robert I and the north of England', *EHR*, lxxiii (1958), 385, 393–4.

[116] Bitterness and grievances 'in abundance' were a central feature of Wales after Edward I's conquest so there were plenty of ingredients for a possible revolt against English rule. There is evidence that in 1316–17 Edward Bruce was negotiating with native Welsh leaders in the hope of provoking one. One important figure, Gruffydd Llwyd, who had previously been and was later again to be a loyal servant of the English crown, seems to have responded and was briefly imprisoned: Davies, *Conquest*, 379–88. For the relationship between events in Ireland and those in England and Wales during this critical period see also Smith, 'Gruffydd Llwyd'; idem, 'Edward II and the allegiance of Wales'; McNamee, 191–4, 204.

[117] Frame, 'The Bruces in Ireland', 3; Frame, *Ireland and Britain, 1170–1450* (London, 1998), 71.

meantime largely neutralized.[118] On 1 September 1315 Bruce defeated an army led, ironically, by Robert Bruce's father-in-law, Richard de Burgh earl of Ulster, at Connor in Down, after which the earl withdrew from Ulster to pursue his other interests in the west of Ireland; in December Bruce defeated Roger Mortimer of Wigmore at Kells, in Meath, although he failed to take Mortimer's great fortress at Trim.[119] The withdrawal from Ireland before the end of 1315 of both Mortimer and of another of the leading magnates, the former justiciar Theobald de Verdon, left both parts of the former de Lacy lordship of Meath to the north of Dublin without resident defenders, and left Dublin itself open to possible attack.[120] Dublin was prepared for a Scottish siege,[121] but was instead bypassed by the Scots, who entered Kildare, where they were confronted at Ardscull near Athy on 26 January 1316 by an Anglo-Irish army whose leaders comprised most of the prominent magnates in the southern half of the lordship. Although no one could have foreseen it at the time, this was a turning-point in the Scottish campaign in Ireland. The Anglo-Irish force was anxious and uncertain, was the last available army for the defence of the lordship of Ireland, and understandably stood on the defensive. The Scottish attack on the other hand appears to have been half-hearted. Exhausted by several months of hard campaigning, far from their base in Ulster, and suffering from food shortages exacerbated by the weather, the Scots did not press the attack. Had they done so and defeated the army of the lordship, they might have gained much greater support among the Gaelic Irish leaders, Dublin would probably have fallen and with it any prospect of continued English rule in Ireland. It is hard to see what Edward II and his government in England could then have done to counter such an outcome. If Ireland had passed out of English control, it is possible that Edward Bruce's desire to raise a revolt in Wales would also have been achieved. Instead, the battle is a classic example of the 'fog of war'. The Scots withdrew into Ulster to fight another day, letting slip an opportunity of victory which they never regained.[122] The battle of Ardscull, in which little happened and few casualties were suffered by either side, may in fact have been a turning-point both in the Scottish campaign in Ireland and in the future political alignments of Britain and Ireland. In its way it was as important an event as Bannockburn less than two years earlier.

Edward Bruce remained in his base in Ulster for the rest of 1316; Carrickfergus finally surrendered in September, but otherwise there was

---

[118] G.O. Sayles, 'The siege of Carrickfergus castle, 1315–16', *IHS*, x, no. 37 (1956–57), 94–100; reprinted in Sayles, *Scripta Diversa* (London, 1982), 212–18; McNamee, 171, 175.

[119] For an account of these episodes see Phillips, 'Mission', 68, 71; McNamee, 171–9.

[120] Phillips, 'Mission', 71. Mortimer went to Glamorgan in South Wales to assist in putting down the revolt of Llywelyn Bren, while Verdon went to England where he pursued his ambition to marry Elizabeth de Clare, one of the heiresses to the earldom of Gloucester.

[121] Phillips, 'Mission', 68.

[122] Ibid., 68–71; Phillips, 'Edward II and Ireland', 10; McNamee, 177–9.

little to show for the year's fighting. In January 1317 Robert Bruce arrived in person, probably to try and restore some momentum to his brother's campaign, and in response to the knowledge that Edward II had sent Roger Mortimer of Wigmore to Ireland as king's lieutenant. In February 1317 Edward and Robert Bruce again advanced out of Ulster, causing devastation as they went. Again Dublin prepared itself for attack but, as in 1316, the Scots changed direction. They advanced through Leinster and Munster, until they approached Limerick in early April. An Anglo-Irish army, led by Edmund Butler, shadowed the Scots but did not attempt to bring them to battle. Failing to take Limerick, lacking anticipated Irish support and short of food, the Scots once more withdrew. Robert Bruce went back to Scotland and the final act of his brother's tragedy began.[123]

Little is known of Edward Bruce's activities between the spring of 1317 and the summer of 1318, but it was during this period that the document commonly but erroneously known as the Remonstrance of the Irish Princes was composed and forwarded to the recently elected pope, John XXII, at Avignon. The Remonstrance was in effect a detailed commentary on the alleged failure of the English crown and its officials, the English clergy, and the English settlers in Ireland to observe the terms of the papal bull *Laudabiliter* of about 1155 in which Pope Adrian IV had authorized Henry II of England to come to Ireland 'to enlarge the boundaries of the church, to reveal the truth of the Christian faith to unlearned and savage peoples, and to root out from the lord's field the vices which grow in it'. The reigning pope, John XXII, was invited to annul *Laudabiliter*, which had been one of the principal legal supports of the English crown's claims to lordship over Ireland since the twelfth century, and to replace it by giving his approval of Edward Bruce's rule as king of Ireland. There is no evidence however that the Remonstrance was either influenced or approved by the native Irish princes of Ireland. In reality the Remonstrance, which was probably composed on Bruce's behalf by a Franciscan from Armagh, was a partisan work of propaganda which can be seen almost as an act of desperation, written in the hope that the pope might give Edward Bruce and his Irish allies the success which military actions alone had not achieved.[124]

Finally in October 1318 Bruce made one last movement out of Ulster, again more in desperation than with any clear plan in mind. This time he was faced by an Anglo-Irish army led by the justiciar Edmund Butler and John de Bermingham, lord of Tethmoy, which had had time to prepare and

[123] McNamee, 179–84; Phillips, 'Edward II and Ireland', 10; R. Frame, 'The campaign against the Scots in Munster, 1317', *IHS*, xxiv, no. 95 (1985, 361–72; repr. in Frame, *Ireland and Britain*, 99–112).

[124] There is a critical edition of the Remonstrance in *Scotichronicon*, vi, pp. xxi–xxv, 384–404, 465–83. In its appeal to history, both real and imaginary, the Remonstrance closely resembles the documents concerning English claims to superiority over Scotland sent to the pope by both Edward I and the Scots in 1301 and the Scottish Declaration of Arbroath of 1320. See Phillips, 'Irish remonstrance of 1317', 121–4.

had confidence in its own abilities. The two armies met at Faughart near Dundalk on 14 October. According to the account in the Lanercost chronicle, 'The Scots were in three columns at such a distance from each other that the first was done with before the second came up, and then the second before the third, with which Edward was marching, could render any aid. Thus the third column was routed, just as the two preceding ones had been. Edward Bruce fell at the same time and was beheaded after death; his body was divided into four quarters, which were sent to the four chief quarters of Ireland',[125] while his head was sent to Edward II in England. In return for this grisly present and one of the few clear-cut victories in battle during his reign, John de Bermingham was made earl of Louth.[126]

The Scottish invasion of Ireland in 1315 had forcibly drawn the attention of Edward II's government to events across the Irish Sea, but this was by no means the first occasion on which Edward had concerned himself with Irish affairs.[127] His appointment in 1308 of Gaveston as his lieutenant in Ireland may have been a convenient way of getting the favourite safely out of England, but it turned out well. Gaveston led successful military expeditions against Irish rebels in the Wicklow mountains to the south of Dublin and saw to the defences of key royal castles in the area. By the time he left Ireland in 1309, Leinster was more securely under English control. Arguably the lordship was better able to defend itself from the Scottish attack when it came in 1315.[128]

The use of Irish resources in Scotland itself, which had begun during the reign of Edward I, continued into that of his son. A planned expedition to Argyll in the west of Scotland by 3,000 Irish troops in the summer of 1310 was frustrated by bad weather; in 1311 another force of 4,000 men from Ireland was intended to land at Ayr in Scotland, but this too failed to materialize.[129] In 1311 or early 1312 Edward ordered that in future Irish revenues should be used in Ireland in order to keep the peace because 'divers Irish of our land of Ireland, our felons and rebels, both because of this same lack of money and their customary pugnacity... [are] day by day perpetrating burnings, homicides, robberies, and other innumerable and intolerable transgressions'.[130] The timing of the letter was probably influenced by the administrative reforms which were then being introduced in England by the Ordainers, rather than by any realization by Edward that he was draining Ireland of its resources, but the wording of the letter suggests that it was also a response to a plea for assistance from the justiciar of Ireland and his

---

[125] *Lanercost*, 225–6; McNamee, 185–6.

[126] Lydon, 'Impact', ii, 293–4.

[127] For a survey of relations between England and Ireland during the reign of Edward II see Phillips, 'Edward II and Ireland', 1–18.

[128] Hamilton, 57–61, 148–9. There is also a detailed treatment of Gaveston's time in Ireland in A.A. Taylor, 'The career of Peter of Gaveston' (MA, London, 1939), ch. 4.

[129] McNamee, 48–9, 52–3, 69; Barrow, 192–3. See also ch. 4 of this book.

[130] Lydon, 'Impact', ii, 201–2; idem, 'Edward II and the revenues of Ireland,' 52–3.

colleagues in Dublin.[131] This did not however bring about any change in government policy. In 1314, the planning for the campaign which came to its disastrous conclusion at Bannockburn included an intended substantial contribution from Ireland. In March Edward wrote summoning twenty-seven of the Anglo-Irish lords to join the campaign, and also to twenty-six of the leading Gaelic Irish chieftains, who could not be required to participate but were nonetheless asked to take part. Four thousand infantry were also summoned from Ireland. All were to be under the overall command of Richard de Burgh, the earl of Ulster and the leading Anglo-Irish magnate.[132] John MacDougall, the ousted lord of Argyll and Lorn, was appointed as admiral of the western fleet to escort this force,[133] and also given the task of preventing any interruption in the supplies of food coming from Ireland to the port of Skinburness near Carlisle.[134] It is likely that this force was intended, as in 1310 and 1311, to land in western Scotland rather than take part in the main campaign to relieve Stirling. Although none of the Irish forces, cavalry or infantry, are known with certainty to have reached Scotland,[135] John of Argyll was instrumental in early 1315 in the partial recovery of the Isle of Man from the Scots. This was soon to prove vital in the struggle to prevent the Scots gaining control of the Irish Sea and thus supporting their attempt to conquer the lordship of Ireland.[136]

After Bannockburn Irish resources were needed more than ever for the English war effort. In August 1314 the English clerk John de Hothum, a former associate of Gaveston and a former chancellor of the Irish exchequer, and soon to become bishop of Ely, was sent to Dublin to discover how much money could be raised there in aid of the Scottish war and to enlist the co-operation of the Anglo-Irish magnates. He apparently met with little success, but on his return to England in November, Hothum was at least able to provide Edward II and his government with an up-to-date report on the situation in Ireland.[137] On 12 March 1315 the Irish administration was

---

[131] The language used in Edward II's letter closely resembles the appeals for assistance which were regularly addressed to the royal government in England by the king's officials in Ireland during the 13th and 14th centuries. This particular letter has not survived but there are many such documents in the National Archives class of Ancient Correspondence, SC 1.

[132] Phillips, 'Mission', 65–6; 79, nn. 34–5; McNamee, 61; Barrow, 204. On 12 March Edward ordered that Robert Bruce's wife, Elizabeth, who was the earl of Ulster's daughter and had been a prisoner in English hands since 1306, should be moved from the custody of the abbess of Barking in Essex to more secure confinement in Rochester castle: *CCR, 1313–18*, 43.

[133] McNamee, 61. For the role of the MacDougalls of Argyll as supporters of the English crown against Bruce see Barrow, 163, 178–82, 192–3.

[134] McNamee, 61.

[135] Phillips, 'Mission', 65–6; Barrow, 204, notes however that the earl of Ulster was with Edward II at Newminster on 29 May 1314, and that 50 years later Barbour recorded that Edward had with him 'a great following from Ireland'.

[136] Phillips, 'Mission', 66. On the chequered history of the Isle of Man at this time see Barrow, 192–3.

[137] Phillips, 'Mission', 66.

ordered to purvey supplies for the English forces on the Scottish border: this was very much in the tradition of employing Irish resources in English wars. But two days later Edward II wrote to sixteen of the leading clergy, twenty-two of the leaders of Gaelic Ireland, thirty-six of the most important Anglo-Irish magnates, and to six urban communities, and the chief officials in the Irish administration, asking them to listen to a message which would be expounded to them orally on his behalf by the justiciar Edmund Butler, the chancellor Richard Bereford, and the treasurer Walter Islip. There is no indication of what the message was to be but it was clearly important. It may have been just another request for assistance in the war against the Scots on the island of Britain, such as had been made in 1314,[138] but there is some evidence that as early as March 1315 Edward II's government had indications that the Scots were planning to invade Ireland and that Edward may therefore have been looking for support against them or in effect warning anyone who might be inclined to join them.[139] This would have given a particular resonance to the proposed contacts with the leaders of Gaelic Irish society; described in Edward's letters as *duces*, some considered themselves kings of their own territories. It was ironic, to say the least, that one of those addressed was Donal O'Neill of Tyrone, the apparent instigator of Edward Bruce's expedition to Ireland.[140]

Although the actual time and place of the Scottish landing in Ireland in May 1315 probably came as a surprise, Edward II and his government acted promptly when news of the invasion reached England. On 10 July 1315 Edward wrote to all the leading Anglo-Norman magnates in Ireland, asking them for information on the activities of the Scots and appealing for their assistance in resisting the invasion.[141] On 1 September the great council of magnates held by Edward II at Lincoln to discuss the

---

[138] *Foedera*, II, i, 245, 262–3; Phillips, 'Mission', 65–6.

[139] Phillips, 'Mission', 66–7. A Scottish envoy/spy named Henry had been a prisoner in Dublin castle since 16 Feb. He may have been circulating copies of a letter in which Robert Bruce spoke of the ties of ancestry between the Irish and the Scots and proposed an alliance between them: R. Nicholson, 'A sequel to Edward Bruce's invasion of Ireland', *SHR*, xlii (1963), 31, 38–9. The letter may however date from as early as 1306–7. For a discussion of it and its date see Frame, 'The Bruces in Ireland', 5, n. 7; and Frame, *Ireland and Britain*, 72, n. 6. The English government also learned that the Scots were planning some kind of venture since at the end of March Sir John Botetourt was ordered to take an English fleet to intercept 13 large cargo ships which the Scots were loading with arms and food at the Flemish port of Sluys: *CCR, 1313–18*, 218–19; *CCW*, 415 (where the date is wrongly given as 26 May instead of 26 March).

[140] According to the Remonstrance, about two years before its composition some of the Irish princes had made a written approach to Edward II, using Hothum as an intermediary, but no details of these contacts have survived. On Gaelic Irish kingship at this period see the recent discussion by B. Smith, 'Lordship in the British Isles, *c.* 1320–*c.* 1360', in *Power and Identity in the Middle Ages*, ed. H. Pryce & J. Watts (Oxford, 2007), 153–6.

[141] Phillips, 'Mission', 65–7; the sending of the letters (though not their contents) and the names of their recipients are recorded in E 101/376/7, f. 74; the replies are recorded in C 81/93/3594. At least 11 of the 30 men written to are known to have replied. This and other

war with Scotland decided to send John de Hothum back to Ireland to report on the situation and to co-ordinate resistance to the Scots.[142] Despite being delayed on his journey at Chester, for fear of the pirate Thomas Dun who had raided the harbour of Holyhead in Anglesey on 12 September and carried off a royal ship, the *James of Caernarfon*, Hothum arrived in Dublin on 5 November.[143] He then carried out his mission with considerable success. Hothum organized the defences of Dublin against a possible Scottish attack during the autumn and winter of 1315–16. At the critical time in early 1316, when it seemed that the Scots were about to overrun the lordship of Ireland, Hothum also applied all his diplomatic skills and experience to the task of encouraging the Anglo-Norman magnates, whose confidence and mutual trust had been severely undermined by the Scottish victories at Connor and Kells in September and November 1315. The drawn battle fought at Ardscull in Kildare on 26 January 1316 was as much the product of Hothum's energies and of the foresight of Edward II's government in sending him to Ireland as it was the result of Scottish exhaustion and hunger.[144]

By early May 1316 Hothum had returned to England, where he reported to the king's council. Between them they then drafted a memorandum for Edward II recommending the rewards to be given to the Irish magnates for their past support and to ensure their continued loyalty, most notably the creation of John Fitz Thomas as earl of Kildare. In November 1316 Roger Mortimer, who was lord of Wigmore and Ludlow in the Welsh March and lord of Trim and Leix in Ireland, was sent to take command in Ireland,[145] but otherwise the defence of the lordship of Ireland *on land* was conducted for the remainder of the war with little reference to England.[146] Even the attempt that had been made in September 1314 to

---

material is edited in Phillips, 'Documents on the early stages of the Bruce invasion of Ireland, 1315–1316', *Proceedings of the Royal Irish Academy*, lxxix, C, no. 11 (1979); see also Phillips, 'Mission', 71–4.

[142] Phillips, 92–3. No replies had so far been received from any of the magnates addressed on 10 July (there were often long delays in the delivery of the king's letters; the three earliest replies of the 11 eventually received were dated 8 Sept. and the latest 2 Nov.) but news of Ireland had been obtained on 25 July from a messenger of the earl of Pembroke and on or just before 21 Aug. from Hugh Canon, an official emissary of the Dublin administration: E 101/376/7, ff. 13, 43; E 101/376/25, m.13; Phillips, 'Mission', 71–3.

[143] Phillips, 'Mission', 67–8. Hothum had to assemble an escort of eight ships and 86 armed men before he could cross in safety. Dun was in Scottish service but may have been from Downpatrick in Ireland.

[144] Phillips, 'Mission', 68–71. For the pledges of loyalty to Edward II which were made by nine of the leading Anglo-Irish magnates on 4 Feb. 1316 and for the reports on the battle by John de Hothum and by one of his clerks see Phillips, 'Documents', 251–7.

[145] The justiciar Edmund Butler had already been made earl of Carrick in Sept. 1315, but this did not take effect partly because he was unable to visit England for his creation: for details of the rewards and privileges granted in May 1316 see Phillips, 'Mission', 63, 74–5; the conciliar memorandum is C 49/File 4, no.19, published in Phillips, 'Documents', 268–9.

[146] Phillips, 'Mission', 76.

send 1,000 marks to Ireland to pay the wages of Irish troops who were supposed to go to Scotland failed when the messenger was robbed near Denbigh in North Wales. Hothum's mission to Ireland cost the English exchequer £1,700 but none of this was available to assist with the defence of the lordship, which had to depend on the inadequate resources of the Irish exchequer. The only money sent from England for use within Ireland during the period of the Bruce invasion was a sum of £400 paid in April 1316, which was borrowed from an Italian merchant company, the Ballardi of Lucca.[147] Instead English financial resources, such as they were, had to be used for the defence of the north of England and also to ensure that all the royal castles in Wales were in good repair and well garrisoned in case of a Welsh revolt in sympathy with the Scots in Ireland.[148]

There was however one other important theatre of English military operations which had a more direct effect on the war in Ireland: the naval campaign in the Irish Sea. As early as June 1315 orders had been given to use all the available Irish revenues to maintain a royal fleet in the Irish Sea, but the orders came too late since the Scots had already landed in Ireland.[149] Shortage of money often hampered naval operations: an elaborate plan agreed with Antonio Pessagno to hire five Genoese galleys, with a total of 1,000 men, to operate in the Irish Sea in the summer of 1317 never came to fruition,[150] while the order for John of Athy to muster fifteen ships to attack the Scots in the seas between Scotland and Ireland at about the same time apparently resulted in the provision of only six ships.[151] But on 2 July 1317 John of Athy did succeed in defeating and killing Thomas Dun, the most notorious of the pirates or privateers in Scottish service.[152] It is difficult to assess the exact contribution of the naval war to the eventual defeat of Edward Bruce at Faughart in October 1318, but it is hard to believe that it had no effect. Although there is little doubt that the Bruce invasion contributed in the longer term to the declining effectiveness of English rule in Ireland, in the short term the defeat and death of Edward Bruce marked one of the few definite military successes of the reign of Edward II.

As to the Irish Remonstrance, this proved to be of no benefit to the Scottish cause in Ireland. Edward II could rely on the papacy for support against the Scots, whose king Robert Bruce had been excommunicated for the murder of his rival John Comyn in 1306. This meant that when a new

[147] Ibid., 66, 70, 74, 76, 82, n. 77. Hothum's account for his mission is published from E 101/309/19 (4) in Phillips, 'Documents', 266–8.

[148] Smith, 'Gruffydd Llwyd', 463–7; McNamee, 191–4, 204; *CCR, 1313–18*, 147, 148; Davies, *Conquest*, 387–8.

[149] Phillips, 'Mission', 67.

[150] McNamee, 181; *CPR, 1313–17*, 603 (16 Dec. 1316). Pessagno was also to supply large quantities of grain and other victuals for use by English garrisons in the north of England.

[151] E 101/531/15: accounts for naval operations in the Irish Sea under the command of John of Athy, 25 April to 24 June 1317.

[152] McNamee, 184.

pope, John XXII, was elected in August 1316, ending the vacancy since the death of Clement V in 1314, Edward II could appeal confidently to him for assistance.[153] In April 1317 the pope issued bulls ordering the Scots to observe a truce in their war with England, until the arrival of two papal envoys[154] in England to negotiate a permanent settlement. The papal orders applied equally to the Scottish campaigning in the north of England and in Ireland.[155] Predictably, Robert Bruce took no notice, and refused even to take delivery of the bulls, on the grounds that the pope did not give him his rightful title of king.[156] This was the very period when the Irish Remonstrance was being composed and transmitted to Avignon. It is hardly surprising that the Remonstrance, with its litany of justifiable complaints against English rule in Ireland, made so little impact at Avignon or that John XXII's admonishment of Edward II amounted to little more than a gentle slap on the wrist.[157] In return for papal support, Edward's own envoys had promised at a meeting held in Avignon in April 1317 that Edward would pay an annual tribute of 1,000 marks for England and Ireland.[158] This tribute (of 700 marks for England and 300 marks for Ireland) had first been promised by King John in 1213 as part of the solution to his dispute with Pope Innocent III[159] and since then had frequently fallen into arrears: by 1317 these amounted to £16,000 (24,000 marks). Edward's envoys paid the tribute for 1316–17; further sporadic payments were made until 1320 when they ceased altogether; but nothing was paid off the arrears. Neither did Edward II take any notice of the pope's further demand that he should render homage and fealty, which was the other part of the package agreed in 1213.[160]

[153] John XXII was personally less favourable to Edward II than his predecessor Clement V, who had a particularly close relationship with the English monarchy, but his overriding interest in preserving the peace of Christendom so that the great military powers, especially France and England, could embark on a new crusade, made him unsympathetic to the Scots. For a discussion of Anglo-papal relations during the pontificates of Clement V and John XXII see Wright, *The Church and the English Crown*, esp. 168–73; Watt, *The Church*, 183–97.

[154] Cardinals Luke Fieschi and Gaucelin d'Eauze.

[155] The English diplomatic mission to Avignon in early 1317 which led to the appointment of the papal envoys and to the issue of the bulls directed against Scottish intervention in Ireland is discussed in Phillips, 107–11.

[156] Barrow, 246–7.

[157] *CPL, 1305–42*, 440; *Vetera monumenta*, ed. Theiner, 201–2. See Phillips, 'Irish Remonstrance of 1317', 112–29.

[158] They met in the chamber of the cardinal of Pellegrue: *Vitae Paparum Avenionensium*, ed. E. Baluze, ii (Paris, 1927), 130.

[159] Watt, *The Church*, 84.

[160] W.E. Lunt, *Financial Relations of the Papacy with England to 1327* (Cambridge, Mass., 1939), 166–9. Since the 1213 agreement between John and Innocent III was a fundamental document in English claims to exercise authority in Ireland, it is surprising that neither Edward II's Scottish nor his Irish opponents appear to have used the failure to pay tribute or to perform homage and fealty as a legal weapon against him at the papal curia. Instead the Remonstrance of 1317 concentrated on the alleged English failure to observe the terms of an even earlier document, Adrian IV's bull, *Laudabiliter*, of c. 1155. On the place of

On a totally different front, Edward II exploited his good relations with the papacy to ensure that whenever possible senior appointments in the Irish Church would not go to native Irishmen. This was partly a reaction to the emergency of the Bruce invasion, but it was also a continuation of a policy which had seen, for example, the appointment since 1306 of a series of archbishops of English origin to the primatial see of Armagh.[161] In 1317 Edward II gained approval of the appointment of the chancellor of Ireland, William Fitz John, as archbishop of Cashel: as in Armagh eleven years earlier, this involved introducing an English prelate into a province which had previously been under Irish control. In contrast, the confirmation of the appointment of an Englishman, the former treasurer, Alexander Bicknor, as archbishop of Dublin, at about the same time, was routine. Edward was also very anxious about the seditious preaching of certain Irish Franciscans on behalf of Edward Bruce: in August 1316 he sent an English Franciscan, Geoffrey of Aylsham, to see Michael of Cesena, the minister-general of the Franciscan order, to persuade him to stop the hostile preaching. In 1317 the pope duly obliged with a denunciation of such friars.[162] There are now grounds for suspecting that one of these disloyal friars, the Franciscan Michael Mac Lochlainn, the unsuccessful Irish candidate for the see of Armagh in 1303 and a future bishop of Derry, was the author of the Irish Remonstrance.[163] In the battle to exert influence at the papal curia Edward Bruce and his allies were no match for Edward II and his government.

LANCASTER COMES TO POWER

In the weeks following the assembly of magnates and senior royal administrators held at Lincoln in late August and early September 1315 the influence of the earl of Lancaster grew rapidly, to the extent that Edward II was communicating regularly both with his council in London and with Lancaster.[164] On 4 October, for example, Edward forwarded to the

---

Laudabiliter in 14th-century Anglo-Irish relations see Phillips, 'The Remonstrance revisited: England and Ireland in the early fourteenth century', in *Men, Women and War, Historical Studies*, xviii, ed. T.G. Fraser & K. Jeffrey (Dublin, 1993), 16–17, 23–4; J.A. Watt., '*Laudabiliter* in medieval diplomacy and propaganda', *Irish Ecclesiastical Record*, 5th ser., lxxxvii (Jan.–June 1957), 420–32.

[161] John Taaffe (1306–7); the Dominican friars, Walter Jorz (1307–11) and Roland Jorz (1311–22); and Stephen Segrave (1323–33)

[162] Watt, *The Church*, 185–6.

[163] For the possible authorship of Mac Lochlainn who had grievances of his own against the English in Ireland, esp. against English members of his own order see Phillips, 'Remonstrance revisited', 17–20, 24–7.

[164] Phillips, 93; Maddicott, 179–80. The king spent the second half of Sept. at Fen Ditton near Cambridge, before settling himself in early Nov. at his manor of Clipstone near Nottingham, where he was to spend most of the time until late Jan. 1316. Lancaster in the meantime stayed at Castle Donington in Leicestershire and elsewhere in the Midlands and in Lancashire.

chancellor in London a letter from Lancaster dated at Castle Donington on 30 September and asking for an inquiry into the death of one of his valets. The chancellor was instructed to do as Lancaster requested.[165] On 19 October Edward sent William Melton and Hugh Audley from Sawtrey to Castle Donington to ask for Lancaster's advice in applying the anti-Scottish measures agreed at Lincoln, and on receiving his replies on 20 October promptly sent them to the council. On the 25th another letter from Lancaster, dated at Castle Donington on 23 October and referring to the affairs of the widowed countess of Lincoln, was passed to the council with instructions for action.[166] In early November the king sent Ingelard Warley, William Melton and William de Montacute from Clipstone to visit Lancaster at Wigan, where Lancaster was engaged in suppressing the revolt by his former retainer Adam Banaster. At the end of November Lancaster's advice was again sought when Edward sent Richard Lovel and Edmund Bacon to visit him, his replies being received at Clipstone on 7 December.[167] In mid-December another meeting between the king and some of the leading magnates was held at Doncaster and was intended, like the earlier assembly at Lincoln, to discuss the state of the realm. Apart from Edward, those attending included the earls of Lancaster, Richmond and Hereford. Scotland and Ireland were certainly high on the agenda, but the presence of Roger Mortimer of Chirk, the leading royal officer in North Wales, shows that Wales was also discussed. The council was also preparing the ground for the parliament which had been summoned on 16 October to begin at Lincoln on 27 January 1316.[168]

Although nominally called to discuss the continuing threat from the Scots, the parliament was to be dominated by the problem of reaching an agreement on Lancaster's future role in the royal government. The result was a game of cat and mouse played between Edward II and his first cousin which first delayed the proceedings of the parliament and then threatened to reduce them to farce.[169] The broad outlines of what

---

[165] SC 1/35/155; C 81/93/3570.

[166] SC 1/34/106, 107; *CCW*, 431–2. The most prominent royal councillors then in London were the archbishop of Canterbury, the chancellor, treasurer, and earl of Hereford. The earl of Pembroke is known to have joined the king on two occasions, at Dalby in Lincolnshire on 26 Oct. and at Clipstone on 16 Nov., with a short return visit to the north of England to free the widow of Robert Clifford from captivity at Barnard's castle, before rejoining the council in London: Phillips, 94.

[167] E 101/376/7, ff. 18, 41; Phillips, 93; Maddicott, 176.

[168] E 101/376/7, f. 11; E 101/376/26, m.5; C 53/102, mm.14,15; *CPR, 1313–17*, 421; *PW*, II, ii, 152–8.

[169] For a detailed account of the parliament and the records of its proceedings see *PROME*, parliament of January 1316. During the parliament Edward stayed in the lodgings of the dean of Lincoln, while the proceedings were held in various locations, including the hall of the dean, the chapter house of the cathedral, and the house of the Carmelites.

happened are recorded on the Parliament Roll but the details of the negotiations between Edward and Lancaster which must certainly have taken place are hidden from us.[170] On 27 January, the day the parliament was supposed to open, Lancaster was still at his castle of Kenilworth in Warwickshire.[171] The political embarrassment this caused was temporarily concealed the following day when the king entered a chamber in the lodgings of the dean of Lincoln and announced to the prelates, earls and others present through William Inge, one of the justices of the Common Bench, that he wished the business of the parliament to be conducted as speedily as possible. On the same day it was agreed that petitions from all the king's dominions, in England, Ireland, Gascony, Wales and Scotland, would be received as was customary until 3 February and arrangements were made to deal with them. The chancellor and treasurer, and the justices of both benches, were also ordered to have business pending before them, which could not be determined outside parliament, set down briefly in writing, and to bring it before the parliament so that appropriate action could be taken on it there. On 29 January it was agreed to proceed with hearing petitions until the arrival of the earl of Lancaster and of other absent magnates, and auditors were appointed for this purpose. On 31 January the earl of Hereford gave answers on behalf of the king to the petitions presented by the clergy. Lancaster was still absent on 1 February when Edward appointed the earls of Pembroke and Richmond, and the bishops of Norwich and Exeter, to act in Edward's place until Lancaster's arrival.[172]

Lancaster arrived in Lincoln only on 9 or 10 February, possibly accompanied by armed retainers, but the real business of the parliament did not begin until his attendance on 12 February.[173] After the enactment of a statute governing the appointment and removal of sheriffs and the repeal on the 14th of the ordinance on the price of victuals issued in the 1315 parliament, the most important matters were reached on 17 February, when the bishop of Norwich announced that the king had agreed to the enforcement of the Ordinances and to the observation of the perambulation of

[170] This is ironic since the record in the Parliament Roll (SC 9/20) of the events leading up to the appointment of the earl of Lancaster as chief councillor is 'the first official narrative account of any parliament to appear': Maddicott, 180. Many of the earlier parliaments of the reign had also dealt with highly contentious and delicate political business (as in 1308, 1309, 1310, etc.) but none of this has left any trace in any surviving official record. Of the 14 parliaments which preceded the Lincoln parliament of 1316, a Parliament Roll exists only for those of Aug. 1312 and Jan. 1315.

[171] SC 8/71/3534. The king was at Lincoln between 27 Jan. and 23 Feb.: E 101/376/26, m.6.

[172] *PW*, II, ii, 169. The chronology of the parliament from 28 Jan. until 14 Feb. is recorded in *PROME*, Parliament of Jan. 1316, SC 9/20, item 1. In *Aymer de Valence*, 95, I wrongly gave the date of the appointment of Pembroke and the others to act for Edward II as 8 Feb.

[173] C 49/File 66/23; *PROME*, Parliament of Jan. 1316, SC 9/20, item 1; Maddicott, 180.

the forest which had been carried out in 1300.[174] On the same day the bishop 'said some things on behalf of the king to the earl of Lancaster'.[175] A week later, on 24 February, their nature became evident when 'some words were further spoken to Thomas earl of Lancaster on behalf of the lord king, to remove a certain doubt which the earl was said to have entertained about the king, informing him that the lord king bore a sincere and wholehearted goodwill towards him and the other magnates of his realm'. Lancaster was then asked on behalf of the king and of the prelates and magnates present in parliament if he would accept appointment as the head of the king's council. Thanking the king for the offer, Lancaster 'humbly begged that he might consider it, and answer later'; the consideration evidently did not last long since Lancaster decided to accept the king's request and was sworn in as chief councillor. In the form of his appointment Lancaster stated that he had agreed to lead the council because of the king's promise to uphold the Ordinances and to reform the administration of his household and government. No major decisions were to be made without the council, and councillors who gave bad advice were to be removable in parliament on the demand of the king and Lancaster. Lancaster's appointment also contained the vital provision that he could discharge himself from the council without incurring any ill-will, if the king did not accept the advice given by him and the council.[176] It followed naturally from the terms of Lancaster's appointment that, at the same time, the king consented to the formation of a commission consisting of the archbishop of Canterbury, the bishops of Llandaff, Chichester, Norwich and Salisbury, the earls of Pembroke, Hereford, Arundel, Richmond and Lancaster, and Bartholomew de Badlesmere, who were instructed to consider means of reforming the realm and the household, as well as the removal from the household of men whom they regarded as unsuitable.[177] Important as Lancaster's position now was, the names of his colleagues on

---

[174] *PROME*, Parliament of Jan. 1316, SC 9/20, item 2; Phillips, 95; Maddicott, 181. The full text of the Statute of Sheriffs was included in the Parliament Roll: *PROME*, Parliament of Jan. 1316, SC 9/19, item 49; SC 9/20, item 8, and the Statute Roll (*SR*, i, 174–5). The statute was the result of 'the representations of the prelates, earls, barons, and other magnates of the realm summoned to that parliament, and through the grievous complaints of the people'. The petition or petitions, which lay behind these representations, have not survived. See Harriss, 120, and 120, n. 1.

[175] *PROME*, Parliament of Jan. 1316, SC 9/20, item 2.

[176] Ibid., item 3 (this contains an enrolled copy of the terms of Lancaster's appointment) & item 4 (the original of the terms of appointment, sewn on to the roll). Although Hilda Johnstone argued that the date of Lancaster's actual appointment was 17 Feb. and not 24 Feb. as stated here and as argued by Tout, the date is clearly given in the Parliament Roll as the Tuesday before Lent, i.e. 24 Feb.: H. Johnstone, 'The Parliament of Lincoln of 1316', *EHR*, xxxvi (1921), 53–7; Tout, *Place of the Reign*, 95.

[177] These details are not recorded on the Parliament Roll and are known only from a letter from Lancaster to the king in July 1317 which is preserved in *Murimuth*, 271–4, and the Bridlington chronicler's *Gesta Edwardi*, 50–2; Phillips, 97, 121; Maddicott, 182. Significantly, Hugh Despenser the Elder was not to be a member of the reform commission.

the reform commission and those of the bishops of Norwich, Chichester, Exeter and Salisbury, who were added to the council on 1 February,[178] show that in practice he would be working with existing royal councillors and sympathizers and not with any of his own supporters. Lancaster's imposition as head of the council might appear a revolutionary step, but he would require personal qualities of a high order if he were to impose himself on long-established royal sympathizers. He would also have to display a degree of application to official business which he had not shown in the past.[179]

THE BUSINESS OF PARLIAMENT

As soon as Lancaster's new status seemed settled, attention could be given to Scotland, the business for which the Lincoln parliament had originally been summoned. On 20 February the king received two separate grants of taxation in aid of the war with Scotland, a sixteenth from the 'magnates and community of the realm', and a fifteenth from the 'citizens, burgesses and knights of the counties'. The service of an armed foot soldier from every vill in the kingdom was also granted by the magnates and community; on the same date the army was ordered to muster at Newcastle on 8 July in readiness for a Scottish campaign,[180] and on 28 February every landholder with land worth £50 or more was ordered to take up knighthood.[181] Whether these military arrangements would have any useful effect would depend in part on how the new political relationship between Edward II and Lancaster worked in practice.

THE KING AND THE CLERGY

The Lincoln parliament also marked a stage in defining the relations between the crown and the English Church. The bargaining between king and clergy was given urgency by the clergy's unwillingness to make any grant of taxation to the king until their grievances had been satisfactorily addressed. These were administrative and jurisdictional in nature and included 'such matters as violent hands upon clerks, royal interference with ecclesiastical property, burdens placed by the crown upon religious houses, and denial of clerical privilege in the correction of criminous clerks . . . royal interference with the process of excommunication, with the rights of sanctuary and abjuration, with the examination of clerks presented to benefices, and with the process of ecclesiastical elections'. On 31 January the earl of Hereford gave answers on behalf of the king and in the king's presence to the petitions presented by the clergy. The responses

[178] *PROME*, Parliament of Jan. 1316, SC 9/20, item 1.
[179] Phillips, 96; Maddicott, 181.
[180] *PROME*, Parliament of Jan. 1316, SC 9/20, item 2; *CCR, 1313–18*, 322.
[181] *PROME*, Parliament of Jan. 1316, SC 9/20, item 2; *PW*, II, ii, 158–9, 161–3, 166–7, 464; *Lay Taxes*, 33; Powicke, *Military Obligation*, 142–3.

of the king and his council, which answered only some of the grievances of the clergy, were later embodied in the *Articuli cleri*, which was issued at York on 24 November 1316. In the meantime, in October and earlier in November, the two provinces of the English Church had finally made the grants of taxation which the king had been looking for at Lincoln.[182]

THE GLOUCESTER INHERITANCE

Many other matters occupied Edward II and his council both during the time of the Lincoln parliament and long after it had ended, some of them time-consuming such as Hugh de Courtenay's claim to the inheritance of Isabella de Forz, countess of Aumale;[183] others both time-consuming and politically sensitive, such as the long-running dispute between the king's chamberlain John Charlton and one of Lancaster's retainers, Gruffudd de la Pole, over possession of the lordship of Welshpool which had been in progress since 1309 and continued until the early 1330s;[184] another lengthy dispute was that between the citizens of Bristol and Bartholomew de Badlesmere, the royal constable of Bristol castle.[185]

Most delicate of all was the fate of the possessions in England, Wales and Ireland of Gilbert de Clare, the late earl of Gloucester, who had been killed at Bannockburn in June 1314, leaving a wife who was thought to be pregnant and lands worth over £6,500 per year.[186] Gilbert also left three sisters, who might each be entitled to a third of the remaining Clare lands, after first allowing for one third as the dower of Gilbert's widow during her lifetime. In 1314 only one of the three sisters was married: Eleanor who had been the wife of Hugh Despenser the Younger since 1307. At the time the marriage was a sign of the royal favour enjoyed by his father Hugh the Elder: the marriage in itself did not bring with it the likelihood that the younger Hugh might one day become a wealthy and powerful man in his own right. In 1314 the other two sisters, Margaret and Elizabeth were both widows, one the former wife of Piers Gaveston and the other of John de

---

[182] Wright, *The Church and the English Crown*, 187–91; J. Denton, 'Walter Reynolds and ecclesiastical politics, 1313–1316', in *Church and Government in the Middle Ages*, ed. C. Brooke et al. (Cambridge, 1976), 262–9; *SR*, i, 171–4, 175–6; *CPR, 1313–17*, 607. This is a greatly simplified account of a very complex set of problems. See also J.H. Denton, 'The making of the "Articuli Cleri" of 1316', *EHR*, ci (1986), 564–95. The clerical *gravamina* presented at Lincoln, together with the royal responses, are printed in Denton, 'Walter Reynolds', 590–5.

[183] *PROME*, Parliament of Jan. 1316, SC 9/19, items 1–19 (this business was still unsettled in 1318). Hugh de Courtenay was the cousin and heir of Isabella who had died as long ago as 1293, leaving a claim to the earldom of Devon which Courtenay finally obtained in 1335.

[184] *PROME*, Parliament of Jan. 1316, SC 9/20, items 11–12. See the article on John Charlton by J.F.A. Mason in *Oxford DNB*, and Maddicott, 140–1, 143–5, 184.

[185] *PROME*, Parliament of Jan. 1316, SC 9/20, item 14.

[186] *PROME*, Parliament of Jan. 1316, SC 9/20, items 7, 9–10; Phillips, 243.

Burgh, the son of the earl of Ulster. The immediate question had been whether Gilbert de Clare's widow was pregnant or not. It was apparent long before January 1316 that she had not been, leaving Gilbert's three sisters as his joint heirs. Hugh Despenser the Younger had been quick off the mark and at some point in 1315 had appeared first in chancery at Westminster and then before the council to ask for his wife's share of the Clare lands. He had been told to raise the matter at the next parliament, and this he duly did at Lincoln in February 1316. A further question was who would marry the remaining Clare heiresses and each scoop a third share of the jackpot. This was of course a political and patronage problem of the highest order and one which Edward II and his council were eager to postpone for as long as possible, knowing that whatever the solution it would cause trouble. On 4 February a leading Anglo-Irish magnate, Theobald de Verdun, seized his opportunity and married Elizabeth de Clare near Bristol castle where she was then living, against the king's wishes and greatly to his annoyance. For his pains Theobald was summoned before the council to explain himself and claimed that he and Elizabeth had been betrothed in Ireland. Theobald did not however live to profit by his act of defiance, dying the following July.[187] In the meantime, although the king and his council could not bring themselves to answer Despenser's claim and delayed a decision on technicalities, the issue could not be postponed indefinitely and would come back to haunt the king and poison English politics.

Despenser was undoubtedly disappointed and this may help to explain an extraordinary incident which occurred during the Lincoln parliament. This was Despenser's attack on John de Roos after the latter allegedly tried to arrest one of his knights, Ingelram Berenger. The attack took place in Lincoln cathedral on Sunday, 22 February in the presence of the king and the prelates and magnates assembled in parliament. The reasons for the animosity between Despenser and Roos are obscure but the incident was an ominous foretaste of the power which Despenser craved and which he was soon to wield.[188]

---

[187] *PROME*, Parliament of Jan. 1316, SC 9/20, item 7; BL, Cotton Ms. Faustina B VI, f. 80; Phillips, 'Mission', 71, 83. Edward II did not let his niece escape his control again. The draft of a royal letter dated 12 Sept. 1316 shows that Elizabeth was under considerable pressure to marry as she was told: SC 1/63/150; Phillips, 132. In Feb. 1317 Elizabeth, who was pregnant at the time of Theobald's death, gave birth to a daughter, Isabella, who was baptized at Amesbury priory in Wiltshire; Edward's sister Mary and Queen Isabella were godmothers: F. A. Underhill, *For her Good Estate* (Basingstoke, 1999), 16–18.

[188] *PROME*, Parliament of Jan. 1316, SC 9/20, items 5, 6. Despenser was pardoned for his offence at the York parliament of Jan. 1320 and the record was cancelled in the Parliament Roll for 1316, SC 9/20. By 1320 Despenser had become, along with his father, one of the most powerful and most hated men in England. John de Roos is probably to be identified with the follower of Henry of Lancaster who became steward of the royal household in Feb. 1327 after Edward II's deposition, so the brawl in Lincoln cathedral could have been connected with the strained relations between Thomas of Lancaster and the king. Another possible explanation is the recent marriage between John de Roos and Margaret Goushill, widow of Despenser's younger brother Philip, who had died in 1313.

WALES

The apparently 'final' conquest of Wales by Edward I in 1282–3 had been followed by revolts in 1287 and especially in 1294–5. As Rees Davies has so eloquently put it, 'the conquest of Wales left a deep legacy of despair and bitterness among Welshmen'.[189] Although the despair and bitterness had dimmed with the passage of time and with the often successful attempts by Edward I and by his son, both as Prince of Wales and as king, to build bridges towards the Welsh community,[190] 'grievances there remained in abundance . . . Wales was still politically volatile. Indeed in 1315–17 the country seemed once more to be on the brink of revolt.'[191] In Glamorgan, for example, a revolt had already broken out in 1314–15 shortly after the lordship was taken into royal hands following Gilbert de Clare's death at Bannockburn.[192] The Scottish invasion of Ireland in the summer of 1315 raised fears that if Edward Bruce succeeded there 'he would at once cross to Wales, and raise the Welsh likewise against our king. For these two races are easily roused to rebellion; they bear the yoke of slavery reluctantly, and curse the lordship of the English.'[193] A letter probably written in the autumn of 1315 indicates that Edward II and his government were acutely aware of the dangers in Wales and were taking urgent measures to prevent trouble. Edward was concerned that the Scots might land in Anglesey or elsewhere in North Wales. He also wanted his officials to provide for the safekeeping of the area 'without stirring the Welsh' and to 'do all in their power to persuade the Welsh to agree to send some of their children and others of their kindred to the king, to be of his company, for the king has long desired it'. 'On the other hand, if they see that the Welsh are inclined to misbehave because of hardship and duress done to them concerning their inheritances and their franchises or in other ways, let them freely promise on the lord's behalf that the matter will be speedily and thoroughly redressed'. In a significant concluding remark, the king's officials were instructed to consult with Sir Gruffydd Llwyd, one of the most influential of Edward II's Welsh supporters.[194]

---

[189] Davies, *Conquest*, 379.

[190] See the discussion in ch. 3 of this book of Edward II's creation as Prince of Wales in 1301 and of his own relations with Wales and the Welsh.

[191] Davies, *Conquest*, 386–7. In a letter to the pope in May 1317, recommending Thomas Charlton as bishop of Hereford, a diocese which lay on the borders of Wales, Edward spoke of his desire to avoid the 'dangers which arose from the accustomed rebellion of the Welsh against himself and his kingdom' (*desiderantes obviae pericula que ex rebellione consueta Wallensium nobis et regno nostro*): C 70/3, m.1. The hardships caused by the severe weather and the famine that followed in its wake made the situation even more volatile.

[192] J. B. Smith, 'The rebellion of Llywelyn Bren', in *Glamorgan County History*, iii, *The Middle Ages*, ed. T.B. Pugh (Cardiff, 1971), 72–4.

[193] *Vita*, 106–7.

[194] SC 1/55, 31: ed. and trans. in *Calendar of Ancient Correspondence concerning Wales*, ed. J.G. Edwards, 2 (Cardiff, 1935), 253–4. The letter bears no address but is clearly from one royal official to another; the editor dates it as probably late July 1315 but Beverley Smith's

Gruffydd Llwyd, another Welsh knight Morgan ap Meredudd, and the bishop of Bangor visited Edward II at Clipstone in early December to discuss the situation in Wales; orders were also given to put the royal castles in North Wales into a state of defence;[195] and during the Lincoln parliament, on 7 February 1316, Edward made a number of concessions to the communities of North, South and West Wales, in answer to the grievances they had expressed in their petitions. Edward also ordered that the ordinances he had issued at Kennington in 1305, when he was Prince of Wales, should be fully observed.[196]

This prompt and energetic response on the part of the king and his council was all the more necessary since they had no recent news of events in Ireland. Details of the battle of Ardscull, fought on 26 January, the day before the opening of the Lincoln parliament, were not received by Edward until 26 February.[197] For all anyone in England knew, the Scots might have won further victories and even taken Dublin. The unsuccessful Scottish attack on Berwick in early January was another sign of just how serious the military situation might become.

Revolt in North Wales was prevented but in Glamorgan the unrest that had existed since the summer of 1314 broke out once more in early 1316 under the leadership of Llywelyn Bren, the grandson of the former lord of Senghenydd who had been dispossessed by the earl of Gloucester in 1266.[198] The royal government had been aware since early December that tensions were rising in Glamorgan and had taken precautions against possible trouble. On 28 January Llywelyn attacked the great castle of Caerphilly, capturing the constable while he was holding a court outside the walls, but failing to take the castle itself. Llantrisant castle was seized and a great deal of damage done elsewhere in the lordship of Glamorgan.[199]

On 6 February the king began his response. William de Montacute and Hugh Audley were appointed to lead a force of men-at-arms into Glamorgan; five days later the earl of Hereford, who was also lord of Brecon, was put in overall command, and was later joined by other marcher lords, including Roger Mortimer of Wigmore, newly arrived

---

suggested date of Oct. is more likely: Smith, 'Gruffydd Llwyd', 464–5; cf. *CCR, 1313–18*, 253. Thirty-three Welsh hostages from North Wales were held in Chester castle from 29 Aug. 1315 until 18 Oct. 1317: E 368/89, m.190.

[195] E 101/376/7, ff. 41, 11v; *CCR, 1313–18*, 267.

[196] *CPR, 1313–17*, 433–4; *Foedera*, II, i, 283–4. The petitions are dated and printed in *Calendar of Ancient Petitions relating to Wales*, ed. Rees, 28–9 (from SC 8/4/187).

[197] *CCW*, 435; Phillips, 'Documents', 250. Hothum's report on the battle was dated 15 Feb.: ibid., 251–3.

[198] For an account of this revolt see Smith, 'Rebellion', 72–86; and R.A. Griffiths, 'The revolt of Llywelyn Bren', *Glamorgan Historian*, ii (1965), 186–96. The author of the *Vita Edwardi Secundi* devoted considerable attention to the revolt: *Vita*, 114–21.

[199] Smith, 'Rebellion', 74–5, 78–9. Ironically, Llantrisant was the castle for which Edward II was heading in Nov. 1326 when he was captured by his enemies.

back from Ireland. The campaign was soon over. On 18 March Llywelyn surrendered and was afterwards sent to the Tower of London, together with his wife and sons. It had taken a force of 150 men-at-arms and 2,000 foot soldiers to suppress the rising, a considerable diversion of resources and of money at a time when these were in short supply.[200]

There is no reason to think that Edward Bruce was in any way connected with the revolt in Glamorgan,[201] and indeed the English government's fears of a Scottish intervention in Wales in 1315–16 were probably much exaggerated. However, in an ironic postscript, there were some contacts during the winter of 1316–17 between Edward Bruce and Gruffydd Llwyd. Some correspondence appears to have passed between them suggesting treasonable intent by Gruffydd.[202] As a result he was arrested in December 1316 and held at Rhuddlan, before being taken to meet the king at Clarendon and then in April 1317 transferred to the Tower of London. The imprisonment seemingly did not last long and Gruffydd later resumed his loyal service of the crown.[203] Wales had not in the event turned against Edward II during the crucial period of the Scottish campaigns in Ireland, while Edward and his government had dealt with Welsh grievances and averted any general revolt.[204]

THE SIEGE OF BRISTOL

While the revolt of Llywelyn Bren was being suppressed, just across the water from Glamorgan another crisis was reaching its climax in the important port town of Bristol. Since 1313 a dispute had been in progress between the people of Bristol and Bartholomew de Badlesmere, the royal constable and warden of the castle and town.[205] Attempts to resolve it in 1315 and at the Lincoln parliament at the beginning of 1316 were unsuccessful.[206] On 13 June the sheriff of Gloucestershire entered Bristol but was

---

[200] Ibid., 79–83, 86.

[201] McNamee, 194; Davies, *Conquest*, 388.

[202] The correspondence, known only from a seventeenth-century source, is discussed and printed in Smith, 'Gruffydd Llwyd', 466–74, 477–8. It is possible, as Smith suggests, that Gruffydd's behaviour was a protest against the oppressive actions of the justice of Wales, Roger Mortimer of Chirk, rather than opposition to the crown; other possibilities are that he was acting as an agent of the crown in replying to Bruce's initial letter and that the plan went wrong, or that 'a reply to Bruce's approaches was fathered upon Gruffydd Llwyd by adversaries bent on discrediting him': ibid., 274–5.

[203] SAL Ms. 120, f. 20v; Smith, 'Gruffydd Llwyd', 466–8; Davies, *Conquest*, 387–8. He was back in royal service by late 1318.

[204] Davies, *Conquest*, 387.

[205] The dispute was a complicated one but a central issue was the reluctance of Bristol to pay the tallage imposed on towns and cities by Edward II at the end of 1312. On the subject of tallage and the history of the Bristol dispute see J.H. Hadwin, 'The last royal tallages', *EHR*, xcvi (1981), 344–58; E.A. Fuller, 'The tallage of 6 Edward II and the Bristol rebellion', *Transactions of the Bristol and Gloucester Archaeological Society*, xix (1894–5), 171–278.

[206] See *PROME*, Parliament of Jan. 1316, SC 9/20, item 14.

prevented from arresting six of the townspeople who had been outlawed because of their defiance of royal authority. When the sheriff returned to carry out the arrests he found the town fortified against him. On 20 June the earl of Pembroke, William Inge one of the royal judges, and others were appointed to inquire into these events and authorized to punish the community if they refused to return to their allegiance to the king.[207] By 7 July Pembroke, Badlesmere and one of Pembroke's retainers, Maurice de Berkeley, the lord of the nearby Berkeley castle, had reached Keynsham close to Bristol. The people of Bristol again defied royal orders, believing wrongly that because the king was planning a campaign in the north against the Scots he would have to withdraw. Instead Pembroke ordered the town to be placed under siege, after which he and Badlesmere returned to London to report to the king. On about 19 July Badlesmere returned to Bristol with William de Montacute and, with the aid of Roger Mortimer of Wigmore and Maurice de Berkeley, began the siege, which ended with the town's surrender on 26 July.[208] In December Bristol was pardoned by the king and its liberties restored. The final outcome was therefore satisfactory for the crown, but it was yet another diversion of energy and resources at a critical time.

LANCASTER IN AND OUT OF GOVERNMENT

In the weeks following his appointment on 24 February 1316 as the head of the king's council Lancaster appears to have been playing an active part in the government of the kingdom. He was being consulted as early as 26 February when John de Hothum's report on events in Ireland and other material relating to Ireland and Scotland was passed to him for comment. Lancaster had not however begun his duties with the council by that date,[209] nor had he done so by 3 March when the king forwarded letters dealing with the situation at Berwick to Pembroke, the archbishop of Canterbury and the chancellor and treasurer.[210] On 6 March Lancaster was at Kenilworth and cannot be traced with the council in London until 14 March, when he was in the company of the archbishop, the bishop of Chichester, the earls of Pembroke and Richmond, and Bartholomew de Badlesmere.[211] On 15 March the king sent two letters from the constable of France to Lancaster, the archbishop and other members of the council

---

[207] *CPR, 1313–17*, 489–90; *CFR, 1307–19*, 286.
[208] SAL Ms. 120, f. 19; *CCR, 1313–18*, 347, 424; *Vita*, 122–7; Fuller, 'Tallage', 188; Phillips, 103; Maddicott, 184–5.
[209] Phillips, 'Documents', 250–65; Phillips, 96. Lancaster was sent the originals of all these documents while the transcripts, now preserved as C 81/93/3594 and edited in Phillips, 'Documents', were sent to the chancellor and treasurer to be put before the council.
[210] C 81/94/3604; Phillips, 'Documents', 265; Phillips, 96.
[211] C 53/102, m.6; *Liber Albus of Worcester Priory*, ed. J.M. Wilson, Worcestershire Historical Society (London, 1919), 46; Phillips, 96.

in London, and further letters were sent to them on 17 and 19 March.[212] On 23 March Lancaster, the chancellor and treasurer and other unnamed members of the council were in session at St Paul's, London.[213] Shortly afterwards Lancaster left London and on 30 and 31 March he and one of his leading retainers, Sir Robert de Holland, were at Langley to report on the work of the council, which had remained in London.[214] After leaving the king, Lancaster moved to his castle at Kenilworth, which he had reached by 8 April, perhaps intending to spend Easter there. There is however no evidence that he rejoined the council after Easter or at any other time in the following months, and by 28 April he had moved on again to Castle Donington in Leicestershire.[215] Ironically, on this same date Lancaster, Robert de Holland, the earl of Pembroke and Badlesmere were authorized to give safe conducts in the king's name to Robert Bruce himself or to other Scottish envoys who were coming to England to discuss a truce or even peace. The meeting was to take place at Leicester, one of Lancaster's own possessions. Yet on the same day the order was cancelled and reissued in the names of two royal clerks and a royal knight.[216] Had Lancaster therefore withdrawn from the council and from an active part in the royal government by the end of April 1316, only two months after his appointment as head of the council?

At some point he did withdraw. In a letter written over a year later, in July 1317, Lancaster claimed that he had done so because Edward had failed to observe the Ordinances, refused to accept the reform proposals drawn up in London by himself and the reform commission established at the Lincoln parliament in January 1316, and had surrounded himself with new favourites.[217] There is however no *prima facie* evidence to support these claims in relation to the events of 1316. There are on the other hand clear indications during Lancaster's association with the council of attempts to enforce the Ordinances. Between 6 March and 12 April orders were given for the sheriffs to publish the Ordinances as often as was necessary, for the resumption of grants that had been made contrary to them, for the prohibition of illegal prises, and for the payment into the exchequer of the entire receipts of the customs.[218] The proposals made to the king by the reform commission at this time are unknown but there is nothing to suggest any abrupt rejection of them, and indeed on 17 March Edward went so far as to express his complete trust in the council and to ask them

---

[212] SC 1/34/156, 157; SC 1/35/126; SC 1/45, 190, 191; Phillips, 96.
[213] *Calendar of the Letter-Books of the City of London: E*, ed. R.R. Sharpe (London, 1900–3), 59–60; Phillips, 96–7.
[214] *CCW*, 440; *CPR, 1313–17*, 476; Phillips, 97.
[215] DL 25/1652; *Liber Albus of Worcester Priory*, 46; Phillips, 97.
[216] *CPR, 1313–17*, 450–1; Maddicott, 183. There is no mention of such contacts in Barrow, and no negotiations are known to have occurred.
[217] *Murimuth*, 271–4; *Gesta Edwardi*, 50–2; Phillips, 97, 121; Maddicott, 182.
[218] *CCR, 1313–18*, 328; *CFR, 1307–19*, 275–7; Phillips, 97.

to continue their work as they had begun.[219] There is no evidence that any new royal favourites were yet conspicuous, unless the ambitions of Hugh Despenser the Younger were causing more disturbance than is shown in the records. It is possible that Lancaster fell out with the king when he visited him at Langley in early April, but if so the records are again silent.

Even if there were some truth in the charges in relation to the spring of 1316, it is more likely that in making the charges over a year later Lancaster was attempting to rationalize his withdrawal in 1316 in the light of more recent events. The underlying hatred and lack of trust between Edward and Lancaster were no doubt part of the explanation, even if there was no spectacular breach between them. But so too was Lancaster's lack of capacity for the role he had undertaken at Lincoln. He had little administrative experience, one contemporary writer noting his habit of leaving even his own affairs in the hands of others.[220] It is likely that he also lacked the ability necessary to act as head of the council and to deal with the complexities of government. It was easier to demand reform of the government while on the outside than to bring it about when in office, even assuming that the king and the other members of the council were wholeheartedly in favour. Lancaster's insistence on the implementation of the Ordinances was little more than a mantra, betraying his lack of any original ideas of his own. The Ordinances had not been a solution to the problems of government when they were first published in 1311, and they were not a solution in 1316. The continuing pressure from the Scots in the north of England and in Ireland, the shortage of money, and the effects both on the government and on the population at large of the bad weather and the resulting hardships indicate the scale of the real burden which Lancaster had naively undertaken to shoulder. It is also very probable that Lancaster found difficulty in his relations with his fellow councillors. As in 1315, he had few if any friends or allies on the council. Lancaster probably also misunderstood his role as head of the council, seeing himself in modern terms as a chief executive officer rather than as chairman of the board. Frustration at his incapacity and poor relations with his colleagues may therefore have caused Lancaster's departure from the council and made him, once he had departed, disinclined to return. It is likely that initially at least neither Edward II nor even Lancaster himself realized that the withdrawal would be final. Fortunately for Lancaster, the condition made at the time of his appointment, which allowed for his possible withdrawal, permitted him to go with some dignity.[221]

[219] SC 1/45/190; Phillips, 97. Although expressions of trust were often formalities, there is no indication of an impending crisis at this time.

[220] *Polychronicon*, 312–15.

[221] Phillips, 96–7. Dr Maddicott agrees that Lancaster withdrew from the court in the spring of 1316 but explains it more in terms of the failure of Edward II to govern effectively than of any inadequacies in Lancaster himself. He also suggests that the final breach between Edward and Lancaster did not occur until July 1316. The essential point is that Lancaster was clearly no longer acting as head of the council from the previous April: Maddicott, 186–7.

EDWARD

In the midst of all the intense politicking and the stresses of warfare, weather and financial problems, it is easy to lose sight of Edward II himself. It was a very bad time for him personally. The burial of his friend and 'brother' Piers Gaveston in January 1315 may have brought closure of a kind but cannot have done much to alleviate the pain Edward had suffered from Gaveston's death or to relieve the humiliation he had experienced at Bannockburn. In early May 1316 he also suffered the loss of his sister Elizabeth, the widowed countess of Holland and currently the wife of the earl of Hereford. Elizabeth and Edward were close in age and also close friends.[222]

Even social events in his life came close to disaster. When he gave a great feast in Westminster Hall, on 20 April 1315, marking the end of parliament and attended by the archbishop of Canterbury and many earls and barons, the hall caught fire.[223] In September 1315, while he was apparently on holiday at Fen Ditton near Cambridge and engaged in rowing, one of his favourite leisure pastimes, Edward had a narrow escape from drowning.[224]

It is probably no coincidence that this low point is the period in which several examples of personal criticism of Edward are recorded. In July 1314, the month after Bannockburn, Robert de Newington in Kent, a messenger in the royal household, remarked that Edward could not be expected to win battles if he spent the time when he should have been hearing mass in 'idling and applying himself to making ditches and digging and other improper occupations'.[225] During the parliament of January 1315 a London goldsmith, John Bonaventure, complained that he had been imprisoned by the marshals of the king's household on an accusation by John of Lincoln of having said 'certain evil and shameful things about the king'.[226] In 1316 a clerk named Thomas de Tynwelle was accused of saying publicly in the park of north Oxford on 19 December 1315 that Edward II was not his father's son. It is not clear whether Thomas meant this to be

---

[222] Elizabeth was born at Rhuddlan in Aug. 1282. On New Year's Day 1316 Edward had given her two items of jewellery worth 17 marks and £30. Gifts were also received by her husband the earl of Hereford and by Gaveston's widow the countess of Cornwall and her sister Eleanor de Clare, the wife of Hugh Despenser the Younger: E 101/376/7, f. 99.

[223] The fire occurred 'at about the ninth hour'. Fortunately the damage does not appear to have been serious: *Ann. Paul.*, 279; *KW*, i, 527. There is no reference to the cost of repairs in the account of the clerk of works for the following year.

[224] *Flores*, 173.

[225] Johnstone, 'The eccentricities of Edward II', 264–7, citing the Memoranda Roll for 1315–16, E 368/86, m.32d. A modern observer might have commented that Edward should have been training for war rather than saying his prayers!

[226] *de rege sinistra aliqua et inhonesta dixisse in contemptu regis*: *PROME*, Parliament of Jan. 1315, SC 9/18, item 145. There is no more detail and the charges were probably used by John of Lincoln to try to blacken the name of his opponent, John of Bonaventure. In any event the latter was found not guilty of any offence against the king. This is part of a series of petitions by Bonaventure against John of Lincoln and his sons concerning events in London and within the palace of Westminster: *PROME*, Parliament of Jan. 1315, SC 9/18, items 140–6. Bonaventure

taken literally or whether he was in effect remarking that Edward II 'was not the man his father was', which was after all a common opinion.[227] In late December 1314, the chancellor of Oxford University, Master Henry Harclay, preached a sermon to commemorate the murder in December 1170 of Archbishop Thomas Becket at the hands of Henry II's knights and implied that final punishment for Becket's death might be visited upon the fourth generation, apparently referring to Edward II.[228] Another ecclesiastical protest, this time in the form of a letter addressed by 'a certain regular of admitted authority' to the king's confessor, is recorded by the author of the *Vita Edwardi Secundi* under the year 1316:

> Since a king is so styled from the fact of ruling, as one who should rule his people with laws, and defend them with his sword from their enemies, he is fittingly called king while he rules well; but when he despoils his people he is rather adjudged to be a tyrant. Indeed our king, passing through the country, takes men's goods and pays little or nothing or badly. In fact, those to whom something is owed from such a cause, in order to save trouble, often make an agreement to remit a percentage, so that the balance may be paid more quickly. Formerly, indeed, the inhabitants rejoiced to see the face of the king when he came, but now, because the people are injured by the king's arrival, they look forward greatly to his departure and as he leaves they pray that he may never return. The king, moreover too often [visits] religious houses ...[229]

---

had a shady past, having been one of a number of London goldsmiths who in 1303 had handled items of royal treasure stolen from the crypt of Westminster Abbey: Doherty, *Great Crown Jewels Robbery*, 126–7.

[227] Memoranda Roll, 9 Edward II, E 368/86, m.94. The episode was first noted by Johnstone in *Edward of Carnarvon*, 130, where it is taken literally. There may have been some grudge at the back of the story, possibility a town/gown dispute. Some of Thomas's accusers seem to have been local tradesmen from Oxford, but some of those in whose presence he made the remarks were from other parts of England and were possibly students at university, as Thomas de Tynwell may himself have been. After a number of hearings in 1316 Thomas was eventually acquitted.

[228] Kemp (the bishop of Chichester), 'History and action', 349–53.

Although Edward II had been on bad terms with Archbishop Robert Winchelsey until the latter's death in 1313, there had never been any question of a violent resolution as in 1170. It is likely that Harclay was more concerned with the controversial appointment by the pope in Oct. 1313 of Walter Reynolds, the royal chancellor and an ally of Edward since he had been Prince of Wales, in place of the renowned scholar, Thomas Cobham, who had been the choice of the monks of Canterbury. Harclay was also an opponent of the privileges exercised in the university by the Dominicans who were favoured by Edward II: Wright, *The Church and the English Crown*, 5, 243–6.

[229] *Vita*, 128–31. The text breaks off at this point. There is nothing to indicate the identity of the 'regular' (i.e. a member of a religious order), but since the king's confessor was always a Dominican friar and had an easy and intimate access to the king, it is worth speculating that the 'regular' was a member of the same order. The letter refers to issues such as the purveyance of goods for the king's household which had been a source of political tension since the time of Edward I.

The one moment of unalloyed joy for Edward during this dismal period was the birth at Eltham on 15 August 1316 of his and Isabella's second child, a boy who was named John. It is likely that he had been conceived during Edward II's long stay at Clipstone in Nottinghamshire at the end of 1315.[230] Lancaster was invited to attend the christening but did not do so.[231] It was yet another indication of the newly embittered state of English politics.

[230] Isabella is known to have been at Clipstone at this time: E 101/376/20, f. 1; Doherty (D.Phil.), 62.
[231] SAL Ms. 120, f. 15.

Chapter 7

PEACE BY ORDEAL, AUGUST 1316 TO AUGUST 1318

AFTER LANCASTER

With Lancaster's withdrawal from the council there now began a new period of political instability. As co-operation between Edward II and Lancaster became increasingly difficult to achieve and hostility between the two men grew, so it also became impossible for over two years, between February 1316 and October 1318, to hold a parliament or to conduct a campaign against the Scots. The instability did not end until a new 'settlement' between Edward II and Lancaster was reached in the Treaty of Leake of August 1318. Lancaster's departure meant of necessity that important actions took place without reference to him. Discussion by the council in May 1316 of the scale of rewards to be given to John Fitz Thomas and other Anglo-Irish magnates in return for their loyalty against the Scots was one such;[1] the siege of Bristol in July 1316 was another. So too was the election on 26 July of Edward II's chancellor, John Sandal, as the new bishop of the important diocese of Winchester.[2]

However, a Scottish campaign was due, the army having been summoned during the Lincoln parliament to meet at Newcastle on 8 July,[3] and if the campaign were to succeed Lancaster would have to play some part.[4] The start of the campaign had already been postponed in May until 10 August, partly because of the distraction caused by Bristol but also because of difficulties in raising the manpower and the taxation which had been promised at Lincoln,[5] but on 20 August it was further postponed

---

[1] C 49/ File 4, no.19; Phillips, 'Documents', 268–9.

[2] Phillips, 103. The earl of Pembroke, acting on the king's behalf, ensured that the monks of Winchester exercised their freedom of election in the desired way: SC 1/49/ 35, 36.

[3] *CCR, 1313–18*, 322.

[4] Lancaster was still formally in overall charge of the defences of the north, as he had been since Aug. 1315: Maddicott, 188.

[5] Commissions for the assessment and collection of the fifteenth granted at Lincoln were issued on 8 June 1316, but no attempt was yet made to levy the tax, because the reforms promised by the king in exchange for these grants and the selection of armed men had been delayed. On 25 June an assembly of knights was summoned to meet at Lincoln on 29 July, and at this assembly, on or before 5 Aug., a grant of a sixteenth was substituted for the earlier grant of foot soldiers. Commissions for the assessment and collection of this sixteenth were issued on 5 Aug., significantly on the same day that concessions made by the king concerning the forest were enacted. The tax was to be paid in two halves, one on

until 6 October.⁶ This decision was made at York after discussions between the king, the bishops of Durham and Carlisle who both had a personal interest in the defence of the north, and the earls of Hereford and Surrey and others. Significantly, Lancaster was present at York and presumably was involved in the discussions.⁷ The pardon issued on 10 October at Lancaster's request to his retainer, Gruffudd de la Pole, for his offences against the royal chamberlain, John Charlton, was an indication that a serious effort was still being made to keep Lancaster happy.⁸

THE DURHAM ELECTION

For a fleeting moment there was now a chance of a much-needed campaign against the Scots, whose attacks on northern England were resumed around midsummer 1316. Raids were made into the bishopric of Durham and into Yorkshire and, for the first time, into Lancashire.⁹ The situation on the English side changed dramatically however with the death on 9 October of Richard Kellaw, the bishop of Durham. As well as being a very wealthy diocese in normal times, Durham was of great strategic importance because of its location close to the border with Scotland. Again, under normal conditions, the rights of election of a new bishop belonged to the monks of Durham. But these were far from normal times and the election was to be hotly contested.¹⁰ On 19 October two monks came to the king at Crayke in Yorkshire to ask for royal licence to elect a new bishop. Licence was duly given, but the king and queen each had their own ideas about the new bishop. Edward wanted the election of Thomas Charlton, keeper of the privy seal since the previous July and brother of his chamberlain John Charlton. Isabella wanted Louis de Beaumont, the brother of Henry de Beaumont, whose removal from court had been sought unsuccessfully by the Ordainers in 1311 and who was deeply detested by Lancaster. Lancaster too had his own candidate, John de Kinardesey, one of his own clerks.¹¹ If Kinardesey were elected, Lancaster

---

3 Nov. 1316, the other on 25 Apr. 1317: *Lay Taxes*, 33; Maddicott, 182, 185; *PW*, II, ii, 158–9, 161–3, 166–7, 464.

⁶ *Foedera*, II, i, 295–6; Maddicott, 186.

⁷ SAL Ms. 120, f. 14; C 53/103, mm.20, 21; Phillips, 104; Maddicott, 187.

⁸ SAL Ms. 120, f. 14; *CPR, 1313–17*, 548; Phillips, 104. The fact that Edward granted the pardon with the advice of four of his most influential and trusted advisers, the earls of Pembroke and Hereford, Bartholomew de Badlesmere and Antonio Pessagno, shows how important this concession was.

⁹ McNamee, 81–4, including map on 83. Although there is no documentary evidence of one, there may have been an informal truce lasting until this time. The Scots had also been heavily engaged in Ireland earlier in the year: McNamee, 81.

¹⁰ For a contemporary account see *Registrum Palatinum Dunelmense*, ed. T. Duffus Hardy, ii, Rolls ser. (London, 1873), 834, 1124, 1310; *Historiae Dunelmensis Scriptores Tres*, ed. J. Raine, Surtees Soc., ix (Edinburgh, 1839), 97–9; Phillips, 105.

¹¹ Maddicott, 204.

could expect a substantial increase in his influence over the north of England.[12] To complicate matters still further, the earl of Hereford supported yet another candidate, John Walwayn. The earl of Pembroke was summoned to see the king at Crayke on 17 or 18 October and was instructed to make sure that either Charlton or Beaumont was elected.[13] But Durham proved to be a far harder problem than John Sandal's appointment to Winchester had been, and by 28 October Pembroke and the other interested parties, Lancaster and Hereford, were at Newcastle, *en route* for Durham.[14] The election took place on 6 November and its result was awaited in the cathedral by Pembroke and several of his retainers, by Lancaster and his leading retainer Robert de Holland, and also by Henry de Beaumont, who was there to advance his brother's candidature on behalf of the queen. Despite the pressure, the monks courageously elected someone of their own choice, Henry de Stamford prior of Finchale near Durham, as the new bishop. Edward II was prepared to accept him, but Isabella was still determined on Beaumont's appointment.[15] In December the pope duly quashed Stamford's election and had provided Beaumont to the see by February 1317.[16]

EDWARD, ISABELLA AND LANCASTER

An open breach now existed between Lancaster and both Isabella and Edward. Isabella's long association with the Beaumonts and the hatred between them and Lancaster had received a powerful new emphasis, which was to have serious consequences in the following year when time came for the new bishop to be consecrated at Durham. Isabella may also have thought that Lancaster had been primarily responsible for the greatly reduced financial support for herself and her household during his years of influence.[17] Edward's own relations with Lancaster were aptly and acutely summed up by the author of the *Vita Edwardi Secundi*:

---

[12] Lancaster had also been building a powerful new castle at Dunstanburgh on the coast of Northumberland since 1313, initially at least without royal licence: ibid., 24–5, 171.

[13] C 81/1706/37; SC 1/49/37.

[14] SAL Ms. 120, f. 72; *Hist. Dunelm. Script. Tres*, App., doc. 95.

[15] *Hist. Dunelm. Script. Tres*, 98–9; Phillips, 105, n. 4; Maddicott, 204.

[16] SC 7/56/5; *Fasti Ecclesiae Anglicanae, 1300–1541*, vi, *Northern Province*, ed. B. Jones (London, 1963), 107. See also the biography of Beaumont by C.M. Fraser in *Oxford DNB*. Edward wrote to the pope on 23 Nov. describing Beaumont as better qualified to defend Durham against the Scots than Stamford: *Foedera*, II, I, 302.

[17] Doherty (D.Phil.), 59–61. It is significant that on 1 Dec. 1316, with the approval of his council, Edward granted Isabella 11,000 marks a year for the expenses of her household; the value of the queen's lands in England was however included in this figure so that the actual amounts she received from the exchequer between then and the summer of 1318 were considerably less: E 403/180, m.7; E 403/181, m.2; E 403/182, m.2; E 403/184, m.12. In March 1318 Isabella was granted permanent dower land to provide her with an income of £4,500: *CPR, 1317–21*, 115–16.

'Whatever pleases the lord king the earl's servants try to upset; and whatever pleases the earl the king's servants call treachery; and so at the prompting of the Devil the followers of each interfere, and do not allow their lords, by whom the land ought to be defended, to come to an agreement.' For his part Lancaster feared 'that the king, mindful of the wrong that the earl did to Piers [Gaveston], is waiting for revenge when he sees the opportunity'. It was also rumoured that whenever the Scots raided the north of England they left Lancaster's estates untouched and that he was secretly in league with Robert Bruce.[18]

NEW DIRECTIONS

With Lancaster's failure to secure his own candidate's election, all hope that he might co-operate in a fresh Scottish campaign vanished. The start of the campaign had already been delayed for a month by the Durham election; it was now abandoned entirely and new arrangements were made for the defence of the north, Wales and Ireland against the Scots. On 19 November the earl of Arundel was appointed as warden of the Scottish March, replacing Lancaster who had nominally held a similar post since the summer of 1315; royal castles in the north were also to be well garrisoned, with the apparent intention of creating a strong line of defence to make up for the English inability to go over to the offensive and fight on Scottish territory. On 23 November Roger Mortimer of Wigmore was appointed to go to Ireland as king's lieutenant and his uncle Roger Mortimer of Chirk was reappointed as justice of North Wales.[19] The following day English envoys were commissioned to seek a truce with the Scots.[20] These new measures were designed to hold the line against the Scots and it remained to be seen whether they would be effective. However, the withdrawal of Lancaster from any pretence of co-operation with the king also meant that for the moment at least Edward II and his government had greater freedom of action than they had possessed at any time since Bannockburn. This made it possible, for example, for Edward

---

[18] *Vita*, 130–1. Other chroniclers also emphasized the distrust between Edward and Lancaster: *Flores*, 341; *Lanercost*, 233; Maddicott, 188. There is no evidence to support the rumours of Lancaster's complicity with the Scots in 1316, but they were to be powerfully renewed in 1319 at the time of Edward II's unsuccessful siege of Berwick and again during the civil war of 1321–2.

[19] E 101/68/2/37; SAL Ms. 120, ff. 44–6; *CPR, 1313–17*, 563; *CFR, 1307–19*, 312; Phillips, 106; Maddicott, 188. For the details of the defensive measures on the Scottish border see McNamee, 149–51. On 4 Jan. 1317, 16 English magnates with lands in Ireland were ordered to go there to assist in their defence against the Scots: *Foedera*, II, i, 309; Phillips, 'Anglo-Norman nobility', in *The English in Medieval Ireland*, ed. J.F. Lydon (Dublin, 1984), 98–9.

[20] E 101/68/2/36; *Foedera*, II, i, 302; *CCR, 1313–18*, 472. The decision was taken with the advice of the earl of Pembroke, Antonio Pessagno and William de Montacute (one of a number of royal knights whose influence was now growing). One of the envoys was John d'Eure, the constable of Pembroke's castle of Mitford in Northumberland: Phillips, 106.

to decide in early December that it was time to proceed with the long-delayed partition of the Gloucester lands.[21] Edward also decided to take advantage of the recent election of a new pope, John XXII, by sending a high-ranking embassy to Avignon to deal with a number of other urgent issues.[22]

THE MISSION TO AVIGNON

The decision to send an embassy was taken at York on 24 November,[23] after which Edward spent the months of December and the first half of January at Scrooby, Clipstone and Nottingham. From these places he kept in frequent contact with his council in London where the detailed planning of the mission was carried out.[24] The embassy, as it finally developed, had three main objectives: firstly to negotiate more favourable terms for the repayment of the loan of 160,000 florins made to Edward II by Clement V in 1314 and so to regain control of the revenues of the duchy of Aquitaine; secondly to persuade the pope to allow a delay in Edward II's fulfilment of the crusading oath he had taken in 1313 and, if possible, to obtain a grant of clerical taxation, nominally in aid of the crusade when it finally took place; and thirdly to obtain papal support against the Scots. The author of the *Vita Edwardi Secundi* added a fourth aim, which is not confirmed by any other source but which is highly plausible: to obtain Edward II's release from his promises to uphold the Ordinances.[25]

In early December the council considered the business to be dealt with by the envoys and then sent a royal clerk to see Edward and obtain his approval.[26] On 16 December Edward gave his envoys full powers to renegotiate the terms of the 1314 loan with the executors of Clement V. Pembroke and Badlesmere however considered these powers insufficient and asked that the envoys should also be allowed to deal directly with Bertrand de Got,

---

[21] *PROME*, Parliament of Jan. 1316, SC 9/20, item 9. The outcome of this decision would soon become apparent.

[22] The pope had been elected on about 7 Aug. 1316 after a vacancy which had lasted since April 1314. News of the election reached Edward II on 17 Aug. via an agent of the Florentine bankers, the Bardi: SAL Ms. 120, f. 48. Edward II sent the pope as gifts 'upon his new creation', two embroidered choir-copes, and a gold ewer and matching gold basin, valued in all at over £360: Wright, *The Church and the English Crown*, App. 2, 283.

[23] E 404/1/6; SC 1/49/38. An embassy was already being considered as early as 16 Sept., shortly after receipt of the official news of John XXII's election: *Foedera*, II, i, 297.

[24] The most prominent members of the council were Walter Reynolds the archbishop of Canterbury, John Sandal bishop of Winchester and chancellor, Walter de Norwich the treasurer, the earl of Pembroke, and Bartholomew de Badlesmere. For the correspondence exchanged between the king and the council see *CCW*, 450–9.

[25] *Vita*, 134–5. Edward had already tried this tactic in 1312 but without success. The Ordinances may have been the subject of the 'secret business' to be explained to the pope by the ambassadors: *Foedera*, II, i, 312.

[26] SC 1/49/ 39; SC 1/45, 192; Phillips, 108.

the marquis of Ancona, who was Clement V's nephew as well as one of his executors. The revised authority was duly given on 21 December.[27] Earlier in the month Edward had even suggested that Bertrand might actually be one of the envoys, which would have involved a conflict of interest and was manifestly absurd. This contribution to the discussion was accordingly rejected by the council, one hopes tactfully.[28] The crusading oath was next to be discussed. After Pembroke and the council had written to Edward about this in mid-December, they were told on 21 December to consider it among themselves and to advise him of the result. On the 28th they replied that Edward should ask for the same period of postponement as Philip V, the new king of France, and on 4 January this was also agreed.[29]

The addition of Scotland to the business of the embassy was rather more complex. Negotiations for a possible truce with the Scots had been in progress since mid-November 1316. On 17 November Master Robert Baldock, a canon of St Paul's and a future chancellor, and Sir Robert Hastang were sent from York to Jedburgh, with powers to negotiate a truce between Edward II and Robert Bruce.[30] On 23 November safe conducts were given for two Scottish knights, Sir Thomas Randolph and Sir John de Menteith, to come to the king, presumably also to take part in negotiations;[31] and on the following day the powers already given to Baldock and Hastang were confirmed.[32] On 26 November, two days after the more general mission to Avignon had been decided on, two more envoys, a royal clerk Master Richard de Burton and a royal judge John Binstead set off for the papal curia to raise the Scottish question there. No sooner had they left than Edward and his advisers changed their minds, and early in December they were recalled after reaching Dover. Their task was then added to the much more elaborate embassy that was already in preparation.[33]

[27] *Foedera*, II, i, 304; *CCW*, 452; Phillips, 108.
[28] SC 1/49/38; Phillips, 110.
[29] SC 1/45/192; *CCW*, 455; *Foedera*, II, i, 309. Philip's elder brother, Louis X, had died in June 1316, leaving his widow Clemence of Hungary pregnant. She gave birth on 15 Nov. to a son John who lived for only five days. Philip then became king.
[30] SAL Ms. 120, f. 15. They returned to the king at Scrooby on 5 Dec.
[31] *Foedera*, II, i, 302.
[32] E 101/68/2/36; *Foedera*, II, i, 302; *CCR, 1313–18*, 472. It is possible that a truce for six months was agreed for the border between England and Scotland. This is suggested by Robert Bruce's departure for Ireland in Jan. 1317: McNamee, 151.
[33] SAL Ms. 120, f. 23v; Phillips, 109. On 19 Dec. Binstead left London for Nottingham at the king's orders to meet Scottish envoys who were expected there. These were not named but were probably Randolph and Menteith. It seems unlikely that any meeting took place since Binstead returned to London on 4 Jan: SAL Ms. 120, f. 25. Between March 1315 and July 1318 the notary Andrew de Tange was engaged in making copies of the documents bearing on England's claims to superiority over Scotland: *Edward I and the Throne of Scotland*, ed. Stones & Simpson, i, 45–7, 81–2; ii, 378–80. These were intended for use in negotiations concerning Scotland and were so used in 1320–21: ibid., ii, 381. One period for which he was paid covered 8 July to 24 Nov. 1316 and raises the question of whether Edward II and his advisers considered making use of this material in 1316–17, either in direct negotiations with the Scots or as evidence to be supplied to the pope.

A great deal of care was given to the organization of the mission to Avignon. Several clerks were employed to transcribe documents stored in the Tower of London and to copy papal bulls for the use of the envoys.[34] On 25 December a number of royal proctors and other English clerks who were already at Avignon were instructed to give whatever assistance they could to the envoys,[35] and at about the same time Pembroke and Badlesmere suggested to the king that the envoys should be allowed to gain influence within the papal curia itself by granting pensions to cardinals. Edward agreed to this on 4 January.[36] No expense was to be spared. The Florentine banking company, the Bardi, was requested to supply ready money and, after consulting Pembroke and Badlesmere, advanced a sum of just under £7,800, of which nearly £3,800 was earmarked for the expenses of the embassy. Out of this sum £1,904 was spent by Edward and Isabella on presents for the pope, on the advice of Pembroke and his colleagues.[37] Edward was concerned above all that the gifts should do honour to himself and Isabella.[38] On 15 December the members of the embassy were formally announced as Pembroke, Badlesmere, Antonio Pessagno, the bishops of Norwich and Ely, and others. In Edward's mind the success that might be achieved at Avignon clearly outweighed the dangers involved in allowing so many of his experienced councillors to leave the country at one time.[39]

The embassy left England in early January 1317. Nothing is known of their midwinter journey which was probably a difficult one, but by the end of March the envoys' labours at Avignon were beginning to show some results. On 28 March the pope agreed to let Edward postpone his crusade, granted him a tenth to be levied upon the English clergy for one year, and also loaned to him for a period of five years part of the proceeds of another clerical tenth which had been imposed in aid of a crusade by the council of Vienne in 1311.[40] On 1 April the envoys also

---

[34] SAL Ms. 120, f. 27; Phillips, 109.

[35] *Foedera*, II, i, 305; Phillips, 109. Eleven people were written to altogether. These included Adam Orleton, the future bishop of Hereford, who was to play a key role in Edward II's eventual downfall; Adam Murimuth, author of an important narrative source for the reign of Edward II; Thomas Cobham, the unsuccessful candidate for Canterbury in 1313; William Melton and Alexander Bicknor, who had been elected as archbishop of York and of Dublin respectively and were awaiting papal confirmation; and two semi-permanent agents of the English crown at the papal curia, Andreas Sapiti and Raymond Subiran.

[36] SC 1/45/192; *Foedera*, II, i, 308; Phillips, 109.

[37] SC 1/45/192; E 404/1/6; SAL Ms. 120, ff. 53v, 54; *CPR, 1313–17*, 608; Phillips, 109.

[38] E 404/1/6. Edward II's stepmother, Queen Margaret, had evidently been consulted, since the presents she had sent to Clement V on a previous occasion were to be used as a guide. The gifts presented to the pope in 1317 included gold plate enamelled in part with the arms of John XXII and Edward II: Wright, *The Church and the English Crown*, App. 2, 283.

[39] *Foedera*, II, i, 302–3; Phillips, 109–10. The bishop of Ely was John de Hothum, who had played such an important role in Ireland in 1315–16.

[40] *Foedera*, II, i, 319–20; Lunt, *Financial Relations*, 166–9. These two sources of revenue yielded the exchequer about £19,500 and £18,500 respectively. Not surprisingly, the loan was never repaid: Lunt, 402–6. These sums were in addition to the subsidies granted to the king by the provinces of Canterbury and York in Oct. and Nov. 1316.

reached an agreement with the executors of Clement V on the repayment of his loan, which would allow Edward to recover control of 80 per cent of the revenues of Aquitaine.[41] As noted earlier, the envoys also made a partial payment of the arrears of the annual tribute for England and Ireland which was owed to the papacy by the English crown: enough to keep the pope happy but no more than that.[42] During their stay at Avignon the envoys and their resident helpers managed to obtain a rich crop of ecclesiastical preferments: the confirmation of William Melton as archbishop of York, Alexander Bicknor as archbishop of Dublin, William Fitz John as archbishop of Cashel, and the provision of Thomas Cobham to Worcester.[43] Edward did not however succeed in achieving the appointment of Thomas Charlton, one of his clerks and his personal choice for Durham in 1316, to the diocese of Hereford. Adam Orleton, an English clerk who was already at Avignon, managed to engineer his own provision instead, much to Edward's annoyance.[44]

If Edward had seriously expected that the pope would agree to quash his oath to uphold the Ordinances, he was to be disappointed. There was no mention of the Ordinances in any of the papal decrees associated with the mission to Avignon: according to the *Vita Edwardi Secundi* the pope refused to absolve Edward since the Ordinances 'had been drawn up, as he had been informed, through the endeavour of trustworthy persons, and it was not likely that they had ordained anything to the prejudice of the kingdom or the church'.[45] On the other hand Edward appeared to have achieved what he wanted in relation to Scotland. On 17 March the pope appointed Gaucelin d'Eauze and Luke Fieschi, the cardinals of SS Marcellinus & Peter and of St Mary in Via Lata, as envoys to negotiate a peace settlement between England and Scotland; on 28 March he excommunicated both Robert and Edward Bruce; and on 1 May he issued bulls promulgating a truce and ordering the Scots to cease their attacks on the north of England and in Ireland.[46] Edward had also gained financially from the great expense and effort put into the Avignon mission; and some of his favourite clergy gained valuable promotions. Not surprisingly the Scots took no notice either of the papal bulls or of the papal envoys, but the presence of the two cardinals in England between the summer of 1317 and the summer of 1318 had an unlooked-for importance when they turned their attention to assisting in a settlement between Edward II and Lancaster.

---

[41] *Foedera*, II, i, 322–4. This was not the end of the story, which contributed to serious problems in the duchy in 1318: Phillips, 182; Vale, 132–4.
[42] Lunt, *Financial Relations*, 166–9.
[43] *Foedera*, II, i, 302–22. The provision of Louis de Beaumont to Durham had already been confirmed by Feb.: ibid., 316.
[44] *Foedera*, II, i, 319, 321; Haines, *The Church and Politics*, 16–19.
[45] *Vita*, 138–9.
[46] *Foedera*, II, i, 321–2, 327–8; *CPL, 1305–42*, 127; Phillips, 111.

THE CAPTURE AND RANSOMING OF THE EARL OF PEMBROKE

The risks attached to the absence of several of Edward II's most trusted advisers from England in the early months of 1317 were shown to be all too real, and in a most unexpected way. The envoys probably left Avignon at some time in early April. The bishops of Norwich and Ely reached London on 11 May,[47] but the return of their fellow envoys was delayed by a dramatic and totally unforeseen event.

After leaving Avignon, Pembroke probably stopped to conduct some private business concerning his French lands before returning to England.[48] Early in May he was travelling between Orléans and Paris when he was waylaid at Étampes and, together with his son and several of his retainers, was taken to an unidentified place in the county of Bar on the River Meuse on the borders of France and the Empire. Here he was held to ransom for the enormous sum of £10,400 sterling.[49] The circumstances of Pembroke's seizure were not immediately understood in England, his captor being named only as 'Jean de la Moiliere'.[50] There is ample evidence to show that the latter's true name was Jean de Lamouilly and to support the statement in the *Scalacronica* that he had once been in the service of the English crown and had a grievance over unpaid wages.[51] He had served Edward I in Scotland and was a member of the garrison of Berwick as late as June 1312, after which he appears to have returned to his home at Lamouilly on the Meuse. He may well have been personally acquainted with Pembroke and have served under his command. Given the financial confusion in England, it is very probable that Lamouilly's wages were still in arrears in 1317 and that this would have given him ample motive to seize Pembroke when he came within easy reach in France.[52] It is likely however that Lamouilly was protected and perhaps even encouraged by his local overlord, Edward count of Bar, who had a grievance of his own against the English crown. The count's mother Eleanor was a sister of Edward II and through this connection Jean de Lamouilly and others from Bar had entered English service in Scotland. Even more significant was the fact that the count's sister Joan had married John de Warenne, the future earl of

---

[47] SAL Ms. 120, ff. 23v, 24; Phillips, 111.

[48] He was lord of Montignac near Angoulême and of other lands in the region: Phillips, 2–3, 338.

[49] *Foedera*, II, i, 329; *CPL, 1305–42*, 240. What follows is traced in more detail in Phillips, 111–17.

[50] *Foedera*, II, i, 329.

[51] *Scalacronica*, 78–9, 230.

[52] Phillips, 111–12. In May 1313, for example, Lamouilly had been assigned the issues of wardships and marriages in royal hands in payment of £711, but the following Aug. Hugh Despenser the Elder was given priority of payment from the same source: *CPR, 1307–13*, 570; *CPR, 1313–17*, 7, 100–1.

Surrey, in 1306. By 1313 the marriage had broken down and Surrey began proceedings for an annulment. Initially the king appears to have taken the side of the countess of Surrey, but in July 1316 the earl of Surrey surrendered his lands to Edward II, who then re-granted them to him with reversion to Surrey's mistress and her two illegitimate sons.[53] In August 1316 Surrey's estranged wife left England and was with her brother the count of Bar by May 1317, when Pembroke was taken prisoner. One of Pembroke's tasks at Avignon had probably been to present a petition on Surrey's behalf asking the pope to annul his marriage. Part of the ransom may even have been an indirect payment of damages by Pembroke on behalf of the earl of Surrey.[54] Edward of Bar would therefore have had ample reason to become involved in Pembroke's capture and ransoming, as a way of punishing his uncle Edward II for the treatment of his sister and at the same time causing the king embarrassment by imprisoning one of his most valued councillors.[55]

The episode was somehow typical of the reign of Edward II, involving as it did both financial confusion and dysfunctional personal relations. Edward was now forced to divert considerable time and diplomatic resources to secure Pembroke's release, as well as contributing £2,500 towards the payment of his ransom.[56] Two of the other members of the embassy to Avignon, Bartholomew de Badlesmere and Antonio Pessagno, who were also important royal councillors who could ill be spared, remained in France to help secure Pembroke's release. On 10 May Edward II wrote to twenty-seven high-ranking members of the French court and magnates from the border lands between France and the Empire, including the count of Bar, asking for their assistance. Guy Ferre, a royal knight, and Eble des Montz, one of Isabella's retainers, were sent to France, while a royal clerk, Master John Hildesle, left for the papal curia at Avignon.[57] It is not known exactly how Pembroke's freedom was achieved, but news of his release was received with delight by Edward II on 17 June.[58] Pembroke arrived in London on 23 June, accompanied by Badlesmere, Pessagno and the French count of Aumale who had been sent with him as an escort to ensure his safety. By 4 July they had all rejoined

---

[53] Phillips, 114–15. For details of Surrey's marriage and his attempts to end it see Fairbank, 'The last earl of Warenne and Surrey', and the article on Surrey by S. L. Waugh in the *Oxford DNB*.

[54] In Oct. 1317 the earl of Surrey granted Pembroke the towns of Grantham and Stamford, to be held until he had recovered a sum of £4,000, which he had paid on Surrey's behalf while overseas: *CPR, 1313–17*, 40, 48; Phillips, 195.

[55] Phillips, 115.

[56] *CPR, 1317–21*, 6, 9; Phillips, 116.

[57] E 403/180, m.5; SAL Ms. 120, f. 27v; *Foedera*, II, i, 329–30; Phillips, 114–16.

[58] The news was brought by one of Pembroke's messengers, who was rewarded with a gold cup. Edward wrote to Pembroke on the same day asking him to hurry back to England as quickly as possible: SAL Ms. 120, f. 93; SC 1/49/40, 41; Phillips, 116.

the king at Northampton and appeared before the council on the following day. The sense of relief which comes through in the records is almost palpable.[59]

ENGLISH POLITICS: EDWARD AND LANCASTER AGAIN

The return of Pembroke and Badlesmere to England came not a moment too soon, since their absence was one of the reasons for the postponement of a planned Scottish campaign due to start on 8 July.[60] To make matters worse, during their absence there had been a sharp deterioration in the relations between Edward II and Lancaster. Although the device of making Lancaster head of the council had been tried and had failed, and much more had happened since the Lincoln parliament of 1316 to embitter Lancaster still further against Edward, the problem of his relations with the king and his government could not be ignored indefinitely. In one way or another it was to continue to dominate politics during both 1317 and 1318.

There are indications that from very early in 1317 attempts were being made to resume contact with Lancaster. This may in part have been due to the advice which Pembroke is known to have given the king before his departure for Avignon,[61] but other prominent members of the council who remained in England, such as Walter Reynolds the archbishop of Canterbury, John Sandal the bishop of Winchester and chancellor, and the earl of Hereford, are likely to have conveyed the same message. Unfortunately, as events would soon show, there were other forces, also close to the king, pulling in the opposite direction.

The first evidence of new efforts to obtain Lancaster's co-operation is associated with two meetings of the council. The first of these was held at Clarendon between 9 and 20 February: in addition to thirteen royal clerks and justices who had been specially summoned, the assembly included all the chief members of the council who had not gone to Avignon, the archbishop, chancellor, treasurer, the bishops of Salisbury and Exeter, the earls of Hereford and Norfolk, and Hugh Despenser the Elder. Lancaster himself was not present, and one chronicler says specifically that he was not invited, but his interests were probably represented by his brother Henry of Lancaster.[62]

It is not known in any detail what was discussed at the council, other than the 'great and arduous affairs touching the king and the state of the

---

[59] SAL Ms. 120, ff. 24, 27v, 54v; E 368/89, m.21; E 101/371/8/30. The council rewarded the count of Aumale with a horse, saddle and £40 in cash. Three of his retainers were also rewarded: E 101/371/8/30; SAL Ms. 121, ff. 28, 66v.

[60] E 101/15/11/4; E 101/15/14/4; Phillips, 117.

[61] SC 1/49/39; Phillips, 117.

[62] C 53/103, mm.12–15; *CCW*, 460; *CCR, 1313–18*, 451; *Trivet (Cont.)*, 20; Phillips, 118; Maddicott, 190–1.

realm' which were referred to in the writs of summons, but it is reasonable to suppose that, in addition to the war with Scotland, relations with Lancaster were high on the agenda.⁶³ It was decided that a further meeting would soon be necessary and on 14 March a formal summons to Westminster on 15 April was sent to the archbishop, the bishop of Exeter, the earl of Hereford and to both Hugh Despenser the Elder and the Younger.⁶⁴ Significantly, on this occasion a summons was also sent to the earl of Lancaster and to his leading retainer Robert de Holland. To give added force to the summons two royal envoys, Robert de la Beche and Robert de Kendale, were sent from Clarendon on 16 March to visit Lancaster at Castle Donington in Leicestershire.⁶⁵ Lancaster and Holland had both moved to Kenilworth by 4 April but they did not appear at Westminster when the council opened on 15 April.⁶⁶ Some at least of those present at the council were still determined to try to consult Lancaster and on 21 April they sent Master Richard de Burton to see him at Castle Donington on behalf of the king.⁶⁷ Again there is no sign that Lancaster responded or offered any co-operation.

Any chance of further efforts to win him over was almost at once ruled out by an act of gratuitous folly which opened an even wider breach between Edward and Lancaster. This was the abduction on 9 May by one of the earl of Surrey's knights of the countess of Lancaster at Canford in Dorset, after which she was taken to the earl in his castle at Reigate in Surrey. This action was seen by Lancaster as a deliberate plot by the king and his supporters, and one usually well informed writer implies that it had been planned at the Clarendon council in February, at which the earl of Surrey had been present.⁶⁸ Although there is no evidence to support such a clear assertion of cause and effect, Surrey may have been encouraged in his intentions by his knowledge of the enmity between Edward and Lancaster. It is more likely that Surrey's abduction of the countess, who was already estranged from her husband and seems to have been a

---

⁶³ Another item which was certainly discussed was the proposal that Edward II should claim a share of the kingdom of France in right of his wife: Chaplais in, 'Un Message de Jean de Fiennes à Édouard II et le projet de démembrement du royaume de France (Janvier 1317)', *Revue du Nord*, xliii (1961), 145–8; repr. in P. Chaplais, *Essays in Medieval Diplomacy and Administration* (London, 1981), item X.

⁶⁴ *CCR, 1313–18*, 449–56, 459; Phillips, 118; Maddicott, 191.

⁶⁵ SAL Ms. 120, f. 26; *CCR, 1313–18*, 459; Phillips, 118–19; Maddicott, 191. The two envoys returned to the king on 5 April.

⁶⁶ *CPR, 1317–21*, 225. Edward probably anticipated a delay in Lancaster's appearance and on 13 April appointed the earl of Hereford, the archbishop of Canterbury and the bishop of Exeter to conduct the council until his own arrival: *CPR, 1313–17*, 634; Phillips, 119; Maddicott, 191.

⁶⁷ SAL Ms. 120, f. 25v; Phillips, 119; Maddicott, 191. Burton returned on 2 May.

⁶⁸ C 53/103, mm.12–15; *Trivet (Cont.)*, 20–1; *Historia Anglicana*, 148 (the date is very clearly given as Monday before the Ascension, 9 May); Phillips, 119; Maddicott, 197 (where the date of the abduction is wrongly given as 11 April). The affair is described in Trivet as '*primus Concilii ramus apud Clarendoniam tenti*'. The king is also accused of complicity in *Flores*, 178.

willing victim, was undertaken by him primarily for personal reasons.[69] The author of the chronicle of Meaux abbey in Yorkshire claimed that the abduction was carried out 'not, however, by way of adultery, but in contempt of the earl'.[70] It is probably also significant that in the negotiations between Edward and Lancaster in 1318 the matter was treated as a private quarrel between Lancaster and Surrey which did not involve the king.[71] Nonetheless it was deeply ironic that twice in the same month, May 1317, the actions of the earl of Surrey had directly or indirectly profoundly disrupted the conduct of royal business and endangered the peace of the realm.

On 29 May Edward sent one of his knights Richard Lovel and a clerk William Hoo to see Lancaster, probably to try to placate him, but with no apparent success.[72] Nothing further happened until after the return from France of Badlesmere and the earl of Pembroke: it is likely that they were shocked by the serious turn of events in their absence and encouraged the king to act promptly before his relations with Lancaster became even more embittered. The arrival of the two papal envoys, Cardinals Gaucelin d'Eauze and Luke Fieschi, who had reached London by 28 June, may also have helped.[73] Although their mission was to make peace between England and Scotland, they soon became just as involved in trying to make peace within England itself. Whatever the motivation, a great council to discuss royal policy in England, Wales, Scotland, Ireland and Gascony was summoned on 1 July to meet at Nottingham on 18 July. All the king's leading councillors were summoned, including the archbishop of Canterbury, the chancellor John Sandal bishop of Winchester, the newly appointed treasurer John de Hothum the bishop of Ely, the bishop of Norwich, the earls of Pembroke and Hereford, Badlesmere and the Elder and Younger Despenser.[74]

As in April, Lancaster was again asked to attend and once again he failed to appear. The beginning of the meeting was delayed for yet another attempt to persuade him to attend, and on 21 July William de Dene delivered two letters from the king to Lancaster at Ashbourne-in-the-Peak in Derbyshire. The first repeated the summons to the council at Nottingham; the second

---

[69] What these were is unknown. They may have had something to do with the rivalry between Lancaster and Surrey over lands in Yorkshire and in North Wales, but this seems to have been a consequence rather than a cause of their enmity.

[70] *Melsa*, 335; Maddicott, 197. According to the chronicle of Dunmow, Essex, Surrey is said to have claimed that the countess of Lancaster had promised to marry him, but given that in 1317 Surrey was deeply involved in trying to marry his mistress, Maud de Neyrford, this proposition is not plausible: BL, Cotton Ms. Cleopatra C. III, f. 295v; Phillips, 120.

[71] Phillips, 120, 170–1, 183; Maddicott, 232–7, 316–18.

[72] SAL Ms. 120, f. 30v; Phillips, 120; Maddicott, 191.

[73] SAL Ms. 120, f. 54; Trinity College, Cambridge, Ms. R.5.41, f. 113v (continuation of the chronicle of Gervase of Canterbury); Phillips, 120. The cardinals were at Canterbury on 24 June.

[74] *CCR, 1313–18*, 482; *PW*, II, ii, 197; Phillips, 120–1; Maddicott, 191.

accused him of gathering armed retainers to disturb the peace.[75] Lancaster's replies are very significant, since they establish the nominal issues of principle which divided him from the king, while at the same time revealing the real nature of their quarrel. In reply to the first letter Lancaster claimed that the business of the Nottingham council ought properly to be dealt with in a parliament. He then claimed that he had withdrawn from attendance at royal council meetings because of Edward's failure to observe the Ordinances, his refusal to accept the reform proposals drawn up in London by himself and the reform commission established at the Lincoln parliament in January 1316, and because he kept at court and made gifts to people who should have been removed under the terms of the Ordinances. Lancaster's insistence upon the Ordinances and his particular emphasis on the position of certain royal associates and on grants of land to them as barriers to any political agreement were a repetition of the demands he had been making since 1311, but they also foreshadowed very closely the demands he would regularly make in the long-drawn-out negotiations which finally resulted in a new settlement between himself and Edward in 1318. However, the real depth of personal hostility and suspicion which lay behind Lancaster's refusal to come to Nottingham is even better described in the account in the *Vita Edwardi Secundi* of the oral message that accompanied his letter. According to this source, Lancaster said he had disobeyed the king's summons for fear of plots against him by the king's favourites, who had already shown their animosity towards him and who, he believed, had caused him disgrace and humiliation through the abduction of his wife. Lancaster promised that if these men were expelled from court, he would come whenever Edward wished.[76] Underlying all Lancaster's talk during 1317 and 1318 of the Ordinances and of reform were his distrust of the king and a well-founded fear of the king's favourites.[77]

In reply to the king's second letter Lancaster admitted that he had been gathering armed retainers, but claimed he was only doing this in readiness for the planned Scottish campaign, which was now due to begin at Newcastle upon Tyne on 11 August.[78] Edward meanwhile had taken the precaution of keeping a well-armed force in his company.[79] The possibility

[75] The letters and Lancaster's replies are known only from the copies in *Murimuth*, 271–4; and *Gesta Edwardi*, 50–2; Phillips, 97, 121; Maddicott, 182, 192.

[76] *Vita*, 136–9.

[77] Phillips, 121–2; Maddicott, 192–3. It is likely that during the periods in 1315 and 1316 when Lancaster was active as a member or as head of the king's council, and was consequently in close proximity to the king, he lived in fear of his life. This would help to explain the brevity of these periods.

[78] *Murimuth*, 271–4; *Gesta Edwardi*, 50–2. There is direct evidence that Lancaster was gathering military force in the indentures made with him by Adam de Swilyngton at Tutbury on 21 June and by Hugh de Meignel at Ashbourne-in-the-Peak on 24 July: Bod., Dodsworth Ms. 94, f. 122v, Dugdale Ms. 778, f. 39v; Phillips, 122; Maddicott, 192.

[79] Edward had the retinues, each of 30 men, belonging to three of his household knights, John Giffard, John Cromwell and John de Somery, who had recently contracted to provide him with military service: SAL Ms. 121, ff. 28v, 29v, 31; Phillips, 122.

of open violence between Edward and Lancaster was a very real one in the summer and autumn of 1317. To make matters worse, in the middle of July ominous reports reached the king that some of the defenders of the Scottish March had abandoned their posts and that the Scots had invaded England on 8 July.[80]

THE KING'S NEW FAVOURITES

Lancaster's suspicions of the king's motives and of those surrounding him were amply justified. In the spring of 1317 there was, as Lancaster claimed, a group of newly influential royal favourites, some of whom are said to have spoken openly of him as a traitor while at Clarendon.[81] The absence on the Avignon mission of the restraining influence of responsible councillors such as Pembroke and Badlesmere probably also contributed to their behaviour. Four individuals can be singled out. The first was Hugh Despenser the Younger, already well established and showing signs of the overweening ambition that was to bring him power and also his own downfall and that of the king. His father, Hugh Despenser the Elder, had been one of Edward II's most influential councillors throughout the reign and had long been an enemy of the earl of Lancaster.[82] There were also three young knights, Roger Damory, Hugh Audley the Younger and William de Montacute.[83] Audley had been a royal household knight since November 1311, Montacute since 1312 or 1313, and Damory since about January 1315.[84] Of the three, Damory appears to have been the most influential. Like Badlesmere, he had originally been a member of the earl of Gloucester's retinue and had first come to Edward II's attention through his bravery at Bannockburn. In December 1314 he was given custody of the important castle of Knaresborough in Yorkshire and in January 1315 Edward ordered specifically that he should stay at court. Between then and early 1317 he received a series of other royal favours.[85] In 1316

---

[80] SC 1/49/42; Phillips, 122. Although Arundel made an incursion into Scotland in March 1317, while Robert Bruce was absent in Ireland, and had also sent ships to raid the east coast, there was little serious fighting in 1317. Bruce returned to Scotland in May to meet these threats from Arundel but there is nothing to suggest a Scottish invasion of England in July: McNamee, 151. The reports probably reflected the nervousness of the time rather than actual events.

[81] *Trivet (Cont.)*, 20; *Flores*, 178; *Vita*, 136–7; *Historia Anglicana*, i, 148, 150; Phillips, 119; Maddicott, 191.

[82] Phillips, 132–3; Maddicott, 195.

[83] Phillips, 131; Maddicott, 192–3.

[84] E 101/373/26, f. 23v; E 101/373/8, f. 35v; C 81/90/3241: *CPR, 1313–1317*, 666; Phillips, 131; Maddicott, 193; A. Tebbit, 'Royal patronage and political allegiance', in *Thirteenth Century England*, x, ed. M. Prestwich, R. Britnell & R. Frame (2005), 200–3. They all came from families closely associated with royal service and probably owed their initial positions in the household to this fact: Phillips, 131–2; Maddicott, 193–4. For further details on all three men see the articles in the *Oxford DNB*.

[85] C 81/90/3241; Phillips, 131–2; Maddicott, 193–4.

Montacute played a leading role in suppressing both the revolt of Llywelyn Bren and disturbances at Bristol, being described as 'captain of the king's knights'; and from November 1316 he was steward of the king's household. In January 1317 both Montacute and Damory contracted to serve the king for life in return for an annuity of 200 marks.[86] Audley's initial career owed much to that of his father, Hugh Audley the Elder, who in 1312 had been one of those commissioned by the king to revise the Ordinances and had briefly been steward of the household in the same year.[87]

By the beginning of 1317 all three had reached a position of great influence. They were the men who allegedly accused Lancaster of treachery at the Clarendon council in February, while the *Flores Historiarum*, whose author was not given to favourable remarks about the king and his supporters, described them as rising up 'in the king's shadow' and being more wicked even than Gaveston.[88]

In the spring of 1317 the status of two of the three men was dramatically enhanced by marriage.[89] The greatest available prizes in the marriage stakes were the three heiresses to the lands in England, Wales and Ireland of the earldom of Gloucester, which were worth about £6,500 a year.[90] After allowing for the dower of the earl of Gloucester's widow, a one-third share of the earldom, even without the title of earl, would propel its holder directly into the senior ranks of the baronage. The partition had already been long delayed because it was such a delicate issue politically but had been decided upon in principle on 13 December 1316. This was nominally in answer to the petition lodged by Hugh Despenser the Younger and his wife Eleanor de Clare at the Lincoln parliament the previous January.[91] But there can be little doubt that Edward had been giving thought to finding suitable husbands for the remaining two sisters, Margaret and Elizabeth, who were both widowed. It is possible that the Gloucester inheritance was one of the topics discussed at Clarendon and, given the presence of Despenser, even more likely that it was discussed at the Westminster council. Damory, Audley and Montacute were probably also present on the fringes of one or both councils.[92] It is even possible that one reason for Edward II's eagerness that Lancaster should attend was to

---

[86] Phillips, 132; Maddicott, 194.

[87] Phillips, 132; Maddicott, 194.

[88] *Trivet (Cont.)*, 20; *Flores*, 178; *Vita*, 136–7, 150–1; *Historia Anglicana*, i, 148, 150; Phillips, 119, 132; Maddicott, 191, 193.

[89] Montacute was already married but in April 1317 his younger son John was married in the royal chapel at Windsor to one of the heiresses of Theobald de Verdon, lord of Alton in Staffordshire and of lands in Meath in Ireland.

[90] On the extended value of the lands in 1317 (at the time of their partition) see J.C. Ward, 'The estates of the Clare family, 1066–1317' (Ph.D., London, 1962), 281; G.A. Holmes, *The Estates of the Higher Nobility in Fourteenth-Century England* (Cambridge, 1957), 35–8; Phillips, 243.

[91] *PROME*, Parliament of Jan. 1316, SC 9/20, item 9.

[92] Maddicott, 190–1.

try to obtain his approval for the marriages of the Gloucester heiresses and the partition of the earldom. On 17 April the decision was taken to proceed with the partition;[93] on 28 April Hugh Audley the Younger married Margaret de Clare, the widow of Gaveston; and on or about the same date Roger Damory married Elizabeth de Clare, the widow of both John de Burgh and Theobald de Verdon.[94] On 22 May Edward ordered new valuations to be made of the lands and on 15 November 1317 he ordered delivery of their shares of the inheritance to the heiresses and their husbands.[95] As an indication of their new status, both Damory and Audley received a summons to parliament as barons.[96]

Lancaster had good reason to be alarmed about the power that was now wielded by the king's new favourites.[97] But he was not the only one. At Pentecost, 22 May 1317, a woman dressed as a theatrical player rode into Westminster Hall while Edward II was feasting with his magnates and presented a letter to the king. She then turned around and left. Edward had the letter opened and read to him, and was angered to discover that he was accused of neglecting knights who had served his father and himself in battle and of promoting others 'who had not borne the heat of the day'. The woman was then searched for and under questioning she revealed that she had been induced to do this by one of Edward II's own household knights. The (unnamed) knight was questioned in turn and said that he had acted for the honour of the kingdom.[98] Up till now Edward had been served with remarkable loyalty by his household knights, but the episode was a serious warning that their loyalty might have its limits.[99]

Significantly, the group of royal favourites and the king himself also realized the potential dangers of their position. On 1 June 1317 the two Despensers, Audley, Damory and Montacute made a series of mutual recognizances for £6,000 each in the king's presence at Westminster. The

---

[93] *PROME*, Parliament of Jan. 1316, SC 9/20, item 10. Formal orders for the partition were given on 12 May: C 81/100/4231.

[94] Audley married in the king's presence at Windsor on the same day as Montacute's son: SAL Ms. 120, f. 10. Damory married between 10 April and 3 May: *CPR, 1317–21*, 641, 644; Phillips, 132; Maddicott, 193.

[95] For a detailed study of the partition see M. Altschul, *A Baronial Family in Medieval England* (Baltimore, 1965), 165–74, 304–5.

[96] Maddicott, 193. Montacute also received a summons. Despenser had been attending parliaments since Sept. 1314.

[97] *Vita*, 136–7, 150–1: the two Despensers and the earl of Surrey were included in the list as well as Audley, Damory and Montacute.

[98] *Trokelowe*, 98–9; *Historia Anglicana*, 149–50; Maddicott, 197; Prestwich, *Plantagenet England*, 203.

[99] Those limits were reached and far exceeded in the civil war of 1321–2. Of 52 household bannerets and knights serving Edward II in 1316 only eight were still in the household by 1322; and 25 knights who had belonged to the household between 1314 and 1321 ultimately fought against Edward in the civil war: Tebbit, 'Royal patronage', 197; M.C. Prestwich, 'The unreliability of royal household knights in the early fourteenth century', in *Fourteenth Century England*, ii, ed. C. Given-Wilson (Woodbridge, Suffolk & Rochester, NY, 2002), 1–12.

purpose of the bonds was not stated, but it is very likely that they were in effect taking out an insurance policy against any future attempts by Lancaster or others to force them from court.[100] If they were to hang, they would surely hang together.

ENGLAND ON THE VERGE OF CIVIL WAR: MAYHEM IN THE NORTH

The late summer and autumn of 1317 was a dangerous period in which passions on both sides of the political divide became very heated and there was a real danger of civil war. Edward was reportedly incensed by Lancaster's refusal to attend the council at Nottingham on 18 July and especially by Lancaster's demand that he should purge his household. Some of Edward's followers, presumably Damory and the others, were ready to persuade Edward to pursue Lancaster and either imprison or exile him. Others, presumably men such as Pembroke, saw the danger that civil war would bring to the kingdom and urged Edward to do everything possible to come to an agreement with Lancaster.[101] The fears of a possible Scottish attack in the north made Lancaster's co-operation more necessary than ever. For this reason the summons for the Scottish campaign, already delayed twice, was again postponed on 28 July from 11 August until 15 September.[102]

After the unsatisfactory end of the council at Nottingham Edward moved further north towards York, and it was during this period that the first fresh contacts were made with Lancaster. It is likely that these moves had been decided upon at Nottingham. At some point between 18 and 30 August while he was at Lincoln Edward sent solemn envoys to visit Lancaster at Pontefract to try to make peace with him, so that the Scottish campaign could proceed. The existence of the mission and its outcome are known only from chronicle sources, where the envoys are identified as the archbishops of Canterbury and Dublin, the bishops of Winchester, Llandaff, Salisbury, Norwich and Chichester, the earls of Pembroke and Hereford, and royal bannerets and clerks. On their arrival at Pontefract the envoys are said to have found no reason why a settlement should not be made; and they reported this to the king, urging him to make

---

[100] *CCR, 1313–18*, 477; E 163/3/6, m.1; Phillips, 133; Maddicott, 195–6; Prestwich, *Plantagenet England*, 203. The bonds were payable on 29 Sept. following. Each bound himself to all the others, except for the Despensers, who did not bind one another. Davies, *Baronial Opposition*, 434, saw the bonds as marking the formation of a court party which later became absorbed in the earl of Pembroke's so-called 'middle party'. It *was* a court party in the sense that it comprised those who had benefited most from royal patronage and had most to lose, but allegiance to the king covered a much wider range of magnates, including Pembroke and others.

[101] *Vita*, 138–9.

[102] *PW*, II, ii, 198.

peace.¹⁰³ According to the *Vita*, the mediators arranged for Lancaster to meet Edward in person, so that they could reach a more rapid resolution of their differences, but before the meeting could take place Lancaster was told that Edward had threatened to kill or imprison him if he came alone, and the negotiations ended amid further recriminations and bitterness. 'From that day forward the earl took care not to approach the king without protection.'¹⁰⁴ Although the Pontefract mission was a failure, it is still of considerable interest and significance. The presence of the two archbishops and five bishops of the Canterbury province suggests a very strong clerical interest in producing a settlement, an impression which was to be strongly reinforced during the tortuous negotiations in 1318. It is not too much to say that without them no agreement would have been possible.¹⁰⁵ The involvement of Pembroke and Hereford, who had probably also urged the king to make peace, shows a concern for a political settlement among an influential group of magnates, which once again is confirmed by later events.

After the abortive mission to Pontefract, Edward continued on his way to York, which he reached on about 4 September, travelling from Lincoln by a circuitous route which took him as far as possible to the east of the direct road passing through Pontefract, which Lancaster could easily block if he wished. This is exactly what Lancaster did after Edward had arrived in York, placing guards on the bridges to the south of the city and preventing any armed reinforcements from reaching the king. Lancaster justified his actions on the grounds that because he held the office of steward of England, granted to him in 1308, Edward should consult him before taking up arms against any enemy.¹⁰⁶ This was a new tactic on Lancaster's part, used now for the first but not the last time.¹⁰⁷

---

¹⁰³ *Trivet (Cont.)*, 23; Phillips, 123–4. Henry de Pateshull, who went to Lancaster on royal business on 18 Aug., was probably sent to announce the mission. The mission to Pontefract is discussed in Maddicott, 208–9, where an undated document preserved in Bod., Dodsworth Ms. 8, f. 262 (text printed in Maddicott, 336–7) is interpreted as the text of an agreement between Lancaster and the prelates made on this occasion, in Sept. 1317. My own interpretation of this document differs substantially. Although there can be no certainty as to the date, I believe that the document is more likely to belong to the negotiations between Lancaster and the prelates held at Leicester in April 1318 and I shall consider it under that date: see Phillips, 155–8, 319–20 (text), and the present chapter.

¹⁰⁴ *Vita*, 138–41; Phillips, 124.

¹⁰⁵ Phillips, 124. During 1317 and 1318, 12 archbishops and bishops were involved as mediators at various stages. In the period 1318–20, 17 out of 23 bishops were active in this way: Maddicott, 214, citing K. Edwards, 'The political importance of the English bishops during the reign of Edward II', *EHR*, lix (1944), 311–47, esp. 331. To this paper should be added R. M. Haines, 'The episcopate during the reign of Edward II and the regency of Mortimer and Isabella', *Journal of Ecclesiastical History*, lvi (2005), 657–709, esp. 674, 678–80.

¹⁰⁶ *Trivet (Cont.)*, 23; *Vita*, 140–1; Phillips, 125; Maddicott, 208.

¹⁰⁷ On Lancaster's use of the stewardship to advance his claims to authority within the kingdom see *Vita*, 140, n. 273; Maddicott, 76–7, 241–3.

Despite Lancaster's precautions, Edward probably had a considerable force with him, amounting to about 1,500 men-at-arms, hobelars, crossbowmen, foot archers and foot soldiers, not counting the retainers gathered for the Scottish campaign by Pembroke, Hereford, Badlesmere and others.[108] In a sinister development, some of the reinforcements which reached Edward from north of the city, where Lancaster's blockade was less effective, came from the Yorkshire lands of Lancaster's opponent, the earl of Surrey.[109] In the meantime Lancaster was gathering his own forces at Pontefract.[110]

Tension and suspicion were greatly increased by an extraordinary act of violence which took place on 1 September near Rushyford on the road between Darlington and Durham. Louis de Beaumont, the successful candidate for the see of Durham in the hotly contested election in October 1316, was travelling to Durham for his consecration as bishop, in the company of his brother Henry, when they were held up and robbed by Sir Gilbert de Middleton, Sir John de Lilburn and others. To make matters worse, the two cardinals who were on their way first to attend the consecration and then to deliver papal bulls to Robert Bruce, were travelling in company with the Beaumonts and were caught up in the robbery. The cardinals were soon released and allowed to continue their journey to Durham but the Beaumonts were taken as prisoners to the castle of Mitford in Northumberland where they were held until October.[111]

The incident was doubly embarrassing for the king since he had shown the pope in the clearest fashion that he could not guarantee the safety of solemn envoys in his own kingdom[112] and also since both Gilbert de Middleton and John de Lilburn were royal household knights;[113] it was also embarrassing for the earl of Pembroke, to whom Mitford castle belonged and whose constable, a local man named John d'Eure, was probably a sympathizer of Middleton and had surrendered the castle to him for his own

---

[108] SAL 121, ff. 19v, 29v, 31; Phillips, 125. Badlesmere, for example, had 32 men with him: C 71/10, m.17.

[109] SAL Ms. 121, f. 43; *Vita*, 140–1; Phillips, 125.

[110] *Vita*, 140–1. Lancaster had, for example, sealed five indentures of retainer with individual knights in June and July 1317: Maddicott, 203, n. 2.

[111] *Reg. Palat. Dunelm.*, iv, 394; *Hist. Dunelm. Script. Tres*, 100; *Melsa*, 334; *Vita*, 142–5; Phillips, 125–6; Maddicott, 204–6. The most detailed treatments of the episode are those of A.E. Middleton, *Sir Gilbert de Middleton* (Newcastle, 1918) and M. Prestwich, 'Gilbert de Middleton and the attack on the cardinals, 1317', in *Warriors and Churchmen in the High Middle Ages*, ed. T. Reuter (London, 1992), 179–94.

[112] On 10 Sept. Edward wrote from York to tell the pope of the attack and to express his horror at what had happened: *Foedera*, II, ii, 341.

[113] Prestwich, 'Gilbert de Middleton', 186–7. Middleton and Lilburn were listed as household knights at Christmas 1315, but their association with the crown was the result of the large-scale recruitment of locally based knights undertaken in 1314–15 to secure the defence of the north rather than any long-term connection. I would not therefore agree with Professor Prestwich's conclusion that 'the events at Rushyford illustrate the consequences of factional disputes in an unhappy court': ibid., 194.

use.[114] It was most embarrassing of all for Thomas of Lancaster, whose hostility to the Beaumonts was well known, and who was understandably assumed by the king and others to be responsible for the attack.[115] It was also believed that Lancaster had acted in collusion with the Scots.[116] While it is true that Lancaster had an interest in stirring up trouble and that John d'Eure was to become one of his retainers in December 1317,[117] there is no evidence that he actually ordered the attack.[118] There is on the other hand some evidence that local interests were closely involved. In April 1317 John d'Eure had made an agreement at Durham with John de Sapy, the keeper of the temporalities of Durham, recognizing a debt of 100 marks, which would become payable only if Louis de Beaumont were consecrated as bishop of Durham or received the temporalities of the diocese before 29 September 1317. The agreement was meanwhile to be kept by the prior of Durham.[119] Eure, de Sapy and the prior clearly all had an interest in preventing Beaumont's consecration, and it can hardly be a coincidence that the attack on the Beaumonts came only three days before the consecration was due to take place.[120] It may also be significant that some London clergy had warned the Beaumonts of the dangers in going beyond York, while the prior of Durham is said to have implied that they would be at risk from a Scottish attack.[121] If Lancaster had any involvement, it was indirect and unintentional, resulting from his attempts to influence local interests and forces which he was not fully able to control.[122] The presence of the cardinals was a further complication that neither he nor anyone else had anticipated.

Lancaster acted swiftly to retrieve both the situation and his own reputation. On 7 September he joined the cardinals at Durham and arranged for Gilbert de Middleton to restore their stolen property. He then escorted them as far south as Boroughbridge in Yorkshire to be met by the earls of Pembroke and Hereford, who conducted them to the king at York, where

[114] Phillips, 126. Pembroke had appointed Eure as constable on 15 Nov. 1316, as part of the arrangements then being made for the defence of the north: E 101/68/2/36.

[115] *Trivet (Cont.)*, 23; Maddicott, 205.

[116] Maddicott, 205–7.

[117] Bod., Dugdale Ms. 18, f. 39v; Maddicott, 203; Phillips, 127. Eure and other retainers of Lancaster were exempted from the general pardon given to Lancaster's followers in 1318 because of the robbery of the cardinals: *CPR, 1317–21*, 233–5; Maddicott, 205.

[118] Prestwich argues convincingly that Lancaster was not directly responsible and that the Scots were not involved: 'Gilbert de Middleton', 183–4, 185–6.

[119] Middleton, *Gilbert de Middleton*, 25, citing Durham Treasury, Misc. Charters 4238; Phillips, 126; Maddicott, 204.

[120] Phillips, 127. Beaumont was eventually consecrated by the bishop of Winchester in Westminster Abbey on 26 March 1318, in the presence of the cardinals: *Ann. Paul.*, 282.

[121] *Trokelowe*, 100; *Hist. Dunelm. Script. Tres*, 100; Maddicott, 205.

[122] Another connection between Lancaster and Middleton's activities and a possible cause of them may have been the arrest in Aug. 1317 of Middleton's cousin, Adam de Swinburne (a royal household knight since 1311), for speaking too *rudement* to the king about the condition of the Scottish March. When Swinburne was released in Oct. 1317 he was delivered to Lancaster: Maddicott, 206; Phillips, 152.

1. Eagle Tower, Caernarfon castle, where, traditionally, Edward is said to have been born in 1284. The tower with its triple turrets, each surmounted by an eagle, was not however finished until much later (Cadw, Welsh Assembly Government; Crown Copyright).

2. Edward I creating Edward Prince of Wales in 1301, from the fourteenth-century Rochester chronicle (BL, Cotton Ms. Nero D.II, f.19v; © British Library Board).

3. Original document from the French chancery recording the betrothal of Edward and Isabella, 1303. It was probably among Edward II's possessions plundered in 1326 (courtesy of the Royal Institution of South Wales, Swansea; held at the West Glamorgan Archive Service RISW DOC 5/3).

4. Isabella kneeling between the shields of England and France. From the Psalter of Queen Isabella of England, made for Isabella either to mark her betrothal or her marriage (Bayerische Staatsbibliothek, Munich, Cod.gall. 16, f. 94r).

5. Silver-gilt casket with arms of Isabella and of her aunt, Margaret of France, wife of Edward I. Probably a gift from Margaret to Isabella either at the time of Isabella's betrothal or of her marriage (© Trustees of the British Museum).

6. Wedding of Edward and Isabella, at Boulogne, January 1308. From Jean de Wavrin's *Chroniques d'Angleterre*, a ms. made in Flanders, *c.*1474–80, for Edward IV (BL, Royal Ms. 15.E.iv, f. 295v © British Library Board).

7. Coronation of a king, in a ms. containing the coronation order of Edward II, 1308 (Corpus Christi College, Cambridge, Ms. 20, f. 68; courtesy of the Master and Fellows).

8. Edward II holding a sword and a sceptre. From the genealogy of English kings known as the Chaworth Roll, probably produced in the early 1320s (courtesy of Sam Fogg, London).

9a and b. Sabrina Lenzi as Isabella, and Wolfgang Stollwitzer as Edward, in David Bintley's ballet, *Edward II* (photographs: Bill Cooper) Birmingham Royal Ballet.

10a, b and c. Miniatures showing Philip IV and Edward II girding Philip's sons with their swords in Paris, June 1313, and the two kings riding out with trumpets preceding them. From a translation of the Book of Kalila and Dimna by Raymond de Béziers, presented to Philip IV in 1313 (Bibliothèque Nationale de France, Paris, Ms. Latin 8504, f. 1v).

11. Miniature showing the opening of the sixth vial: the kings of France and England leading the kings of the East gathered together for the battle of Armageddon. From a ms. of the Apocalypse given to Isabella by Philip IV on the occasion of her visit to Paris with Edward II in 1313, and also marking the taking of the cross by Edward and Philip (Bibliothèque Nationale de France, Paris, Ms. Fr. 13096, f. 50).

12. Representation of the Battle of Bannockburn, 1314, from the fifteenth-century Scotichronicon of Walter Bower (Corpus Christi College, Cambridge, Ms. 171, f. 265; courtesy of the Master and Fellows).

13. Execution of Hugh Despenser the Younger at Hereford, November 1326, from the Chronicles of Jean Froissart (Bibliothèque Nationale de France, Paris, Ms. Fr. 2643, f. 197).

14. Representation of a king and queen kneeling, from the Taymouth Hours, probably made for Isabella between the fall of Edward II in 1326 and 1330 (Yates Thompson Ms. 13, f. 18 © British Library Board).

15. A king and queen, apparently intended to be Edward II and Isabella, looking at one another with unhappy expressions, from Walter de Milemete, *De nobilitatibus, sapientiis, et prudentiis regum*, composed in 1326–7 and presented to Edward III (Christ Church, Oxford, Ms. 92, f. 4v).

16. Berkeley castle, Gloucestershire, the scene of Edward II's imprisonment and death, September 1327 (© Crown Copyright NMR; Wingham Collection).

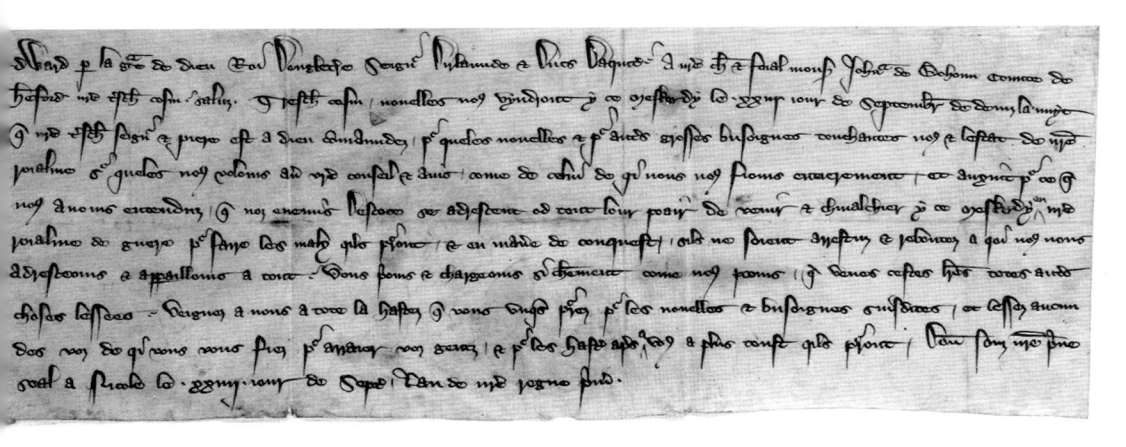

17. Letter of 24 September 1327 from Edward III at Lincoln to John de Bohun, earl of Hereford, in which the young king announces that he had received news *de deinz la nuyt* of the death of Edward II (The National Archives, DL 10/253).

18. Edward II's tomb, Gloucester cathedral (© Angelo Hornak Picture Library).

19. Castle of Melazzo, near Acqui Terme north of Genoa, in which Edward II is alleged to have lived as a hermit (author's photograph).

20. Monastery of S. Alberto di Butrio, near the small town of Cecima, in which Edward II is alleged to have lived after moving from Melazzo (author's photograph).

21. The alleged tomb of Edward II in the monastery of S. Alberto di Butrio (author's photograph).

22. Former cathedral of Saint-Pierre-de-Maguelone, on a sand-spit bounded by the Mediterranean and a lagoon, a few kilometres from Montpellier (photograph © David Merlin).

23. Letter of Manuel Fieschi to Edward III, *c*.1336–8, containing the alleged confession of Edward II. The word 'vacat' ('it is vacant'; i.e., 'it is cancelled') was later inserted in the top right-hand corner of the transcript (Archives départementales de l'Hérault, Montpellier, France, G 1123, Register A of the diocese of Maguelone, f. 86r).

24. The 'Oxwich Brooch': early fourteenth-century set gold ring brooch. Possibly among Edward II's possessions plundered in 1326. Discovered at Oxwich castle in Gower in 1968 (National Museum of Wales).

they arrived on about 8 September.[123] Once in York, the two cardinals and the earl of Pembroke made another attempt to mediate between Edward and Lancaster. They appear to have achieved some success: Edward promised not to take any action against Lancaster or his supporters, while Lancaster agreed to attend a parliament whenever and wherever one was summoned. As an immediate consequence a parliament was summoned on 24 September to meet at Lincoln on 27 January 1318.[124] At the same time the Scottish campaign was finally abandoned.[125] Also on 24 September the earls of Pembroke and Hereford successfully asked Edward to grant a safe conduct to Lancaster and his adherents, and were given powers to free any of Lancaster's men who might be arrested in breach of this guarantee. Two days later the two earls were also authorized at their own suggestion to look after and to safeguard the interests of Lancaster's followers until the opening of the coming parliament. Since both men were prominent members of the king's council it is clear that there was an important element among Edward's close associates who were fully aware of the dangers of the current situation and were working hard for a settlement.[126]

These understandings between Edward and Lancaster reduced the immediate tension. Edward dismissed much of the force he had gathered around him during September, while Lancaster did the same, returning to Pontefract with only a few men and giving up control of the bridges.[127] However, any serious consideration of the real problems outstanding between Edward and his cousin was merely postponed and for there to be any real progress towards a solution both sides would have to act in good faith. This did not happen. On 29 September Edward and his followers left York for London, this time taking the direct route to the south via Pontefract, which was no longer blocked by Lancaster's men. Edward still had a considerable force with him and as he approached Pontefract, which was now weakly defended, he drew up his men and threatened to attack. According to the plausible account of one chronicle, Edward was encouraged by some of his close associates, presumably men such as Damory, Audley and Montacute. For his part Lancaster and his men jeered at Edward from the top of the castle ditch. But for the prompt action of the earl of Pembroke – who reminded Edward that all disputes between himself and Lancaster had been suspended until the coming parliament and told him that if Lancaster were planning to attack the king he would

---

[123] SAL Ms. 121, f. 7; *Hist. Dunelm. Script. Tres*, 100; *Melsa*, 334; Phillips, 128; Maddicott, 206–7. Lancaster then returned to Pontefract: *Trivet (Cont.)*, 23.
[124] SC 1/49/43; *PW*, II, ii, 171; *Trivet (Cont.)*, 23; *Flores*, 180; *Vita*, 140–1; Phillips, 128–9; Maddicott, 209–10. The announcement on 24 Sept. recorded only the intention to hold a parliament on 27 Jan. The formal summons was issued only on 20 Nov.: *PW*, II, ii, 175.
[125] C 17/10, m.16.
[126] E 163/4/7/1; *CPR, 1317–21*, 27, 29; Phillips, 129.
[127] SAL Ms. 121, f. 43; *Trivet (Cont.)*, 23; *Flores*, 180–1; Phillips, 129; Maddicott, 210.

risk the loss of everything he possessed – a full-scale attack on Pontefract might have developed. Fortunately Pembroke managed to persuade Edward, and the king and his men resumed their journey to London.[128]

Lancaster now gave full vent to his fury at Edward's perceived betrayal. On 5 October John de Lilburn seized Knaresborough on his behalf from the constable appointed by Roger Damory; Alton castle in Staffordshire, formerly belonging to Theobald de Verdon and also in Damory's custody, was attacked at the same time. As a precautionary measure Damory's lands in Yorkshire, Herefordshire and Lincolnshire were taken into royal hands on 24 October, in the hope that this would restrain Lancaster from further actions. Lancaster had evidently singled out Damory for attack, since there is no indication that either Audley or Montacute was threatened at this time. Knaresborough was not given up until late January 1318, and then only after a long and expensive siege.[129] Gilbert de Middleton, the captor of the cardinals, also held out at Mitford until January, when he was captured and taken to London for trial and execution.[130] Apart from Roger Damory, Lancaster reserved his special anger for the earl of Surrey. In October he attacked and quickly seized Surrey's Yorkshire castles of Sandal and Conisborough, and held on to them, despite Edward II's protests. In 1318 Lancaster also invaded and threatened to take Surrey's lordships of Bromfield and Yale (Iâl) in the Welsh March, which were close to Lancaster's own lordship of Denbigh.[131]

In an attempt to prevent further outbreaks of violence, in early October Edward forbade the holding of tournaments throughout England in case these were used as a pretext for gathering armed forces. On 1 November the earl of Pembroke was reappointed as constable of the important castle of Rockingham near Lancaster's own castle at Leicester, which Pembroke had held for the king since 1314, while one of his retainers received charge of Gloucester. Badlesmere was put in command of Leeds castle in Kent, the Younger Despenser of Odiham in Hampshire, and the constables of sixteen other royal castles in the Midlands and elsewhere were ordered to prepare their defences.[132] Edward's financial needs were answered on 7 November when Pembroke, Hereford, Badlesmere, the archbishop of Canterbury, and the bishops of Ely and Winchester acted as guarantors for a loan of 10,000 marks by the Florentine banking company, the

---

[128] *Vita*, 140–3; *Trivet (Cont.)*, 24; *Flores*, 181; Phillips, 129–30; Maddicott, 210. The speech attributed to Pembroke in the *Vita Edwardi Secundi* was of course invented but it almost certainly represents the opinions expressed by him.

[129] *CFR, 1307–19*, 225, 346–7; *Foedera*, II, i, 345–6; *CPR, 1317–21*, 34, 38, 46; Phillips, 127, 134; Maddicott, 207. Damory's lands were restored to him on 2 Dec.: *CPR, 1317–21*, 58.

[130] Phillips, 128; Maddicott, 206. The record of Middleton's trial is printed in Middleton, *Gilbert de Middleton*, 57, from *Abbrevatio Placitorum*, Record Commission (London, 1811), 329.

[131] *CCR, 1313–18*, 554, 575; Phillips, 133–4, 165; Maddicott, 207–8, 220.

[132] *Foedera*, II, ii, 343; *CPR, 1317–21*, 46; *CFR, 1307–19*, 344; *CCR, 1313–18*, 504–5; Phillips, 151–2. In March 1318 Edward granted Leeds (previously held for life by Edward I's widow, Queen Margaret) to Badlesmere: *CPR, 1317–21*, 128.

Bardi.¹³³ At about the same the king's personal banker, Antonio Pessagno of Genoa, was appointed as seneschal of the duchy of Gascony with powers to raise a loan there of 20,000 marks and to liquidate what remained of Clement V's loan of 1314.¹³⁴ If civil war were to break out, Edward would at least be prepared.

RESTRAINING THE FAVOURITES

A further way of reducing the likelihood of civil war was to recognize the legitimacy of Lancaster's suspicions of the king's favourites by doing something practical to restrain them. On 24 November 1317 the earl of Pembroke and Bartholomew de Badlesmere made a formal agreement in London with Roger Damory. Damory promised to do his best to persuade Edward to allow himself to be guided by the advice of Pembroke and Badlesmere and to trust their advice above that of anyone else, provided that their counsel was to the advantage of Edward and his kingdom. Damory also promised not to procure or consent to the king's granting of land worth more than £20 without the knowledge and agreement of Pembroke and Badlesmere; nor would he connive at or consent to any action by the king which might be prejudicial to himself or to his crown. Damory would not persuade or allow anyone else to persuade the king to do any of these things in the absence of Pembroke and Badlesmere, and he would also warn them if he discovered that anyone was trying to influence the king against them. Damory also bound himself to keep the agreement by oath and by a pledge of £10,000. In turn, Pembroke and Badlesmere promised to defend and maintain Damory against all men, saving only the king, provided that Damory kept his part of the agreement. As a further guarantee, the two men bound themselves, their heirs, and all their moveable and immoveable goods to the will of Damory. One part of the indenture was sealed by Pembroke and Badlesmere and the other by Damory.¹³⁵

This document was interpreted by nineteenth- and early twentieth-century historians, notably William Stubbs, T.F. Tout and J.C. Davies, as

---

¹³³ E 368/88, m.112; E 159/91, m.40d; Phillips, 152. The Bardi and their sister Florentine company, the Peruzzi, were a major source of credit for the crown and a safe place for magnates such as the Despensers to deposit their accumulated wealth: see E.B. Fryde, 'The deposits of Hugh Despenser the Younger with Italian bankers', in Fryde, *Studies in Medieval Trade and Finance* (London, 1983), item III, 344–62, esp. 355–7.

¹³⁴ C 81/93/3556; C 81/102/4482, 4491, 4495; C 61/32, m.16; *Foedera*, II, ii, 346–7; Phillips, 182. Pessagno was very much in favour, having been given £3,000 in Nov. 1315 when he became a royal knight and a further £3,000 in Oct. 1317. These large payments were probably disguised interest for the loans he made to Edward II, amounting in total between April 1312 and Jan. 1319 to almost £144,000: see the article on Pessagno by E.B. Fryde in *Oxford DNB*.

¹³⁵ E 163/4/6; Phillips, 135; Maddicott, 211–12. The text is printed in Phillips, App. 4, 319–20; and in *PW*, II, ii, App., 120, and Davies, *Baronial Opposition*, App., no. 42.

evidence that in the autumn of 1317 Pembroke and Badlesmere were attempting to form a political alliance which sought to control royal policy and to stand between Lancaster on the one hand and the king's adherents, such as the Despensers and other royal favourites, on the other. This alliance was accordingly described as the 'middle party'[136] and the interpretation then became a standard part of writings on the reign of Edward II,[137] until the early 1970s when a new generation of scholars began to challenge the old certainties.[138] The 'middle party' has, as a result, largely disappeared from historical treatments of the early fourteenth century.[139]

The reality was that, far from trying to create a political following of their own, Pembroke and Badlesmere were experienced and responsible royal councillors of long standing,[140] who were extremely concerned at the deterioration in the relations between Edward II and Lancaster and especially worried by the contribution to the growing political instability of ambitious royal favourites such as Roger Damory. The purpose of the now-famous indenture of 24 November 1317 was therefore to control and to restrain Damory's conduct. In the circumstances of 1317 no one was more likely to try to persuade the king to make excessively generous grants of land than Damory. Damory's recent behaviour and Lancaster's singling him out for special treatment in October showed just how dangerous he had become. A solution to the problem was all the more urgent since on 15 November the king had ordered the delivery of Damory's share of the great Gloucester inheritance.[141] Although there is no reason to believe that

---

[136] For a discussion of how the 'middle party' interpretation came into being and the contribution to it of Stubbs, Tout and Davies see Phillips, 135–41. Cf. Maddicott, 211–12. Some of the major statements of the 'middle party' theory are to be found in Stubbs, *Constitutional History*, ii, 342; Tout, *Place of the Reign* (1st edn), 111–12, 144–5; Davies, *Baronial Opposition*, 429, 433–4, 437.

[137] See, for example, J.G. Edwards, 'The negotiating of the Treaty of Leake, 1318', in *Essays in History presented to R.L. Poole*, ed. H.W.C. Davis (Oxford, 1927), 360–78, esp. 376–7; and B. Wilkinson, 'The negotiations preceding the "Treaty" of Leake, August 1318', in *Studies in Medieval History presented to F.M. Powicke*, ed. R.W. Hunt, W.A. Pantin & R.W. Southern (Oxford, 1948), 333–53, esp. 336–9; B. Wilkinson, *Constitutional History of Medieval England*, ii, *Politics and the Constitution, 1307–1399* (London, 1952), 16–19, 80; McKisack, *The Fourteenth Century*, 51–4.

[138] Notably Phillips, esp. ch. 5, 'The "Middle Party" and the negotiating of the Treaty of Leake, 1318'; Phillips, 'The "Middle Party" and the negotiating of the Treaty of Leake, August 1318', *BIHR*, xlvii (1973), 11–27; and Maddicott, 199, 210–13. In his textbook, *The Later Middle Ages* (London, 1969), 124, Wilkinson described the 'middle party' as 'so-called', while still making use of the interpretation, but otherwise the 'middle party' reigned supreme.

[139] See, for example, Prestwich, *Plantagenet England*, 202–3, where the 'middle party' is described as 'a mirage'; and Raban, *England under Edward I and Edward II*, 148–9, where the events of 1317–18 are discussed without any mention of a 'middle party'.

[140] For a short summary of both men's careers before Nov. 1317 see Phillips, 141–5. Ironically, like Damory, Badlesmere's earlier career had been spent in the service of the earl of Gloucester, until the latter's death at Bannockburn in 1314. This common experience may have given Badlesmere additional influence over Damory in 1317.

[141] *CFR, 1307–19*, 350–1; Altschul, *Baronial Family*, 169.

Pembroke and Badlesmere were acting without the king's agreement and approval,[142] the very fact of their having to make such an indenture with Damory is an indication that their influence over the king and the making of policy had its limits. As Edward II's letters to Pembroke show, including a very remarkable one written in December 1316,[143] Edward was prepared to follow sound advice when it was given to him by men he trusted. But he could just as easily be persuaded to make bad decisions by irresponsible favourites whose company he enjoyed. From this point of view, Edward II was as heavy a cross to bear for his friends as he was for his enemies.[144]

EDWARD II AND THE MAGNATES

The 'middle party' interpretation of Pembroke and Badlesmere's actions in the autumn of 1317 is further undermined by the fact that the two men entered into binding contracts not just with Roger Damory but with the king himself. In Pembroke's case this took place on 1 November 1317, at the same time that precautions were being taken against the possibility of civil war and just over three weeks before the agreement with Damory. Pembroke bound himself to serve the king for life in peace and war in return for land worth 500 marks and an annual peacetime fee of over 1,000 marks. In wartime he was to receive a fee of 2,000 marks (later increased to 2,500 marks) and to supply the king with a retinue of 200 men-at-arms.[145] Badlesmere had already made contracts with the king. On 29 September 1316 he had promised to stay in the king's service in peacetime at an annual fee of 600 marks, and in war with a retinue of 100 men. At a date before 3 August 1317 this was supplemented by an annual sum of 1,000 marks, by which Edward retained him for the value of his

---

[142] Davies, *Baronial Opposition*, 434, wrongly believed that the indenture was kept secret from the king on the grounds of Edward's pardon to Badlesmere in Aug. 1321 for his breach of a certain 'writing': *CPR, 1321–24*, 21. The 'writing' instead referred to the two contracts which Badlesmere made to serve Edward in 1316 and 1317, which he broke by rebelling against the Despensers in 1321.

[143] SC 1/49/39: written on 19 Dec., shortly before Pembroke's departure for Avignon. The text is printed in Phillips, App. 4, 317. Edward promised to follow without default the advice that Pembroke had left him for the conduct of his government during his absence. In a most unusual personal touch, which indicates the respect Edward had for Pembroke, the king offered to act in person as Pembroke's attorney while he was abroad: Phillips, 110.

[144] It is hard, if not impossible, to imagine Edward I, for example, being persuaded to make rash decisions involving royal patronage in the way in which his son was to be influenced: see, for example, Prestwich, *Edward I*, 346–52, 537–40; K.B. McFarlane, 'Had Edward I a "Policy" towards the earls?', *History*, l (1965), 145–59. For a recent examination of the question see A. M. Spencer, 'Royal patronage and the earls in the reign of Edward I', *History*, xciii, no. 309 (2008), 20–46.

[145] E 101/68/2/42D: this is the original indenture, which has suffered damage. For the text see Phillips, App. 3, 314–15. The 500 marks of land were given to him in the form of a grant in tail on 4 Nov. of Haverfordwest and Hertford, both of which he already held for life: *CPR, 1317–21*, 47; Phillips, 142–3.

counsel. On 12 November 1317 he was further rewarded with a grant of land worth 400 marks.[146]

These were not the only contracts made between Edward II and leading magnates. Roger Damory, the other party to the indenture of 24 November 1317, had contracted on 15 January 1317 to serve the king in return for 200 marks per year. The intended size of his retinue in wartime is not known.[147] Damory's co-favourite in 1317, William de Montacute, followed suit on the same date and on the same terms;[148] as did Hugh Audley the Younger.[149] Of the other important magnates, the earl of Hereford promised on 1 September 1316 to serve in peace and war at a fee of 1,000 marks in peacetime and 2,000 marks in wartime, when he would bring 100 men-at-arms. In September 1317 he was granted the lordship of Builth in the Welsh March in return for past and future services, probably as a way of paying his annual fee.[150] On 18 October 1316 Hugh Despenser the Younger contracted to serve in war for two years with thirty men in return for an annual payment of 400 marks but was later given a fee of 600 marks for staying with the king. On 18 November 1317 payment of this increased fee was met by a life grant of 500 marks of land in Wales.[151]

There is evidence between September 1316 and September 1317 of contracts for smaller fees and contingents between Edward II and at least eleven other middle-ranking magnates, some for wartime only, others both in peace and in war.[152] Other magnates of the first rank indicated their co-operation with the king by accepting important military and administrative appointments. In November 1316 the earl of Arundel became warden of the Scottish March, while Roger Mortimer of Wigmore and his uncle Roger Mortimer of Chirk accepted office as king's lieutenant in Ireland and justice of Wales respectively. On 7 October 1317 Mortimer of Chirk was reappointed for life as justice of North and South Wales.[153]

These indications of extensive and apparently unforced co-operation between a large number of magnates and the king are very much at odds with the traditional view of the reign of Edward II as a period of

---

[146] SAL Ms. 120, f. 45; SAL Ms. 121, f. 20v; C 81/101/4339; *CPR, 1317–21*, 14; Phillips, 145, 149, 312.

[147] E 403/180, m.3; *CPR, 1313–17*, 609; Phillips, 149, 313. The annual fee for a royal household knight was 10 marks, and 20 marks for a banneret, so Damory was being paid well above the usual rate.

[148] E 403/180, m.3; *CPR, 1313–17*, 609; Phillips, 149, 313.

[149] *CPR, 1317–21*, 572; *CPR, 1327–30*, 30; Phillips, 149, 314. The full text of Audley's contract was enrolled on the Patent Roll in 1321: C 66/154, m.17.

[150] E 404/1/7; SAL Ms. 121, f. 38; E 101/378/4, f. 16; *CChR, 1300–26*, 367; Phillips, 149, 312.

[151] E 101/13/36/139; *CPR, 1317–21*, 56; Phillips, 149, 312, 314.

[152] John de Mowbray, John Giffard, John de Somery, John de Segrave the Elder, Henry Fitz Hugh, William de Ros of Helmsley (alias Hamelak), John Cromwell, John Botetourt, John de Wysham, Giles de Beauchamp, William de la Zouche of Ashby: Phillips, 149; Maddicott, 203, 210–11. For the details see Phillips, App. 3, 313–14.

[153] E 101/68/2/37; *CPR, 1313–17*, 563; *CFR, 1307–19*, 312, 342; Phillips, 149–50.

prolonged tension between a king intent on preserving his independence of action and on defending his favourites on the one hand, and on the other a baronial opposition led by the earl of Lancaster which was equally intent on imposing upon him both its control and a programme of reform symbolized by the Ordinances.[154] Such a straightforward dichotomy does not however do justice to the history of the reign and to the complexity of the personal interests and relationships which made up political life of the time. For example, once the initial period of tension caused by Edward's devotion to Gaveston was over the majority of the English magnates showed their practical loyalty to the king. In part this was the result of self-interest in such cases as Hugh Despenser the Elder and Henry de Beaumont, who were dependent for their political survival on royal patronage and support. For others, such as Pembroke, Hereford and Badlesmere, it was probably because they felt a duty to aid the king at times of crisis.[155] Many other magnates showed loyalty to the king because this was the natural thing to do: in a monarchy, to whose head they were bound by ties of homage and fealty, there was both legally and practically nowhere else for them to go. What is also apparent is that long before the autumn of 1317 Thomas of Lancaster had become what amounted to a one-man opposition. Once the earl of Warwick had died in 1315 Lancaster had few if any friends, no allies, and an increasing number of critics and real enemies. His interventions in the affairs of the kingdom had failed, both because of these facts, and because he proved to be incompetent. Given this situation there was no incentive for any of the magnates to exchange the rule of the king for that of his first cousin. Lancaster was in consequence reduced to using the Ordinances as a rallying cry which his fellow magnates were no longer prepared to answer, and to impeding the government of the country and the conduct of warfare by using the vast financial and territorial resources at his disposal in the Midlands and the north of England.[156] The willingness of so many of the magnates to rally round the king in 1316 and 1317 was in part due to the critical dangers facing England after the disaster at Bannockburn and the need to ensure that the king had an adequate and guaranteed military force at his disposal. From this point of view the contracts between Edward and the magnates are one aspect of the new military expedients that were tried out in 1314 and 1315.[157] But the

---

[154] Among the classic statements of this view are Tout, *Place of the Reign*, and Davies, *Baronial Opposition*.

[155] Pembroke was also Edward II's cousin and Hereford was Edward's brother-in-law.

[156] Phillips, 283–7. Cf. Maddicott, 198–204, which is a critical but also a much more sympathetic view of Lancaster.

[157] In 1314–15, for example, Edward recruited large numbers of knights to his household. The contracts with the magnates were in essence very similar but on a much larger and politically more significant scale: Tebbit, 'Royal patronage', 203–4. The attempts to extend the bounds of military obligation by obtaining unpaid military service from the northern counties and individual vills however met with mixed success and became a source of grievance: Maddicott, 171–2; Powicke, *Military Obligation*, 142.

contracts were also a political statement. Lancaster's fellow magnates had lost patience with him and regarded his demands for reform as cloaking a demand for supreme political power for himself which they were not prepared to concede.[158] Edward II's attraction of such a wide degree of support and co-operation also suggests that he had a much greater level of political skill than he is usually credited with.[159] However, the willingness of so many magnates to enter into binding contracts to serve the king laid them open to serious dangers, even to the risk of life and limb, if circumstances changed and they found themselves opposing the king. This was to happen to Badlesmere and Hugh Audley in 1321–2 when they joined the rebellion against the Despensers, and to Pembroke when he supported the Despensers' exile.[160]

THE LONG ROAD TO PEACE

Civil war was avoided in the autumn of 1317, partly because of the measures taken by the king and his supporters to prevent it but also because in the last resort no one wanted it. English politics were embittered but had not yet reached this extremity. Instead a process began which led to long-drawn-out and tedious negotiations and ultimately to a treaty of peace between Edward and Lancaster in August 1318. A critical mediating role was played in these negotiations by the English bishops, the archbishop of Dublin,[161] and the papal envoys, while Edward was represented by moderate councillors such as Pembroke, Hereford and Badlesmere. The fact that the archbishop of Canterbury and the bishops of Ely, Winchester and Norwich were members both of the king's council and of the body of clergy also helped the negotiating process.

Contact with Lancaster was apparently resumed in early November when the archbishop of Dublin was sent from London by Edward and his council to visit Lancaster at Pontefract to deliver a message orally on the king's behalf. This mission seems to have provided Lancaster with some reassurance since on 20 November a parliament was formally summoned to meet at Lincoln on 27 January 1318, as had been agreed at York in September.[162]

---

[158] Phillips, 150, 285–7.

[159] He had already shown some of this skill in the way in which he gradually wore down his opponents in 1312–13. This is a more favourable assessment of Edward II's ability than I expressed in my *Aymer de Valence*: Phillips, 150.

[160] Badlesmere lost his life in 1322, while Pembroke was arrested and forced to make a humiliating pledge of loyalty. Hugh Audley survived to become earl of Gloucester in 1337: *CPR, 1321–24*, 21; *CCR, 1318–23*, 563–4; *CPR, 1327–30*, 30; Phillips, 146, 151, 227, 314.

[161] Alexander Bicknor, the former treasurer of Ireland, had been consecrated as archbishop at Avignon in Aug. 1317. He spent the following year in England before returning to Dublin in Oct. 1318.

[162] SAL Ms. 121, f. 30; *CCR, 1313–18*, 585; Phillips, 153; Maddicott, 210. The archbishop was away for 15 days.

On 27 and 28 November the bishops of the Canterbury province assembled at St Paul's, officially to hear the cardinals read out the papal bulls ordering the Scots to cease their attacks on England and Ireland,[163] but, given the imminence of a parliament, they may also have discussed the political situation in England. They certainly had the opportunity to do so at a meeting with the king's council on 30 December, when ten prelates of the Canterbury province, including the chancellor the bishop of Winchester and the treasurer the bishop of Ely, assembled together with the magnate members of the council, who included Pembroke, Hereford and Badlesmere.[164] According to the account of the assembly in the *Vita Edwardi Secundi*, it was agreed that it would be unwise to hold a parliament in January as previously intended, because of the danger of a clash between the large bodies of armed retainers who would certainly accompany Lancaster and the king. They decided that it would first of all be wiser to restore harmony and confidence between the two men by means of mediation, after which a new date could be settled for a parliament. On 4 January 1318 the parliament was accordingly postponed from 27 January to 12 March, while Edward renewed the powers of Pembroke and Hereford to grant letters of safe conduct to Lancaster and his adherents.[165]

A CRUCIAL MEETING AT LEICESTER

Soon afterwards John Salmon, a trusted royal councillor as well as bishop of Norwich, visited Lancaster at Pontefract, presumably to discover if there was any basis for reopening negotiations.[166] On 15 January the bishops of the Canterbury province were summoned to meet at St Paul's on 23 February to discuss the affairs of Church and State. As a result an assembly of clergy and magnates was arranged to meet the earl of Lancaster at Leicester in April.[167] There can be little doubt that the prelates did so with the active encouragement and agreement of the king and his council. In order to clear the way for the negotiations, the meeting of parliament which was due to begin at Lincoln on 12 March was postponed on 3 March until 19 June (although it was still to be held at Lincoln) and the authority of Pembroke and Hereford to give safe conducts to Lancaster and his men was further renewed.[168] The *Vita Edward Secundi*,

[163] *Ann. Paul.*, 281; Phillips, 153–4.

[164] C 53/104, m.9; *CCR, 1313–18*, 586; Phillips, 154. The other prelates present were the archbishop of Canterbury, the bishops of Norwich, Chichester, Coventry & Lichfield, Bath & Wells, St David's, Worcester and Lincoln.

[165] *CCR, 1313–18*, 590; *CPR, 1317–21*, 69; *Vita*, 144–7; Phillips, 154; Maddicott, 213.

[166] Salmon was at Pontefract on 22 Jan.: Norfolk and Norwich Record Office, Register of John Salmon, f. 72; Phillips, 154. See also the article on Salmon by M.C. Buck in the *Oxford DNB*.

[167] Cambridge Univ. Ms. Ee. V. 31, f. 188v (register of H. of Eastry, prior of Canterbury); *Trivet (Cont.)*, 26; *CPR, 1317–21*, 104; Phillips, 155; Maddicott, 214.

[168] *PW*, II, i, 178; *CPR, 1317–21*, 113; Phillips, 155.

which is usually well informed on such matters, confirms that royal representatives were present and put forward proposals in the king's name which had presumably been carefully considered by the council and approved by Edward himself.[169] At least four such representatives can readily be identified. On 29 March John Sandal, bishop of Winchester and chancellor, was sent by Edward from London to Leicester; on 3 April Badlesmere arrived at Northampton with 100 men-at-arms, on the king's orders, and on 5 April went on to Leicester, accompanied by the earl of Pembroke and Walter Reynolds, the archbishop of Canterbury.[170] The conference at Leicester probably began in earnest with the arrival of these four men. Edward II kept in close touch with his envoys: on 7 April a clerk of William de Montacute, the steward of the royal household, was sent to Leicester with private royal letters, and at some stage in the negotiations Pembroke, Badlesmere and the archbishop each sent messengers to the king at Windsor to report on their work.[171]

The meeting at Leicester was of such great importance that it was recorded by several chroniclers, although with varying amounts of detail. According to the author of the *Gesta Edwardi de Carnarvon*, writing at Bridlington, a 'parliament' was held at Leicester on 12 April, attended by the archbishop of Canterbury, the bishops of Norwich, Chichester, Winchester, Llandaff and Hereford, the earls of Lancaster, Pembroke and Hereford, twenty-eight unnamed barons (who may have included some of Lancaster's leading retainers), the chief justice William de Bereford and Walter de Norwich, one of the barons of the exchequer. All those present swore on the Gospels to see that the Ordinances were observed, that evil and unsuitable royal councillors were removed, and that grants of land made by the king contrary to the Ordinances should be rescinded and their holders made to come to parliament for a decision on their possession of the lands. Lancaster's offences against the king in his search for better government of the realm, and his seizure of castles and property, should be pardoned, and any of his men arrested by the king should be freed. Lancaster would also make peace with the Despensers, who for their part would agree to become Lancaster's retainers for life.[172] The *Flores Historiarum* records simply that the magnates, papal envoys and prelates met Lancaster at Leicester and agreed on oath to observe the Ordinances and keep the peace.[173] The Leicester chronicle of

---

[169] *Vita*, 146–7; Phillips, 158.

[170] SAL Ms. 121, f. 20v; *CCR, 1313–18*, 603; Phillips, 158; Maddicott, 215–16. Pembroke, Badlesmere and Reynolds rejoined Edward on about 20 April. The bishop of Norwich was at Leicester from 4 to 12 April: Reg. John Salmon, f. 74.

[171] SAL Ms. 121, ff. 12v, 20v; Phillips, 159; Maddicott, 216.

[172] *Gesta Edwardi*, 54–5; Phillips, 155–6; Maddicott, 216. Lancaster's seizure of Knaresborough had already been pardoned on 19 March: *CPR, 1317–21*, 123. It was highly improbable that the Despensers would ever agree to be bound in this way.

[173] *Flores*, 183–4; Phillips, 155.

Henry Knighton speaks of certain articles which were agreed at Leicester between Lancaster and the prelates and which were afterwards confirmed at London by the cardinals, the archbishops of Canterbury and Dublin, and the other prelates of the Canterbury province.[174] The *Vita Edwardi Secundi* says that the archbishops, earls and barons, acting on the king's behalf, met Lancaster's councillors at Leicester, where they put to Lancaster a number of points, to all of which he refused to give his assent unless the Ordinances were observed. Because of Lancaster's firm stand the archbishop and certain earls promised on their own behalf and on behalf of the king that the Ordinances would be observed and that a document embodying their oath and sealed by each of them should be drawn up. For his part Lancaster promised his due fealty and security to the king and his men, saving only his quarrel with the earl of Surrey over the abduction of his wife.[175]

Further light on the Leicester meeting is thrown by a document preserved as a transcript in the Dodsworth manuscripts in the Bodleian Library in Oxford, which can probably be identified with the articles described by Knighton as being agreed between the clergy and Lancaster.[176] This agreement contains promises by Lancaster that he would not in future commit armed breaches of the peace, that he would come to parliament when summoned and do reverence to the king, and would remit his quarrel with the earl of Surrey until the next parliament. In return the prelates promised on behalf of themselves and the other bishops of the Canterbury province that Lancaster and his men would be given surety for when they came to parliament, and that the agreement would be guaranteed by the authority of the Church. At the same time Lancaster took an oath that he had never wished to deprive the king of his royal power, and that he wished to maintain the Ordinances and see that all land alienated contrary to them was restored to the crown. The document as it is now preserved is undated but the reference to the earl of Surrey shows that it belongs to some time after the abduction of the countess of Lancaster in May 1317. The reference in Lancaster's oath to the Ordinances and the revocation of grants of land also matches other evidence about his demands at Leicester.[177] The prelates are mentioned in the agreement as being those of the province of Canterbury and presumably therefore include the five named in the Bridlington account, while the archbishops named in the heading would be those of Canterbury and of

---

[174] *Knighton*, i, 413; Phillips, 155.

[175] *Vita*, 146–7; Phillips, 156.

[176] The document is headed '*Une accorde entre ercevesques e evesques dune parte e le conte de Lancastre daltre parte de dicto comite veniendo ad parliamentum*': Bod., Dodsworth Ms. 8, p. 262; Phillips, 157. The Latin words in the title were probably added by the transcriber. For the text and other details see Phillips, App. 4, 319–20. It is also published in Maddicott, 336–7, but under the suggested date of Sept. 1317.

[177] *Knighton*, i, 413; Phillips, 157.

Dublin. This identification of the document with the Knighton articles is strengthened by the implication in the agreement that it was made on behalf of the prelates of Canterbury by part of their number and that, as in Knighton's account, it would require confirmation by the remainder of the province's bishops.[178] It is likely that the date of 12 April given by the Bridlington chronicler for the holding of the Leicester meeting marked the end of the negotiations and was possibly also the date on which the articles were agreed between the prelates and the earl of Lancaster.[179]

There is no surviving evidence to confirm the statements of the Bridlington chronicler and the *Vita Edwardi Secundi* that both the clergy and certain of the earls put their seals to another document in which they swore to uphold the Ordinances, but it is certainly possible that some such undertaking was given. At the very least it was now clear to the king and his councillors that Lancaster still saw the Ordinances as the central plank in his demands, together with the removal from court of royal favourites and the resumption of grants.

DEBATES AT WESTMINSTER

Events now moved back to Westminster.[180] The next stage in the negotiations for which there is clear evidence is revealed in a very important series of discussions held at Westminster in June to consider how a fresh round of talks with Lancaster ought to be approached and what concessions should be made to his demands. The Westminster discussions are first of all revealed in two closely related documents, one dated 2 June, and the

---

[178] *Gesta Edwardi*, 54; *Knighton*, i, 413; Phillips, 157.

[179] A case can also be made, as in Maddicott, 208–9, for dating the document to the negotiations at Pontefract in Sept. 1317. However, so far as is known from chronicle sources, those negotiations were restricted to the simple question of Lancaster's attendance at parliament and did not refer to the Ordinances or to gifts made by the king. The document also implies, by Lancaster's promise not to commit armed attacks, that he had already been making these. In Sept. 1317 he had not yet attacked Damory or Surrey but had taken up arms between then and April 1318. In the end the dating comes down to a matter of judgement, with room for differing opinions. If the suggested dating of the document is correct, it adds further valuable evidence on the Leicester meeting and confirms the impression given by Knighton, who in respect of the negotiations in 1318 appears to have had access to material unused by or unknown to other writers, that the clergy played a prominent role at Leicester. This is fully in line with their earlier role both in mediating with Lancaster and in organizing the Leicester meeting.

Although he wrote well after 1318, Henry Knighton came from St Mary's house of Augustinian canons in Leicester which may have preserved evidence of the events of 1318. This was probably also the source of the Tutbury articles of June 1318: *Knighton*, i, 413–21; Phillips, 158. It is even possible, though there is no evidence to confirm this supposition, that the April 1318 meeting was held at St Mary's.

[180] The bishop of Norwich was back in London by 19 May, while the bishop of Winchester was there by 20 April: Reg. John Salmon, f. 75; *Registers of John de Sandale and Rigaud de Asserio, Bishops of Winchester, 1316–23*, ed. F.J. Baigent (Winchester, 1897), lx.

other undated. Both appear to be drafts of a final document which is no longer extant.[181] The document of 2 June lists those present as the archbishops of Canterbury and Dublin, etc., and the earl of Pembroke, etc. and is also endorsed with the names of the bishops of Norwich, Coventry & Lichfield, Chichester, London, Salisbury, Winchester, Ely, Hereford and Worcester, the earl of Hereford, the Elder and Younger Despensers, Roger Damory and William de Montacute. The other version of the document gives the participants only as the archbishops, Pembroke, Hereford, Despenser, and 'other great men of the kingdom'. It is however clear that the prelates were again acting as mediators and that on this occasion they were meeting with members of Edward II's council.[182] The texts reveal the added urgency given to the discussions by the Scots' attack on Yorkshire in May, following their capture of the key border fortress of Berwick in April,[183] since the prelates and magnates of the council had met to advise Edward on the defence of his kingdom as well as to give him prompt counsel and aid on the good government of the realm. They had also agreed that both individually and collectively they would loyally advise the king to the best of their ability.[184] Both texts also agree in seeing Lancaster's actions as a major barrier to the conduct of the king's government and administration, from which he had withdrawn for some time because of the enmity and malevolence of those around the king, 'as one understands'.[185] This statement in the document of 2 June does in passing recognize that Lancaster might have had cause to fear some of the king's associates, but its implied rebuke of Lancaster is made much more explicit in the other text, which says that Lancaster had not counselled or aided his lord the king as was his duty,[186] and that he had gathered men-at-arms at

---

[181] C 49/4/27, dated 2 June, is badly damaged along its right-hand side, contains several erasures and alterations made in the course of drafting, and was added from unsorted Chancery Miscellanea in Sept. 1922. The text is printed in Phillips, App. 4, 320–1. The other document, C 49/4/26, was edited and published by K. Salisbury as 'A political agreement of June 1318', *EHR*, xxxiii (1918), 81–3. For further discussion of the two documents see also Maddicott, 217–18.

[182] '*e autres grandz du roiaume*'; Phillips, 161; Maddicott, 218.

[183] The castles of Harbottle, Wark and Mitford were lost in May, after which the Scots advanced to Ripon, Knaresborough and Skipton, and almost as far as Lancaster's fortress of Pontefract: Maddicott, 216; McNamee, 151–2. See also I. Kershaw, 'A note on Scottish raids in the West Riding, 1316–18', *Northern History*, xvii (1981), 231–9. Edward II's government had tried to anticipate a possible Scottish attack on 22 March 1318 when John Binstead, the earl of Angus and other envoys were sent to the Scottish March to discuss peace with Robert Bruce. They returned on 24 April, without any success: SAL Ms. 121, ff. 8, 8v, 10.

[184] '*touz iointement e chescun de euz li a son poer ben e loialment conseilleront nostre seignur le Roi*': C 49/4/26 (this fills a gap in C 49/4/27); Phillips, 162.

[185] '*des queux il se est esloigne ia une piece pur grosseur e malevolence de ceux qi sont pres du Roi, a ceo que home entente*': C 49/6/ 27; Phillips, 162.

[186] '*ne se est done a conseiller ne aider a nostre seigneur le Roi en ses busoignes come li appent*': C 49/6/26; Phillips, 162.

parliaments and other royal assemblies, creating fear among the people, among whom it was a common opinion that Lancaster was the cause of ills that had befallen the kingdom.[187] Lancaster's peers evidently also saw his failure to co-operate with the king and his use of armed force as chief causes of the present troubles.

Following this general statement on the reasons for the crisis, those present agreed on the terms of a possible solution. Both texts state, in slightly differing words, that Lancaster should not be allowed to gather armed forces under colour of the Ordinances, to which the prelates and the magnates as well as Lancaster had pledged themselves, and that he should not employ force in an inappropriate manner (and to a greater extent than any other great man of the kingdom),[188] except with the consent of the magnates and prelates named above, or the greater part of them. Lancaster should in future come to parliament as a peer of the realm, without trying to claim superiority for himself over the others,[189] a remark which shows that Lancaster's peers had taken strong exception to his past behaviour. It was also agreed that Lancaster should be offered a guarantee by trustworthy men against those he suspected of abducting his wife, but that any of the suspects who did not wish to be involved in this should instead make amends and that because of the urgency of the situation all this should be done without legal process.[190] All those present at Westminster finally assented to be bound by the agreement and to see that it was upheld.[191]

There is, however, evidence that the June discussions went much further than deciding on the demands that would be made of Lancaster and also considered what concessions Edward II was prepared to make to Lancaster. These were very serious issues which would affect not simply Edward himself but also his favourites, Damory, Audley, Montacute and the Despensers. By 8 June the king's reluctance to begin serious negotiations for a permanent settlement had been overcome to the extent that the bishop of Norwich could announce to an assembly of magnates and prelates meeting at St Paul's in the presence of the king that Edward was ready to follow the advice of his earls and barons and that he would confirm the Ordinances;[192]

---

[187] '*en effroi du people, par quoi commune fame e voiz del people . . . est que par les dites enchesons les ditz maux sont avenuz*': C 49/6/26; Phillips, 162.

[188] '*e noun covenable manere (plus que un autre grant du roiaume)*': C 49/4/26 (which fills gap in C 49/4/27). (The text in parentheses was finally erased in the 2 June version); Phillips, 162.

[189] '*sanz sovereinete a li accrocher vers les autres*': C 49/4/27 (one step further would have been to accuse Lancaster of encroaching upon the king's own sovereignty, as was the case in 1322 when he was charged with treason and executed); Phillips, 162, 225. Lancaster had already promised not to use force and to attend parliament when summoned in his agreement with the prelates at Leicester. The point of repeating the promise as a future demand in June was probably to ensure that it had a formal place in any final settlement.

[190] C 49/6/26. This point is not included in C 49/6/27; Phillips, 163.

[191] C 49/6/26, 27; Phillips, 163.

[192] *Ann. Paul.*, 282; *Flores*, 184; Phillips, 164; Maddicott, 218–19.

on the following day the archbishop of Canterbury also noted in a letter that the king was willing to embrace the way of peace discussed at Leicester;[193] and on the same day an order was issued revoking all grants which had been made contrary to the Ordinances.[194]

A third stage in preparing the ground for negotiations was reached on 11 June, in the form of a promise by five of Edward's closest associates and hence the earl of Lancaster's greatest enemies, Hugh Despenser the Elder, Roger Damory, Hugh Audley the Younger, William de Montacute and John de Charlton, that they would not impede or threaten Lancaster or any of his men in any way when Lancaster came to make his peace with the king.[195] In its initial draft the document contained a clause in which Damory and the others admitted that Lancaster had previously failed to appear before the king 'because of us, as it is said',[196] but this was later crossed out, probably because it was too pointed a condemnation of them. In a striking confirmation of the mediating role that had been played by the English bishops and the papal envoys the document stated that Damory and company had given their guarantee to Lancaster with the permission of the king and at the request of Cardinals Gaucelin d'Eauze and Luke Fieschi, the archbishops of Canterbury and Dublin, and the bishops of London, Winchester, Coventry & Lichfield, Norwich, Chichester, Salisbury, Ely, Worcester and Hereford, all of whom promised to ensure that the guarantee was upheld.[197]

The hope that a new campaign against the Scots might at last be possible was shown on 8 June when the delayed parliament which had been summoned as long ago as November 1317 was finally abandoned in favour of a muster of the army at York on 26 July.[198] The commitment of the king's advisers to reaching a political settlement was demonstrated very clearly on 14 June when they replied to a letter from the earl of Surrey asking for royal help to expel the earl of Lancaster's men from his Welsh

---

[193] HMC, *Various Collections*, i, 267; Phillips, 164; Maddicott, 218.

[194] E 159/91, m.64d; E 368/88, m.92. The text of this order is printed in Maddicott, 337. The magnates who had been in receipt of royal patronage as part of their contracts of service with the king were potentially affected by this decision, as well as the obvious royal favourites. This was one area where Lancaster had a strong argument in his favour. Grants to at least three men, Hugh Audley the Younger, John Giffard and Jakinettus de Marigny (a member of Isabella's household), were revoked on 9 June: *CFR, 1307–17*, 374; *CCR, 1318–23*, 51, 64; Phillips, 164; Maddicott, 218–19.

[195] SC 1/63/183. This document was added to the class of Ancient Correspondence from unsorted miscellanea in December 1967. For the text see Phillips, App. 4, 321–2. Hugh Despenser the Younger was probably included in the guarantee by implication under his father's name, but his absence may again suggest that he was not yet recognized as a danger in his own right. John Charlton, the chamberlain of the king's household, was included because of his continuing dispute over possession of the lordship of Powys with Lancaster's banneret, Gruffudd de la Pole: Phillips, 164.

[196] '*par encheson de nous a ce qe home dit*'.

[197] Phillips, 164.

[198] *CCR, 1313–18*, 619, 622–3; Phillips, 167; Maddicott, 218.

lands in Bromfield and Yale. Other than asking Lancaster to desist from his attacks, the council had no intention of being side-tracked by this issue. Instead the earl of Surrey was hung out to dry and told in no uncertain terms to settle the matter himself.[199]

DIFFICULT NEGOTIATIONS

Plans for a personal meeting between Edward and Lancaster were being made as early as 9 June when Lancaster seems to have anticipated that such a meeting would soon take place at Northampton; on 12 June he and his men were given safe conducts to come to the king on 29 June at an unspecified location;[200] and on 22 June the two papal envoys were also given conducts to go to Northampton, confirming it as the intended meeting-place.[201] However, it soon turned out that serious problems remained in the way of any general agreement. On 13 June the bishop of Norwich and the newly appointed chancellor the bishop of Ely set out to visit Lancaster at his castle of Tutbury in Derbyshire. They were accompanied by the archbishop of Dublin and took with them a document drawn up in London by the archbishops of Canterbury and Dublin and containing a series of points which were to be put to Lancaster and his representatives.[202] The negotiations which followed were concluded on 23 June in a garden at Horninglow, between Burton-on-Trent and Tutbury, when Lancaster's knight Stephen Segrave read out the text of a notarial instrument containing his master's replies to each of the points in the presence of the archbishop of Dublin and the bishops of Norwich and Ely.[203]

Lancaster refused to accept the proposal that the recipients of grants made contrary to the Ordinances should restore them to the king without punishment and that a future parliament should decide whether or not the revocation should be made permanent, citing instead the relevant clause

---

[199] SC 8/177/8829–31; *CCR, 1313–18*, 554; Phillips, 165; Maddicott, 220.

[200] DL 34/14; *CPR, 1317–21*, 162; Phillips, 167. However, Lancaster was still deeply suspicious of the intentions of the king and his favourites and instructed the constable of his castle of Bolingbroke to allow no one except members of the garrison to enter until the outcome of the Northampton meeting was known: Maddicott, 219.

[201] *Foedera*, II, i, 366; Phillips, 167. The place is wrongly given as Norham in *CPR, 1317–21*, 166.

[202] *Knighton*, i, 413; *CCR, 1313–18*, 619; Phillips, 165; Maddicott, 219, 221. Lancaster was already at Tutbury on 9 June: DL 34/14.

[203] The document presented by the bishop and now known as the Tutbury articles is preserved in *Knighton*, i, 413–21. The printed text has been checked against both the manuscript copies, BL, Cotton Ms. Claudius E. III, ff. 233–4, and BL, Cotton Ms. Tiberius E. VII, ff. 121v–123, and is correct apart from minor misreadings: Phillips, 165–6. The Horninglow document is preserved in Foljambe Charters, App. 4, Osberton Hall, Worksop, and was made available to me by Dr Maddicott when it was on deposit at the Bodleian Library. The text is printed in Maddicott, App. 1, 337–8, and discussed in Maddicott, 220–3. This relationship between this document and the articles preserved in Knighton is proved by the citing of the first and last lines of the Knighton document.

of the Ordinances.[204] He also rejected the suggestions that the royal favourites should come to parliament and be judged there by their peers for any breach of the Ordinances they might have committed; that instead of being removed altogether from the king's presence, they should absent themselves when Edward and Lancaster met to make peace, so that Lancaster should have no fear of them; and that they should make amends to Lancaster for any injuries they had inflicted on him. Lancaster insisted that they should all be permanently removed under the terms of the Ordinances, of which he again cited the relevant clause.[205] On the question of a surety for his coming to the king, Lancaster said he did not trust the king's promises, since when he had done so in the past he had been imperilled by the king's favourites; nor was he certain of the value of the surety promised by the magnates at Leicester, since he had heard that some of them had since agreed to protect the king's evil councillors; nor did he regard the guarantee of safety given by the prelates and the cardinals to be a sufficient safeguard.[206]

The return of the envoys from Tutbury showed that the earlier optimism was entirely misplaced and that hard bargaining still lay ahead. A new round of negotiations now began, which was conducted by several of the bishops, together with some of the magnate members of the king's council.[207] On 4 July an embassy consisting of the archbishop of Dublin, the bishops of Ely and Norwich, the earl of Pembroke, Badlesmere and the Younger Despenser left Northampton to visit Lancaster at a place which was unnamed, but was probably at or near Tutbury.[208] On 11 July the archbishop of Canterbury wrote from Northampton saying that these envoys had met Lancaster and found him willing to reach a final settlement on a number of points which had earlier seemed likely to destroy any chance of peace, and which were presumably connected with the vexed questions of grants of land and the royal favourites. Lancaster had also agreed to come to the king at Northampton by 21 July in order to make a

---

[204] *Knighton*, i, 413–15; Ordinance 7 of the Ordinances of 1311, under the heading of *Articuli ordinati sunt isti* in the Horninglow document; Phillips, 166; Maddicott, 221. As already noted, some grants had been resumed on 9 June: E 159/91, m.64d; *CFR, 1307–17*, 374; *CCR, 1318–23*, 51, 64.

[205] *Knighton*, 418–21; Ordinance 13, under the heading of *Les poyntes des ordinances sont tiels*; Phillips, 166; Maddicott, 221–2.

[206] *Knighton*, 415–17; Phillips, 166–7; Maddicott, 221. Lancaster was presumably referring to the guarantee of 11 June.

[207] The details of this phase of the negotiations are contained in a number of letters written by the archbishop of Canterbury and by someone in his company: HMC, *Various Collections*, i, 220, 267–8.

[208] Ibid., i, 220; Phillips, 167–8; Maddicott, 223. The bishop of Ely left Northampton on 4 July while the bishop of Norwich was at Burton-on-Trent on 6 July: *CCR, 1313–18*, 620; Reg. John Salmon, f. 76. The presence of the Younger Despenser in the delegation may be another indication that he was not yet regarded as a danger in the same way as his father or Damory and the other favourites.

firm peace agreement.[209] Optimism was still high on 18 July when the archbishop again wrote from Northampton saying that he was now certain that, with the mediation of himself and others, peace between Lancaster, the king and the magnates would be confirmed in a few days.[210]

However, a further letter from the archbishop on 21 July shows that a settlement had not in fact taken place, that the outcome of the negotiations was again uncertain, and that a further embassy, consisting of the archbishop of Dublin, the bishops of Chichester and Ely, the earls of Pembroke and Arundel, Roger Mortimer of Wigmore, and Badlesmere had been sent to see Lancaster on 20 July.[211] Another letter, probably of the same date, and written by someone in the archbishop's company, explains the archbishop's optimism on 11 July and the reasons for the near breakdown of negotiations after that date.[212] This is not just revealing of the tensions that existed between Edward II and his first cousin, Thomas of Lancaster, in the summer of 1318 but is also symbolic of the repeated political crises that had occurred since Edward first became king.

According to this letter, at their first meeting with Lancaster in early July the royal envoys had agreed to Lancaster's two main demands: that gifts made contrary to the Ordinances should be revoked, and that the favourites should be removed from court, with the reservation that they should still be allowed to answer parliamentary and military summonses. In return Lancaster promised to remit all offences against him, except for those committed by Roger Damory and William de Montacute, whom he accused of plotting to kill him and who would have to make amends to him. A further proposal by Lancaster which, with modifications, was finally included in the treaty between Edward and Lancaster in August was that eight bishops, four earls and four barons should remain with the king each year, of whom two bishops, one earl and one baron should stay with the king as part of his council during each quarter.[213] This idea, we are told, was accepted by the envoys, although the prominence of the bishops in the working of such an arrangement suggests that the idea may have been partly inspired by them as a way of ensuring a neutral group on the council. Lancaster also promised to come to the king whenever Edward wished and to join in a campaign against the Scots. The envoys then returned to Northampton and reported to Edward, who agreed with what they had done. The author of the letter then goes on to say that the hopes of peace were shattered by the behaviour of some of the envoys who had just been to see Lancaster, who now went back on their word and persuaded Edward not to confirm the agreement.[214]

---

[209] HMC, *Various Collections*, i, 220; Phillips, 167–8; Maddicott, 223.
[210] HMC, *Various Collections*, i, 220; *CCR, 1313–18*, 620; Phillips, 167–8; Maddicott, 223.
[211] HMC, *Various Collections*, i, 267–8; *CCR, 1313–18*, 620; Phillips, 168; Maddicott, 224.
[212] HMC, *Various Collections*, i, 268; Phillips, 168; Maddicott, 224.
[213] It is not clear whether this was meant to be a permanent arrangement or to last for one year only.
[214] HMC, *Various Collections*, i, 267–8; Phillips, 168–9; Maddicott, 224–5.

Of the envoys who went to Lancaster on 4 July only the Younger Despenser might be described as personally hostile to him, because of Lancaster's long-standing enmity against Despenser's father and perhaps also because acceptance of Lancaster's demands might affect the future development of his own career.[215] Despenser may accordingly have been among those who advised Edward against acceptance. This may explain why Despenser was not a member of the second embassy to Lancaster on 20 July.[216] But it is also highly probable that Edward was even more swayed by the arguments of those others who would lose their influence at court if a settlement were made, namely Damory and Montacute, whom Lancaster had attacked by name during the talks, and probably also by Hugh Audley. The writer then adds that there were differing views among those with the king at Northampton, but that Pembroke and the bishops insisted that the agreement should be upheld, and that because of their determination the second embassy was sent to meet Lancaster on 20 July.[217]

AGREEMENT AT LAST

The embassy returned to Northampton on 29 July, and on 1 August a third and, as it turned out, final mission set out from Northampton, consisting of the archbishop of Dublin, the bishops of Norwich, Chichester and Ely, the earls of Pembroke and Arundel, Roger Mortimer of Wigmore, John de Somery, Bartholomew de Badlesmere, Ralph Basset and John Botetourt.[218] Some progress had evidently been made during the second mission since on 31 July Lancaster's adherents were pardoned all offences committed before 25 July.[219] No more is known until a letter from the archbishop of Canterbury on 8 August, which says that on the previous day Edward II and Lancaster had met between Loughborough and Leicester and had exchanged the kiss of peace in the presence of the two cardinals, the bishops, all the earls except for Surrey, and many of the barons. Edward

---

[215] While Edward II was at Northampton he appointed Despenser as chamberlain of the household. This may have been intended in part to mollify Lancaster since the previous chamberlain, John Charlton, was personally hostile to him. Nonetheless it marked a significant development in the career and influence of Despenser and may also have been objectionable to Lancaster: Phillips, 174, 177; Maddicott, 225.

[216] HMC, *Various Collections*, i, 269; Phillips, 170.

[217] HMC, *Various Collections*, i, 267-9; Phillips, 168-70; Maddicott, 225. Although relying on first-hand information, the author was not actually present at Northampton. Another writer, who may well have been there, was the author of the *Vita Edwardi Secundi* who reports that all of Lancaster's particular enemies, the earl of Surrey, Damory, the Despensers, Audley and Montacute, were at Northampton 'in great strength, so that you would have thought they had come not to parliament, but to battle': *Vita*, 150-1.

[218] HMC, *Various Collections*, i, 268; *CCR, 1313-18*, 620; *CCR, 1318-23*, 112; Phillips, 170; Maddicott, 226. The bishop of Ely dropped out at Leicester because of illness: *CCR, 1313-18*, 620.

[219] *CPR, 1317-21*, 199; Phillips, 170; Maddicott, 226. Some partial agreement had probably therefore been reached on 25 July.

was to meet Lancaster again on 8 or 9 August near Nottingham to discuss measures to protect the north against the Scots until the king could go there in person. This was to take place after a parliament to be held at Lincoln on 13 October.[220] An indenture embodying the final settlement was drawn up at this second meeting at Leake in Nottinghamshire on 9 August 1318.[221] 'So the lord king and the earl met and, speaking together long and intimately, they renewed due friendship and mutual goodwill, and to mark the pact they ate together on that same day; and Roger Amory and the rest, except Hugh Despenser and the earl Warenne [Surrey], humbly presenting themselves before the earl, were received into his grace.'[222]

In the Treaty of Leake itself it was first of all agreed that a standing royal council should be established, consisting of eight bishops (Norwich, Chichester, Ely, Salisbury, St David's, Carlisle, Hereford and Worcester), four earls (Pembroke, Richmond, Hereford and Arundel), and four barons (Hugh de Courtenay, Roger Mortimer, John de Segrave and John de Grey). Lancaster would not be a member, but was to be represented by one of the bannerets of his household. The council would function for one year, with two bishops, one earl and one baron serving for three months at a time. The council would advise the king between parliaments on all matters that could be settled without recourse to parliament. This proposal was put forward by Lancaster during the negotiations in July and was modelled on a scheme originally proposed by Simon de Montfort in 1264. The king and Lancaster promised to issue mutual pardons for all offences committed by their followers, with the exception of the earl of Surrey's offences against Lancaster, which were to be settled privately between the two men.[223] The resumption of all grants made contrary to the Ordinances and the removal

---

[220] HMC, *Various Collections*, i, 269; Phillips, 170; Maddicott, 226–7.

[221] The counterpart of the original indenture containing the treaty is E 163/4/7/2. Lancaster's copy was found among his muniments after his execution in 1322 (DL 41/1/37, m.7) but is no longer extant. The agreement was also enrolled on the Close Roll (*CCR, 1318–23*, 112–14; *Foedera*, II, i, 370) and on the Memoranda Roll (E 368/89, m.84). Those present at Leake were named in the indenture as the archbishops of Canterbury and Dublin; the bishops of Norwich, Ely, Chichester, Salisbury, Chester (i.e. Coventry & Lichfield), Winchester, Hereford and Worcester; the earls of Norfolk (Edward II's half-brother), Pembroke, Richmond, Hereford, Ulster, Arundel and Angus; Roger Mortimer (of Wigmore), John de Somery, John de Hastings, John de Segrave, Henry de Beaumont, Hugh Despenser the Younger, John de Grey, Richard de Grey, Bartholomew de Badlesmere, Robert de Monthaut, Ralph Bassett, Walter de Norwich. The cardinals are not named but there is no reason to doubt the archbishop's statement that they were present.

[222] *Vita*, 152–3. As the archbishop noted (HMC, *Various Collections*, i, 26), the earl of Surrey was not among those who witnessed the Treaty of Leake; neither were Lancaster's other great enemies, Hugh Despenser the Elder and the three favourites, Damory, Audley and Montacute. The Younger Despenser and another long-standing opponent of Lancaster, Henry de Beaumont, were present. It is clear however from the *Vita* that Damory and other favourites were not far from the scene. No one who was recognizably a follower of Lancaster was listed among the witnesses.

[223] *Foedera*, II, i, 371; Phillips, 171–2; Maddicott, 224, 226. Lancaster's adherents had already been pardoned on 31 July of all offences committed before 25 July: *CPR, 1317–21*, 199.

of royal favourites, both of which Lancaster had consistently demanded, were not mentioned directly, although Edward's promise in the treaty to confirm and accept the Ordinances might be taken to imply acceptance of both points.

The kiss of peace between Edward and Lancaster and the Treaty of Leake brought an end to one of the most prolonged periods of tension and certainly the most tortuous set of negotiations since 1307. Whether the king and Lancaster were truly reconciled or whether there would be a new round of suspicion and violence only time would tell.

EDWARD

It is often very difficult to isolate the king's actions and contribution to the making of policy from those of others. There is little doubt that in 1317–18 Edward II was under a variety of pressures, from the favourites who wished to profit from royal patronage and in whose interests it was to foster Edward's hostility to the earl of Lancaster, and from wiser heads, such as Pembroke, Hereford, Badlesmere and other councillors, the leading clergy, and the two papal envoys, who were all too aware of the dangers to the kingdom if the political tensions were left unresolved. Isabella also appears to have played a part in bringing about peace.[224] But, in a very significant passage, the author of the *Vita Edwardi Secundi* implies that amid the impassioned debates that took place in the tense and claustrophobic atmosphere at Northampton in July 1318, when all the king's favourites and more moderate supporters were present, together with their retainers, it was Edward himself who finally decided that peace must be made with Lancaster:

> Thus the king, seeing that he profited nothing, achieved nothing by all the plans he made against the earl, also considering that such discord was dangerous to him, because it encouraged the Scottish rebellion against him, and he could make no headway against the Scots without the help of the earl of Lancaster; considering, too, that the town of Berwick had been disgracefully lost and the town of Norham was on the point of being lost . . .; and considering the enormous expenses he incurred against the earl, asked that, all ill-feeling laid aside, [the earl] should go to a place of his own choosing, where a friendly agreement might be made with him and his men about everything done in his name; moreover all those against whom the earl said that he had any complaint, should make satisfaction at the earl's discretion, and for this should offer sureties, caution money or pledges. And so . . . this was achieved.[225]

For Edward II the year 1318 was also marked by events of personal sadness and joy and by others which can only be described as bizarre and partaking

---

[224] *Vita*, 150–1.
[225] *Vita*, 150–3.

of fantasy. On 14 February his stepmother Margaret of France, the widow of Edward I and aunt of Edward II's own wife Isabella, died at the age of about thirty-eight and was buried in the London church of the Franciscans in the presence of both Edward and Isabella.[226] After her marriage to Edward I in 1299 she appears to have got on well with her stepson, who was only a few years younger than her. She mediated between him and his father during their quarrel in 1305,[227] and attended both his wedding to Isabella in 1308 and the birth of his son, the future Edward III, in 1312.[228] She is not known to have played any direct role in the politics of Edward II's reign but it is likely that her death removed a calming influence and an emotional support from the life of Edward and also from that of Isabella, who was pregnant when Margaret died.[229] Isabella and Edward's third child, a daughter, was born at Woodstock on 18 June, and was named Eleanor after Edward's mother. On 28 June the king and queen left for Northampton.[230]

AN IMPOSTOR APPEARS AT OXFORD

In addition to the heated arguments which preceded the agreement with Lancaster in August, Northampton was to witness the conclusion of another even more extraordinary event. On about 24 June a man, later identified as John Poydras or Powderham, the son of a tanner from Exeter, appeared at the King's Hall in Oxford. In fulfilment of the vow he made after his escape from Bannockburn Edward II had recently granted the building to the Carmelites who were starting to build a church. Ordering the friars to leave 'his house', John 'said that he was the king's son and that the kingdom of England belonged to him by right of blood. He claimed that he had been taken from the cradle, and that the king who now reigned was put in his place . . . Then word reached the king and the man was at once arrested by the king's order, and brought before the lord king the next day. Even brought face to face with the king he did not deny what he had already said, but stated firmly that he was the true heir to the kingdom, and that the king had no right to reign.'[231] In the Lanercost chronicle version of events Edward received John with derision: ' "You are

---

[226] E 101/377/7, f. 6.
[227] Prestwich, *Edward I*, 129–31.
[228] See the article on Margaret by John Carmi Parsons in the *Oxford DNB*.
[229] On 5 March 1318 Isabella was given permanent dower lands to provide her with an income of £4,500, in completion of the dower promised in 1299 in the original agreement for her marriage to the future Edward II. Some of these lands she already held but others came from the former dower of Queen Margaret: *CPR, 1292–1301*, 451–3; *CPR, 1317–21*, 115–16; Doherty (D.Phil.), 66.
[230] SAL Ms. 121, ff. 2, 29v; Doherty (D.Phil.), 67.
[231] *Vita*, 148–9. A full account of this episode can be found in Childs, ' "Welcome my brother." ' Nearly all the evidence is preserved in chronicle sources, such as the *Vita*, the *Ann. Paul.*, the Lanercost and Bridlington chronicles, the French prose *Brut*, and the Meaux chronicle, and many others: see Childs, 149–50.

well come, my brother, yet you are not my brother, but falsely claim the kingdom for yourself, for you have not one drop of the blood of the illustrious Edward, and I am prepared to prove it against you, or any other in your place".'[232] In another account, Edward laughed at John's claim and suggested that he be given a 'bauble' and allowed to go around as a fool;[233] according to the *Vita* Isabella was extremely angry while others realized the danger to the king and to the kingdom as rumours of the event spread rapidly. After Edward was advised very strongly that such a public challenge to his royal status could not go unpunished, John's parents were summoned from Exeter to Northampton to swear at his trial that he was their son; after which he was executed by hanging on or about 23 July.[234] Although the incident took place when the negotiations between Edward II and Thomas of Lancaster were entering their final and most delicate stage, there is nothing to suggest that John of Powderham was in any way connected with Lancaster or that his actions were intended to embarrass Edward II politically.[235] Two chroniclers, those of Osney in Oxford and Meaux in Yorkshire, describe John as *literatus* or *scriptor*, which implies that he may have had some degree of learning and was either connected with the university of Oxford or was pursuing a livelihood on its fringes.[236] The coincidence that John came from Exeter and that Walter Stapeldon the bishop of Exeter had recently founded a new college in Oxford might suggest that the impostor was in some way connected with it; but there is no evidence to support such a conjecture.[237] Many of the chroniclers claim that John was driven to his actions by a pact he had made with the devil: this is interesting in the context of contemporary beliefs in the practice of witchcraft, but does nothing to provide a real explanation of John's behaviour.[238] In the absence of any more specific evidence the most likely

---

[232] ' "*Bene veneris, frater mi*", respondit, "*non es frater meus, sed falso vendicas tibi regnum, nec habes unam guttam sanguinis de Edwardo illustri, et itud sum paratus probare contra te, vel contra quemcunque alium loco tui*" ': *Lanercost*, 236. Edward seems to be offering trial by battle if John persists in his claim.

[233] *Anonimalle*, 94–5.

[234] *Vita*, 148–9; Childs, ' "Welcome my brother" ', 162. The trial, for which there is no official record, was probably conducted summarily in the court of the Marshalsea, presided over by William de Montacute, the steward of the royal household. The only references to the case in record sources are in E 37/4, m.3 (Marshalsea roll) and *CPR, 1317–21*, 273: Childs, ' "Welcome my brother" ', 149, 152.

[235] Childs, ' "Welcome my brother" ', 158–9.

[236] Ibid., 150, 158, 161.

[237] Ibid., 158; Buck, 102–3, 110. Stapeldon was not involved in any of the negotiations which led to the Treaty of Leake in 1318 and was not present at Northampton at the time of John's arrest and trial.

[238] Childs, ' "Welcome my brother" ', 153–5. Accusations of witchcraft were sometimes made against individuals or groups for political reasons, e.g. against Walter Langton bishop of Coventry & Lichfield in 1301, Edward II's brother Edmund earl of Kent in 1330, and the 27 Coventry men accused in 1323 of plotting to murder the king, the Despensers and the prior of Coventry: Childs, 155–6.

answer is that John of Powderham was a deranged individual acting for reasons of his own.[239]

EDWARD II AND THE HOLY OIL OF ST THOMAS OF CANTERBURY[240]

The John of Powderham episode was deeply embarrassing for Edward II, in that it came at such a delicate time in national affairs, in that news of the event spread around the country so fast, and in that it may have suggested to some that a king who indulged in undignified and unkingly pursuits was perhaps not really a king at all.[241] It was even more embarrassing since in the summer of 1318 Edward was also attempting to find an answer to his political troubles by giving renewed emphasis to the sacred character of his kingship which he had acquired at his coronation in 1308.

In the spring or early summer of 1319 Pope John XXII sent a long and circumstantial letter to Edward II in which he recorded a very strange story which he had been told by a Dominican friar, named only as Brother N, who had recently been sent to Avignon as a royal envoy.[242] Since the friar's story was so remarkable the pope wanted to ensure that Edward knew exactly what had been said on his behalf. During a private meeting with the pope Brother N told how the Virgin Mary had appeared to the archbishop of Canterbury Thomas Becket when he was in exile in France after 1164. She had revealed that the fifth king of England from the one then

---

[239] *Gesta Edwardi*, 55, records that it was believed either that John was suffering from a weakness in the head (*debilitate capitis*) or that he was guided by the devil: Childs, ' "Welcome my brother" ', 158.

[240] For what follows see Phillips, 'Edward II and the prophets', esp. 196–201.

[241] Childs, ' "Welcome my brother" ', 160–2.

[242] The text is preserved as a transcript in ASV, Vatican Register 110 (Secreta, i to iv, John XXII), ff. 136r–137v. There is no trace of the original papal letter among the papal bulls preserved in the National Archives at Kew. A transcript of the document and an English translation were published by L.G. Wickham Legg in *Coronation Records* (London, 1901), 69–72 (Latin text), 72–6 (trans.). A partial text of the letter had been in print since the middle of the 17th century in *Annales Ecclesiastici ab Anno MCXCVIII ubi Cardinalis Baronius Desinit Auctore Odorico Raynaldo Tarvisino Congregationis Oratorii Presbytero*, ed. O. Rinaldi (1595–1671), Tomus XV (Rome, 1652), Joannis Papae XXII, no. 20. In his printed edition Wickham Legg concluded what is otherwise an accurate transcript of the letter with the dating clause *Datum Avinonie IIII Nonas Iunii, Anno Secundo* (i.e. 2 June 1318), which is not present in the original register, where the letter is shown without a date. Wickham Legg appears to have assumed that the letter was of the same date as the nearest dated document in the register. This mistake was not made by the editor of *CPL*, ii, *1305–42*, 436–7. As the *Calendar* indicates, Vatican Register 110 which contains the letter is composed of miscellaneous confidential correspondence, *Secreta*, much of it not precisely dated, from the first four years of the pontificate of John XXII, that is, between Aug. 1316 and Aug. 1320. The date of the letter can be roughly worked out from the date of the embassy of Adam Orleton, bishop of Hereford, to Avignon in the early spring of 1319: Haines, *The Church and Politics*, 20–2.

reigning (i.e. Henry II) would be a good man and a champion of the Church (i.e. Edward II); she had also given Becket a phial of holy oil by whose virtue this king would recover the Holy Land from the heathen. Becket had hidden the oil in the monastery of St Cyprian at Poitiers but, as she predicted would happen, it was rediscovered by two Christian subjects of the king of the heathen. According to Brother N, the oil had then come into the possession of the king of Germany and later into that of the duke of Brabant. The duke had brought the oil with him to Edward II's coronation in 1308 but Edward, on the advice of his councillors, had turned down the suggestion that he should be anointed with it in favour of unction with the oil usually employed at English coronations. In order to convince the pope of the miraculous power of the oil, Brother N also told him that a single application of the oil had saved the countess of Luxemburg's life after she had cut herself severely with a knife.

Brother N ended his story by telling the pope that Edward II had reflected on the many misfortunes which had befallen himself and his kingdom and had concluded that these had occurred because of his rejection of the Holy Oil of St Thomas when it was offered to him by the duke of Brabant. Edward had decided that, if he were now to be anointed with the oil, all his troubles would be ended; but he did not wish to do so without papal approval.[243]

Brother N can readily be identified as the English Dominican friar Nicholas of Wisbech, presumably from the vicinity of Wisbech in Cambridgeshire.[244] At some stage in his career he left England, since in 1299 he visited Edward I in England as an envoy of his son-in-law John and daughter Margaret, the duke and duchess of Brabant; he was again in England in April 1303 when he met both the king and Prince Edward and was described as the confessor of the duchess.[245] Nicholas is not recorded in England again with certainty until February 1317 when he was present at Clarendon.[246] In March 1317 he was sent to the papal curia at

---

[243] Phillips, 'Edward II and the prophets', 196–7. The Holy Oil had previously been discussed with passing references to Edward II but mainly in relation to the reigns of Richard II and later English kings in W. Ullmann, 'Thomas Becket's miraculous oil', *Journal of Theological Studies*, new ser., viii (1957), 129–33; J.W. McKenna, 'The coronation oil of the Yorkist kings', *EHR*, lxxxii (1967), 102–4; and T.A. Sandquist, 'The Holy Oil of St Thomas of Canterbury', in *Essays in Medieval History presented to Bertie Wilkinson*, ed. T.A. Sandquist & M.R. Powicke (Toronto, 1969), 330–44.

[244] His identity is apparent from entries in the Roman Roll of 11 Edward II, C 70/4.

[245] *Liber Quotidianus Garderobae*, 167; E 101/363/18, ff. 19v, 21v. It is likely that Nicholas first entered the service of Margaret between the time of her marriage to the future Duke John II of Brabant in 1290 and her departure from England to rejoin her husband in 1297: on the relations between England and Brabant see J. de Sturler, *Les Relations politiques et les échanges commerciaux entre le duché de Brabant et l'Angleterre au moyen âge* (Paris, 1936); and Childs, 'England in Europe', 102.

[246] Nicholas may have been one of the unnamed messengers from Brabant for whose accommodation the royal household paid £5 in Sept. 1316: SAL Ms. 120, f. 101v.

Avignon as a royal envoy and in January 1318 he was ordered to visit both the curia and the duke of Brabant. In June 1318 the pope authorized Nicholas to take another member of his order and to go wherever the king told him; and in July he was appointed as a papal penitentiary.[247]

As to the Holy Oil itself, it was true, as Brother Nicholas was later to inform the pope, that something significant had happened when the duke of Brabant attended Edward II's coronation in 1308. On that occasion the duke restored to Edward a collection of jewels which had once belonged to Edward I but which had come into the hands of the duke in 1297 when Edward I gave them as security during his campaign in Flanders at a time when he was desperately short of money to pay his allies. Payment was completed in 1305, after which the jewels were available to be returned to his son in 1308.[248] One item however was not returned in 1308: a gold cross which seems to have had some connection with the Holy Oil, and may even have contained the ampulla, since in 1318 Nicholas of Wisbech went to collect the cross from Brabant before going to Avignon on behalf of Edward II.[249] If this line of argument is correct, it implies that the story of the Holy Oil of St Thomas was already current in England before the reign of Edward II and that Nicholas of Wisbech could have taken the knowledge with him when he went to Brabant as confessor to Edward I's daughter Margaret, either before or at about the same time as the cross itself was left with the duke.

In his conversation with the pope Brother Nicholas claimed that the Holy Oil had been in the possession of the king of Germany before coming into the hands of the duke of Brabant. Nicholas may simply, of course, have been trying to provide the oil with an impressive-sounding pedigree, but it is possible that he was thinking of Richard of Cornwall, the uncle of Edward I, who was elected king of the Romans and crowned at Aachen in 1257. In 1268 Richard and his son Edmund brought a large collection of relics back to England from Germany, where there was an elaborate cult of St Thomas Becket,[250] and it is possible that the alleged Holy Oil of St Thomas was among them.[251]

As already noted, the future Edward II had met Nicholas of Wisbech as far back as 1303; it is also likely that Nicholas accompanied the duke

---

[247] SAL Ms. 120, f. 9v; C 70/4, m.13d; SAL Ms. 121, f. 33v; *CPR, 1313–17*, 628; *CPL*, ii, 172, 426; Phillips, 'Edward II and the prophets', 198.

[248] C 70/4, m.13d.; Sturler, *Les Relations*, 157–60. Altogether Edward I had promised the duke sums totalling £160,000 *tournois* (£40,000 sterling).

[249] C 70/4, m.13d.

[250] On the development of Becket's cult see, for example, Duggan, 'The cult of St Thomas Becket', esp. 26.

[251] Phillips, 'Edward II and the prophets', 200. This is of course speculation: there is no firm evidence that the Holy Oil of St Thomas actually did come from Germany. One of the relics acquired in Germany by Richard and Edmund was the famous 'Holy Blood' which Edmund of Cornwall gave to Hailes abbey in Gloucestershire: N. Denholm-Young, *Richard of Cornwall* (London, 1947), 92, 174.

and duchess to Edward II's coronation in 1308 and that he had something to do with bringing the Holy Oil to the king's notice on that occasion. Throughout his life Edward was particularly devoted to the Dominican order and its individual members and was probably easily influenced by a plausible holy man who told him a story which seemed to offer an answer to his problems. Edward's piety and his gullibility in religious matters produced a dangerous combination.[252] It is not however until the time of Nicholas's appearance at Clarendon in February 1317 that we can infer that something significant was happening. Since this was also the occasion of an important meeting of the royal council, it is probable that the Holy Oil was discussed, together with the equally unrealistic proposal from Jean de Fiennes, an important magnate in the county of Ponthieu, that Edward II should lay claim to a share of the kingdom of France,[253] and other far more pressing affairs of state, such as Edward II's relations with Lancaster and the war with Scotland.

The likely sequence of events is that when Nicholas of Wisbech went to Avignon in March 1317 he did so in order to inform the pope about the Holy Oil; that the pope refused to believe the story without further evidence; and that when Nicholas was sent back to Brabant in early 1318 to collect the gold cross associated with the Holy Oil and then continued on to Avignon he conveyed a request from Edward to be allowed to receive unction with the Holy Oil. During the summer of 1318 when the negotiations between Edward and Lancaster were at their most critical stage, tension was high among Edward's favourites and allies, and when the impostor John of Powderham made his notorious appearance at Oxford, Edward was also anxiously awaiting news from Avignon. His prayers at the shrine of St Thomas at Canterbury on 13 June, a few days before the birth of his daughter Eleanor, were for more than Isabella's safe delivery.[254]

---

[252] For a detailed examination of this see ch. 2 of this book, 'The nature of a king'.

[253] Fiennes argued that since the count of La Marche had already made a claim to a share of the kingdom of France, as the brother of the late king Louis X, Edward II should now do so in the name of his wife Isabella, Louis X's sister. It seems that the proposal envisaged the division of the lands acquired by the French monarch since (and possibly even before) the accession of Louis IX, and therefore excluded the French crown's ancient demesne lands which were the *droit corps du royaume* and therefore indivisible: SC 8/325/E 672; *CCW*, 460–1. Fortunately Edward II's council did not recommend pursuing the suggestion any further.

[254] SAL Ms. 121, f. 2.

Chapter 8

FROM SETTLEMENT TO CIVIL WAR, 1318–1322

PART ONE
TAKING STOCK

Nebuchadnezzar, that most powerful king of the Assyrians, before the twelfth year of his reign did, we are told, nothing memorable, but in that twelfth year of his reign he began to flourish and to conquer nations and kingdoms... Neither has our King Edward who has reigned eleven years and more, done anything that ought to be preached in the market-place or from the rooftops. Would that, following the example of King Nebuchadnezzar, he would now at least try to attack his enemies, so that he might repair the damage and disgrace which he has borne so long...

Great hope has latterly grown up among us, because God has gladdened king and people with many signs of prosperity.

In the first place, it turned out happily for the English king and people that the lord pope, whose business it is to settle quarrels, imposed upon the Scots and their leaders a two years' truce, so that in the meanwhile he might devise a way to bring harmony, and a form of peace....

Secondly, God gave us victory over our enemies in Ireland, Edward Bruce and his knights, who now for two years had usurped lordship there, approaching Dundalk to take the town, came up against our army; but when battle was joined Edward fell before our men that day, and five hundred stout-hearted men-at-arms with him.

Thirdly, the dearth that had so long plagued us ceased, and England became fruitful with a lavish profusion of all good things. A bushel of wheat, which the year before was sold for forty pence, today is freely offered to the buyer for sixpence...

Fourthly, our king became reconciled with his barons. For putting aside trifles, he listens to the barons' advice, and there is no longer anyone to incite the king to do wrong, because his close supporters who were hostile to the barons have now left the court...[1]

Such was the assessment of the author of the *Vita Edwardi Secundi* of the situation in England in the autumn of 1318.

---

[1] *Vita*, 152–7.

On the whole it was an accurate and shrewd assessment. As the *Vita* also observed, Robert Bruce had ignored the papal truce and had continued his attacks on the north of England. The most significant of these led to the loss of the town of Berwick on the night of 1 to 2 April 1318, when it was betrayed from within. This came after years of Scottish naval blockade and attempts on the town and castle, which had been in English hands since 1296, and were a crucial element in the English defence of the north and in any future campaign in Scotland. The inhabitants of the town (many of whom were still Scottish) and the members of the garrison alike had suffered desperately from a lack of food supplies and money. The castle itself held out for a further eleven weeks, finally surrendering at the end of June. The loss of Berwick was a humiliation for Edward II but also provided an added incentive for reaching agreement with Lancaster. It was certain that as soon as peace was made in England a campaign against the Scots would again be high on the agenda.[2]

The defeat and death of Edward Bruce at Faughart near Dundalk on 14 October 1318 was however a major English victory, which to some degree made up for the loss of Berwick.[3] The people of the lordship of Ireland had suffered greatly since 1315 from the devastation caused by the opposing armies, as well as from the extreme weather conditions and the resulting famine and disease. The government of the lordship had been weakened both for the present and the future by the war, while there was still the risk that at some future date Robert Bruce might renew the attack.[4] For the Scots however the defeat was a disaster. The war in Ireland had diverted experienced manpower and other resources which might have been used to greater effect nearer home: the northern counties of England might not have appreciated this but their suffering would probably have been much worse. Everything had instead been thrown away in a failed attempt to conquer Ireland. 'The Anglo-Irish inflicted on the Scots a reverse the like of which they were not to suffer at the hands of the English until Halidon Hill [1333]: King Robert lost his brother and only male heir; the tide of Scottish expansion, which had flowed strongly since Bannockburn, was stemmed; and Edward II did not completely miss the opportunity that was given him to recover the initiative in the west.'[5]

---

[2] *Bruce*, 617–27. On the situation at Berwick between 1312 and 1318 see McNamee, 216–19. On the north of England more generally in 1318 see *Lanercost*, 235–6; Kershaw, 'Scottish raids'.

[3] *Lanercost*, 225–6; McNamee, 185–6. Bruce's head was sent to Edward II and presumably arrived during the York parliament which began on 20 Oct.: Lydon, 'The impact of the Bruce invasion' 293–4.

[4] Bruce did return to Ulster briefly on two occasions, in 1327 and 1328: R. Frame, *English Lordship in Ireland, 1318–1361* (Oxford, 1982), 140–2.

[5] Ibid., 133. English control over Ulster was recovered after 1318; Edward II also resumed his earlier practice of courting potential allies in south-west Scotland, within Robert Bruce's own kingdom; and in 1322 Edward was again able to draw on Irish manpower for a campaign in Scotland: ibid., 132–5.

The author of the *Vita* was broadly correct in his remarks about the end of the time of famine and high prices. Grain prices fell in 1318 to a lower level than in any year since 1288. Although a severe epidemic among cattle was to occur in 1319 and the harvest failed again in 1321, the worst distress was over by the autumn of 1318, with the exception of the northern counties of England which still experienced Scottish raids.[6]

At first sight the political settlement reached in the summer and autumn of 1318 also showed signs of hope both for the present and for the future. The Treaty of Leake of 9 August was in itself however only a preliminary agreement which had been made after the outlines of a settlement had been sufficiently established to permit Edward and Lancaster to meet and to make their personal peace with each other. The details remained to be worked out at the parliament which was summoned on 25 August to meet at York on 20 October.[7]

THE YORK PARLIAMENT

When the parliament began, the Treaty of Leake was first of all confirmed in its entirety.[8] On 22 October Lancaster and forty-three named followers were pardoned for all their offences up to 7 August.[9] The device of a standing royal council of eight bishops, four earls and four barons, each serving for three months at a time,[10] and with a single banneret to represent Lancaster's views, which was a central feature of the treaty, was also confirmed. It was however modified by the addition of the bishops of Coventry & Lichfield and of Winchester, Hugh Despenser the Younger, Bartholomew de Badlesmere, John de Somery, John Giffard, John Botetourt, Roger Mortimer of Chirk and William Martin.[11] A commission consisting of the earl of Hereford, Badlesmere, Roger Mortimer of Chirk, John de Somery, Walter de Norwich, the archbishop of York, and the bishops of Norwich and Ely was also appointed to conduct a reform of the royal household.[12]

---

[6] Kershaw, 'Great Famine', 13–15.

[7] *PW*, II, ii, 182–95; Phillips, 171. The details of the parliament, which were previously available in *Documents Illustrative of English History in the Thirteenth and Fourteenth Centuries*, ed. H. Cole (London, 1844), can now be found in *PROME*, Parliament of Oct. 1318. The Parliament Roll, SC 9/21, edited by Cole, now contains one additional membrane added from unsorted miscellanea in 1958 and not previously edited; the material from E 175/11/20, E 175/1/22, and BL, Add. Ms. 41612/f. 53 (the 'Liber Eliensis') was previously edited in *Rotuli Parliamentorum Hactenus Inediti*, ed. Richardson & Sayles, 66–80.

[8] *PROME*, Parliament of Oct. 1318, SC 9/21, item 1; *Documents*, ed. Cole, 1–2; Phillips, 171; Maddicott, 229.

[9] *Foedera*, II, i, 373–4.

[10] The bishops of Norwich, Chichester, Ely, Salisbury, St David's, Carlisle, Hereford and Worcester; the earls of Pembroke, Richmond, Hereford, and Arundel; and Hugh de Courtenay, Roger Mortimer, John de Segrave and John de Grey: *PROME*, Parliament of Oct. 1318, SC 9/21, items 57–9; *Documents*, ed. Cole, 12; Phillips, 172.

[11] *PROME*, Parliament of Oct. 1318, SC 9/21, items 57–9; Phillips, 172; Maddicott, 231–2.

[12] *PROME*, Parliament of Oct. 1318, SC 9/21, items 2, 60–1; *Documents*, ed. Cole, 3, 12; Phillips, 173.

Following the confirmation of the Ordinances as had been promised at Leake,[13] a review was undertaken of grants which Edward had made contrary to them and which had been revoked the previous June in the course of the negotiations with Lancaster. It is possible that part at least of this review was carried out in the course of some further negotiations with Lancaster after the making of the agreement at Leake, since on 10 September the restoration of grants made to Hugh Audley the Younger was ordered with the consent of the earl of Pembroke and other magnates who are said to have been recently at Tutbury.[14] The review continued during the York parliament itself, when formal approval was given to grants which had been made to Hereford, Badlesmere, Montacute, the Younger Despenser, Roger Damory and others but with some reductions and modifications in their substance. Lancaster's demand for the complete revocation of all such grants had therefore been effectively side-stepped.[15]

All the major offices under the crown were reviewed during the parliament. The bishop of Ely John de Hothum was confirmed as chancellor and his predecessor, John Sandal the bishop of Winchester, was appointed as treasurer. Badlesmere was advanced to the stewardship of the household in place of William de Montacute, and Hugh Despenser the Younger was confirmed as chamberlain.[16] New sheriffs were also appointed throughout England, except for the northern counties, on 29 November.[17] As to the favourites whose removal Lancaster had been so persistently demanding, a compromise was achieved. Montacute was compensated for his loss of office by his appointment on 20 November as seneschal of Gascony, a move which also conveniently took him away from court.[18] Roger Damory and Hugh Audley the Younger apparently also left court after they and Montacute had made their peace with Lancaster on 23 November by agreeing to pay compensation totalling just over £1,700 for their past hostility to him.[19]

---

[13] *PROME*, Parliament of Oct. 1318, SC 9/21, items 1, 54; *Documents*, ed. Cole, 3, 12; Phillips, 173. Magna Carta was also confirmed and was read out before the clergy, earls and barons. The Ordinances were apparently taken as read.

[14] *CFR, 1307–19*, 374; Phillips, 173.

[15] *PROME*, Parliament of Oct. 1318, SC 9/21, items 37–51; *Documents*, ed. Cole, 9–10; Phillips, 173; Maddicott, 230–1. For example, the grant to Despenser of lands worth 600 marks was reduced to 300 marks.

[16] *PROME*, Parliament of Oct. 1318, SC 9/21, items 6, 12; *Documents*, ed. Cole, 3–4; Phillips, 174; Maddicott, 229–30. Hothum and Despenser had been appointed to their offices in June and July respectively.

[17] *PROME*, Parliament of Oct. 1318, SC 9/21, item 28; *Documents*, ed. Cole, 6–7; *CFR, 1307–19*, 381–3; Maddicott, 230.

[18] *Foedera*, II, i, 377; Phillips, 174. Montacute died in Gascony at the end of Oct. 1319.

[19] *Vita*, 156–7; *CCR, 1318–23*, 109–10; Phillips, 174; Maddicott, 233. Damory recognized a debt of 906 marks 7s 4d; Audley one of 1,229 marks 6s 6d; and Montacute a debt of 413 marks 4s. Damory's debt was certainly paid and in Feb. 1319 an acquittance was sent to Montacute: *CCR, 1318–23*, 109–10; DL 28/1/13, m.1; Maddicott, 233.

On 6 December, three days before the end of the parliament, the very detailed Household Ordinance of York was issued.[20] A statute was also approved, containing six clauses relating to such matters as *novel disseisin*, inquests, justices of *nisi prius*, liberties, and the assize of wine and victuals. Although the statute may have been the result of petitions submitted during the parliament, it is not possible to associate the individual clauses with any commune or private petitions recorded or listed in the surviving records of the parliament.[21]

No subsidy was requested or granted by the parliament, but a tax was levied in Wales in aid of the Scottish war on 22 November 1318 or earlier (probably between June and November). On 25 November the king also ordered the convocation of the clergy of the Canterbury province to grant a subsidy in aid of the coming campaign against the Scots, which it had been decided should begin at Newcastle on 10 June 1319.[22] It was also decided that the next parliament should be held at either York or Lincoln on 6 May 1319.[23]

Apart from the confirmation and amplification of the settlement reached at Leake, the parliament roll records large numbers of petitions. Because of the political uncertainty which had existed since the end of the Lincoln parliament of 1316 this was the first opportunity to submit petitions in parliament and there was therefore a great deal of pent-up grievance to be dealt with. Three bishops, three barons and seven royal judges and clerks were appointed to hear and to answer the bills and petitions from England, Ireland and Wales received during the parliament; and three bishops and one clerk for petitions from Gascony.[24]

---

[20] See Tout, *Place of the Reign*, 118–19 & App. I, A, 241–81.

[21] *SR*, i, 177–8. The statute was also to be sent to Ireland for promulgation there.

[22] *Lay Taxes*, 34; *PW*, II, ii, 196; *PROME*, Parliament of Oct. 1318, SC 9/21, item 17; *Documents*, ed. Cole, 4.

[23] *PROME*, Parliament of Oct. 1318, SC 9/21, item 18; *Documents*, ed. Cole, 4. The next parliament was duly summoned on 20 March 1319 to meet at York on the agreed date of 6 May 1319: *CCR, 1318–23*, 131.

[24] *PROME*, Parliament of Oct. 1318, SC 9/21, items 63, 64; *Documents*, ed. Cole, 13. After the major political business of the parliament, most of the remainder of the roll consists entirely of petitions, items 19–36, 65–293 (items 267–93 are contained in the recently added membrane 12 which was not available to Cole); *Documents*, ed. Cole, 4–9, 13–46. Many more petitions appear in E 175/1/22, mm.2, 3, which lists petitions presented in the parliament of Oct. 1318: *PROME*, Parliament of Oct. 1318; also printed in *Rotuli Parliamentorum Hactenus Inediti*, ed. Richardson & Sayles, 70–80. This document contains lists of petitions in different categories: those for the great council, those for the personal consideration of the king, those concerning the king's debts, those not fully expedited because of various difficulties, and finally petitions that have been expedited. With few exceptions, no petitions save those in the last category can be identified on the Parliament Roll, SC 9/21, but a large number of those expedited correspond with the petitions entered on that roll: *Rotuli Parliamentorum Hactenus Inediti*; 65–6. Over 40 of the petitions listed in E 175/1/22 can be identified with surviving petitions in SC 8/319/E 356–E 417. Another of the sources for the 1318 parliament, E 175/11/20, contains the proceedings on a petition of Hugh de Courtenay, while a fourth source, BL, Add. Ms. 41612/f. 53, is a transcript of a petition from the bishop of Ely, who had been chancellor since 11 June 1318.

Among the petitions was one from Walter Langton, the bishop of Coventry & Lichfield, the former treasurer under Edward I whose arrest and disgrace had been one of the first acts of Edward II when he became king and who had since gradually worked his way back into some degree of favour. Langton now complained bitterly about his imprisonment, bad treatment, and the losses he had allegedly suffered. However, there was no sympathy for him among his fellow bishops and the magnates, and the petition was referred to Edward, who no doubt had vivid memories of his famous dispute with Langton in 1305: with the advice of his council, Edward dismissed Langton's plea.[25]

Edward could be well satisfied with the work of the parliament. None of the members of the standing council was personally objectionable to him, and many of them, men such as the bishops of Norwich, Ely and Winchester, the earls of Pembroke and Hereford, Bartholomew de Badlesmere and Hugh Despenser the Younger, were men with whom he was used to working and could trust. The appointments to the major offices of chancellor and treasurer, steward and chamberlain were equally satisfactory. The grants that he had made to his followers had been substantially confirmed; his household had undergone review but this was essentially a matter of detailed revision of structures that already existed in order to improve their efficiency rather than a revolutionary programme of reform. It was highly significant that the commission appointed at the beginning of the parliament to carry out this duty was content to depute the task to the leading officers of the royal household, Badlesmere the steward, Despenser the chamberlain, Roger de Northburgh the treasurer, and Gilbert de Wigton the controller.[26]

In principle, the earl of Lancaster had got most of what he wanted in relation to royal grants and in the composition of the new standing council, on which one of his bannerets would serve to represent his views and in effect to act as a spy within the government. He also had the satisfaction of being allowed to settle his dispute with the earl of Surrey outside the terms of the Leake treaty. On 29–30 November the earl of Surrey released to him all his lands at Conisbrough, Sandal and other places in Yorkshire and the lordships of Bromfield and Yale and the castle of Holt in North Wales, and pledged to pay Lancaster the vast sum of £50,000 by 25 December. Surrey was first of all held prisoner at Pontefract and threatened with death if he did not give way.[27] Such ruthless behaviour goes far

---

[25] *PROME*, Parliament of Oct. 1318, SC 9/21, item 19; *Documents*, ed. Cole, 4–5.

[26] Cf. Tout, *Place of the Reign*, 118; Maddicott, 231. The king had also been permitted to add the archbishop of York and the bishops of Ely and Norwich, all of them close allies of long standing, to the reform commission: *PROME*, Parliament of Oct. 1318, SC 9/21, item 61; *Documents*, ed. Cole, 12.

[27] *Vita*, 158–61. The details are given in Phillips, 171, 183; Maddicott, 234–7. In Jan. 1319, probably as a result of pressure from the king, the grants of lands in Wales and Yorkshire were modified to allow Lancaster to hold them only for Surrey's life: Maddicott, 235–6.

to explain why Lancaster had no real friends and why during the negotiations of 1318 his fellow earls were unwilling to see him claim superiority over them.[28]

With regard to the king's favourites, Lancaster had apparently achieved their removal from court, semi-permanently in the case of Montacute, and at least temporarily in the case of Damory and Audley. He did not however succeed in obtaining the removal of his old enemy, Hugh Despenser the Elder, although Despenser apparently stayed away from parliament and early in the new year, 1319, went to Spain, ostensibly on pilgrimage to Santiago but probably on a diplomatic mission to the court of Castile.[29]

During the parliament itself Lancaster and several of his bannerets, knights (Robert de Holland, Stephen de Segrave, Fulk Lestrange, John de Clavering and William Latimer) and clerks (Michael de Meldon and Roger Belers) were members of the committee of over fifty archbishops, bishops, earls, barons, knights and clerks who met to decide the order of business.[30] Other than this it is difficult to establish what role he actually played, with the exception of two petitions which he lodged on his own behalf. One concerned his claim to the manor of Levisham in Yorkshire and does not seem to have been of any great significance.[31] The other related to the office of steward of England, which had been held by both Simon de Montfort and Lancaster's own father Edmund as a perquisite of the earldom of Leicester, and to which Edward II had appointed Thomas of Lancaster in May 1308. Lancaster asked that his duties as steward should be clarified for the future.[32] This was deliberately disingenuous on Lancaster's part, since he had already sought in the autumn of 1317 to use the office of steward in order to influence royal policy. On that occasion he had claimed that if the king wished to take up arms against anyone, he had first to notify the steward. At the time this claim had served to justify Lancaster's refusal to co-operate in a campaign against the Scots.[33] Lancaster's petition therefore raised important issues which, if conceded,

---

[28] '*sovereinete a li accrocher vers les autres*': C 49/4/26 (June 1318); Phillips, 162.

[29] *Vita*, 160–1, & 160, n. 113.

[30] *PROME*, Parliament of Oct. 1318, SC 9/21, item 53; *Documents*, ed. Cole, 1; *Foedera*, II, i, 373–4; Maddicott, 232–3. Lancaster was at the parliament from about 26 Oct. to 22 Nov., after which he withdrew to Pontefract. Roger Belers then acted as his agent and kept him informed of what occurred: Maddicott, 229; DL 28/1/15, mm.1, 6. In contrast, Edward II was at York throughout the time of the parliament, before moving to Beverley just after Christmas.

[31] *PROME*, Parliament of Oct. 1318, SC 9/21, item 35; *Documents*, ed. Cole, 8.

[32] *PROME*, Parliament of Oct. 1318, SC 9/21, item 34; *Documents*, ed. Cole, 8. Edward II's charter of 9 May, 1 Edward II, was cited in the petition. On 22 Nov. Lancaster wrote, using his titles of earl of Lancaster and Leicester and steward of England, to the chancellor concerning pardons to be issued to some of his retainers: SC 1/35/189.

[33] *Trivet (Cont.)*, 23; *Vita*, 140–1; Phillips, 125; Maddicott, 208. On Lancaster's use of the stewardship to advance his claims to authority within the kingdom see *Vita*, 140, n. 273; Maddicott, 76–7, 241–3.

might allow him a right of interference in the business of the kingdom far greater than he would achieve from the presence of a single banneret on the council. As a foretaste of what might happen, he objected to the appointment of Badlesmere as steward of the household, before finally giving way.[34] No immediate answer was made to Lancaster's petition. Instead orders were given to make a search of the records of the exchequer and household for any information on the duties and powers of the steward of England and for a report to be delivered in the chancery on 22 April 1319.[35]

One other petition of note was lodged at York, on behalf of Hugh Audley the Younger, who claimed the earldom of Cornwall in right of his wife Margaret, Gaveston's widow. Since Audley was one of the three notorious royal favourites and had already acquired a share of the vast estates of the Gloucester earldom, this was both an audacious and a politically dangerous move. For the moment Audley was persuaded to withdraw his claim in return for lands worth 2,000 marks a year, but was authorized to renew it at the next parliament if a satisfactory agreement had not been reached in the meantime.[36]

The Treaty of Leake and the York parliament had brought about a political settlement and created a framework of government for the future. Both Edward and Lancaster had some reason for satisfaction with the compromise. Neither had won outright, but neither had been humiliated.[37] The settlement had been brought about by the mediation of the archbishops and bishops, the papal envoys,[38] and the determination of moderate baronial figures such as Pembroke, Hereford and Badlesmere. But it had also been achieved by the king's stubbornness and his skill in mobilizing support for himself among the barons and by the fact that Lancaster was increasingly seen by his fellow magnates as unreasonable and self-aggrandizing. Another important factor in producing a settlement was the war with the Scots. Their invasion of Ireland had ended in failure but the loss of Berwick-upon-Tweed was a warning that only active

---

[34] *PROME*, Parliament of October 1318, SC 9/21, item 6; *Documents*, ed. Cole, 3. This section of the roll is in very poor condition.

[35] *PROME*, Parliament of Oct. 1318, SC 9/21, item 34; *Documents*, ed. Cole, 8.

[36] *PROME*, Parliament of Oct. 1318, SC 9/21, item 42; *Documents*, ed. Cole, 9.

[37] The 1318 settlement was certainly not a humiliation for the king, as Tout argued: *Place of the Reign*, 118. Davies on the other hand realized that the members of the standing council were 'nearly all personally acceptable to the King': *Baronial Opposition*, 463, 468; Phillips, 176–7.

[38] Cardinals Luke and Gaucelin left London at the end of their mission on 11 Sept., and returned to Avignon on 5 Nov. 1318: *Ann. Paul.*, 283; Wright, *The Church and the English Crown*, 290. A seventeenth-century transcript of a report on their mission to England and Scotland in 1317–18 by the two cardinals is contained in Biblioteca Apostolica Vaticana, Barberini Ms. 2366. There is a copy of this document in TNA in PRO 31/8/158. Unfortunately, unlike the report of earlier papal envoys (ASV, Instrumenta Miscellanea, 5947) which is so valuable for working out the negotiations of 1312–13, this report consists mainly of copies of papal bulls and throws no light on the politics and negotiations of 1317–18.

co-operation between the king and Lancaster offered any realistic hope of defeating them. The two men had exchanged a kiss of peace and fair words, but whether their reconciliation would last was another question entirely. In the unresolved claims by Lancaster and Audley the settlement had left two more primed and ticking time bombs. This was now the moment when a new figure advanced and proceeded to take centre stage: Hugh Despenser the Younger.[39] Ironically, in his hostility to the elder Hugh Despenser, Lancaster had failed to notice the far greater danger that was developing right under his nose and apparently raised no objections to the appointment of the Younger Despenser as chamberlain. Lancaster, and others too, would soon have cause for regret.[40]

THE WORKING OF THE SETTLEMENT

In some ways the years 1318 to 1321 were a repeat performance of 1317 and 1318. Once again there can be found the rise of a new royal favourite, leading once more to a deterioration in the relations between Edward II and Lancaster. But this time there was no eleventh-hour avoidance of civil war through the mediation of well-intentioned prelates and magnates. By 1321 Lancaster was again bitterly hostile to Edward and, even more sinister than this, a large number of the magnates who had rallied to the king in 1317 and who had helped to make peace in 1318 were now openly ranged against him.[41] Once this point was reached, only violence could resolve the situation.

The central feature of the scheme of government agreed at Leake and confirmed at York was the standing royal council of magnates and prelates. It is very difficult to give a clear description of the working of this council, because of the lack of evidence and the ambiguity of much of what is available.[42] It is not always possible, for example, to say whether an individual prelate or magnate was present at court because it was his turn to serve on the council or whether he happened to be there for entirely different reasons. Important royal officials, such as John de Hothum bishop of Ely and chancellor, John de Sandal bishop of Winchester and treasurer, Bartholomew de Badlesmere the steward of the royal household, and Hugh Despenser the Younger the household chamberlain, were

---

[39] See Phillips, 174–6; and Maddicott, 237–9, for a more sympathetic view of Lancaster.

[40] It is possible, as Dr Maddicott suggests, that Lancaster had objected to Despenser's appointment and (as in the case of the stewardship of the household) had been overruled, but this is not at all certain. Despenser was confirmed as chamberlain '*par consail et a la requeste des grantz*': *PROME*, Parliament of Oct. 1318, SC 9/21, item 12; *Documents*, ed. Cole, 4.

[41] Phillips, 178–9.

[42] The witness lists of royal charters (C 53) are a good guide to those who were at court. For details see *The Royal Charter Witness Lists of Edward II (1307–1326) from the Charter Rolls in the Public Record Office* [TNA], ed. Jeffrey S. Hamilton (Kew, 2001), 288; Hamilton, 'Charter witness lists for the reign of Edward II', in *Fourteenth Century England*, i, ed. N. Saul (Woodbridge, Suffolk & Rochester, NY, 2000), 1–20.

likely to be at court because of their offices. Nor apparently was there any rule or understanding that any prelate or magnate would be required to leave court as soon as his three-month term of office was over.[43]

The only certain information on the serving members of the standing council is that the four councillors deputed to remain with the king during the parliament at York were the bishops of Ely and Worcester, the earl of Pembroke and John de Segrave.[44] The earl of Lancaster's banneret is not named but may have been John de Clavering.[45] It is probable that one of the first two prelates to serve on the council after the parliament was John Salmon, the bishop of Norwich, who wrote on 25 November that he expected to stay with the king at least until the start of Lent. This period fits roughly into the stipulation that each councillor should stay in turn for three months. Salmon's witnessing of charters and details given in his register appear to confirm that he did stay as intended.[46] His colleague was probably Roger Mortival, bishop of Salisbury, whose presence can also be traced until early February. Their two successors may have been the bishops of Chichester and Carlisle, John Langton and John Halton, who both appear as witnesses to royal charters from late February until May.[47] John de Bretagne the earl of Richmond may have been the first earl to serve after the parliament, since he was a regular witness in the early part of 1319; and he was perhaps succeeded by Humphrey de Bohun the earl of Hereford, who starts to appear in early April.[48] The baronial representative on the council is much harder to identify. Hugh Despenser the Younger and Badlesmere were present in February and March, but could have been there in their official capacities, while Roger Mortimer of Wigmore and John Botetourt also appear in mid-March. The most intriguing question is the identity of Lancaster's representative. The only person with recognizable Lancastrian links to appear in early 1319 was his brother Henry. But his

---

[43] Phillips, 179.
[44] *PROME*, Parliament of Oct. 1318, SC 9/21, item 62; *Documents*, ed. Cole, 13.
[45] Maddicott, 231.
[46] HMC, *First Report, Documents of the Dean and Chapter of Norwich*, 88; Phillips, 179. He last witnessed a charter on 4 Feb.: C 53/105, m.9. His register shows that he was at York or Beverley between 15 Nov. 1318 and 21 Jan. 1319 and was back at Norwich on 22 Feb.: Norfolk and Norwich Record Office, Reg. John Salmon, ff. 77v, 78.
[47] C 53/105, mm.9–5. Carlisle was with the king by 4 Feb.: E 101/377/3, m.6.
[48] C 53/105, m.6. Hereford had been in Hainault in the Low Countries from Jan. to March, probably for business connected with Edward II's project for a marriage between his son Edward, the future Edward III, and Margaret the daughter of William, count of Hainault and Holland. Hereford's wife Elizabeth (d. 1316) had previously been countess of Hainault and Holland. Margaret was the sister of Philippa of Hainault, the eventual wife of Edward III: E 404/484/2/1; *Foedera*, II, i, 381. The bishop of Exeter, who accompanied Hereford to Hainault in 1319, included in his register a description of Edward's intended bride, which is often taken to refer to Philippa but seems more likely to be Margaret (my comment): see Buck, 126; article by J. Vale on Philippa of Hainault in the *Oxford DNB*. After his term of service on the council the earl of Pembroke had gone to look after various items of official and personal business in the south and east of England: Phillips, 180–3.

name is recorded only on 4 February[49] and the evidence is therefore inconclusive.[50]

It is probably safe to assume that the standing council established in 1318 was still functioning at the time of the parliament which met as previously agreed at York between 6 and 25 May 1319,[51] and was in many respects a continuation of the York parliament of October 1318. The petition lodged in the previous parliament by Hugh Audley and his wife Margaret, in which they claimed the earldom of Cornwall as Margaret's inheritance, was again considered. 'After a careful discussion of that petition in full parliament, and because record was borne there, both by the prelates and by the earls, barons and the whole community of the realm', it was decided that the request could not be granted since all grants made by the king to Gaveston had been revoked.[52] Audley did not make his claim again,[53] but its rejection must have rankled and was one of the reasons for his change of allegiance in 1321–2.

Lancaster's claim to authority in his capacity as steward of England was also revisited. It had been agreed at the previous parliament that a search was to be made of the records to establish the functions of the steward. It is clear however that nothing had been done, on the specious grounds that Lancaster had not actually sued out the writs necessary to start the search. During the earlier parliament Lancaster had tried to use his position to claim the right to approve the appointment of Badlesmere as steward of the royal household. Now in 1319 he went a stage further and claimed that the office belonged to him by right.[54] Lancaster was in attendance at York with many of his retainers, but whether this was meant to be a show of force is not clear.[55] If the stewardship had been conceded, Lancaster would have gained a position

---

[49] C 53/105, mm.9–6; Phillips, 180.

[50] Phillips, 180. During the early months of 1319 Edward was at York or in its immediate vicinity, while Lancaster was at his castle of Pontefract: Maddicott, 240. Communications between them should have been straightforward, with or without the presence of a formal Lancastrian representative on the council.

[51] Although the holding of a parliament on 6 May 1319 had been agreed during the previous parliament, the summonses for the 1319 assembly were not issued until 20 March: *PW*, II, ii, 197–214. For the records of the parliament see *PROME*, Parliament of May 1319.

[52] *PROME*, Parliament of May 1319, SC 9/ 22, item 7; Maddicott, 240.

[53] To make sure that he could not do so, the judgment was ordered to be entered on the parliament roll and sent to the chancery, exchequer, and the courts of King's Bench and Common Pleas for enrolment there.

[54] *PROME*, Parliament of May 1319, SC 9/ 22, item 3; *Documents*, ed. Cole, 48; Maddicott, 233. This probably meant he had the right to make the appointment rather than marking a desire to hold the office himself. There was an obvious analogy with the rights of the earls of Warwick and Hereford, as hereditary chamberlain and constable respectively, to appoint deputies to represent them at the exchequer: Maddicott, 242. It was no coincidence that in the autumn of 1319 a search of the records was made, at the request of the earl of Hereford, to establish the fees due to the constable. The search went as far back as the *Constitutio Domus Regis* from the reign of Henry I: E 159/93, m.70.

[55] E 368/93, m.12; Phillips, 183; Maddicott, 241.

of control and influence over many of the king's actions.⁵⁶ It is possible that he could even have claimed that the office of steward of England gave him the right to control royal castles, which Edward could not possibly have conceded.⁵⁷ Again he was invited to apply for a search of the records, and there for the moment at least matters rested. Lancaster did not however forget his claim and by 1321 a tract on the office of steward of England had been drawn up on his behalf. This time bomb also continued to tick.⁵⁸

During the parliament the settlement between Lancaster and the earl of Surrey was confirmed. Lancaster was induced to agree to a life tenure of Surrey's lands in Yorkshire and North Wales in place of outright annexation, but this did little to mask the brutality of Surrey's treatment or to conceal the fact that Lancaster was now a major power in the Welsh March, where he already held the lordship of Denbigh, and had greatly strengthened his position in the West Riding of Yorkshire, in the vicinity of his powerbase at Pontefract.⁵⁹

THE HOLY OIL AGAIN

The disappointment of Hugh Audley the Younger and the unresolved demands of the earl of Lancaster are indications that by the summer of 1319 serious tensions were starting to re-emerge. Another, unrelated, cause of disturbance was the serious falling out between two of Edward II's most valuable and experienced advisers, the earl of Pembroke and Antonio Pessagno, the royal financier and former seneschal of Gascony. In earlier years the two men had worked closely together, but in January 1319 Edward wrote to the pope complaining that Pessagno had made false accusations against Pembroke during a recent visit to the papal curia; and a few days later ordered the new seneschal of Gascony, William de Montacute, to send Pessagno (who had apparently not been told of his replacement) back to England at once, if necessary by force.⁶⁰ It is not clear why he and Pembroke had quarrelled but it probably had something to do with Pessagno's treatment of a leading Gascon magnate, Jourdain de l'Isle, on whose behalf the pope had asked Pembroke to intercede

---

⁵⁶ Dr Maddicott suggests that Lancaster's aim was to curb royal extravagance by ensuring the enforcement of the Ordinances and the reform of the royal household: Maddicott, 237–8, 241–2. Although he also argues that 'the events of 1317–18 had shown Lancaster in the best and worst of lights', such a high-minded view of Lancaster is at odds with his behaviour when he had any of his opponents, such as the earl of Surrey, at his mercy. It is far more likely that Lancaster wished to exercise power for his own ends.

⁵⁷ Maddicott, 241–2, citing the precedent of 1268 when the Lord Edward (the future Edward I) had been granted the stewardship and control of the castles. There is no evidence that Lancaster made such a claim on this occasion.

⁵⁸ Phillips, 183; Maddicott, 242–3.

⁵⁹ Phillips, 183; Maddicott, 235–6.

⁶⁰ C 70/4, m.9; SC 1/49/46; C 61/32, mm.3d, 5; Phillips, 181–2.

in 1318.⁶¹ Pessagno did return to England, appearing at the exchequer on 26 April, and was apparently back in favour by the following August.⁶² It is not known whether he repaired his relations with Pembroke, but by April 1320 Pessagno had left England for Paris,⁶³ and played no further direct role in the affairs of England until the reign of Edward III.⁶⁴ With Pessagno's departure Edward II lost access to the expertise which in earlier years had found him the financial resources for the Bannockburn campaign, the defence of the north of England and the successful war against the Scots in Ireland.⁶⁵ However, Pessagno was already yesterday's financier, since by 1319 he was being replaced by the Florentine banking company the Bardi.⁶⁶

Edward II had cause for bitter personal disappointment in the early summer of 1319, for this was when the saga of the Holy Oil of St Thomas of Canterbury reached its final ignominious conclusion. The Dominican friar, Nicholas of Wisbech, who had told Edward II the story of the Holy Oil and had urged him to undergo a ceremony of reanointing as a way of escaping his political troubles, returned to Edward at York in late January or

---

⁶¹ *CPL, 1305–42*, 421; Phillips, 182. Pessagno had been sent to Gascony as seneschal in 1317 in order to recover control of the duchy's revenues which had been pledged to the pope in 1314. Pessagno's term of office as seneschal of Gascony had also been marked by his clumsy attempts to resolve a private war between Jourdain de l'Isle and another local lord, Alexander de Caumont. This and suspicions of peculation and forgery were among the reasons for Pessagno's replacement as seneschal and his recall to England in disgrace in Nov. 1318. Instead he first of all went to Avignon, with the results already mentioned: Vale, 134–6; Phillips, 181–2; E.B. Fryde, article on Pessagno in the *Oxford DNB*.

⁶² E 159/92, Recorda, Easter 12 Edward II; BL, Add. Ms. 17362, f. 13; *Foedera*, II, i, 403 (letters recommending Pessagno to the pope and to Cardinal Luke Fieschi); Phillips, 182.

⁶³ In March 1320 Edward II sent letters of recommendation to the king of France, the pope and the cardinals: *Foedera*, II, i, 420, 429–30; Vale, 155–6. Pessagno had apparently not fallen out personally with the king. The *Oxford DNB* article on Pessagno suggests that he had quarrelled with the Despensers but does not supply any evidence for this.

⁶⁴ Once in France, Pessagno offered his services to, for example, Louis count of Clermont and lord of Bourbon: *Titres de la maison ducale de Bourbon*, no.1604 (Sept. 1321), ed. H. Bréholles (Paris, 1867–82). Later in the 1320s he turned against Edward II and in 1325 was rumoured to be encouraging his brother, Manuel, who was the admiral of Portugal, to send an invasion fleet to England: Tout, *Place of the Reign*; C 61/37, m.12d; Fryde, *Oxford DNB*.

⁶⁵ Between April 1312 and Jan. 1319 Pessagno loaned Edward II almost £144,000: Fryde, *Oxford DNB*.

⁶⁶ The Bardi had done business with the English crown since 1294 but had increased in importance after the expulsion from England of the Frescobaldi in 1311: Prestwich, *War, Politics and Finance*, 212; Fryde, 'Deposits of Hugh Despenser the Younger,' item III, 347. In Aug. 1319 the Bardi were given two gold crowns to keep until Edward had repaid 5,000 marks he owed them and £500 which they had paid to Pessagno out of the king's debts to him: E 159/93, m.77. The crowns were redeemed on 22 Feb. 1320. In Jan. 1320 the Bardi paid Pessagno a further £1,850 on behalf of the king, but it appears that Edward II did not know whether he actually owed Pessagno this much since he had not fully accounted for the time he had been involved in royal affairs (*qil sad medlez de noz busoignes*): E 159/93, m.29d.

early February 1319, bearing with him very unwelcome news, since he had to admit that he had not succeeded in persuading the pope to agree to the proposal. He was then closely interrogated by the chancellor the bishop of Ely and the bishops of Norwich and Salisbury, who wrote down his answers in letters under their seals.[67] On 6 February Edward wrote to the pope, to announce Nicholas of Wisbech's return to England and to say that he was sending the bishop of Hereford and other envoys to Avignon on important business, but without specifying its nature.[68] The bishop left England at the end of February and was in Avignon in early May, when he delivered the letters of the bishops of Ely, Norwich and Salisbury and awaited the pope's reply. He remained abroad on this and other business until February 1320,[69] but John XXII's letter containing his final word on the subject of the Holy Oil was certainly written in May 1319 and reached Edward II at York in early June.[70] The pope recorded that he and the cardinal bishop of Sabina had discussed the matter carefully, having read the letters and interviewed Nicholas, and had concluded: first of all that the Holy Oil was quite different in nature from the oil with which Edward was anointed at his coronation and that it was therefore of no importance one way or another; and secondly that if Edward were to be anointed with the Holy Oil it should be done in secret to avoid public amazement and scandal, and it should not be performed by a bishop. The pope concluded by reminding Edward that neither anointing nor anything else would be of profit to him unless he was well disposed towards God. He earnestly exhorted Edward, as he had often done elsewhere, to obey the divine decrees by leading a virtuous life and cultivating justice in himself and his subjects.[71]

Bitterly disillusioned and no doubt also feeling humiliated, on 8 June 1319 Edward II wrote to the pope asking him to dismiss Nicholas from his office as a papal penitentiary, since he had proved to be unworthy, and to replace him with a fellow Dominican, John de Wrotham.[72] Nicholas was briefly imprisoned, escaped and then disappears from the records. As for Edward II, he was moved in July or August 1319 to send an extraordinary letter to the pope in which he admitted that through his own 'weakness'

---

[67] These details are all stated in or can be inferred from the pope's letter to Edward II containing an account of Nicholas of Wisbech's story: ASV, Vatican Register 110 (Secreta, i to iv, John XXII), ff. 136r–137v; *Coronation Records*, ed. Wickham Legg, 69–72 (Latin text), 72–6 (trans.); *CPL, 1305–42*, 436–7; *Foedera*, II, i, 383. On the date of the letter, see the discussion in the previous chapter and in Phillips, 'Edward II and the prophets', 196–7. The bishops of Norwich and Salisbury were then on duty as members of the standing council.

[68] *Foedera*, II, i, 383, 387; Phillips, 198.

[69] Haines, *The Church and Politics*, 20–2, where Orleton's mission is associated with the canonization of one of his predecessors, Thomas de Cantilupe. It is clear that the Holy Oil was also part of Orleton's business.

[70] *Foedera*, II, i, 399.

[71] Paraphrase of the Wickham Legg translation.

[72] *Foedera*, II, i, 399, 424; Phillips, 198. The king's letter of 8 June also provides a *terminus ante quem* for the date of the pope's own letter.

(*imbellicitatem*) he had allowed the unscrupulous friar to take advantage of his 'dovelike simplicity'.[73]

THE BERWICK CAMPAIGN

All of this was going on against the background of preparations for war. It was implicit in the various agreements reached with Lancaster that he would co-operate in a new military campaign against the Scots. This would be the first since the disastrous campaign of 1314 and, since the fall of Berwick, the need for one had become extremely urgent. There is no reason to suppose that Edward II and his advisers were unaware of this or to suggest that lethargy on the part of Edward was responsible for the long delay in launching a full-scale attack on the Scots.[74] This was quite simply the first occasion during his reign when Edward and the baronage, and most importantly Lancaster, had been united in agreeing on and participating in a campaign.[75]

The two cardinals, Gaucelin d'Eauze and Luke Fieschi, had begun the process on 3 September 1318, in their last official act before leaving England for Avignon, when they published papal bulls excommunicating Robert Bruce and his supporters from the pulpit of St Paul's in London.[76] Orders for a campaign in Scotland to start on 10 June 1319 were issued in November 1318, but on 22 May 1319, three days before the end of parliament, the date was postponed until 22 July, to allow more time for preparations.[77] On 12 May John de Bermingham, the victor over the Scottish army in Ireland in October 1318, was created earl of Louth, as much perhaps *pour encourager les autres* as to reward him for his past services.[78] Orders were issued for the distraint of knighthood and for the levying of £20 fines on all those who did not serve.[79] Purveyance on a large scale was organized in twenty-six English counties and included the collection of grain supplies, which the magnates had agreed at York to loan to the king in aid of the war.[80] The exchequer was also moved from Westminster to York.[81]

---

[73] C 70/ 4, m.6d: '*Hac denique callididate nuper nostram imbellicitatem aggrediens sub columbina simplicitate nostra N. de G.* [Guisbech: i.e. Wisbech] *sue malicie et nequicie tegens sermentum, quedam nobis superstitiosa et Christiane religioni adversa persuasit*'. This letter also refers to Nicholas's escape from custody. The letter is undated but probably belongs to July or Aug. 1319 (the preceding and following letters on the roll belong to these months). There is no suggestion of course that Edward actually wrote the letter, but it is unlikely that anyone else would have used such revealing language if it had not represented the king's own views.
[74] Maddicott, 240.
[75] Ibid., 244.
[76] *Ann. Paul.*, 283.
[77] *PROME*, Parliament of Oct. 1318, SC 9/21, item 17; *Documents*, ed. Cole, 4; *CCR, 1318–23*, 141.
[78] *Foedera*, II, i, 393. On Irish earldoms see Frame, *English Lordship*, 14–16.
[79] *CCR, 1318–23*, 79, 202–3; Phillips, 184.
[80] BL, Add. Ms. 17362, f. 14; E 101/378, ff. 4, 6, 8, 10; Phillips, 184.
[81] E 159/92, m.49; Maddicott, 243.

Great efforts were made to raise as much money as possible for the coming campaign. After Edward II promised to hear the grievances of the city of London against the government, its citizens gave him a loan of 2,000 marks. On 24 March the earl of Pembroke, the king's half-brother Thomas of Brotherton earl of Norfolk, and the treasurer John Sandal bishop of Winchester came to the chapter-house of St Paul's to enquire further and were deluged with complaints against the mayor, John Wengrave. During the York parliament Edward II confirmed all the existing liberties of the city of London in return for another 1,000 marks and granted London a new charter, which was proclaimed on 20 June. This ended a major constitutional crisis by widening the franchise for the elections of aldermen, mayors and sheriffs, and for the moment at least ensured the future loyalty of the city to the crown.[82] The earls of Pembroke and Norfolk performed another valuable service for the king in late April, shortly before the York parliament, when they and Bartholomew de Badlesmere, the steward of the king's household, attended the Canterbury provincial council at St Paul's in London to ask the clergy to grant a subsidy in aid of the war.[83] By the spring of 1320 this source had supplied Edward II's exchequer with £16,366. Before the end of the parliament a grant of taxation for the forthcoming campaign was made by the laity. It took the form of an eighteenth of the value of moveable goods in townships, excluding the clergy but including their villeins; and a twelfth to be levied on moveable goods in cities and boroughs. The assessment of the eighteenth was to be made by men who had not previously done so, because of complaints that earlier assessors and their clerks had embezzled much of the money collected.[84] These subsidies raised the substantial sum of £36,696.[85] A scutage was also ordered on 28 May in aid of the Scottish campaign.[86] On 8 June the king borrowed 6,000 marks from the Bardi to meet the immediate costs of the war and to maintain his household.[87] As in the case of the Bannockburn campaign in 1314, if the king and his army were to fail, it would not be for lack of money.

---

[82] *Ann. Paul.*, 285–6; Williams, *Medieval London*, 281–2.

[83] *Registrum Radulphi Baldock, etc., Bishops of London*, ed. R.C. Fowler, Canterbury & York Series, vii (London, 1911), 207–8; Phillips, 183. The bishops of the province of York had agreed to a subsidy earlier. The Canterbury province preferred not to agree until they were required to do so by the pope, which happened at the end of May. Having learned that it was easier to obtain taxation from the clergy by papal mandate than by clerical grant, in future (from 1320) Edward went directly to the pope when he desired a similar tax in aid of the defence of the kingdom: Lunt, 'Clerical tenths', 173–5.

[84] *Lay Taxes*, 34–5.

[85] J.F. Willard, *Parliamentary Taxes on Personal Property, 1290 to 1334* (Cambridge, Mass., 1934), 344.

[86] *Lay Taxes*, 34–5. Six scutages (one of them double) were now being collected simultaneously, without any agreement between the king and magnates on the basis of collection. There was much resistance, which continued until Edward III finally pardoned arrears of all scutages in 1340.

[87] E 159/92, Brevia Baronibus. Edward also promised to pay the Bardi a further 2,000 marks to cover the late repayment of other sums he owed them and their 'losses' (i.e. interest),

The army was intended to be a large one. Over 23,000 foot soldiers were summoned, although only a little over 8,000 appeared; and even this figure seems to be too high.[88] In addition there were about a thousand lightly armed horsemen or hobelars; and a heavy cavalry force of about 1,400 knights and men-at-arms.[89] The king had fifty-nine household knights at the siege of Berwick,[90] but some of these, such as John Giffard, John de Somery and John Cromwell, were also in command of substantial retinues of their own.[91] Edward knighted his half-brother the earl of Norfolk, whose first experience of war this was to be, and others on 11 July.[92] The earl of Lancaster obtained letters of protection for twenty-eight knights and men-at-arms before the start of the campaign but may have had a following of as many as 140 knights and 350 men-at-arms.[93] The earl of Pembroke had at least seventy-eight knights and men-arms as well as sixty archers;[94] while the earl of Arundel had sixty-one men, Badlesmere ninety-six, Hugh Despenser the Younger ninety-eight, Roger Damory eighty-two, and Hugh Audley the Younger seventy-four.[95] In total the army may have numbered about 10,000,[96] less than in 1314 but still a

---

giving them a 33% return on their investment. The loan was to be repaid out of the receipts of both clerical and lay taxation. Repayment was completed in 1320: E 403/189, m.7. Other details of the repayment can be found in E 403/187 and 189. The largest single amounts they had previously loaned the king were almost £7,800 in Jan. 1317 to meet the costs of the Avignon mission, and 10,000 marks in Nov. 1317, for which they were to receive in return a total of 13,000 marks, repayable from clerical taxation: E 159/91, m.40d; Phillips, 109.

[88] *PW*, II, i, 517–20; Maddicott, 244. Dr Maddicott's calculation (citing *CDS*, ii, nos 663–5, 668) of the number of foot soldiers, including archers and crossbowmen, is about 10,000. My own estimate, using the information in E 101/378/4, ff. 19–37v, was about 11,500: Phillips, 184. Professor Duncan has used another source, E 101/15/27 (calendared in *CDS*, iii, no. 668), which suggests that, although 8,080 men (1,040 hobelars and the rest infantry) mustered at Newcastle, the number of infantry actually paid for from 10 Sep., early in the siege, was only about 5,500, including 456 hobelars: *Bruce*, 630–1, note to ll. 283–4; Maddicott, 245–6.

[89] E 101/378/4, ff.19–37v; Phillips, 184. Dr Maddicott and I are in agreement on the number of hobelars, but his figure for heavy cavalry is only about 500: Maddicott, 244. The figures I cite below for the size of individual retinues suggest that this is a considerable underestimate.

[90] Tebbit, 'Household knights' (Ph.D.), 26–7; Phillips, 149, 312–13.

[91] Phillips, 149, 312–13.

[92] *Ann. Paul.*, 286.

[93] C 71/10, m.4; Phillips, 184; Maddicott, 245.

[94] C 71/10, mm.5, 2; C 81/1736/60; E 101/378/4, f. 36v; Phillips, 185. These are figures for the start of the campaign; other men may have joined him later.

[95] E 101/378/4, ff. 20, 19v, 20v, 29v; Phillips, 185. These are all maximum numbers reached during the campaign.

[96] This figure takes into account the men led by the earl of Lancaster, whose number is unknown but who were not in receipt of pay from the king. The *Vita Edwardi Secundi*, 162–3, notes the presence of the earls and barons, and adds that the infantry and sailors had been encouraged to serve with the promise of the right to plunder in Scotland, without having to make any restitution if there were to be a truce. My previous estimate of about 14,000 (Phillips, 184) was clearly too high.

substantial force. To this should be added a very large naval contingent of seventy-seven ships, commanded by Simon Driby, which was intended both to carry supplies for the advancing army and to break the Scottish blockade.[97]

Edward II clearly harboured ambitions of a major invasion of Scotland, on the lines of his father's great campaigns, since according to the *Vita Edwardi Secundi*, 'the lord king sent envoys to Scotland to claim the kingdom, offer peace and allow safety in life and limb to Robert Bruce. For it is fitting for a king to act thus, and to attack his enemies when peace is refused.'[98] Again according to the *Vita*, Berwick was not the immediate objective of the campaign but was attacked simply because Edward 'came first to Berwick with his whole army, and decided on advice that this should be the first place to be besieged, both because it had withdrawn from his authority, and so that they should not expose themselves to danger by leaving an unconquered enemy in their rear'.[99] This may explain why the army was supplied with prefabricated parts for the construction of two wooden peel towers as the army advanced into Scotland,[100] but lacked siege engines and diggers at the start of the siege.[101] The *Anonimalle Chronicle*, which was written at St Mary's Abbey in York and is very well informed on events in the north, says essentially the same as the *Vita* but with a slightly different emphasis which makes the English plans seem more carefully thought out. In this version of events, Edward II and the magnates held a council at Newcastle before the army set out, and decided that because Berwick was so strongly held by the Scots it should be besieged and taken before the English force advanced further into Scotland. This would also allow them a place of refuge if anything went wrong and they were forced to retreat.[102]

The army reached Berwick on 7 September[103] and launched a determined assault on 8 September both from the landward side and from

---

[97] McNamee, 218, 231. It was ironic that Edward II and his government were able to use naval power in the Irish Sea to great effect: this played a major part in the defeat of the Scots in Ireland. But they were unable to do the same in the North Sea. This was perhaps the result of a lack of resources for a 'two-sea' war and of the proximity of the North Sea to the bases of Scottish allies in Flanders. See McNamee, ch. 6, 'The North Sea theatre of war and the towns'. The Flemish commander John Crabbe was the particular bane of the English: McNamee, 209–11, 213–14, 218–19; H.S. Lucas, 'John Crabbe, Flemish pirate, merchant and adventurer', *Speculum*, xx (1945), 334–50.

[98] *Vita*, 160–1. It is not known when these envoys were sent to Scotland but on 8 March Edward II wrote to the pope asking for permission to treat with the excommunicated Scots: *Vita*, 161, n. 317; *Foedera*, II, i, 381.

[99] *Vita*, 162–3.

[100] *Bruce*, 630, fn., citing BL, Add. Ms. 17362, ff. 25–7. The building materials were carried in eight ships which returned south after the campaign without ever being unloaded.

[101] *CDS*, iii, no. 663; Maddicott, 246–7.

[102] *Anonimalle*, 94–7.

[103] E 101/378/3, m.3; Phillips, 185; Maddicott, 247.

the sea.[104] There was hard fighting between the English and the Scots before the attackers withdrew. Five days later, on 13 September, the English renewed the assault after the arrival of siege equipment from Northampton and Bamburgh.[105] Again there was fierce fighting: the Scots destroyed one of the English siege engines, a device called a sow,[106] and repelled an attack launched from one of the English ships, but by the end of the day the Scottish garrison was exhausted.[107] Another such attack might have been successful, but while Edward II and his commanders were taking stock and preparing to renew the assault events elsewhere intervened and threw the whole campaign into disarray. On the morning of 14 September news reached Edward of the defeat by the Scots on 12 September of another English force at Myton near Boroughbridge in Yorkshire, and that the city of York itself was under threat.[108] The result was confusion and an orgy of suspicion and recrimination which led to the breaking off of the siege and the reopening of all the old wounds in Edward and Lancaster's relationship.

A PLOT TO CAPTURE THE QUEEN

In late August or early September a Scottish force led by Thomas Randolph the earl of Moray and Sir James Douglas, two experienced commanders, entered England by way of Carlisle and moved east via Northumberland and Durham before entering Yorkshire.[109] The main intention of the Scots was probably to draw English attention away from the siege of Berwick. Although the Scottish movement began before the siege started, Robert Bruce certainly knew the English were planning a major campaign and could readily conclude that Berwick was likely to be one of its objectives. As John Barbour, author of *The Bruce*, remarked, Bruce would not take the risk of meeting the king of England in open battle around the walls of Berwick.[110] He had been lucky once, at Bannockburn five years before, but there was no guarantee that the English would make the same mistakes twice.

[104] *Bruce*, 632–3; Phillips, 185; Maddicott, 247; McNamee, 219.
[105] *Bruce*, 632–40; *Anonimalle*, 96–7; Phillips, 185; Maddicott, 247; McNamee, 219. This suggests that the siege was begun prematurely in the hope of a quick victory. Both chronicles are in error in stating that the siege began on 15 Aug. (the feast of the Assumption) instead of 8 Sept. (the feast of the Nativity): *Bruce*, 634, note.
[106] This provided cover for the miners.
[107] *Bruce*, 646–56, and footnotes; *Anonimalle*, 96–7; McNamee, 219; Maddicott, 248.
[108] *Bruce*, 658, and notes to ll. 828 and 858.
[109] *Bruce*, 641–3; *Scalacronica*, 86–7; *Anonimalle*, 96–7; McNamee, 90–1. For a map showing details of the Scottish raid in 1319 see McNamee, 92–3.
[110] *Bruce*, 640–2. Professor Duncan however suggests that the Scots may originally have intended to capture the queen by a clandestine approach to York and that they began to devastate the countryside only after they could no longer move secretly: *Bruce*, 642, note to l. 509.

However, several sources claim that the real objective of the Scots was the capture of Queen Isabella who was staying near York.[111] If successful, this would have changed the whole complexion of the war. As the author of the *Vita Edwardi Secundi* remarked, 'Indeed if the queen had at that time been captured, I believe that Scotland would have bought peace for herself.'[112] The *Flores* also claimed that the Scots hoped to seize the royal administration and all its records which had been moved from Westminster to York, allegedly on the bad advice of John de Hothum, bishop of Ely.[113] According to the *Vita*, a spy captured in York revealed the plot to William Melton the archbishop of York and the chancellor John de Hothum and the leading men of York, claiming that James Douglas would 'come there secretly with his chosen band, to abduct the queen' and giving details of when and where the Scots would hide and lie in wait. Hardly anyone believed the story, since Edward II was already beginning to lay waste to Scotland and it made more sense for the Scots to keep their army closer to home,[114] but as a precaution the queen was brought back into York and taken by water to the safety of Nottingham castle.[115] Whether there really was such a plot, or whether the Scots were simply seeking to take advantage of an opportunity to capture the queen if one should occur, cannot be proved but, given the Scottish expertise at taking well-garrisoned castles and towns by stealth,[116] it should not be ruled out. The *Anonimalle Chronicle*, has no mention of a plot to capture the queen but does emphasize that the Scots hid by day in woods and marshes, moving only at night, so that their movements would not be detected. There is also some evidence that the Scots were guided in their advance by Edmund Darel, a royal household knight from Yorkshire.[117]

THE 'CHAPTER' OF MYTON

It was unfortunate that the local infantry force which would otherwise have been available to defend York had already been ordered to join the

---

[111] *Vita*, 162–3; *Flores*, 189; *Trokelowe*, 103; McNamee, 91.
[112] *Vita*, 162–5.
[113] *Flores*, 189.
[114] *Vita*, 164–5.
[115] *Vita*, 164–5; *Flores*, 189; *Ann. Paul.*, 287.
[116] E.g., Perth, Linlithgow, Roxburgh and Edinburgh in 1313–14: McNamee, 59–60; Barrow, 193–5.
[117] *Flores*, 189; McNamee, 91. Although Darel was a royal household knight from 1315 to 1318, he was one of the many northern knights recruited at a time of serious danger from the Scots, who had no previous connection with the king and whose loyalty was questionable. (The behaviour of Gilbert de Middleton and John de Lilburne in 1317–18 provides other examples.) Darel had earlier been connected with Henry Percy and in 1313 was arrested and briefly held in Tickhill castle. He was apparently arrested at York in Feb. 1320, accused of betraying the queen and taken to London, but was released for lack of evidence. He fought against the king in 1322 and was then imprisoned in the Tower of London for two years: *Ann. Paul.*, 287–8; Phillips, 54–5; Prestwich, 'The unreliability of royal household knights', 8–9.

army besieging Berwick. York castle was kept garrisoned between 4 and 13 September and the vicars choral of York Minster defended their section of the city wall.[118] This time there was no opportunity for John de Hothum to organize a defensive force as he had done so successfully in Ireland in 1316.[119] The archbishop of York and the bishop of Ely were left to take action against the Scots as best they could, and improvised a force composed of citizens of York, including their mayor Nicholas Fleming, local peasantry, clergy and members of the royal administration. No knights or men-at-arms with experience of war were available to stiffen their ranks.[120]

Hoping to take the Scots by surprise, Melton and Hothum led their men out of the city on 12 September and towards the Scots who were encamped on the banks of the River Swale at Myton, about ten miles from York. The Scots were however forewarned and caused confusion among the English by setting fire to bundles of hay.[121] In the resulting smokescreen, the English force lost what little order it possessed and began to flee. Many were killed, including the mayor of York, while others drowned in the Swale or were taken prisoner.[122] The latter included the experienced exchequer clerk William Airmyn and Andrew de Tange, one of the notaries responsible for keeping the records of Anglo-Scottish relations.[123] So many clergy were killed or captured that the Scots named the encounter 'the chapter of Myton'.[124] Melton and Hothum and the other survivors escaped back to York, closed the gates and awaited a siege which never came.[125] Instead the Scots turned around and made their way back to Scotland, causing devastation as they went.[126] Melton and Hothum could scarcely be blamed for the débâcle. They had been placed in an impossible position, resulting from the over-confidence of Edward II and his advisers who yet again fatally underestimated the ingenuity of their opponents.[127] In all of Edward's previous campaigns against the Scots, including the Bannockburn campaign in 1314, his forces had already held

---

[118] *CDS*, iii, no. 664; McNamee, 94, 118.

[119] Phillips, 'Mission of John de Hothum'. Thomas Randolph was one of the Scottish commanders Hothum had encountered in Ireland.

[120] *Vita*, 164–7; *CDS*, iii, no. 665 (18 Sept., a bit late in the day); McNamee, 94. At least one knight was present, Sir John de Pabenham, one of the earl of Pembroke's retainers, who was taken prisoner. There may have been one or two others: Phillips, 185.

[121] *Vita*, 164–7; McNamee, 94.

[122] *Vita*, 166–7; *Anonimalle*, 98–9; *Gesta Edwardi*, 57–8.

[123] *Anonimalle*, 98–9; McNamee, 94.

[124] *Bruce*, 646; Barrow, 239–40.

[125] *Vita*, 164–7; *Anonimalle*, 98–9; McNamee, 94.

[126] Secrecy no longer being necessary: *Bruce*, 642, note to l. 509.

[127] While I would not accept Hugo Schwyzer's assessment that neither Hothum nor Melton had any previous experience of military command or of organizing a defence, it is clear that they had little chance of success on this occasion: 'Northern bishops and the Anglo-Scottish war in the reign of Edward II', in *Thirteenth-century England*, vii, ed. M. Prestwich, R. Britnell & R. Frame (Woodbridge, Suffolk, 1999), 249–50.

strongpoints deep inside Scottish territory. By 1319, with the loss of Berwick and other fortresses, the Scots were right on the English doorstep and capable of counterattacking with ease.

THE END OF THE SIEGE OF BERWICK: DIVISIONS AND DISSENSION

For Edward II and his men who had first arrived at Berwick, 'with trumpets blowing and spent the night in great joy and pleasure [and] music in contempt of their Scottish enemies',[128] the arrival on 14 September of news of the battle of Myton was devastating.[129] Some reports of the Scottish raid into the north of England must already have reached Berwick on 9 or 10 September, since a force of 1,200 hobelars and archers commanded by Sir Andrew Harclay was detached from the besieging army, probably being sent in the direction of Carlisle to cut off the Scottish retreat from Yorkshire.[130]

There were already serious tensions within the senior ranks of the besieging army.[131] If the chroniclers are to be believed, malicious gossip was deliberately spread, causing discord between Edward and Lancaster, and mutual distrust between the king and other magnates.[132] Edward is alleged to have disgusted Lancaster by promising, 'with his usual foolishness' (*fatuitate solita*), that Hugh Despenser the Younger would be made constable of the castle and Roger Damory keeper of the town of Berwick when they were captured.[133] The *Flores Historiarum* also records that Edward made promises of reward to various unworthy men, but without naming any of them, and that he even had two books of blank charters for this purpose. Even worse, Edward began to threaten that if he was victorious, he would avenge the death of Gaveston.[134] Robert of Reading, the author of the *Flores*, was bitterly hostile to Edward II and all his works, but the *Vita Edwardi Secundi* has a very similar report and probably gives a fair picture: ' "When this wretched business is over, we will turn our hands to other matters. For I have not yet forgotten the wrong that was done to my brother Piers". And this remark did not escape the earl; for this reason without doubt he took a less active part at Berwick.'[135]

The news of Myton and the possible threat to the queen's safety made matters worse. *The Bruce* can hardly be described as an impartial account of English affairs but its statement that the king's council was deeply divided over what to do next, the king and the southerners wanting to

---

[128] *Anonimalle*, 96–7.
[129] *Bruce*, 658, and notes to ll. 828 and 858; Maddicott, 248.
[130] *Bruce*, 61, note to ll. 283–4.
[131] Maddicott, 247; Phillips, 185–6.
[132] *Gesta Edwardi*, 57; *Melsa*, 336; Phillips, 186; Maddicott, 247.
[133] *Historia Anglicana*, 155; Phillips, 186; Maddicott, 247.
[134] *Flores*, 188; Maddicott, 247.
[135] *Vita*, 176–9; Phillips, 186; Maddicott, 247.

continue the siege until Berwick was taken while Lancaster and the other northerners were concerned about their lands, carries conviction. Lancaster took offence at this and withdrew himself and his men from the siege.[136] The Lanercost chronicler adds that Edward suggested dividing the army, one part to continue the siege while the remainder pursued the Scots; but that the magnates strongly advised that this would be too risky.[137] This general picture is confirmed by a Canterbury chronicler who speaks of trouble breaking out between Lancaster and the council, leading to his departure.[138]

Lancaster was still at Berwick on 16 September, but may have left on that day or the next.[139] Once he had gone there was no practical possibility of continuing the siege, whatever Edward and the southern magnates may have preferred, and on 17 September Edward and the rest of the army began the return journey to Newcastle,[140] which Edward reached on about 21 September.[141] Edward left on 28 September and was back at York on 5 October.[142] Here he was to remain until the end of January 1320.

THE BLAME GAME

No sooner had the siege been abandoned than the search for a scapegoat began. The story of Edmund Darel's treachery, though never clearly proved, was one small part of what followed. It was even rumoured that Hugh Despenser the Younger had betrayed the queen to the Scots and had then passed the blame on to Lancaster.[143] This report was probably written in hindsight with knowledge of much later events, but Despenser is likely to have been responsible for some of the enmity towards Lancaster. In a letter written to his sheriff in the county of Glamorgan on 21 September Despenser claimed that the Scottish invasion of England during the siege had been carried out at Lancaster's instigation and with his assistance, and that Lancaster's behaviour was responsible for the abandonment of the siege.[144] Despenser was very much an interested party, since the siege of Berwick and its aftermath mark an important

---

[136] *Bruce*, 658.

[137] *Lanercost*, 239; Maddicott, 249.

[138] Trinity College Cambridge Ms. R.5.41, ff. 113v–114; Phillips, 186.

[139] C 53/106, m.8 (the last time he witnessed a royal charter during the siege); Maddicott, 249.

[140] E 101/378/3, m.3; *Bruce*, 660, note; Phillips, 185; Maddicott, 249. It is possible, as Professor Duncan suggests (*Bruce*, 658–60, note to l. 858) that Lancaster left only after the king had decided to break off the siege; but it was really a chicken and egg situation; once it was clear that there was insufficient agreement for the siege to be continued, it did not really matter who made the first move.

[141] *Itinerary*, ed. Hallam.

[142] BL, Add. Ms. 17362, ff. 9, 9d, 14d; Phillips, 187; Maddicott, 251.

[143] Haskins, 'A chronicle', 177; Maddicott, 249–50.

[144] BL, Cotton Ms. Vespasian F.VII, f. 6 (printed in *Cartae et Alia Munimenta de Glamorgan*, iii ed. G.L. Clark (Cardiff, 1910), 1064); Phillips, 186; Maddicott, 249.

stage in his growing power at court. His ambitions and influence over royal patronage were soon to turn not just Lancaster but most of the other leading magnates against both him and the king.[145]

However, the most serious accusations came from the author of the *Vita Edwardi Secundi*, normally unsparing in his criticism of Edward II and his failings, who now turned his ire against Thomas of Lancaster. Having reported that Lancaster was blamed for the raising of the siege, for the plot to seize the queen, and for the Scots' ability to return home unscathed, he added that 'some evidence of treachery was openly spoken of, from which the reputation of the earl and his followers was seriously damaged. For it was commonly said that the earl received 40,000 pounds from Robert Bruce to help him and his men secretly, and that at the siege, while everyone was attacking the wall, none of the earl's retinue assaulted it, and that the town of Berwick would have surrendered if the earl's scheming had not hindered this, and that James Douglas on his way back to Scotland passed through the earl's lines, and that the earl went unarmed through the midst of the Scots.'[146] The author then proceeded to a jeremiad on the themes of treachery, the vices of the rich, and the prospering of the wicked:[147] 'Oh! Earl of Lancaster, whose riches are so great, why for such a sum of money have you lost your reputation and your name for constancy? . . . Oh! What paeans of praise you had while you were constantly upholding the Ordinances! The good will of the people is turned to hatred, and your fame is changed to infamy. Oh! Noble earl, why do you not recall to mind the "chosen generation", your royal family which you disgrace! Why do you not take thought, distinguished earl, how great a charge is the crime of broken faith! . . .'[148]

It was not the first time that rumours of treachery surrounded the earl of Lancaster, and it was not to be the last, but even the author of the *Vita* admitted that there was no evidence to prove his guilt. Lancaster is said to have protested his innocence to the king and to have offered to prove it by ordeal if necessary. In the end he was allowed to purge himself on oath.[149] An open breach between Edward II and Lancaster may have been averted in the autumn of 1319, but there was no possibility of a further settlement between the two men. Whether or not either man really understood it, the final chapter in their relations had been opened and would reach its violent conclusion in the spring of 1322.[150]

[145] Phillips, 186–7.
[146] *Vita*, 166–7; Phillips, 197; Maddicott, 249–50.
[147] Literally so, since he quotes extensively from the Book of Jeremiah (12: 1–2 and 3) and other Old Testament sources: *Vita*, 172–5, nn. 347–8. His outburst covers pp. 166–75 in the latest edition of the *Vita*.
[148] *Vita*, 168–9. There had been rumours, almost certainly malicious, in 1317 at the time of the attack on the cardinals.
[149] *Vita*, 174–5. There is no other evidence that such an event actually took place, but there was certainly an opportunity for Lancaster to communicate with Edward while the latter was still at York.
[150] Phillips, 186–7; Maddicott, 253.

A TRUCE WITH THE SCOTS

Once again Edward II had engaged in a major campaign against the Scots, and once again it had ended, if not in actual defeat on the battlefield, certainly in humiliation. Another campaign was out of the question: the best that could be done was to secure the defences of the north. Badlesmere and other household officers were left behind at Newcastle to see to the munitioning of the towns and castles on the Scottish March; 600 men-at-arms were to stay at York to protect the king, while local levies were raised in Yorkshire.[151] But this could do nothing to prevent the Scots under Sir James Douglas from carrying out 'the most savage raid yet seen on the west side of the Pennines': cruelly they waited until after the harvest and on about 1 November destroyed the corn and seized great numbers of men and animals in Gilsland and Westmorland.[152] Since there was no possibility of renewing the Scottish campaign and in order to save the north from further attacks, Edward had no choice but to make a truce with the Scots, even though some of the magnates were annoyed because they felt that it would add further to the king's humiliation.[153]

On 24 October twelve Scots envoys were given safe conducts to come to Newcastle to discuss either a truce or peace, and on 11 November Robert Baldock left London to go to Berwick with other royal envoys for the same purpose.[154] On 1 December full powers to negotiate a truce were given to the earl of Pembroke, the chancellor the bishop of Ely, Hugh Despenser the Younger, Badlesmere, Henry le Scrope, Robert Baldock, William Airmyn, William Herle and Geoffrey le Scrope. The Scottish and English versions variously date the making of the truce that was eventually agreed to 22 and 24 December.[155] The truce was to last for two years from 29 December 1319, during which time the Scots were to build no new castles in the sheriffdoms of Berwick, Roxburgh and Dumfries, while the English were to garrison Harbottle castle in Northumberland, and later either deliver it to the Scots or destroy it.[156] On 24 January 1320 the chancellor, Pembroke, Badlesmere and Despenser were appointed to perform

---

[151] BL, Add. Ms. 17362, ff. 9, 9d, 14d; Phillips, 187; Maddicott, 251–2.

[152] Barrow, 240, and map on 234–5; McNamee, 95.

[153] *Vita*, 174–7; Maddicott, 252. The author of the *Vita* was fully in sympathy with Edward's decision and added that the people of the March had suffered more from the oppressions of the men sent to guard them than they had from the Scots.

[154] BL, Add. Ms. 17362, f. 9v; *Foedera*, II, i, 404; Phillips, 187; Maddicott, 252.

[155] C 47/22/12/29, 30, 45; *CPR, 1317–21*, 414; *CDS*, iii, 681; Phillips, 187; Maddicott, 252. The envoys were a roll call of Edward II's leading councillors and legal advisers, which is enough to indicate the seriousness of the negotiations. If William Airmyn was taken prisoner at Myton, he had evidently been freed by this time.

[156] *CDS*, iii, 681; *CPR, 1317–21*, 416; Phillips, 187; Maddicott, 252. The full terms of the truce are given in *CDS*, v, no. 657 (from C 47/22/13(6)) and in *Regesta Regum Scottorum*, 433–7, no. 162.

the terms relating to Harbottle, which they had already put into the custody of one of Badlesmere's retainers John de Penrith on 28 December, and keepers of the truce were nominated on the same day.[157]

AN IMPORTANT MEETING AT YORK

On 20 January 1320 a new parliament assembled at York.[158] Its purpose was to confirm the details of the truce with Scotland and to discuss relations with France and the situation in the duchy of Aquitaine, which had been neglected during the Scottish campaign and needed urgent attention. All this business was for the moment however overshadowed by the latest twist in the relations between Edward and Lancaster, who was nearby at his castle of Pontefract[159] but refused to attend because he alleged that the parliament was being held in secret (*in cameris*).[160] This was nonsense; the real reason, as the *Vita* observed, was probably because 'he regarded the king and his supporters as suspect, and he declared, no longer privately but publicly, that they were his enemies'.[161] The tensions raised at Berwick were evidently still very powerful. Another explanation, offered in the unpublished chronicle attributed to Nicholas Trivet, is that Lancaster objected to the truce with the Scots.[162] Perhaps Lancaster was trying to counteract the rumours about his behaviour at Berwick by appearing more bellicose than the king and his fellow magnates. It is possible that Lancaster was induced to attend during the last few days before the parliament ended on 28 or 29 January,[163] but the damage was done. The system of conciliar government established at York at the end of 1318 was clearly at an end. Edward was now able to make his own appointments to important offices without reference to Lancaster. John de Hothum (probably in need of a rest after Myton) was replaced as chancellor by John Salmon the bishop of Norwich; Walter Stapeldon the bishop of Exeter became treasurer in place of John Sandal the bishop of Winchester, who had died in early November 1319; Robert Baldock archdeacon of Middlesex became keeper of the privy seal; and Badlesmere and Hugh Despenser the Younger were confirmed as steward

---

[157] E 101/378/4, f. 21v; *CPR, 1317–21*, 416; Phillips, 187–8; Maddicott, 252.

[158] It had been summoned on 6 Nov. 1319: *PW*, II, ii, 215–16.

[159] DL 42/12, f. 22v; E 368/93, m.12; *CPR, 1317–21*, 431; Phillips, 188.

[160] *Vita*, 176–7; Phillips, 188; Maddicott, 253. The numbers attending would have been smaller than usual, since representatives of the knights, burgesses and lower clergy were not summoned, but still substantial. Altogether the 2 archbishops, 16 bishops, 32 abbots and priors, 9 earls, 73 barons, and 25 royal judges and clerks were summoned. It is not known where they met but it was probably at St Mary's abbey in York. See *PROME*, Parliament of Jan. 1320.

[161] *Vita*, 176–7; Maddicott, 254.

[162] BL, Cotton Ms. Nero D.X, f. 110v (this has valuable material on the events of 1320–3); Maddicott, 253.

[163] Maddicott, 254.

and chamberlain respectively.[164] It was also decided that the exchequer and the lawcourts should return from York to London.[165]

PREPARATIONS FOR FRANCE

Since the end of 1316 Philip V of France had been putting increasing pressure on Edward II to come to France to perform his homage for Aquitaine,[166] both in letters directed to Edward in England and also through communications with his officials in the duchy. In November 1317, for example, two French clerks bearing letters summoning the king-duke to do his homage had been forced to tour the duchy in search of the seneschal, Gilbert Pecche, who was preoccupied by the private war between two Gascon nobles, Jourdain de l'Isle and Alexandre de Caumont. They eventually tracked him down to La Réole near Bordeaux on 20 November and there they formally read out the letters before the seneschal and Edward II's council in Gascony.[167]

Edward II had consistently put off the date of his homage on the grounds either that the political situation in England was too delicate or that the war with Scotland had to take priority, but it could not be delayed any longer.[168] Apart from the act of homage itself, the usual host of problems in Anglo-French relations, which could best be dealt with by a meeting between the two kings, had been steadily accumulating since Edward's last visit to France in 1313,[169] while conditions within the duchy of Aquitaine had also been deteriorating.[170] Edward had formally recognized that he owed homage on 24 May 1319,[171] but nothing further took place because of the imminent Scottish campaign. A visit to France by Edward II was however being considered by the king and his council at York in late November 1319. A royal clerk, Master Richard de Burton, and a knight, Sir John Abel, were sent to visit the king of France, while another clerk, Master John de Hildesle, was sent to Aquitaine. On 30 November Master William de Maldon was sent to London to obtain transcripts of key diplomatic documents in advance of Edward's journey.[172] During the parliament Edward told the assembled magnates that he planned to meet Philip V of

---

[164] *Flores*, 191; Maddicott, 254.

[165] *CCR, 1318–23*, 175; Phillips, 188.

[166] SC 1/35/128, 128A (Nov. 1316); *Foedera*, II, i, 311–12 (Jan. 1317), 360 (April 1318), 390 (March 1319); P. Chaplais, 'Le Duché-pairie de Guyenne', item IV, 149–53.

[167] AN, J 633, nos 36, 37. Cf. Vale, 134.

[168] *Foedera*, II, i, 311–12 (Jan. 1317), 365 (June 1318), 371 (Aug. 1318), 390 (March 1319), 395 (May 1319). There was also of course an element of deliberate delay, since no king of England liked doing homage to the king of France.

[169] See, for example, *Foedera*, II, i, *passim*.

[170] The problems faced by Antonio Pessagno are an indication of the situation: Vale, 134–6.

[171] *Foedera*, II, i, 395. The matter was clearly discussed during the York parliament.

[172] BL, Add. Ms. 17362, ff. 10v, 13.

France at Amiens on 9 March 1320, in order to perform his homage for the duchy of Aquitaine and the counties of Ponthieu and Montreuil. For this reason the parliament was cut short, with the assent of the magnates, but with the intention of holding another one on 1 June to continue its business.[173] During the king's absence the earl of Pembroke was to act as keeper of the realm.[174] In March the king's half-brother, Edmund of Woodstock, Hugh Despenser the Elder, Bartholomew de Badlesmere and the bishop of Hereford left for France.[175] They first went to Paris where they helped to complete the arrangements for Edward's visit, and then to Avignon;[176] Despenser and Badlesmere were then to go on to Gascony to look into allegations of misconduct by royal officials and to try to restore order.[177]

After the end of the parliament at York Edward and Isabella left for Westminster. As they passed Pontefract they were greeted with cries of abuse from Lancaster's retainers.[178] Nothing could have shown better the depth of distrust which again existed between the king and his first cousin. On 16 February the king and queen reached London, where they were met at Kilburn by the mayor Hamo de Chigwell, the sheriffs and aldermen.[179] Almost two weeks later, on 28 February, they rode through the city of London at the beginning of their journey and then spent two weeks waiting at Canterbury for letters of safe conduct from France. Although the letters were issued on 25 March, they did not arrive in time

---

[173] There is no Parliament Roll for the Jan. 1320 assembly; no parliament was held on 1 June because Edward was then preparing to go to France. These details are provided in the speech which was delivered at the opening of the next parliament. See *PROME*, Parliament of Oct. 1320, C 49/43/20. Edward II wrote to Philip V giving details of his plans on 19 Feb.: *Foedera*, II, ii, 417.

[174] He was appointed by the council on 24 Feb.: *CPR, 1317–21*, 425; Phillips, 189.

[175] They left on 19 March: BL, Add. Ms. 17362, f. 11; Phillips, 188; Maddicott, 255.

[176] Haines, *The Church and Politics*, 23–4.

[177] *Foedera*, II, i, 418. On 28 Feb. Edward wrote to the consuls of the town of Castillon near Bordeaux (and probably to other communities as well) asking them to assist his envoys in their work of reform: SC 1/32/84. The appointment on the same date of the greatly experienced Maurice de Berkeley as seneschal of Gascony was another indication that the government wanted to get a grip on the situation there: *Foedera*, II, i, 418. The dispatch to Bordeaux of a royal clerk John de Hildesle in Nov. 1319 was part of the preparation for their visit. He was sent to collect and bring back to England the registers of documents relating to Gascony which had been put together hurriedly and often inaccurately between Nov. 1318 and March 1319 from original documents stored in the wardrobe treasury in the Tower of London. The registers had been taken to Gascony by William de Montacute when he took up office as seneschal. They were never fully revised, if at all, and never returned to Gascony, depriving its governors of valuable information. Their contents were inventoried in the Gascon calendar compiled in 1322: *Gascon Register A* xiv–xvi; *Gascon Calendar*, ed. Cuttino, vii–ix. Despenser and Badlesmere had access to a collection of memoranda and other documents concerning Gascony which were taken by Master Henry of Canterbury: BL, Add. Ms. 17362, f. 12.

[178] Trinity College Cambridge Ms. R.5.41, ff. 113v–114; Phillips, 189.

[179] *Ann. Paul.*, 288; Phillips, 189. No doubt showing gratitude for royal support in the recent revolution in London politics.

and Edward and Isabella were forced to return to Westminster, which they reached on 7 April.[180]

EDWARD IN FRANCE

On 19 June Edward and Isabella crossed to France in the company of Hugh Despenser the Younger, Roger Damory, the bishops of Norwich and Exeter, the countess of Pembroke, and the earl of Pembroke's nephew John de Hastings,[181] the earl of Pembroke himself having been reappointed as keeper of the realm.[182] The royal party reached Amiens on 28 June and two days later Edward performed homage for Aquitaine and Ponthieu in the cathedral.[183] A few days later Philip V issued pardons to those of Edward's subjects who were considered to have committed offences against the French crown.[184]

Edward left Amiens on 9 July, first making his way to Abbeville, the administrative centre of the county of Ponthieu. As far back as February 1317 Isabella had been complaining about the neglect of the government of the county by her seneschal, Jean de Fiennes.[185] The exact issues are not clear but were connected with the opposition within France to Philip V's accession as king in 1316, in which prominent people from Ponthieu including Jean de Fiennes and his brother were involved.[186] This was the probable explanation of Jean de Fiennes's astonishing proposal in January 1317 that Edward II should lay claim to a share of the kingdom of France in right of his wife. The suggestion was discussed at the time by Edward II's council, which was well aware that Fiennes was trying to play politics for his own advantage and did not take any further action.[187] During their meetings at Amiens in

[180] E 101/378/3, mm.7, 8; E 159/93, m.84; *Foedera*, II, ii, 421; *Ann. Paul.*, 288; Phillips, 189. The letters of safe conduct were renewed by Philip V on 11 June: *Foedera*, II, ii, 426.

[181] BL, Add. Ms. 17362, ff. 11, 17v; *CCR, 1318–23*, 238; *Ann. Paul.*, 289; Phillips, 192. Others, notably Edmund of Woodstock, Hugh Despenser the Elder, Bartholomew de Badlesmere and the bishop of Hereford, joined the king at Amiens on 28 June having completed their mission to Avignon: BL, Add. Ms. 17362, f. 11. It is not clear from the chronology of their movements whether Despenser and Badlesmere had also been to Gascony as intended.

[182] Pembroke had been reappointed on 4 June: E 159/93, m.92; *CPR, 1317–21*, 454; Phillips, 191. Edward left Westminster on 5 June. Writs were issued under the testimony of the king until 19 June, the day he left England.

[183] *Chartulary of Winchester Cathedral*, ed. Goodman, 63.

[184] *Registres du Trésor de Chartes*, ii, 509, 731. The details of these alleged offences are not recorded. The records of Anglo-French treaties and of the processes concerning Aquitaine, held at Montreuil in 1306 and Périgueux in 1311, were brought over to France by Master Elias de Jonestone, the keeper of the processes, and were available to aid the discussions: BL, Add. Ms. 17362, f. 13.

[185] *CCW*, 482–3.

[186] Vale, 70–1, 286 (map of Ponthieu).

[187] SC 8/325/E 372; *CCW*, 460–1; P. Chaplais, 'Un message de Jean de Fiennes à Édouard II' repr. in Chaplais, *Essays in Medieval Diplomacy*, item X.

1320 Edward and Philip must have discussed the situation in Ponthieu and Edward was given a free hand to restore order. Several citizens of Abbeville were arrested for disloyalty and taken back to England.[188]

From Abbeville Edward moved to Boulogne, the scene of his marriage to Isabella in 1308, and here he attended the consecration of Bartholomew de Badlesmere's nephew, Henry de Burghersh, as bishop of Lincoln.[189] Edward returned to England on 22 July and reached London on 2 August, where he was given a splendid welcome by the mayor and members of the guilds.[190]

PARLIAMENT

Shortly after Edward's return to Westminster a new parliament was summoned to make up for the brevity of the assembly held at York in January and the impossibility of holding a meeting on 1 July as previously promised. All was intended to be sweetness and light. In the speech delivered at the opening of parliament it was stated on Edward's behalf that, 'in his great desire and wish to do all the things which concern a good lord for the benefit of his realm and of his people', the king had arranged to hold his parliament at Westminster on the octave of Michaelmas (6 October 1320), 'for the greatest convenience of his people and at the most suitable time for his people after the season of August'.[191]

It proved to be a businesslike meeting. On the opening day the king, with the assistance of the archbishop of Canterbury, the bishop of Norwich the chancellor, the bishop of Exeter the treasurer, the bishops of London, Ely, and Coventry & Lichfield, the earls of Pembroke, Edmund of Woodstock the king's half-brother, and several other unnamed magnates, made arrangements for the receipt and answering of petitions from England and Wales, and from Gascony, Ireland and the Channel Islands. One hundred and forty-one petitions with answers are recorded on the Parliament Roll.[192] Several of the items of business (such as the dispute between the abbot and convent of Abingdon, the process between the monks of St Martin's, Dover, and the prior of Christ Church, Canterbury, and the dispute between the abbot of Ramsey and the bishop

---

[188] *Ann. Paul.*, 289. The citizens had written to Philip V claiming that they would prefer to be his subjects than under English rule. Edward II wrote to Philip on the matter on 8 May 1320: *Foedera*, II, ii, 425.

[189] *Ann. Paul.*, 289. The bishops of Norwich, Exeter and Hereford were also present.

[190] E 101/378/10, m.1; *CCR, 1318–23*, 317; *Ann. Paul.*, 290; Phillips, 193; Williams, *Medieval London*, 285.

[191] *PW*, II, ii, 219–30; C 49/43/20: *PROME*, Parliament of Oct. 1320. It is not known by whom the speech was delivered, but it was probably the chancellor.

[192] SC 9/23, *PROME*, Parliament of Oct. 1320. This Parliament Roll was unknown to the editors of *Rotuli Parliamentorum* (who worked from a differently arranged record in the *Vetus Codex*, C 153/1, ff. 78r–93v) and was edited for the first time for *PROME*. See the Introduction to the Parliament of Oct. 1320.

of Ely) involved a lengthy search of the records and take up much space on the roll;[193] there were two petitions concerning the city of London; and several from Ireland. There was also a complaint from the entire community of the realm concerning trespasses and felonies perpetrated in the realm.[194] This petition was presented by the knights, citizens and burgesses present on behalf of the counties, cities and boroughs of the realm. The Statute of Westminster the Fourth, which consists of only two chapters concerning the acquittance of sheriffs and juries of twenty-four, may have been the result of commune or private petitions presented during the parliament.[195]

EDWARD

The parliament was to be the last occasion during the reign of Edward II when the business of receiving and answering petitions was dealt with on such a scale. It was also noteworthy for the extent of Edward II's involvement. In a well-known letter to the pope, Thomas Cobham the bishop of Worcester remarked that the king was rising unusually early and was contributing to the discussions of parliamentary business.[196] The unpublished chronicle attributed to Nicholas Trivet adds that Edward 'showed prudence in answering the petitions of the poor, and clemency as much as severity in judicial matters, to the amazement of many who were there'.[197]

This was not the only occasion in 1320 when Edward conspicuously exerted himself. He may have addressed the York parliament in January on the subject of his homage for Aquitaine;[198] and he most certainly acted with great vigour during his visit to Amiens to perform homage in June–July 1320. Having done so on 30 June, all was at first amicable. On 1 July the two kings dined together and on the 3rd Edward held a *festum generale* with Philip V and other magnates.[199] However, on either 3 or 4 July, when the two kings met to renew the alliance of perpetual friendship concluded between Edward I and Philip IV in 1303, things started to go wrong. A French councillor suggested that in addition to performing

---

[193] SC 9/23, items 4, 5, 14.

[194] SC 9/23, items 6, 7, 9–13, 8.

[195] *SR*, i, 180–1. There is however no trace of such petitions among the records of the parliament.

[196] *Register of Thomas de Cobham, Bishop of Worcester, 1317–27*, ed. E.H. Pearce (Worcester, 1930), 97–8; Maddicott, 257. Cobham was probably right in suggesting that Edward was more active than was his wont, but he also had an axe to grind since in 1313 he had been passed over for appointment as archbishop of Canterbury in favour of the king's close friend and ally Walter Reynolds.

[197] BL, Cotton Ms. Nero D. X, f. 110v.

[198] The speech which opened the parliament of Oct. 1320 implies, though it does not say so directly, that Edward had addressed the earlier assembly: C 49/43/20: *PROME*, Parliament of Oct. 1320.

[199] E 101/378/3.

homage Edward should also swear fealty to Philip. This extra bond of personal allegiance would have indicated that Edward was inferior in status to Philip, and was firmly rejected by Edward in a recorded speech which clearly represents his own views. Without first consulting his advisers, Edward addressed Philip V and his councillors:

> We well remember that the homage which we performed at Boulogne [in 1308] was done according to the form of the peace treaties made between our ancestors, after the manner in which they did it. Your father [Philip IV] agreed to it, for we have his letters confirming this, and we have performed it already in the same fashion; no one can reasonably ask us to do otherwise; and we certainly do not intend to do so. As to the fealty we are certain that we should not swear it; nor was it ever asked of us at that time.[200]

The eyewitness account added that Edward II was visibly angered by the unexpected demand made of him and that the French council reacted with stunned silence. The silence was broken by the councillor who had made the suggestion, now proposing that the two kings should simply swear to maintain the perpetual alliance and agree not to harbour enemies or those banished from either kingdom. Edward agreed to this 'with an amiable countenance'. The necessary promises were then made by Hugh Despenser the Elder on behalf of Edward II and the French king's marshal on behalf of Philip.[201] The incident was an indication that Edward II could be roused to determined action when his majesty as king was under threat; but it was also a warning that Anglo-French relations might be about to enter a more stormy phase.

There was another matter which Edward II considered diminished his royal majesty: the Ordinances. Ever since the Ordinances had been first issued in 1311, he had been trying to evade them or to have them annulled by the pope. They had last been confirmed at the York parliament in the autumn of 1318 as part of the political settlement with the earl of Lancaster. Now that in 1320 the settlement had become a dead letter, Edward may have believed that his promise to uphold the Ordinances was redundant. Ostensibly the purpose of the visit to Avignon by the bishop of Hereford, Edmund of Woodstock, the Elder Despenser and Badlesmere

---

[200] Vale, 51 (the translation is Dr Vale's). The text is taken from C 47/29/9, no. 25, a copy of the original made in 1325. The document was first published in E. Pole-Stuart, 'Interview between Philip V and Edward II at Amiens in 1320', *EHR*, xli (1926), 414–15; and more recently in Chaplais, *Diplomatic Practice*, i, 359–60 (no. 199). See also the record of the five acts of homage performed by English kings between 1259 and 1320 in *Chartulary of Winchester Cathedral*, ed. Goodman, 62–5 (no. 127). Philip V had also come primed with a record of past homages. On 16 June he had a copy made of the homage done by Henry III of England to Louis IX in Dec. 1259: Chaplais, 'Le Duché-pairie de Guyenne', 153.

[201] Vale, 51–2; Chaplais, *Diplomatic Practice*, 360.

in the spring of 1320 was to obtain papal approval for Henry de Burghersh's appointment as bishop of Lincoln, as well as countering the activities of the Scots.[202] But according to the chronicle attributed to Nicholas Trivet the embassy was also intended to seek absolution for Edward from his oath to uphold the Ordinances.[203] It is likely that the royal supporters who had suffered loss when the Ordinances were last enforced in the autumn of 1318 would have been glad to see Edward succeed. An undated papal letter which seems to relate to this mission informed Edward that his petitions had been granted, as his envoys would tell him *viva voce*.[204] Although the chronicler Adam Murimuth, who was very well informed on political matters, remarked of this mission that, despite the alleged expenditure of £15,000, nothing was achieved apart from Burghersh's promotion, it seems likely that Edward did gain absolution from his oath.[205]

SIGNS AND PORTENTS

In the autumn of 1320 there were indications both of a degree of stability and of growing disturbance. On the positive side the king could be reasonably pleased with the outcome of his visit to France. A number of his closest advisers and supporters could also be satisfied with the royal patronage which had come their way. The steward Bartholomew de Badlesmere had seen his nephew consecrated as bishop of the largest diocese in England, while Badlesmere himself was appointed to the key office of constable of Dover; Hugh Despenser the Younger was at the same time made constable of Bristol;[206] the earl of Pembroke's influence had been recognized in his appointment as keeper of the realm during the king's absence in France and by his confirmation in October as keeper of

---

[202] Haines, *The Church and Politics*, 23–5. The bull providing Burghersh to Lincoln was issued on 27 May: SC 7/56/11. His uncle, Bartholomew de Badlesmere had earlier seized the opportunity of the vacancy in the choice see of Winchester to advance the claims of his nephew. Badlesmere's letter to Edward II on 7 Nov. 1319, only five days after Sandal's death, still survives: SC 1/33/10. The pope however got in first and on 26 Nov. provided a papal tax collector, Rigaud d'Assier, as bishop. Edward II was greatly annoyed but Burghersh's appointment to the see of Lincoln, in place of Anthony Bek who had been elected in early Feb., was still a considerable coup.

[203] BL, Cotton Mss, Nero. D.X, f. 110v; Maddicott, 255–6; Haines, *The Church and Politics*, 24. On 28 Feb. Edward II wrote to five cardinals indicating that the business of the mission was of special concern to him (*nos specialiter tangencia*): SC 1/32/78–82.

[204] *CPL, 1305–42*, 445; Haines, *The Church and Politics*, 24.

[205] *Murimuth*, 31; Haines, *The Church and Politics*, 24. One of the purposes of the mission to Avignon in 1322–3 by Rigaud d'Assier the bishop of Winchester and John Stratford was to secure papal absolution of the prelates and magnates from their oaths to uphold the Ordinances. No mention was made of his own oath, which strongly suggests that it had indeed been set aside in 1320: *Foedera*, II, i, 542–3; Haines, *Stratford*, 143; G.O. Sayles, 'The formal judgements on the traitors of 1322', *Speculum*, xvi (1941), 62–3.

[206] *CFR, 1319–27*, 37–8; *CPR, 1317–21*, 514; Phillips, 198.

the forest south of the Trent;[207] and in September Roger Damory had been respited payment of his debts to the crown.[208]

But there were signs of strain both among the baronage themselves and between supporters of the crown. Some of these signs were relatively minor in themselves; others were more serious, but collectively they added up to the makings of a new and graver political crisis than anything that had yet been seen.

The earl of Pembroke's nephew, John Hastings the lord of Abergavenny in the Welsh March, was at odds with the earl of Arundel Edmund Fitz Alan, the lord of Clun and Oswestry, also in the March, over possession of some tenements in Surrey. It was a trivial enough cause of dispute but both Hastings and Arundel had threatened to bring armed retainers to a hearing of the case in April 1320, while the king also took a personal interest in the case. The outcome is unknown but ill feeling is likely to have persisted.[209]

Pembroke was also at odds with Maurice de Berkeley, one of his long-standing retainers, whose followers had attacked Pembroke's manor of Painswick in Gloucestershire in July 1318 and then resisted all attempts to bring them to justice. Pembroke was eventually reduced in 1320 to obtaining compensation by a series of agreements with individuals.[210] It was a significant set of events, since it suggests that the influence of Pembroke was perceived to be waning, and also since Maurice de Berkeley switched his allegiance to what he hoped was a rising political star, Roger Mortimer of Wigmore. Maurice took with him his own retainers: his sons Thomas and Maurice, Thomas de Gurney and John de Maltravers. By a supreme irony three of these men were to be associated in the custody and death of Edward II at Berkeley castle in 1327.[211]

To make matters worse, Pembroke's ability to influence events was affected by the financial problems arising from his imprisonment and holding to ransom by Jean de Lamouilly in 1317. In 1319 and 1320 he was borrowing heavily from the Bardi and other Florentine merchants, as well as from the king. It is probable that he was still in debt when he died in 1324.[212]

---

[207] *CFR, 1319–27*, 23; *PW*, II, ii, 247; Phillips, 191, 198.

[208] E 159/94, m.7; Phillips, 199.

[209] *CCR, 1318–23*, 227; Phillips, 190. In a letter to Pembroke the king even offered to attend the next hearing in person: SC 1/49/48.

[210] For an account of this episode see Phillips, 193–4, 261–7. The basic reason seems to have been Berkeley's displeasure that Pembroke did not support him in a claim to a share in the lands of the earldom of Gloucester through his wife, Isabel de Clare, the half-sister of Gilbert de Clare who had died at Bannockburn.

[211] Maurice's son Thomas married Mortimer's daughter Margaret in May 1319; Maurice and his retainers were already in Mortimer's own retinue in 1318 and joined him in the civil war of 1321–2: Phillips, 266–7.

[212] For the details of his borrowings see Phillips, 194–7. Edward II gave Pembroke £2,500 in 1317; advanced 2,000 marks in payment of his future wages for military service in July 1319; and loaned him £2,000 in Oct. 1319.

His personal life was further affected by the death in September 1320 of his wife, Beatrice de Clermont-Nesle, the daughter of the constable of France, to whom he had been married since 1295. He then became involved in complicated legal proceedings with Beatrice's family in France. Since he had no legitimate male heir, he quickly began the search for a new wife. Soon after 20 November he left England for France, ostensibly to arrange for his remarriage, but probably also because he could not accept the growing power of the Despensers. Apart from a brief visit to England in March to May 1321, he played little direct part in the developing crisis until his return in August, when his role was to be crucial in securing the king's agreement to exile the Despensers.[213] An experienced and trusted royal councillor and a force for moderation had been removed from the scene at a critical time.

Meanwhile the earl of Lancaster's hostility to the king and his followers continued unabated. Lancaster failed to attend parliament in October, although he did send Nicholas de Segrave and others to represent him at Westminster.[214] Those attending parliament were aware of the dangers if Lancaster was not placated in some way and persuaded to resume co-operation with the king. This may explain the order on 14 November for the careful observance of the Ordinances.[215] It was also decided to send the bishops of London and Winchester to visit Lancaster. By 16 November these two had reached St Albans where they were joined by the bishops of Ely and Rochester. Although delayed at Northampton by the bishop of London's illness, the mission continued, the bishop of London returning to Westminster on 6 February 1321.[216] This mission may have represented another attempt at mediation by the prelates, as in 1318, but it is clear that it achieved nothing, and by the time the bishop of London returned events were moving too swiftly for such an intervention to have much hope of success. Against these conciliatory moves in Lancaster's direction it is possible to set the order of 5 November requiring Lancaster to answer for the relief for the lands he had inherited from the earl of Lincoln in 1311. This could only be regarded as provocative, especially since on 20 December Hugh Despenser the Younger was respited payment of the relief for his share of the lands of the earldom of Gloucester.[217]

---

[213] Phillips, 5–6, 190–1, 200–1. Beatrice was buried in the church of the Benedictine priory at Stratford-le-Bow in London.

[214] *Ann. Paul.*, 290; Phillips, 198; Maddicott, 257. On 5 Oct. he was still at Pontefract: E 159/95, m.125.

[215] E 159/94, m.22; Phillips, 198. The pope's apparent annulment earlier in 1320 of Edward II's oath to uphold the Ordinances did not annul the Ordinances themselves: BL, Cotton Ms. Nero.D.X, f. 110v.

[216] *Ann. Paul.*, 290; *Trokelowe*, 106; Phillips, 198. The nominal purpose of the mission was to deliver a papal bull to Lancaster.

[217] E 368/91, m.127; E 159/94, m.27; Phillips, 198–9.

PART TWO

THE RISE AND RISE OF A NEW FAVOURITE

The Younger Despenser was not a new figure on the political scene. The prominence of his father, Hugh Despenser the Elder, among the councillors of both Edward I and Edward II[218] had brought him marriage in 1306 to Eleanor de Clare, one of the sisters of the earl of Gloucester,[219] the right to a share in the lands of the earldom after the earl's death at Bannockburn, and a summons to parliament among the magnates in 1314.[220] Ironically, it seems that initially at least Edward II may have disliked and even hated Despenser.[221] There is however considerable evidence that his wife was a particular favourite of Edward II, and this may have been of great advantage to him in first gaining and then maintaining his influence over the king.[222] In May 1315, at the time when he was trying to hasten delivery of Eleanor's portion of the inheritance, Despenser seized

---

[218] See M. Lawrence, 'Rise of a royal favourite', in *The Reign of Edward II*, ed. G. Dodd & A. Musson (Woodbridge, Suffolk & Rochester, NY, 2006), 205–19; the article by J.S. Hamilton in the *Oxford DNB*; and Fryde, ch. 3, 'The rise of the Despensers'.

[219] The marriage was an acknowledgement of the value of the Elder Despenser's past service and of the Younger Despenser's suitability as a husband for Edward I's granddaughter, Eleanor de Clare, rather than an indication of the Younger Despenser's personal importance at the time. In June 1306 Edward I had paid £2,000 for the right to arrange the marriage: T.B. Pugh, 'The marcher lords of Glamorgan and Morgannwg, 1317–1485', in *Glamorgan County History*, iii, *The Middle Ages*, ed. T.B. Pugh (Cardiff, 1971), 168.

[220] On his career see the article by J.S. Hamilton in the *Oxford DNB*; Fryde, ch. 3. Natalie Fryde is incorrect in stating (p. 36) that in the summons to a council at Northampton in July 1318 the two Despensers led the list of magnates below the rank of earl for the first time. In the list of magnates summoned to the York parliament of Sept. 1314 the Younger Despenser received a personal summons for the first time, appearing with his father immediately after Henry de Percy at the beginning of the list of barons summoned: *RDP*, iii, 241. They appeared at the head of the list of barons summoned to the Westminster parliament of Jan. 1315 (Percy had died in the meantime); again for the Lincoln parliament of Jan. 1316, for the proposed Lincoln parliament of Jan. 1318 (not held), and the York parliament of Oct. 1318: *RDP*, iii, 244, 253, 274, 288.

[221] '*Rex antea nedum minime dilexit immo odivit*': *Le Baker*, 6. This refers to the period before Despenser's appointment as chamberlain, which is incorrectly given by this chronicler as occurring in 1313 and not in 1318. Le Baker was admittedly writing after 1341, many years after the event, and may have been wrong in his chronology while correct in his general view of Edward and Despenser.

[222] Natalie Fryde cites several instances between 1309 and 1312 of Eleanor obtaining financial and other favours from the king: Fryde, 31; 241, n. 16. Michael Prestwich has found several other examples, including in 1319–20 when medicines costing £5 12s 4d were bought 'for the king and Eleanor le Despenser his niece, when ill', and later gifts of caged goldfinches, of sugar to make sweets for her, and a sum of 100 marks: Prestwich, *Plantagenet England*, 214. During the period of Despenser's ascendancy after 1322 Eleanor appears to have been particularly close to her uncle Edward II. The Leicester chronicler, Henry Knighton, reported that while Isabella was absent in France during 1325–6, Eleanor was treated as if she were queen and spoke slanderously of Isabella, while a Hainault chronicler, who recorded events in England in the 1320s in great detail, even claimed that she was

Tonbridge castle from its custodian, the archbishop of Canterbury, and for a month refused to surrender it.[223] Despenser's violent assault on John de Roos in Lincoln cathedral during the parliament of January 1316 may have been another early indication of his future conduct.[224] Although Lancaster regarded Despenser's father as one of his chief opponents and spent a great deal of time and energy in trying to have him removed from the king's council, he does not at first appear to have regarded the Younger Despenser with the same degree of hostility, reserving his venom for other royal favourites, Audley, Damory and Montacute. But the Younger Despenser's power was increasing. One significant moment was the delivery in November 1317 of his wife's portion of the Gloucester lands; another was his appointment as chamberlain of the king's household in 1318, the same office that had been held by Piers Gaveston, giving him ready access to the king. Lancaster had however already concluded that Despenser was a possible threat to him by April 1318, when he suggested during the negotiations at Leicester that the two Despensers should agree to become his retainers for life.[225] This was clearly designed to bring them under his personal control rather than simply augment his military resources.[226] Despenser's role in fostering enmity between Edward II and the earl of Lancaster during the siege of Berwick in September 1319 suggested that Lancaster's judgement was right and was another indication of Despenser's growing power and influence.

The base of Despenser's territorial power lay in the Welsh March. In the partition of 1317 he had acquired the lordship of Glamorgan, valued at almost £1,300 a year and the most important of all the Clare lands. It included several castles, at Cardiff the centre of the lordship, Llantrisant, and the great fortress of Caerphilly, one of the most powerful castles in Britain.[227] In 1326 Llantrisant and Caerphilly were both to play a leading part in the final days of Edward II's reign. The lordship of Gwynllwg, which had previously been dependent on Glamorgan, formed part of Hugh Audley's share of the inheritance and was in future to be organized as a separate lordship. Roger Damory's interests in Wales consisted only of part of the manor of Llangwm in the lordship of Usk, which was held in dower by the widowed countess of Gloucester.[228] Despenser had shown

---

Edward II's mistress and that, after her husband was executed in 1326 she was kept under surveillance in case she might be pregnant by the king: *Knighton*, i, 434; *Willelmi Capellani*, ed. Pijnacker Hordijk, 177. Despenser's influence over Edward II may therefore have had a sexual element to it but not of the kind often assumed in the case of other favourites such as Gaveston.

[223] *CIPM*, v, 351–2; Altschul, *Baronial Family*, 166.
[224] See ch. 6 of this book and *PROME*, Parliament of Jan. 1316, SC 9/20, item 5.
[225] *Gesta Edwardi*, 54–5; Phillips, 155–6; Maddicott, 216.
[226] Lancaster was no doubt aware of the contracts for military service that the Younger Despenser and others had been making with the king.
[227] See D. Renn, *Caerphilly Castle* (Cardiff, 1997).
[228] Altschul, *Baronial Family*, 170; Pugh, *Marcher Lords*, 167–9.

his intentions when he took the homage and fealty of Audley's tenants in Gwynllwg before Audley had a chance to take possession. Although he was ordered to give up control in March 1318 he never did so, and in December 1318 Audley and his wife made a disadvantageous bargain with Despenser by which they surrendered the lordship of Gwynllwg (valued at £458) for six manors in England which were worth considerably less.[229] In November 1318 Edward II had already granted Despenser and his wife all the regalities, liberties and free customs which the de Clares had held in the lordship of Glamorgan. The exchange with Audley meant that after December 1318 Despenser enjoyed as full an authority in the lordship as any of his wife's ancestors.[230] Despenser had also begun to extend his power to the west of Glamorgan in November 1317 when he was granted the castle and town of Dryslwyn and the Cantref Mawr for life.[231] This brought him into contact and into conflict with the tenants of John Giffard of Brimpsfield in Gloucestershire, who held the adjoining Cantref Bychan.[232] In March 1319 one of Despenser's men, John Iweyn, was appointed as sheriff of the neighbouring royal county of Carmarthen, displacing one of Pembroke's men.[233] Despenser was also believed to have his eyes on the castles of Blaenllyfni and Dinas in the lordship of Brecon, which had been granted to Roger Mortimer of Chirk in 1316.[234]

The climax of the Younger Despenser's rise to power in the March appears to have come in the summer and autumn of 1320 as a result of two events, the death of Maud de Clare the dowager countess of Gloucester on 2 July and his acquisition of the lordship of Gower in November. Although the distribution of Maud's share of the de Clare lands did not bring Despenser any more lands in the Welsh March, it did give him a substantial part of the honour of Gloucester including the manor and town of Tewkesbury in Gloucestershire and the castle and manor of Hanley in Worcestershire, as well as lands elsewhere in England. It also brought to Roger Damory the now unified lordship of Usk, making him an uncomfortably near neighbour to Despenser's lordship of Gwynllwg.[235] While the

---

[229] *CCR, 1313–18*, 531–2; Pugh, 'marcher lords', 169.

[230] Pugh, 'marcher lords', 169–70. The exchange was finally confirmed in May 1320: *CPR, 1317–21*, 60, 103, 415, 456.

[231] Pugh, 'marcher lords', 168. For a map of the lordships and other territorial divisions of South Wales see Pugh, 705; Davies, *Conquest*, 393.

[232] SC 1/37/6 (printed in *Calendar . . . concerning Wales*, 184); Pugh, 'marcher lords', 170.

[233] *CFR, 1307–19*, 394; Phillips, 199. In Sept. 1320 Iweyn was also appointed as Despenser's constable of Newport, the administrative centre of Gwynllwg: E 163/21/7/1; E 163/4/9. On the use made by both Despensers of clients such as Iweyn and John Inge to advance their ambitions see S. L. Waugh, 'For king, country and patron', *Journal of British Studies*, xxii (1983), esp. 27–32.

[234] *Vita*, 184–5, and n. 376.

[235] Altschul, *Baronial Family*, 170–1. Tewkesbury was a particularly significant acquisition since the abbey held the tombs of the earls of Gloucester: R. Morris, 'Tewkesbury abbey', *Trans. Bristol and Gloucestershire Archaeological Soc.*, xciii (Gloucester, 1974), 142–55;

partition of the earldom meant in theory that Despenser could never become earl of Gloucester, his intention seems to have been to obtain as much control as possible over the marcher lordships of South Wales and turn them into a virtual earldom[236] independent of all but the ultimate authority of the king himself.

There was one important piece missing between Despenser's lordships in Gwynllwg and Glamorgan and his interests in West Wales: the lordship of Gower, with its administrative centre at Swansea. In 1320 this was held by William de Braose, who had no male heir and had settled the succession upon John de Mowbray, the husband of his elder daughter Alicia. De Braose however kept changing his mind and in effect offered Gower to the highest bidder. Among those who became involved were Humphrey de Bohun, the earl of Hereford and lord of Brecon, and hitherto a reliable supporter of the crown; and Roger Mortimer of Wigmore, nephew of Roger Mortimer of Chirk the justice of Wales, a former royal lieutenant in Ireland and an ambitious man in his own right. By the autumn of 1319 Despenser was also negotiating for the purchase of Gower and seemed likely to be the winner; in order to prevent this in 1320 John de Mowbray took possession of the lordship. Since De Braose had allegedly alienated the lordship to Mowbray without royal licence, on 26 October 1320, at the very end of the Westminster parliament, Edward II ordered Gower to be taken into royal hands.[237] This was regarded by the marcher lords as a direct challenge to the law and customs of the March and they saw the appointment of Despenser as keeper of the lordship on or about 20 November as the prelude to its being granted to him by the king. The attempts by royal officers to enter Gower were resisted and it was not until mid-December that the lordship was under royal control.[238]

THE ROAD TO WAR

By December 1320 the ambitions of Hugh Despenser the Younger in the Welsh March had won him a great deal of valuable territory but with it the enmity of some of the most powerful of the marcher lords, the earl of

---

M. Lawrence, 'Secular patronage and religious devotion', in *Fourteenth Century England*, v, ed. N. Saul (Woodbridge, Suffolk & Rochester, NY, 2008), 78–93.

[236] His rival Hugh Audley had already tried unsuccessfully in 1318–19 to gain the earldom of Cornwall.

[237] *CCR, 1318–23*, 268. For details of the Gower dispute and its connection with the Despenser war of 1321 see Pugh, 'marcher lords', 170, 604; and J.C. Davies, 'The Despenser war in Glamorgan', *TRHS*, 3rd ser., ix (1915), 21–64, esp. 33–42. The events in Gower were seen as especially important by the author of the *Vita Edwardi Secundi*, who wrote a long account of them: *Vita*, 182–5.

[238] *CPR, 1317–21*, 547; *CFR, 1319–27*, 41, 43; Pugh, 'marcher lords', 170. On 20 Nov. the Elder Despenser and Bartholomew de Badlesmere were ordered to inquire into the resistance: *CPR, 1317–21*, 547.

Hereford,[239] the two Roger Mortimers, of Wigmore and Chirk, and John Giffard, as well as Hugh Audley and Roger Damory, and Roger de Clifford.[240] He was also cordially hated by the earl of Lancaster[241] and was probably one of the reasons for the earl of Pembroke's temporary withdrawal from England.[242] The Mortimers had a special cause to hate and to fear him since Despenser threatened to avenge the death of his grandfather, an earlier Hugh Despenser, at the battle of Evesham in 1265, in which their ancestors had fought on opposite sides.[243]

Despenser was also becoming the object of a more general hatred because of the influence that he and his father were perceived to have over the king. An even greater degree of hatred had probably been focused on Gaveston in his day, but then there had been more exaggeration than substance.[244] Now, even allowing for some measure of hindsight in the knowledge of the Despensers' excesses after 1322, there was real substance. 'No baron could approach the king without their [the Despensers, father and son] consent; and then a bribe was usually necessary; they answered petitions as they wished; they removed household officials without consulting the baronage; and any who displeased them or whose lands they coveted they threw into prison. The king would take advice from none but them.'[245] In a very revealing letter written in January 1321 to John Inge, his sheriff in Glamorgan, Despenser remarked that the times changed from one day to another; envy was growing against him, and especially among the magnates, because the king treated him better than any other; therefore it was necessary, while times were good, that his affairs should go well, and that they should be wisely guarded for his honour and good. Therefore Despenser commanded Inge so to watch his affairs that 'we may be rich and may attain our ends'.[246]

---

[239] The earl of Hereford had a special grievance over Gower since William de Braose had assigned Gower to Mowbray and his wife, with reversion to Hereford. The king had apparently agreed to this: *Ann. Paul.*, 293; Davies, 'Despenser war', 36–7.

[240] *Vita*, 186–7. Clifford, the son of the Robert de Clifford killed at Bannockburn, was not a marcher lord but had a grievance over Despenser's interference in an inheritance claimed by his mother: Davies, 'Despenser war', 43.

[241] See Maddicott, 262.

[242] See Phillips, 200–1, 209–10.

[243] *Vita*, 186–7 and n. 382.

[244] See above, Ch. 4 of this book and Hamilton, 38, 139–40; Chaplais, 99–104.

[245] *Le Baker*, 11; *Murimuth*, 33; *Historia Anglicana*, 159; *SR*, i, 182; *Brut*, 212; *Anonimalle*, 92–3; *Melsa*, 337–8; *Ann. Paul.*, 292; Maddicott, 261. Murimuth, for example, claimed that if any of the magnates was allowed to talk to the king, Despenser would listen to the conversation and reply freely on his account. These are all generalized comments, but the newly consecrated bishop of Rochester, Hamo Hethe, recorded that in Dec. 1319 he had to pay the Younger Despenser, in his capacity as chamberlain, a fee of £10 for the restitution of his temporalities, which he rightly regarded as extortion: *Anglia Sacra*, ed. H. Wharton, i (London, 1691), 360–1; Maddicott, 262–3. This story comes from the Historia Roffensis, BL, Cotton Ms. Faustina B.V, an important source for the events of the closing years of the reign of Edward II. Hamo Hethe's experience was minor: much worse was to come.

[246] SC 1/49/143; *Calender . . . concerning Wales*, 219–20.

Edward clearly trusted the Elder Despenser whom he had known and with whom he had worked for many years; the Younger Despenser he probably came to rely on, if not actually to trust. While it is impossible to know the true nature of the relationship between Edward II and the Despensers, it seems as if the king became ensnared by them, especially by the Younger Despenser who was possibly aided by his wife Eleanor de Clare. Edward had, for example, tried at first to prevent Despenser's intrigues against Hugh Audley in Gwynllwg, but proved powerless to stop them.[247] There is also some evidence that the king was personally prepared to allow John de Mowbray to keep possession of Gower and that it was only through Despenser's machinations that this did not happen.[248] Once Despenser got his way, whether it was in Gwynllwg or Gower, or in a host of other matters, Edward had no choice but to follow and to defend him. Little by little the favourite came to dominate his royal master and the fates of both men were to be intertwined. As the unknown author of the *Anonimalle Chronicle* remarked: 'The king loved him dearly with all his heart and mind, above all others, so that there was not in the land any great lord who, against sir Hugh's will, dared to do or say the things he would have liked to have done'.[249] The ultimate disaster of Edward II's reign was still six years away, but its seeds were very firmly planted by the autumn of 1320.

Some attempts were made to reduce the mutual suspicions and avert the slide into civil war. On 5 November Edward II confirmed his father's re-grant of the Gloucester lands in 1290 to Gilbert de Clare and his heirs by his second marriage to Edward I's daughter, Joan of Acre. This was done at the request of Despenser, Damory and Audley, and was probably meant as a guarantee that Despenser would not usurp any more of their rights in their respective shares of the earldom or even claim the title of earl.[250] On 14 November Roger Damory was pardoned the whole of a fine of 2,300 marks which he had agreed to pay in return for the re-grant of certain wardships which had been resumed under the terms of the Ordinances; and on 26 December payment of his debts to the king was respited.[251] It was already too late. When the earl of Hereford and John de Mowbray had protested to the king that the seizure of Gower was a breach of the law of the March, they were outraged when their protest was rejected. Despenser even accused them and anyone who thought like

---

[247] *CPR, 1317–21*, 60, 103, 120–1; Pugh, 'marcher lords', 169; Davies, 'Despenser war', 29–30.
[248] *Ann. Paul.*, 37; Davies, 'Despenser war', 36–7.
[249] *Anonimalle*, 92–3.
[250] *CPR, 1317–21*, 531; Phillips, 199–200. The surrender and re-grant took place on the occasion of Joan's marriage to Gilbert. The confirmation in 1320 would also have had the effect of ruling out once and for all any possible claim by Maurice de Berkeley and Isabel de Clare: Phillips, 263–4.
[251] E 159/94, mm.7, 39d; C 81/113/5509; Phillips, 199. The respite of payment of his debts on 26 Dec. repeated an earlier order on 20 Sept., but it appears that the amount pardoned was now to be only 1,000 marks: *CPR, 1317–21*, 519.

them of treason.[252] England, so often threatened with civil war since the accession of Edward II and so often saved by a last-minute compromise, was on the verge of disaster.

SCOTLAND AGAIN

To the most sincere prince, the Lord Edward, by God's grace illustrious king of England, Robert by the same grace king of Scots, sends greetings in Him by whom the thrones of rulers are governed.

Since while agreeable peace prevails the minds of the faithful are at rest, the Christian way of life is furthered, and all the affairs of holy mother church and of all kingdoms are everywhere carried on more prosperously, we in our humility have judged it right to entreat of your highness most earnestly that, having before your eyes the righteousness you owe to God and to the people, you desist from persecuting us and disturbing the people of our realm, so that there may be an end of slaughter and shedding of Christian blood. Everything that we ourselves and our people by their bodily service and contributions of wealth can do, we are now, and shall be, prepared to do sincerely and honourably for the sake of good peace and to earn perpetual peace for our souls. If it should be agreeable to your will to hold negotiations with us upon these matters, let your royal will be communicated to us in a letter by the hands of the bearer of this present letter.[253]

This letter in high-flown Latin, addressed by Robert Bruce to Edward II, was probably sent in April–May 1320, and indicated Bruce's desire for a final peace between Scotland and England. But the letter was also designed for the eyes of the pope and a copy of it probably accompanied another skilfully composed letter this time addressed directly to the pope and drawn up in April by a body of eight Scottish earls and thirty barons. This document is known today as the Declaration of Arbroath. Pledging their undying loyalty to 'our valiant prince, king and lord, the lord Robert, who that his people might be delivered out of the hands of enemies, bore

---

[252] *Vita*, 184–5; Davies, 'Despenser war', 38–9. In addition to his personal interest in Gower, the earl of Hereford was well aware of an earlier occasion when the crown had broken the custom of the March, Edward I's intervention in 1290 in a dispute in the lordship of Brecon between the earl of Hereford's father and Gilbert de Clare earl of Gloucester: Prestwich, *Plantagenet England*, 136. A further cause for Hereford's hatred of Despenser was the latter's execution in 1318 of Llywelyn Bren, the Glamorgan rebel of 1316, who had been promised safety when he surrendered by both the Mortimers and Hereford. One outcome was that in 1321–2 Llywelyn's seven sons fought for the lord of Brecon: R.R. Davies, *Lordship and Society in the March of Wales, 1282–1400* (Oxford, 1978), 290–1.

[253] Barrow, 314 (Professor Barrow's translation). The Latin text of this undated letter can be found in *Liber Epistolaris of Richard of Bury*, ed. N. Denholm-Young, 325–5, no. 463; and in *Regesta Regum Scottorum*, 698–9. no. 569.

cheerfully toil and fatigue, hunger and danger, like another Maccabeus or Joshua', the Scottish nobles added that 'for as long as a hundred of us remain alive, we will never on any condition be subjected to the lordship of the English. For we fight not for glory nor riches nor honours, but for freedom alone, which no good man gives up except with his life.'[254]

Both documents were part of a diplomatic offensive by Robert Bruce and may have been composed by the same hand.[255] Bruce was attempting to counter the bulls of excommunication which had been issued against him since 1317 and to answer the papal demands for peace by suggesting that Edward II and England were the only barriers to a settlement, and also to demonstrate Scottish unity in the face of English aggression. While the pope knew perfectly well that Scotland was not as united as Bruce wished him to believe,[256] and did not accept the Scottish case for independence, he did go so far as to refer to Bruce in subsequent correspondence as 'Robert, illustrious king of Scotland'.[257] The English were in principle prepared to discuss peace, but any document which described Robert Bruce in this way, whether emanating from the Scottish chancery or from the papal curia, was unacceptable.

In practice they were, at first, more concerned with a continuation of the two-year truce which had been made in December 1319 and would expire in 1321. But Edward II and his advisers now had to allow for the twin possibilities that the pope would weaken his hostility to Bruce even further and that France would lend support to the Scots, either directly or in the guise of mediation. It was known in England in March 1320 that Scottish envoys were present at Avignon and that the pope had cited Robert Bruce to appear before him on 1 May;[258] Edward II and his council were therefore anxious that nothing concerning Scotland should be discussed at Avignon before English envoys had a chance to get there.[259] Had Edward also known of the existence of the Declaration of

---

[254] The Declaration of Arbroath was delivered at Avignon by Scottish envoys in June 1320: Barrow, 303–11. For the text of the Declaration see A.A.M. Duncan, *The Nation of Scots and the Declaration of Arbroath* (London, 1970); or *Bruce*, 779–82. In its appeal to mythical history the Declaration bears some resemblance to the Irish Remonstrance of 1317: Phillips, 'Irish remonstrance of 1317', 121–4.

[255] *Regesta Regum Scottorum*, no. 569.

[256] Within months the Declaration of Arbroath was followed by the conspiracy against Bruce of William de Soules, which was supported by several of those who had put their seals to the Declaration, and indicated the continuing recognition in Scotland of the Balliol family's claim to the throne: Barrow, 309–10.

[257] Ibid., 305–6.

[258] *Foedera*, II, i, 390; Haines, *The Church and Politics*, 22.

[259] *Liber Epistolaris of Richard of Bury*, ed. N. Denholm-Young, 96, no. 209 (before March 1320). The pope's request for letters of safe conduct through England to be issued for Bruce and the bishop of St Andrews was discussed inconclusively by the council in London in April 1320: *Letters from Northern Registers*, 296–8, 302–3. The pope wished to give the impression that the idea of summoning Bruce had come from Edward II and his council, which was not acceptable: Haines, *The Church and Politics*, 22–3.

Arbroath and its imminent arrival at Avignon, his anxiety would have been all the greater.[260]

The English government also became aware that the Scots were being assisted at the papal curia by Odard de Maubuisson, a French lord with long experience of activities against England. This could only have been happening with the approval of Philip V[261] and may help to explain the sending of Master William de Maldon to Paris in May, in advance of Edward II's visit, to ensure that the papal bulls of excommunication against Robert Bruce were properly promulgated.[262] It is very likely that Scotland was discussed while Edward II and his councillors were at Amiens, and that a French offer to send envoys to England was made at this time.[263] For his part the pope wrote to Edward on 10 August urging him to engage in peace talks with the Scots and again on 18 August to tell him of his meetings with Robert Bruce's envoys.[264] The idea of the appointment of a papal envoy probably originated then.[265] Edward was therefore under growing pressure to negotiate seriously with the Scots from both the pope and the king of France. He may not have welcomed their involvement initially but he could not afford to reject it.[266] It was yet another complication to add to the already complicated and tense political situation in England.

The negotiations with the Scots were originally scheduled to begin at Carlisle some time in August and were to be undertaken by three of Edward II's closest advisers: the earl of Pembroke, Bartholomew de Badlesmere and the Younger Despenser. However, on 14 August messengers were sent to Bruce asking for a postponement of the meeting.[267] No reasons were given, but the delay was probably connected with developments in France and at

---

[260] The Declaration and a copy of Bruce's letter to Edward II probably arrived at Avignon in late June: Barrow, 304–5.

[261] Ibid.

[262] BL, Add. Ms. 17352, f. 13; *Foedera*, II, i, 392. Edward was especially concerned that the bulls should be published in the county of Flanders, which was nominally under the suzerainty of the French crown and was also the home of John Crabbe and other Flemings in the service of the Scots. Edward also wrote to his nephew, John duke of Brabant, asking him not to receive the Scots in his territory. The bulls had been brought to England in Feb. 1320 by the bishop of Hereford: Haines, *The Church and Politics*, 22.

[263] The French representatives, who were already in England in early Oct. 1320, were Bertrand Boniface, John lord of Varens, and William bishop of Mende: SC 1/45/197; *Foedera*, II, i, 435, 442, 450.

[264] *Foedera*, II, i, 431–2. The pope also made a point of telling Edward of the involvement of Odard de Maubuisson in these talks.

[265] The papal envoy was to be William de Laudun, OP, archbishop of Vienne, who arrived in England in Feb. 1321: SC 1/45/197; BL, Add. Ms. 9951, f. 21.

[266] On 6 Oct. Edward wrote to Philip V to report the arrival of his envoys but argued that it was not opportune for them to go to Scotland just yet: *Foedera*, II, i, 435.

[267] BL, Add. Ms. 9951, f. 10; Phillips, 203. The messengers included two of Pembroke's retainers, Sir John Darcy, sheriff of Northumberland (not Nottingham as in Phillips, 203) and Percival Simeon; and Sir Andrew Harclay the keeper of Carlisle.

the papal curia. After further contacts with the Scots at Carlisle in September and October a large and impressive English delegation was appointed on 19 January 1321: the archbishop of York, the bishops of Carlisle, Worcester and Winchester, the earls of Pembroke and Hereford, Badlesmere, Robert Baldock the keeper of the privy seal, William Airmyn, and four others, who were to meet Bruce's envoys at Newcastle either to make a final peace treaty or to prolong the existing truce. The French and papal envoys were also expected to participate.[268] Significantly, the four others were all men with Lancastrian connections: Stephen and Nicholas de Segrave, Fulk Lestrange and John de Clavering.[269] Had Edward and his council succeeded in regaining Lancaster's co-operation;[270] had they heard rumours that he might be colluding with the Scots for his own purposes and were trying to discuss his true intentions; or were they hoping against hope that negotiating with the Scots might also help to preserve internal peace? Whatever the intentions, no satisfactory negotiations took place.[271] On 17 February Edward wrote to Badlesmere and his colleagues telling them that the earl of Pembroke had not yet returned from France and to postpone their meeting with the Scots for two or three weeks.[272] On 23 February Edward wrote to them again: Pembroke was still engaged on his private affairs in France and the earl of Hereford had not appeared 'for certain reasons'; on 1 March he reported that Pembroke was still in France.[273] The earl of Richmond was appointed to replace the two absent earls, and then hastened north, taking with him a copy of the records bearing on England's claim to superiority over Scotland.[274] On 26 March an unsatisfactory

---

[268] BL, Add. Ms. 9951, f. 6v; *CPR, 1317–21*, 504, 554; *Foedera*, II, i, 441; Phillips, 203.

[269] *Foedera*, II, i, 441; Maddicott, 232–3. Nicholas de Segrave had been Lancaster's representative at parliament in Oct. 1320: Maddicott, 257.

[270] This may explain the mission of the bishops of London and Winchester to Lancaster in Nov. 1320: *Ann. Paul.*, 290; *Trokelowe*, 106; Phillips, 198.

[271] The actual negotiators on the English side who can be identified from the surviving correspondence between them and the king were the bishops of Worcester and Carlisle, the earl of Richmond, Bartholomew de Badlesmere, Robert Baldock, and William Airmyn. There is nothing to suggest that Lancaster's representatives were in any way involved.

[272] SC 1/45/197; Phillips, 203. On 19 Feb. renewed safe conducts were issued at Roxburgh in the names of all the English envoys, including the absent earls of Pembroke and Hereford: C 47/22/12/31. On 17 and 19 Feb. Edward wrote to his negotiators that the French and papal envoys were in London and would soon be arriving in the north; both sets of envoys were given safe conducts to go to the north on 11 & 16 Feb.: SC 1/45/197, 198 (printed in *Anglo-Scottish Relations, 1174–1328*, ed. E.L.G. Stones (Oxford, 1970), 46–7); *Foedera*, II, i, 442. There is nothing however to suggest that the French and papal envoys played any direct part in the negotiations. On 14 May Edward wrote to the pope explaining that the papal letters addressed to Robert Bruce and carried by the papal envoys were not shown to the Scots because of certain words they contained, i.e. describing Bruce as king, which were not acceptable to the English: *Foedera*, II, i, 450.

[273] SC 1/32/87; SC 1/45, 200, 201.

[274] SC 1/32/87; E 159/93, m.77 (*Anglo-Scottish Relations*, ed. Stones 149). These were the records copied by Andrew de Tange between 1315 and 1318: *Edward I and the Throne of Scotland*, ed. Stones & Simpson, i, 45–7, 81–2; ii, 378–80.

meeting was held with the Scottish envoys at Bamburgh, at which the Scots spoke a lot about their desire for peace, but did nothing to bring it about; rather the contrary. All they were prepared to accept was a long truce, of twenty-six years. It was agreed that another meeting would take place on 1 September when Edward II and Robert Bruce would be able to announce their intentions.[275] There the negotiations ended. On 5 May the earl of Richmond returned the records to the exchequer.[276] English and Scottish envoys were not to meet again for another two years, after a bitter civil war in England and another disastrous English campaign in Scotland.[277]

THE ATTACKS ON THE DESPENSERS

The Scottish negotiations, such as they were, took place against the background of a rapidly deteriorating situation within England. One of the first indications came on 6 January 1321 when Edward informed the chancellor that, allegedly because of illness which prevented him from riding, Lancaster would not be attending the session of the London eyre due to be held on 14 January.[278] In late January and in February the earl of Hereford, Roger Mortimer of Wigmore and other Marchers withdrew to their Welsh lands to gather their forces. In the meantime the king and Despenser were kept well informed of the developing events in the north by Robert Baldock, a member of the delegation based at Newcastle for the Scottish negotiations; by William de Aune, the constable of the royal castle at Tickhill in Yorkshire; and in Wales by John Inge, Despenser's sheriff in Glamorgan.[279] As early as 18 January Despenser told Inge to see that his castles were well garrisoned.[280]

---

[275] '*Et des Escotz avons oi moltz des paroles qil ont dit, qil desiront la pees sur tote rien, mes en fait mostront il rien qui touché a la pees eintz la contraire*': report of the envoys on 8 April: SC 1/21/164 (*Anglo-Scottish Relations*, ed. Stones, 152); Barrow, 241. It appears that by this stage Edward II's initial preference for a truce had changed to one for a peace treaty, presumably as a way of reducing the number of his enemies.

[276] E 159/93, m.77 (*Anglo-Scottish Relations*, ed. Stones, 152).

[277] Because of the failure to make peace by the deadline of 29 Sep. 1321, on 25 Aug. orders were given to destroy Harbottle castle in Northumberland, under the terms of the truce of Dec. 1319: *CPR, 1321–24*, 21.

[278] C 81/113/5551; *CPR, 1317–21*, 562; Williams, *Medieval London*, 286–7, 290–9; Phillips, 201.

[279] For example, on 27 Feb. Baldock wrote separate letters to Edward and Despenser, which they received at Windsor: SC 1/35/8; C 81/114/5602. Despenser also received and replied to letters from Inge on 6 and 21 March: SC 1/58/10 (printed in *Calendar . . . concerning Wales*, 259–60); BL, Cotton Ms. Nero C. III, f. 181 (published by W.H. Stevenson as 'A letter of the Younger Despenser on the eve of the barons' rebellion, 21 March 1321', *EHR*, xii (1897), 755–61); Phillips, 201.

[280] SC 1/49/143 (printed in *Calendar . . . concerning Wales*, 219–20). Despenser wrote to Inge again on 16 Feb.: SC 1/49/144 (*Calendar . . .* 220–1). A file exists of 20 letters under the privy and secret seals from Edward II to William de Aune and covering the period 14 Sep. 1320 to 11 March 1322. Edward regularly asked Aune for news of local events, but Aune's replies have not survived: Maddicott, 264, 306: the copies of these letters are preserved in Sheffield City Library, Jackson Collection, Ms. 1086.

In late February and early March warnings came from both Baldock and Inge that an attack on Despenser's lands in Wales was imminent.[281]

Lancaster's involvement was apparent at a very early stage. On 22 February he held a meeting with other, unnamed, magnates at Pontefract, at which it was decided to attack Despenser.[282] It is likely that Lancaster's plans for such a meeting explain Edward's order on 30 January to the earls of Hereford, Arundel and Surrey, John de Mowbray, Henry de Beaumont and twenty-five others not to join armed assemblies or to make secret treaties.[283] With the exception of Hereford, almost all those named could be described as northerners rather than lords of the Welsh March.[284] Whether Hereford himself attended the gathering is unknown,[285] but it is likely that there was some representation from the March.[286] Lancaster's efforts to stage manage the events of 1321, while staying at Pontefract well clear of any danger, were already apparent.[287]

By 6 March the Younger Despenser had received news that Hereford was gathering troops in Brecon ready to invade Despenser's lands in Wales, and he again ordered John Inge to see that all his castles were well defended;[288] and on 16 March orders were given for Hereford's castle of Builth to be taken back into royal hands, following a last-minute effort by the king's half-brother, the earl of Norfolk, to parley with him.[289] On 21 March Despenser wrote again to Inge from Cirencester, saying that it was no wonder that the earl of Hereford was more than usually gloomy and pensive since he was disloyal to the king who had given him so many goods

---

[281] SC 1/35/8; SC 1/58/10 (*Calendar . . . concerning Wales*, 259–60); Phillips, 201.

[282] SC 1/35/8; C 81/114/5602.

[283] *CCR, 1318–23*, 355; Phillips, 201.

[284] Maddicott, 262–3. Although Mowbray, for example, had a close interest in the fate of Gower, his principal land holdings were in Lincolnshire, at Axholme. The earl of Surrey was virtually at the command of Lancaster since the enforced surrender of his Yorkshire and Welsh lands in 1318–19. Arundel was Surrey's brother-in-law and heir and might have been influenced by his behaviour. Henry de Beaumont's inclusion is strange since he had been loyal personally to Edward II and Isabella and hostile to Lancaster. The names look as if they were an invitation list drawn up by Lancaster of men who were already his allies or who might be induced to join him through hatred of Despenser.

[285] On 22 Feb. Edward wrote to William de Aune, asking him to keep a close watch over what happened at Pontefract and to let him know if Hereford was there: Maddicott, 264; Sheffield City Library, Jackson Collection, Ms. 1086, no. 5.

[286] The king received news of this gathering and the intention to attack Despenser in a letter sent by Robert Baldock from Newcastle on 27 Feb. Baldock mentioned that he had spoken to Sir John Clavering, a Lancastrian retainer and one of those forbidden on 30 Jan. to attend assemblies, who was probably therefore a source of information on Lancaster's plans: SC 1/35/8; C 81/114/5602; Phillips, 201; Maddicott, 264. William de Aune probably also provided information from Tickhill, which was quite close to Pontefract.

[287] It is possible that Lancaster was also intriguing with the Scots, who might then choose to intervene directly in England in the event of trouble between the king and the magnates.

[288] SC 1/58/10 (*Calendar . . . concerning Wales*, 259–60); Phillips, 201; Maddicott, 264–5.

[289] *CCW*, 519; Phillips, 201; Maddicott, 265.

and honours.²⁹⁰ Despenser was no doubt right in his assessment. The earl of Hereford, despite all the reasons he had to distrust and to hate Despenser, was about to sever a long-standing personal alliance and even friendship between himself and his brother-in-law the king. Once the tie was broken there would be no going back.

Two other marcher lords with good reason to consider their position were the Mortimers. Roger Mortimer of Wigmore had returned from Ireland in the autumn of 1320 and arrived at court just after the crisis over Gower erupted.²⁹¹ His reaction to these events is unknown, but can be guessed from his subsequent behaviour. By 11 February he had retired to his stronghold at Wigmore, having been replaced on 1 February as justice of Ireland by one of Despenser's knights, Sir Ralph de Gorges.²⁹² The attitude of Roger's uncle, Roger Mortimer of Chirk, was not yet clear. He had been justice of Wales for much of the reign and had seen to it that Wales remained secure when there was a threat of revolt at the time of the Scottish campaign in Ireland. On 8 March 1321 he was told to inspect and put in order the royal castles in Wales, perhaps as much as a test of his loyalty as as a defensive measure.²⁹³

In their turn, Edward and Despenser reacted swiftly, leaving Windsor for the danger area on 6 March and reaching Gloucester on the 27th.²⁹⁴ On the way Edward seized the castle of St Briavel's in Gloucestershire from Roger Damory and ordered the confiscation of Hugh Audley's lands, including the castle of Montgomery which he held for the crown, because he had broken the terms of his contract with the king.²⁹⁵ Edward's summons on 28 March to the earl of Hereford, the Mortimers and others to attend a council at Gloucester on 6 April to discuss the gathering of armed men in the Welsh March ²⁹⁶ was firmly rebuffed. Hereford informed Edward via two royal knights, John de Somery and Robert de

---

²⁹⁰ '*De ce que vous avez entendu que le counte de Herford est mornes et pensifs plus qu'il ne le soleit, nest mye mervaille s'il est, qar il se ad si portez en contenances devers son lige seignour, q[ui] mult de biens et de honurs luy ad fait, qu'il en deit bien avoir grant pensee*': BL, Cotton Ms. Nero C. III, f. 181, printed in Stevenson, 'A letter' 755–61. Despenser also reported that Hugh Audley was threatening his men at Thornbury in Gloucestershire but was not strong enough to do anything.

²⁹¹ I. Mortimer, *The Greatest Traitor* (London, 2003), 98, 100–1.

²⁹² *CCR, 1318–23*, 360; *CPR, 1317–21*, 558; Phillips, 201. Gorges soon became caught up in the attack on the Despensers and never took up office in Ireland.

²⁹³ *CCR, 1318–23*, 290; Phillips, 201.

²⁹⁴ E 101/378/10, mm.6, 7; Phillips, 201–2; Maddicott, 264. The king's intention to gather an armed force around him is clearly indicated in a letter to the chancellor and treasurer of 6 March: *CCW*, 518.

²⁹⁵ *Vita*, 188–9; *CPR, 1317–21*, 575. The text of Audley's contract is given in full on the original Patent Roll (C 66/154, m.17) and states clearly that if Audley did not observe its terms his lands would be forfeited to the crown. This was the first occasion on which a magnate suffered because of a contract with the king. Badlesmere and Pembroke were both to suffer for the same reason in 1322.

²⁹⁶ *CCR, 1318–23*, 363–4; Phillips, 204; Maddicott, 265. The others included Roger Damory, John Hastings, John Giffard, John Charlton, and Thomas and Maurice de Berkeley. Despenser himself was also summoned to attend.

Kendale, that he would not come while Hugh Despenser the Younger was in the king's company. Hereford then sent the abbot of Dore to Edward with the proposal that Despenser should be put in the custody of the earl of Lancaster and permitted to answer the charges against him in parliament.[297] According to the *Vita Edwardi Secundi*, the barons went even further and threatened to withdraw their allegiance from Edward altogether.[298] Edward sent a cleverly argued reply in which he refused to do as Hereford asked, on the grounds that Despenser had never been accused of any crime, and took his stand upon Magna Carta, the Ordinances, the common law and his coronation oath. Edward ended with another clever move by summoning Hereford and Roger Mortimer of Wigmore to Oxford on 10 May to discuss the date for a parliament.[299] Since this was what they wanted, they could not refuse to attend.

Edward may have hoped that the reappearance at Gloucester on about 28 March of the earl of Pembroke, newly returned from France, might help matters.[300] His reliance on Pembroke's experience and moderation was already apparent in the role he had expected Pembroke to play in the negotiations with the Scots and in Edward's evident disappointment when Pembroke stayed abroad. On 29 March Edward wrote to the pope, seeking a dispensation for Pembroke's intended marriage to the French noblewoman, Marie de St Pol, perhaps hoping in this way to ensure his loyalty and aid in dealing with the Marchers.[301] The Marchers may also have been bidding for his support, since on 19 April he received a letter brought by the abbot of Dore.[302] It is likely that Pembroke was wavering since the usually well informed observer, Adam Murimuth, recorded that Pembroke secretly supported the enemies of the Despensers.[303] Whatever the truth, Pembroke's presence made no difference to the rapidly developing crisis; he was probably glad to have the excuse of his impending marriage to allow him to leave the country again, which he did at the end of May.[304]

By this time it was already far too late for negotiations. The orders to Hereford and the Marchers on 13 April to keep the peace in their own lordships were ignored;[305] while the instructions not to believe false

[297] *CCR, 1318–23*, 364; Phillips, 204; Maddicott, 265–6.
[298] *Vita*, 186–7.
[299] *CCR, 1318–23*, 367–8; Phillips, 204; Maddicott, 266.
[300] C 53/107, m.2; Phillips, 204.
[301] *Foedera*, II, i, 446. On 8 Feb., while Pembroke was still in France, Edward had attended a mass celebrated in the conventual church at Stratford, London, for the soul of Pembroke's late wife, Beatrice. On 14 Sept. 1320 Edward had placed five silk cloths on her body while it was awaiting burial: BL, Add. Ms. 9951, ff. 2v, 45v; Phillips, 190–1.
[302] BL, Add. Ms. 9951, f. 36; Phillips, 205. The letter has not survived.
[303] *Murimuth*, 33; Phillips, 205; Maddicott, 267. Murimuth's opinion was cited by several other chroniclers: Phillips, 204–5, n. 6.
[304] Phillips, 206. He was at Boulogne by 2 June: C 81/1750/21; C 66/154, m.4; *CPR, 1317–21*, 589–91, 596.
[305] *CCR, 1318–23*, 366.

rumours which were issued to over seventy earls and barons on 21 April were little more than fatuous.[306] On 1 May Edward postponed the date of his proposed meeting with the Marchers until 17 May at Westminster.[307] Three days later the earl of Hereford, the Mortimers and other Marchers began their attacks on the Welsh lands of the Younger Despenser. Newport was attacked on 4 May, followed by the capture of Cardiff on 9 May and Swansea on about 13 May.[308] Despenser's lands in Wales were wasted and plundered by the invaders, causing damage estimated afterwards at £14,000.[309] In an attempt to protect his possessions, Despenser surrendered custody of his castles to the king, but with no effect: Glamorgan remained in the hands of Roger Damory, while Hugh Audley recovered Gwynllwg and John de Mowbray regained Gower.[310] Meanwhile Roger Mortimer of Wigmore seized the lands of Despenser's ally, the earl of Arundel, at Clun and elsewhere in the Welsh March.[311] Having finished their work in Wales, the Marchers attempted unsuccessfully to take control of Bristol,[312] before turning their attention in June to the English lands of both Despensers.[313]

---

[306] *Foedera*, II, i, 447–8; *CCR, 1318–23*, 369.

[307] *CCR, 1318–23*, 367–8. Edward was now at Wallingford, having left Gloucester to return to Westminster on about 12 April.

[308] *Flores*, 344–5; BL, Add. Ms. 9951, f. 7v; Phillips, 205; Davies, 'Despenser war', 53–4. An undated letter of about this time and probably addressed to the Younger Despenser by John Inge suggests that Despenser's castles in Glamorgan were less well prepared against attack than he had intended: SC 1/63/185. Apart from Hereford and the Mortimers, the marcher lords who took part in the attacks can be identified as Hugh Audley the Younger and his father, John de Mowbray, Roger de Clifford, John Giffard, Maurice de Berkeley, and others: Davies, 'Despenser war', 53.

[309] *CCR, 1318–23*, 541–2; Davies, 'Despenser war', 57; Pugh, 'marcher lords', 170–1. Details of the campaign against the Despensers and of the destruction caused can be found in *CCR, 1318–23*, 541–3; and in *PROME*, Parliament of 1397, C 65/58, items 56–61. This material forms part of the petition of Hugh Despenser the Younger in Nov. 1321, asking for the annulment of the process against him in July 1321 (*CCR, 1318–23*, 544–6). The petition was recited in the course of the annulment of the processes against the Despensers at the time of the creation of Thomas, lord Despenser, as earl of Gloucester in Sept. 1397.

[310] Davies, 'Despenser war', 56; Pugh, 'marcher lords', 171.

[311] Bod., Laud Misc. Ms. 529, f. 106 (this source is closely related to *Murimuth* but has much local information on the Welsh March); Univ. of Chicago Ms. 224, f. 55v (chronicle of Wigmore abbey); Phillips, 205. Arundel had made his allegiances clear when his son married Despenser's daughter on 9 Feb.: BL, Add. Ms. 9951, f. 45v.

[312] On 25 May a message from Hereford, the Mortimers and others was delivered to the mayor of Bristol by a friar, Brother Maurice de Pencoyt. The mayor immediately informed Edward and promised his loyalty and that of his town: SC 1/33/58, 59; *Foedera*, II, i, 459. The magnates probably hoped that the earlier dispute between the king and Bristol could be turned to their advantage.

[313] *Vita*, 190–1. The Elder Despenser's manor of La Fasterne in Wiltshire, for example, was attacked on 11 June, and other manors at about the same time: *CCR, 1318–23*, 541–3; *PROME*, Parliament of 1397, C 65/58, item 59. The estimated cost of the damage inflicted was £38,000: Davies, 'Despenser war', 56. See also S.L. Waugh, 'The profits of violence', *Speculum*, lii (1977), 848.

LANCASTER TRIES TO TAKE CHARGE

Although Lancaster had had no direct part in the attacks on the Despensers, except for the meeting with some northern magnates and with representatives of the Marchers at Pontefract in February, it was clear to everyone that his was a consenting mind if not the guiding hand.[314] However, once violence had broken out he tried to play a more direct role. On 24 May Lancaster met a group of fifteen northern magnates at Pontefract to discuss the current disturbances and their threat to the peace of the kingdom. If Lancaster was trying to put himself at the head of a northern alliance, he was unsuccessful and all he was able to obtain was a pact for mutual defence.[315]

The next, and critical, stage came on 28 June when Lancaster held a meeting at Sherburn-in-Elmet in Yorkshire with the earl of Hereford, the Mortimers, Roger Damory and Hugh Audley, and the other marcher lords who had attacked the Despensers. The assembly was also attended by northern magnates, by the archbishop of York and the bishops of Durham and Carlisle, and by a large number of Lancaster's own retainers.[316] A document containing a list of seven articles or grievances was read out in French by Sir John Bek, one of Lancaster's knights.[317] Royal officers, such as the chancellor and treasurer, chamberlain and keeper of the privy seal, the justices, escheators and chamberlains had taken office without the approval of parliament and contrary to the Ordinances; those who purchased lands held in chief from the king by accustomed services were being deprived of these lands and suffering forfeiture through the actions of certain evil councillors, while peers of the realm were being prejudged and disinherited, contrary to the law of the land and Magna Carta;[318] the same evil councillors appointed their followers to commissions of trailbaston in various counties, in order to indict both great and lesser men and disinherit them, contrary to common law;[319] they were

---

[314] See Maddicott, 267. Some of Lancaster's retainers were later pardoned for their role in the attacks, while the prisoners taken were sent to Lancaster for safekeeping.

[315] *Gesta Edwardi*, 61–2; Phillips, 205, 207; Maddicott, 269; B. Wilkinson, 'The Sherburn indenture and the attack on the Despensers, 1321', *EHR*, lxiii (1948), 6–7. A proposal for a further meeting to be attended by the northern bishops and other magnates was also agreed to: Wilkinson, 20.

[316] *Gesta Edwardi*, 62; *Flores*, 197; Phillips, 206–7; Maddicott, 274–5. The most detailed discussions of the Sherburn meeting and its significance are those in Wilkinson,'The Sherburn indenture', 1–28, and Maddicott, 268–78.

[317] Wilkinson, 'The Sherburn indenture', Appendix II, 19–21, citing Christ Church, Canterbury, Register I (Wilkinson's Ms. A); Maddicott, 276–7. The Latin version of the articles which is recorded in *Gesta Edwardi*, 62–4, gives Bek's name as the presenter. Maddicott suggests that the document was prepared in advance by Lancaster.

[318] Despenser's acquisitions of Gower and Gwynllwg were probably among the cases in mind.

[319] For example, John Inge, one of the Younger Despenser's men, appears to have influenced an inquest held at Exeter in March 1321 which allowed Herbert de Marisco to regain possession of the island of Lundy in the Bristol Channel. In 1322 Despenser acquired the island in his turn: Stevenson, 'A letter', 760.

responsible for the holding of the eyre in London, by which men were deprived of their franchises;[320] the evil councillors deprived those pleading cases before the court of Common Pleas or elsewhere of access to counsel to assist them in their cases, by encouraging the king to retain the services of the best lawyers;[321] the evil councillors had encouraged aliens to come into the country, to the destruction of Holy Church and of all the people; and they had also forced merchants to sell their wool abroad at the staple of Saint-Omer.[322]

An indenture was drawn up at the meeting, which first recorded that, in the presence of the archbishop of York, the bishops of Durham and Carlisle, and the earls of Lancaster and Angus, it had been claimed that the Despensers had ill advised and guided the king, to the dishonour and damage of the king and his kingdom. Having heard the arguments put forward by the earl of Hereford, the Mortimers, and the other Marchers present,[323] it seemed to the earls of Lancaster and Angus and to thirty-three other named individuals[324] that the actions of Hereford and the Marchers had, as they claimed, been undertaken for the honour of God and for the honour and profit of the king and his kingdom. It seemed to all[325] that the oppressions committed by the Despensers were increasing daily and could not be stopped without force (*reddour*); and it was agreed by all that the quarrel with the Despensers was maintained for the honour of God and of Holy Church, and the profit of the king and his kingdom and the king's children, and for the salvation of the crown and the

---

[320] The eyre, supposedly held to inquire into illegal confederacies, became an inquiry into the franchises of the city of London. On 20 Feb. 1321 the city was taken into royal hands and Robert de Kendale appointed as keeper. It is likely that the eyre was the brainchild of the Younger Despenser but, far from removing possible sources of opposition within London, it had the effect of turning the city against both Edward and Despenser. The consequences were to be very significant in 1326–7 after the invasion of Isabella and Mortimer: *CPR, 1317–21*, 562; Williams, *Medieval London*, 286–7, 290–9.

[321] However, as G.O. Sayles remarked, as far as the King's Bench is concerned, there is no evidence to support Tout's claim that Despenser had packed the courts with his dependants before 1321: *Select Cases in the Court of King's Bench under Edward* II, ed. G.O. Sayles, iv, Selden Soci., lxxiv (London, 1957), xiii, n. 13; Tout, *Place of the Reign*, 130.

[322] The issue of the staple had been discussed in 1319 at two assemblies of merchants summoned by the king. It was considered whether to move the staple from Saint-Omer, in territory obedient to the French crown, where it had been established since 1314, to Bruges in the county of Flanders, which was hostile to France. Bruges would have suited the interests of the merchants better than Saint-Omer, but the interests of good relations between England and France won the day and the staple remained where it was. An alternative suggestion was for the creation of a staple town or towns in England itself. But opinion among the merchants was apparently divided and no general resolution was reached. It was clearly still a live issue in 1321: Tout, *Place of the Reign*, 226–33.

[323] The other Marchers are named as Hugh Audley the Elder and the Younger, Roger Damory, John de Mowbray, Maurice de Berkeley, Roger de Clifford, Henry le Tyeys, John Giffard, Thomas Mauduit, Gilbert Talbot, and 'others of the March'.

[324] Significantly these did not include any of the prelates.

[325] '*Et semblait a tous*', i.e. to those named, but, again significantly, not to all present.

people;[326] the earl of Lancaster and the other great men who had begun the quarrel would maintain the earl of Angus and the twenty-seven others named with all their power; and whenever the earl of Lancaster and the other great men ended their quarrel, the others could also do so without challenge. Finally the earl of Angus and the others named after him had attached their seals.

The Sherburn meeting and the indenture which it produced have been the subject of a great deal of discussion in the past. Both Tout and Davies interpreted the agreement as placing Lancaster at the head of a united coalition of Marchers and northern magnates.[327] Wilkinson, who did most to make the indenture and its variant versions available to scholars, however argued that the indenture was the result of prolonged bargaining, that it was never in fact sealed, and that Lancaster was unsuccessful in trying to unite the Marchers and the northerners.[328] On one point at least the latter interpretation is incorrect, since a copy of the indenture found in Lancaster's muniments in 1322 bore the seals of twenty-five persons.[329] However, since the two versions of the indenture record the presence of forty-eight and thirty-four persons respectively, it is evident that many of those present for some reason either did not or were not prepared to put their seals to it.[330] The prelates are not named at all in the indenture and can certainly be listed among those who did not seal it: William Melton, the archbishop of York, for example, remained a loyal supporter of the crown despite any misgivings he may have had about the Despensers. The Bridlington chronicler explains that the clergy were prepared to give support in resisting the Scots but that all other matters should wait for the holding of the next parliament.[331] It is also apparent that, apart from the Marchers, all of those whose names appear in the Sherburn indenture were retainers of the earl of Lancaster.[332]

This was not, however, the full significance of the meeting at Sherburn.

---

[326] These arguments are very like those put forward in the famous '*Homage et serment*' document first composed in 1308 to justify opposition to Gaveston while not opposing the monarchy as such. Since this document was about to make a spectacular reappearance, it is likely that it was very much in the minds of the magnates in 1321.

[327] Tout, *Place of the Reign*, 128–9; Davies, *Baronial Opposition*, 478–9; Phillips, 206.

[328] Wilkinson, 'The Sherburn indenture', 4, 6; Phillips, 206. No original of the indenture has survived. Its text is known principally from two fourteenth-century copies, one in Canterbury, Register I (Wikinson's Ms. A) and the other in Lambeth Ms. 1213, f. 285 (Wilkinson's Ms. B). The Canterbury version is published with variants from the Lambeth text in Wilkinson, App. III, 21–2. There are also two sixteenth-century summaries derived from the Lambeth version: Wilkinson, 1–2, 22.

[329] DL 41/1/37, m.7; Phillips, 207; Maddicott, 273–4. The names of those who sealed it are not given.

[330] Phillips, 207; Maddicott, 275–6. The names of those who appear are given in Wilkinson, 'The Sherburn indenture' 28.

[331] *Gesta Edwardi*, 64.

[332] These included Robert de Umfraville the exiled Scottish earl of Angus, Robert de Holland, Fulk Lestrange and John d'Eure: Phillips, 207. For the full list see Maddicott, 274, where 27 people are named.

THE STEWARD OF ENGLAND

In the autumn of 1317 the earl of Lancaster had used his alleged authority as steward of England to block the king from direct access to the city of York;[333] during the York parliament in October 1318 he demanded that a search be made of royal records to establish his powers as steward and he attempted to prevent Bartholomew de Badlesmere's appointment as steward of the king's household without his approval;[334] during the York parliament of May 1319 Lancaster had returned to the attack, claiming that the office of steward of the household was his by right.[335] The matter was left unresolved for the time being, but at some point between then and 1321 a treatise was composed in which it was asserted that it was the steward's duty

> 'to supervise and regulate, under and immediately after the king, the whole realm of England and all the officers of laws within the said kingdom in times of peace and war'. He was to determine all cases in which the plaintiff had been unable to obtain a remedy in parliament, or in which there had been a miscarriage of justice. If the law was in doubt, the matter should be decided by a committee of twenty-five, drawn from the nobility and commons and nominated by the Steward and Constable. If the officers of the law were corrupt, the Steward should admonish or remove them. Finally, it was the Steward's special duty to intervene against the King's evil counsellors. Associating with himself the Constable and representatives of the magnates and commons, he should ask such a counsellor to leave the court, and if this was refused, then he should appeal to the King himself and demand the man's expulsion. If this too failed, the Steward, Constable and other magnates, acting for the good of the kingdom, would be justified in taking that counsellor, holding him until the next parliament, and in the meantime confiscating his lands and goods. The tract concluded by citing a series of precedents, ending with Gaveston's execution, to support this argument.[336]

It has generally been assumed that the treatise on the office of the steward played a prominent part in the events of 1321.[337] Yet at first sight it is curiously absent from the surviving records of those events. It might be expected that Lancaster's supposed authority as steward would be referred to in the articles read to the assembly at Sherburn by Lancaster's knight, John de Bek. But there is apparently no direct mention of it. It has also been suggested that the document which was drawn up by the

---

[333] *Trivet (Cont.)*, 23; *Vita*, 140–1; Phillips, 125; Maddicott, 208.
[334] *PROME*, Parliament of Oct. 1318, SC 9/21, items 6, 42; *Documents*, ed. Cole, 3, 9.
[335] *PROME*, Parliament of May 1319, SC 9/22, item 3 *Documents*, ed. Cole, 48.
[336] This summary of the treatise is in the words of Dr Maddicott: Maddicott, 242–3. For the Latin text and a translation of the treatise see L.W. Vernon Harcourt, *His Grace the Steward and the Trial of Peers* (London, 1907), 164–7, 148–51.
[337] Maddicott, 242.

magnates on their way to parliament in 1321 might have been the treatise on the steward.[338] But there is no obvious reference to the powers of the steward of England in the proceedings which led to the exile of the Despensers in August 1321;[339] nor is the treatise on the steward included in the unofficial collections of documents on the events of 1321 which are preserved at Canterbury and at Lambeth.[340] Indeed, Lancaster himself was neither present at nor named as a party to those proceedings.[341]

However, a closer examination of the events at Sherburn suggests a different picture. The French text of the articles read at Sherburn by John de Bek is not a single document but is in two parts. In the first part Bek asked those present at Sherburn on behalf of his lord (i.e. Lancaster) if they knew of any grievances damaging and dishonouring the crown or of any ways in which evil councillors had badly advised the king, and if so they should declare them before Lancaster and the other peers present. The form of the charge echoes the description of the powers and duties of the steward of England in the treatise on the steward and suggests both that composition of the tract was already complete before the Sherburn meeting and that Lancaster had summoned the assembly in his capacity as steward. The articles proper then began with the word, *Sire*, which can only be addressed to Lancaster, suggesting that the articles that follow were the assembly's answers to Lancaster's request.[342]

Both Lancaster and the Marchers were therefore each playing a part in a carefully orchestrated set of events. Lancaster used his powers as steward of England, while Hereford and the Marchers accepted his authority and that it provided them with legitimacy for their actions both in the past and in the future. The earl of Hereford's status as constable of England was additionally significant both at Sherburn and in the weeks that followed because of the role assigned to the holder of this office in the treatise on

---

[338] Maddicott, 242, n.3; *Ann. Paul.*, 293, which refers to '*quidam tractatus ex antiqua consuetudine ordinatus et approbatus*'. Dr Maddicott speculates that the treatise could also have been the *Modus tenendi Parliamentum* or 'some other document'.

[339] *CCR, 1318–23*, 492–4; *PROME*, Parliament of 1321, SC 9/24, item 2. The possibility of the steward acting in association with the constable, which is included in the treatise on the steward, might be held to cover the situation in 1321 when the earl of Hereford was the constable; but one would expect some mention of this in the articles against the Despensers.

[340] These are Canterbury, Register I, f. 376, *et seq.*, and Lambeth Ms. 1213, ff. 285–93, which are also the source of the two texts of the Sherburn indenture. For the details of the documents contained in the two manuscripts see Wilkinson, 'The Sherburn indenture', 19. The famous treatise on the holding of parliament, the *Modus tenendi Parliamentum*, which some writers believe is connected with the events of 1321 and specifically with the earl of Lancaster, is also conspicuous by its absence: cf. Maddicott, 289–92.

[341] I have radically altered the views on the treatise on the steward which I expressed in my Introduction to the 1321 parliament in *PROME.*

[342] The articles were presumably therefore composed at the assembly and not in advance by Lancaster: cf. Maddicott, 270.

the steward.³⁴³ Another feature of the Sherburn assembly which may also be important is that the indenture was sealed by twenty-five persons: this may be no more than coincidence but it is possible that there is a connection with the committee of twenty-five mentioned in the treatise.³⁴⁴

The reluctance of other northern barons to involve themselves in any offensive action, which had already been apparent at the meeting at Pontefract in May, was probably confirmed at Sherburn in June;³⁴⁵ the northern prelates were also unwilling to join Lancaster and the Marchers. Lancaster did not have political control over the north of England,³⁴⁶ but this was not of vital importance for the moment.³⁴⁷ The immediate significance of the Sherburn assembly was that the Marchers had been provided with a legal framework to justify their opposition to the Despensers and to the king. It now remained to be seen how they would develop this framework in the weeks and months to come. Lancaster in the meantime could afford to sit securely in his castle at Pontefract and await events in the south.

EDWARD'S RESPONSE

Edward and the Despensers had arrived back at Westminster from Gloucester in early May, just as the attacks on the Despensers were beginning. On 1 May a meeting of the council was called for the 17th,³⁴⁸ and at this Edward's response to the Marchers and Lancaster was hotly debated. According to the *Vita Edwardi Secundi*, some of Edward's councillors wanted him to attack the Marchers; and Edward would have done so willingly if there had been sufficient support. Other, wiser heads warned that this would lead to a general war, which would destroy the country and ruin

---

³⁴³ Maddicott, 242–4. It is possible that this role was a last-minute addition to the treatise to reflect the earl of Hereford's recent change of sides.

³⁴⁴ However, Michael Prestwich has suggested that the copy of the Sherburn indenture with 25 seals in Lancaster's archive was probably the half sealed by the marcher lords, who would have retained the other half sealed by Lancaster's men: Prestwich, 'The charges against the Despensers, 1321', *BIHR*, lviii (1985), 96, n. 9. Cf. Maddicott, 276, where it is noted that the Lambeth version of the indenture implies that the Marchers did seal it. This also implies that far more than 25 persons sealed the indenture and that my suggestion of a link with the committee of 25 is probably a red herring.

³⁴⁵ All but three of the northerners who had been at Pontefract were also at Sherburn: Maddicott, 274, where the names of the northerners are given.

³⁴⁶ Wilkinson, 'The Sherburn indenture', 4; Phillips, 207; Maddicott, 268, 273–5.

³⁴⁷ The consequences of Lancaster's lack of support in the north were to become all too evident in the early months of 1322 when a northern army, led by Andrew de Harclay of Carlisle, was to bring about his downfall at Boroughbridge.

³⁴⁸ *CCR, 1318–23*, 367–8; *PW*, II, ii, 159. This was the meeting to which Edward also summoned the Marchers, who did not of course attend. The government was so preoccupied with the situation in England that when the bishop of Hereford returned from Gascony in mid-April he was unable for several weeks to obtain answers to urgent questions sent by the seneschal: SC 1/54/139; BL, Add. Ms. 9951, f. 9v; Phillips, 205–6.

the kingdom. They advised Edward to summon the magnates to a parliament where he could hear and settle their complaints according to law.[349]

Three things appear to have emerged from this meeting of the council. First of all Edward followed the moderate advice and on 15 May parliament was summoned to meet at Westminster on 15 July.[350] Secondly, at the end of May preparations were made to send the Younger Despenser to France on royal business: the intention may have been to gain sympathy and perhaps help from the French court, while also keeping Despenser out of the way of the Marchers.[351] Edward accompanied his favourite to the Channel coast at Minster-in-Thanet, which he reached on 12 or 13 June. From here it would have been only a short crossing to France. Minster-in-Thanet was also close to the abbey of Langdon, whose abbot William was a personal friend of Edward II.[352] This gives some plausibility to the statement by a Canterbury chronicler that Despenser went to France disguised in the habit of a monk of Langdon.[353] However, these plans did not work out as intended. The earl of Pembroke, who was supposed to accompany Despenser on the same errand, was in any case returning to France for purposes of his own, his marriage to Marie de St Pol, and by this time his personal opinion of Despenser was almost certainly hostile. According to the same Canterbury chronicler, Despenser went as far as Paris, but left soon after and returned to England for fear of the earl of Pembroke and the information that the latter was spreading about him at the French court.[354] If Despenser was in France at all, it was for a very brief time and it is more likely, as the *Vita* records, that he went first to Dover and then remained at sea in the Channel after the king had put him under the protection of the sailors of the Cinque Ports.[355] During this time he earned himself even greater notoriety by attacking and seizing two Genoese trading vessels and their valuable cargoes.[356]

[349] *Vita*, 190–1.

[350] *PW*, II, ii, 234–43.

[351] C 81/134/7572; *CCW*, 586. He was supposed to be accompanied by Robert Baldock and the earl of Pembroke. On 8 June the king also sent secret instructions, probably concerning Despenser, to the keepers of the Great Seal, with orders that they were not to be enrolled until after the coming parliament: *CCW*, 521.

[352] Haines, *The Church and Politics*, 137–8, 153 n. 95, 188 n. 51.

[353] Trinity College Cambridge Ms. R.5.41, f. 114v; Phillips, 206.

[354] Trinity College Cambridge Ms. R.5.41, f. 114v. Pembroke had crossed to Boulogne by 2 June and reached Paris by the 22nd: Phillips, 206.

[355] This probably explains why Edward was at Dover between 17 and 23 June, and why he appointed his half-brother, Edmund of Woodstock, as constable of Dover on 16 June: *CFR, 1319–27*, 62; Phillips, 207–8.

[356] *Vita*, 196–7, and note 402. In 1336 Edward III paid 8,000 marks' compensation for this attack to the Genoese: Phillips, ' "Edward II" in Italy', 221–2. There is no obvious motive for this attack, but one possibility is that Despenser had a grievance against Antonio Pessagno, the Genoese merchant and banker who had left English service in 1320, and may have seen this as a good way of punishing him.

The third development at the Westminster council was a decision to send Bartholomew de Badlesmere the steward of the household and Walter Reynolds the archbishop of Canterbury, two of Edward II's most experienced and trusted advisers, to Sherburn to appeal to the magnates to call off their attacks on the Despensers and instead to lay their complaints before parliament. While at Sherburn Badlesmere abruptly and dramatically changed sides.[357] This action was undoubtedly a great surprise at the time: Edward was shocked and deeply angered when the archbishop returned to Westminster with the news.[358] It has also caused difficulty for historians searching for an explanation for Badlesmere's behaviour. It is most unlikely that he was seeking to join Lancaster, who had been hostile to him since his appointment as steward of the household in 1318, and who was waiting for an opportunity to destroy him.[359] Badlesmere's action was probably the result of anger at the Younger Despenser's arrogance and monopoly of royal patronage: while Despenser was gathering lordships in South Wales, Badlesmere had hoped for promotion to the earldom of Kent in his native county where his lands were concentrated,[360] and was bitterly disappointed when Edward II's half-brother Edmund of Woodstock was granted the earldom.[361] Badlesmere's replacement by Edmund as constable of Dover on 16 June was probably an additional cause of grievance.[362] His last recorded action as steward was on 18 June, presumably just before his departure for Sherburn.[363] By the time he reached Yorkshire Badlesmere was probably thoroughly disaffected and open to persuasion, not from Lancaster but from Hereford, whom he knew well, and from Roger Mortimer of Wigmore, whose eldest son had married Badlesmere's daughter in June 1316.[364] Badlesmere was unfortunate in the time and place

---

[357] Trinity College Cambridge Ms. R.5.41, f. 114; BL, Cotton Ms. Nero D.X, f. 111; Phillips, 208; Maddicott, 272–3.

[358] *Flores*, 199; Maddicott, 293.

[359] *Vita*, 198–9; Phillips, 208; Maddicott, 264, 272–3. When Badlesmere was in the north to negotiate with the Scots in Feb. 1321 he was warned that ambushes were being set for him, most likely by Lancaster: SC 1/35/8; C 81/114/5602.

[360] Badlesmere's success in getting his nephew appointed as bishop of Lincoln evidently did not satisfy his own ambitions.

[361] Trinity College Cambridge Ms. R.5.41, f. 114; 'A Rochester account concerning disputes during the parliament of 1321', in *Parliamentary Texts of the Later Middle Ages*, ed. N. Pronay & J. Taylor (Oxford, 1980), 163, 168, from the Historia Roffensis, BL, Cotton Ms., Faustina B.V., f. 36. Edmund was not created earl until 28 July, after the beginning of parliament, and perhaps as a way of adding one more earl to the king's side of the equation. But it is likely that his promotion was being discussed earlier, perhaps at the Westminster council in May. The future status of Edmund, who was born in 1301, had been under consideration since Aug. 1320 when he came to Langley to discuss his marriage with the king and the earl of Pembroke. He was first summoned to parliament in Oct. 1320: SC 1/49/49; Phillips, 190–1; Maddicott, 294.

[362] *CFR, 1319–27*, 62; Phillips, 207–8; Maddicott, 293.

[363] C 53/107, m.1; Phillips, 207–8; Maddicott 293 (who gives 14 June).

[364] DL 27/LS 93; BL, Egerton Roll 8724, m.5; BL, Harleian Ms. 1240, f. 113v (the last two are records of Mortimer charters); Phillips, 208.

of his change of allegiance, but as events turned out he was to play a critical role in the drama which led to the exile of the Despensers in August 1321.

THE MARCHERS DEMAND THE EXILE OF THE DESPENSERS

After the meeting at Sherburn, the earl of Hereford and the other marcher lords came south, unaccompanied by Lancaster, in order to present their demands in the parliament which had begun at Westminster on 15 July.[365] They reached St Albans on about 22 July, and there is evidence that during their stay there and in the days that followed there were attempts by bishops of the Canterbury province to mediate between them and the king, as they had done in 1318. The bishops of London, Salisbury, Ely, Hereford and Chichester went to St Albans to try to make peace but achieved no success and had to return to London with the news that the magnates were demanding the exile of the Despensers.[366]

Following this the magnates moved to Waltham, where they spent four days, and on 29 July reached London.[367] This could have been a very dangerous moment for Edward II. Fortunately he had already acted to ensure the city's loyalty. In return for a pledge from the citizens to hold London against his enemies, on 4 July the eyre, which had caused such unrest, was formally closed.[368] The Marchers nonetheless tried to win over the Londoners. On 29 July the earl of Hereford met delegates from the city at Lancaster's Inn in Holborn, where he spoke softly and emphasized the Younger Despenser's responsibility for the recent eyre. The delegates then informed the king of what had happened. Edward's ambiguous reply, in which he promised to punish all enemies, allowed the mayor, Hamo de Chigwell, to assure the Marchers on 1 August of London's goodwill and indifference to Despenser's fate.[369]

This was sufficient for the Marchers. Instead of trying to enter the city they divided their forces, allegedly numbering about 5,000,[370] into three parts and established themselves at various points outside London. Roger Mortimer stayed at Clerkenwell with his followers; the earl of Hereford in Lancaster's Inn; Roger Damory at the New Temple; and Hugh Audley in

---

[365] *Flores*, 197; *Ann. Paul.*, 293; Phillips, 208–9. In the meantime some of Lancaster's retainers, led by Robert de Holland, attacked Despenser's lands in Leicestershire: Maddicott, 279.

[366] *Ann. Paul.*, 293; *Trokelowe*, 109; BL, Cotton Ms. Nero D. X, f. 111; Phillips, 209; Maddicott, 279.

[367] *Ann. Paul.*, 293–4; Phillips, 209.

[368] Williams, *Medieval London*, 287–8.

[369] *Ann. Paul.*, 295–6; Williams, *Medieval London*, 288.

[370] Their supporters wore 'green tunics, of which a quarter part of the right arm was saffron coloured': 'A Rochester account', in *Parliamentary Texts*, 161, 165–6. Cf. *Trokelowe*, 109. The significance of this choice of uniform is not clear.

the priory of St Bartholomew's in Smithfield. The rest of the magnates found lodgings in Smithfield, Holborn and Fleet Street and in neighbouring places; and they all remained peacefully and without causing any disturbance.[371] Further attempts at mediation now took place. On several occasions the archbishop of Canterbury and the bishops of London, Ely, Salisbury, Lincoln, Hereford, Exeter, Bath & Wells, Chichester and Rochester, and others attending parliament, met the magnates at the New Temple and at the house of the Carmelites to try to make a settlement. But the magnates continued to demand the exile of the Despensers, while the king resolutely refused to make any concessions or even to meet his opponents.[372]

The return of the earl of Pembroke from France in late July appears to have helped break the deadlock. Both the king and the Marchers hoped that they could induce Pembroke to give them his support. On 1 August the king wrote to Pembroke asking him to come to Westminster the next day to give his advice on the situation, requesting Pembroke to come via Lambeth so that a boat might be sent for him.[373] According to one apparently well-informed source, the magnates made contact with Pembroke and with three other earls who had so far remained loyal to the king, Richmond, Arundel and Surrey, and put pressure on them to join their ranks, however unwillingly;[374] while the *Vita Edwardi Secundi* suggests that all four took an oath to uphold the magnates' demands.[375] After their meeting with the magnates, Pembroke and the other earls returned to the king in the guise of mediators, bringing with them the baronial ultimatum that, unless the Despensers were removed, the king himself would be deposed. Pembroke told the king to take note of the power of the magnates and not to risk losing his kingdom for the sake of his favourites. He added that the barons had attacked the Despensers for the common good, which the king had sworn to uphold at his coronation. Pembroke concluded with the ominous statement that, if the king refused the magnates' demands, even his loyalty would be lost because of the oath he had taken.[376]

THE 'HISTORIA ROFFENSIS' ACCOUNT

This is a very bare outline of the drama which took place during the parliament of July–August 1322. However, the Historia Roffensis, possibly

---

[371] *Ann. Paul.*, 293–4; Phillips, 209.

[372] *Ann. Paul.*, 294–6; *Vita*, 190–3; Phillips, 209; Maddicott, 279–80.

[373] SC 1/49/50; Phillips, 209. Pembroke had probably just come from Dover via his manors in Kent. His new wife, Marie de St Pol, reached Westminster on 8 Aug.: *Ann. Paul.*, 292.

[374] '*In partem suam licet involuntarie attraxerunt*': BL, Cotton Ms., Nero D.X., f. 111; Phillips, 209–10.

[375] *Vita*, 192–3.

[376] *Vita*, 192–3; *Melsa*, 338; Phillips, 210; Maddicott, 280.

composed by William de Dene, a clerk in the service of Hamo de Hethe, the bishop of Rochester, adds very significant details to this account of events. It records that the four earls met the opposition magnates at Clerkenwell on 27 July and, as in the *Vita Edwardi Secundi* account, agreed to support them.[377] Again like the *Vita*, it stresses the role played by the earl of Pembroke in the final stages of the crisis in persuading Edward to accept the magnates' demands, making it clear that he acted on the side of the barons, since he 'made all his speeches in their interest and against that of the king'. When Pembroke moved that the Despensers should be sent into exile and their heirs disinherited, Edward replied that it was unjust and contrary to his oath that anyone should be disinherited without a hearing, and that it would be better if they went to Ireland for a time until the magnates' anger had cooled. Edward accepted that they had behaved badly towards the magnates but he did not consider them traitors. Pembroke replied that Edward must choose between war with his people or the exile of the Despensers.[378]

The Historia Roffensis also records that a number of bishops were present as mediators at the Clerkenwell meeting on 27 July and therefore refused to take the oath to support the barons. The barons then sent the earls and prelates to the king, together with two knights who carried the magnates' petition. The petition, which is not recorded elsewhere, stated: 'Sire, our masters tell you that they hold both Lord Hugh Despenser, and his son, enemies and traitors to you and to the kingdom, and for this they wish them to be removed from here. And because of this they ask you that you have them brought before parliament to answer, and to restore by award of the peers that which they have destroyed. Ensure that they come, and that they are exiled out of the land for all time and they and their heirs are disinherited as false and traitorous criminals and spies.' Edward refused to accept the petition since the knights did not have written authority for their mission.[379]

In an extraordinary passage, which is not matched in any of the other sources, the Historia Roffensis records that the prelates and barons then reassembled at the house of the Carmelites. Here Bartholomew de Badlesmere took the lead in denouncing Hugh Despenser the Younger as a traitor. Badlesmere claimed that he had conspired against the king and produced as evidence a copy of the *'Homage et serment'* declaration

---

[377] BL, Cotton Ms., Faustina B.V., f. 35v. For the text and a translation of the Historia Roffensis account see 'A Rochester account', in *Parliamentary Texts*, 155–73. For a discussion of the Historia Roffensis see *Parliamentary Texts*, 155–9; and Maddicott, 280–2; and for the career of Hamo de Hethe (Hythe) see the article by M.C. Buck in the *Oxford DNB*. Although Hamo's election as bishop in 1317 had been hotly contested by Giovanni di Puzzuoli, Isabella's chaplain, for whom the pope had reserved the see, Hamo was sympathetic to Edward II in the crises of 1321 and at the end of the reign.

[378] *Parliamentary Texts*, 164, 168.

[379] Ibid., 162, 166.

distinguishing between the authority of the crown and the person of the king, which had originally been composed in 1308 in order to justify the baronial attack on Gaveston. Despenser was alleged to have used the document in his own interest, showing the declaration to two barons, Sir Richard Grey and Sir John Giffard, and a knight, Sir Robert de Shirland, who were now presented as witnesses. Having questioned Grey, the bishop of Rochester concluded that Badlesmere was lying and that he and the magnates were attempting to lay false evidence against Despenser and detested them from that time on.[380]

THE CHARGES AGAINST THE DESPENSERS

Five versions of the charges against the Despensers are now known to exist, all of them in French except for a Latin version in the Bridlington chronicle.[381] The other four are preserved in the archives of the Dean and Chapter at Durham;[382] in manuscripts at Canterbury and at Lambeth,[383] and in the final official version enrolled both on the Parliament Roll[384] and on the Close Roll.[385] The versions probably reflect an initial document drawn up at the Sherburn assembly at the end of June, in the wake of the articles read out by Sir John Bek,[386] and others drawn up in London as negotiations proceeded between the king and his opponents. One important difference between the Canterbury and Bridlington versions and the final indictment of the Despensers is that the barons initially wanted the charges against them and their sentence of exile to be contained in a statute, which required royal consent, and could not be imposed upon the king against his will.[387] This form of the magnates' demands may have been communicated to the king while the barons were still at St Albans and before their arrival in London,[388] or drawn up during the session of

---

[380] Ibid., 162–3, 166–8.
[381] *Gesta Edwardi*, 65–9.
[382] Durham, Dean & Chapter Muniments, Locellus I, no. 61, published in Prestwich, 'Charges'.
[383] Canterbury, Register I, f. 376, *et seq*. (Wilkinson's Ms. A) published in Wilkinson, 'The Sherburn indenture', App. V, 23–7; Lambeth Ms. 1213, ff. 286–90 (Wilkinson's Ms. B), text compared with that in Canterbury in Wilkinson, App. V.
[384] *PROME*, Parliament of July 1321, SC 9/24, item 2.
[385] *CCR, 1318–23*, 492–4; *SR*, i, 181–4.
[386] The St Albans chronicler, John Trokelowe, states that an initial set of articles against the Despensers was composed at Sherburn: *Trokelowe*, 107–8. The Durham text, which is the shortest of the texts, may as Prestwich, 'Charges' 95–6, suggests, be a copy of the earliest version.
[387] Maddicott, 283–4; Prestwich, 'Charges', 97. This prompts the further reflection that the famous additional fourth clause in Edward II's coronation oath of 1308 was, as argued in ch. 4 of this book, not intended to be revolutionary, since it assumed that the king would assent to future legislation not that he could be forced to accept it.
[388] Maddicott, 283–4.

parliament in late July or early August.[389] Edward flatly refused to accept a statute and the indictment was eventually presented to parliament in the form of an award by the peers of the realm which did not require royal assent.[390] The award was consequently recorded on the Parliament Roll and the Close Roll but not on the Statute Roll.[391] The Despensers were given no opportunity to defend themselves. The precedent set by the attack on Gaveston in 1308 had been repeated.[392]

There are other differences between the early drafts of the indictment against the Despensers and the final version. In the Durham version the Younger Despenser was accused of disinheriting peers of the land in order to become earl of Gloucester, whereas in the final document he was charged with trying to obtain the entire earldom of Gloucester but not the title:[393] a small but significant difference which suggests that the magnates had second thoughts and that however ruthless the Younger Despenser was this was one charge which could not be made to stick.

The major difference between the early versions and the final indictment is in their treatment of the '*Homage et serment*' document. In 1321 this was an obvious starting-point and justification for the magnates' actions against the Despensers and for opposing Edward II's support of them without at the same time opposing the crown as an institution. It might therefore be expected that the declaration would be used once more, as it had been in 1308, and it is very likely that this was in the minds of the earl of Lancaster and the other magnates who joined him at Sherburn in late June 1321.[394] It is also interesting to note that the Bridlington chronicler who recorded the articles in French which were drawn up at Sherburn

---

[389] Prestwich, 'Charges', 97, who notes that the Canterbury and Bridlington texts both refer to a statute being made *en ceo parlement*. On the other hand, while a statute could only be made in parliament, the need for one could have been signalled in advance.

[390] Maddicott, 284; Prestwich, 'Charges', 97.

[391] *PROME*, Parliament of July 1321, SC 9/24, item 2; *CCR, 1318–23*, 492–4. There is however considerable confusion on this matter, not helped by the fact that the text printed by the nineteenth-century editors of the *Statutes of the Realm* (*SR*, i, 181–4) relied on the Close Roll. The *Vita Edwardi Secundi* claims that a statute was enacted against the Despensers, while the Historia Roffensis speaks ambiguously about both an award and a statute, and the 1327 Parliament Roll records that the Despensers' exile had been brought about by statute in parliament. However, the contemporary official record in 1321 refers clearly to an award, while the magnates' petition in 1321 for pardon for their attack on the Despensers states specifically that the Despensers' misdeeds could not have been punished by process of law: *Vita*, 194–5; *Parliamentary Texts*, 164, 168; *PROME*, Parliament of 1327, C 65/1, item 1; *PROME*, Parliament of 1321, SC 9/24, item 3; *CCR, 1318–23*, 495; Wilkinson, 'The Sherburn indenture', 16; Maddicott, 283–4.

[392] Maddicott, 285–6. It might be added that the conviction of the Despensers by award provided a precedent for the trial and execution of the earl of Lancaster only a few months later in 1322 and of Roger Mortimer of Wigmore in 1330.

[393] Prestwich, 'Charges', 99.

[394] The original declaration was drawn up in 1308 not far from Sherburn at Pontefract, then one of the castles belonging to the earl of Lincoln and now in the hands of his son-in-law and successor Thomas of Lancaster.

included a Latin translation of the '*Homage et serment*' declaration immediately before entering his version, also in Latin, of the articles against the Despensers.³⁹⁵ However, there is evidence that the '*Homage et serment*' declaration was not made use of in the earliest version of the articles, since it does not appear either in the text preserved at Durham or in the Canterbury version.³⁹⁶ If the suggestion made earlier that the proceedings at Sherburn were undertaken using the treatise on the steward to justify baronial action is correct, then the declaration became surplus to baronial requirements and there was consequently no need to include it in the draft articles against the Despensers.

It is clear however that the declaration re-emerged in the course of the debates after the magnates reached London at the end of July. The statement in the Historia Roffensis that Badlesmere produced a copy of it and alleged that it had been used against the king by the Younger Despenser is apparently inexplicable. One is tempted to agree either with the bishop of Rochester that Badlesmere was engaged in a blatant falsehood or with Wilkinson's argument that because of Edward II's stubborn refusal to accept the barons' demands the opposition magnates were forced to humiliate themselves publicly not only by dropping the declaration but implicitly condemning it by imputing its use to Despenser.³⁹⁷ However, Badlesmere's charge against Despenser is so bizarre that it is unlikely to have been made up. His action reflected recent power struggles within the royal circle between himself in his role as steward of the royal household and would-be earl of Kent on the one hand and Hugh Despenser the Younger as royal favourite, chamberlain of the household and would-be controller of the earldom of Gloucester on the other. Badlesmere's accusation against Despenser may have seemed to lend support to the general allegation against the Despensers of usurping royal power, with which the articles against them began, but it is conceivable that a man of such arrogance and ambition as Despenser may also have thought that he knew better than the king where the king's best interests lay and so have been attracted by the arguments in the '*Homage et serment*'. Since the declaration was no longer required to justify the magnates' own position it could now in effect be recycled and used against Despenser.

The final version of the indictment first of all noted that in the York parliament of October 1318 the Younger Despenser was confirmed as

---

³⁹⁵ *Gesta Edwardi*, 65. The same author also included a Latin version of the declaration in 1308: ibid., 33–4. The two Latin versions are not identical, which suggests that the author made a new translation in 1321, using a French copy of the declaration which was circulating at Sherburn.

³⁹⁶ Prestwich, 'Charges', 95; Maddicott, 284. In Canterbury Register I (Wilkinson's Ms. A) the declaration follows the Sherburn indenture and precedes the articles against the Despensers. In Lambeth Ms. 1213 (Wilkinson's Ms. B) and in the official record the declaration is an integral part of the articles: Wilkinson, 'The Sherburn indenture', 11.

³⁹⁷ Wilkinson, 'The Sherburn indenture', 18.

chamberlain and that 'it was also agreed that certain prelates and other great men of the realm were to remain close to the king season by season, to better counsel our lord the king, without whom no important matter of business ought to be conducted'. Despenser was accused of having drawn 'over to his cause Sir Hugh his father, whose remaining close to the king in this way had not been assented to or agreed to in parliament, and between them usurping to themselves royal power from the king, his ministers and the government of his realm, to the dishonour of the king, the impairment of the crown, and the destruction of the realm, and of the great men and the people, and they committed the misdeeds written below, plotting to distance the affection of our lord the king from the peers of the land, to have sole government of the realm between the two of them'. There then followed the '*Homage et serment*' declaration. Despenser was now alleged to have used the declaration in his own interest, because he 'was angry with the king, and because of this anger made a bill, with the which bill he wished to make an alliance with Sir John Giffard of Brimpsfield, and Sir Richard de Grey, and others, to lead the king to do his will by duress, with the result that he did not forgive him when he did not do it'. 'And also, by their scheming and misdeeds, they led and badly counselled our lord the king, so that his presence, which it is his duty to show to the great men and to his people, and to the graces and right which they might ask him to answer, was not shown by him at all, except at the will and at the bidding of the said Sir Hugh and Sir Hugh, which ousted the king from his duty, against his oath, and the affection of the great men and people from their liege lord'. 'Also, the same men by their false scheming did not allow the great men of the realm, or the good counsellors of the king, to speak with or approach the king, to counsel him well, nor the king to speak with them, except in the presence and hearing of the said Sir Hugh and Sir Hugh, or of one of them, and at their will and bidding and as they chose, alienating the great men and the good counsellors of the king from their good will towards their liege lord, and usurping royal power, mastery and sovereignty over the king's person for themselves, to the great dishonour and peril of the king, of the crown, and of his realm. And also, they wrongly counselled our lord the king to take into his hand the lands and chattels of Sir Hugh Audley the son, and they forejudged him of his lands without due process, according to the law of the land, through the desire to accroach these lands to the said Hugh Despenser the son; and by other false schemes they plotted to have the lands of Sir Roger Damory, to obtain by such false schemes the entire earldom of Gloucester, to the disinheritance of the peers of the land.' The Despensers were also charged that 'they falsely and wickedly counselled our lord the king to go with horses and arms to the region of Gloucester, and they caused him to ride out, and his men to go armed in those parts, to attack his good people, against the terms of the Great Charter, and the judgment of the peers of the land: and thus by their false and wicked counsel they preferred to have war in the land, to the destruction of holy church and of the people, for their own cause'. A number of other charges followed,[398] before the indictment reached its conclusion and the Despensers were sentenced to be exiled.[399]

EDWARD CORNERED

Under intense pressure and in fear that he might even lose his throne if he did not give way, on 14 August Edward came into Westminster Hall, flanked by the earls of Pembroke and Richmond.[400] The earls and barons then declared that if the law of the land did not provide for the exile of the Despensers, 'they had the power, since they were peers of the realm, to promulgate and establish a new law in full parliament in accordance with the custom of the realm, following which custom they immediately afterward determined and decreed that the said Hugh and Hugh should be exiled by due process without hope of returning and with their heirs being disinherited for all time'. The baronial award was then read out by the earl of Hereford, and the Despensers were sentenced to leave England via the port of Dover no later than 29 August, never to return except with the agreement of the king, prelates and magnates in parliament. If they returned without permission they would be treated as enemies of the king and the kingdom.[401] Afterwards the king, 'anxious and sad, went to his chamber having said farewell to the bishops', who had stayed in the large chamber during the proceedings in Westminster Hall.[402] The magnates then petitioned the king for pardon for their attacks on the Despensers;[403] and on 20 August 1321 the pardon was issued in the form of a statute assented to and agreed by the king, prelates, earls and barons.[404]

If Edward had believed that in summoning parliament he might save the Despensers from further attack, he was entirely disappointed. The meeting had instead turned out to be the gravest crisis of his reign to date.

---

[398] Including the appointment of justices who were not sufficiently qualified in the law, such as the Elder Despenser and Sir John Inge (the Younger Despenser's retainer), in order to deprive great men such as the earl of Hereford and Sir John Giffard of their lands; the execution of Llywelyn Bren, the leader of the revolt in Glamorgan in 1316, who had surrendered to the earl of Hereford and Roger Mortimer of Wigmore under guarantee of protection; the seizure of Gower from Sir John de Mowbray.

[399] This is a summary of the indictment as recorded on the Parliament Roll: *PROME*, Parliament of 1321, SC 9/24, item 2.

[400] *Ann. Paul.*, 297; *Vita*, 191–7; *French Chronicle of London*, ed. G. J. Aungier, xxviii (London, 1844), 42; *CCR, 1318–23*, 494; Phillips, 210; Maddicott, 280.

[401] *Parliamentary Texts*, 163–4, 168–9, where the award is mistakenly described as a statute; *Ann. Paul.*, 297; *Vita*, 191–7; *French Chron.*, 42; *CCR, 1318–23*, 494; Phillips, 210; Maddicott, 280–2.

[402] *Parliamentary Texts*, 163–4, 168–9.

[403] *PROME*, Parliament of July 1321, SC 9/24, item 3; *CCR, 1318–23*, 495.

[404] *PROME*, Parliament of July 1321, SC 9/24/ item 4; *SR*, i, 185–7.

The earl of Pembroke, one of Edward's most experienced and trusted councillors had turned against him; even his own wife, Isabella, had allegedly gone down on her knees and urged him to give way for the sake of his throne.[405] Edward's only cause for joy in the summer of 1321 was the birth of his and Isabella's fourth and last child, Joan, at the Tower of London on 5 July.[406] Isabella's own joy at the event was tempered by a leaky roof and the rain which allegedly fell upon her bed while she was in labour.[407]

Edward was determined to avenge his personal humiliation at the earliest opportunity. On 16 August, he whispered to the bishop of Rochester while at dinner, complaining that the Despensers had been condemned unjustly. When the bishop replied that he could totally overcome the defeat, Edward said 'that he would within half a year make such an amend that the whole world would hear of it and tremble'.[408] And so it proved.

PART THREE

THE ROAD TO CIVIL WAR

Edward II was always at his 'best' and most active when faced with a challenge to his personal dignity and that of his crown. As in the case of Gaveston at the beginning of his reign, Edward's one ambition from August 1321 was the return of the Despensers from exile, and there is every indication that he deliberately sought and planned for a clash with the opposition magnates.

Both Despensers had already left England before their sentence of exile was pronounced. The Elder Despenser may have gone to Poitou,[409] while the Younger Despenser remained at sea in the English Channel, under the protection of the men of the Cinque Ports.[410] Edward II's itinerary shows that he was on the isle of Sheppey on 31 August, at Minster-in-Thanet between about 5 and 8 September and finally at Harwich between about 12 and 20 September. Edward and the Younger Despenser could have communicated at any of these places, but it is likely that they met at

---

[405] *Ann. Paul.*, 297.

[406] *Ann. Paul.*, 291. Joan was probably conceived at the time of the Westminster parliament in Oct. 1320. He and Isabella were at Sheen (Richmond) at the beginning of that month. As noted above, Edward appears to have been in particularly good spirits at the time.

[407] *Munimenta Gildhallae Lond.*, ed. Riley, II, i, 409. This accident is given as the reason for John Cromwell's removal as constable of the Tower, but Edward had given Isabella custody of the Tower on 14 June; on 14 July he also gave her custody of the Great Seal: Doherty (D. Phil.), 82; BL, Add. Charter 26,684, *CCR, 1318–23*, 477. He probably hoped that the Marchers would desist from attacking her.

[408] *Parliamentary Texts*, 164, 169.

[409] '*Pictaviam*': *Flores*, 198. The *Vita Edwardi Secundi*, 196–7, says simply that he went overseas. There is no evidence to confirm the statement in Fryde, 49, that he went to Bordeaux.

[410] *Vita*, 196–7; Phillips, 215; Maddicott, 292.

Minster-in-Thanet and that they went by sea to Harwich where they planned their revenge on the magnates.[411] By 25 September Edward was back at Westminster ready to put his plans into effect.

The magnates in the meantime had withdrawn from London only as far as Oxford, from where they could exert pressure on the king if he tried to recall the Despensers. They kept their military skills polished by holding a tournament at Witney in late August or early September, in which the earl of Pembroke and his men took part against Hereford and Badlesmere.[412] Edward was alarmed that Pembroke might remain with the other magnates and sent a messenger to him on 31 August.[413] He need not have worried. However much Pembroke disapproved of the Despensers and their behaviour, he had no option but to rejoin the king, partly because of his past loyalty but also because Lancaster distrusted him and warned the barons that they should not accept his help.[414] Pembroke was with the king at Harwich on 19 September and became heavily involved in what followed.[415]

Hereford and the other magnates were in a difficult position. The treatise on the steward had given them a legal framework justifying their pursuit of the Despensers and the demands for their exile. They had been careful to display banners showing the arms of the king alongside their own when they attacked the Despensers, so as not to incur the charges of rebellion and treason.[416] They had hoped to obtain the king's approval of the charges against the Despensers in the form of a statute; and their case had been presented by the earl of Hereford, the constable of England, possibly representing in that capacity the absent steward of England, the earl of Lancaster.[417] But the king's intransigence meant they had to be satisfied with an award against the Despensers rather than a statute. In

---

[411] *Murimuth*, 33; Maddicott, 292. Murimuth says specifically that Edward met him and they reached Harwich by sea.

[412] Trinity College Cambridge Ms. R.5.41, f. 115; Phillips, 215. Pembroke's manor of Bampton was nearby.

[413] SC 1/49/51; Phillips, 215. The contents of the message are unknown but its bearer, William de Cusaunce, was in the service of the Younger Despenser.

[414] *Vita*, 198–201; Phillips, 215; Maddicott, 326.

[415] C 53/108, m.8; Phillips, 215; Maddicott, 292.

[416] *PROME*, Parliament of July 1321, SC 9/24/ items 3, 4 (petition for pardon and the royal statute of pardon).

[417] It has been suggested that the treatise known as the *Modus Tenendi Parliamentum* was another significant document produced by Lancaster or in his circle in 1321 as part of the preparation for the July parliament. There are as Dr Maddicott has argued (Maddicott, 289–92) some echoes of the treatise on the steward: in, for example, the provision in article 17 that if disputes arise which threaten the peace of the land, the steward, constable and marshal, or any two of them, could appoint a committee of 25 to decide the matter. There are several other references in the *Modus* to the role to be played in parliament by the steward (articles 13, 14). However, the conclusions of recent scholarship suggest that Lancaster's association with the *Modus* is far from certain, and that it was probably a 'procedural tract' produced by a chancery or exchequer clerk around the early 1320s but without

their petition for pardon they had also been forced to admit that they had made alliances without the permission of the king, and had ridden with banners unfurled, and seized and occupied castles, lands and goods, and imprisoned, held to ransom and killed people of the king's allegiance and of others, and committed various other acts while attacking the Despensers and their allies in England, in Wales and in the March, some of which could be called trespasses, and some felonies.[418] Although the pardon they received from the king took the form of a statute,[419] they could not know whether Edward would keep his promise and so remained vulnerable to a royal counterattack. They also had no way of knowing whether Thomas of Lancaster would intervene to help them if the king resorted to force or whether he would again try to guide events from afar while remaining safely behind the walls of his castle at Pontefract.

There were other weaknesses too. Some of the bishops, who had so often played the role of mediators in the past, were unsympathetic to the magnates and in some cases, such as the bishop of Rochester, openly hostile.[420] Several of the prelates, such as the two archbishops, the chancellor the bishop of Norwich, and the treasurer the bishop of Exeter, were

---

any specific connection to the 1321 parliament. Such a clerk might also have had legal training. Possible authors are men such as William Airmyn, keeper of the rolls of chancery from 1316 to 1324, and probably also clerk of the parliament, or an exchequer clerk such as William Maldon, one of the chamberlains of the exchequer who was in the circle of Walter Stapeldon, treasurer for much of the period between 1320 and 1325. 'All we can say with certainty,' argue Pronay and Taylor (*Parliamentary Texts*, 31), 'is that the author was most likely a lawyer, and certainly a person well acquainted with the working of parliament.' The author of the *Modus* considers that 'parliament' is an assembly which comprises the king, the lords, and the representatives of the various communities. He is emphatic that without the presence of these representatives there can be no ' "parliament" . . . [and that] of all the possible forms of assemblies in which the king might choose to meet his subjects, "parliament" is the one in which *all* the representatives of the communities meet the king for such business as lies between them'. Thus many kinds of assembly were held during the first 40 years of the fourteenth century, some of them involving the knights, burgesses and lower clergy as representatives, and others not, and there is no reason to believe either that the author of the *Modus Tenendi Parliamentum* was describing any particular parliament or that he believed that a parliament was the only forum in which important business might be concluded. While it is possible that the author of the *Modus* had access to the treatise on the steward (in seven manuscripts the *Modus* is followed by the treatise: Maddicott, 289), there is nothing in the text of the *Modus* which links it in any obvious way with the political crisis of 1321. As a commentary on current controversy (assuming it was written in 1321) the *Modus* is a curiously silent document. For the text and translation of the *Modus* and a guide to the past debate on the subject see *Parliamentary Texts*, 65–114, and 1–63, esp. 25–31. See also the valuable discussion of the *Modus* in Prestwich, *Plantagenet England*, 224–6. We are in agreement that, while the *Modus* remains a mystery in many respects, it does not fit a Lancastrian agenda in 1321.

[418] *PROME*, Parliament of July 1321, SC 9/24/ item 3; *CCR, 1318–23*, 495.
[419] *PROME*, Parliament of July 1321, SC 9/24/ item 4; *SR*, i, 185–7.
[420] *Parliamentary Texts*, Historia Roffensis, 162–4, 166–7, 169.

actively involved on the king's side. Among the senior magnates Edward could rely upon the support of his two half-brothers, Thomas of Brotherton earl of Norfolk and Edmund of Woodstock the newly created earl of Kent; the earls of Pembroke and Richmond; and probably the earls of Arundel and Surrey. Edward could also call on the services of a relatively small but experienced body of household knights: these were to play a key role in the coming civil war.[421]

THE SIEGE OF LEEDS CASTLE

In September the earl of Hereford, Hugh Audley and Roger Damory were ordered to hand over to royal keepers the Despenser lands which they had occupied. The orders were predictably ignored and were probably designed to provide a *casus belli*.[422] Edward first chose to attack Bartholomew of Badlesmere, both because he regarded Badlesmere's treachery in joining the Marchers as unpardonable and because Lancaster's hostility towards Badlesmere meant there was a good chance of destroying him without baronial intervention.[423] On 26 September Edward ordered Badlesmere to give up custody of Tonbridge castle. Badlesmere reacted by crossing into Kent from Tilbury, putting his castles at Chilham and Leeds into a state of defence, and then rejoining the Marchers at Oxford.[424] In early October Edward and Isabella left Westminster, ostensibly on pilgrimage to Canterbury,[425] but with other things in mind. Instead Isabella went to Leeds to request hospitality from Badlesmere's wife in the hope that she would not admit her and that Badlesmere could then be justifiably attacked. Badlesmere had meanwhile heard of Edward's intentions and rose to the bait.[426] On 3 October Isabella was refused admission, as expected, and several of her followers were killed.[427]

Edward received the news at Witley in Surrey where he was waiting[428] and reacted swiftly but deliberately. He immediately went to rejoin the Younger Despenser, probably at Portchester between Portsmouth and

---

[421] Altogether 33 royal knights fought for him in 1321–2: Tebbit, 'Royal patronage', 197; idem, 'Household knights and military service', 88–91.

[422] *CCR, 1318–23*, 402, 408; Phillips, 216.

[423] Trinity College Cambridge Ms. R.5.41, ff. 114, 114v; *Vita*, 198–9; *CPR, 1321–24*, 47–8; Phillips, 216; Maddicott, 293.

[424] *CFR, 1319–27*, 71; Trinity College Cambridge Ms. R.5.41, ff. 114v, 115; Phillips, 216; Maddicott, 293.

[425] *Ann. Paul.*, 298.

[426] Trinity College Cambridge Ms. R.5.41, f. 115: '*ut negatus sit introitus in castellum*'; BL, Cotton Ms. Nero D.X, f. 111; Phillips, 216; Maddicott, 293.

[427] Trinity College Cambridge Ms. R.5.41, f. 115 (which gives the date as 3 Oct.); *Ann. Paul.*, 298–9 (which gives the date as 13 Oct.); Phillips, 216; Maddicott, 293.

[428] E 101/378/14, m.3.

Southampton,⁴²⁹ and over the next few days they laid their plans. On 16 October Edward announced that he would begin to besiege Leeds on 23 October, sending the earls of Pembroke, Norfolk and Richmond as an advance guard.⁴³⁰ Badlesmere persuaded Hereford and the Mortimers to go to the relief of Leeds,⁴³¹ but the baronial army moved only as far as Kingston upon Thames, where it stopped on 27 October. Its leaders then entered into tentative negotiations with the archbishop of Canterbury, the bishop of London and the earl of Pembroke who promised that if the magnates retreated they would try to mediate with the king. The magnates replied that if Edward raised the siege of Leeds they would surrender the castle after the next parliament. Any chance of success was ended by Lancaster, who wrote from his safe retreat at Pontefract, persuading the magnates to do nothing to help Badlesmere.⁴³² Hereford and his allies withdrew northwards, accompanied by Badlesmere, and on 31 October Leeds castle surrendered.⁴³³ The following day Walter Culpeper the commander of the garrison and twelve others were executed. Badlesmere's wife and children, his nephew Bartholomew de Burghersh (brother of the bishop of Lincoln) and others were sent to the Tower of London.⁴³⁴ Since Edward was at Leeds from 25 October until after the end of the siege,⁴³⁵ there can be no doubt that he was personally responsible for these actions. The battle lines were drawn: those who had already opposed the king were irredeemably his enemies;⁴³⁶ those who might have wavered had no choice but to follow Edward come what may. This was to be a war to the death.

Both sides now prepared for open conflict. Before 11 November Warwick castle had been seized by royal opponents in the Midlands,⁴³⁷ while there were fears that, despite its contribution of 500 men to the siege of Leeds, London might be harbouring enemies of the king. Shortly before 17 November Pembroke was sent there to ensure the city's loyalty in the coming struggle. He met with mixed success: an angry exchange of letters

---

⁴²⁹ Edward was there between 4 and 13 Oct.: E 101/378/14, m.3. This was easily reached from Witley and is far more likely than Thanet, which is usually given as their meeting place: cf. Phillips, 216.

⁴³⁰ *CCR, 1318–23*, 504; *CPR, 1321–24*, 29; *Ann. Paul.*, 299; Phillips, 216–17; Maddicott, 293.

⁴³¹ Trinity College Cambridge Ms. R.5.41, f. 115; Phillips, 217; Maddicott, 293–4.

⁴³² *Murimuth*, 34; *Melsa*, 339; *Vita*, 196–9; *Anonimalle*, 102–3; Phillips, 217; Maddicott, 293–4.

⁴³³ Trinity College Cambridge Ms. R.5.41, f. 115v; *Ann. Paul.*, 299; *French Chron.*, 43; Phillips, 217; Maddicott, 294.

⁴³⁴ *Ann. Paul.*, 299; *Anonimalle*, 102–3.

⁴³⁵ E 101/378/14, m.3.

⁴³⁶ After the fall of Leeds Edward ordered the seizure of lands belonging to the earl of Hereford, Audley and Damory: *Vita*, 198–9. Hereford, for example, held an important manor and castle at Pleshey in Essex, which was within easy reach of royal forces.

⁴³⁷ *CCR, 1318–23*, 503; Phillips, 217.

between Edward and the mayor Hamo de Chigwell ensued. Although the mayor eventually promised a force of 500 men, Edward commented that the citizens 'took the king's affairs less to heart than they were accustomed'. For the moment harmony was restored but the omens were bad, should the king prove victorious and try to impose his will upon the Londoners.[438]

THE STEWARD OF ENGLAND'S LAST THROW

In the north Lancaster was again stirring. On 18 October, acting in his capacity as steward of England, he summoned a meeting of the Marchers and other magnates at Doncaster on 29 November.[439] Although there was once some doubt as to whether the meeting ever took place, it is now clear that a gathering was held.[440] The document which was drawn up, generally known as the Doncaster Petition, began with a justification of the actions of Lancaster and his fellow magnates which clearly draws on the treatise on the steward.[441] After referring to Magna Carta, which had been confirmed by the king, and to the Ordinances which he had granted and which Lancaster and the barons were sworn to maintain,[442] the petition went on to accuse the Younger Despenser of encouraging the king to attack the peers of the realm and to seize their lands, contrary to Magna Carta. Edward was charged with maintaining Despenser, despite his sentence of exile, and of encouraging him in his career of piracy.[443] The

---

[438] *Ann. Paul.*, 299–301; *Calendar of the Letter-Books: E*, ed. Sharpe, 151–6; Williams, *Medieval London*, 289–90; Phillips, 217; Maddicott, 297–8.

[439] G.L. Haskins, 'The Doncaster petition of 1321', *EHR*, liii (1938), 479, 483, citing BL, Cotton Ms. Cleopatra D. IX, f. 81v; Phillips, 217; Maddicott, 295, 297. Copies of the letter of summons to John d'Engayne, dated at Pontefract on 18 Oct., and of the letter addressed to the city of London, dated at Pontefract on 2 Dec., describe Lancaster as steward of England, and clearly show that the stewardship was the basis of his claims to action and authority throughout the events of 1321–2: Haskins, 483; Bod., Kent Rolls 6, f. On 12 Nov. the king wrote to 108 individuals, including the earl of Hereford, Roger Damory, the Audleys and the Mortimers, but significantly not including Badlesmere who was clearly considered to be a pariah by both sides: *Foedera*, II, ii, 459. It is likely that William de Aune, the constable of Tickhill (not far from both Doncaster and Pontefract), was again the source of information on Lancaster's activities.

[440] *Chroniques de Sempringham*, 338; BL, Cotton Ms. Nero D.X, f. 111v; Bod., Kent Rolls 6, f; Phillips, 217–18; Maddicott, 297–8.

[441] It states that 'various grievances have been shown to "us" (i.e. to Lancaster as steward) and to our other good peers of the land ["*a nous e a nos autres bon piers de la tere*"], blemishing the state of the realm and of the crown, which we are sworn to save and maintain according to our powers, by force of which oath we are charged to show these grievances to your lordship'.

[442] In a clear reference to clause 39 of Magna Carta, the petition goes on to say that kings had promised not to take, imprison or disinherit anyone of their franchises; not to outlaw or exile anyone, etc., except by judgment of their peers and the law of the land.

[443] Phillips, 218; Maddicott, 300–1. For the full text of the Doncaster petition, see Haskins, 'Doncaster petition', 483–5. A mutilated text of the petition is contained in Bod., Kent Rolls 6, f.

document was then sent to the king in the names of the earl of Lancaster, steward of England, the earl of Hereford, Roger Mortimer of Wigmore, and 'other good men of the land, in order to maintain the state of the Crown'.[444] Edward was asked to answer the petition by 20 December.[445] His only response was to comment that in making such demands Lancaster was treating him as if he were the earl's subject.[446]

THE RECALL OF THE DESPENSERS

Throughout 1321 Lancaster and the Marchers had followed the forms of legality, and had protested their loyalty to the crown, but they were living increasingly in a world of legal fantasy. It was not at all clear what they proposed to do when, as was now inevitable, the king refused to accept their demands. Violence was the only likely outcome.

Edward had already decided to use force by 15 November, when he announced that he was going to various parts of the realm to deal with the activities of malefactors, although he was careful to deny that he was going to make war. On 28 November Roger Damory and Hugh Audley were again ordered to give up the Despenser lands they had occupied, and Roger Mortimer of Chirk, who was still officially the justice of Wales, was told to join the king at Cirencester in Gloucestershire on 13 December to report on the situation in Wales. On 30 November Edward gave orders for an army to join him at Cirencester on 13 December, a week before the deadline given in the Doncaster petition.[447]

On 14 November the archbishop of Canterbury summoned a provincial council to meet at St Paul's on 1 December, because, as he put it, the realm which had once rejoiced in the beauty of peace was now in danger of shipwreck through civil war.[448] It is likely however that the meeting was intended to set the stage for the return of the Despensers, since on 30 November, the day before the council met, the Younger Despenser delivered to the king a petition outlining the legal flaws in the process of his exile and appealing for its annulment, after which he surrendered himself to the king's custody. Either then or a little later the Elder Despenser followed the same course.[449] On the same day the king announced that he was sending the earls of

---

[444] See the text and translation of the letter, dated 2 Dec. at Pontefract, which was sent, with a copy of the petition, to the mayor and citizens of London, to inform them of current events and presumably also to try to win their support: Maddicott, 297–8; Bod., Kent Rolls 6, f.

[445] Haskins, 'Doncaster petition', 485; Phillips, 218; Maddicott, 300–1.

[446] BL, Cotton Ms. Nero D.X, f. 111v. It is not clear if Edward made any formal response.

[447] *CCR, 1318–23*, 408, 506, 508; *CPR, 1321–24*, 38; Phillips, 218; Maddicott, 303–4.

[448] *Concilia Magnae Britanniae et Hiberniae*, ed. D. Wilkins (London, 1737), ii, 507–8; Cambridge Univ. Ms. Ee.v.31, f. 223v; Phillips, 219; Maddicott, 304.

[449] *CCR, 1318–23*, 541–5; Phillips, 219. It is unlikely that the Despensers appeared in person.

Richmond and Arundel and Robert Baldock the keeper of the privy seal to deliver a message, presumably the Younger Despenser's petition, to the council.[450] The council was not fully representative of the Canterbury province, since apart from Walter Reynolds the archbishop, who was an old friend and ally of Edward, only the bishops of London, Ely, Salisbury and Rochester were present. These were presumably among the bishops who had disagreed with the Despensers' exile in the first place.[451] Ten bishops did not appear, some of them at least, like Adam Orleton the bishop of Hereford and Badlesmere's nephew Henry Burghersh the bishop of Lincoln, because they sympathized with the magnate contrariants.[452] Despenser's petition was read before the prelates, who gave their opinion that the sentence against him was invalid and should be annulled. The petition and this reply were then read again in the presence of the bishops and of the earls of Pembroke, Kent, Richmond and Arundel, all of whom gave the same answer. Pembroke, Richmond and Arundel added, with some truth, that they had consented to the award against Despenser through fear of the other magnates and begged pardon for doing so. Afterwards the royal justices and other members of the king's council gave their opinions to the same effect.[453] In this way the king secured the widest possible consent for Despenser's return. The earls of Pembroke and Richmond, who had been foremost in persuading Edward to accept the exiles of the Despensers, were now bound more closely than ever to the king, no matter what their reservations about the Despensers may have been. So too were the earls of Surrey and Arundel.[454] On 8 December the Younger Despenser was granted a safe conduct, which was renewed, with letters of protection, on 9 January; while the Elder Despenser received a safe conduct on 25 December.[455] On 1 January 1322 the archbishop of Canterbury publicly announced in St Paul's that the process against the Despensers was unlawful, and on 7 January Edward had the Younger Despenser's return to the king's peace proclaimed to the citizens of London. To complete the Despensers' rehabilitation the bishop of Winchester set off for the papal curia on 13 January.[456]

[450] *CPR, 1321–24*, 37; *CCR, 1318–23*, 410, 543; Phillips, 219.
[451] *Parliamentary Texts*, 164, 169.
[452] *Ann. Paul.*, 300; *CCR, 1318–23*, 510–11; Phillips, 219.
[453] *CCR, 1318–23*, 510–11, 543; Phillips, 219.
[454] On 18 Nov. Pembroke received £500 from the king, repayable on demand, for which he gave Edward letters of obligation. This may have been to help Pembroke pay the residue of his ransom dating from 1317, but may also have been in effect a bond for his future loyalty: E 403/196, m.4; E 101/332/13; on 18 Nov. a sum of 1,000 marks was paid to the earl of Surrey as his annual fee, and 400 marks to the earl of Arundel on 9 Dec.: E 403/196, mm.3, 4; *Vita*, 198–201; Phillips, 219–20. The exiled Scottish earl of Atholl formally entered Edward II's service on 29 Nov. in return for a grant of Badlesmere's former castle of Chilham in Kent: *CPR, 1321–24*, 33; *CCR, 1318–23*, 509.
[455] *CPR, 1321–24*, 45, 47; Phillips, 220.
[456] *Ann. Paul.*, 301; *Foedera*, II, ii, 463–4 (8 Dec.). Although the business of the bishop's mission was not spelled out, it was clearly connected with the annulment of the Despensers' exile.

THE CAMPAIGN AGAINST THE CONTRARIANTS

Edward and his supporters left London on 8 December to join the rest of his army[457] at Cirencester for the start of the campaign against Hereford and his allies, who had seized Gloucester at about this time.[458] Edward reached Cirencester on 20 December and remained there over Christmas. While he was there he was rejoined by the earl of Pembroke, who had stayed behind in London on business connected with the recall of the Despensers. Pembroke at once took action to see that his castle of Goodrich in Herefordshire would be able to hold off any marcher attack.[459] Edward was also joined by Pembroke's nephew, John Hastings lord of Abergavenny, the first of the Marchers to make his peace. Hastings had probably been swept into the movement against the Despensers in the summer of 1321: his offence was evidently regarded as slight since he was later sent to take control of Glamorgan for the king.[460] Edward took his first direct action against one of the Marchers when he sent a force to take and destroy the castle of John Giffard of Brimpsfield in Gloucestershire, in retaliation for his attack on some royal supply wagons.[461]

On 27 December the royal army left Cirencester for Worcester, which was reached on 31 December.[462] Because the crossing of the River Severn there was held by the Marchers, a royal advance guard of cavalry and infantry, led by Fulk Fitz Warin, Oliver Ingham, John Pecche and Robert le Ewer, was sent to seize and hold the crossing at Bridgnorth. However, on the night of 5 January Bridgnorth castle was attacked by the men of the earl of Hereford and the Mortimers, shouting 'Wassail' (*Wesseheil*) in English as they did so. The bridge was burned and the royal garrison forced to withdraw to Worcester.[463] Still unable to cross the Severn,

---

[457] It is difficult to estimate the size of the army but Edward had the services of six earls (Norfolk, Kent, Pembroke, Richmond, Arundel, Surrey) with their retainers, plus his own household knights. The *Vita*, 198–201, makes particular note of the part played in the king's army by Robert le Ewer, who was in command of the infantry, and Fulk Fitz Warin in command of the cavalry. The forces that joined the king at Cirencester were mainly infantry.

[458] Bod., Laud Ms. Misc. 529, f. 106v (this chronicle, which is related to that of Adam Murimuth, has much valuable material on events in the Welsh March in 1321–2); Phillips, 220.

[459] *CCR, 1318–23*, 620.

[460] BL, Cotton Ms. Nero D.X, f. 111v; Bod., Laud Ms. Misc. 529, f. 106v; *CFR, 1319–27*, 115; Phillips, 220; Maddicott, 304. Hastings however had a family connection with the Despensers since his father, John Hastings senior (d. 1313), had been married to the Younger Despenser's sister Isabel: N. Saul, 'The Despensers and the downfall of Edward II', *EHR*, xcix (1984), 9–10.

[461] Trinity College Cambridge Ms. R.5.41, f. 116v; R. Butler, 'The last of the Brimpsfield Giffards and the rising of 1321–22', *Trans. Bristol & Glos. Arch. Soc.*, lxxvi (1958 for 1957), 75–97; Phillips, 220; Maddicott, 304; Fryde, 53, 243. A valuable insight into the activities of Giffard and his followers can be found in Waugh, 'The profits of violence', 855–8.

[462] E 101/378/13, m.5; Phillips, 220; Maddicott, 304–5.

[463] Bod., Laud Ms. Misc. 529, f. 107; Trinity College Cambridge Ms. R.5.41, ff. 116v, 117; Phillips, 220–1; Maddicott, 304–5.

Edward left Worcester on 8 January, heading for the next possible crossing-place at Shrewsbury, where he arrived on 14 January 1322.[464]

THE MORTIMERS SURRENDER

So far the Marchers had done well. They had already taken Gloucester and Bridgnorth, and were to add Worcester on 14 January,[465] and had forced Edward into a long detour before he could cross the Severn. However, events now took a sharp turn in the king's favour. The first break in the Marchers' ranks came just as Edward was approaching Shrewsbury. On 13 January at Newport in Shropshire a safe conduct until the night of 17 January was issued for Roger Mortimer of Wigmore and twenty of his companions to come to Betton Lestrange near Shrewsbury to treat with the earls of Pembroke, Richmond, Arundel and Surrey. The safe conduct was granted at the request of these four earls and the king's half-brothers, the earls of Kent and Norfolk. The conduct was renewed at Shrewsbury on 17 January until 20 January to allow for further meetings with the royalist earls at Betton, and was again extended on 21 January until the following day.[466] Badlesmere was specifically excluded from all of these guarantees because of Edward's implacable hatred of him. Since Lancaster was also implacably opposed to Badlesmere and refused to offer any assistance to the Marchers while he remained in their company, the former steward of the royal household was in total isolation.[467]

On 22 January both Roger Mortimer of Wigmore and his uncle, Roger Mortimer of Chirk, came in to Shrewsbury and submitted themselves to Edward's will.[468] Some chroniclers argued that Pembroke and the other royalist earls had negotiated in bad faith with the Mortimers, since they had come to make peace but they were imprisoned rather than being pardoned as they had been promised.[469] The initiative for negotiations with the king had however certainly come from them since a Welsh force led by Sir Gruffydd Llwyd had captured the Mortimer-controlled castles of Welshpool, Chirk and Clun, and Lancaster's castle at Holt, on behalf of the king.[470] Both Mortimers were deeply loathed by their Welsh tenants,[471] so much so that later in 1322 the communities of North and

---

[464] E 101/378/13, m.5; Phillips, 221; Maddicott, 305.

[465] Bod., Laud Ms. Misc. 529, f. 107; BL, Cotton Ms. D.X, f. 111v; Phillips, 222; Maddicott, 305–6.

[466] *CPR, 1321–24*, 47–51; Phillips, 221.

[467] Trinity College Cambridge Ms. R.5.41, ff. 116v; Phillips, 221.

[468] Davies, *Baronial Opposition*, 561 (App. 35); E 159/95/m.17d., E 368/92, m.49; *Calendar of Letter-books: E*, 150; Phillips, 221; Maddicott, 305.

[469] *Murimuth*, 35; *Melsa*, 340; *Anonimalle*, 104–5; Phillips, 221.

[470] BL, Cotton Ms. D.X, f. 111v; Phillips, 221. This was the same Gruffydd Llwyd who had been a loyal supporter of the crown in Wales until suspicions over his behaviour in 1317 after the Bruce invasion of Ireland had earned him a temporary period of imprisonment.

[471] On both Gruffydd Llwyd and the Mortimers see Davies, *Conquest*, 409–10.

South Wales warned the king that if the Mortimers were restored to royal favour they would be forced to flee their lands.[472] The Welsh attack on the Mortimers in 1322 was no accident. There is evidence that Edward had been in communication with Gruffydd Llwyd, who was sheriff of Merioneth in North Wales, since November 1321 and had ordered him to raise an army to suppress rebellion.[473] Gruffydd also devastated the earl of Hereford's lands in Brecon, while his nephew did likewise in Cantref Bychan, Gower, Narberth and Builth.[474] Some of the other Marchers were apparently prepared to confront the royal army at Shrewsbury, but the Mortimers refused to do so both because of the Welsh attacks and because their own men were starting to desert. The Mortimers therefore had ample reasons for throwing themselves on the king's mercy, and with their departure others were also ready to surrender.[475]

In a skilfully managed and determined campaign, Edward wasted no time in pursuing his remaining enemies. Edward left Shrewsbury on 24 January, travelling via Ludlow and Hereford[476] before arriving at Gloucester on 6 February.[477] Here Maurice de Berkeley and Hugh Audley the Elder surrendered, and at the request of Pembroke and others safe conducts were issued for those who might wish to follow their example.[478] Edward's ruthlessness now began to show itself once more. Although Maurice de Berkeley was received into the king's grace, he was arrested and his castle of Berkeley was confiscated; the Mortimers were sent to the Tower of London, in case they changed their minds and returned to their baronial allies.[479] Ironically Edward was to end his days as a prisoner in Berkeley castle and as a victim of Roger Mortimer of Wigmore. Three knights, who had ridden with the barons, possibly including a former sheriff of Herefordshire, were hanged at Gloucester.[480]

---

[472] *CCW*, 556–7; Davies, *Conquest*, 410. This may partly explain why the Mortimers were imprisoned rather than pardoned.

[473] J.G. Edwards, 'Sir Gruffydd Llwyd', *EHR*, xxx (1915), 593.

[474] Fryde, 54, 244.

[475] *Vita*, 202–3; *Melsa*, 340; Phillips, 222; Maddicott, 305–6.

[476] While at Hereford Edward appears to have confronted the bishop of Hereford, Adam Orleton, who was an experienced royal diplomat, with his suspected sympathies with the Mortimers. Although no charges were brought against him until 1323, he was to prove a key member of the growing opposition to Edward II in the closing years of his reign: *Vita*, 202–3, and n. 420; Haines, *The Church and Politics*, 135–7.

[477] Edward made his intentions plain in a letter written from Shrewsbury to his exchequer officials at Westminster on the day of the Mortimers' surrender, reporting this event and announcing that he was about to leave for Ludlow to bring justice and comfort to his people: Davies, *Baronial Opposition*, 561 (App. 35); E 159/95/m.17d, E 368/92/m.48d.

[478] Bod., Laud Ms. Misc. 529, f. 107; BL, Cotton Ms. D.X, f. 111v; *Vita*, 202–5; Phillips, 222; Maddicott, 306.

[479] *Vita*, 202–3; *Anonimalle*, 104–5.

[480] *Vita*, 202–5, and note 422; *Flores*, 203. The Mortimers were brought to the Tower on 13 Feb. by the earl of Surrey, Robert le Ewer and others: *French Chron.*, 43.

THE FLIGHT OF THE MARCHERS

The earl of Hereford was apparently also tempted to surrender but changed his mind when he heard that the Mortimers had been imprisoned. After first returning to Gloucester,[481] he fled with Hugh Audley the Younger and Roger Damory to join Lancaster at Pontefract.[482] It is not clear whether any plans for joint action existed by this time or whether this was no more than an act of desperation. Lancaster had however already entered the fray by 10 January when he began the siege of the royal castle at Tickhill near Doncaster, whose constable William de Aune had been the eyes and ears of the crown since September 1320.[483] News of the siege gave Edward the perfect excuse to move against Lancaster but on 8 February he gave his cousin one final chance when he wrote telling him of the rebellion of the Marchers and ordering him on pain of forfeiture not to receive or assist them. Lancaster's response – no doubt he was still trying to draw on his supposed authority as steward of England – was to claim that he knew of no rebels but if he saw any he would kill them or expel them from the kingdom.[484]

Edward now had to move swiftly, both in order to catch Lancaster and the Marchers before they could organize their resistance but also because the Scots had appeared on the scene when they raided the lands of the bishopric of Durham in January, after the expiry of the truce made in 1319.[485] The Scots might simply have been taking advantage of the disturbances in England but Edward also feared, and soon had good reason to believe, that they were coming to the aid of Lancaster and the Marchers.[486] According to the *Vita Edwardi Secundi* Edward was visited at Gloucester by Sir Andrew de Harclay, the sheriff of Cumberland, who warned him of the danger from the Scots.[487] Whether this is literally true or not, Edward was certainly in contact with Harclay, who was authorized on 9 February to make a truce with the Scots.[488] Instead of fighting the Scots, Harclay raised a force of hobelars that, just over a month later on 16 March, turned the scale of battle and brought about the defeat and death of many of the king's opponents.[489]

---

[481] Bod., Laud Ms. Misc. 529, f. 107; BL, Cotton Ms. D.X, f. 111v; Phillips, 222; Maddicott, 305–6.

[482] Bod., Laud Ms. Misc. 529, f. 107; BL, Cotton Ms. D.X, f. 111v; *Vita*, 202–3; *CPR, 1321–24*, 70; Phillips, 222; Maddicott, 307.

[483] *CPR, 1321–24*, 47; Maddicott, 306–7.

[484] *Foedera*, II, ii, 472–3; *Melsa*, 341; Maddicott, 307.

[485] *Lanercost*, 241; *Gesta Edwardi*, 73; Phillips, 222; McNamee, 96–7 (including a map of the raids).

[486] McNamee, 96.

[487] *Vita*, 204–5; Maddicott, 307–8.

[488] *Foedera*, II, ii, 473; Phillips, 223. There is no evidence that any truce was made.

[489] The queen is said to have written to the sheriff of Yorkshire and to Harclay asking them to intercept the rebels: *Flores*, 346; Maddicott, 311. It is implausible however that their army had not already been gathered.

On 11 February Edward issued safe conducts for the Despensers and their men;[490] and on the 14th ordered the mustering of a substantial force of over 12,000 infantry from Wales and several thousand more from adjoining English counties at Coventry on 5 March.[491] He even sought military assistance from his subjects in the duchy of Gascony, and wrote to the king of France and the pope informing them of what was taking place.[492] Edward left Gloucester on 18 February, captured Lancaster's castle of Kenilworth on 26 February and arrived at Coventry to join his gathering army on the following day.[493]

On 1 March the ground was further cut from under Lancaster by the publication of treasonable correspondence exchanged since January 1321 between Lancaster and the Scottish magnates Sir James Douglas and the earl of Moray in which Lancaster was referred to as 'King Arthur'.[494] Copies of the letters had come into the hands of William Melton, the archbishop of York and a loyal ally of Edward, and had been sent by him to the king.[495] The archbishops, bishops and sheriffs were all ordered to have the letters read publicly. They could not have been more damning of Lancaster and his cause and served to confirm the rumours of collusion which had long been circulating.[496] Although Robert Bruce is said to have remarked, 'How will a man who cannot keep faith with his own lord keep faith with me?'[497] an indenture found on the body of the earl of Hereford after the battle of Boroughbridge recorded an agreement between Lancaster, Hereford and Bruce in which the Scots promised to help the magnates in their quarrel anywhere in England, Wales and Ireland, without claiming any rights of conquest. In return the magnates would not serve Edward II in any future campaign against the Scots and would do everything they could to make peace between England and Scotland.[498]

LANCASTER'S DEFEAT

On 3 March Edward arrived at Lichfield where he was met by the Despensers and a large force of troops.[499] Hearing of the king's advance,

---

[490] Bod., Laud Ms. Misc. 529, f. 107; *CPR, 1321–24*, 64; Phillips, 222; Maddicott, 307.

[491] *CPR, 1321–24*, 73–4; Phillips, 222–3; Maddicott, 307.

[492] *Foedera*, II, ii, 475–6.

[493] E 101/378/13, m.6; Bod., Laud Ms. Misc. 529, f. 107; Phillips, 223; Maddicott, 308.

[494] Phillips, 223; Maddicott, 301–3. The texts were enrolled on the Close Roll and have been published in calendared form in *CCR, 1318–23*, 525–6 and in *CDS*, iii, no. 746 (pp. 139–40), and in full in *Foedera*, II, ii, 463, 472, 474. See also *Regesta Regum Scottorum*, 692–3, no. 559.

[495] This is stated in Edward's letter to the archbishop ordering him to publish the letters: *CCR, 1318–23*, 525. My earlier suggestion in Phillips, 223, that the letters might have been found at Kenilworth is clearly incorrect.

[496] See Maddicott, 301–3.

[497] *Lanercost*, 241–2; Barrow, 242.

[498] *Foedera*, II, ii, 479; *Gesta Edwardi*, 78; Maddicott, 302–3.

[499] Bod., Laud Ms. Misc. 529, f. 107; Phillips, 223.

Lancaster's forces broke off the siege of Tickhill; he and Hereford left Pontefract and took up defensive positions on 1 March at the river-crossing at Burton-on-Trent near Lancaster's castle at Tutbury.[500] After three days' unsuccessful fighting around the bridge and fords at Burton,[501] Edward decided to try to outflank the rebel army. On 10 March the earl of Surrey was sent to cross the river by a bridge three miles further downstream, while Pembroke and Richmond with 300 men crossed by a ford discovered at Walton, followed by the main body of the army. Robert le Ewer meanwhile kept the contrariants busy by an attack on the bridge at Burton itself.[502] At first Lancaster was prepared to give battle and unfurled his banners, a fatal move which effectively declared open rebellion against the king. He and Hereford changed their minds when they saw the scale of the forces ranged against them, and fled to Pontefract, leaving Tutbury to be captured by Edward.[503] The mortally wounded Roger Damory was also captured, but this did not save him from Edward's vengeance. On 13 March he was tried and, without any opportunity to defend himself, was declared to be a traitor; he was however spared the sentence of execution because of the king's former affection for him and because he was married to Edward's niece; shortly afterwards he died at the neighbouring abbey.[504]

On 11 March the fate of Lancaster, Hereford and the rest was sealed: with the advice and consent of the earls of Pembroke, Kent, Richmond, Arundel, Surrey and Atholl, Edward formally declared Lancaster and his allies to be traitors and ordered his half-brother the earl of Kent and the earl of Surrey to take Pontefract.[505] In the meantime a desperate debate took place there among the remaining contrariants. Some wanted to go to Lancaster's castle of Dunstanburgh in Northumberland, and stay there until the king's anger cooled; others wanted to throw themselves on the king's mercy; Lancaster, still clinging to the belief that as steward of England he had acted against the Despensers and not against his cousin the king, also thought that his close kinship to Edward would save him from harm.[506] He argued that if they went to Northumberland they would

---

[500] *Chroniques de Sempringham*, 340; *Melsa*, 341; BL, Cotton Ms. Nero D.X, f. 112; Phillips, 223; Maddicott, 309.

[501] *Gesta Edwardi*, 74; *Vita*, 206–9; Phillips, 223; Maddicott, 309–10.

[502] BL, Cotton Ms. Nero D.X, f. 112; Bod., Laud Ms. Misc. 529, f. 107v; *Chroniques de Sempringham*, 340; *Gesta Edwardi*, 74; *Vita*, 206–9; *Anonimalle*, 104–5; Phillips, 223; Maddicott, 309–10.

[503] *CCR, 1318–23*, 522; BL, Cotton Ms. Nero D.X, f. 112; Bod., Laud Ms. Misc. 529, f. 107v; *Chroniques de Sempringham*, 340; *Melsa*, 341–2; *Gesta Edwardi*, 74; *Vita*, 206–9; *Anonimalle*, 104–5; Phillips, 223; Maddicott, 309–10. Despenser is said to have dissuaded Edward from unfurling his own banners, which would have put the kingdom in a state of open war: p.645 *Gesta Edwardi*, 75; M. Keen, 'Treason trials under the law of arms', in M. Keen, *Nobles, Knights and Men-at Arms in the Middle Ages* (London, 1996), 156–7, 164–5.

[504] *PW*, II, i, 284; *Vita*, 208–9, and n. 436.

[505] *Foedera*, II, ii, 479; *CCR, 1318–23*, 522; Phillips, 224; Maddicott, 310.

[506] *Le Baker*, 13; Phillips, 224; Maddicott, 310.

appear to be seeking help from the Scots, and eventually agreed to leave Pontefract only after Roger de Clifford threatened him with a sword.[507]

The magnates got no farther than Boroughbridge in Yorkshire. On 16 March they were met and defeated by Andrew Harclay's northern army of about 4,000 men.[508] Hereford was killed when a Welsh infantryman lying in wait under the bridge stabbed him with a spear; had he lived he had planned to seek refuge in Hainault in the Low Countries.[509] Lancaster was captured the next day, while trying to escape on foot, and taken to York where he was placed under guard in the tower of York castle.[510] On 18 or 19 March Edward, accompanied by the Despensers and Pembroke, reached Pontefract and received its surrender.[511] All the leading fugitives from the battle were captured, including the wretched Badlesmere, who was taken a few days later at Stow Park in Lincolnshire.[512]

THE DEATH OF LANCASTER

On 21 March Lancaster was taken to Pontefract, 'a place the earl loved more than any other town in the land'. There he was met by the Younger Despenser and by Edward who 'contemptuously insulted him to his face with malicious and arrogant words'.[513] Lancaster was then shut up for the night in a new tower which he had had built as a prison for Edward if he ever laid hands on him.[514] The following day, 22 March, Lancaster was brought before Edward, the Despensers and the earls of Pembroke, Kent, Richmond, Surrey, Arundel, Atholl and Angus,[515] and one of the king's justices, Robert Mablethorp.[516] A lengthy indictment was read out against

---

[507] *Brut*, i, 217; BL, Cotton Ms. Nero D.X, f. 112; Phillips, 224; Maddicott, 311.

[508] *Ann. Paul.*, 302; *Gesta Edwardi*, 75–6; *Melsa*, 342; *Flores*, 205; *Vita*, 210–11; BL, Cotton Ms. Nero D.X, ff. 112–112v (this includes the text of Harclay's report on the battle to the king); Phillips, 224; Maddicott, 310.

[509] DL 34/25; *Le Baker*, 13–14; Phillips, 224; Maddicott, 310. Hereford had contacts there through his late wife, Edward II's sister Elizabeth, who was previously married to the count of Hainault.

[510] *Gesta Edwardi*, 76; *Flores*, 347; *Anonimalle*, 106–7; *Vita*, 210–13; Haskins, 'A chronicle', 78; Phillips, 224; Maddicott, 311.

[511] E 101/378/13, m.7; *Chroniques de Sempringham*, 342; *Anonimalle*, 106–7; Phillips, 224; Maddicott, 311.

[512] BL, Cotton Ms. Nero D.X, f. 112v; BL, Cotton Ms. Cleopatra C.III, f. 296; *Brut*, i, 221; Phillips, 224.

[513] *Anonimalle*, 106–7; *Gesta Edwardi*, 76; *Flores*, 347; Phillips, 225; Maddicott, 311.

[514] *Vita*, 212–13. The author however adds, 'this was the common story, but I have not heard witness to its truth'.

[515] *Vita*, 212–15; *Anonimalle*, 106–7; *Gesta Edwardi*, 76; *Flores*, 347; *Foedera*, II, i, 478–9; Phillips, 225; Maddicott, 311–12.

[516] He is not named in the official record of Lancaster's condemnation (*Foedera*, II, i, 478–9) but is mentioned by several chroniclers: e.g., *Ann. Paul.*, 302; *Melsa*, 342; *Brut*, i, 222. Ironically, he was one of a number of future royal justices who had earlier received fees of retainer from Lancaster: Maddicott, 49.

him, listing every cause of offence against the king from his seizure of the king's jewels and horses at Newcastle in 1312, and his bringing armed men to parliaments, to the recent capture of Gloucester and Bridgnorth, the siege of Tickhill, and the treasonable correspondence with the Scots.[517] Lancaster, who was not allowed to say anything in his defence, was declared guilty of treason and sentenced to be hanged, drawn and beheaded. Because of his royal blood the first two stages of the sentence were remitted, possibly following a plea from Isabella.[518] Without delay Lancaster was taken outside his castle and beheaded by the executioner with two or three blows.[519] Gaveston was not mentioned by name in the indictment, but it was clear to everyone that Edward had at last avenged himself on Lancaster: 'the earl of Lancaster once cut off Piers Gaveston's head, and now by the king's command the earl of Lancaster has lost his head'.[520]

---

[517] *Foedera*, II, i, 478–9; Maddicott, 311–12.
[518] *Brut*, i, 222–3.
[519] *Foedera*, II, i, 478–9, 493; *Vita*, 212–15; *Gesta Edwardi*, 76; *Flores*, 347; Phillips, 225; Maddicott, 312.
[520] *Vita*, 214–15; cf. *Anonimalle*, 108–9.

Chapter 9

EDWARD VICTORIOUS, 1322–1324

EDWARD'S REVENGE

'It is not safe to rise up against the king, because the outcome is often likely to be unfortunate. For even Simon, Earl of Leicester, was at last laid low in battle at Evesham;[1] the Earl Ferrers lost his estates;[2] the king himself succeeded the Earl Marshal;[3] each of these had resisted the king, and each of them in the end succumbed'; 'What does it serve, to resist the king, save to throw away one's life and lose all one's goods as well. For an islander to rebel against an island king is as if a chained man were to try his strength with the warden of his prison.'[4] These were the comments of the author of the *Vita Edwardi Secundi* on the dangers for a magnate, however great and powerful, when he resisted the king. Even over three hundred years later, during the English Civil War, the earl of Manchester was to express a reality that any fourteenth- or fifteenth-century opponent of the crown would have understood all too well: 'If we beat the king nine and ninety times he is king still, but if the king beat us but once we shall be hanged and our posterity made slaves.'[5]

Lancaster was only the first to die. Six others were pronounced guilty by the king's record on the same day and immediately executed.[6] On the following day John de Mowbray, Roger de Clifford and Gaucelin d'Eyville were hanged in chains at York.[7] Justices were also appointed to pass judgment

---

[1] Simon de Montfort was killed at the battle of Evesham in 1265 during the civil war between Henry III and the barons. His earldom was given to Henry III's younger son, Edmund earl of Lancaster, the father of Thomas of Lancaster.

[2] In 1266 William de Ferrers, earl of Derby, forfeited his lands, which were also given to Edmund of Lancaster.

[3] Roger Bigod, earl of Norfolk, was one of Edward I's opponents in the 1297 crisis. On his death in 1306 Edward I took his lands for the crown. The earldom was revived by Edward II in 1312 in favour of his half-brother Thomas of Brotherton.

[4] *Vita*, 76–7, *sub* 1313; *Vita*, 128–9, *sub* 1316.

[5] In 1644: C. Carlton in 'Three British revolutions and the personality of kingship', *Three British Revolutions, 1641, 1688, 1776*, ed. J.G.A. Pocock (Princeton, 1980), 165, cited in J.R.S. Phillips, 'Simon de Montfort (1265), the Earl of Manchester (1644), and other stories' in *Violence in Medieval Society*, ed. R. W. Kaeuper (Woodbridge, Suffolk & Rochester, NY, 2000), 79–80.

[6] William Tuchet, Henry de Bradbourne, Warin de Insula, Thomas Mauduit, William Fitzwilliam, and William Cheyny: *Foedera*, II, i, 479; Maddicott, 312.

[7] *Gesta Edwardi*, 78; *Melsa*, 342–3; *Brut*, i, 224.

on ten others at various places ranging from the Tower of London, Windsor and Winchelsea to Bristol, Cardiff and Swansea. In each case the justices were supplied with a document outlining the judgment expected from them.[8] The most notable victims were John Giffard of Brimpsfield who was hanged at Gloucester in late April or early May, and Bartholomew de Badlesmere[9] who was taken back to his native Kent and executed with especial cruelty on 14 April: after being dragged through the city of Canterbury he was first hanged and then beheaded and his head stuck on the Burgate at Canterbury.[10] The bodies of those executed were left on the gallows as an example to other potential rebels. They remained there until 1324 when Edward finally allowed them to be buried.[11]

There was shock at the manner in which Lancaster and the other contrariants were condemned simply by a royal record of their alleged crimes, without any permitted questioning of the evidence or anything being said in their defence.[12] The Lanercost chronicler, for example, commented that Lancaster had been executed '*sine parliamento et sine majori et saniori consilio*' and that no earl had ever been treated in this manner before; the *Anonimalle Chronicle* stated that the king's record was now taken for law; while the *Vita Edwardi Secundi* reported what its author claimed were the only words Lancaster was allowed to utter: 'This is a powerful court, and very great in authority, where no answer is heard nor any mitigation admitted.'[13] Another perceptive writer, Adam Murimuth, was later to remark with bitterness that from the execution of Lancaster in 1322 to that of Roger Mortimer in 1330 no noble condemned to death had been allowed to speak in his own defence.[14] While the procedures used against Lancaster and the other contrariants could be justified under the law of arms covering acts of war which were not justiciable under the common law[15] and under the

---

[8] A copy of the document sent to the justices is preserved in *PW*, II, ii, App., 261–7, and in G.L. Haskins, 'Judicial proceedings against a traitor after Boroughbridge', *Speculum*, xii (1937), 509–11. A record of the individual judgments was enrolled in Jan. 1325 on the roll of the King's Bench (KB) 27/259 (Hilary 1325), mm.173d, 34–35d (Crown Roll): Sayles, 'The formal judgments,' 58.

[9] *CPR, 1321–24*, 148–9; *Melsa*, 342–3; *Murimuth*, 36; *Brut*, i, 224.

[10] Trinity College Cambridge Ms. R.5.41, f. 118; *Anonimalle*, 108–9. See also Fryde, 61; and the article on Badlesmere by J.R. Maddicott in the *Oxford DNB*.

[11] *Murimuth*, 43. The short chronicle in BL, Cotton Ms. Cleopatra D.IX, ff. 83r–85r, published by Haskins as 'A chronicle of the civil wars of Edward II', has lists of those who were killed at Boroughbridge (three: including the earl of Hereford), who died beforehand (one: Roger Damory), or were executed afterwards (22).

[12] Maddicott, 312.

[13] *Lanercost*, 244; *Anonimalle*, 108–9; *Vita*, 214–15.

[14] *Murimuth*, 56; see also McKisack, *The Fourteenth Century*, 103.

[15] Keen, 'Treason trials'. It could however also be argued (and was so argued by Thomas of Lancaster's brother Henry in 1327) that Thomas had been condemned in time of peace since Edward had not unfurled his own banners: Keen, 164–5. The same argument was also put forward by Roger Mortimer of Wigmore in Feb. 1327 and accepted in July that year: *CPR, 1327–30*, 142.

developing law of treason,[16] allowance must also be made for the depth of bitterness which had entered English politics since the death of Gaveston in 1312. Just as Gaveston had been condemned to death unheard and undefended, and in 1321 the Despensers had been sentenced to exile by the award of the magnates, so Edward wished to adopt a similar procedure when he in turn had his enemies at his mercy.[17] The author of the *Flores Historiarum* later wrote that Edward II 'hated all the magnates with such mad fury that he plotted the complete and permanent overthrow of all the great men of the realm together with the whole English aristocracy', while the writer of the *Brut* remarked that Edward 'had brought the flower of chivalry unto death'.[18] They were both exaggerating but it must have seemed the case in 1322.

Edward had achieved his longed-for revenge. In 1324 Master John of St Albans painted the walls of the Lesser Hall of Westminster Palace with scenes, probably martial and heroic in character, from the life of his father: Edward perhaps felt that in destroying his internal enemies during the civil war of 1321–2 he had somehow at last matched Edward I's greatness in war.[19] But it proved to be a pyrrhic victory. The effect was to raise the stakes to such heights that in future anyone wishing to engage in violent opposition to the king had to be prepared to end the king's reign and even his life. By acting with such ruthlessness against his enemies Edward II had only made himself vulnerable to a greater degree than ever before.

Other contrariants were condemned to imprisonment. Hugh Audley the Younger was spared because he was married to Edward's niece and Gaveston's widow, Margaret de Clare.[20] Roger Mortimer of Wigmore and his uncle Roger Mortimer of Chirk, who had been in the Tower of London since February,[21] were brought out to face their judges in Westminster Hall, where on 2 August they were sentenced to death for their roles in the capture of Gloucester and Bridgnorth. For once Edward relented and on the following day their sentences were commuted to life

---

[16] Phillips, 'Simon de Montfort', 87–8.

[17] Matthew Strickland has also argued convincingly that the executions of William Wallace in 1305, Simon Fraser in 1306, and many other Scottish opponents under Edward I formed a major precedent for Edward II's actions in 1322 and that, having sat in judgment on several of his father's victims, Edward II himself would have been well aware of this: Strickland, 'Treason, feud,' 109–13. John Gillingham has drawn attention to the role of professional judges, such as Robert Mablethorp in Lancaster's trial, and of others such as Geoffrey le Scrope, suggesting that they were prepared to pass judgment on Lancaster and others by the king's record rather than by judgment of their peers: Gillingham, 'Enforcing old law in new ways', in *Law and Power in the Middle Ages*, ed. P. Andersen, M. Münster-Swendsen & H. Voght (Copenhagen, 2008), 199–220.

[18] *Flores*, 200; *Brut*, i, 224–5; Gillingham, 'Enforcing old law', 199–200.

[19] Binski, *Painted Chamber*, 112; *KW*, i, 508, n. 7.

[20] See the article on Audley by J.R. Maddicott in the *Oxford DNB*.

[21] *French Chron.*, 43.

imprisonment.²² They were joined in the Tower by at least fifteen others, including Thomas Gurney (who was to play a sinister role in the imprisonment and death of Edward II in 1327), Badlesmere's son Giles and John de Mowbray's son John.²³ Maurice de Berkeley and Hugh Audley the Elder were both sent to Wallingford castle.²⁴ Wives, widows and children were consigned to castles and convents around the country.²⁵ All the contrariants, both those who died in battle or were executed and those who were imprisoned, were also liable to forfeiture of all their lands and other property.²⁶ At least 117 men were to suffer permanent loss of their possessions.²⁷

In July 1322 Edward introduced a procedure by which former rebels or suspected sympathizers could regain their lands on payment of a fine. This was not all, since each individual also had to promise payment of a sum to be decided by the king if he should ever reoffend.²⁸ One hundred and fifty-eight men promised payment of fines totalling £15,000, often payable in instalments both as a way of ensuring collection and also to provide yet another guarantee of their future behaviour.²⁹ There were many cases in 1321-2 of families with divided sympathies, causing some members to suffer while others survived to flourish under the new regime. Two outstanding examples of the latter were Thomas of Lancaster's brother Henry who had played no part in Thomas's rebellion and Richard Damory the elder brother of Roger Damory. Henry soon regained his lands and in March 1324 was recognized as earl of Leicester, one of the

---

²² *PW*, II, ii, App., 216; *CPR, 1327-30*, 141-3 (July 1327); Mortimer, *The Greatest Traitor*, 126 (where the date of their conviction is wrongly given as 21 July 1322). The judges had been appointed by the king on 14 July and provided with a copy of the charges against the Mortimers, which they used to pronounce judgment on 2 Aug. Edward had however already ordered on 22 July that the sentences of death should be commuted: *CPR, 1327-30*, 142.

²³ Fryde, 63; KB 27/254, Rex, m.37.

²⁴ *Vita*, 218-19. Haskins, 'A chronicle', 80-1, lists the names of 85 men (including the Mortimers who gave themselves up) who were imprisoned. Five others escaped (including four who went overseas).

²⁵ Including the widow and mother-in-law of Lancaster, the wife, sons and daughters of Roger Mortimer of Wigmore and the sons of the earl of Hereford: Fryde, 63-4, 245; Mortimer, *The Greatest Traitor*, 121.

²⁶ See Fryde, 69-86, for a general view of the confiscation of land which followed the king's victory in 1322.

²⁷ Ibid., 70; List in PRO, Lists and Indexes, v, *Ministers' Accounts*, part 1, 441-62. Many of these were apparently poor men who could not afford to pay fines or from whom it was not worth trying to collect anything.

²⁸ The form of the procedure and an example of how it was applied in one case, that of Richard le Waleys, a former supporter of the earl of Lancaster in Yorkshire, are given in Fryde, 70-1, citing *CFR, 1319-27*, 152-3; C 47/34/9, an original file of submissions. The names of over 1,000 suspects were entered on the rolls of the court of King's Bench: Fryde, 70; KB 27/262, Rex, mm. 13-14.

²⁹ Fryde, 75-6.

five earldoms which Thomas had held at his death; while in July 1322 Richard Damory was appointed to the important and highly influential office of steward of the royal household.[30] The successful rehabilitation of such men only gave further emphasis to the plight of those who had suffered loss and who might suffer once more at the whim of the king. The insecurity and enmity engendered by the 1322 'settlement' contributed mightily to Edward's own insecurity in the closing years of his reign and to the ultimate loss of his throne.

Edward II's victory in 1322 over Thomas of Lancaster, the wealthiest and most powerful of the English magnates, and his marcher allies, the earl of Hereford and the Mortimers and the rest, at first sight appears almost inexplicable, especially after the relative ease with which Edward and the Despensers had been overcome in the spring and summer of 1321. However, the magnates seriously underestimated Edward's determination to avenge himself upon them, the extent and quality of the intelligence supplied to him by his informants in Wales, the Marches and the north of England, and the speed with which he and his own supporters would act. The failure of the Marchers and Lancaster to produce any concerted plan of action once Edward's intentions became clear and the panic which then entered their ranks were to prove fatal.

Edward's decision to attack Badlesmere first was a very shrewd move, since his lands in Kent were close to Westminster and easily reached, while there was a strong likelihood that Lancaster's enmity towards him would ensure that no baronial force came to his rescue. On the other hand Edward undertook the campaign with very limited financial and material resources. Between December 1321 and March 1322 the royal household spent about £8,000, of which just over £5,000 came from the exchequer. The rest was raised from a variety of sources, including local and foreign merchants,[31] and the lands of contrariants such as Badlesmere and Roger Damory.[32] It is likely that royal use of the contrariants' own resources made a significant contribution to their defeat.[33] Royal purveyance of food supplies in Gloucestershire and Herefordshire met with some resistance, partly for political reasons but also because of the poor harvest in the autumn of 1321. The winter of 1321–2 was also particularly harsh.[34] The barons too met resistance. The damage they inflicted on the lands of the Despensers in 1321 did not endear them to the inhabitants of those areas. In December 1321 both Roger Mortimer of Wigmore and Maurice

---

[30] Ibid., 72–3; Maddicott, 319. On Henry's career see the article by S.L. Waugh in the *Oxford DNB*. He was apparently abroad at the time of the rebellion: *CPR, 1321–24*, 69; Phillips, 228.

[31] The Bardi, for example, provided loans totalling £2,000: Fryde, 92; E 159/95, m.32; E 403/202.

[32] Fryde, 92; E 372/171, m.43v; E 101/15/38; E 404/484, file 30.

[33] Fryde, 55, 244, n. 57; Tebbit, 'Household knights', 89.

[34] Waugh, 'The profits of violence', 851–3.

de Berkeley had to resort to pillage when their demands for food were refused. These and other acts by the Marchers cut away any local support they might otherwise have enjoyed.[35] Something very similar happened in the north where Lancaster's attempts to gather supplies and to raise infantry forces in Yorkshire and Lancashire were also resisted.[36] His death left many creditors desperately pleading with the king to pay what Lancaster had owed them. Edward rejected their petitions out of hand with the words: 'The king does not pay the earl's debts.'[37]

Recent scholarship has placed considerable emphasis upon the unreliability of royal household knights during the reign and especially in the crisis of 1321–2.[38] It has also been noted that twenty-five knights who had served in the royal household between 1314 and 1321 ultimately fought against Edward in 1321–2.[39] There is a considerable amount of truth in this argument. There are obvious examples such as the behaviour of Gilbert de Middleton and John de Lilburn in 1317–18, and Edmund Darel in 1319.[40] More spectacular was the defection in 1321 of prominent individuals who had contracted to serve the king, such as the earl of Hereford, Badlesmere, Roger Damory, Hugh Audley the Younger, John Giffard, John de Mowbray and others.[41] However, many of the knights who joined the royal household were northerners who did so when it was greatly expanded to meet the threat from Scottish raids after the battle of Bannockburn in 1314. These were not men with any tradition of royal service and it is not surprising that some of them also had other allegiances, in a number of cases as retainers of the earl of Lancaster.[42] What was ultimately far more significant was the fact that in 1321–2 thirty-three others fought for Edward. Men such as John de Somery, John de Segrave the Elder, Oliver Ingham, Robert de Sapy, John and Walter de Beauchamp played a leading role in taking control of lands confiscated from the contrariants, and in raising and commanding troops. The force led by the Welsh knight Gruffydd Llwyd cut the ground from under the Mortimers and undermined both the earl of Hereford's and the earl of Lancaster's holdings in Wales.[43] The Cumberland

---

[35] Ibid., 848–51.

[36] Maddicott, 308–9, 314.

[37] '*Le roi ne paye mie les dettes le conte*': petition of John de Ripon, a merchant of Pontefract: SC 8/5/212. Other examples are SC 8/6/252 (Walter de Shirburn, vicar of Wyston); SC 8/7/336 (Constance, widow of William Haliday of Pontefract, responsible for 15 children '*qe perissent par defaute*').

[38] Prestwich, 'The unreliability of royal household knights', 1–11, esp. 5–7.

[39] Tebbit, 'Royal patronage', 197.

[40] Prestwich, 'The unreliability of royal household knights', 7–9.

[41] Ibid., 5–6; Tebbit, 'Royal patronage', 197, 206–8.

[42] Prestwich, 'The unreliability of royal household knights', 7; Tebbit, 'Royal patronage', 204.

[43] Phillips, 221; Davies, *Conquest*, 409–10; Edwards, 'Sir Gruffydd Llwyd', 593. However, the earl of Hereford's own Welsh tenants in the lordship of Brecon remained loyal and fought for him in 1321–2: Davies, *Lordship and Society*, 290–1.

knight Andrew de Harclay showed that the barons also lacked local support in the north-west of England and, crucially, raised the army which brought defeat to the contrariants at Boroughbridge.[44] These and other royal knights were an essential part of Edward's victory and one that has usually been overlooked.[45]

While Edward II retained the active loyalty of a significant number of his household knights, the earl of Lancaster's experience was quite different. Not only did his attempts to raise troops prove unsuccessful,[46] but many of his retainers deserted him, either because they could not in the last resort bring themselves to fight against the king or because they feared the consequences if Lancaster were defeated. At least ten of his retainers, such as Peter de Mauley, John de Clavering, Fulk Lestrange, William Latimer and, most significantly of all, Robert de Holland, Lancaster's most trusted follower, changed sides in 1321–2.[47] Holland was in negotiations with the king from about 4 March, nearly two weeks before Boroughbridge, and even attacked some of Lancaster's men fleeing from Burton-on-Trent before giving himself up to the king.[48] With friends such as these Lancaster had no need of enemies.

A TIME FOR REWARDS

It was now time for Edward to divide the spoils of victory. Some of his largesse involved no more than reversing territorial gains which Lancaster had made during his lifetime and cost Edward little or nothing. The earl of Pembroke, for example, regained the New Temple in London and the manor and castle of Thorpe Waterville in Northamptonshire, both of which Lancaster had forced him to give up in 1314, while on 15 March, the day before Boroughbridge, he was granted Lancaster's valuable honour of Higham Ferrers as a reward for services rendered.[49] Another of Lancaster's victims, the earl of Surrey, regained his lordships of Bromfield and Yale in the Welsh March, but not the Yorkshire lands seized from him by Lancaster in 1318–19.[50] On 25 March the services of Andrew de Harclay were rewarded with the earldom of Carlisle, the first such new creation in England during the reign of Edward II, who personally girded Harclay with the belt signifying his new status. He was also to receive lands worth 2,000 marks per

[44] On Harclay see the article by Henry Summerson in the *Oxford DNB*.
[45] Tebbit, 'Household knights', 88–93.
[46] Maddicott, 308–9, 314–15.
[47] Maddicott, 295–6; Phillips, 225. Latimer had been a royal knight before joining Lancaster in 1319. On Holland's career see Maddicott, 'Thomas of Lancaster and Sir Robert Holland', *EHR*, lxxxvi (1971), 449–72.
[48] *CPR, 1321–24*, 77; *CCR, 1318–23*, 525; BL, Cotton Ms. Nero D.X, f. 112; *Brut*, i, 216; *Vita*, 208–9; Phillips, 224.
[49] *CPR, 1321–24*, 87; *CChR, 1300–26*, 441; Phillips, 77–82, 227. Higham Ferrers was close to Thorpe Waterville.
[50] *CCR, 1318–23*, 455, 561.

annum.[51] Others who gained were the earl of Richmond who was given a number of manors in May; the earl of Arundel, now appointed justice of Wales, who was given his predecessor Roger Mortimer's lordship of Chirk to add to his own lordships of Oswestry and Clun; the king's half-brother, Edmund earl of Kent, who received the castle of Oakham in Rutland and two castles in Wales; the king's younger son John of Eltham, who gained Lancaster's former castle of Tutbury; and Robert Baldock, keeper of the privy seal and soon to be chancellor, who was granted some of the possessions of Roger de Clifford.[52]

These were minor gains compared with the stream of patronage which came the way of the Despensers and continued to flow almost until the end of the reign. Hugh Despenser the Elder was given the earldom of Winchester on 10 May during the parliament at York which followed the king's victory.[53] In April and May he received four separate grants of lands to maintain his new rank, and in July was given the lordship of Denbigh in North Wales, previously held by the earl of Lancaster.[54] Hugh Despenser the Younger was not made earl of Gloucester, but the virtual earldom which he had created for himself in the Welsh March before 1321 was quickly reconstituted. He regained the lordships of Glamorgan, the Cantref Mawr, and Gower, which had been the immediate cause of the crisis in 1321; and added the strategically placed Lundy Island in the Bristol Channel which he had tried to obtain from Herbert de Marisco in 1321; Roger Damory's former lordship of Usk; and the lordship of Is Cennen with the castle of Carreg Cennen which had previously been held by John Giffard.[55] This last acquisition allowed him to link the Cantref Mawr with Gower and Glamorgan. He also had custody of the lordship of Brecon from July 1322; in August 1323 the earl of Norfolk, the king's half-brother, leased his lordship of Chepstow to him for life; and after the death of the earl of Pembroke in 1324 he obtained custody of the county of Pembroke as well as the former Hastings lordships of Cilgerran and Abergavenny. By the end of the reign Despenser had reunited all the lands of the earldom of Gloucester in South Wales and ruled over almost everything from

---

[51] *Foedera*, II, i, 481. New earldoms had however been created in Ireland, those of Carrick (for Edmund le Botiller) in 1315; Kildare (for John Fitz Thomas) in 1316; and Louth (for John de Bermingham) in 1319.

[52] *CChR, 1300–26*, 441–3, 448; *CPR, 1321–24*, 98, 144, 183–4. Arundel had been closely allied with the Despensers since his son married the Younger Despenser's daughter in Feb. 1321: BL, Add. Ms. 9951, f. 45v.

[53] The Despenser family held lands in Wiltshire; and it has recently been suggested that Hugh Despenser the Elder could have made a distant claim to the earldom of Winchester through his descent from an earlier earl of Winchester, Saher de Quency (d. 1219): M. Lawrence, 'Edward II and the earldom of Winchester', *Historical Research*, lxxxi (2008), 732–9.

[54] *CChR, 1300–26*, 442–4, 448; *CPR, 1321–24*, 128.

[55] *CChR, 1300–26*, 444, 448–51; SC 1/49/144 (printed in *Calendar . . . concerning Wales*, 220–1).

Pembroke to Chepstow.[56] Why the Younger Despenser did not go the whole hog and persuade Edward II to make him earl of Gloucester is something of a puzzle. The lands held by the husbands of the other two Gloucester heiresses, Hugh Audley the Younger and Roger Damory, had come into royal hands through the forfeiture and imprisonment of the one and the forfeiture and death of the other and were technically available to be given to Despenser together with the title of earl. One possible explanation is that Despenser had only to bide his time, since his father, who was already aged sixty-one in 1322, could be expected to die of natural causes before many more years passed, leaving his son the title and vast possessions of the earldom of Winchester, to add to those he had already acquired. It was scarcely through moderation or restraint, as Tout suggested, that the Younger Despenser did not become earl of Gloucester.[57]

Tout's other suggestion – that Despenser was waiting until some other more grandiose dignity could be devised, such as the title of earl of March which Roger Mortimer of Wigmore was to acquire in 1328 – is unproven but is another possible explanation.[58] Moderate or not, it has been estimated that Despenser's Welsh lands, including those he held in custody, brought him an annual revenue of almost £5,000, making him one of the richest landowners of his day.[59] 'Between them, the king, the two Despensers and the earl of Arundel held almost three-quarters of Wales under their sway in the years 1322–6.'[60]

A succession of grants of lands in England added substantially to Despenser's holdings and the income derived from them.[61] The survey of his English lands made after his fall in 1326 valued them at £2,100 per annum, while his father's English possessions were assessed at £2,500.[62] This did not take account of moveable goods, which were valued at £2,300 for the Younger Despenser and £6,600 for his father.[63] There were also very large sums in ready cash, which the Younger Despenser deposited with

[56] *CFR, 1319–27*, 143 (Brecon); *CPR, 1321–24*, 341 (Chepstow); Pugh, 'Marcher lords', 171–2. For a map showing Despenser's territorial control in Wales, 1322–6, see Davies, *Conquest*, 406. The only important exception was the lordship of Kidwelly, held by the former earl of Lancaster's brother, Henry.

[57] Tout, *Place of the Reign*, 15.

[58] Ibid., 138. One wonders if the notion of an earldom of March had already been considered before the fall of Despenser only two years earlier.

[59] Davies, *Conquest*, 405.

[60] Ibid.

[61] At least 17 grants of lands in England are recorded between March 1322 and March 1324: *CChR, 1300–26*, 441, 443–4, 448–52, 461, 464; *CPR, 1321–24*, 129, 132.

[62] Both figures are derived from the records of the survey in E 142/33. My figure for the Younger Despenser's income differs from that of £1,827 which Dr E.B. Fryde derived from the same source. He noted however that the figure probably did not include all the English estates in Despenser's possession in 1326: Fryde, 'Deposits of Hugh Despenser the Younger', item III, 348. For a detailed examination of the value of the Despensers' lands and other possessions see Fryde, *Tyranny*, App. 1, 228–32.

[63] Again derived from E 142/33.

the London branches of two firms of Florentine bankers, the Bardi and the Peruzzi. In September 1324 they held £5,886 between them in Despenser's name.[64] With the addition of the revenues of his Welsh lands and the unknown but certainly substantial value of his moveable goods there, the Younger Despenser was an immensely wealthy man. His wish expressed in January 1321 that 'we may be rich and may attain our ends' had been achieved, probably even beyond his dreams of avarice.[65]

EDWARD IS WEALTHY

The Despensers were not the only ones to benefit by Edward II's victory over the contrariants: Edward himself also became immensely wealthy.[66] Throughout his reign Edward had been short of money. He had begun with the debts and the administrative confusion inherited from his father's war with Scotland; and had experienced the political resistance and social tensions which followed his attempts to finance his own campaigning through prises and purveyance. When he did briefly achieve a measure of solvency, in 1313–14, he immediately threw it all away in the disastrous Bannockburn campaign; the same pattern was repeated in 1318–19, culminating this time in the failure at Berwick. His victory in 1321–2 was achieved by hand-to-mouth finance, by which the contrariants in effect bore much of the cost of their own defeat.

In early May 1322 the treasury held no more than £1,195 in ready cash,[67] but this was only a part of the money available to Edward since the revenue generated from the confiscated possessions of some of the contrariants and from the payment of fines by others was being paid directly into the king's chamber rather than the exchequer. Between July and September the chamber handled sums totalling at least £14,724, some paid out on behalf of the exchequer and some delivered to the wardrobe.[68] Even after Edward's campaign against the Scots in August

[64] Fryde, 'Deposits of Hugh Despenser the Younger', 348. For details of Despenser's deposits and withdrawals from his account with the Peruzzi, 1322–6, see ibid., 360–2.

[65] Letter to John Inge, sheriff of Glamorgan: SC 1/49/143 (*Calendar . . . concerning Wales*, 219–20).

[66] What follows is greatly indebted to Fryde, *Tyranny*, ch. 7, 'Royal finance, 1321–6'; and to Buck, *Politics, Finance and the Church*, ch. 8, 'The Exchequer'. See also W. Childs, 'Finance and trade under Edward II', in *Politics and Crisis in Fourteenth-century England*, ed. J. Taylor & W. Childs (Gloucester, 1990), 19–21; Prestwich, *Plantagenet England*, 210.

[67] Fryde, 92; E 401/239. Walter Stapeldon, bishop of Exeter, took office as treasurer on 10 May 1322.

[68] Fryde, 92; E 401/239; BL, Stowe Ms. 553, f. 18v. Dr Fryde suggests that this was only a part of the revenues obtained from the contrariants and that other receipts were being paid into the reserve that Edward was starting to build up. This is possible but more evidence is needed. Payment into the chamber was however only a temporary measure and from July the revenues from contrariant lands were ordered to be paid into the exchequer: Buck, 164.

and September 1322 the wardrobe still had £7,000 in hand.[69] The taxation granted by the York parliament in November 1322 brought in at least another £42,000,[70] much of which was not needed because of the thirteen-year truce made with the Scots in May 1323. In July 1323, £27,500 in fifty-five barrels, each holding £500, was sent from York for storage in the Tower of London.[71] A further £34,172 was received in 1323 and 1324 from the proceeds of clerical subsidies granted by the pope in April 1322 in aid of the Scottish war,[72] and much of this probably also went into Edward's growing reserve in the Tower of London, to which £44,000 was added in May 1324.[73] Even after the expenditure of over £65,000 on war with France in 1324–5,[74] £69,000 remained in the treasury.[75]

In January 1324 an official estimate was made of the royal revenue. The total was £60,549, of which £13,000 came from Gascony, £16,000 from customs duties, £24,385 (?) from royal lands and the county farms, and £12,643 from the revenues of confiscated lands in England.[76] This estimate resulted from a request by Edward in April 1323 for a statement of his revenues,[77] and was part of a reorganization of the working of the exchequer which had begun in July 1322 when control over the revenues of confiscated lands was passed to it from the chamber.[78] This led to a great increase in the work of the exchequer, especially when in 1324 Edward also ordered the collection of all outstanding debts owed to contrariants.[79] One consequence was the division of the exchequer into two sections, one for the counties south of the Trent and one for those to the north.[80]

---

[69] Fryde, 93; BL, Stowe Ms. 553, f. 27.

[70] Fryde, 93–4; Willard, *Parliamentary Taxes*, 344–5. See also *Lay Taxes*, 36. The total assessment for the tax was £42,394.

[71] Fryde, 94; E 403/202. Dr Fryde reasonably suggests that much of this money was the proceeds of the lay tax, together with money seized from the contrariants.

[72] Fryde, 94; Lunt, *Financial Relations*, 411.

[73] Fryde, 94; E 403/207, m.13.

[74] Fryde, 94. The detailed breakdown of this figure is given in ibid., 250, nn. 38, 39.

[75] Fryde, 94; E 101/332/20; Buck, 193; E 101/332/18.

[76] Fryde, 97–8; Bod. Library, Ms. North C.26, no. 4. I have not had an opportunity to examine this at first hand. It has also been discussed by Dr G.L. Harriss, in *King, Parliament and Public Finance*, 146, App. B, 523–4. As Dr Fryde points out, the condition of the document makes it very difficult to read so that her figures differ from those of Dr Harriss. Both scholars agree on the total of £60,549, but give the figure for royal lands and the shires as £24,385 and £19,496 respectively. Dr Fryde's reading would bring the total to £66,028.

[77] Fryde, 97; E 159/96, m.26v.

[78] Fryde, 101; E 159/95, m.35v; C 47/35/21.

[79] Fryde, 102–3; E 159/97, m.32.

[80] Fryde, 103; T.F. Tout, 'The Westminster chronicle attributed to Robert of Reading', *EHR*, xxxi (1916), 461–3, where a copy of the writ ordering the division is recorded. The writ is also recorded in E 159/97, m.4.

The royal treasure continued to accumulate until the very end. When the new regime of Isabella and Mortimer took control at the close of 1326 it inherited almost £62,000 in ready money and treasure,[81] a far cry from the debt of about £200,000 with which Edward II had begun his own reign and which had hampered his government at every turn.[82] After his victory in 1322 Edward was determined that he would never again face such problems. Like the Younger Despenser, Edward II wanted to be wealthy and, again like Despenser, he did not hesitate to say so. In an order to his exchequer officials in September 1323 he told them that it was their duty to make him rich.[83] There is ample evidence from 1322 that Edward took a strong personal interest in the collection of revenue and the accumulation of treasure from all available sources.[84] The shared interest in money was probably one of the things that bound Edward most closely to Despenser. Like the archetypal miser Edward not only gathered every penny he could but was remarkably loath to spend any more than he had to. It is ironic that in his final years expenditure on his household, which the Ordainers and the earl of Lancaster had once sought to curtail, was lower not only than at any time in his own reign but for generations past and to come.[85] Edward's meanness even extended to trying to persuade parliament in February 1324 to contribute to the ransom of the earl of Richmond, who had been taken prisoner by the Scots in October 1322 and whose loyalty to the crown had never wavered since 1307. Parliament firmly turned down both this request and Edward's attempt to obtain a subsidy, knowing full well that he was wealthy and they were poor.[86] In 1324 Edward even still owed over £400 for the repairs carried out to Westminster Palace before his coronation in 1308.[87]

According to the *Brut* chronicle, Edward II 'was the richest kyng that ever was in Engeland after William Bastard of Normandy', while the *Vita*

---

[81] Fryde, 105; E 159/103, m.24; *Calendar of Memoranda Rolls, Michaelmas 1326–Michaelmas 1327*, ed. R.A. Latham (London, 1968), no. 212; Buck, 193; E 101/332/21.

[82] See Prestwich, *Plantagenet England*, 175–7. Although about £60,000 of this remained outstanding in the 1320s, it is not clear whether Edward thought it his duty to pay off all his father's debts.

[83] Fryde, 102; E 159/97, m.17: '*et mettez votre peine qe nous soioms riches*'. Prestwich, *Plantagenet England*, 209–10, is however sceptical that this represents Edward's personal wishes, precisely because of its resemblance to Despenser's remark in Jan. 1321 that 'we may be rich and may attain our ends': SC 1/49/143; *Calendar . . . concerning Wales*, 219–20.

[84] See examples given in Fryde, 98–103.

[85] Ibid., 97: the wardrobe receipts for 1325–6 (19 Edward II) were £6,175, the lowest recorded for any year between 1224 and 1399: citing Tout, *Chapters*, vi, 74–101, esp. 86–7. This low figure was also the result of the wardrobe being restricted to its household role and giving up wider responsibilities. In 1319–20 these wider responsibilities (largely military in nature) were reflected in wardrobe receipts of over £50,000: Prestwich, *Plantagenet England*, 209.

[86] *Flores*, 219–20; Buck, 145–6; W.M. Ormrod, 'Agenda for legislation, 1322–*c*.1340', *EHR*, cv (1990), 8.

[87] SC 1/17/28 (certificate from Walter Stapeldon, the treasurer).

commented that many of his predecessors had accumulated money but he had surpassed them all. 'However the king's hardness is blamed on Hugh, like the other evils that take place at court.'[88] 'This sir Hugh was full of evil and wrongdoing, and he was also greedy and covetous while he was in office. He was also proud and haughty, more inclined to wrongdoing than any other man, so that no one was able to approach the king without the consent of the said sir Hugh and even then only through making large gifts.'[89] The financial pressures and the sheer greed of the regime of Edward and the Despensers were apparent to all and were to play a large part in the regime's sudden collapse in the autumn of 1326.

THE YORK PARLIAMENT OF MAY 1322

In order to complete Edward's victory there were certain things for which only a meeting of parliament would suffice. On 14 March, even before the battle of Boroughbridge, Edward summoned a parliament to meet at York on 2 May. Edward's elder son Edward earl of Chester was summoned for the first time, together with his uncles the earls of Norfolk and Kent, the king's half-brothers, and the other earls who had remained loyal, Richmond, Pembroke, Arundel, Surrey, and the earls of Angus and Atholl who were in exile from Scotland. The earls of Lancaster and Hereford who were in rebellion against the king and would both soon be dead were not of course invited. The seventy-two barons summoned also excluded those who had rebelled and would also soon be dead in battle, executed or imprisoned. Ironically, Thomas of Lancaster's brother Henry was among those called to attend. For the first time representatives were summoned from the Cinque Ports in recognition of the assistance they had given to Hugh Despenser the Younger during his exile; and also from the principality of Wales, where the revolt against the Marchers had played such a large part in undermining Edward II's opponents at the beginning of 1322.[90]

On the opening day of parliament the legal process against Lancaster was confirmed and the processes against the two Despensers formally annulled.[91] The Ordinances, from which Edward had been trying to escape since 1311, were formally revoked in the Statute of York, on the grounds that they improperly restrained royal power. In future any such ordinances would be null and void unless they were 'discussed, agreed and ordained in parlia-

---

[88] Buck, 193; *Brut*, i, 225; *Vita*, 136 (Denholm-Young edn), 230–1 (Childs edn).

[89] *Anonimalle*, 92–3, cited in Prestwich, *Plantagenet England*, 205. The remark was made in the context of the period 1318–21 but would have applied with even greater force after 1322.

[90] For the writs of summons to these and to the earls, barons, etc., see *PW*, II, ii, 245–60. For the proceedings of the York parliament of May 1322 see also my introduction in *PROME* on which I have drawn here. There is no surviving Parliament Roll for this assembly.

[91] *Foedera*, II, ii, 478–9; *CPR, 1321–24*, 115; *CCR, 1318–23*, 544–6; Phillips, 228.

ments, by our lord the king and with the assent of the prelates, earls and barons and the community of the realm, as has been the custom in times past'.[92] Much of the speculation about the significance of the Statute of York has been anachronistic. Edward II was trying to turn the clock back to before 1310–11, rather than to introduce a new emphasis on the authority of parliament or on the role of the 'community' in its future sense of the 'commons'.[93] No king in his hour of victory was likely to tie his hands for the future by introducing a new constitutional doctrine.[94] As a way of emphasizing that the Ordinances had originally been imposed upon him and that he was not opposed to reform in principle, Edward had six clauses reissued and confirmed as 'good points'. The rights and liberties of the Church, as contained in Magna Carta and other statutes, were to be observed; the king's peace was to be firmly kept throughout the land; Edward I's establishment concerning prises in the *Articuli super Cartas* of 1300 was to be upheld (this was the issue which lay behind many of the crises at the beginning of the reign of Edward II); sheriffs and the officials in charge of hundreds were to be appointed according to the Statute of Sheriffs of the 1316 Lincoln parliament; Edward I's grant in his Westminster parliament of 1306 concerning his forests was to be upheld; another of the *Articuli super Cartas*, concerning the estate of the steward and marshals of the household and of pleas to be held there was to be upheld in all its points (cf. Ordinances 26, 27); and the ordinances concerning the statute of merchants, outlawry and appeals, which were given verbatim as in the Ordinances of 1311 (cf. Ordinances 33, 35, 36).[95] However, the promulgation by Edward II of the 'good points' of the Ordinances was not, as has been suggested, a sign of 'the magnanimity of the king in adopting the good reforms of his bitterest enemies'; neither was it 'a good augury for the new era'.[96] Just as Edward's determination to defeat and destroy his enemies had inspired the Boroughbridge campaign in 1321–2, so now it dictated the ruthless zeal with which Edward and his

---

[92] *SR*, I, 189–90; *Select Documents*, 31–2 (French text); *English Historical Documents*, 543–4 (English trans.).

[93] Prestwich, *Plantagenet England*, 205–6, argues that by this date 'community of the realm' was coming to mean 'Commons'. My own view is that Edward's intention is that all those concerned in parliaments, from the king downwards, should approve legislation and that no one element, in this case the magnates, should be allowed to claim superiority over the rest.

[94] Cf. Phillips, 228, citing McKisack, *The Fourteenth Century*, 71–2; D. Clementi, 'That the Statute of York is no longer ambiguous', in *Album Helen Maud Cam*, ii (Louvain & Paris, 1961). See also Fryde, 65–6; Davies, *Baronial Opposition*, 511–17; Tout, *Place of the Reign*, 136–7.

[95] Davies, *Baronial Opposition*, 492–4. For the text of the 'good points' see *CCR, 1318–23*, 537–8. Edward was however giving with one hand and taking with the other, since one of the consequences of the repeal of the Ordinances was that he could again levy the 'new custom' on the imports and exports of foreign merchants. This began to be collected on 21 July 1322 and could be expected to add several thousand pounds annually to the king's ordinary revenue: Fryde, 64.

[96] Davies, *Baronial Opposition*, 492.

agents exploited the confiscated lands of the contrariants for the advantage of the royal treasury.

The surviving agenda of matters referred by the king to the council before the parliament met shows that the business of parliament was determined in advance.[97] Altogether fourteen items were discussed by the council, beginning with the statutes to repeal the Ordinances and give effect to the 'good points', and including the treatment of chattels belonging to felons and fugitives, and the creation of a staple for wool and cloth in England. Edward charged his councillors to give thought as to whether each of these matters, other than the first two, should be dealt with by statute or by other measures, in order that those attending parliament need not stay any longer than necessary. This last statement could be taken to mean either that Edward was considering the convenience of his subjects or that he intended to allow parliament as little initiative as possible. The answer probably lies in both. The one item on which Edward did not get his way was in relation to the goods of fugitives and felons, which he wished to turn into an annual revenue for his own use, and suggests that the proposal met considerable opposition.[98]

Scotland was also high on the agenda. Edward was determined to avenge his past defeats at the hands of the Scots as well as their recent raids. A Scottish campaign had already been ordered on 25 March to begin on 13 June, but during the parliament, on 11 May, the start of the campaign was postponed until 24 July at the request of the magnates and prelates.[99] The clergy granted an aid for the war in Scotland[100] but, so far as is known, the laity was not asked for a grant of taxation on this occasion. Edward did however revert to an expedient, which had already been tried in 1316 and 1318, for the service for forty days of one foot soldier from each vill, which was apparently approved at the parliament.[101] On 18 May an assembly of wool merchants was summoned to meet at York on 13 June, in order to discuss the wool staple but probably also in the hope that they might provide Edward with financial help for the coming campaign.[102]

---

[97] C 49/4/20: printed in Davies, *Baronial Opposition*, 582–3.

[98] Fryde, 65. Edward III tried the same policy in 1337 and was soon forced to abandon it: E.B. Fryde, 'Parliament and the French war, 1336–40', in *Historical Studies of the English Parliament*, i (London, 1970), 252–3.

[99] *CCR, 1318–23*, 532; *PW*, II, ii, 296; Phillips, 228.

[100] Lunt, *Financial Relations*, 410.

[101] Powicke, *Military Obligation*, 152–3.

[102] J.C. Davies, 'An assembly of wool merchants in 1322', *EHR*, xxxi (1916), 596–606. The meeting of merchants was part of the lengthy process by which the staple town was moved by 1324 from Saint-Omer in territory loyal to France to Bruges in the county of Flanders: Tout, *Place of the Reign*, 232–4. In the interest of preserving good relations with France Edward preferred to leave the staple at Saint-Omer but was meeting with growing pressure either to move it to Bruges or to establish staple towns in England.

A SIGN OF THE TIMES

The completeness of the Despensers' victory was vividly demonstrated shortly after the end of the York parliament. The earl of Pembroke was arrested by royal knights on the king's orders and taken back to York, but at the suit of some leading magnates he was pardoned, after making a pledge of loyalty on 22 June at Bishopsthorpe near York.[103] In this document Pembroke witnessed that Edward had been 'aggrieved against him for certain reasons that he was given to understand' and that 'desiring to obtain the king's grace and good will' so that Edward might assure himself of him 'as his faithful and loyal liegeman in all points', he had sworn upon the Gospels of his own free will to obey, aid and counsel the king in all matters, to come to him whenever ordered, to aid him in peace and war, not to ally with anyone against the king or anyone maintained by him, and to repress all alliances against him. For security Pembroke pledged his body and all his lands and goods, and also found guarantors.[104] The Despensers had obvious motives for wishing to see Pembroke humiliated and wishing to make him pay the penalty for his hostility towards them in 1321, but Edward had not forgiven him for his role in the Despensers' exile. He probably also believed that in 1320–1 Pembroke had used his planned remarriage as a pretext for staying abroad as long as possible. Pembroke was now a spent force politically. Short of outright opposition, which was unthinkable, he had no choice but to follow on the path marked out by Edward and the Despensers. He was one of the first noble men and women to suffer from the Despensers' greed; he was by no means the last.

DEFEAT IN SCOTLAND

As in 1314 and 1319, extensive and careful preparations were made for Edward's latest attempt to defeat the Scots. On 25 March, shortly after Lancaster's execution and while Edward was still at Pontefract, 38,000 infantry were summoned from throughout England; in early April a force of 6,000 infantry, 1,000 hobelars and 300 men-at-arms was ordered from Ireland; over 10,000 infantry from Wales; and 400 crossbowmen and lancers were to come from Gascony.[105] Orders were given for the purveyance in England, Ireland and Gascony of enormous quantities

---

[103] BL, Cotton Ms. Nero D.X, f. 112v; *CCR, 1318–23*, 563–4; Phillips, 227.

[104] Phillips, 227–8. The pledge was in effect a repetition by Pembroke and a reminder of the terms of his indenture with Edward II on 1 Nov. 1317. There is no positive evidence that Pembroke did pay a fine as stated in BL, Cotton Ms. Nero D.X, f. 112v.

[105] *CPR, 1321–24*, 96–8; *Foedera*, II, i, 482. In Feb. over 13,000 infantry from Wales and 4,000 from neighbouring English counties had been summoned for service against both the rebels and the Scots: *CPR, 1321–24*, 73–4. At this stage Edward evidently imagined that he would be able to proceed directly from defeating one enemy to tackling the other. There was some overlap between these plans and those of March and April.

of food for this army;[106] and a large fleet of ships was engaged to carry these supplies and to support the advance of the army into Scotland.[107]

Edward's plans were on the grandest, one might even say megalomaniac, scale. Victory had clearly gone to his head. The enormous army that he envisaged would have been unmanageable and, as events turned out, even more difficult to keep supplied. The army as finally assembled was much smaller than planned and consisted of nearly 20,000 infantry together with 2,100 hobelars.[108] In addition, the heavy cavalry force provided by the leading magnates, such as the earls of Arundel, Pembroke, Norfolk, Kent, Surrey, Carlisle, Richmond and Winchester, the earl of Louth from Ireland, the Scottish earls of Atholl and Angus, and the Younger Despenser and Henry of Lancaster, amounted to about 1,250.[109] Even so, it was bigger than the army which Edward had taken to Scotland in 1314 and the largest since his father's army at Falkirk in 1298. Edward himself remarked that the army was 'such as never had been seen in our time, or in the times of our ancestors'.[110] The sheer size of the army generated tensions: even before the campaign began a riot at Newcastle between English and Welsh troops left one royal knight, John de Penrith, and seven Welsh injured; while other Welsh foot soldiers caused considerable damage to a local convent for which Edward later paid the nuns compensation.[111]

Edward left York on 22 July and joined his army at Newcastle on or before 3 August. He was in a particularly angry mood since Robert Bruce had personally led a raid into England on 1 July, passing through Cumberland into Furness, and then into Lancashire, where he burned the towns of Lancaster and Preston before returning to Scotland on 24 July.[112] The advance into Scotland began on 10 August and the army reached Roxburgh on 13 August and Musselburgh near Edinburgh on 19 August.[113] If Edward hoped to bring Bruce's army to battle, he was sorely disappointed. Bruce withdrew northwards, clearing Lothian of all its livestock and other food supplies as he did so. As Edward himself remarked later in a letter to the archbishop of Canterbury, having taken the road on the sea coast to do more

---

[106] *CPR, 1321–24*, 93–4.

[107] BL, Stowe Ms. 553, ff. 51, 77–8; McNamee, 214; Prestwich, *Armies and Warfare* 117. The fleet numbered either 36 or 25 ships, depending on how many were engaged in the Scottish expedition and how many in other royal service. Although it was half the size of that employed in 1319, the fleet was still very valuable: McNamee, 214, 230.

[108] BL, Stowe Ms. 553, 56–62, 80–4; McNamee, 124–5, 158; Prestwich, *Armies and Warfare*, 117.

[109] Prestwich, 'Cavalry service', 155; Phillips, 228. The earl of Pembroke, for example, brought a total of 108 men-at-arms, including three bannerets and 25 knights: BL, Stowe Ms. 553, f. 56. The service of the magnates as a whole is recorded in ibid. ff. 56–62. There is a photograph of part of this record in Prestwich, *Armies and Warfare*, 50.

[110] McNamee, 124–5; Prestwich, *Armies and Warfare*, 117, 246; E 163/4/11, no.42.

[111] McNamee, 224, 232; BL, Stowe Ms. 553, f. 23d; N. Fryde, 'Welsh troops in the campaign of 1322', *Bulletin of the Board of Celtic Studies*, xxvi (1974–5), 85.

[112] Phillips, 228; Barrow, 243; McNamee, 98–9.

[113] Edward's movements can be followed in BL, Stowe Ms. 553 and *Itinerary*, ed. Hallam; McNamee, 99.

damage, he found neither 'man nor beast'. Bruce then crossed the Forth and established himself at the Cistercian abbey of Culross to await developments.[114] Edward's army spent three days, from 23 to 25 August, at Leith, the port for Edinburgh, while it waited for the ships carrying supplies to appear.[115] Some store ships may have arrived but not enough to feed the increasingly hungry army, the rest of the fleet having been scattered by stormy weather and by the activities of Flemish sailors allied to the Scots.[116] English attempts to forage for food met with little success. Allegedly all the soldiers found was one lame bull, provoking the remark by the earl of Surrey: 'In truth, I'm quite sure that this is the dearest beef that I've ever seen up to now; for a fact, it cost a thousand pounds or more'.[117] Edward and his army, many of them starting to die of hunger and disease,[118] had no choice but to abandon Scotland: they were followed by the Scots under Sir James Douglas who surprised them when they were trying to sack Melrose abbey and inflicted severe casualties. After the English crossed the border, the Scots infiltrated Northumberland provoking floods of refugees.[119] On 10 September Edward was back at Newcastle, having achieved nothing and added only to his reputation for military incompetence.

The campaign was ill conceived from the beginning. Edward realized well enough that if he brought together very large numbers of troops, they would have to be fed and that a fleet of supply ships would be needed to ensure this. He was also aware of the dangers that might be posed to a campaign by Flemish sailors in Scottish service and took action beforehand to try to prevent this happening.[120] When the campaign had ended he was quick to place the blame on 'these evil Flemings' for preventing his supply ships from getting through.[121] On the other hand, Edward's army was far too large and inflexible and consisted of the wrong kind of troops for the situation faced in

---

[114] *Bruce*, 678–9; *CDS*, iii, 144; Barrow, 243; Phillips, 228–9.

[115] Edinburgh castle, which had earlier been an English-held stronghold, had been destroyed by the Scots after they captured it in 1314 and was of no use to Edward in 1322: Barrow, 196.

[116] *Bruce*, 680–1; McNamee, 99; Fryde, 129. There is a record of payments in money and wheat flour to members of the army at Leith on 23 Aug. which may indicate the arrival of supplies by sea: *CDS*, iii, 142.

[117] *Bruce*, 680–1.

[118] See, e.g., Trinity College Cambridge Ms. R.5.41, f. 118d. In 1326 the Younger Despenser was accused of bringing about the deaths of more than 20,000 men in the 1322 campaign through neglect: *Gesta Edwardi*, 88. This is certainly greatly exaggerated. It is difficult to distinguish losses through death from desertions, which were certainly substantial: see Fryde, 'Welsh troops', 82–9.

[119] Barrow, 243; McNamee, 99; Phillips, 229.

[120] In April and May he had tried to improve relations with the count of Flanders and had also ordered Great Yarmouth and the Cinque Ports to provide ships for defence against Flemish attack: *Foedera*, II, i, 483–5. Edward's dealings with Flanders were part of a diplomatic campaign that had begun in early 1319 when the earl of Hereford and the bishop of Exeter had visited Flanders, Brabant and Hainault to try to ensure that the Scots received no help from their rulers: Buck, 126.

[121] Prestwich, *Armies and Warfare*, 246; E 163/4/11, no. 73; *CDS*, iii, 144.

Scotland. Unlike his father, Edward no longer possessed strongpoints in Scotland under English control which could support and reinforce the actions of a large invading army. A smaller army with greater numbers of hobelars and other mobile forces, such as the new earl of Carlisle Andrew Harclay had successfully employed at Boroughbridge, might have achieved better results.[122] The armoured infantry, used experimentally in the 1322 campaign, had no opportunity to show their worth.[123] As it was, all the Scots had to do was wait for the English to starve and begin their inevitable retreat.

Edward decided to stay in the north for the winter to protect it from further Scottish attacks. He appointed Andrew Harclay as warden of the entire Scottish March, both east and west, and ordered local commanders, such as Sir Thomas de Grey the constable of Norham and Louis de Beaumont the bishop of Durham, to see to the defence of their own regions. He showed irritation at the behaviour of the bishop's brother, Henry de Beaumont, and also took out his displeasure on other commanders, such as the constables of Bamburgh, Dunstanburgh, Warkworth and Alnwick, for failing to challenge the Scots who had entered Northumberland and were infesting the neighbourhood of their castles.[124]

A PERSONAL LOSS

As Edward told the archbishop of Canterbury on 17 September, after his return from Scotland, he was then in good health.[125] This may in part have been the result of the large stock of medicines worth over £9 and provided by the king's surgeon, Master Stephen of Paris, which was carried by land from London to Newcastle, and thence by sea to Edinburgh, before being shipped back again to '*Halyeland*'.[126] However, Edward experienced a personal loss in the death of Adam, the mysterious illegitimate son, who had his first and last experience of campaigning in the summer of

---

[122] Harclay had also made use of the Scottish tactic of the schiltrom, soldiers armed with long spears in close formation: Prestwich, *Armies and Warfare*, 333.

[123] Powicke, *Military Obligation*, 152–3; Prestwich, *Armies and Warfare*, 134.

[124] *CDS*, iii, 143–6. This may be a first sign of the tensions which led to Henry storming out of a council meeting at York in May 1323: C 49/45/15 (printed in Davies, *Baronial Opposition*, 584–5).

[125] *CDS*, iii, 144.

[126] *CDS*, iii, 142. '*Halyeland*' is probably Holy Island off the coast of Northumberland. The 'medicines' included such items as *Oxerocrosin, Dyatarascos, Apostolicon, dyaculon, Terbentyn, Agrippa*, white and dark ointments, *Gracia Dei, Apoponak, Mastyk, Saunguys Draconis, Mirre, Calamine, Tutie* and *litarge. Saunguys Draconis*, or Dragon's blood, for example, was a resin used for treating wounds.

One of the places passed by the English army on its journey to and from Edinburgh was the Augustinian house and hospital at Soutra near Edinburgh. Recent archaeological investigations conducted by Dr Brian Moffat for the SHARP project (Soutra Hospital Archaeoethnopharmacological Research Project) have revealed extensive evidence of the medical and surgical treatment provided by the friars to men and women caught up in the Anglo-Scottish wars of the late 13th and 14th centuries.

1322.[127] Although there is no known reference to Adam before 1322, he was evidently openly recognized by Edward as his son and was held in some degree of affection. Hugh Chastilloun, a squire of the royal household, was Adam's master, while Sir John Sturmy, one of the king's household knights, decided what Adam would need by way of arms and other equipment for the war. Adam was at York on 6 June and can be traced there again on 4 and 10 July. On 3 August he was at Newcastle, at Musselburgh in Scotland on 19 August, and again at Newcastle on 18 September, all dates which match his father's itinerary.[128] Adam was probably one of the many members of the army who became sick, and he died before 30 September when a silk cloth with gold thread was placed upon his body at his burial in the conventual church of Tynemouth priory.[129] That is all that can be said with certainty, but there is a possible mention of Adam in a letter addressed to Edward and datable to the summer of 1322. The unnamed author of the letter notes that Edward had ordered him to bring 'the king's son' safely to York, and adds that 'all good qualities and honour are increasing' in him.[130] The son in question could have been Edward of Windsor, Edward II's elder legitimate son, who was summoned as earl of Chester to join the army preparing for Scotland. But Edward was only nine years old and unlikely to have been present in person even if he sent military service in his name. The reference in the letter simply to 'the king's son', rather than to the earl, suggests that Adam was meant and that the author of the letter might have been Adam's master, Hugh Chastilloun.

TWO NARROW ESCAPES

On the day of Adam's burial his father was at Barnard Castle near Durham helping to gather forces to meet an expected Scottish attack. His wife, Isabella, meanwhile had been sent to Tynemouth for safety:[131] it proved to be anything but safe. On about 30 September Robert Bruce entered England, reaching Northallerton in Yorkshire on about 12 October, only 15 miles from where Edward was staying at Rievaulx abbey.[132] Although Bruce may have been hoping to take Edward by surprise and to capture him, Edward was warned by his spies of the proximity of the Scots and on 13 October wrote to the earl of Pembroke, asking him to come to Byland on the following day with all the force he could muster. There he would find the earl of Richmond

---

[127] Nothing is known of Adam's mother but I suggested in ch. 3 that, assuming he was at least as old as Edward II had been when he first went to war (i.e. in his seventeenth year in 1300), Adam could have been born in about 1305 or 1306. F.D. Blackley first drew attention to Adam's existence in his paper, 'Adam, the bastard son', BL, Stowe Ms. 553, f. 27.

[128] BL, Stowe Ms. 553, f. 27. Blackley did not notice this later reference to Adam.

[129] BL, Stowe Ms. 553, f. 113.

[130] SC 1/63/177: '*tutes bountes e honours sount en lui cressaunt*'.

[131] *CDS*, iii, 146 (letter to the constable of Norham castle; undated but probably Sept.). Isabella was presumably present at Adam's funeral.

[132] *Bruce*, 683–4; *Lanercost*, 247; SC 1/49/52; Barrow, 243; Phillips, 229.

and Henry de Beaumont, to whom Edward had already explained his intentions, and he was to make all the necessary plans with them.[133] Pembroke and Richmond carried out their orders and on 14 October stationed their men on the summit of Blackhow Moor near Byland. Here they were attacked by Sir James Douglas and the earl of Moray, and in the rout which followed they were defeated and the earl of Richmond and a French nobleman, Henry de Sully the butler of France, were captured.[134] Pembroke escaped from the battle to York with some of his retainers.[135] The encounter itself did not however come as a surprise since as early as 2 October Edward had summoned forces to assemble at Blackhow Moor.[136] On the day the English were defeated by more determined leadership and by the ferocity of the Scottish attack up a steep hillside which left them outflanked and in a desperate position.[137] Edward was warned of the danger while he was eating his breakfast and made his escape just in time, accompanied by his half-brother the earl of Kent, the Younger Despenser and others, first to Bridlington priory and Burstwick, and then to York, hotly pursued by the Scots until he reached the gates of the city.[138] As had happened at Bannockburn, Edward again lost his privy seal, together with other valuables and equipment.[139] When news of the battle reached London on 28 October it caused great alarm.[140]

Even now Edward's humiliation at the hands of the Scots was not complete, since Isabella was cut off behind enemy lines and also in danger of capture by the Scots. To be fair to Edward, the Benedictine priory of Tynemouth, in which he had placed her for security, was situated in a strongly fortified position on a headland overlooking the North Sea. He had also told the constable of Norham to look after her safety,[141] and he had ordered the earls of Atholl and Richmond to gather men from among those commanded by the Younger Despenser and to take them to defend the queen. Edward later had second thoughts and decided that Henry de Sully and his men should undertake the defence of Tynemouth since they would be *'plus greables que autres'* to Isabella.[142] This could be interpreted to

---

[133] SC 1/49/52; *CDS*, iii, 146–7; Phillips, 229. For safety, the letter was sent in duplicate by different messengers.

[134] *Melsa*, 345–6; *Lanercost*, 247; *Bruce*, 684–8; *Flores*, 210; BL, Stowe Ms. 553, ff. 68v, 69; Phillips, 229; Barrow, 244; McNamee, 101. For a map showing the Scottish raids in 1322 see McNamee, 102.

[135] *Chroniques de Sempringham*, 345; Phillips, 229.

[136] *Foedera*, II, i, 497; McNamee, 100.

[137] Barrow, 244, 371, n. 45.

[138] *Gesta Edwardi*, 79–80; *Lanercost*, 247–8; *Melsa*, 346; *Bruce*, 691–2; Barrow, 244.

[139] *Foedera*, II, i, 498; *Lanercost*, 247–8; *Bruce*, 691–2; *CDS*, iii, 147; Barrow, 244. The privy seal was merely mislaid in the confusion and had been found again by 19 Oct.: E 159/96, mm.96, 140.

[140] SC 1/63/169 (letter from the bishop of Ely to Edward).

[141] *CDS*, iii, 146.

[142] Doherty (D.Phil.), 93; E 163/4/11, no. 15 (a set of drafts of privy seal letters). In one of the drafts the reference to Despenser and his men is erased, which may be significant.

mean either that Isabella already disliked Despenser so much that she could not bear to have any of his men around her or that Henry de Sully, freshly arrived with news of her family and of the French court, would be better company.[143] These plans of course came to nothing because of the débâcle at Blackhow Moor and in the end Isabella and Eleanor de Clare, Despenser's wife who was with her, were taken to safety by a number of squires of the royal household.[144] It is not clear how they escaped, probably by sea, or just how close Isabella and Eleanor came to capture by the Scots.[145] But there can be little doubt of Isabella's anger and humiliation. She had been forced to flee on three occasions during her marriage to Edward: from Tynemouth in 1312 when she, Edward and Gaveston had escaped from the advancing forces of the earl of Lancaster; in 1319 from Scottish raiders at the time of the battle of Myton; and now, once again from Tynemouth in 1322.

A SCOTTISH SETTLEMENT AT LAST

On 28 October Edward gave his minstrel, William de Morley, alias the King of the North, property at Pontefract which had belonged to one of Thomas of Lancaster's minstrels, John le Boteler, alias King Bruaunt. This action could be seen either as an example of Edward II's preference for trivial matters over affairs of state or, more positively, as a reward to a man who had served him loyally since 1299 and whose playing of the harp was helping him to get over the humiliation and tragedy he had just experienced.[146]

Whatever the truth, there is no doubt that in the winter of 1322–3 Edward was as heavily concerned as ever with the Scots. Having come so close to capturing Edward on 14 October, the Scots took their revenge on the canons of Bridlington priory and their possessions before raiding other parts of the East Riding and returning across the border on 2 November. The Scots had been one month and three days in England, the longest time they had yet spent there. In the meantime they had ravaged the area around Carlisle, preventing Andrew Harclay from bringing his cavalry forces to aid Edward at Blackhow Moor, as intended.[147]

On 18 September, immediately after his return to Newcastle from his disastrous Scottish campaign, Edward summoned a parliament first to

---

[143] Isabella's brother, Philip V, king of France had died in Jan. and been succeeded by her remaining brother Charles as Charles IV. So there would have been plenty of news to catch up on.
[144] BL, Stowe Ms. 553, ff. 45, 134.
[145] If the account in *Recueil des Historiens des Gaules*, xx, 632, cited in Doherty, *Isabella*, 77–8, is correct, the two women were in real danger; one of Isabella's ladies was killed and another died later of her injuries.
[146] *Foedera*, II, i, 498; Bullock-Davies, *Register*, 18–19, 125–8.
[147] *Gesta Edwardi*, 79–81; *Lanercost*, 241; McNamee, 99–101, 104. The canons did at least manage to send their treasures to safety in Lincolnshire.

Ripon on 14 November, and then under pressure of events to meet at York. Edward announced his intention of spending the winter in the north with a strong force to restrain the attacks of the Scots, before returning to Scotland in the coming summer to defeat the Scots once and for all, 'with God's aid'.[148] When the parliament met on 14 November the chief topics were probably recriminations and money. The failure in Scotland was one of the things which weakened Edward II's hold on power in the closing years of his reign.[149] On 27 November, two days before the end of the parliament, it was decided that the king and the leading magnates should remain in the north over the winter and on 2 December a fresh muster was ordered to take place at York on 2 February 1323.[150] In order to finance this new campaign a tenth and a sixth of the value of moveable goods were granted to the king, to be payable in two parts, on 3 April and 1 July 1323. This tax, which proved to be both the last and the heaviest of Edward II's reign, yielded over £42,000.[151] On 27 November the archbishops of Canterbury and York were ordered to summon the clergy, who had not attended the parliament, to meet at Lincoln on 14 January 1323 to discuss a subsidy in aid of the Scottish war.[152]

However, there was no reason to believe that a new campaign in Scotland would be any more successful than its predecessor. The futility of Edward's policy towards Scotland was further demonstrated on 3 January 1323 when the earl of Carlisle, Andrew de Harclay, the victor of Boroughbridge, acted on his own initiative in meeting Robert Bruce at Lochmaben and making a draft peace treaty recognizing Scottish independence.[153] Two versions of the treaty exist, one now in the Royal Library in Copenhagen which Professor Barrow considers to be the best text;[154] and the other, of which there are two copies, in England: one in the National Archives in London and one in the *Gesta Edwardi de Carnarvon* composed at Bridlington priory.[155] England and Scotland would be separate kingdoms,

---

[148] *PW*, II, ii, 261–80.

[149] Military incompetence was to be one of the primary charges brought against Edward in 1327. While Professor Michael Powicke observed that at least seven of the knights who served in the 1327 parliament during which Edward was deposed had also played a part as arrayers of infantry troops in 1322, and no doubt had strong views on the failure of the campaign, he overestimates the part played by the 'commons' in 1327: M.R. Powicke, 'The English commons in Scotland in 1322 and the deposition of Edward II', *Speculum*, xxxv (1960), 556–62, esp. 556–8.

[150] *CCR, 1318–23*, 687, 690; Phillips, 229.

[151] *Lay Taxes*, 36. The form of taxation is in *PW*, II, ii, 279–80.

[152] For the summons to the clergy see *PW*, II, ii, 280–1. Forty-four abbots and three priors were also summoned to this assembly.

[153] *Lanercost*, 248; *CCR, 1318–23*, 692; Phillips, 229; Barrow, 248.

[154] Barrow, 248, 372. The text (text A) is printed with a commentary in *Regesta Regum Scottorum*, no. 215, 480–3, 485.

[155] E 159/96, m.70 (French), printed in *Anglo-Scottish Relations*, ed. Stones, no. 39; *Gesta Edwardi*, 82–3 (Latin); and (as texts B & C) in *Regesta Regum Scottorum*, 483–5, no. 215; Barrow, 249; Phillips, 229. A summary of the treaty also appears in *Lanercost*, 248–9.

each with its own king and with its own laws and customs. Harclay promised to do everything in his power to ensure that the treaty was implemented and to secure the independence of Bruce and his kingdom; in return Bruce would promote and maintain the common advantage of the kingdom of England. If Edward accepted the terms within one year, Bruce would pay him 40,000 marks in ten annual instalments, would found a monastery in Scotland for the souls of those killed in the war, and allow Edward to choose a wife from his own family for Bruce's heir. Neither king would be forced to accept back into his kingdom anyone who had fought against him or to restore his lands.[156] Harclay sought to obtain the support of the mayor and community of Newcastle for the proposed treaty.[157] Harclay's motives are uncertain. According to the author of the Lanercost chronicle, he said that since Edward could neither govern nor defend his kingdom against the Scots, whose devastations were growing year by year so that in the end the entire kingdom would be lost, the lesser of two evils was for the two kingdoms to exist together in peace.[158] On the other hand, the mutual guarantees given by Harclay and Bruce that neither would harm the other's lands in any future campaign suggest that Harclay had given up on Edward II altogether and was also looking to his own interests.[159]

Edward already had his suspicions on 8 January when he forbade Harclay and the communities of the Scottish March to engage in any truce negotiations with the Scots.[160] When he heard the details of Harclay's draft treaty, Edward at once repudiated it and declared Harclay a traitor. His arrest was ordered on 1 February and on 25 February Harclay was taken by surprise and captured in Carlisle castle by Sir Anthony de Lucy.[161] Two days later the earl of Kent, Sir John Hastings, three royal knights and a royal judge, Sir Geoffrey le Scrope, were appointed to pass judgment on Harclay, which they duly performed at Carlisle on 3 March. Harclay was to be degraded from his title as earl and from knighthood before being hanged, drawn and quartered. The quarters were then to be displayed at Carlisle, Newcastle, York and Shrewsbury, as a warning to other possible traitors.[162] The savagery of his sentence marked not only Edward's feelings of betrayal by the very man who had defeated Lancaster less than a year

[156] Based on the summary of the terms in Barrow, 248–9. Some details have been omitted here.
[157] *Gesta Edwardi*, 83.
[158] *Lanercost*, 248. Barrow, 248, suggests the chronicler may have recorded Harclay's final words on the scaffold. Coming so soon after the recently held parliament, which he attended, Harclay's actions suggest that there had been discussion, perhaps heated, about whether or not to negotiate with the Scots and that those in favour of peace had for the moment been overruled, leading to Harclay taking matters into his own hands.
[159] Barrow, 248.
[160] *Foedera*, II, i, 502.
[161] BL, Stowe Ms. 553, f. 18v; *Lanercost*, 250–1; *Foedera*, II, i, 504; *CPR, 1321–24*, 240; Phillips, 230.
[162] *CPR, 1317–24*, 260; *Foedera*, II, i, 509; Phillips, 230.

earlier but also the depths of violence and confusion into which the kingdom was now beginning to descend and which would soon be beyond anyone's control.

Although in early April Edward ordered troops to assemble at York before the 24th in case the Scots resumed their attacks, he had already entered into negotiations of his own.[163] The first steps in dealing with the Scots had been taken early in February, even before Harclay's arrest and execution, when some of the retainers of Henry de Sully who had been captured at Blackhow Moor came to the king as intermediaries. As a result a temporary truce lasting until 22 May was made on 14 March, and on 1 April, following an appeal from Robert Bruce to Sully, three Scottish envoys were given safe conducts until 5 May to come to Newcastle. On the same date Sully was asked to prolong the truce until after 22 May and English envoys were appointed to meet the Scots. Soon after this, all the orders issued on 1 April were cancelled, perhaps to give more time to prepare for the talks. On 29 April the truce was extended until 2 June, and on 30 April the Younger Despenser's son Hugh, Pembroke's nephew John Hastings and two others were sent from Newark to stay at Tweedmouth as hostages while the Scottish envoys, the bishop of St Andrew's and the earl of Moray, came to Newcastle and York to discuss a longer truce.[164] Since December 1322 negotiations for a truce had also been under way with the count of Flanders, in the hope that this would remove one of the most persistent and intractable sources of external support for the Scottish cause. On 5 April a truce with Flanders was finally proclaimed.[165]

On 1 May the earl of Pembroke, bishop of Exeter, the Younger Despenser and Robert Baldock were given authority to make a final peace treaty with the Scots, whom they met at Newcastle a few days later.[166] The negotiations did not go well at first.[167] A letter from Robert Bruce to Henry de Sully, written from Berwick on 21 March, gives a good idea of the problems. In it Bruce expressed his desire to make peace with England but said that Edward's refusal even to address him by name, let alone as king, had so far made peace impossible. Bruce concluded by saying that 'it does not seem advisable to us to accept a truce in which no more mention is made of us than of the humblest man in our kingdom, so that we could demand no more than any other if the truce were to be infringed wholly or in part'.[168]

---

[163] *Foedera*, II, i, 512.

[164] *CPR, 1321–24*, 236, 268, 277–9, 281; *Foedera*, II, i, 511; BL, Stowe Ms. 553, f. 27; Phillips, 230–1. The accident of Sully's capture by the Scots contributed considerably to smoothing the way for serious negotiations between the English and the Scots. The reason for Sully's presence in England in 1322–3 is not clear, but it may have been in response to Edward II's appeal to the French king in Feb. 1322 for help against Lancaster: *Foedera*, II, i, 475.

[165] *Foedera*, II, i, 500, 508, 511.

[166] *CPR, 1321–24*, 279; E 159/96, m.27d; *Lanercost*, 252; *Gesta Edwardi*, 84; Phillips, 231.

[167] *Foedera*, II, i, 521; Phillips, 231.

[168] Barrow, 245, citing *Foedera*, II, i, 511.

This was disingenuous on Bruce's part, since the English refusal to recognize him as the king of an independent kingdom was at the heart of the Anglo-Scottish conflict. On 11 May Edward wrote to the earl of Pembroke, telling him that the existing truce had been extended until 5 June, but also advising him to be ready to answer the military summons to Newcastle on 1 July if the talks should break down. Edward then indulged in a tirade against the malice of the Scots and the innumerable killings and acts of devastation they had committed against the people of his kingdom, whose welfare he claimed was always close to his heart:[169] fairly standard language in terms of past conflict, but not at all the words to be expected from a king who seriously intended to make peace.

No peace treaty was made, but Edward had his way, at least with regard to Bruce's title. In late May the English and Scottish negotiators agreed on a truce between Edward and 'Sir Robert de Bruce' and their respective subjects, lasting thirteen years; after which both sets of envoys came to Bishopsthorpe near York, where on 30 May the truce was confirmed by Edward and the council.[170] The final recognition of an independent Scotland by the English crown had to wait until the Treaty of Northampton concluded in the name of Edward III by Isabella and Mortimer in 1328. Although the 1323 truce had been born out of Edward's humiliation, England was at least at peace with all its external enemies for the first time since 1294.

However, an indication that all was not well occurred during the Bishopsthorpe council. Fifty councillors were present, including the archbishop of York, the bishops of Norwich and Exeter, the earls of Kent, Pembroke, Winchester and Atholl, as well as the Younger Despenser and Henry de Sully, newly released by the Scots. Henry de Beaumont, one of Edward's closest advisers since the beginning of the reign, was also present but disagreed so strongly with the proposed truce that he refused to take part in the discussion. Edward angrily dismissed Beaumont from the council and had him committed to prison, from which he was released only after the intervention of eight other councillors.[171] Henry had a personal interest in Scotland since the terms of the truce prevented him from pursuing his claim to the Scottish earldom of Buchan, in right of his wife Alice Comyn.[172] In

---

[169] SC 1/49/53; Phillips, 231. The summons had been issued on 23 Feb.: *PW*, II, ii, 346.
[170] *Foedera*, II, i, 521; Phillips, 231; McNamee, 236–7.
[171] *Foedera*, II, i, 520. A list of those present at Bishopsthorpe, entitled *Les nouns de ceux qi furent au conseil a Thorp y ceo Lundi a Lendemayn as oytaves de la Trinite*, is preserved in C 49/45/15 and printed in Davies, *Baronial Opposition*, 584–5. Beaumont was related to Edward II through his great-grandfather, Alfonso IX, king of Leon, while his service to the crown went back as far as 1297, which made the breach in 1323 all the more serious: M. Prestwich, 'Isabella de Vescy and the custody of Bamburgh castle', *BIHR*, xliv (1971), 148–52.
[172] This was an early indication of the problem of 'the disinherited' (whose ranks included other northern families such as the Wakes and Percys and David of Strathbogie, earl of Atholl) which was to be of great importance in the early years of Edward III's reign: W.M. Ormrod, *The Reign of Edward III* (New Haven & London, 1990), 8; R. Nicholson, *Edward III and the Scots* (Oxford, 1965), 57–74.

February Edward had also criticized his brother Louis, the bishop of Durham for allegedly not doing enough to defend the lands of his diocese from the Scots.[173] To make matters worse, the Beaumonts were related to Isabella, who had pressed strongly for Louis's appointment as bishop of Durham in 1316. Although Henry's relations with Edward were later patched up,[174] the episode was a sign of the times and may have been another cause of estrangement between Edward and his wife.

SIGNS AND PORTENTS

There were many indications that England itself was only superficially at peace. In September 1322 miracles were said to have taken place at Thomas of Lancaster's tomb in Pontefract priory, where the deaf, the dumb and the blind all found cures; and to make sure that the greatest possible political mileage could be obtained miracles were also said to have occurred in May 1323 at the painted plaque which Lancaster had set up in St Paul's cathedral in London to commemorate Edward II's granting of the Ordinances in 1311. In response Edward forbade anyone to go near Lancaster's place of execution or burial on pain of punishment; while on Edward's orders Robert Baldock the keeper of the privy seal and archdeacon of Middlesex removed the plaque and the candles which had been left burning there in Lancaster's honour.[175] In September 1323 the mayor of Bristol inquired into a riot which had recently taken place at the gallows on which the bodies of Henry de Montfort and Henry de Wilyngton had been hanging since their execution in March 1322, and told the king that Reginald de Montfort and others had fraudulently reported miracles.[176] It was probably a fear of further politically inspired miracles rather than just the pleading of the Church which in March 1324 finally induced Edward to allow the burial of the men executed in 1322.[177]

The 'miracles' were only one example of local unrest and disturbance. Some of this had been caused by the passage of the rival armies of the

---

[173] *Foedera*, II, i, 506.

[174] But only for a time since in 1326 Henry was to be one of Isabella's leading supporters against her husband.

[175] E 163/4/11/16 (draft of privy seal letter, dated at Durham on 28 Sept., from the king to the archbishop of York); *Foedera*, II, i, 525–6; *Flores*, 213–14; *Brut*, i, 228–30; *Anonimalle*, 114–15. The incident at St Paul's probably reflected the hostility to the king and to the Younger Despenser within the city of London just as much as any more general support for the memory of Lancaster: see Williams, *Medieval London*, 291–3.

[176] JI 1/291, m.61; *CCW*, 543; *CPR, 1321–24*, 148, 378. A poor child, for example, had been given 2s to claim that he had recovered his sight.

[177] *Foedera*, II, i, 546;-*Murimuth*, 43. But at the same time Edward made sure that the evidence of their guilt was preserved by ordering the enrolment in Jan. 1325 of the judgments recorded against them on the roll of the King's Bench (KB) 27/259 (Hilary 1325), mm.173d, 34–35d (Crown Roll): Sayles, 'The formal judgments', 58.

contrariants and king during the civil war of 1321–2.[178] In many places the fighting between the king and the magnates was followed by an orgy of looting as individuals carried away as much as they could of property belonging to former contrariants before royal officials could take charge;[179] in other cases fugitive contrariants fought on.[180] The civil war and its aftermath also provided the cue and opportunity for men to engage in law-breaking and brigandage, secure in the knowledge that the government did not have the resources or the energy to bring them to book.[181]

One such individual was Robert le Ewer, a royal yeoman with a reputation for unruly and unscrupulous behaviour, which had caused a demand from the Ordainers for his expulsion from the king's service in 1311, and petitions to be lodged against him in 1314–15 and 1320.[182] One chronicler even described him as 'the prince of thieves'.[183] In February 1320 he was replaced as constable of Odiham castle in Hampshire by the Younger Despenser, and the following August his arrest was ordered, for defying and threatening violence against royal officials.[184] He was again put in charge of Odiham in July 1321 when Despenser's lands were taken into royal control to protect then from attack; and was active in the civil war of 1321–2 during which he helped to seize control of rebels' lands and raised and commanded troops for the crown. He appears to have served in the Scottish campaign but in September 1322 left the king secretly and without permission and headed for his home county of Hampshire, where he allegedly acted like a Robin Hood, distributing the goods of executed contrariants to the poor as alms for their souls; in November the king ordered Robert's arrest after he attempted to seize Odiham and raided a royal manor, and sent the earl of Kent south to capture him.[185] Robert le Ewer's motives are obscure but he appears to have had had a particular enmity against Hugh Despenser the Elder, the new earl of Winchester, whose Hampshire manors he attacked, and who was allegedly forced to

---

[178] Waugh, 'The profits of violence'.

[179] Examples can be found in the commissions of oyer and terminer appointed by the government in May 1322 as it attempted to get a grip on the situation: *CPR, 1321–24*, 151–61 (May 1322).

[180] Fryde provides several examples of this: 151–2.

[181] See, for example, E.L.G. Stones, 'The Folvilles of Ashby-Folville in Leicestershire, and their associates in crime', *TRHS*, 5th ser., vii (1957), 117–36; J.G. Bellamy, 'The Coterel gang', *EHR*, lxxix (1964), 698–717.

[182] *Ann. Lond.*, 199 ('*Roberd le Ewer archers et tieu manere de ribaudaille*', serving in castles and elsewhere); SC 8/4/190–1; SC 8/92/4562A, 4562B (the latter concerned a particularly devious and heartless attempt by le Ewer and an accomplice, William de Bentworth, to gain possession of a watermill near Basingstoke from its rightful owners).

[183] *Princeps ipse latronum*: *Flores*, 211.

[184] *CFR, 1319–27*, 15, 18; *CCR, 1318–23*, 260, 326.

[185] BL, Stowe Ms. 553, f. 63; *CFR, 1319–27*, 64; *CPR, 1321–24*, 40, 44, 199, 206, 221–3, 254; *CCR, 1318–23*, 597; *Vita*, 200–1, 216–17, and n. 412. Le Ewer had been replaced as constable on 19 Sept.: *CFR, 1319–27*, 178.

withdraw for safety to Windsor castle. Despite the efforts of the earls of Winchester and Kent to track him down, Robert le Ewer was eventually captured by chance in Southampton on about 13 December 1322, after first attempting to flee with his wife to France. Refusing to answer his judges, he was consigned to prison in Winchester, deprived of food and water, and so loaded with chains that he died there a few days later.[186]

PLOTS AND COUNTERPLOTS

Robert le Ewer's revolt caused considerable anxiety to the king, especially since it included an attempt to seize a royal castle and also endangered one of his closest supporters, the earl of Winchester. So far as is known, Robert was acting on his own account and was not part of any more general conspiracy. Two far more serious events took place in 1323, not only involving the security of other important royal castles but also showing that the contrariants still had influential and determined supporters. The first of them occurred on 11 January 1323, when an attempt was made to free Maurice de Berkeley and other prisoners, including Hugh Audley the Elder, from captivity in Wallingford castle in Berkshire, where they had been held for almost a year.[187] According to the *Vita Edwardi Secundi*, one of Berkeley's squires, later identified as Roger Wauton, who had visited him regularly in prison, one day entered the castle with several companions, with the guard's permission and without arousing any suspicion. That night Maurice invited the constable and all the doorkeepers and watchmen to dine with him. While they were dining the squire and his companions rose and demanded the keys of the castle; the squire then opened a postern gate and let in twenty more men. All this was done in complete silence and the conspirators might have escaped with all the prisoners, but for a young boy who realized that something was wrong and warned the mayor of the town that the castle was lost. When the local sheriff arrived, the conspirators tried to buy time by claiming that they had entered the castle with the king's authority. The earls of Winchester and Kent then came and threatened to attack the castle. On about 25 January, the conspirators opened the gates and withdrew to the castle chapel in search of sanctuary: 'Thus, having entered, the earls found Maurice

---

[186] BL, Stowe Ms. 553, ff. 63, 68; *Vita*, 214–19; *Flores*, 211; *Murimuth*, 39. Control of Odiham castle was probably the root cause of his behaviour, since its custody had alternated between himself and the Despensers.

[187] *CPR, 1321–24*, 257; *Chroniques de Sempringham*, 346. Edward learned of the event on 17 Jan. at Stowe Park in Lincolnshire: BL, Stowe Ms. 553, f. 27v. On the same date he wrote to the constable of Skipton castle in Yorkshire (and probably other constables too) to tell him to see to the castle's safety and to report any news, 'because of some strange and diverse news we have heard'; ('*par ascuns estranges et diverses novelles qe nous avons oy*'): SC 1/45/206.

in custody as usual, and the rest in the chapel.'[188] Of those involved, the ringleader Roger Wauton, and two others, Sir Edmund de la Beche and Sir John de '*Goleinton*', were taken to the king at Pontefract, where Wauton was hanged and the others imprisoned.[189] It had been a close call and was a foretaste of the attempts made in 1327 to release Edward II from captivity in Maurice de Berkeley's own castle.[190]

The attempt on Wallingford occurred just as Andrew Harclay's conspiracy was developing in the north. The king's suspicions that the Londoners were complicit in the Wallingford affair were not allayed when they refused to send fifty crossbowmen to help in the siege, on the pretext that their prime duty was to hold London for the king, as surety for which the queen and her children were living among them.[191] Isabella had come south after Christmas and since 12 January had been staying in the Tower of London, where she was apparently joined by her elder son, Edward earl of Chester.[192] Because of the Harclay conspiracy Edward was unable to come south until late March, but was preceded by Harclay's head which on 13 March was stuck on a spike on London Bridge, as a warning to the Londoners.[193] Edward first spent a few days at King's Langley before reaching Westminster on 1 April. On 4 April he removed the mayor of London, Hamo de Chigwell, from office, replacing him with Nicholas de Farndon.[194] Edward (and probably Isabella) then made a short visit to Canterbury, on 10 April, perhaps to give thanks for past victories and pray for assistance in his present difficulties, before returning to the Tower of London on the 15th. Within a few days they were again on their travels, taking with

---

[188] *Vita*, 218–23; *Chroniques de Sempringham*, 346 (the only source to give a date for the start – 11 Jan. – of the occupation, which it says lasted for about two weeks). Roger Wauton was identified as the ringleader of the attackers in records dated 14 Nov. 1323 and 24 May 1324: E 159/97, m.187d; *CPR, 1321–24*, 349; *Foedera*, II, i, 537–8. The first men sent to besiege the castle were Hugh Chastilloun and Richard Damory the steward of the royal household, who left Stowe Park for Wallingford on 24 Jan.; it is clear that they then awaited the arrival of other men-at-arms: BL, Stowe Ms. 553, f. 60.

[189] E 159/97, m.187d; *Foedera*, II, i, 537–8; *Brut*, i, 231; *Chroniques de Sempringham*, 346. Sir John de '*Goleinton*' was probably John de Wilyngton, a former adherent of John Giffard of Brimpsfield, who was pardoned for his support of the rebels in Nov. 1323: *CPR, 1321–24*, 9, 353. According to the Sempringham chronicle Sir John Maltravers was also involved. If this is meant to refer to John Maltravers the Younger, it is quite possible, but it is also believed that he escaped to the continent and there made contact with Roger Mortimer of Wigmore after the latter's escape in Aug. 1323: see Haskins, 'A chronicle', 80, and the article on Maltravers by C. Shenton in the *Oxford DNB*.

[190] Maurice died in prison in May 1326. On 5 Feb. the king ordered an inquiry into the incident: *CPR, 1321–24*, 257. The account in the *Vita* breaks off at just the point where more information was about to be revealed.

[191] Williams, *Medieval London*, 293.

[192] Isabella can be traced there on 12 Jan., 3 Feb. (when she dined with her son) and 17 Feb.: Doherty (D.Phil.), 96; E 101/379/9, m.4; SC 1/37/45. It is not clear where the younger Edward had been previously.

[193] *Ann. Paul.*, 304.

[194] *Ann. Paul.*, 305; Williams, *Medieval London*, 293.

them Hamo de Chigwell and three other London citizens, who were forced to follow the court wherever it went as if they were prisoners.[195] Edward and Isabella were back at Bishopsthorpe outside York in early May, just as the negotiations with the Scots were coming to their conclusion.[196] Edward left an angry London behind him. One likely consequence was the outbreak of Lancastrian miracles in St Paul's during May; another was to appear with great drama on 1 August.

The interrogation of Mortimer's close associate Maurice de Berkeley after the recapture of Wallingford may have given some indications of a plot to free Mortimer from the Tower of London.[197] But if so, no special precautions seem to have been taken to ensure that Mortimer was securely held: when he made his escape a full six months later it appears to have come as a complete surprise. Although there is no documentary evidence to support the claims by two of the chroniclers that Edward had decided to carry out the death sentence originally passed on Mortimer in August 1322, and that news or rumour of this precipitated Mortimer's escape, it is quite possible.[198] In any case the longer Mortimer remained in prison and the more conspiracies grew around him, with or without his active connivance, the more likely it became that he would be put to death,[199] so he had every incentive to escape at the earliest opportunity. On 1 August 1323 he did so, with the aid of Gerard d'Alspaye, the deputy constable of the Tower. After drugging the constable, Stephen de Segrave, and the guards, while they were dining, Gerard let Mortimer out of his cell; both men escaped through the kitchens and let themselves down the outer wall using a rope ladder, to the banks of the river where other conspirators were waiting with a boat. They crossed the Thames, to a mill where Mortimer was met by several more men with horses and made his way to the coast and safety.[200]

---

[195] *Ann. Paul.*, 305; Williams, *Medieval London*, 293. Chigwell was restored to office by the king in Nov. 1323: *CCW*, 547.

[196] Isabella was with Edward at Selby in Yorkshire on 10 June, which makes it very likely that she had returned from London at the same time: Doherty (D. Phil.), 97; E 159/96, m.344.

[197] Berkeley and several of his followers, notably Thomas de Gurney and John Maltravers, had become retainers of Roger Mortimer in 1319 and served with him in the civil war of 1321–2. In May 1319 Berkeley's son Thomas married Mortimer's daughter Margaret: Phillips, 266.

[198] *Anonimalle*, 116–17, states that Mortimer would have been drawn and hanged within four days if he had remained in the Tower; and the *Flores*, 217, says that Edward intended to produce Mortimer before the people and execute him. The author of the *Flores* was however consistently hostile to Edward II and all he stood for and the claim comes immediately before a comparison of Mortimer's escape with that of St Peter as recorded in the New Testament: Acts, 12: 4, 6–11. Mortimer is said to have built a chapel at Ludlow castle dedicated to St Peter, on whose feast day (St Peter ad Vincula) he had made his escape: E.L.G. Stones, 'The date of Roger Mortimer's escape from the Tower', *EHR*, lxvi (1951), 98. Cf. Fryde, 142–3; Mortimer, *The Greatest Traitor*, 130–1, 282, n. 18.

[199] Mortimer's situation was remarkably like that of Edward II when he was Mortimer's prisoner in Berkeley castle in 1327.

[200] *Knighton*, 429; *Ann. Paul.*, 305–6; *Murimuth*, 40; *Flores*, 217; *French Chron.*, 47; *Blaneford*,

Mortimer's escape was certainly planned, and he had helpers both inside and outside the Tower. It is very likely, as in the case of Wallingford, that visitors were able to smuggle correspondence in and out of the Tower. Although the constable was so badly affected by the drug he had been given that he was unable to resume his duties,[201] he inevitably came under suspicion and was later questioned about Mortimer's escape. He appears to have cleared himself, but admitted that 'he could have kept Mortimer in deeper and closer imprisonment than he did'.[202] Edward replaced him as constable on 6 August, when the treasurer the bishop of Exeter was appointed. Edward however suspected that there might be resistance from within the Tower and told the bishop to visit the Tower on the pretext of examining the royal treasure which was stored there and to show his royal commission only after he and his household had entered.[203] There is also evidence that several prominent Londoners – Richard de Bethune, John de Gisors and a London merchant Ralph de Bocton – were actively involved in the plot.[204] Edward II was now paying the price for his interference in London politics. [205]

THE DESPENSER REGIME

One chronicler, Robert of Avesbury, writing in the reign of Edward III, called Despenser a 'second king', just as Gaveston had been described early in the reign of Edward II; while Thomas de la More, the author of the *Vita et Mors Edwardi Secundi*, added Hugh Despenser the Elder and wrote of there being three kings at once.[206] The Younger Despenser certainly behaved like one. In the 1320s he established a family mausoleum in Tewkesbury abbey, modelled in part on the royal mausoleum at Westminster in which the tombs of the Clare earls of Gloucester were located. If Despenser could not himself be earl of Gloucester, he evidently intended to go one better.[207] At his fortress of Caerphilly in Glamorgan he built a great hall,

---

145–6. Blaneford's is the most detailed account, except that it wrongly gives the year as 1324: Stones, 'The date of Roger Mortimer's escape', 97–8.

[201] *CCR, 1323–27*, 13–14.

[202] Fryde, 161; KB 27/254, Rex, m.37.

[203] *CCR, 1323–27*, 13–14. Edward was no doubt also worried that if the Tower were held against him, he would lose control of a vast sum of ready money.

[204] Williams, *Medieval London*, 291–4. Gisors owned the mill to which Mortimer crossed from the Tower; while Bocton supplied the ship in which Mortimer crossed to France.

[205] Ibid., 285–91: Gisors was one of those who had lost power at this time.

[206] '*Qui se gessit ut alter rex*': Robertus de Avesbury, *De Gestis Edwardi Tertii*, ed. E.M. Thompson, Rolls Series (London, 1889), 280; *Vita et Mors*, 305. For comparisons with Gaveston see *Ann. Paul.*, 259; *Vita*, 4–5; Chaplais, 103, n. 62.

[207] Morris, 'Tewkesbury abbey'; Phillip Lindley, 'The later medieval monuments and chantry chapels', in R. Morris & R. Shoesmith, eds, *Tewkesbury Abbey* (Logaston, Herefordshire, 2003), 161–5; Lawrence, 'Secular patronage.' Fragments of a carved figure painted with the arms of Hugh Despenser the Younger were discovered amidst rubble flooring in Tewkesbury abbey in 1824: Morris & Shoesmith, 174 (illust.).

constructed by Master Thomas de la Bataille, a mason who had worked for the crown and may also have worked at Tewkesbury, and by Master William Hurley the craftsman who a few years later built the elaborate timber 'lantern' inside the famous octagon at Ely cathedral. The stone corbels supporting the timber roof bear carved heads, probably depicting Despenser himself and Edward II together with Isabella and Despenser's own wife Eleanor de Clare.[208] It was a hall fit for a king: in the autumn of 1326 Despenser had his only opportunity to entertain Edward here but not in circumstances he would have chosen. In the charges laid against him before his exile in 1321 Despenser was accused of accroaching royal power to himself and of usurping royal power, mastery and sovereignty over the king's person.[209] Similar language reappeared in the list of accusations made before his execution in November 1326, when he was charged with riding against the peers of the realm with force of arms, and of seizing and exercising royal power.[210] He was also accused of being a traitor, of having badly advised the king, and of having acted as a tyrant.[211]

Compared with Gaveston, whose influence seems to have been over the person of the king rather than in the day-to-day business of government, there was much more reason to accuse Despenser of acting as if he were king. Although his official title was never more than that of chamberlain of the royal household, or Hugh Despenser lord of Glamorgan, there was no doubting the power and influence he exercised. In November 1323, for example, Edward singled out three men – his chamberlain Despenser; Geoffrey le Scrope, chief justice of King's Bench; and Robert de Ayleston, keeper of the privy seal – as his most intimate advisers, to whom he committed and communicated all his most private business.[212] To these three could be added Master Robert Baldock, archdeacon of Middlesex the former keeper of the privy seal and chancellor since August 1323, and Walter Stapeldon, bishop of Exeter and treasurer since 1322. Hugh Despenser the Elder, an experienced royal councillor since the days of Edward I, was also influential in his new role as earl of Winchester.[213]

But it was the Younger Despenser who played the leading part. Evidence of his power is apparent throughout the records. There are

---

[208] Renn, *Caerphilly Castle*, 41–4 (incl. photographs). On the possible involvement of Thomas de la Bataille and the influence of other royal masons, such as Michael of Canterbury (*fl.* 1275–1320) and Thomas of Canterbury (*fl.* 1323–35) at Tewkesbury see Morris, 'Tewkesbury abbey', 150–5.

[209] *SR*, i, 181–4; *PROME*, Parliament of July 1321.

[210] '*votre Roial poer que aviez purpris contre notre seignour le Roi*': G.A. Holmes, 'Judgement on the Younger Despenser, 1326', *EHR*, lxx (1955), 264.

[211] '*tyrant*': ibid., 265–6.

[212] '*Secretarios nostros,*' *quibus secretoria negotia nostra committimus et communicamus*: *Foedera*, II, i, 541–2: letter to John de Stratford.

[213] Baldock ('a false pilede clerc': *Brut*, I, 240) and Stapeldon were especially unpopular and paid the price at the end of the reign. See the articles on them by R.M. Haines and M.C. Buck in the *Oxford DNB*.

many instances of royal letters under the privy seal being sent together with covering letters from Despenser to the same persons and on the same date: on 23 September 1323, for example, royal letters to Edmund Passele and the bishop of Exeter were matched by letters from Despenser; two days later letters were sent in the same way to the earl and countess of Pembroke;[214] there are similar examples in November and December of 1323, and in January 1324.[215] On other occasions Despenser appears to have sent letters of his own on important royal business, as if he were acting as a chief minister.[216] There are examples of letters being addressed to Despenser rather than the king[217] and of Despenser acting as the king's agent.[218] The accident of the survival of part of Despenser's personal archives shows that he was centrally involved with the administration of Gascony during the time of the Anglo-French War there in 1324–5.[219] As Davies noted, in some of the correspondence there appears to be an assumption of regality. A draft letter from Despenser to Robert de Waterville, for example, said that Despenser had shown Waterville's letters to the king and the council, and 'it seems to our lord the king and to us that you have acted wisely'. Even though the words 'to us' were cancelled, Davies is surely right in commenting that 'Despenser had an exalted view of his own importance'.[220] The pope also knew that Despenser was the avenue to influencing the king and wrote to him on numerous occasions after 1322, asking him for example to be watchful in the king's service, to try to remove causes of difference between Edward and the pope, to cause the bishop of Winchester (John Stratford) to be received with favour, and in 1326 asking him to retire from participation in the government so that Isabella could return to her husband without fear, and asking him to promote good relations between Edward and Isabella.[221]

Despenser has traditionally been credited with overall responsibility for the extensive programme of administrative reorganization and reform of

---

[214] BL, Stowe Ms. 553, ff. 130, 131v.

[215] E 101/379/19, ff. 2, 2v, 3v, 4, 5v.

[216] E 101/379/19, f. 2 (letter to Geoffrey le Scrope), f. 4 (letter to Richard Damory, steward of household).

[217] C 81/128/7027 (letter, 1324, from bishop of Exeter concerning Scotland); SC 1/49/58 (letter concerning the Scottish March); Davies, *Baronial Opposition*, 337–8.

[218] C 81/125/6744 (interview with a royal envoy returned from Avignon); SC 8/39/1944 (dispute concerning priory of Bermondsey); Davies, *Baronial Opposition*, 338.

[219] Despenser's personal archives were delivered to the exchequer on 25 March 1327: *The War of Saint-Sardos (1323–1325)*, ed. P. Chaplais, Camden 3rd ser. lxxxvii (London, 1954), vii; E 101/332/27.

[220] SC 1/49/152 (? end of April 1325: *Saint-Sardos*, 171–2); Davies, *Baronial Opposition*, 339–40.

[221] *CPL, 1305–42*, 444, 457, 459, 475, 477–8; Davies, *Baronial Opposition*, 337. Many of the documents edited by Chaplais in *Saint-Sardos* consist of newsletters and other correspondence sent by officials in Gascony to the Younger Despenser or from Despenser to recipients in Gascony. Of the 218 documents published, 126 fall into these two categories: see Chaplais, *Saint-Sardos*, Table of Documents, xv–xxi.

the royal household and the exchequer which took place after 1322.[222] There is however little to support this conclusion. Reforms and reorganization there certainly were, but this was a pattern that had already been established with the collection of documents relating to Scottish affairs made by Andrew de Tange between 1315 and 1318;[223] the household ordinance of York in 1318;[224] the register of Gascon documents drawn up by John Hildesle and Elias de Joneston in 1318–19;[225] the sorting of exchequer records begun in August 1320;[226] the calendar of Gascon documents produced under the overall supervision of Walter Stapeldon the bishop of Exeter between 1320 and November 1322;[227] the ordering of the muniments relating to Scotland, Ireland and Wales which was decided on by the council in July 1321;[228] and perhaps even the mysterious *Modus Tenendi Parliamentum* which was possibly a 'procedural tract' composed by a member of the royal administration.[229] This process continued after the York parliament of 1322. The personal archives of Walter Langton, bishop of Coventry & Lichfield, who had died in November 1321, were delivered to the exchequer in November 1323, while a listing was also made of Thomas of Lancaster's muniments.[230] In November 1322 Stapeldon delivered to the treasury three books containing details of royal gifts, forest rentals and parliaments;[231] copies of the registers of clerical taxation were delivered to the exchequer; and detailed records of contrariant lands and their revenues were also made.[232] All these labours and the exchequer ordinances of 1323, 1324 and 1326, and the household ordinances of 1323 and 1324 took place on Despenser's 'watch', but there is no reason to suppose that he was personally involved in any of them. Walter Stapeldon in his capacity as treasurer was the prime mover, while the division of the exchequer into northern and southern departments in 1324 is said to have been the idea of Roger Belers, one of the barons of

---

[222] Tout, *Place of the Reign*, 142–6 (though he does not ascribe exclusive responsibility to Despenser); Davies, *Baronial Opposition*, 103–4.
[223] *Edward I and the Throne of Scotland*, ed. Stones & Simpson, i, 45–7, 81–2; ii, 378–80.
[224] Tout, *Place of the Reign*, 118–119 & App. I, A, 241–81. In his capacity as chamberlain Despenser had played some part in drawing up this ordinance.
[225] *Gascon Register A*, ed. Cuttino; Buck, 167.
[226] *CCR, 1318–23*, 258; Buck, 168; E 159/93, m.53d. See *Antient Kalendars*, ed. Palgrave.
[227] *Gascon Calendar*, ed. Cuttino; Buck, 167–8.
[228] *CPR, 1321–24*, 7; Buck, 168.
[229] See the discussion in the previous chapter; *Parliamentary Texts*, 65–114, and 1–63, esp. 25–31; and Prestwich, *Plantagenet England*, 224–6.
[230] Buck, 168; E 159/96, m.81; Phillips, 171; DL 41/1/37.
[231] *Antient Kalendars*, ed. Palgrave, iii, 437; Buck, 169. While it is tempting to imagine that this was something to do with the *Modus Tenendi Parliamentum*, it is more likely to have been the *Vetus Codex* (C 153/1), containing transcripts of the Parliament Rolls for some of the parliaments of Edward I between 1290 and 1307, the 1320 parliament, and brief references to the 1318 and 1319 York parliaments: see *PROME*, General Introduction and Parliaments of 1318, 1319, 1320.
[232] Buck, 169.

the exchequer.²³³ These measures were all carried out in the interests of efficient accounting for, collection and distribution of revenue. Both Despenser and Edward II had a close interest in money and its accumulation, but it is unlikely that their interest went further than urging the financial administration to gather as much of it as possible and by whatever means was available.²³⁴

It has been observed that 'the Despensers carried out their policies with the aid of a sprawling clientele of retainers, administrators and servants', and by their systematic exploitation of the 'double allegiance' of men who served both them and the crown.²³⁵ Although double allegiance was not a new phenomenon or necessarily an indication of corruption,²³⁶ the Despensers, and especially the Younger Despenser, brought it to an altogether new level. In the Younger Despenser's case over seventy individuals in personal and royal service have been identified. Some were figures, such as John Inge, John Iweyn and Ralph de Gorges, already familiar from before 1321; but the majority of them, including royal administrators such as Robert Baldock, Roger Belers and Adam de Lymbergh, dated from 1322.²³⁷ At least three of the four controllers of the royal wardrobe between 1320 and 1327 were clients of the Younger Despenser;²³⁸ eight of the county sheriffs appointed between 1320 and 1326, about one in ten, can be identified as retainers of the Despensers;²³⁹ and there are many examples of humble members of the royal administration who also acted as Despenser clients.²⁴⁰ Despenser also acquired the services as retainers of a number of men who had previously been followers of other magnates, such as the earl of Pembroke, several of whose men joined Despenser after

---

²³³ Ibid., 165: Prestwich, *Plantagenet England*, 208–9. On Stapeldon's role see Buck, 163–96.

²³⁴ As Nigel Saul has put it, 'The notion that the two favourites and their clerical advisers were deeply preoccupied with the day-to-day minutiae of household reform or the keeping of exchequer records seems a faintly dated one': Saul, 'The Despensers', 3.

²³⁵ Waugh, 'For king, country and patron', 24, 26.

²³⁶ It was common, for example, for retainers of magnates such as the earls of Pembroke and Lancaster to hold royal offices such as sheriff: ibid., 27; Phillips, 310–11. Lancaster also made a practice of retaining royal justices and legal experts: Waugh, 'For king, country and patron', 27; Maddicott, 48–51.

²³⁷ Waugh, 'For king, country and patron', Table 2, 49–56. Table 1, 47–8, lists 18 individuals who were clients of his father, more than half of whom had connections with him dating from before 1322–6.

²³⁸ Baldock (1320–3), Holden (1323–6), Huggate (1326–7): ibid., 28.

²³⁹ Saul, 'The Despensers', 18: e.g., Ingelram Berenger, Ralph de Wedon, John Inge.

²⁴⁰ Such as William de Aylmer, John de Dunstaple and Richard de Tyssbury, who were all royal clerks and acted as stewards or auditors for Despenser: Waugh, 'For king, country and patron', 28–30. Although there is evidence that before 1321 Despenser had placed some of his clients on judicial commissions, there is no evidence that he had packed the central royal courts with his dependants: Waugh, 27, n. 12; *Select Cases*, ed. Sayles, iv, xiii, n. 13; Tout, *Place of the Reign*, 130. Saul reaches broadly the same conclusion: 'The Despensers', 24–5.

Pembroke's death in 1324.[241] Even men who had been actively opposed to Despenser in 1321–2, notably Roger Belers who had been a retainer of Thomas of Lancaster, joined him after the victory over the contrariants.[242] Altogether, over two dozen individual knights have been identified as serving one or both of the Despensers in the 1320s.[243]

It is initially surprising to discover that, despite the value to them of their clients and retainers, the Despensers did not go out of their way to intrude their followers into official positions, such as that of sheriff or judge. Their failure to do so when the opportunity offered has even been identified as one of the reasons why their power and Edward II's regime collapsed so swiftly at the end of 1326. When Isabella and Mortimer came to make changes in shrieval appointments in February 1327, they found it necessary to replace only nine sheriffs out of twenty-four; while most of the justices of the central courts of King's Bench and Common Pleas were quickly reappointed or even promoted.[244] What gave the Despensers their authority was their influence over the king and the knowledge that whatever they wanted they were likely to get. Their network of clients and informers, spread over many counties of England and much of Wales, then ensured the desired result.

The lordship of Gower, whose seizure by the crown in 1320 had provoked the attacks on the Despensers in 1321, provides a very good illustration of how the Despensers achieved their ends. In July 1322 Gower was granted to the Younger Despenser, who then proceeded to use the lordship as a means of gaining further territory in South Wales. He first of all exchanged Gower for the lordships of Usk and Caerleon, which belonged to Roger Damory's widow, Elizabeth de Clare. In April 1324 and at Despenser's instigation, the former lord of Gower, William de Braose, began legal action to recover the lordship from Elizabeth by means of an assize of *novel disseisin*. Having succeeded, in June 1324 De Braose then granted Gower to the Elder Despenser, who passed it on to his son, so completing the circle.[245] The appearance of legality hid the reality of fraud, threats of violence and abuse of legal process.[246] In this case we know much of what occurred since in May 1326 Elizabeth de Clare lodged

---

[241] Waugh, 'For king, country and patron', 25–7; Phillips, 257. Examples are Thomas de Goodrichcastle, William Lovel and Constantine de Mortimer.

[242] Waugh,'For king, country and patron', 25: other examples are the contrariants, Edmund Pinkenny, Robert de Wateville (although Saul, 'The Despensers', 13, thinks this is incorrect), and Thomas Wyther.

[243] Saul, 'The Despensers', 6–8.

[244] Ibid., 19–22, 24–5. The nine sheriffs all had apparent or likely connections with the Despensers or with the court.

[245] Pugh, 'Marcher lords', 171–2.

[246] G.A. Holmes, 'A protest against the Despensers, 1326', *Speculum*, xxx (1955), 210. Saul, 'The Despensers', 23, quotes R.W. Kaeuper's apt remark that 'The two Despensers were probably the masters in malicious prosecution': Kaeuper, 'Law and order in fourteenth-century England', *Speculum*, liv (1979), 778.

a petition protesting against her treatment by the Younger Despenser. In March 1322 Elizabeth had been captured at her castle of Usk and taken to Barking abbey where she was held throughout the summer of 1322. While she was there the king tried to persuade her to give Caerleon and Usk to the Younger Despenser in exchange for Gower. Elizabeth was unwilling to do so, believing that Usk was more valuable than Gower, but she eventually agreed through fear. At the end of 1322 she was summoned to the king at York, where she was imprisoned apart from her council and forced to promise that she would not remarry or grant any of her remaining lands away without Edward's permission. This was of course intended to preserve the Younger Despenser's position. She was threatened that if she refused, she would lose all the lands of her inheritance. Then came the final straw in 1324 when Gower was also taken away from her.[247]

This was typical of the way in which the Despensers achieved their ends. It shows too how completely Edward II supported them and aided them in their demands. If his niece Elizabeth de Clare could not withstand them, there was no hope for anyone else, whether high or low. Even Edward's own half-brother, Thomas earl of Norfolk, suffered in August 1323 when he was forced to grant the Younger Despenser a lifetime lease of the valuable lordship of Chepstow.[248] Elizabeth and Thomas were not the only victims. Alice de Lacy, the widow of Thomas of Lancaster, and daughter of Henry de Lacy the earl of Lincoln and therefore also an heiress in her own right, was, like Elizabeth, summoned to York in 1322 and imprisoned until she released her lands to the king. These were then granted to the Despensers: to make this possible even Joan de Lacy, the widow of Henry de Lacy, was forced to give up some of her dower lands.[249] After the earl of Pembroke's death in 1324 the Younger Despenser was given custody of the lordships of Pembroke in Wales and Wexford in Ireland. Pembroke's widow, Marie de St Pol, complained to the king that the Younger Despenser refused to allow the escheator to return an inquest on Pembroke's lands in Hertford and Haverfordwest because he wanted them for himself, and that Robert Baldock would not allow her to have dower in either of these places or in Pembroke's lands in Monmouth unless she produced the original royal charters. The countess of Pembroke gave up her rights in Little Monmouth, which in July 1325 was granted to Despenser.[250] One of Pembroke's heirs, John Hastings of

---

[247] Holmes, 'A protest', 207–9. The text of Elizabeth's protest is in ibid., 210–12.

[248] *CPR, 1324–27*, 52. Despenser was to pay an annual rent of £200; in Nov. 1323 this was changed to a single payment of 1,200 marks in cash. There is no overt indication of pressure but there can be little doubt that it was applied.

[249] *CCR, 1318–23*, 574–6; *CPR, 1321–24*, 179–80, 194; Holmes, 'A protest', 209. Alice's own later protest is contained in DL 42/11, ff. 66v–67. The Elder Despenser gained the lordship of Denbigh, while the Younger Despenser obtained the constableship of Chester and the reversion of the honour of Bolingbroke in Lincolnshire: Holmes, 'A protest', 209.

[250] SC 8/294/14690–2; SC 8/277/13819; *CCR, 1323–27*, 288, 395; *CChR, 1300–26*, 478; Phillips, 235.

Abergavenny, was forced to make an obligation for £4,000 to Despenser in August 1324; while another of his heirs, Elizabeth Comyn, was imprisoned by the Despensers until in March 1325 she released to them her rights in the former Pembroke lands at the valuable castle of Goodrich in Herefordshire and Painswick in Gloucestershire.[251]

The regime established in England after the victory over the contrariants in 1322 acted within a framework of legality but in reality was arbitrary and brutal. Edward II was implicated in everything that was done in his name and with his acquiescence. In 1325 the author of the *Vita Edwardi Secundi* told the truth when he remarked: 'The king's harshness has indeed increased so much today that no one, however great and wise, dares to cross the king's will. Thus parliaments, consultations and councils decide nothing these days. For the nobles of the realm, terrified by threats and the penalties inflicted on others, let the king's will have free rein. Thus today will conquers reason. For whatever pleases the king, though lacking in reason, has the force of law.'[252] This was a situation which could not last for long without further challenge. Even as early as 1323 the signs of the regime's ultimate dissolution were there for those with the will to read them. Although seeming all-powerful, it was severely restricted in its ability to control a deeply divided and disturbed kingdom which its own behaviour had done much to bring about. The regime of Edward II and the Despensers was indefensible and in the last resort there were few who were prepared even to try to defend it.

EDWARD FALLS OUT WITH THE CHURCH

With the exception of the dispute with Archbishop Winchelsey of Canterbury which he had inherited from his father and his hostility to Walter Langton bishop of Coventry & Lichfield, his father's former treasurer, for most of his reign Edward II had been on good terms with both the English Church and the papacy.[253] Since 1313 he had a loyal and compliant archbishop of Canterbury in Walter Reynolds; the other English archbishop, William Melton of York, was also a loyal servant of the crown, as was Alexander Bicknor, archbishop of Dublin in Ireland. Edward had generally been successful in securing the appointment to English dioceses of men who were royal servants and were personally acceptable to him: Walter Reynolds to Worcester in 1307, Walter Stapeldon to Exeter in 1308, John Droxford to Bath & Wells in 1309, John de Hothum to Ely and John Sandal to Winchester in 1316 were all examples. In November 1321 his old antagonist Walter Langton had finally died, allowing Edward to plunder

---

[251] *CCR, 1323–27*, 309, 357; Phillips, 235. See also Fryde, 113–15.
[252] *Vita*, 230–1.
[253] For a general view of Edward II's relations with the Church see Menache, *Clement V*; Wright, *The Church and the English Crown*; Edwards, 'Political importance'; Haines, 'The episcopate'.

his possessions in aid of the war effort and to scrutinize his accounts for any sums that might be collected by the crown.[254] The English bishops and the papacy had also played a key role during most of the reign in mediating between Edward and his baronial opponents.

In 1321–2 this all started to change. Signs of the change were already apparent in Edward's hostility to Henry Burghersh the bishop of Lincoln, the nephew of Bartholomew de Badlesmere, whose appointment he had vigorously supported in 1320 but who had sympathized with the contrariants in 1321–2. In retaliation Edward took control of the temporalities belonging to the diocese. Burghersh did not help himself in the eyes of the king when in 1323 he appealed to Charles IV of France to intercede with the pope on his behalf.[255] Adam Orleton, a former royal diplomat, whose appointment as bishop of Hereford in 1317 over a preferred royal candidate had been accepted by Edward only under protest, was suspected of having supported the Mortimers in 1321–2. This was very much in the nature of unfinished business and was to come to a head spectacularly in the early months of 1324.[256] Another bishop under a cloud of suspicion was John Droxford of Bath & Wells, who had been in royal service since as early as 1290. The cause of his offence is less clear than in the cases of Burghersh and Orleton, but in February 1323 Edward demanded that the pope remove both Burghersh and Droxford from the realm, which the pope refused the following September, together with Edward's further demand that Droxford should be replaced by his friend and confidant, William the abbot of the Premonstratensian house of Langdon in Kent.[257] Louis de Beaumont, the bishop of Durham whose appointment Isabella had championed in 1316, was in uncertain favour too in 1322–3 because of his alleged failure to defend his diocese against the Scots, even before his brother Henry quarrelled with the king over the Scottish truce in May 1323.[258]

Edward was also finding it increasingly difficult to persuade the pope to appoint his nominees to English sees. This had already happened in 1319 when the pope appointed one of his tax collectors, Rigaud d'Assier, as bishop of the extremely wealthy diocese of Winchester and ignored Edward's pleas on behalf of Badlesmere's nephew, Henry Burghersh. It occurred again in the autumn of 1321 when the pope appointed Roger Northburgh as bishop of Coventry & Lichfield, in place of Edward's preferred candidate, Robert Baldock, the archdeacon of Middlesex and a close ally of the Despensers.[259] Northburgh's appointment would

---

[254] Fryde, 103; E 159/97, m.42v.
[255] *Foedera*, II, i, 38–9; Haines, *The Church and Politics*, 137–8.
[256] Ibid., 17–19, 134–6, 144–5.
[257] SC 7/24/16; SC 7/25/1; *Foedera*, II, i, 515, 537, 542–3; Haines, *The Church and Politics*, 137–8, 144. On the respective careers of Burghersh and Droxford see the articles by N. Bennett and M.C. Buck in the *Oxford DNB*.
[258] *Foedera*, II, i, 506.
[259] Ibid., 452–3, 462, 468–9.

ordinarily have been a very acceptable one to the king since Roger was treasurer of the royal household and a royal servant of long standing, on whose behalf Edward had written to the pope earlier in 1321 asking for him to be made a cardinal. The pope refused the request and made Roger a bishop as a consolation prize.[260]

Edward did not complain too loudly on this occasion but the disappointment was swiftly followed by another in April 1323, when the bishop of Winchester Rigaud d'Assier died while at the papal curia. The news reached Edward in less than two weeks and this time he was determined that Baldock should be appointed.[261] On 26 April Edward wrote to the pope, pressing the claims of Baldock to the see in the strongest terms. Further letters of recommendation followed, culminating on 7 June in a letter in which Edward expressed his concern at rumours he had heard about the pope's intentions. Edward's fears were well founded. On 20 June the pope appointed an English royal clerk John Stratford to be the new bishop of Winchester.[262] Stratford was a trusted royal councillor who had long experience of dealing with royal business at Avignon. He spent several months there in early 1322, seeking papal support against the contrariants and the Scots, before returning to England in July to report to Edward. Before the end of July he was again on his way to Avignon, with a long list of favours to be sought on behalf of the king,[263] not least the advancement of Robert Baldock.

When Edward learned that Stratford had been made bishop of Winchester he was furious. The development was all too reminiscent of Adam Orleton's appointment as bishop of Hereford in 1317 when he too had been a royal envoy at Avignon and had seemingly taken advantage of the opportunity to advance his own career. Despite the pope's protestations to the contrary,[264] Edward assumed that Stratford had done the same and bombarded the pope and cardinals with letters demanding that the appointment be revoked and attacking Stratford's integrity. Meanwhile

---

[260] Northburgh had been keeper of the privy seal at the time of Bannockburn and had been captured there, together with the seal. On his career see the article by R.M. Haines in the *Oxford DNB*.

[261] Haines, *Stratford*, 136.

[262] *Foedera*, II, i, 517–20, 522, 525; Haines, *Stratford*, 136–7. As well as stressing Baldock's personal qualities, Edward emphasized the value of his services to the crown. On Stratford's appointment and its repercussions see also N. Fryde, 'John Stratford, bishop of Winchester, and the crown, 1323–30', *BIHR*, xliv (1971), 153–61.

[263] Haines, *Stratford*, 128–31. These included several matters of close personal interest to Edward. One concerned a prospective marriage, whose details were not specified but probably related to the young Edward, earl of Chester. Another matter with which Stratford was charged was obtaining a papal bull in favour of the Dominican priory at Langley where Gaveston was buried.

[264] In Aug. 1323 the pope told Edward that he had appointed Stratford because of his personal qualities; he added, significantly, that certain information regarding Baldock had reached the curia, but that Stratford knew nothing about this: *Foedera*, II, i, 533; Haines, *Stratford*, 140.

the authorities at Dover and other English ports were to seize any papal letters relating to Stratford's promotion. In September Edward was even forced into making an embarrassing apology to the pope when the clerks of Cardinal Raymond de Roux were arrested and gaoled at Dover.[265]

In November 1323 the new bishop of Winchester returned to England and was summoned to appear before the Younger Despenser, Geoffrey le Scrope and the keeper of the privy seal to explain himself.[266] Having refused to answer their questions he was held in contempt and summoned again, finally appearing before Hervey de Staunton and other royal justices at Nottingham on 28 November. Stratford then underwent a lengthy examination of his conduct of royal business at Avignon, which gives striking evidence of the pope's growing reluctance to do Edward's bidding.[267]

Stratford and his fellow envoys had been charged in 1322 with asking the pope to confirm and strengthen earlier papal sentences of excommunication and interdict against the Scots. The pope had initially been prepared to do this but on learning of the thirteen-year truce between England and Scotland[268] decided to go no further in the matter, especially since one of the terms of the truce bound Edward II not to object to any relaxation of the sentences.[269] The pope also refused Edward's request that no Scot should be appointed to a Scottish diocese on the grounds that, since a bishop of English origin could not function in Scotland, Scottish souls would be imperilled.[270] The pope was under growing pressure from the Scots themselves. Late in 1323 the earl of Moray went to Avignon to argue the case for Bruce's recognition as king of Scots. The pope agreed and in January 1324 wrote to Edward II explaining that doing so 'could not diminish your right and honour, nor add to Bruce's'.[271]

Another important issue raised during Stratford's mission to Avignon related to the Ordinances. Edward's oath to uphold the Ordinances had been annulled by the pope in 1320, while the Ordinances themselves had

---

[265] *Foedera*, II, i, 526–9, 531–3, 535; Haines, *Stratford*, 138–41.

[266] *CCW*, 546; Haines, *Stratford*, 142.

[267] Haines, *Stratford*, 142–5. The record of the 'process' against Stratford, which contains details of the issues raised by him at the papal curia together with the papal replies, is printed in *Foedera*, II, i, 541–4.

[268] News of this arrived at Avignon while Stratford was there and rendered his initial instructions out of date: *Foedera*, II, i, 542.

[269] Ibid.; Haines, *Stratford*, 142–3. There is an understandable confusion on this issue in Barrow's *Robert Bruce*, 250, where it is stated that Stratford's mission asking for the strengthening of papal sentences took place in 1324 (i.e. *after* the 1323 truce) instead of in 1322–3. The record of his mission appears in *Foedera* under the date 1324 since the proceedings against Stratford went on until Jan. 1324.

[270] *Foedera*, II, i, 542; Haines, *Stratford*, 142–3.

[271] *Foedera*, II, i, 541, 549–50, 561; Barrow, 250. Edward's protest on 1 April 1324 made no difference but in 1325 the pope did confirm earlier sentences of excommunication and interdict: *Foedera*, II, i, 613; Barrow, 250.

been revoked during the York parliament in May 1322. However, there remained the question of the oaths taken by the prelates and magnates to uphold the Ordinances. Stratford had considerable difficulty over this matter. The pope pointed out that many people had endangered themselves by their adherence to the Ordinances and reminded Edward through his envoy that, although he could revoke and alter statutes, he had no jurisdiction over oaths: it was only with some reluctance that the pope gave authority to the archbishop of Canterbury to set aside the oaths, if he deemed it in the interests of the king and the kingdom.[272]

The pope had also expressed his reluctance or inability to do Edward's bidding with regard to certain unnamed bishops (clearly the bishops of Lincoln and Hereford), the appointment of cardinals and other matters.[273] The latter included Edward's request for papal assistance in his pursuit of King Robert of Sicily for a share in the counties of Provence and Forcalquier, a claim stemming ultimately from Edward's grandmother Eleanor of Provence, the queen of Henry III.[274] Edward was unsuccessful in his claim, which served only to demonstrate the world of fantasy in which he was living as his kingdom began to collapse around him.

The record of Stratford's examination by the royal justices showed that he had in fact carried out his diplomatic duties at Avignon with great skill and had adapted his instructions to meet with changes in circumstances, such as news of the truce with Scotland. But this did not satisfy Edward, who summoned Stratford to appear before him in person on 7 December 1323. Nothing is known about the outcome of this meeting but Stratford was later ordered to present himself at parliament in February 1324.[275]

THE 'TRIAL' OF ADAM ORLETON

Edward's anger against Stratford may have begun to subside because of his growing fears about Roger Mortimer's activities in France and his suspicion that the bishop of Hereford, Adam Orleton was in some way involved with Mortimer. The matter went back to the civil war of 1321–2 when Orleton was suspected by the king of having sympathized with the Mortimers and even

---

[272] *Foedera*, II, i, 542–3; Haines, *Stratford*, 43. The Statute of York which annulled the Ordinances was enrolled on the Statute Roll in 1322 and again enrolled in the court of King's Bench and on the Memoranda Roll of the exchequer in 1324. This was clearly done in reaction to the pope's decision on the oaths: Sayles, 'The formal judgments', 62–3. Although Sayles argues that Edward had sought papal annulment of his own oath to uphold the Ordinances, it is clear that it was the oaths taken by others that were at issue.

[273] *Foedera*, II, i, 542–3 (contains a list of the nine items of business to be raised at Avignon together with the replies, article by article, of the pope); Haines, *Stratford*, 142–5.

[274] *Foedera*, II, i, 507–8, 543. The claim to Provence was yet another consequence of the death of Edward II's first cousin, Thomas of Lancaster, since Eleanor of Provence had settled her share of Provence on Thomas and Henry of Lancaster in equal shares: Maddicott, 4.

[275] What, if anything, happened during the parliament is unknown; Stratford's case was probably overshadowed by that of the bishop of Hereford.

of sending them military help. There is some evidence for the former but nothing to prove the latter. Nor is there evidence that in 1322 Orleton helped to persuade Edward to commute the death sentences on the Mortimers to life imprisonment or that he played any part in Roger Mortimer of Wigmore's escape from the Tower of London in August 1323.[276] Nonetheless Edward's distrust of Orleton continued to fester. Orleton was ordered to appear before royal justices at Hereford on 23 January 1324, when the charges of collusion with the Mortimers in 1321–2 were rehearsed. Orleton refused to answer the charges on the grounds that he was the bishop of Hereford at the will of God and of the supreme pontiff and that the substance of the articles alleged against him was so serious that he ought not to answer in court on the matters alleged against him, nor could he answer thereon without offence to God and Holy Church.[277] Orleton then appeared before the king at Westminster on 24 February, the day after the beginning of parliament.[278] Again the charges were read out and again Orleton refused to answer them; whereupon the archbishop of Canterbury claimed Orleton for the Church and was ordered to produce him again on 19 March. The archbishop and bishop duly came on that date, when Orleton was convicted on the evidence of a jury from Hereford of having given aid to the Mortimers. His lands and goods were seized by the king and Orleton himself was delivered to the custody of the archbishop.[279] According to another and even more dramatic version of events, Orleton's conviction took place in his absence after the archbishops of Canterbury, York and Dublin and ten other unnamed bishops had taken Orleton under their protection and warned those present not to lay hands on him under pain of anathema. Only after this was Orleton convicted, and then by specific order of the king.[280]

By the early months of 1324 Edward II had succeeded in quarrelling openly with at least three of his bishops, Lincoln, Winchester and Hereford, and in causing offence to the archbishops and to the pope. It was time for Edward to mend some fences. In March he restored the temporalities of the diocese of Lincoln which had been in royal hands since 1322, thus depriving the bishop of most of his income.[281] In the same month Henry of Lancaster was restored to his brother's earldom of Leicester. Edward's attitude towards John Stratford was also starting to soften and the two men were reconciled at Tonbridge in Kent on 24 June

---

[276] Haines, *The Church and Politics*, 140–4.

[277] *Select Cases*, ed. Sayles, iv, 145 (from KB 27/255, m.87d) (the detailed charges are ibid., 143–4); Haines, *The Church and Politics*, 144. There is a partial record of the proceedings in *Chartulary of Winchester Cathedral*, ed. Goodman, no. 441 (p. 185). The summons to Orleton was part of the investigation into possible contrariants and their sympathizers which was launched after Mortimer's escape in Aug. 1323.

[278] See *PROME*, Westminster Parliament of Feb. 1324. Unfortunately there is no surviving roll for this parliament.

[279] *Select Cases*, ed. Sayles, iv, 145–6; Haines, *The Church and Politics*, 145.

[280] *Blaneford*, 140–2; Haines, *The Church and Politics*, 146–7.

[281] Article on Henry Burghersh by N. Bennett in the *Oxford DNB*.

1324.²⁸² Edward however remained resolutely unreconciled with Adam Orleton: the breach remained unhealed to the very end of the reign and was to have a profound impact on Edward's own fate.²⁸³

In 1324 Edward had the strongest of reasons for wishing to restore some semblance of harmony to his kingdom: for the first time since 1298 England and France were rapidly approaching open war in Gascony.

---

²⁸² *Foedera*, II, i, 543; Haines, *Stratford*, 147 and n. 143. The reconciliation was recorded in the Historia Roffensis which added that in the meantime Robert Baldock, the chancellor and Stratford's defeated rival for Winchester, had continued to persecute him: ibid., 147, n. 143. Stratford was however forced to enter into a bond with the king for £10,000, £2,000 of it payable on demand: ibid., 149.

²⁸³ Even the papal envoys who visited England in Nov. 1324 could do nothing to soften Edward's attitude to Orleton: Haines, *Stratford*, 151–2.

Chapter 10

EDWARD VANQUISHED, 1324–1326

PART ONE

THE ROAD TO WAR WITH FRANCE

During the earlier years of Edward II's reign relations between England and France 'possessed many of the characteristics of *détente*'.[1] The multitude of problems caused by the earlier war in the 1290s both within the duchy of Aquitaine and in the relations of the king-duke and his French overlord had never been fully resolved, even when peace was made in 1303. The processes of Montreuil in 1306 and of Périgueux in 1311, which were conducted by expert representatives of both sides and were intended to remove outstanding problems, did not succeed in doing so. The personal visits to France by Edward II at the time of his marriage in 1308, in the summer of 1313 and again in 1320, helped to ease the difficulties but did not end them, partly because of 'the tendency of the French to conduct their meetings as if they were part of a lawsuit between unequals rather than between two sovereigns of equal authority'.[2] The determination of the French monarchy to exercise its sovereignty as widely as possible, especially through its encouragement of Edward II's subjects in Gascony to take their grievances on appeal to the *Parlement* of Paris, meant that however many problems were settled or shelved fresh ones kept appearing to take their place. The turbulent nature of Gascon politics, sometimes amounting to acts of private war, such as the long-standing rivalry between the counts of Foix-Béarn and of Armagnac, the disputes between Jourdain de l'Isle and Alexandre de Caumont in 1318–19, and between Bernard-Jourdain de l'Isle and Amanieu d'Albret in 1322–3, made English rule in the duchy all the more difficult and created opportunities for French intervention.[3] Throughout the reign of Edward II the problems of Aquitaine with their potential for renewed conflict between England and France were, so to speak, the elephant in the room.

The danger signs were already apparent in June 1320 when Edward II performed homage for Aquitaine at his meeting with Philip V at Amiens

---

[1] Vale, 228; Lalou, 'Les Négociations', 325–55.
[2] Vale, 228. On the processes see Cuttino, *English Diplomatic Administration*, 62–111.
[3] Vale, 124–6, 132–7. For a detailed study of the politics of Gascony see ibid., ch. 4, 'Politics and society in Aquitaine'.

and brusquely rejected the French suggestion that he should also swear fealty.[4] But worse was to follow after the death of Philip V in January 1322.[5] First of all the question of homage returned to the agenda: the new king of France, Charles IV, proved to be much less accommodating of Edward II's desire to delay its performance for as long as possible. Charles IV was prepared to withhold his summons while England and Scotland were still openly at war, but as soon as news of the Anglo-Scottish truce in May 1323 reached Paris he acted. In July 1323 Charles sent envoys to England summoning Edward to be at Amiens at Candlemas (2 February) or at Easter (15 April) 1324. As he had done in the past, Edward played for time and in December 1323 asked for a postponement on the spurious grounds of a new Scottish invasion.[6] This was a dangerous tactic since a determined king of France might interpret it as a disguised refusal to perform homage and use it as an excuse to seize control of Gascony: and the new king of France was determined.[7] Charles had begun his reign by removing his predecessor's advisers, including Henry de Sully the butler of France who had acted as an intermediary between France and England before going to England in 1322.[8] There were now fewer influential voices with a desire to restrain or to avoid conflict. The death in 1319 of Louis count of Évreux, with whom Edward II had been on terms of friendship, had already removed one such from the scene, while the death in June 1324 of Aymer de Valence the earl of Pembroke, who had close personal ties with both Edward II and the French court, removed another.[9] One of the 'new' men in 1322 was Charles count of Valois, Charles IV's uncle and half-brother of Louis of Évreux, who had played a leading part in the previous Anglo-French conflict in the 1290s and had personal scores to settle with the English crown.[10]

By the summer of 1323 the situation in Gascony was becoming dangerous. At least thirty-seven separate appeals involving Gascon subjects of the English crown were pending before the *Parlement* of Paris; in the past both central and local officials of the French crown had been amenable to pressure or even to bribes, but no more.[11] The French showed what they were capable of in May 1323 when Jourdain de l'Isle's career ended with his execution in Paris for persistent acts of defiance of Charles IV's sovereignty.[12] The

---

[4] Ibid., 51; Chaplais, *Diplomatic Practice*, part 1, i, 359–60 (no. 199).

[5] Like his predecessor, Louis X, Philip died young and without a male heir. He made his will in Aug. 1321 and added a codicil on 2 Jan. 1322 when he must have been aware that he was dying: AN, J 404, nos 26, 27. There is no mention of Philip's sister Queen Isabella of England in either document.

[6] *Saint-Sardos*, ix, 176–80.

[7] Ibid., ix.

[8] Vale, 129, 136, 228–9; *Saint-Sardos*, 56–8.

[9] Vale, 136, 229; Phillips, 233–4.

[10] Vale, 229.

[11] Vale, 229; *Saint-Sardos*, ix, 183.

[12] Vale, 137–8; *Saint-Sardos*, ix.

brief war between the count of Foix and Arnaud-Guillaume de Marsan between April and June 1323 may or may not have been instigated by Charles of Valois, but was yet another distraction for the English authorities in the duchy. The seneschal, Fulk Lestrange, had to mobilize local forces to deal with the outbreak; which meant in turn that Gascon troops were not available for use in Scotland as Edward II had intended. The war was ended by the mediation of John de Hothum the bishop of Ely, another indication of the increasing engagement of English resources in Gascony. A further disturbing development was the partial occupation of the island of Oléron by French troops in October.[13]

Edward II's government was well aware of the growing problems relating to the duchy of Aquitaine. In April and June 1322 Edward had complained to Charles IV about the actions of French officials in the duchy;[14] in January 1323 he gave notice to his subjects there that he was sending Amaury de Craon, a leading Gascon nobleman and former seneschal, and the bishop of Ely who was also to visit the French king; in February he complained again about French 'excesses' and in the same month issued a set of ordinances for the future government of the duchy; further complaints to Charles IV followed in April.[15] In May Edward sent instructions to the bishop of Ely and Amaury de Craon on the safekeeping of the ducal castles in Gascony.[16] If war broke out, the duchy would at least be defended. The French reply was a proposal that Edward II's elder son, Edward earl of Chester, should marry the daughter of Charles count of Valois, to which Edward II replied on 6 June that this would have to be discussed in a parliament, which he did not intend to hold until 29 September.[17]

ENGLAND AND THE SCOTS

By the autumn of 1323 the situation in Gascony was threatening. One big unanswered question was how far the French were prepared to go, even as far as an invasion. But there were two more unanswered questions: would the French take advantage of the growing tension between the two kingdoms to draw in the Scots, and would they offer refuge and assistance to Roger Mortimer of Wigmore after his escape from the Tower of London in August?

Although the French had made an alliance with the Scots under their then-king John Balliol in 1295, the alliance was in effect suspended when

---

[13] Vale, 230–2; *Saint-Sardos*, ix, 183.

[14] *Foedera*, II, i, 483, 488–9. The details of Edward's complaints are contained in AN, J 634, no. 1.

[15] *Foedera*, II, i, 503, 505–6, 510, 512–13, 515.

[16] *Foedera*, II, i, 519. This was part of a programme of surveying and repair of these castles which had been under way since 1320: Vale, 230.

[17] *Foedera*, II, i, 524. No parliament was in fact held until Feb. 1324. By Jan. 1324 Charles of Valois's proposals had changed to a double marriage between Edward II's two daughters, Eleanor and Joan, and his own two sons: *Saint-Sardos*, 16.

England and France made peace in 1303. In future the French confined their activities to encouraging truce negotiations between England and Scotland.[18] In return the English did nothing to impede the French king in his bitter conflict with his rebellious vassal the count of Flanders. As long as the French had a greater interest in maintaining good relations with England than in offering assistance to the Scots, nothing happened to change this situation. By the summer of 1324 however Edward II had good reason to fear that if war did begin in Gascony the Scots would attack England, either on their own initiative or with French encouragement.[19] When Robert Bruce proposed negotiations to turn the thirteen-year truce of May 1323 into a permanent peace Edward therefore had every incentive to oblige, in the hope of reducing the number of his enemies.[20] The bishop of St Andrews and earl of Moray met English envoys at York on 18 November 1324.[21] According to the *Vita Edwardi Secundi*, which provides the only information on the negotiations, the Scots demanded that the kingdom of Scotland should be free from every exaction of the kingdom of England; that they should be allowed to retain by right of conquest and lordship all the land they had traversed as far as the gates of York; that Robert Bruce should be given back the family lands in Essex which he had forfeited through rebellion; and that the Stone of Scone on which the kings of Scots had been inaugurated and which had been taken to Westminster Abbey by Edward I and placed by the tomb of St Edward the Confessor, should be restored to the Scots. Robert Bruce also proposed a marriage between his daughter and Edward, earl of Chester; and finally that the treaty should be confirmed by the king of France in the presence of the pope.[22] These were terms which the English could not possibly accept. Edward II is said to have commented when he heard them: 'The Scots have come not to draw us towards a peace, but to seek opportunity for further discord and for unprovoked breaches of the truce.'[23] If the proposals are accurately recorded, it appears they were terms that were meant to be rejected, perhaps providing a pretext for renewing war. The mention of the king of France as a guarantor would also have raised suspicions as to Scottish motives.

Although on this occasion the Scots and the French did not act together openly, it was reported in April 1325 that in the event of a French invasion

---

[18] Barrow, 63–5, 128, 183, 200.

[19] In May 1324 Hugh d'Angoulême, the papal envoy who was then in London, wrote to the pope that he believed Bruce would join an Anglo-French war: Barrow, 251, 372, n. 71; ASV, Instrumenta Miscellanea 944. If Hugh believed this, Edward II would certainly have done so.

[20] *Vita*, 222–3.

[21] *Foedera*, II, i, 577–8; *Saint-Sardos*, 76.

[22] *Vita*, 222–5. See also *Vita*, 224–5 nn. 465–8. There is no mention of these negotiations in Barrow or in *Regesta Regum Scottorum*.

[23] *Vita*, 224–9.

of England the Scots would probably join in.²⁴ It is unknown whether the Scots and the French were in contact at this time, but in April 1326 the Franco-Scottish alliance of 1295 was to be revived in the Treaty of Corbeil in which the two countries promised mutual assistance in any war against England.²⁵ Edward was probably right to have his suspicions and he took precautions. In or shortly before July 1324 Edward summoned to England his namesake Edward Balliol, the son of John Balliol, who had been living on his ancestral lands at Bailleul in Picardy since his father's death there in 1314.²⁶ Edward II knew Edward Balliol, who had been resident in his own household as far back as the 1290s and had lived in honourable custody in England until his departure for France.²⁷ Since Balliol had a claim to be the rightful king of Scots, his recall to England suggests that Edward II was considering intervention in Scotland if the Scots allied themselves with the French or if the peace talks broke down.²⁸ Edward also used his agents at the papal curia to ensure in 1325 that the pope did not accept Scottish petitions and instead confirmed his earlier sentences of excommunication and interdict upon them.²⁹

ROGER MORTIMER IN FRANCE

Although Edward's government knew as early as 10 August 1323 that Mortimer had escaped to France, and that a ship had been specially brought across in advance from Normandy to Portsmouth,³⁰ they were deeply concerned about his future plans. By late August there were fears that Mortimer meant to sail from the continent to Ireland,³¹ where he had extensive possessions, including the great fortress of Trim in Meath and where he had held office as king's lieutenant between 1317 and 1320. By November 1323 Edward had learned that the seizure of Wallingford in January had been only the first stage of a much greater plot designed to seize two other royal castles, Windsor and the Tower of London, as well as to free Roger Mortimer.³² Correspondence was also passing via the Staple at Saint-Omer between Mortimer and his sympathizers in England; and on 21 November the gates of the city of London were ordered to be closed to

---

²⁴ *Saint-Sardos*, 164–5.
²⁵ Barrow, 251.
²⁶ *Foedera*, II, i, 558, 567; Barrow, 251.
²⁷ See the articles on John and Edward Balliol by G.P. Stell and B. Webster in the *Oxford DNB*.
²⁸ It is not known if Balliol did return to England at this stage, but he did so in 1327 after Edward III became king and was placed on the Scottish throne by Edward in 1332.
²⁹ *Foedera*, II, i, 613; Barrow, 250.
³⁰ An inquisition held at Portsmouth on that date uncovered the details of Mortimer's passage to the continent: *Ann. Paul.*, 306. On 6 Aug. officials in all the English ports were ordered to look out for him and any of his accomplices: *CCR, 1323–27*, 132–3.
³¹ *CCR, 1323–27*, 133–4.
³² *Foedera*, II, i, 537–8 (14 Nov. 1323); *CPR, 1321–24*, 349; E 159/97, m.187d (24 May 1324); Phillips, 266.

prevent the entry of conspirators.[33] Even more alarming were reports that Mortimer had sent agents to murder the king and the Despensers.[34] Mortimer's hand was seen everywhere,[35] and prompted a search for any contrariants and their sympathizers who remained at large.[36]

Edward's agents and correspondents on the continent kept him informed of news and rumour concerning Mortimer and his activities. In September Edward heard that Mortimer had been given shelter by John and Robert de Fiennes in Picardy and forbade them to do so.[37] There is no further information on this but Roger Mortimer's mother Margaret de Fiennes was a close relative of the two men, so it is plausible that Roger should have sought refuge with them. It also raises the question of whether they had also been involved in some way in the planning of his escape. In November Master John de Shoreditch and two other envoys were sent to Paris. Among other matters, they were instructed to ask Charles IV to arrest Mortimer and his accomplices and either send them back to England or banish them from the kingdom, in the same way that Edward II had dealt with Flemish enemies of France in the past.[38] They evidently achieved some success, since on 13 December John de Shoreditch and his colleagues wrote from Paris with the news that Mortimer and his fellow rebels had been forbidden to remain within the domains of the king of France, but had been favourably received by the count of Boulogne. The envoys had not however been able to deliver Edward's letters to the count or to speak to him in person since they understood that he had gone to Toulouse with the king of France,[39] so leaving open the question of where Mortimer actually was. On 6 December 1323 Ralph Basset wrote from Saint-Émilion in Gascony telling Edward that his spy had reported that

---

[33] *Ann. Paul.*, 306; Williams, *Medieval London*, 294.

[34] *PW*, II, ii, 374 (24 Nov. 1323). The earl of Arundel, Robert Baldock the chancellor, and Geoffrey le Scrope one of the royal judges were also the intended victims.

[35] It was ironic that in early Sep. 1323, just a month after Mortimer's spectacular escape, Edward paid 5s to Eleanor Rede and Alice de Whorlton for chanting songs to him about an earlier opponent of the crown, Simon de Montfort, while he was at Whorlton castle in Yorkshire: J.W. Walker, 'Robin Hood identified', *Yorks. Arch. Journal*, xxxvi (1944), 30; Taylor, *English Historical Literature*, 267.

[36] Haines, *The Church and Politics*, 144; KB 27/255/Rex m.87r; JI 1/1388.

[37] *Foedera*, II, i, 536 (1 Oct.). The letter refers to Picardy rather loosely, since the Fiennes family were prominent in the county of Ponthieu, which was one of Edward II's hereditary domains. Robert de Fiennes had also been seneschal of Ponthieu from 1316 to 1320.

[38] *Saint-Sardos*, 177–9.

[39] Ibid., 5; C 81/125/6788, no. 1; *CCW*, 548. This does not match the suggestion that Roger 'was welcomed with great honour' by Charles IV when he first arrived in France: *Melsa*, 348; Mortimer, *The Greatest Traitor*, 136; Doherty (D.Phil.), 99. What the chronicle actually says is that Mortimer was held in great honour and favour '*apud proceres Franciae*', which could be interpreted to mean the members of his various family connections in France, Fiennes, Joinville, Lusignan. The county of Boulogne was close to the lands of John and Robert de Fiennes, which might help to explain Mortimer's temporary association with the count.

Mortimer and others were going to 'Germany'.[40] In February 1324 Pierre de Cussac told Edward among many other things that Roger Mortimer's son Geoffrey, the new lord of Couhé near Poitiers, had recently been in Paris, but without indicating whether Roger had also been there.[41] Whatever else, Geoffrey was at least in a position to help support his father financially. In early October 1324 the Younger Despenser wrote to John Sturmy, the admiral of the royal ships in the North Sea, that he had certain information about a large fleet of ships gathered in Holland and Zeeland, with the assent of the king of Bohemia (who was also count of Luxemburg) and the count of Hainault, and preparing to land a force of men-at-arms and other troops in Norfolk and Suffolk under the command of Roger Mortimer.[42] This was strikingly similar to what eventually transpired when Mortimer invaded England in 1326. Nothing more came of this report, but it suggests that Mortimer was already looking for military assistance in the Low Countries. Some support for this suggestion came on 21 November 1324 when Nicholas Hugate wrote to the Younger Despenser from Bordeaux, telling him that Mortimer's son Geoffrey had pledged his French lands to Charles IV in return for 16,000 *livres*, repayable in three years, and that he and his father had gone towards 'Germany'. Despenser was warned of Mortimer's malice and of the peril that he represented.[43] Mortimer was clearly up to something but his plotting was about to become absorbed into a chain of events which led England and France directly into war in the summer of 1324 and then almost inexorably to the downfall of Edward II and the Despensers two years later.

THE WAR OF SAINT-SARDOS

On the night of 15–16 October 1323 a band of armed men hanged a French serjeant from a post bearing the fleurs-de-lys of France, which had been

---

[40] *Saint-Sardos*, 2; BL, Cotton Ms. Caligula D III, no. 6/1. This is very vague and could mean anywhere in the Empire, including parts of the Low Countries, which would tie in geographically with the references to Picardy, Boulogne and Hainault/Holland.

[41] *Saint-Sardos*, 22; SC 1/47/102. Geoffrey inherited Couhé, which was a portion of the vast estates of the former Lusignan counts of La Marche and Angoulême, through his mother Joan de Joinville (Geneville): Phillips, 14; G.W. Watson, 'Geoffrey de Mortemer and his descendants', *Genealogist*, new ser., xxii (1906), 1–16.

[42] *Saint-Sardos*, 72; CPR, *1324–27*, 31. This 'certain information' was probably based on the letter from the archbishop of Canterbury to the chancellor on *c.* 20 Sept. in which the archbishop spoke of 180 German cogs and 60 French vessels assembled by the count of Hainault in Zeeland ready for an invasion of England in Oct.: *Saint-Sardos*, 59. Any large gathering of vessels, including such innocent ones as the annual Genoese trading fleet from the Mediterranean to the Low Countries, was likely to be interpreted as an invasion fleet: Fryde, 145. However in 1324 Antonio Pessagno, Edward II's former Genoese financier, was suspected of plotting some kind of attack on England with the aid of his brother Manuel, the admiral of the kingdom of Portugal. Edward wrote to his cousin Dinis of Portugal, asking him to put a stop to Pessagno's plans: Childs, 'England in Europe', 109.

[43] *Saint-Sardos*, 102–3; SC 1/50/95.

driven into the ground to mark the foundation of a new *bastide* at Saint-Sardos in the Agenais. The proposal by the monks of the nearby abbey of Sarlat to establish a *bastide* on the lands adjoining their priory at Saint-Sardos had been hotly debated for several years past, since its construction would have created a French-controlled enclave in an area which owed allegiance to the English crown, whose agents could be expected to oppose it. It was also opposed by local interests in the city of Agen and by Raymond-Bernard of Montpezat, the secular lord of the area and a vassal of Edward II.[44] When news of the killing of one of his officials reached Charles IV at Angers on 1 November it was assumed with some justification that Raymond-Bernard's men were responsible, and with less justification that Ralph Basset, Edward II's seneschal of Aquitaine, was complicit.[45] The news arrived in England in early December and was received with shock and consternation by Edward II and his council who were already deeply engaged in trying to resolve the existing disputes between England and France and immediately understood the seriousness of the situation. Edward himself termed the attack an outrage.[46]

In his letter to Charles IV on 7 December Edward said that he had no knowledge of or involvement in anything that had taken place at Saint-Sardos and would instruct his own officials in the duchy to inquire diligently into the facts. He could not openly apologize for something that had happened in his own territory, but this came close. It was deeply unfortunate that at the same time Edward was also asking for a postponement of his homage.[47] Charles IV exploited the situation with great skill. In February 1324 Ralph Basset and Raymond-Bernard of Montpezat were banished from the kingdom of France after failing to answer a summons to appear before the king at Toulouse, and orders were given to seize the castle of Montpezat.[48] When the English garrison refused to surrender, Charles ordered a local proclamation of arms for 1 April, which was suspended when an English embassy led by the archbishop of Dublin and Edward II's half-brother the earl of Kent came to Paris. They were received coldly, being told of Edward's folly in thinking that he, a mere duke, vassal and subject could presume to address the king of France, who was emperor in his own realm and sovereign under God.[49] Under extreme pressure from the French side,

---

[44] For the details see *Saint-Sardos*, xi–xii; Vale, 233–4. For the location of Sarlat, Agen and Montpezat see the excellent map of the duchy of Aquitaine, *c.* 1307 (and therefore not including Saint-Sardos itself) in Vale, 284–5.

[45] *Saint-Sardos*, xii; Vale, 234–5.

[46] *Saint-Sardos*, 179. This forms part of a recital of Anglo-French negotiations from 17 Aug. 1323 until 3 May 1325, printed in *Saint-Sardos*, xii, 176–207. News of the attack arrived within days of the departure for Paris of John de Shoreditch and other English envoys with a long agenda of business, including ironically the plans for the new *bastide* at Saint-Sardos.

[47] *Saint-Sardos*, xii, 179–80.

[48] *Saint-Sardos*, xii; Vale, 235–6.

[49] *Saint-Sardos*, 186.

the envoys first of all promised to give up Montpezat, and then changed their minds. At the same time they asked for a further postponement of Edward II's homage until 1 May 1325 or at the earliest 6 October 1324 at Boulogne.[50]

The slow fuse continued to burn.[51] In England one last attempt to avoid disaster was made at a meeting of the council at Westminster on 27 May 1324.[52] Aymer de Valence, the earl of Pembroke and lord of Montignac near Angoulême, with a unique experience of Anglo-French diplomacy and personal contacts with the French court,[53] was chosen to go to Paris. No details of his commission have survived but his mission was clearly connected with the Gascon crisis.[54] He left London for Paris shortly before 13 June, but never reached his destination. On 23 June somewhere close to Saint-Riquier on the road from Boulogne he died suddenly after dining.[55] His death was almost certainly natural, but it was a sign of the times that one chronicler suggested that he had been murdered because of his part in the judgment of Thomas of Lancaster in 1322.[56] The news reached Edward II at Tonbridge in Kent on 26 June. In a show of gratitude to his cousin and one of his most loyal supporters, but whose influence had recently been eclipsed by the Despensers,[57] Edward sent his confessor Robert de Duffeld to break the news to the countess of Pembroke at Hertford.[58] Pembroke's body was received with honour in London on 31 July and was buried in Westminster Abbey near the high altar and the royal tombs on 1 August.[59]

It is unlikely that the earl of Pembroke's mission would have made any difference, even had he lived. Edward and his advisers had badly underestimated French determination. To Charles IV and his advisers the prevarication over Montpezat and the delay in doing homage looked like a refusal by Edward to recognize his obligations to the French crown. Shortly before 25 April 1324 Charles IV ordered a general proclamation

---

[50] The full account of the mission is given in *Saint-Sardos*, xiii, 27–38, 181–8; see also Vale, 235–6.

[51] This is Malcolm Vale's very apt choice of image: Vale, 235.

[52] SC 1/49/56; *CCR, 1323–27*, 184; Phillips, 233. Though the date of the meeting, nearly a month after it was summoned on 1 May, does not suggest any great sense of urgency.

[53] See Phillips, 1–8; Vale, 27–33.

[54] *Ann. Paul.*, 307; *Chroniques de Sempringham*, 350; *Melsa*, 348; *Blaneford*, 150; Phillips, 233.

[55] Phillips, 233.

[56] BL, Royal Ms. 20. A. III, f. 216v; *Brut*, I, 252; Phillips, 233. If Roger Mortimer or any of his associates were suspected of such a killing, there would certainly be some mention of it.

[57] Nonetheless a memorandum of April 1324, in which the unknown author discussed how Edward II should respond to the French over Saint-Sardos, described Pembroke and the Younger Despenser as the king's closest advisers ('*les plus privetz le roi*'): *Saint-Sardos*, 42; SC 1/60/126.

[58] *CFR, 1319–27*, 427; E 101/379/19, f. 15v; Phillips, 233.

[59] *Ann. Paul.*, 307; Phillips, 233. His burial at Westminster was decided upon by the council at his widow's request: C 81/1329/6925. Aymer's father, William de Valence, and his brother John and sister Margaret were already buried at Westminster. Aymer's own tomb, which was constructed within a few years of his death, is particularly fine. See Binski, *Westminster Abbey*, 113–14, 118–19.

of arms for 10 June,[60] as a preliminary to invading and confiscating the duchy.

Edward reacted to the news of French mobilization by appointing his half-brother, Edmund earl of Kent, as his lieutenant in Gascony on 20 July. Orders also went out for the arrest of all French citizens in England and for the gathering of shipping and an army to go to Gascony under the leadership of John de Segrave and Fulk Fitz Warin.[61] But it was already too late. On 13 August a French army of about 1,000 men-at-arms and 6,000 infantry commanded by Charles of Valois was assembled at Moissac ready to carry out Charles IV's orders. To resist them were 400 men-at-arms and 4,000 infantry recruited locally.[62] Charles of Valois then advanced into the Agenais, where the city of Agen surrendered on 15 August, followed by Valence-d'Agen, Aiguillon, Nicole, and other places in the valley of the Garonne. The French army reached the important town of La Réole on the approaches to Bordeaux, the administrative centre of the duchy, on 25 August and began to besiege it, taking care to prevent any reinforcements reaching it from Bordeaux.[63]

Closed up inside La Réole were the earl of Kent himself and his colleague, Alexander Bicknor the archbishop of Dublin. The town was well supplied and defended and should have been able to sustain a long siege if necessary, tying down a large proportion of the French forces in the process. As the siege progressed the French suffered casualties, including the marshal of France; they also suffered from lack of food and disease.[64] In Bordeaux itself great efforts were made to ensure its safety from any French attack, which in the event never occurred.[65] In early September 1324 the greater part of the duchy, including the ports of Bordeaux and Bayonne and other key centres such as Bourg, Blaye, Saint-Émilion and Libourne in the vicinity of Bordeaux, and Dax and Saint-Sever further south, was still in Anglo-Gascon hands and remained so for the rest of the war.[66] There was also the prospect of the arrival in Gascony of reinforcements from England.

---

[60] *Saint-Sardos*, xiii, 186–7; Vale, 236.

[61] *Foedera*, II, i, 560–2, 564–5. It is likely that Edmund had not returned to England after his unsuccessful mission to Paris in April.

[62] *Saint-Sardos*, 49–52; Vale, 237–8. This and much else is recorded in a very detailed report from the constable of Bordeaux John Travers to the Younger Despenser, written from Bordeaux on 1 Sept. For details of the Gascon nobility who served Edward II with their followers during the war see Vale, 239–40.

[63] *Saint-Sardos*, 49–52.

[64] Ibid., 50, 52; Vale, 238.

[65] Vale, 238–9.

[66] Ibid. The war of Saint-Sardos was characterized by the loyalty of most of Edward II's subjects in Gascony, who preferred the lighter and more distant hand of Plantagenet rule to the more severe form of government practised by the French crown and its officials. The main exception was Amanieu d'Albret, whose loyalty to the English crown had been put under strain much earlier in the reign by the behaviour of Gaveston and his relatives in the county of Béarn: Vale, 240. Amanieu gave the French valuable assistance at the siege of La Réole.

But these potential advantages were offset both by the confusion and uncertainty caused by the French invasion[67] and by the distance and time which separated Gascony from England. Although, for example, the council in England discussed the war in great detail during the autumn of 1324,[68] its decisions could have no immediate effect and might be seriously out of date by the time they reached Gascony. By the end of the war the English government had succeeded through a major administrative effort in mobilizing and transporting several thousand men, hundreds of horses, food supplies and munitions, but all this took nearly a year to achieve.[69] Altogether the war of Saint-Sardos cost the English crown about £65,000, much less than the average annual cost of £72,000 in 1294–8, the previous occasion of Anglo-French hostilities in Gascony; and unlike the earlier war, Edward's financial reserves were such that he could fight this one without recourse to borrowing.[70] This did not however mean that cash was readily available to the defenders of Gascony. The first assistance for the duchy did not reach Bordeaux until 3 October, when a sum of £8,000 was delivered, but another payment of 14,600 marks and a force of about 300 men-at-arms and several hundred foot soldiers were delayed by unfavourable winds and did not arrive until November.[71] Further reinforcements, amounting to about 4,000 infantry and 300 men-at-arms, and the large sum of £20,441 did not reach Bordeaux until 10–11 May 1325, long after the immediate fighting had ceased but ready for a possible renewal.[72] As has been aptly remarked, the attackers were exposed to fewer risks than the defenders.[73]

On 28 September the Younger Despenser wrote from Porchester to the earl of Kent saying that no news had been received from him between 10 August when his valet John Daspale had arrived in England and 24 September when two vessels, one from Bordeaux and the other from Bayonne, had brought news of the duchy.[74] He could not know that

---

[67] In his long report to the Younger Despenser John Travers stated that the entire duchy was on the point of being occupied by the French: *Saint-Sardos*, 50.

[68] Ibid., 65–8: datable only as between the end of Sept. and Dec. 1324.

[69] F. Bériac-Lainé in 'Une Armée anglo-gasconne vingt ans avant la guerre de Cent Ans', in *Guerre, pouvoir et noblesse au Moyen Âge*, ed. J. Paviot & J. Verger (Paris, 2000), 92. This is however a much more positive assessment of the English war effort than Fryde, 144–5. A good comparison is with the communication and logistical difficulties which faced the British government during the American War of Independence: see Piers Mackesy, *The War for America, 1775–1783* (London, 1964).

[70] Vale, 236.

[71] BL, Add. Ms. 7967, ff. 4r, 7v, 17v; 30r–39v; Fryde, 144; Bériac-Lainé, 'Une Armée', 84–5 (this includes a valuable graph showing the size of the forces available for the defence of Gascony at various dates between May 1324 and Dec. 1325).

[72] BL, Add. Ms. 7967, ff. 4r, 17r, 20v, 20v; *Saint-Sardos*, 210, n. 1, 221–2; Bériac-Lainé, 'Une Armée', 83–4. The reinforcements consisted of two separate fleets of 80 and 53 ships, which had left Portsmouth and Harwich on 22 April and 3 May.

[73] Bériac-Lainé, 'Une Armée', 92.

[74] *Saint-Sardos*, 64.

on 22 September the earl of Kent had agreed to surrender La Réole to Charles of Valois in return for a six-month truce.[75]

EDWARD'S RESPONSE

Even before news of the truce was received in England measures were being taken to intensify and to extend the war. On 18 September Queen Isabella's English lands were taken into royal hands; a few days later the arrest of all French subjects in the kingdom was ordered, even including members of Isabella's household; at the end of September Edward appealed individually to the lords and urban communities of Gascony for support against the French; he also requested military assistance from the rulers of Aragon and Castile, and proposed a marriage between his elder son, Edward earl of Chester, and the daughter of the king of Aragon.[76] In a letter from the Younger Despenser to Ralph Basset the seneschal of Gascony in early October more details of Edward's plans were given, including the very significant information that Edward intended to go to Gascony the following summer in person and at the head of as large an army drawn from England, Wales and Ireland as he could muster.[77]

On 20 October, by which time the news of La Réole had arrived, an assembly of magnates, bishops and knights was held at London.[78] Edward personally delivered a very interesting opening speech, demonstrating an insistence on his rights and duties as king but also claiming somewhat disingenuously that he had always sought and followed the advice of his magnates:

> Lords, I have shown you certain things which concern the crown which have come under debate, as one who is your chief and who has the sovereign keeping of it, and as one who is ready to maintain the crown in all its rights, with your counsel and aid, and to defend it as far as a

---

[75] AN, J 634, no. 2; *Saint-Sardos*, 61–3; Vale, 238. Both sides had probably by this stage fought one another to a standstill. The French were also distracted by the anti-French revolt which had recently broken out in Flanders: Fryde, 143; Vale, 236. The English extension of their existing truce with the count of Flanders in Aug. 1324 was likely to have been an attempt to take advantage of this situation: *Foedera*, II, i, 566.

[76] *Foedera*, II, i, 568–73. In Feb. 1325 this plan for an Aragonese marriage was abandoned in favour of a proposed double marriage alliance between the young Edward and Eleanor the sister of king Alfonso XI of Castile, and Alfonso and Edward II's daughter Eleanor: *Foedera*, II, i, 586–7. For a report on these and other Anglo-Castilian negotiations see *Saint-Sardos*, 214–17. On relations between England and Castile and Aragon see esp. Childs, 'England in Europe', 104–9, 111–12.

[77] *Saint-Sardos*, 75–7. Edward even imagined that Robert Bruce would accompany him, if the peace talks with the Scots succeeded. This document is wrongly dated as 1323 in Fryde, 145.

[78] *PW*, II, ii, 317–25: this assembly was not designated in the writs as a parliament. For details see *PROME*, Parliament of Oct. 1324.

man can, by the power of all your might, on which matter I have always asked for your counsel, and have done nothing in the said business without counsel, in which I believe that I have done my part; whereupon I have demanded your counsel, aid and might on this, which you should do, give, and show to me at your peril, exactly as you would wish to acknowledge it, now and in the future, and that each of you, individually and independently, should give me his counsel and his advice on what I ought to do; which given, I wish it to be entered for perpetuity in the roll of parliament: because of which I again ask you, on your faith and your allegiance, to give it to me again orally, each of you individually and independently. For although you have shown me in a bill all your advice and arguments in general, this could be drawn up and put in a bill on the advice and counsel of one or two of you, who know best how to lead and win you over to their opinion, so I nevertheless wish to have your answers individually and from each one independently, and for each one to tell me orally what he thinks, so that I may be fully advised on the said business and on all the circumstances in detail: and I wish to be answered in such a manner, both by clerks and by laymen, that in future each one can answer in his own words without a general cover, and that your answers should be put down in writing: both what I have shown you and what you answer. For I do not want any concealment or sly evasion between us on such an important matter but to be answered orally, clearly and distinctly, just as the matters are distinctly and openly shown to you.[79]

A group of prelates and magnates was chosen to advise Edward on his plans to go to Gascony, and they presented their recommendations to him at a meeting at Mortlake on 1 November: at least 1,000 men-at-arms should accompany him, and 10,000 infantry, 6,000 from England and 4,000 from Wales; Edward earl of Chester should act as his father's lieutenant in England during his absence in Gascony and should be assisted by a council consisting of two archbishops, four bishops, two earls and four barons; and before Edward's departure fealty should be sworn to his son, in the same way as when Edward I went to Flanders in 1297. But they added a word of warning: if so many men left England, there would not be enough left to protect the kingdom, 'the times being as they are', a significant choice of phrase encompassing every possibility from foreign invasion to internal disorder, rebellion or conspiracy.[80] For the moment the plans went ahead. Orders went out for troops to muster at Portsmouth on

---

[79] For the text and translation, edited from E 30/1582, see *PROME*, Parliament of Oct. 1324. The text was previously published in *Rotuli Parliamentorum Hactenus Inediti*, ed. Richardson & Sayles, 94–8, but incorrectly dated as belonging to the parliament of June 1325. The speech is also edited in *Saint-Sardos*, 95–8, with a note as to the correct date. E 30/1582 includes the detailed replies of the magnates present to the king's questions.

[80] '*a temps qe ore est*': *Saint-Sardos*, 89; SC 1/49/89.

17 March 1325. But soon signs started to appear of a change of mind. On 20 February it was announced that, at the request of certain prelates and magnates, Edward had decided to delay his own departure for Gascony until 20 May and that the March expedition would be led by the earl of Surrey.[81] This was the force that arrived in Bordeaux on 10–11 May.[82] Edward himself was never to leave England.

NEGOTIATIONS FOR PEACE

Edward's change of plan was the result of the peace talks which had been under way since the previous autumn under the auspices of the pope. John XXII had been anxious to preserve the peace before the war broke out, appealing to both Charles IV and Edward II.[83] From Edward's perspective it was important to obtain the pope's goodwill. This was one reason for Edward's reconciliation with John Stratford, the new bishop of Winchester: Stratford's experience in dealing with the papal curia was to be needed again. In July Edward had already written to the pope presenting his case against France; and in late September a proposal was made to him that Stratford should be asked to review the operation of previous peace treaties between England and France in order to demonstrate to the pope that Edward had not failed to perform his homage or other services required of him.[84] At about the same time news arrived in England that the pope intended to send two envoys, Guillaume de Laudun, archbishop of Vienne, and Hugh, bishop of Orange, to mediate.[85] The envoys arrived on 8 November and dined with Edward at the Tower of London on 11 and again on 20 November, just before their departure.[86]

The main outcome of their visit was Edward's decision on 15 November to send an embassy to negotiate with Charles IV. This was to consist of the bishops of Norwich and Winchester, the earl of Richmond now released from captivity in Scotland, and Henry de Beaumont.[87] They were authorized to tell the French king that Edward had never refused to perform homage since he had not been properly summoned to do so; to negotiate for the return of the lands in Gascony and Ponthieu occupied by the French king's forces; to be prepared to discuss a marriage alliance if the king of France were to make the suggestion, but to agree to nothing

---

[81] *Foedera*, II, i, 580, 583, 591.
[82] Bériac-Lainé, 'Une Armée', 83.
[83] *Foedera*, II, i, 547; Vale, 236.
[84] *Foedera*, II, i, 563–4; *Saint-Sardos*, 68–9.
[85] *Foedera*, II, i, 567–8 (30 Aug.).
[86] *Ann. Paul.*, 308; *Saint-Sardos*, 192, n. 1.
[87] *Saint-Sardos*, 192. Richmond, the brother of the duke of Brittany, and Beaumont both had close family connections with the French court. Beaumont however seems to have dropped out since he is not named in the recital of Edward II's letters patent in the agreement of 31 March 1325 between English and French representatives: AN, J 634, nos 3, 3 bis. Beaumont was probably still angry about the 1323 truce with the Scots.

without consulting Edward. They were also empowered to propose that Edward should grant all the land he held from the king of France to his elder son Edward and that the young Edward should then perform homage for all these lands and those now under French occupation; if that proposal was unacceptable, then homage should be performed by Edward II on a date to be agreed but as near as possible to All Saints following (1 November 1325) and at a place as close to the coast as possible. Edward II was prepared to confirm the six-month truce agreed by the earl of Kent and authorized his envoys to extend it until 29 September; and last but not least that Roger Mortimer and his accomplices should be expressly excluded from any treaty.[88] These instructions are of particular interest in showing that the suggestion that the young Edward should receive Gascony and go to France to perform homage for it originated from the English side and not from the French, as is sometimes argued.[89] Nor was it an original idea: it was in essence a repetition of the situation in the closing years of the reign of Edward I when the then Prince of Wales was first supposed to go to France to perform homage on behalf of his father and then in 1306 was granted the duchy of Aquitaine in his own right.

The English envoys arrived in Paris during December, and in early January 1325, after preliminary negotiations with Charles IV and his council, they sent the bishop of Winchester to report to Edward II and his advisers.[90] The news was not encouraging. The French had objected to the English attempts to make alliances with Aragon and Castile against the count of Hainault and the French crown, which were considered to be acts of treason; they did not consider themselves bound by the agreement entered into by the earl of Kent, which they claimed was more to the advantage of the king of England than the king of France; they also objected to Edward II's reception of men who had been banished from France, such as Ralph Basset the former seneschal of Gascony; and they were annoyed by the removal of the French members of the queen's household. The envoys had also heard that Charles IV had summoned another army and intended to enter the duchy of Gascony on 1 May, accompanied by the king of Bohemia and the count of Hainault.[91] No mention was made of Roger Mortimer.

On the other hand, John Stratford brought with him a set of proposals for discussion by Edward II and his council. Firstly the king of France promised that if Edward were to come to him without preconditions

---

[88] *Saint-Sardos*, 192–4.

[89] Cf. Mortimer, *The Greatest Traitor*, 138. Since the ambassadors' instructions were drawn up in England before they began their mission, there is nothing to support Natalie Fryde's argument that the bishop of Winchester was responsible for this suggestion: Fryde, 146.

[90] Haines, *Stratford*, 153–4. After a very difficult journey because of violent storms in the Channel he reached Dover on 13 Jan. and London on the 17th: *Saint-Sardos*, 195, n. 1.

[91] *Saint-Sardos*, 129–32: the famous king John of Bohemia who was killed fighting for France against Edward III and the Black Prince at Crécy in 1346, and William count of Hainault, who was to become Edward III's father-in-law.

concerning his lands in Gascony, he would do him justice fairly and speedily. The two papal envoys, the archbishop of Vienne and bishop of Orange, who had also been in Paris, had put forward three further proposals after discussions of their own with Charles IV's council. If Edward granted the Agenais and the county of Ponthieu to the king of France, he could then hold the duchy of Gascony on the same terms as before; if this was not acceptable, the king of France would be satisfied with the Agenais alone and would restore the duchy and county in return for homage; alternatively, if Edward gave up the Agenais, Charles IV would grant him lands elsewhere in France and restore the duchy and county. But there was one more proposal, which seems to have originated with Charles IV in person, but was supported by the members of his council who were negotiating with the English and via the papal envoys. This was to prove a fateful one: if Isabella and the young Edward were to come to France, then there was an excellent chance that Charles would extend the truce and would restore all Edward II's lands either to him or to the young Edward on performance of homage; in which case the alliances between England and France would be restored.[92] It was a tempting offer but a dangerous one. Charles IV may genuinely have been offering peace but Edward II and his advisers could not be certain that he had no ulterior motives.

Edward first summoned a meeting of prelates, magnates and others to Westminster in early February and informed them of the French proposals.[93] As for the suggestion that Isabella and the young Edward should go to France together, 'all with one voice' advised that Edward should not go until peace had been settled; but it was agreed that Charles IV should be asked if it was acceptable for Isabella to go on her own to make peace; and if this was the case, the English envoys should ask for an extension of the truce until 24 June or at least until Pentecost (26 May), to allow Isabella time to discuss and make peace and to return to England. The envoys were also to ask for the expulsion of '*le Mortimer*' and other traitors and royal enemies from France, before the queen's arrival, 'lest she and her followers suffer peril and dishonour upon the road'.[94] This reflected a fear

---

[92] Ibid., 195.

[93] Ibid.; this must be the assembly decided on by the council when it was discussing Gascon affairs in Jan. ('*vii: Item qe les grantz soient somounz dy estre pur conseiller etc. et noun pas pur parlement*'): ibid., 134–5; E 175/2/10. From this reference Natalie Fryde (Fryde, 67) concluded, I think wrongly, that Edward II did not like parliaments. They had not always of course been to his liking, but Edward needed advice quickly and this was the best way to obtain it. Councils of prelates and magnates were just as regular a feature of Edward's dealings with his subjects as were parliaments: see General Introduction to *PROME*. The changes in date and meeting place of parliaments and other assemblies, esp. in 1324–5, reflected the changing fortunes of the war in France and the state of the peace negotiations rather than an unwillingness to hold such meetings: cf. Fryde, 67.

[94] *Saint-Sardos*, 195–6: '*pur perils et deshonurs qe a lui ou as soens purroient avenir sur chimyn, qe Dieu defende*'.

that Isabella might be held up and abducted by Mortimer.[95] Edward fully expected that Isabella would return from France after her mission and he made it clear to the prelates and magnates both that he still intended to go to Gascony if the negotiations failed and that he wanted Isabella to accompany him.[96]

Armed with these detailed instructions, Thomas de Astley was first of all sent back to the bishop of Norwich and earl of Richmond in Paris on 7 February. On 16 February Edward received news from his envoys advising him that Isabella should be sent to France and the following day Edward confirmed that she would go. However, Edward also told both his own and the papal envoys, the archbishop of Vienne and bishop of Orange, who had also advised him to send Isabella, that her stay in France and her return to England were subject to his will, and that he would not accept the outcome of any negotiations if this meant his disinheritance or dishonour. As with the earlier instructions concerning Roger Mortimer, there is nothing here to suggest that Isabella might refuse to return after her mission was ended, simply a well justified apprehension about the terms which Charles IV and his team of legal advisers might seek to impose.[97] At the same time Edward made sure that, if anything untoward were to happen, he would be kept fully informed of Isabella's activities. The retinue of thirty which was to accompany her was selected by Edward and included the countess of Surrey, whose husband was about to lead an expedition to Gascony.[98] Perhaps he was simply anxious about the outcome of the negotiations, but it is also possible that he had reservations about letting Isabella out of his control. Whatever the truth of the matter, on 14 February the bishop of Winchester set off once more for Paris.[99]

ISABELLA'S FATEFUL JOURNEY

On 8 March 1325 Edward wrote to the pope, informing him that Isabella was going to Paris.[100] In fact she was already well on her way, crossing to Wissant on 9 March and reaching Pontoise on 20 March. On 21 March

---

[95] The areas in which he was reported to be lurking and where he had friends were uncomfortably close to the road she would have to follow from Wissant in the Pas-de-Calais to Paris. The fear was probably increased by the memory of Isabella's narrow escapes from capture by the Scots in 1319 and 1322, and by the problems caused in 1317 when the earl of Pembroke was seized and held to ransom in France.

[96] *Saint-Sardos*, 196.

[97] Ibid., 197–8.

[98] *CPR, 1324–27*, 44, 91–2; Doherty (D.Phil.), 114; E 101/381/3, f. 1v. Another of her company was a certain William le Galeys, who may be the same man who claimed he was Edward II at Koblenz in 1338.

[99] The bishop had left even before the arrival at Westminster of the latest dispatches from Paris and crossed to France on 18 Feb., the same date as his letters of instruction. Fast messengers would have caught up with him and delivered the letters: see Haines, *Stratford*, 155–6.

[100] *Foedera*, II, i, 595.

she was at Poissy where she met the three English envoys, the bishops of Norwich and Winchester and the earl of Richmond,[101] and it was here on the same date that she also met her brother Charles IV.[102] The serious business of her mission now began. According to the letter, dated 31 March, in which she reported on the negotiations to her husband, Isabella found her brother harsh and unyielding.[103] The English envoys faced the same attitude when they tried to negotiate with Charles IV's representatives, to such an extent that they failed to find any common ground. The papal envoys were present throughout and tried to break the deadlock, but with little success, the talks veering from day to day between hope and despair. The English envoys even refused to attend a meeting with the French arranged by the papal envoys. This situation lasted until 29 March when the French announced that they would agree only to an extension of the existing truce in Gascony, which was due to expire on 14 April. The English envoys rejected this and Isabella wrote that she was so despondent that she was on the point of returning to her husband as fast as she could. But on the following day, 31 March, she intervened directly and managed to persuade her brother to agree to a new truce lasting from 14 April until 9 June.[104] The bishop of Winchester and William Airmyn, a chancery clerk, then crossed to England and reported to Edward and his council at Beaulieu in Hampshire soon after 10 April.[105]

The terms for a permanent settlement were agreed at Poissy on 31 March between the two papal envoys and Charles IV's representatives and presumably conveyed to the English envoys but they were not given them to deliver. Instead the terms were to be transmitted in letters which would be brought to England by the bishop of Orange and Henry de Sully.[106] They were severe: Edward should first surrender all his lands in Gascony, which would be restored only after Edward had personally performed homage,[107] which Charles IV promised he was prepared to receive 'through love of his sister';[108] Edward was additionally asked to pay an indemnity to cover the

---

[101] These details are supplied in Isabella's itinerary: *Saint-Sardos*, App. III, 267, using E 101/380/9 & 10.

[102] *Saint-Sardos*, 199. This contradicts the statement in Fryde, 147, that she did not meet her brother until 30 May, apart allegedly from another brief meeting at Bois-de-Vincennes in April (this latter detail is not confirmed by Isabella's itinerary: *Saint-Sardos*, 267).

[103] *Saint-Sardos*, 199: '*lui trovai deur*'. Edward was so anxious to learn the outcome of the negotiations that on 2 April he gave strict orders that any news from either Isabella or the other envoys was to be brought directly to him and not to be revealed to anyone else first: *Foedera*, II, i, 596. This does necessarily imply that Edward actually distrusted Isabella.

[104] AN, J 634, nos 3, 3 bis; *Saint-Sardos*, 201–2.

[105] *Saint-Sardos*, 199–205. Edward II was at Beaulieu for most of that month, ready either to respond quickly to news from Paris or to cross to Gascony if the talks failed. The bishop reached Dover on that date: *Saint-Sardos*, 197, n. 1.

[106] Ibid., 204.

[107] Ibid., 202–5.

[108] Ibid., 202: '*pur lamur et la contemplacion de sa soer, la roigne Dengleterre*'. Cf. *Vita*, 228–9.

costs of the French campaign; he should not maintain any armed forces in the duchy other than those recruited locally; and Charles IV would also retain possession of the lands in the Agenais occupied by his army, while promising to do Edward justice. To make matters worse, Charles IV allowed only one month after Easter (5 May) for Edward to reply to these terms, and when the bishop of Orange and Henry de Sully came to Edward II at Winchester three weeks had already elapsed.[109]

There were understandable fears on the English side about what might happen if the negotiations failed. On 9 April Ralph Basset wrote to the Younger Despenser from Bordeaux, telling him that after Isabella's arrival in Paris the earl of Kent and his fellow envoys had tried to discover as much as they could about French intentions and had learned that, in the event of war, they planned to divide their forces, one army entering Gascony while another would go to Normandy and from there cross to England, where they would be assisted by a Scottish attack.[110]

On 2 May the French envoys and the bishop of Winchester and William Airmyn appeared at Winchester before the king and a hastily summoned gathering of prelates and magnates.[111] Edward was faced with an almost impossible situation. His councillors considered that if he accepted the terms offered, he would be both disinherited and still run the risk of war; while outright rejection would bring about immediate war. They dared not advise Edward any further because such a decision should be taken only with the assent of the great men of the realm in parliament. However, they strongly defended Edward against the charge that he had been unwilling to perform homage to the French king.[112] It was therefore decided to send the bishop of Winchester and William Airmyn back to France to continue negotiations, while on 6 May a parliament was summoned to meet at Westminster on 25 June.[113] Edward showed the depth of his anxiety and his suspicion that he was being betrayed when he wrote to the pope on 14 May complaining bitterly that he had been led to believe that if he sent Isabella to France, her brother Charles IV would refuse her nothing.[114]

The extreme nervousness of all present was only added to by a row which took place while Edward was at Winchester. According to the *Vita*

---

[109] *Saint-Sardos*, 204–7. If literally three weeks elapsed, this would place their arrival at around 28 April. The bishop of Orange and Henry de Sully did not leave for England until 4 April at the earliest: *Saint-Sardos*, 202. Edward also included a summary of the terms in his letter of complaint to the pope on 14 May: *Foedera*, II, i, 599.

[110] SC 1/49/114; *Saint-Sardos*, 164–5. Basset assumed that Despenser would already have heard this news more directly, but he added that he had also been told by the earl of Kent that his messengers were being intercepted and imprisoned by the French wherever they were found. The plans for a possible new attack on Gascony had been reported to Edward II by the earl of Kent as far back as Jan. 1325: *Saint-Sardos*, 129–32.

[111] *Saint-Sardos*, 202–7.

[112] *Saint-Sardos*, 205–6; *Foedera*, II, i, 599.

[113] *Saint-Sardos*, 206–7; *PW*, II, ii, 328–33.

[114] *Foedera*, II, i, 599.

Edwardi Secundi, the earl of Leicester, Henry of Lancaster, aroused the king's anger by showing sympathy for the plight of the bishop of Hereford, Adam Orleton, who was still unreconciled to Edward; and also by using the arms of his brother Thomas of Lancaster and setting up a cross outside the town of Leicester in his brother's memory. Henry was ordered to attend the forthcoming parliament and to answer there for his behaviour.[115]

PEACE AT LAST

Meanwhile Isabella was in Paris, where she attended mass in Notre Dame on 7 May. On 18 May she was joined at Bois-de-Vincennes by William Airmyn, and on the 26th she dined at Fontainebleau with the queen of France, the two papal envoys, the bishop of Norwich, the earl of Richmond and Henry de Sully.[116] This was not just a social occasion, since on that same day the truce in Gascony was extended until 22 July.[117] On 30 May Isabella and the other English envoys appeared before the council of Charles IV in the palace of the Louvre to discuss peace terms, which were agreed on the following day by the papal, French and English envoys including the '*treshaute et tresnoble dame madame Isabel Reyne Dengleterre*'.[118] On the same day it was decided that peace would be publicly declared in Gascony on 4 July, and on 1 June that Edward II should come to Beauvais on 15 August: and 'if the king of England offers to do homage, the king of France will receive it'.[119] On 5 June William Airmyn left Paris to bring the news to England.[120]

Under the treaty Edward's lands in the duchy of Gascony would come under the control for the time being of Charles IV, who would appoint a seneschal acceptable to Edward, and other officials throughout the duchy; the duchy would be governed according to local laws and customs; troops in Edward's service who were already in the duchy should withdraw to Bayonne as soon as possible; and French troops would also withdraw, except for the garrisons of castles and other strongpoints. Edward would come to Beauvais to perform homage as agreed; afterwards Charles IV would restore his lands in the duchy and the county of Ponthieu, and Edward would then appoint his own officials; but if either king were unable to go to Beauvais because of sickness, he would inform the other as soon as

---

[115] *Vita*, 232–5. This dispute probably explains why on 6 May Henry was not summoned to the forthcoming parliament as an earl but instead was listed among the barons, coming after the Younger Despenser. In late April and early May Orleton was at Middleton in Hampshire, within easy reach of Winchester, should Edward wish to make his peace with him: Haines, *The Church and Politics*, 108, 152. Edward's response was to write to the pope on 28 May, making a further denunciation of Orleton: *Foedera*, II, i, 601.

[116] *Saint-Sardos*, 267–8.

[117] AN, J 634, no. 4.

[118] *Saint-Sardos*, 268; AN, J 634, no. 6; *Foedera*, II, i, 601–2.

[119] AN, J 634, nos 8, 9; *Foedera*, II, i, 601–2.

[120] *Saint-Sardos*, 268.

possible. If Edward asked Charles to do him justice concerning the lands in the duchy which were held by the king of France, he would do so; within a year Edward would pay the costs of the French actions in the duchy; but if the king of France were to retain the land he had occupied (i.e. the Agenais), he would remit these costs. No mention was made in the treaty either of Roger Mortimer and other English exiles or of Ralph Basset and others who had been exiled from France.[121]

These were harsh terms, but made to appear less so by the language employed. Charles IV was at pains to emphasize that his restoration of the duchy was an act of generosity, and that he was also acting out of love of his sister Isabella. It was clear however that come what may Charles IV meant to keep the Agenais, which was what he had probably wanted from the beginning.[122] Much would also depend on whether the French acted in good faith once homage had been performed.

In England Edward laid the terms of the proposed treaty before the prelates and magnates who had gathered for parliament. Each group in turn stated that they considered the terms reasonable and that Edward would not suffer disinheritance or dishonour. They advised him to accept the terms,[123] and on 13 June Edward did so, confirming the treaty; but in order to allow time for further details to be worked out the date of his homage was postponed until 29 August 1325.[124]

HOMAGE

Preparations went ahead for Edward II's journey to Beauvais to perform homage on 29 August. It was to be a visit on a grand scale. Over 300 people were to accompany the king, one of them being Hugh Despenser, the son of the Younger Despenser; and a small fleet of ships including the king's personal barge the *Saint Mary of Westminster* was assembled at Dover, ready to cross to Wissant on 18 August. Other preparations for Edward's coming were made at Le Crotoy in Ponthieu and at Beauvais itself.[125] Edward left his manor at Havering-atte-Bower in Essex on about 11 August, heading for the coast, but he got no farther than the Premonstratensian abbey of Langdon near Dover, where his old friend William was abbot. Here he was suddenly taken ill and was unable to continue his journey, or so he wrote to

---

[121] *Foedera*, II, i, 601–2.

[122] A French conquest of the whole of Gascony was probably beyond their resources and would have met with local resistance. In 1327 the estimated cost of a proposed invasion of Aquitaine amounted to more than three times the annual revenues of the French monarchy, and would have required heavy and unpopular taxation to carry out: Vale, 247–8.

[123] *Saint-Sardos*, 277–8.

[124] AN, J 634, no. 9 bis; *Foedera*, II, i, 601–2.

[125] *Foedera*, II, i, 604–6; J. Hunter, 'Journal of the mission of Queen Isabella to the court of France, and of her long residence in that country', *Archaeologia*, xxxvi (1855), 248.

Charles IV on 24 August. He expressed his continued willingness to come to Beauvais if arrangements could be agreed and said that he would depute John Stratford the bishop of Winchester and Master John de Bruton a canon of Exeter to see to this.[126]

Edward may have been genuinely unwell, but it is far more likely that his illness was a diplomatic one and designed to take advantage of the provision in the Anglo-French treaty which allowed for postponement of the ceremony of homage if either monarch were unable to attend.[127] Crucially, it also gave Edward and his council time for further thought. Indeed there is evidence that further thought had already being given to Edward's crossing to France only three weeks after his confirmation of the treaty. On 5 July the bishop of Winchester, the earl of Richmond and William Airmyn were authorized to propose that the duchy of Aquitaine should be granted by Edward II to his son, who would then perform homage for it in his father's place and in his own right.[128] This repeated the proposal that Edward II's ambassadors had made in December 1324 and which the French had then been prepared to accept on condition that both the young Edward and Isabella should go to France.[129] At the time the English council had refused to agree to the absence from England of both Edward and Isabella. But now with peace agreed it was time to revive the suggestion: the only problem was that Isabella was still in France. Would she return to England in advance of her son's arrival in France; and was there as yet any indication that she might be unwilling to do so? It was a risk, but one that Edward II was prepared to take. It had the advantage that Edward would not have to meet Charles IV in his inferior capacity of duke of Aquitaine and a vassal of the French crown. After his bad experience when he last performed homage at Amiens in July 1320 and the haughty reception given to his half-brother the earl of Kent in Paris in March 1324, he knew that the intended ceremony at Beauvais was likely to be deeply offensive. The author of the Historia Roffensis probably expressed the fears of Edward and his advisers when he remarked that if Edward went to France he would find the French ready to threaten him with war.[130] If on the other hand Aquitaine were held by the heir to the English throne the young Edward, the danger of public embarrassment and a possible renewal of conflict might be reduced.

But there were other reasons for Edward II's lack of enthusiasm for crossing to France. According to the Historia Roffensis Edward and his advisers were also worried that if he crossed to Wissant a trap might be laid to capture him and take him somewhere outside the kingdom of

---

[126] *Foedera*, II, i, 606. The date of 21 Aug. given in Haines, *Stratford*, 159, n. 2, comes from a different edition of *Foedera*, and may be incorrect.

[127] *Foedera*, II, i, 602.

[128] *Calendar of Treaty Rolls preserved in the Public Record Office*, i., *1234–1325*, ed. P. Chaplais (London, 1955), 256–8; *CPR, 1324–27*, 129; Haines, *Stratford*, 158.

[129] *Saint-Sardos*, 192–5.

[130] BL, Cotton Ms. Faustina, B.V, f. 45v; Haines, *Stratford*, 159.

France.¹³¹ This sounds fanciful but it was very like the fear expressed at the time of Isabella's journey to Paris in March.¹³² The reason was the same: anxiety verging on paranoia about Roger Mortimer's whereabouts and intentions. Edward would be passing close to an area in which Mortimer might be lurking and, if seized, could easily be taken to a nearby imperial territory such as the county of Holland, where Mortimer was already rumoured to have support.¹³³

According to the *Vita Edwardi Secundi*, the prelates and magnates who had advised him to go to France during the June parliament were clearly uneasy about their decision but had done so because they felt they had no other choice.¹³⁴ That was not enough in itself, for there were still anxieties about possible plots against Edward within England itself. If Mortimer might reach him on the continent, there was also the danger that he might do so at home. There were also the current tensions between Edward and Henry of Lancaster which had not been addressed during parliament in June and remained unresolved; there was the matter of the bishop of Hereford; and the archbishops of Canterbury and York, Walter Reynolds and William Melton, were at odds since the latter's appointment as treasurer in July and their consequent row over Melton's right to carry his cross of office in the Canterbury province when on royal business.¹³⁵ Recriminations were starting to be heard about the war in Gascony. Edward blamed Alexander Bicknor, the archbishop of Dublin for the advice to the earl of Kent which had led to the loss of La Réole in September 1324 and for subsequently accusing the Younger Despenser of treachery. In May 1325 Edward asked the pope to remove Bicknor from office and in December seized his lands and goods in England and Ireland, thereby adding one more to the growing list of disaffected prelates.¹³⁶ A further complication was that although the young Edward would nominally be in charge of the kingdom in his father's absence, his chief advisers would have to be Henry of Lancaster, 'because he was of better blood than the others', and the Elder Despenser the earl of Winchester, 'shrewder than all and more experienced' but 'hated by everyone and even by the king's son'.¹³⁷

It was probably the position of the Despensers as much as anything else that finally determined Edward not to go to France. While it is incorrect to

---

¹³¹ BL, Cotton Ms. Faustina, B.V, f. 45v; Haines, *Stratford*, 159.

¹³² *Saint-Sardos*, 195–6.

¹³³ *Saint-Sardos*, 72; *CPR, 1324–27*, 31. This must also be the reason for Edward's expression in Nov. 1324 of his willingness to do homage, provided the scene was near the coast: *Saint-Sardos*, 194.

¹³⁴ *Vita*, 234–7.

¹³⁵ *Vita*, 236–9. Melton replaced Walter Stapeldon, who is accused by the *Vita* of greed and extortion, but who probably removed because in the king's eyes he was not sufficiently active in raising revenue: *Vita*, 236–7; Buck, 210–15; Fryde, 103.

¹³⁶ *Foedera*, II, i, 600–1; see also the article by J.R.S. Phillips on Bicknor in the *Oxford DNB*.

¹³⁷ *Vita*, 236–9.

say that the Younger Despenser had been banished from the kingdom of France and could not have accompanied Edward for this reason, nonetheless he could scarcely have gone there in safety.[138] If Mortimer really were laying traps for Edward, Despenser would have been an even more welcome quarry.[139] Two well-informed chroniclers, Adam Murimuth and the author of the *Vita*, record that the Despensers were afraid to accompany the king to France but were also terrified of what might happen to them if they were left behind in England.[140] Although it would take more than the sorcery of John of Nottingham, the Coventry magician, and other 'magical secret dealings' to bring an end to the careers of the Despensers, there is little doubt that by 1325 they were deeply insecure and perhaps, as Natalie Fryde remarked, living 'in a nightmare of fear'.[141]

A letter from Henry of Eastry the prior of Christ Church, Canterbury, to his archbishop on 15 August reveals that Edward II had convened a gathering of prelates, earls and barons at Sturry near Canterbury, at which a final decision on whether the king should go to France in person or send his son would be taken.[142] This meeting, which was probably a stormy one, was clearly the source of Edward II's 'illness'. So it was decided that Edward would not after all go to France. To put the best face upon it, in September the archbishop of Canterbury circulated a letter in his province which stated that Isabella, the earl of Richmond, the bishop of Winchester and the papal envoys had advised Edward that it would be better for him to stay in England governing his kingdom in peace and justice and to send his son in his place.[143]

Events now moved quickly. On 2 September the bishop of Winchester visited Charles IV at Châteauneuf-sur-Loire, where Isabella and the earl of Richmond were also present.[144] Two days later Charles IV signified his acceptance of the proposal, 'at the request of his dear sister', that the duchy

---

[138] The *Vita*, 240–3, comments that because of their treatment of Isabella 'there are four greater persons among the men of England [the bishop of Exeter, Robert Baldock, and the Despensers] who if they are found within the kingdom of France will certainly not lack bad quarters'.

[139] Mortimer, *The Greatest Traitor*, 283, n. 10, wrongly concludes that, because Despenser was apparently unwelcome in France when he went there briefly in exile in 1321, he had therefore been banished from France. The men banished who were referred to in Charles IV's letter to Edward II in Dec. 1323 were Ralph Bassett the former seneschal of Gascony and Raymond-Bernard of Montpezat who were held responsible for the attack on Saint Sardos: *Saint-Sardos*, xii, 180–1; Vale, 235–6.

[140] *Murimuth*, 44; *Vita*, 234–5.

[141] The incident which began in Nov. 1323 is recorded in *Select Cases*, ed. Sayles, iv, 154–7, from which Fryde has worked out a very entertaining account: Fryde, 162–4. The Younger Despenser had earlier complained to the pope about being 'threatened by magical and secret dealings', to which the pope replied that he should 'turn to God with his whole heart, and make a good confession': *CPL, 1305–42*, ii, 461. It is clear that the Younger Despenser at least was deeply superstitious.

[142] *Literae Cantuarienses*, ed. Sheppard, i, 145–6. Edward was at Sturry on 19 and 20 Aug.

[143] Haines *Stratford*, 160.

[144] *Saint-Sardos*, 268–9.

of Aquitaine should be transferred to Edward, the elder son and heir of Edward II. He undertook to receive Edward's homage in the usual form for the duchy, with the exception of the land which he himself controlled, i.e. the Agenais. In return Edward would have to pay a relief of 60,000 *livres parisis* (about £15,000).[145] Even before Charles IV's letter reached England, Edward II had acted: on 2 September he granted the county of Ponthieu to his son; and on 10 September he granted him the duchy of Aquitaine, following a form of words received from the bishop of Winchester and presumably reflecting the requirements of Charles IV.[146] On the same date Edward formally remitted all causes of rancour that had arisen between himself and his brother-in-law Charles IV and informed him that the new duke of Aquitaine would soon be crossing to France, accompanied by Henry de Beaumont and the bishop of Exeter.[147] The young Edward duly crossed the Channel on 12 September and joined his mother Isabella in Paris ten days later.[148] The great event took place on 24 September at Vincennes. After first granting Edward a dispensation because he was still only twelve years old, Charles IV received Edward's homage for Aquitaine and for Ponthieu. The ceremony was attended from the English side by Isabella, the bishops of Winchester, Exeter and Norwich, the earl of Richmond, Henry de Beaumont, John Cromwell and Gilbert Talbot; by the papal envoys, the archbishop of Vienne and bishop of Orange, and the bishop of Viviers; and by a large number of royal administrators and French nobles, including the count of Clermont and the duke of Burgundy.[149]

PART TWO

THE ENDGAME BEGINS

Much would now depend on whether Charles IV kept his side of the bargain. The Anglo-French peace negotiations in 1325 had been long and difficult and the advantage had lain throughout with the French. In October 1325 the duchy of Aquitaine was duly restored to the control of a new seneschal appointed by Edward: Oliver Ingham, an English knight

---

[145] *Foedera*, II, i, 607. Edward undertook to pay this sum on 2 Oct. 1325: AN, J 634, no. 22.

[146] AN, J 634, nos 11, 12; *Foedera*, II, i, 607–8. Since Edward was never granted the principality of Wales, strictly it is incorrect to describe him as Prince Edward: cf. Fryde, 294; Mortimer, *The Greatest Traitor*, 141–3; Buck, 156.

[147] AN, J 633, no. 1; J 634, no. 12; *Foedera*, II, i, 608; *Saint-Sardos*, 241. Charles IV did the same but the document was left in the custody of the young Edward's treasurer William de Cusance and never reached Edward II: Buck, 157.

[148] *Foedera*, II, i, 609; *Saint-Sardos*, 269.

[149] AN, J 634, nos 13, 14; *Saint-Sardos*, 241–5, 269. There is a photograph of AN, J 634, no. 14, in A. Wathey, 'The marriage of Edward III and the transmission of French motets to England', *Journal of the American Musicological Society*, xlv (1992), 6.

and close associate of the Younger Despenser.[150] It should however have been clear all along to Edward II and his council that, regardless of whatever settlement was ultimately agreed, Charles IV had no intention of relinquishing control of the Agenais.[151]

Recriminations were inevitable. The archbishop of Dublin had already been one victim; another was William Airmyn, who was blamed for Charles IV's failure to return the Agenais.[152] This was unfair, but Airmyn was guilty in Edward II's mind of another offence, that of blocking yet again the promotion to bishop of the chancellor, Robert Baldock archdeacon of Middlesex. The death of John Salmon, the bishop of Norwich and one of Edward's envoys in Paris, on 6 July 1325, should have opened the way for Baldock's appointment to the vacancy. The monks of Norwich duly obliged by electing Baldock on 23 July, and on 12 August Edward restored the temporalities of the diocese. Unfortunately for him, the pope had also quickly learned of Salmon's death and on 19 July appointed William Airmyn as bishop. With Airmyn's consecration by the papal envoys in Paris on 15 September, there was nothing left for Baldock to do but to resign. For the third and last time Edward II failed to get Baldock made a bishop; he retaliated by withholding Airmyn's temporalities, which were not restored until February 1327 shortly after Edward III's coronation.[153]

The most serious problem was Isabella herself. Edward clearly expected Isabella and Edward duke of Aquitaine to return promptly to England once their business was concluded.[154] Although it is known that between 9 March and 29 September 1325 Isabella received expenses from the English exchequer amounting to £2,841, no direct payment was made to her after 17 June, just after Edward II's confirmation of the Anglo-French treaty.[155] This implies that Edward already had suspicions about her intentions and this was a way of ensuring that she returned home.[156] If this was Edward's own intention, he simply played into the hands of his brother-in-law Charles IV. A note in Isabella's accounts reveals that on 18 July she

---

[150] Vale, 247; *Saint-Sardos*, 235–6. He succeeded Henry de Sully, who had been appointed by Charles IV as a seneschal acceptable to the English crown while the duchy was in French hands.

[151] The dangers implicit in the negotiations had been spelled out in the summer of 1325 in a memorandum addressed to the council by one of Edward II's clerks, Elias de Joneston, an expert on Anglo-French relations: *Saint-Sardos*, 238–9.

[152] *Foedera*, II, i, 622; *Saint-Sardos*, 277, n. 1; Haines, *Stratford*, 161.

[153] *Vita*, 238–40 & n. 503. Airmyn had been elected as bishop of Carlisle in Jan. 1325, with support from both Edward and Isabella. John XXII had then appointed John Ross, while promising to look after Airmyn in due course. The pope may have thought that in appointing Airmyn to Norwich he was acting according to Edward II's wishes. However, he would have known of Edward's desire to promote Baldock, of whom the pope clearly disapproved; so he acted to forestall any further royal requests on Baldock's behalf.

[154] He made this clear in his letter to Charles IV on 1 Dec. 1325: *Foedera*, II, i, 614.

[155] Doherty (D.Phil.), 123; E 101/380.

[156] As suggested by Doherty (D. Phil.), 124.

dined with the queen of France at Châteauneuf-sur-Loire and that from that day Charles paid the living expenses of herself and her ladies.[157] No more money came to her from England until the arrival of Walter Stapeldon, the bishop of Exeter and treasurer, in Paris on 22 September: the money was to be handed over to her on condition that she returned to England at once.[158]

But she did not return.

EDWARD AND ISABELLA

While there is no way of gauging the true nature of the relations between Edward and Isabella, until at least 1322 they appear to have been close. As the Bridlington chronicler remarked, their marriage had been intended to maintain and to improve relations between England and France,[159] but there was nothing unusual in this. Royal marriages were invariably arranged for reasons of political advantage or to advance a diplomatic agenda. Although Isabella was little more than a child when she married Edward in 1308, again there was nothing unusual in this by the standards of the time nor is there anything to suggest that Edward was in any way reluctant to contract the marriage for which he had been preparing since 1303. Edward's relationship with Gaveston, although almost certainly non-sexual in nature, was a major distraction of her husband's time and energies in the early years of their marriage, but with Gaveston's removal in 1312 and Isabella's growing physical and emotional maturity Edward and Isabella's own relationship appears to have flourished. Edward and Isabella produced four children at regular intervals between 1312 and 1321.[160]

---

[157] *Saint-Sardos*, 268.

[158] Buck, 156, 158; SC 1/49/106 (the text of this is given in Buck, App., iii, 228–9: it is wrongly given as SC 1/49/100 in Doherty (D. Phil.), 124).

[159] *Gesta Edwardi*, 32 (*sub* 1308). In April 1324 the suggested instructions for Isabella's reply to a French knight on his return to Charles IV emphasized the same point: *Saint-Sardos*, 42. While these were not of course Isabella's own words, it is unfair to imply that this was the only basis for their marriage or that Edward held her partly responsible for the difficulties in Anglo-French relations during his reign: cf. Fryde, 146; Mortimer, *The Greatest Traitor*, 135. For most of the reign relations with France were good, and for this Isabella certainly could take some of the credit. It was only after 1320 that the situation began to change and this reflected a growing insistence by the French crown on its rights of overlordship and sovereignty.

[160] The suggestion by Trease, in 'The spicers and the apothecaries', 46, that Isabella may have had a miscarriage in 1313 has been discounted (Doherty (D.Phil.), 53) since the medical treatment she was undergoing was the result of burns sustained in an accident in France. Nonetheless there may have been other pregnancies apart from the four known ones. The document published by C.J.S. Thompson as 'Rules of health prescribed for an English queen in the fourteenth century', Wellcome Historical Medical Museum (London, 1921), was drawn up for the use of Isabella by her brother Louis X, but consists only of general advice and does not refer to any specific form of illness from which she may have suffered.

Edward appears to have been considerate of her welfare: he did not for example abandon the pregnant Isabella at Tynemouth in May 1312, as is sometimes alleged. As part of her marriage contract Isabella was also well provided for financially, even though for much of the reign money was in very short supply. Although she played some role as a mediator between Edward and his baronial opponents in, for example, 1312, 1313, 1318 and 1321, she was not particularly active in politics. She was loyal to her husband, giving her services as a negotiator with the French crown in 1314, and in 1321 allowing herself to be used as the bait to secure the defiance of Badlesmere's wife at Leeds castle and so begin the process of destroying Badlesmere and the other contrariant magnates.[161]

The king's victory in 1322 was to lead to a change in his relations with his wife as in much else. If Isabella had not distrusted or even hated the Younger Despenser before 1322,[162] there can be little doubt that she did so afterwards. Despenser's increasing ascendancy over Edward, his behaving as if he were the real king, and his greed and lack of scruple were also an affront to her status as queen of England and the daughter of one king of France and the sister of three others. This was bad enough, but Despenser also had to bear some part of the blame for Edward's humiliation in Scotland in 1322, his near capture at Byland and her own near capture at Tynemouth. For the third time in her married life she had been forced to flee her husband's enemies.[163] Whether her experiences in 1322 also marked the beginning of an estrangement from Edward there is no way of knowing, but it seems likely.

Isabella was further humiliated in September 1324 by the seizure of her English lands in Cornwall and other western counties because of the alleged risk of a French landing in these remote districts.[164] Superficially this was a plausible excuse since the small ports of the west of England were a favourite route through which English exiles, such as John Maltravers and others came and went;[165] and if they could do it, so might the French or, most dreaded of all, Roger Mortimer himself. But it was no more than plausible since it was impossible to control clandestine comings

---

[161] Isabella also had a personal reason for wanting Badlesmere's expulsion from Leeds, since Edward had settled the reversion of Leeds on her after the death of Edward I's widow Queen Margaret in 1318.

[162] The charge that Despenser instigated the Scottish attempt to capture Isabella near York in Oct. 1318 appears to have been a slander directed against him and without substance: Haskins, 'A chronicle', 177; Maddicott, 249–50.

[163] In 1326 the Tynemouth incident was included in the charges laid against Despenser: *Gesta Edwardi*, 88.

[164] *Foedera*, II, i, 569. Fryde, 146, wrongly implies that Isabella's lands had been seized before April 1324. In lieu of these revenues, Isabella was granted 1,000 marks a year plus eight marks a day for her food and drink. As Dr Doherty points out, this was not generous treatment and was in any case a breach of the agreement on dower made in 1308 between Edward II and her father, Philip IV: Doherty (D. Phil.), 101–3; E 403/201, m.4.

[165] See Phillips, ' "Edward II" in Italy', 209–11.

and goings from England. In reality it was a petty move on the part of Edward, as was the removal and imprisonment of French members of Isabella's household.[166] She blamed the Younger Despenser for both actions,[167] which also caused serious annoyance at the French court.[168] Even more humiliating was the removal from her household of her children, John, Eleanor and Joan, into the custody of the Younger Despenser's wife Eleanor de Clare.[169]

By the time Isabella departed for France in March 1325 she apparently had ample reason to wish to leave England. According to the *Vita Edwardi Secundi*, 'The queen departed very joyfully, happy with a twofold joy; pleased in fact to visit her native land and her relatives, pleased to leave the company of some of those whom she did not like. Certainly she does not like Hugh . . .; consequently many think she will not return until Hugh Despenser is wholly removed from the king's side.'[170]

Her dislike and even fear of Despenser are not in doubt, but this passage may not be strictly contemporary:[171] even a few months' delay in writing would be enough for hindsight to affect the chronicler's opinion. In the late autumn of 1325 Isabella gave Despenser as the reason for her

[166] *Foedera*, II, i, 570. Twenty-seven French members of her household, including her chaplains and physician, were sent to religious houses around the country: Doherty (D. Phil.), 101; E 403/201, mm.14–15.
[167] It was another of the charges against him in 1326: *Gesta Edwardi*, 89; cf. *Vita*, 242–3.
[168] *Saint-Sardos*, 128, 130.
[169] Doherty, (D. Phil.), 103; E 403/201, mm.14–15. If there were any truth in the rumour that Eleanor also became Edward II's mistress, these indignities would have been particularly galling: *Willelmi Capellani*, ed. Pijnacker Hordijk, 177. According to the highly coloured account given by the author of the Lanercost chronicle, this was not all that Isabella had to put up with. Eleanor de Clare was allegedly also given custody of Isabella's personal seal so that she could read all her private correspondence; while at the instigation of the Younger Despenser a certain religious named Thomas Dunheved and Robert Baldock were sent to the papal curia in order to procure a divorce between Edward II and Isabella; these were further reasons for Isabella's desire to leave England: *Lanercost*, 254.

Although Dunheved did go to Avignon in 1325 and was appointed as a papal chaplain in Sept., his mission was to support Edward II's actions against the archbishop of Dublin; there is no evidence to support the story of a divorce: *CPL, 1305–42*, 474, 479. If such a scheme was ever considered it is more likely to have been in the summer of 1326 when the breach between Edward and Isabella was becoming unbridgeable. Thomas Dunheved was however to be involved in a plot to release Edward from his prison at Berkeley castle in 1327. In describing Dunheved's arrest the author of the *Ann. Paul.*, 337, also referred to his alleged role in trying to secure a divorce, so the story or rumour must have circulated widely. Haines, *Stratford*, 156, is probably correct in describing the Dunheved story as apocryphal. An attempted divorce in the conditions of 1325 would have been political madness, since it would have meant the repudiation of all agreements between England and France, which Edward and Isabella's marriage had been intended to strengthen, and would have plunged England into an immediate war with France: see also F.D. Blackley, 'Isabella and the bishop of Exeter', in *Essays in Medieval History presented to Bertie Wilkinson*, ed, T.A. Sandquist & M.R. Powicke (Toronto, 1969), 226.
[170] *Vita*, 228–9.
[171] See Given-Wilson, '*Vita Edwardi Secundi*', 175–6.

refusal to return to England,[172] but whether this was her intention all along is less certain. On 31 March, at the conclusion of the draft treaty with France, Isabella told her husband that, with the consent of the other English envoys, she would stay in France, unless Edward ordered otherwise.[173] This may of course have been a subterfuge, designed to ward off suspicion, but it was also true that the negotiations were not fully complete until August when Charles IV agreed to the young Edward's taking the place of his father in the performance of homage. Until then she could plausibly justify a longer stay in France.

It has also been alleged that Isabella's departure in March 1325 was part of a carefully contrived plot to get her out of England. The claim by the chronicler Geoffrey le Baker that Adam Orleton, the disgraced bishop of Hereford, somehow engineered her departure as the first part of a carefully stage-managed plot to bring about the downfall of Edward II has been shown to be entirely spurious.[174] John Stratford, who had fallen out with Edward II over his appointment as bishop of Winchester in 1323, and took a leading part in the peace negotiations of 1324–5, has also been suggested as being behind this.[175] However, the plan certainly originated in the set of proposals drawn up by the French negotiators and papal envoys and brought back to England by Stratford in January 1325.[176] From the French point of view it was a way of offering Edward II something tangible while still maintaining that he could claim nothing as of right. From the English point of view it offered a way of breaking the deadlock in the negotiations. The idea that Isabella should take some part in the negotiations was not an entirely new one in England. As far back as April 1324 someone close to Edward II had drawn up a detailed memorandum of the words she should use in replying to a French knight visiting England before his return to Charles IV.[177] It was not a great step from this to Isabella's actually going to France herself. She had, after all, done so successfully in 1314. In early February 1325 Edward II's council discussed the proposal and approved the idea in principle.[178] Although it is possible that in doing so Edward and his advisers were falling into a trap carefully prepared by Charles IV with the unwitting connivance of the papal envoys in Paris,[179] it is more likely that what followed when Isabella did go to France was a prime example of the law of unintended consequences.

---

[172] *CCR, 1323–27*, 580–1.
[173] *Saint-Sardos*, 200: '*tantque jeo ei vostre comandement*'.
[174] *Le Baker*, 16–17, 19; Haines, *The Church and Politics*, 104–5, 158; Blackley, 'Isabella', 227.
[175] Fryde, 162. This view is argued but finally rejected in Doherty (D. Phil.), 107–12.
[176] *Saint-Sardos*, 195.
[177] Ibid., 42.
[178] Ibid., 195–6.
[179] Cf. Mortimer, *The Greatest Traitor*, 138–9, 283, n. 14; Doherty (D.Phil.), 113.

ISABELLA REFUSES TO RETURN TO ENGLAND

By the end of September 1325 Isabella had been in France for over six months. Even without any ulterior motives on her part, she had good reason for staying in France for as long as possible. She was away from the tense atmosphere of the English court and especially away from Hugh Despenser; since 22 September her elder son and heir to the English throne, the new duke of Aquitaine had been with her; and she was probably enjoying herself in the company of her brother the king of France and other members of her family. During June 1325 Isabella remained in Paris, where she dined on occasions with her sister-in-law Clemence of Hungary the widow of Louis X, the countess of Foix, the Dominicans and Minoresses, as well as the earl of Richmond and the two papal envoys who were evidently still engaged in negotiations with the French crown. In July she went on a tour of places outside Paris, including Chartres and Étampes, before reaching Charles IV's palace at Châteauneuf-sur-Loire where she spent much of the rest of July and August. She was still at Châteauneuf in early September when she dined with the French queen and the earl of Richmond and bishop of Winchester: this was the time when the arrangements for the young Edward to perform homage were being settled. On 9 September she was back at Bois-de-Vincennes and from then until late October she remained in Paris. Her social life continued: she dined, for example, with the queen, the countesses of Saint-Pol, Évreux and Boulogne, and the abbot of Cluny. On 22 September her son joined her, and although he had his own household arrangements he ate with her on 7, 14 and 17 October. On 16 October she went to Saint-Denis to visit her uncle, Charles of Valois, just two months before his death on 16 December. Isabella was also in contact with some of the envoys who had helped to negotiate the unsatisfactory peace between England and France: she met the archbishop of Vienne, the bishop of Orange and the earl of Richmond on 1 October and the earl on 5–7 October.[180]

Significantly there is no mention of any social dealings with another English envoy, Walter Stapeldon the bishop of Exeter who had come to Paris for the young Edward's performance of homage on 24 September.[181] He was also charged with trying to persuade Isabella to return to England with her son, and he failed utterly. If the dramatic account in the *Vita Edwardi Secundi* is to be believed, Stapeldon's message was delivered publicly in the presence of both Isabella and her brother, Charles IV, to which she delivered herself of a dramatic and equally public reply: ' "I feel", she said, "that marriage is a union of a man and a woman, holding fast to the practice of a life together, and that someone has come between my husband and myself and is trying to break that bond; I declare that I will not return until that intruder is removed, but, discarding my marriage garment, shall put on the robes of widowhood and mourning until I am avenged of this

---

[180] *Saint-Sardos*, 267–70.
[181] Buck, 156–7; Blackley, 'Isabella', 229–30.

Pharisee". And the king of France, not wishing to seem to detain her, replied, "The queen", he said, "has come of her own free will, she may return freely if she wishes. But if she prefers to remain in these parts, she is my sister, I will not expel her." '[182] No one needed to be told who had come between Isabella and Edward. The bishop of Exeter was so shaken by his hostile reception at the French court and so fearful of being attacked there that he fled back to England as soon as he was able.[183] The opportunity came when Isabella and her son left Paris on 22 October. Against Isabella's express orders, the bishop also left, crossed the Channel as fast as he could and rejoined Edward II at Cippenham near Windsor on 30 October.[184] When Stapeldon tried to justify his conduct to Isabella, she reacted furiously and on 8 December sent him an angry letter from Paris in which she accused him of dishonouring both Edward and herself and of acting in the interests of the Younger Despenser.[185]

EDWARD II REACTS

The news from Paris was depressing in the extreme. Even before the bishop of Exeter's return, it was clear that Isabella had no intention of coming home, and that the Younger Despenser's position was the reason for her behaviour. What was not yet clear, however, was whether she was acting solely on her own initiative or with the support and prompting of others.

In the bishop of Exeter's absence a parliament had been summoned on 10 October to meet on 18 November.[186] It was appropriate that he should be chosen to open it with a sermon on the theme of the battle between the giants Gog and Magog, representing the kings of England and France.[187] Edward was still obsessed with the failure, as he saw it, of Charles IV to

---

[182] *Vita*, 242–3. The statements in the *Vita* and in the *French Chronicle of London*, ed. G.J. Aungier, Camden Soc. London, 1844, 49 that Isabella dressed in widow's clothes are probably to be taken figuratively rather than literally.

[183] *CCR, 1323–27*, 580–1 (Edward's letters of 1 Dec. to Isabella and to Charles IV); Buck, 157, esp. n. 207; Blackley, 'Isabella', 230. The *Vita Edwardi Secundi*, 240–3, stresses the hostility to Stapeldon at the French court because he was allegedly responsible for advising Edward II to seize Isabella's lands and to arrest her French servants.

[184] Buck, 157–8. In the angry letter which Isabella wrote to Stapeldon from Paris on 8 Dec. she said that Stapeldon claimed to have left on orders from Edward II but refused to show her the instructions. Significantly however she also said that she had promised to protect the bishop from any harm, which confirms that he was in some danger while in Paris: Blackley, 'Isabella', 230–1 (incl. a photograph of Isabella's letter, SC 1/49/ 118). Buck, 158, misreads Isabella's letter as stating that Stapeldon had promised to protect her rather than the other way round.

[185] Blackley, 'Isabella', 231; Buck, 158–9. Although Stapeldon did not forward Isabella's letter to the king until 15 Jan. 1326 from Morton in Somerset, it is unlikely that there was anything in it that Edward did not already know: Buck, 158.

[186] *PW*, II, ii, 334–47.

[187] BL, Cotton Ms. Faustina B. V, f. 45v; Buck, 157.

honour the peace treaty by returning the Agenais; and on 15 October he complained bitterly about this to the papal envoys.[188]

But the real business of the parliament revolved around two people: the Younger Despenser and Queen Isabella. In the chapel of the Tower of London, according to the *Historia Roffensis*, Despenser announced that anyone who failed to counsel the king truly was either a traitor or a fool; but received no reply, since everyone was afraid to speak the truth publicly.[189] According to the *Vita*, Edward then gave a short speech in which he said:

> 'You know all the long-standing disputes and processes between the King of France and us over the land of Gascony, and how, wisely enough as it seemed at the time, the queen crossed to France to make peace, and she had instructions to return at once when her mission was accomplished. And this she promised with a good will. And on her departure she did not seem to anyone to be offended. For as she took her leave she bade farewell to everyone and went away joyfully. But now someone has changed her mind; someone has filled her with extraordinary stories. For I know that she has not invented any affront out of her own head, although she says that Hugh Despenser is her adversary and enemy.'

And he added this: 'It is surprising that she has conceived this grudge against Hugh, for when she left, towards no one was she more agreeable, myself excepted. For this reason Hugh has been made very unhappy; but he is nevertheless prepared to prove his innocence in any way whatsoever. Hence I firmly believe that the queen has been led into this error at the suggestion of someone else and, in truth, whoever he may be he is a man who is wicked and is an enemy. Now therefore deliberate wisely so that she, whom the teaching of evil men directs and incites to deceit, may be urged and brought back to rightful harmony by your sensible and kindly reproof'.[190] At the request of the king's council, each of the bishops then wrote to Isabella, telling her that Despenser had proved his innocence before them and appealing to her as a dutiful wife to return to her husband. While there was no mention of Mortimer in the letter, the bishops were aware, allegedly from the queen's own letters, that a landing in England to remove Despenser was being considered and they begged her to spare the country the evils of foreign invasion, lest the innocent should suffer along with the guilty.[191]

---

[188] *Foedera*, II, i, 611.
[189] BL, Cotton Ms. Faustina B. V, ff. 45v–46r; Buck, 158.
[190] *Vita*, 242–5.
[191] *Vita*, 244–7: 'But notwithstanding these mother and son refused to return to England'. This is the very last entry in the *Vita*. The text of the bishops' letter is generally similar to those addressed by Edward II on 1 Dec. to Isabella and Charles IV: *CCR, 1323–27*, 580–1.

EDWARD'S APPEAL TO ISABELLA

While the parliament was still in session, John Stratford the bishop of Winchester returned from Paris where he had briefly met Isabella on or soon after 12 November.[192] Stratford could only confirm what everyone already knew: that Isabella was staying in France. Armed with the latest news, on 1 December 1325 Edward II wrote to his errant wife and to Charles IV, as well as to sixteen of the leading clergy and nobility of France. He noted that he had frequently ordered her, both before and after the act of homage, to come back with all speed. Edward professed to be surprised that she was afraid of Despenser, since she had always behaved amiably to him, and he to her, especially at the time of her departure for France. Edward also claimed he had always treated her with honour since their marriage, except for a few times when he had occasion to reprove her in private. He told her that it would be unfortunate if her visit to France, which had been intended to bring peace between himself and her brother Charles IV, should instead be a cause of difference between them. Edward appealed to her to put aside all feigned reasons and excuses and come back to him with their son as quickly as possible.[193] On the following day, 2 December, Edward also addressed a short letter to his son, asking him, although he was young and of tender age, to remember what he had promised when they parted at Dover, and to come home, if necessary without his mother: they had much to talk about.[194]

ISABELLA AND MORTIMER

On 29 November the bishop of Rochester was travelling towards Stone near Dartford in Kent when he met some members of Isabella's household returning from France.[195] Others came back to England on 23 December and during January and February 1326.[196] Some of them may have come home simply because Isabella no longer had enough money to pay them;[197] some because they did not approve of her refusal to rejoin her husband or because they were aware of a liaison between her and Edward II's greatest enemy, Roger Mortimer of Wigmore.[198]

The first clear reference in England to a connection between the two was in a royal proclamation on 8 February 1326 when it was claimed that

---

[192] Haines, *Stratford*, 161–2. Stratford left England from Dover on 28 Oct. and returned from Wissant on 18 Nov. It is possible that during his outward journey he met Walter Stapeldon on his hasty return from Paris: from a review of Buck by R.M. Haines in *Speculum*, lx (1985), 131.

[193] *CCR, 1323–27*, 580–2; the original French texts are in *Foedera*, II, i, 615.

[194] *Foedera*, II, i, 616.

[195] BL, Cotton Ms. Faustina B. V, f. 46r; Buck, 158.

[196] SC 1/49/58; SAL Ms. 122, pp. 46, 49, 52; Doherty (D.Phil.), 127.

[197] Trinity College Cambridge Ms. R.5.41, f. 120v; Doherty (D.Phil.), 127.

[198] BL, Cotton Ms. Faustina B. V, f. 46r; *Murimuth*, 45–6.

Isabella was adopting the counsel of 'the Mortimer' and other rebels.[199] A closer and more personal relationship was hinted at on 18 March when Edward II wrote to his son and accused Isabella of openly and notoriously keeping Mortimer in her company and of associating with him 'within and without house'.[200] Mortimer's attendance in the company of Isabella and the young Edward, and wearing Edward's livery, at the coronation of the new queen of France on 11 May was a further humiliation for her husband.[201]

There has been much debate about the nature of the relationship between Isabella and Mortimer and when it started. One writer has suggested that it began as early as the autumn of 1321; another that it 'was not of sudden growth';[202] while Ian Mortimer, the biographer of Roger Mortimer, describes their relationship as 'one of the great romances of the Middle Ages', suggesting that it already existed early in 1323.[203] On the other hand both F.D. Blackley and Natalie Fryde see the relationship as developing only after her departure for France,[204] while Isabella's biographer, Paul Doherty, argues that there is no evidence of any liaison existing before December 1325 when some of Isabella's followers began returning to England.[205]

Mortimer was three years younger than Edward II, had been knighted at the same time during the great ceremonies at Westminster in 1306, and also took part in Edward's coronation in 1308. Although Mortimer was absent for long periods in Ireland or in Wales, he and Isabella would have come to know one another socially. But that is all one can say. It is possible that Isabella sympathized with Mortimer's plight after his imprisonment in the Tower in 1322 and that this explains the letter she wrote on 17 February 1323 asking the acting treasurer to treat Mortimer's wife, Joan, with greater generosity.[206] Since Isabella was staying in the Tower at the time, it has

---

[199] *Foedera*, II, i, 619; *CCR, 1323–27*, 543.

[200] *Foedera*, II, i, 623 ('*a lui se acompaigne en houstel et de hors*'); *CCR, 1323–27*, 578.

[201] *Foedera*, II, i, 630–1; *CCR, 1323–27*, 576–7. Charles IV had recently married Jeanne d'Évreux as his third wife. Another important occasion attended by Isabella and Edward in 1326 was the laying by themselves and Louis X's widow, Clemence of Hungary, of the foundation stone of the church of the Holy Sepulchre in Paris on 18 May. There is no mention of Mortimer's presence: R. Cazelles, *Nouvelle Histoire de Paris de la fin du règne de Philippe Auguste à la mort de Charles V* (Paris, 1972), 62. Ironically Edward II had made a contribution towards the building of the church: J. Sumption, *Trial by Battle* (London, 1990), i, 4, 6.

[202] Blackley, 'Isabella', 221, citing N. Denholm-Young's introduction to his edition of the *Vita Edwardi Secundi* (London, 1957), xiii, n.1, and Davies, *Baronial Opposition*, 107.

[203] Mortimer, *The Greatest Traitor*, 129, 145, 284.

[204] Blackley, 'Isabella', 221–4; Fryde, 147.

[205] Doherty (D. Phil.), 125–6; but in his book, *Isabella and the Strange Death of Edward II*, 87–8, he suggests that it could have begun earlier. This is a good place to acknowledge the insights I have gained from Dr Doherty's very thorough and scholarly researches.

[206] Blackley, 'Isabella', 223–4 (where the date is wrongly given as 1322), citing SC 1/37/45 (the full text is given in 223, n. 16); Davies, *Baronial Opposition*, 107; Mortimer, *The Greatest Traitor*, 129; Doherty (D.Phil.), 98–9. Joan was being held by the sheriff of Hampshire.

been suggested that Mortimer was able to communicate with her from his prison cell and that she may even have assisted his escape the following August.[207] There is nothing however to support this conclusion. Although one French chronicler does seek to implicate Isabella in Mortimer's escape, there is not a hint of such collusion in any of the English sources.[208] There is also the inconvenient fact that the Younger Despenser's wife, Eleanor de Clare, wrote a very similar letter to the acting treasurer on the same date.[209]

A connection between Isabella and Mortimer before she left England cannot of course be ruled out absolutely, but it seems unlikely. What is more interesting is the point at which she first made contact with Mortimer after her arrival in France. The one thing which both Isabella and Mortimer certainly had in common was their desire to see the Younger Despenser removed from power. It did not automatically follow that they both wished to see Edward II removed from the throne or that they were also involved romantically. Initially at least, their relationship may have been solely one of business.

There is no mention of Mortimer anywhere in the record of Isabella's stay in France between 9 March and 14 November, when it ends.[210] This is hardly surprising, since if there were any contact Isabella would have tried to keep it secret from members of her household who might pass on the news to Edward in England. However, on 22 October she was joined by her son, who then stayed with her until 12 November. The two set off from Paris for Reims where they stayed between 30 October and 1 November, before returning to Paris on 12 November.[211] While they were at Reims Isabella visited all the major churches, including the cathedral, and made offerings especially at the Ampulla containing the holy oil with which the kings of France were anointed at their coronation.[212] Reims was within easy reach of Valenciennes, the chief city of the county of Hainault in which Roger Mortimer may have been staying,[213] secure in the knowledge that he was outside the power of the kings of France and of England and yet able to communicate with both kingdoms whenever he chose.[214] While there is no

---

[207] Mortimer, *The Greatest Traitor*, 129.

[208] Blackley, 'Isabella', 222–3; *Chronographia Regum Francorum*, ed. H. Moranville, i (Paris, 1891), 267–8.

[209] Doherty (D.Phil.), 99; SC 1/37/4. As Blackley points out, Isabella's letter could have been simply an act of kindness, but since Joan was also a member of the great French noble family of de Joinville, representations may have been made on her behalf from France: Blackley, 'Isabella', 224; Doherty (D.Phil.), 99–9.

[210] *Saint-Sardos*, 267–70; Hunter, 'Journal', 242–57.

[211] *Saint-Sardos*, 270.

[212] Hunter, 'Journal', 254. It is tempting to think that this symbol of kingship was somehow connected with the purpose of her visit.

[213] *Saint-Sardos*, 5, 72, 102–3. Hainault was under the jurisdiction of the emperor, at this time Ludwig of Bavaria, and hence part of 'Germany'.

[214] His relatives in Ponthieu, from the family of his mother Margaret de Fiennes, were another possible point of contact between Mortimer and both France and England.

firm evidence to support this suggestion, it is possible that Isabella made contact with Mortimer while she and Edward were at Reims and that this was the real purpose of their visit.

However, on 5 February 1326 Isabella wrote a remarkable letter from Paris in reply to Walter Reynolds, the archbishop of Canterbury, who had pleaded with her to return to England and had tried to persuade her that Hugh Despenser was not malevolent and that he wished her no harm.[215] Isabella said that no one should think that she would have left the king, whom she described as her 'beloved and sweet lord and friend',[216] 'without very great and justifiable cause',[217] and if she were not escaping from danger to her life.[218] For she was afraid of Hugh Despenser who 'governs our lord [the king] and his entire kingdom', and who 'wished to dishonour us by all means in his power'. Isabella admitted that for long she had kept secret her dislike of Hugh, but only to escape from danger.[219] She went on: 'We desire, above everything else, after God and the salvation of our soul, to be in the company of our said Lord and to die with him',[220] but could not return to her husband without endangering her life.[221] Although Isabella wrote the letter in the midst of a very tense and dangerous political situation, it appears that she was still sincerely attached to her husband Edward. If this was so, it must cast some doubt on whether her relationship with Mortimer was more than just an alliance against the Younger Despenser. It is yet another of the riddles in which the reign of Edward II abounds.[222]

Another line of communication was with the city of Bruges in Flanders in which the wool staple for English merchants had been established in 1324. In May 1325 Edward II appointed the London merchant Richard de Béthune as mayor of the staple, a move which has been described as 'a political error of the first magnitude' since Béthune had been involved in Roger Mortimer's escape from the Tower in 1323. In Sept. 1326 he came out openly in support of Mortimer and Isabella: Williams, *Medieval London*, 291–5.

[215] The letter is described in Blackley, 'Isabella', 234, citing *Historiae Anglicanae Scriptores Decem*, ed. R. Twysden (London, 1652), col. 2766 (*recte* 2767–8), where it is printed in full. Although it forms part of Adam Orleton's *Apologia* of 1334, defending his conduct in 1326–7, there is no reason to doubt its authenticity. The letter also appears in the copy of the *Apologia* entered in the Winchester Cathedral Cartulary, but is only briefly calendared in the printed edition: *Chartulary of Winchester Cathedral*, ed. Goodman, 107. Some of the letter's contents appear in Edward II's letter to Charles IV on 18 March: *Foedera*, II, i, 622–3; *CCR, 1323–27*, 578–9.

[216] '*nostre treschier et tresdouche seignur et amy*'.

[217] '*saunz trop graunt cause et resonable*'.

[218] '*et si ceo ne fust pur le peril de nostre corps eschuver*'.

[219] '*et pur la doute de dit Hughe qad le government de noster dit seignur et de tout son Roialme, et qi nous voudrait deshonurer a son poair sicome nous esumes bien certaings et bien lavoms esp, coment qe nous layoms dissimule longtemps pur le peril eschuver*'.

[220] '*Et certes nous desyroms sur toutes riens, apres Dieu et la sauvete de nostre alme, estre en la compaignie de nostre dit seignur et vivre et morir en icele*'.

[221] '*Car en nule manere nous ne porroms retourner en la compaignie de noster dit seignur saunz nous mestre en peril de mort, dount nous sumes en plus graves meschief qe escrivre ne poems*'.

[222] It is of course possible or even likely that Isabella was concealing her real feelings, since she could scarcely admit publicly to a relationship with Mortimer. Nonetheless I am inclined to take the letter at face value.

RUMOURS OF INVASION

Isabella was not the only person under stress. The situation for Edward and his followers in England in early 1326 was much worse: all around them were signs of danger. The murder on 19 January near Melton Mowbray in Leicestershire of Sir Roger Belers, a baron of the exchequer, and one of the most hated supporters of the Despensers, struck at the heart of the regime. Although the murder may have been associated with a local feud, Belers, a former retainer of Thomas of Lancaster, had deserted him in 1322. The facts that it took place while Belers was riding to meet Henry of Lancaster and that some of the attackers afterwards fled to France were probably therefore significant.[223]

Meanwhile in France Isabella was starting to become the centre of a group of exiles from England. One was John of Brittany, the earl of Richmond and brother of the duke of Brittany, who had been one of Edward II's envoys to Paris. Despite orders from Edward, the earl refused to return to England.[224] She was also joined by Edward's half-brother, Edmund of Woodstock the earl of Kent, who had been in France since 1324, and by Henry de Beaumont and John Cromwell, who had accompanied her son Edward to France in September 1325.[225] The new bishop of Norwich, William Airmyn, was another recruit. In early 1326 he was summoned to appear before the King's Bench in England to explain himself: he did not attend, fled abroad and joined Isabella.[226] Worst of all, Roger Mortimer of Wigmore was also in her company, and plotting.

Edward II and his government became obsessed with the danger from the continent. On Christmas Day 1325 commissioners of array throughout England were told to see that every able-bodied man was properly armed and to erect beacons and appoint sentinels.[227] Royal castles were also to be properly supplied and garrisoned.[228] On 3 January 1326 Edward, fearing that she might be in communication with her son, ordered the removal of Roger Mortimer's mother, Margaret de Fiennes, from Worcester to the abbey of Elstow near Bedford.[229] On the same date orders were given to look out for any suspicious correspondence entering England. A month later, on 8 February, Edward ordered the coast to be carefully guarded against any

---

[223] Stones, 'The Folvilles', 119–20. See also the article on Belers by J. Röhrkasten in the *Oxford DNB*. Fryde also describes another attack on a member of the regime: the brutal murder in July 1325 of the deputy keeper of contrariant castles in Wales and the theft of his records: Fryde, 176.

[224] Blackley, 'Isabella', 234–5; Buck, 161. On 2 Jan. 1326 Edward ordered the seizure of his lands; and his arrest on 13 March:, E 159/102/m.71d; *Foedera*, II, i, 622, 630.

[225] Buck, 161. Their lands were seized in March: *CCR, 1323–27*, 463–4; *CFR, 1319–27*, 374.

[226] *Saint-Sardos*, 277, n. 1; *Foedera*, II, i, 622. On Airmyn's career see the article by M.C. Buck in the *Oxford DNB*.

[227] *CPR, 1323–27*, 216–18. The order was repeated on 24 Jan.: ibid., 220–1.

[228] Buck, 160; E 159/102.

[229] *CPR, 1323–27*, 206.

possible landing by foreigners in the service of Isabella and Mortimer:[230] this was in response to a rumour reported to the king by the archbishop of Canterbury that Isabella was preparing to invade England from Normandy, accompanied by the count of Hainault and the king of Bohemia.[231] This may also have been the occasion of the archbishop's appeal to Isabella to come home, and her reply on 5 February.[232] On 12 March Henry of Eastry, the dean of Christ Church, Canterbury, told the archbishop that the return of Isabella and her son was imminent, but was not clear whether this would be as part of an invasion or not. He advised that if they did return, they should be met with reverence and not hostility.[233]

Edward was also alarmed by other news. On 2 January the archbishop of Canterbury wrote telling the king that Charles IV had written to Count William of Hainault proposing a marriage between the young Edward and one of the count's daughters and asking for his assistance in an invasion of England.[234] Edward II was still planning a Spanish marriage between his son and heir and Eleanor the sister of Alfonso XI of Castile, as a counterbalance to the power of France.[235] He reacted angrily and on 3 January wrote asking the pope not to grant a dispensation for his son's marriage without consulting him first.[236] A marriage between the young Edward and the count of Hainault's daughter was all too plausible. Edward II had himself pursued such a scheme between 1319 and 1321,[237] when a Hainault marriage would have helped to improve commercial relations between the two sides. But Edward had not worked hard enough at preserving relations with Hainault and may have caused offence when he broke off the marriage negotiations in favour of potentially more

---

[230] *Foedera*, II, i, 617, 619; *CPR, 1323–27*, 208–10.

[231] Reported by the archbishop of Canterbury on 22 Jan.: SC 1/49/92; *CDS*, v, 256.

[232] *Historiae Anglicanae Scriptores Decem*, ed. Twysden, cols 2767–8.

[233] *Literae Cantuarienses*, ed. Sheppard, i, 172–4. It is possible that there was some ground for hope of a peaceful resolution, since on 8 March Edward still thought that Isabella and their son Edward would come home of their own accord in royal ships: *Foedera*, II, i, 619. On 11 March a messenger claiming to be sent by the earl of Kent came to Canterbury with letters for the king in which the earl said he would return to England if he could do so without penalty but would otherwise stay where he was and await better times: *Literae Cantuarienses*, i, 173.

[234] SC 1/49/91. The indefatigable Henry of Eastry had picked up this news or gossip from travellers passing through Canterbury.

[235] *Foedera*, II, i, 611–12. On these negotiations, which were still in progress as late as the summer of 1326, see Childs, 'England in Europe', 107–9.

[236] *Foedera*, II, i, 618.

[237] The original plan for Edward to marry Margaret, the daughter of the count of Hainault and Holland, had long since lapsed: Buck, 126. In Nov. 1320 Edward II asked the pope for a dispensation for the marriage of Edward and Margaret, but in March 1321 wrote to tell the count that he had not yet had a reply and that the king of Aragon and others (not named) were making proposals for the marriage of Edward: *Foedera*, II, i, 437, 446. Margaret instead married the emperor Ludwig of Bavaria in 1324. On English relations with Hainault and Holland see Childs, 'England in Europe', 102–4.

advantageous arrangements with Aragon or Castile. This may also help to explain why Mortimer appears to have found refuge there after his escape from England in 1323 and the persistent rumours of invasion plans with the assistance of Count William of Hainault. A revival of the Hainault marriage plans was thus an obvious tactic for Isabella and Mortimer to employ. Although Hainault was under imperial rather than French overlordship, there were close personal links between France and Hainault. The countess of Hainault was the daughter of Charles of Valois and therefore also a cousin of Isabella. The autobiography of Charles of Luxemburg, the son of King John of Bohemia and the future emperor Charles IV, records that Charles of Valois actively promoted a marriage between Isabella's son and a daughter of Count William.[238] Negotiations could have been started in December 1325 when the countess and her daughter Philippa were in Paris to visit Charles of Valois on his deathbed. Since the countess is also known to have met Isabella, the young Edward may even have met his future wife.[239] From Count William's point of view a marriage to the heir to the English throne and a successful invasion of England by Isabella and Mortimer could bring many advantages for Hainault. In January 1326 Edward II tried to improve his relations with Hainault but it was already too late.[240]

Charles IV's role was probably the passive one of providing sanctuary for his sister Isabella; there was no need for him to involve himself directly in an invasion of England, as was rumoured.[241] This would have been even further beyond his resources than a full-scale invasion of Gascony and would certainly have met with fierce resistance and rallied support around Edward II. For the moment it suited him that Edward's attention was distracted by news and rumours of Isabella and Mortimer's plans, allowing him to digest more fully his recent gains in Gascony. Since the war of Saint-Sardos, the valley of the Garonne, up to and including the great fortress of La Réole, had remained in French hands, undermining the eastern defences of the duchy. Saint-Macaire was now the only important stronghold before Bordeaux.[242] The war had also left a large number of outstanding claims for restitution of lands and for compensation which could not be settled speedily and caused tensions both within the duchy and between England and France.[243] Edward

[238] *Autobiography of Emperor Charles IV and his Legend of St Wenceslas*, ed. B. Nagy & F. Schaer (Budapest, 2001), 26–7; Fryde, 180–1. Charles was brought up at the French court.

[239] K. Petit, 'Le Mariage de Philippe de Hainaut, reine d'Angleterre (1328)', *Le Moyen Age*, lxxxvii (1981), 375. There is also evidence that the countess wrote to Isabella in Feb. 1326: Doherty (D.Phil.), 142. Isabella's visit to Charles of Valois on 16 Oct. might therefore have been more than a visit to a sick uncle. Her journey to Reims in Nov. 1325 could also have been connected with the marriage plans.

[240] *Foedera*, II, i, 618.

[241] SC 1/49/92 (22 Jan.); *Literae Cantuarienses*, ed. Sheppard, i, 172–3 (12 March).

[242] Sumption, *Trial by Battle*, 204.

[243] Vale, 241–4. Before 1 Oct. 1327 the English submitted a long list of requests for the restitution of lands occupied by the French in 1324–5 and later: *Saint-Sardos*, 257–66.

was forced to prepare for a possible resumption of hostilities. In April 1326 orders were given for the urgent completion of a new city wall for Bordeaux. As a precaution, the castles along the Scottish border were put in a state of defence, in case the Scots also joined in. War was resumed in Gascony between June and August 1326: in June Edward resumed the government of Gascony in his own name and in July was even considering sending an army there. Drift into a more general war in the region was a very real possibility and was avoided only by Isabella and Mortimer's invasion of England in September and the rapid disintegration of Edward II's rule.[244] The problem of Aquitaine was left for the new regime in England to deal with. Edward II could do no more.[245]

EDWARD'S DESPERATION

On 18 March 1326 Edward wrote both to his son and to his brother-in-law Charles IV. He reminded the young Edward that he had promised when he left England in 1325 that he would always follow his father's orders; told him that he was not to marry without his father's permission, threatening him with forfeiture if he did so; and said he was to return home as soon as possible, accompanied if he wished by the earl of Richmond and John Cromwell. Edward said that he understood his son's desire not to leave his mother while she was suffering such distress and unhappiness, but told him that her fear of Hugh Despenser, the king's dear and faithful servant, was merely feigned, and that she had shamed her husband by her open association with Roger Mortimer. Edward's letter to Charles IV was in the same vein, reminding him that he had earlier banished Mortimer from France, and asking him to send the young Edward back to England. Of Isabella, he said that if she truly loved him she would want to be in his company, as she had claimed; 'she who ought to be a mediator between England and France should not seek new forms of dissension'. Edward concluded by asking his brother-in-law to make his decisions 'according to reason, good faith, and fraternal affection, without having regard to the wilful pleasure of women'.[246]

THE POPE INTERVENES

During 1325 and 1326 the pope kept a very close watch on events in France and England. His envoys, the archbishop of Vienne and the bishop of Orange, had played a central role in the tortuous negotiations in Paris

[244] *Foedera*, II, i, 626, 632–4; Vale, 244–7.
[245] The future Edward III's experiences in France in 1325–6 and his knowledge of the intense diplomatic pressures placed upon his father by Charles IV and the French negotiators may have contributed to his determination to assert his own rights and claims against the French when he became king in 1327.
[246] *Foedera*, II, i, 622–3; *CCR, 1323–27*, 578–9: '*volentrine pleisaunce de femmes*'.

which led to the unsatisfactory peace between Edward II and Charles IV in June 1325 and were probably partly responsible for the proposal that Isabella should go to France. On 15 February 1326 the pope intervened when he wrote to both Edward and Isabella to say that he had heard with grief of the dissension between them and was sending his envoys to talk to them, begging that they would each listen to their advice. Two days later the pope went to the heart of the matter when he wrote to the Younger Despenser, suggesting that, since his role in the king's government was given by the queen as the reason for her fearing to return to her husband, he should retire and find a way of removing Isabella's fear.[247] The pressure on Edward was also increased by the rumours circulating in France and reported to him in April by the papal envoys in Paris that he had banished both Isabella and his son from England and was refusing to let them return.[248]

On 19 May Edward issued instructions for the reception of the papal envoys at Dover and their safe conduct.[249] When they arrived they were accompanied by messengers from the French king and were kept waiting at Dover for eight days before being taken to meet the king and Despenser at Saltwood castle near Hythe on the Kent coast. Here they arrived 'in fear and trembling', not knowing how they would be received, and delivered their bulls and other letters in a sealed box. In the event they were received honourably and spent the next two days in discussion with the king and Despenser before crossing back to France on 10 June.[250] There was much business to transact. The pope was concerned about payment of the accumulated arrears of the annual census of £1,000 owed to the papacy, the repayment of the clerical tenth which had been loaned to Edward II in 1322 in aid of the war in Scotland, and the plight of the archbishop of Dublin and the bishops of Hereford, Lincoln and Norwich; while Edward for his part was still pressing the case of Robert Baldock for promotion.[251]

The real business of the meeting was of course Isabella, and Edward's willingness to create the necessary conditions for her return. For this to be possible he would have to promise to treat her honourably and see to her safety; he had promised both when he wrote to Isabella on 1 December 1325 and might be expected to do so again.[252] But the central and abiding problem had been and remained the Younger Despenser. Unless Edward

---

[247] *CPL, 1305–42*, 473, 475.
[248] Edward denied these rumours in a letter to the pope on 15 April: *Foedera*, II, i, 625.
[249] *Foedera*, II, i, 628–9; *CPL, 1305–42*, 478.
[250] *Ann. Paul.*, 312: '*trepidi et timorati accesserunt*'. Edward was at Saltwood between around 1 and 6 June 1326. Although Saltwood belonged to the archbishop of Canterbury, he and the other bishops were not allowed to meet the envoys: Doherty (D.Phil.), 134; *HMC, Various Collections*, i (1901), 271–2.
[251] *Foedera*, II, i, 629 (this can all be gleaned from Edward's reply to the pope on 10 June).
[252] *CCR, 1323–27*, 580.

was prepared to give him up, which would mean in effect sending him into exile to a safe place, if there was such a place, no settlement was possible. And Edward was not prepared to give up Despenser: by this stage in the reign each was dependent on the support of the other; if one fell, the other was likely to follow. There is no formal record of what took place but on 10 June Edward wrote to the pope that the Younger Despenser had been questioned by the papal envoys and had replied to each point orally.[253] On the matter of Isabella there is some information. Edward II attached a schedule to his letter[254] in which he rehearsed the history of Isabella's going to France at the suggestion of the pope and of many others in order to make peace, and how Edward in all the sweetness of true love and with heart and mind had sent her;[255] he told of her refusal to return to England; of her association with his mortal enemy the convicted traitor '*le Mortimer*'; and of her detention in France of his elder son and heir Edward, whom she forced to associate with Mortimer who wore Edward's livery at the coronation of the queen of France, in contempt and disparagement of the king; it was also rumoured that Isabella was planning to invade the kingdom in alliance with various magnates. Edward concluded by saying that if she came to England, and showed herself obedient to him, he would act towards her in a fitting manner; and he did not believe that the Holy Father himself, the king of France or any other man would do otherwise.[256] Edward was very angry with Isabella: if she were to be allowed home she would have to break with Mortimer and allow her son to return to England; and Edward clearly had no intention of breaking with Despenser.

A few days later, on 15 June, the bishop of Rochester met both Edward and Despenser on the road between Leeds castle and Rochester, while they were on the way back to the Tower of London, and in conversation he asked about the talks with the papal envoys. Despenser told him that he was not the real obstacle to Isabella's return: she could have returned long ago but was prevented by Mortimer, who had threatened to kill her if she came back Edward.[257] It is possible, as Paul Doherty has suggested, that Edward II was now so angry that he was seriously contemplating divorcing Isabella.[258] Later, in the prior's chamber at Rochester, Edward

---

[253] *Foedera*, II, i, 629.

[254] *Foedera*, II, i, 629. Edward said his responses to the envoys were given in French but to enable the pope (who was a speaker of the Occitan rather than northern French) to understand them better they had been translated into Latin.

[255] '*in omni dulcedine veri amoris, cordis, et animi, quoad nos, Deus novit*'.

[256] *Foedera*, II, i, 629.

[257] BL, Cotton Ms. Faustina B.V, ff. 46v–47r, printed in Historia Roffensis, *Anglia Sacra*, i, ed. Wharton, 365. The date is given by Edward's itinerary. The record was composed by William Dene, one of the bishop's clerks, and the author of the Historia Roffensis. Hamo de Hethe, the bishop of Rochester, was one of the few people who could speak to the king with complete frankness.

[258] Doherty (D.Phil.), 138.

spoke of a queen who was deposed from her royal dignity for refusing to obey her lord the king.[259] In reply the bishop told the story of a councillor who was hanged for trying to estrange a king from his queen.[260] With great boldness the bishop added that he would have preached to this effect in the king's presence at Tonbridge if he had been summoned to do so. Despenser commented that this would have been a marvellous sermon, since it was about him; to which Edward replied that the bishop spared no one.[261] The bishop said that it was the duty of a priest to tell the truth about everyone, great or small, whether in the confessional or in preaching. The following afternoon, while the bishop escorted the king to Gravesend, Edward said: 'You have not asked me for anything. For you have done many things for me and the Lord Hugh, and I have not rewarded you. I have done much for those who are ungrateful, whom I promoted to high rank, and are now my chief enemies.' And Edward told Despenser to let the bishop have whatever he wished. When the party reached Hallings, the bishop asked Edward and Despenser's permission and departed, 'and he never saw the king again'.[262]

ISABELLA'S NEXT MOVE

This was the immediate background to Edward's appeal on 19 June to his son, to Charles IV, and the bishop of Beauvais. Edward spoke of his own shame and humiliation at Isabella's refusal to leave France and her association with Mortimer. Again he ordered his son not to marry without permission and begged him to return to England, and ended with a threat that if he disobeyed, he would feel it for the rest of his life and be an example to all other disobedient sons.[263] If Edward also wrote to Isabella, there is no record of it.

Isabella was now in a quandary, since her position in France was becoming difficult. There is some evidence that the support given to her by her uncle, Charles of Valois, was continued after his death by his son Philip, who was aware that the king of France was ailing and likely to die without a male heir.[264] In this case Philip of Valois and Isabella's son

---

[259] This was a reference to the Saxon queen Eadburga who murdered her husband Beorhtric, king of Wessex, in 802: Doherty (D.Phil.), 137–8.

[260] This was a reference to the Persian king Ahasuerus and his Jewish queen Esther: Doherty (D.Phil.), 138; Book of Esther, 7: 10.

[261] '*Et Rex ait: Non pepercisset tibi, Domine Hugo, episcopus in predicando*': *Anglia Sacra*, ed. Wharton, i, 365. The bishop was certainly not teasing Despenser: cf. Doherty (D. Phil.), 138.

[262] *Anglia Sacra*, ed. Wharton, i, 365–6.

[263] *Foedera*, II, i, 630–1; *CCR, 1323–27*, 576–7. It is not clear what Edward meant by this threat, but it may have referred to the resumption of control over the administration of Gascony which he announced on 27 June: *Foedera*, II, i, 632–3. It is possible however, as Paul Doherty has argued, that Edward was thinking of barring his son from the succession to the throne by divorcing Isabella: Doherty (D.Phil.), 137.

[264] Charles IV made wills in Oct. 1324 and just before his death in Jan. 1328: AN, J 404, nos 29, 29bis. In neither of them is there any mention of Isabella.

Edward would each have a strong claim to the French throne. At some point Philip of Valois made an agreement to help Isabella, for which the quid pro quo may have been that Isabella would support his claim over that of her son.[265] On the other hand, by the summer of 1326 her welcome from the king of France, her brother Charles IV, was starting to wear thin. Charles did not approve of her conduct in abandoning her husband and in associating herself so openly with Roger Mortimer.[266]

Charles IV may have been tempted to send Isabella home[267] and she may herself have been tempted to return. But this could quickly be ruled out. If the Younger Despenser's statement to the bishop of Rochester that Mortimer had threatened to kill her if she tried to return had any substance,[268] then she was in danger in France; while Mortimer was later alleged to have tried to persuade her that if she returned to her husband, Edward would kill her.[269] There is also evidence that the Younger Despenser tried to bribe some of Charles IV's councillors into withdrawing their support,[270] while one chronicler claimed that Edward plotted to have Isabella murdered, using the earl of Richmond as his agent.[271] Whatever the explanation, the simple truth was that Isabella was now both an embarrassment and in serious danger, and she had to move on.[272] If she had had doubts earlier in 1326 about the wisdom and feasibility of launching an invasion of England with the assistance of Roger Mortimer, she now laid all doubts aside. Her destiny was as closely linked with that of Mortimer as Edward II's was with Despenser.

According to the highly coloured accounts of the Liège chronicler Jean le Bel and his successor Jean Froissart, Isabella left France after she was warned by Robert d'Artois, one of Charles IV's councillors, that she was about to be expelled. Accompanied by her son, the earl of Kent and

---

[265] Fryde, 181–2, citing J. Viard, 'Philippe de Valois avant son avenement au trône', Bibliothèque de l'Ecole des Chartes, xci (1930), 324. Isabella duly obliged after Edward II's overthrow by renouncing her son's claim.

[266] Edward II referred to these opinions in his letter to Charles on 12 June: *Foedera*, II, i, 631; *CCR, 1323–27*, 577.

[267] Doherty (D. Phil.), 141; *Chronographia Regum Franciae*, ed. Moranville, i, 280; *Recueil des Historiens des Gaules et de la France*, xxiii, ed. H. Welter (Paris, 1894), 419–20.

[268] Historia Roffensis, *Anglia Sacra*, ed. Wharton, i, 365.

[269] This was one of the charges against Roger Mortimer at his trial in Nov. 1330: *PROME*, Parliament of Nov. 1330, C 65/2, item 1. This evidence is misunderstood in Mortimer, *The Greatest Traitor*, 147, 285, n. 33, where it is argued that Mortimer and not the king would have killed her.

[270] Doherty (D.Phil.), 140–1, 266. The author of the *Scalacronica*, Sir Thomas Gray, claimed that Despenser had bribed the French council to have her sent back to England: *Scalacronica*, 90–3. In the indictment against him in Nov. 1326 Despenser was accused only of sending large sums overseas to procure the destruction of Isabella. But there was no direct mention of Charles IV's councillors: Holmes, 'Judgement', 266.

[271] *Historia Anglicana*, i, 179, which also claimed that Edward tried bribery.

[272] Natalie Fryde may be technically correct that Isabella was not forced to leave France, but in practice life was clearly becoming increasingly difficult for her: Fryde, 181.

Roger Mortimer, she went first to Cambrai, outside the borders of France, and then to Buignicourt in Hainault where she lodged with a simple knight, Eustace d'Aubrecicourt. Here she met Jean de Beaumont, a young knight 'in the flower of his age', who took pity on her and took her to his brother Count William of Hainault at Valenciennes. William offered to help her at the price of a betrothal between his daughter and the young Edward, and the invasion plans grew from there.[273]

Isabella may well have left France in a hurry but the truth was probably less dramatic.[274] The only direction in which she could realistically go was the county of Hainault with whose count both she and Mortimer had long been in contact and in negotiation. It was now time to put those contacts to good use and complete the negotiations. Isabella had begun to plan the invasion of England even before she left France. On 10 June 1326 she was still in Paris, where she began arrangements to pledge the revenues of the county of Ponthieu to the count of Hainault to cover the costs of hiring ships and supplies.[275] It is likely that she then went to Ponthieu and reached Hainault in early August.[276] Mortimer had preceded her and before the end of July was gathering ships and supplies in her name and with the approval of the count. The ships were to be ready at ports between Rotterdam and Dordrecht by 1 September.[277] On 3 August Isabella was at Mons in Hainault, where she confirmed and guaranteed an agreement made between Mortimer and the count for the supply of 132 ships and eight warships.[278]

BETROTHAL

On 27 August 1326 Edward, duke of Aquitaine, count of Ponthieu and earl of Chester, and Philippa, the daughter of William, count of Hainault,

---

[273] *Le Bel*, 13–17; *Froissart*, 43–51.

[274] Eustace d'Aubrecicourt probably did provide some kind of assistance to Isabella since in Oct. 1330 he was rewarded by Edward III: *Froissart*, ii, 504.

[275] Doherty (D.Phil.), 144–5; AN, J 237, no. 105. There is also evidence that Isabella obtained some financial and other help from Gascony, including sailors from Bayonne and possibly even from Oliver Ingham, the seneschal of Gascony: *Foedera*, II, i, 647; Doherty, 145–6. A further agreement with the men of Ponthieu was made at Ostrelte on 17 Aug. and confirmed by Isabella in Brabant on 5 Sept. In it they provided security for the invasion fleet and agreed to pay Isabella £3,000 in return for certain concessions: Doherty (D.Phil.), 146, n. 5; BN, Paris, Collection Moreau, vols 225, f. 84, 255, f. 89. There is no evidence to support Fryde's statement that Philippa's dowry paid for the invasion of England; this would not in any case have been payable until the marriage actually took place: Fryde, 182.

[276] Doherty (D.Phil.), 145; *Recueil des Historiens des Gaules*, ed. Welter, 66.

[277] Petit, 'Le Mariage', 376; Doherty (D. Phil.), 144; *Table chronologique des chartes et diplomes*, ed. A. Wautier (Brussels, 1896), 220.

[278] Doherty (D. Phil.), 145; *Groot Charterboek der Graven van Holland*, ed. F. Mieris (Leiden, 1754), ii, 393–4. Isabella also pledged compensation for any losses against the revenues of Ponthieu. If she defaulted, Charles IV was to be the ultimate guarantor. There is no indication however as to whether Charles was aware of his potential liability.

Holland and Zeeland, were formally betrothed at Mons. Edward engaged himself to marry Philippa within two years, to obtain the necessary dispensation from the pope, and to give her a dower worthy of a queen of England; if the marriage did not take place he would pay the count £10,000 sterling. In return for all these promises the count of Hainault undertook to provide troops for the planned invasion of England. On the same occasion Isabella promised that if the marriage had not occurred within two years she would send ten knights of noble lineage to Valenciennes, to stay there until the ceremony was completed. In two separate documents, Edward's uncle Edmund earl of Kent and Roger Mortimer also undertook to see that the marriage took place.[279] This was no romantic engagement. The count of Hainault had driven a hard bargain and stood to gain, whatever the outcome.

GATHERING THE FLEET

After the betrothal Isabella left Hainault and travelled through Holland, Zeeland and Brabant, to arrange further details of the planned invasion, before joining the count of Hainault at Dordrecht on 7 September.[280] Isabella, Edward and her companions then moved between the Hague, Rotterdam and Brill, where their presence is last recorded on 20 September.[281] The core of the army was a force of 700 mercenaries raised by Philippa's uncle Jean de Beaumont in Hainault and in Germany.[282] There were also a number of English exiles, who had escaped soon after Boroughbridge or who had left England later, men such as John de Kingston, John Maltravers, John Botetourt, William Trussell, and others; as well as Henry de Beaumont and John Cromwell who had accompanied the young Edward to France;[283] there were the leaders of the force, Queen Isabella, her son Edward, Roger Mortimer, the earl of Kent, the earl of Richmond, and their own personal retainers. In total the army probably came to no more than between 1,000 and 1,500,[284] but what the army lacked in size it made up

---

[279] *Inventaire analytique du chartrier de la Tresorerie des comtes de Hainaut*, ed. G. Wymans (Brussels, 1985), nos 574–6, pp. 128–9; Petit, 'Le Mariage', 376–7. The texts of two of the four documents, Edward's marriage contract and the undertaking by the earl of Kent, are also printed in *Froissart*, ii, 502–4. On 13 April 1981 the contract was sold for £16,000 at Sotheby's, London, as Lot 41 of *Bibliotheca Phillippica: Catalogue of English Charters and Documents*: M. Michael, 'The iconography of kingship in Walter de Milemete's treatise', *Journal of Warburg & Courtauld Institutes*, lvii (1994), 38, n. 26; Given-Wilson & Curteis, *Royal Bastards*, 22. So far as I have been able to discover, the marriage contract is not preserved in English records.

[280] Doherty (D. Phil.), 146; *Rekeningen van de Herberge van Joanna van Valois, 1319–1326*, ed. H. Smit, Koninklijk Nederlands Historisch Genootschap, 3rd ser., xlvi (1924), 260.

[281] Petit, 'Le Mariage', 377; Archives du Nord, Lille, série B 3271, ff. 1, 9, 10; Doherty, (D. Phil.), 148; *Rekeningen*, ed. Smit, 261.

[282] Petit, 'Le Mariage', 377–8.

[283] *PW*, App., p. 201, no. 191; *Ann. Paul.*, 314; *Knighton*, i, 431–2; Doherty (D.Phil.), 149.

[284] Various figures are quoted, ranging from 500 to as high as 2,500: see Doherty (D.Phil.), 148; Mortimer, *The Greatest Traitor*, 149.

for in professional skill and in determination to bring down the hated Despensers. The fleet when finally assembled came to only ninety-five ships, far fewer than the original 140 which had been summoned.[285] But they were enough to carry the men, horses and supplies. On 21 or 22 September 1326 the invasion force set sail for England from Dordrecht or Brill.[286]

D-DAY, 24 SEPTEMBER 1326

The long-awaited and long-feared invasion had begun at last. Although safeguards against an invasion by Roger Mortimer had been being put in place since January, the main perceived threat in the summer of 1326 was of a French invasion of England from Normandy in conjunction with the resumption of war in Gascony. On 10 August Edward ordered the setting up of a system of coastal beacons and watchers, and two days later, on the 12th, the assembling at Portsmouth on 31 August of all ships of more than 50 tons from the mouth of the Thames westwards; on 26 August he ordered the arrest of French subjects; and on 3 September that all ships of over 30 tons' burden from the mouth of the Thames northwards were to be assembled at the port of Orwell in Suffolk on 21 September.[287] The chief enemy against which the ships were to be directed was the French: in the order of 12 August the French were the only enemy mentioned but on 3 September they were joined by 'others', unnamed but a clear indication that Edward had learned something of the plans of Isabella and Mortimer.

By coincidence or not, Orwell was close to the very spot at which Isabella and her followers landed on 24 September. This was an obvious destination for an invasion fleet coming from the Netherlands: two years earlier, in October 1324, it was believed that Mortimer was preparing to land in Norfolk or Suffolk from precisely this direction.[288] Although Isabella and Mortimer probably took care to prevent news of their plans from leaking out,[289] it seems likely that Edward had some knowledge, not just of their general plans, but also of the intended place and approximate date of their landing. On 2 September, orders were given for a force of 2,000 men, comprising 1,300 archers and 700 infantry, to be at Orwell by 21 September

---

[285] See Doherty (D.Phil.), 150, for a detailed breakdown of the figures.

[286] The 21 Sept. was the day after Isabella's last appearance at Brill in the accounts of the countess of Hainault. However Petit, 'Le Mariage', 378, n. 13, apparently using the same sources, gives Dordrecht and 22 Sept. as the place and date of departure. Dordrecht, which was upstream from Brill, is given as the place of departure by both Jean le Bel and Froissart and seems the more likely: *Le Bel*, 18; *Froissart*, ii, 66.

[287] *Foedera*, II, i, 636–9.

[288] *Saint-Sardos*, 72; *CPR, 1324–27*, 31.

[289] One possible source of information, William Weston, was detained at Antwerp in Brabant. Although the duke of Brabant, John III, appears to have been sympathetic to Isabella, his mother Margaret, the widow of John II, was also a sister of Edward II and was apparently still alive in Sept. 1326: *Foedera*, II, i, 643; *CCR, 1323–27*, 648.

and to stay there for a month;[290] and on 10 September a squadron of twelve ships from Harwich and Ipswich was ordered to be at Orfordness, not far from Orwell, on 24 September, ready to repel an enemy landing if the main fleet was absent on other duties. On 10 and 12 September two other squadrons were ordered to take up positions off Hunstanton in Norfolk and the Isle of Thanet in Kent.[291]

However, if Edward knew something of Isabella's invasion plans and took precautions against them, he completely underestimated their chances of success. Instead he took his eyes off the real danger and continued to give his attention to the non-existent threat of a French invasion of England. Edward's presence at Portchester near Portsmouth from about 30 August until 17 September must be connected with the attack on Normandy in the early days of September by 133 ships manned by 4,200 sailors and carrying about 1,600 soldiers.[292] The attack was led by John Felton, one of the Younger Despenser's knights, who was later to take part in the defence of Despenser's fortress of Caerphilly in Wales.[293] It appears to have been in the nature of a commando-style raid, which was undertaken either to forestall a French attack or even in the mistaken belief that Edward II's son, Edward, was in Normandy and might be brought back to England.[294]

At about midday on 24 September Isabella landed in the port of Orwell and seized a position on the Colvasse peninsula a few miles from Harwich. She was accompanied by her son Edward the duke of Aquitaine, John de Beaumont the brother of the count of Hainault, Edward II's half-brother Edmund of Woodstock the earl of Kent and his wife,[295] Roger Mortimer, John Cromwell, William Trussell, and other knights and men-at-arms. The ships were quickly unloaded and with a fair wind departed before sunset, all except the ship in which Isabella had crossed to England, which either deserted her or was captured as it left the harbour. The vessel was sailed to London where the crew

---

[290] *CPR, 1324–27*, 315–16.
[291] *CCR, 1323–27*, 612–13.
[292] Trinity College Cambridge Ms. R.5.41, f. 120v; SAL Ms. 122, p. 84; Fryde, 184; E 403/218, m.18; E 101/17, nos 24–7.
[293] *CPR, 1327–30*, 10; *CPR, 1324–27*, 344.
[294] Fryde, 184–5; *CPR, 1327–30*, 10: Edward III's pardon to Felton for the damage he caused in Normandy '*dum eramus in partibus illis*', which could imply, as Dr Fryde suggests, that Edward was there at the time of the attack. However, *in partibus illis* could also refer in a more general way to Edward's sojourn on the continent. Dr Fryde's statement that Edward was not with Isabella when she landed in England on 24 Sept. is contradicted by, for example, *Foedera*, II, i, 643–4; *Ann. Paul.*, 313. *French Chroni.*, 51, refers to the attack on Normandy but makes it appear the action of a force which went to plunder Normandy rather than defend England and Despenser's cause.
[295] *Ann. Paul.*, 313–14. The earl's wife, Margaret Wake, was the daughter of Joan de Fiennes, the sister of Roger Mortimer's mother. Their marriage, probably in Paris in Dec. 1325, cemented the earl's alliance with Mortimer: Mortimer, *The Greatest Traitor*, 147, 285.

broke the news of Isabella's landing to Edward II at the Tower of London,[296] probably on 27 September.[297]

Isabella spent the first night at the nearby village of Walton,[298] before moving on to Bury St Edmunds, 'as if she were on a pilgrimage'. Here she found 800 marks left there by one of the king's judges, Hervey de Stanton, which she borrowed to pay for the costs of her household.[299] Her next stop was Barnwell priory near Cambridge, where she spent several days, before going on to Baldock in Hertfordshire, which she had reached by 6 October; then on to Dunstable in Bedfordshire, before starting her pursuit of the king in his flight from London.[300]

Isabella's advance appears to have met no resistance.[301] Of the 2,000 troops ordered to assemble at Orwell only fifty-five are known to have appeared.[302] All the evidence suggests that, as news of her landing spread,[303] supporters flocked to her, united by their common hatred of the Despensers. She was joined soon after the landing by Edward II's other half-brother, Thomas of Brotherton the earl of Norfolk,[304] and by Henry of Lancaster the earl of Leicester, who 'by chance' had already begun to gather troops at Leicester. He immediately came south and met Isabella at Dunstable.[305] Several of the prelates who had fallen out with Edward II, the bishops of Lincoln, Hereford and Ely, and the archbishop of Dublin, also joined her.[306]

---

[296] *Ann. Paul.*, 313–14. If the ship was captured, the landing may have been a closer run thing than it appears.

[297] *Foedera*, II, i, 643–4: this is the first indication that Edward knew.

[298] This may have been a possession of the earl of Norfolk.

[299] *Ann. Paul.*, 314.

[300] *Ann. Paul.*, 314–15; *Anonimalle*, 126–7 (this dates her presence at Baldock).

[301] *Anonimalle*, 122–5.

[302] Doherty (D.Phil.), 153; E 101/17/20.

[303] It is very likely that Isabella had contacted potential supporters even before her arrival: *Foedera*, II, i, 642. After the landing Isabella sent letters to London and other towns announcing her arrival; her status as queen of England and the presence of her son, the heir to the throne, gave her appeals greater authority than if Mortimer had been their author. It was therefore much easier for anyone with a grievance against Edward II and the Despensers to join Isabella without appearing to commit an act of treason.

[304] *Historia Anglicana*, 180; *Murimuth*, 46; *Lanercost*, 255; *Le Baker*, 21. It is not known when and where this took place, but the earl had lands in the area and may well have had advance warning of Isabella's arrival. The earl of Norfolk had personal grievances against the Younger Despenser who had forced him to give up his valuable lordship of Chepstow in 1323, and against his brother the king who had temporarily deprived him of the office of marshal of England: see the article on Thomas of Brotherton by S.L. Waugh in the *Oxford DNB*.

[305] *Knighton*, i, 435; *Murimuth*, 46; *Lanercost*, 255; *Le Baker*, 21. He had multiple grievances against Despenser, beginning with the execution of his brother Thomas of Lancaster in 1322 and most recently Edward II's refusal to restore him to the earldom of Lancaster.

[306] The dioceses of Lincoln and Ely were near to the landing place so their bishops, Henry de Burghersh and John de Hothum, did not have far to go. Burghersh had suffered since 1322 from being Bartholomew de Badlesmere's nephew. Hothum had previously been a loyal servant of the crown. Adam Orleton, the bishop of Hereford, came from Hereford and joined her at Oxford in mid-Oct.: Haines, *The Church and Politics*, 165, 227. It is not known when and where Alexander Bicknor the archbishop of Dublin joined her.

EDWARD'S RESPONSE

On 27 September Edward gave orders to raise forces against the invaders; on the following day he put a price of £1,000 on the head of Roger Mortimer, 'his mortal enemy', while ordering that no harm should come to Isabella, or to his son and the earl of Kent.[307] This proclamation was received with open hostility when it was read out in London.[308] On 30 September the archbishop of Canterbury, the bishops of London and Winchester, and the abbots of Westminster and Waltham gathered in St Paul's cathedral and solemnly republished a seven-year-old papal bull excommunicating all invaders of the realm and originally directed against the Scots. But a letter from Isabella and her son Edward announcing their landing and their purpose had already been widely circulated in the city. Although they had not replied because of fear of the king and the Despensers, the citizens realized what the archbishop was doing and showed their support of Isabella's cause by shouting down the archbishop's clerk Thomas de Stowe when he tried to read the bull in public.[309]

For Edward II the message was all too clear. Since his return from Portchester he had been staying in the Tower of London and could probably hear and see what was going on around it. On 2 October Edward abandoned London, heading west and accompanied by the Despensers, the chancellor Robert Baldock, a great company of men-at-arms, and with a large sum of money.[310] Edward left behind him most of his administration,[311] his ten-year-old son John of Eltham and Despenser's wife Eleanor de Clare in the Tower, and a city seething with discontent.[312] Nonetheless, there was still much to play for. The south and east of England already appeared to be a lost cause, but if Edward could use the money available to him to good effect, and if Wales was to prove its loyalty again as it had in 1321–2, a victory might still be possible.

---

[307] *Foedera*, II, i, 643–5; *CPR, 1324–27*, 327–31. If the forces had actually been raised they would have amounted to over 50,000 men. Over 100 men guilty of homicide and other felonies were also pardoned on condition they served the king.

[308] Williams, *Medieval London*, 295.

[309] *Ann. Paul.*, 315; *French Chroni.*, 51; *Anonimalle*, 124–5; Williams, *Medieval London*, 295.

[310] *Anonimalle*, 126–7 ('*grant compaignie des gentz darmes*'); *Melsa*, 351–2 ('*cum copia armatorum*') (the Meaux chronicle appears to be drawing on the Anonimalle at this point). There is no indication of the size of the force Edward had with him. However, he had had at least £29,000 when he left London: Fryde, 105; E 101/17/18; E 159/103, m.24. Large sums continued to be paid out by the exchequer for several days after Edward left London: Buck, 218, n. 17; E 403/219, mm.1,2.

[311] As well as the exchequer, under the recently appointed treasurer Walter de Norwich, the royal justices such as Geoffrey le Scrope and Hervey de Stanton, were still in London: Buck, 220.

[312] *Historia Anglicana*, 181; *French Chroni.*, 54; *Knighton*, 434. Knighton also remarked that Eleanor had been behaving as if she were queen during Isabella's absence abroad.

LONDON IN REVOLT

On 9 October a second open letter from Isabella and her son, sealed with their pendant seals and asking the citizens to help them in the destruction of the Younger Despenser, arrived in London and was widely publicized.[313] The Londoners, who deeply hated Despenser for his attacks on their liberties since 1321 and were already sympathetic towards Mortimer, needed no further encouragement.[314] From this moment any hope that the king might retain some sort of control of the city vanished.

A last attempt at mediation was made on 13 October when the archbishop of Canterbury and the bishops of Winchester, Exeter, Worcester, London and Rochester assembled in convocation.[315] It was a measure of how dangerous London had become that they met at the archbishop's palace at Lambeth, south of the River Thames, instead of in St Paul's cathedral as originally planned. A very nervous group of bishops decided on 14 October to send two of their number to Isabella to mediate between her and Edward. John Stratford, the bishop of Winchester, volunteered to go but only if another bishop would join him.[316]

On the following day and while Stratford was still trying to persuade the bishop of Rochester to accompany him, the Londoners rose in revolt. A great crowd gathered at the Guildhall and at what may have been a prearranged signal began to attack anyone associated with Edward II's regime. John le Marshal, a London citizen and a close ally of the Younger Despenser, was dragged out of his house and beheaded; the mayor of London, Hamo de Chigwell, saved his life only by swearing to support Isabella; and in one final act of barbarity Walter Stapeldon, the bishop of Exeter and former treasurer, was seized in the porch of St Paul's cathedral where he had sought sanctuary, beaten and savagely beheaded with a bread-knife. Afterwards Stapeldon's head was sent to Isabella at Gloucester. Stephen Gravesend, the bishop of London was lucky to avoid the same fate.[317]

This was only the beginning of an orgy of plunder and mayhem. The chief justice, Geoffrey le Scrope, who had earlier tried to raise forces to

---

[313] *Anonimalle*, 124–7 (this includes the French text of the letter, dated at Baldock on 6 Oct.); *Ann. Paul.*, 315; *French Chroni.*, 51–2; Williams, *Medieval London*, 295; Buck, 218–19.

[314] See Williams, *Medieval London*, 290–5.

[315] On 29 Aug. 1326 the king had summoned a council of prelates and magnates to meet at Stamford on 13 Oct. 1326 to discuss the growing emergency. On 14 Sept. he wrote from Portchester to the archbishop of Canterbury asking him to be at Stamford on 13 Oct. and to cancel his provincial council summoned for the same date. The archbishop had duly obliged and postponed his council until 3 Nov. but evidently decided to stick to his original plan after the news of Isabella's landing: *PW*, II, ii, 349.

[316] Haines, *Stratford*, 171–3, citing the very detailed account in the Historia Roffensis, BL, Cotton Ms. Faustina B.V, ff. 47v–48r.

[317] BL, Cotton Ms. Faustina B.V, f. 48r; Trinity College Cambridge Ms. R.5.41, ff. 121v–122r; *French Chron.*, 51–2; *Ann. Paul.*, 315–16; *Anonimalle*, 126–9; *Murimuth*, 48; Williams, *Medieval London*, 295–6; Haines, *Stratford*, 173; Buck, 220–1.

assist the king, was another of the mob's targets. Scrope escaped across the Thames from Blackfriars, where he had been meeting the bishops of Exeter and London and other royal councillors in a vain effort to find a way out of the crisis, and rode for his life on one of the archbishop's horses. Walter Reynolds, the archbishop and one of Edward II's oldest and closest allies, rode off into Kent, leaving Hamo de Hethe the bishop of Rochester to follow on foot as best he could.[318] The treasuries belonging to the earl of Arundel at St Paul's and Robert Baldock at Holy Trinity were looted; and the offices of the Florentine bankers the Bardi, with whom Despenser had deposited large sums, were attacked.[319]

On the following day, 16 October, the constable of the Tower, John de Weston, was forced to hand over the keys. All the prisoners who had been held there since 1322 were released, including Roger Mortimer's two sons, Badlesmere's widow and son, and others. The king's son, John of Eltham, was then appointed as the nominal guardian of the city after swearing loyalty to the city's cause.[320] One who did not live to regain liberty was Mortimer's uncle, Roger Mortimer of Chirk, who had died in the Tower on 3 August.[321] The completeness of the victory was symbolized on 17 October when Thomas of Lancaster's plaque marking the publication of the Ordinances in 1311 was restored to its former place in St Paul's from which it had been removed in 1323.[322] In a quite different symbolic act, nearly all the London Dominicans, whose order was very close to Edward II, fled the city.[323]

The seizure of control of London by partisans of Isabella and Mortimer had not been quite as straightforward or certain as the outcome suggested. The collapse into anarchy was almost as dangerous to Isabella's cause as it was to her husband's. Nonetheless, London's allegiance to Edward II was now definitively at an end: a letter read at the Guildhall and claiming that Edward and Isabella had been reconciled and the enemies of the kingdom captured was immediately treated as a forgery.[324] When the bishop of Winchester arrived on 15 November with letters from Isabella appointing Richard de Béthune and John de Gisors as joint keepers of the Tower, and

---

[318] BL, Cotton Ms. Faustina B.V, f. 48r; Trinity College Cambridge Ms. R.5.41, ff. 122r; E.L.G. Stones, 'Sir Geoffrey le Scrope (*c.* 1285–1340), Chief Justice of the King's Bench', *EHR*, lxix (1954), 4, n. 1; Haines, *Stratford*, 173; Buck, 220–1.

[319] *French Chron.*, 53–4; Williams, *Medieval London*, 296; Buck, 221.

[320] Trinity College Cambridge Ms. R.5.41, f. 122v–123r; *French Chron.*, 54; *Knighton*, 434; Buck, 222. John of Eltham was still however in considerable danger until the end of October when his mother sent eight men-at-arms to see to his safety: Doherty (D.Phil.), 162; E 101/382/3.

[321] Haines, *The Church and Politics*, 161, 227: he was buried at Wigmore on 14 Sept. by Adam Orleton the bishop of Hereford, who thus gave a clear indication of his loyalties, even before Isabella's return to England.

[322] *French Chron.*, 54; Buck, 222.

[323] Trinity College Cambridge Ms. R.5.41, f. 123r; *French Chron.*, 54; Buck, 222.

[324] *French Chron.*, 55.

Richard de Béthune replaced Hamo de Chigwell as mayor, order began to be restored.[325] All that remained was the Londoners' noisy participation in the parliament of January 1327 during which Edward II was deposed.

EDWARD VERSUS ISABELLA

Edward and the Despensers did not waste any time in their journey westwards. Pausing at Wallingford on 6 October, they were at Gloucester between 9 and 12 October. They were not however fleeing aimlessly. Edward believed that he could trust the principality of Wales to offer him military support against the invaders; while the Younger Despenser also disposed potentially of enormous resources in money and manpower in the lordships he held or controlled in South Wales all the way from Chepstow in the east to Pembroke in the west. Whatever sympathy Roger Mortimer may have enjoyed in England, he was still cordially hated in Wales. Unfortunately for Edward's cause, the Younger Despenser was also loathed by his Welsh tenants.[326] One of Edward's first acts on hearing of the invasion was to order two of his most loyal Welsh subjects, Rhys ap Gruffudd in South Wales and Gruffydd ap Rhys (otherwise known as Gruffydd Llwyd), to gather all the available forces of South, West and North Wales, and bring them to him.[327] This strongly suggests that Edward and the Despensers were planning to fight in Wales even before their departure from London on 2 October. These two men had been largely responsible for the defeat of Roger Mortimer and the other Marchers in 1321–2 and Edward clearly hoped that they would do so again in 1326. However, events in the autumn of 1326 moved so fast that neither man was able to intervene in time to save Edward II from capture by his enemies. The knowledge that they would also be helping to save the Despensers from their well-deserved punishment may have somewhat dampened their enthusiasm and made them slower to react.[328]

While he was at Gloucester Edward sought to add to these anticipated forces by summoning men from Wigmore and Ludlow and other places under royal control with orders to join him at Gloucester on the following Wednesday, 15 October.[329] But when that day came he had already moved to Tintern, and then on the following day to the great castle of Chepstow

---

[325] *Ann. Paul.*, 318; *French Chron.*, 55; Williams, *Medieval London*, 296–7.

[326] Davies, *Conquest*, 410.

[327] *CPR, 1324–27*, 325. On the careers of these two men see Davies, *Conquest*, 409–10 (Gruffudd Llwyd), 410, 415–16 (Rhys ap Gruffudd); R.A. Griffiths, *The Principality of Wales in the Later Middle Ages* (Cardiff, 1972), 99–102 (Rhys ap Gruffudd).

[328] Griffiths, *Principality*, 100; Fryde, 189–90. The chamberlain of North Wales, Robert Power, was active in ensuring the security of North Wales: this may have included preventing Gruffudd Llwyd from bringing any assistance to the king: Fryde, 189–90; *List of Welsh Entries in the Memoranda Rolls, 1282–1343*, ed. N. Fryde (Cardiff, 1974), 81, no. 693.

[329] *CPR, 1324–27*, 326.

on the borders between England and Wales. Events were moving rapidly and Edward could not afford to wait until the troops he had summoned began to arrive. Perhaps he already knew that they were not coming.

Isabella meanwhile was hot on his heels. On 9 October she was at Dunstable where she placed a reward of £2,000 on the head of the Younger Despenser.[330] On 15 October she was at Wallingford and here, on the same day as the rising in London, a proclamation was issued in the names of Isabella 'queen of England, lady of Ireland, and countess of Ponthieu'; Edward, 'the elder son of the noble king of England', duke of Guyenne,[331] earl of Chester, and count of Ponthieu and Montreuil'; and Edmund, 'the son of the noble king [Edward I]', earl of Kent.[332] No mention was made of Roger Mortimer. This was a crucial moment, since it was still uncertain whether she and her followers had enough support to attain their objectives. In order to consolidate that support it was now essential for her to spell out exactly what those objectives were and to convince any waverers that her actions were legitimate. Isabella, Edward and the earl of Kent began by claiming that the state of the Church and of the kingdom had been greatly diminished by the evil counsel of Hugh Despenser the Younger, who had seized royal power for himself, against right and reason, with the aid and evil counsel of Robert Baldock and others; the crown of England had been destroyed in various ways, disinheriting the king and his heirs; many of the great men of the realm had been shamefully put to death, and others imprisoned, banished or exiled; widows and orphans had been wrongfully deprived of their rights; the people of the land had been ruined by various tallages and undue exactions; and for all these offences Hugh 'showed himself to be a tyrant and enemy'[333] of God and the Holy Church, of 'our beloved lord the king',[334] and of the whole kingdom. Isabella, Edward and Edmund went on to say that, having been deprived of the goodwill of the king by the false suggestions and evil procurement of Hugh, Robert and their adherents, they had come into the land to relieve the Holy Church and the realm and all the people of the realm of these oppressions, and in order to guard and maintain the honour of the Holy Church, of 'our lord the king', and of the entire kingdom to the best of their ability. Therefore they called upon each and every one, for the common profit of all, to give them every assistance; since their actions were undertaken for the honour and profit of the Holy Church and the whole kingdom, as would appear in time.

The emphasis throughout was on the legitimacy of their cause and the many crimes and acts of oppression committed by the 'tyrant' Hugh Despenser and his adherents. Nowhere was it suggested that the king was himself a tyrant or that he was anything but a victim of Despenser's

---

[330] *Historia Anglicana*, 181.
[331] Reflecting the fact that he did not hold all of Aquitaine.
[332] *Foedera*, II, i, 645–6.
[333] '*se monstre apert tyrant et enemy*'.
[334] '*nostre treschier seigneur le Roy*'.

machinations. A few days later, in order to ram home Despenser's culpability, Adam Orleton the bishop of Hereford preached before the university at Oxford on the text 'I will put enmity between thee and the woman, and between thy seed and her seed; it shall bruise thy head . . ..'[335]

EDWARD ALL AT SEA

On 20 October Edward and Despenser sailed from Chepstow: they were to be at sea for the next four days.[336] Their immediate destination was Lundy Island in the Bristol Channel, which had been in Despenser's hands since 1322, but this tiny windswept island was not a feasible refuge, and it is very likely, as several chronicle sources suggest, that they were hoping to escape from there to Ireland.[337] Edward II did not reach Ireland in 1326, but it is interesting to speculate as to what might have happened had he succeeded. Although the English government had been worried in 1323 that Roger Mortimer of Wigmore might go to Ireland after his escape from the Tower of London, there is no evidence to show that he had a significant following in Ireland by the time he and Isabella invaded England in 1326.[338] On the other hand, if Edward II had landed in the south-east of Ireland, in for example Waterford or Wexford,[339] he might have found a friendly reception in the lordship of Wexford, which had been in royal hands since the death of the earl of Pembroke in 1324; and in the lordship of Kilkenny, two-thirds of which was in royal control, while the remainder was held by Despenser.[340] More importantly, he would probably have been well received in Dublin, the centre of the government of the lordship. Alexander Bicknor,

---

[335] Genesis, 3:15. The reference was to the enmity between Despenser on the one hand and Isabella and her son, the young Edward, on the other: Haines, *The Church and Politics*, 164–5. Orleton later had to defend himself against the charge that he caused enmity between Isabella and her husband: ibid. Professor Haines's explanation of the purpose of Orleton's sermon and his argument that Isabella's stay in Oxford occurred after she had been at Wallingford and not before are both convincing. Cf. Mortimer, *The Greatest Traitor*, 154–5; Doherty, (D. Phil.), 158–9; Buck, 122.

[336] E 101/382/1; SAL Ms. 122, p. 90.

[337] *Lanercost*, 256–7; *Murimuth*, 49; *Anonimalle*, 130–1; Frame, *English Lordship*, 138–9; Phillips, 'Edward II and Ireland', 14–15. Geoffrey le Baker speaks only of Edward's attempt to reach Lundy, but says nothing about Ireland: *Le Baker*, 23. See also P. Dryburgh, 'The last refuge of a scoundrel?', in *The Reign of Edward II*, ed. G. Dodd & A. Musson (Woodbridge, Suffolk & Rochester, NY, 2006), 119–39, esp. 119, 134–9. Dr Dryburgh is more sceptical about Edward II's possible escape to Ireland, but does not appear to rule it out.

[338] *CCR, 1323–27*, 133–4; Frame, *English Lordship*, 165–8. In March and July 1326 Edward II had tried to contact Edmund and Hugh de Lacy, Irish magnates who had a potential claim to Mortimer's lordship of Trim and his other Irish lands. Nothing came of these approaches: Dryburgh, 'Last refuge', 132.

[339] These were likely destinations for any crossing of the Irish Sea beginning in the Bristol Channel.

[340] Phillips, 233–4; Frame, *English Lordship*, 169. The lordship of Carlow might also have been sympathetic, although it belonged to the earl of Norfolk, who had joined Isabella.

the archbishop of Dublin, who was on bad terms with both Despenser and the king, was in England; while the justiciar, John D'Arcy, a former retainer of the earl of Pembroke who had been a loyal supporter of the king, would almost certainly have been sympathetic to Edward.[341]

A strong indication of the possible attitude of the Dublin government can be found in the fact that, although Edward III was proclaimed king in England on 25 January 1327, the new king's authority was not proclaimed in Ireland until 13 May. D'Arcy had been replaced as justiciar and left Ireland twelve days earlier, on 1 May, but his successor, the earl of Kildare, found difficulty in asserting his authority for some time afterwards.[342] If Edward II really had been alive and well and living in Ireland, his position as the legitimate crowned king of England and lord of Ireland would have been extremely strong: no amount of manoeuvring in England by Mortimer and Isabella could have concealed this fact. Edward II could then have been removed from office only by another round of bloody civil war. From a base in Ireland Edward in his turn might have raised an army to restore his authority in England.[343] He would certainly have found allies in Wales,[344] and probably in Scotland[345] as well as in England itself.[346] Edward would also have had the money to pay an army, since it is known that the sum of £29,000 which had been brought from the treasury in the Tower of London when he left London on 2 October was formally delivered to him at Chepstow on 20 October, the day he put to sea.[347]

---

[341] Phillips, 261, 268.

[342] Frame, *English Lordship*, 139, 174–82. The inauguration in 1327 of Donal Mac Murrough as king of Leinster, the first such inauguration since the 12th century, may have been an Irish reaction to the events in England, based perhaps on a belief that the deposition of Edward II had removed the legitimacy of English rule in Ireland: J. Lydon, 'The impact of the Bruce invasion', *New History of Ireland*, ii, *Medieval Ireland, 1169–1534*, ed. A. Cosgrove (Oxford, 1987), 302.

[343] Frame, *English Lordship*, 138–40. The well informed Lanercost chronicler recorded the fears of Edward II's opponents 'that if the king could reach Ireland and gather an army there, he might cross to Scotland and, with the help of the Scots and the Irish, invade England': Frame, citing *Lanercost*, 256–7.

[344] Such as Gruffudd Llwyd in the north and Rhys ap Gruffudd in the south. Rhys was with Edward at Neath abbey on 11 Nov.: *Foedera*, II, i, 647.

[345] Rhys ap Gryffudd: Griffiths, *Principality*, 100; McNamee, 240. Another ally was the Scottish earl, Donald of Mar: McNamee, 240; Barrow, 252. A third potential ally may have been none other than Robert Bruce himself: Barrow, 252–5.

[346] The situation in England was probably far more fluid than the rapid fall of Edward II in the autumn of 1326 would seem to suggest. Although Edward II and Despenser had many enemies, not all of them were certain that exchanging the rule of the king and his favourite for that of Isabella and Mortimer was a good bargain. The hostilities between Henry, earl of Lancaster, and Mortimer in the winter of 1328–9, the execution of Edward II's half-brother the earl of Kent in March 1330, and Mortimer's own fall and execution in Oct. 1330 show how close England was to a renewed civil war. The persistent rumours that Edward II was still alive and might be restored to his throne only served to stir the pot even more vigorously.

[347] *CMR, 1326–27*, 36, no. 212. The sum of £10,000 which John Langton sent by water from Gloucester, and which was received at Chepstow by 17 Oct., was probably part of the

Edward's successful escape to Ireland would therefore have been fraught with all kinds of possibilities. But it was not to be. Instead of getting even as far as Lundy Island, the fugitives were held up by unfavourable winds in the Bristol Channel. Their prayers to St Anne went unanswered and they were forced to land at Cardiff on 25 October,[348] before seeking refuge in Despenser's almost impregnable fortress at Caerphilly. From here on 28 and 29 October Edward summoned the forces of South and West Wales to his aid in the hope of a last-minute rescue from his enemies.[349]

EDWARD IS DEPRIVED OF HIS AUTHORITY

Edward's flight into Wales had handed Isabella and her allies a political opportunity. By 18 October she had reached Bristol, whose defence had been entrusted to the earl of Winchester Hugh Despenser the Elder.[350] The city and castle surrendered after a brief siege and here on 26 October, at about the same time that Edward returned to dry land in Wales, the first stage in divesting him of his crown took place. A carefully worded statement placed on the Close Roll recorded that since Edward II had left his kingdom,[351] accompanied by Despenser and Baldock and other notorious enemies of the queen and her first-born son, and the kingdom had been left without government, the archbishop of Dublin, the bishops of Winchester,[352] Ely, Lincoln, Hereford and Norwich, and other prelates, the earls of Norfolk, Kent and Leicester,

---

overall total of £29,000 rather than an addition to it: Fryde, 189 & 267, n. 67. The 26 barrels, each containing £500 in silver pennies, which were later found among Edward II's possessions in Despenser's castle at Caerphilly near Cardiff, were probably the residue of the sum of £29,000: E 352/120, mm.39r, 39v (1 Ed. III): account of John de Langton, clerk, for the treasure, goods and chattels found at Caerphilly. Langton was the exchequer official who had delivered the £29,000 to Edward II on 20 Oct.

[348] SAL Ms. 122, p. 90; *Lanercost*, 256–7; *Murimuth*, 49; *Anonimalle*, 130–1; *Le Baker*, 23.
[349] *Foedera*, II, i, 646; *CPR, 1324–27*, 333–5.
[350] *Murimuth*, 47–8; *Anonimalle*, 130–1; *Flores*, 233. Edward learned of her arrival before Bristol on 18 Oct.: SAL Ms. 122, f. 90. On the way there she had taken Berkeley castle and restored it to its owner, Thomas de Berkeley, but not before her men had done considerable damage to some of its neighbouring properties. Ironically, Edward II's future prison was now ready: *Murimuth*, 48; Berkeley Castle Muniments, Select Rolls 41 (steward's account) & 42 (account of Ham manor).
[351] '*a regno suo Anglie . . . recedente*': *Foedera*, II, i, 646; *CCR, 1323–27*, 655–6.
[352] The archbishop of Canterbury meanwhile was keeping out of sight and dithering over whether to maintain his loyalty to the king or to join the queen: Wright, *The Church and the English Crown*, 273–4; Haines, *Stratford*, 175. William Melton, the archbishop of York, and apparently still loyal to Edward II, was engaged on business in the north. He did not take any role in Edward's deposition and did not attend Edward III's coronation in Feb. 1327, but he did perform the marriage of Edward III and Philippa of Hainault in York Minster in 1328: see article on Melton by R. Hill in the *Oxford DNB*.

Thomas Wake,[353] Henry de Beaumont, William la Zouche of Ashby, and other barons and knights, then at Bristol, in the presence of the queen and Edward duke of Aquitaine, and 'with the assent of the whole community of the realm there present', unanimously chose the duke to be guardian of the kingdom, and to rule and govern the kingdom in the name of the king and during his absence.[354] The young Edward put his new authority to use for the first time on 28 October when he summoned a parliament to meet at Westminster on 14 December 1326.[355] Edward II was still recognized as king and would formally resume his authority as soon as he returned to England, but the writing was on the wall.

It was now time for rewards and punishments, as appropriate. On 26 October Henry of Lancaster, already recognized as earl of Leicester since March 1324, was styled earl of Lancaster;[356] and on 27 October the Elder Despenser appeared before Sir William Trussell, who had been assigned to act as judge, the earls of Lancaster, Norfolk and Kent, Roger Mortimer, Thomas Wake and others to hear his sentence. In a procedure which was deliberately modelled on the trial of Thomas of Lancaster, Despenser was told that since he had made a law which allowed men to be condemned without being given any right of reply he would be treated in the same way. As an attainted traitor he had been banished and exiled, he had returned without being reconciled, and had usurped royal power and had advised the king to break the laws, namely in the putting to death of Thomas of Lancaster without cause; he was a robber, against whom the people cried out for vengeance; and he had treacherously advised the king to act against prelates of the Church. For his treason he was to be drawn; for robbery to be hanged; and for his acts against the Church to be beheaded; since he had dishonoured the rank of earl his head was to be taken to Winchester for display; and for having dishonoured the order of chivalry by hanging knights wearing coats quartered with their arms, he should be hanged in the same way and his arms destroyed for ever. And so he was executed on the public gallows at Bristol, the first victim of Isabella and Mortimer's revenge.[357]

---

[353] The arrival from the north of England of Thomas Wake, the earl of Leicester's son-in-law, Henry de Percy, and others showed that Edward II had no hope of support from that part of the country: *Murimuth*, 47. The earl of Surrey's attempt earlier in Oct. to gather forces in Yorkshire to help Edward had clearly failed: Fryde, 105, 189.

[354] *Foedera*, II, i, 646; *CCR, 1323–27*, 655–6. The duke began to exercise authority on the same day, using his own privy seal, since the king still had custody of the Great Seal.

[355] *PW*, II, ii, 350–66; *CCR, 1327–30*, 101–2; *RDP*, iii, 369–72. The legality of both the original summons of 28 Oct. and of the prorogation of 3 Dec. until 7 Jan. is highly questionable.

[356] His formal restoration to the earldom occurred on 3 Feb. 1327, as one of Edward III's first acts after his coronation.

[357] Trinity College Cambridge Ms. R.5.41, f. 123v; *Ann. Paul.*, 317–18 (which includes the French text of his judgment).

EDWARD'S LAST DAYS OF FREEDOM

Edward and Despenser could have stayed at Caerphilly, which was well supplied and capable of withstanding a long siege.[358] Instead after nearly a week they left on 2 or 3 November and moved westwards to the Cistercian abbey of Margam. After two days here Edward moved on again to the neighbouring Cistercian abbey of Neath, where his presence is recorded until at least 10 November.[359] After this there is no certainty as to his whereabouts until the fateful day, 16 November.

Edward's departure from Caerphilly has no obvious logic. He left behind him at least £13,000 in twenty-six barrels, each containing £500 in silver pennies, together with a large number of personal items, including his bed, drinking cup, armour and swords, privy seal and household records, and a vast amount of other material.[360] However he still had with him at least £6,000, the Great Seal and the rolls of chancery and other possessions, some of which he deposited in Neath abbey and in Neath castle, while some other items were left in the nearby Swansea castle.[361] While he was at Margam he placed the ports of Glamorgan in the care of four custodians, including a certain John Joseph, the master of the king's ship the *Goodyear of Cardiff*.[362] Edward might have left Caerphilly because his servants were deserting him;[363] or because of the failure of more of his Welsh allies to join him; or because even at this stage he still had hopes of escaping by sea to Ireland or indeed anywhere he could reach. More likely he was in despair. But even now he made one last attempt to avert final disaster. On 10 November while he was still at Neath abbey he appointed the abbot of Neath, Rhys ap Gruffudd the only Welsh ally to have reached him, his nephew Edward de Bohun, and two others to go to his 'most beloved consort', Isabella queen of England, and

---

[358] As it did under the command of the Younger Despenser's son, also named Hugh: *Historia Anglicana*, 183–4. The siege lasted from Dec. 1326 until 20 March 1327: W. Rees, *Caerphilly Castle and its Place in the Annals of Glamorgan* (Caerphilly, 1974), 81–4. The inventory of Edward's goods drawn up after the siege also shows that the castle contained £1,000 in cash belonging to Despenser and large quantities of weapons and food supplies belonging to him and the king: Rees, 109–21.

[359] For Edward's movements see *Itinerary*, ed. Hallam. There is also a useful account in R.W. Banks, 'King Edward II in South Wales', *Archaeologia Cambrensis*, 5th ser., iv (1887), 161–82.

[360] E 352/ 120, mm.39r, 39v (1 Ed. III); Rees, *Caerphilly Castle*, 84–6. The full details of all the items found after the fall of Caerphilly in 1327 are given in the inventory in E 352/ 120, mm.39r, 39v, printed in Rees, 109–21.

[361] Rees, *Caerphilly Castle*, 78–9. The money was found in Neath castle by the earl of Leicester, who retained it for several years: *CCR, 1327–30*, 445; W.M. Ormrod, 'Edward II at Neath Abbey, 1326', *Neath Antiquarian Society Trans. 1988–89* (Neath, 1988), 110–12.

[362] *CPR, 1324–7*, 336–7; Rees, *Caerphilly Castle*, 78.

[363] The ending of Edward's chamber account and of his daily household roll on 31 Oct. (SAL Ms. 122, p. 90; E 101/380/1, m.6) may signify, as Paul Doherty has suggested, that his household clerks had left him (Doherty (D.Phil.), 164), or that they had given up in despair.

Edward his first-born son on business especially concerning him and his kingdom.[364] It was his last recorded act as a free man.

There is nothing to suggest that the deputation ever departed or that it would have been received by Isabella and her son Edward if it had reached them. However, Isabella and Mortimer understood the dangers that might still arise if the king remained at large and had sent a search party to find him. This consisted of the earl of Leicester, who wanted to avenge his brother's death and was also lord of Monmouth and of Kidwelly in the Welsh March;[365] William la Zouche, Master Rhys ap Hywel newly released from prison in London, and two sons of Llywelyn Bren whose father had been treacherously executed by the Younger Despenser. Edward abruptly left Neath on 11 November, probably after discovering that he was being pursued and, accompanied by Despenser, Baldock and a few others, tried to make his way back to the relative safety of Caerphilly. It is likely that they followed a mountain road leading from Neath to Caerphilly via another of Despenser's castles at Llantrisant. On 16 November, after a stormy night, Edward was betrayed and captured by some Welshmen and taken to Llantrisant, before being handed over to the earl of Leicester. Despenser, Baldock and others were found in a nearby wood and taken to Hereford.[366] The place where Edward was made prisoner became known locally as Pant-y-brad or the Vale of Treachery.[367]

THE TRANSFER OF POWER

Edward was first taken to the earl of Leicester's castle of Monmouth, where the next stage of his humiliation took place. Since the young Edward's authority as guardian of the kingdom ceased with his father's return to England, on 20 November Isabella and her son sent the bishop of Hereford from Hereford to Monmouth to ask the king to give up the Great Seal. This scene took place in the presence of Henry of Lancaster, the archdeacon of Hereford and others. After some hesitation Edward II gave the seal to Sir William Blount, who delivered it to Isabella and her son at '*Martleye*' on 26 November. Four days later at Cirencester abbey Isabella and Edward appointed William Airmyn the bishop of Norwich as keeper of the Great Seal in the presence of Roger Mortimer and others, and he began to act as such, returning the seal to Isabella and Edward at the end of each day's work.[368] The chancery rolls which Edward II had left in Swansea castle were handed over to the queen at Hereford on

---

[364] *Foedera*, II, i., 647; *CPR, 1324–27*, 336.
[365] Kidwelly, with its powerful castle, was not far to the west of Neath.
[366] *Ann. Paul.*, 319; *Anonimalle*, 130–1; *Murimuth*, 49; *Flores*, 234; *Historia Anglicana*, i, 184.
[367] Rees, *Caerphilly Castle*, 80: it is not certain that this place-name is connected with Edward II's capture, but it is likely.
[368] *Foedera*, II, i, 646; *CCR, 1323–7*, 655. Possibly Martley in Worcestershire but more probably Much Marcle in Herefordshire: Haines, *The Church and Politics*, 166.

22 November,[369] while the records of the privy seal and chamber were found at Caerphilly when the castle fell in March 1327.[370] Even before the Great Seal had been recovered, steps had been taken to gain control of the other great organ of state, the exchequer. On 6 November John Stratford the bishop of Winchester was appointed treasurer by the guardian of the kingdom, arrived at the exchequer in London on 14 November with some ceremony and began to exercise his office three days later.[371] All that remained now was to decide what to do with Edward.

THE THEATRE OF VENGEANCE: THE TRAITORS ARE PUNISHED[372]

The Younger Despenser and the former chancellor Robert Baldock were taken to Hereford, where they were met by great crowds amidst much noise and vilification.[373] Edmund Fitz Alan, the earl of Arundel, who had been closely associated with Despenser and whose son had married Despenser's daughter, had earlier been arrested in Shropshire and brought to Hereford where he was beheaded on 17 November.[374] Baldock was accused of many of the same crimes as the Younger Despenser and also suffered public humiliation but, as a clerk, was spared execution. He was handed over to the custody of the bishop of Hereford but suffered a miserable fate. He was first taken to London and imprisoned in the bishop's house in the parish of St Mary Mounthaw. Since the bishop had no right to have a prison within the city of London, some of the Londoners used this as a pretext to seize Baldock, and threw him into the Fleet prison where he died a few months later.[375]

The worst fate was suffered by Despenser, after several days reflecting upon his inevitable fate and allegedly trying to starve himself to death.[376] On 24 November he was brought before William Trussell, the justice who had sentenced his father at Bristol, as well as the earls of Leicester, Norfolk and Kent, Roger Mortimer and other magnates.[377] As in the trials of his

---

[369] *CFR, 1319–27*, 422.

[370] Rees, *Caerphilly Castle*, 111.

[371] *CMR, 1326–27*, no. 832; Tout, *Place of the Reign*, 298; Davies, *Baronial Opposition*, 568, no. 49.

[372] Here I have borrowed from Matthew Strickland's description of the Feast of the Swans, 1306: Strickland, 'Treason, feud', 104.

[373] *Knighton*, 436.

[374] *Anonimalle*, 130–1. *Ann. Paul.*, 321; *Knighton*, 436. Arundel had also been concerned in the execution of Thomas of Lancaster and had allegedly caused harm to the queen during her absence: *Knighton*, 436.

[375] *Knighton*, 436–7; *Ann. Paul.*, 320–1: he died on 28 May 1327, but despite the odium in which he had been held his fellow canons of St Paul's received his body honourably and buried him in the canons' cemetery on 30 May.

[376] *Brut*, 239–40.

[377] *Ann. Paul.*, 319–20; *Gesta Edwardi*, 87; *Knighton*, 437.

father and Thomas of Lancaster before him, the charges and judgment were all of a piece: Despenser was allowed to say nothing in his defence.[378] He was accused of returning to England after his exile as a traitor in 1321; of robbing two galleys worth £60,000 and so dishonouring the king and his kingdom and hindering merchants; of urging the king to ride against the peers of the realm and other faithful subjects, in order to disinherit them, contrary to Magna Carta and the Ordinances; of bringing about the death of the earl of Hereford and two others at the battle of Boroughbridge; of usurping royal power and committing an act of tyranny by causing the death through a false record of Thomas of Lancaster, the cousin of the king and queen and of the king of France; of the execution of eighteen other named individuals and the imprisonment of others, including the Mortimers, Maurice de Berkeley and the Elder and Younger Hugh Audley, and the king's nephews the sons of the earl of Hereford; of treating widows and orphans tyrannically; of traitorously embracing royal power in company with the Elder Despenser and Robert Baldock and inducing the king to fight in Scotland with the loss of 20,000 men; of leaving the queen in danger from the Scots at Tynemouth priory and of endangering the king at Blackhow Moor; of destroying the franchises of the bishops of Hereford, Lincoln, Ely and Norwich; of falsely advising the king to create the Elder Despenser earl of Winchester and Andrew Harclay earl of Carlisle; of seizing the Cantref Mawr and other lands rightfully belonging to the crown; of seizing the lands which the king had assigned to the queen in dower and promoting discord between the king and queen; of sending a great sum of money to bring about the destruction of the queen and her son, the rightful heir to the kingdom, while they were in France trying to make peace and preventing their return to England; of forcing great and lesser men to swear to support him against their allegiance and the estate of the king and his crown; of usurping royal power by imprisoning others such as Henry de Beaumont who were not prepared to swear to support him; and of leading the king out of the realm after learning of the arrival of the queen and her son, risking the safety of the king and dishonouring him and his people, and feloniously taking the treasure of the kingdom and the Great Seal out of the realm. All the good people of the realm, great and small, rich and poor, regarded Despenser as a traitor and a robber: for which he was sentenced to be hanged. As a traitor he was to be drawn and quartered and the quarters distributed around the kingdom; as an outlaw he was to be beheaded; and for procuring discord between the king and the queen and other people of the kingdom he was sentenced to be disembowelled and his entrails burned; finally he was declared to be a traitor, tyrant and renegade.

---

[378] The charges and judgment are printed in Holmes, 'Judgement', 264–7; the known manuscript copies of the text are discussed ibid., 263. There is another printed version in *Knighton*, 437–41.

Despenser was then taken out for execution on a specially built gallows 50 feet high.[379] On the way to execution he wore a ' "chapelette of sharpe nettles" upon his head to reflect his crime of "accroaching royal power" ',[380] and a tunic with his coat of arms reversed, on the front of which was written the text of Psalm 51, beginning with the words '*Quid gloriaris in malicia qui potens est in iniquitate?*'[381] Despenser allegedly bore all the grisly rituals, including castration,[382] with patience, confessing his crimes to those who witnessed his death. Afterwards his head was carried to London where it arrived amid great rejoicing on 4 December. It was carried through Cheapside and impaled on London Bridge.[383]

EDWARD

By early December 1326 Edward II had been taken from Monmouth via Ledbury to the earl of Leicester's castle of Kenilworth,[384] where for the time being he stayed. He left behind him a kingdom of which he was still nominally the ruler, an orgy of bloodletting as the Despensers and others paid the price for their crimes, and a large quantity of personal possessions scattered over South Wales between Caerphilly, Neath and Swansea. Many of these possessions were recovered but goods worth over £3,000

---

[379] Trinity College Cambridge Ms. R.5.41, ff. 123v–124; *Historia Anglicana* 185; *Anonimalle*, 130–1; *Ann. Paul.*, 320. One of Despenser's knights, Simon de Reading, who had been captured with him and had been a particular enemy of the queen, was executed immediately after him on a gallows 10 feet lower: *Historia Anglicana*, 185.

[380] *Brut*, 240; *Knighton*, 436; Strickland, 'Treason, feud', 97 (similar imagery was used when Wallace and Simon Fraser were executed by Edward I in 1305 and 1306).

[381] 'Why do you glory in malice, you who are mighty in iniquity?' (Psalm 51 in the Vulgate; Psalm 52 in King James Bible): BL, Arundel Ms. 17, f. 40r. This comes from the annals of the Cistercian abbey of Newenham, near Axminster in Devon which provide valuable information on the events between 1326 and 1330. The annals appear in BL, Arundel Ms. 17, ff. 40–4, under the title *Memorabilia facta tempore Regis Edwardi secundi in Anglia*. The psalm is also referred to in *Historia Anglicana*, 185, and *Knighton*, 437.

[382] The cutting off of his genitals marked not only Despenser's own death but also the intended destruction of his family line. This can be compared with the mutilation of Simon de Montfort's corpse after the battle of Evesham in 1265 when his head and genitals were removed and sent as a trophy to the then Roger Mortimer's wife at Wigmore: Prestwich, *Edward I*, 51; Maddicott, *Simon de Montfort*, 342; Strickland, 'Treason, Feud', 87. 'Barbarous yet highly symbolic multiple punishments such as hanging, drawing, disembowelling, beheading and quartering as the potential penalty for treason' already existed by the 1320s and were not devised specially for Despenser in 1326, having been undergone for example by William Wallace and Simon Fraser: Strickland, 86–7. However, Despenser's castration was seen in a different light by the Hainault chronicler, Jean le Bel, who was in England in 1327 (though not it seems in 1326 when Despenser was executed) and wrote that Despenser's genitals were cut off because 'he was a heretic and a sodomite, even, it was said, with the king': *Le Bel*, 28.

[383] *Anonimalle*, 130–1; *Ann. Paul.*, 320; *Knighton*, 441.

[384] The 5 Dec. is the first date on which Edward can be placed at Kenilworth: *CPR, 1324–27*, 337.

fell victim to looters, especially from the lordship of Gower, and were never restored to the crown.³⁸⁵ Of the items lost in 1326 a few have been found in modern times: some silver pennies discovered in Swansea and at Neath abbey;³⁸⁶ a gold brooch, set with jewels and cameos found at Oxwich castle in Gower in 1968;³⁸⁷ and, most intriguing of all, the document recording the betrothal of the future Edward II and Isabella in 1303 which came to light in the 1830s and is now preserved by the West Glamorgan Archive Service, Swansea.³⁸⁸ That Edward should lose this of all documents at the time of his final separation from queen, crown and kingdom was somehow appropriate.

³⁸⁵ Inquests were held at Swansea on 3 Oct. 1328, 23 April 1331 and 15 June 1339; various individuals were named as suspects but the authorities were evidently only partially successful in recovering the items plundered in 1326: E 368/111, m.35d (13 Ed. III, 1338–9); E 159/115, mm.235d, 255 (13 Ed. III); E 159/107, m.350d (5 Ed. III, 1330–1); *List of Welsh Entries*, ed. Fryde, no. 922. For details of some of the items lost both at Neath and Swansea at this time and the crown's attempts to recover them see C.H. Hartshorne, 'Inquisition on the effects of King Edward II', *Archaeologia Cambrensis*, 3rd ser., ix (1863), 163–7; Rees, *Caerphilly Castle*, 92–5; Ormrod, 'Edward II at Neath Abbey', 110.

³⁸⁶ A hoard of 150 silver pennies, mostly from the reigns of Edward I and Edward II, was found while demolishing an old manor house at the Plas in Swansea in the 1850s, and two more small hoards of the same period, wrapped in cloth and evidently abandoned in a hurry, were found while 1956–7 in the ruins of Neath Abbey during restoration work: Rees, *Caerphilly Castle*, 95; Ormrod, 'Edward II at Neath Abbey', 110–11. Neither of course was necessarily left by Edward II himself but there is a strong possibility.

³⁸⁷ D. M. Williams, *Gower* (Cardiff, 1998), 36. The brooch is dated *c.* 1320–40, and the cameos to *c.* 1250. See Alexander & Binski, eds, in *Age of Chivalry*, no. 653, p. 456 (with a colour photograph). While there is no certainty that the brooch belonged to Edward II, its date is about right and one of the men suspected of plundering Edward II's possessions was Robert de Penres, from Penrice, which is very close to Oxwich castle.

³⁸⁸ It was formerly on display in the Royal Institution of South Wales, Swansea (now the Swansea Museum). The document is in the form of letters patent of the count of Évreux, duke of Burgundy and duke of Brittany, dated 20 May 1303 and rehearsing the details concerning the proposed marriage. It seems to be the counterpart of the letters patent of the English envoys. It was discovered when a local physician, Dr Nichol of Swansea, was given it in lieu of payment by a patient who produced it in a small box, containing this and other documents, from a hiding-place in the thatch. It was presented to the Royal Institution by Dr Nichol shortly after it opened in 1835. See Francis, 'Original contract'; R.W. Banks, 'The marriage contract of King Edward II', *Archaeologia Cambrensis*, 5ᵗʰ ser., iv (1887), 53–7; Rees, *Caerphilly Castle*, 95–6.

Chapter 11

DEPOSITION AND DEATH

A CHRISTMAS CELEBRATION

Isabella, her son Edward, Roger Mortimer and their followers spent Christmas 1326 at Wallingford castle, once the property of Piers Gaveston, earl of Cornwall and more recently the prison of Maurice de Berkeley. Here they were joined by Isabella's younger son John of Eltham and a party of Londoners.[1] This was no mere social visit since John Stratford the bishop of Winchester, the newly appointed treasurer, and the earl of Leicester's son-in-law Thomas Wake had already met the mayor and aldermen of London on business 'touching the king':[2] Edward II, who spent his own Christmas at Kenilworth 'in great sadness',[3] was the unseen presence at the festivities.

Two big problems had to be addressed by the gathering at Wallingford. One was Isabella's future relations with her husband. The tone of her reply in February 1326 to the archbishop of Canterbury's plea for her to come home from France suggests that she still had a strong attachment to Edward.[4] However, even supposing that she was not actually Roger Mortimer's mistress, she could hardly return to Edward as his wife, for this in itself would imply that Edward still had some status as king and make it almost impossible to remove him from the throne.[5] Nonetheless her failure to do so required some public explanation. According to Adam Orleton's later defence of his conduct, composed in 1334, comments about Isabella's failure to visit her husband were already being made at Wallingford, and presumably elsewhere, in December 1326. The question was discussed there by the archbishop of Canterbury,[6] the bishops of Winchester and Norwich, the

---

[1] Trinity College Cambridge Ms. R.5.41, f. 124v; *Anonimalle*, 132–3.
[2] *Ann. Paul.*, 318; *CMPR*, 17; Williams, *Medieval London*, 297; *Calendar of the Letter-Books . . . : E*, ed. Sharpe, 215.
[3] '*In ingenti tristitia*': *Flores*, 235.
[4] *Historiae Anglicanae Scriptores Decem*, ed. Twysden, col. 2766 (*recte* 2767–8). See the discussion of this letter in Ch.10.
[5] Cf. Haines, *The Church and Politics*, 176.
[6] After his flight from London on 15 Oct. Reynolds had remained in Canterbury or other places in Kent, keeping his distance from the turmoil in London and from the events in Oxford, Bristol and Hereford. However, he ventured back as far as Lambeth on 23 Dec. and was at Newington near Wallingford on the 29th: Wright, *The Church and the English Crown*, 410. The exact process by which Reynolds decided or was induced finally to desert Edward II and to throw in his lot with the new regime is unknown: cf. Haines, *Stratford*, 175.

earls of Leicester and Kent, and others and it was decided that in order to protect Isabella's reputation Orleton should deliver a sermon explaining the reasons. This he did, 'neither adding to nor diminishing what was laid upon me', stating that Edward's cruelty to Isabella made it impossible for her to return to him.[7] Orleton later vigorously defended himself against the charge that he had said that Edward 'carried a knife in his hose to kill queen Isabella, and that if he had no other weapon he would crush her with his teeth', admitting only to saying that Edward's anger was increased by Despenser's death.[8] However, if the Historia Roffensis is to be believed, during the parliament of January 1327 Orleton, with the support of other bishops, did then say that if the queen were to return to the king, he would kill her.[9]

Even this did not end Isabella's attachment to Edward. Again according to Orleton, in April 1327 Isabella told a council held at Stamford that she was ready and willing to visit her husband but was told firmly by the prelates and magnates present that it was out of the question.[10] Although Orleton was abroad at the time, on a mission to Avignon to explain to the pope the recent dramatic events in England,[11] his account is generally borne out by the mandate of the archbishop of Canterbury Walter Reynolds to the English bishops on 5 May 1327. Reynolds was anxious to quell the rumours about Isabella's failure to return to her husband, stating that until the kingdom was fully at peace it would be dangerous for her to do so.[12] Edward was probably desperate to see both his wife and his children,[13] but in the light of the archbishop's mandate Adam Murimuth's claim that Isabella hypocritically refused to see him, while sending Edward delicacies and friendly letters, is not believable.[14] It was of course very much in the interests of those who had gained most by Edward's deposition, especially Roger Mortimer of Wigmore, that once in prison he should stay there without any possibility of restoration or reconciliation, but these facts also offer some defence to Mortimer against the charge in 1330 that he 'falsely and maliciously initiated discord' between Edward and Isabella.[15] If Mortimer

[7] *Historiae Anglicanae Scriptores Decem*, ed. Twysden, cols 2767–8; *Chartulary*, ed. Goodman, 106–7. Interestingly, Orleton makes no mention of Roger Mortimer, who was certainly present at Wallingford.

[8] *Chartulary*, ed. Goodman, 105–7; *Historiae Anglicanae Scriptores Decem*, ed. Twysden, col. 2767.

[9] BL, Cotton Ms. Faustina B.V, f. 49: '*si Regina Regi adhereret occideretur ab eo.*'

[10] *Historiae Anglicanae Scriptores Decem*, ed. Twysden, cols 2767–8; *Chartulary*, ed. Goodman, 106–7.

[11] Haines, *The Church and Politics*, 228.

[12] R.M. Haines, 'The Stamford Council of April 1327', *EHR*, cxxii (2007), 141–8, esp. 145–8.

[13] *Brut*, i, 252.

[14] *Murimuth*, 52.

[15] 'Also, the said Roger falsely and maliciously initiated discord between the father of our lord the king and the queen his consort, and he caused her to believe that if she came to him he would have killed her with a knife or murdered her in another manner. Because of which, for that reason, and by his other subtle scheming, he caused the said queen not to come to her said lord, to the great dishonour of the king and of the queen his mother, and

did so, he was merely repeating and perhaps exaggerating a commonly held opinion of the time.[16]

PLANS FOR EDWARD

The other and even bigger question raised during the Christmas council at Wallingford was what to do with Edward II. Now that he had finally been separated from the Younger Despenser he could in principle have been restored to some semblance of power. But Edward's ability to escape control and to exploit any evidence of disunity among his opponents had been shown too often before. The tensions that may already have existed between Roger Mortimer and Henry of Lancaster and which almost led to a renewal of civil war in 1328–9 would probably have surfaced even sooner if Edward II had been freed from Kenilworth. It is unlikely that anyone during that Christmas at Wallingford ever seriously considered this option.

Although Edward II had allegedly already been threatened with deposition both in 1310 and 1321,[17] achieving this with some semblance of legality and consent was far more difficult than removing him from the company of his wife. This was an action for which there was no precedent since 1066 and consequently no procedure. According to a late version of Froissart's *Chroniques* those present at the Wallingford council were each asked whether Edward should be put to death or imprisoned. The first to be asked was Jean de Beaumont, the brother of the count of Hainault and commander of the mercenary troops who had assisted Isabella's invasion, who replied that Edward was king of England and, although he had acted badly, he had done so as the result of bad advice; it was not for Jean or anyone else to condemn Edward to death. He advised that Edward should be put in a castle, with proper regard to his rank, there to live in reasonable comfort for the rest of his life, and in the hope that he would be able to make amends. All those present accepted this advice and Edward was spared death.[18] It is improbable that Jean de Beaumont's role was quite as prominent as Froissart later made out, or that there were no voices calling

---

perhaps the great damage of all the realm in future, which God forbid': *PROME*, Parliament of Nov. 1330, C 65/2, item 1.

[16] The claim that Edward would have killed Isabella, and even their son, if they had come to visit him in prison, was also repeated by the author of the *Brut* chronicle: *Brut*, i, 252–3.

[17] *Vita*, 18–21, 192–3.

[18] *Froissart*, 85: this is from the fourth redaction of Froissart's chronicle. One of Froissart's patrons was Jean de Beaumont (d. 1356) who was able to tell him about his role in events in England nearly 30 years before. Although the early part of Froissart's chronicle was based very closely on the work of the Liège chronicler Jean le Bel who was in England in 1327 and acquired a great deal of first-hand information, this story does not appear in le Bel's account. On Jean le Bel (c. 1290–1370) and Froissart (? 1337–c. 1404) see the articles by J. Vale and M.C.E. Jones in the *Oxford DNB*.

for Edward's execution, but it is clear that everyone agreed on at least one thing: Edward II had to be removed from the throne.

The first step in detaching Edward's subjects from their allegiance and preparing the way for the act of deposition which followed also formed part of the bishop of Hereford's sermon delivered at Wallingford. Echoing the sermon he had preached at Oxford in October, when he had publicly explained the reasons for the return to England of Isabella and her son, Orleton allegedly accused Edward of being both a tyrant and a sodomite.[19] Although Orleton subsequently denied having used these words about Edward II, or inciting his subjects to rebellion, claiming instead that he was referring to the Younger Despenser,[20] even their indirect use would be enough to suggest to his hearers that Edward was not a fit person to be king. Accusations or suggestions of sodomy, which was considered tantamount to heresy, were a familiar method of blackening the character of one's enemies: they were used, for example, by Philip IV of France against both Pope Boniface VIII and the Templars, and in the previous generation had been used against Philip's own father Philip III. They were also employed in 1311 by James II of Aragon against one of his subjects, the count of Ampurias.[21] The hint, if such it was, that Edward engaged in unnatural vice was readily picked up and disseminated by chroniclers, especially those on the continent.[22]

---

[19] '*tyrannus et sodomita*': see Mortimer, 'Sermons of sodomy', 50–2; and Ormrod, 'The sexualities of Edward II', 39. However, the articles of his deposition in 1327 did not accuse him of either tyranny or sodomy. Orleton's alleged remarks about Edward II are contained in the charges laid against Orleton by John Prickehare in April 1334 as part of the attempt to prevent his translation from Worcester to the diocese of Winchester: *The Register of John de Grandison, Bishop of Exeter*, ed. F.C. Hingeston-Randolph, iii (London, 1899), 1542 (this has the full Latin text of the charges, including the offending words '*tyrannus et sodomita*'); *Chartulary*, ed. Goodman, 104–5. There is a new edition of Prickehare's charges in R.M. Haines, 'Looking back in anger', *EHR*, cxvi (2001), 398–404.

[20] *Historiae Anglicanae Scriptores Decem*, ed. Twysden, cols 2763–4; *Chartulary*, ed. Goodman, 106. Out of delicacy perhaps, Twysden inserted 'etc' after the word '*tyrannus*' and made no reference to sodomy, which is similarly absent from Goodman's edition of the Winchester cartulary. In his refutation of the charges against him, Orleton also spoke of Edward's immoderate and inordinate love for Despenser: '*quem Rex immoderato et inordinato amore dilexit*': *Historiae Anglicanae Scriptores Decem*, col. 2767. This detail is also omitted by Goodman.

[21] Mortimer, 'Sermons of Sodomy', 52–3; Brown, 'The prince is father of the king', 525–6; J.A. Brundage, 'The politics of sodomy: Rex v. Pons Hugh de Ampurias (1311)', in *In Iure Veritas: Studies in Canon Law in Memory of Schafer Williams*, ed. S.B. Bowman & B.E. Cody (Cincinnati, 1991), 3–10; see also the Introduction to this book. The very interesting discussion of Edward II's sexuality by C.T. Wood in 'Queens, queans and kingship', in Wood, *Joan of Arc and Richard III* (Oxford, 1988), 12–17, does not allow for the possibility that his character was deliberately blackened in 1326–7. Sodomitical acts were also among the charges laid against Richard II in 1399: Evans, *The Death of Kings* (London, 2003), 130–1, 245.

[22] See, e.g., *Chronographia Regum Francorum*, ed. Moranville, 285, under the year 1326: '*sese sodomitane immundicie, ut sibi imponebatur, tradidit, innaturalem venerem naturali libidini preferens*'; *Le Bel*, 28, writing about the cutting off of Despenser's genitals at his execution, '*pour tant qu'il estoit herites et sodomites, ainsi comme on disoit, et mesmement du roy mesmes*'. Jean le Bel's opinion was quoted almost verbatim by his successor and fellow Hainaulter, Jean Froissart: *Froissart*,

It is likely that the Wallingford council took two further significant actions: firstly the composition of the articles of deposition, or at least of a first draft of the articles which were to be read out by the archbishop of Canterbury in Westminster Hall on 13 January;[23] and secondly the decision to send two bishops, the bishop of Hereford and either the bishop of Winchester or London, to Kenilworth to request Edward II's attendance at the parliament[24] which was due to begin on 7 January.[25]

SCENES AT WESTMINSTER

On 31 December Isabella and her followers left Wallingford for London, where they arrived on 4 January and were received with great solemnity by the Londoners.[26] Nonetheless the chaos and anarchy in London were still of very recent memory and precautions were taken against any repetition.

87–8. The only example I have found among English writers is the chronicle of Meaux abbey in Yorkshire which was composed before 1399: '*Ipse quidem Edwardus in vitio sodomitico nimium delectabat, et fortuna ac gratia omni suo tempore carere videbatur*': *Melsa*, 355.

[23] *French Chron*, 57; *Historiae Anglicanae Scriptores Decem*, ed. Twysden, cols 2765–6 (where the full text of the articles is given); *Chartulary*, ed. Goodman, 106 (where only the opening lines are given). According to Orleton's later defence, the decision of the prelates and magnates that the king should be removed was embodied in a document drawn up by John Stratford the bishop of Winchester and set down in writing by Stratford's secretary and public notary William Mees. Given the nature of the debate at Wallingford, it is very unlikely that the composition of the articles would have been delayed until after the beginning of parliament at Westminster on 7 Jan.

[24] *Literae Cantuarienses*, i, ed. Sheppard, 204–5: a letter from Henry of Eastry, prior of Christ Church, Canterbury, to the archbishop, which indicates that a delegation had been sent before the start of parliament, but does not name the two bishops. The Lanercost chronicle names them as Orleton and Stratford: *Lanercost*, 257; while the so-called Pipewell chronicle names them as Orleton and Stephen Gravesend of London: BL, Cotton Ms. Julius A.1, f. 56, printed in M.V. Clarke, *Medieval Representation and Consent* (London, 1936; repr. New York, 1964), 194. Since they returned from Kenilworth on 12 Jan., it is most unlikely that they had departed only on the 7th, the day parliament formally began, and far more probable that they left from Wallingford at the same time that Isabella left there for London: cf. Valente, 'Deposition', 855.

[25] There is no record of the writs of summons issued on 28 Oct. in the name of Edward II's son as guardian of the kingdom for a meeting of parliament on 14 Dec. On 3 Dec. 1326 further writs were issued at Ledbury in the name of Edward II, postponing the meeting of the parliament 'for certain necessary causes and utilities' to Westminster on 7 Jan. 1327, and recording the alleged basis on which the original summons was issued. Edward II is recorded as stating that, through the agency of his 'most beloved consort Isabella queen of England' and of Edward his 'firstborn son keeper of the kingdom', he himself being outside the kingdom, he had wished to hold a parliament at Westminster on 14 Dec. to have a '*colloquium*' and '*tractatum*' with those present 'upon various affairs touching himself and the state of his kingdom': *PW*, II, ii, 350–66; *CCR, 1327–30*, 101–2; *RDP*, iii, 369–72. Since in reality Edward II did not summon the parliament which met in his name and during which he lost his throne, the legality of both the original summons of 28 Oct. and of the prorogation of 3 Dec. is highly questionable.

[26] Trinity College Cambridge Ms. R.5.41, f. 124r; *Anonimalle*, 132–3.

On 30 December every citizen was required to take an oath by 6 January to keep the peace, and on 2 January orders were issued forbidding anyone to bear arms in the city, except for the guards appointed by the mayor and aldermen and the queen's escort of men-at-arms from Hainault.[27]

The bishop of Hereford and his colleague returned to Westminster on 12 January, with the news that Edward adamantly refused to attend, saying that he did not wish to venture among enemies and traitors.[28] If Edward believed that his absence invalidated the assembly at Westminster as a parliament, whose legality was in any case doubtful, he underestimated the determination of his opponents. They may indeed have preferred Edward's absence to the embarrassment of having in their midst a crowned and anointed monarch whose very presence might pose awkward questions about the legitimacy of their proceedings, as well as attracting sympathy. It was no secret, for example, that the bishop of Rochester and some other bishops were deeply unhappy at the turn of events.[29] There was also the proximity of two papal envoys, William of Laudun the archbishop of Vienne, who already had long experience of Edward II and English affairs, and Master John de Grandison the archdeacon of Nottingham. They had arrived in England on 10 December 1326, nominally to assist in making peace between England and France, but had they been given the chance they might also have tried to mediate between Edward II and his enemies and to save him from deposition.[30]

In Edward II's absence matters now proceeded quickly. On 12 January, the day of his return from Kenilworth, the bishop of Hereford asked those present whether they wanted Edward II to remain as king or whether he should be replaced by his son, Edward duke of Aquitaine. It appears that there were differing opinions on this, so parliament was dismissed until the following morning, 13 January, to allow for further thought and persuasion.[31]

---

[27] *CPMR*, ii, 18.

[28] *Lanercost*, 257. For what follows I am greatly indebted to the sequence of events worked out by Dr Claire Valente in 'Deposition'. Her chronology is generally both clearer and more convincing than, for example, that of Haines, in *Stratford*, 179–86 (who appears to conflate the events of 7 and 13 Jan. and also places the critical sermons by the bishops of Hereford and Winchester and the archbishop of Canterbury on three separate days, 13, 14, and 15 Jan., following the Lanercost chronicle); and Fryde, 196–200 (who has the sermons of the bishop of Winchester and archbishop of Canterbury occurring *after* the return of the delegation sent to Kenilworth to renounce homage rather than *beforehand*); Williams, *Medieval London*, 298. My main difference from Dr Valente's chronology is in placing the Guildhall oaths *after* rather than *before* the proceedings in parliament on 13 Jan.

[29] BL, Cotton Ms. Faustina B.V, f. 49v.

[30] The envoys were kept at Canterbury and did not reach London until 4 Jan. Although there is no record of their participation in the events that followed, and they left England on 26 Jan., they would certainly have been able to inform the pope of Edward II's fate: *Foedera*, II, i, 647; Haines. *Stratford*, 177.

[31] BL, Cotton Ms. Faustina B.V, f. 49r, 49v. Dr Valente is surely correct in placing this address by Orleton on 12 Jan., when the real business of the parliament began, rather than on 7 Jan., the official opening day of the assembly, as implied in the

At this point the mayor and citizens of London intervened, either on their own account or in concert with Edward II's opponents, by writing to the prelates and magnates asking them to ally with them, to swear to maintain Isabella and her son, and 'to crown the latter, and to depose his father for frequent offences against his oath and his Crown'.[32] On the evening of 12 January there was a meeting of prelates and magnates, probably in Westminster Hall, at which the articles of accusation against Edward II were either drawn up or an existing draft refined, and at which it was agreed that Edward should no longer reign and that he should be be replaced by his son.[33]

Up to this point it is possible to be reasonably confident about the sequence of events. However, apart from the formal proclamation of Edward II's 'abdication' and Edward III's accession in London on 24 January,[34] there is a distinct lack of any official record of the events connected with the end of Edward II's reign in January 1327. The Parliament Roll for January–February 1327 records only the petitions which were presented when parliament resumed in February after the coronation of Edward III. Although there are many references to current events, there is no direct explanation of how Edward III had come to succeed his father. Edward II is referred to only in euphemisms such as 'Edward his father, when he was king'.[35] Even the six articles of accusation against Edward II do not now survive in any official form, although they may once have so existed.[36] One official or quasi-official document is the *Forma deposicionis Regis Edwardi post Conquestum Secundi*, which is preserved in a Canterbury chronicle contained in Trinity College Cambridge Ms. R.5.41. It has been plausibly argued that the document was composed by a supporter of Queen Isabella

---

Historia Roffensis: Valente, 'Deposition', 855, n. 4; 858, n. 2. However, her argument that the parliament was dismissed until the following afternoon is incorrect. The reference in the Historia Roffensis to the meeting reassembling '*hora tercia*' after everyone had had food and drink clearly means the morning, at about 9 a.m.: cf. Mortimer, *The Greatest Traitor*, 167, 287, n. 9.

[32] *CPMR*, 11–12; Valente, 'Deposition', 855–6.

[33] The meeting is described by Jean le Bel: *Le Bel*, 29; and is referred to in the *Forma deposicionis*.

[34] *CCR, 1327–30*, 1. The full French text from the Close Roll is given in *Foedera*, II, ii, 683, and in *Select Documents*, 38.

[35] See *PROME*, Parliament of Jan. 1327, C 65/1, *passim*.

[36] For the text of the articles of deposition see *Historiae Anglicanae Scriptores Decem*, ed. Twysden, col. 2765–6 (where the full text of the articles is given); *Chartulary*, ed. Goodman, 106 (where only the opening lines are given). The articles are more conveniently published in *Foedera*, II, i, 650, and in *Select Documents*, 37–8, using the text derived from Lambeth Palace Ms. 1213. A better text, drawn from the *Winchester Chartulary*, is now available in Valente, 'Deposition', 878–81. One significant correction in interpretation is in clause 6, where the meaning of the word '*deguerpist*' is shown to be 'abandoned' (because Edward had left England for Wales, and probably intended going to Ireland) rather than 'neglected' or 'stripped'. An official version of the articles apparently existed in the time of Richard II, when it was used by his opponents in 1386–7, and was probably destroyed by Richard after his coup of 1397: Valente, 856–7.

and Roger Mortimer and designed to provide a description of events which would make it appear that Edward II had voluntarily resigned the throne instead of acting under the threat of force. Edward III's accession was presented as a substitution for the inadequate rule of his father. The author of the *Forma deposicionis* recorded only one deputation to Edward II at Kenilworth and not two, and implied that Edward II had already consented to his replacement by his son before the events at Westminster on 13 January. The second visit to Kenilworth was therefore made redundant and was not mentioned.[37] Nonetheless, if used with care, the *Forma deposicionis* is still a valuable source.

According to the *Forma deposicionis* Roger Mortimer of Wigmore was deputed by the gathering of prelates and magnates on the evening of 12 January to announce the results of their deliberations to those assembled in parliament[38] when they reconvened in Westminster Hall on the following day, as the bishop of Hereford had asked them to do.[39] Then followed a speech from Roger Mortimer and three sermons, by the bishops of Hereford and Winchester and the archbishop of Canterbury, and including the reading by the archbishop of the set of six articles, agreed on the night of 12 January, outlining Edward's defects as king.[40] Roger Mortimer cleverly told the gathering that he was not speaking for himself but on behalf of the magnates who had unanimously agreed that the king should be removed from the government of the realm because he was inadequate (*insufficiens*), and because by accepting evil counsel he was the destroyer of the magnates and the Church, in breach of his coronation oath. Therefore Edward's first-born son the duke of Aquitaine should reign in his place if the people gave their approval (*si populus preberet assensum*). Thomas Wake, Henry of Lancaster's son-in-law, then replied in a clearly prearranged move and, raising his hands, announced that so far as he was concerned Edward should not remain king (*dico pro me numquam*

---

[37] Trinity College Cambridge Ms. R.5.41 is a late 14th-century continuation of the chronicle of Gervase of Canterbury down to the year 1385. It is particularly valuable for the events of 1320–2 and later: see Phillips, 206–22, *passim*. The *Forma deposicionis*, which is contained on ff. 125–6, and is followed by William Trussell's renunciation of homage, is clearly a separate document which had come into the hands of the continuator, who was probably working at Canterbury. Given the important role played by the archbishop of Canterbury in the events of 1327, it is not surprising that a copy of the document should have been preserved there. Another copy may also have reached St Albans and been known to the St Albans chronicler, Thomas Walsingham: *Historia Anglicana*, 186; Valente, 'Deposition', 872. For a printed text see Fryde, App. 2, 233–5. There are however some errors in Fryde's transcription: e.g., '*rundit*' and '*rundebat*' for '*respondit*' and '*respondebat*', and three *Fiats* at the end of the document instead of two: Valente, 871, n. 3. Another transcript of the document is published, together with the Historia Roffensis (BL, Cotton Ms. Faustina B.V) account of Edward II's deposition, in Haines, *King Edward II*, App. A, 343–5. For discussions of the *Forma deposicionis* see Valente, 871–5; Haines, *Stratford*, 184–6.

[38] *Forma deposicionis*, Fryde, 233; Valente, 'Deposition', 856.

[39] BL, Cotton Ms. Faustina B.V, ff. 49r, 49v (Historia Roffensis).

[40] *Forma deposicionis*, Fryde, 233; Valente, 'Deposition', 858–9.

regnabit). Mortimer was followed by Adam Orleton the bishop of Hereford, who took as his theme the text from chapter 11 of the Book of Proverbs (*ubi non est gubernator populus corruet*) ('Where there is no governor the people shall fall').[41] He described his mission to Kenilworth and how he had spoken frankly to the king. He had addressed the king, citing the text, *audi preces populi tui* ('hear the prayers of thy people'),[42] and speaking of the great and intolerable defects in Edward's government, his adherence to evil and treacherous counsel, his destruction of the magnates and his loss of the lands which his father had left him. For these reasons the prelates and magnates wished Edward's son to rule in his place. Although, according to Orleton, the king had replied that he had followed the counsel ordained for him by the magnates, he showed himself penitent for the misdeeds which the envoys explained to him, and the homages of the magnates were annulled.[43] This version of events, as described in the *Forma deposicionis*, may well reflect words exchanged with the king when Orleton was sent to Kenilworth to try to persuade Edward to attend parliament, but the implication that Edward II had accepted the transfer of sovereignty to his son even before the dramatic events of 13 January is to say the least doubtful, and as already indicated suggests that the *Forma deposicionis* is not an impartial record.[44] Orleton was followed by John Stratford the bishop of Winchester who preached on the text *caput meum doleo* ('my head aches'),[45] arguing that since the king was as it were the head of the kingdom, any weakness in the king produced a weakness in the kingdom; expounding on the many *indecencia*[46] and evils which had been brought upon the Church and the kingdom; and concluding that the magnates were unanimous that the king should be replaced by his

---

[41] Proverbs, 11: 14. Given as ch. 13 in the *Forma deposicionis*, Fryde, 233–4.

[42] Paralipomenon II, ch. 6, verse 21 (i.e. Second Book of Chronicles).

[43] *Forma deposicionis*, Fryde, 234. *Lanercost*, 257, has another text for Orleton's sermon, from Ecclesiastes 10: 3, *Rex insipiens perdet populum suum*, in which he dwelt on the king's unwise and foolish behaviour, and his puerilities, 'if they can be called such' (*si tamen puerilia dici debent*). The Historia Roffensis records a different text from the same chapter of the Bible: *vae terra cuius Rex puer est* (10 : 16), an unfortunate choice perhaps since the replacement for Edward II was still only fourteen years old: BL, Cotton Ms. Faustina B.V, f. 49v.

The Lanercost chronicler also states that the three sermons were delivered on three successive days, which seems unlikely given the way in which the excitement of the occasion was deliberately built up by those who orchestrated it: see Valente, 'Deposition', 858–60; cf. Haines, *Stratford*, 183.

[44] The contents of this sermon are more appropriate to the second mission to Kenilworth after 13 Jan. and the withdrawal there of homage from Edward II, rather than to the events of 13 Jan. when the withdrawal of homage was signalled but had not yet occurred. See Valente, 'Deposition', 873, and more generally 871–5. Perhaps the text given in the Lanercost chronicle and referred to in the Historia Roffensis represents the actual sermon delivered by Orleton on 13 Jan.

[45] 2 Kings, 4 : 19; *Forma deposicionis*, Fryde, 234. This text is confirmed in *Lanercost*, 258, and in the Historia Roffensis, BL, Cotton Ms. Faustina B.V, f. 49v.

[46] 'improprieties' or 'things that were unfitting' rather than 'indecencies' in the modern sense.

first-born son in the government of the kingdom, provided that this decision of the prelates and magnates was supported by the people. With this, Thomas Wake stretched out his arms and asked the people if they consented to this decision, and with a loud voice they acclaimed it. Speaking in French, Walter Reynolds the archbishop of Canterbury then began to address the people, taking as his text the proverbial saying *Vox populi vox dei* ('the voice of the people is the voice of God'): 'Dearly beloved, you know that for a long time you have been afflicted by various oppressions on the part of the king and his evil councillors; and you have called upon God for a remedy. Now it appears that your voice has been heard, since by the unanimous consent of all the magnates the lord King Edward has been deprived of the government of the kingdom and his son put in his place, if you consent to this unanimously. He [i.e. the young Edward] has accepted the counsel of the wise men of the kingdom, after the inadequacy (*insufficiencia*) of the king, as outlined earlier [i.e. in the articles of deposition], and the offences he had brought upon the Church and kingdom were explained to him.' The whole people with one accord then raised their hands again and shouted '*Fiat, fiat, Amen*'.[47] After which the young Edward was presented to his future subjects, with the words 'Behold your king', followed by the singing of 'Glory, laud and honour'.[48]

THE ARTICLES OF DEPOSITION

At some point in the proceedings on 13 January, either during the archbishop of Canterbury's concluding sermon or, more probably, at an earlier stage in the day, the articles of deposition were presented to the assembly.[49] The document was a simple one, without any of the circumstantial detail which had accompanied the charges against, for example, the Younger Despenser. Edward II was accused of being personally incapable of

---

[47] *Forma deposicionis*, Fryde, 234: not three *Fiats*: Valente, 'Deposition', 871, n. 3. The archbishop's text is confirmed by *Lanercost*, 258, and BL, Cotton Ms. Faustina B.V, f. 49v. My translation of the archbishop's words differs in places from that in Fryde, 200, especially in the emphasis that consent was still to be sought from all those in attendance at parliament and had not already been obtained; and that the young Edward had accepted the advice of the wise men of the kingdom.

[48] '*Ecce Rex vester*'; '*Gloria laus et honor*': BL, Cotton Ms. Faustina B.V, f. 49v; Valente, 'Deposition', 859. Although the chronicle speaks of homage being performed to Edward, this cannot have been the case since homage had not yet been withdrawn from his father: cf. Valente, 859. The young Edward was apparently not prepared to accept the crown while his father remained unwilling to give it up: *Historiae Anglicana*, 186.

[49] References to the king's failings in the reports of the sermons given on 13 Jan. suggest that the audience had already heard the articles. The words '*ut prius*' towards the end of the archbishop's sermon also suggest that the articles had previously been read out. The *Forma deposicionis* does not specifically refer to the reading of the articles by the archbishop; the French chronicle of London, the Anonimalle chronicle, and the Pipewell chronicle account all record that the archbishop read the articles while not saying at what point in the proceedings he did so: *French Chroni.*, 57; *Anonimalle*, 132–3; Clarke, *Medieval Representation*, 194.

governing, of allowing himself to be led and governed by others who advised him badly, and of refusing to remedy these defects when asked to do so by the great and wise men of the kingdom or allowing anyone else to do so; of devoting himself to unsuitable work and occupations, while neglecting the government of his kingdom; of exhibiting pride, covetousness and cruelty; of losing, for lack of good government, the kingdom of Scotland, and other lands and lordships in Gascony and Ireland (which had been left to him in peace by his father) and of forfeiting the friendship of the king of France and of many other great men; of destroying the Church and imprisoning churchmen, and of putting to death, imprisoning, exiling and disinheriting the great men of his kingdom; of failing to observe his coronation oath through the influence of his evil counsellors; of abandoning his kingdom and doing all in his power to cause the loss both of it and of his people; and of being incorrigible and without hope of improvement. All of which was said to be so notorious that it could not be denied.

Even allowing for the vagueness of these charges and for the simplistic nature of some, such as his alleged personal responsibility for the failure to hold Scotland (which had been far from peaceful in 1307) and for the war in Ireland (which in reality was the scene in 1318 of one of the few definite English military successes), Edward II was depicted as an incompetent ruler and as a man who could not command any respect, whose government in the last resort could only be ended, not mended. He was not however, and very significantly, described as a tyrant. Although the word was freely used of the Younger Despenser,[50] it was not employed for Edward II[51] any more than it was applied to Richard II in 1399.[52]

---

[50] E.g., in Isabella's proclamation at Wallingford on 15 Oct. 1326, and in the judgment against Despenser before his execution at Hereford on 24 Nov.: *Foedera*, II, i, 645–6; Holmes, 'Judgment', 264–7. Mortimer was later described in similar fashion: e.g. the Lanercost chronicler wrote that in 1329 Thomas Wake and others fled to France 'fearing the cruelty and tyranny of the earl of March': *Lanercost*, 265.

[51] In 1334 Adam Orleton had to defend himself against the charge of having described Edward II as a tyrant in his sermon delivered at Oxford in Nov. 1326, arguing that he was referring to the Younger Despenser and not the king: *Historiae Anglicanae Scriptores Decem*, ed. Twysden, cols 2763–4; *Chartulary*, ed. Goodman, 105–6. The only chronicle references I have found to Edward II as a tyrant are in the *Flores*, a notably hostile source, which describes the king as giving way to 'insane tyranny' *(vesanae tyrannidi: sub* 1322; and in the *Vita* where a letter from an unidentified religious sent in 1316 to the king's confessor noted that a king 'is fittingly called king while he rules well; when he robs his people he is rather adjudged to be a tyrant. Indeed our king, passing through the country, takes men's goods and pays little or nothing or badly': *Flores*, 214–15; *Vita*, 128–31. It is surprising that there is no discussion of the subject in Fryde's *Tyranny and Fall*.

[52] See C. M. Barron, 'The tyranny of Richard II', *BIHR*, xli (1968), 1–18; T. Jones, 'Was Richard II a tyrant?', in *Fourteenth Century England*, v, ed. N. Saul (Woodbridge, Suffolk & Rochester, NY, 2008), 130–60. In Richard II's case, he was accused of tyranny only by the chronicler Thomas Walsingham, but not directly in any of the articles of deposition. His attacks on the property of his subjects could however be construed as tyrannical behaviour, even if not openly described as such: Barron, 1.

Although concepts of tyranny had long been discussed by political theorists such as John of Salisbury in the twelfth century[53] and Bracton in the thirteenth,[54] and were treated almost contemporaneously by the dissident Franciscan William of Ockham,[55] the implications of using accusations of tyranny to remove a legitimate and anointed king were too contentious and divisive to be of any practical use.[56] Edward was instead condemned for his inadequacy and for lacking in those qualities necessary in a king,[57] an approach which even some of those sympathetic to him would have had to admit carried conviction. The fact that Edward had a son and heir available to succeed him on the throne made his removal easier to contemplate, even if still difficult to perform in practice. It was little wonder that at the same time as his father was being deprived of his throne, his son and successor, Edward duke of Aquitaine, was receiving plentiful advice from writers such as Walter Milemete and William of Pagula on how to conduct himself as king.[58]

---

[53] R. H. Rouse & M. A. Rouse, 'John of Salisbury and the doctrine of tyrannicide', *Speculum*, xlii (1967), 693–709, esp. 695, ' "Between a tyrant and a prince there is this single or chief difference, that the latter obeys the law", while the former "brings the laws to nought".'

[54] F. Schulz, 'Bracton on kingship', *EHR*, lx (1945), 136–76, esp. 151–3: 'the king who violates his duty to maintain justice automatically ceases to be king. He is no longer a king, but a tyrant'. Bracton does not however seek to justify tyrannicide.

[55] See A.S. McGrade, ed., *A Short Discourse on Tyrannical Government* (Cambridge, 1992). This was written some time between 1334 and Ockham's death in 1347.

[56] For a general discussion of the themes of kingship and tyranny see C. Valente, *The Theory and Practice of Revolt in Medieval England* (Aldershot, Hants & Burlington, VT, 2003), 14–15, 19–25; and the chapter on government by J. Dunbabin in J.H. Burns, ed., *The Cambridge History of Political Thought, c.350–c.1450* (Cambridge, 1988), 495–6.

[57] See the discussion of the notion of the *princeps inutilis* with reference to the resignation of Pope Celestine V in 1298, and the depositions of Adolf of Nassau in 1298 and Edward II in 1327 in Peters, *The Shadow King*, 213–42; Prestwich, *Plantagenet England*, 217–18.

[58] The betrothal in 1326 of Philippa of Hainault and the young Edward was probably also the occasion of the production of two illuminated manuscripts which were presented by Philippa to Edward between the time of their betrothal and their marriage in 1328: Paris, BN, Ms. Fr. 571 (containing among other texts Brunetto Latini's *Livre dou Tresor*), and Harvard Law School Ms. 12 (containing a set of statutes): M.A. Michael, 'Towards a hermeneutics of the manuscript' in *Freedom of Movement in the Middle Ages*, ed. P. Horden (Donington, Lincs, 2007), 308–11, 313–16; Wathey, 'The marriage of Edward III', 14–22. Soon after Edward arrived back in England in Sept. 1326 he was presented with a text of the *Secretum Secretorum* by a clerk, Walter Milemete, who had also written a separate treatise, *De Nobilitatibus, Sapienciis et Prudenciis Regum*, for the young Edward by the time he was crowned in Jan. 1327: Michael, 'Towards a hermeneutics', 314–15, and idem, 'The iconography of kingship'. The Milemete ms, which is also elaborately illuminated, is preserved as Christ Church, Oxford, Ms. 92. F. 4v of this ms has a drawing of a king and queen, possibly intended to be Edward II and Isabella, looking at one another with an unhappy expression. On both William Milemete and William of Pagula (whose work, *The Mirror of Edward III*, was composed no later than 1332) see also *Political Thought in Early Fourteenth-century England*, ed. C. J. Nederman (Tempe, Ariz., 2002). The future Edward III would certainly be given a better grounding in the theory of good government than his father had received.

THE GUILDHALL OATH

After the dramatic events in Westminster Hall on 13 January a gathering was held at the Guildhall in the City of London. In the presence of the mayor, aldermen and 'a great commonalty' many of those attending parliament[59] took an oath to safeguard Isabella, queen of England, and Edward, the son of the king of England, to give good counsel, to safeguard the liberties of the city, and to keep the ordinances made, or to be made, in parliament by the peers of the land.[60] The wording of the oath makes it clear that although Edward II was on the way out, he was still technically king, and it was less extreme in form than the oath demanded by the citizens of London the day before.[61] Over the next three days the oath was taken by Edward II's half-brothers, the earls of Norfolk and Kent, the earls of Hereford[62] and Surrey, and their retainers; by Roger Mortimer and twenty-three other barons including the earl of Leicester's son-in-law Thomas Wake; fifty-six knights and ten serjeants 'of the court',[63] four royal justices,[64] and four others; twelve or thirteen knights of the shire currently attending parliament; the archbishops of Canterbury and Dublin; John Stratford the bishop of Winchester and treasurer, the bishops of Salisbury, Bath & Wells, Chichester and Llandaff, William Airmyn bishop of Norwich the chancellor, and the bishops of Coventry & Lichfield, Ely, Lincoln, Rochester,[65] Worcester, and Adam Orleton of Hereford;[66] the abbots of Westminster, St Albans, Waltham, Bury St Edmunds and Peterborough;

---

[59] Many of those who took the oath were not participating in the parliament in any formal capacity: e.g. the household knights of the earls, Isabella and the young Edward, as well as many of the barons of the Cinque Ports, and the men from Bury St Edmunds and St Albans. A lot of people were clearly in London for the excitement of the occasion.

[60] *CPMR*, 12. The oath in its original French form is given in *Literae Cantuarienses*, i, ed. Sheppard, 204–7. The *Ann. Paul.*, 323, contains a different version of the oath, which refers to Isabella and to '*Edward ore rey d'Engleterre*' (i.e. 'Edward, now king of England') in a context which implies that the young Edward was already regarded as king. It is likely that this oath is the one taken at the Guildhall on 20 Jan. by the archbishop of Canterbury and other prelates: *CPMR*, 11, n. 2.

[61] *CPMR*, 11–12: in which the prelates and magnates were asked to crown the young Edward as king and to depose his father 'for frequent offences against his oath and his Crown'. The names of those who took the oath are listed in *CPMR*, 12–14.

[62] John de Bohun was the son and heir of Humphrey de Bohun who had been killed at Boroughbridge in 1322. John was restored to his earldom and lands on 1 Nov. 1326.

[63] Henry of Lancaster the earl of Leicester was not among those who took the oath, presumably because he was keeping Edward II secure at his castle of Kenilworth. His son-in-law Thomas Wake clearly represented his interests during the parliament. The knights were presumably the followers of Isabella and the young Edward: their names included Edward, Roger and John, the sons of Roger Mortimer.

[64] Including the chief justice Geoffrey le Scrope, and Robert Mablethorp who had presided over Thomas of Lancaster's judgment in 1322.

[65] This confirms the statement in the Historia Roffensis that the bishop was undecided about how to act: BL, Cotton Ms. Faustina B.V, f. 49v.

[66] William Melton, the archbishop of York, was conspicuous by his absence.

three priors, twenty-three priests and clerks;[67] thirty barons of the Cinque Ports, five men from Bury St Edmunds, and thirteen burgesses from St Albans.[68]

THE END COMES

A second delegation then went to Kenilworth,[69] probably leaving London on 15 or 16 January.[70] There are differing accounts of its membership. According to the Historia Roffensis, the bishops of London, Ely and Hereford, two earls, two barons, and representatives from the counties, cities and Cinque Ports were sent to renounce the homage of the realm;[71] the Canterbury chronicle which preserves the *Forma deposicionis* speaks simply of three bishops, two earls, two barons, two abbots and two justices, without giving any names, apart from that of William Trussell;[72] the *Brut* chronicle states that the earl of Surrey went to act for the earls, John de Hothum the bishop of Ely for the clergy, Henry de Percy for the barons, and William Trussell for the knights.[73] The most detailed accounts of the delegation are given in the Lanercost and Pipewell chronicles. Lanercost states that the delegation was composed of the bishops of Winchester and Hereford, the earls of Leicester and Surrey, William de Roos and Hugh de Courtenay for the barons, two abbots, two priors, two justices, two Dominicans, two Carmelites, four knights (two from north of the Trent and two from south of the Trent), two citizens of London, and two citizens of the Cinque Ports, numbering twenty-four persons in all. No Franciscan friars were included in the delegation, allegedly at the request of Isabella, who had a particular affection for the order, so that they would not be the bearers of so displeasing a message. There is no mention in this account of William Trussell, although it is certain that he was a member, nor of the bishops of London and Ely.[74] The Pipewell chronicle gives the composition

---

[67] Including Master Gilbert de Middleton the official of Canterbury; the dean of the court of Arches; and the dean of St Paul's.

[68] Williams, *Medieval London*, 298; Clarke, *Medieval Representation*, 181–2. The full list of names is given in *CPMR* 12–14.

[69] Earlier Henry of Eastry, the prior of Christ Church, Canterbury, had written to the archbishop of Canterbury suggesting that a second deputation, consisting of two earls, two barons, four persons from the cities and borough, and four knights, should be sent to Kenilworth to make a further attempt to persuade the king to attend parliament. This was not done but may have had a bearing on the composition of the delegation which did in the end go to Kenilworth: *Literae Cantuarienses*, i, ed. Sheppard, 204–5 (the letter is undated but clearly belongs to the period of the parliament).

[70] One of the delegation's members, the earl of Surrey, did not take the Guildhall oath until 15 Jan.: *CPMR*, 12; Valente, 'Deposition', 860.

[71] BL, Cotton Ms. Faustina B.V, f. 49v.

[72] Trinity College Cambridge Ms. R.5.41, f. 125v.

[73] *Brut*, i, 241–2.

[74] *Lanercost*, 258; Valente, 'Deposition', 860.

as the bishops of London, Winchester and Hereford; the abbots of Glastonbury and Dover; the earls of Surrey and Lancaster (i.e. Leicester); the barons Hugh de Courtenay and Richard de Grey; two royal justices, Geoffrey le Scrope and John Bourchier; two (?) barons of the Cinque Ports; four burgesses of London; and four knights to represent the community of the land.[75] While there is no agreement on the exact composition of the delegation sent to Kenilworth, it is clear that it was large in number and intended to be as widely representative of the kingdom as possible, and not just of those who were attending parliament.[76]

The delegation reached Kenilworth or its immediate vicinity on 20 January,[77] when according to the chronicle of Geoffrey le Baker, which has the most detailed account of the mission, the bishops of Winchester and Lincoln[78] went ahead of the rest and spoke to Edward in private, accompanied only by Henry of Lancaster. They tried to persuade him to resign his crown to his elder son, Edward, promising that he would be honoured as before and suggesting that he would obtain merit in the sight of God and bring peace to his subjects. But they also threatened that, if Edward did not resign his crown, 'the people' would withdraw their homage and fealty, repudiate his sons, and place someone of non-royal blood upon the throne. After many tears and much sighing, Edward gave way, prepared, as the chronicler put it, to lay down his life for Christ rather than witness his sons' disinheritance or the disturbance of the kingdom, and knowing that a good shepherd would give his soul for his sheep. The bishop of Hereford then arrived with the other members of the delegation, whom he gathered in order of rank in the king's chamber. At length Edward emerged from an inner room, dressed in a black robe, and so affected by grief that he could barely stand and had to be helped by the earl of Leicester and bishop of Winchester. The bishop

---

[75] Clarke, *Medieval Representation*, 194.

[76] The fact that it was not simply a parliamentary delegation but something much wider in scope is emphasized in ibid., 190–1; and in B. Wilkinson, 'The deposition of Richard II and the accession of Henry IV', *EHR*, liv (1939), 225–7. The most detailed analysis of the sources relating to the delegation is in Clarke, *Medieval Representation*, 186–90, where it is also suggested that the size of the delegation might have followed the procedure in ch. xvii of the famous *Modus Tenendi Parliamentum* for choosing a committee of 25 in order to settle discord between the king and the magnates: Clarke, 189–90. As argued earlier, there is no evidence that the *Modus* was used or intended to be used in any of the political controversies earlier in the reign, specifically in 1321. However another possibility is that the procedure for a committee of 25 contained in the treatise on the steward was a model for 1327, since there is strong evidence that the treatise was made use of by the earl of Lancaster in 1321–2: Vernon Harcourt, *His Grace the Steward*, 164–7, 148–51; Wilkinson, 'The Sherburn indenture', App. II, 19–21; *Gesta Edwardi*, 62–4. Whether or not either of these possible models had any bearing on the events of 1327, the essential point was that the delegation was large, thereby sharing out the responsibility (and any possible future blame or recrimination) for the king's removal from the throne.

[77] The Pipewell chronicle: Clarke, *Medieval Representation*, 194.

[78] *Le Baker*, 27. This is the only mention of the bishop of Lincoln as a member of the delegation.

of Hereford explained the reason for the delegation's presence and demanded that he resign his crown to his first-born son. Again Edward was threatened that if he did not agree, someone more suitable would be chosen as king. Weeping and crying out, Edward said that he was deeply saddened that his people were so angry with him, but was pleased that his son would at least succeed him as king.[79] It is possible that a notary, as was later to be the case with Richard II in 1399, formally recorded Edward's acceptance, but there is no clear evidence of this.[80] The threat to disinherit Edward's sons from the succession is not recorded by any of the other chroniclers and would in any case have been an empty one, since the placing on the throne of anyone other than the young Edward would scarcely have met with general acceptance and would have been a recipe for civil war.[81] There is also a strong element of propaganda attaching to the account of Geoffrey le Baker, who was seeking here and elsewhere to portray Edward II as a suffering saint and martyr.[82] However, there can be little doubt about Edward's grief at being deprived of his throne and reduced to an imprisoned subject of a new king, even if that king was his own son.[83] On the following day, 21 January, Sir William Trussell formally withdrew homage on behalf of the kingdom from Edward, now once more Edward of Caernarfon,[84] and Sir Thomas Blount, steward of the household, broke his staff of office.[85] The reign of

---

[79] *Le Baker*, 27.

[80] Valente, 'Deposition', 860, n. 6. The author of the *Gesta Edwardi de Carnarvon* reported that it was put in writing, as did the St Alban's chronicler, Thomas Walsingham: *Gesta Edwardi*, 90; *Historia Anglicana*, 187. It is reasonable to suppose that the proclamation on 24 Jan. announcing Edward's resignation was based on a document just received from the delegation at Kenilworth.

[81] Making either Edward II's first cousin Henry of Lancaster or even Roger Mortimer king could never have worked as long as Edward II's two sons, Edward and John, and his two half-brothers, the earls of Norfolk and Kent, were alive. There is no reason to believe that such a move was ever seriously considered.

[82] See Haines, *Stratford*, 178–9.

[83] See, e.g., BL, Cotton Ms. Faustina B.V, f. 49v; Clarke, *Medieval Representation*, 195; *Knighton*, i, 442; *Murimuth*, 51.

[84] *Le Baker*, 28; *CMR, 1326–27*, 29, no. 155 (letters patent of a citizen of London, 6 Feb. 1327). For the text of the renunciation of homage, see *Foedera*, II, I, 650; *Rotuli Parliamentorum Hactenus Inediti*, ed. Richardson & Sayles, li, 100–1; *Select Documents*, 38; *Knighton*, i, 441–2; *Ann. Paul.*, 324; *Anonimalle*, 132–3. See also Fryde, 234–5, where the text is taken from Trinity College Cambridge Ms. R.5.41, f. 126r, following the *Forma deposicionis*.

Although the renunciation of homage is not recorded in the Parliament Roll for 1327 (C 65/1) there is a copy in C 49/83, m.2r, a roll whose heading describes it as 'the Points of the Parliament'. This is the source of the text published by Richardson & Sayles. In addition to Trussell's renunciation, it includes the petitions of the community of the realm which bear a close relation to the material contained in the Parliament Roll; the 1321 articles against the Despensers, which were confirmed in 1327; and a form of coronation office (although no specific mention is made of Edward III). C 49/83 was probably one of a number of unofficial rolls produced to satisfy a public demand for information on the events surrounding the deposition of Edward II. For further details see *PROME*, Parliament of Jan. 1327, Introduction and the edn of C 49/83.

[85] *Le Baker*, 28; Valente, 'Deposition', 860–1.

Edward II was ended, having lasted, as the Canterbury chronicler noted, for nineteen years, twenty-nine weeks and five days.[86] For the unknown author of the *Brut* chronicle the downfall of Edward II and the disasters of his reign were the fulfilment of the prophecies of Merlyn:[87] 'and ever afterwards he lived his life in much sorrow and anguish'.[88]

ABDICATION OR DEPOSITION?

The delegation probably arrived back in London from Kenilworth on 25 January, but their news had preceded them.[89] On 24 January it was proclaimed in London that 'Sir Edward, late king of England, has of his good will (*de sa bone volunte*) and by the common counsel and assent of the prelates, earls and barons, and other nobles, and of all the commonalty of the realm, resigned the government of the realm (*sen est ouste del gouvernement du roialme*), and has granted and wills that the government of the realm shall come to Sir Edward, his eldest son and heir, and that [Edward] shall govern, reign and be crowned king.' The peace of the new king was proclaimed at the same time;[90] the first official acts in the name of Edward III were dated on the same day as the proclamation; and his first regnal year began officially on the following day, 25 January.[91]

Everything looked neat and tidy. One king had willingly divested himself of his office; a new king, the elder son of the old one and with an unquestioned right to succeed him, had been proclaimed and would soon be crowned. But was it quite so straightforward? Not everyone was happy at the events of January 1327. It is known, for example, that the archbishop of York, one of Edward II's oldest friends and allies, another close friend the bishop of Rochester, and the bishops of London and Carlisle did not consent on 13 January to Edward II's replacement as king by his son.[92] Many others attending parliament tacitly accepted what was being done because of fear of the Londoners, whose clamour both inside and outside Westminster Hall punctuated the whole proceedings,[93] which were carefully

---

[86] Trinity College Cambridge Ms. R.5.41, f. 126v.
[87] *Brut*, i, 242–7; Phillips, 'Edward II and the prophets', 191–2.
[88] 'and ever he levede his lif aftirward in miche sorw and anguisse': *Brut*, i, 247.
[89] Valente, 'Deposition', 861.
[90] *CCR, 1327–30*, 1; *Foedera*, II, ii, 683; *Select Documents*, 38. Orders to proclaim Edward III's accession in the rest of England, Wales and Ireland were sent out on 29 Jan.: *CCR, 1327–30*, 1.
[91] The last dated enrolments of acts in the name of Edward II were on 21 and 23 Jan.: *CCR, 1323–7*, 629 (21 Jan.); *CMR, 1326–27*, 206 (23 Jan.); Valente, 'Deposition', 860, n. 3.
[92] However, the bishop of Rochester appears to have done fealty to the young Edward, sending the archbishop to perform it in his name: BL, Cotton Ms. Faustina B.V, f. 49v; cf. Valente, 'Deposition', 859; Haines, *Stratford*, 182.
[93] BL, Cotton Ms. Faustina B.V, f. 49v: '*quidam metu ducti nonnulli tacite propter metum London*'. The Londoners had a special interest in seeing that Edward II was removed from the throne, since they wanted immunity for their murder of the bishop of Exeter and other violent acts of Oct. 1326 and also confirmation of the liberties of their city: BL, Cotton Ms. Faustina B.V, ff. 49v–50r; Williams, *Medieval London*, 297–9.

stage-managed by Roger Mortimer and Thomas Wake. William Trussell, who withdrew allegiance from Edward II on behalf of the whole community of the realm, was also part of the management team: he was not an elected member of parliament,[94] but like Thomas Wake was a follower of Henry of Lancaster, earl of Leicester and Edward II's gaoler at Kenilworth. The taking of the Guildhall oath to support Isabella and the young Edward on 13 January and in the days following added further pressure, which some apparently resisted. Of the forty-seven men summoned to the parliament as barons only seventeen are recorded as having taken the oath.[95] It is also noticeable that only twelve or thirteen knights of the shire out of sixty-eight who were elected,[96] and a handful of abbots out of the nineteen who were summoned took the oath. The only burgesses who subscribed were eighteen men from Bury St Edmunds and St Albans, but none of these was an elected member of parliament;[97] of the 108 elected burgesses none is recorded as subscribing.[98] Earls and barons and their knightly retainers, on the other hand, were especially prominent.[99] The representatives of North and South Wales were not even summoned to parliament until it had already begun: and one of the most prominent Welshmen, Sir Gruffydd Llwyd the sheriff of Merioneth, appears to have refused to attend, probably out of loyalty to Edward II and hatred of Roger Mortimer.[100] The pressure was maintained after the deputation had left London for Kenilworth: on 20 January the archbishop of Canterbury and seven bishops took a new oath in support of the young Edward, which this time described him as king. Others may have done the same.[101]

[94] Clarke, *Medieval Representation*, 190–1.

[95] *RDP*, iii, App. i, Part i (London, 1829), 370; *CPMR*, 12 (24 men are described here as barons but only 15 of them were actually summoned to parliament as barons; two more men who were summoned as barons are listed here among the knights who took the oath). Because a baron did not apparently take the oath, it should not be assumed that he did not approve of Edward II's deposition, but many probably did not.

[96] Of the 13 knights described as knights of the shire in *CPMR* only nine can be identified in the list of knights returned to the parliament; however, three more elected knights appear in the list of 'knights and serjeants of the court' and were probably retainers of the crown or other lords: *CPMR*, 13; *Members of Parliament*, part i, *Parliaments of England, 1213–1702* (London, 1879), 75–7.

[97] *CPMR*, 11, n. 3. Both Bury St Edmunds and St Albans had given special support to Isabella and her followers after their landing in Sept. 1326: *Ann. Paul.*, 314–15. Their burgesses probably came to London to join in the excitement.

[98] *Members of Parliament*, Part i, 75–7.

[99] *CPMR*, 12–14.

[100] Edwards, 'Sir Gruffydd Llwyd', 594–6. Welsh representatives had been summoned in 1322, in gratitude for their role in suppressing the revolt of the Mortimers and the other Marchers. Twenty-three out of the 24 representatives (both Welsh and English) summoned from North Wales attended. The one missing was presumably Gruffydd Llwyd. No returns exist for those summoned from South Wales: *Members of Parliament*, Part i, 77.

[101] *CPMR*, 11; *Ann. Paul.*, 323; *French Chron.*, 58. The archbishop of Canterbury also gave the Londoners 50 tuns of wine, presumably to try to buy their goodwill. The seven bishops are not named.

It was made to seem as if Edward II had willingly resigned or abdicated his throne. But it was obvious to everyone that he had done so under extreme pressure. Earlier in his reign the Ordinances had been imposed upon him against his will and in 1320 he had won support from the pope for the annulment of his personal oath to uphold them: an oath made unwillingly was no oath, in the eyes of the Church. How much greater was the offence when an anointed king was forced to leave his throne; and how great the urgency to bundle the old king quickly out of sight and crown his successor. The chroniclers knew perfectly well that Edward II had been deposed, and several of them said so.[102]

But deposed by whom? Was Edward II deposed by parliament or during parliament? Some of the major events, such as those of 13 January, the presentation of the six articles against Edward II, the speech by Roger Mortimer, the sermons by the archbishop and bishops, and the acclamation of Edward II's elder son, certainly took place in parliament, in Westminster Hall, and in the presence of those who had been summoned to attend. But these were really only the public formalities, and were supplemented by other actions which occurred separately, such as the oath-taking at the Guildhall of the city of London between 13 and 15 January, or the meeting of the magnates and prelates on their own in Westminster Hall on the night of 12 January. The reservations and fears of some of those within Westminster Hall, the careful management of the events that took place there, and the intimidation of any possible opponents by the Londoners both inside and outside Westminster Hall must all be taken into account. What really brought about Edward II's downfall was the combined determination of the leading magnates, their personal followers and the Londoners that he must go. It has aptly been said that if 'the magnates and prelates had deposed a king in response to "the clamour of the whole people", that clamour had a distinct London accent'.[103]

The one certainty is that Edward II was still king when the month of January 1327 began, even if held a prisoner, but that he had ceased to be king before the month had ended. Although the deposition of Edward II did not attack kingship itself, the actual process of deposing a legitimate and anointed king involved an attempt to square the circle. That process had in practice taken place during, in, on the margins of and outside an assembly whose own legitimacy was to say the least doubtful. Edward II may in the end have given the appearance of abdicating his throne in

---

[102] Most notably the unknown Canterbury chronicler who inserted the title *Forma deposicionis Regis Edwardi post Conquestum Secundi* at the beginning of the document which was otherwise designed to preserve a version of events favourable to Isabella and Mortimer: Trinity College Cambridge Ms. R.5.41, ff. 125r–126r; Fryde, 233–5. See also *Ann. Paul.*, 322; *Lanercost*, 258, 260; *Flores*, 235. The chronicler Adam Murimuth, who was a canon of St Paul's and had acted as a royal diplomat at the papal curia and emphasized that Edward II gave up his throne only because he had no choice: *Murimuth*, 51.

[103] Williams, *Medieval London*, 298.

favour of his son, but he had done so under intense pressure and while he was a prisoner. It was essential, both for propaganda purposes and for the future peace of the kingdom, that Edward II's deposition should have been agreed to 'by the prelates, earls, barons, and the whole community of the realm'. The real nature of what had happened did not bear too close an examination.[104] It is hardly surprising that a Parliament Roll for the period before 1 February 1327 does not exist: it is more than likely that one never existed.[105] Edward II had been airbrushed out of the record.

EDWARD IN CAPTIVITY

On 1 February the new king was knighted, together with many other young men, by John de Beaumont, the brother of the count of Hainault, and John de Bohun earl of Hereford.[106] On the following day Edward III was crowned in Westminster Abbey by the archbishop of Canterbury, who had known and worked with his father since at least 1297; and he took the same oath which had been administered to Edward II in 1308.[107] The bishops present included John de Hothum of Ely, Adam Orleton of Hereford, John Stratford of Winchester, Henry Burghersh of Lincoln and William Airmyn of Norwich, all of whom had fallen out with the former king.[108] The former Edward II's two half-brothers, Thomas of Brotherton earl of Norfolk and

[104] See the valuable discussions in Valente, 'Deposition', 862–8; Wilkinson, 'Deposition', 223–9; Clarke, *Medieval Representation*, 173–95; W.H. Dunham & C.T. Wood, 'The right to rule in England', *American Historical Review*, lxxxi (1976), 738–61, esp. 738–44; Prestwich, *Plantagenet England*, 216–18. The medal struck to mark Edward III's coronation, with the motto '*Populi dat iura voluntas*' ('The will of the people gives rights') indicated one contemporary view of the events which had taken place since 7 Jan. 1327: see Valente, 866.

[105] Various explanations have been offered for the lack of a Parliament Roll covering the events up to Edward III's coronation on 1 Feb. 1327. It has been suggested that a roll once existed and that it was removed by Richard II after he was threatened with deposition in 1386; that the absence of a roll proves that the assembly was not legally a parliament at all; or that the new king did not want a record of a parliamentary deposition which might set a precedent: Valente, 'Deposition', 862–3, citing Clarke, *Medieval Representation*, 177; Wilkinson, 'Deposition' 224; and G.T. Lapsley, *Crown, Community and Parliament*, ed. H. Cam & G. Barraclough (Oxford, 1951), 311. The Jan. 1327 assembly is unambiguously described as a parliament in the writs of summons; members of parliament were paid from 7 Jan; and although there was a break between the proclamation of Edward III as king and the reassembly of parliament after his coronation, there was no prorogation and the assembly was treated all as one. Yet although the parliament was nominally summoned by Edward II and he was deposed in the course of it, the Parliament Roll (C 65/1) is described as the *Rotulus Parliamenti Edwardi Tertii* and not the roll of the twentieth year of the reign of Edward II.

[106] Trinity College Cambridge Ms. R.5.41, f. 126r. Roger Mortimer's three sons were among those knighted: Mortimer, *The Greatest Traitor*, 170; 288. nn. 15, 16.

[107] *CCR, 1327–30*, 100; *Foedera*, II, ii, 684.

[108] The others present were the bishops of Chichester, Worcester and Llandaff. The absentees included the bishop of Carlisle and William Melton, the archbishop of York, another of Edward II's oldest allies, who, it is likely, both still disapproved of the change of king; Melton's absence was probably also connected with the difficulties which always arose when an archbishop of York travelled in the province of Canterbury. The presence of

earl marshal, and Edmund of Woodstock earl of Kent, were present, as were the earls of Surrey and Hereford, Roger Mortimer, Henry de Beaumont, 'and other magnates of the realm'.[109] On the day after the coronation the work of parliament was resumed: political debts were repaid in the confirmation of the 1321 articles of accusation against the Despensers; the judgment against Thomas of Lancaster in 1322 was reversed; Henry of Lancaster was confirmed as earl of Lancaster and steward of England; and there were moves to have both Thomas of Lancaster and Robert Winchelsey archbishop of Canterbury, another former opponent of Edward II, canonized.[110] Roger Mortimer also petitioned for the reversal of the judgment against him in 1323, which was duly granted in July 1327, four months after the end of the parliament.[111] The other winners in 1327 were the citizens of London, whose actions had done so much to undermine the power of Edward II in the autumn of 1326 and had helped to ensure his deposition in January 1327. The Londoners' petition for the restoration of their liberties could not be refused and on 7 March they were rewarded with a comprehensive charter confirming all the ancient liberties they had held before 1321 and granting them important new privileges.[112]

The change in regime was further signified by the choice of a council to advise the new king. 'Because,' according to the *Brut* chronicle, 'Edward was so young and his father had been misled by false councillors' he should be governed by twelve great lords of the land: four prelates (the archbishops of Canterbury and York, the bishops of Winchester and Hereford), four earls (Lancaster, Norfolk, Kent and Surrey), and four barons (Thomas Wake, Henry Percy, Oliver Ingham and John de Roos). It may be significant that Roger Mortimer was not among them.[113]

---

the bishops of London and Rochester, who had earlier disapproved of Edward II's removal, is not mentioned in the official record, but according to the Historia Roffensis both men took part in the coronation ceremony: BL, Cotton Ms. Faustina B.V, ff. 49v, 50r.

[109] *CCR, 1327–30*, 100; *Foedera*, II, ii, 684.

[110] See *PROME*, Parliament of Jan. 1327, C 65/1 items 1 (the Despensers), 2 (Lancaster; and Winchelsey); *CCR, 1327-30*, 105–6. Henry of Lancaster, earl of Leicester was styled earl of Lancaster on 26 Oct. 1326 and formally restored to the earldom on 3 Feb. 1327.

[111] *CPR, 1327–30*, 142. Although he lodged his petition in Feb., there is no mention of Mortimer in the Parliament Roll for 1327. Nor is it clear why he had to wait until July when Henry of Lancaster's petition in respect of his brother Thomas was answered at once. Possibly Mortimer was less powerful at this stage than he may appear: cf. Mortimer, *The Greatest Traitor*, 170–2.

[112] For the petitions of the citizens and the replies of Edward III and his council see *PROME*, Parliament of Jan. 1327, C 49/43/173. The text of the charter is in *Ann. Paul.*, 325–32. See also Williams, *Medieval London*, 298–9.

[113] This is recorded in a manuscript of the *Brut* in Corpus Christi College, Cambridge, Ms. 174, ff. 152v–153r, cited in Haines, *Stratford*, 188. The appointment of such a council was one of the things asked for in the commune petition submitted at the 1327 parliament, but it is likely that it had already been decided before parliament reconvened after Edward III's coronation: *PROME*, Parliament of Jan. 1327, C 65/1, item 5; Haines, *Stratford*, 188.

EDWARD

The former Edward II, now simply 'Edward, the king's father', or 'Edward of Caernarfon'[114] was still at Kenilworth. Little is known about his stay there, except that he was apparently well treated; but even the gift of two tuns of Rhenish wine by his son the new king can have been of little consolation.[115] Later, while Edward was at Berkeley, his keepers, Thomas de Berkeley and John Maltravers, were allowed £5 a day for his maintenance;[116] altogether they were paid £700, of which £200 came directly from the exchequer, while in May 1327 they received a further £500 in cash, equivalent to one hundred days' maintenance, which was part of the £13,000 in silver pennies found in Caerphilly castle after its surrender by the son of the Younger Despenser.[117] It was not lavish but was enough to keep Edward in modest comfort.[118] However, if Murimuth is correct, Thomas de Berkeley and John Maltravers took turns in looking after Edward, one month at a time: Berkeley allegedly treated him humanely but Maltravers 'otherwise'.[119] Several of the chroniclers remark on the misery experienced by Edward while he was at Berkeley, though whether he was actually placed in a room adjoining a pit filled with rotting flesh there is no way of knowing.[120] Regardless of any physical mistreatment, it was to be expected that he should continue to miss the company of his family and could not understand why they still refused to visit him.[121] Any anger he had felt against Isabella

---

[114] The former description was used a number of times in the Parliament Roll for Jan.–March 1327; the latter appears, e.g., in the letters close of 20 Aug. 1327 referring to the recent attempt to release him from Berkeley castle: *CCR, 1327–30*, 158.

[115] *PROME*, Parliament of Nov. 1330, E 175/2/216, item 19.

[116] *CCR, 1327–30*, 27 (15 May 1328). This contradicts the claim by Adam Murimuth that only 100 marks a month were allowed: *Murimuth*, 52.

[117] E 352/ 120, m.39r (1 Ed. III): account of John de Langton, clerk, for the treasure, goods and chattels in Caerphilly; Berkeley Castle Muniments, Select Roll 39; J. Smyth of Nibley, *The Lives of the Berkeleys*, ed. Sir J. Maclean (Gloucester, 1883), i, 293; Rees, *Caerphilly Castle*, 113. The enrolled accounts of Thomas de Berkeley and John Maltravers, for custody of Edward II, from 3 April to 21 Sept. 1327, and of his body from 21 Sept. to 21 Oct. 1327 are contained in E 352/120, m.25r. There is also a heading for these accounts at the top of m.25v, as if more material was to go there. The original accounts do not appear to be extant. See also S.A. Moore, 'Documents relating to the death and burial of King Edward II', *Archaeologia*, (1887), 223–4.

[118] Rolls 39, 41, 42 of the Berkeley accounts contain references to the supply of wine, wax, spices, eggs, cheese, capons, cattle, etc. for Edward's use. I should like to thank Mr David Smith, honorary archivist at Berkeley castle, for enabling me to see these and other material at Berkeley in 1998. See also I.H. Jeayes, *Descriptive Catalogue of the Charters and Muniments at Berkeley Castle* (Bristol, 1892), 274–7. Edward did not however have the use of the personal effects which he had left behind in Caerphilly castle. His bed and clothing and other items were given by Isabella and the newly crowned Edward III to the hospital of St Leonard at York, whose recently appointed warden was a royal clerk: Rees, *Caerphilly Castle*, 86–7.

[119] *Murimuth*, 52.

[120] *Brut*, i, 252–3; *Le Baker*, 33.

[121] See, e.g., *Brut*, i, 252–3; *Le Baker*, 29.

and any possibility that he might do her harm had probably dissipated by this time and been replaced by feelings of loss and unhappiness. However, there is little reason to believe that Edward's despair was reflected in the Anglo-Norman poem in which Edward laments his fate and shows repentance for his past misdeeds. This was almost certainly composed by an anonymous fourteenth-century writer, making use of the familiar theme of the wheel of fortune and trying to cast Edward in a favourable light.[122]

A MULTIPLICITY OF PLOTS

Edward II was gone but not forgotten. No sooner had he been deposed than his friends and allies began plotting to free him from his imprisonment.

The first signs came in early March when a commission was appointed to inquire into the activities of a number of Warwickshire men, including Stephen Dunheved or Dunhead from Dunchurch, a few miles from Kenilworth, and two local priests both named William Aylmer.[123] At this stage there was no mention of any plot to release the former king, but a strong hint of something more serious came on 28 April when the earl of Lancaster wrote from Leicester to the chancellor, John de Hothum bishop of Ely, telling him that he had heard that Brother John de Stoke, a Dominican friar from Warwick, had been plotting with others unnamed to 'betray' the earl's castle of Kenilworth, and asking for a commission to arrest him: this was duly issued on 1 May, significantly with orders to bring John to the king in person. Three days later further orders were issued for the arrest of Stephen Dunheved, who was to be taken to Wallingford for imprisonment. These apparently unconnected facts, together with the arrest of William Aylmer which was ordered on 23 April,[124] suggest that the earl of Lancaster's anxiety about Edward's security, expressed in his letter and recorded by the Leicester chronicler Henry Knighton, was well founded and that the earl was eager for his royal charge to be moved somewhere safer.[125] Although in 1328 the quarrel between the earl of Lancaster and Mortimer almost led to a renewal of civil war and in 1330 Roger Mortimer was accused of seizing Edward from Kenilworth and taking him to Berkeley with the intention of murdering him,[126] there is nothing to suggest any unwillingness on the earl's part in 1327[127]

---

[122] For the latest discussions of the fascinating text see Valente, 'The "Lament of Edward II" ', and Tyson, 'Lament for a dead king'. See also Ch. 1 of this book.

[123] *CPR, 1327–30*, 79–81.

[124] SC 1/29/64; *CPR, 1327–30*, 99–100. The author of the Anonimalle chronicle was however aware of a plot to rescue Edward from Kenilworth and states that this was the reason for his transfer to Berkeley: *Anonimalle*, 134–5.

[125] The earl of Lancaster was particularly aware of the danger to Kenilworth whenever he was away on other business: *Knighton*, i, 444.

[126] *Knighton*, i, 447–8, 450–1, 454–5; *PROME*, Parliament of Nov. 1330, C 65/2, item 1.

[127] Cf. Mortimer, *The Greatest Traitor*, 173, where it is suggested that Mortimer had indeed schemed to obtain control of the former king.

or that there was any deliberate intention to exchange Edward's relatively comfortable imprisonment for a harsher regime under Mortimer's control.[128] Nonetheless, that was to be the effect.

On 3 April 1327 Edward was formally transferred to the custody of two of Roger Mortimer's leading followers, his son-in-law Thomas de Berkeley and Berkeley's brother-in-law John Maltravers.[129] On 5 April Edward arrived, with a heavily armed escort, either at the abbey of Llanthony in Gloucester or at Gloucester castle which was close by; and on the same day, or very soon afterwards, he was delivered to Berkeley castle.[130] Within a short time of his arrival at Berkeley a second plot to release him was being hatched, involving some of the same cast of characters as at Kenilworth together with numerous other individuals. The evidence suggests that the conspirators were very determined but at the same time had little or no idea of what they expected to happen if they succeeded in freeing Edward. If they were acting with other more powerfully placed conspirators, there is nothing to suggest this.[131]

---

[128] Tout, 'Captivity and death', 156–7. Tout's paper is the classic account and the starting-point for all later writing. The most recent discussions are R.M. Haines, *'Edwardus redivivus'*, *Trans. Bristol and Gloucestershire Archaeological Soc.*, cxiv, for 1996 (1997), 65–86; idem, *Death of a King* (Lancaster, 2001); idem, *King Edward II*, 219–38; Doherty, *Isabella*, 113–215; Haines, 'Sir Thomas Gurney of Englishcombe in the county of Somerset, regicide?', *Somerset Archaeology and Natural History*, cxlvii (2004), 45–65; Mortimer, *The Greatest Traitor*, 244–64; idem, 'The death of Edward II in Berkeley castle', *EHR*, cxx (2005), 1175–214; idem, *The Perfect King* (London, 2006), App. 2, 'The fake death of Edward II', and App. 3, 'A note on the later life of Edward II'; and J.S. Hamilton, 'The uncertain death of Edward II', *History Compass* (2008). See also the historical novel by Doherty, *The Death of a King*, and an account by a local historian, R. Perry, *Edward the Second* (Wotton-under-Edge, Glos., 1988). There is also an excellent survey of the controversies by G. Marchant, *Edward II in Gloucestershire* (Gloucester, 2007), which was published in aid of the Edward II tomb conservation project.

[129] E 352/120, m.25r; Trinity College Cambridge Ms. R.5.41, f. 126v; Phillips, 262, 264–5. According to the historian of the Berkeleys, John Smyth of Nibley, the handing-over of Edward was recorded in an indenture made between Henry of Lancaster and Berkeley and Maltravers: *Lives of the Berkeleys*, i, 291–2. On the other hand, as Tout pointed out, neither man was very likely to be sympathetic towards the deposed king. After 1322 Berkeley had been imprisoned until his release in Oct. 1326; after the Younger Despenser's execution at Hereford he had been briefly reunited at Wigmore with his wife who had also been imprisoned and whom he had not seen for six years; and in Jan. 1327 had made a short visit to his ancestral home at Berkeley before attending parliament: ibid., 288; Tout, 'Captivity and death', 156–7. Maltravers had spent much of the time since 1322 in exile on the continent before returning with Isabella and Mortimer in Sept. 1326, and had also just regained his forfeited lands: article on Maltravers by C. Shenton in the *Oxford DNB*.

[130] *Ann. Paul.*, 333; *Murimuth*, 52. The 5 April is the date given for his arrival at Berkeley in the Canterbury chronicle, Murimuth and by Smyth: Trinity College Cambridge Ms. R.5.41, f. 126v; *Murimuth*, 52; *Lives of the Berkeleys*, i, 291. The 70 miles between Kenilworth and Berkeley could have been covered between 3 and 5 April without too much difficulty. Presumably his escort was on guard for any possible rescue attempt. A list of repairs needed to Gloucester castle in Jan. 1331 referred to a little chapel opposite Llanthony called *'Edwardes chaumbre'* and to a latrine called *'Kyngeswardrobe'*: *CIM*, ii, 286, no. 1166. This suggests that Edward was held in the castle rather than the abbey; given the need for security, this makes more sense.

[131] The annals of St Paul's speak of the support of *'quibusdam magnatibus'* without specifying who they were: *Ann. Paul.*, 337.

On 27 July Thomas de Berkeley wrote to the chancellor John de Hothum reminding him of an earlier letter in which he named a number of men who had approached Berkeley castle in force, had seized 'the father of our lord the king' from his custody[132] and had plundered the castle.[133] Exactly when this had occurred is not stated but it was probably earlier in July.[134] Neither is it clear whether Edward had actually been taken out of the castle by the conspirators or whether he had only been freed from his prison within the castle. However, the names of those indicted for the offence are of great interest. They include Stephen Dunheved, the two parsons named William Aylmer who had been involved in the earlier attempt on Kenilworth, and thirteen others from the counties of Warwick, Stafford and Gloucester.[135] Among the others were Stephen's brother, the Dominican Thomas Dunheved, two other Dominicans, John de Newminster and Henry de Ryhale, a monk from Hailes abbey in Gloucestershire, a canon of Llanthony, and the parson of Huntley in Gloucestershire. Thomas de Berkeley added that his men had also learned that a large number of men had gathered for the same purpose in the county of Buckingham and other adjoining counties, and that two of their leaders were another friar John de Redmere and John Norton. Berkeley said that he would do his best to apprehend Edmund Gacelyn and the others named in the commission. The fate of the Dunheved brothers is uncertain. Thomas is said to have died in prison after an unsuccessful attempt to escape, while his brother Stephen was captured at London. However, Thomas's imprisonment is said to have taken place around 11 June, which does not fit with his involvement at Berkeley in July; his brother apparently escaped and was still at large in 1329.[136]

The striking things about this list of names are the number of clergy, especially Dominican friars, and the number of men who had in one way or another served Edward as king. Edmund Gacelyn had been a royal household knight before 1321 when he had opposed the Despensers; while

---

[132] '*ravi le pere nostre seignor le roi hors de nostre garde*'.

[133] The original letter is preserved as, SC 1/35/207. It was first noticed and published by F.J. Tanquerey as 'The conspiracy of Thomas Dunheved, 1327', *EHR*, xxxi (1916), 119–24, where the author was wrongly identified as John Walwayn. This identification was accepted by Tout in 'Captivity and death', 160–1, and in Fryde, 201. However, it is now known that the letter was sent by Thomas de Berkeley, who was appointed as a commissioner of the peace on 11 July and on 1 Aug. was ordered to arrest 21 named persons: *CPR, 1327–30*, 154, 156–7. There is no evidence that John Walwayn had any connection with Berkeley castle or Edward's imprisonment there. Significantly, the commission of 1 Aug. mentions the plundering of Berkeley castle but says nothing about Edward and accuses the men instead of having refused to join Edward III's expedition against the Scots.

[134] Fryde, 201, gives the date as 9 July, citing Tout, 'Captivity and death', 166, which does not mention any date. Her source may be KB 27/272, m.2v, which records the trial of some of the conspirators 'for trying to seize the king', but without adding any significant details: Fryde, 269, n. 26.

[135] Thomas de la Hay and William atte Hulle had also been involved at Kenilworth.

[136] *Ann. Paul.*, 337; *CCR, 1327–30*, 146, 549; Tout, 'Captivity and death', 163; Tanquerey, 'Conspiracy', 123–4. Redmere and Norton were arrested at Dunstable: SC 8/69/3444.

John de Redmere had, as the letter stated, been the keeper of the king's stud; William Aylmer and John le Botiller had probably also been in royal service.[137] Of particular significance is the Dominican friar Thomas Dunheved. He had been one of Edward II's confessors and a papal chaplain and he it was who allegedly tried to obtain a divorce between Edward and Isabella while he was at Avignon in 1325;[138] he may even have been with Edward in Wales in 1326.[139] Thomas had probably been involved with his fellow Dominican, John de Stoke, and his own brother Stephen in the earlier plot against Kenilworth. Although the royal government understandably did not make the attempt to release Edward public, both the plot and Thomas Dunheved's part in it were known to the writers of the *Anonimalle Chronicle* and the *Annales Paulini*.[140]

The support given to the former Edward II by lowly members of the clergy and religious orders suggests that Edward's reputation for holiness which later gave rise to a campaign for his canonization had some kind of substance. But the appearance of so many Dominicans in their ranks is especially significant since the English Dominicans had a close relationship with and a fierce loyalty to Edward II both before and after he became king.[141] Edward in his turn had expressed 'a great affection for the order of friars preacher, for many reasons'.[142] They provided his confessors and, in the case of the schemer and trickster Nicholas of Wisbech, supplied him with 'evidence' to support his belief in the miraculous powers of the Holy Oil of St Thomas.[143] The Dominicans who protected Gaveston's body after his death in 1312 may have been from Oxford but it is also likely that they were from the Dominican house in Warwick.[144] In June 1317 these friars told the king in a petition that they and their property had been attacked by the local population on account of *monsire Piers*.[145] It was then hardly a coincidence that in March–April 1327 John de Stoke and perhaps other Warwick Dominicans plotted to free Edward from his imprisonment nearby at Kenilworth; or that other men from the same area should have been involved in the July plot against Berkeley castle. The attacks planned or carried out against Kenilworth and Berkeley were all too reminiscent of the seizure of Wallingford and of Mortimer's own escape from the Tower in 1323 for the authorities not to take them seriously.

---

[137] Tanquerey, 'Conspiracy', 123–4. On Aylmer see also Waugh, 'For king, country and patron', *Journal of British Studies*, xxii (1983), 30.

[138] *Ann. Paul.*, 337; *Lanercost*, 254. The story of the divorce is probably apocryphal: Haines, *Stratford*, 156.

[139] SAL Ms. 122, p. 34; Haines, *Stratford*, 209, n. 90.

[140] *Anonimalle*, 134–5; *Ann. Paul.*, 337. The author of the Anonimalle chronicle also knew about the earlier plot against Kenilworth and the friars' part in it. A closely related text, Bod., Lyell Ms. 17, f. 118v, also mentions the friars, but without giving any names.

[141] See the discussion in ch. 2 of this book.

[142] *Letters of Edward Prince of Wales*, 1 & 21.

[143] Phillips, 'Edward II and the prophets', 196–201.

[144] Hamilton, 99.

[145] C 81/100/4276–7; *CCW*, 472; Bullock-Davies, '*Multitudo*', 180, n. 8.

The July plot came at a very difficult and dangerous time for the government of the young Edward III, since England and Scotland were again at war. The Scots had reopened hostilities, which had been dormant since the thirteen-year truce of 1323, when they attacked Norham castle on 1 February 1327, the very day of Edward III's coronation.[146] In retaliation the English launched a campaign in July which resulted only in humiliation for the young king, who came close to capture at Stanhope Park in Weardale near Durham. It also resulted in the dissipation of much of the financial reserve which had been built up under Edward II; and in quarrels and recriminations between Roger Mortimer, the earl of Lancaster and Edward II's half-brother, Thomas of Brotherton the earl of Norfolk and earl marshal.[147] The Scots then launched a savage and very determined attack on the main castles and the countryside of Northumberland during August and September.[148] It was nothing less than a replay of Edward II's campaigns against the Scots and, to make matters worse, there were worrying signs from Ireland. Edward III's rule there was not formally proclaimed until 13 May 1327 and in February the justiciar, John D'Arcy, had sent an emissary to Scotland on 'certain confidential business touching the lord king', who was still considered to be Edward II. Robert Bruce's landing in Ulster around Easter 1327 (12 April) may have been connected with this mission, but Bruce certainly had ambitions of his own which may have amounted to a scheme to invade England with the assistance of Edward II's former ministers in Ireland and Edward's supporters and Mortimer's enemies in Wales.[149] The government in England could not have known all of this but by July they had learned enough to be deeply worried about the situation in Ireland.[150] Had they also known that two of Edward II's closest personal allies, Rhys ap Gruffudd[151] and Donald earl of Mar,[152] were also in Bruce's ranks, they would have been even more concerned.

By the late summer of 1327 England was under external attack and riddled with internal conspiracies, some of which were aimed at freeing Edward from captivity and perhaps even restoring him to the throne. For all anyone knew, Robert Bruce, now an ailing man and soon to die, might also have seen this as a way to gain the English recognition of Scottish

---

[146] *Foedera*, II, ii, 649; *Lanercost*, 256.

[147] For an account of the Stanhope Park campaign see Nicholson, *Edward III and the Scots*, 26–41; Barrow, 252–4; Fryde, 210–14.

[148] Barrow, 254.

[149] Frame, *English Lordship*, 139–41, 175–6.

[150] Ibid., 179.

[151] Rhys fled to Scotland after the fall of Edward II, was involved in Sept. 1327 in the unsuccessful plot to free him from captivity, and then fled once more to Scotland: Griffiths, *Principality*, 100; McNamee, 240.

[152] Donald had spent most of his life at the English court and had a close personal loyalty to Edward II. After Edward's fall he too went to Scotland where he involved himself in schemes to restore Edward II to his throne: McNamee, 240; Barrow, 252.

independence which had eluded him ever since Bannockburn. Not surprisingly, Edward's guards took extra precautions. He was apparently moved around secretly by night from place to place, including Corfe castle in Dorset, so that no one could be sure of where he was being held, before finally being brought back to Berkeley.[153]

ANOTHER CONSPIRACY

The precautions were not sufficient: within weeks of Edward's return to Berkeley news came of yet another conspiracy to free the deposed king. On 14 September 1327[154] William Shaldeford, Roger Mortimer's lieutenant in North Wales, wrote to Mortimer from Rhosfair[155] in Anglesey to report a plan to release Edward from Berkeley on the part of Rhys ap Gruffudd and others in South and North Wales, and with the support of certain unnamed magnates. The letter was sent to Mortimer at Abergavenny,[156] and one of Mortimer's retainers William Ockley was allegedly then sent to Berkeley with instructions to Edward's guardians John Maltravers and another of Mortimer's men, Thomas Gurney, to read the letter 'and to take speedy action to avoid greater danger':[157] 'thereupon William Ockley and the others who had Edward in their custody treacherously slew and murdered Edward, the father of our lord the king, in destruction of the royal blood'.[158] If Edward had been successfully released, the conspirators also intended to bring about the destruction of Roger Mortimer and his followers. Although the story is known today only from a court case in

---

[153] *Murimuth*, 52. This episode is probably a source of Geoffrey le Baker's story that Edward was moved from place to place. Corfe also figures in Le Baker's account, as does Bristol: *Le Baker*, 30–1. Another likely source is the version of the French *Brut* contained in Corpus Christi College, Oxford, Ms. 178, ff. 169r, v: V.H. Galbraith, 'Extracts from the Historia Aurea and a French "Brut" (1317–1347)', *EHR*, xliii (1928), 216. Smyth, *Lives of the Berkeleys*, i, 291, interprets the stays in Corfe and Bristol as taking place during the initial movement of Edward from Kenilworth to Berkeley rather than as a consequence of the escape attempt in July.

[154] Monday after the Nativity of the BVM. Tout misread the date as the Monday before, i.e. 7 Sept: Tout, 'Captivity and death', 165, 184.

[155] Rhosfair on the Menai Straits is now known as Newborough: ibid., 184, n. 4. Mortimer had been appointed as justice of both North and South Wales on 20 Feb. 1327. On Shaldeford see ibid., 166–7. On 8 Sept. Mortimer was ordered to arrest all those breaking the peace in Wales, so there was clearly already some concern: *CCR, 1327–30*, 217–18; *CPR, 1327–30*, 207.

[156] Shaldeford believed Mortimer to be at Abergavenny, but he may have been somewhere else in the Welsh March, such as his castle at Ludlow. The Berkeley castle records show that a number of (undated) letters from Thomas de Berkeley were directed to Mortimer at Ludlow. Berkeley Castle Muniments, Select Roll 39: Berkeley steward's accounts, 1 Jan.–29 Sept. 1327.

[157] '*et qils feissent hastive remedie pur greindre peril eschuer*': *Select Cases*, ed. Sayles, v, 59. I have preferred my own translation to the accurate but rather clumsy rendering in Sayles, 'and to furnish speedy remedial measures in order to eschew greater peril'.

[158] '*Sur quoi le dit William Docleye et les autres qavoient le dit sire Edward en garde trayterousement oscirent et murdrirent le dit sire Edward, pier noster seigneur le roi, en destruccion du saunc real*': *Select Cases*, ed. Sayles, v, 59.

March 1331, when a man from North Wales, Hywel ap Gruffudd, accused William Shaldeford of aiding and abetting the murder of Edward II,[159] it is very plausible that in 1327 men like Rhys ap Gruffudd in South Wales and his counterpart Gruffydd Llwyd in North Wales, in whom loyalty to the former king was joined with hatred of Mortimer, really were planning to release Edward from his captivity. It is also worth remembering that Rhys ap Gruffudd had been with Edward at Neath abbey in his last days of freedom in 1326 and it also appears that he was involved in the earl of Kent's conspiracy in 1330. Hywel himself had probably been one of the men who joined Rhys ap Gruffudd in Scotland after the fall of Edward II.[160] If Hywel's accusations are true, the news of this latest plot to free the former king had come not to Edward III's government but directly and personally to Roger Mortimer, who was then in Wales and therefore able to decide how to react without reference to Edward III and his council.[161] This would therefore seem to be an open and shut case: Roger Mortimer had the opportunity to murder the former king and his agents Gurney and Ockley duly carried it out.

On 22 September Thomas Gurney was sent to the king and Isabella with letters from Thomas de Berkeley informing them that Edward had died on the previous day, 21 September, only seven days after the dispatch of Shaldeford's letter from Anglesey.[162] Gurney may have been expecting to find Edward III at Nottingham[163] but it is more probable that he did so at Lincoln, where a parliament had been meeting since 15 September. The young Edward III was told of his father's death on Wednesday, 23 September, 'during the night'.[164] The news was clearly made public

---

[159] The full text in the original French and Latin is published with an English translation ibid., 58–63. It is also transcribed in Tout, 'Captivity and death', 185–9. The original source is KB 27/285, m.9, although Tout gives the reference as KB 27/285, m.188. The case was not however brought to a conclusion in the court of King's Bench, on the grounds that because the charges related to acts both in the principality of Wales and in England they could not finally be determined in England: *Select Cases*, ed. Sayles, v, 63.

[160] *CCR, 1327–30*, 212; *CFR, 1319–37*, 169; *CCR, 1330–33*, 51; Griffiths, *Principality*, 100; McNamee, 240.

[161] There is nothing to suggest that Edward III and the council knew of this plot at the time. If they had, the near coincidence of the warning message and Edward's death might have been too much to believe.

[162] The date of Edward's death is very clearly given as 21 Sept. in the accounts of Hugh de Glaunville: E 101/383/1, and in their enrolled form, E 352/125, m.46v, and E 372/177, m.45d.

[163] Gurney was paid 31s 1d for this duty: Berkeley Castle Muniments Select Rolls 39; Jeayes, *Descriptive Catalogue*, 274; Smyth, *Lives of the Berkeleys*, i, 293, 296–7. The record says that Nottingham was Gurney's destination.

[164] '*Trescher cosin novelles nous vyndront y ce meskerdy le xxiii iour de Septembre de deinz la nuyt qe nostre trescher seignur e piere est a dieu comaundez*': DL 10/ 253: letter dated at Lincoln on 24 Sept. The news probably came during the night of 23/24 Sept. rather than 22/23 Sept. The Historia Roffensis (BL Ms. Cotton Faustina B.V, f. 51r), confirms that Gurney brought the news to Lincoln, but gives the date as 22 Sept., which was the date of his departure from Berkeley.

without delay:[165] for the moment there was no suspicion that the death was other than natural.[166]

PEACE AT LAST

Even if there had been any suspicion of foul play, there was no time to look more closely or even for the young Edward III to go to Berkeley to pay his respects.[167] On 24 September Edward wrote to the earl of Hereford (and presumably other magnates) informing him of the death of his father but also warning him that the Scots were reported to be on the point of invading England.[168] Resisting the Scots had to take precedence over grieving for the old king, for whom nothing could now be done. The Scots were continuing their raids in the north, but these were for the moment at least to be the last of their kind, since the English had decided to negotiate for a final peace with Scotland. The failure of the latest Scottish campaign, along with near-bankruptcy[169] and the growing disturbances within England[170] made peace unavoidable. The regime of Mortimer and Isabella also no longer had the (very expensive) support of the force of Hainaulters under John of Hainault, which had left England for home at the end of August.[171] In early October envoys were sent to seek out Robert Bruce and to discover his terms. These were received on 18 October and formed the basis of negotiations at Newcastle during November and December 1327. On 1 March 1328 Edward III recognized the independent existence of the kingdom of Scotland and the legitimacy of Robert Bruce as its king; and on 17 March a formal treaty was concluded. It was in many respects the same as the

---

[165] Although, according to the Berkeley historian, the news of Edward's death was not announced locally until 1 Nov. It is not clear whether this was an order brought back by Gurney from Lincoln or an order by Thomas de Berkeley, Edward's keeper: Smyth, *Lives of the Berkeleys*, i, 297.

[166] On 23 Oct. Edward's old friend and ally William Melton, archbishop of York offered an indulgence to all who prayed for the soul of the former king: *Letters from Northern Registers*, ed. Raine, 355–6 (where the date is wrongly given as 1328). Melton describes Edward's death as a *fatalis casus*, 'a fatal happening'. I don't think it means anything as literal as a fall, as suggested by Ian Mortimer: 'The death of Edward II', 1192.

[167] In 1307 one of Edward II's first acts had been to go to Burgh-on-Sands near Carlisle 'to weep for his father': *Lanercost*, 207.

[168] DL 10/ 253.

[169] The war cost over £67,000 and exhausted the treasure built up by Edward II in his later years: A.E. Prince, 'The payment of army wages in Edward III's reign', *Speculum*, xix (1944), 138. Edward III's coronation had cost a further £13,550: Vale, *The Princely Court*, 81; E 101/382/9.

[170] Apart from the plots to release the former king, there were serious riots in Abingdon in April and in Bury St Edmunds in July 1327; London was also very disturbed: *Foedera*, II, ii, 711.

[171] Doherty (D.Phil.), 220–1; the Hainaulters' wages amounted to nearly £55,000.

abortive treaty for which the earl of Carlisle Andrew Harclay had lost his head in 1323.[172]

A ROYAL FUNERAL

While the preliminaries of peace were taking place the body of the former king lay at Berkeley. The long delay between Edward's death on 21 September and his burial on 20 December was not the result of indifference or callousness on the part of the young king, but rather of the pressure of events. Relations with France remained tense and had to be improved,[173] while there was also the matter of Edward III's marriage to Philippa of Hainault, whose details had still to be negotiated.[174] The situation was not unlike that at the beginning of the reign of Edward II, when the continuing war in Scotland and the arrangements for Edward and Isabella's own marriage took precedence over the burial of Edward I, who had died on 7 July and whose funeral took place on 27 October.

Such state events in any case took time to organize and there are indications that Edward II's funeral was intended to be a significant event: he was not going to be bundled quickly out of sight and promptly forgotten. The first question to be answered was where he was to be buried. The obvious place was Westminster Abbey, which Henry III had rebuilt to hold the shrine of the royal saint, Edward the Confessor, as well as his own tomb and those of his successors. The abbey was clearly intended to become a royal mausoleum to rival that of the kings of France at Saint-Denis.[175] Both Edward I and his first queen, Eleanor of Castile, had been buried there and it might be expected that Edward II would also be laid to rest there. However, Edward had been on bad terms with Westminster Abbey since the beginning of his reign,[176] while the political

---

[172] For details of the negotiations see Barrow, 254-60. As Professor Barrow has argued, the treaty showed what Edward II might have achieved if he had been prepared to act with generosity and to make the necessary leap of faith. On the other hand Edward II perceived – probably rightly – that such a treaty would have been regarded as a humiliation. There was also the question of the 'disinherited', those Scottish magnates who had fought against Bruce and English magnates with claims to lands in Scotland. This was not settled in 1328 and was one of the causes of renewed war between England and Scotland in 1333, as well as a cause of serious tension within England itself.

[173] One of the first actions of Edward III's government after the coronation in Feb. 1327 was to send an embassy to Paris to try to resolve the continuing tensions over Gascony. The details are recorded in *Foedera*, II, ii, 180, 185-6; AN, J 634, nos 15-17, 19, 20. There was also of course the need for the new king of England to do homage for the duchy of Aquitaine, as his father had done in 1308 and 1320 and as he himself had done in 1325. Edward III performed his homage at Amiens on 6 June 1329: AN, J 634, nos 21, 21bis.

[174] Further negotiations took place in Hainault in early Aug. 1327 and the papal dispensation for the marriage was issued on 30 Aug.: *Inventaire analytique*, ed. Wymans, nos 583-4, p. 130.

[175] See Palliser, 'Royal mausolea', 1-8; Binski, *Westminster Abbey*, ch. 3, 'A royal fellowship of death: the royal mausoleum under Henry III and Edward I'.

[176] See Ch. 1 of this book, 'The reputation of a king'.

turbulence shown by the Londoners at the end of his reign and which had contributed so much to his deposition in January 1327 might have been expressed once more if the hated king's body were to be brought into their midst.[177] It is known however that the monks of Westminster were anxious for Edward II to be buried there, no doubt for reasons of prestige. Two monks, Robert de Beby and John de Tothale, were sent to Nottingham during October 1327 'to seek the body of the dead king':[178] not to find out where the body of the dead king was, but to obtain it for burial. They were not successful and Westminster Abbey was ruled out in favour of the great Benedictine abbey of St Peter's, Gloucester. The story that John Thoky, the abbot of Gloucester, transported the body on a richly decorated wagon from Berkeley to Gloucester where it was solemnly received by the monks of St Peter's and a procession of the local people, can be only partly true since the orders for the body's removal to Gloucester came directly from the king and the journey was paid for by the exchequer.[179] However the claim in the history of St Peter's, Gloucester, that the monasteries of St Augustine in Bristol, Kingswood near Bristol and Malmesbury in Wiltshire had all refused to accept Edward's body for burial because they were afraid of Roger Mortimer and Isabella and their followers is patently untrue.[180] St Peter's, Gloucester, was deliberately chosen by Edward III and Isabella as Edward's resting place, partly because it was not Westminster but also because it had the merits both of proximity to Berkeley and of some previous connections with the English ruling house: the nine-year-old Henry III had undergone his first coronation there after his accession in 1216, and in 1134 Duke Robert of Normandy, the eldest son of William the Conqueror and one of the leaders of the first crusade,

---

[177] London was already in a very disturbed state in the autumn of 1327: *Foedera*, II, ii, 711, 723. In 1326 the Londoners had also shown their continued sympathy with the memory of Thomas of Lancaster: *French Chron.*, 54.

[178] '*pro corpore Regis defuncti petendo*': Westminster Abbey Munimenta, WAM 20344, for the revenues of the church of Oakham in Rutland. They were away for a total of 21 days (not 31 days as given in Tout, 'Captivity and death', 169, n. 1) which would place their mission in the period between news of Edward II's death reaching Westminster and the order to remove his body from Berkeley. As the current or past infirmerer (1321–2), John de Tothale might have possessed the necessary skills for preserving a body before burial. He was however of some importance since he had been present at and taken a part in Edward III's coronation in Jan. 1327: Westminster Abbey, Liber Niger, f. lxxvi v. On the careers of the two monks see E.H. Pearce, *The Monks of Westminster* (Cambridge, 1916), 71–2, 77–8.

[179] E 368/100, m.8r; E 101/383/1.

[180] *Historia et Cartularium*, ed. Hart, 44–5. Both Mortimer and Isabella attended the funeral in Dec. The history was written for or by abbot Walter Frocester in the late 14th century at a time when the abbey had benefited substantially from the cult which had developed around the dead king and from the offerings of pilgrims at his tomb. There is a translation of the parts of the chronicle relating to Edward II in Welander, *The History . . . of Gloucester Cathedral*, 628–30, 634.

had been buried there.[181] It was not a royal abbey in the same sense as Westminster but it had the makings of one.

Little is known in detail about the treatment of Edward II's body while it still lay at Berkeley. According to Adam Murimuth, various abbots, priors, knights and burgesses from Bristol and Gloucester were summoned to view the body but were able to do so only superficially.[182] It was looked after by a royal serjeant, William de Beaucaire, and it was eviscerated and embalmed by an unnamed woman, who was taken to see Isabella at Worcester in the days immediately following the funeral at Gloucester.[183] Edward's heart was placed in a specially made silver vase costing 37s 8d:[184] after Isabella's own death in 1358 this was placed inside the breast of the effigy on her tomb in the choir of the church of the London Franciscans in Newgate.[185] It is clear that Edward was being regarded and treated with dignity. Instead of such euphemisms as 'Edward, the king's father' or even 'Edward of Caernarfon', Edward was referred to as king throughout the financial records of his funeral; and this was consistent with the lavish display of the funeral arrangements themselves. It was clearly to be a ceremony which, like a coronation, emphasized the continuity of the monarchy and the legitimacy of both the present and the previous incumbents of the English throne. The ambiguities and untidiness of the events surrounding Edward II's deposition in January were to be made up for

---

[181] See also Palliser, 'Royal mausolea', 8–9; D. Verey & A. Brooks, *Gloucestershire*, ii, *The Vale and the Forest of Dean; The Buildings of England* (London, 2002), 397.

[182] *Murimuth*, 53–4. This seems to refer to the time when Edward's body was still at Berkeley but it is not clear.

[183] Hugh de Glaunville's original accounts for the custody of Edward's body and for his funeral are preserved in E 101/383/1, and were also enrolled on the Chancellor's Roll for 6 Ed. III, E 352/125, m.46v, and on the Pipe Roll for the same year, E 372/177, m.45d. A transcript of this material was published in 1887 by Moore, 'Documents', 224–6. There is an earlier edition by J. Hunter, 'Expenses of conveying the body of King Edward II from Berkeley Castle to the Abbey of Gloucester', *Archaelogia*, xxvii (1838), 294–7. There is also important material in the accounts of Thomas de Useflete, E 361/3, m.8d, and in the accounts of the great wardrobe for 1 Edward III, E 101/383/3 (both published in W. St John Hope, 'On the funeral effigies of the kings and queens of England', *Archaelogia*, lx (1907), 530–1).

[184] Smyth, *Lives of the Berkeleys*, 293, citing the Berkeley receiver's account for 1327, which is no longer extant. There is no mention of this in the funeral accounts. It was common for the heart to be removed and sometimes given separate burial. In the case of Edward II's mother, Eleanor of Castile, there were three separate burials: of her body at Westminster, her entrails at Lincoln, and her heart at the Blackfriars in London: Binski, *Westminster Abbey*, 107–10; Parsons, *Eleanor*, 59–60.

[185] E.B.S. Shepherd, 'The church of the Friars Minor in London', *Archaeological Journal*, lix (1902), plan between 248 & 249, and 259, 267. Isabella's tomb and other monuments were sold in 1547 at the time of the Reformation and the church was destroyed in the Great Fire of 1666: *The Grey Friars of London: their History with the Register of their Convent and an Appendix of Documents*, ed. C.L. Kingsford (Aberdeen, 1915; repr. 1965), 7, 74–5; F.D. Blackley, 'Isabella of France, Queen of England, 1308–1358, and the late medieval cult of the dead', *Canadian Journal of History*, xv (1980), 30; idem, 'The tomb of Isabella, wife of Edward II of England', *Bulletin of the International Soc. for the Study of Church Monuments*, viii (1983), 161–4.

by the splendour of his funeral in December, and reinforced within a few years by the construction of an elaborate tomb above his burial place in Gloucester abbey.[186]

On 21 October, a month after Edward's death, his body was moved from Berkeley castle to Gloucester abbey,[187] where it was initially placed upon a hearse brought from London. This was then replaced by a specially built one constructed by eight carpenters between 24 November and 11 December. It included four gilded lions painted by the king's painter, John de Eastwick, which stood around the hearse and wore mantles bearing the royal arms, and standing figures of the four evangelists. Eight figures of angels and two lions rampant completed the decoration.[188] A great many people were evidently expected to come to view Edward lying in state, and a great many did so; four stout oak beams were placed around the hearse to control the crowds.[189] The body in its coffin was not visible, being also surmounted by a specially made wooden image of the dead king, which bore a copper crown and was probably dressed in the pieces of armour which were brought from London.[190] This was the first occasion on which a royal effigy was employed in England, but it started a tradition which was followed until the eighteenth century.[191] The image of a warrior king was presented for the lying in state but for the actual burial the effigy was adorned with Edward II's coronation robes, which were returned to the great wardrobe in London after the funeral; the body itself was clothed in the undergarments which

---

[186] There is a very valuable discussion of Edward II's funeral and its significance in J. Burden, 'Re-writing a rite of passage', in *Rites of Passage*, ed. N. F. McDonald & W.M. Ormrod (Woodbridge, Suffolk & Rochester, NY, 2004), 13–29.

[187] Moore, 'Documents', 224–5.

[188] E 101/383/3, m.6; Moore, 'Documents', 221; Burden, 'Re-writing', 17–18.

[189] Moore, 'Documents', 226. The account specifically mentions the crush of people.

[190] E 101/383/3, m.6; E 101/624/14 (enrolled on E 372/181, m.38, 10 Ed. III, 1336–7). Even if the body was not fully enclosed it is unlikely that the face would have been visible, perhaps helping to give rise to later suspicion that the body was not that of Edward II. This mistake was not repeated in the case of Richard II, whose body lay 'with the face uncovered so that all could see it': Evans, *The Death of Kings*, 135, citing Adam of Usk.

[191] See Burden, 'Re-writing', 17 and n. 16; St John Hope, 'Funeral effigies', 517–50; A. Harvey & R. Mortimer, eds, *The Funeral Effigies of Westminster Abbey* (Woodbridge, Suffolk & Rochester, NY, 1994), 4–6, 30–6. Edward II's funeral effigy has not survived but those of later rulers, starting with Edward III (St John Hope, 532) and ending with Queen Anne, are displayed in the undercroft of Westminster Abbey. See also the discussions in Lindley, *Gothic to Renaissance*, who suggests that Edward II's funeral effigy was designed to draw attention away from the body itself and any rumours of foul play or even that the former king was still alive and in custody: Lindley, 110–12. In this case one might ask why the same procedure was followed for Edward III and other kings whose deaths were not mysterious. It seems more likely that the wooden effigy was a natural development from the practice followed since the time of the death of King John of displaying the embalmed body of the king dressed in his coronation robes: Lindley, 99–101. As Lindley points out, the battle against the forces of putrefaction changed the form of royal funerals, especially if they were delayed for any reason.

Edward had worn at his coronation in 1308.[192] While it was awaiting burial the body was again attended by William de Beaucaire, together with the bishop of Llandaff John Eaglescliff, who was a Dominican friar and therefore especially sympathetic to the memory of the late king; two royal chaplains Bernard de Bergh and Richard de Potesgrave; two royal knights Edmund Wasteneys and Robert Hastang; two royal serjeants Bertrand de la More and John de Enfield; and Andrew the king's candle-maker.[193]

The funeral took place on 20 December. Although it was attended by Edward III, Isabella and Mortimer, nothing is known about it. There are no official records and the English chroniclers barely mentioned the occasion.[194] If there were any doubts or suspicions about the circumstances of Edward's death, they were not voiced on that day. On 27 November the archbishop of Canterbury Walter Reynolds, who had known Edward for thirty years but had betrayed him at the last, preceded him to the grave.[195]

A ROYAL MAUSOLEUM OR A ROYAL SHRINE?

Edward III and the court had to hasten away. Edward's future bride Philippa of Hainault was about to arrive at Dover prior to their marriage at York on 24 January;[196] and the peace negotiations with Scotland were still in progress. But this was not the end of Edward III's interest in Gloucester, since it appears that he now intended to turn St Peter's abbey into a royal mausoleum or rather a shrine to the memory of his father, and in the process replace the ignominy of Edward II's deposition and imprisonment by a powerful advertisement for the English crown. This in turn raises the question of whether Edward III considered making Gloucester rather than Westminster the usual burial place for English kings. The answer is probably negative: when his brother John of Eltham, earl of Cornwall died in 1336 he was buried at Westminster and a fine tomb later erected in his memory; and when Edward III himself died in 1377 it was to Westminster that his body was conveyed for burial.[197]

---

[192] E 361/3, m.8d; E 403/232, m.2; St John Hope, 'Funeral effigies', 530–1, 564, Burden, 'Re-writing', 17.

[193] Moore, 'Documents', 224–6; Tout, 'Captivity and death', 169.

[194] *Lanercost*, 260, for example remarked simply that Edward was not buried with other kings in London since he had been deposed and was not a reigning king. The St Paul's annalist noted that he was buried in Gloucester abbey in the presence of his first-born son and many magnates, but said no more: *Ann. Paul.*, 337–8. The Charter Roll witnesses for 20 Dec. included the bishops of Ely and Norwich and the earl of Kent; a charter dated at Worcester on Christmas Day named the earl of Lancaster and Roger Mortimer: C 53/114, mm.6, 5.

[195] He died at Mortlake on 16 Nov.: *Ann. Paul.*, 338.

[196] She landed on 23 Dec. accompanied by her father, Count William of Hainault: *Ann. Paul.*, 339; *Knighton*, i, 446–7.

[197] In both cases Edward III gave specific orders that Westminster was to be chosen.

On 20 December 1328, the first anniversary of his father's burial, Edward III visited Gloucester and showed his gratitude to the people of the town for their respect to the body of his father by confirming their charters; he also granted privileges to the abbey.[198] He was there between 13 August and 4 September 1329, and again from 14 to 26 September, after a few days spent at Hereford; and between 22 and 26 June 1330. In September 1332 Edward wrote to the abbots of Gloucester, Hailes, Winchcombe and Tewkesbury, reminding them that his father's anniversary was about to occur and asking them and religious persons from Gloucester and the surrounding area to celebrate it in Gloucester abbey with all due devotion and honour.[199] This was probably an annual occurrence both at Gloucester[200] and in the king's own private chapel, or wherever he happened to be.[201] Edward visited Gloucester again on 14 September 1337, and in March 1343 presented the abbey with a gold ship in honour of his victory over a French fleet at Sluys in 1340 and his recent narrow escape from shipwreck in the Channel: this was offered at the high altar but later attached to Edward II's tomb. In 1353 Edward III's sons also visited Gloucester to pay their respects to their grandfather's memory.[202] There is also ample evidence that Edward III encouraged others outside his family to pray for the soul of his father,[203] sometimes as a quid pro quo for a royal grant.[204]

---

[198] *CChR, 1327–41*, 97; Welander, *History*, 144. The movements of the privy seal also place Edward III at Gloucester on 4–7 Oct. 1328; 13 Aug.–4 Sept. and 14–26 Sept. 1329; 22–26 June 1330; 14 Sept. 1337; and again in March 1343: C. Shenton, *The Itinerary of Edward III and his Household, 1327–1345* (Kew, 2007), 36, 48–9, 60, 168, 249.

[199] E 368/104 (5–6 Ed. III), m.120d.

[200] For other examples, in 1338 and the 1340s, see Ormrod, 'The personal religion of Edward III', 871.

[201] On 21 Sept. 1338, e.g., he attended mass at the conventual church of St Andrew in Antwerp for the soul of Edward II on the anniversary of his father's death. Masses in memory of Edward II were also celebrated on that date by the Dominicans of Antwerp and by the Carthusians just outside the city: *The Wardrobe Book of William de Norwell*, ed. Lyon et al., 207.

[202] Murimuth, 135; Welander, *History*, 630 (trans. of *Historia et Cartularium*, using Gloucester Cathedral Ms. 34); Ormrod, 'The personal religion of Edward III', 860, 871 (a similar gift was made to four other shrines, at Walsingham, St Paul's and Canterbury (chapel of St Thomas and Lady Chapel); Evans, *English Art*, 164–5.

[203] Mark Ormrod argues however that while Edward III was not indifferent to the memory of Edward II, he did not go out of his way to encourage veneration of his father: Ormrod, 'Personal religion', 870–1.

[204] E.g., 4 March 1334: grant to the abbey of Stratford in return for saying mass for the soul of Edward II and others: *CChR, 1327–41*, 306; 13 July 1338: grant to Thomas de Sibthorp, parson of Bekyngham, diocese of Lincoln, who had set up chantries in honour of the Blessed Virgin Mary and of the soul of Edward II in the churches of Sibthorp, diocese of York, and Bekyngham: *CChR, 1327–41*, 450; 3 May 1341: Bishop Wulstan of Worcester (1339–49) was excused attendance at parliaments on grounds of age and in return for the annual celebration of Edward II's anniversary at Gloucester: *CPR, 1340–3*, 431; 13 March 1345: confirmation of grants made by Queen Isabella to Peter de Eltham, clerk, for saying mass in the manor chapel for the souls of Edward II and John of Eltham before she surrendered the manor to Edward III: *CPR, 1343–45*, 445. Isabella's original grant was probably made in about 1336, at the time of her son John's death. It is significant that she included her former husband in the prayers.

But Edward II himself was the main attraction at Gloucester. Large numbers of pilgrims came to visit the site of his burial and probably in even larger numbers after the construction of his tomb. It is traditionally believed that the offerings by visitors to the tomb helped to finance the extensive reconstruction of the Norman abbey during the course of the fourteenth century:[205] the south transept was rebuilt between 1331 and 1336 in a style modelled on that of St Stephen's Chapel at Westminster;[206] a new choir screen and choir were added between 1337 and 1367;[207] and the great east window was built between 1350 and 1360, with paintings of the coronation of the Virgin, saints, angels and kings, but also including the arms of Edward II as well as those of Edward III and the Black Prince and other men who had fought at Crécy and Calais in 1346–7.[208]

The result was a magnificent recreation of the Norman abbey church in the new architectural style known today as perpendicular, and the perfect setting for the royal tomb which was constructed inside it. Although a great deal has been written about the tomb, many uncertainties remain. It is not known, for example, who ordered and paid for it, who designed and constructed it, and exactly when. The tomb effigy is made of alabaster probably from a quarry in Nottinghamshire, and may have been intended to emulate the white marble effigies of French kings of the same period. Edward is shown holding the orb and sceptre and 'with a fine bearded head, calm and typically Plantagenet, flanked by angels',[209] which has led one commentator to suggest that the tomb was designed to emphasize the

---

[205] The *Historia et Cartularium* claims that the offerings enabled Abbot Wigmore to rebuild the transept in six years; Welander, *History*, 628 (trans.); Verey & Brooks, *Gloucestershire*, 397.

[206] Welander, *History*, 151–60; Verey & Brooks, *Gloucestershire*, 397, 401, 407–8.

[207] Welander, *History*, 161–76; Verey & Brooks, *Gloucestershire*, 397–8, 408–10.

[208] Welander, *History*, 183, 192–7; Verey & Brooks, *Gloucestershire*, 401–2, 416–17.

[209] Verey & Brooks, *Gloucestershire*, 420. Although it is tempting to think that the face of Edward II might have been modelled from a death mask, there is no evidence that this was the case: the effigy was an idealized representation of the king rather than an attempt at portraiture: Welander, *History*, 147. The tomb was restored at the expense of Oriel College, Oxford, on three occasions in the 18th century, in 1737, 1789 & 1798; a major restoration was undertaken by the Board of Works in 1875; it was cleaned in 1940 and some repairs carried out in 1963 and 1968. The recent study and conservation of the tomb, completed in 2007, have revealed that the grave was marked initially by a slab of dark grey-green Purbeck stone from Dorset, on which the painted wooden effigy of the king used in his funeral may have been laid; the grave was first enclosed with a kerb of limestone, after which a Purbeck plinth was added to the top of the slab; a solid core of limestone with deep inset arches was then built on it, with a surrounding set of Purbeck arches keyed in and carved in intricate detail with plant forms; above these arches were metal coats of arms of Edward's relatives; the larger niches held statues of them, the so-called 'weepers'; 12 smaller arches may have held the 12 Apostles; amid these symbolic figures was laid the life-sized alabaster effigy of the king: R. M. Bryant, G. N. H. Bryant & C. M. Heighway, *The Tomb of Edward II: a Royal Monument in Gloucester Cathedral* (Stonehouse, Glos., 2007), 1–16.

saintliness of Edward II, and the idea of the king as a type of Christ.[210] The effigy lies on a tomb-chest of Purbeck marble and is surmounted by a canopy of fine-grained Cotswold oolitic limestone, which has been described as 'the work of a genius and arguably the most thrilling of all tomb canopies'.[211]

It was certainly in the interests of the monks of Gloucester to have a king buried in their midst, especially one whose supposed saintly qualities attracted streams of visitors seeking miracles. Gloucester abbey was no doubt well aware of Hereford cathedral only about 30 miles away which possessed the shrine of the recently canonized Thomas Cantilupe and had been making a steady income from pilgrims since his death in 1282.[212] Gloucester was now in a position to offer competition and appears to have done so: the number of pilgrims to Hereford had declined steeply by the mid-1330s.[213] It might therefore have made good business sense for the monks of Gloucester abbey to invest in an elaborate shrine to Edward II without any involvement on the part of the crown. This may have been what happened[214] but it seems unlikely. In the first place the tomb was clearly the work of a master and not of a local craftsman or architect. It was work of the very highest quality with both a national and an international significance.[215] Two possibilities have been suggested, both men

---

[210] A. McG. Morganstern, *Gothic Tombs of Kinship in France, the Low Countries and England* (University Park, Penn., 2000), ch. 5, 'The royal English tomb during the minority and reign of Edward III', 83–4; Evans, *English Art*, 164–5.

[211] Verey & Brooks, *Gloucestershire*, 420; C. Wilson, entry on the tomb of Edward II in Alexander & Binski, eds, *The Age of Chivalry*: catalogue entry 497 (pp. 416–17). There is also a detailed description of the tomb in Morganstern, *Gothic Tombs*, 83–91.

[212] He was canonized in 1320. See R.C. Finucane, 'Cantilupe as thaumaturge', and Morgan, 'Effect of the pilgrim cult', in *St. Thomas Cantilupe Bishop of Hereford*, ed. M. Jancey (Hereford, 1982), 137–44 and 145–52.

[213] Morgan, 'Effect of the pilgrim cult', 150. There may of course have been other reasons for the decline.

[214] Mark Ormrod suggests that the erection of Edward II's tomb in Gloucester abbey was the work of 'relic-hungry monks' anxious to claim 'their very own royal saint' and that they rather than Edward III paid for it: Ormrod, 'Personal religion', 870–1. The same view is expressed by G.P. Cuttino & T.W. Lyman in their important paper, 'Where is Edward II?', *Speculum*, liii (1978), 525, n. 20, in which they cite the reply of Dr Howard Colvin to their query: 'It [the tomb] was certainly not paid for by the king [Edward III] and was presumably commissioned by the abbot and convent of Gloucester. So far as I know there are no Gloucester accounts for this period, so the tomb is almost certainly undocumented.'

[215] There are close similarities in general design between Edward II's tomb at Gloucester, his son John of Eltham's at Westminster, and the tomb of Pope John XXII in Avignon cathedral: Binski, *Westminster Abbey*, 92, 177–80; C. Wilson in Alexander & Binski, eds, *Age of Chivalry*, cat. entry 497 (pp. 416–17); Morganstern, *Gothic Tombs*, 91–5. John XXII's tomb, which was built c. 1335–45, was designed by an English mason, possibly John the Englishman who was active at Avignon between 1336 and 1341: P. Binski & D. Park, 'A Ducciesque episode at Ely', in *England in the Fourteenth Century*, ed. W.M. Ormrod (Woodbridge, Suffolk, 1986), 39. There are also parallels in the quality of the work with the

who had worked on royal building projects at Westminster: Thomas of Canterbury, who was in charge of St Stephen's chapel, Westminster, between about 1323 and *c.* 1335–6, and was also familiar with the latest developments in London and Canterbury, with a suggested building date for the tomb of about 1330;[216] and William Ramsey, surveyor of the king's works from 1336, with a construction date of 1336–9.[217] Secondly, it was very much in the interest of Edward III that his father should not only be buried amid splendour but that his tomb, when it was built, should convey a message of quiet but dignified majesty. If pilgrims wished to visit the tomb in search of miracles, so much the better. The English royal house could do with a saint from its own ranks, to add to the cult of St Edward the Confessor which was national rather than dynastic in nature, and also to counter the miracles attributed to Edward II's old opponent and deadly enemy, Thomas of Lancaster. In the quality and power of the effigy the tomb has no contemporary parallel and has aptly been described as 'a remarkable example of theatrical statecraft', and 'a monument *fit* for a saint . . . that remains to-day a powerful manifestation of the evocative power of great architecture'.[218] It is hard to believe that an object of such subtlety and importance could have been created without both the approval and the involvement of Edward III. There is also the possibility that the king was concerned in and contributed to the rebuilding of the abbey church, especially the south transept which has close architectural parallels with the tomb.[219] If we were to guess at a possible date for the dedication of the tomb, it might be September 1337, the occasion of a visit

---

tomb of Aymer de Valence, earl of Pembroke, in Westminster Abbey, which was made between his death in 1324 and 1330: Morganstern, 68, 73–80. It has been suggested that the three-bay design and tiered superstructure of the tomb in Tewkesbury abbey of Hugh Despenser, the son of the Younger Despenser, who died in 1349, was loosely based on that of Edward II: P. Lindley, 'The later medieval monuments and chantry chapels', in Morris & Shoesmith, eds, *Tewkesbury Abbey*, 166.

[216] Binski, *Westminster Abbey*, 176, 178. The attribution to Thomas of Canterbury is accepted by Wilson in Alexander & Binski, eds, *Age of Chivalry*, cat. entry 497 (pp. 416–17). On St Stephen's chapel see ibid., cat. entries 324, 325 (pp. 337–9), also by Dr Wilson. Using other work by Dr Wilson, Morganstern suggests a date very soon after Edward's burial in 1327 for the tomb and that Isabella was responsible for having it built: *Gothic Tombs*, 83. I am not convinced by Ormrod's suggestion that even if Thomas of Canterbury was the architect responsible, this does not necessarily mean that the tomb was either commissioned or paid for by Edward III: Ormrod, 'Personal religion', 870, n. 123. It is unlikely that such an important royal servant would have been diverted to work in which his employer Edward III was not involved in some way.

[217] Mortimer, *The Perfect King*, 460, n. 87. On Thomas of Canterbury and William Ramsey see *KW*, i, 514–16; J.H. Harvey, 'The origins of the perpendicular style', in *Studies in Building History*, ed. E.M. Jope (London, 1961), 135–58.

[218] Morganstern, *Gothic Tombs*, 83.

[219] C. Wilson has suggested that the architect of the tomb was also responsible for the south transept: Alexander & Binski, eds, *Age of Chivalry*, cat. entry 497 (pp. 416–17).

by Edward III[220] and the year following the completion of the south transept.

Another question is who paid for the tomb. Pilgrims and visitors no doubt made a contribution as the Abbey chronicle claimed, but there are no extant financial records of the medieval abbey to show whether or not this was so.[221] It is also possible that the town of Gloucester made its own contribution in return for the confirmation of its charters in December 1328, but again there is no evidence to support this. On the other hand, if Edward III contributed wholly or largely to the cost,[222] there should be documentary proof of this. Unfortunately this is not the case either.[223] By the time that Edward III took over the rule of his kingdom from the regime of his mother Isabella and Roger Mortimer in late 1330, the treasury was almost empty.[224] He was reduced to raising money by extraordinary measures and did so, for example, for the wedding of his sister Eleanor to Count Reginald of Guelders in 1332, when he sent out what amounted to begging letters to the heads of nearly 300 religious houses: these brought in over £1,300.[225] It is conceivable that Edward III also raised money by special measures for the construction of his father's tomb. In his account for 1332–3 the sheriff of Gloucestershire recorded a sum of £1,521 received from the lands at Cheltenham and Slaughter belonging to the great Benedictine abbey of Fécamp in Normandy.[226] These had been in royal

[220] Ormrod 'Personal religion', 871; E 101/388/5. One might further speculate that Edward III's long visit to Gloucester in Aug.–Sept. 1329 was concerned in part with the making of his father's tomb: Shenton, *Itinerary of Edward III*, 48–9.

[221] The records and manuscripts belonging to the abbey were dispersed at the time of the Reformation. The manuscripts now in the cathedral library are later acquisitions. For example, Gloucester Cathedral Ms. 34, containing abbot Walter of Frocester's Historia Monasterii Gloucestriae, which includes material on the pilgrims who visited Edward II's tomb (ff. 18r–19v; Welander, *History*, 629), was bought by the dean and chapter in 1879 from a dealer in Berlin: S. M. Eward, *A Catalogue of Gloucester Cathedral Library* (Gloucester, 1972), 5; I. M. Kirby, *Diocese of Gloucester* (Gloucester, 1967), 2, 30. W.H. Hart's Rolls Series edition of the Historia Monasterii Gloucestriae (London, 1863) was produced from manuscripts in the British Library and the Queen's College, Oxford.

[222] Palliser, 'Royal mausolea', 8–9, considers that Edward III was primarily responsible both for the building of the shrine and for the rebuilding of the abbey, and that these were not just a local initiative based on pilgrims' offerings at the tomb of Edward II.

[223] I have examined a substantial amount of financial material for the early years of the reign of Edward III without finding any mention of his father's tomb.

[224] C. Shenton, 'Edward III and the coup of 1330', in *The Age of Edward III*, ed. J.S. Bothwell (Woodbridge, Suffolk & Rochester, NY, 2001), 24. As already noted, the enormous surplus inherited from Edward II in 1326 had almost all been spent by the end of 1327.

[225] A.K. McHardy, 'Paying for the wedding', in *Fourteenth Century England*, iv, ed. J.S. Hamilton (Woodbridge, Suffolk & Rochester, NY, 2006), 43–60.

[226] E 352/125, no membrane number; E 372/177/m.30 (6 Ed. III); E 106/7/4 (extent of lands of Fécamp, Glos., 18 Ed. II); SC 6/bundle 1125/no. 15 (accounts for lands of alien priories in Glos., 18 Ed. II to 3 Ed. II, including those of Fécamp). Edward III took the fealty of the new abbot on 20 April 1332, when the financial obligations of the abbey to the English crown would have ceased.

custody for several years, arising first from the seizure of the lands of alien religious houses in 1324 during the war of Saint-Sardos and then from the vacancy which arose when the abbot Pierre Roger was appointed as archbishop of Rouen. Pierre Roger was well known to the English court through his close involvement in Anglo-French relations: in 1328 and again in 1329 he was sent to England to demand that Edward III should perform homage; and in between these two missions he was sent to Gascony to sequester Edward's revenues until he agreed to pay homage, which was eventually performed at Amiens on 6 June 1329.[227] It might have seemed appropriate to Edward III that in turn the abbey's own sequestered revenues should be used to help pay for his father's tomb: £1,521 would have gone a long way towards this.[228] But there was another reason why Fécamp might have made a contribution: this was the close connection which had existed between England and the abbey since the time of Edward the Confessor, who had been a generous benefactor to the abbey, including granting it land in Sussex.[229] The monks of Fécamp had retained their interest in Edward the Confessor and England and in about 1308 had installed stained glass depicting the lives of St Louis and St Edward, possibly to mark the marriage of Edward II and Isabella at nearby Boulogne.[230] If they were interested in Edward II at the beginning of his reign, perhaps they were still interested in him after his death. This is of course highly speculative and there is no proof of any of these suggestions. Nonetheless a link between two famous Benedictine abbeys, one in Normandy and the other in Gloucester, remains an intriguing possibility.

HOW DID EDWARD II DIE?

The sources are generally in agreement that Edward died on 21 September 1327 and at Berkeley castle, with the exception of some versions of the *Brut* chronicle which place his death at Corfe castle in Dorset.[231] There is

---

[227] Chaplais, *Le Duché-pairie*, 157–8; Sumption, *Trial by Battle*, i, 109–10, 119–20. In 1342 Pierre Roger also became pope as Clement VI.

[228] The restoration of the tomb completed in 2007 cost £152,000.

[229] F. Barlow, *Edward the Confessor* (London, 1970), 39, 180, 230; P.H. Sawyer, *Anglo-Saxon Charters* (London, 1968), no. 1054. In 1247 Henry III forced the monks to exchange their lands at Rye and Winchelsea for Cheltenham and Slaughter in Glos.: *CChR, 1226–57*, 321–2; D. Matthew, *The Norman Monasteries and their Possessions* (Oxford, 1962), 76.

[230] M. Harrison, 'A life of Edward the Confessor in early fourteenth-century stained glass at Fécamp in Normandy', *Journal of Warburg & Courtauld Institutes*, xxvi (1963), 22–37; M. Kauffmann, 'The image of St Louis', in *Kings & Kingship in Medieval Europe*, ed. A. J. Duggan (London, 1993), 265.

[231] *Brut*, i, 253. This may be a significant detail, possibly reflecting the development of the story of Edward II's death in the years after 1327, since in 1330 Corfe was the scene of the earl of Kent's vain attempt to free Edward II, who he had been led to believe was still alive and held there: *Brut*, i, 263–4. A version of the French *Brut*, ending in 1333 (Trinity College Dublin, TCD Ms. 500, f. 191) also seems to imply that Edward died at Corfe.

however a much wider variety of explanations for his death.[232] Some sources recorded simply that he died, but made no attempt at any further explanation; one that he died naturally; others that he died of grief; others claimed that he was murdered, but without much elaboration; and a final category had the lurid red-hot iron story. The first group includes the initial announcement of his death during the parliament assembled at Lincoln in September 1327; the *Annales Paulini* say no more than that he died at Berkeley and was buried at Gloucester;[233] the short annals composed at the Cistercian abbey at Newenham near Axminster in Devon in the early 1330s say only that Edward died and lay at Gloucester;[234] the Canterbury chronicle says that Edward '*Migravit ad Christum*' at Berkeley and was buried at Gloucester;[235] while the author of the Wigmore chronicle went out of his way to insist that Edward died a natural death, whatever was said to the contrary.[236] Other examples could also be given, although some express doubt.[237] The shorter continuations of the French *Brut* chronicle, ending in the early 1330s, use language which suggests that Edward died of grief but which might also be taken to mean that he died in pain.[238] The *Anonimalle Chronicle*, another continuation of the French *Brut*, says simply that Edward became ill and died.[239] But there were also doubters. Adam Murimuth,

---

[232] Ian Mortimer has published a very useful guide to the sources in his paper 'Sermons of sodomy', Table 1, 'Principal accounts which mention the death of Edward II, 1327–1400', 58–60. He lists 21 such sources, both in manuscript and in published form, but several more manuscript sources can be added: the Canterbury chronicle, Trinity College Cambridge, Ms. R.5.41, f. 126v; the Historia Roffensis, BL, Cotton Ms. Faustina B.V, f. 51r; the Wigmore chronicle, Univ. of Chicago Ms. 224, f. 35; Memorabilia facta tempore Regis Edwardi secundi in Anglia (contained in the Register of the Cistercian abbey of Newenham, near Axminster, Devon), BL, Arundel Ms. 17, f. 44r; and two more versions of the French *Brut*, Bod. Lyell Ms. 17, f. 118v, and TCD Ms. 500, f. 191. Yet another version of the *Brut* is the text edited from Corpus Christi College, Oxford, Ms. 178: Galbraith, 'Extracts from the Historia Aurea', esp. 216–17.

[233] *Ann. Paul.*, 337–8.

[234] BL, Arundel Ms. 17, f. 44r: it makes no mention of Berkeley.

[235] Trinity College Cambridge, Ms. R.5.41, f. 126v.

[236] Univ. of Chicago Ms. 224, f. 35: '*quicquid aliter pacis mundi ablocuntur morte naturali moriebatur*'. This was, however, written about 40 years later, at Wigmore priory, of which the Mortimers were patrons, and is not an unbiased witness. See Gransden, ii, 61.

[237] See Mortimer, 'Principal accounts' in 'Sermons of sodomy'; Woburn chronicle, BL, Cotton Ms. Vespasian E ix, ff. 80r–80v; *Lanercost*, 260; *Le Baker*, 172; and *Scalacronica*, 94–5, which said he died but that the manner of death was unknown.

[238] E.g., Edward '*enmaladist en le dit chastel de Berkelee grevousement de grant dolour et morust*': Bod. Lyell Ms. 17, f. 118v; '*tost après le Roi par cas de maladie en le chastel de Berkeleie grevousement de grant dolour e morust*': Trinity College Dublin, TCD Ms. 500, f. 191. Mortimer also cites three other *Brut* mss: BL, Cotton Ms. Cleopatra D.VII, f. 174v; BL, Harleian Ms. 6359, f. 83r; BL, Cotton Ms. Domitian A.X, f. 87r (which also suggests that his death was finally brought about by murder). On the French *Brut* and its value for the reign of Edward II see Taylor, *English Historical Literature*, ch. 6, esp. 120–7, and App. I, 274–84.

[239] *Anonimalle*, 134–5: see the Introduction. Also Taylor, *English Historical Literature*, ch. 7, esp. 133–9.

another writer connected with St Paul's, who wrote his final account twenty years after the event but was certainly working from much earlier notes, was shrewd and generally well informed; he was also the administrator of the vacant diocese of Exeter when Edward died and so not a great distance away. He too said that Edward died at Berkeley; but then added that it was commonly said that Edward had been murdered 'by a trick';[240] later when writing of Mortimer's execution in 1330 he says that Mortimer was accused of having Edward suffocated.[241] The Lanercost chronicler hedged his bets, saying that Edward died either naturally or through the violence of others;[242] the author of the *Gesta Edwardi de Carnarvon*, writing at Bridlington in the 1330s, noted that he did not believe what was then being written;[243] an annotation in the Peterborough chronicle records that 'Edward was in good health in the evening but was found dead on the morrow';[244] and the French chronicle of London remarked that he was 'vilely murdered'.[245] Some writers were more specific as to the mode of death. Strangulation was cited by the Lichfield chronicler,[246] while suffocation combined with the insertion of a red-hot iron into Edward's bowels was offered by a number of writers. This appears in the longer continuations of the *Brut* chronicle;[247] Ranulph Higden's *Polychronicon*;[248] the *Chronicon* of Geoffrey le Baker;[249] the chronicle of Meaux abbey in Yorkshire;[250] and in Henry Knighton's chronicle written at Leicester;[251] one version of the *Brut* adds that Edward was first of all drugged while he sat at dinner before being killed.[252] Through the sheer horror of the account and by dint of repetition the red-hot iron has become the classic explanation of Edward's death.

There were also plenty of suggestions as to both the instigators and the actual murderers. The author of the Historia Roffensis, in recording that

---

[240] '*per cautelam occisus*': *Murimuth*, 53–4. The Latin word *cautela* literally means 'a trick' or 'a device'. Perhaps the sense here should be metaphorical, such as 'by treachery' or 'treacherously'. Cf. Mortimer, 'Principal accounts' in 'Sermons of sodomy', 58.

[241] '*suffocatus*': *Murimuth*, 63.

[242] *Lanercost*, 260.

[243] *Gesta Edwardi*, 97–8.

[244] Haines, '*Edwardus redivivus*', 72; BL, Cotton Ms. Claudius A.V ('*Edwardus vespere sanus in crastino mortuus est inventus*').

[245] *French Chron.*, 58.

[246] Mortimer, 'Principal accounts' in 'Sermons of sodomy', 58; BL, Cotton Ms. Cleopatra D.IX, f. 63r.

[247] *Brut*, i, 248–9, 253. On the English version of the *Brut* see Taylor, *English Historical Literature*, 127–31.

[248] *Polychronicon*, 324.

[249] *Le Baker*, 33–4.

[250] *Melsa*, 354–5.

[251] *Knighton*, i, 448, says he was killed ('*occisus*') but on p. 446 also gives the suffocation and red-hot iron story.

[252] Galbraith, 'Extracts', 216–17. The English *Brut* says he was killed after he had gone to bed and did not suspect any treachery: *Brut*, i, 253.

Thomas Gurney brought the news of Edward's death to Lincoln, spoke volumes when he described Gurney as 'the follower of Satan' and added that Edward had died while in the hands of enemies who had long planned to kill him, 'saying we shall put him to a most shameful death'.[253] John Maltravers and Thomas Gurney were named as the killers by Adam Murimuth, the *Brut*, and Geoffrey le Baker, among others; the *Brut* added that they were acting on orders received by Thomas de Berkeley from Roger Mortimer; Geoffrey le Baker claimed that Berkeley was deliberately kept away from Edward because he was too kindly disposed towards him,[254] but that the orders for Edward's death were sent by Isabella through the medium of a deliberately ambiguous message composed by Adam Orleton, the bishop of Hereford.[255]

It is possible that Edward did die a natural death. Although he was described as a man of outstanding strength,[256] there is no way of knowing his physical condition during the time of his imprisonment at Kenilworth and Berkeley and how far he was affected by confinement and possible ill-treatment. However, the mental condition of a man who had so recently been in a position of power with all the trappings of royalty and was now separated from family, friends and dignity is likely to have been very poor. It is easy to believe that Edward was deeply depressed by September 1327.[257] If there were any underlying physical illness as well this might have been enough to bring about or accelerate his death. However, nearly all the references to a natural death or death from illness come from soon after Edward's presumed death and before new information came to light or other explanations had time to be elaborated. It seems more likely that he was murdered, probably by suffocation, and with the intention of leaving no outward mark on his body. A violent death, allegedly accompanied by the dying screams of the victim, is at odds with such a plan. The gruesome story of the red-hot iron may be true, or simply be a dramatic way of accounting for Edward's death from a painful illness. But it is also possible that it was a later addition: once the story began to circulate it quickly took on the status of undisputed fact. It has been plausibly argued that the story, with its implications of anal rape, was developed later as propaganda by his enemies, specifically in order to blacken his reputation still further[258] and probably

---

[253] '*Sathanae satellitem*'; '*Obiit itaque in manibus hostium qui multo tempore mortem illi inceptanates et dicentes morte turpissima occidamus eum*': BL, Cotton Ms. Faustina B.V, f. 51r.

[254] Murimuth, 53–4; *Brut*, i, 253; *Le Baker*, 32–4; Galbraith, 'Extracts', 216–17.

[255] '*Edwardum occidere nolite timere bonum est*', which could be interpreted as either 'Do not fear to kill Edward. It is good', or 'Do not kill Edward. It is good to fear': *Le Baker*, 31–2.

[256] *Polychronicon*, 298–300. The description was written after his death.

[257] As the account in the *Brut*, i, 252–3, would strongly suggest.

[258] Mortimer, 'Sermons of sodomy', 53–6, 58–60. See also Evans, *The Death of Kings*, 124–34, where the story is treated as originating in rumour 'modelled to fit his supposed homosexuality and passivity', rather than propaganda, and Ormrod, 'The sexualities of Edward II', in Dodd & Musson, eds, *The Reign of Edward II*, 37–9.

also to counter any attempts to portray him as a potential saint.[259] There is also a parallel, which may be significant, between this story and the twelfth-century chronicle accounts of the murder in 1016 of an earlier English king, Edmund Ironside.[260]

There is no definite evidence of any initial suspicions about the manner of Edward II's death. As already mentioned, it is known that the woman who eviscerated Edward's corpse visited Isabella at Worcester a few days after the funeral. This could be interpreted as Isabella wanting to know more about the manner of her husband's death, either because she had a guilty conscience or because she suspected foul play; or the purpose may simply have been for her to receive Edward's heart.[261] Although it is impossible to prove that Isabella had nothing to do with her husband's death, one part at least of the accusations against her can be rejected. The ambiguous message allegedly sent to Edward's gaolers on her behalf by the bishop of Hereford was pure fiction, since the bishop was not even in England at the time and so could not possibly have done this. A similar literary device has been traced via the St Albans chronicler Matthew Paris writing in the mid-thirteenth century to the early thirteenth-century French chronicler, Alberic des Trois Fontaines, who recorded a message allegedly written in 1213 by the archbishop of Gran/Ezstergom in Hungary, instigating the murder of Queen Gertrude the wife of Andrew II of Hungary: *Reginam interficere nolite timere bonum est.*[262]

---

[259] Geoffrey le Baker's account seems designed to establish Edward II's credentials as a potential saint. Some of the details in Le Baker are very similar to those in the account of Edward's ill-treatment and murder to be found in *Brut*, i, 252–3; Galbraith, 'Extracts', 216–17.

[260] Chaplais, 16–17, 112–13; Mortimer, 'Sermons of sodomy', 51. Godfrey II, duke of Lower Lorraine, is said to have been murdered in the same way in 1076: Chaplais, 112, n. 18. Two 12th-century examples of death by impalement are cited in Evans, *The Death of Kings*, 132–3. In 1447 Duke Humphrey of Gloucester was also allegedly murdered by the insertion of a red-hot iron: Evans, 124–34. Another parallel is the death of the earl of Hereford at the battle of Boroughbridge in 1322, when a spear thrust through a gap in the planking of the bridge entered his body by the anus and spilled his bowels: *Brut*, i, 219. The red-hot iron story might have been a literal or poetic revenge for the earl's death.

[261] E 101/383/1; E 352/125, m.46v; E 372/177, m.45d; Moore, 'Documents', 224–6. The only important difference between the original and the enrolled versions of Henry de Glaunville's accounts is that the reference to the woman who disembowelled Edward II after death is only in the enrolments, E 352 and E 372. This was noted in Moore, 218. The evisceration of the corpse could also have contributed to the growth of the red-hot iron legend, if that is what it was.

[262] Matthew Paris, *Chronica Majora*, ed. H.R. Luard, Rolls Series, iii (London, 1876), 51; Matthew Paris, *Historia Anglorum*, ed. F. Madden, Rolls Series, ii (London, 1866), 233–4; *Chronica Albrici Monachi Trium Fontium*, MGH, SS.23, ed. G.H. Pertz (Hanover, 1874; repr. 1963), 898. See Tout, 'Captivity and death', 164, n. 1. The origins of the literary device were originally revealed by S.H. Cassan in his *Lives of the Bishops of Winchester*, i (London, 1827), 185: Haines, *The Church and Politics*, 109.

It was not until the fall and execution of Roger Mortimer in October–November 1330 that Edward's death was first publicly described as murder and that anyone was named as responsible. In the indictment laid before parliament in November 1330 Mortimer was accused of having Edward moved from Kenilworth to Berkeley castle where he was 'traitorously, feloniously and falsely murdered and killed by him and his followers'.[263] Two of these followers, Thomas Gurney and William Ogle or Ockley, were also judged guilty of the murder of 'King Edward, the father of our present lord the king' and sentenced to death in their absence.[264]

THE PRISONER AT CORFE

The execution of Roger Mortimer and the conviction of Ockley and Gurney were the continuation and climax of another drama which had been working itself out since 1327. No sooner had Edward II been buried than tales began to circulate that he was not dead after all and that someone else was buried in his place. The usual cast of fantasizing friars reappeared on stage, together with former friends and allies of the departed king, and at least some leading magnates.

On 16 March 1330 Edward II's half-brother, Edmund of Woodstock the earl of Kent, was brought first before Robert Howel, the coroner of the king's household, and then before the magnates who were assembled in parliament at Winchester. After interrogation by Howel and Roger Mortimer Edmund made a remarkable confession: that the pope had asked him to free the former king from imprisonment, offering to pay the costs of doing so; that a Dominican friar from the London convent had come to him at Kensington near London and told him that he had raised the devil, who had told him for certain that the former king was still alive;[265] that William Melton, the archbishop of York, sent Robert de Taunton, one of his chaplains, to him with an offer of £5,000 to aid in Edward's delivery. In a long and circumstantial confession Edmund gave the names of a number of people who he said were also involved, who

---

[263] *PROME*, Parliament of Nov. 1330, C 65/2, item 1: '*et ordina q'il feust mande au chastell de Berkle, ou par lui et ses soens feust treterousement, felonessement, et falsement murdre et tue*'. No evidence was presented to support this and none given in defence of Mortimer, who was judged guilty by the earls and barons present and sentenced to death. Mortimer was in prison during the proceedings.

[264] *PROME*, Parliament of Nov. 1330, C 65/2, item 5: 'and that whoever can take the said Thomas alive will have £100, and that whoever brings the head 100 marks. In addition that whoever can take the said William alive will have 100 marks, and that whoever brings the head, if it happens that he be not taken alive, will have £40 of the king's gift'.

[265] *Murimuth*, 253–7. The Lanercost chronicle claims that this was none other than Thomas Dunheved, but he was probably dead by then: *Lanercost*, 265. According to Geoffrey le Baker, the Dominican was sent to Corfe by Edmund to confirm the story and, after bribing a doorkeeper, made his way inside and even claimed to have seen Edward dining splendidly: *Le Baker*, 44.

believed that Edward was still alive and wanted to see him freed: four knights, Ingelram Berenger, William de la Zouche, John Pecche and Fulk Fitz Warin; William de Cliff; Hugh Despenser; two Dominican friars, Edmund and John Savage, who were 'out of their order';[266] and the bishop of London. On a journey to France he had met Sir Henry de Beaumont and Sir Thomas Roscelyn in the chamber of the duke of Brabant, the former Edward II's nephew. The two exiles had said they planned to launch an invasion of England via Scotland, with the aid of Donald, earl of Mar. A Cistercian monk from Quarr abbey on the Isle of Wight had also arranged a barge to bring Edward and Edmund from Corfe to Arundel castle, and from there to wherever they decided. Edmund also admitted that he had written to Sir Bogo de Bayouse and Sir John Deveril concerning Edward's release from captivity.[267] The lengthy account of the affair in the *Brut* chronicle appears to be based in part on Edmund's confession, but it adds that certain Dominicans had told him not just that Edward was alive but that he was being held by Thomas Gurney in Corfe castle, whose constable was John Deveril.[268] When approached by Edmund, Deveril had admitted to him that he had Edward in his custody but was under strict orders not to allow anyone to see him. Edmund gave Deveril a letter addressed to his brother in which he promised to release him and claimed that he had the support of many prelates, earls and barons. Deveril betrayed him and took the letter directly to Roger Mortimer.[269] The earl of Kent's confession was then repeated before a deputation of peers attending parliament. The result was a foregone conclusion, and the earl was executed outside the gate of Winchester castle on 19 March, but only after a delay in finding someone willing to perform the execution.[270]

A month later it was the turn of William Melton, archbishop of York, who was interrogated before the king and his council at Woodstock on 23 April and again at Banbury on 30 April. Melton was charged that on 10 October 1329 a certain William de Kingsclere had come to him at Sherburn, 'announcing to him and emphatically asserting that Edward, the late king of England, the father of the present king, was alive and in good health in the prison of Corfe Castle and asking him if he would furnish any advice or help in releasing him'. Melton had allegedly replied that he would have sold all his goods and chattels, except for a single vestment and a single

---

[266] The Lanercost chronicle claims that three Dominicans, in addition to Thomas Dunheved, were involved, Edmund and John (presumably the Savage brothers) and a certain Richard: *Lanercost*, 265.

[267] *Murimuth*, 59–60, and App., 253–7 (the text and translation of the earl of Kent's confession); *Brut*, i, 266 (this mentions the direct involvement of Mortimer).

[268] *Brut*, i, 263–7.

[269] The text of the letter (whether it is genuine is another matter) is in ibid., i, 265.

[270] *CCR, 1330–33*, 132. *Foedera*, II, ii, 783, 787; *Murimuth*, 60; *Brut*, i, 267; Mortimer, *The Greatest Traitor*, 231–2.

chalice, in order to bring this about. It was claimed that Melton had then sent William de Kingsclere to Scotland to obtain the assistance of Donald, earl of Mar, who replied that when he was notified by the archbishop he would enter England with an army of 40,000 men. The archbishop denied all the charges and was to have been tried before Henry le Scrope, together with the bishop of London and William, the abbot of Langdon in Kent.[271] These three men, William la Zouche 'and many others' petitioned the king during the parliament of November–December 1330 on the grounds that John de Haltby from Ipswich and Martin Love had tried to implicate them in the rebellion of the earl of Kent,[272] and the proceedings ended abruptly on 12 December 1330 when Edward III ordered the justices not to take any further action since he held the archbishop completely guiltless of adherence to Edmund of Woodstock.[273]

In the end the only person to suffer death for his adherence to the alleged plot was the earl of Kent himself, and he won little sympathy because of his past behaviour and that of his followers.[274] William Melton's clerk Robert de Taunton and various unidentified Dominican and Carmelite friars were put into prison;[275] the provincials of the two orders, the distinguished scholar Simon de Boraston and John de Baconthorpe, may have been exiled for a time;[276] and four knights, Fulk Fitz Warin, John Pecche, Ingelram Berenger and George de Percy, had their lands seized as the earl's adherents.[277]

It is easier to construct some kind of narrative than to explain exactly what was going on in 1330; to what extent those engaged in the plot really believed that Edward II was still alive; or whether they were simply entrapped by their own wishful thinking and by Mortimer and his agents; or whether they used the opportunity to further their own political agendas. An element of all these was probably involved. Part of the explanation was certainly the activities of friars concerned to demonstrate their continued loyalty to the former king, prepared to clutch at any straws and to persuade others of the truth of their stories. If Thomas Dunheved himself was no longer alive to lend his own special brand of fanatical

---

[271] Trinity College Cambridge Ms. R.5.41, f. 129v; *Select Cases*, ed. Sayles, v, 43–5; KB 27/280, m.38.

[272] SC 8/173/8613; SC 8/172/8555; *PROME*, Parliament of Nov. 1330, C 65/2, item 7. SC 8/50/2485 identified Haltby as a former adherent of the Younger Despenser.

[273] *Select Cases*, ed. Sayles, v, 45. A similar order was given with regard to the bishop of London.

[274] *Murimuth*, 60; *Le Baker*, 44. Edmund has won little sympathy from historians either, being regarded as unreliable in his political allegiances, as well as stupid and gullible, which is probably a fair assessment: see, for example, Tout, 'Captivity and death', 172–3.

[275] Including Thomas Dunheved, if the Lanercost writer is to be believed: *Le Baker*, 44; *Murimuth*, 60; *Lanercost*, 265.

[276] See S. Tugwell's article on Boraston in the *Oxford DNB*. Boraston was certainly back in favour in 1333; Baconthorpe was in Paris for a time in 1330.

[277] *CPR, 1327–30*, 565. Pecche's lands were restored on 9 Aug. 1330: *CCR, 1330–33*, 52.

loyalty, then other friars certainly did so. Several of the names of those identified by Edmund of Woodstock in his confession are men who had been connected with the Younger Despenser before 1327: Sir Ingelram Berenger was a former Despenser retainer; William de Cliff a chancery clerk had also been a Despenser adherent;[278] the Carmelite Richard de Bliton had been the Younger Despenser's confessor;[279] and Hugh Despenser was the son and heir of the Younger Despenser who had defended Caerphilly castle during the siege of 1326-7. Then there were the old and loyal friends of the former king, William Melton the archbishop of York, Stephen Segrave the bishop of London and William abbot of Langdon. All of these groups were hostile in varying degrees to the regime of Mortimer and Isabella.[280] Particular attention has been drawn to the possible role of Sir John Pecche, one of the knights implicated by the earl of Kent. It has been suggested that he was in a position to know whether or not Edward II really was alive and being held at Corfe, since he had been constable of the castle.[281] Pecche had been appointed as constable in December 1325 but it is not clear when he left office. He and his wife appointed attorneys prior to going overseas in February 1327 and again in February 1328.[282] Whether he did go overseas or not is unknown but it is very unlikely that he remained as constable until 1329, as has been argued.[283] John Maltravers was formally appointed as constable in September 1329, but was already described as keeper in the previous month, while there is evidence that he was also at Corfe in or about September 1327.[284] This suggests that he may have replaced John Pecche much earlier than the date of his formal appointment. Earlier in his career Pecche had had associations both with the Younger Despenser and, interestingly enough, was also acquainted with the Dunheved family;[285] Pecche and Fulk Fitz Warin, another knight named by the earl of Kent, had also played an important part in the war against the

---

[278] Tout, *Place of the Reign*, 123; Fryde, 225.

[279] *Le Baker*, 44; Haines, *Stratford*, 213, n. 109.

[280] The list of over 40 men whose arrest was ordered on 31 March 1330 as adherents of the earl of Kent included the familiar figures of Rhys ap Gruffudd and Stephen Dunheved, four friars (Richard de Pontefract, Richard Vavasour, Henry Domeram and Thomas de Bourne), and two former members of Edward II's chamber, a squire John Harsik and the usher Peter Bernard: *CFR, 1319-37*, 169-70; *CCR, 1330-33*, 51; J.C. Davies, 'The first journal of Edward II's chamber', *EHR*, xxx (1915), 670, 676, 662-80.

[281] Mortimer, 'The death of Edward II', 1201-2.

[282] *CPR, 1324-7*, 202; *CPR, 1327-30*, 11, 234.

[283] Mortimer, 'The death of Edward II', 1201: the reference cited, *Complete Peerage*, x, 343, n. b., does not support this statement.

[284] *CFR, 1327-37*, 149; *CCR, 1327-30*, 487; Mortimer, 'The death of Edward II', 1190, citing Berkeley Castle Muniments, Select Roll 39.

[285] Saul, 'The Despensers', 27, 29. Pecche was a Warwickshire man and evidently a neighbour of the Dunheveds; he had a dispute with Margery de Dunheved, against whom he invoked Despenser's help.

Mortimers in the Welsh March in 1321–2.[286] Far from knowing that Edward II was alive and well in Corfe castle, Pecche may have been as much influenced by rumour and disinformation as anyone else.

Another source of hostility was Henry, earl of Lancaster. Although Lancaster and his son-in-law Thomas Wake had helped to orchestrate the events which led to Edward II's deposition in January 1327, and he had apparently willingly acquiesced in Edward's transfer from Kenilworth to Berkeley in April that year, tension between him and Mortimer was increasing. This arose in part from the peace treaty with Scotland in 1328 to which he was bitterly opposed, together with others such as Henry de Beaumont who had claims to lands in Scotland; but it also stemmed from the growing influence and arbitrary behaviour of Roger Mortimer. Mortimer's power, symbolized by the title of earl of March which he was granted in October 1328, exceeded even that of the Younger Despenser against whom he had fought in the closing years of Edward II's reign. In the summer and autumn of 1328 the situation deteriorated so far that Lancaster began raising an army; among his sympathizers were the former king's two half-brothers, the earls of Kent and Norfolk. Open conflict was avoided and most of the rebels were pardoned, with the exception of Henry de Beaumont, Thomas Wake and Thomas Roscelyn who were forced into exile and fled to France.[287] It was deeply ironic that some of those who invaded England with Isabella and Mortimer in 1326 were once again abroad and plotting, this time Mortimer's downfall.

There is a hint of things to come as early as November 1328 when the earl of Lancaster wrote to the mayor of London telling him that the earl of Kent had made certain communications with him, which he could not put into writing but which the bearer would report by word of mouth. Although it has been suggested that these concerned rumours that Edward II was still alive and that Lancaster was implicated in the earl of Kent's plot,[288] this probably indicates no more than a growing sympathy between the two earls. The earl of Kent did however go to France in June 1329 on royal business connected with the canonization of Thomas of

---

[286] Bod., Laud Ms. Misc. 529, f. 107; Trinity College Cambridge Ms. R.5.41, ff. 116v, 117; Phillips, 220–1. There is no confirmation of Ian Mortimer's statement that Pecche had sided with Mortimer during the initial stages of the Despenser war before being reconciled with the king: Mortimer, 'The Death of Edward II', 1201.

[287] For a short summary of events see Ormrod, *The Reign of Edward III*, 4–5; Fryde, 216–24; Nicholson, *Edward III and the Scots*, 61–3.

Another sign of the times was the murder in Oct. 1328 of Sir Robert de Holland, the former retainer of Thomas of Lancaster, who had betrayed him in 1322: Maddicott, 'Thomas of Lancaster and Sir Robert Holland', 469.

[288] *CPMR*, i, 72; V.B. Redstone, 'Some mercenaries of Henry of Lancaster, 1327–1330', *TRHS*, 3rd ser., vii (1913), 160–1, 166 (this has the French text of the letter). Paul Doherty has however shown a possible link between William Aylmer and the earl of Lancaster in relation to the Dunheveds' attack on Berkeley in 1327: Doherty, *Isabella*, 123–5.

Lancaster[289] and it was evidently during this period that he contacted the Lancastrian exiles living in Paris as well as visiting Avignon.[290] If the account in the *Brut* is to be believed, Edmund told the pope that he thought his brother Edward was still alive. Although this account then says that the pope gave Edmund encouragement in releasing his brother from captivity,[291] it seems unlikely that the pope would have committed himself to such a rumour: it is more probable that he fobbed Edmund off with polite words, but no more. In fact John XXII appears to have been profoundly embarrassed when he discovered that Edmund had engaged in a plot, and when John Walwayn, canon of Salisbury, came to Avignon in 1330, shortly after the execution of the earl of Kent,[292] he expressed his unease very forcibly and made it clear that he did not and never had believed that Edward II was still alive. On 5 September 1330 the pope wrote to both Isabella and Edward III, thanking them for the news that John Walwayn had just brought and expressing his amazement that the earl of Kent could have asserted that the pope believed something so incredible: 'that he for whom such solemn funeral ceremonies had been held was alive'.[293] The pope added that he believed firmly that those who were present at the funeral were not deceived and did not attempt to deceive. If the funeral had been secret, there might be some justification for the report, but as it was held in public there was none. Had the pope believed such a report, he would have dealt not with the earl of Kent or anyone else, but with the queen and her son concerning the restoration to liberty and the production in public of the man said to be alive.[294]

---

[289] *CPR, 1327–30*, 397, 415. He was accompanied by William Melton's clerk Robert de Taunton who was later implicated in his plot. This may imply that Melton knew something of the rumours about Edward II's survival even before Oct. 1329. On the other hand, Melton had been closely involved since Feb. 1327 in the attempt to have Thomas of Lancaster canonized, so there was a good reason for his clerk to go to Avignon with the earl of Kent: *Letters from Northern Registers*, ed. Raine, 339–42.

[290] The earl cannot be found again in England until 3 Dec. 1329: C 53/116, m.27.

[291] *Brut*, i, 263.

[292] Walwayn was probably sent to explain what had recently been occurring in England: see *Foedera*, II, iii, 40–1.

[293] *CPL*, 499. This letter is no longer extant in The National Archives but I have checked the original papal register in which it is recorded without finding any material which is not in the calendared version: ASV, Vatican Register 116, f. 41: the relevant passage is '*miramur quomodo nobilis ille* [i.e. the earl of Kent] *assere potuit quod nos rei tam incredibili fidem dederimus credulam videlicet illum vivere pro quo facte fuerunt exequie tam solemnes*'.

[294] Ibid. The pope was very well and speedily informed about events in England: on 7 Nov. he wrote to Edward III about the arrest of Roger Mortimer on 19 Oct. (which he had probably heard of on 3 Nov.), asking that he should be treated justly and shown mercy: *CPL*, 498. On the same day he told Edward III that he had heard Edward was not showing signs of filial affection to his mother; should she have done anything to justify his behaviour, the pope exhorted him to remember what she had done for him, and what enmity and ill-will against herself she had provoked in his service. He begged Edward to show mercy, that he might find mercy on the Day of Judgment: *CPL*, 498.

The pope had not believed that Edward II was still alive in 1330 and, just as significantly, some of the chroniclers did not believe it either. The author of the Lanercost chronicle expressed his amazement that the Dominican friar who began the rumour, or indeed any educated person, should have believed the devil, the father of lies;[295] while Geoffrey le Baker remarked that the whole thing was false and a fantasy.[296] Roger Mortimer and his agents must have learned of the existence of rumours being spread by certain friars and had then used them to entrap their enemies.[297]

THE END OF ROGER MORTIMER

Mortimer's success in snaring Edmund of Woodstock contributed to his own downfall only a few months later. Edward III was furious and ashamed: he had been very reluctant to order the execution of his uncle Edmund of Woodstock and had done so only under great pressure, from both his mother Queen Isabella and from Mortimer.[298] There were other reasons for what followed but it is likely that the death of the earl of Kent was the last straw for the eighteen-year-old king. Mortimer and his mother between them had usurped the power which was rightfully his as king; they had bankrupted the treasury; humiliated him in his first and unsuccessful campaign against the Scots in 1327; imposed upon him a hateful treaty with the same enemy and, without his approval, married his sister

---

[295] *Lanercost*, 265: '*Mirum vero est quod dictus frater, vel aliquis multum literatus, voluit credere diabolo, cum a Deo dicatur in sancto Evangelio secundum Johannem, quod mendax est et pater eius, id est, inventor eius mendacii*'.

[296] *Le Baker*, 44: '*totum hoc fuisset falsum et fantasiatum*'.

[297] It has been suggested that the two mysterious Dominicans, Edmund and John Savage who were never arrested, were *agents provocateurs*: Doherty (D.Phil.), 296. John Deveril and Bogo de Bayouse belonged to the garrison at Corfe and were certainly Mortimer's agents. At the time of writing, a paper by Roy Haines, 'Roger Mortimer's scam', was awaiting publication in *Trans. Bristol and Glos. Archaeological Society*. This has now appeared in cxxvi (2008), 139–56, and has been followed by a second paper, 'Sumptuous apparel for a royal prisoner: Archbishop Melton's letter, 14 January 1330', *EHR*, cxxiv (Aug. 2009), 885–94, in which a letter from William Melton to a London draper, Simon Swanlond, is published and discussed. The letter, whose existence was first noted by J.H. Bloom in 'Simon de Swanland and King Edward II', *Notes and Queries*, 11th ser., iv (1911), 1–2, confirms that Melton had been led to believe that Edward was still alive in 1330 but provides no evidence that this was the case. The letter also shows that the William de Cliff, whom I identified above with the chancery clerk of that name, was in fact another friar. Professor Haines has also shown that the clerk Robert de Taunton is properly identified as Robert de Tauton ('Roger Mortimer's scam', 150). William de Kingsclere, who was accused of being responsible for persuading William Melton that Edward II was alive (*Select Cases*, ed. Sayles, v, 43–5), was captured in Rochester on 25 July 1332 and imprisoned in the Tower of London: E 101/310/34; J. Hunter, 'On the measures taken for the apprehension of Sir Thomas de Gournay, one of the murderers of King Edward the Second', *Archaeologia*, xxvii (1838), 283, 290.

[298] *Brut*, i, 267.

Joan to David Bruce, the son and heir of Robert Bruce;[299] and there was also the question of relations with France. With the aid of one of his most trusted followers, William de Montacute, Edward began to plot the overthrow of Mortimer. In early September Mortimer and Isabella moved, with Edward III, to Nottingham castle. Despite Mortimer's suspicions of a plot against him, Edward III and his supporters held their nerve, and on 19 October Montacute and a group of armed men entered the castle by an underground passage during the night and placed Mortimer under arrest.[300] The following month Edward III gained his revenge. Mortimer was indicted before parliament for the murder of Edward II at Berkeley castle in September 1327 and for other crimes, was duly convicted, and was drawn and hanged at Tyburn on 29 November.[301]

PUNISHING THE GUILTY

Several of Mortimer's followers were dealt with at the same time. Simon de Bereford was convicted of aiding and abetting Mortimer in all his crimes;[302] William Ockley and Thomas Gurney were convicted of the murder of Edward II;[303] and two others, the Yorkshire knight Bogo de Bayouse and John Deveril, who had been at Corfe when the earl of Kent tried to find the former king, were both found guilty of the earl's entrapment.[304]

However, neither of Edward's former keepers at Berkeley castle, John Maltravers and Thomas de Berkeley, was charged with responsibility for his death. Maltravers was instead sentenced to death in his absence for his alleged leading role in plotting against the earl of Kent. He was charged with knowing that Edward was dead but not with his murder.[305] Thomas de Berkeley was present in parliament and must have known in advance that it was reasonably safe for him to be there, since he was treated quite differently. He may have been encouraged by the fact that his son Maurice de Berkeley

---

[299] Edward III had even refused to attend the wedding at Berwick in July 1328: Nicholson, *Edward III and the Scots*, 51–3.

[300] Mortimer *The Greatest Traitor*, 236–9; Haines, *Stratford*, 214.

[301] *PROME*, Parliament of Nov. 1330, C 65/2, item 1; Mortimer, *The Greatest Traitor*, 239–40.

[302] *PROME*, Parliament of Nov. 1330, C 65/2, item 2: 'the murder of a liege lord, and the destruction of the royal blood line' were included among his offences but there is no suggestion that he was directly involved in Edward II's death.

[303] *PROME*, Parliament of Nov. 1330, C 65/2, item 5.

[304] *PROME*, Parliament of Nov. 1330, C 65/2, item 4. William de Montacute was appointed as constable of Corfe in Dec. 1330: *CFR, 1327–37*, 211. If anything untoward was happening there, he would soon have known.

[305] *PROME*, Parliament of Nov. 1330, C 65/2, item 3: 'All the peers, earls and barons assembled at this parliament at Westminster have also closely examined, and have assented and agreed thereupon that John Maltravers is guilty of the death of Edmund, earl of Kent, the uncle of our present lord the king, in that he principally, traitorously and falsely plotted the death of the said earl, since he knew of the death of King Edward [*le dit Johan savoit la mort le roi Edward*], nevertheless the said John by ingenious means and by his false and evil subtleties led the said earl to understand the king was alive, which false plotting was the cause of the death of the said earl and of all the evil which followed'.

and Thomas de Bradeston, a royal household knight but with Berkeley connections, were among the conspirators who had arrested Roger Mortimer on the night of 19–20 October.[306] Thomas de Berkeley accepted that Edward had been delivered into the safe-keeping of himself and John Maltravers at Berkeley, and that Edward was murdered there while in their custody, but said that 'he was never an accomplice, a helper or a procurer in his death, nor did he ever know of his death until this present parliament'.[307] He also claimed that when Edward was murdered he was absent from the castle at Bradley and was so ill that he could remember nothing of what took place. When he was asked why he did not take better care of the king, he replied that he had appointed other keepers and officials to act in his place, and again denied any part in Edward's death. On 20 January 1331 a jury of twelve knights appeared before the king in parliament and declared that Thomas de Berkeley was not guilty of any part in Edward's murder, that they believed that he had been ill, that Thomas Gurney and William Ockley had been acting in his place, and that they had carried out the murder. The king was evidently not fully convinced, since Berkeley was left in the custody of the steward of the royal household to await a decision on his fate at the next parliament.[308]

The jury which advised Edward III on the guilt or innocence of Thomas de Berkeley was no ordinary body of county knights attending parliament, but included well-connected and experienced men, such as the royal household bannerets Roger Swynnerton, John D'Arcy and John de Wisham (seneschal of Gascony from 1324 to 1327; and currently justice of North Wales), and a royal household knight, William Trussell (who had formally renounced the community's homage to Edward II in January 1327).[309] Such men knew perfectly well that anyone who had committed treasonable acts could expect no mercy: if they had disbelieved Berkeley's story, there is little doubt that they would have said so.[310] But the men who were best placed to tell the jury and the king about Thomas de Berkeley's guilt or innocence were William Ockley, Thomas Gurney and John Maltravers, who were not to be found, having already fled the country each with a sentence of death and a price on his head hanging over him.[311]

---

[306] Shenton, 'Edward III', 24–6; Phillips, 262, 265.

[307] *PROME*, Parliament of Nov. 1330, C 65/2, item 16: '*dicit quod ipse nuncquam fuit consentiens, auxilians, seu procurans, ad mortem suam, nec unquam scivit de morte sua usque in presenti parliamento isto*'.

[308] Ibid.

[309] See list of household bannerets and knights in 1330 in *CMR, 1326–27*, 377. Swynnerton and Trussell had previously been the earl of Lancaster's retainers; there were several John Darcys, all closely related, but this Darcy is probably the man who had been one of the earl of Pembroke's chief retainers until his death in 1324 and until recently had been justice of Ireland.

[310] *PROME*, Parliament of Nov. 1330, C 65/2, items 3, 5.

[311] Maltravers was valued at 1,000 marks if taken alive and brought to the king and at £500 (wrongly given as £50 in the English translation in *PROME*) for his head; while Gurney and Ockley respectively were worth £100 and 100 marks alive or 100 marks and £40 for the head alone.

THE EXILES

Nothing was heard again of William Ockley and his fate remains a mystery. Maltravers could in principle have gone to Ireland, where his younger brother Edward held the valuable family manor of Rathkeale in Co. Limerick, but he would have been far too conspicuous there and would have invited arrest by the royal authorities.[312] Instead Maltravers and Gurney, who both had close family connections with the south-west of England, probably escaped to the continent from the small Cornish port of Mousehole, with the aid of two local men, Benedict Noght and John le Taverner. The authorities believed that these two remained in contact with Maltravers and Gurney after their escape and continued to supply them with food and arms.[313] Even this was not the end of the story. Maltravers appears to have gone to the Low Countries, where he had spent a previous period of exile after 1322, and worked hard at rehabilitating himself by acting as an English agent at the time when Edward III was busily building alliances there against France.[314] In 1332 Maltravers's wife Agnes went abroad, allegedly on pilgrimage but probably in order to join her husband. In 1334 Maltravers contacted Edward III because he 'was desirous to reveal to him many things concerning his honour and the estate and well-being of the realm'. It is likely that he wished to tell what he knew about the death of Edward II, with which he had not been charged but about which he certainly knew more than was good for him. William de Montacute, the same knight who had been instrumental in the overthrow of Roger Mortimer in 1330, was sent to the continent to meet him.[315] If Maltravers did tell his side of the tragedy of Edward II, no record has survived but, as will appear, it is likely that his evidence was closely linked with the exoneration of Thomas de Berkeley in 1335.[316] In 1339 Maltravers was granted a life annuity of £100; in 1342 his wife was authorized to stay with him for as long as she wished; in 1345 Maltravers

---

[312] Frame, *English Lordship*, 61–2. Control of Rathkeale passed to Maltravers in 1351 after his return from exile: Frame, 68.

[313] On 15 July 1331 a commission of oyer and terminer was appointed to inquire into the activities of Noght and Taverner: *CPR, 1330–34*, 144.

[314] See Sumption, *Trial by Battle*, i, ch. 7, 'Grand strategy'.

[315] *CPR, 1330–34*, 535. In March 1335 Edmund Bereford (Maltravers's brother-in-law), Maurice de Berkeley (the son of Thomas de Berkeley), John Moleyns and Nicholas Beche were all pardoned by Edward III for receiving Maltravers, apparently when he had briefly slipped back into England. Montacute was separately pardoned for receiving Maltravers: *CPR, 1334–38*, 88–9. Berkeley's presence is very significant in relation to the decision in 1335 to pardon his father. See also J.S. Bothwell, 'Agnes Maltravers (d. 1375) and her husband John (d. 1364)', in *Fourteenth Century England*, iv, ed. J.S. Hamilton (Woodbridge, Suffolk & Rochester, NY, 2006), 84–5.

[316] W.M. Ormrod, 'Richard de Bury and the monarchy of Edward III', in *War, Government and Aristocracy in the British Isles, c. 1150–1500*, ed. C. Given-Wilson, A. Kettle & L. Scales (Woodbridge, Suffolk & Rochester, NY, 2008), 172–4.

submitted to Edward III in Flanders;[317] in 1351 he was pardoned and eventually returned to England, where he died in 1364.[318] Even more extraordinary than the real-life story of John Maltravers is the outside possibility that he was so well known in the Low Countries as an Englishman who had fled his country after being involved in the death of a nobleman that he became an inspiration for the fictional English knight, Sir John Mandeville, the hero of one of the most widely read works of travel literature of the late medieval and early modern period.[319]

The fate of Thomas Gurney was very different. Since Gurney had been convicted of playing a direct role in the murder of Edward II, Edward III was determined to capture him and discover the truth about his father's death. In 1331 Gurney was found in Spain, and held prisoner in Burgos by the king of Castile,[320] but escaped before Edward III's agents could take charge of him.[321] He then made his way to Italy and was discovered in Naples, where an English agent, William of Cornwall, held him. Gurney was taken back to Collioure near Perpignan, then into Spain, and finally to Bayonne, in Edward III's duchy of Gascony. There he died in the early summer of 1333.[322]

---

[317] *CPR, 1330–34*, 535; *CPR, 1343–45*, 535.

[318] The pardoning of Maltravers is all the more remarkable given the size of the reward offered for his capture. Edward III was however trying to clear the decks politically in the mid-1330s by pardoning both former supporters of Edward II who had suffered in his downfall and former allies of Mortimer. Another remarkable detail is that as early as Feb. 1331 Edward III's queen Philippa had obtained an income for Maltravers's wife, Agnes (d. 1375) from the dowers of John Nerford (d. 1329) and John Argentine (d. 1318), her former husbands, in order to maintain her family, now destitute following the confiscation of Maltravers's lands. For the career of John Maltravers and his activities after 1330 see Phillips, ' "Edward II" in Italy', 210; the article by C. Shenton in the *Oxford DNB*; and Bothwell, 'Agnes Maltravers', 80–92.

[319] See Phillips, 'The quest for Sir John Mandeville', esp. 251–2.

[320] According to a version of the French *Brut*, both Gurney and Maltravers had gone to Spain, ostensibly as pilgrims to Compostella, but were recognized at Burgos by an English lady, Isolda de Belhouse, who denounced them to the local authorities. Maltravers escaped but Gurney was arrested. This account may be partially true but does not include Gurney's own escape: Galbraith, 'Extracts', 217. See also Haines, 'Sir Thomas Gurney', 58–9.

[321] Diplomatic relations between England and Castile had been very close ever since the marriage of the future Edward I and Eleanor of Castile at Burgos in 1254: see Childs, 'England in Europe', 104–10; and Phillips, 'Plantagenet Ireland, England and Castile: from Burgos (1254) to Batalha (1385)', in *Spanish–Irish Relations through the Ages*, ed. D. M. Downey & J. Crespo MacLennan (Dublin, 2008), 5–11.

[322] J. Hunter, 'On the measures taken for the apprehension of Sir Thomas de Gournay, one of the murderers of King Edward the Second', *Archaeologia*, xxvii (1838), 274–94; Haines, '*Edwardus redivivus*', 76–9, 85 (incl. map on p.78 which shows the pursuit and capture of Gurney); Haines, 'Sir Thomas Gurney', 45–65. The French *Brut* account claims that Gurney was beheaded by the seneschal of Gascony Sir Oliver Ingham after he had confessed that he had 'assented' to the death of Edward II and had told how he died: Galbraith, 'Extracts', 217; Haines, 'Sir Thomas Gurney', 61. However, it is clear from the records published by Hunter that Gurney had been sick and had been given medical treatment which failed to save his life: Hunter, 285, 292–3. The exact date of Gurney's death is not recorded.

Another fugitive from justice was the Yorkshire knight Bogo de Bayouse, who, like Maltravers and John Deveril, was sentenced to death for the entrapment of the earl of Kent at Corfe castle.[323] He fled to France, travelled via the Rhône valley, and ended up in Rome where he was joined by his wife Alice and lived in rooms rented from an unnamed countess. Bogo died in Rome on 26 July 1334 and was buried in the local parish church of San Celso, near the Ponte Sant' Angelo. The English authorities were certainly interested in his whereabouts but so far as is known they did not succeed in tracing him. Nonetheless, although Bogo and his wife may have lived in reasonable comfort, they must have been in constant fear of discovery.[324]

The ultimate fate of Thomas de Berkeley depended in part on the fugitives. It is unlikely that Bogo de Bayouse knew anything at first hand about what had happened at Berkeley in 1327, but Gurney and Maltravers were another matter. When parliament next met in September 1331 the prelates and magnates informed the king that since Thomas Gurney, who knew fully how the murder had been committed, was still alive, so far as they knew, the king and his council should wait until the following parliament before taking any decision on Berkeley's fate.[325] In fact it was several parliaments later before the king and his council returned to the subject of Thomas de Berkeley, and in the meantime Gurney had died, taking his secrets with him to the grave. Although Berkeley was not formally pardoned for his neglect of his royal prisoner until the parliament of March 1337,[326] a recent discovery has shown that two years earlier, during the York parliament of May–June 1335, Berkeley was declared by the king to be 'quit of the death of the king his father and without culpability'. The reason for the decision was not given but it is likely that it was the result of newly acquired information about Edward's death and that it had come from none other than John Maltravers.[327]

Edward II was dead and buried, and the men guilty of his murder had been punished. But it was not the end of the story.

---

[323] Bayouse (whose name is wrongly given as '*Bayons*' in *RP*, ii, 53) was sentenced in his absence, as was Deveril; a price of £100 and 100 marks was put on them if taken alive, and 100 marks or £40 for their head: *PROME*, Parliament of Nov. 1330 (C 65/2), item 4.

[324] The details of Bogo's death are contained in C 49/45, no. 30 (proceedings on a petition of his brother William de Bayouse for restitution of the family lands in Helperby, Yorkshire) and KB 27/301, rotulus 25. Bogo had enough money to be able to leave four florins to pay the priests of S. Celso to say masses for his soul and 16 florins in aid of the Holy Land. For the strange tale of Bogo de Bayouse see my paper ' "Edward II" in Italy', 210–11; I have discussed the topic further in 'An Englishman in Rome, 1330–1334', in *Dublin and the Medieval World*, ed. A. Simms & A. Fletcher (Dublin, 2009), 422–32. It is not known what happened to John Deveril.

[325] *PROME*, Parliament of Sept. 1331, C 65/2, item 18: '*depuis qe Monsir Thomas de Gourneye, qi savoit pleynement coment le murdre se fist, par qi nostre seignur le roi et son conseil ent poeient estre enfourme, feust en vevant a ce q'ils entendeient*'.

[326] *Foedera*, II, iii, 160; *PROME*, Parliament of March 1337, Introduction.

[327] Ormrod, 'Richard de Bury', 172–4; C 81/1708/34.

Chapter 12

AFTERLIVES

WAS EDWARD II REALLY DEAD IN 1330?

It has recently been argued that Thomas de Berkeley lied about the death of Edward II; that the body buried as that of Edward II was that of some other unidentified individual; and that the former king was secretly kept at Corfe, under the control of Roger Mortimer and his most trusted followers.[1] Could this be true?

Certainly there are problems with the evidence relating to Edward II's death and burial in 1327. Because of the press of other business, there was no opportunity for the king or anyone close to him to view the body before it was disembowelled and embalmed by the unnamed woman who later visited Isabella at Worcester.[2] According to Adam Murimuth, the only people who saw the body were the abbots, priors, knights and burgesses from Bristol and Gloucester who were summoned to view it but could do so only superficially.[3] Some of them may however have seen the former king in life, on his various visits to those parts, and have been able to recognize him.[4] Although Edward II's tomb was briefly opened in October 1855, the inner coffin containing the body was not opened,[5] unlike the

---

[1] Mortimer, 'The death of Edward II', esp. 1175–6, 1193–4; and Mortimer, *The Perfect King*, App. 2, 'The fake death of Edward II'.

[2] Moore, 'Documents', 226. Edward II's personal physician Pancius da Controne left his service in March 1327, was not with him at Berkeley and could not have testified to the cause of death. Controne however transferred his services to Edward III, and was to be one of the conspirators involved in Mortimer's overthrow in 1330: *CCR, 1327–30*, 446, 448, 485; *CChR, 1327–41*, 190; Shenton, 'Edward III', 13–34.

[3] *Murimuth*, 53–4.

[4] He visited Gloucester in 1321, 1322, 1324, and in May and Oct. 1326; and Bristol in 1308 and 1321. Much would depend on whether or not the face was covered with cerecloth. Mortimer makes much of this possibility in 'The death of Edward II', 1182–3.

[5] The occasion was recorded by the sub-sacrist of the cathedral, Marshall Allen: 'King Edward's Tomb: On the second day of October, 1855, in the presence of Dr Jeune, Canon in Residence, Mr Waller, architect, Marshall Allen, sub-sacrist, and Henry Clifford, the master mason. The tomb of King Edward the Second, in the Cathedral, was opened by removing the floor on the south side of the tomb, and excavating about two feet, then working under the tomb; and only just below the flooring immediately under the tomb we came first to a wood coffin, quite sound, and after removing a portion of this, we came to a leaden one, containing the remains of the King; the wood, although light as cork, was still very perfect, and the lead one quite entire, and made with a very thick sheet of lead,

treatment accorded to the body of Edward I when his tomb was opened for one hour in 1774 and a learned antiquarian had to be prevented from making off with a royal finger bone.[6] If it were possible to investigate the tombs of Edward I and Edward II, and perhaps Edward III for good measure, and to perform DNA tests upon the remains, it might be proved whether the body now at Gloucester really is that of Edward II. But even if Edward II's presence in the tomb could be proved definitively, this would still leave the possibility that someone else had been buried there in 1327 and that the body of Edward II had been placed there subsequently.[7] In any case it is improbable in the extreme that permission would ever be given for such an invasion of royal tombs, even using non-intrusive methods.[8]

The chronicle evidence relating to Edward II's death is also, as already indicated, problematic, with a wide variety of explanations being offered, from that of natural death to murder in various forms. It is also evident that the stories surrounding Edward's alleged murder were elaborated in the telling and as one writer borrowed from another. This is certainly the case with the story of the red-hot iron, with the strong possibility that this account was given weight by writers with the contradictory aims of blackening Edward's reputation or of laying the groundwork for possible canonization.[9]

Thomas de Berkeley's role in the events of 1327 is another problem. Ian Mortimer has argued that he lied when he 'claimed in 1330 not to have heard of the ex-king's death in his custody'.[10] The short answer to this is that he almost certainly did lie, but not in the way suggested. The Berkeley family historian, John Smyth of Nibley, who was writing in the seventeenth

---

its shape very peculiar, being square at bottom, and rising on each side like an arch, and so turned over the body in an oval or arched form, and seemed to have been made to set nearly close upon the body. The tomb was never known to have been opened before this. It remained open but the space of two hours, and was then closed again, without the slightest injury being done to the tomb, – the fact of his interment being now 528 years since, it was considered to be in a wonderful state of preservation.

    Oct. 3rd, 1855,   Marshall Allen,
    Cathedral, Gloucester   Sub-sacrist'

:'Account Book of Marshall Allen, Subsacrist, 1835–1858', Gloucester Cathedral Ms. 55, ff. 82v–81v (the book was the wrong way up when the account was entered, which explains the odd foliation). A transcript is published in David Welander, *History*, 150.

[6] J. Ayloffe, 'An account of the body of King Edward the First, as it appeared on opening his tomb in the year 1774', *Archaeologia*, iii (1786), 376–413; J. Steane, *The Archaeology of the Medieval English Monarchy* (London, 1993), 55.

[7] Mortimer believes that Edward did not die until the autumn of 1341 and that his burial at Gloucester would have followed: Mortimer, *The Perfect King*, App. 3, 'A note on the later life of Edward II', 417.

[8] Techniques, analogous to those used in keyhole surgery, might now be available.

[9] Mortimer, 'Sermons of sodomy', 53–6; *Le Baker*, 9, 27, 30, 33–4.

[10] Mortimer, 'The death of Edward II', 1175.

century, thought that Thomas was economical with the truth. He observed that if Thomas really was at Bradley and so sick that he had no memory of events, it would have been surprising if he were able to send Thomas Gurney to Edward III and Isabella with letters announcing the former king's death.[11] John Smyth also noted that the Berkeley household accounts for that period showed that Thomas did not arrive at Bradley until 28 September, seven days after the presumed death of Edward II, and implies that he was either at or very near to Berkeley itself.[12] Smyth also speculated that Gurney was sent to announce Edward's death in order 'to take him from the earth, for telling of tales in the world',[13] presumably on the principle of 'shoot the messenger' who might otherwise be able to reveal information inconvenient to its sender. Berkeley allegedly kept Edward's death a secret until 1 November, 'by which time and longe before hee had so well recovered his health, as hee attended the kings body to Gloucester, and spent many of the intervenient days in huntings hawkings and other sports of the field'.[14] Finally, Smyth claims that Thomas concealed Gurney until after his trial in parliament and then gave him money and other things to enable him to flee, in return for a transfer of lands. Smyth certainly considered Thomas de Berkeley to be devious and self-serving and to have 'shuffled his cards' with great art but at the last he also defended him from 'the treason of murdering his kinge, Edward the second'.[15]

Berkeley emerges as a liar, but did he lie about the king's death because, as Ian Mortimer has suggested, he knew that the king was in fact still alive,[16] or did he know perfectly well that the king was dead and instead lie about the extent of his knowledge of the crime? The key lies in the interpretation of Berkeley's statement during the November 1330 parliament that he did not know about Edward II's death until the present parliament (*'nec unquam scivit de morte sua usque in presenti parliamento isto'*).[17] Is 'the most obvious meaning' that Berkeley was claiming 'that he had not at any time heard *of* the death',[18] or does it mean that he did not know about

---

[11] Berkeley Castle Muniments, Select Roll 39; Jeayes, *Descriptive Catalogue*, 274; Smyth, *Lives of the Berkeleys*, i, 293, 296–7. Since Berkeley never denied having sent the letters to the king, there is no possibility of someone else having written in his name or using his seal.

[12] Smyth, *Lives of the Berkeleys*, i, 296. The relevant roll for 1 Ed. III (Jan. 1327–Jan. 1328) is no longer extant. Berkeley Castle Muniments, Select Roll 60, Household Accounts, 2 Ed. III, has no information.

[13] Smyth, *Lives of the Berkeleys*, i, 296–7.

[14] Ibid., 297. This does not make sense since the body was moved to Gloucester on 21 Oct.

[15] Ibid.

[16] Mortimer, 'The death of Edward II', 1186–7.

[17] *PROME*, Parliament of Nov. 1330, C 65/2, item 16.

[18] Mortimer, 'The death of Edward II', 1186. Although this corresponds with my translation in my edn of the 1330 Parliament Roll in *PROME* ('nor did he ever know of his death until this present parliament'), my intention there was to avoid over-interpretation of the text, since I was aware that it was open to different meanings.

the *circumstances* of the death until 1330? The latter meaning is more consistent with the language employed, especially when taken in conjunction with the immediately preceding statement that 'he was never an accomplice, a helper or a procurer in his death' (*'ipse nuncquam fuit consentiens, auxilians, seu procurans, ad mortem suam'*):[19] this can only mean that Berkeley knew that the death had occurred but that he claimed he had no part in it.

It is highly significant that neither of the men who were supposed to be guarding Edward II at Berkeley was ever charged with his murder. As already noted, John Maltravers was charged instead with the entrapment of the earl of Kent. This must suggest either that it was already known for certain that Maltravers was not present when Edward was killed or that the authorities had a better chance of making the second charge 'stick'. In the case of Thomas de Berkeley, there was room for doubt. Far from Edward III consciously allowing Berkeley 'to lie his way out of trouble',[20] the king was clearly suspicious. Even the favourable opinion of the jury of knights in January 1331 was not enough, and it was another four years before Thomas de Berkeley was cleared, and a further two years before he was fully pardoned, not of suspected murder but of having neglected his royal charge. The information received from John Maltravers in 1335 and Thomas Gurney's death in 1333 was probably sufficient to convince Edward III and his advisers that there was no point in pursuing the matter further. In any case by 1337 the king was concentrating on rewarding friends and pardoning former enemies so that he could turn his attention to the looming conflict with France.

The arguments that Roger Mortimer deliberately arranged for false reports of Edward II's death, staged an elaborate and very public funeral for the corpse of some other person, kept the former Edward II in secret custody after 1327 to prevent any further attempts at rescue and to use as 'a potent threat to the young Edward III', and that he also informed Edward III of his father's survival shortly after the funeral[21] are puzzling. It is hard to see what advantage would have been gained by such a tactic. Given the number of people with an interest in Edward II's fate, it was questionable whether any secret imprisonment would have remained secret for long. If Edward II had really been alive and had been released, it is very unlikely that 'Edward III would . . . have had to contest with his father as to his right to be king':[22] Edward II had ceased to be king in January 1327; he was now once more 'Edward of Caernarfon' or 'Edward, the king's father'. However questionable the means by which that end had been achieved, Edward III was king and fully recognized as such. To adapt a familiar line, to lose one anointed and crowned monarch might

---

[19] *PROME*, Parliament of Nov. 1330, C 65/2, item 16.
[20] Mortimer, 'The death of Edward II', 1186.
[21] Ibid., 1188–9, 1193–4.
[22] Ibid., 1193.

just be acceptable; to lose two in swift succession would be more than carelessness. It is equally implausible to imagine that Mortimer could have revealed to Edward III that the funeral in December 1327 had been completely fraudulent without dire consequences for himself. The affront to the royal dignity would have been such that the king and the growing number of Mortimer's opponents would have combined to see that he was sent to a 'gallows even higher than the one on which he was eventually hanged in 1330'.[23]

So what did happen in September 1327? We shall never know the whole truth, but the simplest explanation is surely the best one: that Edward II did die at Berkeley on 21 September and that he was murdered or helped on his way to death, either from a pre-existing illness or from physical decline and depression. The story told after Mortimer's fall by Hywel ap Gruffudd in his accusation against William de Shaldeford in 1331[24] probably holds the key, even allowing for the enmity which existed between the Welsh and the Mortimers and all their followers. Roger Mortimer may simply have wanted William Ogle and Thomas Gurney to take greater care of the imprisoned king rather than risk his release from Berkeley by the latest group of conspirators; or he may have intended Edward to be murdered but carefully refrained from saying so specifically in writing, relying on an oral message to convey his wishes; or Ogle and Gurney may have panicked and exceeded their orders, in which case Mortimer was not after all directly responsible for Edward's death.[25] As for Thomas de Berkeley and John Maltravers, it is possible, if Adam Murimuth's statement that they took turns to have custody of the former king is correct, that Maltravers was absent from Berkeley when Edward died and therefore guiltless of direct involvement in the crime.[26] Thomas de Berkeley was clearly close to the scene, but was either negligent or given a hint that he should stay out of the way.[27]

---

[23] Quoted from 'What happened to Edward II?', David Carpenter's review of Mortimer's book, *The Perfect King*, in the *London Review of Books*, 7 June 2007.

[24] *Select Cases*, ed. Sayles, v, 58–63.

[25] Although the judgment against Roger Mortimer in Nov. 1330 was annulled in the parliament of 1354, this was done because the procedure adopted in 1330 was defective in that Mortimer 'was put to death and disinherited without any accusation and without being brought to judgment or to answer'. Nothing was said as to the veracity of the charge of murdering Edward II. The 1326 judgment against the earl of Arundel was annulled on the same grounds: see *PROME*, Parliament of 1354, C 65/18, items 8–14, and the Introduction to the same parliament.

[26] *Murimuth*, 52. There is some evidence that Thomas de Berkeley sent letters to Maltravers at Corfe at the relevant time: Mortimer, 'The death of Edward II', 1190, citing Berkeley Castle Muniments, Select Roll 39. I missed this detail when I examined the roll at Berkeley in 1998: the roll is however badly faded and difficult to read.

[27] Although I disagree with the conclusions reached by Mortimer, the issues he raises needed to be addressed.

EDWARDUS REDIVIVUS[28]

Edward II died in September 1327 and was buried in Gloucester abbey in the following December. But that was not the end of stories about his survival,[29] since there are two separate pieces of evidence which show that in the mid- to late 1330s someone claiming to be Edward II was travelling around Europe. Although the two are at first sight unrelated, they are in fact very closely connected. The first is contained in the records of the royal household which report that in September 1338 a man named William le Galeys or le Waleys was 'arrested' at Cologne in Germany after apparently declaring that he was Edward II, and was then escorted to Koblenz where Edward III was meeting the emperor, Ludwig IV.[30]

The other evidence is an undated letter addressed to Edward III by a papal notary named Manuel Fieschi. In the letter Fieschi tells of a meeting with a man who had identified himself as Edward II, and who had then made a confession in which he told Fieschi a long and circumstantial tale. According to this, Edward II had escaped from Berkeley castle with a servant, after killing a sleeping doorkeeper whose body was later buried as if it were his; Edward had gone to Corfe and with his servant had then crossed to Ireland, where he had spent nine months. We are not told what Edward did in Ireland, where he went or if he met anyone. Then, fearing that he would be recognized, he took the habit of a hermit and returned to England, where he arrived at the port of Sandwich. Still dressed as a hermit, he crossed to Sluys in Flanders. From there he went to Normandy, and then to many other places. Having travelled through the Languedoc, he came to Avignon, where he gave a florin to one of the pope's servants to take a letter to Pope John XXII. The pope summoned him and kept him honourably and in secret at Avignon for fifteen days. Finally, 'after various discussions, and all things considered', the pope gave Edward permission to leave. Edward then went to Paris, from there to the duchy of Brabant in the Low Countries, and to Cologne, where he visited the shrine of the Three Kings 'for the purposes of devotion'. He crossed Germany to Milan in Lombardy and entered a hermitage belonging to the castle of '*Milasco*', where he stayed for two and half years. When this castle was overrun by war, Edward moved to another hermitage, in or connected with the castle of Cecima in the diocese of Pavia in Lombardy, and was in this hermitage for about two more years, 'always the

---

[28] I have borrowed from the title of Haines's excellent paper, '*Edwardus redivivus*', 65–86.
[29] What follows draws heavily on my paper, ' "Edward II" in Italy'.
[30] Cuttino & Lyman, 'Where is Edward II?', 530, n. 43, citing refs in the Wardrobe book for 1338–40, E 36/203, ff. 178, 179. This source is available in print as *The Wardrobe Book of William de Norwell*, ed. Lyon et al. For the refs to William le Waleys see 212, 214. These refs were originally discovered by Dr P. Chaplais. For the meetings between Edward III and the emperor see *Vitae Paparum Avenionensium*, ed. E. Baluze, new edn, ed. G. Mollat, ii, 303–6; *Knighton's Chronicle, 1337–1396*, ed. G.H. Martin (Oxford, 1995), 9–10.

recluse, doing penance', and praying to God for Edward III and other sinners.[31]

A distinguished French scholar, Alexandre Germain, who was a pupil of Michelet in Paris, found the letter in the 1870s. In 1838 he was appointed as the first professor of history in the newly created faculty of letters at the university of Montpellier; became dean of the faculty in 1861 and remained so until his retirement in 1881. Germain published many works based on the extensive medieval records preserved in the Archives départementales de l'Hérault and in the municipal archives at Montpellier.[32] In the 1870s he was examining a mid-fourteenth-century register of documents belonging to the diocese of Maguelone, of which Montpellier formed a part, when he found the letter from Manuel Fieschi to Edward III. The document is preserved in the middle of an unrelated collection of charters concerning the bishop's property rights in the small town of Cournonterral, to the south-west of Montpellier.[33] Just how the

---

[31] Archives départementales de l'Hérault, Series G 1123, f. 86r (Cartulaire de Maguelone, Register A) (the text of the letter is given in Cuttino & Lyman, 'Where is Edward II?', App. i, 537, where the reference is wrongly given as GM 23). The extremes of possible dating are 1329 and 1343 when Fieschi gave up his post at the papal curia and became bishop of Vercelli in north-eastern Italy. As will be argued below, a date between about 1336 and 1338 seems more likely.

[32] Born in Paris, 14 Dec 1809; died at Montpellier, 26 Jan. 1887. For his career and publications see M. Prévost et al., eds, *Dictionnaire de biographie française*, v (Paris, 1982), cols 1307–8. It is important to emphasize Germain's importance as a scholar since one modern commentator has described him rather dismissively simply as 'an archivist named Germain': Fryde, 203, 295.

[33] The register covers six vols, A to F: Series G, 1123–8, followed by a contemporary index volume, Register G (Series G, 1129). Register A is a large bound parchment volume, written clearly in a consistent hand or hands. According to the *Répertoire numérique des archives départementales antérieures à 1790, Herault, archives ecclésiastiques, series G, clergé séculier*, ed. M. Gouron (Montpellier, 1970), Register A was begun by Bishop Jean de Verdale of Maguelone (1339–52) and finished by Bishop Gaucelm de Deaux (1367–73). The *Inventaire* of the records of the diocese of Maguelone says that the cartulary was started under Bishop Jean de Verdale and finished in six '*recueils*' under Bishop Gaucelm de Deaux. It could be then that the whole of Register A was composed under Verdale, since the latest document is one from the 1350s (1359: doc. 247, is the latest date); there is one from 1351 and possibly one from 1352). The document from 1387 at the end of the volume is a later addition. All the others come from earlier and few are from the 1340s. The first document in the volume (f. 1r) is dated 1293 and is headed *Libertates Ville Nove*. On f. 3 there is some material written in a seventeenth- or eighteenth-century hand. On f. 4r are written some apparent dedications: '*A Monseigneur le Marquis de Louvoys ministre et secretaire d'Estat; A Monseigneur; Monseigneur Lafon premier duc et pair de France A La Cour.*' The register proper begins on what would have been f. 5, but the foliation starts again from f. 1. The previous four folios were evidently blank and were therefore filled in by various persons at a later date.

F. 1 is headed as follows: *In isto cartulario continetur recogniciones recepte per reverendum in Christo patrem dominum A. dei gratia Episcopum Magalon a personis et nobilibus infrascriptis suis et Ecclesie predicte vassallis*. The documents which follow all appear to be recognitions of obligations or grants of property by lay vassals of the bishops of Maguelone. Throughout the volume documents are dated both by the year of grace and by the name of the French king then

document, which is otherwise entirely unknown, had reached Maguelone is uncertain.[34] The clerk who was compiling the register was evidently intrigued by the extraordinary story told in the letter and copied it along with more routine material. However, the clerk later added the single word, *'vacat'* ('it is vacant'; i.e. 'it is cancelled'), in the top right hand corner of the transcript, and the contemporary index volume to the registers of the diocese of Maguelone omits the Fieschi letter altogether.[35]

---

reigning (the range of French kings noted is from Louis VII to John II (one example)); sometimes in the fourteenth century the name of the reigning pope is also given.

The seat of the diocese was at Maguelone, on a sand-spit overlooking the Mediterranean in one direction and a large freshwater lagoon in the other. Here it was reasonably secure from outside attack. During the thirteenth and fourteenth centuries Maguelone was coming under increasing pressure from the French monarchy, through its seneschals at Beaucaire and Nîmes; the important trading centre of Montpellier, some miles from Maguelone, was under the control of the kingdom of Aragon from 1204 until its acquisition by France in 1349. When the seat of the diocese moved to Montpellier in 1536, the 12th-century basilica of Maguelone ceased to be a cathedral and is now an intact but empty shell.

[34] Copies of the letter could have been circulating at the papal curia at Avignon, which was near Maguelone and with which its bishops had close connections. Pope Urban V's stay of two months in Maguelone, starting on 9 Jan. 1367, at the time when the newly appointed bishop, Gaucelm de Deaux (who was also papal treasurer), was overseeing the completion of Register A, offers one possible explanation of the Fieschi letter's appearance in Maguelone: A. Germain, *Maguelone sous ses évêques et ses chanoines* (Montpellier, 1869), 139.

[35] There is a photograph of the document in Mortimer, *The Greatest Traitor*, between 188 and 189. The photograph does not show the entire width of the folio, thereby omitting *'vacat'*. The text of the Fieschi letter is written in its entirety on one side of G 1123, Register A, f. 86r. The hand is no different from that of the documents entered before and after. There is nothing to suggest the document was added after the completion of the register in a previously blank space, or that it could be a clever modern forgery. Blank folios are very rare in the register. The ink is pale brown and may have faded slightly over time. The folio containing the letter has a fold in it where the folio has clearly been bent over at some past time. There is nothing in the immediate appearance of the document to draw attention to it, apart from the lack of a date, which is usually the case in this register only with very early documents. The fourteenth-century documents always have date of incarnation and the name of the ruling king of France (though not the year of his reign). The document is not part of any chronological sequence which would help to date it; it has nothing to do with the documents before and after; it is the only document in the register (really a cartulary) which has nothing to do with the secular business of the diocese of Maguelone. There is none of the business one would expect in a bishop's register of the usual kind.

The Fieschi letter, doc. 120 on f. 86r, is preceded and followed by documents relating to Cournonterral: 119 (1264), 121 (1299), 122 (1317), 124 (1286), 125 (1315). These are all entirely typical of the kind of material elsewhere in the cartulary. No. 120 is entirely untypical (except for being in Latin), since it is a document of outside origin, it is undated, and there is no indication of where it was drawn up.

The original documents which were transcribed into the six volumes of the register are no longer extant, removing the possibility that the Fieschi letter in the form in which it reached Maguelone might still be available for study. Large-scale destruction of ecclesiastical archives occurred at Montpellier in 1566 and later, and again in 1621 and 1623: *Répertoire numérique*, ed. Gouron, 1.

Alexandre Germain communicated his discovery to the Académie des inscriptions et belles-lettres in Paris on 21 September 1877 (by coincidence or perhaps design, the 550th anniversary of Edward II's death), and published it in Montpellier in the following year.[36] The document first became known in England in 1880 and has been republished and discussed on a number of occasions since.[37] Until the spring of 2003, the latest treatments of the letter were the papers published by George Cuttino and Thomas P. Lyman in 1978 and by Roy Haines in 1997, and a short book by Haines published in 2001. However, a large amount of new material on Edward II and his fate has recently appeared, in the books by Paul Doherty on Queen Isabella and by Ian Mortimer on Roger Mortimer and Edward III, as well as in Roy Haines's detailed study of Edward II.[38]

Opinions on the Fieschi letter have varied. Neither Stubbs nor Tout was convinced by the story of Edward II's survival but neither offered any definitive explanation of the letter's purpose and significance. Cuttino was impressed by the evidence, as he saw it, that Edward II did not die in 1327 and was not buried at Gloucester, while also expressing strong reservations about many of the Italian aspects of the story.[39] Doherty and Mortimer also argue that Edward II escaped death in 1327. Mortimer believes that the story told in the letter was genuine, and that the Genoese used the letter as a means of forcing the English crown to pay outstanding debts; while Doherty thinks it was a clever forgery put together by Manuel Fieschi, with the intention of embarrassing or even blackmailing Edward III. On the other hand Haines does not believe that Edward II survived after 1327. He suggests that the letter was a forgery, to which the name of Manuel Fieschi was attached to give it plausibility, that its purpose was to foster a reputation of sanctity on behalf of the former king, and that Edward III, to whom the letter was nominally addressed, never received it.[40]

---

[36] The document was published by the local learned society, the Société Archéologique de Montpellier in 1878: A. Germain, 'Lettre de Manuel Fiesque concernant les dernières années du roi d'Angleterre Édouard II', repr. in *Mémoires de la Société Archéologique de Montpellier*, vii (1881), 109–27. For a transcription of the Latin text of the letter and a good translation see Cuttino & Lyman, 'Where is Edward II?' 537–8 and 526–7.

[37] J. T. Best, 'Where did Edward the Second die?', *Macmillan's Magazine*, xli (March 1880), 393–4; Best, 'Where did Edward II die?', with a reply by J.H. Cooke, *Notes and Queries*, lxii (13 and 20 Nov., 18 Dec. 1880), 381–3, 401–3, 489–90. The document was discussed by William Stubbs in *Chronicles of the Reigns of Edward I and Edward II*, Rolls Series, ii (London, 1883), cvi–cviii, and Tout in 'Captivity and death', 179.

[38] The most recent discussions of the Fieschi letter can be found in Haines, '*Edwardus redivivus*', *Death of a King*, and *King Edward II*, 219–38; Doherty, *Isabella*, 183–215, Mortimer, *The Greatest Traitor*, 251–61; and again in Mortimer, *The Perfect King*, App. 3, 'A note on the later life of Edward II'.

[39] Cuttino & Lyman 'Where is Edward II?', 522–43. For a summary of the views of Stubbs and Tout see ibid., 527–8.

[40] Mortimer, *The Greatest Traitor*, 251–63 (esp. 259–63), 301–3; Doherty (D.Phil.), 185–215 (esp. 207–13); Haines, '*Edwardus redivivus*', 63–86, esp. 65, 79–80; idem, *King Edward II*, 220–38.

The Fieschi letter took longer to become known in Italy. The first reference to it in print was in a paper published in April 1901 by Count Costantino Nigra, a former diplomat of the kingdom of Savoy and a member of the Italian Senate, who had spent a considerable part of his service in Paris.[41] This probably explains how he came to know of Germain's publication of the document in 1878.[42] While not dismissing the authenticity of the Fieschi letter out of hand, and drawing attention to the political importance and connections of the Fieschi family, he was nonetheless sceptical. Nigra however added to Germain's research by proposing an identification of the two castles in which the supposed Edward II had stayed as Melazzo (near Acqui Terme, north of Genoa) and Cecima south of Voghera in the diocese of Tortona,[43] although more recent research has suggested that the Fieschi letter's '*Milasco*' may be better identified with Mulazzo near Pontremoli in Liguria.[44] In the same year in which Nigra's paper appeared, a priest of the cathedral of Tortona, Canon Vincenzo Lege, published a history of the abbey of Sant' Alberto di Butrio, a short distance from Cecima, in which he also referred to the Fieschi letter and tentatively suggested that Edward II's second place of refuge was this abbey rather than Cecima.[45] In his history of Cecima, published in 1906, Count

---

[41] C. Nigra, 'Uno degli Edoardi in Italia', *Nuova Antologia: Rivista Lettere Scienze*, xcii, ser. 4, fascicle for 1 April 1901, 403–25.

[42] Costantino Nigra (1828–1907) was first a soldier and then a prominent diplomat in the service of the kingdom of Savoy. He played a very important role in Franco-Italian relations from 1855 and was in Paris continuously from 1861 until the end of 1876, when he was moved to St Petersburg. He would not therefore have been in Paris when Germain first publicly announced his discovery of the Fieschi letter in 1877. However, he was also a considerable scholar in his own right (including published work in the field of Celtic studies), and so was probably familiar with the cultural scene in Paris during and after his time in France: A. Horne, *The Fall of Paris* (London, 1965), 57; *Enciclopedia Italiana* (repr. of the 1934 edn, Rome, 1951), xxiv, 818–19.

[43] Nigra, 'Uno degli Edoardi in Italia', 413–15, 419–25. The castle of Melazzo still exists as a private residence. The castle of Cecima no longer exists, apart from the street name, Via Castello, and some overgrown ruins on the top of the hill on which Cecima stands. There was however a castle there in the fourteenth century. Cecima came under the secular lordship of the diocese of Pavia and the ecclesiastical jurisdiction of the diocese of Tortona: A. C. Sangiuliani, *Cecima* (Milan, 1906), 37, 39; idem, *Dell' Abazia S. Alberto di Butrio* (Milan, 1865), 245–6.

[44] Mortimer, *The Perfect King*, 414. Pontremoli had associations with the Fieschi family, which Melazzo did not. In his will, dated at Avignon on 31 Jan. 1336, Cardinal Luke Fieschi asked for prayers in memory of the emperor Henry VII who had given the castle and town of Pontremoli to Federico Fieschi: ASV, Avignon Register 49, f. 440v.

[45] V. Lege, *Sant' Alberto Abate e il suo culto*, repr. from *Atti dell'Accademia Tortonese Leone*, xiii (Tortona, 1901), 83–6. Lege however makes it clear that his source was Nigra's paper 'Uno degli Edoardi in Italia', and not any local tradition. Nigra's work came to his notice while his own was in the press. It appears then that in the late nineteenth century Germain's paper was beginning to become known in the areas of northern Italy associated with the Edward II story.

The abbey of Sant' Alberto was founded in the eleventh century and had a continuous existence until its suppression in the early nineteenth century. Since the beginning of the

Antonio Cavagna Sangiuliani accepted this identification of Sant' Alberto.[46] The work of Nigra and Lege was then developed by another Italian scholar, Anna Benedetti, who published a paper in 1924 in which she sought to prove not only that the exiled Edward II had been at the abbey of Sant' Alberto di Butrio, but that he had also been buried there, before finally being transferred to his resting place at Gloucester.[47] Since the publication of the conclusions of Benedetti it has become accepted historical fact in Italy that Edward II was indeed in the country. There is a plaque in the main entrance hall of the castello at Melazzo recording his 'presence' there from 1330 to 1333;[48] while Sant' Alberto di Butrio displays an empty medieval tomb as that of the English king.[49]

---

twentieth century a religious community has again occupied the monastery, which is visited for Sunday mass by large numbers of people from the nearby town of Pontenizza. There is a short history of the abbey by a member of the present community, Domenico Sparpaglione, FDP, *Una Gemma d'Oltrepo* (4th edn, Tortona, 1990).

[46] Sangiuliani, *Cecima*, 36–8.

[47] A. Benedetti, *Edoardo II d'Inghilterra all'Abbazia di S. Alberto di Butrio* (Palermo, 1924). She had visited the abbey in 1919. She also published a study of the French poem supposedly composed by Edward II after his deposition: 'Una canzone francese di Edoardo II d'Inghilterra'.

[48] Nigra noted in his 1901 article, 'Uno degli Edoardi in Italia', that the owners of Melazzo had recently erected two plaques recording the supposed stay of Edward II in the castle, but remarked that there was no local tradition of such a stay and that the evidence was derived from Germain's paper on the Fieschi letter: 413, n. 1. Nigra had visited Melazzo in 1890 in the course of his researches and had presumably told the owners about Germain's paper: Nigra, 414. The short history of the castle refers to the Fieschi letter and contains a photograph of the memorial plaque: C. Violono, *Melazzo nella storia* (Melazzo, 1995), 70–2. In the first half of the fourteenth century the castle may have been in the possession of the bishops of Acqui: Violono, 22. But, as already indicated, Mulazzo may be a better identification.

[49] For details of the treatment of the 'Edward II' story in modern works on the abbey see Sparpaglione, *Una Gemma d'Oltrepo*, 57–65, 82–3 (Cuttino & Lyman, 'Where is Edward II?', 531–2, cited the 3rd edn, 1973). There is also an earlier and longer edition with the same title, published in Tortona (n.d.). In this version the material relating to 'Edward II' appears on 131–54, 186–7. The text is substantially the same as that in the later editions, but does not, for example, include a reference to Sparpaglione's 1958 conversation with the eighty-eight-year-old man, Zerba Stefano. The text on the plaque above the tomb of 'Edward II' and a photograph of the tomb appear in Cuttino & Lyman, 531 and fig. 3. The most recent book about the abbey of Sant' Alberto is F. Bernini, *La Badia di S. Alberto di Butrio tra Storia, Arte e Fede* (Pontenizza, 1993): the section dealing with Edward II appears between 165 and 176. Bernini's account adds nothing of significance, except that the tomb now displayed as that of Edward II was opened in 1900 by a local parish priest, Paolo Cassola, when only a portion of a cranium was found: Bernini, 169 (citing Benedetti, *Edoardo II*, 23–4). If the date is correct, this was another consequence of the growing knowledge locally of the Fieschi letter at that time. Benedetti met Cassola when she visited Butrio in 1919; Cassola wrote to her in May 1923 about the opening of the tomb, without seemingly giving a date for when this occurred: Benedetti, *Edoardo II*, 23–4. The investigation of the tomb evidently took place at or about the same time as the opening of that of the abbey's founder, Sant' Alberto, on 9 July 1900. This was also the time when the revival of the abbey as a religious house was being seriously proposed: Sparpaglione (3rd & 4th edns), 67–8.

The evidence for Edward II's presence at Melazzo, and at Cecima or Sant' Alberto, is however questionable. Much of the material that Benedetti put forward to prove her thesis in relation to the tomb at Sant' Alberto was shown by Cuttino and Lynam to be entirely wrong. 'Neither the cloister sculpture nor any other sculpture at Sant' Alberto di Butrio can be dated on the basis of style or in relation to archaeological evidence of the building sequence much beyond the twelfth century, and could not therefore have been designed with Edward in mind. The sepulchre itself appears to be even older than the sculpture and probably contemporaneous with Sant' Alberto's own funerary chapel built by his successor, Benedict, shortly after 1073. Only common decency, of course, would prevent appropriating the tomb of a former abbot for a prestigious visitor.'[50] Nor has a pair of thirteenth-century Limoges candlesticks, supposedly presented to the abbey in memory of Edward II and now in the civic museum in Turin, anything to do with the English king.[51]

The available evidence suggests that the tradition that Edward II was at Sant' Alberto goes back no further than the decade between 1890, when Costantino Nigra visited the castle of Melazzo, and 1901, when he published his findings and when the alleged tomb of Edward II was first examined. Don Domenico Sparpaglione's conversation in 1958 with an eighty-eight-year-old man, Zerba Stefano, whose grandfather allegedly 'well before 1900, had spoken of an English king who had taken refuge in the hermitage', does not carry conviction.[52] Sparpaglione himself asks whether there was any local tradition of an English king having been buried at Sant' Alberto di Butrio and concludes emphatically that no document written before 1901 and the publication of Nigra's paper drawing attention to the Fieschi letter makes any such reference.[53] The history of the abbey of Sant' Alberto, which was published in 1865 by Count Antonio Cavagni Sangiuliani, before Alexandre Germain revealed the Fieschi letter, has no mention of Edward II. Neither is there any reference in the second edition of Sangiuliani's book, published in 1890.[54] If there were any medieval tradition of an exiled king or of an unusual holy man living and perhaps dying at Sant' Alberto di Butrio, some trace of it should appear in the history of the abbey. At the very least, one would expect the fourteenth-century monks of Sant' Alberto to have turned a

---

[50] Cuttino & Lyman, 'Where is Edward II?', 537, and more generally, 531–7.

[51] Ibid., 532, citing Benedetti, *Edoardo II*, 24.

[52] Cuttino & Lyman, 'Where is Edward II?', 531, citing Sparpaglione, *Una Gemma d'Oltrepo* (3rd & 4th edns), 62. 'Well before 1900' could apply just as easily to the knowledge of Germain's article that was beginning to circulate from 1890.

[53] Sparpaglione, *Una Gemma d'Oltrepo* (3rd & 4th edns), 62–3.

[54] Sangiuliani, *Dell' Abazia S. Alberto di Butrio*. Sangiuliani knew of the Edward II legend and of the suggested connection with Sant' Alberto by 1906 when he published his history of Cecima, but only through his reading of Nigra's 1901 paper and Lege's 1901 history of the abbey: Sangiuliani, *Cecima*, 32–8.

healthy profit from pilgrims, if they possessed the body or other relics of such a distinguished stranger.[55] One may go even further and argue that, while it is possible to accept the identification of Melazzo/Mulazzo and Cecima with the places named in the Fieschi letter, the modern introduction of Sant' Alberto di Butrio into the story is ill-founded and best discarded altogether.

So what about the letter itself? The story it tells is superficially plausible, but ultimately unbelievable. It is plausible in that the author of the letter, Manuel Fieschi, was a member of an important family, prominent in the politics of Genoa and with territorial interests in Lombardy, Piedmont and Liguria.[56] The Fieschi were especially prominent in the Church, providing two thirteenth-century popes (Innocent IV and Adrian V), numerous cardinals and a great many bishops.[57] Manuel himself was a papal notary at Avignon from 1329 to 1343; a collector of papal taxes in Lombardy, in the same area as Melazzo (although not of Mulazzo)[58] and Cecima; and bishop of Vercelli from 1343 until his death in 1348.[59] In the 1330s a relative of his, Percival Fieschi, was bishop of Tortona, the diocese in which Cecima and Sant' Alberto were situated;[60] and his uncle, Cardinal Luke Fieschi, had been a papal envoy in England in

---

[55] If a portion of a cranium really were discovered when the tomb ascribed to Edward II was opened in 1900, this would also tell against the belief that Edward II had ever lain in the tomb. A piece of bone would scarcely have been left behind when the body was later transferred to Gloucester abbey: Benedetti, *Edoardo II*, 23–4 (cited by Bernini, *La Badia*, 169).

[56] The Fieschi were counts of Lavagna in Liguria; they also appear to have had influence or control over places such as Voghera and Vercelli, both of which figure in the story of the Fieschi letter. On the history of the Fieschi family see F. Federici, *Della Famiglia Fiesca Trattato* (Genoa, 1645), 7–9; G. P. Balbi, *I 'Conti' e la 'Contea' di Lavagna* (Genoa, 1984); B. Bernabo, 'I Fieschi e la Val di Vara', and M. Macconi, 'I Fieschi e l'Impero nel XIV e XV secolo', in D. Calcagno, ed., *I Fieschi tra medioeve ed età moderna* (Genoa, 1999). Manuel Fieschi was the son of Andrea, count of Lavagna, and nephew of Cardinal Luke Fieschi: Haines, '*Edwardus redivivus*', 68. He was also an executor of Cardinal Luke's will (made at Avignon on 31 Jan. 1336) and was present in Avignon on 4 Aug. 1336 when the performance of the terms of the will was recorded: ASV, Avignon Register 49, f. 439v. Nicolino Fieschi (discussed below) was the brother of Francesco, count of Lavagna, which probably also made him the brother of Manuel: Sumption, *Trial by Battle*, 163.

[57] Federici, *Della Famiglia*, 49–52; Nigra, 'Uno degli Edoardi in Italia', 418–20. Bernabo, 'I Fieschi e la Val di Vara', *passim*.

[58] Mulazzo is not in Lombardy but it was in an area of interest to the Fieschi as a family.

[59] For Manuel Fieschi's career and family connections see Cuttino & Lyman, 'Where is Edward II?', 529–30, 540–2; Germain, 'Lettre de Manuel Fiesque', 10–11, 13; Nigra, 'Uno degli Edoardi in Italia', 418–20; B. Guillemain, *La Cour pontificale d'Avignon (1309–1376)* (Paris, 1962), 314; Haines, '*Edwardus redivivus*', 68. The diocese of Vercelli appears to have been a Fieschi preserve for much of the 14th century: Federici, *Della Famiglia*, 52. Manuel's successor was Giovanni Fieschi who was bishop from 1349 until his death in Rome in 1380: *Libro delle investiture del vescovo di Vercelli Giovanni Fieschi (1349–50)* (Turin, 1934), ed. D. Arnaldi, 249–51. Several other members of Giovanni's family are mentioned in this volume: see 254–62.

[60] Bernini, *La Badia*, 167–8.

1317–18.[61] Manuel Fieschi held a number of benefices in the English Church between 1329 and 1343 (exactly the period for which he was a papal notary); [62] and he was also distantly related to the English royal house.[63] Another of his close relatives, Nicolino Fieschi, was a confidential agent of Edward III in his dealings with the city of Genoa and with the papacy, and was also a member of Edward's council from April 1336.[64] So important was he, that on 13 April 1340 the French sent a small force across the Rhône to Avignon, captured Nicolino and one of his sons in their lodgings, and held them in French territory until the following June.[65] The episode caused a major scandal, which is referred to in a second Fieschi-related document in the register of the diocese of Maguelone, dated 14 May 1340.[66]

The story in the Fieschi letter is also plausible in that many of the circumstantial details of Edward II's capture and imprisonment in 1326–7 (which

[61] Phillips, esp. chs 4 & 5. On Luke's career see Federici, *Della Famiglia*, 38–9; Guillemain, *La Cour pontificale*, 185, 212, 219; and esp. the detailed account in Z. Hledíková, *Raccolta Praghese di Scritti di Luca Fieschi* (Charles University, Prague, 1985).

[62] For details see Cuttino & Lyman, 'Where is Edward II?', 529–30, 539–42.

[63] Ibid., 529, 544. Manuel was Edward II's third cousin once removed.

[64] There is a lot of information on Nicolino, who, although he was married and had two sons, Gabriel and Anthony, was commonly known as 'the cardinal of Genoa', even in papal records: e.g. Codex Vaticanus Latinus 10883, f. 221, Avignon, 13 Jan. 1331, at the start of the arbitration by the pope between Genoa and the king of Cyprus, in which Nicolino was a proctor on behalf of Genoa. Officially Nicolino's duties on behalf of Edward III involved such matters as the hiring of shipping to assist Edward in transporting and defending his forces in the Low Countries in the late 1330s. He was active from at least Oct. 1336 in this role, which also involved preventing the French from gaining access to the same resources to use against England's interests. It is clear from the way he is described in the English records that Nicolino's real role was often that of a royal agent dealing with extremely delicate affairs of state: *CPR, 1334–38*, 247; *Foedera*, II, ii, 941, 946–8, 1058, 1066, 1068, 1104, 1107. There is some interesting material on Nicolino in Sumption, *Trial by Battle*, 163, 249, 319–20, 437–8, 444. Nicolino is also discussed in Mortimer, *The Greatest Traitor*, 261, 263, 303, where he is however wrongly described as a cardinal, and in Haines, 'Edwardus redivivus', 68–9.

Nicolino was not the first member of his family to be a member of the royal council in England. In Aug. 1315 his relative Charles Fieschi had been appointed by Edward II: *Foedera*, II, ii, 274. It is not clear what services Edward II expected from his 'cousin'. Genoa however provided invaluable financial services to the English crown for much of Edward II's reign through the activities of the merchant and banker Antonio Pessagno: see N. Fryde, 'Antonio Pessagno of Genoa, king's merchant of Edward II of England', in *Studi in Memoria di Federigo Melis*, ii (Naples, 1978).

[65] See Sumption, *Trial by Battle*, 319–20; *Vitae Paparum Avenionensium*, ed. Baluze, i, 205–6, 213–14.

[66] Pope Benedict XII was particularly angry because the incident occurred on the night of Maundy Thursday, and on 17 April issued a bull against those who had captured Nicolino and thrown him into prison: *Vitae Paparum Avenionensium*, ed. Baluze, iii (Documents), 483–6. The document, which is preserved in the second volume of the register containing Manuel Fieschi's letter, records the reaction at Montpellier to the seizure of Nicolino: Archives départementales de l'Hérault, ser. G 1124, Cartulaire de Maguelone, Register B, no. 429, ff. 54v–55r. Germain noted the existence of this additional Fieschi document in his paper on the Fieschi letter: Germain 'Lettre de Manuel Fiesque', 11, n. 2.

are omitted from the summary above) can be confirmed from other sources; and in that several genuine plots to free Edward II from captivity did take place, so that one more might appear a distinct possibility. Yet the story as told by Fieschi has obvious flaws. The earl of Arundel, for example, was no longer with Edward II when he reached Wales, as claimed in the letter. The two knights sent to Berkeley to kill Edward are named as Thomas Gurney (which corresponds with the role ascribed to him in other sources) and Simon Bereford (which does not).[67] Edward II's alleged escape from Berkeley past a doorkeeper, who is conveniently asleep and whom he kills at the very time when the two knights have just arrived to kill him, also defies credibility. It is very reminiscent of the stories told in the Acts of the Apostles of the miraculous release from prison of St Paul and Silas, and of St Peter; and, more specifically, of the chronicler Robert of Reading's account of the escape of Roger Mortimer of Wigmore from the Tower of London in August 1323, which uses the same literary device.[68] There are also close parallels with the escape of Sir Robert Walkefare from Corfe castle in 1326 after killing a porter and with Thomas Dunheved's attempted escape from Pontefract in 1327.[69] One might also ask how the real Edward II would have travelled to places like Paris, Avignon and Brabant where he would have been in danger of being recognized, and then revealed himself only to the pope at the moment he chose; and where a poor travelling hermit would get a gold florin with which to tip the pope's servant; and so on.

Despite such objections, the Fieschi letter itself is almost certainly genuine. Manuel Fieschi almost certainly did meet someone who either claimed to be or thought he was Edward II. One explanation is that Fieschi could have encountered 'Edward II' by chance while in Italy on official business. Although he had links with England and with Edward himself, it is unlikely that Fieschi had any first-hand knowledge of the former king's true appearance, since he had probably never been in England and would never have met the real Edward II.[70] Manuel Fieschi

[67] Simon Bereford was one of Roger Mortimer's leading followers and was executed as such in Nov. 1330, but he was not directly accused of having murdered Edward II.

[68] Acts, 16:22-8 (St Paul and Silas: who did not take advantage of the opportunity to escape); Acts, 12: 6-11 (St Peter). Robert of Reading used the story of the escape of St Peter from Herod's prison (the words in italics are quoted from Acts): 'The king sent his detestable cruel officials to the Tower of London, *intending to bring forth* the younger Roger after a few days *to the people* and condemn him to a violent death. *And when* the king *would have brought him forth*, behold *on the night* of St Peter ad Vincula, the Holy Ghost came . . . and touching Roger's heart *raised him up, saying, "Arise up quickly and follow me"*. And Roger, leaving, *followed him, which was done by* Christ; thus it was not that *he thought he saw a vision. When they were past the first and second ward* they came to the river Thames': Gransden, ii, 20, citing *Flores*, 217.

[69] *CPR, 1327–30*, 42, 125; *Ann. Paul.*, 337; Haines, '*Edwardus redivivus*', 72; idem, *Stratford*, 208, n. 9.

[70] The benefices he was given in England did not involve the 'cure of souls' and in practice could be held *in absentia*. The letters of attorney he was granted from time to time by the English crown (e.g. 8 June 1335, *CPR, 1333–38*, 116) probably imply that he was already out of England rather than that he was about to leave the country.

could have written down the confession of the alleged Edward II and sent it to Edward III with a covering letter, saying in effect 'I think you had better know the following story.' [71] Edward III already knew that his father had been murdered in 1327 and by whom, but would have been curious to know more and replied, again saying in effect, 'I should like to meet the impostor; send him to me by return. By the way, I shall be in Germany, so send him there.'

This is one explanation of the origins of the Fieschi letter, but there is another more likely answer, one which involves the papal curia, Luke, Manuel and Nicolino Fieschi, as well as Edward III himself. Assuming that the impostor really did visit Avignon on his travels, as recorded in the letter, the conclusion that he was not the real Edward II could have been reached very quickly. There were too many people at the papal curia or in its vicinity who had been papal envoys to England and had known Edward II personally, and would readily have determined whether the traveller was genuine or not. These included Manuel Fieschi's uncle, Cardinal Luke Fieschi, who was alive at Avignon until 1336; Cardinal Gaucelin d'Eauze, the other envoy to England in 1317–18, who was alive until 1348;[72] Guillaume de Laudun, OP, archbishop of Vienne (1321–7) and later archbishop of Toulouse (1327–45); and possibly Hugh, the bishop of Orange, who together with Guillaume had made several visits to England between late 1324 and January 1327 in a last desperate attempt at mediation.[73] Since the pope had already stated in his letters to Edward III and Isabella in September 1330 that he did not believe Edward II was still alive, he would have needed little persuading that his strange visitor was an impostor, and so have sent him on his way. However by the time the impostor's wanderings brought him to northern Italy his claims had became so embarrassing both to the Church and potentially to the legitimacy of Edward III as king of England,[74] that he was sent for safe custody first to Melazzo/Mulazzo and then to Cecima. Both places were under the

---

[71] Some kind of covering letter would have been necessary, since the 'Fieschi letter' is not strictly a letter in itself but more in the nature of a notarial instrument (although not, strictly speaking, that either). Any covering letter would presumably have been dated.

[72] Guillemain, *La Cour pontificale*, 219 (Fieschi), 214, n. 72 (d'Eauze). There is a short account of Gaucelin d'Eauze's career by G. Mollat in R. Aubert, ed., *Dictionnaire d'histoire et de géeographie ecclésiastiques*, xx (Paris, 1984), 18. Although Luke Fieschi had been in England in 1317–18, he was not there in May 1325, as suggested in Mortimer, *The Perfect King*, 416. The letters of protection issued to him in his capacity as the absentee parson of the church of *Tiryngton* (probably Tirrington, near Peterborough) were simply a formality to protect him from legal actions in his absence and do not imply that he was in the country: *CPR, 1324–27*, 119.

[73] For their missions in England see the Index below and Haines, *Stratford*, 151, 153, 155, 157, 160, 168, 170, 177. On Guillaume de Laudun's later career as archbishop of Toulouse see *La Papauté d'Avignon et le Languedoc (1316–1342)*, Cahiers de Fanjeaux, xxvi (Toulouse, 1991), 152, 212, 219. It is not clear whether the bishop of Orange might still have been alive in the 1330s.

[74] If the impostor and his story had become public knowledge, they could have reflected on Edward III's legitimacy as king of England and so provided the French monarchy with an excellent propaganda weapon just as England and France were going to war over the

control of the local bishop and within an area of influence of the Fieschi family, who were connected both with the papal curia and with the English royal house, and whose discretion could therefore be relied upon. [75]

However discreetly the pope and his agents attempted to deal with the situation, at some stage Edward III would have to be informed. It is likely that Manuel Fieschi was directed to go to Italy from Avignon in order to receive the 'confession' of the impostor and to put the information into a document which could then be sent to Edward III. Nicolino Fieschi, Manuel's close relative, could have played a key role in these proceedings.[76] Nicolino had been in direct personal contact with Edward III as early as July 1336, when he brought a letter from Genoa to Edward at Perth in Scotland. Fieschi's official role on this occasion was to seek compensation from the English crown for Hugh Despenser the Younger's seizure and plundering of a Genoese cargo vessel in the English Channel in 1321. This was a long-running dispute, which Edward III wisely settled by the payment of 8,000 marks in order to ensure future access to Genoese naval resources. Edward III was impressed by Nicolino, whom he described in his reply to the Genoese as *vir eloquens et industrius*.[77] However, Nicolino was working for Edward III before this: he was made a member of the royal council on 15 April 1336, which in turn implies that he had already come to the notice of Edward III. Nicolino also acted as Edward III's proctor at the papal curia from 24 June 1336 until 12 July 1338. Although Nicolino was not personally present at Avignon throughout this period, it is likely that at some point he became directly aware of reports circulating in Avignon of 'Edward II's' wanderings. It is even possible that he was personally involved in the choice of Melazzo/Mulazzo and later Cecima as places of detention for the impostor, and that he had a direct role both in Manuel Fieschi's composition of his letter and in its onward transmission to Edward III.[78] This would place the date of the Fieschi letter somewhere between the summer of 1336 at one extreme and the summer of 1338 at

---

rights of succession to the French monarchy. Although, as Stubbs suggested, the story in the Fieschi letter could conceivably have been a French plot, there is no evidence to suggest that France was in any way involved either in the production of the letter or in its aftermath.

[75] For ecclesastical purposes Cecima was in the diocese of Tortona, of which Percival Fieschi was bishop in the 1330s, while it came under the secular lordship of the bishop of Pavia: Bernini, *La Badia*, 167–8; Sangiuliani, *Cecima*, 37, 39. It is possible, though not certain, that the castle of Melazzo was under the jurisdiction of the bishop of Acqui: Violono, *Melazzo nella storia*, 22.

[76] Here I am in agreement with Ian Mortimer: *The Greatest Traitor*, 261, 263, 303; *The Perfect King*, 413–17.

[77] *Foedera*, II, ii, 941; Fryde, 49, 243; Mortimer, *The Greatest Traitor*, 259–60.

[78] *CPR, 1334–38*, 247. Nicolino's account as king's proctor in the papal curia, for 747 days from 24 June, 10 Ed. III (1336) to 12 July, 12 Ed. III (1338), for expediting the king's affairs at the curia and elsewhere overseas, is preserved in E 372/184, m.48 (13 Ed. III). He was owed £44 4s but received only £13 6s 8d at York in Nov.: 10 Ed. III (1336).

the other. If the Fieschi letter had some kind of official status as a document produced with the knowledge and approval of the pope, this would also help to explain how a copy of it came to be preserved in Register A of the diocese of Maguelone.

Nicolino's involvement in English affairs probably did not end there. Edward III's wardrobe book for 1338–40 records in September 1338 that William le Galeys, 'who asserts that he is the father of the lord king' and who was recently 'arrested' (*arestati*) at Cologne, was taken to meet Edward III at Koblenz by Francis the Lombard, a king's sergeant. On 18 October a sum of 13s 6d was paid at Antwerp to Francekino Forcet (almost certainly the same man) for three weeks' expenses in 'December', during which he had custody of William le Galeys 'because he named himself as king of England and the father of the present king'.[79] It is most unlikely that William le Galeys had turned up in Cologne by coincidence at a time when Edward III happened to be in the vicinity, and then proceeded to make a public demonstration which led to his arrest.[80] The word 'arrested' in the wardrobe book record should probably be understood as meaning 'confined' or 'in custody'.[81] The most likely explanation is that William le Galeys was none other than the pious hermit whose confession was contained in the letter of Manuel Fieschi to Edward III, that he had been brought from Italy specifically in order to meet Edward III and that he had been in the custody all the time of Francis the Lombard, probably acting on the orders of Nicolino Fieschi who is known to have been with Edward III at Koblenz.[82] William could have been brought overland from

---

It is possible, as Ian Mortimer suggests, that Nicolino brought with him Manuel Fieschi's letter as early as July 1336: Mortimer, *The Greatest Traitor*, 259–60. Nicolino was again (or still) in England on 30 Oct. 1336, when he came into the chancery at York to confirm his letters patent of 16 Oct. in which he stated that he was acting as a special envoy of the city of Genoa in its dealings with Edward III. Earlier, on 6 Oct., Edward III had appointed him as his proctor and envoy to arrange for the hire of galleys and men-at-arms: *Foedera*, II, ii, 947–8. These were his official functions, but there was plenty of room left for him to engage in more sensitive and highly confidential activities.

[79] *The Wardrobe Book of William de Norwell*, ed. Lyon et al., 212, 214. The reference to Dec. in the second entry is surely a mistake for Sept.: three weeks' expenses would scarcely be paid in Oct. for a date two months ahead. The meeting between Edward III and the emperor took place at Koblenz on 3, 4 Sept.: *Vitae Paparum Avenionensium*, ed. Baluze, ii, 304.

[80] This is the way in which both Chaplais and Cuttino & Lynam interpreted the event: Cuttino & Lyman, 'Where is Edward II?', 530, n. 43. Cuttino & Lyman did not however pursue the question of William le Galeys and his possible identity.

[81] See R.E. Latham, *Revised Medieval Latin Word-list* (London, 1965), 31. The second wardrobe book reference does use the word 'custody'. Mortimer also considers that William was not 'arrested' in the modern sense of the word: Mortimer, *The Greatest Traitor*, 260.

[82] This is also Mortimer's opinion: *The Greatest Traitor*, 261, 303. Although Francis Forcet is described as a royal serjeant-at-arms and therefore technically a member of the royal household, this was probably, as Mortimer suggests, to give him status. Forcet may in fact have been an associate of Dino Forcetti, of the Florentine banking company the Bardi,

northern Italy, but the fact that he first appeared at Cologne and then had to be taken south to Koblenz tells against this argument and suggests that he may have come by sea, most probably in one of the Genoese galleys which Nicolino Fieschi was engaged in hiring for Edward III. Nicolino's kinsman, Nicholas Blank de Fieschi, who was a master of galleys and had recently been sent to Edward III in England, had evidently caught up with the king instead in the Low Countries. At Koblenz on 6 September 1338 Nicholas was given licence to return home and was freed from all obligations that he had made to Nicolino at Marseilles. Some of those obligations were certainly to do with the hire of shipping, but it is possible that one of them had been to transport William le Galeys by sea from Marseilles to England and then on to Antwerp. From there it would have been a short journey overland first to Cologne and then to Koblenz.[83] This is all of course hypothetical, but it seems very probable that the appearance of the man claiming to be Edward II at Cologne in September 1338 was not a surprise to Edward III. It is also significant that there is nothing in the English records to suggest that the impostor was tried and summarily executed, as one might have expected.[84] It is known that he was escorted to Antwerp by Francekino Forcet and perhaps taken back in Nicholas Blank's galley from there to Italy, to end his days.[85] At Antwerp on 6 January 1339 Nicolino Fieschi was reappointed a member of Edward III's council at an annual fee of £20, which would continue to be paid to his sons Gabriel and Anthony after his death. The letters patent state that the appointment had been made because of the purity of his affection for Edward III and his royal house and the circumspection with which he had carried out royal business.[86] It is hard to resist the conclusion that Nicolino's services to the English crown did not consist only of the hiring of Genoese galleys, however important these were to the English war

---

who was also with Edward III at this time and was closely involved in Edward's credit operations in the Low Countries and Germany: Mortimer, *The Greatest Traitor*, 303; *The Wardrobe Book of William de Norwell*, ed. Lyon et al., lxxv, 216. Nicolino Fieschi was probably at Antwerp on 24 Sept. when he was authorized to obtain shipping for use by Edward III and at the same time to prevent others (i.e. France) from doing so: *CPR, 1338–40*, 190.

[83] *Foedera*, II, ii, 1058.

[84] One important clue to Edward III's opinion of William le Galeys is the fact that on 21 Sept. 1338 he attended mass at the conventual church of St Andrew in Antwerp for the soul of Edward II on the anniversary of his father's death. Masses in memory of Edward II were also celebrated on that date by the Dominicans of Antwerp and by the Carthusians just outside the city: *The Wardrobe Book of William de Norwell*, ed. Lyon et al., 207. Edward III would scarcely have done this if he had any doubt about the real identity of William le Galeys, unless he was being extraordinarily devious.

[85] Despite being given licence to depart on 6 Sept., Nicholas Blank was still in Antwerp on 29 Oct.: *The Wardrobe Book of William de Norwell*, ed. Lyon et al., lxv, 275.

[86] '*Cum nuper attendentes affectionis puritatem, quam dilectus et fidelis noster, Nicholinus de Flisco, dictus cardinalis de Janua, ad nos et domum nostram regiam optinuit, necnon ipsius circumspectionem providam, quam nobis in agendis nostris fore credidimus oportunam*': *Foedera*, II, ii, 1066.

effort, and that he was centrally involved in the events which led both to the writing and delivery of the Fieschi letter and to the custody and delivery of William le Galeys.[87]

There remains the question: who was William le Galeys? Ian Mortimer suggests that William was no less than Edward II himself, while Paul Doherty argues for William Ockley or Ogle, one of the men accused of Edward II's murder who had fled England in 1330.[88] Edward II was certainly dead, while there is no evidence relating to Ockley one way or the other. It is however worth searching for someone named le Galeys who might fit the known evidence, even though 'le Galeys' or 'le Waleys', or in its various other forms, such as 'Wallace' or 'Walsh, was a common enough name, meaning simply 'the Welshman'.[89]

By coincidence one of the *armigeri* of Queen Isabella's household was named William le Galeys and was eventually buried in the church of the Grey Friars in London, where Isabella herself was buried in 1358. In 1347 William founded a chantry at Cheylesmore near Coventry for the repose of the souls of Isabella and others, including interestingly enough Edward II. By a further coincidence Cheylesmore is only a few miles from Dunsmore and Dunchurch, the home of the Dunheveds who were so active in trying to free Edward II from prison while he still lived.[90] But there is nothing more. If this William had been the wandering hermit of the Fieschi letter in the 1330s, then he made an extraordinary change of career later in life. So he can be ruled out of any further consideration.

There is one other candidate who fits some of the requirements of the wanderer, while at the same time falling short in at least one crucial aspect. This is William le Walsh, son of William le Walsh (d. 1303) and stepson of Andrew de Beauchamp, who held the manor of Woolstrop in Quedgeley just outside Gloucester from the earldom of Pembroke.[91] William was a

---

[87] Given Nicolino's value to the English crown, it is hardly surprising that the French went to the trouble of seizing him from Avignon in April 1340. There is nothing to suggest that this episode was in any way connected with William le Galeys.

[88] Mortimer, *The Greatest Traitor*, 260–2; Doherty, *Isabella*, 213–14.

[89] For example, the Waleys family of Glynde in Sussex and that of Henry le Waleys, alderman and mayor of London under Edward I: see N. Saul, *Scenes from Provincial Life* (Oxford, 1986); B. Breslow, 'Henry le Waleys', *The Historian*, Phi Alpha Theta (2009).

[90] *The Grey Friars of London*, ed. Kingsford, 100–1; *CPR, 1345–48*, 429.

[91] William le Walsh was the stepson of Andrew de Beauchamp who had married William's mother: *RP*, i, 311. He was a commissioner of array in 1322 and 1324; in 1322 the sheriff of Gloucester included William Walsh in a list of 'men-at-arms in his bailiwick aged between sixteen and sixty who were able in body and could wield arms'; in 1324 the sheriff returned that W. Walsh was one of 14 men holding lands in his bailiwick who were eligible to become knights (but Saul thinks that W. Walsh managed to evade actually taking up knighthood): N. Saul, *Knights and Esquires* (Oxford, 1981), 27, 31–2, 44–5.

Woolstrop in Quedgeley is now on the outskirts of the city of Gloucester. As heir of Robert Pont de l'Arche (d. 1246) and of his son William, William le Walsh held Woolstrop from Aymer de Valence, earl of Pembroke, whose own manors of Whaddon, Moreton Valence and Painswick were close at hand. In 1312 and again in 1315 William le Walsh,

partisan of Roger Damory against the Despensers in the civil war of 1321–2; he appears to have had some connections with Edward II's wife Queen Isabella;[92] and possibly also with the Berkeley family, whose castle nearby was the prison and place of death of Edward II.[93] While not of great importance in himself, William was the head of one of those locally well connected gentry families who were on the verge of knighthood and performed many of the functions of that rank.[94] Anyone living in Gloucester and its vicinity in and around 1327 would certainly have heard the stories and rumours both about the manner of Edward II's death and about his supposed escape from captivity. William le Walsh would have been no exception, and perhaps better informed than most. But to transform William's role from that of an interested observer of events to that of a wanderer claiming to be Edward II is another matter entirely. Here there is no direct evidence; only speculation is possible. If William le Walsh of Woolstrop really was the William le Galeys who appeared at Cologne in 1338, it is possible that he was so affected by the events of 1327 that he took to religion in a big way and abandoned his possessions for a life of wandering and prayer; or that he was simply deranged and suffered from delusions; or that he was a confidence trickster who knew enough to create

---

supported by the earl of Pembroke, petitioned in parliament over a disputed 10s a year service owed to the manor of the Barton, adjacent to Woolstrop and held by Queen Margaret, the widow of Edward I: *RP*, i, 311 (the original petition is SC8/145/7245). See also *VCH, Gloucestershire*, x, ed. C.R. Elrington (Glos., 1972). 218–19.

[92] On his role in 1321–2 see *CPR, 1321–24*, 163–4. Queen Isabella had an interest in Woolstrop, which, as noted above, owed some service to the manor of the Barton, which formed part of Isabella's dower. William may have had other connections with the queen, since on 20 Feb. 1325 a certain William le Galeys was given letters of protection (with 29 others) for going overseas on the king's service with Queen Isabella: *CPR, 1324–27*. This may mean that William was with the queen in France and the Low Countries before her invasion of England in Sept. 1327. Although William opposed the Despensers in 1321–2, in 1324–5 he was acting as receiver of revenues from the lands of Thomas of Lancaster and other rebels in Wales: see *List of Welsh Entries*, ed. Fryde, 59, no. 495, citing E 368/96/m.108d (Hilary term, 18–19 Ed. II).

[93] William le Walsh gave evidence at Gloucester at the proof of age of Thomas de Berkeley of Coberley, son of Giles de Berkeley in Feb. 1311: *CIPM*, v, no. 280, pp. 164–5. This does not prove that he was a close associate of the Berkeleys of Berkeley castle, but does place him in a general Berkeley orbit. The Berkeleys of Coberley, Glos., were a junior but important branch of the main Berkeley family: see B. and M. Gittos, 'Motivation and choice', in *Heraldry, Pageantry and Social Display in Medieval England*, ed. P. Coss & M. Keen (Woodbridge, Suffolk & Rochester, NY, 2002), 153–8. In 1335 Andrew le Walsh acquired land in Woolstrop from Thomas de Berkeley: *VCH, Gloucestershire*, x, 219. One of William le Walsh's immediate descendants (probably a younger son), Ralph le Walsh of Woolstrop (and of Llanwern and Dinham in South Wales) was certainly a 'Berkeley man'. He was receiver of the Berkeleys in 1373–4; escheator in 1376–7; sheriff of Gloucestershire in 1379–80 and 1383–4; member of parliament for Gloucestershire in Oct. 1383: Saul, *Knights and Esquires*, 72, 117, 128, 138, 154, 288.

[94] Saul, *Knights and Esquires*, 226–7: table of manors held by Glos. knights and esquires in 1316.

a plausible story and hoped that his real identity would not be discovered. One small clue is that he also held two manors in south-east Wales, just across the Bristol Channel from Berkeley and close to Gloucester: the manor of Dynan (Dinham) held from the earl marshal's lordship of Chepstow, and the manor of Llanwern near Newport, the site of the present-day steelworks, which was held from the Pembroke lordship of Goodrich.[95] Llanwern was next door to Goldcliff priory, a daughter house of the famous abbey of Bec in Normandy.[96] There is ample evidence that William le Walsh was closely interested in Goldcliff, and through this he had contacts with Bec.[97] This might perhaps be an explanation for the statement in the Fieschi letter that the alleged Edward II spent some time in Normandy during his travels.

Unfortunately there is one fundamental problem with this chain of speculation: William le Walsh of Woolstrop and Llanwern apparently died in 1329 and was succeeded not by another William, but by his son Andrew. But did William really die in 1329[98] or was he only dead in the eyes of

[95] *CIPM*, vii, no. 207, p. 156, where he is named as William le Walsshe of 'Wolvesthrop', i.e. Woolstrop. There is a full translation of the inquisitions in *The Index Library*, v, *1302–1358*, ed. E.A. Fry, The British Record Society, xl (London, 1910), 226–7. Transcripts of the original inquisitions are preserved in C 135/15. The inquisitions make it clear that the W. le Walsh who held Woolstrop was the same man who held Llanwern and Dynan. The editor of the *CIPM*, vii, 335, mistakenly identified *Lanwaryn* in Netherwent, as it appears in the inquisition, with the present-day Llanwarne in Hereford and Worcester, because of its connection with Goodrich castle in the same county. However the fact, as will appear below, that W. le Walsh of *Lanwaryn* was closely involved with the adjoining Goldcliff priory makes it certain that the identification should be with Llanwern.

[96] See R. Graham, 'Four alien priories in Monmouthshire', *Journal of British Archaeological Association*, 2nd ser., xxxv (London, 1927), 104–5, 108–9, 112–13, 115–19.

[97] In 1319 William held a water-mill from Goldcliff priory: *CPR, 1317–21*, 376. In May 1322 William and other former partisans of Roger Damory were accused of having tried to force the prior of Goldcliff to answer pleas in Roger Damory's court and not in a royal court; and in the same month he and others were accused of having supported the former prior, Ralph de Rounceville, in his refusal in 1318 to accept the appointment by the abbot of Bec of William de St Albin as prior: *CPR, 1321–24*, 157, 163–4. These matters are also described in two petitions from William de St Albin to the king and council: *Calendar of Ancient Petitions relating to Wales*, ed. Rees, 102–4 (SC 8/68/3360); and 118–19 (SC 8/83/4101). In 1319 the abbot of Bec, supported by the king of France, petitioned Edward II on behalf of the new prior: F.D. Logan, *Runaway Religious in Medieval England, c.1240–1540* (Cambridge, 1996), 104, n. 30 (citing *CPR, 1317–21*, 544–5, and *Registrum Ade de Orleton, Bishop of Hereford*, ed. A.T. Bannister, Canterbury & York Ser., V (London, 1908), 104). Ralph de Rounceville's arrest was ordered on 15 Jan. 1319: Logan, *Runaway Religious*, 187 (citing *CPR, 1317–21*, 268). William le Waleys was clearly in the thick of a long-running dispute over the prior of Goldcliff. Whether he would have received a welcome had he arrived at Bec as a wanderer is therefore debatable.

[98] *CIPM*, vii, no. 207, p. 156. Andrew, who was aged 24 years or more, was named after William's stepfather, Andrew de Beauchamp. Perhaps Andrew had an illegitimate brother named William, who could have been the wanderer, but there is no evidence to support this. There is no suggestion in the original material in The National Archives (C 135/15) that William le Walsh did not die in 1329. Each return says that he held the piece of land in question on the day that he died. No date of death is given. The Woolstrop inquest was

the law, and free to go where he wished?[99] This is surely one speculation too many.

SURVIVAL LEGENDS

Kings who lost their throne or who died mysteriously were often rumoured to be alive somewhere or other, perhaps living as hermits to do penance for their sins or waiting for the moment when they could return as the saviour of their people; the burial of a substitute body and the appearance of impostors also often formed part of such legends.[100] They were attached, for example, to Harold the last Anglo-Saxon king of England,[101] to the Holy Roman Emperors Henry V in the twelfth century and Frederick II in the thirteenth;[102] and to the emperor Baldwin of Constantinople in the 1220s.[103] Similar rumours of survival were also to be associated with Edward II's great-grandson Richard II after his deposition in 1399.[104]

---

held at Gloucester on 9 Nov., 3 Ed. III (1329), so that William would have died in the late summer or early autumn of 1329.

[99] If a man became 'professed in religion', his heir immediately inherited from him any land that he had, and, if he had made a will, it took effect at once as though he were naturally dead: Logan, *Runaway Religious*, 6, n. 108; F. Pollock and F.W. Maitland, *The History of English Law before the Time of Edward I* (2nd edn, Cambridge, 1968), i, 434. There is nothing to prove either that William le Walsh became a professed religious in 1329 and so passed on his lands to his heir, or that he decided to divest himself of his lands for some other reason, but it is not impossible. It is not clear whether, in either of these situations, an inquisition *post mortem* would have been held, as if he were really dead. But there must have been such situations. In the case of William le Walsh, the only lands he held in chief were a messuage and a carucate in the manor of Woolstrop, which were held from the king's barton in Gloucester, which was of the king's ancient demesne: *CIPM*, vii, no. 207, p. 156. The lords who would have been principally concerned in giving their assent were the heirs to the earl of Pembroke in the manors of Woolstrop and Llanwern and the earl marshal in the case of Dinham. There is one notable precedent, involving one of the most famous medieval persons, Peter Abelard. Both his parents retired to monasteries. 'This form of retirement was a way of ensuring that the family property was passed on to the next generation under parental supervision, as well as giving husband and wife the chance to prepare for the next world . . . Although Abelard had already surrendered his interest in Le Pallet (his family home in Brittany), confirmation of this was probably required. Unsuccessful clerics like him, who had not irrevocably committed themselves to celibacy by becoming priests, might return home unexpectedly like the Prodigal Son and get the fatted calf': M.T. Clanchy, *Abelard* (Oxford, 1997), 71.

[100] What follows is based on Evans, *Death of Kings*, ch. 6, 'Once and future kings'; see also Tout, 'Captivity and death', 171–2.

[101] Evans, *Death of Kings*, 147–8, 155, 157–9 (hermit).

[102] Ibid., 152–3, 155 (Frederick II: penitent pilgrim, hermit, impostors), 157 (Henry V: hermit; impostors).

[103] Ibid., 155 (impostor).

[104] Saul, *Richard II*, 427. See also P. McNiven, 'Rebellion, sedition and the legend of Richard II's survival in the reigns of Henry IV and Henry V', in *Bulletin of the John Rylands Library*, lxxvi (1994), 93–117, esp. 94, 98; P. Strohm, 'The trouble with Richard', *Speculum*, lxxi (1996), 87–111, esp. 91–101.

Another fourteenth-century example is John I, king of France, and the posthumously born son of Louis X, who lived for a few days in 1316. Forty years later, after the defeat of his namesake, John II, at the battle of Poitiers, a certain Giannino Baglioni of Siena in Italy was astonished to be told that he was none other than the lost John I and that he should vindicate his claim by invading France.[105]

Given the atmosphere of intrigue and conspiracy which surrounded the last days of Edward II, and which was really the culmination of the intrigues and conspiracies that had been rife in the kingdom of England ever since 1322, it is hardly surprising that after his death Edward II should become the focus of fresh rumours; it would have been more surprising if he had not.

'SAINT' EDWARD

It was not uncommon for the deaths of great men to be followed by moves for their canonization, sometimes popular, sometimes politically inspired. This had happened, for example, after the death of Simon de Montfort, earl of Leicester in the battle of Evesham in 1265.[106] It happened again after the execution in 1322 of Simon's self-styled political heir, Thomas of Lancaster, when 'miracles' were reported both at his tomb in Pontefract and around the plaque he had set up in St Paul's cathedral in London to mark the publication of the Ordinances. Edward II and his advisers had been forced into taking swift action before events got out of hand.[107] Edward II's deposition in January 1327 was followed by a move for the canonization both of Thomas of Lancaster and of another of Edward's former opponents, Robert Winchelsey, archbishop of Canterbury who had died in 1313.[108] On 15 February Henry of Lancaster wrote from London

---

[105] C.T. Wood, 'Where is John the Posthumous?', in *Documenting the Past*, ed. J.S. Hamilton & P.J. Bradley (Woodbridge, Suffolk & Wolfeboro, NH, 1989), 99–117.

[106] The manner of Simon de Montfort's death contributed to a popular movement for his canonization which made him a potential threat to the political stability of the kingdom. This movement has been studied by T.J. Heffernan: 'Dangerous sympathies', in *The South English Legendary*, ed. K.P. Jankofsky (Tübingen, 1992), 1–17, esp. 4; and ' "God hath schewed ffor him many grete miracules" ', in *Art and Context in Late Medieval English Narrative*, ed. R.R. Edwards (Woodbridge Suffolk & Rochester, NY, 1994), 177–91. See also J.C. Russell, 'The canonisation of opposition to the king in Angevin England', in *Haskins Anniversary Essays in Medieval History*, ed. C.H. Taylor (Boston & New York, 1929), 279–90.

[107] E 163/4/11/16 (draft of privy seal letter, dated at Durham on 28 Sept. from the king to the archbishop of York); *Foedera*, II, i, 525–6; *Flores*, 213–14; *Brut*, i, 228–30; *Anonimalle*, 114–15. On political canonization and on concepts of sanctity see J.E. Bray, 'Concepts of sainthood in fourteenth-century England', *Bulletin of John Rylands Library*, lxvi (1983–4), 40–77; J.M. Theilmann, 'Political canonization and political symbolism in medieval England', *Journal of British Studies*, xxix (1990), 241–66; and M.A. Stouck, 'Saints and rebels', *Medievalia et Humanistica*, new ser., xxiv (1997), 75–94.

[108] *PROME*, Parliament of Jan. 1327, C 65/1, item 2 (Lancaster and Winchelsey).

asking William Melton the archbishop of York to request the pope to begin an inquiry into the miracles attributed to Thomas of Lancaster. On 24 February the archbishop duly obliged, sending the pope a very flattering estimate of Thomas's character and claims to sanctity.[109] Although no formal canonization process was ever ordered by the pope, the cult of 'St Thomas of Lancaster' flourished in England and even on the continent and has left many traces.[110] A miniature in the copy of the Sarum Hours made for use in the diocese of Lincoln between about 1325 and 1330 depicts Thomas of Lancaster facing St George;[111] the Luttrell Psalter, made somewhere between 1320 and 1340, has a marginal illustration of Lancaster's execution;[112] in the church of South Newington in Oxfordshire there is a wall painting of Lancaster's 'martyrdom', dated to before 1340 and shown in conjunction with the martyrdom of St Thomas of Canterbury;[113] a Latin office composed late in the reign of Edward II or early in that of Edward III also treats Thomas of Lancaster as imitating the sacrifice made by St Thomas;[114] the Liber de Reliquiis produced in Durham in 1383 includes a pair of *bedys* of 'St Thomas of Lancaster';[115] the British Museum possesses a number of pilgrims' badges depicting scenes from Lancaster's life and death;[116] and an anonymous life of 'St Thomas' is preserved in two late fifteenth-century continental manuscripts.[117]

Any attempt to present Edward II as a martyr and as worthy of canonization therefore had to compete with a substantial amount of support for the cause of his first cousin Thomas of Lancaster. Yet there is considerable

---

[109] *Letters from Northern Registers*, ed. Raine, 339–42. The fact that Melton did so suggests that he had at last recognized the fact of the change of regime; while his composition of the document at Southwell in Nottinghamshire may imply that he was distancing himself from the business of the parliament still in progress at Westminster. For a much less flattering opinion of Lancaster see *Polychronicon*, viii, 313–15.

[110] This is fully discussed in Echerd, 'Canonization and politics' (Ph.D.); J. Edwards, 'The cult of "St" Thomas of Lancaster and its iconography', *Yorks. Arch. Journal*, lxiv (1992), 103–22; and idem, 'The cult of "St" Thomas of Lancaster and its iconography: a supplementary note', *Yorks. Arch. Journal*, lxvii (1995), 187–91.

[111] Bod. Library, Douce Ms. 231, f. 1r; Edwards, 'The cult of "St" Thomas' (1992), 109–11 (incl. photograph). The bishop of Lincoln, Henry Burghersh, was an opponent of Edward II and might have been sympathetic to the cause of Lancaster.

[112] Edwards, 'The cult of "St" Thomas' (1992), 112–13; BL, Add. Ms. 42130, f. 56.

[113] E.W. Tristram, *English Wall Painting of the Fourteenth Century* (London, 1955), 70, 72–3, 228–9, and plate 18; Edwards, 'The cult of "St" Thomas' (1992), 118–20 (incl. photograph).

[114] *Political Songs*, ed. P. Coss, 268–72; Edwards, 'The cult of "St" Thomas' (1992), 118–19.

[115] *Extracts from the Account Rolls of the Abbey of Durham*, ii, ed. J.T. Fowler (Durham 1899, for the year 1898), 427. The beads had presumably been sanctified by proximity to his tomb.

[116] Edwards, 'The cult of "St" Thomas' (1992), 113–17 and plates 3 & 4.

[117] The life is printed in *Anecdota ex Codicibus Hagiographicis Iohannis Gielemans* (Brussels, 1895), 80–100. The MSS are from the Charterhouse of St Barbara, Cologne, and the Augustinian abbey of Rouge-Cloître near Brussels, where Johann Gielemans was a canon: Echerd, 'Canonization and politics' (Ph.D.), 237, 174–5, 268–71.

evidence to show that Edward II was so presented. He had certain advantages over his cousin in that he had been a king and not just an earl, however powerful. Another advantage was the cult of the royal saint, Edward the Confessor (canonized in 1162 during the reign of Henry II), which had been consciously developed by the English monarchy in the years before 1307, and which was given significant emphasis in Edward II's coronation in 1308.[118] The cult of Edward the Confessor also helped to inspire the otherwise unknown Adam Davy to write his English poem, *Five Dreams of Edward II*, with its hints of future martyrdom, at about the time of Edward II's coronation in March 1308.[119] Edward's fondness in life for the company of monks and friars, especially the members of the Dominican order,[120] had sometimes led him into trouble, as in the case of Nicholas of Wisbech and his promotion of the virtues of the Holy Oil of St Thomas,[121] but it also won him their enduring loyalty. Many of the individuals who sought to free him from captivity in 1327 or who believed in 1330 that he was still alive in Corfe castle were drawn from these groups.[122]

Among the chroniclers Ranulf Higden, the author of the *Polychronicon*, remarked that some people thought that Edward II should be placed among the saints, while countering this view with an account of Edward's vices and the failure of his government.[123] The author of the *Annals of Osney* commented shrewdly that no one should be considered a saint on the grounds of the squalor of his imprisonment and the vileness of his death, unless these were matched by the holiness of his life.[124] In contrast, Geoffrey le Baker's account of Edward II's death, written in the 1340s, seems positively designed to prepare the way for a cult of royal sanctity. The literary device of the bishop of Hereford's ambiguous message is followed by the terrible details of Edward's murder, by a comparison of his sufferings with those of Christ and a description of him as a glorious martyr.[125] Geoffrey also asserted that at the time of his deposition Edward

---

[118] This theme is more fully discussed in Chs 2 & 4. See Binski, *Westminster Abbey*; and two important unpublished papers by Parsons, 'Saints' cults and kingship', and 'Rethinking English coronations'. I am grateful to Professor Parsons for allowing me to see these papers.

[119] See Phillips, 'Edward II and the prophets', 191–4, and Ch. 1 of this book.

[120] See ch. 2 of this book.

[121] Phillips, 'Edward II and the prophets', 196–201, and Chs 1 & 7 of this book.

[122] It may be more than a coincidence in the formation of a story of martyrdom that Corfe was also associated with the life and death of an earlier murdered king and saint, Edward the Martyr, who was foully murdered there in the year 978: Stenton, *Anglo-Saxon England*, 367–8; Fell, *Edward, King and Martyr*.

[123] *Polychronicon*, 300.

[124] *Annals of Osney*, ed. Luard, iv, 348.

[125] '*Clamor ille expirantis multos de Berkeleya et quosdam de castro, ut ipsi asseruerunt, ad compassionem et oraciones pro sancta anima migrante evigilavit. Sic quem mundus odivit, suumque magistrum Iesum Christum prius odio habuit, primo preceptorem de regno Iudeorum reprobatum, deinde discipulum regno Anglorum spoliatum recepit celsitudo regni angelorum. Gloriose atque bone finis Edwardi proditorios ministros*' (i.e. Gurney and Maltravers). Le Baker then says that Edward of Windsor became

was prepared to end his life for Christ, knowing that a good shepherd should place his soul at the service of his sheep.[126] When he was imprisoned in Berkeley castle the 'ministers of Belial' attempted to end the life of 'the servant of God' by poison, but failed, either because of Edward's natural strength or, which Geoffrey believed was the truth, because 'the Most High reserved his confessor for a more manifest martyrdom'.[127] Geoffrey also claimed that Edward had escaped from the disaster at Bannockburn in 1314 through the intervention of the Mother of God.[128]

Another writer who tried to promote Edward's cause was the Dominican scholar Thomas Ringstead, who was bishop of Bangor between 1357 and 1366, but who had taught in Cambridge in the 1340s. In her study of Ringstead's lectures on the Book of Proverbs, Dr Beryl Smalley found an intriguing story about Prince Edward of Caernarfon and his father Edward I, which must have had its roots in their famous quarrel in 1305: Edward I 'had cast him off under the influence of evil counsellors. He bore the injury patiently and came to his father's help on a winter's night, when the king was riding along a muddy, dangerous road. Fearing for his safety, Prince Edward took the horse's bridle and walked beside him until the danger was over. The king did not know who had come to his rescue.' And so, according to Ringstead, *Talis filius fuit Christus*.[129]

The magnificent tomb erected in memory of Edward II in Gloucester abbey, the pilgrims it attracted and the miracles which were enacted around it no doubt contributed to his reputation for sanctity but there is no evidence of any attempt, whether by Dominican enthusiasts or by royal authority, to start a formal process for the canonization of Edward II[130] until the reign of

---

king '*postquam gloriosus rex Edwardus regni diadema, ut prescriptum est, suo primogenito, domino Edwardo de Wyndesore, resignaverat*': *Le Baker*, 30–4, esp. 33–4. This passage reads like the conclusion to a saint's life. In contrast the much shorter *Chroniculum Galfridi le Baker* says simply that Edward II died at Berkeley on 20 Sept. and was buried at Gloucester on 21 Dec.: in *Le Baker*, 172.

[126] '... *paratior pro Christo vitam finire ... sciens quod bonus pastor animam suam poneret pro ovibus suis*': *Le Baker*, 27; *Vita et Mors*, 313.

[127] '*Venenum quampluries propinaverunt servo Dei ministry Belial, quod aut fortitudine naturali evacuavit, ... aut, quod verius credo, manifestiori martirio, suum confessorem Altissimus reservavit*': *Le Baker*, 30. The language of martyrdom also appears in the chronicle of Walter of Guisborough: the account of the beginning of reign of Edward II is preceded by the rubric, '*De coronacione regis Edwardi secundi et martiris*': *Guisborough*, 380. Even if this rubric was added much later, it still indicates someone's opinion of Edward II.

[128] *Le Baker*, 9; *Vita et Mors*, 300: Edward also later fulfilled his promise to found a house for 24 Carmelites to study theology at Oxford, in gratitude for his escape, despite the Younger Despenser's attempt to dissuade him because of the cost: *Vita et Mors*, 300.

[129] Smalley, *English Friars*, 211–15, 219, 338. As Dr Smalley points out, the story must be apocryphal since, although Edward did follow his father around in 1305, their quarrel and final reconciliation took place in the summer and autumn, not in winter.

[130] Although Edward III wrote to the pope on three occasions to request the canonization of Thomas of Lancaster, he never did so on behalf of his own father: see Given-Wilson, 'Richard II', 568.

Richard II, who had his own dynastic and political reasons for wanting a royal saint in the family.[131] Richard's interest in Edward II and his canonization may have begun in October 1378 when he visited Edward's tomb during a parliament held in the abbey of St Peter's, Gloucester, leaving his personal badge of the white hart painted on the adjoining pillars as a mark of his visit.[132] In 1383 he exempted the abbots of Gloucester from attending parliament in person, in return for the celebration of mass for Edward II's soul on the anniversary of his death.[133] So far this was little more than the recognition given to Edward II's place of burial by Edward III, but in 1385 Richard sent a delegation to the curia to press Urban VI for his great-grandfather's canonization;[134] and two years later he sent William Brut, a monk of Gloucester abbey, to ask Urban VI for an inquiry into Edward's miracles.[135] Richard's work bore fruit on 4 December 1389 when the newly elected pope Boniface IX ordered the archbishop of Canterbury to examine the life, merits and miracles of Edward II.[136] In October or November 1390 Richard II went to Gloucester in company with the archbishop and Richard Braybrooke, bishop of London, to supervise the beginning of this work.[137] The resulting book of miracles, together with a gold cup and a gold ring set with a ruby, was delivered to the pope in Florence by Peter Merk and James Monald early in 1395.[138] Between then and 1399 Richard II pursued the process with determination through his agents, Master William Stortford

---

[131] The best and most detailed study of the reign is Saul, *Richard II*; see esp. ch. 13, 'Piety and orthodoxy'. See also Given-Wilson, 'Richard II', 553–71; Saul, 'Richard II and the vocabulary of kingship', *EHR*, cx (1995), 854–77. The canonization of Edward II was just one of a number of strategies employed by Richard II to glorify his own kingship and to overcome his political opponents. The Wilton Diptych, made in the 1390s, shows Richard kneeling with St Edmund the Martyr (another royal saint), John the Baptist and St Edward the Confessor standing behind him. It has been suggested that St Edmund may represent Edward II; Richard may also have tried to make use of the Holy Oil of St Thomas, as Edward II had done: Theilmann, 'Political canonization', 257–61; Sandquist, 'Holy Oil', 337–8; Shelagh Mitchell, 'Richard II', in *The Regal Image of Richard II and the Wilton Diptych*, ed. D. Gordon, L. Monnas & C. Elam (London, 1997).

[132] Welander, *History . . . of Gloucester Cathedral*, 148, 634.

[133] *CPR, 1381–85*, 273.

[134] *Polychronicon*, ix, App., 79 (from a continuation of the *Polychronicon*, made at Westminster); now re-edited as *The Westminster Chronicle, 1381–1394*, ed. L.C. Hector & B. F. Harvey (Oxford, 1982), 158–9; *The Diplomatic Correspondence of Richard II*, ed. E. Perroy, Camden, 3rd ser., xlviii (London, 1933), 62–3.

[135] *Diplomatic Correspondence*, ed. Perroy, 210. This was done at a time of political weakness when Richard needed all the support he could get in his struggle with his baronial opponents, the Appellants.

[136] ASV, Indice 320, f. 35v; L. E. Boyle, OP, *A Survey of the Vatican Archives and of its Medieval Holdings* (Toronto, 1972), 140–1 (where Edward is wrongly identified as Edward the Confessor).

[137] *Polychronicon*, ix, App., 237; *The Westminster Chronicle*, 436–9.

[138] *Issues of the Exchequer*, ed. F. Devon (London, 1837), 247–8, 259; Perroy, *L'Angleterre*, 342, n. 1. The envoys were paid their expenses on 24 April 1395, presumably after their return to England.

the bishop of London's clerk, Richard Scrope bishop of Coventry & Lichfield, and the monk William Brut.[139] Nothing was achieved and Richard even appears to have fallen out with Brut.[140] Despite further English diplomatic pressure nothing had come of the attempted canonization when Richard II was deposed in 1399, and the new king Henry IV had no interest in the matter.[141]

Although there was certainly a devotion to Edward II in Gloucester, expressed through the gifts of visitors and the occasional miracle, there is no material evidence of the kind associated with Thomas of Lancaster's cult: no pilgrims' badges, no office of the 'saint'. It is hard to resist the conclusion that Edward II's cult flourished only in Gloucester and in the mind of Richard II. The report in 1389 by the St Albans chronicler, Thomas Walsingham, that Lancaster had been canonized may have been wishful thinking, but was probably intended to counter Richard II's efforts on behalf of Edward II.[142] Ironically, the cult of Thomas of Lancaster continued to flourish until the Reformation,[143] while that of Edward II disappeared from sight.

But Edward II has had the last word, if not the last laugh. While Thomas of Lancaster is now mainly the subject of specialized academic

---

[139] Perroy, *L'Angleterre*, 342, n. 2.

[140] A.L. Brown, 'The Latin letters in All Souls Ms. 182', *EHR*, lxxxvii (1972), 571–3: in 1399, in a letter to the pope, Richard II accused Brut of forging royal letters on behalf of the archbishop of Canterbury, Thomas Arundel, who had fled to the curia in 1398.

[141] I have found no sign of the book of Edward II's miracles in the Vatican Archive, the Vatican Library, in the Italian National Library in Florence and other libraries in Florence, or in The National Archives, the British Library, and elsewhere in England. The medieval holdings of Gloucester Cathedral Library are very limited in scope and contain no trace of the book. It may yet turn up, perhaps in some very unlikely place, and throw light on 14th-century popular religion, the politics of sanctity, and the scale of devotion to Edward II. In contrast, the book of miracles ascribed to Henry VI has survived in BL, Royal Ms. 13 c. viii, while his cause was still active at Rome when Henry VIII broke with the papacy: *The Miracles of King Henry VI*, ed. R. Knox & S. Leslie (Cambridge, 1923).

[142] Walsingham may also have been trying to counter the opinion in his own abbey that Edward II was especially blessed by God and deserved to be numbered among the saints: '*Edwardus Karnerivan, cui Dominus nostris temporibus benedixit specialiter, ac inter sanctos merito numeretur*': *Liber de Benefactoribus Monasterii Sancti Albani*, in *Trokelowe*, 433. The *Book of Benefactors* was compiled at about the same time that Richard II was promoting the cause of Edward II's canonization. All royal benefactors, even King John ('*etsi suis exstitit minus bonus, Beato tamen Martyri devotus fuit*') were spoken of in glowing terms, although Edward II was the only one considered as a possible saint: xlii–xliii, 430–4. Edward II's gifts to the abbey consisted of a gold cross containing precious stones and relics of the saints; timber for the repair of the choir; and a large silver and gold cup for the refectory. See also Given-Wilson, 'Richard II', 569–70.

[143] For examples collected by Nicholas Rogers of the continuation of Lancaster's cult in the 15th century see Edwards,'The cult of "St" Thomas' (1995), 189–91. Lancaster's hat and belt were still preserved at Pontefract on the eve of the Reformation as remedies respectively against headaches and the dangers of childbirth: Maddicott, 329.

interest, Edward II has in a sense experienced a series of afterlives which have lasted down to the present.[144] For good or ill, there is probably as much interest in him today as a deeply flawed and tragic personality as there was in him as king in his own time.[145]

[144] See ch. 1 of this book.
[145] There is, e.g., no website devoted to the life and times of Thomas of Lancaster as there is to Edward II (http://edwardthesecond.com/).

CONCLUSION

Two royal proclamations from the early months of 1312 provide a very clear idea of the nature of Edward II's kingship, as he saw it, and of his relations with his kingdom. The first was issued at York on 18 January and referred to the laws and usages of the kingdom which Edward had sworn to uphold at his coronation.[1] Five weeks later, on 24 February, a second order was issued at York, containing a proclamation of the peace in the following words:

> We desire, as befits our royal majesty, and are bound by our oath to maintain and preserve whole and unharmed the rights of our royal crown, our royal dignity, and the peace and tranquillity of the Holy Church and whole people committed to our rule, and to resist with God's help all things that might occur to weaken the aforesaid rights or our royal dignity, or in breach or disturbance of the peace, or terror of our people.[2]

These two proclamations suggest that Edward II had a very strong sense of his royal status and of his rights and duties as king. This was the case throughout his reign, from the time of his coronation in 1308, which was carefully prepared and clearly meant a great deal to him, until the very end. Even in his last independent action, at Neath abbey on 10 November 1326, he still saw himself as king.[3] Others did too: the difficulty with which he was finally removed as king in January 1327 and the reluctance with which many of those present accepted his removal show the durability of kingship however unsatisfactory or unworthy its holder.

Edward II could never be represented as one of the greatest of medieval English kings. There are no enduring legal reforms; no successful wars of conquest. There is no court as a centre of culture:[4] despite his interest in architecture there are no great building projects to match the castles of his father's reign. The administrative reforms which marked his

---

[1] *CCR, 1307–13*, 448–9. The original French text is printed in *Foedera*, II, i, 153.
[2] *Foedera*, II, i, 158, has the full original Latin text, as does *PW*, II, ii, App. 46–7. The calendared version in *CCR, 1307–13*, 450, has none of the significant detail.
[3] *Foedera*, II, i, 647.
[4] See Prestwich, 'The court of Edward II'.

own reign came either as the result of pressure from opponents or as part of a general exercise in administrative tidying up with which he had little to do.

Whether he performed his duties as king as seriously as he regarded his status as king is more difficult to determine. The first proclamation may throw some light on that: it was evidently an unusual document since the chancery clerk noted that 'this form was made by the king himself, and that he took the writs as soon as they were sealed and put them on his bed'.[5] The remark of the bishop of Worcester in October 1320 that the king was rising unusually early and was contributing to the discussions of parliamentary business[6] also suggests that he did not do so as a matter of course. As this book has attempted to show, Edward resisted with remarkable stubbornness and tenacity any attempt to restrict the powers of the monarchy. Although his voice does not echo through the records of government in the imperious way that his father's had done, it is unwise to assume that Edward II was neither interested in nor involved in the day-to-day business of government.[7] But his activity was inclined to be sporadic and unpredictable and gave ample scope both for favourites as well as for others with better intentions (such as the earl of Pembroke) to exert influence over him.

Edward was however fortunate in having a number of able administrators at his command, men such as William Melton who had been with him since his youth, John de Hothum and Walter Stapeldon; nor was Walter Reynolds, his chancellor and then archbishop of Canterbury, who had also served him in his early years, as lacking in ability as the chroniclers would have us believe. Such men remained loyal to him and it was only in the final crisis of 1326–7 that they finally accepted the inevitability that Edward would lose his throne. Edward also inspired a remarkable degree of loyalty among the military members of his household, many of whom had served him when he was Prince of Wales or had known him well before he became king.[8] Despite recent work on the unreliability of royal knights, it was only after Edward's victory in the civil war of 1321–2, and the brutality with which that victory was maintained, that royal knights deserted Edward's cause in significant numbers. As the plots to release Edward from captivity and the later attempts to portray him as a saint

---

[5] *CCR, 1307–13*, 448–9.

[6] *Register of Thomas de Cobham*, ed. Pearce, 97–8.

[7] One of Edward's practices was to issue orders orally. This could cause problems if the person concerned had to seek payment of a debt owed by the king and was unable to provide a written warrant: this was the case in 1330 when Edward's former butler Benedict of Fulsham sought payment for supplying wine; the same thing had happened to Stephen of Abingdon an earlier butler of Edward II: *PROME*, Parliament of Nov. 1330, E 175/2/216, items 19, 20. Edward's son and successor apparently followed a similar practice: Ormrod, 'Richard de Bury', 168–9.

[8] See Tebbit, 'Household knights' (Ph.D.), ch. 1, 'Recruitment and function'.

show, loyalty to him persisted in certain quarters after his deposition and even after his death.

Edward had considerable skill when it came to dividing his enemies and wearing down opposition until he got his way, as he did in the protracted negotiations with Thomas of Lancaster and his allies after the execution of Gaveston in 1312, and again in the negotiations in 1317–18. He was certainly helped by the calibre of his leading opponent, his first cousin the earl of Lancaster, whose character won him enemies and whose capabilities meant that he was even less suited for the work of government than Edward. Some may have thought of Lancaster as worthy of canonization after his defeat and death in 1322: few if any would have thought him worthy of veneration while he lived.

Edward also showed great determination at some moments of crisis, most especially in the civil war of 1321–2, but then threw away the fruits of victory by his vindictive treatment of his opponents. On other occasions, such as the Scottish campaigns of 1314, 1319 and 1322, his eagerness to go to war led to disaster and humiliation. His one major military success, against the Scots in Ireland in 1318, should not however be underrated since it removed the very real possibility of a profound reshaping of political structures and relationships within and between the islands of Britain and Ireland. The victory owed something to the skill and application of his advisers in England but more to his supporters in Ireland.

Just as he enjoyed a surprising degree of loyalty until the closing years of the reign, so he was loyal to those he considered to be his friends. Unfortunately these friends sometimes became favourites, a danger which any medieval king was wise to avoid, and they diverted patronage and royal attention from others whose support Edward should also have cultivated. While Edward I had been if anything too niggardly in his distribution of patronage, his son was often too generous and succeeded only in creating resentment in those who went unrewarded and in making his court 'a hotbed of political intrigue'.[9] Edward's loyalty to Piers Gaveston may well have been based on a relationship of brotherhood, as Pierre Chaplais has argued, but whatever its basis it greatly embittered the politics of the early years of the reign and, after Gaveston's death in 1312, poisoned the politics of the next ten years as well. The two proclamations with which this conclusion began were not just resounding statements of Edward II's status and duties as king: they were also issued in the context of Edward's declaration that the sentence of exile upon Gaveston in 1311 had been contrary to law and that Edward was exercising his authority as king in recalling him to England.

---

[9] Prestwich, 'The court of Edward II', 73. Tensions were created, e.g., by Hugh Audley the Younger's failure to obtain the earldom of Cornwall in 1318–19 and Bartholomew de Badlesmere's ambition to become earl of Kent in 1320–1, while the ambitions of their rival Hugh Despenser the Younger were promoted.

Edward's loyalty and attachment to Gaveston were unwise and were pursued to an extreme which alienated many potential allies. Their relationship obscured the fact that Edward II had inherited many serious problems from the reign of his father, especially a heavy burden of debt and administrative confusion, both largely caused by the war with Scotland; and he inherited the war itself which was already going badly, which it was politically unthinkable to abandon, and which was to dominate much of his own reign. Edward II also inherited a deep-seated distrust among his leading subjects of the monarchy's good faith in accepting and implementing demands for reform, and a growing degree of popular disorder and resistance to taxation. Even though Edward was probably more ready to accept reform in 1308 than he has usually been credited with being, his willingness was soon overtaken by events. It has been well said that 'Edward II sat down to the game of kingship with a remarkably poor hand, and he played it very badly'.[10] In fairness to him, however, even a more able king would have found the task a formidable and perhaps impossible one. It is also arguable that the political and administrative problems involved in governing the kingdom were starting to exceed the capacity of any king, other than the most able, especially if warfare added to their complexity, and that Edward II was unfortunate to be the first ruler fully to experience this.

His loyalty and attachment to Hugh Despenser the Younger had far more serious consequences. Edward's desire to destroy Lancaster blinded him to the dangerous ambitions of Despenser. Edward became ensnared by those ambitions and after 1322 had no choice but to follow the course set out for him by Despenser. Both men destroyed their enemies in 1322; both prospered and became immensely wealthy with the spoils of victory or royal patronage. What followed was not so much tyranny (of which Edward was never directly accused, even at the end of his reign) as a rapacious and harsh regime, which exploited the legal and administrative systems to its own advantage but also operated in a climate of conspiracy, intrigue and incipient revolt. The fates of both men became inextricably linked and they fell together in 1326–7. Much ink has been spilled on whether or not a sexual relationship existed first between Edward and Gaveston and secondly between him and Despenser.[11] It seems to this writer unlikely that there was such a relationship with either favourite. While sodomy was used as a charge to blacken Despenser's name in 1326 and indirectly to blacken that of the king, there is no recorded gossip about such practices at Edward II's court. All the complaints about Edward's engagement in 'improper pastimes' relate to quite different

---

[10] *Vita Edwardi Secundi*, ed. Denholm-Young, Introduction, ix.

[11] See the discussion in ch. 3 of this book and J. Burgtorf, ' "With my life, his joyes began and ended" ', in *Fourteenth Century England*, v, ed. N. Saul (Woodbridge, Suffolk & Rochester, NY, 2008), 31–51.

activities, which today would be regarded as hobbies or mild eccentricities rather than matters for opprobrium.[12]

Edward's loyalty to and dependence on Despenser ultimately alienated his wife, Isabella, with whom he appears to have enjoyed a happy and fruitful marriage up to about 1322. Her liaison with Roger Mortimer of Wigmore in France and later in England may or may not have been sexual, but it is significant that Isabella appears to have retained affection for her husband, even after his deposition. It is certainly significant that many years later when her own turn came to die she chose to be buried in her wedding clothes[13] and that Edward's embalmed heart was placed within her funeral effigy.[14]

The fall of Edward II was also a consequence of his alienation after 1322 of an important section of the English nobility, including his own half-brothers, and of several of the leading clergy whose role earlier in the reign had generally been one of mediation. But it was brought about by foreign war too: not with Scotland, since that conflict had been contained since the truce agreed in 1323, but with France. Hitherto Edward had worked with considerable success to maintain good relations with France, whose kings were his queen's father or brothers, to enable him to use French mediation against his opponents at home and to ensure that French interference in the lands of the English crown in Gascony was kept in check. The accession to the French throne in 1322 of a new king who was determined to exercise his own rights in Gascony ended that policy and led to a war in which France had the strategic advantage. Although the English administration did quite well in organizing the defence of Gascony, Edward could not prosecute the war by leading an army to France as he intended, since he could not afford the risk of revolt in England against himself and Despenser during his absence. He could not even afford to cross to France for long enough to perform homage, and so was forced to allow his wife Isabella and his elder son and heir Edward to go to France in an attempt to make peace. The outcome was the invasion of England, followed by Edward II's imprisonment, deposition and death. Without the war with France, Edward II's rule might have lasted considerably longer than it did. The war however had one other consequence. Although France 'won' in the 1320s, the intense legal and military pressure it exerted on the English monarchy and in particular on the young Edward III, who spent a very formative period in France in 1325–6, probably contributed to the outbreak of the greater conflict between the two kingdoms ten years later and to the devastation of France which followed.[15]

---

[12] See ch. 2 of this book and Prestwich, 'The court of Edward II', 70–1.
[13] Fryde, 269, n. 28; Tout, *Chapters*, v, 249; E 101/393/4.
[14] *The Grey Friars of London*, ed. Kingsford, 7, 74–5.
[15] Phillips, 'Simon de Montfort', 89.

Within England itself the politically inspired violence which led to the destruction of Gaveston, and to the executions, confiscations and violent deaths that marked the closing years of Edward II's reign, continued into the new reign: the St Paul's chronicler Adam Murimuth noted with bitterness that from the execution of Lancaster in 1322 to that of Roger Mortimer in 1330 no noble condemned to death had been allowed to speak in his own defence.[16] The political fabric of England broke down in the 1320s so far that no magnate, and in the last resort not even the king himself, was safe. In 1330 the nobles who passed judgment on Roger Mortimer were clearly uneasy, and they were even more uneasy at judging men who were not their peers, asking that this should not be made a precedent.[17] Edward III's revision of the law of treason in 1352 was undertaken to avoid similar situations arising in the future.[18]

So what in the end can we make of Edward II?[19] It is fair to say that he was probably underrated in his own time and has certainly been underrated since. His personality was complicated, which made (and makes) it all the more difficult to assess him fairly. He was not lacking in physical or moral courage. He was not stupid; he was probably at least as well educated as his father Edward I and his son Edward III; on occasions he spoke in public with eloquence and firmness, most notably perhaps at Amiens in July 1320 when his refusal to perform fealty in addition to homage for Aquitaine apparently reduced Philip V of France and his council to stunned silence. He was religious in a conventional way in much of his life, but there was also something of the holy man about him, which made the later story of his wanderings around Europe in the guise of a hermit and the attempt by Richard II to have him canonized at least seem plausible.[20]

As a king he was too able to be ignored but had too many weaknesses of character and behaviour to be a success. His ultimate legacy lay not in any constitutional formulas[21] or in any growth in the importance of parliamentary institutions,[22] but rather in the precedent set by his deposition,

---

[16] *Murimuth*, 56; McKisack, *The Fourteenth Century*, 103.

[17] *PROME*, Parliament of Nov. 1330, C 65/2, item 4; Phillips, 'Simon de Montfort', 79–89.

[18] Ormrod, *The Reign of Edward III*, 48–9; *PROME*, Parliament of Jan. 1352, Introduction.

[19] For a more detailed assessment see Phillips, 'The place of the reign of Edward II'.

[20] Phillips, ' "Edward II" in Italy'.

[21] The events of the reign had finally shown that the finely wrought programmes of reform and high-sounding declarations of principle, which had punctuated the political history of England since 1307 and which have so fascinated historians down to the present, counted for nothing when there was deep distrust and even loathing between the opposing sides.

[22] For an assessment of the role of parliament during the reign of Edward II see, e.g., the General Introduction to *PROME* and *passim*. As argued in ch. 11 of this book, the deposition of Edward II in 1327 was essentially the work of a powerful section of the magnates, whatever attempt there may have been to obtain as broad a range of consent (and complicity) as possible.

which poisoned English politics for generations to come.[23] Edward II was an enigma in his time and in some respects he remains an enigma now,[24] despite the vast quantity of available record and chronicle sources and the efforts of historians over the past century and more. Instead of Cuttino and Lyman's question 'Where is Edward II?',[25] perhaps we should echo Jacques Le Goff's magisterial study of another complex and enigmatic monarch, St Louis, and ask in its place 'Who was Edward II?'[26]

[23] See Phillips, 'Simon de Montfort (1265)', 79–89.

[24] There is no indication that he suffered from any mental illness, other than understandable depression after his deposition, but it is worth considering whether Edward II might, for instance, have been manic-depressive. This could account for his sudden fits of application to work, as noticed in 1320. It is however very dangerous to speculate on the mental state of any medieval monarch without clear and convincing evidence, as Nigel Saul has pointed out in his discussion of the problem of Richard II's mental condition in another Yale English Monarchs volume, *Richard II*, 462–4.

As I have indicated in ch. 1 there has been some speculation as to Edward II's sanity: Robinson, 'Was Edward the Second a degenerate?' This was answered very effectively by Dr Vivian Green in *The Madness of Kings*, 47–53, where he comments that 'While his personality had abnormal traits and to many of his contemporaries seemed unfitting for a king, Edward II was not a madman', and that 'Edward II was surely neither mad nor degenerate but the complexities of his private life found a public expression'. No one is likely to go as far as the French scholar Brachet in his study of the kings of France, *Pathologie mentale des rois de France*, including an examination of the mental state of Edward II's father-in-law, Philip IV: Brachet, 443–54.

[25] Cuttino & Lyman, 'Where is Edward II?', 522–43. As I argued in ch. 11, Edward II is in the tomb in Gloucester Cathedral and has been since 1327.

[26] Jacques Le Goff, *Saint Louis* (Paris, 1996), part 2, 'La production de la mémoire royale: Saint Louis a-t-il existé?'

BIBLIOGRAPHY

MANUSCRIPT SOURCES
ENGLISH ARCHIVES
Berkeley Castle Muniments

Select Roll 39: Berkeley steward's accounts, 1 Jan.–29 Sept. 1327.
Select Roll 41: Steward's account, 1326–7.
Select Roll 42: Account of Ham manor, 1326–7.
Select Roll 60: Household accounts, 2 Edward III.

Bodleian Library

Dodsworth Mss. 8, 94: Volumes of Yorkshire and Northern charters.
Dugdale Mss. 12, 15, 18: Original notebooks of William Dugdale.
Kent Rolls 6: A fourteenth-century roll of documents from Tonbridge priory, Kent.
Ms. Latin Hist. C.5: Daily account roll of royal household, 2 Edward II.
Laud Misc. Ms. 529: Chronicle of English history, 1066–1390.
Lyell Ms. 17: A Ms. of the Brut chronicle.
Tanner Ms. 90: A miscellaneous collection of mainly sixteenth-century material.
Tanner Ms. 197: Record of wardrobe expenses of Edward II at Berwick-upon-Tweed, 1311, compiled by John de Ockham.

British Library
Additional Manuscripts and Charters

Add. Ms. 7966A: Material from Wardrobe Book, 29 Edward I.
Add. Ms. 7967: Accounts of Nicholas Hugate, Keeper of King's Wardrobe, 1 March 1324–31 May 1326.
Add. Ms. 9951: *Liber Cotidianus Garderobae*, 14 Edward II.
Add. Ms. 17362: Wardrobe Book of 13 Edward II.
Add. Ms. 22923: Account of Walter Reynolds, Prince Edward's treasurer, for 35 Edward I.
Add. Ms. 24509, f. 61: Vol. 1 of Joseph Hunter's collections.
Add. Ms. 28024: Beauchamp cartulary.
Add. Ms. 35293: Wardrobe Account Book, 32 Edward I (1303–4).
Add. Ms. 41612: the 'Liber Eliensis'.
Add. Charter 11241 (formerly Archives Nationales, J 655, no. 28): Record of appointment of Ordainers, 1310.

Arundel Manuscripts

Arundel Ms. 17, ff. 40–4: *Memorabilia facta tempore Regis Edwardi secundi in Anglia*. Annals from Newenham abbey, Devon.
Arundel Ms. 57, ff. 4v–5v: the *Verses of Gildas*.

Burney Manuscripts

Burney Ms. 277, f. 5v: Articles presented by the earl of Lincoln in 1308.

Cotton Manuscripts

Cotton Ms. Julius A.I, ff. 51–63: Pipewell chronicle and other documents.
Cotton Ms. Julius E.I, f. 45: A register of Gascon documents.
Cotton Ms. Cleopatra, C.III: Extracts from the Dunmow chronicle.
Cotton Ms. Cleopatra D.iii: Extracts from the Hailes abbey chronicle.
Cotton Ms. Faustina B.V: Historia Roffensis.
Cotton Ms. Faustina B.VI: Croxden abbey chronicle.
Cotton Ms. Claudius E.III: Text of *Chronicon Henrici Knighton*.
Cotton Ms. Nero C.VIII: Wardrobe Book, 4 Edward II.
Cotton Ms. Nero D.X: Chronicle 1287–1323, attributed to Nicholas Trivet.
Cotton Ms. Tiberius E.VII: Text of *Chronicon Henrici Knighton*.
Cotton Ms. Vespasian F.VII, f. 6: letter of Younger Despenser, 1319.
Cotton Charter XVI.58: Notarial certificate of appointment of Ordainers, 1310.

Egerton Manuscripts and Rolls

Egerton Roll 8724: Roll of Mortimer charters.

Harleian Manuscripts

Harleian Ms. 636: *Polistorie del Eglise de Christ de Caunterbyre*.
Harleian Ms. 1240: Mortimer charters.
Harleian Ms. 2901: Coronation Order of 1308.
Harleian Ms. 5001: Wardrobe Accounts of Prince Edward for 35 Edward I, 1306–7.

Stowe Manuscripts

Stowe Ms. 553: Account Book of the Wardrobe, 15–17 Edward II.

Cambridge

Cambridge Univ. Ms. Ee.V.31, f. 188v: Register of Henry of Eastry, prior of Canterbury.
Trinity College Cambridge Ms. R.5.41: A Canterbury chronicle from AD 303 to 1385: A continuation of the chronicle of Gervase of Canterbury.

Foljambe Charters, Osberton Hall, Worksop

Appendix 4.

Gloucester Cathedral Library

Ms. 34: Walter of Frocester, *Historia Monasterii Gloucestriae*.
Ms. 55: Account Book of Marshall Allen, Sub-sacrist, 1835–58.

Lambeth Palace Library

Lambeth Ms. 1213: Collection of documents on the major political events of the reign of Edward II.
Register of Walter Reynolds, archbishop of Canterbury (1313–27).

The National Archives (TNA)

Chancery

C 47: Chancery Miscellanea.
C 49: Parliamentary and Council Proceedings.
C 53: Charter Rolls.
C 54: Close Rolls.
C 57: Coronation Roll.
C 60: Fine Rolls.
C 61: Gascon Rolls.
C 65: Parliament Rolls.
C 66: Patent Rolls.
C 70: Roman Rolls.
C 71: Scottish Rolls.
C 81: Chancery Warrants.
C 135: Inquisitions *post mortem* (Edward III).
C 145: Miscellaneous Inquisitions.
C 153/1: Vetus Codex.
C 219: Parliamentary Election Writs and Returns.

Duchy of Lancaster

DL 10: Royal Charters.
DL 25: Deeds, Series L.
DL 27: Ancient Deeds, Series LS
DL 28: Various Accounts.
DL 34: Ancient Correspondence.
DL 41: Miscellanea.
DL 42: Miscellaneous Books.

Exchequer

E 30: Diplomatic Documents.
E 101: Accounts Various.
E 106: Extents of Alien Priories.
E 159: Memoranda Rolls (KR).
E 163: Exchequer Miscellanea.
E 175: Parliamentary and Council Proceedings.
E 329: Ancient Deeds, Series BS.
E 352: Pipe Office, Chancellor's Rolls.
E 361: Enrolled Wardrobe and Household Accounts.
E 368: Memoranda Rolls (LTR).
E 372: Pipe Rolls.
E 401: Receipt Rolls.
E 403: Issue Rolls.
E 404: Wardrobe Debentures and Warrants for Issues.

Justices Itinerant

JI 1: Assize Rolls.

King's Bench

KB 27: Coram Rege Rolls.

Special Collections

SC 1: Ancient Correspondence.
SC 7: Papal Bulls.
SC 8: Ancient Petitions.
SC 9: Parliament Rolls (Exchequer series).

TNA Transcripts from other Archives

PRO 31/8/158: Copy of Biblioteca Apostolica Vaticana, Barberini Ms. 2366: a seventeenth-century transcript of a report on the mission of cardinals Luke and Gaucelm to England and Scotland in 1317–18.
PRO 31/9/59: Transcript of Instrumenta Miscellanea, 5947: report on the mission of papal envoys in England, 1312–13.

Norfolk and Norwich Record Office

Institutions Register of John Salmon, bishop of Norwich.

Society of Antiquaries of London

Ms. 119: Wardrobe Book, 28 Edward I (1299–1300).
Ms. 120: Wardrobe Book, 10 Edward II (1316–17).
Ms. 121: Wardrobe Book, 11 Edward II (1317–18).
Ms. 122: Chamber Account Book, 18–20 Edward II (1324–26).

Westminster Abbey Munimenta

WAM 20344: Account roll of Brother Robert de Beby, Michaelmas, 1 Edward III, until Michaelmas, 2 Edward III, for the revenues of the church of Oakham in Rutland.
Liber Niger.

French Archives

Archives départementales de l'Hérault, Montpellier

Series G 1123–1129: Cartulaire de Maguelone, Registers A to G.

Archives Nationales, Paris

J 356: (1309) Documents concerning the subsidy for the marriage of Isabella and Edward II.
J 404: Royal Wills.
J 408: Marriage Treaties.
J 633: Documents on Anglo-French Relations, 1299–1317.
J 634: Documents on Anglo-French Relations, 1322–30.
J 654: Various rolls, thirteenth to fourteenth centuries.
J 918: Documents on Anglo-French relations, thirteenth to fifteenth centuries.
JJ 44: Documents relating to the marriage of Edward II and Isabella.

Bibliothèque Nationale, Paris

Latin Ms. 8504: Latin translation of *Kalila et Dimna*, 1313.

BIBLIOGRAPHY

ARCHIVES IN ROME
Archivio Segreto Vaticano

Archivum Arcis, Arm. C, fasc.79: 'Pater Sancte' letter of Edward III.
Avignon Register 49 (ii, Benedict XII (1335–6)).
Indice 320: Summary of register of Boniface IX (1389).
Instrumenta Miscellanea, 5947: Report of mission of papal envoys in England, 1312–13.
Vatican Register 110 (Secreta, i to iv, John XXII).
Vatican Register 116 (xv–xvi, John XXII (1330–2)).

Biblioteca Apostolica Vaticana

Barberini Ms. 2366: A seventeenth-century transcript of a report on the mission of Cardinals Luke Fieschi and Gaucelm D'Eauze to England and Scotland in 1317–18.
Barberini Latini, Ms. 2126: Notebook of Andreas Sapiti.
Codex Vaticanus Latinus 10883: Record of business at papal curia.

OTHER DEPOSITORIES

Trinity College Dublin TCD Ms. 500: A version of the French Brut to 1333.
University of Chicago Ms. 224: Chronicle of Wigmore abbey.

PRINTED SOURCES
Calendars and Transcripts

Abbrevatio Placitorum, Record Commission (London, 1811).
Additiones agli 'Instrumenta Miscellanea' dell'Archivio Segreto Vaticano (7945–8802), ed. S. Pagano, Collectanea Archivi Vaticani, 57 (Vatican City, 2005).
Ancient Libraries of Canterbury and Dover, ed. M.R. James (Cambridge, 1903).
Anecdota ex Codicibus Hagiographicis Iohannis Gielemans, Subsidia Hagiographica, iii, Société des Bollandistes (Brussels, 1895).
Anglo-Norman Political Songs, Anglo-Norman Texts, xi, ed. I.S.T. Aspin (Oxford, 1953).
Anglo-Scottish Relations, 1174–1328, ed. E.L.G. Stones (Oxford, 1970).
The Antient Kalendars and Inventories of His Majesty's Exchequer, ed. F. Palgrave, 3 vols (London, 1836).
Calendar of Ancient Correspondence concerning Wales, ed. J.G. Edwards, Board of Celtic Studies, History and Law Series, 2 (Cardiff, 1935).
Calendar of Ancient Petitions relating to Wales (Cardiff, 1975), ed. W. Rees, Board of Celtic Studies, History and Law Series, 28 (Cardiff, 1975).
Calendar of Chancery Warrants, 1244–1326 (London, 1927).
Calendar of Charter Rolls (1903—)
Calendar of Close Rolls (1892—)
Calendar of Documents relating to Ireland, iv, *1292–1301*, ed. H.S. Sweetman (London & Dublin, 1881).
Calendar of Documents relating to Scotland, ii, iii, iv, ed. J. Bain (Edinburgh, 1884–87); v, ed. G.G. Simpson & J.D. Galbraith (Edinburgh, 1986).
Calendar of Fine Rolls (1911—)
Calendar of the Letter-Books of the City of London, ed. R.R. Sharpe (London, 1900–3).
Calendar of Memoranda Rolls (Exchequer), Michaelmas 1326–Michaelmas 1327, ed. R.A. Latham (London, 1968).
Calendar of Inquisitions, Miscellaneous (1916—)
Calendar of Inquisitions Post Mortem (1898—)
Calendar of Papal Letters, 1305–42, ed. W.H. Bliss (London, 1895).
Calendar of Patent Rolls (1891—)

BIBLIOGRAPHY

Calendar of the Plea and Memoranda Rolls of the City of London, 1324–1457, ed. A.H. Thomas, i (London, 1926).
Calendar of Treaty Rolls preserved in the Public Record Office, i, *1234–1325*, ed. P. Chaplais (London, 1955).
Cartae et Alia Munimenta de Glamorgan, iii, *c. 1271–1331*, ed. G.L. Clark (Cardiff, 1910).
Chartulary of Winchester Cathedral, ed. A.W. Goodman (Winchester, 1927).
The Chaworth Roll: A Fourteenth-century Genealogy of the Kings of England, ed. A. Bovey (London, 2005).
Cheshire in the Pipe Rolls, 1158–1301, ed. R. Stewart Brown, Lancashire & Cheshire Record Society, xcii (Manchester, 1938).
Concilia Magnae Britanniae et Hiberniae, ii, ed. D. Wilkins (London, 1737).
Coronation Records, ed. L.G. Wickham Legg (London, 1901).
Councils and Synods, ed. F.M. Powicke & C.R. Cheney, ii, part 2 (Oxford, 1964).
'Deeds enrolled on the de Banco Rolls', ed. E.A. Fry (National Archives typescript, 1927).
The Diplomatic Correspondence of Richard II, ed. E. Perroy, Camden, 3rd. series, xlviii (London, 1933).
Documents and Records illustrating the History of Scotland, ed. F. Palgrave, i (London, 1837).
Documents Illustrating the Crisis of 1297–98 in England, ed. M. Prestwich, Camden, 4th series, xxiv (London, 1980).
Documents Illustrative of English History in the Thirteenth and Fourteenth Centuries, ed. H. Cole (London, 1844).
'Documents on the early stages of the Bruce invasion of Ireland, 1315–1316', ed. J.R.S. Phillips, *Proceedings of the Royal Irish Academy, section C*, lxxix (1979), 247–70.
Edward I and the Throne of Scotland, 1290–1296: An Edition of the Record Sources for the Great Cause, ed. E.L.G. Stones & G.G. Simpson, 2 vols (Oxford, 1978).
Edward II, the Lords Ordainers and Piers Gaveston's Jewels and Horses, ed. R.A. Roberts. Camden 3rd series, xli (London, 1929).
English Historical Documents, 1189–1327, ed. H. Rothwell (London, 1975).
English Royal Documents: King John – Henry VI, 1199–1461, ed. P. Chaplais (Oxford, 1971).
Extracts from the Account Rolls of the Abbey of Durham, ii, ed. J.T. Fowler, Surtees Society Publications, c (Durham 1899, for the year 1898).
Fasti Ecclesiae Anglicanae, 1300–1541, vi, *Northern Province*, ed. B. Jones (London, 1963).
Five Dreams about Edward II, ed. F.J. Furnivall, Early English Text Society, old series, lxix (1878).
Fleta, ed. H.G. Richardson & G.O. Sayles, Selden Society, lxii (1953; London, 1955).
Foedera, Conventiones, Litterae et Acta Publica, ed. T. Rymer, Record Commission edition, vols I, II (London, 1816–20).
The Gascon Calendar of 1322, ed. G.P. Cuttino, Camden, 3rd series, lxx (London, 1949).
Gascon Register A (Series of 1318–19), ed. G.P. Cuttino, with the collaboration of J.T. Trabut-Cussac, 3 vols (Oxford, 1975).
Gascon Rolls, 1307–1317, ed. Y. Renouard (London, 1962).
The Grey Friars of London: their History with the Register of their Convent and an Appendix of Documents, ed. C.L. Kingsford, British Society of Franciscan Studies, vi (Aberdeen, 1915; repr. 1965).
Historical Manuscripts Commission, First Report, Documents of the Dean and Chapter of Norwich (London, 1870).
Historical Manuscripts Commission, Tenth Report (London, 1885).
Historical Manuscripts Commission, Various Collections, i (London, 1901).
Historical Poems of the XIVth and XVth Centuries, ed. R.H. Robbins (New York, 1959).
The Household Book of Queen Isabella of England for the Fifth Regnal Year of Edward II, ed. F.D. Blackley & G. Hermansen (Edmonton, Alberta, 1971).
The Index Library: Abstracts of Inquisitiones Post Mortem for Gloucestershire, part v, *1302–1358*, ed. E.A. Fry, The British Record Society, xl (London, 1910).
Inventaire analytique du chartrier de la Trésorerie des comtes de Hainaut, ed. G. Wymans, Archives générales du Royaume (Brussels, 1985).
Issues of the Exchequer, ed. F. Devon (London, 1837).

The Itinerary of Edward II and his Household, 1307–1327, ed. E.M. Hallam, List and Index Society, ccxi (London, 1984).
John of Gaddesden and the Rosa Medicinae, ed. H.P. Cholmeley (Oxford, 1912).
Letters of Edward Prince of Wales, 1304–1305, ed. H. Johnstone, Roxburghe Club (Cambridge, 1931).
Letters from Northern Registers, ed. J. Raine, Rolls Series (London, 1883).
Liber Albus of Worcester Priory, ed. J.M. Wilson, Worcestershire Historical Society (London, 1919).
Liber de Antiquis Legibus, ed. T. Stapleton, Camden Society, xxxiv (London, 1846).
Liber Epistolaris of Richard of Bury, ed. N. Denholm-Young, Roxburghe Club (Oxford, 1950).
Liber Quotidianus Garderobae, 28 Edward I, ed. J. Topham (Society of Antiquaries, London, 1787).
Libro delle investiture del vescovo di Vercelli Giovanni Fieschi (1349–50), ed. D. Arnaldi, Biblioteca della Società Storica Subaplina, vol. LXXIII, ii (Turin, 1934).
List of Welsh Entries in the Memoranda Rolls, 1282–1343, ed. N. Fryde (Cardiff, 1974).
Literae Cantuarienses, i–iii, ed. J.B. Sheppard, Rolls Series (London, 1887–9).
Materials for the History of the Franciscan Province of Ireland AD 1230–1450, ed. E.B. Fitzmaurice & A.G. Little (Manchester, 1920).
The Miracles of King Henry VI, ed. R. Knox & S. Leslie (Cambridge, 1923).
Munimenta Gildhallae Londoniensis, ed. H.T. Riley, II parts i & ii, containing *Liber Custumarum*, Rolls Series (London, 1860).
Parliament Rolls of Medieval England (PROME), 1275–1504, vol. 3 (1307–27), ed. J.R.S. Phillips; vol. 4 (1327–48), ed. J.R.S. Phillips & W.M. Ormrod: general editor C. Given-Wilson, digital edition (CD-ROM and online), Scholarly Digital Editions & The National Archives (Leicester, 2005). Printed edition in 16 vols (Woodbridge, Suffolk & Rochester, NY, 2005).
Parliamentary Texts of the Later Middle Ages, ed. N. Pronay & J. Taylor (Oxford, 1980).
Parliamentary Writs and Writs of Military Summons, Edward I and Edward II, ed. F. Palgrave, Record Commission (London, 1827–34).
The Political Songs of England from the Reign of John to that of Edward II, ed. T. Wright, Camden Society (London, 1839), republished by the Royal Historical Society with an introduction by Peter Coss (Cambridge, 1996).
Political Thought in Early Fourteenth-century England: Treatises by Walter of Milemete, William of Pagula, and William of Ockham, ed. C.J. Nederman (Tempe, Arizona, 2002).
Proceedings of His Majesty's Commissioners on the Public Records, i, ed. C.P. Cooper (London, 1833).
The Record of Carnarvon, ed. H. Ellis, Record Commission (London, 1838).
Records of the Trial of Walter Langton, Bishop of Coventry and Lichfield, 1307–1312, ed. A. Beardwood, Camden, 4th series, vi (London, 1969).
Records of the Wardrobe and Household, 1285–1286, ed. B.F. & C.R. Byerly (London, 1977).
Regesta Regum Scottorum, v, *The Acts of Robert I*, ed. A.A.M. Duncan (Edinburgh, 1988).
The Register of John de Grandison, Bishop of Exeter, ed. F.C. Hingeston-Randolph, iii (London, 1899).
Register of Thomas de Cobham, Bishop of Worcester, 1317–27, ed. E.H. Pearce, Worcestershire Historical Society (Worcester, 1930).
Register of Walter Stapeldon, Bishop of Exeter, 1307–1326, ed. F.C. Hingeston-Randolph (London, 1892).
Register of William Greenfield, Archbishop of York, 1306–1315, ed. W. Brown & A. Hamilton Thompson, Surtees Society, cxlv (Durham, 1931).
Registers of John de Sandale and Rigaud de Asserio, Bishops of Winchester, 1316–23, ed. F.J. Baigent, Hampshire Record Society (Winchester, 1897).
Registres du Trésor des chartes, 2 vols, ed. R. Fawtier (Paris, 1958, 1960).
Registrum Ade de Orleton, Bishop of Hereford, ed. A.T. Bannister, Canterbury & York Series, v (London, 1908).
Registrum Palatinum Dunelmense, ed. T. Duffus Hardy, ii, Rolls Series (London, 1873).
Registrum Radulphi Baldock, etc., Bishops of London, ed. R.C. Fowler, Canterbury & York Series, vii (London, 1911).
Registrum Ricardi de Swinfield, Bishop of Hereford, ed. W.W. Capes, Canterbury & York Series, vi (London, 1909).

Registrum Simonis de Gandavo, Bishop of Salisbury, ed. C.T. Flower & M.C.B. Dawes, Canterbury and York Series, xl (London, 1934).
Répertoire numérique des archives départementales antérieures à 1790, Hérault, archives ecclésiastiques, series G, clergé séculier, ed. M. Gouron (Montpellier, 1970).
Reports from the Lords' Committees touching the Dignity of a Peer of the Realm, iii (London, 1829).
Roll of Arms of the Princes, Barons and Knights who attended Edward I at the Siege of Caerlaverock, ed. T. Wright (London, 1864).
Rotuli Parliamentorum, i, ii, ed. J. Strachey, et al. (London, 1767).
Rotuli Parliamentorum Hactenus Inediti, ed. H.G. Richardson & G.O. Sayles, Camden, 3rd series, li (London, 1935).
Rotuli Scotiae, Record Commission, 2 vols (London, 1814–19).
The Royal Charter Witness Lists of Edward II (1307–1326) from the Charter Rolls in the Public Record Office [TNA], ed. J.S. Hamilton, List & Index Society, 288 (Kew, 2001).
Select Cases in the Court of King's Bench under Edward II, ed. G.O. Sayles, IV, V, Selden Society, lxxiv, lxxvi (London, 1957, 1958).
Select Documents of English Constitutional History, 1307–1485, ed. S.B. Chrimes & A.L. Brown (London, 1961).
Statutes of the Realm, i, Record Commission (London, 1810).
Titres de la maison ducale de Bourbon, ed. Huillard Bréholles (Paris, 1867–82).
The Treatise of Walter de Milemete, De Nobilitatibus, Sapientiis, et Prudentiis Regum, ed. M.R. James, Roxburghe Club (Oxford, 1913).
Tudor Royal Proclamations, i, *The Early Tudors, 1485–1553*, ed. P.L. Hughes & J.F. Larkin (New Haven & London, 1964).
Vetera monumenta Hibernorum et Scotorum historiam illustrantia, ed. A. Theiner (Rome, 1864).
The War of Saint-Sardos (1323–25): Gascon Correspondence and Diplomatic Documents, ed. P. Chaplais, Camden, 3rd series, lxxxvii (London, 1954).
The Wardrobe Book of William de Norwell, 12 July 1338 to 27 May 1340, ed. M. Lyon, B. Lyon, H.S. Lucas & J. de Sturler, Commission Royale d'Histoire (Brussels, 1983).
William Twiti: The Art of Hunting, ed. B. Daniellsson, Stockholm Studies in English, xxxvii, Cynegetica Anglica, i (Stockholm, 1977).

Narrative Sources

Adæ Murimuth Continuatio Chronicarum, ed. E.M. Thompson (London, 1889).
Anglia Sacra, 2 vols, ed. H. Wharton (London, 1691).
Annales Ecclesiastici ab Anno MCXCVIII ubi Cardinalis Baronius Desinit Auctore Odorico Raynaldo Tarvisino Congregationis Oratorii Presbytero, ed. Odoricus Rinaldi (1595–1671), Tomus XV (Rome, 1652).
Annales Londonienses, in *Chronicles of the Reigns of Edward I and Edward II*, i, ed. W. Stubbs (London, 1882).
Annales Minorum, vi, by Luke Wadding (Rome, 1733).
Annales Monasterii de Waverleia, Annales Monastici, ii, ed. H.R. Luard, Rolls Series (London, 1865).
Annales Paulini, in *Chronicles of the Reigns of Edward I and Edward II*, i, ed. W. Stubbs (London, 1882).
Annales Prioratus de Dunstaplia, Annales Monastici, iii, ed. H.R. Luard, Rolls Series (London, 1869).
Annales Regis Edwardi Primi, Fragmentum I, in *Chronica Monasterii S. Albani*, ed. H.T. Riley, Rolls Series (London, 1865).
Annals of Osney, Annales Monastici, iv, ed. H.R. Luard, Rolls Series (London, 1869).
Anonimalle Chronicle 1307 to 1334, ed. W.R. Childs & J. Taylor, Yorkshire Archaeological Society, Record Series, cxlvii, for the year 1987 (Leeds, 1991).
Autobiography of Emperor Charles IV and his Legend of St Wenceslas, ed. B. Nagy & F. Schaer (Budapest, 2001).
The Bruce, ed. W. W. Skeat, 2 vols, Scottish Text Society, 31–3 (1894).
The Bruce, ed. A.A.M. Duncan (Edinburgh, 1997).

The Brut, ed. F.W.D. Brie, Early English Text Society, cxxxi, part i (London, 1906).
Chronica Albrici Monachi Trium Fontium, MGH, SS.23, ed. G.H. Pertz (Hanover, 1874; repr. 1963).
Chronica Monasterii de Melsa, ed. E.A. Bond, ii, Rolls Series (London, 1867).
Chronicle of Pierre de Langtoft, ed. T. Wright, Rolls Series (London, 1886).
Chronicle of Walter of Guisborough, ed. H. Rothwell, Camden, 3rd series, lxxix (London, 1989).
Chronicles of the Reigns of Edward I and Edward II, ed. W. Stubbs; 2 vols, Rolls Series (London, 1882–3).
Chronicon Galfridi le Baker de Swynebroke, ed. E.M. Thompson (Oxford, 1889).
Chronicon Henrici Knighton, ed, J.R. Lumby, i, Rolls Series (London, 1889).
Chronicon de Lanercost, ed. J. Stevenson, Maitland Club (Edinburgh, 1839).
Chronique métrique de Godefroy de Paris, ed. J.-A. Buchon, Collections des Chroniques Nationales Françaises, ix (Paris, 1827).
Chroniques de Sempringham: Livere des Reis de Britannie, ed. J. Glover, Rolls Series (London, 1865).
Chronographia Regum Francorum, ed. H. Moranville, i (Paris, 1891).
Commendatio Lamentabilis, in Transitu Magni Regis Edwardi, in *Chronicles of the Reigns of Edward I and Edward II*, ed. W. Stubbs, ii, Rolls Series (London, 1883).
Cotton, Bartholomew, *Histaria Anglicana*, ed. H.R. Luard, Rolls Series (London, 1859).
Flores Historiarum, iii, ed. H.R. Luard, Rolls Series (London, 1890).
French Chronicle of London, ed. G.J. Aungier, Camden Society, xxviii (London, 1844).
Froissart, Jean, *Oeuvres de Froissart*, ed. K. de Lettenhove, ii (Brussels, 1867).
 Chroniques de Jean Froissart, ed. S. Luce, i, Société de l'Histoire de France (Paris, 1869).
Gesta Edwardi de Carnarvon Auctore Canonico Bridlingtoniensi, in *Chronicles of the Reigns of Edward I and Edward II*, ii, ed. W. Stubbs, Rolls Series (London, 1883).
Grandes Chroniques de France, ed. J. Viard, viii (Paris, 1934).
Gray, Sir Thomas, *Scalacronica, 1272–1363*, ed. and trans. A. King, Surtees Society, ccix (Woodbridge, Suffolk & Rochester, NY, 2005).
Historia Coenobii Burgensis auctore Waltero de Whitlesey, Historiae Coenobii Burgensis Scriptores, ed. J. Sparks (London, 1723).
Historiae Anglicanae Scriptores Decem, ed. R. Twysden (London, 1652).
Historiae et Cartularium Monasterii Sancti Petri Gloucestriae, i, ed. W.H. Hart, Rolls Series (London, 1863).
Historiae Dunelmensis Scriptores Tres, ed. J. Raine, Surtees Society, ix (Edinburgh, 1839).
Holinshed, R., *The Chronicles of England, Scotland and Ireland*, 2 vols (London, 1577).
Johannis de Trokelowe et Henrici de Blaneforde, Chronica et Annales, ed. H.T. Riley, Rolls Series (London, 1866).
Knighton's Chronicle, 1337–1396, ed. G.H. Martin, Oxford Medieval Texts (Oxford, 1995).
Le Bel, Jean, *Chronique de Jean le Bel*, ed. J. Viard & E. Deprez, i, Société de l'Histoire de France (Paris, 1904).
Le Livere des Reis de Brittanie, ed. J. Glover, Rolls Series (London, 1862).
Myreur des Histors by Jean d'Outremeuse, ed. S. Bormans, 7 vols (Brussels, 1964–8).
Nicolai Triveti Annalium Continuatio, ed. A. Hall (Oxford, 1722).
Paris, Matthew, *Historia Anglorum*, ed. F. Madden, Rolls Series, ii (London, 1866).
Paris, Matthew, *Chronica Majora*, ed. H.R. Luard, Rolls Series, iii (London, 1876).
Polychronicon Ranulphi Higden, ed. J.R. Lumby, viii, Rolls Series (London, 1882).
The Recovery of the Holy Land, by Pierre Dubois, ed. W.I. Brandt (New York, 1956).
Recueil des Historiens des Gaules et de la France, xxiii, ed. H. Welter (Paris, 1894).
Robertus de Avesbury De Gestis mirabilibus Regis Edwardi Tertii, ed. E.M. Thompson, Rolls Series (London, 1889).
Scalacronica of Thomas Gray of Heton, ed. J. Stevenson, Maitland Club (Edinburgh, 1836).
Scotichronicon by Walter Bower, ed. D.E.R. Watt, vi, viii (Aberdeen, 1991, 1987).
Trevet, Nicholas, *Annales Sex Regum Angliae*, ed. Th. Hog, English Historical Society Publications, ix (London, 1845).
Vita Edwardi Secundi, ed. N. Denholm-Young (London, 1957).
Vita Edwardi Secundi, ed. W.R. Childs (Oxford, 2005).

Vita et Mors Edwardi Secundi, in *Chronicles of the Reigns of Edward I and Edward II*, ii, ed. W. Stubbs, Rolls Series (London, 1883).
Vitae Paparum Avenionensium, ed. E. Baluze, new edition, ed. G. Mollat, ii, iii (Paris, 1921, 1927).
Walsingham, Thomas, *Historia Anglicana*, ed. H.T. Riley, Rolls Series, i (London, 1863).
The Westminster Chronicle, 1381–1394, ed. L.C. Hector & B.F. Harvey (Oxford, 1982).
Willelmi Capellani in Brederode postea Monachi et Procuratoris Egmondensis Chronicon, ed. C. Pijnacker Hordijk, Werken uitgegeven door het Historisch Genootschap, 3rd series, xx (Amsterdam, 1904).
William of Rishanger, *Chronica et Annales*, ed. H.T. Riley, Rolls Series London, 1865).

Secondary Sources

Ackerlind, S.R., *King Dinis of Portugal and the Alfonsine Heritage*, American University Studies, series ix, History, lxix (New York, 1990).
Alexander J. & Binski, P., eds, *Age of Chivalry: Art in Plantagenet England, 1200–1400*, Catalogue (London, 1987).
Altschul, M., *A Baronial Family in Medieval England: the Clares, 1217–1314* (Baltimore, 1965).
Anon., *Histoire Remarquable de la Vie et Mort d'un Favory du Roy d'Angleterre* (Paris, 1649).
Anon., *The People Informed of their Oppressors and Oppressions with a Remedy Against Both* (London, 1648).
Anon., *The Prime Minister and King, with Political Remarks, by Way of Caution to all Crowned Heads and Evil Ministers* (London, 1720).
Aubert, R., ed., *Dictionnaire d'histoire et de géographie ecclésiastiques*, xx (Paris, 1984).
Ayloffe, J., 'An account of the body of King Edward the First, as it appeared on opening his tomb in the year 1774', *Archaeologia*, iii (1786), 376–413.
Ayton, A., *Knights and Warhorses: Military Service and the English Aristocracy under Edward III* (Woodbridge, Suffolk & Rochester, NY, 1994).
Badham, S., 'Edward the Confessor's chapel, Westminster Abbey: the origins of the royal mausoleum and its Cosmatesque pavement', *Antiquaries Journal*, lxxxvii (2007), 197–208.
Balbi, G.P., *I 'Conti' e la 'Contea' di Lavagna* (Genoa, 1984).
Banks, R.W., 'The marriage contract of King Edward II', *Archaeologia Cambrensis*, 5th series, iv (1887), 53–7
—— 'King Edward II in South Wales', *Archaeologia Cambrensis*, 5th series, iv (1887), 161–82.
Barber, M., 'The world picture of Philip the Fair', *Journal of Medieval History*, viii, no. 1 (*Amsterdam, March 1982*), 13–27.
—— *The Trial of the Templars* (2nd edition, Cambridge, 2006).
Barber, R., *The Knight and Chivalry* (Woodbridge, Suffolk & Rochester, NY, revised edition, 1995).
Barlow, F., *Edward the Confessor* (London, 1970).
Barnes, J., *The History of that Most Victorious Monarch Edward III, King of England and France, and Lord of Ireland, and First Founder of the most Noble Order of the Garter etc.*, etc. (Cambridge, 1688).
Barraclough, G., *The Medieval Papacy* (London, 1968)
Barron, Caroline M., 'The tyranny of Richard II', *BIHR*, xli (1968), 1–18.
Barrow, G.W.S., *Kingship and Unity: Scotland, 1000–1306* (London, 1981).
—— *Robert Bruce and the Community of the Realm of Scotland* (2nd edition, Edinburgh, 1976; and 3rd edition, Edinburgh, 1988).
—— 'A kingdom in crisis: Scotland and the Maid of Norway', *SHR*, lxix (October 1990), 121–41.
Baudon de Mony, C., 'La Mort et les funérailles de Philippe le Bel', *Bibliothèque de l'École des Chartes*, lviii (1897), 5–14.
Beardwood, A., 'The trial of Walter Langton, bishop of Lichfield, 1307–1312', *Trans. of the American Philosophical Soc.*, new series, liv, part 3 (Philadelphia, 1964), 1–45.
Bellamy, J.G., 'The Coterel gang: an anatomy of fourteenth-century criminals', *EHR*, lxxix (1964), 698–717.

Benedetti, A., 'Una canzone francese di Edoardo II d'Inghilterra', *Nuova studi medievali*, i, part 2 (1923), 283-94.
—— *Edoardo II d'Inghilterra all'Abbazia di S. Alberto di Butrio* (Palermo, 1924).
Bériac-Lainé, F., 'Une Armée anglo-gasconne vingt ans avant la guerre de Cent Ans', in *Guerre, pouvoir et noblesse au Moyen Âge*, ed. J. Paviot & J. Verger (Paris, 2000), 83-92.
Bernabo, B., 'I Fieschi e la Val di Vara', in *I Fieschi tra medioeve ed età moderna*, ed. D. Calagno (Genoa, 1999), 1-28.
Bernini, F., *La Badia di S. Alberto di Butrio tra storia, art e fede* (Edizioni Eremo di S. Alberto, Pontenizza, 1993).
Best, J.T., 'Where did Edward the Second die?', *Macmillan's Magazine*, 41 (March 1880), 393-4.
—— 'Where did Edward II die?', with a reply by J.H. Cooke, *Notes & Queries*, lxii (13 and 20 November, 18 December 1880), 381-3, 401-3, 489-90.
Biddle, M., ed., *King Arthur's Round Table* (Woodbridge, Suffolk 2000).
Bingham, C., *The Life and Times of Edward II* (London, 1973).
Binski, P., *The Painted Chamber at Westminster*, The Society of Antiquaries of London, Occasional Papers, new series, ix (London, 1986).
—— *Westminster Abbey and the Plantagenets: Kingship and the Representation of Power, 1200-1400* (New Haven & London, 1995).
Binski, P. & Park, D., 'A Ducciesque episode at Ely: the mural decoration of Prior Crauden's chapel', in *England in the Fourteenth Century*, ed. W.M. Ormrod (Woodbridge, Suffolk 1986), 28-41.
Blackley, F.D., 'Adam, the bastard son of Edward II', *BIHR*, xxxvii (London, 1964), 76-7.
—— 'Isabella and the bishop of Exeter', in *Essays in Medieval History presented to Bertie Wilkinson*, ed. T.A. Sandquist & M.R. Powicke (Toronto, 1969), 220-35.
—— 'Isabella of France, Queen of England, 1308-1358, and the late medieval cult of the dead', *Canadian Journal of History*, xv (1980), 23-47.
—— 'The tomb of Isabella, wife of Edward II of England', *Bulletin of the International Soc. for the Study of Church Monuments*, viii (1983), 161-4.
Bloch, M., *The Royal Touch: Sacred Monarchy and Scrofula in France and England* (London, 1973) (first published as *Les Rois thaumaturges*, Paris, 1961).
Bloom, J.H., 'Simon de Swanland and King Edward II', *Notes & Queries*, 11th series, iv (1911), 1-2.
Boehm, J.L., 'The maintenance of ducal authority in Gascony: the career of Sir Guy Ferre the Younger, 1298-1320', in *Essays in History*, xxxiv (University of Virginia, Charlotteville, 1992, on line version).
Borenius, C.T., *St Thomas Becket in Art* (London, 1932).
Boswell, J., *Christianity, Social Tolerance, and Homosexuality* (Chicago, 1980).
Bothwell, J.S., 'Agnes Maltravers (d. 1375) and her husband John (d. 1364): rebel wives, separate lives and conjugal visits in later medieval England', in *Fourteenth Century England*, iv, ed. J.S. Hamilton (Woodbridge, Suffolk & Rochester, NY, 2006), 80-92.
Boucher, J., *Histoire tragique et memorable de Pierre de Gaverston, gentilhomme Gascon jadis le mignon d'Édouard 2 Roy d'Angleterre* (Paris, 1588).
Boyle, L.E., OP, *A Survey of the Vatican Archives and of its Medieval Holdings*, Pontifical Institute of Mediaeval Studies, Toronto, *Subsidia Mediaevalia*, 1 (Toronto, 1972).
Brachet, A., *Pathologie mentale des rois de France* (Paris, 1903).
Bray, J.E., 'Concepts of sainthood in fourteenth-century England', *Bulletin of John Rylands Library*, lxvi (1983-84), 40-77.
Breeze, A., 'A manuscript of Welsh poetry in Edward II's library', *National Library of Wales Journal*, xxx, part 2 (Winter 1997), 129-31.
Breslow, B., 'Henry le Waleys: London merchant and royal servant', *The Historian*, Phi Alpha Theta (2009), 431-49.
Brown, A.L., 'The Latin letters in All Souls Ms. 182', *EHR*, lxxxvii (1972), 565-73.
Brown, E.A.R., 'Gascon subsidies and the finances of the English dominions, 1315-1324', *Studies in Medieval and Renaissance History*, viii (Lincoln, NB, 1971), 33-163.

—— 'The prince is father of the king: the character and childhood of Philip the Fair of France', *Mediaeval Studies*, xlix (Toronto, 1987), 282–334.
—— 'The case of Philip the Fair', in *Persona et Gesta: the Image and Deeds of the Thirteenth-century Capetians*, *Viator*, xix (Berkeley & Los Angeles, 1988), 219–46.
—— 'The political repercussions of family ties in the early fourteenth century: the marriage of Edward II of England and Isabelle of France', *Speculum*, lxiii (Cambridge, Mass., 1988), 573–95.
—— 'The marriage of Edward II of England and Isabelle of France: a postscript', *Speculum*, lxiv (1989), 373–9.
—— 'Diplomacy, adultery, and domestic politics at the court of Philip the Fair: Queen Isabelle's mission to France in 1314,' in *Documenting the Past: Essays in Medieval History presented to George Peddy Cuttino*, ed. J.S. Hamilton & P.J. Bradley (Woodbridge, Suffolk & Wolfeboro, NH, 1989), 53–83.
—— *Customary Aids and Royal Finance in Capetian France: The Marriage Aid of Philip the Fair* (Cambridge, Mass., 1992).
—— 'Introduction' and 'Ritual brotherhood in western medieval Europe', in *Ritual Brotherhood in Ancient and Medieval Europe: A Symposium*, *Traditio*, lii (New York, 1997), 261–83, 357–81.
Brown, E.A.R & N.F. Regalado, 'La Grant feste: Philip the Fair's celebration of the knighting of his sons in Paris at Pentecost of 1313', in *City and Spectacle in Medieval Europe*, ed. B.A. Hanawalt & K.L. Reyerson (Minneapolis, 1994), 56–86.
Brown, R.A., Colvin, H.M. & Taylor, A.J., *The History of the King's Works*, i, ii, *The Middle Ages* (London, 1963).
Brückmann, J., 'The *Ordines* of the Third Recension of the medieval English Coronation Order', in *Essays in Medieval History presented to Bertie Wilkinson*, ed. T.A. Sandquist & M.R. Powicke (Toronto, 1969), 99–115.
Brundage, J.A., 'The politics of sodomy: Rex v. Pons Hugh de Ampurias (1311)', in *In Iure Veritas: Studies in Canon Law in Memory of Schafer Williams*, ed. S.B. Bowman & B.E. Cody (Cincinnati, 1991), 3–10.
Bryant, R.M., Bryant, G.N.H. & Heighway, C.M., *The Tomb of Edward II: a Royal Monument in Gloucester Cathedral* (Stonehouse, Glos., 2007).
Buck, M., *Politics, Finance and the Church in the Reign of Edward II: Walter Stapeldon Treasurer of England*, Cambridge Studies in Medieval Life and Thought, 3rd series, xix (Cambridge, 1983).
—— 'The reform of the exchequer, 1316–1326', *EHR*, lxcix (1983), 241–60.
Bullock-Davies, C., *'Menestrallorum Multitudo': Minstrels at a Royal Feast* (Cardiff, 1978).
—— *A Register of Royal and Baronial Minstrels, 1272–1327* (Woodbridge, Suffolk & Dover, New Hampshire, 1986).
Bullough, V.L., *Sexual Variance in Society and History* (New York & London, 1976).
—— 'The sin against nature and homosexuality', in *Sexual Practices and the Medieval Church*, ed. V.L. Bullough & J. Brundage (Buffalo, NY, 1982), 55–71, 239–44.
Bullough, V.L. & Brundage, J.A., eds, *Handbook of Medieval Sexuality* (New York & London, 1996).
Burden, J., 'Re-writing a rite of passage: the peculiar funeral of Edward II', in *Rites of Passage: Cultures of Transition in the Fourteenth Century*, ed. N. McDonald & W.M. Ormrod (Woodbridge, Suffolk & Rochester, NY, 2004), 13–29.
Burgtorf, B., ' "With my life, his joyes began and ended": Piers Gaveston and King Edward II of England revisited', in *Fourteenth Century England*, v, ed. N. Saul (Woodbridge, Suffolk & Rochester, NY, 2008), 31–51.
Burns, J.H., ed., *The Cambridge History of Political Thought, c.350–c.1450* (Cambridge, 1988).
Burns, R.I., ed., *The Worlds of Alfonso the Learned and James the Conqueror: Intellect and Force in the Middle Ages* (Princeton, 1985).
Butler, R., 'The last of the Brimpsfield Giffards and the rising of 1321–22', *Trans. Bristol & Glocs. Arch. Soc.*, lxxvi (1958 for 1957), 75–97.

Calcagno, D., ed., *I Fieschi tra Medioeve ed Età Moderna: Atti del ciclo di conferenze tenute in occasione del 450 anniversario della Congiura dei Fieschi* (Genoa, 1999).
Calmette, J., *Textes et Documents d'Histoire* (2nd edition, Paris, 1953).
Carlton, C., 'Three British revolutions and the personality of kingship', in *Three British Revolutions, 1641, 1688, 1776*, ed. J.G.A. Pocock (Princeton, 1980), 165–207.
Carpenter, D., 'What happened to Edward II?', *London Review of Books*, 7 June 2007.
Cary, E., *The History of the Most unfortunate Prince King Edward II, with Choice Observations on Him and his unhappy Favourites, Gaveston and Spencer* (London, 1680).
—— *The History of the Life, Reign, Deposition and Death of King Edward the Second, with an Account of his Favourites, P. Gaveston and the Spencers* (London, 1689).
Cassan, S.H., *Lives of the Bishops of Winchester*, i, (London, 1827).
Cazelles, R., *Nouvelle Histoire de Paris de la fin du règne de Philippe Auguste à la mort de Charles V* (Paris, 1972).
Chaplais, P., 'Chartes en déficit dans les cartons "Angleterre" du trésor des chartes', *Bibliothèque de l'École des Chartes*, cix (1951), 96–103.
—— 'Le Duché-pairie de Guyenne: l'homage et les services féodaux de 1303 à 1337', *Annales du Midi*, lxix (Toulouse, 1957), 5–38; repr. in Chaplais, *Essays in Medieval Diplomacy and Administration* (London, 1981).
—— 'Un Message de Jean de Fiennes à Édouard II et le projet de démembrement du royaume de France (janvier 1317)', *Revue du Nord*, xliii (1961), 145–8; repr. in Chaplais, *Essays in Medieval Diplomacy and Administration* (London, 1981).
—— *Essays in Medieval Diplomacy and Administration* (London, 1981).
—— *English Medieval Diplomatic Practice*, part 1, 2 vols (London, 1982).
—— *Piers Gaveston: Edward II's Adoptive Brother* (Oxford, 1994).
Childs, W.R., 'Finance and trade under Edward II', in *Politics and Crisis in Fourteenth-century England*, ed. J. Taylor & W. Childs (Gloucester, 1990), 19–37.
—— ' "Welcome my brother": Edward II, John of Powderham and the chronicles, 1318', in *Church and Chronicle in the Middle Ages: Essays presented to John Taylor*, ed. I. Wood & G.A. Loud (London, 1991), 149–63.
—— 'England in Europe in the reign of Edward II', in *The Reign of Edward II: New Perspectives*, ed. G. Dodd & A. Musson (Woodbridge, Suffolk & Rochester, NY, 2006), 97–118.
Clanchy, M., *From Memory to Written Record: England, 1066–1307* (2nd edition, Oxford, 1993).
—— *Abelard: A Medieval Life* (Oxford, 1997).
Clarke, D., ' "The sovereign's vice begets the subject's errour": the Duke of Buckingham, "sodomy" and narratives of Edward II, 1622–28', in *Sodomy in Early Modern Europe*, ed. T. Bettridge (Manchester, 2002), 46–64.
Clarke, M.V., *Medieval Representation and Consent* (London, 1936; repr. New York, 1964).
Clementi, D., 'That the Statute of York is no longer ambiguous', in *Album Helen Maud Cam*, ii (Louvain & Paris, 1961), 93–100.
Cobban, A.B., 'Edward II, Pope John XXII and the university of Cambridge', *Bulletin of the John Rylands Library*, xlvii (1964–5), 49–78.
—— *The King's Hall within the University of Cambridge in the Later Middle Ages* (Cambridge, 1969).
—— *The Medieval English Universities: Oxford and Cambridge to c.1500* (Aldershot, 1988).
Coldstream, N., 'The commissioning and design of the Eleanor Crosses', in *Eleanor of Castile, 1290–1990*, ed. D. Parsons (Stamford, 1991), 55–67.
Colvin, H.M., *A History of Deddington* (London, 1963).
Cosgrove, A., ed., *A New History of Ireland*, ii, *Medieval Ireland, 1169–1534* (Oxford, 1987).
Coulton, G. C., *Medieval Panorama* (Cambridge, 1943).
Crook, D., 'Clipstone peel: fortifications and politics from Bannockburn to the Treaty of Leake, 1314–1318', in *Thirteenth Century England*, x, ed. M. Prestwich, R. Britnell & R. Frame (Woodbridge, Suffolk & Rochester, NY, 2005), 187–95.
Crooks, P., ed., *Government, War and Society in Medieval Ireland: Essays by Edmund Curtis, A.J. Otway-Ruthven and James Lydon* (Dublin, 2008).

Curtis, E., *A History of Medieval Ireland* (London, 1938).
Cuttino, G.P., *English Diplomatic Administration, 1259–1339* (2nd edition, Oxford, 1971).
Cuttino, G.P. & Lyman, T.W., 'Where is Edward II?', *Speculum*, liii (1978), 522–43.
Daly, P.H., 'The process of canonization in the late thirteenth and early fourteenth centuries', in *St. Thomas Cantilupe, Bishop of Hereford: Essays in his Honour*, ed. M. Jancey (Hereford, 1982), 125–36.
Davies, J.C., 'The first journal of Edward II's chamber', *EHR*, xxx (1915), 662–80.
—— 'The Despenser war in Glamorgan', *TRHS*, 3rd series, ix (1915), 21–64.
—— 'An assembly of wool merchants in 1322', *EHR*, xxxi (1916), 596–606.
—— *The Baronial Opposition to Edward II: Its Character and Policy* (Cambridge, 1918; repr. London, 1967).
Davies, R.R., 'Colonial Wales', *Past & Present*, lxv (Oxford, 1974), 3–23.
—— *Lordship and Society in the March of Wales, 1282–1400* (Oxford, 1978).
—— *Conquest, Coexistence and Change: Wales, 1063–1415* (Oxford & Cardiff, 1987).
—— *The First English Empire: Power and Identities in the British Isles 1093–1343* (Oxford, 2000).
D'Avray, D.L., *Death and the Prince: Memorial Preaching before 1350* (Oxford, 1994).
Denholm-Young, N., *Richard of Cornwall* (London, 1947).
—— 'The authorship of the *Vita Edwardi Secundi*', *EHR*, lxxi (1956), 189–211 (repr. in his *Collected Papers* (Cardiff, 1969), 267–89).
—— *History and Heraldry, 1254–1310* (Oxford, 1965).
—— *The Country Gentry in the Fourteenth Century* (Oxford, 1969).
Denton, J.H., 'Walter Reynolds and ecclesiastical politics, 1313–1316', in *Church and Government in the Middle Ages: Essays presented to C.R. Cheney on his Seventieth Birthday*, ed. C. Brooke et al. (Cambridge, 1976), 247–74.
—— *Robert Winchelsey and the Crown 1294–1313: a Study in the Defence of Ecclesiastical Liberty*, Cambridge Studies in Medieval Life and Thought, 3rd series, xiv (Cambridge, 1980).
—— 'The making of the "Articuli Cleri" of 1316', *EHR*, ci (1986), 564–5).
Dictionary of the Middle Ages, 13 vols, ed. J.R. Strayer (New York, 1982–89).
Dodd, G. & Musson, A., eds, *The Reign of Edward II: New Perspectives* (Woodbridge, Suffolk & Rochester, NY: York Medieval Press in association with the Boydell Press and with the Centre for Medieval Studies, University of York, 2006).
Doherty, P.C., 'The date of the birth of Isabella, queen of England (1308–58)', *BIHR*, xlviii (London, 1975), 246–8.
—— *The Death of a King: A Mediaeval Mystery Story* (London, 1985).
—— *Isabella and the Strange Death of Edward II* (London, 2003).
—— *The Great Crown Jewels Robbery of 1303: The Extraordinary Story of the First Big Bank Raid in History* (London, 2005).
Doran, J., *The Book of the Princes of Wales* (London, 1860).
Drabble, M., *The Oxford Companion to English Literature* (Oxford, 1995)
Druon, M., *Les Rois maudits*, 6 vols (Paris, 1955–60); published in English as *The Accursed Kings* (London, 1956–61).
Dryburgh, P., 'The last refuge of a scoundrel? Edward II and Ireland, 1321–7', in *The Reign of Edward II: New Perspectives*, ed. G. Dodd & A. Musson (Woodbridge, Suffolk & Rochester, NY, 2006), 119–39.
Duffy, M., *Royal Tombs of Medieval England* (Stroud, 2003).
Duffy, S., 'The Gaelic account of the Bruce invasion *Cath Fhochairte Brighite*: medieval romance or modern forgery?', *Seanchas Ard Mhacha*, xiii, no. 1 (Dundalk, 1988–89), 59–121.
—— 'The "Continuation" of Nicholas Trevet: a new source for the Bruce invasion', *Proceedings of the Royal Irish Academy*, xci, Section C, no. 12 (Dublin, 1991), 303–15.
—— 'The Bruce brothers and the Irish sea-world, 1306–29', *Cambridge Medieval Celtic Studies*, xxi (1991), 55–86.
Duggan, A.J., 'The cult of St. Thomas Becket in the thirteenth century', in *St Thomas Cantilupe, Bishop of Hereford: Essays in his Honour*, ed. M. Jancey (Hereford, 1982), 21–44.

Duncan, A.A.M., *The Nation of Scots and the Declaration of Arbroath*, Historical Association pamphlet (London, 1970).
—— 'The Scots' invasion of Ireland, 1315', in *The British Isles, 1100–1500: Comparisons, Contrasts and Connections*, ed. R.R. Davies (Edinburgh & Atlantic Highlands, NJ, 1988), 100–17.
Dunford, M., *Rough Guide to Rome* (NY & London, 2005).
Dunham, W.H. & Wood, C.T., 'The right to rule in England: depositions and the kingdom's authority', *American Historical Review*, lxxxi (1976), 738–61.
Edwards, J., 'The cult of "St" Thomas of Lancaster and its iconography', *Yorkshire Archeological Journal*, lxiv (1992), 103–22.
—— 'The cult of "St" Thomas of Lancaster and its iconography: a supplementary note', *Yorks. Arch. Journal*, lxvii (1995), 187–91.
Edwards, J.G., 'Sir Gruffydd Llwyd', *EHR*, xxx (1915), 569–601.
—— 'The negotiating of the Treaty of Leake, 1318', in *Essays in History presented to R.L. Poole*, ed. H.W.C. Davis (Oxford, 1927), 360–78.
Edwards, K., 'The political importance of the English bishops during the reign of Edward II', *EHR*, lix (1944), 311–47.
Egbert, D.D., 'Sister to the Tickhill Psalter: the Psalter of Queen Isabella of England', *Bulletin of the New York Public Library*, xxxix (1935), 759–88.
Elliott, J.H. & Brockliss, A.W.B., eds, *The World of the Favourite* (New Haven & London, 1999).
Enciclopedia Italiana (repr. of the 1934 edition, Rome, 1951).
Evans, J., *English Art, 1307–1461* (Oxford, 1949).
Evans, M., *The Death of Kings: Royal Deaths in Medieval England* (London, 2003).
Eward, S.M., *A Catalogue of Gloucester Cathedral Library* (Gloucester, 1972).
Fairbank, F.R., 'The last earl of Warenne and Surrey', *Yorkshire Archeological Journal*, xix (1906–7), 193–264.
Favier, J., *Un Conseiller de Philippe le Bel: Enguerrand de Marigny* (Paris, 1963).
Federici, F., *Della Famiglia Fiesca Trattato* (Genoa, 1645).
Fell, C., *Edward, King and Martyr*, Leeds Texts and Monographs, new series (Leeds, 1971).
Finucane, R.C., 'Cantilupe as thaumaturge: pilgrims and their "miracles" ', in *St. Thomas Cantilupe Bishop of Hereford: Essays in his Honour*, ed. M. Jancey (Hereford, 1982), 137–44.
Fisher, A., *William Wallace* (Edinburgh, 1986 & 2002).
Frame, R., 'The Bruces in Ireland, 1315–18', *IHS*, xix, no. 73 (March 1974), 3–37 (revised version repr. in Frame, *Ireland and Britain, 1170–1450* (London, 1998), 71–98).
—— *English Lordship in Ireland, 1318–1361* (Oxford, 1982).
—— 'The campaign against the Scots in Munster, 1317', *IHS*, xxiv, no.95 (1985), 361–72, repr. in Frame, *Ireland and Britain*, 99–112.
—— *Ireland and Britain, 1170–1450* (London, 1998).
Francis, G.G., 'Original contract of affiance between Edward Prince of Wales and Isabella of France', *Archaeologia Cambrensis*, iii (Cardiff, 1848), 150–5.
Fraser, C.M., *A History of Anthony Bek* (Oxford, 1957).
Fryde, E.B., 'Parliament and the French war, 1336–40', in *Historical Studies of the English Parliament*, ed. E.B. Fryde & E. Miller, i (London, 1970), 242–61.
—— 'The deposits of Hugh Despenser the Younger with Italian bankers', in Fryde, *Studies in Medieval Trade and Finance* (London, 1983), item III, 344–62.
—— 'Financial resources of Edward III in the Netherlands, 1337–40', in Fryde, *Studies in Medieval Trade and Finance* (London, 1983), item vii, 1142–1216.
Fryde, E.B., Greenway, D.E., Porter, S. & Roy, I., *Handbook of British Chronology*, 3rd edition, Royal Historical Society (London, 1986).
Fryde, N., 'John Stratford, bishop of Winchester, and the Crown, 1323–30', *BIHR*, xliv (1971), 153–61.
—— 'Welsh troops in the campaign of 1322', *Bulletin of the Board of Celtic Studies*, xxvi (1974–75), 82–9.
—— 'Antonio Pessagno of Genoa, king's merchant of Edward II of England', in *Studi in Memoria di Federigo Melis*, ii (Naples, 1978), 157–78.

—— *The Tyranny and Fall of Edward II, 1321–1326* (Cambridge, 1979).
Fuller, E.A., 'The tallage of 6 Edward II and the Bristol rebellion', *Transactions of the Bristol and Gloucestershire Archeological Society*, xix (1894–95), 171–278.
Galbraith, V.H., 'Extracts from the Historia Aurea and a French "Brut" (1317–1347)', *EHR*, xliii (1928), 203–17.
—— 'The literacy of the medieval English kings', *Proceedings of the British Academy*, xxi (1935), 78–111 (repr. in Galbraith, *Kings and Chroniclers: Essays in English Medieval History* (London, 1982)).
—— 'The St Edmundsbury Chronicle, 1296–1301', *EHR*, lviii (1943), 51–78.
Germain, A., *Maguelone sous ses évêques et ses chanoines* (Montpellier, 1869).
—— 'Lettre de Manuel Fiesque concernant les dernières années du roi d'Angleterre Édouard II', Société Archéologique de Montpellier (Montpellier, 1878); repr. in *Mémoires de la Société Archéologique de Montpellier*, vii (1881), 109–27.
Gillingham, J., 'Enforcing old law in new ways: professional lawyers and treason in early fourteenth-century England and France', in *Law and Power in the Middle Ages*, Proceedings of the Fourth Carlsberg Academy Conference on Medieval Legal History 2007, ed. P. Andersen, M. Münster-Swendsen & H. Voght (Copenhagen, 2008), 199–220.
Gittos, B. & Gittos, M., 'Motivation and choice: the selection of medieval secular effigies', in *Heraldry, Pageantry and Social Display in Medieval England*, ed. P. Coss & M. Keen (Woodbridge, Suffolk & Rochester, NY, 2002), 143–67.
Given-Wilson, C., 'Richard II, Edward II, and the Lancastrian inheritance', *EHR*, cix (June 1994), 553–71.
—— '*Vita Edwardi Secundi*: memoir or journal', in *Thirteenth Century England*, vi, ed. M. Prestwich, R. Britnell & R. Frame (Woodbridge, Suffolk, 1997), 165–76.
—— *Chronicles: The Writing of History in Medieval England* (London & New York, 2004).
—— 'Legitimation, designation and succession to the throne in fourteenth-century England', in *Building Legitimacy: Political Discourses and Forms of Legitimacy in Medieval Societies*, ed. I. Alfonso, H.N. Kennedy & J. Escalona, The Medieval Mediterranean, liii (Leiden and Boston, 2004), 89–105.
Given-Wilson, C. & Curteis, A., *The Royal Bastards of Medieval England* (London, 1984).
Graham, R., 'Four alien priories in Monmouthshire', *Journal of British Arch. Association*, 2nd series, xxxv (London, 1927).
Gransden, A., *Historical Writing in England*, i, *c.550–c.1307* (London, 1974).
—— *Historical Writing in England*, ii, *c.1307 to the Early Sixteenth Century* (London, 1982).
—— 'The uses made of history by the kings of medieval England', in *Collection de l'École française de Rome*, lxxxii (Rome, 1985).
—— 'The continuation of the *Flores Historiarum* from 1265 to 1327', in Gransden, *Legends, Traditions and History in Medieval England* (London, 1992).
Gray, D., 'Songs and Lyrics', in *Literature in Fourteenth-century England*, ed. P. Boitani & A. Torti (Tübingen & Cambridge, 1983).
Green, M.A.E., *Lives of the Princesses of England*, ii (London, 1850).
Green, V., *The Madness of Kings* (Stroud, 1993).
Griffiths, R.A., 'The revolt of Llywelyn Bren', *Glamorgan Historian*, ii (1965), 186–96.
—— *The Principality of Wales in the Later Middle Ages: the Structure and Personnel of Government*: I: *South Wales, 1277–1526* (Cardiff, 1972).
Guillemain, B., *La Cour pontificale d'Avignon (1309–1376)* (Paris, 1962).
Gwynn, A., 'The medieval university of St. Patrick's, Dublin', *Studies*, xvii (Dublin, 1938), 199–212 & 437–54.
Hadwin, H., 'The last royal tallages', *EHR*, xcvi (1981), 344–58.
Haines, R.M., *The Church and Politics in Fourteenth-century England: The Career of Adam Orleton, c.1275–1345*, Cambridge Studies in Medieval Life and Thought, 3rd series (Cambridge, 1978).
—— *Archbishop John Stratford: Political Revolutionary and Champion of the Liberties of the English Church, c. 1275/80–1348*, Studies and Texts, 76, Pontifical Institute of Mediaeval Studies (Toronto, 1986).

—— '*Edwardus redivivus*: the "afterlife" of Edward of Caernarvon', *Transactions of the Bristol and Gloucestershire Archeological Society*, cxiv, for 1996 (1997), 65–86.
—— *Death of a King: An Account of the Supposed Escape and Afterlife of Edward II, King of England, Lord of Ireland, Duke of Aquitaine* (Lancaster, 2001).
—— 'Looking back in anger: a politically inspired appeal against John XXII's translation of Bishop Adam Orleton to Winchester (1334)', *EHR*, cxvi (2001), 389–404.
—— *King Edward II: Edward of Caernarfon, His Life, His Reign, and its Aftermath, 1284–1330* (Montreal & London, 2003).
—— 'Sir Thomas Gurney of Englishcombe in the county of Somerset, Regicide?', *Somerset Archaeology and Natural History*, cxlvii (2004), 45–65.
—— 'The Episcopate during the Reign of Edward II and the Regency of Mortimer and Isabella', *Journal of Ecclesiastical History*, lvi (2005), 657–709.
—— 'The Stamford Council of April 1327', *EHR*, cxxii (2007), 141–8.
—— 'Roger Mortimer's scam', *Transactions of the Bristol and Gloucestershire Archaeological Society*, cxxvi (2008), 139–56.
—— 'Sumptuous apparel for a royal prisoner: Archbishop Melton's letter, 14 January 1330', *EHR*, cxxiv (August 2009), 885–94.
Hallam, E.M., *English Royal Marriages: The French Marriages of Edward I and Edward II: 1299 and 1307* (London, 1981).
—— *The Plantagenet Encyclopaedia* (London, 1990).
—— 'The Eleanor crosses and royal burial customs', in *Eleanor of Castile, 1290–1990*, ed. D. Parsons (Stamford, 1991), 9–21.
Hallam, H.E., ed. *The Agrarian History of England and Wales*, ii (Cambridge, 1988), 1042–1350.
Hamilton, J.S., *Piers Gaveston: Earl of Cornwall, 1307–1312: Politics and Patronage in the Reign of Edward II* (Detroit & London, 1988).
—— 'Another daughter for Piers Gaveston? Amie de Gaveston, damsel of the Queen's Chamber', *Medieval Prosopography*, xix (Kalamazoo, 1998), 177–86.
—— 'Charter witness lists for the reign of Edward II', in *Fourteenth Century England*, i, ed. N. Saul (Woodbridge, Suffolk & Rochester, NY, 2000), 1–20.
—— 'The character of Edward II', in *The Reign of Edward II: New Perspectives*, ed. G. Dodd & A. Musson (Woodbridge, Suffolk & Rochester, NY, 2006), 5–21.
—— ed., *Fourteenth Century England*, iv (Woodbridge, Suffolk & Rochester, NY, 2006).
—— 'The uncertain death of Edward II', *History Compass* (electronic publication, 2008).
Harrison, M., 'A life of Edward the Confessor in early fourteenth-century stained glass at Fécamp in Normandy', *Journal of Warburg & Courtauld Institutes*, xxvi (1963), 22–37.
Harriss, G.L., *King, Parliament and Public Finance in England to 1369* (Oxford, 1975).
Hartshorne, C.H., 'Inquisition on the effects of King Edward II', *Archaeologia Cambrensis*, 3rd series, ix (1863), 163–7.
Harvey, A. & Mortimer, R., eds, *The Funeral Effigies of Westminster Abbey* (Woodbridge, Suffolk & Rochester, NY, 1994).
Harvey, J.H., 'The origins of the perpendicular style', in *Studies in Building History: Essays in Recognition of the Work of B.H.St.J. O'Neil*, ed. E.M. Jope (London, 1961), 134–65.
Harwood, T., *The History and Antiquities of the Church and City of Lichfield* (Gloucester, 1806).
Haskins, G.L., 'Judicial proceedings against a traitor after Boroughbridge', *Speculum*, xii (1937), 509–11.
—— 'The Doncaster petition of 1321', *EHR*, liii (1938), 476–85.
—— 'A chronicle of the civil wars of Edward II', *Speculum*, xiv (1939), 73–81.
Hederman, A.D., *The Royal Image: Illustrations of the Grandes Chroniques de France, 1274–1422* (Berkeley, 1991).
Heffernan, T.J., 'Dangerous sympathies: political commentary in the *South English Legendary*', in *The South English Legendary: A Critical Assessment*, ed. K.P. Jankofsky (Tübingen, 1992), 1–17.
—— ' "God hath schewed ffor him many grete miracules": political canonization and the *Miracula* of Simon de Montfort', in *Art and Context in Late Medieval English Narrative: Essays*

in Honor of Robert Worth Frank, Jr., ed. R.R. Edwards (Woodbridge, Suffolk & Rochester, NY, 1994), 177–91.
Hinnebusch, W.A., *The Early English Friars Preachers* (Rome, 1951).
Hledíková, Z., *Raccolta Praghese di Scritti di Luca Fieschi* (Charles University, Prague, 1985).
Hollaender, A., 'The pictorial work in the "Flores Historiarum" of the so-called Matthew of Westminster', *Bulletin of the John Rylands Library*, xxviii (Manchester, 1944), 361–81.
Holmes, G.A., 'A protest against the Despensers, 1326', *Speculum*, xxx (1955), 207–12.
—— 'Judgement on the younger Despenser, 1326', *EHR*, lxx (1955), 261–7.
—— *The Estates of the Higher Nobility in XIV-Century England* (Cambridge, 1957).
Horne, A., *The Fall of Paris: the Siege and the Commune, 1870–71* (London, 1965).
Horne, P., 'The besotted king and his Adonis: representations of Edward II and Gaveston in late nineteenth-century England', *History Workshop Journal*, xlvii (Oxford, 1999), 31–48.
Housley, N., *The Avignon Papacy and the Crusades, 1305–1378* (Oxford, 1986).
Howard, R., *Historical Observations upon the Reigns of Edward I, II, III, and Richard II. With Remarks upon their Faithful Counsellors and False Favourites* (London, 1689).
—— *The History of the Life and Reign of Edward II, containing a Full Account of the Tyrannical Government of his Favourites and Minions* (London, 1713).
Howell, M., *Eleanor of Provence: Queenship in Thirteenth-century England* (Oxford & Malden, Mass., 1998).
Hoyt, R.S., 'The coronation oath of 1308: the background of "Les leys and les custumes" ', *Traditio*, xi (1955), 235–57.
—— 'The coronation oath of 1308', *EHR*, lxxi (1956), 353–83.
Hubert, F., *The Deplorable Life and Death of Edward the Second, King of England, together with the Downefall of the two Unfortunate Favorits, Gavestone and Spencer, Storied in an Excellent Poem* (London, 1628).
Hughes, A., 'Antiphons and acclamations: the politics of music in the coronation service of Edward II, 1308', *Journal of Musicology*, vi, no. 2 (Spring 1988), 150–68.
—— 'The origins and descent of the Fourth Recension of the English Coronation', in *Coronations: Medieval and Early Modern Monarchic Ritual*, ed. J.M. Bak (Berkeley, 1990), 197–216.
Hughes, J.B., 'Walter Langton, bishop of Coventry and Lichfield, 1296–1321, and his register', *Staffordshire Studies*, ix (1997), 1–8.
Hunter, J., 'On the measures taken for the apprehension of Sir Thomas de Gournay, one of the murderers of King Edward the Second', *Archaeologia*, xxvii (1838), 274–94.
—— 'Expenses of conveying the body of King Edward II from Berkeley Castle to the Abbey of Gloucester', *Archaeologia*, xxvii (1838), 294–7.
—— 'Journal of the mission of Queen Isabella to the court of France, and of her long residence in that country', *Archaeologia*, xxxvi (1855), 242–57.
Hutchison, H.F., *Edward II: The Pliant King* (London, 1971).
Jack, R.I., *Medieval Wales: The Sources of History* (London, 1972).
James, E., *Britain in the First Millennium* (London, 2001).
Jancey, M., ed., *St Thomas Cantilupe, Bishop of Hereford: Essays in his Honour* (Hereford, 1982).
Jarman, D., *Queer Edward II* (London, 1991).
Jeayes, I.H., *Descriptive Catalogue of the Charters and Muniments at Berkeley Castle* (Bristol, 1892).
Johansson, W. & Percy, W.A., 'Homosexuality', in *Handbook of Medieval Sexuality*, ed. V.L. Bullough & J.A. Brundage (New York & London, 1996), 155–89.
Johnson, C., 'The homage for Guienne in 1304', *EHR*, liii (1938), 728–9.
Johnstone, H., 'The county of Ponthieu, 1279–1307', *EHR*, xxix (1914), 435–52.
—— 'The Parliament of Lincoln of 1316', *EHR*, xxxvi (1921), 53–7.
—— 'The eccentricities of Edward II', *EHR*, xlviii (1933), 264–7.
—— 'Isabella, the she-wolf of France', *History*, xxi (1936), 208–18.
—— *Edward of Carnarvon, 1284–1307* (Manchester, 1946).

Jones, M.C., 'The feudal barons of Powys', *Collections relating to Montgomeryshire*, i (1868).
Jones, T., 'Was Richard II a tyrant? Richard's use of the books of rules for princes', in *Fourteenth Century England*, v, ed. Nigel Saul (Woodbridge, Suffolk & Rochester, NY, 2008), 130–60.
Jordan, W.C., *The Great Famine: Northern Europe in the Early Fourteenth Century* (Princeton, 1996).
Jurkowski, M., Smith, C.L. & Crook, D., *Lay Taxes in England and Wales, 1186–1688*, Public Record Office Handbook no. 31 (London, 1998).
Kaeuper, R.W., 'The Frescobaldi of Florence and the English crown', *Studies in Medieval and Renaissance History*, x (Lincoln, Nebraska, 1973), 41–95.
—— 'Law and order in fourteenth-century England: the evidence of special commissions of oyer and terminer', *Speculum*, liv (1979), 734–84.
—— *War, Justice and Public Order* (Oxford, 1988).
—— ed., *Violence in Medieval Society* (Woodbridge, Suffolk & Rochester, NY, 2000).
Kauffmann, M., 'The image of St. Louis', in *Kings and Kingship in Medieval Europe*, ed. A.J. Duggan (London, 1993).
Keen, M., 'Treason trials under the law of arms', in Keen, *Nobles, Knights and Men-at-Arms in the Middle Ages* (London, 1996), 149–66 (first published in *TRHS*, 5th series, xii, 1962).
—— 'Brotherhood in arms', in Keen, *Nobles, Knights and Men-at-Arms in the Middle Ages*, 43–62 (first published in *History*, xlvii, 1983).
—— *Chivalry* (New Haven & London, 1983).
Kemp, E.W. [the bishop of Chichester], 'History and action in the sermons of a medieval archbishop', in *The Writing of History in the Middle Ages: Essays presented to Richard William Southern*, ed. R.H.C. Davis & J.M. Wallace-Hadrill (Oxford, 1981), 349–65.
Kershaw, I., 'The Great Famine and Agrarian Crisis in England 1315–1322', *Past & Present*, lix (May, 1973), 3–50.
—— 'A note on Scottish raids in the West Riding, 1316–18', *Northern History*, xvii (1981), 231–9.
King, A., 'Thomas of Lancaster's first quarrel with Edward II', in *Fourteenth Century England*, iii, ed. W.M. Ormrod (Woodbridge, Suffolk, & Rochester, NY, 2004), 31–45.
Kirby, I.M., *Diocese of Gloucester: A Catalogue of the Records of the Dean and Chapter, including the former St. Peter's Abbey* (Gloucester, 1967).
Knowles, D. & Hadcock, R.N., *Medieval Religious Houses: England and Wales* (London, 1953).
Kurth, G., *Étude critique sur Jean d'Outremeuse*, Classe des Lettres et des Sciences morales et politiques et Classe des Beaux-Arts, Mémoires, 2nd series, vii (Brussels, 1910).
Lalou, E., 'Les Négociations diplomatiques avec l'Angleterre sous le règne de Philippe le Bel', in *La 'France Anglaise' au Moyen Age*, Colloque des historiens médiévistes français et britanniques, Actes du IIIe congrès national des sociétés savantes (Poitiers, 1986), Section d'histoire médiévale et de philologie (Paris, 1988), 323–55.
Lambert, M., *Franciscan Poverty: the Doctrine of the Absolute Poverty of Christ and the Apostles in the Franciscan Order 1210–1323* (2nd edition, Oxford, 1998).
Lang, H.R., *Das Liederbuch des Königs Denis von Portugal* (Halle, 1894; repr. Hildesheim & New York, 1972).
Lapsley, G.T., *Crown, Community and Parliament*, ed. H. Cam & G. Barraclough (Oxford, 1951).
Latham, R.E., *Revised Medieval Latin Word-List* (London, 1965).
Lawrence, M., ' "Too flattering sweet to be substantial": the last months of Thomas, Lord Despenser', in *Fourteenth Century England*, iv, ed. J.S. Hamilton (Woodbridge, Suffolk & Rochester, NY, 2006), 146–58.
—— 'Rise of a royal favourite: the early career of Hugh Despenser the Elder', in *The Reign of Edward II: New Perspectives*, ed. G. Dodd & A. Musson (Woodbridge, Suffolk & Rochester, NY, 2006), 205–19.
—— 'Secular patronage and religious devotion: the Despensers and St. Mary's abbey, Tewkesbury', in *Fourteenth Century England*, v, ed. N. Saul (Woodbridge, Suffolk & Rochester, NY, 2008), 78–93.
—— 'Edward II and the earldom of Winchester', *Historical Research*, lxxxi (2008), 732–9.
Le Goff, J., *Saint Louis* (Paris, 1996).

Lege, V., *Sant' Alberto Abate e il suo culto* (repr. from *Atti dell'Accademia Tortonese Leone*, xiii, Tortona, 1901).
Lehmann-Brockhaus, O., *Lateinische Schriftquellen zur Kunst in England, Wales und Schottland vom Jahre 901 bis zum Jahre 1307*, 5 vols (Munich, 1955–60).
Lewis, J.M., 'A medieval ring-brooch from Oxwich castle, West Glamorgan', *Antiquaries Journal*, lxii (1982), 126–9.
—— 'The Oxwich brooch', *Jewellery Studies*, ii (1985), 24–8.
Lewis, S., 'The Apocalypse of Isabella of France: Paris, Bibl. Nat. ms. Fr. 13096', *Art Bulletin*, lxxii (New York, 1990), 224–60.
Libro delle investiture del vescovo di Vercelli Giovanni Fieschi (1349–50), ed. D. Arnaldi, Biblioteca della Società Storica Subaplina, vol. LXXIII, ii (Turin, 1934).
Lindley, P., *Gothic to Renaissance: Essays on Sculpture in England* (Stamford, 1995).
—— 'The later medieval monuments and chantry chapels', in *Tewkesbury-Abbey: History, Art and Architecture*, ed. R.K. Morris & R. Shoesmith (Logaston, 2003), 161–82, 303–6.
Linehan, P., 'The English mission of Cardinal Petrus Hispanus, the chronicle of Walter of Guisborough, and news from Castile at Carlisle (1307)', *EHR*, cxvii (June, 2002), 605–21.
List of Documents relating to the Household and Wardrobe: John to Edward I (London, 1964).
Lloyd, S.D., *English Society and the Crusade, 1216–1307* (Oxford, 1988).
Logan, F.D., *Runaway Religious in Medieval England, c.1240–1540* (Cambridge, 1996).
Loomis, R.S., 'Edward I: Arthurian enthusiast', *Speculum*, xxviii (1953), 114–27.
Lopez, R.S., *The Birth of Europe* (New York, 1967).
Lucas, H.S., 'John Crabbe, Flemish pirate, merchant and adventurer', *Speculum*, xx (1945), 334–50.
—— 'The great European famine of 1315, 1316, and 1317', in *Essays in Economic History*, ii, ed. E.M. Carus-Wilson (London, 1962), 49–72.
Lumsden, A., 'The fairy tale of Edward II', *Gay and Lesbian Review*, xi, no. 2 (London, March–April 2004), 27–9.
Lunt, W.E., 'Clerical tenths levied in England by papal authority during the reign of Edward II', in *Anniversary Essays in Mediaeval History by Students of Charles Homer Haskins*, ed. C.H. Taylor (Boston & New York, 1929), 166–71.
—— *Financial Relations of the Papacy with England to 1327* (Cambridge, Mass., 1939).
Lydon, J., 'Edward II and the revenues of Ireland in 1311–12', *IHS*, xiv (1964), 39–57.
—— 'Edward I, Ireland and the war in Scotland, 1303–1304', in *England and Ireland in the Later Middle Ages: Essays in Honour of Jocelyn Otway-Ruthven*, ed. J. Lydon (Dublin, 1981), 43–61.
—— 'The impact of the Bruce invasion', in *A New History of Ireland*, ii, *Medieval Ireland, 1169–1534*, ed. A. Cosgrove (Oxford, 1987), 275–302.
Macconi, M., 'Fieschi e l'Impero nel XIV e XV secolo', in *I Fieschi tra medioeve ed età moderna* ed. D. Caccagno (Genoa, 1999), 29–50.
McFarlane, K.B., 'Had Edward I a "Policy" towards the earls?', *History*, l (1965), 145–59.
McGrade, A.S., ed., *A Short Discourse on Tyrannical Government* (Cambridge, 1992).
McHardy, A.K., 'Paying for the wedding: Edward III as fundraiser, 1332–3', in *Fourteenth Century England*, iv, ed. J.S. Hamilton (Woodbridge, Suffolk & Rochester, NY, 2006), 43–60.
McKenna, J.W., 'The coronation oil of the Yorkist kings', *EHR*, lxxxii (1967), 102–4.
Mackesy, P., *The War for America, 1775–1783* (London, 1964).
McKisack, M., *The Fourteenth Century, 1307–1399* (Oxford, 1959).
McNamee, C., *The Wars of the Bruces: Scotland, England and Ireland, 1306–1328* (East Linton, 1997).
McNiven, P., 'Rebellion, sedition and the legend of Richard II's survival in the reigns of Henry IV and Henry V', *Bulletin of the John Rylands Library*, lxxvi (1994), 93–117.
McQuillan, J.T., 'Who was St Thomas of Lancaster? New manuscript evidence', in *Fourteenth Century England*, iv, ed. J.S. Hamilton, (Woodbridge, Suffolk & Rochester, NY, 2006), 1–25.
Maddicott, J.R., *Thomas of Lancaster, 1307–1322: A Study in the Reign of Edward II* (Oxford, 1970).

—— 'Thomas of Lancaster and Sir Robert Holland: a study in noble patronage', *EHR*, lxxxvi (1971), 449–72.
—— *The English Peasantry and the Demands of the Crown, 1294–1341*, Past & Present Supplement, No. 1 (Oxford, 1975).
—— 'Poems of social protest in early fourteenth-century England', in *England in the Fourteenth Century, Proceedings of the 1985 Harlaxton Symposium*, ed. W.M. Ormrod (Woodbridge, Suffolk, 1986), 130–44.
—— *Simon de Montfort* (Cambridge, 1994).
Maitland, F.W., *Constitutional History of England* (Cambridge, 1908).
Marchant, G., *Edward II in Gloucestershire: A King in our Midst* (Gloucester, 2007).
Marlowe, C., *Doctor Faustus and Other Plays*, ed. D. Bevington & E. Rasmussen (Oxford, 1995).
Masschaele, J., 'The public space of the marketplace in medieval England', *Speculum*, lxxvii (2002), 383–421.
Matthew, D., *The Norman Monasteries and their Possessions* (Oxford, 1962).
Members of Parliament, part i, *Parliaments of England, 1213–1702* (London, 1879).
Menache, S., *Clement V*, Cambridge Studies in Medieval Life and Thought, 4th series, 36 (Cambridge, 1998).
Michael, M.A., 'The iconography of kingship in Walter de Milemete's treatise', *Journal of Warburg & Courtauld Institutes*, lvii (1994), 35–47.
—— 'Towards a hermeneutics of the manuscript: the physical and metaphysical journeys of Paris, BNF, Ms. Fr. 571', in *Freedom of Movement in the Middle Ages*, Harlaxton Medieval Studies, XV, Proceedings of the 2003 Harlaxton Symposium, ed. P. Horden (Donington, 2007), 305–17.
Middleton, A.E., *Sir Gilbert de Middleton* (Newcastle, 1918).
Mitchell, S., 'Richard II: kingship and the cult of saints', in *The Regal Image of Richard II and the Wilton Diptych*, ed. D. Gordon, L. Monnas & C. Elam (London, 1997).
Moore, S.A., 'Documents relating to the death and burial of King Edward II', *Archaeologia*, 50 (1887), 215–26.
Morgan, P.E., 'The effect of the pilgrim cult of St. Thomas Cantilupe on Hereford cathedral', in *St. Thomas Cantilupe, Bishop of Hereford: Essays in his Honour*, ed. M. Jancey (Hereford, 1982), 145–52.
Morganstern, A.M., *Gothic Tombs of Kinship in France, the Low Countries and England* (University Park, Pennsylvania, 2000).
Morris, J.E., *Bannockburn* (Cambridge, 1914).
Morris, R., 'Tewkesbury abbey: the Despenser mausoleum', *Transactions of the Bristol and Gloucestershire Archeological Society*, xciii (Gloucester, 1974), 142–55.
Morris, R.K. & Shoesmith, R., eds, *Tewkesbury Abbey: History, Art and Architecture* (Logaston, 2003).
Mortimer, I., *The Greatest Traitor: The Life of Sir Roger Mortimer, 1st Earl of March, Ruler of England, 1327–1330* (London, 2003).
—— 'The Death of Edward II in Berkeley Castle', *EHR*, cxx (2005), 1175–214.
—— *The Perfect King: The Life of Edward III, Father of the English Nation* (London, 2006).
—— 'Sermons of sodomy: a reconsideration of Edward II's sodomitical reputation', in *The Reign of Edward II: New Perspectives*, ed. G. Dodd & A. Musson (Woodbridge, Suffolk & Rochester, NY, 2006), 48–60.
Mountford, W., *King Edward the Third, with the Fall of Mortimer Earl of March. An Historicall Play, as it is Acted at The Theatre Royall, by their Majesties Servants* (London, 1691).
Newdigate, B.H., *Michael Drayton and his Circle* (Oxford, 1961).
Nicholson, R., 'A sequel to Edward Bruce's invasion of Ireland', *SHR*, xlii (1963), 30–40.
—— *Edward III and the Scots: The Formative Years of a Military Career, 1327–1335* (Oxford, 1965).
Nigra, C., 'Uno degli Edoardi in Italia. Favola o Storia?', *Nuova Antologia: Rivista Lettere Scienze*, xcii, series 4, fascicle for 1 April 1901, 403–25.
Nussbacher, A., *The Battle of Bannockburn, 1314* (Stroud, 2000).

Oggins, R.S., *The Kings and their Hawks: Falconry in Medieval England* (New Haven & London, 2004).
Ormrod, W.M., 'Edward II at Neath Abbey, 1326', *Neath Antiquarian Society Transactions for 1988-89* (Neath, 1988), 107-12.
—— 'The personal religion of Edward III', *Speculum*, lxiv (1989), 849-77.
—— *The Reign of Edward III: Crown and Political Society in England, 1327-1377* (New Haven & London, 1990).
—— 'Agenda for Legislation, 1322-c.1340', *EHR*, cv (1990), 1-33.
—— 'The sexualities of Edward II', in *The Reign of Edward II: New Perspectives*, ed. G. Dodd & A. Musson (Woodbridge, Suffolk & Rochester, NY, 2006), 22-47.
—— 'Richard de Bury and the monarchy of Edward III', in *War, Government and Aristocracy in the British Isles, c.1150-1500: Essays in Honour of Michael Prestwich*, ed. C. Given-Wilson, A. Kettle & L. Scales (Woodbridge, Suffolk & Rochester, NY, 2008), 163-78.
Owen, E., ed., *A List of those who did Homage and Fealty to the First English Prince of Wales in AD 1301* (privately printed, 1901).
Owen, R., 'Welsh Pool and Powys-Land', *Collections relating to Montgomeryshire*, xxix (Welshpool, 1929), 257-60.
Palliser, D.M., 'Royal mausolea in the long fourteenth century (1272-1422)', in *Fourteenth-century England*, iii, ed. W.M. Ormrod (Woodbridge, Suffolk & Rochester, NY, 2004), 1-16.
La Papauté d'Avignon et le Languedoc (1316-1342), Cahiers de Fanjeaux, xxvi (Toulouse, 1991).
Parsons, J.C., 'The year of Eleanor of Castile's birth and her children by Edward I', *Mediaeval Studies*, xlvi (1984), 245-65.
—— 'Eleanor of Castile (1241-1290): legend and reality through seven centuries', in *Eleanor of Castile, 1290-1990*, ed. D. Parsons (Stamford, 1991), 23-54.
—— *Eleanor of Castile* (New York & London, 1995).
Partner, P., 'Florence and the papacy, 1300-1370', in *Europe in the Late Middle Ages*, ed. J. Hale, R. Highfield & B. Smalley (London, 1965).
Pearce, E.H., *The Monks of Westminster: Being a Register of the Brethren of the Convent from the Time of the Confessor to the Dissolution* (Cambridge, 1916).
Pépin, G., 'Le Sirventés El dugat... Une chanson méconnue de Pey de Ladils sur l'Aquitaine Anglo-Gasconne', *Les Cahiers du Bazadais*, clii (Bazas, 2006), 5-28.
Perroy, E., *L'Angleterre et le Grand Schisme d'Occident* (Paris, 1933).
Perry, R., *Edward the Second: Suddenly at Berkeley* (Wotton-under-Edge, Glos., 1988).
Peters, E., 'I Principi negligenti di Dante e le concezioni medievali del *Rex Inutilis*', *Rivista Storica Italiana*, lxxx (1968), 741-58.
—— *The Shadow King: Rex Inutilis in Medieval Law and Literature, 751-1327* (New Haven & London, 1970).
—— 'Henry II of Cyprus, *Rex inutilis*: a footnote to *Decameron* 1.9', *Speculum*, lxxii (1997), 763-75.
Petit, K., 'Le Mariage de Philippa de Hainaut, reine d'Angleterre (1328)', *Le Moyen Age*, lxxxvii (1981), 373-85.
Phillips, J.R.S., *Aymer de Valence, Earl of Pembroke, 1307-24: Baronial Politics in the Reign of Edward II* (Oxford, 1972).
—— 'The "Middle party" and the negotiating of the Treaty of Leake, August 1318: a re-interpretation', *BIHR*, xlvi (1973), 11-27.
—— 'The mission of John de Hothum to Ireland, 1315-1316', in *England and Ireland in the Later Middle Ages: Essays in Honour of Jocelyn Otway-Ruthven*, ed. J.F. Lydon (Blackrock, Co. Dublin, 1981), 62-85.
—— 'The Anglo-Norman nobility', in *The English in Medieval Ireland: Proceedings of the first joint meeting of the Royal Irish Academy and the British Academy, Dublin, 1982*, ed. J.F. Lydon (Dublin, 1984), 87-104.
—— 'Edward II and the prophets', in *England in the Fourteenth Century: Proceedings of the 1985 Harlaxton Symposium*, ed. W.M. Ormrod (Woodbridge, 1986), 189-201.
—— *The Medieval Expansion of Europe* (Oxford, 1988; 2nd edn, 1998).

—— 'The Irish Remonstrance of 1317: an international perspective', *IHS*, xxvii (1990), 112–29.
—— 'The Remonstrance revisited: England and Ireland in the early fourteenth century', in *Men, Women and War, Historical Studies*, xviii, ed. T.G. Fraser & K. Jeffrey (Dublin, 1993), 13–27.
—— 'The quest for Sir John Mandeville', in *The Culture of Christendom: Essays in Medieval History in Memory of Denis Bethell*, ed. M.A. Meyer (London & Rio Grande, 1993), 243–55.
—— 'The outer world of the European Middle Ages', in *Implicit Understandings: Observing, Reporting, and Reflecting on the Encounters between Europeans and Other Peoples in the Early Modern Era*, ed. S.B. Schwartz (Cambridge, 1994), 23–63.
—— 'Simon de Montfort (1265), the Earl of Manchester (1644), and other stories: violence and politics in thirteenth- and early fourteenth-century England', in *Violence in Medieval Society*, ed. R.W. Kaeuper (Woodbridge, Suffolk & Rochester, NY, 2000), 79–89.
—— 'Edward II and Ireland (in fact and in fiction)', *IHS*, xxxiii (May 2002), 1–18.
—— 'The reputation of a King: Edward II from chronicle and written record to compact disc and internet', in *European Encounters: Essays in Memory of Albert Lovett*, ed. J. Devlin & H.B. Clarke (Dublin, 2003), 37–54.
—— ' "Edward II" in Italy: English and Welsh political exiles and fugitives in continental Europe, 1322–1364', in *Thirteenth Century England*, x, *Proceedings of the Durham Conference, 2003*, ed. M. Prestwich, R. Britnell & R. Frame (Woodbridge, Suffolk & Rochester, NY, 2005), 209–26.
—— 'The place of the reign of Edward II', in *The Reign of Edward II: New Perspectives*, ed. G. Dodd & A. Musson (Woodbridge, Suffolk & Rochester, NY, 2006), 220–33.
—— 'Plantagenet Ireland, England and Castile: from Burgos (1254) to Batalha (1385)', in *Spanish–Irish Relations through the Ages: New Historical Perspectives*, ed. D.M. Downey & J. Crespo MacLennan (Dublin, 2008), 5–16.
—— 'An Englishman in Rome, 1330–1334', in *Dublin and the Medieval World*, ed. A. Simms & A. Fletcher (Dublin, 2009), 422–32.
Phillips, J.R.S. & Stones, E.L.G., 'English in the public records: three late thirteenth-century examples', *Nottingham Medieval Studies* (1988), 1–10.
Pole-Stuart, E., 'Interview between Philip V and Edward II at Amiens, 1320', *EHR*, xli (1926), 412–15.
Pollock, F. & Maitland, F.W., *The History of English Law before the Time of Edward I*, 2 vols (2nd edition, Cambridge, 1968).
Powel, D., *The Historie of Cambria* (London, 1584).
Powicke, F.M., *Henry III and the Lord Edward: the Community of the Realm in the Thirteenth Century* (Oxford, 1947).
Powicke, M.R., 'The English commons in Scotland in 1322 and the deposition of Edward II', *Speculum*, xxxv (1960), 556–62.
—— *Military Obligation in Medieval England* (Oxford, 1962).
Prestwich, M., 'Isabella de Vescy and the custody of Bamburgh castle', *BIHR*, xliv (1971), 148–52.
—— *War, Politics and Finance under Edward I* (London, 1972).
—— *The Three Edwards: War and State in England, 1272–1377* (London, 1980).
—— 'Parliament and the community of the realm in fourteenth-century England', in *Parliament and Community, Historical Studies*, xiv (Irish Conference of Historians), ed. A. Cosgrove & J.I. McGuire (Belfast, 1983), 5–24.
—— 'A new version of the Ordinances of 1311', *BIHR*, lvii (1984), 189–203.
—— 'Cavalry service in early fourteenth-century England', in *War and Government in the Middle Ages: Essays in Honour of J.O. Prestwich*, ed. J. Gillingham & J.C. Holt (Woodbridge, Suffolk & Totowa, NJ, 1984), 147–58.
—— 'The piety of Edward I', in *England in the Thirteenth Century: Proceedings of the 1984 Harlaxton Symposium*, ed. W.M. Ormrod (Grantham, 1985), 120–8.
—— 'The charges against the Despensers, 1321', *BIHR*, lviii (1985), 95–100.
—— *Edward I, King of England* (London, 1988; new edition, New Haven & London, 1997).

—— 'Edward I and the Maid of Norway', *SHR*, lxix (October 1990), 157–74.
—— 'The Ordinances of 1311 and the politics of the early fourteenth century', in *Politics and Crisis in Fourteenth-Century England*, ed. J. Taylor & W.R. Childs (Gloucester, 1990), 1–18.
—— 'Gilbert de Middleton and the attack on the cardinals, 1317', in *Warriors and Churchmen in the High Middle Ages: Essays presented to Karl Leyser*, ed. T. Reuter (London, 1992), 179–94.
—— *Armies and Warfare in the Middle Ages: The English Experience* (New Haven & London, 1996).
—— 'The unreliability of royal household knights in the early fourteenth century', in *Fourteenth Century England*, ii, ed. C. Given-Wilson (Woodbridge, Suffolk & Rochester, NY, 2002), 1–11.
—— *Plantagenet England, 1225–1360*, New Oxford History of England (Oxford, 2005).
—— 'The court of Edward II', in *The Reign of Edward II: New Perspectives*, ed. G. Dodd & A. Musson (Woodbridge, Suffolk & Rochester, NY, 2006), 61–75.
Prevost, M., d'Amat, R. & Tribout de Morembert, H., eds, *Dictionnaire de Biographie Française*, v (Paris, 1982).
Prince, A.E., 'The payment of army wages in Edward III's reign', *Speculum*, xix (1944), 137–60.
Pryce, H. & Watts, J.L., eds, *Power and Identity in the Middle Ages: Essays in Memory of Rees Davies* (Oxford, 2007).
Pugh, T.B., 'The marcher lords of Glamorgan and Morgannwg, 1317–1485', in *Glamorgan County History*, iii, *The Middle Ages*, ed. T.B. Pugh (Cardiff, 1971), 167–204.
Raban, S., *England under Edward I and Edward II, 1259–1327* (Oxford, 2000).
Redstone, V.B., 'Some mercenaries of Henry of Lancaster, 1327–1330', *TRHS*, 3rd series, vii (1913), 151–66.
Rees, W., *Caerphilly Castle and its Place in the Annals of Glamorgan* (Caerphilly, 1974).
Regalado, N.F., '*Kalila et Dimna, Liber regius*: the tutorial book of Raymond de Béziers (Paris, BNF Ms. Lat. 8504)', in *Satura: Studies in Medieval Literature in Honour of Robert R. Raymo*, ed. N.M. Reale & R.E. Sternglantz (Donington, 2001), 103–23.
Reid, W.S., 'The Scots and the Staple Ordinance of 1313', *Speculum*, xxxiv (1959), 598–610.
Renn, D., *Caerphilly Castle* (Cardiff, 1997).
Renouard, Y., 'Édouard II et Clément V d'après les rôles gascons', in Renouard, *Études d'histoire médiévale*, ii (Paris, 1968), 935–57.
Rhodes, W.E., 'The inventory of the jewels and wardrobe of Queen Isabella (1307–8)', *EHR*, xii (1897), 517–21.
Richardson, A., ' "Hedging, ditching and other improper occupations": royal landscapes and their meaning under Edward II and Edward III', in *Fourteenth Century England*, iv, ed. J.S. Hamilton (Woodbridge, Suffolk & Rochester, NY, 2006), 26–42.
Richardson, H.G., 'The Parliament of Carlisle: some new documents', *EHR*, liii (1938), 425–37.
—— 'The English coronation oath', *TRHS*, 4th series, xxiii (1941), 129–58.
—— 'The *Annales Paulini*', *Speculum*, xxiii (1948), 630–40.
—— 'The English coronation oath', *Speculum*, xxiv (1949), 44–75.
—— 'The coronation in medieval England: the evolution of the office and the oath', *Traditio*, xvi (1960), 111–202.
Richardson, H. G. & Sayles, G. O., 'Early coronation records', *BIHR*, xiii (1936), 129–45; xiv (1936–7), 1–9, 145–8; xvi (1938–9), 1–11.
Rigg, A.G., 'Antiquaries and authors: the supposed work of Robert Baston, O. Carm.', in *Medieval Scribes, Manuscripts and Libraries: Essays presented to Neil Ker*, ed. M.B. Parkes & A.G. Watson (London, 1978), 317–31.
Robinson, C., 'Was Edward the Second a degenerate? A consideration of his reign from that point of view', *American Journal of Insanity*, lxvi (1909–10), 445–64.
Rouse, R.H. & Rouse, M.A., 'John of Salisbury and the doctrine of tyrannicide', *Speculum*, xlii (1967), 693–709.
Russell, J.C., 'The canonisation of opposition to the king in Angevin England', in *Haskins Anniversary Essays in Medieval History*, ed. C.H. Taylor (Boston & New York, 1929), 279–90.
Saaler, M., *Edward II, 1307–1327* (London, 1997).

St John Hope, W., 'On the funeral effigies of the kings and queens of England', *Archaelogia*, lx (1907), 517–50.
Salisbury, K., 'A political agreement of June 1318', *EHR*, xxxiii (1918), 81–3.
Sams, E., ed., *Shakespeare's Edward III* (New Haven & London, 1996).
Sandquist, T.A., 'The Holy Oil of St. Thomas of Canterbury', in *Essays in Medieval History presented to Bertie Wilkinson*, ed. T.A. Sandquist & M.R. Powicke (Toronto, 1969), 330–44.
Sandquist, T.A. & Powicke, M.R., eds, *Essays in Medieval History presented to Bertie Wilkinson* (Toronto, 1969).
Sangiuliani, A.C., *Dell'Abazia S.Alberto di Butrio* (Milan, 1865; 2nd edition, 1890).
—— *Cecima* (Milan, 1906).
Saul, N., *Knights and Esquires: The Gloucestershire Gentry in the Fourteenth Century* (Oxford, 1981).
—— 'The Despensers and the downfall of Edward II', *EHR*, xcix (1984), 1–33.
—— *Scenes from Provincial Life: Knightly Families in Sussex, 1280–1420* (Oxford, 1986).
—— 'Richard II and the vocabulary of kingship', *EHR*, cx (1995), 854–77.
—— *Richard II* (New Haven & London, 1997).
Sawyer, P.H., *Anglo-Saxon Charters* (London, 1968).
Sayles, G. O., 'The formal judgments on the traitors of 1322', *Speculum*, xvi (1941), 57–63.
—— 'The siege of Carrickfergus castle, 1315–16', *IHS*, x, no. 37 (1956–57), 94–100; repr. in Sayles, *Scripta Diversa* (London, 1982), 212–18.
Scammell, J., 'Robert I and the north of England', *EHR*, lxxiii (1958), 385–403.
Scattergood, V.J., 'Adam Davy's *Dreams* and Edward II', in *Archiv für das Studium der neueren Sprachen und Literaturen*, ccvi (Braunschweig, 1970), 253–60, repr. in Scattergood, *Reading the Past: Essays on Medieval and Renaissance Literature* (Dublin, 1996).
Schein, S., *'Fideles Crucis': The Papacy, the West and the Recovery of the Holy Land, 1274–1313* (Oxford, 1991).
Schulz, F., 'Bracton on kingship', *EHR*, lx (1945), 136–76.
Schwyzer, H., 'Northern bishops and the Anglo-Scottish war in the reign of Edward II', in *Thirteenth-century England*, vii, Proceedings of the Durham Conference, 1997, ed. M. Prestwich, R. Britnell & R. Frame (Woodbridge, Suffolk, 1999), 243–54.
Shenton, C., 'Edward III and the coup of 1330', in *The Age of Edward III*, ed. J.S. Bothwell, York Medieval Press (Woodbridge, Suffolk & Rochester, NY, 2001), 13–34.
—— *The Itinerary of Edward III and his Household, 1327–1345*, List and Index Society, cccxviii (Kew, 2007).
Shepherd, E.B.S., 'The church of the Friars Minor in London', *Arch. Journal*, lix (1902), 238–87.
Simpkin, D., 'The English army and the Scottish campaign of 1310–1311', in *England and Scotland in the Fourteenth Century: New Perspectives*, ed. A. King & M. Penman (Woodbridge, Suffolk & Rochester, NY, 2007), 14–39.
Smalley, B., *English Friars and Antiquity in the Early Fourteenth Century* (Oxford, 1960).
Smallwood, T., 'The lament of Edward II', *Modern Language Review*, lxviii (1973), 521–9.
Smith, B., 'Lordship in the British Isles, *c*.1320–*c*.1360', in *Power and Identity in the Middle Ages: Essays in Memory of Rees Davies*, ed. H. Pryce & J. Watts (Oxford, 2007), 153–63.
Smith, J.B., 'The rebellion of Llywelyn Bren', in *Glamorgan County History*, iii, *The Middle Ages*, ed. T.B. Pugh (Cardiff, 1971), 72–86.
—— 'Gruffydd Llwyd and the Celtic alliance, 1315–1318', *Bulletin of the Board of Celtic Studies*, xxvi, part 4 (May, 1974–6), 463–78.
—— 'Edward II and the allegiance of Wales', *Welsh History Review*, viii (1976–77), 139–71.
—— *Llywelyn ap Gruffudd, Prince of Wales* (Cardiff, 1998).
Smith, K., 'History, typology and homily: the Joseph Cycle in the Queen Mary Psalter', *Gesta*, xxxii (1993), 147–59.
Smyth, J., of Nibley, *The Lives of the Berkeleys*, ed. Sir John Maclean, 2 vols (Gloucester, 1883).
Society of Antiquaries of London: Annual Report: Proceedings 1997 (London, 1997).
Sparpaglione, D., FDP, *Una Gemma d'Oltrepo: S. Alberto di Butrio: Storia, Arte, Fede* (4th edition, Tortona, 1990).

Spencer, A.M., 'Royal patronage and the earls in the reign of Edward I', *History*, xciii, no. 309 (2008), 20–46.
Stanton, A. Rudloff, *The Queen Mary Psalter: A Study of Affect and Audience, Transactions of the American Philosophical Society*, xci, part 6 (Philadelphia, 2001).
Steane, J., *The Archaeology of the Medieval English Monarchy* (London, 1993).
Stenton, F.M., *Anglo-Saxon England* (Oxford, 1955).
Stevenson, W.H., 'A letter of the Younger Despenser on the eve of the barons' rebellion, 21 March 1321', *EHR*, xii (1897), 755–61.
Stones, E.L.G., 'The date of Roger Mortimer's escape from the Tower', *EHR*, xvi (1951), 97–8.
—— 'Sir Geoffrey le Scrope (c. 1285–1340), Chief Justice of the King's Bench', *EHR*, lxix (1954), 1–17.
—— 'The Folvilles of Ashby-Folville in Leicestershire, and their associates in crime', *TRHS*, 5th series, vii (1957), 117–36.
Stouck, M.-A., 'Saints and rebels: hagiography and opposition to the king in late fourteenth-century England', *Medievalia et Humanistica*, new series, xxiv (1997), 75–94.
Strayer, J.R., *Medieval Statecraft and the Perspectives of History* (Princeton, 1971).
—— *The Reign of Philip the Fair* (Princeton, 1980).
Strickland, M., 'A law of arms or a law of treason? Conduct of war in Edward I's campaigns in Scotland, 1296–1307', in *Violence in Medieval Society*, ed. Richard W. Kaeuper (Woodbridge, Suffolk & Rochester, NY, 2000), 39–77.
—— 'Treason, feud and the growth of state violence: Edward I and the "War of the Earl of Carrick, 1306–7",' in *War, Government and Aristocracy in the British Isles, c.1150–1500: Essays in Honour of Michael Prestwich*, ed. C. Given-Wilson, A. Kettle & L. Scales (Woodbridge, Suffolk & Rochester, NY, 2008), 84–113.
Strohm, P., 'The trouble with Richard: the reburial of Richard II and Lancastrian symbolic strategy', *Speculum*, lxxi (1996), 87–111.
Stubbs, W., *Constitutional History of England*, ii (Oxford, 1875).
—— ed., *Chronicles of the Reigns of Edward I and Edward II*, 2 vols, Rolls Series (London, 1882–3).
Sturdy, D., ' "Continuity" versus "change": historians and English coronations of the medieval and early modern periods', in *Coronations: Medieval and Early Modern Monarchic Ritual*, ed. J.M. Bak (Berkeley, 1990), 228–45.
Sturler, J. de, *Les Relations politiques et les échanges commerciaux entre le duché de Brabant et l'Angleterre au moyen âge* (Paris, 1936).
Sumption, J., *Trial by Battle: The Hundred Years War*, i (London, 1990).
Tanquerey, F.J., 'The conspiracy of Thomas Dunheved, 1327', *EHR*, xxxi (1916), 119–24.
Taylor, A.J., 'Royal alms and oblations in the late thirteenth century', in *Tribute to an Antiquary: Essays presented to Marc Fitch by some of his Friends*, ed. F. Emmison and R. Stephens (London, 1976), 93–125.
—— *Caernarfon Castle* (4th edn, Cardiff, 1997).
Taylor, J., 'The French prose *Brut*: popular history in fourteenth-century England', in *England in the Fourteenth Century: Proceedings of the 1985 Harlaxton Symposium*, ed. W.M. Ormrod (Woodbridge, 1986), 247–54.
—— *English Historical Literature in the Fourteenth Century* (Oxford, 1987).
Tebbit, A., 'Royal patronage and political allegiance: the household knights of Edward II, 1314–1321', in *Thirteenth Century England*, x, ed. M. Prestwich, R. Britnell & R. Frame (Woodbridge, Suffolk & Rochester, NY, 2005), 197–208.
—— 'Household knights and military service under the direction of Edward II', in *The Reign of Edward II: New Perspectives*, ed. G. Dodd & A. Musson (Woodbridge, Suffolk & Rochester, NY, 2006), 76–96.
Theilmann, J.M., 'Political canonization and political symbolism in medieval England', *Journal of British Studies*, xxix (1990), 241–66.
Thompson, C.J.S., 'Rules of health prescribed for an English queen in the fourteenth century', Wellcome Historical Medical Museum (London, 1921), 7 unnumbered pages.

Thomson, W.S., *A Lincolnshire Assize Roll for 1298*, Lincolnshire Record Society, xxxvi (Lincoln, 1944).
Tierney, B., *The Crisis of Church and State, 1050–1300* (New York, 1964; repr. Toronto, 1988).
Tomkinson, A., 'Retinues at the tournament of Dunstable', *EHR*, lxxiv (1959), 70–89.
Tout, T.F., *The Political History of England, 1216–1377* (London, 1905).
—— 'The Westminster chronicle attributed to Robert of Reading', *EHR*, xxxi (1916), 450–64.
—— 'The captivity and death of Edward of Caernarvon', in *Collected Papers of Thomas Frederick Tout*, iii (Manchester, 1933–34), 145–90.
—— *Chapters in the Administrative History of Mediaeval England*, ii, vi (Manchester, 1933, 1937).
—— *The Place of the Reign of Edward II in English History* (Manchester, 1914; 2nd edition, revised by H. Johnston, 1936).
Trabut-Cussac, J.P., *L'Administration anglaise en Gascogne sous Henry III et Edouard I de 1254 à 1307* (Paris & Geneva, 1972).
Trease, G.E., 'The spicers and apothecaries of the royal household in the reigns of Edward I and Edward II', *Nottingham Medieval Studies*, iii (1959), 19–52.
Tristram, E.W., *English Wall Painting of the Fourteenth Century* (London, 1955).
Trueman, J.H., 'The personnel of medieval reform: the English Lords Ordainers of 1310', *Mediaeval Studies*, xxi (1959), 247–71.
Tupling, G.H., *South Lancashire in the Reign of Edward II*, Chetham Soc., 3rd series, i (Manchester, 1949).
Turville-Petre, T., *Alliterative Poetry of the Later Middle Ages* (London, 1989).
—— *England the Nation: Language, Literature, and National Identity, 1290–1340* (Oxford, 1996).
Tyson, D., 'The *Siege of Caerlaverock*: a re-examination', *Nottingham Medieval Studies*, xlvi (2002), 45–69.
—— 'Lament for a dead king', *Journal of Medieval History*, xxx, no. 4 (December 2004), 359–75.
Ullmann, W., 'The curial exequies for Edward I and Edward III', *Ecclesiastical History Review*, vi (1955), 26–36.
—— 'Thomas Becket's miraculous oil', *Journal of Theological Studies*, new series, viii (1957), 129–33.
Underhill, F.A., *For her Good Estate: The Life of Elizabeth de Burgh* (Basingstoke, 1999).
Vale, M., *The Angevin Legacy and the Hundred Years War, 1250–1340* (Oxford, 1990).
—— *The Princely Court: Medieval Courts and Culture in North-West Europe* (Oxford, 2001).
Valente, C., 'The deposition and abdication of Edward II', *EHR*, cxiii (1998), 852–81.
—— 'The "Lament of Edward II": religious lyric, political propaganda', *Speculum*, lxxvii (2002), 422–39.
—— *The Theory and Practice of Revolt in Medieval England* (Aldershot, Hants., & Burlington, VT, 2003).
Verbruggen, J.F., *The Art of Warfare in Western Europe during the Middle Ages: from the Eighth Century to 1340* (Woodbridge, 1998).
—— *The Battle of the Golden Spurs (Courtrai, 11 July 1302)* (Woodbridge, Suffolk, 2002).
Verey, D. & Brooks, A., *Gloucestershire, ii, The Vale and the Forest of Dean; The Buildings of England* (London, 2002).
Vernon Harcourt, L.W., *His Grace the Steward and the Trial of Peers* (London, 1907).
Viard, J., 'Philippe de Valois avant son avènement au trône', Bibliothèque de l'École des Chartes, xci (1930), 307–25.
Victoria County History, Hertfordshire, iv, ed. W. Page (Oxford, 1971).
Victoria County History, Gloucestershire, x, ed. C.R. Elrington (Gloucester, 1972).
Violono, C., *Melazzo nella storia* (Melazzo, 1995).
Wagner, A.R., *Catalogue of English Medieval Rolls of Arms* (Oxford, 1950).
Walker, J.W., 'Robin Hood identified', *Yorkshire Archeological Journal*, xxxvi (1944).
Wathey, A. 'The marriage of Edward III and the transmission of French motets to England', *Journal of the American Musicological Society*, xlv (1992), 1–29.
Watson, G.W., 'Geoffrey de Mortemer and his descendants', *Genealogist*, new series, xxii (1906), 1–16.

Watt, J.A., '*Laudabiliter* in medieval diplomacy and propaganda', in *Irish Ecclesiastical Record*, 5th series., lxxxvii (January–June 1957), 420–32.
—— *The Church and the Two Nations in Medieval Ireland*, Cambridge Studies in Medieval Life and Thought, 3rd series, iii (Cambridge, 1970).
Waugh, S.L., 'The profits of violence: the minor gentry in the rebellion of 1321–22 in Gloucestershire and Herefordshire', *Speculum*, lii (1977), 843–69.
—— 'For king, country and patron: the Despensers and local administration, 1321–1322', *Journal of British Studies*, xxii (1983), 23–58.
Weiler, B., 'The *Commendatio Lamentabilis* for Edward I and Plantagenet kingship', in *War, Government and Aristocracy in the British Isles, c.1150–1500: Essays in Honour of Michael Prestwich*, ed. C. Given-Wilson, A. Kettle & L. Scales (Woodbridge, Suffolk & Rochester, NY, 2008), 114–30.
Welander, D., *The History, Art and Architecture of Gloucester Cathedral* (Stroud, 1991).
Wheatley, A., *The Idea of the Castle in Medieval England* (Woodbridge, Suffolk & Rochester, NY, 2007).
Wilkinson, B., 'The coronation oath of Edward II', in *Historical Essays in Honour of James Tait*, ed. J.G. Edwards, V.H. Galbraith & E.F. Jacob (Manchester, 1933), 405–16.
—— 'The deposition of Richard II and the accession of Henry IV', *EHR*, liv (1939), 215–39.
—— 'The coronation oath of Edward II and the Statute of York', *Speculum*, xix (1944), 445–69.
—— 'The Sherburn indenture and the attack on the Despensers, 1321', *EHR*, lxiii (1948), 1–28.
—— 'The negotiations preceding the "Treaty" of Leake, August 1318', in *Studies in Medieval History presented to Frederick Maurice Powicke*, ed. R.W. Hunt, W.A. Pantin & R.W. Southern (Oxford, 1948), 333–53.
—— *Constitutional History of Medieval England*, ii, *Politics and the Constitution, 1307–1399* (London, 1952).
—— *The Later Middle Ages: England, 1216–1485* (London, 1969).
Willard, J.F., *Parliamentary Taxes on Personal Property, 1290 to 1334* (Cambridge, Mass., 1934).
Willett, J. & Manheim, R., eds, *Bertolt Brecht: Collected Plays*, i (London, 1970).
Williams, B., 'The coronation oath of Edward I', in *Medieval Dublin*, ix, Proceedings of Friends of Medieval Dublin Symposium, 2007, ed. S. Duffy (Dublin, 2009), 84–90.
Williams, D.M., *Gower* (Cardiff, 1998).
Williams, G.A., *Medieval London: From Commune to Capital* (2nd edn, London, 1970).
Willis, D., 'Marlowe our contemporary: *Edward II* on stage and screen', *Criticism*, xl, no. 4 (Detroit, 1999), 599–622.
Wood, C.T., 'Queens, queans and kingship', in Wood, *Joan of Arc and Richard III: Sex, Saints and Government in the Middle Ages* (Oxford, 1988), 12–28.
—— 'Where is John the Posthumous? or Mahaut of Artois settles her Royal Debts', in *Documenting the Past: Essays in Medieval History presented to George Peddy Cuttino*, ed. J.S. Hamilton & P.J. Bradley (Woodbridge, Suffolk & Wolfeboro, NH, 1989), 99–117.
Wright, J.R., 'The supposed illiteracy of Archbishop Walter Reynolds', *Studies in Church History*, v (1969), 58–68.
—— *The Church and the English Crown, 1305–1334*, Studies and Texts, 48, Pontifical Institute of Mediaeval Studies (Toronto, 1980).

Unpublished dissertations

Clarke, R.D., 'Some secular activities of the English Dominicans during the reigns of Edward I, Edward II and Edward III, 1272–1377' (MA, London, 1930).
Doherty, P.C., 'Isabella, Queen of England, 1296–1330' (D.Phil., Oxford, 1977).
Echerd, A.R., Jr., 'Canonization and politics in late medieval England: the cult of Thomas of Lancaster' (Ph.D., University of North Carolina, Chapel Hill, 1983).

Taylor, A.A., 'The career of Peter of Gaveston' (MA, London, 1939).
Tebbit, A., 'The household knights of Edward II, 1307–1326' (Ph.D., Bristol, 2006).
Ward, J.C., 'The estates of the Clare Family, 1066–1317' (Ph.D., London, 1962).

Online Sources

Grove Dictionary of Art.
JSTOR
Oxford Dictionary of National Biography: references to individual articles are given in the footnotes.
Parliament Rolls of Medieval England (PROME), 1275–1504.
(See also Printed Sources)

INDEX

Abernethy, Alexander de 95, 168
Acton, Ralph 19
Adam (illegitimate son of Edward II) 82, 102, 428–9
Adam of Usk 25 n.89
administration, royal
    abuses 138
    at accession of Edward II 129, 138
    and household of Edward of Caernarfon 47–50
    and Ordinances 177–80
    reforms 243, 258, 265, 293, 443–4, 607–8; and Ordinances of 1311 177–80, 239–40; pressures for 49, 68, 138–9, 141–3, 155–7, 158–60, 191, 610; reform commission 267–8, 275
Adrian IV, Pope (1154–9), *Laudabiliter* 257, 263 n.160
Agenais
    and Charles IV 464, 470, 473, 475, 479–80, 483, 487
    as dower for Isabella 134
    held by Edward II 109, 462, 464
Airmyn, William
    and Anglo-French peace negotiations 472–3, 474, 476, 480
    and battle of Myton 348
    as bishop of Norwich 480, 492, 520–1
    and coronation of Edward III 539
    and Guildhall oath 532
    as keeper of the Great Seal 515
    and *Modus Tenendi Parliamentum* 395–6 n.417
    and Scottish War 352, 372
Albret, Amanieu d' 180 n.296, 208 n.94, 212, 455, 464 n.66
Alexander III of Scotland 41
Alexander of Argyll 168
Alfonso X 'the Wise' of Castile 39, 57, 60, 109–10 n.188
Alfonso XI of Castile 120, 466 n.76, 493

Alfonso (3rd son of Edward I) 35, 39–40, 42, 84 n.31
allegiance, double 445–6
Amesbury, convent 41, 42, 43–4, 50, 52, 64, 192
Amy/Amie de Gaveston (illegitimate daughter of Gaveston) 101–2, 192
Anglo-French War (1294) 5–6, 77–9, 80–1, 91, 465
Anglo-French War (1324–5) 18, 252 n.93, 420, 461–79, 560
    cost 420, 465
    and Despenser the Younger 443
    French gains 494
    and Isabella 471–4, 475, 476, 483
    peace negotiations 468–71, 474–5, 479, 484, 495–6
    truce 466, 469–70, 472, 474
Angus, Robert de Umfraville, earl
    at Bannockburn 234, 237
    and Despensers 379–80
    loyalty to Edward II 168, 169, 171, 237, 313 n.183
Annales Londonienses 8 n.15, 164–5, 181 n.30
    and Bannockburn 234
    and execution of Gaveston 191 n.375
    and negotiations for treaty 198 n.43
    and opposition magnates 244
    and pursuit and capture of Gaveston 185–6, 188 n.357
Annales Paulini 8 n.15
    and coronation of Edward II 144, 146 n.112
    and death of Edward II 561
    and divorce of Edward and Isabella 483 n.169
    and funeral of Edward II 554 n.194
    and Gaveston 97 n.118, 100–1, 127, 135–6, 141, 146, 181
    and Guildhall oath 531 n.60
    and imprisonment of Edward II 543 n.131, 545
    and marriage of Edward II 145 n.110

Annales Paulini (cont.)
    and Northampton meeting with
        magnates 151
    and Westminster parliament
        (April 1308) 148
Annals of Dunstable 49
Annals of Osney 602
Anonimalle Chronicle
    and articles of deposition 529 n.49
    and death of Edward II 561
    and Despenser the Younger 368
    and Mortimer of Wigmore 440 n.198
    and plots to rescue Edward II 542
        n.124, 545
    and Scottish War 345, 347
    and trial of Thomas of Lancaster 411
Apocalypse 211–12, Pl. 11
Aquitaine, duchy
    appeals from 208–9, 222, 247
    and Edward III 476, 478–9
    English control 6, 10, 86, 108, 455
    and Gaveston's second exile 150
    homage for: to Charles IV 456,
        462–3, 468–70, 472, 474–9; to
        Louis X 248; to Philip IV 91, 103,
        110, 134, 138, 359; to Philip V 61,
        134 n.57, 354–5, 356, 359–60, 455
    loans secured against 218, 284, 287
    and Louis X 247, 248
    and marriage of Edward II and
        Isabella 116–18, 132, 146, 202, 208
    and Philip IV 77–8, 117–18, 141 n.95,
        146, 222
    and Philip V 61, 118, 134 n.57, 354,
        356, 358–9
    see also Agenais; Edward III; Gascony
Arcy, John D' *see* Darcy
Ardscull, battle (1316) 225, 232–3, 256,
    261, 272
Argentein, Giles d' 225, 232–3
Argyll and Lorn, John MacDougall, lord
    of 259
armour and equipment 92–3
army, Anglo-Irish 256, 257–8
army, English
    against Isabella and Mortimer 502–3,
        504, 505
    against Marcher rebels 402
        n.457, 406
    for Anglo-French War 467–8
    at Bannockburn 226–37, 251
    infantry and cavalry 235–6, 344
    size 226–9, 251, 344–5, 425–6, 427–8,
        467–8

    and supplies 425–7
    see also Scottish War
army of Isabella and Mortimer 501–2, 522
Arthur, king 6–7, 34–5, 41, 111 n.199
Articuli cleri (1316) 269
Articuli super Cartas (1300) 156–7, 159, 162,
    195 n.28, 423
Artois, Robert d', and Isabella 499–500
Arundel, Edmund Fitz Alan, earl
    armed retainers 182, 344
    arrest and execution 516, 581 n.25
    and civil war 400, 407, 417
    and Despensers 374, 377, 393, 400,
        417 n.52
    and Edward II: coronation 145;
        negotiations with 199; and royal
        pardon 216; and standing royal
        council 320; support for 166, 245,
        246, 397, 417, 591
    and Gaveston 127, 154, 162, 184;
        pursuit and capture 185, 190
    and John Hastings 361
    as justice of Wales 417
    knighting 112
    and London revolt (1326) 507
    and Mortimer of Wigmore 460 n.34
    and opposition magnates 387
    as Ordainer 166, 176
    and papal authority 160
    and parliament of July 1309 158
    and reform commission 267
    and Scottish War 227, 294 n.80, 344
    and Thomas of Lancaster 318,
        319, 407
    as warden of Scottish March 283, 306
Arundel, Richard Fitz Alan, earl 88
Ashridge, Walter de (Dominican friar) 241
Assier, Rigaud d', as bishop of Winchester
    360 nn.202, 205, 449–50
Atholl, David de Strathbogie, earl
    and Isabella 430
    loyalty to Edward II 237, 401
        n.454, 407
Audley, Hugh the Elder
    and Despenser the Younger 375, 377
        n.308, 379 n.323
    and Scottish campaigns 169
    surrender and imprisonment 404,
        413, 438
    and Thomas of Lancaster 265
    and Welsh revolt 272–3
Audley, Hugh the Younger
    and change of allegiance 338,
        405, 415

INDEX 645

claim to earldom of Cornwall 335,
    338, 366 n.236, 609 n.609
contract with Edward II 306
and Despensers 308, 364, 365, 367–8,
    377, 378, 379 n.323, 386–7, 392,
    397, 400
and Gloucester inheritance 308
    n.160, 335, 365
imprisonment 412
marriage to Margaret de Clare 17,
    296, 335, 338, 412, 418
as royal favourite 98, 294–5, 331, 334
and Scottish War 344
and Thomas of Lancaster 301, 315,
    319, 331
Aumale, count of 289, 290 n.59
Aune, William de, constable of Tickhill
    castle 373, 374 n.285, 399 n.439, 405
Aux, Arnaud d', bishop of Poitiers 152, 153,
    160 n.181, 194–5, 197, 200, 201, 205, 208
Ayleston, Robert de, keeper of the privy
    seal 442
Aylmer, William 542, 544–5, 569 n.288

Bacon, Edmund 265
Badlesmere, Bartholomew de
    and citizens of Bristol 245, 269,
        273–4, 295
    and civil war 403, 408, 414–15
    as constable of Dover 360, 385
    and Damory 303–5
    and defence of the north 249, 251, 352
    and Despensers 308, 385, 388–9, 391,
        393, 397–8
    and desertion of Edward II 385–6,
        388–9
    embassies to John XXII 284, 286,
        289–90, 294, 359–60
    execution 411
    and Gaveston 242
    and hostility of Edward II 379, 403
    indenture to Edward II 305–6, 415
    and king's council 284 n.24, 292
    and Leeds castle 302, 382, 397–9
    and opposition magnates 385–6, 388
    and Ordainers 166
    and reform commission 267
    and reform of royal household 330
    and Scottish War 18, 90, 169, 238, 298,
        344; and peace negotiations 371–2
    and standing royal council 330, 333,
        336–7
    as steward of royal household 331,
        333, 335, 339, 353–4, 381, 385, 391
    and support for Edward II 307
    and Thomas of Lancaster 281 n.8,
        292, 310, 317–18, 319, 339, 385,
        398, 403, 414
    and truce discussions 352
    visit to France (1320) 355
Badlesmere, Giles de 413
Baldock, Ralph, bishop of London and
    chancellor 125–6, 129 n.27
Baldock, Robert
    capture 515, 516
    as chancellor 442, 454 n.282
    and Despensers 373–4, 384 n.351,
        401, 445, 447, 449
    and possible divorce of Edward II
        and Isabella 483 n.169
    and Edward's flight from London 505
    and Isabella 509
    as keeper of the privy seal 353, 436
    and London revolt (1326) 507
    and Mortimer of Wigmore 460
    rewards for support of Edward II 417
    and Scottish peace negotiations 285,
        352, 372, 373, 434
    and see of Coventry & Lichfield 449
    and see of Norwich 480
    and see of Winchester 449–50
Balliol, Edward 51–2, 79, 112 n.203, 459
Balliol, John, king of Scots 52, 79, 457
Bamburgh castle, Gaveston in 171
Banaster, Adam 250, 265
Bannockburn, battle (June 1314) 18, 170,
    219, 228–37, 419, Pl. 12
    aftermath 238–40, 243, 277
    and chronicles 7
    courage of Edward II 11, 229
    English losses 234–5
    English prisoners 239–40, 249
    escape of Edward II 232–4, 322
    loss of privy seal 233, 234, 237
    and siege of Stirling 223, 228–9
    size of English army 226–9, 251
    terrain 229–31
Bar see Edward, count of Bar; Henry,
    count of Bar; Joan de Bar
Barbour, John, archdeacon of Aberdeen
    83, 114, 225, 232 n.244, 234, 346,
    349–50
Bardi (Florentine bankers) 286, 302–3,
    340, 343, 361, 414 n.31, 419, 506
Barnes, Joshua, *The History of Edward III*
    27–8
Barrow, Geoffrey 128, 229 nn.221,225, 231,
    432, 433 n.158, 451 n.269, 550 n.172

Basset, Ralph
  and Anglo-French war 473, 475
  and Mortimer 460–1
  as seneschal of Gascony 462, 466, 469, 478 n.139
  and Thomas of Lancaster 319
Baston, Robert (poet) 18–19, 235 n.264
Bataille, Thomas de la (mason) 441–2
Bath & Wells, bishop of *see* Droxford
Bayouse, Bogo de 572, 576
Beaucaire, William de 552, 554
Beauchamp, Giles de 306 n.152
Beauchamp, Guy de *see* Warwick, Guy de Beauchamp, earl
Beauchamp, John de 415
Beauchamp, Walter de 52, 64, 415
Beaumont, Henry de 183 n.318, 195, 210, 492
  and Anglo-French War 468, 479
  and attack on Despensers 374
  and coronation of Edward III 540
  and dismissal from council 435–6
  and Gaveston 242
  and Isabella 203, 436, 492, 501, 513, 517
  mission to France (1314) 221–2
  and opposition to Mortimer 569
  and Ordinances 179 n.291, 193, 200, 215–16, 240
  and plot to free Edward II 566
  and royal patronage 307
  and Scottish War 169, 230, 238, 569; defence of the north 251, 428, 430; peace negotiations 435–6
  and see of Durham 282, 299
  and Thomas of Lancaster 300
  and York parliament (1314) 239 n.5
Beaumont, Jean de 500, 501, 503, 522–3
  and knighting of Edward III 539
Beaumont, Louis de, as bishop of Durham 281–2, 299–300, 428, 436, 449
Becket, Thomas *see* Thomas of Canterbury, St
Bek, Anthony, bishop of Durham and patriarch of Jerusalem 51, 74, 107
  and accession of Edward II 126
  death 174
  and funeral of Edward I 131
  and Gaveston 122 n.256
  and marriage of Edward II 133, 134
Bek, John de 378, 381–2, 389
Belers, Sir Roger 334, 444–6, 492
Benedetti, Anna 587–8
Bereford, Edmund 574 n.315
Bereford, Richard, as chancellor of Ireland 260

Bereford, Simon de 572, 591
Bereford, William de 151 n.140, 310
Berenger, Ingelram 270, 445 n.239, 566, 567–8
Berkeley castle (Glos.) Pl. 16
  confiscation by Edward II 404
  and death of Edward II 3, 14, 547–9, 550, 552, 553, 560–5
  imprisonment of Edward II 37, 65, 90, 439, 541, 542–3, 547, 582
  release attempts 483 n.169, 543–4, 547–8, 565–6, 591
  taken by Isabella 512 n.350
Berkeley, Maurice de
  and Bristol revolt 274
  and civil war 414–15
  and defence of Berwick 250, 252
  and Despenser the Younger 377 n.308, 379 n.323
  and Maltravers 574 n.315
  and Mortimer 572–3
  and Pembroke 361–2
  and Scottish War 90, 226, 235 n.263
  as seneschal of Gascony 355 n.177
  surrender and imprisonment 404, 413, 438–40
Berkeley, Maurice the Younger 361
Berkeley, Thomas
  and death of Edward II 548, 563, 577, 578–81
  exoneration 572–3, 574, 576
  and imprisonment of Edward II 541, 543–4
  and Isabella 512 n.350
  and Mortimer 361, 440 n.197, 563
Bermingham, John de 257–8, 342
  as earl of Louth 417 n.51
Bermingham, Peter de 90
Bermingham, Walter de 116 n.222, 174 n.259
Berwick
  army muster at (1314) 223, 226, 228–9
  Edward II's escape to 233–4, 238
  English siege (1319) 283 n.18, 345–6, 350–1, 364, 419
  Isabella at 223, 233–4
  Scots attacks on 252, 272, 274, 313, 321, 328
  Scots siege (1318) 249–50, 329, 335, 342
  strategic importance 248, 250
Berwick, John de 51, 52
Berwick castle, English control 224, 328
Béthune, Richard de 441, 490–1 n.214, 507

Bever, John *see* John of London
Bicknor, Alexander
    and Anglo-French War 464, 477
    as archbishop of Dublin 264, 286
        n.35, 287, 308, 311–12, 315
    and Edward III 532
    and Isabella 504, 512
    loyalty to Edward II 448, 511
    mission to France (1324) 462–3
    and Thomas of Lancaster 297, 313,
        316–18, 319
Binski, Paul 145 n.115
Binstead, John 95, 194 n.19, 251, 285, 313 n.183
Bintley, David, *Edward II* (ballet) 31, Pl. 9
Bishop, William 14 n.39
bishops
    and deposition of Edward II 525–9,
        532–6, 538
    and Edward III 537
    Edward II's enmity towards 450–1,
        452–4
    and Gaveston 185, 188
    and Isabella 487, 504, 506, 512
    and king's council 318, 320
    and opposition to Despensers 386–8,
        396–7, 401
    and Ordainers 166–7, 176
    petition to Edward II 164–5
    and standing royal council 320, 330,
        333, 336–7, 392
    support for Edward II 159, 396–7,
        448–9, 536
    and Thomas of Lancaster 297–8,
        308–12, 313, 315, 317–19, 362,
        372 n.270
Blackfriars priory 193–4
Blackhow Moor, battle (1322) 430, 431, 517
Blackley, F.D. 429 n.127, 489, 490
Blacklow Hill (Warwick), and execution of Gaveston 190–1
Bloch, Marc 61 n.171, 71
Blount, Thomas, as steward of the household 535
Blount, Sir William 515
Blunsdon, Henry (king's almoner) 106
Blyborough, William (royal administrator) 48, 79 n.13, 80, 126
Bohun, Edward de 514
Bohun, Henry de, at Bannockburn 230
Bohun, Humphrey de *see* Hereford, Humphrey de Bohun, earl
Bohun, John de *see* Hereford, John de Bohun, earl

Bonaventure, John 15, 277
Boniface VIII, Pope 2, 81 n.19, 105 n.160
Boroughbridge, battle (1322) 383 n.347,
    406, 408, 411 n.11, 416, 517
    and death of Hereford 408, 411 n.11,
        517, 564 n.260
    tactics 236 n.268
Botetourt, John
    contract to serve Edward II 306 n.152
    and English fleet 260 n.139
    and French and papal mediators 197,
        200, 206–7
    and Gaveston 186, 189–90
    and Isabella and Mortimer 501
    negotiations with Robert Bruce 240
    and Ordainers 166, 173
    and royal pardon 216
    and standing royal council 330, 337
    and Thomas of Lancaster 319
Bothwell castle 90, 234
Boucher, Jean 25
Boulogne Declaration (1308) 138–9, 142, 164
Bourchier, John 534
Bower, Walter, *Scotichronicon* 16, 18,
    235 n.264, Pl. 12
Brabant, John de *see* John II, duke of
Bradeston, Thomas de 573
Braose, William de 105 n.161, 366, 446
Brechin castle, siege (1303) 93–4
Brecht, Bertolt 30
Bren, Llywelyn 272–3, 294, 369 n.252, 393 n.398, 515
Bristol
    dispute with Badlesmere 245, 269,
        273–4, 280, 295
    and Isabella 512–13
brotherhood 100–3, 123, 126, 146, 149, 609
Brotherton, Thomas of (half-brother of Edward II) *see* Thomas of Brotherton, earl of Norfolk
Brittany, John of *see* Richmond, John of Brittany, earl
Bruce, Alexander (brother of Robert Bruce) 113
Bruce, David (son of Robert Bruce) 571–2
Bruce, Edward (brother of Robert Bruce)
    death 258, 329
    excommunication 287
    invasion of Ireland 21 n.74, 253–8,
        262, 264, 328
    negotiations with Edward II 240
    raids into England 224
    and Stirling castle 223
    and Wales 254 n.116, 256, 262, 271, 273

Bruce, Elizabeth (wife of Robert Bruce) 185 n.335, 237, 240
Bruce, Mary (sister of Robert Bruce) 115, 237
Bruce, Neil (brother of Robert Bruce) 113
Bruce, Robert, king of Scots 21, 109, 111–12, 113–15, 164
    defeat at Methven (1306) 113–14, 229
    defeats of English 123, 151
    and Edward II 170, 185, 193, 225, 228, 240, 369–73, 511 n.345
    excommunication 262, 287, 342, 370–1, 451
    and France 160, 167, 458–9
    and Gaveston 170, 185, 187
    and Hereford 406
    in Ireland 257, 260 n.139, 285 n.32, 329, 546
    and papal envoys 263, 299
    and pope 262–3, 369–71, 451
    peace negotiations 432–5, 458, 549–50
    raids into England 224, 226, 237, 248, 250–1, 254, 281, 283, 287, 330, 346–79, 405, 426, 429–30, 546–7, 549
    safe conduct offered to 275
    successes 167, 169 n.225, 170–1
    tactics 236
    and Thomas of Lancaster 283, 351, 406
    truce negotiations 285, 327–8, 352–3, 370
    see also Bannockburn
Bruce, Thomas (brother of Robert Bruce) 113
Brut chronicle 11–12, 14 n.39, 72, 126, 412, 421, 522 n.16, 533, 536
    and attempts to free Edward II 566
    and death of Edward II 547 n.153, 560, 561, 562–3, 575 nn.320, 322
    and Edward III 540
    and rumours of Edward's survival 570
Brut, William 604–5
Bullock-Davies, Constance 75 n.257
Burgh, John de 269–70
Burghersh, Henry de, bishop of Lincoln 357, 360, 401, 449, 453, 505 n.306, 539
    and coronation of Edward III 539
    and deputation to Kenilworth 534
    and Guildhall oath 532
    and Isabella 504, 512
Burton, Richard de 285, 291, 354
Burton, Thomas, chronicle of Meaux Abbey 10 n.22, 24

Butler, Edmund, justiciar of Ireland 257, 260, 261 n.145
Byland, battle (1322) 203 n.66

Caerlaverock, siege (1300) 83–4
Caernarfon castle
    and birth of Edward II 33–4, 87
    Eagle Tower 33, 36 n.19, Pl. 1
    significance 35–6
Caerphilly castle 69, 272, 364
    construction at 441–2
    and flight of Edward II 512, 514–15
    and possessions of Edward II 511–12 n.347, 514 n.358, 541
    siege 503, 514, 516
Caillau, Arnaud 182
Caillau, Bertrand (nephew of Gaveston) 152, 153, 180 n.298, 182
Cambridge university 62–3
Canterbury, archbishop of *see* Reynolds; Winchelsey
Canterbury, Henry de 187 n.350, 247, 355 n.177
Canterbury chronicler 97 n.114, 533, 536, 537 n.102, 561
Cantilupe, Thomas, bishop of Hereford 70 n.215, 341 n.69, 557
Carlisle
    army muster at (1308) 151, 154 n.151
    castle 186
    Scots siege (1315) 250, 251
    strategic importance 248, 253
Carlisle, bishop of *see* Halton; Ross
Carlisle, earl of *see* Harclay, Andrew
Carrickfergus castle, siege (1315) 254–5, 256
Cary, Elizabeth, *The History of the Most unfortunate Prince King Edward II* 27
Castile, Edward II as possible heir to 119–20
Castre, John de 252
Caumont, Alexandre de 340 n.61, 354, 455
cavalry, and infantry 235–6
Cecima, abbey of S. Alberto di Butrio 30, 586–8, Pls 20 and 21
    castle (Lombardy) 582–3, 586–9, 592–3
Chaplais, Pierre 15 n.48, 127, 137, 155 n.157, 183, 187 n.351, 241 n.21, 594 n.80
    and brotherhood 100, 609
chapter of Myton (1319) 346, 347–9, 431
Charles I of England 26
Charles IV of France 145, 431 n.143
    and Agenais 464, 470, 473, 475, 479, 480, 483, 487

and Anglo-French War 462–71,
    472–3, 474–5
and Aquitaine 457, 476, 478–9
and Burghersh 449
death 498
and Isabella 472, 479–81, 484, 485,
    488, 494, 499
and Mortimer 460
and threat of invasion of England 493
Charles of Valois (brother of Philip IV)
    456–7, 464, 466
    and Anglo-French War 456, 464, 466
    and coronation of Edward II 141
        n.95, 145
    and future Edward III 494
    and Isabella 485, 498
    knighting 210
    and marriage of Edward II 134
Charlton, John
    as chamberlain 205, 216, 281, 319 n.215
    and Gruffudd de la Pole 161, 205,
        216, 246 n.56, 269, 281
    and lordship of Powys 161, 246
        n.56, 269
    and Thomas of Lancaster 216,
        281, 315
Charlton, Thomas
    and see of Durham 281–2
    and see of Hereford 271 n.191, 287
Chastilloun, Hugh 429
Chaworth Roll 22 n.80, Pl. 8
Chester castle 70, 73, 271–2 n.194
Chichester, bishop of *see* Langton, John
Chigwell, Hamo de, mayor of London
    355, 399, 439–40, 506, 508
Childs, Wendy 12–13 n.32, 120 n.248
Chronicon de Lanercost see Lanercost chronicle
Church
    and clerical taxation 78, 130, 153, 218,
        219, 243, 249, 252–3, 268–9, 284,
        286, 332, 343, 420, 424, 432, 496
    and crown 268–9
    and Edward II 448–52, 477, 504,
        509, 527
    and Ordainers 172
civil war, danger of 101, 147–51, 152 n.141,
    182, 184, 192–3, 209, 297
    and Thomas of Lancaster 301–3,
        305–8
    and Edward I 46, 80
civil war (1321–2) 29, 37, 46, 97, 115
    n.219
    campaign against Marcher lords 402–4
    and defeat of Lancaster 406–8

execution of enemies 115 n.219, 398,
    408–9, 410–12
and household knights 296 n.99, 402
    n.457, 415
looting and civil unrest 437
and recall of Despensers 400–1, 406
and royal finances 414, 419–22
settlement 412–16
and spoils of victory 416–19
and Thomas of Lancaster 283,
    399–400, 405–9, 414
Clanchy, Michael 58 n.151, 59
Clare, Eleanor de (wife of Hugh Despenser
    the Younger) 98, 112, 242, 431
    and Edward II 363 n.222, 368
    and Gloucester inheritance 269–70,
        295, 363
    and Isabella 483, 505
    and Mortimer 490
    as possible mistress of Edward II
        483 n.169
Clare, Elizabeth de 63, 256 n.120
    and Gloucester inheritance
        269–70, 295
    and lordships of Usk and Caerleon
        446–7
    marriage to Roger Damory 17, 296
    marriage to Theobald de Verdun 271
Clare, Gilbert de *see* Gloucester, Gilbert
    de Clare, earl (d. 1295); Gloucester
    Gilbert de Clare, earl (d. 1314)
Clare, Gilbert, lord of Thomond (Ireland)
    89, 99 n.131, 107
Clare, Isabel de (half-sister of earl of
    Gloucester) 361 n.210
Clare, Margaret de
    birth of daughter 183, 203
    and death of Gaveston 192, 201
    and Edward II 192, 295
    and Gloucester inheritance
        269–70, 295
    marriage to Gaveston 17, 101, 128,
        161 n.187, 182, 269
    marriage to Hugh Audley the
        Younger 296, 335, 338, 412, 418
Clarendon council (1317) 290–1, 294–5, 327
Clarke, M.V. 534 n.76
Clavering, John de 249, 334, 372, 374
    n.286, 416
Clemence of Hungary (widow of Louis X)
    485, 489 n.201
Clement V, pope (1305–14)
    coronation 108–9, 145 n.112
    and crusades 263 n.153

Clement V (*cont.*)
    and Edward I 131, 141 n.98
    and Gaveston 152, 153, 154–5, 156–8, 180, 188–9, 241
    loan to Edward II 218–19, 252, 284–5, 287, 303
    and marriage of Edward II and Isabella 116–19
    and Ordinances 180, 194–5, 198, 200
    and see of Canterbury 130 n.32, 214
    and university of Dublin 62
Clermont, Louis de 134, 208–9, 341 n.64, 479
Cliff, William de 566, 568
Cliff, William de, O.P., 571 n.297
Clifford, Robert de 126, 138, 142, 417
    and Bannockburn 226, 229, 234, 237
    and Boulogne Declaration 138, 142
    death 249
    as marshal 142–3, 143 n.104
    and Gaveston 185, 187
    and marriage of Edward II 135
    and negotiations for treaty with Edward II 197, 198 n.41, 200, 205–7
    and Ordainers 166
    and Robert Bruce 170
    and royal pardon 216
    widow 265 n.166
Clifford, Roger de
    and Despenser the Younger 367, 377 n.308, 379 n.323
    execution 410
    and Thomas of Lancaster 408
Clipstone palace 247, 264 n.164, 265, 272, 279
Cobban, Alan 63 n.180
Cobham, Thomas 187 n.350, 209, 214, 278 n.228, 286 n.35
    as bishop of Worcester 287, 320, 358, 608
    and standing royal council 337
Commendatio Lamentabilis 5, 131 n.40, 415
Comyn, Alice (wife of Henry de Beaumont) 435
Comyn, Elizabeth 448
Comyn, John (the elder), of Badenoch 95, 109, 111, 262
Comyn, John (the younger), death at Bannockburn 112 n.203, 234
Conisborough castle, seized by Thomas of Lancaster 302
constable of England 88, 110, 228, 230, 381–3
constables of royal castles 156, 159

constitutionalism
    and City of London 343
    and historians 29–30, 612–13
    and magnates 29–30, 423
Continuatio Chronicarum 8 n.15
contrariants 401
    campaign against 402–8
Corbeil Treaty (1326) 459
Corfe castle
    and death of Edward II 547 n.153, 560
    and supposed survival of Edward II 565 n.265, 566–8, 572, 577, 582
Cornwall
    earldom *see* Edmund, earl of Cornwall; Gaveston, Piers; John of Eltham
    Isabella's lands in 482
Coronation Order (1308) 142, 143 n.104
coronation Pl. 7
    oath 54–6, 69, 141–3, 148–9, 198, 389 n.387, 527, 539, 607
    and sacred character of monarchy 71, 143
Cotton, Bartholomew 78 n.6
Council of Northampton (1308) 143 n.104
council, standing 318, 320, 330, 333, 336–7, 349–50, 392, 424
Courtenay, Hugh de 268, 320
    and deputation to Kenilworth 533–4
    as Ordainer 166, 182
Courtrai, battle (1302) 235–6
Coventry & Lichfield, bishop of *see* Langton, Walter; Northburgh
Crabbe, John (pirate) 345 n.97, 371 n.262
Craddock, William (minstrel) 210
Cromwell, John 479
    as constable of Tower of London 196, 394 n.407
    contract to serve Edward II 306 n.152
    and Isabella 492, 501, 503
    and Ordainers 166–7
    and Scottish campaigns 169, 344
    as steward of the household 239, 293 n.79
crusades
    and Edward I 4, 51 n.110, 108, 131
    financing 219
    in prophetic writings 21
    taking of the cross by Edward II 21 n.76, 51 n.110, 210–13, 219, Pl. 11; release from crusading oath 284–6

customs
    of 1303 156, 159, 177
    and financing of royal household
        172, 177–8, 253, 275, 420
Cuttino, George and Lyman, Thomas P.
    585, 588, 594 n.80, 613

Dafydd ap Gruffudd 34
Dalderby, John, bishop of Lincoln
    and coronation of Edward II 131
    and reform 166
Damory, Richard 413–14, 439 n.188
Damory, Roger
    and civil war 400, 405, 407, 415
    contract with Edward II 306, 375
    death 411 n.11
    and Despenser the Younger 365–6,
        367, 375, 377, 378, 379 n.323, 386,
        392, 397, 417, 446, 597
    and Gloucester inheritance 296, 364,
        365, 368, 418
    marriage to Elizabeth de Clare 17, 296
    as royal favourite 98, 294–5, 297,
        303–5, 331, 334, 349, 360
    and Scottish War 344
    and Thomas of Lancaster 301–2,
        313, 315, 318–19, 331, 349, 378
    visit to France (1320) 356
Dante Alighieri, *Divine Comedy* 2, 3
Darcy, John 371 n.267, 511, 546, 573
Darel, Edmund 205, 347, 350, 415
Davies, J.C. 29, 244 n.43, 296 n.100,
    303–4, 305 n.142, 335 n.37, 380, 443
Davies, Rees 255, 271
Davy, Adam, *Five Dreams of Edward II*
    20–1, 602
De la Beche, Robert 291
De la Pole, Gruffudd
    and Charlton 161, 205, 206, 216, 246
        n.56, 269, 281
    and Lestrange 200, 205, 216
De la Zouche, William 306 n.152, 513,
    515, 566–7
De l'Isle, Jourdain 339–40, 354, 455, 456
De Vere, Hugh 51, 166, 247 n.63
Declaration of Arbroath (1320) 369–71
Dene, William de 292–3
    and *Historia Roffensis* 388, 497
        n.257
Denholm-Young, N. 12–13 n.32
Denton, Jeffrey 160–1 n.183
deposition of Edward II 3–4, 9, 522–49,
    552–3
    accusations 19
    articles of 15, 72, 98 n.120, 523 n.19,
        524, 527, 529–31
    and deputation to Kenilworth 533–6
    early threat of 165, 387
    legality 71, 522, 536–9
    and parliament of Jan. 1327 29,
        524–9, 538–9
Despenser, Hugh the Elder 108, 147,
    288 n.52
    and Anglo-French War (1324–5) 477–8
    charges against 389–93, 395,
        509–10, 540
    and coronation of Edward II 145
    Despenser regime 441–8
    as earl of Winchester 417, 437, 438, 442
    execution 513
    exile 362, 386–8, 389, 393–4, 412,
        513; and recall 400–1, 406
    in France (1313) 210
    and French marriage negotiations 117
    and Gaveston 160, 193, 242
    as godfather of future Edward III 201
    and king's council 292, 294, 363–4
    and Le Ewer 437–8
    and marriage of Edward II 135
    and negotiations with opposition
        magnates 197, 200, 206
    and Northampton meeting
        (Aug. 1308) 151
    and Ordinances 176, 240
    and parliament of Jan. 1315 143
    and parliament of Sept. 1313 215
    political influence 362, 363, 367–8
    rebellion against 308
    and reform commission 267 n.177
    and royal patronage 307, 417
    and Scottish campaigns 94, 226,
        238, 344
    seen as second king 441
    surrender to Isabella 512
    and Thomas of Lancaster 294, 310,
        313, 315, 319–20, 334, 336, 364,
        367, 378–80, 396, 513
    and threat of civil war 196
    treason accusations 388–93, 513
    unpopularity 217 n.151
    visit to France (1320) 355
Despenser, Hugh the Younger 9, 14, 68
    ambition 242, 270, 276, 294, 351,
        367–8, 391, 610
    and Anglo-French War 443
    armed retainers 445–6, 567–8
    attack on John de Roos 271, 364
    and Audley the Younger 364–5

Despenser, Hugh the Younger (*cont.*)
  capture 515
  as chamberlain of royal household 137, 264, 319 n.215, 331, 333, 336, 353–4, 391–2, 442
  charges against 389–93, 395, 399, 477, 540; tyranny 442, 509, 517, 530
  as constable of Bristol 360
  contract to serve Edward II 306, 364 n.226
  and Damory 365–6, 367, 375, 377, 378, 379 n.323, 386, 392, 597
  Despenser regime 441–8
  execution 98, 516–18, Pl. 13
  exile 362, 386–8, 389, 393–5, 412; and recall 400–1, 406
  and exploitation of double allegiances 445–6
  flight to Wales (1326) 58, 69, 187, 510
  in France (1320) 356
  in France (1321) 384
  and Gascony 443, 465–6
  and Gloucester inheritance 269–70, 295–6, 363–6, 390, 417
  hostility of magnates towards 366–75, 386–93, 394–6
  and Isabella 394, 431, 443, 482–4, 486, 487–8, 491, 495–7, 499, 508, 611
  and king's council 292, 330
  knighting 112
  marriage 98, 112, 269, 363
  and Mortimer of Wigmore 460–1, 478, 487, 490
  and Ordinances 517
  and Orleton 510, 523
  political power 362, 364, 367, 441–8, 451
  proceedings against 149
  rebellion against 308
  and revenge on magnates 397–8
  and royal administration 443–5
  as royal favourite 98, 107, 240, 349, 363–8
  and Scottish War: battle of Blackhow Moor 430, 517; campaign of 1322 427 n.118, 482; peace negotiations 371–2, 434; siege of Berwick 350–1; truce discussions 352
  seen as second king 136 n.67, 441–3, 482, 517
  and standing royal council 333, 336–7, 392
  and Thomas of Lancaster 302, 310, 313, 317, 319, 336, 349, 350, 364, 373–5, 378–83, 396, 408, 517, 610
  wealth 418–19, 421–2
  Welsh Marcher lordships 364–9, 373–7, 385, 417–18, 508

Despenser, Hugh (son of Younger Despenser) 475, 514 n.358, 557–8 n.215, 568

Despenser, Philip (brother of Hugh the Younger) 270 n.188

Deveril, John, constable of Corfe castle 566, 571 n.297, 572

Dinis, king of Portugal 13 n.34, 60

Doherty, Paul 30 n.111, 213 n.128, 514 n.363
  and Edward II and Isabella 81 n.20, 118 n.236, 497
  and Edward II's survival 585, 596
  and Isabella's English lands 482 n.164
  and Mortimer 489
  and Thomas of Lancaster 569 n.288

Dominican friars
  attempts to free Edward II from captivity 65, 543–4, 565–6
  and Edward's religious formation 64–5, 327, 507, 602
  and Eleanor of Castile 43, 57, 64–5
  and Gaveston 191, 545
  prayers for Edward II 145 n.111
  as royal confessors 65
  and university of Oxford 278 n.228
  see also King's Langley

Doncaster, council of magnates (1315) 265

Doncaster Petition (1321) 399–400

Doran, J. 33 n.1

Douglas, James 233, 346, 347, 351, 352, 406, 427, 430

Dover castle 194, 384 n.355, 385

Drayton, Michael, *The Barons' Wars* 26

Droxford, John
  as bishop of Bath & Wells 67, 158, 532
  as keeper of the wardrobe 105 n.158
  support for Edward II 159, 448–9

Druon, Maurice 30 n.111

Dublin, and Scottish invasion 261, 256, 257

Dublin, archbishop of *see* Bicknor

Dublin university 62

Dubois, Pierre 5–6 n.2

Duffeld, Robert de (Edward II's confessor) 65, 463

Dumfries castle, Scots recapture 224

Dun, Thomas (pirate) 261, 262

Dunbar castle 233

Dunbar, Patrick, earl, and Edward II 233

Duncan, Archie 223, 231 n.233, 254 n.108, 344 n.88, 346 n.110, 350 n.140

Dunheved, Stephen 542, 544–5, 568 n.280
Dunheved, Thomas 483 n.169, 544–5, 565 n.265, 567, 591
Dunstable, tournament (1309) 155
Dunstanburgh castle 282 n.12, 407–8
Durham, election of bishop (1316) 281–2, 283, 449
Durham, bishops of *see* Beaumont, Louis de; Bek, Anthony

Eaglescliff, John, bishop of Llandaff 532, 539 n.108, 554
Eauze, Card. Gaucelin d' 263 n.154, 287, 299, 315, 335 n.38, 342, 592
Edinburgh castle, Scots recapture 224, 427 n.115
Edmund, earl of Cornwall 64, 84, 110 n.193, 122, 326
Edmund Ironside, murder 564
Edmund of Lancaster (brother of Edward I) 9, 40 n.48, 51, 84
Edmund of Woodstock (half-brother of Edward II) *see* Kent, Edmund of Woodstock, earl
education, and Edward II 27, 53–7, 61–3, 124
Edward the Confessor
    cult 20, 35, 39, 53, 59, 69–70, 140, 458, 550, 560, 602
    laws of 143
    Life 58, 59
Edward, count of Bar 288–9
Edward I of England
    children 39–40
    coronation oath 141–2
    criticisms of 2–3
    and crusades 4, 51 n.110, 108, 131
    death 123–4, 125, 128; eulogy of 5–6, 131; funeral 130–2, 550; tomb 131
    devotion to Thomas of Canterbury 70–1
    and Edward II: creation as Prince of Wales 85, Pl. 2; as father 45–7; and Gaveston 97, 99–100, 107; marriage negotiations 116–17; quarrel and reconciliation 23, 81, 99–100, 103–7, 322, 603; succession 41, 44 n.70, 77–8, 103–4
    Edward II compared with 5–7, 277–8
    health 108, 110 n.192, 112, 116
    and relics 34–5, 63, 83, 121
    revenues 254; debts 129, 162–3, 419, 421, 610; and taxation 49, 78–9, 85, 109–10 n.188, 420
    temper 46, 81, 107, 115 n.219, 116, 120–1
    and Wales 34–6, 271
    war with Scotland 5–6, 7, 79, 80, 90, 91–5, 112–16, 123, 128–9; and Robert Bruce 109, 111–12
    wars with France 5–6, 77–9, 80–1, 91
Edward II as Edward of Caernarfon
    birth 33–6, Pl. 1
    coat of arms 84 n.31
    as count of Ponthieu and Montreuil 77, 88 n.56, 104, 105 n.157, 120, 134
    as earl of Chester 85–7, 104, 105 n.157
    education 53–7, 57–60, 61, 124
    and Edward I 45–7
    and family 39–45, 124
    health 40–1, 90 n.72, 93
    household 47–53
    imprisonment 541–7
    public career 77–80, 84–8
    as Regent of England 48–9, 104, 124
    travels 50, 52–3, 86–7
    and Wales 36–9
    see also Edward II as king of England; Edward II as prince of Wales
Edward II as prince of Wales 2, 36–9, 84–8
    and allegations of cruelty 114–15
    banishment from court 105–6
    creation as prince of Wales 84–8, Pl. 2
    homage paid to 87–8
    household 89
    and kingdom of Castile 119
    knighting 20, 99, 109–12, 145 n.112
    revenues 104–5
    and Scottish War 83–4, 88–90, 91–5, 96, 105, 112–16
Edward II as king of England Pls 8 and 15
    accession to throne 123–4, 125–6, 130–2, 138–9
    alleged confession Pl. 23
    alleged life as hermit 1, 23, 30 n.112, 62, 66, 582–99, Pls 19 and 20
    appearance 10, 13, 220
    brotherhood 100–3, 123, 126, 146, 149, 609
    character: courage 11, 213, 229, 612; cruelty/ruthlessness 114–15, 404, 410–11, 433–4, 530, 609; eccentricity 16 n.50, 76; as inspiring loyalty 608–9; loyalty to friends 76, 124, 191, 609–10; piety 22, 63–4, 66, 67, 327; as

Edward II as king of England (*cont.*)
  public speaker 61, 194, 359, 466–7, 612
  and Charles IV of France 462–9
  and the Church 448–52, 477, 504, 509, 527
  coronation 140–6, Pl. 7; banquet 145–6; Coronation Order 142, 143 n.104; and cult of Edward the Confessor 20, 69, 140, 602; guests 145, 489; and Holy Oil of Thomas of Canterbury 143–4 n.108, 325–7, 545; oath 54–6, 69, 141–3, 148–9, 165–6, 198, 207, 389 n.387, 527, 607; and oaths of allegiance 148–9; preparations 133, 139–40
  death 1, 4, 14, 560–5; alleged tomb 30, 587–8, Pl. 21; and Edward III 125 n.2; effigy 556–8; funeral 131 n.39, 550–4; and lying in state 553; as martyrdom 22, 535, 601–3; as murder 547–8, 561–5, 572–3, 575, 578–81; as natural 548–9, 561, 563; rumours of survival 511 n.346, 565–71, 577–81, 582–99
  deposition 3–4, 9, 522–49, 552–3; articles of 15, 72, 98 n.120, 523 n.19, 524, 527, 529–31; charges against 19, 527; and deputation to Kenilworth 533–6; legality 71, 522, 536–9; and parliament (Jan. 1327) 29, 524–9, 538–9; sermons preached against 16–17, 509–10, 521, 528–9
  early life *see* Edward II as Edward of Caernarfon
  and Edward I, quarrel and reconciliation 23, 81–100, 103–7, 322, 603
  favourites *see* Andley, Hugh the Younger; Damory, Roger; Despenser, Hugh the Younger; Gaveston, Piers; Montacute, William de
  finances 217–19, 253, 511; and confiscation of contrariants' land 413, 414, 419–22, 423; debts 158, 177, 191, 243, 245, 419, 421, 610; from fines on contrariants 413, 419; loans from Bardi 302–3, 340, 343, 414 n.31; papal loans 195, 218–19, 252, 284, 286, 303; revenues 124, 129–30, 167, 175, 178, 179, 180, 217–19
  and France: state visit (1313) 209–13 state visit (1320); 356–7, 455; war with (1324–5) 420, 455–7; *see also* Aquitaine; Gascony
  health 30, 428, 613
  and household knights *see* knights, household
  imprisonment: in Berkeley castle 37, 65, 90, 439, 483 n.169, 541, 542–3, 547; in Kenilworth castle 16, 65, 87, 518, 520, 522, 527–8, 541, 542, 545; release attempts 483 n.169, 542–8, 565–6, 591, 608
  and invasion of England (1326) 502–5; capture 515; English army 502–3, 504, 505 and flight to Wales 36, 58, 69, 505, 508–9, 510–12; and revolt in London 506–8; rumours of 492–5, 497
  legitimacy 15–16, 277–8, 322–4
  leisure activities 72–6, 123–4; animals 74–6, 93; building 72–3; gambling 75; hunting 74–6; music 37, 74; rowing 72, 277; rustic pursuits 10, 11, 13, 15, 19, 72–3, 220, 277, 324, 610–11
  and magnates: death of Gaveston 192; and French and papal envoys 194–6, 197, 206–9, 215, 217 n.154; hatred of 412; negotiations between 194–6, 197–201, 221; possibility of civil war 101, 147–51, 182, 184, 192–4, 301–3, 305–8, 388; *see also* Hereford, Humphrey de Bohun; Ordinances of 1311; parliament; Pembroke, Aymer de Valence; Thomas of Lancaster; Scotland; Warwick, Guy de Beauchamp
  marriage: alienation of Isabella 5, 138, 436, 611; alleged cruelty to Isabella 521; betrothal 91, 132, 519, Pl. 3; and children 102, 201–2, 279, 322, 327, 394, 481, *see also* Edward III of England; Eleanor (daughter of Edward II); Joan (daughter of Edward II); John of Eltham (son of Edward II); delay 107–9, 132, 202; and possible divorce 483 n.169, 497, 498 n.263, 544; Flemish marriage plans 77–8, 81; Isabella's refusal to return 481–8, 491, 492, 498–500, 520–1;

negotiations 116–20, 132–4; and
papal envoys 495–7; settlement
109; wedding 134–5, Pl. 6;
wedding gifts 135, 136, 137
and Philip IV of France 101, 108,
138–9, 141 n.95, 146, 149–50,
160, 187 n.350, Pl. 10; loans
from 218; and opposition
magnates 208; state visit to
France (1313) 21 n.76, 209–13,
217, 221, 455, Pl. 11
and Philip V of France 354,
356–7, 358–9
and religion 27, 63–9; and
Dominicans 64–5, 67, 554;
personal devotions 50, 68, 69–72,
175, 324–7; religious foundations
67–8; visits to monasteries 66–7, 83
reputation 1–4; in sixteenth- to
eighteenth-century literature 25–8;
in nineteenth and twentieth
centuries 28–31; in twenty-first
century 31–2; canonization moves
4, 14, 20, 23–4, 31, 545, 578,
600–6, 612; in chronicles 5, 7–15,
24, 25; compared with Edward I
5–7, 23, 277–8; in early years 49;
as holy figure 20–5, 31, 65, 535,
557–8, 564, 585, 608–9; and
personal criticisms 15–19, 277–9;
as *rex inutilis* 1, 5, 531
sexuality 3, 24, 25–6, 28–9, 32,
97–103, 481, 523, 610
taking of the cross 21 n.76, 51 n.110,
210–13, 219, 284, 286, Pl. 11
talents and abilities 220, 609
horsemanship 53, 57, 74, 83
tomb *see* Gloucester cathedral
and war with Scotland *see*
Scottish War
and Westminster Abbey 7–9, 110, 550
see also civil war (1321–2); favourites;
parliament; prerogative, royal
Edward III of England
accession to throne 123, 125 n.2,
526–7, 536
baptism 70, 201
birth 201–2, 322
burial 554
claim to French throne 499,
592–3 n.74
coronation 55, 512 n.352, 539
and death of Edward II 548, 549,
Pl. 17
and deposition of Edward II 526
and Dominicans 68
as duke of Aquitaine 476, 478–9,
480, 484, 485, 513, 550 n.173
as earl of Chester 422, 439
as Edward II's lieutenant in
England 467
finances 559
funeral effigy 553 n.191
as guardian of the kingdom 513,
515–16, 524 n.25
and Isabella 489–91, 497, 500, 520
and Isabella's invasion 503, 505, 509
and council 540
knighting 539
literacy 60
and Ludwig IV 582
marriage proposals 337, 457, 458,
466, 493–4, 498, 500
and overthrow of Mortimer 571–2
petitions of the community 157
and Philippa of Hainault 46, 337 n.48,
494; betrothal 500–1, 531 n.58;
marriage 512 n.352, 550–1, 554
proclamation as king 511
and Scottish War 546, 549–50, 571
and tomb of Edward II 23–4, 554–60
Edward the Martyr 20, 602 n.122
Eleanor of Brittany (cousin of
Edward II) 44
Eleanor of Castile (wife of Edward I)
34–5, 119
children 39–40
and county of Ponthieu and
Montreuil 77
death 42, 43, 46, 550, 552 n.184
and Dominicans 43, 57, 64–5
and education of Edward II 57, 65
Eleanor (daughter of Edward II) 102, 322,
327, 466 n.76, 559
Eleanor of Provence (mother of Edward I)
40, 41, 42, 43–4, 50, 57–8, 192, 452
Eleanor (sister of Edward II) 36, 40–1,
43, 112
literacy 57
marriage to Henry of Bar 42, 50, 52,
53, 78 n.4, 288
Elizabeth (sister of Edward II) 40–1, 47
nn.85,86
as countess of Hereford 43, 88, 107,
228, 240, 337 n.48, 408 n.509
as countess of Holland 43, 44–5,
78 nn. 4,6
death 277

Ellis, Havelock 28
Eltham palace 202, 215, 279
Ely, bishop of *see* Hothum
English, royal use of 60
Eure, John de 249, 283 n.20, 299–300, 380 n.332
Evans, Joan 59, 140 n.93
Evesham, battle (1265) 3 n.14
exchequer
　　and Isabella 516
　　and maintenance of royal household 177–8, 414
　　and payment of customs 177–8, 275
　　reorganization 420, 444–5
Exchequer Memoranda Roll (1315–16) 15
Exeter College, Oxford 62
Eyndon, Philip de 192

Faleise, John (Isabella's tailor) 203
Falkirk, English victory (1298) 80, 227, 232, 237
famine and agrarian crisis 19, 238, 253–4, 271 n.191, 327, 328, 330
Farndon, Nicholas de (mayor of London) 439
Faughart, battle (1318) 258, 262, 329
favourites, royal 1, 5, 10, 98, 124, 275–6, 293, 294–7, 608–9
　　restraining 303–5, 331
　　and Thomas of Lancaster 294–7, 303, 312, 317–18, 320–1, 331, 334
　　see also Audley, Hugh the Younger; Damory, Roger; Despenser, Hugh the Younger; Gaveston, Piers; Montacute, William de
Felton, John 503
Ferdinand III of Castile 57
Ferdinand IV of Castile 91 n.77, 119–20
Ferre, Guy ('master' of Edward of Caernarfon) 53–4, 64, 89, 92, 93, 97
Ferre, Guy the Younger 54, 289
Ferre, John (steward of Eleanor of Castile) 53
Ferrers, John de 208 n.94
Fiennes, Jean de 88 n.56, 327, 356, 460
Fiennes, Margaret de (mother of Mortimer of Wigmore) 490 n.214, 492
Fiennes, Robert de 460
Fieschi, Charles 252 n.96, 590 n.64
Fieschi, Luke, cardinal 74, 263, 287, 292, 299, 315, 335 n.38, 342, 586 n.44, 589–90, 592

Fieschi, Manuel, letter to Edward III 23, 66, 582–94, 596, 598, Pl. 23
Fieschi, Nicolino 590, 593–6
Fieschi, Percival 589, 593 n.75
Fitz Alan, Edmund *see* Arundel, Edmund Fitz Alan
Fitz Gilbert, Walter, constable of Bothwell castle 234
Fitz John, William, archbishop of Cashel 264, 287
Fitz Payn, Robert 95, 160, 166–7, 170
Fitz Roger, Robert, as Ordainer 166
Fitz Warin, Fulk 403, 464, 566, 567, 568–9
Fitz William, Ralph 166
Flanders
　　assistance to Scotland 212 n.123, 248 n.64, 345 n.97, 427, 434
　　French campaigns in 248, 253, 458, 466 n.75
fleet
　　English 260 n.139, 262, 345, 502–3
　　of Isabella and Mortimer 502
Fleta 5–6 n.2
Flores Historiarum 193 n.11, 221
　　and Edward II and magnates 412
　　and John of London 7 n.8
　　and Langton 184 n.330
　　and Mortimer 440
　　and Robert of Reading 8–9, 591
　　and royal favourites 295, 349
　　and Scottish War 347
　　and Thomas of Lancaster 310
Foix, Gaston de Béarn, count 187
food shortages 253
　　and Scots invasion of Ireland 256–7
Forcet, Francekino 594–5
Forma deposicionis Regis Edwardi post Conquestum Secundi 526–8, 529 n.49, 533, 537 n.102
Frame, Robin 329 n.5
France
　　and Edward I 5–6, 80–1
　　and Edward II 124, 194–5, 247–8, 455–7, 611; state visit (1313) 21, 21 n.76, 209–13, 217, 245, Pl. 11; state visit (1320) 356–7, 455
　　English exiles in 492
　　fears of invasion from 492–5, 497, 502
　　and Scotland 90, 91, 94, 153–4, 160, 167, 213, 240, 370–1, 457–9
　　war with (1294) 5–6, 77–9, 80–1, 91, 465
　　war with (1324–5) 18, 252 n.93, 420, 461–79, 560

see also Aquitaine; Flanders; Gascony;
    Philip IV of France
Franciscans
    and Isabella 533
    preaching in Ireland 264
    Spiritual 3, 21 n.76
Fréauville, Nicholas de 211
French
    and Latin 54–6, 60, 65
    as literary language 75
Frescobaldi (bankers) 163, 178, 179 n.291,
    181, 219, 340 n.66
Froissart, Jean (chronicler), *Chroniques* 98
    n.124, 128 n.20, 499–500, 502 n.286,
    522, 523 n.22, Pl. 13
Fryde, Edmund 418 n.62
Fryde, Natalie
    and Anglo-French War 469 n.89
    and deposition of Edward II 525 n.28
    and Despensers 363 nn.220, 222, 478
    and Edward II and parliament
        470 n.93
    and imprisonment of Edward II 544
        n.134
    and Isabella 482 n.162, 489, 499
        n.272
    and revenues of Edward II 419 n.68,
        420 n.71

Gabaston, Arnaud de (father of
    Gaveston) 96
Galbraith, V.H. 54–5, 57 n.143, 60 n.163,
    61 n.171
Galeys, William le 596–9
Gascony
    aid to Isabella 500 n.275
    and Anglo-French War 18, 252 n.93,
        461–74, 487, 494
    appeals to Paris *parlement* from 132,
        221, 248, 455, 456
    armed support sought from
        187, 406
    as bargaining counter 188–9
    and Despenser the Younger 443
    disputes over 208–9, 212, 221,
        494–5
    and Edward III 550 n.173
    English control 21, 91, 132, 456–7, 611
    Gaveston exiled to 121–2
    homage for 560
    and royal revenues 303, 420
    and support for Scottish campaigns
        251–2, 425, 457
    see also Agenais; Aquitaine

Gaveston, Joan (daughter of Piers
    Gaveston) 101, 183, 192, 200
Gaveston, Piers 13–14, 96–103, 610
    in sixteenth- to eighteenth-century
        literature 25–6
    accusations: as evil counsellor 178–9;
        of misappropriation 136–7, 205;
        of treason 173, 190, 200–1, 205–6
    and brotherhood 100–3, 123, 126,
        146, 149, 609
    and coronation of Edward II
        141–2, 145
    and county of Ponthieu 46–7 n.84,
        77, 99, 120–3, 150
    death 18, 100, 189–91, 192; burial
        at King's Langley 65, 67–8, 192
        n.2, 240–2, 277, 545; Edward's
        revenge for 241, 283, 349, 409,
        412, 414
    as earl of Cornwall 84, 99,
        122–3, 126–8, 145, 149,
        182, 338; reinstatement
        159, 182, 184
    excommunication 150, 152, 154–5,
        157–8, 185, 191, 241
    first exile (1307) 77, 99, 100, 120–4;
        return 126–9
    Flemish campaign (1297) 96
    honours and positions: as *camerarius*
        (chamberlain) 137, 364; as
        constable of Nottingham castle
        174; as *custos regni* 133, 135–8; as
        justice of the forest 173, 186;
        knighthood 112, 123, 190
    hostility of Philip IV 137–8,
        141 n.95, 149–50, 155, 180
        n.298, 182–3
    in household of Edward Prince of
        Wales 89, 96–7, 107
    and Isabella 149, 181, 187, 202,
        203, 481
    knights 193, 208, 220
    and magnates: burial of Gaveston
        241–2; execution 190–1, 192–3,
        198–200, 206, 412; hostility of 101,
        136–8, 141, 145, 146–50, 151–2,
        154, 161–2, 164, 169, 184–5;
        pursuit and capture by 185–7,
        195–9, 203, 216, 390; support
        from 126–8
    and Ordainers 136 n.75, 166–7, 172,
        176, 178–9, 181–2
    and patronage 98, 136, 161
    private life: daughter 101, 183, 192,

Gaveston, Piers (cont.)
    200, 203; and sexuality 25–6,
    97–103, 481, 610; marriage 101,
    128, 136, 161 n.187, 269
  and Robert Bruce 170, 185, 187
  and Scottish campaigns
    116, 168–71
  second exile (1308) 127, 148–51; as
    Edward's lieutenant in Ireland
    150–1, 258; return 61, 153–5,
    156, 157–8
  seen as second king 13, 135–8
  and taxation 163
  third exile (1311) 179, 180–2;
    return 182–5
  and Thomas of Lancaster 127–8,
    147, 152, 154, 161–2, 175, 184,
    205–6, 609
Geoffrey of Monmouth (chronicler),
  Historia regum Britanniae 58, 59
Germain, Alexandre 583–4, 586, 588
Gervase of Canterbury (chronicler),
  Chronica 12 n.31, 292 n.73, 527 n.37
*Gesta Edwardi de Carnarvon Auctore Canonico
Bridlingtoniensi*
  and Bek, bishop of Durham 51 n.109
  and charges against Despensers
    389, 390–1
  and death of Edward II 562
  and Edward II's resignation of the
    crown 535 n.80
  and John of Powderham 324 n.239
  and marriage of Edward and
    Isabella 481
  and Ordinances 243 n.34
  and reform commission 267 n.177
  and reputation of Edward II 10 n.22,
    14–15, 24
  and Scottish peace treaty 432–3
  and Thomas of Lancaster 310–12, 380
  and Wales 37 n.27
Gibson, Mel, *Braveheart* (film) 31
Giffard, John 315 n.194
  and Bannockburn 235
  and civil war 402, 415
  contract to serve Edward II 293 n.78,
    306 n.152, 344, 415
  and Despenser the Younger 365, 367,
    377 n.308, 379 n.323, 389, 392, 417
  execution 411
  and king's council 80
  and standing royal council 330
Giles, archbishop of Narbonne 91
Giles of Oudenarde (royal clerk) 47–8

Gillingham, John 412 n.17
Girovart, Br Pierre 2, 3
Gisors, John de 196, 441, 507
Given-Wilson, Chris 12–13 n.32
Given-Wilson, Chris and Curteis,
  Alice 102 n.144
Glamorgan, revolt (1316) 272–3, 393 n.398
Glaunville, Henry de 548 n.162, 553 n.183,
  564 n.261
Gloucester cathedral, tomb of Edward II
  9, 28 n.103, 551–3, 554–60, Pl. 18
  effigy 131, 556–7
  and Oriel College, Oxford 62
  opening (1855) 577–8
  pilgrimage to 23–4, 25 n.90, 556,
    559, 603
Gloucester, Gilbert de Clare, earl (d. 1295),
  marriage to Joan of Acre 41, 42
Gloucester, Gilbert de Clare, earl (son of
  above; d. 1314)
  armed men 182, 226
  as *custos regni* 174
  death 232, 237, 271; and inheritance
    269–70, 284, 295–6, 304, 335,
    363–6, 368, 390, 417
  and Gaveston 101, 159, 161; pursuit
    and capture 185, 190 n.371; return
    from exile 154, 184
  knighting 112
  mission to France (1314) 221–2
  and Northampton meeting (Aug.
    1308) 151–2
  and opposition magnates 197,
    199–200, 206, 207, 215
  as Ordainer 166, 174, 176
  and papal authority 160
  and parliament of July 1309 157
  and parliament of July 1313 214
  and Scottish War: campaign of 1306
    113, 116 n.222, 123; campaign of
    1310–11 154, 168–70; campaign of
    1314 226, 230–2, 237
  support for Edward II 41, 159, 164,
    166, 197
  and taxation 163
  and Thomas of Lancaster 174–5
Gloucester, Maud de Clare, countess,
  269–70 365
Godefroy de Paris (chronicler) 210, 211
  n.114, 213, 222
Gorges, Ralph de
  and double allegiance 445
  as justice of Ireland 375
Got, Bertrand de 284–5

Gower, lordship, and Despenser 365–6, 368, 375, 377, 393 n.368, 417, 446–7, 519
Grandison, John de 525
Grandison, Otto de 180 n.296
Gransden, Antonia 7
Gravesend, Stephen, bishop of London 506, 534, 536, 539–40 n.108, 566–8
Gray, Sir Thomas 230, 233 n.246, 428
Gray, Sir Thomas the Younger, *Scalacronica* 10–11, 233 n.246, 235 n.265, 288, 499 n.270
Great Cause 245, 444
Great Seal
   in control of Edward II 184 n.324, 514
   in control of Isabella 394 n.407, 515
   and death of Edward I 125–6, 127
   and Gaveston 127, 135, 150
   and Ordinances 176, 177 n.275
Green, Vivian 613 n.24
Grey, John de 166, 320
Grey, Reginald de 80, 88, 89
Grey, Richard de 249, 252, 389, 392, 534
Guildhall oath 532–3, 537, 538
Guillaume de Villeneuve 213
Gurney, Thomas
   in exile 574, 575
   imprisonment and death of Edward II 413, 547, 563, 565, 566, 572–3, 576, 579–81, 591
   and Mortimer 361, 440 n.197, 547–8
   and Scottish campaign of 1301 90
Guy, bishop of Soissons 152

Haines, Roy Martin 483 n.169, 510 n.335, 525 n.28, 571 n.297, 585
Halton, John, bishop of Carlisle 337
Hamilton, Jeffrey 73 n.240, 102 n.145, 161 n.184, 168 n.218, 241 n.21
Harbottle castle 352–3, 373 n.277
Harclay, Andrew 349, 371 n.267, 431
   arrest and execution 433–4
   and battle of Boroughbridge 236 n.268, 408, 416
   and civil war 405
   draft peace treaty with Bruce 432–3, 439, 550
   as earl of Carlisle 416, 428
   and rewards of victory 416–17
   and siege of Carlisle 250
   and Thomas of Lancaster 383 n.347
   as warden of Scottish March 428
Harclay, Henry 17, 278
Hastang, Robert 285, 554
Hastings, John
   and Arundel 361
   and Despenser the Younger 447–8
   and Harclay 433
   as lord of Abergafenni (Abergavenny) 88–9, 226
   and Pembroke 402
   as seneschal of Gascony 150 n.136, 356
Haustede, John de (valet) 99 n.131, 107
hawking 74
Henry III of England 39, 46, 69, 85–6, 109 n.188, 123, 551
Henry III of France, favourites 25
Henry VII, Holy Roman Emperor 109, 145
Henry (deceased son of Edward I) 40, 47
Henry, count of Bar 5, 42, 52, 53, 78 n.4
Henry of Eastry (prior of Christ Church Canterbury) 74, 478, 493, 524 n.24, 533 n.69
Henry of Lancaster
   and Clarendon council (1317) 290
   and defence of the north 250
   and deputation to Kenilworth (1327) 533–4
   and Despensers 513, 516
   as earl of Lancaster 513, 540
   as earl of Leicester 413–14, 453, 474, 512, 521
   and Edward II 88, 474, 477, 515
   and Edward III 540
   and household of Edward of Caernarfon 45, 51–3
   and Isabella 504, 512
   and Mortimer 511 n.346, 522, 542, 546, 569
   and Ordainers 166
   and parliament 422
   and Scottish War 426
   and standing royal council 337–8
   as steward of England 540
   and Thomas of Lancaster 411 n.15, 600–1
Henry of Luxembourg *see* Henry VII
Hereford, bishop of *see* Orleton
Hereford, Humphrey de Bohun, earl 45 n.76
   armed retainers 164, 182, 226
   and Boulogne Declaration (1308) 138, 142
   and civil war 404, 405–6, 407–8, 414
   as constable of England 88, 110, 228, 230, 382–3, 395
   death 408, 411 n.11, 517, 564 n.260
   and defence of the north 250, 281

Hereford, Humphrey de Bohun (*cont.*)
    and Despensers 366–7, 374–7, 378–9, 382, 385, 386, 393, 397, 517
    and Edward II: contract to serve 306, 415; coronation 145; marriage 135; as member of king's council 245, 265–6, 292, 301; negotiation with 197, 199–200, 205–7, 217, 228; opposition to 164, 197, 393, 395, 400, 402–3, 415; and royal pardon 216; and standing royal council 320, 333, 337; support for 159, 246, 307
    and Gaveston 127–8, 242; pursuit and capture 185–6, 190, 192; return from exile 154, 159, 184
    and knighting of Edward Prince of Wales 110
    and lordship of Gower 366
    marriage to Elizabeth (sister of Edward II) 43, 88
    and Northampton meeting (Aug. 1308) 151–2
    as Ordainer 166, 172, 176, 194
    and papal authority 160
    and parliament 158, 268
    and reform of royal household 267, 330
    and Scottish War 113, 116 n.222, 130, 154, 169, 298; battle of Bannockburn 226, 227–30, 234, 237, 240; peace negotiations 372
    and see of Durham 282
    and siege of Leeds castle 398
    and Thomas of Lancaster 290, 297–8, 301, 309, 313
    and Welsh revolt 272–3
Hereford, John de Bohun, earl 532, 539, 540, 549, Pl. 17
Herle, William 352
Herwynton, Adam de 197
Heslarton, John de 197
Hethe, Hamo, bishop of Rochester
    and coronation of Edward III 539–40 n.108
    and deposition of Edward II 536
    and Despenser the Younger 367 n.245, 388–9, 391, 394
    and Guildhall oath 532
    and Isabella 497–8
    and London revolt 507
    and opposition magnates 396
    and parliament of Jan. 1327 525
Higden, Ranulf (chronicler), *Polychronicon*
    and death of Edward II 14 n.39, 22, 562

    and Edward's rustic pursuits 10, 15, 72
    judgement of Edward II 9–10, 22, 24, 61, 602
Hildesle, John 289, 354, 355 n.177, 444
Historia Roffensis 497 n.257
    and Anglo-French War 476–7
    and coronation of Edward III 539–40 n.108
    and death of Edward II 548 n.14, 562–3
    and delegation to Edward at Kenilworth 533
    and deposition of Edward II 521, 524–5 n.31, 528 n.43
    and Despensers 387–9, 390 n.391, 391, 487
    and Orleton 454 n.282
hobelars 8, 236, 344
Holland, Robert de 216, 275, 282, 291, 334, 380 n.332, 386 n.365, 416
Holcot, Robert 16
Holinshed, Raphael, *Chronicles* 14 n.39, 25–6
Holy Land, Moslem conquest (1291) 108
Holy Oil *see* Thomas of Canterbury, St
Homage et serment document 148, 380 n.326, 389, 390–2
Hoo, William 292
Horn, Andrew 8 n.15
horses, seized at Newcastle 187, 200, 205, 206, 207 n.87, 409
Hothum, John de
    as administrator 608
    as bishop of Ely 286 n.39, 308, 316–18, 319, 352, 448
    as chancellor 331, 353, 542, 544
    and chapter of Myton 348
    and coronation of Edward III 539
    and deputation to Kenilworth 533
    and Gascon disputes 457
    and Guildhall oath 532
    and Ireland 259, 260 n.140, 261–2, 272 n.197, 274
    and Isabella 504, 512
    and king's council 292
    and Scottish War 259, 347, 348
    and standing royal council 320, 333, 336–7
household of Edward of Caernarfon 47–53, 89
    almsgiving 64
    expenses 47–50, 52, 99, 104, 421
household of Edward II
    clerks 514 n.363

financing 177–8, 219, 343, 414
and government 29, 98
reforms 166, 172, 239–40, 243, 267, 293, 330, 443–4
see also knights, household; marshal of the royal household; prises; purveyance; steward of the royal household
household of Isabella 202–3, 596
costs 282, 504
French members 469, 483
and Isabella's refusal to return to Edward II 488, 490
Household Ordinance
of York (1318) 332, 444
of 1323 444
of 1324 444
Howard, Sir Robert
Historical Observations 27
The History of the Life and reign of Edward II 27
Hoyt, R.S. 142
Hubert, Sir Francis, *The Deplorable Life and Death of Edward II* 26
Hugh, bishop of Orange
and Anglo-French War 468, 470–1, 472–3, 479, 485
mission to Edward II and Isabella 495–7, 592
hunting 73–4, 76
Hurley, William (craftsman) 441–2
Hywel ap Gruffudd 548, 581

impostors 37
see also John of Powderham; Richard de Neueby; Tynwelle
infantry
armoured 428
and cavalry 235–6
unpaid service 251, 268, 280, 424
Inge, John 378 n.319
as Despenser's sheriff in Glamorgan 367, 373–4, 377 n.308, 393 n.398
and double allegiance 445
Inge, William 151 n.140, 190, 266, 274
Ingham, Oliver 402, 415, 540
as seneschal of Aquitaine 479–80, 575 n.322
Innocent III, pope (1198–1216) 263
Ireland
Edward II attempts to reach 510–12, 514
and Edward III 546
Gaveston as lieutenant 150–1, 258

preaching against English rule 16–17
and purveyance of supplies 163, 260
Remonstrance of Irish princes 257, 260, 262–4
and Scottish War 169, 252, 258–60, 327
Scottish invasion 21, 237, 248, 250, 253–64, 271–2, 274, 546, 609
Irish Sea, fleet 262, 345
Isabella Casket Pl. 5
Isabella of Castile (sister of Ferdinand IV) 91 n.77, 119
Isabella of Flanders 78
Isabella (daughter of Philip IV of France and wife of Edward II) 15, Pl. 4
and Anglo-French War 8, 470–4, 475, 476, 478–9, 483, 496
and coronation 145–6
death 552
and Despensers 394, 443, 482–4, 486, 487–8, 491, 495–7, 499, 508, 611
in France: 1313 209–13; 1314 221–3, 247, 482; 1320 356–7, Pl. 11; 1325–6; and English exiles 492, 501; and peace negotiations 8, 471–4, 475, 476, 478–9, 483; refusal to return to England 481–8, 491, 492, 498–500
and Guildhall oath 532–3, 537
handover of power to 515–16
health 213
and hunting 74
invasion of England: and excommunication 505; fleet 501–2; landings 503–4; plans 499–500; and revolt in London 506–8; rumours 492–5, 497; Wallingford proclamation 509
and William Le Galeys 596
and Marcher rebellion 405 n.489
marriage: alienation 5, 138, 436, 611; attachment to Edward II 520–2; betrothal 91, 132, Pl. 3; and children 102, 201–2, 279, 322, 327, 394, 481, 483, *see also* Edward III of England; Eleanor (daughter of Edward II); Joan (daughter of Edward II); John of Eltham (son of Edward II); death of Edward 548–9, 563–4; and possible divorce 483 n.169, 497, 498 n.263, 544; dower 91, 121, 133–4, 139 n.84, 146, 149, 202, 204, 322 n.229, 482;

Isabella (daughter of Philip IV of France and wife of Edward II) (*cont.*)
  Edward's alleged cruelty towards 521; and Gaveston 149, 181, 187, 202, 203, 242, 481; and papal envoys 495–7, 525; wedding 134–5, Pl. 6
  and Mortimer: acts of revenge 513; and burial of Edward II 551–2; early relationship 488–91, 497, 611; in France 492, 499, 611; Hainault support for 500, 501, 549; opponents 568; and political power 8, 446, 571–2
  and opposition magnates 203
  and John of Powderham 323
  Scots plot to capture 347, 349, 351
  and see of Durham 281–2, 436, 449
  and Thomas of Lancaster 282–3, 321, 409
  and treaty of Montreuil 80–1
  in Tynemouth (1322) 429, 430–1, 482, 517
  will 204
  and see household of Isabella
Isabella Psalter 58–9, 135, Pl. 4
Islip, Walter, as treasurer of Ireland 260
Iweyn, John, and double allegiance 445

Jarman, Derek (film director) 31
Jean de Wavrin, *Chroniques d'Angleterre* 134 n.59, Pl. 6
Jeanne d'Évreux (wife of Charles IV) 489 n.201
jewels, seized at Newcastle 187, 200, 205, 206–7, 409
Joan of Acre (sister of Edward II) 36, 40, 47 n.86
  as countess of Gloucester 41, 42, 51, 75, 88, 106, 161 n.187
  death 132
  and Gloucester inheritance 368
Joan de Bar (niece of Edward II) 112, 227, 288–9
Joan (daughter of Edward II) 102, 394, 572
Joan (wife of Mortimer of Wigmore) 489
John XXII, pope (1316–34) 55–6, 241 n.19
  and Anglo-French War 468, 471, 495–8
  assessment of 2
  and death of Edward II 570–1, 592
  and Despenser the Younger 496
  and English Church appointments 449–51, 481

  English mission to (1317) 284–7
  English mission to (1320) 359–60
  English mission to (1322–3) 450–2
  and English universities 62
  and Holy Oil of Thomas of Canterbury 22, 324–7, 340–2
  and Irish Church appointments 264
  and Irish Remonstrance 257, 262–3
  and mission to England (1317–18) 287
  and mission to England (1326–7) 495–7, 525
  and royal oath to uphold Ordinances 359–60, 451–2, 537
  and Scottish War 263, 309, 369–71, 451, 459
  and see of Durham 282
  and supposed survival of Edward II 582, 593–4
  See also Eauze; Fieschi, Luke
John of Athy 262
John of Bridlington 14, 24
John of Brittany *see* Richmond, John of Brittany
John, count of Holland and Zeeland (brother-in-law of Edward II) 43, 44–5, 78 n.4
John (deceased son of Edward I) 40
John of Eltham (son of Edward and Isabella) 505, 520
  birth 102, 279
  death 555 n.204, 557 n.215
  as earl of Cornwall 554
  as guardian of London 507
  and Tutbury castle 417
John, king of England, and tribute to papacy 263
John of Hainault 549
John I, duke of Brabant 41
John II, duke of Brabant 41, 42, 45, 51–3, 77, 78 n.4
  and coronation of Edward II 145, 325–7
  and Gaveston 181
  and marriage of Edward II and Isabella 134
  and Scottish War 371 n.262
John III, duke of Brabant
  and Isabella 501 n.289
  and plot to free Edward II 566
John of Lenham (Edward II's confessor) 65
John of Lincoln 15, 277
John of London
  Commendatio Lamentabilis 5, 131 n.40, 415
  and *Flores Historiarum* 7 n.8

John of Monmouth, bishop of Llandaff 267, 297, 310
John of Ockham, cofferer of the wardrobe 239
John Pater Noster 3
John of Powderham (impostor) 11 n.25, 15–16, 322–4, 327
John of St Albans (painter) 46, 412
John of Warefield (Edward II's confessor) 65
Johnstone, Hilda
　　and Edward I 46 n.79, 278 n.227
　　and Edward II: as Edward of Caernarfon 30 n.109, 33 n.1, 38 n.35, 45 n.77, 50 n.103, 124; and Gaveston 122; knowledge of languages 36 n.20, 56; Scottish campaigns 114
　　and marriage agreement with France 117 n.234, 118 nn.236–7
　　and Thomas of Lancaster 267 n.176
Joneston, Elias de 247 n.60, 356 n.184, 444, 480 n.151

Kalila and Dimna 211, Pl. 10
Kellaw, Richard, bishop of Durham 281
Kendale, Sir Robert de 291, 375–6, 379 n.320
Kenilworth castle
　　capture by Edward II 406
　　delegations to 524, 525, 527–8, 533–6
　　Edward II imprisoned in 16, 65, 87, 518, 520, 522, 527–8, 541, 542, 545
　　and Thomas of Lancaster 190, 206
Kent, Edmund of Woodstock, earl (half-brother of Edward II)
　　and Anglo-French War 18, 464–6, 469, 473
　　and battle of Blackhow Moor 430
　　conspiracy to free Edward II (1330) 67, 548, 565–8, 570, 572, 576
　　as constable of Dover 384 n.355, 385
　　and coronation of Edward II 145
　　and Despensers 513, 516
　　and Edward III 202, 355, 501, 540
　　execution 81, 511 n.346, 566
　　and Guildhall oath 532
　　and Harclay 433
　　and Henry of Lancaster 569–70
　　and Isabella 492, 493 n.233, 500, 521; invasion of England 501, 503, 509, 512
　　and Marcher rebellion 407
　　mission to France (1324) 462–3, 492
　　and support for Edward II 397, 417

Kildare, John Fitz Thomas, earl 90, 261, 280, 417 n.51, 511
Kinardesey, John de 281–2
King's Hall, Cambridge 63
King's Langley
　　Dominican priory 27, 62, 65, 67–8, 73, 186–7, 240–2, 450 n.263
　　royal manor 49–51, 67, 73, 80, 128, 162, 186, 241, 439; Edward and Gaveston at 164
Kingston, John de 501
Kirkstall abbey chronicle 25 n.89
Knaresborough castle 73, 183, 187
　　seized by Thomas of Lancaster 302, 310 n.172
Knighton, Henry (chronicler)
　　assessment of Edward II 10 n.22, 24
　　and death of Edward II 562
　　and Eleanor de Clare 363 n.222, 505 n.312
　　and plots to release Edward II 542
　　and Thomas of Lancaster 316 n.203, 319–20
　　and Welsh attachment to Edward II 37 n.27
Knights Hospitaller, and Templar revenues 218 n.160
knights, household 299, 307 n.157, 397
　　and civil war 402 n.457, 415, 608
　　desertion of Edward II 608
　　neglect of 17, 296
　　and opposition magnates 193
　　reliability of 299, 415–16, 608
　　and Scottish War 226, 234, 244
Knights Templar *see* Templars

La Réole, siege (1325) 18, 464, 466, 477, 494
Lacy, Henry de *see* Lincoln, Henry de Lacy
Lamberton, William, bishop of St Andrews 153
Lament on the Death of Edward I 20 n.72, 22–3 n.80
Lamouilly, Jean de 288, 361–2
Lancaster, Alice de Lacy, countess 174
　　abduction 291–2, 293, 311, 314
　　and Despensers 447
Lancaster, Henry of *see* Henry of Lancaster
Lancaster, Thomas of, earl *see* Thomas of Lancaster, earl of Lancaster
Lanercost chronicle 11, 125 n.2
　　and Edward II: assessment 16, 72; death 562, 565 n.265, 566 n.266; deposition 524 n.24, 528 n.43;

Lanercost chronicle (*cont.*)
> funeral 554 n.194; supposed survival 571
> and English magnates 150, 221
> and Gaveston 100, 150
> and Harclay 433
> and Ireland 511 n.343
> and Isabella 483 n.169
> and John of Powderham 322–3
> and Scottish War 258, 350
> and Thomas of Lancaster 411
> *see also* Thomas of Otterbourne

Lanercost priory 113, 116
> oaths taken by Gaveston and Prince Edward 100–1, 120–1, 126

Langdon, Premonstratensian house 67, 384, 449, 475–6

Langley *see* King's Langley

Langtoft, Peter (chronicler) 93, 111 n.199

Langton, John, bishop of Chichester
> as chancellor 129 n.27, 159, 167, 511 n.347
> and Guildhall oath 532
> as Ordainer 166–7
> and standing royal council 320, 337
> and Thomas of Lancaster 318, 319

Langton, Walter, bishop of Coventry & Lichfield
> archives 444
> charges against 3, 6, 130, 153, 323 n.238
> and Edward I 5–6, 108
> and Edward II 107, 117–18, 120–1, 129–30, 183 n.318, 333, 448–9
> and Gaveston 136
> as keeper of royal household 52, 99 n.129, 243
> as treasurer 104–5, 107, 120, 129, 185, 186

Latimer, William 334, 416

Latin, knowledge of 54–6, 60, 65

Laudun, William (Guillaume) de, archbishop of Vienne 592
> and Anglo-French War 371 n.265, 468, 470–1, 472, 474, 479, 485
> mission to Edward II and Isabella 495–7
> and parliament of 1327 525

Launge, John 204

Le Baker, Geoffrey, of Swinbrook (chronicler) 562–3, 564 n.259, 565 n.265, 571
> *Chronicon* 5, 13–14, 68 n.205, 363 n.221
> and deputation to Kenilworth 534–5
> and flight of Edward II to Wales 510 n.337
> and imprisonment of Edward II 547 n.153
> and Isabella 484
> and royal sanctity 22–3, 602–3

Le Bel of Liège, Jean (chronicler), *Chronique* 6–7, 499–500, 502 n.286, 518 n.382, 522 n.18, 523 n.22, 526 n.33

Le Carré, John, *The Deadly Affair* 30

Le Ewer, Robert 402, 407, 437–8

Le Galeys, William 37 n.28, 471 n.98, 582, 594–8

Le Goff, Jacques 613

Leake, Treaty (1318) 16, 280, 318, 320–1, 330–1, 333, 335, 336

Leeds castle 302, 398, 482

Lege, Vincenzo 586–7

Leicester, earl *see* Henry of Lancaster; Thomas of Lancaster

Leicester meeting (1318) 309–12, 315, 318, 364

Lenzi, Sabrina Pl. 9

Lestrange, Fulk
> and Gruffudd de la Pole 200, 205, 216
> as seneschal of Gascony 457
> and Thomas of Lancaster 334, 372, 380 n.332, 416

Lewis, Suzanne 135 n.64

Leygrave, Alice de (nurse) 47

Liber Custumarum 181 n.306

Lilburn, John de 299, 302, 415

Lincoln, council of magnates 1315 8 n.16, 250, 260–1, 264–5

Lincoln, bishop of *see* Burghersh; Dalderby

Lincoln, Henry de Lacy, earl 52, 88 n.56, 108, 447
> and Boulogne Declaration (1308) 138, 142
> as *custos regni* 169, 173
> death 174
> and Edward II: accession 126; coronation 145; marriage 133, 135
> and Gaveston 126, 127–8, 147–9, 154, 159, 161–2
> and Northampton meeting (1308) 151
> as Ordainer 166, 173–4
> and papal authority 160
> and Scottish campaigns 88, 169
> support for 106, 107, 110, 152, 159, 164, 166
> and taxation 163

Lincoln, Joan de Lacy, countess 265, 447

Linehan, Peter 119
Linlithgow castle, Scots recapture 224
Literae Cantuarienses 188 n.357
Little London, Langley 67–8
Llandaff, bishop of *see* Eaglescliff; John of Monmouth
Llantrisant castle 272, 364, 515
Llwyd, Gruffydd 271–3
    and civil war 403–4, 415
    and Edward Bruce 255 n.116, 271, 273
    and Isabella's invasion 508, 511 n.344
    loyalty to Edward II 39, 88, 255 n.116, 548
    and Mortimer of Wigmore 537, 548
Llywelyn ap Gruffudd 34–5, 85
London, bishop of *see* Gravesend; Stratford
London (city)
    and baronial army 195–6
    and Edward II: deposition 536, 538–9, 551; flight from 505; hostility towards 398–9, 439–41, 505, 540; loyalty to 193–4, 196, 202, 343, 355–6, 532–3
    and eyre 373, 379, 386
    and financing of Scottish War 343
    loyalty to Isabella 506–8, 520, 524–6
    and opposition to Despensers 386–7, 436 n.175, 506
    and Ordainers 172
London, Thomas de 192
Louis, count of Évreux (half-brother of Philip IV) 38–9, 210
    and French throne 45 n.78
    and coronation of Edward II 145
    death 456
    as friend of Edward II 38–9, 152, 195
    as godfather of Edward III 201
    and marriage between Edward II and Isabella 107, 109, 132 n.48, 134
    and negotiations between magnates and Edward II 195, 197, 200, 215
Louis IX, king of France 198, 213, 613
Louis X, king of France
    council 245–6
    death 285 n.29
    and Flanders 212 n.123
    as king of Navarre 210–11
    Pembroke's mission to (1315) 247–8
Lovel, John 166
Lovel, Richard 265, 292
Lucy, Anthony de 234, 249, 433
Ludwig IV, Holy Roman Emperor, and Edward III 582

Lughtebergh, William de 180
Luke of Wodeford (Edward II's confessor) 65
Lumet, Sidney, *The Deadly Affair* 30–1
Lundy Island, and Despenser the Younger 378 n.319, 417, 510
Lymbergh, Adam de 445

Mablethorp, Robert 408, 412 n.17, 532 n.64
Mac Lochlainn, Michael, likely anthor of Irish Remonstrance 264
Mac Murrough, Donal, as king of Leinster 511 n.342
McCabe, John (composer) 31
MacDougall, John 259
McNamee, Colm 170 n.232
Maddicott, John 18 n.61, 156, 276 n.221, 339 n.56, 344 n.88
Magna Carta
    breaches 165, 378, 392, 517
    confirmation 79, 172, 331 n.13, 399
    and Ordinances 198, 423
magnates, Anglo-Irish, and Scottish campaigns 258–61, 280
magnates, English
    and Anglo-French War (1324–5) 466–7, 473–5
    Boulogne Declaration (1308) 138–9, 142, 165
    and defence of the north 248–51, 280, 432
    and Despensers 366–77, 378–93, 394–8
    divisions among 361–2
    and Edward I 141–2
    and Edward II: and armed support 195–6; contracts between 305–8; defences against 193–4; deposition 524–9, 538–9; homage to 126, 148, 207; and Isabella 203, 482; negotiations with 194–6, 197–201, 204–8, 215–17, 221, 398; opposition to 164, 191, 193–6, 336, 349, 361–2, 378–92, 412, *see also* Marcher lords; Thomas of Lancaster; Warwick, Guy de Beauchamp; reconciliation with 151–4, 155, 160, 327–8; renunciation of homage 528, 533, 535; safe conducts 196–7, 200, 204–5, 301; support for 164, 166–7, 193, 201, 305–8, *see also* Hereford, Humphrey de Bohun; Pembroke, Aymer de Valence; and visit to France 209

magnates, English (*cont.*)
    and Gaveston: burial 241–2; execution 190–1, 192–3, 198–200, 206; opposition to 101, 136–8, 141, 145, 146–50, 151–2, 154, 161–2, 164, 169, 184–5; pursuit and capture 185–9, 216; and royal pardon 200–1, 207–8, 215–17; support for 126–8
    Northampton meeting (Aug. 1308) 151–3
    northern 249
    and papacy 160
    and parliament 146–9, 214
    and pressure for reform 138–9, 141–3, 151–4, 155–7, 158–60, 166–7, 240
    protests against taxation 78–9, 80, 85
    and royal administration 178
    and Scottish War 89–90, 93 n.85, 94, 124, 128, 130, 151, 168–70, 199, 342, 352
    and standing royal council 318, 320, 333
    and Thomas of Lancaster 333–4, 335
    and threat of civil war 176, 184–5, 192–3, 388
    see also Marcher lords; Ordainers; Ordinances of the Staple; Ordinances of 1311
magnates, French, opposition to Gaveston 141, 145
magnates, Scots
    loyalty to English crown 95, 126, 231, 233, 236–7
    and Robert Bruce 167–8, 369–70
    and Thomas of Lancaster 406, 409
Malachy of Limerick 17 n.56
Maltravers, Agnes 574
Maltravers, John 112, 361, 439 n.189, 482, 501, 568
    and death of Edward II 563, 572–3, 576, 580–1
    in exile 574–5
    and imprisonment of Edward II 541, 543, 547
Mar, Donald, earl of 237, 511 n.345, 546, 566–7
Marcher lords
    attacks on Despensers 364–9, 373–86
    confiscation of lands 413, 414, 415, 423
    Despensers' revenge on 397–8
    flight 405–6
    support for 414–15
    see also civil war (1321–2); Wales, Marcher lordships
Marcher rebellion *see* civil war (1321–2)
Margaret, duchess of Brabant (sister of Edward II) 22, 40–1, 47 n.85, 65, 181, 501 n.289
    and coronation of Edward II 145
    and Holy Oil of St Thomas 143–4 n.108, 325–7
    marriage 41, 45, 51, 75, 77, 78 n.4, 812
    and marriage of Edward II and Isabella 134
Margaret of France (wife of Edward I) 38 n.34, 45 n.78, 286 n.38, Pl. 5
    children 34 n.6, 81
    death 322
    dower 85, 105 n.159, 134 n.56
    and Edward II 45 n.78, 81–2, 106–7, 112, 134, 322
    and Gaveston 149
    and Isabella Psalter 59 n.154, 135 n.64
    marriage 70, 75, 81
    as mediator between Edward I and Edward of Caernarfon 81, 322
Margaret of Hainault 337 n.48
Margaret of Norway
    proposed bride of Edward II 41–2, 77
    and Scottish succession 245
Marie de Brabant (wife of Philip III of France) 2, 45 n.78, 107
Marigny, Enguerrand de 215, 217
Marisco, Herbert de, and Lundy 378 n.319, 417
Marlowe, Christopher, *Edward II* 14 n.39, 26, 28, 30–1
marshal of the royal household 156, 159
Marshal, William, as Ordainer 166, 234
Martin, William 88, 166, 182, 330
Mary (sister of Edward II) 40, 42, 43–4, 50, 52–3, 74, 82
    and coronation of Edward II 145
    debts 105 n.159
    literacy 57
Maubuisson, Odard de 371
Mauduit, Thomas 379 n.323, 410 n.6
Mauléon castle 109, 116–17, 118
Mauley, Edmund (royal steward) 11, 193, 196, 200
    and Cockermouth castle 226
    death at Bannockburn 233, 239
Maunsel, Mariota (Mary, wet-nurse) 37, 47
Meaux abbey chronicle 10 n.22, 24, 37 n.27, 292, 323, 523 n.22, 562

Melazzo castle 1, 30, 586–9, 592–3, Pl. 19
see also Mulazzo
Meldon, Michael de (steward of Lancaster) 197, 245, 334
Meldon, William de 354, 371, 372, 395–6 n.417
Melton, William
  as administrator 608
  as archbishop of York 87, 239, 286 n.35, 287
  and chapter of Myton 348
  and Edward II: as chamberlain to earl of Chester 86–7; death 549 n.166, 565, 566–7, 570 n.289; loyalty to 380, 448, 512 n.352, 536, 539 n.108, 568
  and Edward III 540
  and Guildhall oath 532 n.66
  as keeper of the privy seal 87, 129 n.27, 177 n.275
  as keeper of the wardrobe 239
  and reform of royal household 330
  and Scottish War 347
  and Thomas of Lancaster 265, 406, 601
  as treasurer 477
Memorabilia facta tempore Regis Edwardi secundi in Anglia 12 n.31, 98 n.123, 561
Menteith, Sir John de 285
Methven, battle (1306) 113–14, 229
middle party thesis 296 n.100, 304, 305
Middleton, Master Gilbert de 533 n.67
Middleton, Gilbert de 299–300, 302, 415
minstrels 74–5, 111, 431
miracles
  associated with Thomas of Lancaster 9, 436, 440, 558, 600–1
  book of Edward II's miracles 604–5
Mitford castle 249, 283 n.20, 299–300, 302, 313 n.183
Modus Tenendi Parliamentum 395–6 n.417, 444, 534 n.76
Molay, Jacques de, Templar Grand Master 222
monarchy
  rights and duties 607–8
  sacred character 69, 71, 143, 324–7
  and sacred touch 71
monasteries, Edward II's visits to 66–7
Mongols, in Persia 213
Monmouth castle, Edward II held at 515–16
Montacute, John de 295 n.89
Montacute, William de 265

  as advisor 283 n.20
  and Bristol revolt 274, 295
  contract with Edward II 306
  as royal favourite 98, 294–5, 334
  as seneschal of Gascony 331, 339, 355 n.177
  as steward of royal household 310, 323 n.234, 331
  and Thomas of Lancaster 301, 313, 315, 318–19
  and Welsh revolt 272–3
Montacute, William de (son of the above)
  and overthrow of Mortimer 572, 574
  and constable of Corfe castle 572 n.304
  and Maltravers 574 n.315
Montfort, Simon de 174, 320, 334, 410, 518 n.382, 600
Monthaut, Robert de 90, 230 n.221, 249
Monthermer, Ralph de 88, 161 n.187, 234, 237
Montreuil Process (1306) 208 n.95, 356 n.184, 455
Montreuil treaty (1299) 80–1, 132
Montz, Eble des 289
Moray, Thomas Randolph, earl 254, 346, 406, 430, 434, 451, 458
More, Sir Thomas (Laurence) de la (chronicler) 13, 441
Morgan ap Meredudd 272
Morgan, Nigel 59 n.157
Morganstern, A.M. 558 n.216
Morley, William de (minstrel) 431
Morris, J.E. 227 n.210, 229 n.221
Mortimer, Edmund 88, 98
Mortimer, Geoffrey 461
Mortimer, Ian 489, 578, 579, 585, 594 n.82, 596
Mortimer, Roger (of Chirk) 88, 90 n.68
  death 507
  and Despenser the Younger 365, 367, 375, 377, 378–9
  as Justice of North Wales 250, 265, 283, 306, 400
  and reform of royal household 330
  and siege of Leeds castle 398
  and standing royal council 330
  surrender 403–4
  trial and imprisonment 412–13, 453, 507
Mortimer, Roger (of Wigmore) 90 n.68
  and Anglo-French War 469, 470–1, 475, 477–8, 482

Mortimer, Roger (of Wigmore) (cont.)
  arrest and execution 562, 565, 572, 573
  and Bristol siege 274
  and civil war 403–4, 414–15, 452–3
  and Despenser the Elder 513
  and Despenser the Younger 365, 375–7, 378–9, 385, 386, 400, 460–1, 478, 487, 490, 516
  as earl of March 418, 569
  and Edmund earl of Kent 566, 571
  and Edward II: burial 551–2; coronation 145, 489; death 112, 547–8, 563, 565, 572, 580; deposition 527, 537; imprisonment at Berkeley 542–3, 547; supposed survival 570–1, 577, 580–1
  and Edward III 571–2; coronation 540; and Guildhall oath 532; and king's council 540
  escape 9, 440–1, 453, 457, 490, 510, 591; in France 459–61, 492, 499
  followers 572–6
  and Henry of Lancaster 511 n.346, 522, 542, 545, 569
  and Isabella 488–91, 492, 495, 611; and Edward II 520–2; invasion of England 8, 99 n.126, 492–5, 497, 499–500, 501–2, 503–4
  knighting 489
  and Leeds castle, siege of 398
  as lieutenant in Ireland 283, 306, 459
  and lordship of Gower 366, 375, 393 n.398
  opponents 527, 568–9, 581
  political power 361, 540, 569, 571–2
  and Scots invasion of Ireland 256, 257, 261
  and Scottish War 116 n.222, 169
  and standing royal council 337
  and Thomas of Lancaster 318, 319
  trial and imprisonment 390 n.392, 412–13, 453, 540
  and Welsh revolt 272–3
  and Westminster Palace 137 n.80
Mortival, Roger, bishop of Salisbury
  and Guildhall oath 532
  and standing royal council 337
Mountford, William, *King Edward the Third* 28 n.103
Mowbray, John 168, 306 n.152, 415
  and attack on Despensers 279 n.323, 374, 377, 393
  execution 410
  and lordship of Gower 366, 368, 393 n.398
Mowbray, John (the Younger) 413
Mowbray, Philip de
  invasion of Ireland 254
  and siege of Stirling 223, 228, 231 n.231, 233
Mulazzo 586
  see also Melazzo
Murimuth, Adam (chronicler) 8 n.15, 286 n.35
  and civil war 402 n.458
  and Despensers 367 n.245, 376, 395 n.11, 478
  and Edward II: death 552, 561–3, 577, 581; deposition 537 n.102; imprisonment 541
  and English mission to John XXII (1320) 360
  and Isabella 521
  and trial of rebels 411, 612
music
  for coronation 143
  Welsh 37, 74
Myton, Scots victory at (1319) 346, 347–9, 431

Newcastle
  army muster at (1316) 268, 280
  army muster at (1317) 293
  army muster at (1319) 332, 343–5
  and draft peace treaty with Scots 433
  Edward II's flight from 187, 200, 203, 205, 206–7
Newington, Robert de 15, 180, 277
Nicholas III, pope 2
Nicholas of Wisbech 22, 65–6, 325–7, 340–2, 545, 602
Nigra, Costantino 586–8
Norfolk, earl *see* Thomas of Brotherton
Normandy, English attack on 503
Northampton meeting (Aug. 1308) 151–3
Northampton Treaty (1328) 435
Northburgh, Roger de
  as bishop of Coventry & Lichfield 62, 449–50
  and Guildhall oath 532
  as keeper of the privy seal 233, 237 n.274, 239, 450 n.260
  as treasurer 333
Norwich, bishop of *see* Airmyn; Salmon
Nottingham castle 73, 186, 347, 572
Nottingham council (1317) 292–3, 297
Nouvel, Arnaud 194–5, 197, 201

Novo Castro, William de 195, 198
Nussbacher, A. 229 n.221, 231 n.233

Ockley (Ogle), William 547–8, 565, 572–3, 574, 581, 596
O'Neill of Tyrone, Donal 254, 260
Ordainers
  appointment 163, 165–7
  and Edward II 168, 173–4
  and Gaveston 136 n.75, 166–7, 172, 176, 181
  and parliament 172, 175–7
  and reform of royal administration 49, 68, 166–7, 171–5, 191, 258, 267
Ordinance of the Staple 212 n.123, 379 n.322, 424
Ordinances of 1311 56, 156, 172–5, 176–80, 221
  evasion of 179, 182, 185, 194–6, 201, 216, 275–6, 293, 307
  and Gaveston 178–9, 181–2, 190, 198–9
  held in abeyance 239
  and Henry de Beaumont 179 n.291, 193, 200, 215–16, 240
  oath to uphold 284, 287, 359–60, 362 n.215, 451–2, 538
  objections to 198–9
  observance 243–4, 246, 266–7, 310–11, 314, 331, 362
  revocation 184, 422–4, 452
  and revocation of grants 177, 243, 246, 275, 293, 310–12, 315, 316–18, 320–1, 331, 333
  and royal administration 177–80, 239–40
  second set of articles 181–2
  and Thomas of Lancaster 194, 198–9, 239, 275–6, 293, 307, 310–12, 314, 316–18, 321, 333, 359
Oriel College, Oxford 28, 62, 556 n.209
Orleton, Adam 532
  as bishop of Hereford 16, 287, 341, 355
  and canonization of Thomas Cantilupe 70 n.215
  and contrariants 401, 474
  and Council of Vienne 180 n.296
  and deputation to Kenilworth 533–5
  and Despenser the Younger 510, 523
  and Edward II: breach with 452–4; capture 515; charges of tyranny against 98, 523; death 563; deposition 16, 509–10, 524, n.23, 525, 528

  and Edward III 539, 540
  and Isabella 484, 504, 512, 520–1
  mission to John XXII 286 n.35, 287
  and Mortimers 449, 452–3, 507 n.321
  and parliament of Jan. 1327 525, 527–8
  and standing royal council 320
Ormrod, Mark 71 n.221, 555 n.203, 557 n.214, 558 n.216
Owen, Edward 87 n.52
Oxford
  Carmelite priory 28, 62, 68, 233, 235 n.264, 322, 603 n.128
  Dominican priory 191, 192, 241
Oxford castle 194
Oxford, Robert de Vere, earl
  and Gaveston 162, 184
  and Ordainers 166, 176
  support for Edward II 147, 160
Oxford university 62, 523
Oxwich castle, and possessions of Edward II, 519, Pl. 24

papacy
  annual tribute paid to 263, 287
  and crusades 108
  and Edward I 90
  and Edward II 448–51, 468, 495–8
  and Holy Oil of St Thomas of Canterbury 22, 65–6, 324–7, 340–1
  and Philip IV 211
  protest against abuses of authority 160
  and Spiritual Franciscans 3, 21 n.76
  and taxation of the Church 78, 286, 420
  see also Clement V; John XXII
Paris, court scandal 222–3
Paris, Matthew (chronicler), *Flores Historiarum* 7
Paris *parlement*
  appeals from Aquitaine/Gascony 132, 208–9, 221–2, 247–8, 455
Paris treaty (1303) 6, 86, 91, 103, 132, 134
parliament
  armed retainers banned from 164, 182, 200, 207, 216
  Edward II's addresses to 61, 104, 358–9
  frequency 178, 470
  Lincoln, July 1312 189; Jan. 1316 8–9 n.16, 246 n.54, 253, 265–7, 268–9, 270, 272, 273, 275, 280, 293, 295, 364, 423; 1318 301, 308–9, 315, 320; Sept. 1327 548, 561
  role of 29, 411, 423, 448, 470, 612

parliament (*cont.*)
    and royal prerogative 163, 216
    Stamford July 1309 153, 158–60, 161, 165
    and standing royal council 318, 320, 336
    and taxation 130, 163, 199, 200, 207, 252, 268, 332, 420, 432
    Westminster 1306 423; March–April 1308 146–9, 158; Oct. 1308 152–4; April 1309 153, 154, 155, 159, 167, 178; Feb. 1310 164–6; Aug. 1311 175–7; Dec. 1311 183; Aug. 1312 195–6, 201, 244; March 1313 205, 207–8; July 1313 208, 214, 225; Sept. 1313 215–16, 227; Jan. 1315 243–5, 249, 253, 277; Aug. 1320 357–60; Oct. 1320 357–8, 362; July 1321 384, 386–9, 390, 393–4; Feb. 1324 452, 453; June 1325 473–4; Nov. 1325 486–7; Dec. 1326 513; Jan. 1327 508, 521, 524–9, 536–9, 540; Nov.–Dec. 1330 567, 579; Sept. 1331 576
    York, Sept. 1314 239, 242 n.28, 243, 246; Oct. 1318 329 n.3, 330–6, 337, 359, 381, 391–2; May 1319 338–9, 342–3, 381; Jan. 1320 270 n.188, 353–5, 359; Nov. 1322 420, 431–2; May–June 1335 576
Parsons, John 81 n.20
Pateshull, Henry de 298 n.103
patronage, and royal favourites 98, 136, 161, 321, 351, 360, 385, 417, 609, 610
Pecche, Gilbert 56 n.136, 354
Pecche, John 402, 566, 567–9
Pembroke, Aymer de Valence, earl 29, 52 n.113
    armed retainers 164, 182, 193, 226, 234–5, 344, 445
    and Boulogne Declaration (1308) 138, 142
    and Bristol 274
    capture and ransoming 288–90, 361–2
    as constable of Rockingham 302
    and Damory 303–5
    death 417, 456, 463
    debts 361
    and Despensers 367, 376, 384, 387–8, 393–4, 401, 425, 447
    and Edward II: campaign against Marcher lords 402–3, 404, 407; coronation 145; indenture to 305; and king's council 245, 265 n.166, 274, 284 n.24, 292, 301; marriage 133, 134–5; and middle party 296 n.100, 304, 305; opposition 164, 384, 387, 393–4, 395; and standing royal council 320, 333, 337; support for 152, 154–5, 159, 190, 191, 193, 196, 246, 307, 393–4, 395, 397–9, 416, 425
    and embassies to France 195, 247
    and embassy to John XXII 284–6, 294
    in France (1313) 209–10
    and Gaveston 149, 152, 199; burial 241–2; and Edward I 126, 137; nickname 161; pursuit and capture 185–8, 189–90; return from exile 154–5, 159, 184
    as godfather of Edward III 201
    marriage 362
    and Maurice de Berkeley 361–2
    mission to France (1324) 463–4
    as Ordainer 166, 172, 176
    and papal authority 160
    and Pessagno 339–40
    political influence 361–2, 608; and opposition magnates 196, 197–200, 206, 215; and parliaments of 1313 214–15; and reform commission 267
    positions: as keeper of the forest (south) 360–1; as keeper of the realm 355, 356, 360; as keeper of Scotland 226
    and Scottish War 95; Bannockburn and aftermath 228–9, 232–3, 234, 238–9; campaign of 1306 113, 114–15, 123, 128; campaign of 1310–11 168 n.217, 169; campaign of 1317 299; campaign of 1319 344; and defence of the north 248–52, 283 n.20, 429–30; and peace negotiations 371–2, 434–5; truce discussions 352–3
    and see of Durham 282
    and Leeds castle, siege of 398
    and Thomas of Lancaster 246, 250, 267, 290, 292, 297–8, 301–2, 309–10, 313, 317–19, 395, 416
    tomb 557 n.215
Pembroke, Beatrice de Clermont-Nesle, countess 362, 376 n.301
Pembroke, Marie de St Pol, countess 63, 376, 384, 384 n.351, 447
Penrith, John de 353, 426
The People Informed of their Oppressors and Oppressions 26
perambulations of the forest 244, 246, 266–7

Percy, George de 567
Percy, Henry de 105, 160
  death 246, 249
  and Gaveston 185, 187–8, 189, 193
  and Ordainers 166–7, 176
  restoration of lands 200, 205, 207
  and royal pardon 216
  and Scottish campaigns 169, 171
Percy, Henry de (son of the above)
  and deputation to Kenilworth 533
  and Edward III 540
  and Isabella 513 n.353
Périgueux Process (1311) 208–9, 247, 356 n.184, 455
Perth castle, Scots recapture 224
Peruzzi (bankers) 419
Pessagno, Antonio (banker) 218–19, 225, 243, 247, 252, 253, 262, 590 n.64
  as advisor 281 n.8, 283 n.20
  and Despenser the Younger 384 n.356
  and embassy to John XXII 286, 289
  and Pembroke 339–40
  and plots to attack England 461 n.42
  as seneschal of Gascony 303, 339, 354 n.170
Peter of Spain, cardinal
  and funeral of Edward I 131 n.38
  and marriage of Edward II and Isabella 116–17, 119, 120, 132 n.48
petition of 1310 164–5
petitions to parliament 244, 266, 272, 332–5, 338, 357–8, 526
Pey de Ladils 18
Philip III of France 2
Philip IV of France Pl. 10
  and Aquitaine 77–8, 117–18, 146, 208, 222
  childhood 45
  and court scandal 222–3
  criticisms of 19 n.69
  death 223
  and Edward II 101, 108, 138–9, 146, 152, 187 n.350, Pls 10 and 11; embassy of 1312 195; loan to 218; marriage to Isabella 77–8, 117–18, 132–5, 149–50; and opposition magnates 208, 215; and Ordinances 194; state visit to France 1313 209–12, 218, 221; wedding gifts 135, 136, 137
  and Gaveston 137–8, 141 n.95, 149–50, 155, 180 n.298, 181, 182–3, 188
  knighting of sons 209, 210, Pl. 10

and papacy 2, 211
royal propaganda 7
and Scotland 154, 160, 240
taking of the cross 21 n.76, 210–13, Pl. 11
and Templars 101 n.139, 135 n.62, 139 n.84, 149, 150 n.136, 153, 211, 222
Philip V of France
  and Aquitaine 61, 118, 134 n.57, 354, 356, 358–9, 455
  and crusading oath 285
  death 431 n.143, 456
  homage to 359, 456
  and Scotland 371
Philip of Valois, and Isabella 498–9
Philippa of Flanders 78
Philippa of Hainault 46, 337 n.48, 494, 512 n.352, 575 n.318
  betrothal 500–1, 531 n.58
  marriage to Edward III 550–1, 554
Pipewell chronicle 524 n.24, 529 n.49, 533–4
poetry
  prophetic 20–1
  of protest 18–19, 72
  Welsh 38, 58
Polistorie del Eglise de Christ de Caunterbyre 97 n.114, 100, 137 n.77
politics, constitutional development 29–30, 343, 423, 612–13
Pontefract castle 299, 301–2, 339, 355, 396
  capture 407
  royal missions to Thomas of Lancaster 297–8, 308, 309, 312 n.179
  Thomas of Lancaster held at 408
  and York parliament 353
Ponthieu and Montreuil, county
  and Anglo-French War 470
  armed men sought from 194
  as dower of Isabella 2–4, 121, 134, 150, 181, 202, 356, 500
  and Edward II 77, 88 n.56, 104, 105 n.157, 134
  and Edward III 479
  and Gaveston's first exile 46–7 n.84, 77, 99, 120–3, 126, 150
  homage for 248, 355, 356
  and Mortimer of Wigmore 490 n.214
Powel, David, *The Historie of Cambria* 36
Powicke, M.R. 542 n.149
prerogative, royal 157, 198, 201, 216, 607–8
  see also prises; purveyance; tallage
Prestwich, Michael
  on community of the realm 423 n.93

Prestwich, Michael (*cont.*)
    on Edward I 128
    on Edward II: character 47 n.85;
        coronation oath 141 n.98; and
        Despensers 363 n.222, 390 n.389;
        household knights 299 n.113
    on Gaveston 100 n.133
    on Ordinances 172–3, 178 n.283,
        179–80
    on Sherburn indenture 383 n.344
    on Thomas of Lancaster 300 n.118
prices, royal ordinance (1315) 243–4, 253, 266
Prima Tractatio ad Pacem Confirmandam 198–9
The Prime Minister and the King 27
prises 217, 419, 423
    abolition 175, 177
    abuses 158, 162, 172
privy seal writs, and common law 156, 159
prophesy, prophetic writing and preaching 14, 16, 20–1, 123
Psalter of Queen Isabella of England 58–9, 135, Pl. 4
purveyance 217, 225–6
    abuse 17, 49, 156, 244
    and civil war 414
    reforms 157, 159–60, 162–7
    and Scottish campaigns 162–3, 342, 419, 425–6
Puzzuoli, Giovanni di, chaplain to Isabella 388 n.377

Queen Mary Psalter 59

rainfall, 1314–20, effects 238, 252–3, 276
Ramsey, William (architect) 558
Randolph, Sir Thomas 285
Rationes Baronum 198, 200, 201
Raymond de Béziers, *Kalila and Dimna* 211, Pl. 10
Redmere, John de 544–5
reform
    11 articles 156–9
    commission 267–8, 293
    pressure for 138–9, 141–3, 151–4, 155–7, 158–60, 610
    of royal administration 49, 68, 166–7, 171–5, 191, 258, 267, 443–4
    of royal household 166, 172, 239–40, 243, 267, 330
Reginald of Guelders, marriage to Eleanor (sister of Edward III) 559
relics
    and Edward I 34–5, 63, 83, 121
    and Edward II 63, 68–9, 228

Remonstrance of the Irish Princes 257, 260 n.140, 262–4
revolt, fears of 163–4, 177
Reynolds, Walter
    as administrator 608
    as ally of Edward II 16, 153, 167, 214, 401, 505, 507
    as archbishop of Canterbury 16, 214–15, 217, 239, 241, 246, 278 n.228, 448, 477
    as bishop of Worcester 153, 159, 201, 207, 213
    as chancellor 167, 172, 174, 177 n.275, 215
    death 554
    and deposition of Edward II 16, 521, 524, 527, 529–30
    and Despensers 385, 401
    and Edward III 537, 540
    and Guildhall oath 532
    and household of Edward of Caernarfon 56–7, 89, 92, 106–7, 108, 126
    and Isabella 491, 507, 520–1
    and king's council 284 n.24, 292, 308
    and Ordainers 167, 173–4
    and reform commission 267
    and Thomas of Lancaster 290, 297, 310–12, 313, 315, 317–18, 319–20
    as treasurer 129, 154–5
Rhys ap Gruffudd 39, 508, 511 n.344, 514, 546, 547–8, 568 n.280
Rhys ap Hywel 515, 548
Rhys ap Meredudd 85
Richard of Cornwall 326
Richard de Neueby (impostor) 15
Richard II
    and canonization of Edward II 4, 14, 604–5, 612
    and Edward II 24–5, 26–7, 539 n.105, 553 n.190
    survival legend 599
Richard the Rhymer 37
Richardson, H.G. 141 n.98, 142, 145 n.109
Richardson, H.G. and Sayles, G.O. 55
Richmond, John of Brittany, earl 94, 492
    and Anglo-French War 468, 471, 472, 474, 476, 478–9
    and civil war 398, 401, 407, 417
    and defence of the north 250, 429–30
    and Despensers 387, 393, 401; and Edward II 145, 147, 154–5, 159, 164, 166, 196, 245, 397

in France (1313) 210
and Gaveston 127, 154, 161
as godfather of Edward III 201
and Isabella 485, 492, 499, 501
as member of king's council 265
and negotiations with opposition
  magnates 197, 199–200, 206, 208
and Northampton meeting (Aug.
  1308) 151
as Ordainer 166
and papal authority 160
and parliaments of 1313 214–15
and reform commission 267
and Scottish War 128, 168–9,
  429–30; capture 421; and defence
  of Isabella 430; peace negotiations
  372–3
and standing royal council 320, 337
Rigg, A.G. 235 n.264
Ringstead, Thomas, bishop of Bangor
  23, 603
Rishanger, William (chronicler) 36–7, 82
  n.26, 113, 114–15
Robert of Avesbury (chronicler) 441
Robert I, king of Scots *see* Bruce, Robert
Robert of Newington *see* Newington
Robert of Reading (chronicler) *Flores
  Historiarum* 8–9, 591
Robert of Scotland *see* Bruce, Robert, king
  of Scots
Rochester, bishop of *see* Hethe
Rockingham castle, and Pembroke 302
Roderick of Toledo, chronicle 119 n.247
Rodriguez, Pedro *see* Peter of Spain
Roos, John de
  and Despenser the Younger 271, 364
  and Edward III 540
Roos, William de 533
Rosary, royal house 3 n.16
Roscelyn, Thomas 566, 569
Ross, John, bishop of Carlisle 536, 539
  n.108
Roxburgh castle 224

Saint Sardos, war of (1324–5) 18, 461–6,
  494, 560
Saint-Pierre de Maguelone cathedral
  583–4, Pl. 22
St Alban's abbey 68–9, 228
St Albans chronicle 7, 36–7, 97 n.118,
  189, 203, 535 n.80, 605
St John, John de 83, 89, 169
St Mary's Hall, Oxford 28
Saisset, Bernard, bishop of Pamiers 2

Salisbury, bishop of *see* Mortival
Salmon, John, bishop of Norwich 309,
  314, 316–17, 319
  and Anglo-French War 468, 471,
    472, 474, 479
  as chancellor 353
  death 480
  and Isabella 512
  and standing royal council 320,
    333, 337
Salveyn, Gerard (escheator) 152 n.143, 181,
  182–3
Sandal castle, seized by Thomas of
  Lancaster 302
Sandal, John
  as bishop of Winchester 280, 282,
    308, 401, 448
  and citizens of Bristol 245
  and defence of the north 249
  and king's council 284 n.24, 292
  negotiations with opposition
    magnates 206
  and standing royal council 336–7
  and Thomas of Lancaster 290,
    297, 310
  as treasurer 173 n.249, 177 n.275, 205,
    207, 239, 331, 353
Sangiuliani, Antonio Cavagna 586–8
Sant' Alberto di Butrio abbey 30, 586–9,
  Pls 20 and 21
  see also Cecima
Sapiti, Andreas 286 n.35
Sapy, John de 300
Sapy, Robert de 415
Saul, Nigel 445 n.234, 596 n.91, 613 n.2
Sauviac, Bertrand de 195 n.22
Sayles, G.O. 379 n.321, 452 n.272
Scalacronica 10–11, 233 n.246, 235 n.265,
  288, 499 n.270
Scarborough castle, and Gaveston 186,
  187–8, 193
Schwyzer, Hugo 348 n.127
Scotichronicon of Walter Bower 16, 18, 235
  n.264, Pl. 12
Scotland
  and Edward I 5–6, 7, 79, 80, 82–4,
    128; and Robert Bruce 109,
    111–12, 151
  and Edward II 79, 82–4,
    128–9, 151
  Flemish assistance to 212 n.123,
    248 n.64
  and France 90, 91, 94, 160, 213, 240,
    270, 370–1, 457–9

Scotland (cont.)
  and invasion of Ireland 21 n.74, 237,
    248, 250, 253–64, 271–2, 274,
    328–9, 609
  threat of invasion of England 209, 240
  war with England (1296) 78
Scottish War 82–4, 123, 138
  and defence of the north 249–53,
    262, 280–1, 283, 320, 328, 352–3,
    428, 432, 546
  and Edward I 5–6, 7, 79, 80, 90,
    91–5, 112–16, 123, 128–9
  and Edward II as Prince of Wales
    83–4, 88–90, 91–5, 96, 105, 112–16
  and Edward III 546
  English campaigns: 1300 83–4, 96;
    1301 88–90; 1303 91–5; 1304 105;
    1306 112–16, 123, 128; 1307 123,
    128–9; 1308 151; 1309 160;
    1310–11 167–71, 177, 223–4;
    1314 223–8, 609; 1315 249–51;
    1316 268, 280–1, 283; 1317 290,
    293–4, 297–8, 301; 1318 332;
    1319 342–52, 609; 1322 419–20,
    424, 425–8, 432, 482, 609
  and English finances 168–9, 171, 178,
    217–19, 340, 342–3, 549; and
    clerical subsidies 219, 243, 249,
    252–3, 286, 424, 432, 496; and
    Gascon subjects 251–2; and
    Ireland 169, 252; and parliament
    199, 200, 207, 252; and prises and
    purveyance 162–3, 260, 342, 419;
    and taxation 138, 165, 218, 225,
    243, 268, 280, 332, 343, 420, 432
  and English magnates 89–90, 93
    n.85, 94, 124, 128, 130, 151,
    168–70
  invasions of England 294, 297,
    347–51, 429–31; Durham 405;
    Yorkshire 313, 429–31
  and papal envoys 263, 287, 292,
    299, 309
  peace negotiations 369–73, 432–5,
    440, 458, 549, 554, 569
  and Scots magnates 167–8
  truces 213, 240, 263, 283, 373, 405,
    451; 1308 153–4, 163–4; 1323 420,
    434–5; local 224; papal 285, 287,
    328–9, 352–3, 370
  see also Bannockburn; Bruce, Robert
Scrope, Geoffrey le 505 n.311, 506–7
  and deputation to Kenilworth 534
  and Guildhall oath 532 n.64
  and Harclay 433
  as leading adviser 442, 451
  and Mortimer of Wigmore 460 n.34
  and Thomas of Lancaster 412 n.17
  and truce negotiations 352
Scrope, Henry le 352, 567
scutage 244, 245, 343
Segrave, Henry de 174 n.259
Segrave, John de (elder) 169, 234, 306
  n.152, 320, 337, 415, 464
Segrave, Nicholas de
  as marshal of the household 196
  and negotiations with opposition
    magnates 197, 200
  as retainer of Lancaster 151 n.140,
    334, 362
  and Scottish peace negotiations 372
Segrave, Stephen (knight of Thomas of
  Lancaster) 316, 372, 440–1
Sempringham chronicle 439 n.189
sermons, and criticism of Edward II
  16–17, 509–10, 521, 523, 528–9
Seton, Sir Alexander 231
Shakespeare, William, *Edward III*
  26 n.94
Shaldeford, William 547–8, 581
Sheen (Richmond)
  Carmelite priory 64
  royal manor 68, 206, 394 n.406
Sherburn indenture 378–80, 381–3, 385,
  389, 390–1
sheriffs
  appointment 178, 239, 245, 331, 423
  publication of Ordinances 275
Skillehare, Hugh (chaplain of Thomas of
  Lancaster) 205
Smalley, Beryl 23 n.81, 603
Smith, J. Beverley 271–2 n.194, 273 n.202
Smith, Kathryn 59 n.157
Smyth, John 543 nn.129,130, 547 n.153, 552
  n.184, 578–9
socius, Gaveston as 96
sodomy, accusations of 24, 102 n.146,
  523, 610
Somer Soneday 22 n.80, 60
Somery, John de 293 n.79, 306 n.152, 319,
  330, 344, 375
  and civil war 415
  and reform of royal household 330
songs and poems, political 17–19
Soules, John 254
Spain, and Edward II 119–20
Sparpaglione, Domenico 587 n.49, 588
Spigurnel, Henry 190

Stamford, Henry de, and see of Durham 282
Stapeldon, Walter, bishop of Exeter
   and administrative reforms 444, 608
   as constable of the Tower 442
   death 506, 536 n.93
   embassy to France 247
   in France 479, 481, 485–6
   and Ordainers 167
   and Oxford university 323
   and Paris *parlement* 208–9
   and peace negotiations with Scotland 434
   support for Edward II 159, 442, 448
   as treasurer 58, 62, 353, 395–6 n.417, 419 n.67, 477 n.135
   and York parliament 1314 239
'Statute of Prises' (1309) 158
Statute of Sheriffs (1316) 267 n.174, 423
Statute of Stamford (1309) 158, 159–60, 162–3
Statute of Westminster I (1275) 158, 244
Statute of Westminster IV (1320) 358
Statute of Winchester (1285) 251
Statute of York (1322) 29, 422–3, 452 n.272
Staunton, Hervey de 451, 504, 505 n.311
Stefano, Zerba 587 n.49, 588
steward of England 149, 298, 334–5, 338–9, 381–3, 385, 391, 399–400
steward of the royal household 156, 159
Stirling Bridge (1297), English defeat at 79, 236
Stirling castle
   English control 96, 168, 223
   English siege (1304) 95
   Scottish siege (1314) 223, 224–5, 228–30, 233, 236, 259
Stoke, John de 542, 545
Stollwitzer, Wolfgang Pl. 9
Stone, Marcus 28
Stratford, John
   and Anglo-French War 468–71, 472–3, 476, 478–9, 484
   as bishop of Winchester 16, 443, 450–1, 453–4, 484, 485, 507
   and city of London 520
   and deposition of Edward II 16, 520, 524 n.23, 528
   and deputation to Kenilworth 533–4
   and Edward III 539, 540
   and Guildhall oath 532
   and Isabella 484, 488, 506, 512
   mission to John XXII 450–2, 468
   and parliament of 1327 527–9
   as treasurer 516
Strathearn, earl of, loyalty to Edward II 168, 169
Strickland, Matthew 412 n.17, 516 n.372
Stubbs, William 29, 55, 198 n.43, 303–4, 585, 592–3 n.74
Sturmy, John 429, 461
Subiran, Raymond 195, 198, 286 n.35
Sully, Henry de 430–1, 434–5, 456, 472–3, 474, 480 n.150
Surrey, John de Warenne, earl
   and Anglo-French War 468, 471
   and civil war 407, 416
   and defence of the north 250, 281
   and Despensers 374, 393
   and Earl of Pembroke 187–8, 191, 289
   and Edward II: deputation to Kenilworth 533–4; marriage 135; and royal pardon 216; support for 164, 191, 193, 227 n.213, 246, 397, 401, 513 n.353
   and Edward III 532, 533 n.70, 540
   and Gaveston 127, 161; pursuit and capture 185–8, 189, 216; return from exile 154, 159, 184; homage to Edward as Prince of Wales 88
   knighting 112
   marriage 288–9
   and opposition magnates 199, 387
   and Ordainers 166
   and papal authority 160
   and Scottish War 168–71, 227
   and Thomas of Lancaster 246 n.56, 291–2, 293, 299, 302, 311, 315–16, 319 n.217, 320, 333–4, 339
survival legends 599–600
Swynnerton, Roger 573

Talbot, Gilbert 379 n.323, 479
tallage 201, 273 n.205
Tange, Andrew de 285 n.33, 348, 444
Taunton (*recte* Tauton), Robert de 565, 567, 570 n.289, 571 n.297
taxation
   of the Church 78, 130, 153, 218, 243, 249, 268–9, 284, 286, 332, 343, 420
   under Edward I 49, 78–9, 85, 109–10 n.188
   under Edward II 80, 130, 136, 155, 160, 201, 420; and war with Scotland 138, 165, 218, 225, 243, 268, 280, 332, 343, 432
Taymouth Hours Pl. 14

Tebbit, Alistair 193 n.11
Templars
    and Philip IV of France 101 n.139, 135 n.62, 139 n.84, 149, 150 n.136, 153, 211, 222
    suppression in England 58, 139 n.84, 153, 197–8, 218 n.160
Testa, Cardinal William (papal chancellor) 218
Thomas of Brotherton, earl of Norfolk (half-brother of Edward II)
    birth 34 n.6, 81
    and city of London 343
    and coronation of Edward II 145
    and coronation of Edward III 539–40
    and Despensers 447, 513, 516, 610
    as earl marshal 546
    as earl of Norfolk 82, 84 n.31, 202, 374, 410 n.3
    and Edward III 202, 540
    and Guildhall oath 352
    and Isabella 504, 512
    knighting 344
    lands 110 n.193
    and Leeds castle, siege of 398
    and Mortimer of Wigmore 546
    and support for Edward II 397
Thomas of Cambridge 251
Thomas of Canterbury (architect) 558
Thomas of Canterbury, St
    devotion to 50, 70, 82, 175, 601
    and Holy Oil 21–2, 58 n.148, 63, 65–6, 71, 143–4 n.108, 324–7, 340–2, 545, 602
    Life 58, 70
Thomas of Lancaster, earl of Lancaster
    armed retainers 164, 182, 196, 266, 293, 299, 309, 415–16, 446
    awarded safe conduct 164, 196–7, 200, 204–5, 208, 301, 309, 316
    and Badlesmere 281 n.8, 292, 310, 317–18, 319, 339, 385, 398, 403, 414
    and *Brut* chronicle 12
    and civil war 405–9, 414, 415
    and constitutionalism 29–30
    cult of 540, 569–70, 600, 605–6
    and defence of the north 249–50, 280–1, 283, 320
    and Despensers 373–7, 378–80, 393
    and earldom of Leicester 174, 334
    and Edward II: coronation 145; estrangement from 152, 175, 191, 270 n.188, 276, 279; hostility between 195–6, 221, 243, 280, 282–3, 290–4, 299–301, 307, 349, 362, 414; mediation between 301, 308–19; negotiations with 197–201, 204–7, 217, 293, 327, 329, 331, 334, 609; opposition to 61, 164, 307–8; and political influence 264–8, 275–6; reconciliation 319–21, 327–8, 335–6; and royal favourites 294–7, 303, 312, 317–18, 320–1, 331, 334; royal pardon 216, 330; support for 147, 149
    enemies 609
    and Gaveston 127–8, 161–2, 175, 185, 205–6; absence from burial 242; and danger of civil war 147, 152; execution 191, 192, 198–9, 206, 609; pursuit and capture 187–8, 190–1; return from exile 154, 184
    and Gloucester 174–5
    and household of Edward of Caernarfon 45, 51–3
    march on London 196–7
    and miracles of healing 9, 436, 440, 558, 600–1
    muniments 444
    and Northampton meeting (Aug. 1308) 152
    as Ordainer 160, 166, 172, 176, 179, 181–2
    and Ordinances 194, 198–9, 239, 275–6, 293, 307, 310–12, 314, 316–18, 321, 333, 359, 362, 507
    and papal authority 160
    and parliament 158, 265–7, 353–4, 362
    and Pembroke 246, 250, 267, 290, 292, 297–8, 301–2, 309–10, 313, 317–19, 395, 416
    political influence 264–8; as chief councillor 267–8, 274–6, 290; departure from council 276, 280–1, 313; desire for 307–8; as member of king's council 244–7, 264–6; and reform commission 267–8, 275, 293; refusal to attend council 290–3, 297; and see of Durham 281–2; and standing royal council 318, 320, 337–8, 349–50; as steward of England 149, 298, 334–5, 338–9, 381–3, 399–400, 405, 407
    and pressure for reform 155–6, 166, 267
    and Robert Bruce 185, 283, 351, 406

royal mission to (1317) 297–8
  and Scottish War 88, 113, 169, 227,
    228, 300, 318, 334, 344; siege of
    Berwick 349–50
  and Surrey 246 n.56, 291–2, 293,
    299, 302, 311, 315–16, 319 n.217,
    320, 333–4, 339
  treason accusations 295, 351, 407,
    409, 411
  and Treaty of Leake 16, 280, 318,
    320–1, 330–1, 333, 335, 336
  trial and execution 18, 390 n.392,
    409, 411, 513, 517, 540
Thomas of Otterbourne (chronicler)
  chronicle of Lanercost 11, 16
Thomas of Westminster (king's painter)
  139–40
Thorp, Walter de 206
Tickhill castle, siege 405, 407, 409
touch, royal 71
tournaments 40–1, 73, 158, 185, 215,
  302, 395
Tout, T.F.
  on Despenser the Younger 418
  on Edward I 141 n.98
  on Edward II: imprisonment 543
    n.129; and magnates 29, 244 n.43,
    303–4, 335 n.37; and Ordinances
    212 n.123; revenues 105 n.157;
    rumours of survival 585
  on Thomas of Lancaster 380
Tower of London
  and Edward II 505
  and Isabella 439, 489–90
  and Mortimers 412–13, 440–1,
    489–90, 507, 591
Tranchell, Peter (composer) 31
Travers, John, constable of Bordeaux 464
  n.62, 465 n.67
Trease, H. 213 n.128, 481 n.160
Trivet, Nicolas (chronicler) 12 n.31, 25
  n.92, 234 n.258, 291 n.68, 353, 358, 360
Trokelowe, John (chronicler) 97 n.118,
  189, 203
Trussell, William, Justice of Chester 86–7
Trussell, William
  and deputation to Kenilworth 533
  and Despensers 513, 516
  and Isabella and Mortimer 501, 503
  knighting 112
  renunciation of homage 527 n.37,
    533, 535, 537, 573
Turnberry castle, siege (1301) 90
Tutbury castle 316–17, 407, 417

Tweng, Sir Marmaduke de 237
Tybetot, Payn 166, 234
Tynemouth
  flight from (1312) 187, 203, 431, 482
  Isabella in (1322) 429, 430–1, 482, 517
Tynwelle, Thomas de 15, 277–8
tyranny, charges
  against Despenser the Younger 442,
    509, 517, 530
  against Edward II 8–9, 98, 278, 448,
    523, 530–1, 610

Ulster, Richard de Burgh, earl
  and Edward Bruce 256
  as lieutenant in Ireland 150–1
  and papal authority 160
  and Scottish campaigns 96, 169, 259
Umfraville, Ingram de 231 n.231, 234
Umfraville, Robert de see Angus
universities, development 61–2

Vale, Malcolm 75, 112 n.200
Valence, Agnes de 52
Valence, Aymer de see Pembroke, Aymer
  de Valence
Valente, Claire 525 nn.28, 31
Varennes, Matthew de 160
Verdon, Isabella de 270 n.187
Verdon, Theobald de 89, 256, 270, 302
Verdon, Thomas de 116 n.222
Verses of Gildas 21
Vescy, Isabella de 179 n.291, 203, 216, 221
Vescy, William de 2–3
Vienne, Council of 180, 210 n.109, 219, 286
Villani, Giovanni (chronicler) 2, 19 n.69
Vita Edwardi Secundi
  and Anglo-French War 477
  and civil war 405, 410, 438
  and Despensers 376, 383–4, 387, 394
    n.409, 396, 478
  and Edward II: assessment 12–13, 17,
    72, 220, 328; coronation 144; flight
    from Newcastle 187 n.351; and
    Henry of Lancaster 474; marriage
    145 n.110; and Thomas of
    Lancaster 321; as tyrant 278, 448,
    530 n.51; visits to religious houses
    278; wealth 421–2
  and Gaveston 168 n.218, 182 n.311,
    220; and brotherhood 100, 102
    n.147; burial 241; as *custos regni*
    135–6; execution 191, 192, 198;
    and magnates 152 n.141, 164–5;
    pursuit and capture 188, 189–90;

Vita Edwardi Secundi (*cont.*)
    and Robert Bruce 185; as second king 13, 135–6; and Thomas of Lancaster 161
    and Isabella 61, 483–4, 485–6, 487
    and magnates 328; and Gaveston 152 n.141, 164–5; opposition 196 n.30, 243, 387–8, 390 n.391; and royal pardon 215
    and Ordinances 175–6, 199–200, 239, 284, 287
    and Pembroke 302 n.128
    and Powderham 323
    and Scottish War 169–70, 327–8, 344–5 n.96; 345, 347; battle of Bannockburn 227, 229, 231, 235, 240; defence of the north 249, 330; peace negotiations 458
    and Thomas of Lancaster 298, 319 n.217; assessment 19; and Edward II 321, 353; and Leicester meeting (1318) 309–12; and Robert Bruce 185, 282–3, 351; and royal favourites 161, 293; trial 411
Vita et Mors Edwardi Secundi 13–14, 441

Wake, Thomas 513, 520, 540
    and deposition of Edward II 527–9, 537
    exile 569
    and Guildhall oath 532, 537
Wales
    and Despenser the Younger 364–5, 373–7, 417
    and Edward Bruce 254 n.116, 256, 262, 271, 273
    and Edward I 34–6, 271
    and Edward II 36–9, 265, 271; flight to 36, 58, 59, 505, 508–9, 510–12; lands granted to 85–6; loyalty to 547; revenues from 104–5, 254; and Scottish campaigns 169, 229, 234, 425–6
    Marcher lordships 364–9, 373–7, 378–83, 385–6, 417–18, 508
    petitions from 104
    revolts 271–3
    and taxation 332
    Welsh music 37, 74
    Welsh poetry 38, 58
    see also Mortimer, Roger (of Chirk)
Waleys, William le *see* Galeys
Walkingham, Thomas de 168 n.218

Wallace, William 80, 95, 107, 109, 236, 412 n.17, 518 n.382
Wallingford castle 194, 459
    contrariant prisoners 413, 438–9, 440
    council 520–4
    and Gaveston 136, 147, 182 n.311, 189
    and Isabella and Mortimer 520
    and Langton 130
Walsh, William le *see* Galeys
Walsingham, Thomas (chronicler) 25 n.91, 37 nn.23,27, 69 n.207, 530 n.52, 535 n.80, 605
Walter de Milemete, *De Nobilitatibus, Sapientiis, et Prudentiis Regum* 23 n.82, 531, Pl. 15
Walter of Guisborough (chronicler) 46 n.81, 96, 100, 120–2, 126, 130 n.28, 171, 603 n.127
Walter of Norwich
    and reform of royal household 330
    as treasurer 177 n.275, 239, 284 n.24, 310, 505 n.311
Walwayn, John 544 n.133, 570
    and Scottish War 170
    and see of Durham 282
    and *Vita Edwardi Secundi* 12–13 n.32
Ward, Simon 250 n.80
wards, royal 89, 96
Warenne, John de *see* Surrey
Warley, Ingelard, as keeper of the wardrobe 205, 239, 265
Warwick, castle 190, 398
Warwick, Guy de Beauchamp, earl
    and armed retainers 164, 182
    death 245, 246, 248, 307
    and defence of the north 249
    and Edward II: coronation 145; and king's council 244–6; negotiations with 197, 199–201, 205–7, 217 n.153; opposition to 164, 191, 243; royal pardon 216; support for 152
    and Gaveston 128, 160, 162, 199; burial 242; pursuit and capture 185, 189–90, 192; return from exile 126, 154, 184; use of nicknames 161
    and Northampton meeting (Aug. 1308) 151
    as Ordainer 166, 172, 176, 181–2, 194
    and papal authority 160
    and parliament of July 1309 158
    and Scottish War 169, 227
Wauton, Roger 438–9
Waverley abbey annals 35

weather *see* rainfall
Westminster Abbey
    and burial of Edward III 554
    and Edward II 7–9, 110, 550–1;
        coronation 133, 140–6
    and funeral of Edward I 131
    and Gaveston 136, 137 n.76
    shrine of Edward the Confessor 20,
        35, 39, 69, 143, 458, 550
    and Stone of Scone 35 n.14, 140, 458
Westminster council (1317) 291, 295–6
Westminster Hall 17, 111, 140, 216, 277, 296
Westminster Palace
    building work 73, 139, 421
    Lesser Hall 46, 139, 412
    privy palace 137 n.80
Weston, John de (constable of
    the Tower) 507
Weston, John de (valet) 99 n.131, 107
wheel of fortune imagery 22–3 n.80,
    59–60, 542
Wigton, Gilbert de, as controller of royal
    household 333
Wilde, Oscar 28
Wilkinson, B. 304 n.138, 380, 391
William of Gloucester 3
William of Hainault, count
    and Charles IV 493–4
    and Edward III 500–1
    and Isabella 500, 501
William of Langdon 67, 449, 475, 567–8
William of Pagula 19, 531
Williams, Bernadette 142 n.102
Winchelsey, Robert, archbishop of
    Canterbury 52, 448
        canonization attempts 540, 600
        and coronation of Edward II 140
        death 214, 278 n.228
        excommunication of Gaveston 152,
            154–5, 157–8, 185, 241

    as Ordainer 160, 166–7, 172
    reconciliation with Edward II
        78, 130
    and Thomas of Lancaster 246
Winchester, bishop of *see* Assier; Sandal;
    Stratford; Woodlock
Winchester, earl of *see* Despenser, Hugh
    the Elder
Windsor castle
    chapel of St Edward 69–70
    defences 147, 149
    Edward II and Gaveston at
        101, 149
Wisham, John de, seneschal of Gascony 573
Wishart, Robert, bishop of Glasgow 153,
    218 n.160, 240
Wonderful Parliament (1387) 24–5
Woodlock, Henry, bishop of Winchester
    and Edward II's coronation 131
    and reform 166
Woodstock, Edmund of *see* Kent, Edmund
    of Woodstock, earl
Worcester, bishop of *see* Cobham;
    Reynolds
Wrotham, John de (Edward II's confessor)
    65, 341

York
    army muster at (1318) 315
    army muster at (1323) 432, 434
    council (Oct. 1309) 162
    defences 352
    Edward II in (1314) 238–9
    flight to (1322) 430
    St Mary's abbey 188, 345
    threat from Scots invaders 346–8
    see also parliament, York
York, archbishop of *see* Melton
York castle, Thomas of Lancaster held
    in 408